POETIC HEROES

POETIC HEROES

Literary Commemorations of
Warriors and Warrior Culture
in the Early Biblical World

Mark S. Smith

William B. Eerdmans Publishing Company
Grand Rapids, Michigan / Cambridge, U.K.

Published 2014 by
Wm. B. Eerdmans Publishing Co.
2140 Oak Industrial Drive N.E., Grand Rapids, Michigan 49505 /
P.O. Box 163, Cambridge CB3 9PU U.K.

Library of Congress Cataloging-in-Publication Data

Smith, Mark S., 1955-
Poetic heroes: literary commemorations of warriors and warrior culture
in the early biblical world / Mark S. Smith.
pages cm
Includes bibliographical references and index.
ISBN 978-0-8028-6792-6 (pbk.: alk. paper)
1. War in literature.
2. War and literature — History.
3. War stories — History and criticism.
I. Title.

PN56.W3S65 2014
809'.933581 — dc23

2014009184

www.eerdmans.com

In memory of my beloved teacher and friend,

Aloysius Fitzgerald, F.S.C. (1931-2003)

Contents

Preface xi

Acknowledgments xiv

Abbreviations and Sigla xvii

INTRODUCTION Warriors between Poetry and Practice 1

1. The Subject of This Study 1
2. The Scope of This Study 3

I: The Literary Commemoration of Warriors and Warrior Culture

ONE Considerations of Evidence and Method 15

1. The Central Topics of Warrior Poetry: Pre- and Postbattle Practices and the Values of Warriors in Early Biblical Literature 15
2. Archaeological and Iconographical Material for Warriors 24
3. A Central Problem in the Topic: Warrior Culture between Literary Representation and Cultural Reality 33

II: Three Warrior Pairs in Mesopotamia, Greece, and Israel

TWO Brothers in Arms 51
1. Gilgamesh and Enkidu 52
2. Achilles and Patroklos 59
3. David and Jonathan 64

THREE Gender Inversion in the Poetry of Heroic Pairs 68
1. Introduction 68
2. The Goddesses 73
3. Human Females 76
4. Brotherly Bonds 79

III: Human and Divine Warriors in the Ugaritic Texts

FOUR Heroes in the Story of Aqhat 99
1. Introduction 99
2. Hero Father, Would-be Hero Son 101
3. The Son's Gift of the Hunt to the Goddess and His Weapons Withheld 106
4. The Hero's Death by the Goddess and the Rituals for the Hero 115
5. The Heroic Daughter's Revenge 124
6. The Heroic Code of Honor and the Gender of Human and Divine Warriors 127

FIVE The Commemoration of the Dead Rephaim Warriors 137
1. The Eponymous Ancestor of Heroic Rephaim Warriors 138
2. The Journey and Late Summer Feast of the Rephaim 141
3. Royal Commemoration: Calling on Dead Heroes and Kings 154

SIX Divine Warriors in the Baal Cycle 162
1. Baal, Yamm, and Mot 163
2. ʿAthtar 168
3. Anat 170
4. The Warrior's Feast: Music, Gender, Sex 176
SEVEN ʿAthtart among the Divine Warriors 183
1. Introduction 183
2. Goddess of the Hunt and Warfare 187
3. ʿAthtart's Relations with Other Deities 197
4. The Warrior Attribute Animal of ʿAthtart 204

IV: Israelite Warrior Poetry in the Early Iron Age

EIGHT Introduction to Early Israelite Poetry: The Problem of Dating "Old Poetry" and the Poem of Judges 5 211
1. Introduction to "Old Poetry" and Its Dating 211
2. Assessment of Criteria and Method 212
3. Features of Antiquity in Judges 5 220
NINE Human and Divine Warriors of Israel in Judges 5 234
1. Traditional Material in Judges 5 234
2. The Composition of Judges 5 in Diachronic Perspective 242
3. The Synchronic Structure of the Poem 251
4. The Poem and Its Performance: The First Person Voice 259
5. Divine and Human Warriors in Judges 5 262
TEN The Lamentation over Fallen Warriors in 2 Samuel 1:19-27 267
1. Translation of 2 Samuel 1:19-27 with Notes 267
2. Traditional Warrior Motifs in the Lament 270
3. The Poetic Voice(s) of David 275

ELEVEN The Cultural Settings for Warrior Poetry in Early Israel 284

1. The Represented Oral Settings of Warrior Poetry 285
2. Inscribing the Warrior Songs 295
3. The Iron II Written Reception of Warrior Poetry 300

TWELVE The Passing of Warrior Poetry in the Era of Prosaic Heroes 308

1. The Biblical Record and the Ugaritic Classics in Counterpoint 309
2. Legendary Warriors and Rephaim in the Era of the Philistine Wars 314
3. The Fading of the Warrior Goddesses and the Rise of the National God 322
4. The Social Dislocation of Heroic Poetry in Ancient Israel 326

Notes 333

Index of Subjects 577

Index of Texts 591

Index of West Semitic Key Words, Grammatical Features, and Poetic Terms 617

Index of Select Iconography 620

Index of Modern Authors 622

Preface

"The myth of war entices us with the allure of heroism."[1] With these words, the news correspondent Chris Hedges offers a distillation of his experience of war around the globe. Warfare and warriors hold a powerful grip on our imaginations. It is not only that we have witnessed wars on several continents, or that as Americans we have found our nation regularly engrossed in military conflicts abroad.[2] There is something about the violence of war itself and about claims made about its necessity that make it feel all the more problematic — and palpable. We use the language of sacrifice for war, as if life lost in war is a sacred loss.[3] Modern societies are hardly immune to claims of divine support for wars, and they may even accept claims of divine involvement. When warfare is given a divine casting, "the gods beautify death."[4]

The problem extends to our study of war in the past. Here Hedges observes: "The mythical heroes of the past loom over us."[5] There have been laudable efforts to counteract biblical images of violence (and here I have in mind especially a fine book by Susan Niditch).[6] However, those images still surround us.[7] In our culture, biblical images inform the idea of future apocalyptic battles that are supposed to decide the course of human matters once and for all.[8] Biblical paradigms of violence are basic elements in many movies and novels.[9] In the film *Pulp Fiction*, the character Jules recites Ezek. 25:17 before executing his victims.[10] Featuring a paradigmatically messianic main character, the *Matrix* movies draw on a number of biblical terms: Zion is the name of the underground refuge for humans; Trinity is the main female character; the Seraph character is an emissary of the Oracle, as well as her protector; and the *Nebuchadnezzar* is the name of the heroes' ship. Appearing in both print and film, *The Chronicles of Narnia* are famous conflict narratives inspired by the Bible. In his novel *Waiting for the Barbarians,* the South African writer J. M. Coetzee casts the end of civilization in terms that echo the Bible: "Is there any better way to pass these last days than in dreaming of a saviour with a sword who will scatter the enemy hosts and forgive us the errors that have been made by others in our name and grant us a second chance to build our earthly paradise?"[11]

The dream of great warriors who serve as society's saviors is an ancient one. The Bible offers a succession of saviors in the book of Judges and in the figures of royal protectors, most famously David. The English word "messiah" derives from the Hebrew for "anointed," part of the ancient coronation ritual that marked David and his successors as kings. Great literary classics of Mesopotamian and Greek traditions, in particular *Gilgamesh* and Homer's *Iliad,* present their audiences with an array of heroes displaying attitudes about war and warriors found also in the biblical world. In view of the ancient concern for war and warriors as well as our own, a study of ancient heroic poetry, both in the Bible and beyond, provides an opportunity for critical reflection.[12]

At first glance, the ancient classics glorify war and its warriors. At the outset of *Gilgamesh,* glory is the name of the game. Gilgamesh wishes to defeat the monster Huwawa in order to establish his name forever (OB III, col. iv, lines 148-49): "If I fall, I should have made my name: (men will say) 'Gilgamesh joined battle with ferocious Huwawa.'" In the same speech (OB III, col. iv, line 160), Gilgamesh declares: "[A name that] is eternal I will establish for myself," a line that he repeats later (OB III, col. v, line 188 = MB Bogh 1, frg. d, line 4). The theme is echoed also in SBV (IV.248): "It is they who have established a name [for] future [*time*]!" Enkidu later tells Gilgamesh: "We shall join forces and do a thing unique, a feat that does not (yet) exist in the land!" (OB Harmal-1, rev., line 15).[13] Gilgamesh has smiths make decorative horns to celebrate the glory of his defeat of the Bull of Heaven and brags to the serving-girls of his house: "Who is the most glorious of fellows?" (SBV VI.160-75). However, the story of Gilgamesh also offers comments that disparage the heroic quest for glory. The elders of the city criticize the undertaking against the monster, now called Humbaba (SBV II.287-301). Later, in lamenting his dead friend (SBV VIII.3-56), Gilgamesh says nothing of glory. The glories of Gilgamesh, recalled later in conversations, have turned him into a wasted, sorrowful figure (SBV X.29-52, 112-48).

A positive sense of glory in war in the *Iliad* likewise gives way to a negative viewpoint. Achilles is ready for war so that his exploits would be sung for the ages to come. Indeed, later tradition would admire him.[14] Alexander the Great was reputed to have said at Achilles' tomb (Cicero, *Pro Archia* 24): "How fortunate you were, young man, to enjoy a great proclaimer of your deserts!"[15] This is the picture of the hero that the *Iliad* largely recalls. Yet in the story, Achilles comes to doubt the heroic code of honor when Agamemnon takes his trophy of war away from him (*Iliad* 9.308-429).[16] Odysseus praises Achilles: if he were only to return to battle, the Acheans "will honor you as though you were a god, for surely you will win great glory in their eyes" (9.302-3). In his response, Achilles sketches out two options, either glory in battle ending in death or a quiet life at home that postpones death (9.411-16); glory in battle is not greater. The hero "calls the entire code into question" in "saying that he would rather live quietly at home than pursue glory in the Trojan war."[17] The fear that Hector, donned in his armor, inspires in his infant son (6.466-81) signals the terrible cost of war for families.

At times, the Bible also offers a bleak view of war. In the battle that takes the life of Jonathan, this son of Saul is represented as being doomed (1 Sam. 28:16-19). Saul's patron god has removed his support and become Saul's "adversary" (NJPS, 1 Sam. 28:16). Not only Saul, but "his sons" as well, will join those in the underworld (1 Sam. 28:19). As this biblical narrative of 1 Samuel traces the paths of Saul's demise and David's rise, Jonathan is caught tragically in the middle. He will not leave his father's side in death, even from a battle that Saul knows cannot be won.

Whether in ancient or modern contexts, warfare seems to exert a magnetic power, even a terrible attraction, not only by its valorization of glory, but also by its call to honor and duty. These values are supported by a separation and division of genders, with warfare and its planning largely considered the domain of men and with women left on the side to endure its effects, to sing its praise, or to lament its losses. A male military also turns men into fictive brothers drawn together by ties of experience in victory and in defeat. While women have entered the military in the United States in modern times, the male military as well as its gender attitudes remain very much with us, and the effects of this situation have been a matter of considerable controversy since the 1980s.[18] To address warfare — or more precisely, its glorification through its poetic commemorations of warriors — represents an opportunity to face what is a central problem in our society and to help root out what is represented as attractive about war. To face war's terrible nature, it is arguably necessary to face how our biblical traditions have made it attractive, even alluring. This book undertakes an exploration of "poetic heroes" across a number of ancient cultures to understand their attitudes about war and warriors.

Acknowledgments

I would like to begin by thanking New York University, and especially the Skirball Department of Hebrew and Judaic Studies. I received strong encouragement from both our former departmental chair, Larry Schiffman, and his successor, David Engel. My colleagues in the field, Daniel E. Fleming and Beate Pongratz-Leisten, generously responded to my queries about Assyriological matters. They also commented extensively on an early draft of the book. I also thank my predecessor, Baruch A. Levine, for his support and humor. I would also mention a final NYU faculty member, and that is the late Seth Benardete. This study draws on his insightful book, *Achilles and Hector: The Homeric Hero* (South Bend: St. Augustine's Press, 2005). I met Professor Benardete the year before his death in 2001.

This study began in 2008, but only reached fruition in the spring term of 2011, thanks to appointments as Annual Professor at the Albright Institute of Archeological Research and as a Lady Davis Visiting Professor at the Hebrew University. I benefitted from many conversations with fellows at the Albright. I particularly thank Andrea Berlin and Jonathan Greer, as well as Sy Gitin, director of the Albright. I received valuable suggestions from the members of a Ugaritic reading group at the Hebrew University: Steve Fassberg, Ronnie Goldstein, Shalom Paul, Alex Rofé, Michael Segal, Nili Wazana, Noga Ayali, Richard Medina, and Tania Notarius. A number of archaeologists also helped me with various aspects of material culture: Avi Faust, Liora Kolska Horwitz, Amihai Mazar, Tallay Ornan, Ilan Sharon, and Sam Wolff.

During the 2011 spring term, this work strongly benefitted thanks to the archaeologist Elizabeth Bloch-Smith, my wife and also an Albright fellow that term. We worked many mornings together on a commentary on the book of Judges. Our conversations often veered into matters pertaining to this book, and Liz offered many fine observations and references. In addition, she gave me invaluable feedback on this book. That term, our son Ben, his wife Elizabeth, and our daughter Rachel were working in the United Arab Emirates, while our daughter Shula and her friend, Howie Stanger, were living in Israel. They have been a constant source of strength and wonder to me, as they find their ways in the world. In the spring, the seven of us realized the dream of being together in Jerusalem for Passover.

The 2012 spring semester of Ugaritic at New York University was devoted largely to the study of Aqhat and the Baal Cycle. I wish to express my appreciation to the students in the course: Seth Chalmer, Julie Deluty, Ryan Higgins, Yael Landman, David Moster, and Phillip Strosahl. A number of scholars provided critical and thoughtful readings of various chapters: Deborah Beck, Sarah Morris, Saul Olyan, and Stephen Russell. On a variety of matters, I was helped by Susan Ackerman, Steve Fassberg, Jan Joosten, Israel Knohl, Ross Kraemer, Peter Machinist, Susan Niditch, and Stanley Stowers. I add my great thanks to Mahri Leonard-Fleckman and Julie Deluty, who corrected many errors and infelicities in this book. I wish to express my appreciation to Eerdmans for accepting this manuscript and bringing it to publication. I am deeply grateful to Allen Myers, my wonderful Senior Biblical Editor at Eerdmans, and to Michael Thomson, Acquisitions and Development Editor at Eerdmans, for his great interest in this book.

This study also improved thanks to institutions that provided a forum for various chapters presented in 2008-12: the Albright Institute of Archaeological Research; Baylor University; Brown University; the Catholic Biblical Association; the Colloquium for Biblical Research; the Columbia University Seminar for Hebrew Bible; the Department of Hebrew Language, the Hebrew University; the Department of Bible, the Hebrew University; Keio University, the Society of the Near Eastern Studies in Japan; Simposio de la Asociación Española de Estudios Hebreos y Judíos; the Old Testament Colloquium; the Society of Biblical Literature; and Yale Divinity School.

In reaching the end of my acknowledgments, I return to the beginning. Decimus Magnus Ausonius, a fourth-century *rhetor* (professor) at Burdigala (Bordeaux) and later tutor to the son of Emperor Valentinian I, opened his recollection of his professors with these words: "It is not enough that I think of you often, gentle men/who were not my kin but as dear to me: my teachers/who shared with me their love of learning and culture."[1] These words remind me of my many wonderful professors of decades ago. This book has allowed me to return to the study of Homer, first introduced to me by

Gregory Nagy at The Johns Hopkins University. The pages that follow also show the monumental influences of Frank Cross of Harvard University (who passed away this past autumn, on 16 October 2012), Marvin Pope of Yale University (who died on 15 June 1997), and Jonas Greenfield of the Hebrew University (who died on 13 March 1995). The poetic analyses of Michael Coogan and Kyle McCarter, both teachers of mine when I was at Harvard, were most helpful for this study, as has been the work of my teacher at Yale, Robert Wilson, especially in his efforts to reconstruct Israelite society. My first professor of Old Testament at Catholic University, Peter Kearney, was kind enough to read this work. I would like to end by acknowledging my enormous debt to another teacher of mine from Catholic University, Aloysius Fitzgerald, F.S.C. (1931-2003), to whose memory this book is dedicated. As I was finding my way into biblical studies in 1977, I found Aloysius's love for the material deeply affecting, whether it concerned biblical poetry, the Hebrew verbal system, or the east and west winds. His great insight and spirit for all of these matters are captured in his beautiful book *The Lord of the East Wind* (CBQMS 34; Washington: The Catholic Biblical Association of America, 2002). His love for students was no less evident week in and week out. It also extended well beyond, for the quarter-century after I left his classroom in December of 1978 until he passed away in June of 2003, now almost a decade ago.

MARK S. SMITH

Addendum

The ms. was submitted at the very end of 2012. I regret being unable to use works that appeared in the meantime. Some of these were added in page proofs to footnotes, but such citations hardly do them justice. This lack includes the third edition of KTU (2013).

Abbreviations and Sigla

AASOR	Annual of the American Schools of Oriental Research
AB	Anchor Bible
ABD	*Anchor Bible Dictionary.* Ed. David Noel Freedman. 6 vols. Garden City: Doubleday, 1992.
ABL	*Assyrian and Babylonian Letters Belonging to the Kouyunjik Collections of the British Museum.* Ed. Robert Francis Harper. 14 vols. Chicago: University of Chicago Press, 1892-1914.
ABR	*Australian Bible Review*
ABRL	Anchor Bible Reference Library
AbrN	*Abr-Nahrain*
AcOr	*Acta orientalia*
ADAJ	*Annual of the Department of Antiquities of Jordan*
AEM	*Archives épistolaires de Mari.* ARM 26. 2 vols. Paris: Editions Recherche sur les Civilizations, 1988.
AfO	*Archiv für Orientforschung*
AHw	Wolfram von Soden, *Akkadisches Handwörterbuch.* 3 vols. Wiesbaden: Harrassowitz, 1965-81.
AJA	*American Journal of Archaeology*
AJSL	*American Journal of Semitic Languages and Literature*
ALASP	Abhandlungen zur Literatur Alt-Syrien-Palästinas und Mesopotamiens
ANEP	*The Ancient Near East in Pictures Relating to the Old Testament.* Ed. James B. Pritchard. 2nd ed. Princeton: Princeton University, 1969.
ANET	*Ancient Eastern Texts Relating to the Old Testament.* Ed. James B. Pritchard. 3rd ed. Princeton: Princeton University Press, 1969.
AnOr	Analecta orientalia
AnSt	*Anatolian Studies*

AOAT	Alter Orient und Altes Testament
ARES	Archivi Reali di Ebla, Studi
ARM	Archives royales de Mari
ASOR	American Schools of Oriental Research
ATANT	Abhandlungen zur Theologie des Alten und Neuen Testaments
AuOr	*Aula orientalis*
BA	*Biblical Archaeologist*
BAR	*Biblical Archaeology Review*
B.A.R.	British Archaeological Reports
BASOR	*Bulletin of the American Schools of Oriental Research*
BBB	Bonner biblische Beiträge
BDB	Francis Brown, S. R. Driver, and C. A. Briggs. *A Hebrew and English Lexicon of the Old Testament.* Oxford: Clarendon, 1907.
BETL	Bibliotheca ephemeridum theologicarum lovaniensium
BFCT	Beiträge zur Förderung christlicher Theologie
BH	Biblical Hebrew
BHS	*Biblia Hebraica Stuttgartensia.* Ed. Karl Elliger and Wilhelm Rudolph et al. 5th rev. ed. Stuttgart: Deutsche Bibelgesellschaft, 1997.
Bib	*Biblica*
BibOr	Biblica et orientalia
BIW	The Bible in Its World
BJS	Brown Judaic Studies
BK	*Bibel und Kirche*
BM	British Museum number
BN	*Biblische Notizen*
BO	*Bibliotheca orientalis*
Bogh	Boghazköy
BRev	*Bible Review*
BRS	Biblical Resources Series
BSV	Pierre Bordreuil and Dennis Pardee with Robert Hawley. *Une bibliothèque au sud de la ville: Textes 1994-2002 en cunéiforme alphabétique de la maison d'Ourtenou.* RSO 18. Lyon: Maison de l'Orient et de la Méditerranée — Jean Pouilloux, 2012.
BZAW	Beihefte zur Zeitschrift für die alttestamentliche Wissenschaft
CAD	*The Assyrian Dictionary of the Oriental Institute of the University of Chicago.* Chicago: Oriental Institute, 1956-.
CahRB	Cahiers de la Revue Biblique
CANE	*Civilizations of the Ancient Near East.* Ed. Jack M. Sasson. 4 vols. New York: Scribner's, 1995.
CBQ	*Catholic Biblical Quarterly*
CBQMS	Catholic Biblical Quarterly Monograph Series

CDA	*A Concise Dictionary of Akkadian*. Ed. Jeremy Black, Andrew George, and Nicholas Postgate. Wiesbaden: Harrassowitz, 2000.
CHANE	Culture and History of the Ancient Near East
CIS	Corpus inscriptionum semiticarum
ConBOT	Coniectanea biblica: Old Testament Series
COS	*The Context of Scripture*. Ed. W. W. Hallo and K. Lawson Younger. 3 vols. Leiden: Brill, 1997-2002.
CRRAI	Comptes Rendus, Rencontre Assyriologique Internationale
CT	Cuneiform Texts from Babylonian Tablets in the British Museum
CTA	*Corpus des tablettes en cunéiforms alphabétiques découvertes à Ras Shamra-Ugarit de 1929 à 1939*. Ed. Andrée Herdner. MRS 10. Paris: Imprimerie Nationale, 1963.
DCH	*Dictionary of Classical Hebrew*. Ed. David J. A. Clines. Sheffield: Sheffield Academic, 1993-2011.
DDD	*Dictionary of Deities and Demons in the Bible*. Ed. Karel van der Toorn, Bob Becking, and Pieter W. van der Horst. 2nd ed. Leiden: Brill and Grand Rapids: Eerdmans, 1999.
DJD	Discoveries in the Judaean Desert. Oxford: Clarendon, 1955-.
DMOA	Documenta et monumenta Orientis antiqui
DN(s)	divine name(s)
DNWSI	*Dictionary of the North-West Semitic Inscriptions*. Ed. J. Hoftijzer and K. Jongeling. 2 vols. Leiden: Brill, 1995.
DSD	*Dead Sea Discoveries*
DULAT	G. del Olmo Lete and J. Sanmartín. *A Dictionary of the Ugaritic Language in the Alphabetic Tradition. Part One [('a/i/u–k]; Part Two [l–z]*. Trans. W. G. E. Watson. 2nd ed. HO 67. Leiden: Brill, 2003. Continuous pagination between the two volumes.
EA	El Amarna texts. Numbering as found in William L. Moran, *The Amarna Letters*. Baltimore: Johns Hopkins University Press, 1992; and Shlomo Izre'el, *The Amarna Scholarly Tablets*. Cuneiform Monographs 9. Groningen: Styx, 1997.
EBH	Early Biblical Hebrew
EBib	Etudes bibliques
Emar	Daniel Arnaud. *Recherches au pays d'Aštata. Emar VI.4: Textes de la bibliothèque-transcriptions et traductions*. Paris: Editions Recherche sur les civilisations, 1987. Cited by text number.
ErIsr	*Eretz-Israel*
FAT	Forschungen zum Alten Testament
FB	Forschung zur Bibel
FRLANT	Forschungen zur Religion und Literatur des Alten und Neuen Testaments

GKC	*Gesenius' Hebrew Grammar.* Ed. E. Kautsch. Trans. A. E. Cowley. 2nd ed. Oxford: Clarendon, 1910.
GN(s)	geographical name(s)
HALOT	Ludwig Koehler, Walter Baumgartner, and Johan Jakob Stamm. *Hebrew and Aramaic Lexicon of the Old Testament.* Trans. and ed. M. E. J. Richardson. 5 vols. Leiden: Brill, 1994-2000.
HAR	*Hebrew Annual Review*
HKAT	Handkommentar zum Alten Testament
HO	Handbuch der Orientalistik
HR	*History of Religions*
HS	*Hebrew Studies*
HSM	Harvard Semitic Monographs
HSS	Harvard Semitic Studies
HTKAT	Herders Theologischer Kommentar zum Alten Testament
HTR	*Harvard Theological Review*
HTS	Harvard Theological Studies
HUCA	*Hebrew Union College Annual*
IAA	Israel Antiquities Authority
ICC	International Critical Commentary
IEJ	*Israel Exploration Journal*
Int	*Interpretation*
IOS	*Israel Oriental Studies*
JAAR	*Journal of the American Academy of Religion*
JANES	*Journal of the Ancient Near Eastern Society of Columbia University*
JAOS	*Journal of the American Oriental Society*
Jastrow	Marcus Jastrow. *A Dictionary of the Targumim, the Talmud Babli and Yerushalmi, and the Midrashic Literature.* New York: Judaica, 1971.
JBL	*Journal of Biblical Literature*
JBQ	*Jewish Bible Quarterly*
JCS	*Journal of Cuneiform Studies*
JHS	*Journal of Hebrew Studies*
JJS	*Journal of Jewish Studies*
JNES	*Journal of Near Eastern Studies*
JNSL	*Journal of Northwest Semitic Languages*
Joüon-Muraoka	Paul Joüon, S.J. *A Grammar of Biblical Hebrew.* Rev. Takamitsu Muraoka. 2 vols. Subsidia Biblica 14/I-II. 2nd ed. Rome: Pontificio Istituto Biblico, 2009. Cited by paragraph.
JPOS	*Journal of the Palestine Oriental Society*
JQR	*Jewish Quarterly Review*
JR	*Journal of Religion*
JSem	*Journal of Semitics*
JSOT	*Journal for the Study of the Old Testament*

JSOTSup	Journal for the Study of the Old Testament: Supplement Series
JSQ	*Jewish Studies Quarterly*
JSS	*Journal of Semitic Studies*
JTS	*Journal of Theological Studies*
K	Kethib
KAI	Herbert Donner and Wolfgang Röllig. *Kanaanäische und aramäische Inschriften*. 3rd ed. Wiesbaden: Harrassowitz, 1971-76. Cited by text number.
KAT	Kommentar zum Alten Testament
KB	Ludwig Koehler and Walter Baumgartner. *Lexicon in Veteris Testamenti libros.* 4th ed.
KTU	*The Cuneiform Alphabetic Texts from Ugarit, Ras Ibn Hani, and Other Places (KTU: 2nd enlarged ed.).* Ed. Manfried Dietrich, Oswald Loretz, and Joaquín Sanmartín. ALASP 8. Münster: Ugarit-Verlag, 1995. Texts cited by number.
Lane	E. W. Lane. *An Arabic-English Lexicon.* 8 vols. London: Williams and Norgate, 1863-1893. Repr., Beirut: Librairie du Liban, 1968.
LAPO	Littératures anciennes du Proche-Orient
LBH	Late Biblical Hebrew
LCL	Loeb Classical Library
Leš	*Lešonénu*
Leslau	Wolf Leslau. *Comparative Dictionary of Geʿez (Classical Ethiopic).* Wiesbaden: Harrassowitz, 1987.
LHB/OTS	Library of Hebrew Bible/Old Testament Studies
LXX	Septuagint
MARI	*Mari: Annales de recherches interdisciplinaires*
MB	Middle Babylonian
MIO	*Mitteilungen des Instituts für Orientforschung*
MLC	Gregorio del Olmo Lete. *Mitos y leyendas de Canaán: según la tradición de Ugarit.* Institución San Jerónimo para la Ciencia Biblica. Valencia: Institucion San Jeronimo; Madrid: Ediciones Cristiandad, 1981.
MRS	Mission de Ras Shamra
ms(s).	manuscript(s)
MT	Masoretic Text (text of the Bible in Jewish tradition)
MuE	Manfried Dietrich and Oswald Loretz. *Mythen und Epen IV.* TUAT 3. Gütersloh: Gütersloher, 1997.
Mus	*Le Muséon*
MUSJ	*Mélanges de l'Université Saint-Joseph*
NAB	New American Bible translation
NABRE	New American Bible Revised Edition
NEA	*Near Eastern Archaeology* (formerly *Biblical Archaeologist*)

NEAEHL	*The New Encyclopedia of Archaeological Excavations in the Holy Land.* Ed. Ephraim Stern. 4 vols. Jerusalem: Israel Exploration Society/Carta; New York: Simon & Schuster, 1993.
NEAEHLSup	*The New Encyclopedia of Archaeological Excavations in the Holy Land 5: Supplementary Volume.* Ed. Ephraim Stern. Jerusalem: Israel Exploration Society; Washington: Biblical Archaeology Society, 2008.
NICOT	New International Commentary on the Old Testament
NIDB	*The New Interpreter's Dictionary of the Bible.* Ed. Katharine Doob Sakenfeld et al. 5 vols. Nashville: Abingdon, 2006-2009.
NJPS	*TANAKH: The Holy Scriptures: The New JPS Translation According to the Traditional Hebrew Text.* Philadelphia: Jewish Publication Society, 1988.
NRSV	New Revised Standard Version
OB	Old Babylonian
OBO	Orbis biblicus et orientalis
OIP	Oriental Institute Publications
OLA	Orientalia lovaniensia analecta
Or	*Orientalia* (new series)
ORA	Orientalische Religionen in der Antike
OTL	Old Testament Library
OTP	*Old Testament Pseudepigrapha.* Ed. James H. Charlesworth. 2 vols. New York: Doubleday, 1983-85.
OtSt	*Oudtestamentische Studiën*
PEFQS	*Palestine Exploration Fund Quarterly Statement*
PEQ	*Palestine Exploration Quarterly*
PN(s)	personal name(s)
PRU III	Jean Nougayrol. *Le palais royal d'Ugarit.* Vol. 3. MRS 6. Paris: Imprimerie Nationale/Librairie C. Klincksieck, 1955.
PRU IV	Jean Nougayrol. *Le palais royal d'Ugarit.* Vol. 4. MRS 9. Paris: Imprimerie Nationale/Librairie C. Klincksieck, 1956.
Q	Qere
Qad	*Qadmoniot*
RA	*Revue d'assyriologe et d'archéologie orientale*
RB	*Revue biblique*
RCU	Dennis Pardee. *Ritual and Cult at Ugarit.* SBLWAW 10. Atlanta: Society of Biblical Literature, 2002.
RES	*Répertoire d'épigraphie sémitique*
RHR	*Revue de l'histoire des religions*
RINAP	Royal Inscriptions of the Neo-Assyrian Period
RS	Ras Shamra (number of object found at the site of Ras Shamra — Ugarit)

RSO	Ras Shamra — Ougarit series
RSV	Revised Standard Version
RTU	Nicolas Wyatt, *Religious Texts from Ugarit: The Words of Ilimilku and His Colleagues.* The Biblical Seminar 53. Sheffield: Sheffield Academic, 1998.
SAA	State Archives of Assyria
SANT	Studien zum Alten und Neuen Testaments
SAOC	Studies in Ancient Oriental Civilization
SBH	Standard Biblical Hebrew (Classical Biblical Hebrew)
SBLCP	Society of Biblical Literature Centennial Publications
SBLDS	Society of Biblical Literature Dissertation Series
SBLEJL	Society of Biblical Literature Early Judaism and Its Literature
SBLMS	Society of Biblical Literature Monograph Series
SBLRBS	Society of Biblical Literature Resources for Biblical Study
SBLSBS	Society of Biblical Literature Sources for Biblical Study
SBLSymS	Society of Biblical Literature Symposium Series
SBLWAW	Society of Biblical Literature Writings from the Ancient World
SBT	Studies in Biblical Theology
SBV	Standard Babylonian Version (Gilgamesh)
ScrHier	Scripta hierosolymitana
SEL	*Studi epigrafici e linguistici sul Vicino Oriente antico*
Sem	*Semitica*
SJLA	Studies in Judaism in Late Antiquity
SJOT	*Scandinavian Journal of the Old Testament*
SMEA	*Studi Micenei ed Egeo-Anatolici*
SMSR	*Studi e materiali di storia delle religioni*
SSI	John C. L. Gibson, *Textbook of Syrian Semitic Inscriptions.* 4 vols. Oxford: Clarendon, 1971-2009.
SSN	Studia semitica neerlandica
STDJ	Studies on the Texts of the Desert of Judah
TA	*Tel Aviv*
TDOT	*Theological Dictionary of the Old Testament.* Ed. G. Johannes Botterweck, Helmer Ringgren, and Heinz-Josef Fabry. Grand Rapids: Eerdmans, 1977–.
TO 1	A. Caquot, M. Sznycer, and A. Herdner. *Textes ougaritiques.* Vol. 1: *Mythes et legendes.* LAPO 7. Paris: Cerf, 1974.
TO 2	A. Caquot, J. M. de Tarragon, and J. L. Cunchillos. *Textes ougaritiques.* Vol. 2: *Textes religieux, rituels, correspondance.* LAPO 14. Paris: Cerf, 1989.
TSAJ	Texte und Studien zum antiken Judentum
TUAT	Otto Kaiser et al., eds. *Texte aus der Umwelt des Altes Testament.* Gütersloh: Gütersloher, 1984-.

TZ	*Theologisches Zeitschrift*
UBC 1	Mark S. Smith. *The Ugaritic Baal Cycle.* Vol. 1: *Introduction with Text, Translation and Commentary of KTU 1.1-1.2.* VTSup 55. Leiden: Brill, 1994.
UBC 2	Mark S. Smith and Wayne Pitard. *The Ugaritic Baal Cycle.* Vol. 2: *Introduction with Text, Translation and Commentary of KTU 1.3-1.4.* VTSup 114. Leiden: Brill, 2009.
UF	*Ugarit-Forschungen*
UG	Josef Tropper. *Ugaritische Grammatik.* AOAT 273. Münster: Ugarit-Verlag, 2000.
Ugaritica V	J. Nougayrol, E. Laroche, C. Virolleaud and C. F. A. Schaeffer. *Ugaritica 5.* MRS 16. Paris: Imprimerie Nationale /Libraire orientaliste Paul Geuthner, 1968.
UNP	*Ugaritic Narrative Poetry.* Texts and Translations by Mark S. Smith, Simon B. Parker, Edward L. Greenstein, Theodore J. Lewis, and David Marcus. Ed. Simon B. Parker. SBLWAW 9. Atlanta: Scholars, 1997.
UT	Cyrus H. Gordon. *Ugaritic Textbook.* AnOr 38. Rome: Pontifical Biblical Institute, 1965.
VT	*Vetus Testamentum*
VTSup	Vetus Testamentum Supplements
WdM	H. W. Haussig, ed. *Wörterbuch der Mythologoie.* Stuttgart: Klett, 1965-97.
Wehr	Hans Wehr. *A Dictionary of Modern Written Arabic.* Ed. J. Milton Cowan. 3rd ed. Ithaca: Spoken Language Services, 1976.
WO	*Die Welt des Orients*
WTJ	*Westminster Theological Journal*
WUNT	Wissenschaftliche Untersuchungen zum Neuen Testament
ZA	*Zeitschrift für Assyriologie und Vorderasiatische Archäeologie*
ZAH	*Zeitschrift für Althebräistik*
ZAW	*Zeitschrift für die alttestamentliche Wissenschaft*
ZDPV	*Zeitschrift des deutschen Palästina-Vereins*
1QM	*Serek ha-Milḥamah (War Scroll)* from Cave 1 at Qumran
D-stem	Verbal stem with doubled second root-letter corresponding to the Hebrew *Piel*
C-stem	Causative verbal stem (corresponding to the Hebrew *Hiphil*)
G-stem	Basic verbal stem in Semitic languages corresponding to Hebrew *Qal* stem
Gt-stem	*t*-form of the *G*-stem
N-stem	Verbal stem corresponding to the Hebrew *Niphal*

INTRODUCTION

Warriors between Poetry and Practice

1. The Subject of This Study

Traditional warrior or heroic poetry has been long recognized in the Hebrew Bible[1] and ancient Near Eastern sources,[2] not to mention Homer.[3] The poetic commemoration of heroes in what we may call "the early biblical world" is known today, thanks primarily to the Hebrew Bible and its literary forebears in the Ugaritic texts. This book constitutes the results of my efforts to understand a number of key heroic poems in Ugaritic and the Bible as well as the cultural practices, attitudes, values, and worldview that they enshrine. In addition, two poetic classics from further afield, *Gilgamesh* and the *Iliad,* are included for their notable similarities with Ugaritic and biblical warrior poetry. The project offered here builds on several strands of modern scholarship. With new data and fresh insights emerging from various quarters, it seems timely to offer an appraisal of heroic poetry and its representations of warriors.

At its core, heroic poetry sounded warriors to battle and celebrated their exploits and victories; it also lamented their defeats and named their losses.[4] Poetic heroes, the main title of this study,[5] include both divine and human figures, sometimes battling alone, at other times acting in tandem. The ideal warrior is a leader who strengthens followers. To paraphrase a third-millennium hymn praising Shamash as the leader of the Anunna-gods: "to the young men, he gave great strength."[6] These and other ideas about heroic warriors are captured by the words used for them in ancient literatures. Important terms include Greek *hērōs,* "hero" or "lord"[7] (forebear of the English word, hero); Hebrew *gibbôr,* "warrior, strong one";[8] Ugaritic *ǵzr,* "hero, warrior";[9] and Akkadian *qarrādu*, "hero, warrior."[10] These words denote physical strength and size as well as psychological values and dispositions.

The practices as well as values, attitudes, and worldviews expressed in heroic poems constitute the core elements of what the subtitle labels as "warrior culture."[11] This culture is expressed not only by texts of war, but also by its tools.[12] In anthropological terms,[13] both texts and tools represent fundamental "practices"[14] of "warrior culture." Tools and texts express and give agency to this culture.[15] Poetry about warriors not only reflects notions about heroes and war;[16] it also reinforces these ideas. These descriptive and prescriptive dimensions are important aspects of poetic commemoration, as the subtitle of this book highlights.

It is not clear that warrior practices and attitudes issued in a specific "warrior subculture"[17] within the larger societies at the time when heroic poetry was produced (at least, in the Ugaritic and Israelite contexts). In the case of ancient "warrior culture," we know rather little about the actual situation on the ground. Many studies of modern subcultures view them as nonconforming or dissenting. According to what heroic poetry represents, it was largely conforming and supportive of the societal structure. Some Levantine contexts specify their relationships to monarchic or tribal structures, not to mention designations for warriors (e.g., the much-discussed *maryannu*, "chariot warrior");[18] these, too, might have conditioned the nature of warfare and warrior poetry in some contexts. At ancient Ugarit, the important social context for texts about warriors was the monarchy,[19] while for early Israel, the critical milieu was tribal and early royal leadership.

The difference between the actual situation for ancient warriors and what heroic poems say about them constitutes a major issue for this study, a question to which we will return at a number of points. When I use the expression "warrior culture" in this book, it is in the first moment what is commemorated in its poetic representations. Heroic poetry constitutes a literary representation of "warrior culture" (it involves, in that sense, "literary culture"). Heroic poetry commemorates a represented past that allows its audiences to participate in it.[20] What is represented in this literary evidence is clearly not fully representative of warfare. Several topics of war receive little or no treatment in heroic poetry, and in many warrior texts, no mention at all: for example, torture and the mutilation of genitals,[21] displaced populations, and psychological trauma to combatants[22] among the defeated and victors alike.[23] Rape and enslavement are mentioned, but little narrated.[24] Omissions of these sorts arguably show one of warrior poetry's purposes, namely to divert attention from war's atrocities and to valorize it, even to "prettify" it. Although the terrible cost of war may be in view in a poem such as the *Iliad,* heroic poetry nonetheless makes warriors and their conflicts appear poignant and attractive.[25] It may mask the horror of warfare behavior relative to routine life.[26]

What ancient warrior poetry perhaps most fundamentally represented about "warrior culture" was its crossing of routine boundaries.[27] War and warriors in this poetry often entailed an inversion of the customary practices and ideas of life, and the cultural expressions of warrior culture regularly inverted the paradigms of routine existence.[28] I would mention only three brief illustrations of this point. First, violence was prized in battle, but shunned in normal life. Second, the brotherhood of warriors substituted for one's own kin, even to the point of using love language associated with the relationship of men and women. Third, the gender-marked roles of human male warriors were often paralleled on the divine level by warrior goddesses. These sorts of inversions are paradigmatic for warrior culture as represented in heroic poetry.

2. The Scope of This Study

This study proceeds in four parts. Part I offers preliminary considerations of matters of evidence and method surrounding the study of warrior culture and its commemorative poetry. Part II offers a broad first look at warrior culture in comparing and contrasting three great warrior pairs known from Mesopotamia (Gilgamesh and Enkidu), Greece (Achilles and Patroklos), and Israel (David and Jonathan). This part serves to introduce some of the main themes studied in considerable depth in the warrior texts of Ugarit examined in Part III, and in the early heroic poetry in the biblical texts addressed in Part IV. I would like to explain these parts in detail.

Part I, Chapter One, describes the contours for the landscape of this study. Three matters are fundamental for this study. First, it is important to signal the basic core of warrior activities and their cultural associations.[29] Second, it seems that before launching into an intense study of heroic literature, it would be worth trying to offer some appreciation of the material realities witnessing to warfare and its related activity, hunting. This means looking at archaeological evidence and iconography. Third, this topic requires some consideration of what is in some ways the most difficult aspect of this study, namely the interplay between the poetic commemoration of warrior life and the possible social or cultural realities behind it and informing it. The focus here will fall on the problems of studying Iron I Israel.

Part II, consisting of Chapters Two and Three, takes up the literary study of "poetic heroes" from a broad, comparative perspective. This entails the study of three heroic pairs: Achilles and Patroklos in the *Iliad;* David and Jonathan in the Hebrew Bible; and Gilgamesh and Enkidu in the story of Gilgamesh. Part II is dedicated to looking at these three pairs in tandem, as there are many lines of connection between them. Even if there is little direct literary influence between the three pairs of heroes,[30] their shared literary and cultural features may suggest how a comparative, literary approach may advance our understanding.[31] The basic themes involving these three pairs are explored in Chapter Two. In addition, it seems important to locate these heroic pairs within the larger context of their relationships not only with goddesses and human women (a task admirably carried out by a number of scholars, especially Susan Ackerman), but also to recognize the place of the hero's major oppositional figure in these narratives: Ishtar for Gilgamesh; Agamemnon for Achilles; and Saul for David. Sexual issues have dominated discussion of the story of Gilgamesh, but it has also affected the understanding of David and Jonathan. These are the subjects of Chapter Three.

Part II builds on a considerable body of prior research. Thankfully, serious work comparing David and Jonathan with Gilgamesh and Enkidu has been undertaken over the past decade. Here I have in mind studies especially by Susan Ackerman, Thomas Römer and Loyse Bonjour, and Jean-Fabrice Nardelli.[32] At the same time, I feel it necessary to add Achilles and Patroklos to this discussion, as their story in the *Iliad* provides further parallels as well as instructive differences. To be clear, Part II does not provide an examination of the "warrior culture," as represented specifically in either *Gilgamesh* or the *Iliad.* (These would be book projects in themselves, as is evident by the work on Homeric "status warriors" by Hans van Wees.)[33] At this point, we may note some contrasts among these texts. First, warrior violence as well as wealth and gift exchange play major roles in the *Iliad,*[34] but figure considerably less in the other traditions. Second, status and honor play a considerably greater role in Homer than in Ugaritic poetry. There is no such representation of the clash over status as such between human warriors in the known Ugaritic corpus. The story of Gilgamesh as well as the biblical narrative about David, Saul, and Jonathan arguably stand closer to Homer in their concern for status. However, even on this score, a contrast may be noted: the referencing of status is considerably less conspicuous in the biblical narrative about David, Saul, and Jonathan and in the story of Gilgamesh, which presume their superiority over other human males; the *Iliad* dramatizes the point over and over again in its narrative. Third, the story of Gilgamesh also stands apart as the adventures of two heroes rather than combat. The journeys of Gilgamesh and Enkidu likewise demarcate their story from the others. Fourth, sexual activity and expression are much more common in the Gilgamesh story compared with the others, as discussed in Part II. The survey in Part II offers broad scope for the themes discussed in a rather detailed way in Part III in the Ugaritic texts.

Part III turns to what the Ugaritic literary texts indicate about activities and ideas associated with warriors: hunting and feasting, music and song; honor and intimacy, attraction and intensity; and of course, military victory as well as loss, life and death. Again, scholars have noted many of these points. At the same time, it seems that the various representations of warrior activities and themes in Ugaritic poetry have not been studied sufficiently in tandem with the poems' production and transmission as warrior song. With the focus often falling on biblical texts,[35] there has not been sufficient analysis of the Ugaritic poems that offer some of the best background for the biblical material. The Ugaritic poems' ideas about warriors, the manner of their representation and their cultural enshrinement in poetic form constitute a constellation of interrelated themes deserving greater attention in the context of a broader study.

The necessity of reading biblical and Ugaritic warrior poetry together particularly struck me, as I noted many words and expressions that occur in both biblical warrior poetry and the Ugaritic narrative poems of Aqhat and the Baal Cycle. What has emerged with particular poignancy for me in Chapter Four on Aqhat is the importance, arguably even the centrality, of this story's warrior themes. For this reason, I have devoted considerable attention to this narrative. Aqhat is not simply a family story or even a royal story; it is a narrative about a father, his son, and his daughter, three human warriors forever altered by the son's encounter with yet another warrior, the goddess Anat. The representation of warrior themes in this text, it now seems to me, is key to understanding this narrative poem. The story of Aqhat is concerned with warriors: their social success is represented by Danil; their failure is conveyed by Aqhat's inability to reach maturity as a warrior; and their potentially devastating effects are expressed by the ritual responses of the father and the revenge sought by the sister. (We might even say that the poem implies a certain view of warriors, namely that combatants that endure conflict or suffer losses together are like family.) This consideration of the poem's warrior features, as far as I know, has played an insufficient role in the literary criticism devoted to Aqhat.[36] The reading of Aqhat that this perspective provides needs to be explicated in some detail, and it deserves to be included with a consideration of warrior poetry in the larger context of early Israel, or what we may call "the early biblical world." Indeed, given its many lexical and thematic links to biblical warrior poetry, the story of Aqhat is particularly important for the study of warriors in early Hebrew poetry.

This approach to the poem of Aqhat also holds implications for reading the so-called Ugaritic "Rephaim texts," discussed in Chapter Five. These are the poems about the dead heroes known in Ugaritic *rp'um/rp'im*. These texts include a mention of Aqhat's father, Danil. As a result, many scholars once believed that they constituted a sequel to the story of Aqhat. While few hold this view today, the Rephaim texts' commemoration of dead warriors does fit the warrior reading of Aqhat that I am suggesting. The Rephaim texts may not represent a narrative sequel to Aqhat, but we may regard them as a sort of thematic sequel: if the story of Aqhat is concerned with warriors in life, then the Rephaim texts offer a representation of the postmortem destiny of warriors. It is in this thematic sense that Aqhat and the Rephaim texts go together.

Divine warriors are also in abundance in the Ugaritic texts. While the goddess Anat plays a major role in the story of Aqhat, her representation in the Baal Cycle is no less noteworthy, as is Baal's. For this reason, Chapter Six is devoted to divine warriors in the Baal Cycle. This text provides insight into not only Baal and Anat, but also the gods Yamm, Mot, and ʿAthtar; these serve ultimately as foils to Baal in this text. The representation of divine warriors in the Baal Cycle is hardly news — perhaps apart from the particular attention to gender that is paid in this study to Baal's victory feast (in the opening column of the third tablet, KTU 1.3 I). Another divine warrior making a passing appearance in the Baal Cycle is the goddess ʿAthtart (attested in the Bible as ʿAshtoreth and in the plural form as ʿAshtarot, and better known in classical sources as Astarte). There is new material for the goddess ʿAthtart, especially from Emar and to a lesser extent from Ugarit. Thus, Chapter Seven is devoted to her. All in all, the Ugaritic texts show a tradition of narrative poetry largely devoted to divine and human conflict, as well as a commemoration of the heroes in life and death. All the major literary cycles presently known from Ugarit (including the story of King Kirta, which is not addressed in this study) revolve around warriors, a concern of particular interest to the monarchy.[37] In all, the material investigated in Part III provides a rich background for the early biblical poems studied in Part IV. Indeed, the Ugaritic texts furnish not simply parallels for the biblical texts, but a broader backdrop for the literary world of early Israelite warrior poetry.

Part IV turns to warrior literature in early Israel (Iron I down to the tenth or ninth century). I want to be clear that in addressing biblical material, this study focuses on early heroic poetry and not on heroic prose. The prose traditions enshrined especially in the stories in the books of Judges, Samuel, and Kings (not to mention even later biblical works) are not the subjects of this work. Indeed, several scholars such as Stanley Isser, Susan Niditch, Gregory Mobley, and Jacob L. Wright have been engaged in telling this side of the biblical story.[38] Isser focuses on Davidic "heroic" traditions, Niditch provides a broad anthropological perspective on warfare in ancient Israel, Mobley focuses on figures in the prose stories of Judges, and Wright covers a massive amount of ground for the prose traditions of the Iron II period (ca. 1000-586) and later. Presently there is no study that examines in detail the earlier heroic poetry in Israelite literature (Iron I, ca. 1200-1000, and down through the tenth century)[39] and situates it in its cultural context. While these authors have nicely covered the heroic prose of ancient Israel, there still seems to be a need for a study devoted specifically to the older heroic poetry of Israel.

To be sure, Niditch has stressed the problem of making sharp distinctions between the prose and poetic heroic traditions. Still some benefit may come from separate analyses of the poetic material. The reception of the poetic heroic traditions in their larger prose contexts arguably comes into sharper relief when the poetry and prose are handled separately. Treating early biblical poetry separately also facilitates comparison with the Ugaritic poetic texts studied in Part III, which share many specific literary features and references pointing to a larger, shared literary tradition. We may sense literary and even cultural commonality between the Ugaritic texts and the older biblical literature on the topic of warfare and warriors. As literary pieces and cultural artifacts, early Hebrew heroic poetry (and even some of the older prose narratives) seems to stand closer to the Ugaritic texts than to much of later biblical prose literature in the Hebrew Bible. Indeed, it has not been noted sufficiently that a major part of the older poetry from early Israel is devoted to war and warriors. In focusing on the older poetry, it would appear that textual production in early Israel included warfare and warriors in a significant way.

This is a central point about early Israelite literature that has often not been addressed in the scholarly discussion. It is also critical for trying to understand early Israel itself. In recent years, the premonarchic period has largely fallen out of the discussion of Israelite textual production, as exemplified by recent introductions to biblical literature. For example, what Alexander Rofé calls "the epic poetry" receives only brief notices in his monumental work, *Introduction to the Literature of the Hebrew Bible*.[40] The early period is likewise the only phase of Israelite textual production not addressed by the detailed and otherwise comprehensive survey of David M. Carr, *The Formation of the Hebrew Bible: A New Reconstruction.*[41] Carr offers textual or literary "profiles"[42] for different periods in Israel's history, with the exception of the premonarchic period.[43] For Carr,[44] the early monarchic period is as far as scholars can go. The consideration of the earliest Israelite literature is also missing from Konrad Schmid's period-by-period survey of biblical literature, *The Old Testament: A Literary History.*[45] In these scholarly works, it is as if Israelite literature in this period never existed. At the moment, this is the state of the question, which I seek to reopen in Part Four.

The current — and I would add well-placed — skepticism about the early dating of biblical texts involves the so-called "old poetry." Appeals about "old poetry" dating to the Iron I (ca. 1200-1000) and Iron IIA (ca. 1000-925), as made in the 1950s and 1960s (for example, by Frank Moore Cross and David Noel Freedman),[46] are rarely heard in biblical scholarship today. Such claims have come to be viewed as overconfident, in part because they were based on debatable criteria, as even Cross came to acknowledge.[47] Another objection involved the exaggerated claims made for old poetry as a source or series of sources for reconstructing early Israelite history, a problem perhaps most prominently on display in Johannes C. de Moor's detailed 1990 study, *The Rise of Yahwism.*[48] Research on the subject from David Noel Freedman[49] was likewise not immune from the temptation to reconstruct early Israelite history based on old poetry. Between the problem of dating "old poetry" and its appropriateness as source material for reconstructing early Israelite history, it came to be viewed as problematic material. Whether the rejection of the high dating of "old poetry" today is justified in all instances requires close examination, which is attempted in Part Four of this study, in particular in Chapters Eight through Ten. It is part of my argument that heroic poetry represents a significant component in the literary profile of early Israelite textual production beginning in the premonarchic period (Iron I). Chapter Eight introduces the problems involved in trying to date Judges 5, the old poem examined further for its diachronic development and formation in Chapter Nine. Chapter Ten offers an analysis of the development of 2 Sam. 1:19-27. The two poems, especially in their early parts (or at least the traditions lying behind them), offer insight into the world of Israel's earliest literature, which I would date from the Iron I down through the tenth century (ca. 1200-900).

For the specimens of early Israelite heroic poetry treated in Chapters Eight through Ten, the Ugaritic texts furnish some valuable backdrop. At present, there is little available scholarship comparing heroic poetry in the

Ugaritic texts and the Hebrew Bible.[50] In the comparative study of these poetic corpora, this omission may be due to a focus on their formal features. Yet it is evident to many scholars who work on both Ugaritic and biblical texts that the two corpora belong to a shared or overlapping tradition.[51] At the same time, this is not the only important point in this comparison between the Ugaritic texts and the Hebrew Bible's early literature.[52] Indeed, the comparison also points to an important contrast: the biblical warrior poems do not show the same sort of length and scale as their Ugaritic counterparts.[53] In this respect, the biblical poems are hardly "epic" by comparison. While epic motifs and themes are spread broadly across the Bible's poetry and prose, the genre of epic, narrative poetry is not represented in the extant literature of ancient Israel. At best, one might suggest that such epic is adapted in shorter heroic poems, but this remains a major assumption, one that is not accepted in this study. Instead, the early poems examined in Chapters Eight through Ten seem to echo and adapt an old tradition of heroic poetry, which later took little hold as a genre in ancient Israel after the tenth century.[54]

As a related matter, the investigation of heroic poetry involves gender roles. The inclusion of men as warriors and the exclusion of women often mark warrior poetry. In addition, women play a further role in the support structures of battle.[55] Finally, both women and men played significant roles in the oral production and transmission of heroic poetry. Like other ancient literature studied in this work, several verses within Judges 5 and 2 Samuel 1 reveal Israelite constructions of masculinity and femininity as understood for early Israel,[56] but they also illustrate the gendered roles of men and women in the very performance of warrior song.[57]

In Chapter Eleven, the discussion shifts to an exploration of what can be reasonably said about the production of Israelite heroic poetry. There are serious, ongoing theoretical challenges to reconstructing the past, especially for a period as little known as 1200-900 B.C.E.[58] Such an enterprise might be thought to be doomed from the outset in view of "the postmodern challenge,"[59] involving "the denial that historical writing refers to an actual historical past."[60] I do not doubt that primary sources and modern scholarship are fraught with interpretational difficulties. However, the view that primary evidence (material culture, inscriptions, and the specimens of heroic poetry), as studied in this work, does not witness in some way (or ways) to an actual past remains undemonstrated. This is an *a priori* assumption, a philosophical stance rather than the results of analysis.[61]

As discussed in Chapter Eleven, both inscriptions and early heroic poetry point to textual production in Iron I and the tenth century. As noted in

Chapter One, this work stands in a long line of efforts to study early Israel (or, in my case, one aspect of this culture), based on material culture, inscriptions, and the surviving heroic poetry. This sort of effort has also been made in Homeric studies, which at the same time offer a salutary cautionary note. Here I would mention the formulation of the problem, as it applies to the *Iliad* and the *Odyssey* for Hans van Wees: ". . . the epics are a peculiar source, and . . . any reconstruction based on epic material is precarious. Ancient historians thus cannot use the epics as they would any other sources, nor can they easily afford to leave them to one side. They have little choice but to confront the problems and look for acceptable ways of squeezing out of the poems what information they can. One purpose of this book is to do just that."[62] Heroic poetry in early Israel is no less difficult, and ancient historians of this material can neither use them at face value nor afford to discard them. To some extent, I, too, will try to work with the poems to see what can be reasonably used for understanding Israel's early heroic poetry and the warrior culture that it represents.

At the same time, what may be "squeezed out" is not necessarily nearly as much as some earlier commentators assayed. In Chapter Eleven, I will not be building any sort of detailed history around particular persons or events mentioned in the poetic sources,[63] what the *Annales* historian Fernand Braudel (following François Simiand) called "l'histoire événementielle."[64] Instead, heroic poetry as well as inscriptions and other material culture from early Israel can be ascertained for longer-term conditions of life (Braudel's "conjonctures"),[65] and in particular for what I am calling in this book its "warrior culture." The work of *Annales* historians is appealing for the study of the data pertaining to ancient Israel because it is capable of including evidence of material culture with textual data. Moreover, while this study is driven by data, its emphasis falls on the variety of types of data, and certainly not on any sort of claim to gaining statistical representativeness. In addition, the approach combines the study of broad conditions of life with a sense of how these are remembered — and forgotten — in the written sources. The *Annales* approach addresses the memory of experience of the past and moves toward human experiences of broader conditions.[66] In this respect, it is compatible with, and is also advanced by, German "historical social science" (with its study of masses of records and other sources), as modified by a social historian such as Dorothee Wierling[67] and by other social historians of "everyday life" (with its emphasis on the conditions of life as experienced).[68]

It is true that for ancient Israel we have neither masses of written records nor much biographical or autobiographical material (cf. the Lachish letters in the first person voice of officials). Ancient literature hardly offers "the history of everyday life,"[69] as it was experienced in its particulars by early Israelites, but some effort at ascertaining some aspects of their general cultural conditions does seem feasible.[70] To alleviate the difficulty, one might engage in exercises of historical imagination[71] or "virtual history."[72] However, these are not the approaches taken in this work. Instead, the effort is cultural in orientation, as I discuss in Chapter One. There I outline the elements of "warrior culture" that may be gleaned broadly from early Israelite sources. In addition, an effort is made in Chapters Nine and Ten at exploring "the poetics of culture"[73] and the "warrior politics"[74] in the two heroic poems studied in Chapters Eight through Ten.

Scholarly attention has not been paid to one aspect of the cultural history of "old poetry," namely the fact that a considerable number of so-called early Hebrew poems are devoted particularly to warfare and warriors. What also seems to be lacking in the discussion is not just *that* warfare and warriors constitute an important topic of this poetry, but also *how* postbattle practices provide an arena of activity that inspired the composition of several of these relatively early poems. In other words, postbattle practices played a significant role in generating a significant portion of textual production in early Israel. In turn, these poems offer insights into the early culture of Israel that gave rise to these textual artifacts. Chapter Eleven focuses on these matters. It also takes a look at the settings represented for the production and performance of heroic poetry.

The final chapter of this study, Chapter Twelve, offers an epilogue to the story of heroic poetry after the tenth century. Warrior poetry, as far as we can tell from the biblical record, was displaced from Israel's centers of textual production. Warrior poems were transmitted and added to, but it would seem that after the tenth century new heroic poems were not being created — or at least these new ones were not preserved — within the social setting that yielded these old warrior poems ca. 1200-900 B.C.E. Instead, the later period seems to show imitations of these older poems or their parts,[75] or incorporations of their motifs[76] in monarchic and later contexts.[77] In addition, prose legend emerged, for example in the David and Goliath story. In short, warrior poetry of the older tradition seems to be displaced among Israel's text-producers. On this score, Ugarit offers an interesting counterpoint: where the Ugaritic monarchy was a primary patron of this warrior literature, in ancient Israel it was early Israel's pre- or nonmonarchic culture that supported the production of early heroic poetry. Unlike the royal patronage for Ugaritic warrior literature, there is little evidence for the support for warrior poetry in the monarchic circles of ancient Israel and Judah after the tenth century.

Chapter Twelve also examines what seem to be a number of developments concomitant with the evident social displacement of the production of warrior poetry. The warrior goddesses seem to fade in Israel, just as the national god comes into particular prominence. Where the warrior goddesses play a clear role in the literature of Ugarit, by contrast the warrior, the national god of Israel, seems to step into their roles. An analogous contrast can be seen also in how the Rephaim are regarded in the Ugaritic and Israelite literary traditions. The Rephaim are a treasured part of the Ugaritic monarchy's cultural identity of its ancient past; indeed, the Ugaritic dynasty understands the Rephaim as the ancient beginnings of its own lineage. By contrast, the biblical record shows a "disidentification" with the traditions of the Rephaim. The biblical traditions about the Rephaim are not only "fractured" into different aspects (such as deceased figures and ancient giants) by comparison to what we see in the Ugaritic texts. In biblical material, the Rephaim are represented as entirely "other," decidedly not Israelite; they are not even "pre-Israelite." It is quite possible that the cultural "disidentification" of which I am speaking was an inner Israelite development, and hardly an older or general Israelite view. The developments involving the demise of warrior poetry, traditional goddesses, and the Rephaim may be interrelated. Still, it is hard to know, and we leave this issue for the final chapter of our story. At this point, we may turn to Part I, with its presentation of basic information about "warrior culture," as well as its consideration of methodological concerns that inform Parts II-IV.

PART I

The Literary Commemoration of Warriors and Warrior Culture

CHAPTER ONE

Considerations of Evidence and Method

This introductory chapter begins with basic information about battle practices and values enshrined in the heroic poetry of ancient Ugarit and early Israel.[1] The discussion then turns to archaeological and iconographical evidence relevant to warrior practices. Finally, this chapter addresses issues of literary and historical method, especially as they bear on early Israel. Before entering into the basic description of the central topics of warrior practice, let me note one point: heroic poetry does not focus much on the nuts and bolts of warfare itself,[2] such as its strategies and methods, travel and provisioning, or the political goals and results of warfare.[3] Since heroic poetry does not usually concentrate on these matters, this study follows suit. Instead, this work focuses on warrior practices before and after battle as well as the attitudes and values emphasized in heroic poetry. With this clarification in mind, we may begin.

1. The Central Topics of Warrior Poetry: Pre- and Postbattle Practices and the Values of Warriors in Early Biblical Literature

Practices

The practices that we see in older warrior poetry of the Bible[4] occur in four phases surrounding battle: formation of warriors through the traditional practice of hunting; prebattle preparations; postbattle practices and ritual; and postbattle commemoration.[5] Some basic older sources are provided below for the components of the four phases of prebattle and postbattle acts. This brief listing of major pre- and postbattle phenomena also serves to highlight the major motifs that this work addresses in different chapters.

Before entering into this summary listing, let me make a brief methodological comment about the procedure here. For each feature, an older source (either Ugaritic or old biblical poetry down into the tenth century[6] or both) is provided in order to indicate a practice for the Iron I (ca. 1200-1000)–tenth century (1000-900). An effort is also made at including extra-biblical material that dates to this period; in this matter, there is a further complication of knowing what evidence counts as Israelite or not.[7] In some instances, the early evidence may be further complemented by later biblical sources or other material (e.g., Neo-Assyrian annals), but such later texts are mentioned for illustrative purposes only and do not serve as the basis for Israelite evidence in the Iron I–tenth century. Citation in this manner is designed to indicate that these warrior practices belong to older Ugaritic or biblical literature (even when they perdure in later periods). To be clear, this discussion does not presuppose that later texts in themselves can be used to establish an early practice for ancient Israel.[8]

The first phase in prebattle practices involves warrior training (**lmd*, cf. Song 3:8;[9] Isa. 2:4 = Mic. 4:3).[10] This role is attributed to the patron deity of warriors. For example, Anat is presented as Aqhat's "teacher" or "trainer" for the hunt (*ʾalmdk*, KTU 1.18 I 29).[11] Yahweh is likewise a divine "trainer" in warfare (*mĕlammēd*, 2 Sam. 22/Ps. 18:35,[12] the apparent inspiration for Ps. 144:1; cf. Judg. 3:2).[13] Hunting may play a role in the early development of skills and thus in the formation of prospective warriors (Aqhat, in KTU 1.17 II and 1.18 I).[14] Hunting activity more broadly serves to acculturate would-be warriors to bloodshed.[15] The passage from youth into manhood is a signal transition for the emergence of a warrior.[16] Hunting may be a practice of a warrior from his youth.[17] Hunting,[18] not to mention auxiliary roles in battle (such as "arms bearer"),[19] contributed toward the training of warriors. Hunting also serves as a literary image for warfare.[20] It is within the context of training for the hunt and warfare that we might locate the literary theme of the divine gift of the bow made to the father of Aqhat, who in turn gives it to his son for hunting (KTU 1.17 V; cf. *Iliad* 15:441).[21] Some males would prosper as warriors (Danʾil); other would-be warriors would not (Aqhat).

Training in weapons is an important aspect of warrior preparation. Thanks to training with bows (Aqhat, in KTU 1.17 V-VI),[22] warriors enjoy facility in weaponry (Gen. 49:24; 1 Sam. 2:4; 2 Sam. 1:22).[23] They may also display capability with spears (the Baal Cycle, KTU 1.6 I 51;[24] 2 Sam. 23:8; cf. 1 Sam. 18:11; 20:33; 2 Sam. 23:18; Song 3:8).[25] Ability with the short sword (sometimes, dagger)[26] is likewise developed; indeed, it may serve as a way to name warriors (**šlp ḥrb*, in Judg. 20:2, 15, 17, 25, 35, 46) and their training (Song 3:8). Weapons not only mark hunter-warriors; they are also extensions of their bodies, in other words, "those objects that are in closest contact with their owners" which "become, as it were, 'extra-somatic body parts.'"[27] For warriors, weapons are the "extra-somatic" markers of their identity. In addition, the ideal warrior excels in running (the Baal Cycle, KTU 1.6 I 52;[28] Ps. 19:5; Job 16:14; cf. 2 Sam. 15:1; 2 Sam. 22:34/Ps. 18:34[33]; 1 Kgs. 1:5; Jer. 23:10),[29] and in scaling walls (2 Sam. 22:30/Ps. 18:30[29]). Not only physical capacity, but also physical strength is a core aspect for the *gibbôr*.[30] The physical may be emphasized further by reference to a warrior's size (see KTU 1.6 I 56-62; cf. 1 Sam. 10:23-24).[31]

The second major group of warrior practices involves prebattle behaviors. These include the preparation of weapons,[32] notably sharpening swords (as suggested by the imagery for divinities in the Baal Cycle, in KTU 1.2 I 33[33] and Deut. 32:41; see also Ezek. 21:9, 11; Pss. 7:12; 64:3); stringing bows (Ps. 7:12);[34] sharpening arrows (Isa. 5:28; Ps. 45:5); and oiling shields (2 Sam. 1:21; Isa. 21:5).[35] Warrior clothing and weapons are donned (see Pughat in KTU 1.19 IV and Deut. 22:5).[36] Before battle, vows may be voiced (Kirta, KTU 1.14 IV 34-43; cf. Judg. 11:30; Ps. 76:11-12),[37] blessings offered to the deity (Kuntillet ʿAjrud plaster inscription;[38] see also Judg. 5:2, 9), divine oracles taken via intermediaries (Num. 24:15-19;[39] Judg.4:9, 21 [?]; Deut. 33:20),[40] and the battle cry raised (see Num. 23:21; cf. Exod. 32:17).[41] Warriors may refrain from cutting hair (Judg. 5:2; cf. KTU 1.4 VII 53-56), thus marking their war activity as a departure from and thus an inversion of routine life.[42] Fitting into this sort of profile for prebattle preparation, but known only from later passages, is consecration (**qdš*) of personnel and their vessels (see Josh. 3:5; 1 Sam. 21:6; Jer. 6:4; Mic. 3:5; Joel 3:9; cf. Deut. 23:9-14),[43] in contrast to nonsacred march (see *derek ḥōl* in 1 Sam. 21:5[6]). There may be other practices involved at this stage, but they are not enshrined in early Israelite poetry.[44] In short, these represent ritual behaviors that demarcate warfare from routine life.

The third phase, which is often referenced in warrior poetry, consists of postbattle rituals. Postbattle washing involves warriors cleaning themselves with water (KTU 1.3 II 38-40) and also their weapons (cf. washing weapons in Lugal-e[45] and the weapons sullied in 2 Sam. 1:21). Some passages suggest the picture of warriors washing in the blood of the vanquished enemies (Anat in KTU 1.3 II 34-35, and Yahweh's warriors in Ps. 68:23; cf. the metaphorical use of the imagery in Ps. 58:10). Biblical representations also present the victor that "feeds on the flesh" of captives (Deut. 32:42) and "drinks the blood of the slain" (Num. 23:24; cf. Gen. 49:11?).[46] While these seem to be images for complete victory[47] (apparently assumed by Anat's postbattle treatment of her captives at her house in KTU 1.3 II 17-30),[48] it has been suggested that such postbattle behaviors are not to be dismissed as fantasy.[49] For the victors, body-parts served as trophies for purposes of display (see KTU 1.3 II 11-13; cf. Josh. 10:26-27; 1 Samuel 17:54; 31:8-13 with 1 Chr. 10:10; and 2 Sam. 4:12).[50]

Weapons of war collected from the defeated may become dedicatory objects and trophies given to temples, for example the dedication of the shield of metal in KTU 1.123.2.[51] While neither Ugaritic literary texts nor early Israelite poetry mentions this practice, early ancient Near Eastern texts[52] would suggest that it is traditional. Similarly, biblical passages attest to the practice. Saul's armor is said to have been placed in the temple of Ashtarot (1 Sam. 31:10), and Goliath's sword is said to have been given by David to the priests at Nob (1 Sam. 22:10). In this connection, we may note the axe found in a temple at Tell Qasile; it is thought to have been an offering.[53] As Abraham Malamat noted,[54] the deposition of weapons in a temple served the purpose of communal memory of martial exploits. Writing of 1 Sam. 31:10, Jordi Vidal comments similarly: "Those weapons were originally ordinary weapons that became renowned for historical reasons (they reminded the Philistines of their victory over the Israelites at Mount Gilboa). Thus the weapons became a suitable votive offering, not for their material value, but for their historical associations, as well as functioning as a war memorial."[55]

The counterpart to dividing the spoils of war or depositing enemy weapons as trophies for display is the destruction of enemy property, specifically in the form of Ugaritic **ḫrm*/BH *ḥērem* (Anat in KTU 1.13.3-7; cf. 1.3 II for Anat as well as biblical instances of this type of warfare). As an aside, it might be suggested that destruction of humans after warfare corresponds to sacrifice of humans within the context of warfare: both represent efforts to meet the demands of the warfare situation as perceived of the deities that receive both sets of offerings. Child sacrifice as known from 2 Kings 3 and Philo of Byblos entails an extreme measure to appease deities in warfare, while postwarfare *ḥerem* is to offer proper thanks to deities for their help in warfare (see also the postbattle context of Judges 11; cf. Genesis 22 and Mic. 6:7).[56] In sum, the two sets of war trophies, body-parts as well as their weapons, serve to evoke the defeated warriors as well as what their bodies wield in battle. In this postbattle practice, the body and weaponry put on display "re-perform" the defeat and death of the opponents.

For the defeated, it was important to avoid the desecration of slain bodies of their comrades by providing proper burial when possible (Anat's burial of Baal with offerings in KTU 1.6 I 8-31; 1 Sam. 17:44, 46; and the archaeological evidence, which I will mention below). Failure to do so would leave corpses vulnerable to destruction by animals (Mot's corpse in KTU 1.6 II 35-37, left for the birds; cf. 1 Sam. 17:44, 46),[57] or to desecration by an enemy (Anat's treatment of Mot in 1.6 II 33-35; Achilles' treatment of Hector's corpse in *Iliad* 23:395f.; cf. 1 Sam. 31:8-13).[58]

In cases of victory, the postbattle acts of cleaning would mark a transition to celebration rituals. The most dramatic postbattle practices may be war song and dance in the battle camp.[59] Celebration with food and wine[60] as well as song may be the occasion for marking the kingship of a battle leader, for example, Baal feasting in the Baal Cycle (KTU 1.3 I).[61] As in this case, celebration after battle may involve the recognition of a male leader as being fit for kingship. For this point, the cases of Saul and David[62] come to mind. The victory feast may entail excessive drinking (KTU 1.3 I),[63] even to the point to falling into a drunken stupor (cf. Ps. 78:65, "like a warrior shaking off wine," NJPS; cf. Gen. 49:12 and Jer. 23:9). The division of persons and goods taken in battle was also a matter of celebration. Prisoner soldiers in the aftermath of battle are depicted on the Megiddo ivory (dated to the Late Bronze Age or early Iron I).[64] This piece shows a procession of feasting and music along with captives presented before a seated figure, presumably a king; they are tied up and naked, a sign of their shaming. The capture of civilian women (Judg. 5:30; cf. 1 Sam. 30:2-3) is likewise a trope of victory, like spoils of war more broadly (Gen. 49:27).[65]

In cases of defeat, lament following battle would ensue, performed by family members (the laments of El and Anat over Baal, in 1.5 VI 11-25 and 1.5 VI 31–1.6 I 6-8), by other warriors (the lament over Saul and Jonathan in 2 Sam. 1:19-25),[66] and by weeping women (cf. Anat over Aqhat in 1.18 IV 39; 2 Sam. 1:24; see also *Iliad* 19:287-300).[67] Thomas M. Greene emphasizes the community formed by the performance of laments in epic literature: "In the common field of performance, . . . the grief of the poet merges with the performer's, and the character's, and the audience's."[68] Viewed in light of Green's observations, postbattle laments may be understood as a ritualized behavior that serves "to create a community of shared mourners."[69] As 2 Sam. 1:20 and 24 suggest, women play a central role in this community-building activity.

In cases of victory, women welcome men home from battle and celebrate their victory (1 Sam. 18:6-7; 2 Sam. 1:20; 6:20; cf. Exod. 15:20-21; Judg. 11:34).[70] It is also a role of women to spread the good news of triumph in battle (see Ps. 68:11-12 and the image of Zion in Isa. 40:9-10; cf. 2 Sam. 1:20).[71] A good deal of heroic poetry in early Israel is arguably to be situated in the context of oral women's song.[72] A victory parade might also ensue (see Ps. 68:24-25; cf. *ANEP*, #305 and #332). These traditional elements of postbattle practice can be found in older iconography.[73]

Fourth and finally, postbattle warrior song involves later commemoration of warriors. Examples are seen in the song of Achilles in *Iliad* IX[74] and Judges 5.[75] These texts present song about warriors after battle and away from the battlefield. This may be the situation sometimes for the song and lamentation for leaders at their burials (see 2 Sam. 3:32-34). Another form of postbattle commemoration involves postmortem recollection of great leaders, such as Deborah and David.[76] The recollection of leaders known as the Rephaim seems to involve different forms of commemoration in Ugaritic and the Bible.[77]

The cumulative experience would eventually produce warriors, with some given names (or nicknames) that would reflect their military reputation.[78] Some instances of this practice involve common nouns used as monikers. Examples might include the two Israelite heroes of Judges 4–5. The word Baraq ("Lightning") is a common figure of warfare.[79] Given his connection to Deborah ("Bee"), her name is perhaps to be understood in these terms as well.[80] The Midianite leaders, Zeeb ("Wolf") and Oreb ("Raven"), likewise have common nouns for their names (Judg. 7:25; 8:3), potentially understood as terms for warfare and scavenging.[81] The name of Nahash ("Serpent") the Ammonite king may fall into this category (1 Sam. 11:1-2; 12:12).[82] It is tempting to understand other names in this light, such as Gideon in Judges 6-8 (**gdʿ*, "to cut down") or Labayu of Shechem in the Amarna letters ("Lion").[83] These names may be largely legendary elements of folkloric tales. Even if the names were fictional, their literary usage may reflect a cultural practice of giving martial nicknames to warriors. Such emblematic names, fictional or not, may denote the military success of leaders.

Values and Attitudes

Warrior practices are informed by a constellation of values and attitudes. First, a heightened sense of honor (Aqhat) is accompanied by a deep concern with mortality (Aqhat, Achilles, Enkidu).[84] Indeed, martial aggression may be pursued on the battlefield, as it says in a number of biblical passages, even to the point of putting one's own life at grave mortal risk ("to die").[85] We will return to these basic points in Chapters Two and Three.

Second, the exclusion of human women (Baal Cycle, KTU 1.3 I)[86] corresponds to the patronage of human male warriors by divine warrior females (Aqhat, KTU 1.17 VI; Gilgamesh).[87] Human women are generally excluded from participating in battle,[88] and the death of a warrior at the hands of a woman is considered dishonorable (Judg. 9:54; cf. Judg. 4:9; Jdt. 13:15). Weapons are not for human women (KTU 1.17 VI 39-41).[89] This gender contrast, noted in a number of the following chapters in this study, constitutes one of the cornerstones of "warrior culture."

Third, great positive value is placed on various expressions of martial aggression when manifest in combat. The terms involved constitute a virtual "lexicon" of warrior aggression in Ugaritic and the older Hebrew poetry. Within this "lexicon," there are three sets of sometimes overlapping semantic terms used to denote martial aggression: (i) fierceness *(ʿz* and *qšh);* (ii) perhaps the most complex, anger (*ʾap* and its related expression, **rûaḥ ʾap),* as well as the later comparable terms, *qinʾâ* and *ḥēmâ;* and (iii) lack of satiety (Ugaritic **šbʿ*/BH *śbʿ*). All three sets involve fundamentally physically-based terms with psychological associations, and they may be used together. Let me address these three sets of terms in turn.

The first is *ʿz.* The word may certainly denote "strength, might."[90] At its core, it is essentially a physical term.[91] When used in the context of conflict, it may further denote fierceness, which involves the interface of the physical and the psychological.[92] Baal and Mot are both "strong" *(ʿz)* in KTU 1.6 VI 16-20.[93] The BH term *ʿaz* is parallel with *qāšâ* in Gen. 49:7 (cf. *qāšâ* used to describe the war in 2 Sam. 2:17). In modern terms, the term evokes the physical and psychological effects of adrenaline produced by the "flight or fight" response in the face of a serious threat.[94] Fierceness is the response of readiness and disposition to fight.

The second and related set of terms largely revolves around *ʾap,* "anger" (< "nose").[95] The noun is used commonly with the verb "to burn" (**ḥrh*), which is grounded in the physical experience of anger in the face (i.e., increase in facial temperature accompanied by an increase in rate of breathing).[96] Baal is sometimes thought to be "angry" in KTU 1.2 I 38.[97] Mot shows his *ʾap* in 1.6 V 20-21.[98] Chemosh manifests anger (**ʾnp*) against his people, according to the Mesha stele (KAI 181.5-6).[99] Yahweh's *ʾap* is directed against Yamm in Hab. 3:8 and against the peoples in Hab. 3:12 (cf. Deut. 32:22; Ps. 110:5).[100] The word is used sometimes in conjunction also with *rûaḥ* ("force"). The divine force/breath of the nostrils, **rûaḥ ʾap,* is attested in Exod. 15:8 and 2 Sam. 22:16//Ps. 18:16(15). This is at once an expression of anger and its accompanying bodily response. Accordingly, this image for the divine warrior may provide conceptual backdrop to the "force" *(rûaḥ)* that comes upon a warrior from the deity at the outset of conflict (Judg. 3:10; 6:34; 11:29; 14:6, 19; 15:14; 1 Sam. 11:6; 16:13-23; cf. Judg. 13:25; Job 33:4).[101] Parallel to *ʾap* is **ʿebrâ* ("overflow"[?])[102] in Gen. 49:7 and Amos 1:11. Yahweh's *ʿebrâ* is manifest also in Hab. 3:8. Later terms semantically related to *ʾap* and *ʿebrâ* include "rage" (so NJPS for *qinʾâ* of the warrior in Isa. 42:13; cf. Isa. 59:17; Ezek. 23:25; Ps. 79:5-6)[103] and fury (or "heat," *ḥēmâ*, for divine and humans in Ps. 76:10).[104] Comparable with these terms is Achilles' notorious *mēnin* (often rendered "anger, fury") in the *Iliad;* this is the very first word of the *Iliad,* which signals its epic theme[105] and shows "the importance of being angry"[106] in warrior culture in Homer. The word not only applies to Achilles' fury on the battlefield; this warrior rage also expresses and characterizes his response to Agamemnon.

This second group of terms seems to go well beyond "strength, fierceness." The basic analogy is a bodily condition of "burning" or "heat."[107] It involves an excess of physical energy directed at a perceived enemy. The terms involved express an intense martial aggression. Indeed, such aggression may be pursued on the battlefield, as it says in biblical passages, to the point of putting one's own life at grave mortal risk ("to die").[108]

The third of the three sets of terms involves insatiability, which is somewhat different in nature. It is a major term for the representation of Anat in battle (*šbʿt,* KTU 1.3 II 19-20 and 29-30).[109] This usage is evidently reflected in the New Kingdom Egyptian name labelling a royal horse: "Anat is content."[110] The sated (**śbʿ*) divine sword also appears in Jer. 46:10 (cf. Isa. 34:5-6). The same root **śbʿ* is applied to Yahweh in Hab. 2:15-16 (there in association with divine **ḥēmâ* and *ʾap*).[111] Death is likewise a personified force that is insatiable (Hab. 2:5; Prov. 30:15-16), an image that is congruent with the images of his massive appetite in the Ugaritic Baal Cycle.[112] In this text, Death is represented as a formidable warrior, as we will see in Chapter Six.[113]

In its physical and psychological bearings, the notion of not being satisfied is quite different from the others.[114] The attitude in warfare described in these terms is analogized implicitly as a fundamental physical lack (cf. the four things that are "not satisfied" in Prov. 30:15-16). The state of not being "satisfied" is a curse in ancient Near Eastern texts (e.g., the Sefire inscription, in KAI 222A 21-24).[115] It further involves a psychological need (perhaps akin to the modern term "blood-lust," an extreme desire for violence and carnage). Such a picture of combat is evident in Anat's battling in KTU 1.3 II, where she is said not to be satisfied (line 19) until she has destroyed her captives (line 29).[116] A comparable scene appears in the Middle Kingdom story sometimes called "The Destruction of Mankind."[117] In this text, the goddess called the Eye, and named Hathor as well, is insatiable[118] in her destruction of humanity. Its annihilation is averted only by a divine ruse that tricks her into drinking seven thousand jars of beer-mash mixed with red ochre that she thinks is human blood. At the sight, "her gaze was pleased by it."[119]

In the context of battle, all of these terms express a positive quality. To be sure, aggression in other contexts could get out of control, which was recognized as a social danger (see Gen. 49:4-7;[120] 2 Sam. 3:39; cf. Amos 1:11).[121] In the case of divine warriors, this quality too is potentially dangerous (Anat in KTU 1.17 VI–1.18 IV; Yahweh in Ps. 74:1; Lam. 2:3-4; 4:11).[122] Yet when directed against enemies, it is prized (Anat in KTU 1.13; Yahweh in Isa. 42:13; Lam. 3:66). Ritual before battle and after it demarcates the boundaries of martial aggression. The consecration of weapons before battle signals the beginning of such prized martial behavior, while the washing and storage of weapons after battle mark its closure.[123] With the weapons of war locked or dedicated in the temple, warriors are to follow suit and to reenter the "normal mode" of society. Within these boundaries, negative attributes (fierceness, jealousy, cruelness — perhaps even cannibalism) become positive attributes for both humans and deities.

Finally, there is the matter of fame and glory. While I have not found such a notion expressed in West Semitic warrior poetry, an additional warrior value entailed winning fame or renown or glory, which as we noted in the first section above occurs in *Gilgamesh* several times, for example, in SBV IV.248: "It is they who have established a name [for] future [*time*]!" The classic biblical term is likewise gaining a "name" (2 Sam. 8:13; 23:19, 22; cf. Gen. 6:4),[124] with terminology of "glory" (**kbd*) also found (1 Sam. 22:14; 2 Sam. 23:19).

As this range of practices and attitudes perhaps suggests, warriors in literary texts do not refer primarily to professional soldiers at one end of the spectrum or only to conscripts at the other end. Rather, warriors in the literary context refer broadly to those males who stand out for their physical capacities for fighting and battle. For Iron I Israel, the situation involves tribal militias[125] marshaled for battle (Judges 5), as well as other fighting forces led by local leaders pitted against one another (as recalled in such figures as Gaal and Abimelekh in Judges 9), or even smaller forces (emblemized by the five Danite scouts in Judges 18). Individual males might stand out as potential warriors (cf. 1 Sam. 14:52: "whenever Saul noticed any strong man or warrior, he would collect him to himself"). The evidence from material culture helps to fill out this picture.

2. Archaeological and Iconographical Material for Warriors

Material evidence suggests that warrior attitudes and ideals are not entirely confined to their literary representations. Nontextual material also reveals a great deal. The evidence beginning in earlier periods and moving down into the Iron Age provides a backdrop for this study of early Israelite warrior culture. This artifactual information is drawn from burials, arrowheads, and animal bones as well as iconography. The following discussion notes each briefly in turn.

Burials and Warriors

Most periods of Levantine history attest to burials with weaponry.[126] To provide some idea of the finds from a long-term perspective, I offer a very brief listing of some major finds for each period beginning with the Chalcolithic period and going down into the Iron II period. Tamar Schick published what she calls a "cave of the warrior" discovered in the Jericho area.[127] This cave burial included arrows, as well as a blade fragment and a nearly complete prismatic blade (over 300 mm. in length and 31 mm. in maximal width).[128] Based on radiocarbon dating of the skeleton and other finds, Yorke M. Rowan argues for a Chalcolithic date rather than Schick's Early Bronze I date.[129]

From the Early Bronze, a hoard of metal objects known as the Kfar Monash hoard was discovered on the coastal plain 3.3 km southeast of Tel Hefer (Tell Ibshar).[130] The collection comprised thirty-five tools and weapons, including two long curved knives (60 cm. in length), four dagger blades (22 cm. to 25.5 cm in length), four spearheads (33.3 cm. to 66 cm long), and one mace-head. In addition, over eight hundred small, thin, ridged copper plates were found. Ruth Hestrin interpreted these pieces as scales of armor.[131]

In the Middle Bronze Age, the Levant attests to what is characterized by archaeologists as warrior burials,[132] defined as "burials interred with artifacts whose design indicates 'weapon' as their primary function."[133] Whether or not this particular characterization is accurate, "the treatment of the corpse depended on the selection and the marking of a number of the social identities which an individual had achieved in life."[134] One of the "social identities" in these burials involved warfare, to judge from the weaponry. It is debated what further conclusions are to be drawn about the significance of weapons in these burials. For Graham Philip, the inclusion of weapons is important for marking status,[135] while for Yosef Garfinkel, the percentages of warrior burials at different sites suggests that there was no "segregated social class of warriors; it rather suggests that most of the adult population carried arms."[136] In his discussion of warrior burials, Philip notes "the complete absence in the succeeding Late Bronze Age."[137] In conjunction with this trend, Philip notes that axes decline sharply.[138] Marguerite Yon has pointed to a thirteen-century burial chamber at Minet el-Bheida that included funerary offerings, pottery, bronze weapons, and tools.[139]

The Late Bronze–Iron Age transition offers considerable information. The Late Bronze–Iron I burials at Tell es-Saʿidiyeh (Jordan) yielded burials with battle gear with swords beneath the heads.[140] In addition, contemporary Late Bronze–Iron I pithos burials at Tel Nami and Tel Kinrot (Israel) included short swords.[141] In the case of the unpublished Tel Kinrot double-pithos burial, the sword has a design with a scorpion and a caprid (gazelle?) on one side and a squiggly line on the other side. Samuel Wolff has considered the possibility that these are to be understood as warrior burials.[142] This type of double-pithos burial with a sword is relatively rare. This information may be supplemented by weapons found apart from burials, for example, in the Late Bronze–Iron I transition at Tell el-ʿUmayri.[143]

The Iron Age evidence for weapons in burials in Israel has been summarized by Elizabeth Bloch-Smith in her important 1992 work, *Judahite Burials and Beliefs about the Dead.*[144] Javelin heads and spearheads were found in Iron I burials, specifically in Tell Zeror jar and cist burials, Tell es-Saidiyeh simple and cist graves, and Tell el-Farah South bench tombs. For Iron I burials with weapons, Bloch-Smith's 1992 survey may be supplemented by the arrowheads and blade/knives founds in tombs 39 and 1101B Upper in stratum VI at Megiddo, published in 2004 by Patricia Paice.[145] Spearheads appear in Iron II burials from Megiddo, Beth Shan, Gibeon, Tell es-Saidiyeh, and Tell el-Farah South, but none in coastal or Shephelah burials. Bloch-Smith summarizes the finds in these burials: "Half the assemblages with spearheads included Mycenaean or Philistine vessels, all had jewelry, and virtually all had personal items, Egyptian amulets and additional tools, either a blade or an arrowhead."[146] Burials in the Iron II period containing weaponry seem to be quite rich in associated material compared with Iron I burials with weaponry.

Before leaving the evidence for weapons, we may mention a Phoenician tomb from Achzib.[147] It contained one of the very few long swords known from the early Iron II period. There are no long swords attested in Iron I Israel, and besides the Achzib sword, there are only two known Iron II long swords, from Vered Jericho[148] and Tel Rehov (itself in an Assyrian burial).[149] The Achzib tomb also contained a dagger, knife, spearhead, axe, and several arrowheads.[150] For the excavator, Eilat Mazar, this tenth/early ninth century burial bespeaks "a great hero."[151] The finds from this tomb seem to span the entire Iron Age IIA (or even I) to the very end of the Iron Age. No skeletons were found in phase 1. Mazar supposes they were removed (and the grave goods pushed against the walls), in order to make space for later burials. From this tomb, it might appear that the practice of honoring a deceased warrior perdured in some instances.

Thanks to excavations, we have a material picture of weapons mentioned in the texts. While the available mortuary evidence may be insufficient for positing "warrior culture" in early Israel,[152] even minimal weaponry in burials is suggestive of a cultural commemoration of men at the time of their deaths. Whether or not they died from warrior activity that may have dismembered them, their burials honored them and marked the "remembering" of their association with weaponry.

Arrowheads and Battle

If burials witness to warriors at the end of their lives, then arrowheads provide a picture during their lives. Before proceeding, it must be noted that the corpus of arrowheads with inscriptions[153] has grown dramatically in recent years, raising concerns about their authenticity.[154] For this reason, the discussion here is based on the uninscribed arrowheads discovered *in situ* or on the inscribed arrowheads prior to their entry into the market in larger numbers.[155] To be clear, in focusing on information from the inscribed arrowheads published in earlier decades, it is not my intention to cast aspersions on any particular examples; rather, I am trying to exercise caution. I would also add that arrowheads are also known prominently in more distant contexts, for example, in Babylonia[156] as well as southeastern Arabia.[157]

The purpose of the inscribed Iron I arrowheads from the Levant is difficult to determine. J. T. Milik and Frank Moore Cross believed that the arrowheads pointed to hereditary guilds of warriors. Cross also viewed them as prizes in archery contests.[158] For P. Kyle McCarter, arrowheads were used in battle; the retrieval of arrowheads from defeated enemies would serve to help determine the successful archer, and thus his share in postbattle plunder.[159] Undermining these sorts of theories, Emile Puech expresssed his view that many came from tombs.[160] Christopher A. Rollston thinks that they are inscribed prestige objects.[161] This view would fit with McCarter's further observation that some arrowheads bear the name of a high-status individual (e.g., "king of Amurru"): "the arrows fired by the archers in a nobleman's personal retinue would bear their lord's name, thus claiming a portion of the spoils for him."[162] (We will return to this matter in Chapter Eleven.) Whatever their precise function, the inscribed arrowheads are suggestive of a social acknowledgment of the place of archery within the society. In addition, the inscribed arrowheads of the Iron I period contain information that may reflect the notion of martial goddesses as divine military patrons.[163] Because this notion seems to find broad expression in the Ugaritic texts, perhaps it should not be considered simply a literary fiction (though its considerable elaboration as in Aqhat may well be). We will return to the question of the arrowheads and warrior goddesses in Chapter Seven.

According to Bloch-Smith, arrowheads in burials appear more frequently in the Iron II than in the Iron I. With the exception of two simple graves and two urn burials, all arrowheads from burials were reported from cave or bench tombs. Beginning in the tenth century, arrowheads appear in coastal burials and also in the Shephelah and hill country, including Lachish, Jerusalem, Tell en-Nasbeh, and Khirbet el-Qom, and in Transjordan at the sites of Tell el-Farah South, Meqabelein, Amman, and Sahab.[164]

We will return to the arrowheads and their cultural significance in Chapters Nine and Eleven. For the moment, it is to be noted that arrowheads provide a vivid witness to the practice of warfare as well as some associated notions. Like other sources, arrowheads tell a story about military men.

Animal Bones and Hunting

Bones of undomesticated species offer an archaeological perspective into hunting, a practice complementary to warfare. As noted above, it may be surmised that hunting was part of the training of young men, which would also help to prepare them for handling weaponry in warfare and the experience of conflict.[165] The role of hunting in the story of Aqhat (discussed in Chapter Four) is suggestive of hunting as a socio-religious practice that males learn as part of their upbringing. It points specifically to the use of bows and arrows in hunting. Other means were deployed as well in hunting deer or gazelle (such as snares or nets). I have not found evidence for the use of nets or snares for hunting these animals in Iron I Israel, much less for Iron IIA Israel.[166] However, nets for capturing gazelles and stags (as well as birds) are known earlier, for example, at Mari,[167] and so this practice might be operative elsewhere in Syria-Palestine, including early Israel.

It is interesting to note the cultural picture in the legislation of Deut. 12:15 and 14:5: one may eat meat of undomesticated species, including deer and gazelle, apart from sacrificial practice.[168] These passages acknowledge the consumption of undomesticated species outside the sacrificial system. It seems important to observe that Deuteronomy 12, as well as the list of wild animals permitted to eat found in Deuteronomy 14, date no earlier than the Iron II period (at best).[169] Thus, judgment about the sacral use of undomesticated species in Iron I Israel should not be premised on what these texts have to say about hunting. Instead, in the absence of Iron I texts, it is the Iron I archaeological record that should be considered for understanding the Iron I situation.

The archaeological evidence confirms the practice of hunting in the Iron I period, and to some degree it cuts against the impression given by later biblical texts that undomesticated species were not used for sacrifice. According to Brian Hesse and Paula Wapnish, deer and gazelle are well documented for the diet from the Late Bronze Age through the Roman period.[170] Steven Rosen has asserted: "Judging from the osteological data, hunting played a secondary, but surely not insignificant role in the economic system of the Iron Age I highlands peasant."[171] A number of sites point to the practice of hunting in both Iron I and II Israel. For example, bones of fallow deer from the Iron I site on Mount Ebal are well attested, comprising about 10 percent of the total diagnostic bone sample.[172] These may be part of a sacrificial cult in what has been regarded as a shrine with an altar by Adam Zertal,[173] but as a tower by Anson Rainey and Aaron Kempinsky.[174] Whether this structure is an altar or a tower, the bones represent important evidence. The nature of the sacrificial cult in this case is controversial in view of the location of the bulk of the bones, as noted by Amihai Mazar:

> The bones are of ritually acceptable young animals (with the exception of some bones of fallow deer); they are butchered near the joints and are burned, as in the biblical descriptions of animal sacrifices . . . the bones were found in the fill of the structure; if they are bones of sacrificial victims, they must have been offered in the phase preceding the large structure or during its construction.[175]

It is to be noted that almost 20 percent of the bones of undomesticated species were found not in the fill, but outside of it, mostly in Area B.[176] If the animal bones belonging to domesticated species found outside of the fill represent sacrificial offerings, then there is no reason not to suppose that the bones of undomesticated species in the same locale were likewise sacrificial in character. In any case, it is evident that for this site, hunting was a considerable activity. At the late eleventh–tenth century site of Khirbet Qeiyafa, bones of undomesticated species are also attested according to the excavator, though their sacral use remains undetermined.[177] Red deer bone was discovered at Kinrot, Dor, and Shiloh.[178]

Iron II sites in the Israelite highlands also attest to the hunting of undomesticated species, apparently with sacrificial use operative in some instances. A tenth-century "cultic" structure at the site of Taanach attests to bones of some gazelle and/or roe deer and some fallow deer.[179] More specifically, the cultic site yielded twenty-one astragali from gazelles and/or roe deer and three from fallow deer.[180] Deer and gazelle bones have also been noted at the Iron II Dan sacred precinct.[181] No sacrificial altar as such was discovered.[182] However, the excavators did find one very large horned altar stone, apparently from a very large altar, as well as a large square stone construction interpreted as an altar later enclosed within its own temenos. Paula Wapnish and Brian Hesse also note a bowl with various bones of sheep, goat, and gazelle found with an incense stand and incense burners just to the south of "Bamah A."[183] At smaller northern sites, such as Horvat Rosh Zayet,[184] bones of undomesticated species have been found in what have been regarded as cultic structures. We may also note the sacrifice of undomesticated species also at southern Iron II sites, for example, Lachish.[185] In addition to the evidence for these Cisjordanian sites, there are indications of fallow deer and gazelle at Iron Age Transjordanian sites, such as Hesban,[186] Tall Abu Al-Kharaz (Jordan Valley),[187] and Khirbet al-Mudayna.[188] In these cases, sacrificial use is lacking for evidence.[189] However, at some sites, it would appear that undomesticated species — contrary to later biblical norms — were used in sacrificial cult.

What Paul Croft states about the situation there may well represent the larger picture in ancient Israel:

> Hunting was never of great importance in the economy, although the occurrence throughout the sequence of wild animals and birds indicates that it was a perennial pursuit. The numerous species of wild bird and a few species of wild mammal which are represented moderately frequently in the faunal assemblage were probably hunted reasonably locally. Such mammals include fallow deer, gazelles, hartebeest, and fox.[190]

The situation has been summarized by Justin Lev-Tov, Benjamin Porter, and Bruce Routledge in these terms: "Hunting is evident at most settlements, with those in the foothills and highlands sharing a primary focus on large ungulates (esp. gazelle and fallow deer), and a secondary focus on wild boar in a number of cases."[191] Despite problems in interpretation,[192] it is apparent that hunting constituted an Israelite practice during the Iron Age. The further dimensions of the practices in the Iron I period, for example, the degree to which it was sacralized in the sacrificial cult, cannot be determined. Nonetheless, it would seem that the sacrificial cult included undomesticated species at some Israelite sites. The bones of undomesticated animals may provide a glimpse into social and religious life in the face of the near silence of texts bearing on the topic.

Further help comes from the iconography of undomesticated species, such as deer and gazelle.[193] For example, the Late Bronze–Iron I cemetery at Tell es-Saʿidiyeh yielded a lovely gazelle head constituting the handle of a bronze cup.[194] Tel el-ʿOreimeh produced a poetry sherd incised with a stag.[195] Horned animals (gazelle, ibex, or deer) are a feature for the early Iron Age stamp seals,[196] as well as tenth–eighth-century Israel miniature art[197] and eighth–sixth century Hebrew seals.[198] These sorts of depiction would seem to point to a societal awareness of the role that hunting wild animals played. In contrast to the iconography, not to mention the archaeology, the near silence of the textual record on hunting remains an issue.

Iconography of Human Warriors

Iconography provides evidence for the representation of warfare and hunting in Syro-Palestine.[199] There is a particularly rich iconography of divine warriors for this region (particularly in the Late Bronze Age),[200] which cannot be surveyed properly in this context. The following remarks focus on depictions of human warfare and hunting from the Early Bronze onwards.

Royal Palace G at Ebla (Tel Mardikh IIB1, ca. 2400) yielded a series of limestone inlays with scenes portraying, among other subjects, prisoners in chains, the killing of captured enemies, heaps of cut-off heads, and the spoils taken from the enemy.[201] A hunting scene thought to date to the Early Bronze Age has been detected on rock art in the central Negev highlands.[202] Moving to the Middle Bronze Age, an iconographic source for weapons is the alphabet. The invention of West Semitic alphabetic writing was pictographic, and its pictographic repertoire of letters gives iconographic prominence to weaponry. According to Gordon J. Hamilton, "West Semitic chose five Egyptian signs for weapons to represent Proto-Canaanite letters: **giml-/*gaml-*, 'throw-stick'; **zayn-/*zên-*, 'weapon (axe)'; **ṯann-*, 'bow'; and **waw*, '[mace].' "[203] The axe and throw-stick may also be used for hunting, and so these signs suggest both of these spheres of activity. The alphabet's letters reflect common spheres of life,[204] such as the human body[205] and architecture,[206] as well as the basic necessity of water[207] and the pastoralism that it supports.[208] Accordingly, the letters informed by weaponry show how the alphabet attests not only to some of the basic lexicon of weaponry, but also to its social importance in the Middle Bronze context and beyond: warfare and hunting are as "at home" symbolically as the other spheres of the human condition expressed by the alphabet. As long as the signs remain pictographic or were recognized as such (perhaps even into the Iron I period), the symbolic freight of such letters may have remained as well.

The symbolism of warriors is evident also in iconography as we move into New Kingdom Egypt and the Levant in the Late Bronze Age. The relevant iconographic evidence has been surveyed for this period,[209] and the following instances are particularly telling. Egyptian art provides portrayals of Levantine warriors. A Syrian carrying a bow and arrows appears on a wall painting in the tomb of Rehkmire (TT109), dating to Dynasty Eighteen (reigns of Thutmose III–Amenhotep II).[210] A fine example of a human warrior appears in a particularly stunning depiction painted on limestone (29.5 cm. height, 24 cm. width), thought to be from Tell el-Amarna in the reign of Akhenaten (ca. 1353-1336).[211] The warrior's name, Tarura, as supplied by the inscription, is thought to be foreign, as is his wife's, Arbura.[212] "His bulging forehead, small nose, and full beard are not consistent with the features of an Egyptian native. His hairstyle and white headband are also foreign to Egypt, as is his colorful tasseled kilt."[213] Based on these features as well as the foreign names, the warrior is thought to be Syrian (the vessel from which he drinks may also be "Canaanite").[214] The warrior is seated, with his spear standing up behind his seat and a dagger in his belt. He is drinking from a tube connected to a vessel holding a liquid. This tube is held by a second, smaller figure. Behind the server sits Arbura, who is identified as his wife *(nbt pr)*. With the attention of the server and the female directed at the warrior, he along with his weaponry stands out. Whatever else may be taken from this representation, the figure's status as a warrior is central.

Late Bronze Levantine cylinder seals show figures with various weapons, including the bow and the mace.[215] One seal includes a hunting scene: the hunter with his bow taking aim at an equid and a stag.[216] The Late Bronze iconographic material from Ugarit is also particularly rich. The famous bed panel of carved ivory from the royal palace of Ugarit (room 44 to the northwest of Garden III) includes a series of plaques showing the king in various activities, including warfare and hunting.[217] One panel on a libation chimney-pipe shows a figure ready to strike with one hand and a bird in the other hand; the other panels on the object show a bull, stag, and a bird.[218] In other cases, the nature of the figure in question is unclear. For example, the figure on a gold bowl (RS 5.032), discovered on the acropolis to the southwest of the Baal Temple, may be divine or human. According to Marguerite Yon, "the decoration consists of mythological heroes in a hunting scene."[219] Yet another object from the acropolis, a gold plate, shows a hunting scene, this time with two separate fields.[220] An inner circle of the plate depicts wild goats, while the outer circle with the principal scene shows a hunter in a two-wheeled chariot with his bow drawn and a supply of arrows on his back; three wild bulls are shown along with two dogs and a gazelle.[221] From these scenes, it is evident that warriors and hunters represented a recognized dimension for kings and gods at Ugarit.

An ivory plaque, .26 m. in length and 1-1.5 mm. in thickness, was discovered at Late Bronze Age Megiddo (stratum VIIA). It shows a celebration scene with a king, seated before a procession of soldiers and captives returning from battle.[222] This plaque is of further importance, as it evidently was affixed to a blade handle.[223] The message of the plaque's depiction thus goes hand-in-hand with the medium of the blade handle. Less well known from the same stratum at Megiddo is an ivory piece with battle scenes with chariots.[224] A second chariot scene on ivory shows an army on the march.[225]

For the Iron Age, there is iconography relevant to human warriors. A number of stamp seals for early Iron Age Israel show chariot scenes and archer scenes that include various weapons. Seals with Aramaic and Phoenician legends include combat scenes.[226] The iconography of deities in the Iron I context also represents an important resource for this study. In Chapter Seven, we will take a look at one of the goddesses on one cult stand from Tell Taanach and possibly another on a terracotta model shrine from Tel Rehov. Both arguably point to the portrayal of the warrior goddess in some form. We may also note the later Bethsaida stele, which provides a most interesting combination of deity as emblem animal shown as armed with a sword or dagger.[227]

The evidence for hunting in Iron I Levant is more sparse.[228] A few examples may suffice to illustrate.[229] Karatepe yielded reliefs with a hunter with his bow and arrows, as well as a warrior carrying a calf on his shoulders.[230] Zinjirli attests to a deer-hunting scene carved on stone orthostats.[231] Finally, the site of Tell Halif has yielded an ovoid cube incense altar (Obj. 3191) depicting a hunting scene; the object is dated to the late eighth century.[232] There are other artifactual representations that provide "snapshots" of activity related to topics of warrior practice.[233]

Taken together, these various sources point to the larger context of warrior practices. While I do not see these as directly explaining many, if not most, of the problems raised by texts or vice-versa (though each one may occasionally offer some help for understanding the other), the artifactual material may suggest that pre- and postbattle practices are not simply literary constructions imagined by their authors. Rather, these practices were apparently grounded in the ancient societies that produced and transmitted the texts that represent them, even if the texts may elaborate what was the cultural reality. And where textual sources remain silent or "quiet," archaeological sources may be eloquent by comparison. (For example, the animal bones of undomesticated species in Israel are suggestive by comparison with the textual record.) In most cases, it is impossible to determine with much confidence what is to be deduced from the artifactual evidence, much less what to posit about the relationship between textual and archaeological data. Accordingly, I draw on the artifactual evidence cautiously. The investigation that follows remains largely a textual study. The limits of the literary sources for discerning the situation on the ground remain a central problem, one that I would like to address further at this point.

3. A Central Problem in the Topic: Warrior Culture between Literary Representation and Cultural Reality

In these introductory comments, I find it necessary to point out the various problems of any cultural investigation into Ugarit or premonarchic Israel, including one about warriors in these cultures. While the texts have been illuminated, thanks to a long and venerable tradition of philology and literary analysis, the additional study of the cultural reality behind such texts has been fraught with difficulty.[234] In this regard, warrior poetry is both the topic at hand and also a problem. Let me explain, beginning with the Ugaritic texts.

The information about warriors in Ugarit reviewed below in Part III of this study is confined largely to literary texts. These poetic texts do not offer recordings of a warrior culture, expressing its own values and attitudes within ancient Ugarit's society. Instead, the texts provide a series of literary representations and commemorations of warriors, sponsored by the Ugaritic monarchy. As several colophons in the literary texts show (e.g., KTU 1.4 VIII 49; 1.6 VI 54-58),[235] the monarchy supported the transmission of the literary texts that we will examine. It is evident that these texts were not all final literary editions, since they contain occasional instructions for their recitation (e.g., KTU 1.4 V 42-43; 1.19 IV 63, left hand-edge at line 23),[236] a point that is sometimes overlooked.[237] From the colophons, it would seem that the monarchy was the setting for recitations of the literary texts.[238] Thus, the cultural reality that Ugaritic literature would reflect (if it does) was the monarchy.[239] Presumably these texts convey representations of the present and commemorations of the past that the monarchy found useful, including their warrior values and themes.

The Ugaritic texts under examination include one ritual text that we will address in Chapter Five (section 3). It includes the names of old premonarchic leaders and yet it is also patently royal, containing names of kings and an invocation of blessing for the king and his household (KTU 1.161).[240] In this text, ancient heroes called the Rephaim and the recently deceased kings appear as a single body participating in a ritual designed to promote the dynasty's well-being. This ritual representation coheres fairly well with the literary representation of the same cultural material.[241] (It is unfortunate that the administrative texts do not provide much information relating to "warrior culture," apart from some minor details.)[242] In view of the royal themes in the literary texts as well as the thematic coherence between the royal ritual of KTU 1.161 and the literary texts likewise mentioning the Rephaim, it is evident that the literary representations of warriors enshrine cultural values or ideals upheld by the monarchy. Whether from traditional values or monarchic endorsement or both, military personnel may have favored these ideals as well.

Even if many such practices and values are expressed in heightened or even mythological forms in the Ugaritic texts or other literature, it seems quite plausible that they would have resonated for men in military service. At Ugarit, the recitation of such texts may have served to reinforce, if not to inculcate, such values. Thus, such texts may have exercised a certain agency in the reinforcement and perhaps formation of "warrior culture" (perhaps at a rather high elite level where they might have been recited). Accordingly, the values expressed in the literary texts may have informed the attitudes of the military. Still, we can hardly be sure, and to some extent it may be a historical illusion. As the preceding section suggests, texts, archaeology, and iconography may provide different perspectives on a larger cultural reality that I call "warrior culture." Still I find it necessary to be mindful of the fact that what is mostly considered in this study is a matter of literary representation and commemoration, which in many, if not most, respects may have stood at quite a distance from the lived reality of ancient soldiers. Thus the study of the Ugaritic texts, and most especially the literary texts, for the subject of warrior poetry remains a problematic basis for discerning historical realities behind these texts. Archaeological and iconographical sources may help, yet these too may have been no less subject to potential conceptual constructions in antiquity.

Similar issues affect the study of the biblical literature that we will examine in Part IV. The biblical poems discussed in Chapters Eight through Ten explore some warrior themes that we see in Ugaritic poetry, and to this extent the Ugaritic texts show the traditional character of biblical language about warriors. In this sense, the Ugaritic texts help to indicate the antiquity of these ideas and ideals even if the biblical texts examined are not all of high antiquity. The Ugaritic material furnishes a limited backdrop for the literary representation of warriors, as recalled for early Israel. At the same time, this help from the Ugaritic texts hardly alleviates the perennial problem for biblical scholars, namely the lack of Hebrew texts in the twelfth through the tenth century.

This gap in our textual knowledge is hardly a new problem. Over a half century ago, it was addressed by a wonderful biblical scholar in his book on early Israelite society and warfare. In the introduction to his *Jahwekrieg und Stämmebund* (originally published in 1963), Rudolf Smend offered the following comments, and with good reason:

> Concerning the demonstrability of the presentation, I have no illusions. The phenomena with which one can work are for the most part of a hypothetical nature. In this area one can surmise much, but prove little. It lies in the nature of the matter and for the present cannot be changed. In view of the importance of the subject, conjectures are thus necessary if one does not wish to be satisfied with ignorance. In the following, I have nowhere aimed at a general investigation of the earliest history of Israel.[243]

Smend's study involved an effort at describing the social and cultural situation of earliest Israel via its literature. In view of the sorts of difficulties that Smend wisely recognized, my effort in this study focuses more on specific older texts for understanding the representation of Israel's early situation, and it draws on the Ugaritic texts (where appropriate) to gain some backdrop to the situation in early Israel. As a result of this effort, I do not preclude the possibility of recovering some limited sense of what we might call "warrior culture" as enshrined in this literature. I have also enlisted the aid of the Ugaritic texts to help get at the putatively early biblical record on this subject (something that most biblical scholars today do not use sufficiently, to my mind). At the same time, it must be said that this use of Ugaritic is hardly a guarantee for understanding many matters involved in the study of the biblical texts. Indeed, such comparison entails difficulties of its own.

Readers may regard my efforts at recovering the largely "lost world" of early Israel's warrior culture as quixotic. Perhaps they will respond to it with a similar sense of "greatest reservation" expressed by the great scholar, Isac Leo Seeligmann. In 1959, Seeligmann responded to Smend's book, *Jahwekrieg und Stammebund,* while he was working on it. As Smend recalled, Seeligmann "did not like the . . . subject at all, and asked if I had forgotten that we had as good as no reliable sources for the pre-state period, so that a work of this kind would inevitably be purely hypothetical."[244] Smend did not forget. Indeed, Seeligmann's question seems to be echoed in the very words of Smend from his book's introduction that I quoted above. Like Smend, I have not forgotten.

I see two basic choices. Either scholars can prescind from textual studies of early Israel, as many have done, and thus abdicate our responsibility to study this past; or, we may take on this sort of investigation and run a certain risk, with the hope and expectation that present and future colleagues will do better, perhaps spurred on and assisted by investigations (such as this one) despite their lacks or failures. In choosing the second alternative, I may — to echo Martin Luther — sin boldly, perhaps, but also carefully, I hope. Despite the outstanding problems, my sense is not that the goal or task is hopeless, but that there are major obstacles to be met, along with some ancient hints to be recognized and appreciated. To be sure, whatever conclusions are drawn, they are not to be built on weak conceptual categories, or on highly reconstructed sources for early Israel, or on citations of considerably later texts for Israel. Conclusions are also to remain proportionate to the degree of evidence that we have for early Israelite textual and archaeological material.

To illustrate the sort of difficulties that this study faces, I would turn to the work of two of the very best scholars who have worked on early Israel. One is a famous textual scholar, the other a well-known archaeologist. In many respects, each one represents the best scholarship of his generation. The first is Frank Moore Cross, for decades the doyen of Hebrew Bible and

West Semitics at Harvard University. The second is Avraham Faust, presently professor at Bar Ilan University in Tel Aviv. Both have produced superb and important work, and their studies raise a number of methodological difficulties faced in any reconstruction of early Israel.

Cross's highly influential and seminal 1973 book, *Canaanite Myth and Hebrew Epic: Essays in the History of the Religion of Israel,*[245] offered a major synthesis of early Israelite traditions drawing in large measure on early Hebrew poetry as well as the Ugaritic texts. (In this respect, my study stands in the tradition of Cross's research, which I gratefully acknowledge.) Cross relied on conceptual constructs that affected the way that he reconstructed early Israelite literature and culture. Central to Cross's discussion was the notion of a fundamental dichotomy between epic with its focus on human heroes and myth with its focus on divinities. This accompanied the idea that the category of epic serves as the basic representation of Israel's self-understanding in its textual sources, while myth serves as the opposing term for the Canaanites, with the Ugaritic texts considered the primary exemplar of their literature.[246] At the same time, Cross viewed the mythic and the historical as standing in an ongoing tension in biblical tradition, sometimes tending toward the mythic (such as later apocalyptic), sometimes tending more to the historical (e.g., the books of Kings). As Cross himself conceded, both Israelite and Ugaritic literatures show elements of both myth and epic; it was difficult to fully posit a strong contrast between the two in either corpus.[247]

For the issue of early Israelite literature and society, there was more to Cross's theorizing. Cross built his reconstruction of Israelite epic on three pillars.[248] First, he posited an epic, poetic source lying behind the so-called Yahwist and Elohist sources (essentially, Martin Noth's *Grundlage*)[249] and also informing "old poetry." Second, Cross argued that the Ugaritic myths showed a long tradition of epic poetry transmitted orally and set down into writing. Thus, for Cross, Ugaritic narrative poetry bolstered a comparable understanding of his Israelite epic. Third, Cross applied to this Israelite epic Albert B. Lord's theory comparing the production and transmission of Homeric epic with oral epic in modern Serbia and Croatia.[250]

It is not my intention to review all of the dimensions of Cross's theory in great detail, but it is evident that the strength of these pillars has suffered in the past two decades. First, few, if any, biblical scholars today would accept either Noth's *Grundlage* or Cross's epic based on the so-called sources.[251] The existence of these written sources as such has come under fire in recent years.[252] Even if some claim of older oral tradition could be mounted for some prose material[253] or poetic passages, it hardly tallies up to an old epic source.[254] Similarly, the high dating of the so-called "old poetry" has been called into question in a serious way. I have devoted Chapter Eight below to this thorny issue. For now, I would say that the basis for such datings is not simply (and perhaps primarily) linguistic, and that even as some basis may be offered for dating material relatively early, the dates proposed by Cross and others for "old poetry" seem too high. Second, the Ugaritic myths show signs of oral performance, but it is hardly clear that they are the result of oral dictation to the scribes who wrote down the versions of the Ugaritic narrative poems that we have. Contrary to Cross's view, it is not evident that a Ugaritic narrative poem such as the Baal Cycle was dictated by a bard to a scribe.[255] Third, the applicability of Lord's theory to other corpora, not to mention the theory as applied to Homer itself, has come under fire.[256]

Despite some defense of epic in ancient Israel,[257] for many scholars poetic epic simply did not exist in ancient Israel. The title of Shemaryahu Talmon's provocative article on the subject posed the crucial question, "Was There a Biblical National Epic?" Talmon was unequivocal in his answer: "Biblical Israel did not produce, nor did it foster, the epic genre."[258] Volkmar Fritz[259] and Simon Parker[260] denied epic for ancient Israel. I have noted some difficulties bearing on this matter.[261] At one level, the problem is a matter of scale; epic is generally considered a poem of considerable length,[262] and there simply is no such epic poem attested in the Hebrew Bible.

Scholars sympathetic to the notion of epic in ancient Israel would qualify the application of this term. In his discussion of epic and Exodus 15 and Judges 5, Cross says of these poems: "I am not claiming that these two poems are 'epics in miniature.' They are lyric pieces."[263] Michael David Coogan spoke in these terms: "The poet is able to present a battle without elaborating it in epic style."[264] Andrés Piquer Otero labels Judges 5 "un canto épico desde ángulos indirectos."[265] Surely there was a wider oral tradition, but this need not point to a national epic as envisioned by Cross and others. Even Cross seems to be saying that this early war poetry is not so much epic as lyric, which at most draws on known epic elements. Moreover, it has not served Cross's cause well that epic seems to be poorly understood for the Levant in this period.[266]

At this point, I pause to mention the suggestion that epic has been viewed primarily as a genre of men's song and the lyrical as a genre of women's song.[267] If so, the elements of the two domains of usage may have influenced one another. A possibility that is entertained in this study is that the early heroic poetry as we have it in the Bible is no less the activity and domain of women (the Song of Deborah[268] and the couplet in 1 Sam. 18:7; 21:11; 29:5),[269] as it is of men (e.g., David's lament over Saul and Jonathan in 2 Sam. 1:19-27).[270] By contrast, the heroic poetry in Ugaritic that we explore in Part III seems to have overwritten women's perspectives and activities, even as it occasionally mentions them. Still it is notable how goddesses play important roles in the great heroic poetry such as the Baal Cycle, in contrast to a work such as Enuma Elish with which it is often compared.[271]

Prior to Cross, Israelite epic had been discussed by scholars such as Cyrus Gordon[272] and Umberto Cassuto.[273] As Cassuto observed, biblical tradition, especially in many Psalms as well as the older poetry, shares much in common with older West Semitic traditions as attested in the Ugaritic texts and other sources. Accordingly, Cassuto perceived an epic tradition that could be traced in both Ugaritic and biblical poetry.[274] Cassuto's view reflected a certain apologetic in suggesting that the Israelite poetic epic further constituted a certain anti-Canaanite reaction. Whatever the merits of this particular perspective on this epic tradition (and I find them lacking for evidence), Cassuto's arguments and the massive data that he marshaled from Hebrew poetry posed a serious case in favor of some sort of early Israelite epic. These sources for Cassuto represented early Israel's epic.

Cross knew the data presented by Cassuto, yet he did not engage Cassuto's work on this score in any detail.[275] Given the relative antiquity of the sources as well as their shared features with earlier Ugaritic literature,[276] Cassuto's poetic epic (and a rather mythical-looking one, to say the least) arguably represented a plausible candidate for Israelite epic compared with the biblical prose sources that Cross attempted to use to reconstruct it. In any case, biblical prose historiography represents a dubious source for hypothesizing an Iron I Israelite epic in the massive way that Cross suggested. This is not to say that it is impossible to identify some older traditional literary formulary in the prose texts.[277] Even as biblical prose material may seem distant from the manner of epic as found in Homer or Gilgamesh, I would sympathize with Cross's conviction that biblical books such as Samuel were "interpreting the later history of Israel in Epic patterns."[278] Many type-scenes and expressions known from traditional works are to be found in biblical prose cycles, as noted by many commentators.[279] I would thus affirm with Cross the possible value of comparisons of Homeric epic diction and type-scenes with Ugaritic literary texts.[280] Nonetheless, this is not enough to reconstruct an Israelite epic behind the so-called "Yahwist" and "Elohist" sources, as suggested by Cross. Indeed, the prose cycles of the Pentateuch and the so-called historical books constitute in many respects an "anti-epic,"[281] designed to create an image of ancient Israel in light of thinking in the late Iron II period (and later), in reaction to Israel's older origins story or stories, which among other notions had featured the idea of Israel's god as one among seventy national gods in a divine family (as reflected in a fairly summary fashion in Deut. 32:8-9 LXX and 4QDeuteronomy^{j}).[282] Other elements in this older origins story include Yahweh's conflict against mythological enemies, as seen in Ugaritic and as discerned by Cassuto in the poetic corpus of the Hebrew Bible. In short, Cross's theorizing about epic, not to mention myth, constituted a questionable scaffolding for reconstructing the development of early Israelite literature.

The lesson for this study is that biblical prose sources cannot be readily used as a major pillar for reconstructing the Iron I period. I would not state categorically that it is impossible to use them,[283] but sufficient reasoning needs to be provided for doing so; the same applies to later poetry as well. For example, my decision not to use prose stories in the book of Judges does not mean that I think that it may not contain some old tradition (e.g., Judges 9). Still the issue of monarchic overwriting of these traditions[284] remains a critical problem. An appeal to prose sources in the present study would run the risk of weakening the argument here; thus little appeal is made to prose material for reconstructing Iron I Israel. To understand early Israel, it is necessary to rely as much as possible on Iron I sources, aided in the first moment by even older sources that show connections with them. It is for this reason that this study relies primarily on early biblical poetry (which I will discuss further), in conjunction with Iron I archaeological sources as well as Late Bronze Age sources (especially the Ugaritic texts) that can be shown to have linguistic and thematic associations.

The other author whose work illustrates the challenges involved in reconstructing early Israel from archaeology and biblical texts is Avraham Faust, in particular in his well-known book, *Israel's Ethnogenesis: Settlement, Interaction, Expansion and Resistance.*[285] In this work, Faust attempts to understand early Israel by taking an anthropological approach, which represents a significant step forward.[286] The approach, it should be said, is also occasionally biblical, and the use of biblical texts is an issue. Before mentioning further specifics, I want to note that Faust's mention of biblical texts does not constitute a major part of the evidence presented.[287] Moreover, I applaud Faust's working against the trend of scholarly claims denying early historical possibilities for Iron I Israel.[288]

At a number of points in the discussion, Faust enlists biblical texts as support, yet the passages often derive from the Iron II or later periods. Faust uses later texts to describe Israel in "the Iron Age" (which by definition includes Iron I Israel), but with little or no methodological explication for why such texts provide evidence for the Iron I period. For example, for the idea of the Canaanites as traders "in Iron Age society,"[289] no text before Hosea is marshaled, and no chronological distinction is made. The use of the so-called priestly source,[290] even if it were preexilic as Faust prefers, is a questionable source for reconstructing Iron I cultural realities without some further basis and argumentation. No support is given for the claim that "the stories relating to the Iron I in 1-2 Samuel are at least very old."[291] Some may be or may contain old elements or traditions,[292] but Faust's cause is not well served by generalization without documentation. A less egregious instance involves Faust's claim that Judges 4-5 relates to the same time and region as Iron I Israel;[293] I agree for much of the poem of Judges 5.[294] However, Faust prescinds from any discussion of the historicity of Judges 4 or 5; he suggests viewing Judges 4–5 "as an illustration for the circumstances evident here" (regarding the ethnic reality of Iron I Israel). The methodological procedure presupposed in this claim is fallacious if "the ethnic reality of Iron I Israel" is a contested issue in Judges 5[295] or if Judges 4 reflects a later period of Israelite social history. To use Judges 4 or 5 in this manner, further argumentation or evidence would be helpful.[296]

In these cases,[297] Faust does not provide a provenance for textual evidence, and so he does not show that the concepts in such texts were operative in the Iron I period (even down to the ninth century). The arguments become circular, with the textual data presumed to correspond to the archaeological evidence and vice-versa.[298] In general, claims about early Israel that use biblical texts as support would ideally include at least some early biblical texts. It is also notable that while Faust turns to biblical texts on any number of points, there is no comparable marshaling of other early textual sources with cultural similarities. For example, some of the "Proto-Canaanite"[299] and Akkadian[300] inscriptions from the southern Levant in the Late Bronze and Iron I periods or the Late Bronze Ugaritic texts[301] stand closer to the Iron I period than many if not most of the biblical sources cited by Faust. Here, too, iconographical evidence deserves a place in the discussion.[302] The Ugaritic texts, especially where they clearly share commonalities with early biblical texts, often represent a more proximate resource for understanding themes and concepts expressed in early Israelite literature or society than many biblical texts that date to the eighth century or later. Other texts, such as the Amarna letters[303] or Egyptian historiographical sources bearing on the Levant,[304] too, may serve for background information.[305]

A further problem bearing on the relationship between biblical and archaeological sources can be detected in an article that Faust co-authored with Shlomo Bunimovitz.[306] In this study, the Bible is said to offer "answers" to problems raised by archaeological data of the Iron Age (with no distinction made about Iron I versus Iron II). To derive these biblical "answers," the article draws conceptual generalizations from the Bible. Again, insufficient attention is paid to the problem of dating such biblical evidence for generalizations about early Israel or how well they hold. Faust derives his "answers" from different biblical sources dating to a number of periods. Faust's use of the Bible to "answer questions" raised by archaeology looks like a newer form of biblical archaeology. Unlike the older biblical archaeology,[307] Faust does not use archaeological data to support biblical claims. Instead, he applies — and arguably constructs — biblical notions,[308] rarely if at all attested in early biblical material, to explain archaeological data from the early period. As a result, the procedure throws into some doubt Faust's broad claim that the four-room house is an ethnic marker for early Israel, much less that its features "reflect Israelite values and ethnic behavior: e.g. egalitarian ethos, purity, privacy, and cosmology."[309] In short, the archaeology needs a description either with contemporary textual sources (biblical or otherwise) or with later sources that are cogently argued to be relevant to the early Israelite context.[310] To be clear, it is not my view that archaeologists should not use biblical texts, only that they should do so with restraint[311] and with some interaction with biblical scholarship on the biblical passages that they would use. Indeed, more attention to biblical texts might have been helpful for the discussion of early Israelite ideology of "egalitarianism." The claim for the existence of an ideology of egalitarianism is not affirmed by early Israelite literature (e.g., Judg. 5:2a, 3a, 9-11, 14c, 14d, 15a, 25b, and 29a), according to Ernest Axel Knauf.[312]

This discussion of the important works by Cross and Faust suggests some guidelines for using biblical texts in addressing early Israel. In general, the procedure in this book is to build a reconstruction first by using texts that reflect traditions or even textual composition in the tenth century (or perhaps ninth century) or earlier.[313] The basic biblical texts that I use for this purpose are the core of Judges 5 for Iron I proper and 2 Sam. 1:19-27 for the tenth century. In Chapter Eight, I will argue that the evidence supports the conclusion that at least the tradition of the poetic core of Judges 5 did not originate in the Iron II period; rather, its tradition, if not much of its core composition, is to be dated in the Iron I period (I will also make a case for a tenth-century date for the poem's overall composition). Similarly, I will argue in Chapter Ten that the tradition of 2 Sam. 1:19-27, if not the composition of its core (vv. 19-25) or even its entire composition, may be set in the tenth century. In addition, I also use some of the sayings in Genesis 49 for early Israel[314] (based on some of the vocabulary items,[315] as well as the reference to the El Shadday, Heaven, and Deep and the goddess of "Breasts and Wombs" in v. 25, which I take to be a reference to Asherah).[316] There are also oral variants in Genesis 49 that are traditional and presumably older than the possibly later date of the poem as a whole.[317] Psalm 68 also strikes me as having older material in it.[318]

I am not claiming that all of these were composed in their basic written form[319] before the tenth or ninth century, only that their traditions go back to the period of early Israel or that parts of these poems were composed in some form by then.[320] Indeed, it is important to note that a number of poems often included as "old poetry" date down into the ninth or even eighth century. For example, Baruch Levine has argued for the first half of the ninth century for the date of the Balaam oracles in Numbers 23–24.[321] With its reference to monarchy (v. 10), 1 Samuel 2 likewise shows the trending of old poetry down into the monarchy.[322] The same may be said of Habakkuk 3 (see v. 13). (I am hesitant about dating Exodus 15 to the Iron I or even to the tenth or ninth century.)[323]

My core extrabiblical texts are Iron I inscriptions from what is emerging as Israel and its environs in this period.[324] A necessary complement in this effort to build a picture of Iron Age Israel consists of the iconographic and archaeological data from Iron I Israel. To be sure, the complex relationships between texts, iconography, and archaeology in the Iron I period require their own case-by-case discussion.[325] As we have seen, the archaeological evidence for Iron I Israel may point to information that the available texts may not provide.

The second step is to draw on earlier extrabiblical texts with evident cultural connections to the early biblical material. For example, some motifs in the core older biblical poems can be seen in the Ugaritic literary texts, suggesting that the traditions of the biblical poems predate them. (The list of prebattle and postbattle practices listed in the opening section of this chapter generally includes citations from early Hebrew poems and Ugaritic material.) Other older West Semitic texts, for example at Mari and Emar as well as the Amarna letters, also provide information potentially bearing on early Israel. By the same token, continuity from earlier periods cannot be assumed; rather, continuity of literary tradition or continuity of material culture needs to be argued. For the historical enterprise, the burden of providing literary or cultural evidence falls on me in trying to build the picture of Iron I Israel. To posit a feature for Iron I Israel, it would be ideal to have the feature attested in an older biblical poem and in a contemporary or prior West Semitic text. In the past, discontinuity between early Israel and Late Bronze Age corpora from elsewhere has been assumed in large measure from a perception that the culture and society of ancient Israel was discontinuous from its Canaanite forebears or neighbors. Thanks to the work of many scholars, such as H. L. Ginsberg and Frank Moore Cross, literary continuity between the Ugaritic and biblical literary corpora has been demonstrated in several cases. Even after all these efforts of successive generations of scholarship, continuity still needs to be argued, because it is a proper procedure for historical research and because the lesson of the work of these scholars (and many others as well) has still not been fully assimilated in biblical scholarship. It seems to me that many biblical scholars and archaeologists continue to treat the attestations of biblical motifs in such extrabiblical West Semitic texts generally as "parallels" and not as markers of literary or cultural continuity. When the same feature can be identified in prior or contemporary extrabiblical texts and an early biblical poem, it is a matter of at least some literary continuity. This procedure is different from identifying parallels from other ancient Near Eastern cultures that are not in literary or cultural continuity with early Israel. For the picture of early Israel that I am trying to sketch, I have also used some parallels from other Near Eastern cultures largely for illustrative purposes, though in themselves they do not constitute the basis for the reconstruction of early Israel in this study. Parallels may be illuminating, and they may serve to explain details of ancient Israel or the Bible, but they are not part of the data set itself for early Israel.

As a third step, there is the matter of whether or not to use texts from the Iron II period or later for reconstructing Iron I Israel. In the past, it has not been uncommon for scholars to draw on later biblical texts for reconstructing the Iron I period without offering an accompanying argument for literary or cultural continuity of the later texts or their traditions with early Israel. (As we have just seen, Cross and Faust used later sources to generalize about the Iron I period.) To be sure, there is considerable cultural continuity between the Iron I and Iron II periods in many matters. Accordingly, I would hardly exclude the use of later biblical texts when literary or cultural continuity from the earlier biblical material to later biblical material can be shown. Indeed, it is true that there may be continuity with Iron I, but it may not be immediately perceptible at this point in scholarly investigation. Still, there is a way to get at this problem.

Let me illustrate. Many of the warrior practices or notions that are listed in the first section of this chapter are attested in the Ugaritic texts and in later biblical prose texts, suggesting that these also existed in early Israel. "*Ḥērem*-warfare" is a good example. Examples from other realms of life also suggest the broader reality of the point for early Israel. To illustrate, I would mention three instances. First, biblical terminology concerning social organization ("house of the father," *bêt ʾāb;* "family," *mišpāḥâ,* etc.) may find expression only in later texts, and an argument can be made for the antiquity of such concepts in early Israel based on archaeology,[326] together with prebiblical textual sources, such as materials from Mari and Ugarit.[327] Second, the language of "divine sons" *(bĕnê ʾēlîm)* may not appear in Iron I Israel (depending on when one dates Ps. 29:1), but it does appear in Iron II Israel. It is likely to be an early motif for early Israel, since it is standard in both later Hebrew poetry and earlier Ugaritic literature (*bn ʾilm,* e.g., KTU 1.4 III 14; cf. for an individual *bn ʾilm* in 1.4 VII 45; 1.4 VIII 16, 30, etc.; see also *bn ʾil* in 1.40.7, 8, etc.). Third, the very specific references to the Leviathan in Ugaritic (*ltn,* in KTU 1.5 I 1) and later biblical poetry (Isa. 27:1; Ps. 74:14; Job 3:8; 41:1) point to the likelihood that this motif was known also in early Israel.[328] These cases could be multiplied many times over. It is quite feasible to argue for a feature in Iron I Israel if the feature can be shown in sources before Iron I and in sources after Iron I. This sort of triangulation of sources from before and after Iron I is in many instances a sufficient basis for positing a feature for Iron I Israel.[329] However, a motif could appear independently in two different time periods, and so a case for literary continuity needs to be made; it cannot be assumed for a proper historical picture of early Israel. In short, to reconstruct a picture of Iron I Israel, it is necessary to build the case with evidence and argument, and not to presuppose continuity without discussion.

There is a further methodological consideration when it comes to making a case for a feature in Iron I Israel: it can be argued by means of literary discontinuity with the same motif in Iron II Israel, when the motif displays a distinctive alteration. In Chapter Eight, we will discuss leaving hair long (**prʿ*) for battle represented in Judg. 5:2 as a warfare practice for tribal militia. The BH nominal form is attested elsewhere only in Deut. 32:42, "from the head the locks of the enemy" *(mērōʾš parʿôt ʾôyēb).* In this passage, the idiom of the long hair appears in the Iron II context in a clichéd manner. There seems to be some literary development of the motif. The development of this motif in Deut. 32:42 compared with the usage in Judg. 5:2 would seem to indicate an older background in the tradition embedded in the latter verse. In other words, the discontinuity between Judg. 5:2 and Deut. 32:42 is suggestive of an Iron I setting for the tradition of the practice in Judg. 5:2. Tracing the development of a motif between the Iron I and Iron II may provide some aid in trying to build the picture of Iron I Israel.

Literary and cultural discontinuity is not only an issue; it additionally offers a helpful, critical perspective on the task of studying early Israel. The gap between the traditions of earlier texts and their later biblical historiographers is itself an important datum for this study. Iron II biblical historiography seems to show a sense of the temporal distance between its own times (perhaps from the ninth-eighth centuries and following) on the one hand and on the other hand the early world of Israel (perhaps prior to the ninth century).[330] The transmission of heroic poetry in written form in turn allowed the preservation of this early world that oral transmission perhaps did not meet in the ninth century and afterwards. This was, in a sense, a "lost world" for these later historiographers. Their incorporation of older poetic texts lent to their prose reconstructions of the past a sense of the older time that they narrate.[331] (The sort of gap between the older poetic sources in the Bible and the later prose historiography may have an analogy in the gap in settlement distribution between the Iron I and II attested in the archaeological record, noted by Faust.[332]) Scholars of Israel's texts need to draw on what archaeology can provide, both as a check on their textual research and as a source for possible suggestions for the cultural realities represented in the texts and those omitted from the texts. In turn, archaeologists interested in ancient Israel are to be applauded for using textual sources, yet these sources need to be used for understanding ancient Israel in the time frames in which the texts were composed, unless some further argumentation can be brought to bear that suggests their relevance for an earlier period within ancient Israel. Biblical texts involve no little amount of "excavating" for their time frames and for their correlation with archaeological evidence of the same time periods. Without such controls, overly optimistic use of texts in conjunction with archaeology seems to recall old-fashioned "biblical archaeology." And if no effort is made to sift between Iron I and II literary and cultural realities, then the outcome will be little different from what has come from either the older or newer biblical archaeology that has been criticized here.

The chapters on early Israelite warrior poetry in Part IV are suggestive of the possibilities in this regard. At the same time, it is to be emphasized that the sketchy nature of the available earlier evidence, especially on the textual side, is not simply a problem, but is itself an interesting part of the larger Iron I picture, one that this study will address (in Chapter Twelve).

As we go through the evidence, there is a further effort to address methodological issues as they arise (especially in Chapters Seven and Eight). Finally, there is so much textual evidence to investigate and to understand that the effort made here falls decidedly on trying to comprehend how the ancients understood their "warrior culture." In other words, this study does not look first for guidance from modern theorizing, but hews closely to the ancient evidence for signs of its own theory or preunderstandings. This project in part retraces the steps of Iron II (and later) Israelite historiographers back to the Iron I situation, aided by Ugaritic texts as well as great heroic poems from Mesopotamia and Greece. I am not aiming for a broad reconstruction of these cultures (including Iron I Israel),[333] only for a particular part of the picture. It is my hope that some helpful results may emerge from this effort to understand this one aspect of ancient Israel's early culture.

In order to understand the wider scope of ancient warrior culture, we turn at this point to Part II and its consideration of three great warrior pairs of ancient literature: Gilgamesh and Enkidu; Achilles and Patroklos; David and Jonathan.

PART II

Three Warrior Pairs in Mesopotamia, Greece, and Israel

CHAPTER TWO

Brothers in Arms

When we look across the ancient world, we see the commemoration of ancient heroes spanning from east to west. Three notable cultures of antiquity fashioned famous pairs of heroes in their great literary works. In ancient Mesopotamia, the single best-known figure of literature is the great Gilgamesh, king of Uruk. The immortalization of this warrior-king is closely intertwined with the name of his wild warrior companion, Enkidu. These two figures go on heroic adventures, not on the battlefield against other men; they journey to faraway places and engage in conquests against monsters that are mythic in scale. In ancient Greece, the *Iliad* commemorates the great warrior-king Achilles, son of Peleus and Thetis,[1] and ruler of Phthia in southern Thessaly. He is recalled by the title "best of the Achaeans" (*Iliad* 1.244, 412; 16.271).[2] He is closely connected with another great warrior companion, Patroklos, whom Achilles recognizes "in all things like his very self, in stature and fair eyes and in voice" (*Iliad* 23.66-67). In the *Iliad,* both warriors meet the enemy on the battlefield, and in the *Odyssey,* the two are linked in eternity in the underworld. The Bible's recollection of a great warrior-king lies at the center of Israel's national memory. This is the hero and king David, who cherishes his dear companion, Jonathan, the son of King Saul. Like Patroklos, Jonathan meets death on the battlefield, without his heroic counterpart.

These ancient classics recall the great warriors as mythic figures,[3] human icons attributed heroic labors not only in conflict, but also well beyond. The devotion of these brothers in arms marks each of these warrior narratives, with each greater warrior in these pairs deeply affected by his lesser counterpart. What experiences the pairs of heroes share — and do not share — make them who they are. Each literary tradition offers a reflection on heroic life and death. The three texts also differ, not only over the circumstances of the death of the lesser warrior in each pair, but also over its impact on the surviving and ultimately greater warrior brother.

In this chapter we will focus on how the slightly lesser companion contributes to the making of the great hero. For all three literary traditions, the story of the lesser figure informs the great hero's life and character. It is part of the epic plotline that while equal in some respects, the second member of the pair also remains second in status, and in turn the first of the pair appears greater by comparison.[4] In each instance, the hero repeats elements in the life of his lesser friend and thereby becomes the great hero as he is later remembered. By contrast, the slightly lesser member of each pair, interestingly, seems hardly — or at least less — changed by the greater hero. By comparison with their greater counterparts, Enkidu, Patroklos, and Jonathan seem more fully formed as characters before they come to meet their slightly greater brother in arms.

1. Gilgamesh and Enkidu

We may begin the discussion of heroic pairs with Gilgamesh and Enkidu.[5] This story is not summarized easily, as it exists in multiple editions spanning about two millennia. A number of scholars, not only Jeffrey H. Tigay in his well-known 1982 work, *The Evolution of the Gilgamesh Epic*,[6] but also Thorkild Jacobsen, William L. Moran, Andrew R. George, and most recently Daniel E. Fleming and Sara J. Milstein, have approached the literary developments in these editions from a diachronic perspective, in particular the separate Sumerian tales, the Old Babylonian Version (OB) of the early second millennium, and the Standard Babylonian Version (SBV) of the first millennium.[7] The Middle Babylonian (MB) version has assumed new importance in the scholarly discussion, thanks in particular to the version of the introduction from Ugarit published in 2007.[8] There are also artistic representations of the story's figures from different periods, which fortunately have been surveyed in a recent volume dedicated to the iconography of Gilgamesh.[9] I will not offer a diachronic description here, but I remain aware of the differences in the various versions, and in the discussion that follows, several are noted.

The description that I attempt here will not concentrate so much on the story's overall trajectory and structure,[10] or its general themes,[11] or even its literary genre,[12] approaches that have been ventured by scholars of Assyriology. Rather, I will focus on what the story's plot and themes represent about the relationship between Gilgamesh and Enkidu, who are more sportsmen rather than warriors on the battlefield.[13] This discussion is particularly informed by several acute observations on this score made by William L. Moran as well as Rivkah Harris and Benjamin Foster.[14]

Gilgamesh and Enkidu begin as near equals. In contrast to the Sumerian version, which presents Enkidu as Gilgamesh's servant,[15] the Akkadian versions represent the two as counterparts with high status, as denoted by the initial element in each of their names. Gilgamesh's name has been thought to have two Sumerian components, *pa,* meaning "senior, first-born," and *bilga,* "offshoot, fruit," thus "the ancestor/the chief is a young man."[16] Enkidu's name is Sumerian for "lord (of) the pleasant place."[17] Moreover, Enkidu appears as a divine creation made in response to Gilgamesh's physical strength and aggression (SBV 1.94-104; see below for further nuances in the OB version[s]). Enkidu is literally made for Gilgamesh, as one who can rival him, in the SBV (1.98). As Ninsun the mother of Gilgamesh[18] says about Enkidu, he is "one like yourself" (*ittika,* OB II.17; see *ittiya,* SBV I.285). With this creation, Gilgamesh finally has *šá-ni-nam-ma,* an "equal" that he never had before (SBV 1.82).[19] The gods commission Aruru to create another: "let them rival each other and let Uruk be rested" (SBV I.98). Gilgamesh repeatedly addresses Enkidu as his *ibru,*[20] "companion,"[21] or as the Sumerian Bilgames and the Netherworld characterizes him (line 247), *ku.li,* a Sumerian equivalent for Akkadian *ibru* regarded by Andrew R. George as indicating "an informal relationship bordering on equality."[22] The noun seems to denote a relationship across kinship boundaries; it is related to the abstract noun *ibrūtu,*[23] referring to a "relationship between persons of the same status or profession," "alliance," or "collegium."[24] The Akkadian usage seems to denote the kind of relationship called in biblical terms *bĕrît,* "covenant,"[25] the very sort of social tie that David and Jonathan enjoy. Enkidu is also called Gilgamesh's *meḫrum,* his equal or counterpart[26] (OB II, col. v, line 194; see also OB II, col. ii, line 43) and his *talīmu,* his "preferred brother" (SBV VIII.137).[27]

The corresponding companionship of the two heroes is cast in terms of brotherhood. This is intimated already in the OB version in Gilgamesh's second dream about the axe, a figure for Enkidu. Gilgamesh says about the axe (OB II.35): "I took it up and put it at my side *(a-ḫi-a).*" Jerrold S. Cooper has suggested that the line involves wordplay: "the pun 'side/brother' (both = Akkadian *aḫu*) foreshadows his future relationship with Enkidu."[28] He is Gilgamesh's friend at his side. The SBV is more explicit by comparison.

After they butcher the Bull of Heaven,[29] "the two brothers sat down" (SBV VI.150).[30] Later their *ibru*-relationship is qualified by brotherhood. Shamash tells Enkidu when the council of the gods has pronounced judgment on his life: "Now Gilgamesh, your friend and brother (**talīmu*)/[will] lay you out on a great bed" (SBV VII.139-40). Here the word *talīmu* stands in construct to and qualifies *ibru;*[31] literally, Gilgamesh is "friend of your brother," that is, "friend who is your brother." According to the *CAD, talīmu* is "often in apposition to *aḫu,* rarely to another word, such as *ibru.*"[32] The construct usage is not common according to the *CAD,* and perhaps its usage at this point in the narrative is notable. It occurs as Gilgamesh prepares Enkidu for death that he is called his friend and brother. Interestingly, it is not the death on a battlefield together that glorifies them as brothers, but a death caused by illness decreed by the gods (see SBV VII.255-67). In this context, Enkidu mentions his fear; his death is no glorious fall in battle. In the Hittite version, it is Enkidu who calls Gilgamesh "my dear brother," just after the divine decree when he "lay down to sleep."[33]

The narrative ties their status to their shares of divinity: "for Gilgamesh, like a god, a rival was appointed" (OB II, col. v, lines 194-95). The text further defines both figures in terms of divinity. Gilgamesh is famously two-thirds divine and one-third human (according to SBV 1.48), with Ninsun as his mother (cf. the Hittite prose summary version's understanding of Gilgamesh as made by the gods).[34] The Old Babylonian version presents not only Gilgamesh as divine (OB II, col. v, line 194), but also Enkidu as godlike ("I look at you, Enkidu, you are like a god" (OB II, col. ii, line 53). Over the course of Gilgamesh's later adventures in the SBV, the various parties who receive him also perceive his divine nature. The scorpion-man tells his wife about Gilgamesh: "He who has come to us, flesh of the gods is his body" (SBV IX.49). Echoing SBV I.48, the wife retorts: "Two-thirds of him are god but a third of him is human" (SBV IX.51). Later when Siduri, the alewife who lives by the seashore, sees Gilgamesh, "he had the flesh of the gods in [*his body*]" (SBV X.7), and Utnapishti still later tells Gilgamesh that he is "[built] from the flesh of gods and men" (SBV X.268).

These descriptions of divinity fall more emphatically on Gilgamesh than on Enkidu. Indeed, even as the narrative stresses correspondences between the two heroes, the heroes are not quite symmetrical. Enkidu is more accurately understood as Gilgamesh's near equal. Enkidu's physique compares to Gilgamesh's, but they are also different: "This fellow — how similar to Gilgamesh he is in build"[35] (SBV II.40; cf. OB II, col. ii, lines 80-81 and MB Bogh 1, frg. a, obverse, lines 10-11, reconstructed as, "In build he is the equal of Gilgamesh, but shorter in stature and sturdier of bone").[36] In George's words, the story here "presents the picture of the archetypal heroic pair of mythology, the dominant partner tall and slim, his helpmate not quite so tall, but stockier."[37] The iconography of the heroes sometimes points to their difference in stature. For example, a terracotta plaque in the British Museum, thought by Wilfred Lambert to be an Old Babylonian representation of the two heroes together, depicts Enkidu as the shorter figure.[38] This asymmetry is crucial to the epic plot not only here, but also for Achilles and Patroklos as well as David and Jonathan. It is clear which member of each heroic pair is put forward as the superior partner. The figures of Gilgamesh, Achilles, and David loom over Enkidu, Patroklos, and Jonathan. On the narrative level of Gilgamesh SBV, the asymmetry is particularly central. Each member of the heroic pair serves as a vehicle for the other's self-realization, but this process is hardly even. As Benjamin Foster has emphasized,[39] Enkidu's self-discovery is facilitated by his sexual experience with Shamhat (her very name thought to denote a "prostitute").[40] By contrast, it is over the length of the narrative — in both life and death — that Gilgamesh's experience with and of Enkidu serves as the crucible of what Foster calls the former's ascent to self-knowledge.[41]

The sense of the two as near equals is related further to their character as polar opposites, or what Foster calls the "definition of opposites."[42] Each is the supreme male exemplar of his domain. Referring to Gilgamesh's urban home, Daniel E. Fleming and Sara J. Milstein state: "According to the perspective of the epic author, Enkidu represents the physical power of untamed nature; this is what renders him the ultimate match for Gilgamesh."[43] In this reading, the text constructs these figures as the full male potential of the urban versus the wild, of culture versus nature: Gilgamesh is the great king ruling the great urban center of Uruk, while Enkidu is a man of the hinterlands, a wild-man *(lullû)*[44] of the steppeland (*ina ṣeri* [*edin*]) in both OB Penn tablet (OB II i 18, 54) and the SBV (1.103, 178-79). Fleming and Milstein have argued that the OB Yale tablet understands Enkidu somewhat differently. He is an *awilum,* which they translate as "gentleman," who works with "herds" (*būlum,* OB II, col. iii, lines 112-16; see also III iii 107). In their view, Enkidu is an experienced herdsman working livestock in the steppeland.[45] In either reading, the spatial contrast between Gilgamesh and Enkidu and the social-cultural contrast that it implies are clear.

The trajectories of their lives not only mirror but also invert their identities in relation to these domains. Each hero passes from his own zone of life into the other's. Enkidu, the man of the wild,[46] is socialized before meeting Gilgamesh in the city. Enkidu hardly remains the man of the wild, but becomes the opposite, as he moves to Gilgamesh's city. Similarly, following Enkidu's death Gilgamesh leaves Uruk to roam the steppeland (SBV IX.2; X.45) and eats wild animals (SBV X.259-60).[47] Gilgamesh takes on the appearance that Enkidu had (SBV I.105; cf. II.176): "And I, after you are gone, [I shall have] myself bear [the matted hair of mourning,]/I shall don the skin of a [lion] and [go roaming the wild]" (SBV VIII.90-91, reconstructed in part on the basis of SBV VII.146-47).

A corollary element of these journeys involves the figures of Shamhat and Siduri, as noted in an instructive essay by Rivkah Harris.[48] The two women help Enkidu and Gilgamesh, respectively. In Harris's view, both women are also wise, and their words uphold "the social norms of Mesopotamian society."[49] Enkidu's socialization into society, thanks to Shamhat,[50] brings him "wisdom" (SBV 1.202, *ḫasisu*). For Gilgamesh, it is first the wisdom of his mother that teaches him the meaning of his dreams and then his search beyond society that brings him wisdom.

As these observations suggest, Enkidu's story anticipates Gilgamesh's own, even as it inverts it. William L. Moran has noted an important temporal usage marking the inversion of the heroes' condition, specifically the periods of "six days and seven nights."[51] As Moran observed, this time period characterizes Enkidu's sexual intercourse with Shamhat (OB II, col. ii, line 48; SBV I.194), later Gilgamesh's mourning for Enkidu (OB Meissner, col. I, line 8′; cf. SBV X.58, 135, 235), and finally Ut-napishti's challenge to Gilgamesh not to sleep (SBV XI.209; it is also a detail of Ut-napishti's own story of the flood, SBV XI.128). For the SBV, the three usages mark transitions in Gilgamesh's development.[52] The first signals Enkidu's socialization,[53] the second the beginning of Gilgamesh's journey toward accepting mortality, and the third his acceptance of his mortality, as noted by Moran.

The inversion of their journeys, first together and then by Gilgamesh alone, is signaled by a spatial detail, the ascending parallelism of "twenty leagues"//"thirty leagues." This length is given for the journeys three times in SBV IV.1-2, 120-21, 163-64, and then twice again in XI.301-2 and 319-20 (cf. SBV VII.41). The journey in SBV IV takes the two out to the far west, while the journey in XI returns Gilgamesh to Uruk.

Finally, the two sets of dreams mark two stages in the lives of the heroes. The first set of dreams portends their meeting, while the second set of dreams portends Enkidu's death.[54] In a sense, these details literarily relate Enkidu's story to Gilgamesh's, a connection marked in tablet X when Gilgamesh tells Enkidu's story in his lament over him. Even in death, Enkidu in Gilgamesh's memory never leaves him.

The literary force of Gilgamesh's journeys is captured in the somewhat asymmetrical trajectories of the stories of its two heroes. For while it is true that upon Enkidu's death Gilgamesh on one level assumes his identity, this is no return to nature free of the knowledge and experience of the human world as it had been early on for Enkidu; for the SBV, it is to escape its haunting effects as well as its limitations. Nor is Gilgamesh's journey limited to the realms of Enkidu's earlier wild existence. In the long period after Enkidu's death, Gilgamesh "scoured the world-regions ever searching for life," as SBV puts it (I.41).[55] It is the memory of Enkidu's death — and the prospect of his own death — that haunts Gilgamesh's search: "I shall die," complains Gilgamesh who then asks, "and shall I not then be like Enkidu?" (SBV IX.3). As Foster and others observe, Gilgamesh's self-knowledge comes in part through his experience of his corresponding companion's death.

Tablet XI marks the end of Gilgamesh as a figuration of Enkidu. Perhaps echoing Enkidu's reception of clothing in OB II, col. iii, line 110 and SBV II.35, Ut-shanabi follows Ut-napishti's commands to wash Gilgamesh's matted hair, to remove Gilgamesh's hides, and to clad him "in a royal robe, the attire befitting his dignity" (SBV XI.253-58, 263-70). Moran rightly notes that here bathing and clothing are " 'rites of passage,' symbols of an inner transformation."[56] With his bathing and new clothing, Gilgamesh becomes his royal self once again, or as Moran puts the point, "this would-be god, the anti-man, is no more. . . . Thus he is ready for the journey back, back from the rim of the world, where the immortals dwell, back from the steppe, the haunt of animals and death, Uruk, where he as a man belongs."[57]

The episode with Ut-napishti may mark Gilgamesh's transformation in another way. Earlier it was clear that it is Enkidu who is Gilgamesh's equal: the mother of Gilgamesh says about Enkidu, he is "one like yourself" (*ittika*, OB II i 17; see *ittiya* in Gilgamesh's dream, in SBV 1.285).[58] But now Gilgamesh offers another comparison to himself when he perceives Ut-napishti, "As I look at you, Ut-napishti, your form is not different, you are just like me *(ki-i ia-ti-ma at-ta),* you are not different at all, you are just like me" (*ki-i ia-ti-ma at-ta,* SBV XI.3-4). While these lines sound like a recognition that Ut-napishti is as human as any other human, this human characterization of this immortal figure here may also represent a new insight for Gilgamesh's self-perception, that he has come to the other side of the world where the legendary Ut-napishti dwells, that even as his experience of the world and now himself has exceeded what he had experienced with Enkidu, he like Ut-napishti is just as human after all.[59]

The journey of Gilgamesh goes one last step, in the final episode with "the plant of heartbeat," as Andrew George understands *šam-mu ni-kit-ti* (XI.295),[60] the plant lost to the snake (XI.305-7). This episode marks Gilgamesh's knowledge of his mortality. This experience perhaps also marks his becoming fully wise, as enshrined with a refrainlike quality in the SBV prologue (SBV I.2, 4, 6), culminating in line 6 with the summary statement that "he [knew] the totality of wisdom about everything," the line now known in the older MB version attested at Ugarit (line 6).[61] Overall for the SBV, Enkidu's death, and the journey that it impels Gilgamesh to take, gain for him an experience of the world beyond any mortal. At the same time, Enkidu's demise impels his heroic friend to pursue a superhuman goal that contains the seeds of his own failure; Gilgamesh cannot escape his mortality. In the experience of the superhuman quest and its ultimate failure, Gilgamesh becomes his great self, returning from beyond the edge of the world to the city of Uruk where, as Moran says, "he as a man belongs."[62] The command to go up and note the city wall, commanded at the end (SBV XI.323-28), as at the beginning (SBV I.18-23),[63] marks the story coming full circle.[64] In returning to Uruk where he belongs as king, Gilgamesh completes his journey, and he becomes the man as he would later be remembered, namely by the city that he had built and left for future generations. Both this text and the city wall that it holds up for the audience's view mark Gilgamesh in later memory.[65]

In his observations about the end of the SBV, Moran emphasized Gilgamesh's return to the city, and the proper work of the human person that the city represents. Moran stressed that with Uruk as the beginning and end point of the SBV narrative, Gilgamesh ultimately belongs in a man-made world. "There seems," Moran wrote, "to be an intuitive if inarticulate perception that this is the work proper to man and his destiny: to build, to create a world of his own, as well as to die."[66] Gilgamesh in his unsurpassable wisdom[67] is immortalized by the city that he has built. Benjamin Foster and Piotr Michalowski would stress that this commemoration of the hero with his city is ultimately literary in character.[68] In other words, it is the text itself and not only the urban center that "extends" Gilgamesh's life beyond his days. The arc of Gilgamesh's life does not end with his death; no death is narrated. Instead, the narrative of his human life ends in what the hero leaves behind in texts and in the city, the two ancient realities through which Gilgamesh was largely remembered and experienced. The end of this person is not the end of his story.[69]

The narrative likewise enshrines the memory of Enkidu, yet it does so as a matter within Gilgamesh's story. The memory of Enkidu lies, in a sense, "inside" the narrative commemoration of Gilgamesh. Overall, Enkidu's story is recounted within Gilgamesh's and then echoed later in his lament. The companion's story is not only intertwined with Gilgamesh's; it also casts a long shadow over Gilgamesh's own story in the wilderness and beyond. Like the slight asymmetry in their physiques and shares of divinity, there is a literary asymmetry between the two figures: Enkidu is really part of Gilgamesh's story, and Enkidu helps to make Gilgamesh the greater figure. By comparison, Enkidu's character is not as strongly altered as a result of his relationship with Gilgamesh. Enkidu's character changes little after the two heroes meet. In short, the narrative commemorates the dead Enkidu within Gilgamesh's larger story.

Both figures are recalled as having lived in an older era. In the case of Gilgamesh and Enkidu, this is not only clear from the epic story that recalls Gilgamesh in particular as a king of long-ago days, but also from other texts that the epic tradition influenced. Emar, located on the Euphrates above Mari, and Ugarit, due west of Emar on the Mediterranean coast, preserved versions of a ballad about heroes of old. The Sumerian-Akkadian bilingual version from Ugarit asks: "Where is Enkidu? Where are the great kings?"[70] The longer version from Emar asks: "Where is Gilgamesh?" "Where is Huwawa?" "Where is Enkidu?" "Where are the great kings?"[71] The answer is clear: they are long gone. This sense of the earlier times of the great heroes can be felt also in the *Iliad.*

2. Achilles and Patroklos

The narrative arc of the *Iliad,*[72] though no less complex than that of the *Epic of Gilgamesh,* moves in a very different direction. The very first line of the *Iliad*[73] names its theme as Achilles' "wrath" *(mēnin).*[74] The invocation closes with the epithet *dios Achilleus,* "godlike" or "noble" Achilles (*Iliad* 1.7), a title that marks this figure elsewhere in the story (see 1.131, 179; 9.485, 494; 19.279; 24.59, 486, etc.).[75] Fury or anger is the state of the deity in warfare, and the descriptions of Achilles once he has returned to the battlefield in Book 19 are of near theophanic fury. Indeed, the wrath of Achilles is near to the martial fury of gods like Ares and Apollo.[76] The wrathful side of Achilles is complemented by his characterization as "pitiless" *(nēlēs/nēlees),* a trait that belongs only to him (9.497, 632; 16.33, 204).[77] "We hardly see Achilles apart from his wrath. . . . Achilles is his wrath, and his wrath is his fate," writes Seth Benardete.[78] With the application of images of fire to Achilles, his wrath is nothing less than a force of nature and perhaps even a natural disaster; his wrath devours all around him.[79] Yet his wrath is not the end of the story. Rather, the *Iliad* charts a long and painful path from Achilles' wrathful, merciless actions to a certain emotional completion of his character.[80] His dear comrade Patroklos, in life and in death, is central to this development.[81]

The story of the pair begins with Achilles suffering the indignity of losing to his rival Agamemnon the prize of war, the beautiful Briseis. Offended, Achilles sits out repeated engagements of battle.[82] Achilles stays in his tent, away from the fighting *Iliad* 1.488-92):

> But he raged as he sat beside his swift-faring ships, the heaven-sprung son of Peleus, Achilles, swift of foot. Never did he go to the place of assembly, where men win glory, nor ever to war, but allowed his heart to waste away, as he remained there; and he longed for the war cry and battle.[83]

The pained Achilles elects to remain away and apart from the company of his fellow soldiers, with the notable exception of his comrade Patroklos. The narrative provides Patroklos with no background information. The audience presumably knows his royal lineage (11.785),[84] just as they know Achilles' royal — and divine — descent (21.187-89; 24.538-40).[85] The audience also knows how the two spent their youth together (*Iliad* 23.85). Compared with Gilgamesh and Enkidu or with David and Jonathan, Achilles and Patroklos are quite alike; Gregory Nagy goes as far as to characterize Patroklos as the "surrogate of Achilles, his alter ego."[86] Their differences are notable as well. Generally Achilles is the nobler and "in might . . . the better far," while Patroklos is the elder (*Iliad* 11.786-87).

In his first narrative appearance, Patroklos is present at Achilles' side. After Achilles commands him to bring Briseis out to Agamemnon's messengers, Patroklos does not speak, and the narrative adds nothing to his response to Achilles' command: "Patroklos obeyed his dear comrade" (*Iliad* 1.345; see also 9.190). Later, Patroklos acts as a virtual servant going and obeying, as Achilles commands him (*Iliad* 9.190; 11.612-848). His own voice only emerges when faced with the potential defeat of his fellow Achaians in Book 11; he poignantly asks: "How will these things be?" (11.838). In Book 16, this all changes thanks to the sudden, shocking death of Patroklos. He has gone to battle dressed in Achilles' armor; for a moment, this clothing marks him as a second — but ultimately lesser — Achilles.[87] Achilles is pointedly not present when Patroklos meets his death, a central theme of the later lament that Achilles pronounces: "my dear comrade is dead, Patroklos, whom I honored above all my comrades and equally with myself" (18.80-81;

cf. 24.274).[88] Achilles then states: "let me die, since I was not to protect my comrade at his slaying" (18.98). At this point for Achilles, "his whole psychology has been transformed by the death of Patroklos."[89] Up to this point in the story, the behavior of Agamemnon has driven Achilles from the field of battle against the enemy Trojans led by Hector.

Now the pathos evoked in Achilles by Patroklos' death unleashes the former's notorious fury against Hector and the Trojans.[90] While the death of Enkidu compels Gilgamesh to leave society, the death of Patroklos impels Achilles to rejoin the society of warriors of which he is its singular example. Like Gilgamesh, Achilles is changed. On Patroklos' death, Benardete comments: "it cuts him off completely, binds him more closely to Achilles than he ever was bound in life."[91] And as in Gilgamesh, the death of his colleague brings awareness of his own death. Thetis herself warns Achilles following his vow to avenge Patroklos' death (*Iliad* 18.94-96) that he is "doomed to a speedy death." The ghost of Patroklos, too, tells Achilles of his destiny: "godlike Achilles, it is fate *(moira)* to die beneath the wall of the wealthy Trojans" (23.80-81).[92] This is one fact of life that this great warrior comes to know of himself, as Achilles himself acknowledges: "over me too hang death and resistless fate *(moira)* . . . my life too will some man take in battle" (*Iliad* 21.110, 112). It is not despite this knowledge of his *moira*, but rather with his sense of it that the death of Patroklos impels Achilles to return to the battlefield and drives him to achieve his greatest glory as a warrior.

And it is not out of soft-heartedness that Achilles returns to battle.[93] When he receives the weapons from Thetis, "then wrath *(cholos)* came on him still more" (19.15-16). Achilles is "not at all soft of heart or gentle of mind . . . but exceedingly fierce" when he kills Tros (20.467-68). He is likewise without pity when he dispatches Lycaon. His voice is "ungentle" (21.98) when he addresses this defeated warrior who begs for mercy and receives none (21.97-119; see also 21.147). Later in battle Achilles appears as "a wild man" (*agrion andra*, 21.314; see also 21.542-43) and "a hard man" (or "hardhearted," *schetlios*, 22.41). His battling exceeds the "'heroic' desire for revenge," particularly in "his contemptuous maltreatment of Hector's corpse."[94] In battle, Achilles "carries the savage ethical code of the Homeric hero to its ultimate and terrifying conclusion."[95]

This is not the end of the story of Achilles and Patroklos. His debt to Patroklos, as much as it can be repaid, is repaid: with Hector slain and his corpse dishonored by Achilles, Patroklos is avenged and his body given a proper burial.[96] To echo his words first spoken to Patroklos' ghost (23.95-96) and then addressed to him both before and at the funeral (23.20-21, 180),

Achilles has accomplished all that he promised to Patroklos. Now with the funeral games, Achilles further commemorates Patroklos. Instead of competing as he had in battle, Achilles oversees the games. The games in his friend's memory signal Achilles' return to the society of warriors.[97] He now takes his place in the assembly (23.448, 798-99), which he had sworn off at the outset of the *Iliad* (1.488-92, quoted above). Only in this moment in honoring his heroic comrade does the narrative honor Achilles as hero, as he gives to others their prizes of victory in the games (23.824, 896). For the first time in the text,[98] he is now the hero.

At this point, Achilles' furious behavior is not entirely behind him, and there remains a final, stunning emotional moment involving the memory of Patroklos. At the outset of Book 24, thoughts of Patroklos still plague Achilles, and it seems that this memory cannot be eased (24.3), which leads immediately to Achilles' dragging Hector's corpse from his chariot (24.3-21). Under the advice of the gods, the Trojan king Priam undertakes the protracted process of ransoming the body of his son Hector from Achilles (24.159-484). As seen in a touching depiction of Achilles and Priam on a bronze relief on a mirror,[99] the hero stands with his head slightly bowed to Priam; it is Achilles who in a sense is redeemed in their meeting. In one of the *Iliad*'s rare "one-on-one conversations" outside of battle,[100] Priam and Achilles come before each other as enemies, yet give each other something only the other can provide. Rather than rejecting the piteous plea of Priam (24.485-506) or perfunctorily accepting his gifts of ransom, Achilles responds emotionally to Priam's appeal to remember his own father (24.504). Priam's plea "in Achilles roused his desire to weep for his father; and he took the old man by the hand and gently pushed him away from him. So the two remembered" (24.506-9). Then Achilles and Priam openly lament for those dearest to them, in a manner represented with a notable symmetry: Priam for his son, Achilles for his father — and also for his Patroklos.[101] As they stand together, the two, Priam and Achilles, are linked in the single sound that they jointly make: "the sound of their moaning went up through the house" (24.512).[102] Achilles' response marks not so much the transformation of his character as its completion or integration through an act of emotional commemoration undertaken with his enemy. Priam literally reminds Achilles of his father not only with his words, but also with his very person; he, too, is a great king and father of a great son.[103] The memory of Achilles' own father and the fresh wound of his loss of Patroklos drive his emotions in this scene. For Achilles, Patroklos was the driving force from the moment of his death to the very end. This is true not only of Achilles, but also of Gilgamesh and David: their emotional responses appear with full force only after being separated from their heroic counterparts, Enkidu and Jonathan.

After Priam makes his request for Hector's body, Achilles remains capable of shooting Priam what A. T. Murray translated as "an angry glance"[104] (*Iliad* 24.559), more literally "fiercely, sternly" *(hypodra)*. This is the very same demeanor that Achilles demonstrates when he speaks exultingly over the dying Hector (22.260; 22.344). As a result of Achilles' response to Priam, "the old man was seized with fear" (24.571). Still, Achilles' anger is channeled into a swift response to Priam's request, made not with any violence or reproach of Priam. Achilles can be fierce here at this point; he is also moved by Priam. Here he moves quickly to act on his behalf: "he sprang like a lion" (24.572).[105] Just as Patroklos' death marks the return of Achilles to the battlefield, and the games in his friend's memory signal his return to the society of warriors, Achilles' honoring the process of ransom marks his further social reincorporation. Emily Vermeule comments: "Learning respect for the body of the dead is one of the principal lessons of the *Iliad,* a training for heroes to drop the carnivore mask and express courtesy to mortality."[106] Thus, in Sarah P. Morris's words, Achilles "has reentered the social tradition that his μῆνις ('anger') rejected; he pronounces the reconciliation of the two enemies, prepares a meal, and provides his guest a bed for sleep."[107] Here at the end of the *Iliad,* Achilles achieves what Agamemnon could not in Book 1. Achilles' adversary could not accept the ransom offered by Chryses for his daughter (1.8-32), but in the final book, Achilles can accept the ransom offered for the body of his Trojan enemy.

The issue of Achilles and his anger appears one last time in this scene, but in a touching reversal. As he returns the corpse of Hector, Achilles calls on the dead Patroklos not to be angry with him (*mē moi Patrokle skudmainemen,* 24.592). The address here is telling. Strikingly, it is Achilles, the one infamous for his furious anger, who now asks Patroklos not to be angry with him. Here he can turn to his dearest and deceased comrade and plead with emotional concern, perhaps even deference. The scene perhaps highlights the full meaning of this reversal, with the memory of the dead Patroklos bringing Achilles to a capacity for affective expression. The narrative refers to Patroklos here in 24.591 as *philon . . . hetaron,* "his beloved companion," in Richmond Lattimore's translation.[108] This is the same wording used of Patroklos when the narrative first introduces him in 1.345 *(philō . . . hetairō)* and when Achilles refers to him later in 18.81 *(philos . . . hetairos)*. The Greek term *hetairos* may denote a particular role of a chief's or king's "friend."[109] With his touching consideration of king Priam and the memory of his "beloved companion," the narrative has come full circle in the relationship of Achilles and Patroklos. With these final acts of devotion to his enemy in life and his dearest friend in death, Achilles has become what he fully is and what he earlier claims for himself. Now he is not only the greatest hero; Achilles and not Agamemnon is indeed "the best of the Achaeans" *(aristos Achaiōn),* the issue signaled at the outset of the *Iliad* (1.91, 244, 412; see also 2.82; 5.103, 414; 13.313; 16.271-72, 274).[110] This is the completion of Achilles as well as the story of the *Iliad.*

That this episode with Priam marks the completion of Achilles' story in the *Iliad* may be seen further in what might seem to be an omission. The *Iliad* ends with Hector's funeral, but modern students raised on summaries of "Homer" may recall what later tradition supplied about Achilles' death between the *Iliad* and the *Odyssey:* the Trojan horse, the sacking of Troy, and Achilles felled by Paris' arrow.[111] As noted above, the death of Achilles is predicted by several figures — Thetis, Hector, and even the ghost of the dead Patroklos. However, the description of Achilles' death is not part of the *Iliad*'s narrative trajectory, which instead concludes with the encounter between Priam and Achilles. Nor does the *Odyssey* offer a description of Achilles' death. Instead, Achilles has been joined in death to his friend Patroklos, who in his ghostly form had earlier begged him: "Lay not my bones apart from yours, Achilles, but let them lie together" (*Iliad* 23.83-84). In the memory of the *Odyssey,* the two slain heroes reached their shared destiny "around the great city of king Priam . . . there Achilles, there Patroklos" (*Odyssey* 3.107, 109-10; cf. 24.36-37); the bones of the two heroes lie together (24.76).[112] Odysseus in his descent to the underworld gives witness to the final destiny of the two rejoined in Hades (*Odyssey* 11.467-68; cf. 24.15-16). At this point, the two are linked in life and death as glorious heroic brothers at the end of the Homeric era.

While the events of the *Iliad* may not stand nearly so distant in time from its classical audience as the traditions of the *Epic of Gilgamesh* do from later Mesopotamian tradition, there seems to be a sense of a bygone age in the *Iliad,*[113] that the Homeric era has passed and its audience lives in a later and rather different time.[114] In this respect, the *Iliad* is not unlike the story of David and Jonathan.

3. David and Jonathan

The literary medium presenting the biblical pair differs from the other cases. The biblical story offers only one seminal moment in the poetic medium, unlike the poetic texts of *Gilgamesh* or the *Iliad.* Prose storytelling dominates the presentation of David and Jonathan, which is complex and layered, thanks to the harmonization of different traditions centered on a number of events in their lives. As with the Gilgamesh story, this is a complex matter beyond the scope of this discussion.[115] The story of David and Jonathan breaks out in the poetic form of lamentation only with the emotional highpoint of 2 Sam. 1:19-27, itself originally independent of the prose material; the poem's purpose is not a continuation of the prose's or vice-versa.[116] For this reason I have decided to devote a separate chapter to the poem in Chapter Ten. Here I will offer only a short overview of the warrior pair, David and Jonathan, as it relates to the epic pairs of *Gilgamesh* and the *Iliad.* Not only in the poem, but also in the prose, echoes of epic sensibilities may be discerned.[117] It has been thought that the models of heroic love from Mesopotamia and Greece may have influenced the prose rendering of the biblical pair.[118]

The arc of the overall biblical narrative is different from what we see in either *Gilgamesh* or the *Iliad.* First of all, David at the beginning of his story is not royalty, unlike Gilgamesh or Achilles. Instead, it is David's dear friend Jonathan who enjoys royal lineage; in this respect Jonathan is certainly more like Patroklos than the wild-man Enkidu. The biblical story ends with David becoming what Jonathan was supposed to become. In this respect, David will become Jonathan. Initially an outsider to the monarchy,[119] David enters the king's service and wins the hearts of the king's daughter and son (1 Samuel 18), another dynamic alien to the stories of Gilgamesh and Achilles. At the time of the Philistine war in which Jonathan dies with his father, David resides at a distance. He is not present at war, not even in the Israelite camp, and he belatedly receives the news of the deaths of the royal father and son.

The prose narrative of Samuel attends closely to David's many steps in his rise to kingship, and it notes various figures that attend to him in different ways, whether it is Saul, Jonathan, or Michal. I do not view David entirely in the sorts of politically cynical terms that recent scholars have suggested for the prose representation of David,[120] though these critics have a point. Looking at the emotional tenor that the narrative conveys, a different nuance in David's relationships might be discerned. He seems to take everything of the royal family, including marriage to the king's daughter and friendship with the king's son — initially, at least. As David gains Michal as his wife and Jonathan as his devoted friend, David also comes to anger the king, and in doing so, David arguably takes the sanity of the very king who was the first to favor him (see 1 Samuel 16). In taking from the family of the king, David positions himself to become king. He steals the affections of Saul and his family, as they come "to love" (*'hb) David: first Saul (1 Sam. 16:21), then Jonathan (18:1, 3) and Michal (18:20, 28), as well as all Israel and Judah (1 Sam. 18:16). Yet David seems hardly to reciprocate on the affective level. Even with Jonathan, the affection of David is hardly symmetrical.[121] This can be seen in two important details. According to the longer recension in 1 Sam. 18:1-4,[122] even as the text tells us that the two loved each other dearly, it is Jonathan who is said to love David as himself (see also 20:17).[123] It is also Jonathan who gives to David his clothing and weapons, as noted by Christophe Nihan.[124] In his speech to David in 1 Sam. 20:16,[125] Jonathan declares that it is he who has made a covenant with the house of David, again signaling that up to this point in the story, it is Jonathan who is incorporated into David's household. To highlight the terms of their relationship, the narrative in the very next verse reiterates Jonathan's love for David. Up to this point in the story of their relationship, there seems to be a certain affective asymmetry.

Some shift may be detected shortly thereafter, in 1 Sam. 20:41-42, when the two warriors separate. They kiss each other and weep together "until," as the very end of v. 41 tells us, "David did so greatly *('ad-dāwîd higdîl).*" This unparalleled expression has troubled commentators,[126] but if it may be taken more or less at face value, this turn of phrase suggests a turn in the representation of David's emotional life. At this point, David appears the greater in emotional expression; in affect David now surpasses Jonathan. While David had Jonathan in his life, it was Jonathan's emotional expression that was the more pronounced; now that David faces the prospect of losing Jonathan, his emotional expression exceeds his beloved friend's. Here David and Jonathan exchange places; David becomes by comparison the emotional one. There is something poignant in this development: Jonathan's emotions for David have been fully expressed in their time together, but David's come into their own only when facing life without Jonathan. The same might also be said for Achilles and Gilgamesh. These three great heroes seem to find their affective selves only as they face the prospect of losing their beloved companion; until that point, their emotional selves appear muted by comparison. The small signal here at 1 Sam. 20:41 perhaps heralds the completion of the warrior as companion. David has been already a great hero in battle; now David becomes a great hero in expressing his devotion to his warrior companion.

David's emotional devotion is expressed more fully in the wake of Jonathan's death. The news of his death seems to reveal in this passing moment a side of David that otherwise is rare up to this point in the prose narrative. The poetic words in 2 Samuel 1, most certainly in the final lines of the poem (in vv. 26-27), reveal a David never seen before in the prose narrative. Here David emotionally voices his recognition of Jonathan's love for him:

> 26I am in pain over you, my brother;
> O Jonathan, you were so desirable to me,
> Wondrous was your love for me,
> Greater than the love of women.
> 27How the warriors fell,
> The weapons of war perished!

I will devote Chapter Ten to this poem. For now we may observe that David up to this point in the prose narrative is almost prosaic by comparison with this poetic David.

With David's separation from Jonathan and then at his death, the text shows David's rising emotional expression, which will recur later in his family tragedies, in particular in his lament over his dead son, Absalom (2 Sam. 19:1-5). In rapid succession in 2 Samuel 19, David's emotional capacity appears on display: he can be accused by Joab of misplaced compassion; he can offer mercy to Shimei;[127] he can adjudicate in favor of the grandson of his old enemy, Saul; and he treats Barzillai the Gileadite well. We might suspect that the David of the text feigns his emotions for the audience (or his textual "spinners" do), perhaps as part of his chameleonlike abilities, as scholars have suspected. Or, we may see the personal David overtaking the political David.

Like Gilgamesh's narrative, David's story hardly ends with the conflict of war and the resulting loss of his comrade. He, too, rules the kingdom after the death of his beloved friend. This long prose story of David and Jonathan offers ongoing reflections on kingship and friendship. It is, at least in part, a series of reflections on the meaning of heroic friendship put most poignantly in the poetic expression of 2 Sam. 1:19-27, which we will examine in detail in Chapter Ten. The pairs of warriors discussed in this chapter find their identities in the relationships that they have with one another. Other figures that the heroes encounter also play a role in shaping their characters. The wider web of relationships in each of the three stories is the subject of the next chapter.

CHAPTER THREE

Gender Inversion in the Poetry of Heroic Pairs

1. Introduction

The *Epic of Gilgamesh*, the *Iliad*, and the biblical book of 1 Samuel present their heroic pairs within a larger web of relationships. These involve a number of peripheral human women,[1] as well as an initial opponent or adversary of the greater member of the heroic pair.[2] In all three classic texts, human women stand at the edge of the hero's life, while his relationship with his close companion remains central. The situation with goddesses in these traditions ranges considerably, contributing in large measure to the differences across these narratives.[3]

In *Gilgamesh*, human women, the goddess, and the heroic pair form a series of relationships that drives the narrative. *Gilgamesh* is particularly rich in its descriptions of Ishtar and her involvement with the hero. In the first half of the epic, the two figures are often at odds in the story, but Ishtar's role fades in the epic's second half. Moreover, as we will see, the story links Gilgamesh's rejection of Ishtar to his choice of Enkidu as his companion. Unlike Ishtar, the named human women, Shamhat and Siduri, stand in important transitional and supportive roles in *Gilgamesh*.[4]

For the *Iliad*, several goddesses are crucial in the human-divine synergy, as seen in various military engagements. In contrast to *Gilgamesh*, the *Iliad* is well stocked with both gods and goddesses, yet no deity is Achilles' opponent or adversary. In fact, warrior goddesses and gods generally support one army or the other: Athena and Hera on the side of the Achaians, versus Ares and Apollo on the side of the Trojans (see especially 4.439; 5.35, 825-34; 7.17-42; 10.515-16). Hera refers to those deities supporting the Achaians (including herself) as "all we who are aiders of the Danaans" (*Iliad* 8.205). Deities also have their favorites: Athena is partial to Odysseus (2.279); Aphrodite favors Paris (3.374-76); and Menelaus is called "dear to Ares" (3.206, 438, 457; 4.150, etc.). Divine mothers also hold their warrior sons in special regard, for example, Thetis, the mother of Achilles,[5] and Aphrodite, the mother of Aeneas. Achilles does not come into conflict with a goddess[6] as Gilgamesh does. Human women in the *Iliad* are also important for the story. Helen of Troy is the original cause of the war between the Trojans and the Achaians (*Iliad* 9.339), while the dispute over Briseis[7] causes the initial conflict between Achilles and Agamemnon (*Iliad* 1.8-412; 9.131-34, 273-74).[8] To some degree, the females function as pawns; they are almost pretexts for the conflict[9] between Achilles and Agamemnon over which one is the "best of the Achaians" *(aristos Achaiōn).*[10]

The biblical story of David is entirely different in lacking a goddess. Instead, central to the narrative is the national patron god's support, signaled by the divine "spirit" given to David and removed from Saul (see 1 Samuel 16). The biblical case figures a god in this important divine role, in contrast to the *Epic of Gilgamesh* and the *Iliad* where the central divine figures include supportive goddesses. To be sure, gods figure prominently in the literatures of Mesopotamia, Israel, and Greece, but the biblical case is distinctive for the god as the hero's mainstay.[11] This situation of the national god instead of a warrior goddess[12] seems to correspond to the status of David, who is construed as the new head of national dynasty.[13] As we will also see, David has a number of wives, the most prominent being Michal, the daughter of Saul, who has her role to play in the web of relationships.

The opponent within the larger story drives much of the initial narrative. For Gilgamesh, it is his conflicts with Ishtar; for Achilles, it is his rivalry with Agamemnon; and for David, it is his troubles with Saul. In all three cases, conflict with the opponent initially structures the larger situation of the hero and his warrior companion. Yet over the course of each story, the adversary fades in importance submerged by the greater partner's attachment to his companion in the wake of his death. The human relationships in the three stories vary considerably. These may be viewed in schematic form in the diagram on page 70, which outlines the heroic pairs, their opponents, and the females central to the story.[14] As this diagram suggests, there is considerable variation in the opponent in the three narratives. By contrast to Gilgamesh's opponent, Ishtar, David's is neither divine nor female. It is King Saul, the father of his beloved friend, who is potentially deadly to him. Similarly, there is no goddess but a king, Agamemnon, who is Achilles' great opponent. The key women likewise vary in the three narratives. In David's story it is the

OPPONENT
Ishtar (goddess of the city)

HERO
Gilgamesh (city king)

COMPANION
Enkidu (man of outback)

KEY HUMAN FEMALE
Shamhat/Siduri (versus unnamed women of the city)

OPPONENT
Agamemnon (warrior-king)

HERO
Achilles (warrior-king)

COMPANION
Patroklos (royal warrior)

KEY HUMAN FEMALE
Helen/Briseus (objects of male conflict)

OPPONENT
Saul (king)

HERO
David (commoner)

COMPANION
Jonathan (king's son)

KEY HUMAN FEMALE
Michal (king's daughter)

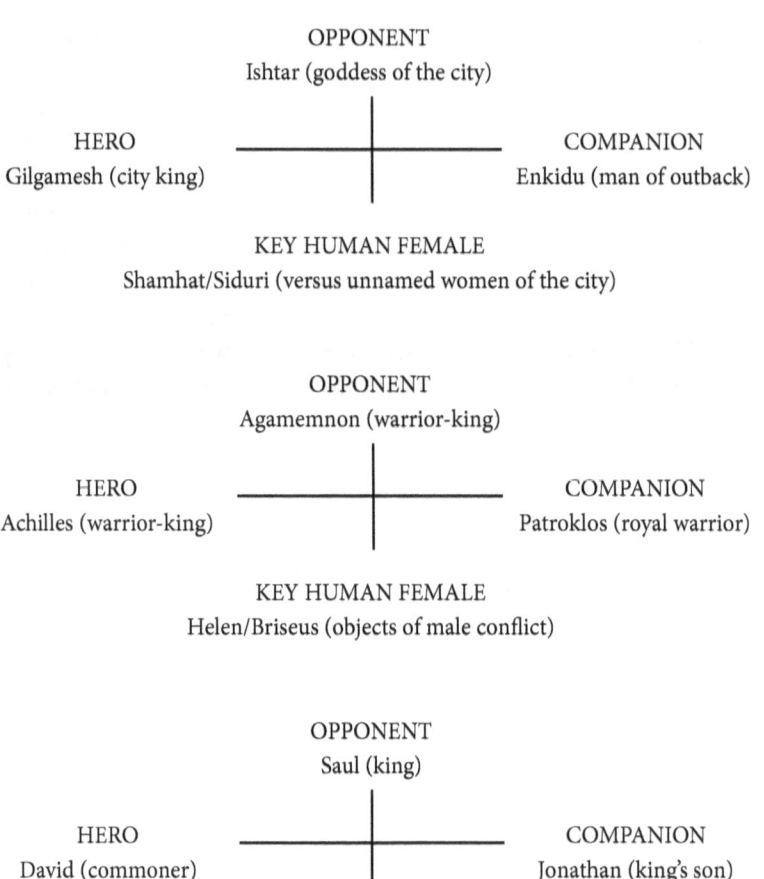

king's own daughter, while within the conflict between Achilles and Agamemnon it is the figure of the captive woman. To be sure, the larger context of the *Iliad* likewise places the famous Helen of Troy at the center of the cause of the Trojan War, but it is Briseis who lies at the center of the animosity between Achilles and Agamemnon. By contrast, no such human woman drives the narratives of Gilgamesh and David in a comparable manner.[15] This relative gap in the gender role perhaps corresponds to the dominant place of Ishtar as the divine opponent in the story of Gilgamesh.

The diagram on page 70 suggests that in each story, three of the four figures share something in common that the fourth figure lacks. This feature may suggest an important emphasis in each case. The biblical account highlights just how much David's narrative is a family story, or more precisely a royal family story, in which the nonroyal David will become what the others are. He is not yet a royal, but will become what Saul already is and what Jonathan is supposed to become, namely the successor to the throne. By contrast, Gilgamesh operates in the narrative tension created between the patron goddess of his city on the one hand, and on the other hand, his friendship with the man of the wild. Yet like David, Gilgamesh becomes what these other two protagonists are. As we have already seen in the preceding chapter, Gilgamesh's relationship with Enkidu makes him into something of an Enkidu figure; after Enkidu's death, Gilgamesh like Enkidu becomes a figure of the wilderness. With respect to Ishtar, Gilgamesh's rejection of the goddess figures as a central moment at the heart of the epic, but the story also begins and ends with Gilgamesh in her city functioning as he is supposed to. He, like Ishtar,[16] is ultimately a figure of the city. In the case of the *Iliad,* the three major figures are all warriors and royals,[17] while the fourth is the figure of Briseis; the dispute over her initially drives the dynamics of the warrior men. Winning Briseis back, Achilles becomes his great self by successfully taking up Patroklos' quest to defeat Hector and thereby displacing Agamemnon as "best of the Achaians." In all these cases, it is not only the companion, but also something of the adversary that the hero becomes.

Each story also includes an enemy — or something of an enemy — who defeats the lesser member of the heroic pair. On this score, the three stories differ sharply. Hector is the clearest and most direct example of the enemy. He defeats Patroklos (*Iliad* 16.818-22), who is in turn avenged by Achilles (*Iliad* 22.326-30). By contrast, the enemy in the story of David and Jonathan is unnamed Philistine archers (1 Sam. 31:3). Interestingly, the prose account in this chapter is centered more on Saul, and Jonathan is mentioned only in a list of his sons ("Jonathan, Abinadab, and Malchi-shua," v. 2). The narrative of 1 Samuel 31 is focused on Saul, quite in contrast to the poem of 2 Sam. 1:19-27, where Jonathan is highlighted along with Saul; there the enemy is named indirectly (in v. 20). *Gilgamesh* differs in lacking a military enemy altogether, and in part this reflects *Gilgamesh* as a story of heroic ventures, not one of war in a conventional sense. The enemy of Enkidu is the judgment of the gods against him (SBV VII.1, 85-89), sadly revealed to him in a dream (SBV VII.165-210). It takes the form of sickness and death (SBV VII.255-

67), a rather unheroic end. In short, for all their differences, all three lesser members of the heroic pairs die.

We may also note the varying landscapes for the narrative action in each case. The *Epic of Gilgamesh* involves no battlefields, no armies. The pair largely acts as heroic sportsmen and not as warriors. The conflicts of Gilgamesh and Enkidu are conquests of mythic monsters and journeys to faraway and mythic lands. The geography of the Gilgamesh story is particularly vast[18] (we might even say it is "epic" in scale).[19] For the *Iliad*, a narrow physical landscape of battle surrounds the heroic pair, as they stand initially removed from it and later enter it. The battlefield, with its scores of heroes and armies, is the scene of repeated engagements. The text is strewn over and over again with the bodies of warriors: "Then were heard alike the sound of groaning and the cry of triumph of the slayers and the slain, and the earth flowed with blood" (*Iliad* 4.450-51 = 8.64-65; cf. for the final clause, 10.484; 15.715; 20.494; see also 10.297-98). The text is packed with many famous warriors, with Achilles surpassing them all. Against the vast landscape of multiple conflicts and seemingly innumerable warriors,[20] the pattern of brothers in arms is not limited to Achilles and Patroklos. Other, lesser pairs likewise appear in battle: Idomeneus and his comrade, Meriones, in *Iliad* 7.165-66; Odysseus and Diomedes fighting together in 11; the two Lapiths in 12.127; Sarpedon and Glaucus in 12.307-30; and Aias and Teucer, in 12.344-70. Achilles and Patroklos emerge in the second half of the *Iliad* as the pair above the heroic pairs mentioned in the first half. They, as well as the other heroes who surround them in conflict, are warriors to the core. Many of them have their own epic story told about them. Indeed, as Deborah Beck has noted,[21] the *Iliad* is one-half speech. The *Iliad* is epic in its warriors and in their stories — or we might say, because of the stories told about them. Above them stands Achilles. Seth Benardete put the point this way: "Achilles is a hero in a world of heroes; he is of the same cast as they, though we might call him the first impression which has caught each point more finely than later copies. He holds within himself all the heroic virtues that are given singly to others, but his excellence is still the sum of theirs."[22] One caveat: Hector is considerably more than this quotation implies, and as the title of Bernadete's work would suggest (and as he himself seems to concede).[23] Still, he was right to point to Achilles as the Iliadic epitome of the hero, with a particular genius revealed in his near theophanic fury.

The biblical figures of David and Jonathan are also warriors, but their battles lie somewhat to the side of their relationship. The two comrades in their relationship stand between the two armies and their largely unnamed warriors, between the Philistines on one side and the Israelite army on the other side. David and Jonathan battle, but not together, in contrast to the victory of Saul and David lauded in 1 Sam. 18:7; 21:11; and 29:5,[24] and the defeat of Saul and Jonathan lamented in 2 Sam. 1:19-27.[25] After 1 Samuel 19, when Saul urges Jonathan and his servants to kill David, he never enters the fray on either side. David, like Achilles, will not be present in battle when his beloved companion falls, and David, like Achilles, will take up and end the conflict successfully. If this biblical story can be called an epic analogous to *Gilgamesh* and the *Iliad*,[26] then it is the story of David's kingship emerging in the era of the Philistine wars, with him becoming what or who Jonathan was supposed to become.

What we will see in the discussion that follows is a number of interesting inversions in terms of gender roles.[27] As we will observe, most gods and goddesses exhibit the same roles as men and women in human society,[28] but in a number of important instances, there is an inversion of goddesses' roles relative to their human female counterparts. In these stories, gender inversion is an important feature, which emerges in different ways. We begin with a gender inversion associated with goddesses in the literary traditions of the *Iliad* and *Gilgamesh*.

2. The Goddesses

We may begin this section by making a general observation about warrior goddesses in the *Iliad* and *Gilgamesh*. As I have noted above, a goddess does not play a role in the case of the biblical narrative, but as suggested in Parts III and IV of this study, warrior goddesses are evident in Ugaritic and also appear in early Israelite warrior culture. The *Iliad* and *Gilgamesh* show the warrior goddesses in a manner inverse to the roles of human women. In their roles, the warrior goddesses are not generally parallel with human women, who are not customarily cast in any warrior role. In other roles manifest by deities, there is often consistency in gender relative to their human counterparts. To state what is well known on this score, divine fathers are male and divine mothers are female; divine kings are male and divine queens are female. In the arena of warfare, both gods and goddesses are warriors, yet in the texts of Mesopotamia, Ugarit, and early Israel, and Greece, it is goddesses who are linked to human warfare and hunting and the men that conduct it. With gender, warfare shows an inversion of divine roles compared with humans.[29] Why?

Let me begin with three possible — and possibly interrelated — reasons. First, this difference about gender and war on the divine and human levels may signal a broader cultural understanding of warfare as an inversion of what otherwise was considered as "regular" or "routine" human existence: warrior life and warfare are represented as an inversion of routine life without war. For example, it is evident that the military camp is consecrated (1 Sam. 21:5), with sexual activity with women absent (1 Sam. 21:4; 2 Sam. 11:11-13); this stands in contrast to routine human life.[30] The warrior goddesses compared with human females also capture this cultural sensibility, which may also mask the basic reality of war as a common matter for ancient societies.[31] Second, gender inversion may also further glorify war or at least make it appear attractive with the presence of goddesses, sometimes even in an alluring manner. Third and finally, the goddess may reflect not simply a model for male warriors, but as suggested by the Ugaritic story of Aqhat that we will study in the following chapter, the goddess is a patron and mentor of warriors.[32] This relationship may assume a certain sexual tension, which informs the stories of Gilgamesh and Aqhat. Both warriors, the goddess and the human male, stand in a relationship signaled and arguably heightened by a female-male dynamic.

We may begin the survey of goddesses in the three literary works with the *Iliad*. In the case of Achilles, he is aided by a number of goddesses. Athena provides divine counsel in restraining Achilles' anger against Agamemnon (1.194-95), and in concert with Hera, Athena appears in battle on behalf of the Greeks (5.736-37; 8.387). Athena is a warrior goddess unlike Aphrodite, described as "a weakling goddess and one of those goddesses who lord it in the battle of warriors — no Athena she, nor Enyo, sacker of cities" (5.592; cf. 5.348-51). Zeus distinguishes between goddesses of war and goddesses of marriage; Athena belongs to the former, Aphrodite to the latter (5.426-30). Still Aphrodite intervenes to help Paris (3.37-38). Thetis, the divine mother of Achilles, likewise appears before Achilles (1.357-58; 18.85-86), approaches Zeus on his behalf (1.502-3), and provides her son with armor (18.368-69; 19.3-4). In the *Iliad*'s denouement that we explored in Chapter Two, Thetis tells Achilles to accept the ransom for the body of his enemy, Hector (23.137).[33] Thetis, in her support of her son as well as her advice to him and her advocacy on his behalf, somewhat resembles Ninsun, the divine mother of Gilgamesh.[34] Within the wide array of Greek goddesses, it is to be noted that none is the warrior's mortal foe. On the contrary: not only his mother, Thetis, but also the divine warrior, Athena, offers crucial help to Achilles. This situation contrasts sharply with the situation in the story of Gilgamesh.

The portrayal of goddesses in *Gilgamesh* is important, as it is in the *Iliad*. However, where goddesses offer strong help to the hero, in *Gilgamesh* the roles of the central goddesses are polarized. On the one hand, important in the narrative are the nurturing goddesses, Ninsun, the hero's mother, and Aruru, who creates Enkidu.[35] In their creative capacities, Ninsun and Aruru are somewhat parallel female presences. Ninsun further hears Gilgamesh's request for blessing, and in turn she beseeches Shamash on his behalf (SBV III.23-115).[36] She further inducts Enkidu ceremonially into the ranks of her cultic personnel and thereby adopts him, as she says (SBV III.120-27): "I myself hereby adopt Enkidu, whom [I love] as a son." On the other hand, the central goddess in *Gilgamesh* is Ishtar, and her role vis-à-vis the hero is sharply conflictual compared with any goddess in the *Iliad*. She is first seen in her efforts to court Gilgamesh; and when he rejects her advances, she acts as his adversary. Rivkah Harris observes that the goddess at once shows the warfare attributes associated with human males and the sexual roles characterized by human females — and in superabundance in both.[37] Gilgamesh captures both sides of the goddess in his encounter with her, first as would-be sexual lover and then as his adversary.[38] If polar opposites are expressed in the relationship of the two heroes (for example, as emblems of the city and the wild),[39] polar opposition is located within the figure of the goddess herself. Stated differently, she embodies a duality of her own in alternating between affective connection to the hero and aggression towards him, as she is attracted to yet rejected by the hero.

No goddess informs the story of David as we see in the *Iliad* or *Gilgamesh*. Instead, it is David's family and personal god who help him succeed on most every front. This divinity is no opponent to David, as we see with Ishtar in *Gilgamesh*. In this respect, David more closely resembles Achilles, for while goddesses play significant roles through the *Iliad*, there is little sense that any one in particular opposes the hero to the death. In *Gilgamesh* and the *Iliad*, the encounters between warrior goddesses and human warrior men provide important scenes for tracking the larger flow of the narrative and for offering a charged contrast with the hero's other relationships. While no goddess enters the narrative world of David and Jonathan, traces of goddesses in Israel's early warrior culture as known from outside of the Bible can be discerned. Viewed in this light, the evidence of the Bible says as much, if not more, about the loss of this feature of warrior culture, as the Israelite monarchy became established and the national god perhaps takes up the warrior role of the goddess in human warfare.[40] The situation, as it seems from the Bible, concerns not only the absence of the warrior goddess, but also a shift within ancient Israel's polity.[41] This manner of Israel's "social disidentification" with its past[42] may be situated within an effort to charter Israelite distinctiveness, as part of the later proclamation of Yahweh as Israel's singular national god.

3. Human Females

Warfare is not only a matter of physical conflict. In going to war, heroes perform social roles defined in large measure by gender.[43] It is the cultural expectation that human females are generally not part of combat,[44] in contrast to the paradigmatic presence of goddesses in warfare. As we will see, human females in the three stories are not portrayed as warriors, but play other roles. In turn, the paradigm accusation of weakness aimed at men at war is to compare them with women or to be defeated by them, as we will note below.

Gilgamesh presents human women as objects of sexual satisfaction,[45] figures of culture or acculturation, or sources of wisdom, but not as figures of combat.[46] This seems to be a broadly held attitude in ancient Near Eastern literature. In Egypt, where the martial role of royal women is known, its wisdom literature could pose the question, "Had women ever marshaled the battle array?"[47] In the Tale of the Two Brothers, one of the divine brothers shrinks from conflict with the Sea when he says to his new wife: "I cannot rescue you from it, because I am a woman like you."[48] The Seven of the Erra Epic, "the ones who are in fury," ask: "Shall we eat woman food, like noncombatants?"[49] The Epic of Creation (as *Enuma Elish* is commonly called) shows Ea declaring: "A woman's force may be very great, but it cannot match a man's."[50] Neo-Assyrian sources commonly disparage male enemies by recourse to their feminization, as Cynthia R. Chapman has observed.[51] One well-known instance involves a curse in a treaty between Ashur-nerari V and Mati-ilu, king of Arpad: "let the same (Mati'ilu) be a prostitute, his soldiers be women."[52] Chapman notes as well the disparagement of male warriors by comparison with women also in the Bible (e.g., Nah. 3:13; cf. 2 Sam. 3:29;[53] Jer. 31:32; 48:41; 49:22; 51:30; see also Judg. 4:9; 9:54).[54]

The *Iliad* refers to men as women in order to reproach allies, to taunt enemies, or to indicate their unsuitability for battle. Thersites "of measureless speech" (*Iliad* 2.212) reproaches his fellow Greeks for their support of Agamemnon at Achilles' expense: "Soft fools! Base things of shame, you women of Achaea, men no more" (*Iliad* 2.235-36; cf. 7.96-100).[55] It did not bode well for Nastes when "he came to battle all decked in gold, like a girl, fool that he was" (*Iliad* 2.872). Menelaus reproaches his fellow Achaians when they shrink from Hector's challenge to single combat with him: "Ah me, you braggarts, you women of Achaea, men no more!" (*Iliad* 7.96). Put in the mouth of Hector are several images of women intended to denote inability in battle. He declares that Aias should not try to frighten him "like some puny boy or a woman who knows not the deeds of war" (*Iliad* 7.235-36).[56] Hector taunts Diomedes: "now they will scorn you; you are, it appears, no better than a woman" (8.163). Later Hector fears that Achilles will "slay me out of hand unarmed, as if I were a woman" (22.124-25).[57] Women are set in huts, away from battle (*Iliad* 19.280).[58]

Beyond Homer, the disparagement of warriors by comparison with women is hardly uncommon. Polybios (32.15.9) criticizes the "unmanly" behavior of King Prousias II of Bithynia in connection with a disastrous war against Pergamon: "After doing nothing worthy of a man in his attacks on the town, but behaving in a cowardly and womanish manner both to gods and men, he marched his army back to Elaia."[59] Sexual language informs the language of battle. "Get pregnant (with this)," reads an inscription on a lead sling bullet found on Cyprus, thought to have been projected by Ptolemaic soldiers at their enemy.[60] The inverse notion is applied to Amazons, women regarded as "the peers of men" (*Iliad* 3.189; 6.186, etc.).[61]

At the same time, women have a significant cultural role to play in warfare. As we noted earlier, the Trojan War is driven by one woman, Helen of Troy, and it is extended on the Greek side by the dispute between Achilles and Agamemnon over Briseis, herself a captive of battle. Briseis is in effect a trophy of war[62] — and Helen herself is not entirely different. As noted by Angelos Chaniotis,[63] women as war plunder is a regular trope in Greek literature (*Iliad* 2.225-29; 3.301; 6.454-55, 465; 8.164-66, 291; 9.129, 139, etc.), as it is in elsewhere (e.g., Judg. 5:30). In *Iliad* 9.663-68, the only sex scene that mentions Achilles and Patroklos locates the two men on "the opposite side" from one another, each with a woman at his side; Patroklos' woman in this scene is said to have been given to him by Achilles. Women as war plunder is not only a literary trope in epic literature.[64] The Greek historian Phylarchos styles the war in Sparta in 272 B.C.E. between its former ruler and his successor as a fight not only for the city, but also for the king's wife.[65] No women are taken as captives in *Gilgamesh,* but they are treated as little more than objects of sexual gratification (SBV I.72, 76, 91; see also the serving girls in SBV VI.171 to whom Gilgamesh brags about himself).

In the context of warfare, women are more than captives. They serve other functions as well. Their role in lamenting military defeat is well known. For example, Briseis and the other women lament Patroklos (*Iliad* 19.282-302), and Andromache, Hecabe, and the other women lament Hector (22.315; 24.725-45, 746-47).[66] Similarly, the lament over Saul and Jonathan is commanded of the women by David (2 Sam. 1:24). Gilgamesh couches his lament for his Enkidu in terms of lamenting women (SBV VIII.44-45): "I shall mourn, Enkidu, my friend,/like a professional mourning woman I shall lament bitterly."

Fokkelien van Dijk-Hemmes, following S. D. Goitein,[67] has noted a further role for women as offering "comments on political occurrences."[68] Van Dijk-Hemmes has pointed to 1 Sam. 18:7; 21:11; 29:5 as an example of women's song particularly championing David.[69] The women told to weep over Saul in 2 Sam. 1:24 might be viewed in this light.[70] Chaniotis notes women's roles as spectators at battle and judges of military valor. Chaniotis comments:

> One of the typical images of besieged cities in ancient art and literature — for example, in the *Iliad* or in the Nereid Monument at Xanthos (ca. 400 BC . . .) — represent women anxiously watching from the city walls a battle that might determine their fate. . . . Their role is, nevertheless, not just that of the passive spectator. Very often they pass judgment upon the warriors. Again, this goes back to very early tradition. In a famous scene in the *Iliad* (3.161-242), Priam and Helena — an old man and the prospective booty of the besiegers — watch the battle and Helena recognizes the Achaian warriors and gives information about them. Later, when Paris retreats, she is the one who castigates his behavior as cowardly (3.426-36).[71]

Chaniotis proposes other cases of women who sing the praises of brave soldiers. The communicative function of women, as claimed by Chaniotis, has been appreciated by biblical commentators, yet the evaluative role of women may suggest a further perspective on the biblical material.

The celebration of victory also elicits another response from women, specifically in their being attracted to the successful warriors. Michal is reported to be in love with David (1 Sam. 18:20, 28), shortly after the report of his great victories (1 Sam. 18:7).[72] The report of Phylarchos (noted above) states that upon seeing the young Akrotatos "covered with blood and triumphant, the Spartan women thought that he had become taller and more beautiful than ever and envied Chilionis her lover."[73] Chaniotis asserts that the Spartan women loved Akrotatos not despite his bloody appearance, but because of it.[74] In this case, blood serves as the male cosmetics of war. The notion may seem unlikely, but it is to be remembered that the red of cosmetics and the red of blood mark the warrior goddess, Anat. In KTU 1.3 II, she puts on cosmetics of red henna before battle (lines 2-3) and she washes in the blood of warriors following battle (lines 34-35).[75] In these cases of Akrotatos and Anat, the blood of enemies is a powerful and perhaps attractive mark of triumph.[76]

4. Brotherly Bonds

Informing the exclusion of human females and the inclusion of divine females is the bond between brothers. In Chapter Two, we surveyed the heroic pairs and the bonds between them. The specific nature of this bond was discussed in antiquity, as it is today. In the case of Achilles and Patroklos, later Greek writings, such as the speech of Phaedrus in Plato's *Symposium* (179e-80b), affirm their relationship as a model for lovers.[77] In Aeschylus' lost play *Myrmidons,* they are lovers.[78] By contrast, other ancient authors, such as Xenophon in his *Symposium,* argued that it was inaccurate to label their relationship as a romantic one.[79]

The modern discussion of warrior-pairs has followed suit, with the debate focusing on whether or not the pairs of warriors engage in physical sexual activity.[80] There is no doubt that the bond between brothers is emotionally strong and physically palpable. As the survey below indicates, our texts are highly suggestive of intimacy between men. At the same time, same-sex physical relations are hardly pronounced in the three stories.[81] Achilles and Patroklos are bound by family history and then by battle, but they are never described by Homer as lovers as such. As noted above, the only sex scene depicts Achilles and Patroklos, the two men on "the opposite side" from one another, each with a woman at his side (*Iliad* 9.663-68). Hans van Wees suggests that this explicit expression of heterosexual physical relations distinguishes it from other warriors' sexual relations acceptable in Homer's time.[82] In contrast, Daniel Ogden surmises that the two were lovers, based on circumstantial evidence.[83] Achilles may be "yearning for the manhood and valiant might of Patroclus" (*Iliad* 24.6), yet this does not necessarily point to a picture of physical, sexual relations. Still it cannot be disproven.

David and Jonathan are joined by a covenant (1 Sam. 20:16; 23:18) that links them across family lines and serves as an expression of their love. Even more, the comparison "more than the love of women" for Jonathan's love for David (2 Sam. 1:26) is unusual and differs significantly from other expressions of covenantal "love," as Saul Olyan has noted.[84] For Olyan, this expression is not one of "covenantal love." The love of Saul (1 Sam. 16:21; cf. 18:22) for David sounds like the standard sort of covenantal love. However, the love expressed in 2 Sam. 1:26 stands in a wide web of the expressions of "love" that build on — yet also exceed — covenantal love: not only Jonathan's (1 Sam. 18:1, 3), but also Michal's (1 Sam. 18:20, 28). All Israel and Judah likewise "love" David (1 Sam. 18:16). Olyan notes that the expression in 2 Sam. 1:26 stands closer to Jacob's love for Rachel ("he loved Rachel more than Leah") in Gen. 29:30 than to the more common expression of covenant loyalty that the biblical text uses elsewhere (it is also notably different in that it is Jonathan's great love for David that David is acclaiming and not David's own love for Jonathan).[85] Römer and Bonjour note the multileveled nature of their "love": it is at once personal, political, and religious.[86] This complex expression of love may be understood as homoerotic.[87] There is strong attraction and attractiveness in the expressive lament in 2 Sam. 1:26, and it may convey a relationship that is "sexual or sexual-psychological," in Olyan's terms.

At the same time, the biblical story does not provide a clear sense of the physical-sexual side of this relationship. The biblical narrative does not represent the two heroes as having sexual relations, much less particular physical proximity or shared battle experience. It is not possible to rule out this possibility; after all, the scholarly dictum holds that absence of evidence is not evidence of absence. Still these texts generally differ in the manner in which they present the explicit male-female sexual relations on the one hand, and on the other hand, the largely indirect representation of the male-male relationship. While scholars often see some cultural reason at work for this difference, it itself may be an important literary difference worthy of further exploration. To anticipate, the erotic language of 2 Sam. 1:26 suggests a highly charged relationship of physical and psychological magnetism, one that we see David exercising on many around him in 2 Samuel. The poem of 2 Samuel 1 recognizes Jonathan's particular attachment, which David only seems to fully understand now that he has lost him. David recognizes that Jonathan was more attached to him than to any woman. Indeed, 1 Samuel 18 describes the love that both Jonathan and Michal feel toward David. The biblical story seems to create a very special space for this male-male relationship between psychological-sexual attraction and physical expression. We will return to this issue after we examine the comparable language for the other pairs of heroes.

The most involved case of sexual language and imagery involves Gilgamesh and Enkidu. Gilgamesh is arguably the most sexualized hero of all three narratives. At the center of the story is Gilgamesh in all his magnetic attractiveness; he is the model of the well-formed body of the king, according to Irene J. Winter.[88] In this regard, Winter points to four aspects of Gilgamesh's "physique, shape" (*gattu*, SBV I.29): it is well built or well formed (**banû*, SBV I.236); it is "good" or auspicious (*damqu*, SBV I.62); it has "life force, vigor, vitality" (*baštu*, SBV I. 236); and it is "attractive" (*kuzbu*, SBV I.237). This last attribute that Gilgamesh is said to have, namely "seductive allure" in Andrew George's translation,[89] also belongs to Shamhat (SBV I.164, 181).[90] The physical picture of the hero is a sort of physical attractiveness that can be associated with either males or females, and in Gilgamesh's case this entails a physical appeal to members of both sexes. Achilles (*Iliad* 1.673-74, 17.279-80) and David (1 Sam. 16:12, 18), too, are attractive.[91] All three figures embody a royal ideal[92] of masculinity put on textual display.[93] Gilgamesh is further said to be "so tall, perfect, and terrible" (SBV I. 37; see also I.61-62), as well as "powerful, pre-eminent, expert" (SBV I.90; see also line 75) and "perfect in strength" (SBV I.211). This physical model is often attributed as well to deities, perhaps suggesting that the ideal physique of Gilgamesh as well as other monarchs places them in the company of the gods. As Winter stresses, the story adds an emphasis on Gilgamesh's physique as the object of others' visual gaze. For example, the description of the hero in SBV I.234-39 begins with Shamhat's command to Enkidu: "look at him, regard his face." The powerful allure of the great physique is clearly expressed in Gilgamesh, compared with the possible hints at same-sex physical relations suggested by modern critics, as discussed below.

The relationship between Gilgamesh and Enkidu involves not only physical attraction, but also passionate attachment. This point is expressed in Gilgamesh's lament to Siduri, as beautifully rendered by Moran:

> [My friend, whom I still love so very much,]
> Who journeyed through all hardships with me,
> Enkidu, whom I still love so very much,
> Who journeyed through all hardships with me,
> Did journey to the fate of all mankind.[94]

The bond is deep on multiple levels. What more precisely seems to be the nature of the two heroes' relationship?

The evidence has been thoroughly studied by a number of biblical scholars, most notably Neal Walls, Susan Ackerman, and Jean-Fabrice Nardelli, as well as a number of Assyriologists, including Thorkild Jacobsen, Jerrold Cooper, Rivkah Harris, and Martti Nissinen. In addition, theories of gender and sexuality for the ancient world have been addressed admirably by a number of these scholars, in particular by Nissinen, Walls, and Ackerman.[95] This research rightly cautions against using modern labels and categories for the relationship between Gilgamesh and Enkidu, and the following discussion accordingly refrains from imputing modern notions of sexual orientation to the figures.[96] Much of the discussion of the relationship between Gilgamesh and Enkidu has focused on whether they engaged in full physical same-sex relations, which was a possibility for ancient Mesopotamia.[97]

Modern scholarship has expended considerable energy on trying to peek behind the narrative via various tantalizing details. As a result, we have perhaps been seduced into an approach that largely opts between maximal or minimal conclusions influenced by modern issues. A number of commentators have raised the question whether or not the modern discussion of homosexual relationships has played a role in favor of a maximal reading.[98] At the same time, the current cultural climate[99] has also arguably helped to extend scholarly horizons in order to understand better what is in or behind the narrative. So perhaps more should be seen behind the allusive sexual language and imagery.

The issue is important. At the same time, it may also miss a fundamental point, to be explored below, about how the text represents the matter of the heroes' relations. At the outset, let me say this: while the *Iliad* and the story of David and Jonathan contain fewer sexual expressions compared with the *Epic of Gilgamesh,* overall these two texts resemble Gilgamesh in showing explicit male-female sexual relations on the one hand, and on the other hand, largely indirect and often analogical language for the male-male relationship. As Römer and Bonjour put the point, the texts in the first place do not address sex, but love.[100] On this point there seems little dispute. To be sure, future discovery of Gilgamesh texts might alter the picture on this score, but this is where the textual evidence currently stands.

Building on the works of many scholars, I will explore how the *Epic of Gilgamesh* represents the intimacy and attraction of the warrior pair. The basic point is this: the narrative creates a magnetic zone of charged emotional intimacy and physical attraction between and around the heroic pair. It achieves this representation of heroic love between the highly explicit sexual relations between male and females (as well as the expressions of sexual allure of some human males and females) on the one hand, and on the other hand, the deliberately evocative female imagery representing male-

male relations. Before spelling out this contrast, it is necessary first to address the evidence in the text for the relationship between Gilgamesh and Enkidu, as well as the views of Assyriologists concerning this language. There are five main sorts of information that are suggestive of a picture of physical intimacy and attraction.[101] Building on the work of other scholars, I will address each piece of evidence in turn and offer some comments for each one that contribute to the larger picture, as I see it.

1. The dreams and their narrative realizations. We begin with the two dreams of Gilgamesh about Enkidu, as these have particularly fueled the issue.[102] Their evocative love images are unmistakable and important, and scholars have rightly emphasized them in the discussion. In Gilgamesh's dreams, the "axe" *(ḫaṣṣinu)* and the "lump of rock *(kiṣru)* from the sky" engender his physical affection "like a wife":

> "[I loved it] like (*kīma* [gim]) a wife and I caressed it and embraced it." (SBV I. 256)

> "I saw it and became glad.
> I loved it like *(ki-ma)* a wife, caressing it and embracing it,
> I took it up and put it at my side *(aḫu)*."
> (OB II, col. i, lines 32-35; cf. SBV I.283-84)

For each of these dreams, Ninsun confirms their meaning. In both cases, her interpretation repeats her prediction that "you will love him like a wife, and will caress and embrace him" (SBV I.267, 288-89). There is no doubt that the dreams concern Enkidu for the SBV, as made explicit by the description of Enkidu in I.150-52: "There was a certain fellow who [came by the watering-hole,]/mightiest in the land, [he possesses strength.]/His strength is] as mighty as a lump of rock of Anu from the sky (literally, "of Anu," *ki-ma ki-ṣi-ri šá* ^{d}*a-nim;* see also SBV VIII.48, for the third line). All of these passages involve analogy expressed by *ki-ma*, "like."

Given these passages, it is hardly surprising that several Assyriologists view the dreams as portending sexual relations. For example, Thorkild Jacobsen early in his career viewed this passage in sexual terms: "the dream cannot mean anything but that homosexual intercourse is going to take place between Gilgameš and the newcomer."[103] A. Leo Oppenheim seems to concede the point in an understated way: "an erotic interest is permitted to affect the friendship of the two heroes of the epic."[104] In his magisterial commentary on Gilgamesh, George concludes: "the language of the dreams is clear. Gilgameš will love Enkidu as a wife."[105] Moreover, these dreams take place, as Susan Ackerman has noted,[106] at the same time as the sexual relations between Enkidu and Shamhat. The SBV makes this connection explicit when Shamhat is instructed in the same terms found in Gilgamesh's dreams: "His 'love' will caress and embrace you" (SBV I.186). In this episode with Shamhat and in Gilgamesh's dream, Enkidu is involved: he will do sexually to Shamhat what Gilgamesh will do to Enkidu, according to the dream. In this view, the audience is supposed to understand that the dream interpretations herald the men's physical relations like those of Enkidu and Shamhat. As commentators have noted, the larger context of the story arguably reinforces the point: Gilgamesh has already chosen Enkidu, and he rejects Ishtar's proposal of marriage.

As these considerations suggest, there is something quite sexy about the dreams and their larger context. In the Mesopotamian context, Gilgamesh's dreams are symbolic rather than literal, in Oppenheim's terms.[107] Francesca Rochberg has related the dreams of Gilgamesh to dream omens.[108] While the narrative of Gilgamesh's dreams and their interpretation lack the signs of mantic practice,[109] their literary representation does exhibit three features known from omens. First, the verb used for Gilgamesh's "reporting" his dreams (**pašāru,* OB II, col. i, line 1 = SBV I.245; OB II, col. ii, line 44) is common in dream omina.[110] Second, his mother Ninsun plays the role of the interpreter, as Oppenheim noted.[111] Third, the subject of the first dream, the *kiṣru* from the sky, is suggestive of a celestial omen. The word serves as an analogue for a meteor in an omen text: "if a meteor flashes and disappears (on the horizon) like a *kiṣru* from west to east. . . ."[112] More broadly *kiṣru* is known for its celestial origins.[113]

I would like to explore the meanings of the dreams within the narrative arc of the story. The dreams provide an analogy between the content of the dream and the life of the dreamer. Both dreams are notable for their explicit simile, "like" *(kima)* a wife; this particle marks the image as an analogy.[114] The verbs, "to love," "to caress," and "to embrace," as a man does with a wife, do indeed sound like sexual relations. However, the narrative realizations of the terms of the dreams are no less important for understanding their sexual imagery. Gilgamesh's first dream sounds like an omen specifically for the wrestling match that the two undertake upon meeting.[115] The lump of rock in the second dream refers to the appearance of Enkidu into Gilgamesh's life, while the axe further signals their later adventures in the story, namely, axes used in the cedar forest (SBV II.248; V.55; cf. Gilgamesh's axe in SBV

IX.15; X.93). The force of the second dream has been unpacked by Jerrold S. Cooper with his insightful observation about the pun in the last line of the second dream (OB II i 35): the word for "side" here is *aḫu,* better known as the Akkadian word for "brother." The equation of the two terms and their application to Enkidu is explicit in Gilgamesh's lament over the dead Enkidu when he calls him "the axe at my side" (*ḫaṣṣinu aḫiya,* SBV VIII.46).[116] In other words, the image of lovers in the dream portends the later relationship of the two heroes who join forces in meeting conflicts together.

The question, as I see it, is whether the language is to suggest that Gilgamesh and Enkidu are lovers in the same physical sense as a husband and wife or whether being a warrior-pair is analogous in some way. The use of *aḫu,* "side/brother," suggests a brotherly life. In other words, warrior life may be analogous to brotherhood even as the text may charge the relationship with intimations of physical intimacy. The differing details in the dreams and their interpretation refer to events in the course of the two heroes' relationship, while the image of caressing found in both dreams speaks to the general nature of their relationship. The image of Gilgamesh caressing Enkidu, as stated in Ninsun's interpretation of the hero's dreams, hovers over the story. Gilgamesh's love for Enkidu marks their entire relationship, as Gilgamesh later refers to his deceased friend as the one "whom I love mightily *(ša arammušu danniš),* who with me went through every danger" (OB Meissner = Sippar, col. ii, line 2′; see also SBV X.55, 56; cf. 68-69).[117] The love that is expressed in physical, male-female terms in the dream is characterized here by Gilgamesh as a matter of two men who shared experiences of danger. We cannot and should not preclude the possibility of sexual relations between the two men, but if we work with what is preserved in our text, then Ninsun's interpretation of the image of Gilgamesh loving and caressing Enkidu as a wife finds its expression in their shared experience, according to Gilgamesh's own words. The image of male-female relations with its erotic overtones is played out in Gilgamesh's experience first in his meeting and wrestling with Enkidu,[118] and then in their shared adventures and companionship. If the interpretation of the dream is not fulfilled literally (and thus far there is no evidence that it is), it still charges the relationship with a certain magnetic attractiveness. The evidence of the dreams is important, and I will return to them below.

2. The analogy of Enkidu with a bride. Another love image between the two men informs the narrative later at Enkidu's death. At this point, Gilgamesh "felt his heart, but it was not beating any more. He covered (his) friend, (veiling) his face like a bride *(kallati)*" (SBV VIII.58-59).[119] Here again it is Enkidu who is implicitly compared with a woman, in turn suggestive of Gilgamesh as a possible husband figure. At the same time, this image is also followed by further similes of the eagle circling and of the lioness deprived of her cubs (SBV VIII.60-61); both are parent-child images. As these additional similes suggest, the text uses the analogy of relations between men and women as the point of reference for the feelings of warrior men for one another. The text uses particles of comparison, in particular "like" *(kima)*.[120] For these images, the text marks them as analogical in nature.

3. Kissing and hugging. The story of Gilgamesh shows the two men kissing and hugging: "You will hug him" (OB II, col. I, line 22); "they kissed and formed a friendship" (OB III i 18); and "they hugged each other, kissing one another" (SBV XII.88; note also Bilgames and the Netherworld 244-47).[121] So why not see further physical intimacy? This is what George has done in his reconstruction of SBV XII.96-97: "*'[My friend, the] penis* that you touched (so that your heart rejoiced, grubs devour [(it) . . . like an old *garment.*'"[122] George's italics in this translation reflect the broken nature of the text, which includes *išaru,* the word that he renders as "*penis.*" Every sign of this word is reconstructed, either wholly or in part.[123] George sees this expression as a reworking of a new Sumerian piece (MS rr), which shows Enkidu describing the corruption of the corpse of a woman who had been the sexual partner of Gilgamesh.[124] This alignment of the old Sumerian text with these lines from Gilgamesh suggests to George that in SBV XII.96-97 a sexual sense of the relationship of the two warrior-men is acknowledged. In addition, it is to be noted that the verb in question, *lapāṭu,* "to touch," is used in a sexual sense. In view of several rather different understandings of this broken line offered by scholars,[125] this particular passage will remain *sub iudice* for the issue of same-sex relations.

With judgment on this particular line suspended, we may return to the matter of the heroes kissing. OB III i 18-19 indicates the meaning of the physical act: "they kissed each other and formed a friendship." A few lines later, the significance of the kissing is put in these terms: "I have acquired a friend, a counselor/the one that I kept seeing in dreams" (OB Schøyen obv. 1′-2′ = OB III i 24-25). Later, in SBV XII.88, "they hugged each other, kissing one another." These kisses are arguably brotherly acts (see *Enuma Elish* II.1-5;[126] cf. Gen. 33:4; Exod. 4:27), or perhaps more broadly familial (see *Enuma Elish* I.54, III.132;[127] Gen. 27:26-27; 50:1; 1 Kgs. 19:20; cf. male-male kissing also in 2 Sam. 14:33; 19:39; 20:9). In other words, kissing may signal that the two warriors regard each other as brothers.[128]

4. The physical appearance of the heroes. Another marker of the heroes' physical relationship involves the language used for their physical appearance. Both men are said to be *damqu,* translated "fine" by George[129] (see SB I.207, VII.38). The same word is translated "handsome" in the *CAD.*[130] Perhaps closer to the mark is "attractive," as this word is used also for the beauty of women. Furthermore, Gilgamesh is said to be "perfect in beauty" (SBV 1.61). This is language of physical appeal used more commonly for women.[131] Similarly, Enkidu is described as being "adorned with tresses like a woman" (SBV I.106). Physical appeal is important in the story of these heroes.[132]

The image of Enkidu is designed to evoke an element in the relationship with Gilgamesh. Here as in the dreams, Enkidu is figured as a wifelike man for Gilgamesh. More broadly, Gilgamesh's attractiveness is a key element in the textual representation; all are to be drawn to him. His physical magnetism is a key force in the literary construction of the text — not only is he to be attractive to Enkidu, but also to everyone else in the text — and also, I suspect, to the audience. More specifically, Enkidu forms an inner circle of attractiveness with Gilgamesh. The other figures in the story — and perhaps the audience as well — are drawn to the beauty of these heroes. Like Enkidu, the audience is attracted to the great king as they follow the hero on his adventures. This physical magnetism among males is generated by competition and conflict as well as their success.

5. Sexual wordplay. A final marker of sexual relations between the heroes may underlie a number of words used in the narrative. In a well-known article, Anne D. Kilmer has proposed seeing an evocation of the heroes' sexual relationship by various terms in the story.[133] For Kilmer, *ḫaṣṣinu,* "axe," is suggestive of *assinnu,* a word for male prostitute; and the meteorite *kiṣru* may conjure up *kezru,* a male counterpart to the *kezertu,* a sort of cultic prostitute. In addition, the sexual symbolism of *pukku* and *mekkû* is thought by Kilmer likely to contribute as well.[134] Such wordplay and symbolism, if correctly ascertained,[135] charge the narrative presentation of the relationship with a sexual energy. Kilmer concludes that a full sexual relationship is in view, with Gilgamesh taking a sexual interest in Enkidu. Elsewhere Kilmer compares Enkidu's role vis-à-vis Gilgamesh with the Greek male youths adopted by high-status men for educational and sexual relations.[136]

Kilmer's observations about the wordplay in the text have found acceptance,[137] though not always with the conclusions that she draws. Noting the wordplays cited by Kilmer, Nissinen sees an implied analogy: "The roles of Enkidu and *assinnu* do not appear at first glance to be similar, but they have certain things in common: a divinely sanctioned 'otherness' compared with ordinary people, the role of the guarding of life, lifelong devotion and, finally, also of their appearance demonstrating the sexual aspect of 'otherness.'"[138] The final issue is whether or not the wordplay noted by Kilmer should be seen as indicative of sexual relations between Gilgamesh and Enkidu. According to Nissinen, it should not. The role of the *assinnu*, Nissinen observes, "was characteristically asexual rather than homosexual."[139]

It is difficult to confirm the force of such possible wordplay. It might be argued that such wordplay might be more in the eye of the beholder than operative for the ancient audience; it is hard to know either way. To illustrate the problem, let us return to one of Kilmer's proposals. She suggests in the case of *kiṣru* that it involves wordplay on *kezru*. At the same time, one may ask: if wordplay is involved, why not associate this use of *kiṣru* in the meaning of "lump" (meteorite) with the same word *kiṣru* in its meaning of "contingent of soldiers or troop"?[140] In this reading, Enkidu will appear like a military force, perhaps like those serving under the king, in this case Gilgamesh. I am not militating for this particular reading. Rather, I raise it in order to suggest something of the difficulty inherent in discerning the force of wordplay. Certainly, wordplay was a highly literate activity perfectly expected of such a literary great work as *Gilgamesh*. The issue is not so much whether wordplay is there or not; the question is what wordplay is actually involved for the ancient audience. For the purposes of this discussion, this sort of information remains unverifiable.

These five sorts of information are important, even if they are lacking as evidence for an explicit picture of same-sex relations. It is to be noted as well that description of further sexual relations between men is missing from our narrative poems, not only *Gilgamesh*, but also the *Iliad* and the Bible. One might conclude that none of these ancient texts understand these male warriors as engaging in physical sexual activity such as intercourse. Indeed, it might be argued that the pairs should not be understood as physical lovers, since when the texts describe actual sexual relations, they are explicit. As we have noted, Enkidu enjoys very explicit, sexual relations with Shamhat (OB II, col. ii, lines 46-49; SBV 1.191-95, 300).[141] The sexual relations that Gilgamesh and David enjoy with women are clear, even if presented in summary fashion. Gilgamesh frequently enjoys sex in the city. He is said to "meet with the young woman by night" in the OB version (II, col. v., line 198) and in the later SBV not to let the girl go to her bridegroom (SBV I.76, 91, II.113).[142] David "lay with" Bathsheba (2 Sam. 11:4; 12:24 — the twofold use of the expression serves as the frame for this episode).[143] Moreover, Gilgamesh is said to have wives waiting for him back in Uruk when he is about to set off on his journey with Enkidu to the Cedar Forest (SBV III.225): "let him bring his person back to his wives *(ḫi-ra-a-tu)!*"

Scholars have viewed the relationship between Gilgamesh and Enkidu in different ways. There are those scholars who see a relationship of full physical, sexual expression, as noted above. Other scholars see this as a possibility, but are unsure.[144] Still others do not see such physical relations. Let me offer a sample of Assyriologists who view the text in this way; each one makes interesting and important points. As noted above, Jacobsen early on interpreted their relationship as sexual love.[145] Jacobsen later changed his mind. Instead, he saw their relationship as a competition with marriage and as a replacement for it.[146] On this score, Harris and Ackerman, as noted above, largely follow suit. Jacobsen goes further. The relationship is, for Jacobsen, "a boyhood friendship," belonging to "preadolescence," suggesting a lack of physical, sexual relations. Gilgamesh is said to be "young" (*ṣeḫēru*, SBV II.289; V.145) and counts himself among the young men (*eṭlu*, SBV VI.172, 174; see also 180; cf. XI.213),[147] but Gilgamesh is hardly in "preadolescence." This characterization by Jacobsen is not how the text presents Gilgamesh's progression. Instead, it depicts Gilgamesh moving from sexual relations with women to a lack of sexual relations with his male companion. Contrary to Jacobsen's reading, Gilgamesh reverts from sexual relations with women to apparently no sexual relations as such with his male companion. It is not clear that Gilgamesh is "preadolescent."

Wilfred G. Lambert errs on the side of caution on the issue: "Babylonian texts do not avoid explicit language, so until further and less ambiguous language evidence is forthcoming the present writer does not assent to the proposal."[148] Indeed, Lambert's point is true of the sexual relations between men and women in the story of Gilgamesh. Benjamin Foster similarly suggests that their friendship "has no sexual basis at all."[149] By "sexual basis," Foster seems to be referring to physical relations beyond hugging and kissing. Foster continues: "This union seems the closer for being asexual and of near equals. . . ."[150] This formulation does not address either the physical attractiveness that the two are said to have or the interpretation of the dreams that refer to physical caressing. At the same time, Foster makes an interesting point that the friendship seems closer for not being one of intimate physical relations.

Harris sees an analogy of husband-wife in the relationship, but also without literal sexual relations: "What is noteworthy is that the relationship between them is not simply that of male and female, but that of husband and wife. Theirs then was a reversal of normal societal relations. . . . It is an example of category reversal — male acts like female."[151] This approach has generally been taken also by Ackerman, and with good reason given the striking language.[152] Indeed, Harris has rightly emphasized the inversion of gender in Gilgamesh. Harris further offers a view of matters behind the text: "I think that on a subliminal level, if not overtly, the composers of the epic were critical of so intense a relationship between men."[153] This sort of reading is possible and interesting; it is hard to confirm or disprove it.

In his discussion, Nissinen points to a range of attitudes toward male-male sexual relations.[154] On the one hand, the Middle Assyrian Laws seem to show disapproval: "If a man has sex with his comrade and they prove the charges against him and find him guilty, they shall have sex with him and turn him into a eunuch" (par. 20). On the other hand, the omen series known as *šumma ālu* shows no such attitude between equals: "If a man copulates with his equal from the rear, he becomes the leader among his peers and brothers."[155] Nissinen notes that the positive view taken here is reserved for equals; in other omens involving sexual relations between men of unequal rank, the omens are disapproving.[156] Finally, Nissinen notes a Mesopotamian almanac of incantations corresponding to heavenly constellations, which correlates Scorpio with the "love of a man for a man."[157]

Within this context, Nissinen has studied the question of the relations of Gilgamesh and Enkidu in considerable detail. He concludes: "Homoeroticism is certainly not a central theme in the *Epic of Gilgameš*."[158] Nissinen also suggests that the sexual relations enjoyed with women by both heroes are replaced by a relationship of loving tenderness between the two of them that is not expressed in sexual activity. Gilgamesh's sex in the city, Nissinen notes, is "now replaced by an accentuated masculine asceticism."[159] By asceticism here, Nissinen is apparently not referring to later practices of religious celibates; rather, he is capturing something of the state of warriors in battle (cf. Uriah the Hittite refraining from sexual relations with his wife Bathsheba while engaged in war, in 2 Sam. 11:11-13). Gilgamesh and Enkidu, by their friendship, perhaps place themselves in a warrior state involving what Nissinen calls "homosocial bonding," standing apart from the routine social institution and practices of family. Nissinen puts the relationships of Achilles and Patroklos and of David and Jonathan in the same category of "homosocial bonding," although according to Nissinen these two other pairs "do not share the sexual pessimism and masculine ascetism of the *Epic of Gilgameš*."[160]

The notion of the warriors refraining from sexual relations also fits another contour of the Gilgamesh story. Sexual relations mark Enkidu's way to the city and Gilgamesh's life in the city. In her essay on "Sex as Symbolic Form," Zainab Bahrani has remarked upon this feature of Enkidu's induction into human society, that sex is equated with culture and women: "Sex was not equated to nature but to culture. . . . Sex in the symbolic order of Mesopotamia, is in the realm of Woman."[161] The trajectory of the two heroes' relationship largely takes place beyond the zone associated with culture and women. Their travels together take them away from the city and evidently from what it means in terms of full sexual relations. Ackerman's understanding of the heroes as liminal figures seems to comport with this approach.[162] Ackerman goes further. According to her, the conflict between "the Epic's unrelieved insistence on the two heroes' egalitarianism" and its "frequent use of the hierarchically dependent language of erotic and sexual relationships in its descriptions of Gilgamesh's and Enkidu's interactions . . . *is precisely the point*."[163] For Ackerman, the liminal status of the two heroes allows them to be represented in terms of the superior-inferior/active-passive sexual paradigm without their interactions being limited to this paradigm. There is much in the text to support this "liminal interpretation." At the same time, it leaves open the possibility of full sexual relations. The text is ambiguous on the issue, for Ackerman.

It is this ambiguity — or more precisely, the construction of this ambiguity — that I wish to explore. To do so, I would like to focus attention again on how the narrative differs in its representation of male-female and male-male relations. The difference on this score is not simply an issue or interpretational problem; rather, it is arguably a significant datum for understanding the heroes' relationship. The crucial question is not whether or not the various sorts of information noted above point to same-sex physical relations between the two warriors, or whether it should be seen as ambiguous, as Walls and Ackerman have suggested.[164] Rather, it is also why the narrative represents the sexual side of this relationship in a suggestive manner rather than by more explicit indicators. Scholars who do not see full sexual relationships in or behind the language of the text need to account for this important metaphorical discourse, as underscored by Hanne Løland's cautions on gendered language when it is used analogously (in the case of her discussion, with respect to divinity).[165] Gendered language is critical to the representation of the heroes' relationship. Walls captures the textual "sexual tension" in his summary statement on the issue: "the epic's use of marital and gendered imagery to describe the heroes' intense relationship may be an attempt to depict the unorthodox relationship between two warriors who love each other as male-identifying men. Their intimate bonds of loyalty are likened to those of a married couple, while their passionate devotion is described with images that blur the distinction between platonic and sexual love."[166] Building on the work of scholars discussed up to this point, I would like to highlight two crucial dynamics at work, as I see it.

The first is literary. The female sexual imagery for the men's relationship conveys the magnitude of passion and the magnetism of attraction, with Gilgamesh especially presented as the center of attention. As noted above, the image of Gilgamesh's love for Enkidu, as stated in Ninsun's interpretation of the hero's dreams, hovers over the entire narrative of his relationship with Enkidu, and at the textual level it reaches expression only late, when Gilgamesh characterizes his love for Enkidu as a matter of experiences of shared danger (OB Meissner = Sippar, col. ii, line 2′; see also SBV X.55, 56; cf. 68-69).[167] Even if the physical intimacy is not fulfilled literally (and thus far there is no evidence that it is), male physicality still charges the relationship; it is homoerotic. As Foster suggests,[168] the narrative field of male attraction and attractiveness is arguably heightened by the actual lack of description or narration of actual sexual relations. It is precisely this combination of the presence of love language and the absence of explicit sexual relations that charges the relationship with a particular potency. Both the presence of such language for pairs of warrior men and the absence of actual full sexual relations between them infuses the characters with physical magnetism and emotional intimacy. It is in the narrative space between the presence of the love language and the absence of sexual action between the heroes where the text constructs a magnetic zone of male intimacy.[169] The heroes are attractive physically to both women and men: women get to respond to the heroes with physical proximity to this magnetic attraction differently from men, while the two heroes get to respond to one another with shared experience and intimacy differently from women. There is a certain eroticism involved for both women and men in relation to the hero. Indeed, the text constructs the two sets of gendered relations in relation to one another, but also in contrast with one another.

The second dynamic involves the cultural construction and representation of relations that are not simply male-male, but more specifically involve two human warriors. The claim that I want to explore is this: on the physical level, conflict shared by warrior males is like sexual relations shared between men and women. Both, in a sense, involve clashes of bodies: women and men with one another in sexual relations, heroes together in physical combat at each other's side. Let us return briefly to the dream report about the hero's encounter with the man who will become his beloved companion. The text characterizes the new companion as a meteorite that Gilgamesh says he could not pick up or push (OB II, col. i, lines 8-9). This physical resistance foreshadows their initial meeting, as the dream's interpretation by Gilgamesh's mother suggests (lines 17-22). Walls suggests that the wrestling match is sexualized, as it takes place outside the door of a bridal chamber: "The intimate bodily contact of wrestling . . . and the threshold symbolism of the doorway all contribute to the scene's sexual symbolism. The bridal chamber provides an erotically charged setting for their tussle."[170] In other words, the initial meeting narrated as a wrestling match, the text perhaps suggests, is analogous to sexual relations between a man and a woman. More broadly, Gilgamesh refers to Enkidu, the one whom he loved so greatly, as also the one who shared every danger with him. In the representation of warrior life in Gilgamesh, wrestling and combat, the physical activity undertaken by warriors together is akin to sexual activity.[171]

If shared male-male military experience is analogous to male-female sexual relationships, then the inverse is perhaps true as well: male-female relationships may be cast in military terms. The series Shaziga characterizes sex in terms of battle: "let the battle of my love-making be waged, let us lie down by night."[172] It is perhaps no accident that we find the image of "the dance of the two camps" for the lover's dancing in Song of Songs (7:1),[173] or that Nike, the goddess of military victory, was represented on Greek vases with wedding scenes, thought to represent "the victory of the bridegroom over the bride."[174] The *Iliad* refers to combat as *oaristus* (13.291; 17.228), translated as "dalliance" by Murray and Wyatt (LCL) but as "tender conversation" by van Wees. As van Wees observes, the term is "otherwise applied to relations between lovers and spouses."[175] Emily Vermeule notes further examples from Aeschylus and observes, "Aischylos shares the general fifth-century delight in the inter-penetration of war and love."[176]

It is perhaps in light of this analogy that we may also view metaphors of warfare as dance[177] or of battle as a feast or festival (*isinnu*) for men — and for Ishtar:[178]

> "battle is a feast for her (Ishtar)" (Agushaya)
>
> "battle and struggle are a feast for us"
> (Tikulti-Ninurta Epic ii 4; cf. iv 20)

"Should we fear and tremble like one who is not used to battle?
Going to war is nothing but a festival for men!" (Erra I:51)[179]

"at the clash of weapons, the festival of men" (Lugale IV 1)

For warriors, combat is a feast, not only for human warriors, but for divine ones as well. The battle of the warrior goddess Anat gives joy in her heart, and it culminates in a feast in her house where she may be cannibalizing her warrior captives (KTU 1.3 II 17-30).[180]

The transfer of metaphors between warfare and sexual relations, as well as dancing and feasting, points to a literary and cultural sensibility. Both conflict and sexual relations express hierarchy and love. As in sexual relations as understood in the ancient world, these heroic pairs also express hierarchy. As noted in Chapter Two, the stories never lose sight of who the greater of the heroic pairs is in each instance. At the same time, love and affection loom large in the picture. Gilgamesh's love for his deceased friend is on prominent display when he refers to Enkidu as the one whom "I love mightily *(ša arammušu danniš),* who with me went through every danger" (OB Sippar, col. ii, line 2′; see also SBV X.55, 56; cf. 68-69).[181] For warriors the shared experience of combat and companionship may be, as David says, "greater than the love of women" (2 Sam. 1:26), an expression that we will revisit in Chapter Ten. It is the experience of close conflict shared by brothers in arms. It may not involve full-fledged physical, sexual relations as such (though this is hardly impossible in view of our present knowledge). The picture in *Gilgamesh* entails close physical contact, energy, and eroticism, analogous with and suggestive of sexual relations, and as many modern readers have often thought, a similar situation seems to obtain in the case of David and Jonathan. "The profound love, devotion, and loyalty between comrades-at-arms," Walls writes, "are seemingly difficult to convey without recourse to the erotic language of passion and desire."[182]

In the end, we may ask whether the modern focus on the same-sex sexual relations of the heroic pairs was a significant issue or question for any of the heroic texts under examination in this chapter. What the texts emphasize in all three cases is the intense attraction that the heroic leaders hold for both men and women. As suggested by the density of gendered language in heroic poetry and its emphasis on the physical beauty of the heroes, the literary representations of heroes stand as textual monuments to the ideal physical magnetism of the male leader, a point stressed at various points above. It seems that the question of same-sex sexual relations may have been of relatively little interest. It may be a misplaced and perhaps an anachronistic concern on the part of modern readers.

With this reappraisal of gendered and sexual language, we have reached the end of our broad consideration of the heroic pairs. To understand warrior themes in greater depth, especially in the Bible, it will be helpful now to undertake in Part III a lengthy treatment of the warrior texts known from the Ugaritic corpus. This examination will help to elucidate the background of early Israel's heroic poetry, particularly David's lament over Saul and Jonathan, to which we will return in Part IV.

PART III

Human and Divine Warriors in the Ugaritic Texts

CHAPTER FOUR

Heroes in the Story of Aqhat

1. Introduction

Of all the Ugaritic texts about human warriors examined in this study, the story of Aqhat is the longest.[1] When we enter the world of Aqhat, we meet a family drama rich in heroic ideas and values. The story's defining event is the execution of Aqhat, which sets the parameters for the characters' roles. On one side of the narrative are the members of a human family: Danil; his son, Aqhat, and his daughter, Pughat; the mother Danatayu, who appears in only one extant scene. The three main family members in the story are all presented as warriors. Danil is the patriarch and hero. Aqhat, his son, is killed without reaching maturity and achieving the status of his father.[2] Pughat, the daughter and sister, sets out to avenge her brother's death. Against the expectations of her gender, she acts as a stealthy warrior. On the other side of the story are the warrior goddess Anat and Yatpan, a human military leader who works for her.[3] In taking Aqhat's life, Anat and Yatpan serve as the literary opposites of Danil, Aqhat, and Pughat.

This divide informs the literary construction of the narrative. As Shirly Natan-Yulzary's recent study of Aqhat has nicely demonstrated,[4] part of the story's literary effect is to cast the human family members and their divine counterparts as antitypes. Both Anat and Pughat lament the death of Aqhat. Pughat sets out to avenge this death instigated by Anat. Pughat would kill the very follower of Anat who had killed her brother in a manner that promises to be no less violent. El and Danil are both patriarchal figures who offer blessings and support their daughters in the execution of their enemy. Other deities who appear in the story, such as Baal and Kothar, remain largely on the sidelines. In general, the deities in the story support Danil and his family until the fateful meeting of Anat and Aqhat (1.17 VI); after that point, only the family god Baal shows any act of sympathy (1.19 III), yet he remains in the background.

Scholars have focused on different aspects of the story of Aqhat. For Simon B. Parker, this narrative is about family and the value of familial piety.[5] For this family tale, David P. Wright has brilliantly emphasized the key importance of ritual.[6] Although Aqhat is indeed a family story, this narrative so far as it is preserved shows little of the mother or her maternal role. Instead, this story highlights warrior titles, behavior, and values, as Baruch Margalit has suggested.[7] It has not been appreciated sufficiently that the story of Aqhat focuses on three warriors related by blood who experience and avenge the bloody death of one of their own. In her book, *The Ethics of Violence in the Story of Aqhat,* Chloe Sun focuses on the various responses of the different figures to the violent attack on Aqhat perpetrated by Anat,[8] the central moment of the narrative that we will examine below.

At the outset, it is important to emphasize that this is not the story of a royal family.[9] This text does not depict the royal realm, with kingship and its privileges and power. The tale involves no great journeys involving known cities, only the family home, local shrines and towns, as well as the fields and lands in between.[10] What we have here is a family story, and a fairly rural-looking one in general. It evokes a family household negotiating its basic needs, its ritual duties to its ancestral line, its attention to the patriarch and the household. As we will see in the following section, the list of filial duties, iterated four times in the opening two columns (KTU 1.17 I 16–II 23),[11] marks the identity of the would-be heroic son, including repairing the roof of the family house when it is muddy and washing the father's clothing when it is dirty. These are not exactly duties for a royal son. This is not to say that the monarchy was disinterested in this narrative. On the contrary, the Ugaritic king was evidently the patron of this version of the story, as suggested by the damaged colophon barely surviving on the first of its three tablets.[12] While the heroic world depicted in this story is not royal, it is one that royalty — and perhaps also its scribal, priestly, and military elite — perhaps looked to for values and for its sense of the past.[13] In short, Aqhat may represent a royal commemoration of a nonroyal heroic past.

The story begins with the divine help that Danil receives in Aqhat's conception and birth (KTU 1.17 I-II), followed later by the divine gift of the bow and arrows (1.17 V). The central scenes dramatize Aqhat's conflict with Anat over these superlative weapons and the hero's subsequent death instigated by the goddess (1.17 VI–1.18 IV). The remainder of the tale relates the family's mourning rituals and vengeance of Aqhat's murder (1.19 I-IV). Because the third tablet ends without this vengeance achieved, it has been thought that a fourth tablet may have detailed its successful conclusion.[14]

Readers should be aware of some additional facts about the three tablets of the story of Aqhat. Of the six columns in the first tablet (KTU 1.17), the middle two are missing (1.17 III and IV), and of the four columns in the second tablet (1.18), its two middle columns are lost (1.18 II and III). In addition, the three tablets suffer from damage to various lines. As a result of these problems, it is difficult to be sure what the story of Aqhat is entirely about.[15] At the same time, what has survived of this text shows a deep exploration of heroic values.

Before turning to an examination of the story's focus on warriors and their cultural attitudes in section 6, it is necessary to provide a reading of the story's major parts. The text bears many difficulties crucial to understanding the story as a whole. Thanks to recent work on Aqhat as well as the publication of several new Ugaritic texts, it is possible to clarify some matters and thus to ground the overall interpretation offered here. It is to the description of the story's parts that we now turn.

2. Hero Father, Would-be Hero Son

Missing from the top of the first tablet is the very first word of the text, which would have been its prose superscription, "to Aqhat."[16] This label, as it is attested at the top of the third tablet, points to Aqhat as the character at the center of the story. Following some ten missing lines, the story seemingly begins "in the middle of things" *(in medias res),* with the figure of Danil performing a night ritual offering to the gods conducted six times over a week (1.17 I 1-15),[17] perhaps in a temple or sanctuary.[18] Line 1 is reconstructed with the particle *ʾapnk* ("then, thereupon") in parallelism with *ʾaph⟨n⟩* ("then, thereupon") preserved in line 2, based on the parallelism of these two particles in KTU 1.17 II 27, V 4 and elsewhere.[19] These particles commonly mark the beginning of a new section. This usage may even introduce a character,[20] but it does not begin any text in Ugaritic as far as we know. In using the particles in this manner, the narrative marks the initial scene as a story in the middle of Danil's life.

Danil is first called "man of Rp'u" *(mt rpʾi),*[21] a title that is prominent in the first and third tablets of the story (KTU 1.17 I 2, 17, 18, 35, 36, 37, 42; II

28; V 4-5, 14, 33-34; VI 52; 1.19 I 20, 36-37, 38-39, 47; II 41; IV 13, 17, 18, 36). This appellation names Danil as a devotee[22] to the divinity, Rp'u, evidently regarded as the head of the line of deceased, divinized ancestors similarly named *rp'um*. (Rp'u is known from KTU 1.108, a text discussed in the following chapter in connection with these *rp'um*.) Parallel to the name of Danil is the title "hero" *(ǵzr)*, a label that is prominent in this story and one to which we will return in section 6. Parallel to the title *mt rp'i* is *mt hrnmy*, which is obscure by comparison. It has been associated with a place in Syria known from Egyptian sources.[23] While the significance of this title remains unclear, it places the family at some distance from the center of Ugarit and its royal power. Finally, the common word *mt* here bears a further significance in two later contexts. In 1.17 VI 35-36 and 38, the use of *mt*, "man," is followed by the fourfold use **mt*, "die/death." In 1.19 II 41-42, the two words are brought together, and together they express the fate of the death *(mt)* of this man's son *(mt)*: "Hear, O Danil, man *(mt)* of [Rapiu]: 'Dead *(mt)* is Aqhat the Hero!'"[24] At these two critical junctures in the story, this wordplay names its tragic theme. With this listing of names and titles, the very first attested lines of Aqhat locate the family among those devoted to the eponymous ancestor of the premonarchic predecessors of the monarchic line. The figure of Danil hails from distant antiquity from the perspective of the story's royal patrons, much as this figure is understood in Ezek. 14:14, 20 and 28:3, where he is presented as a worthy of old along with Noah and Job.[25] From the perspective of the text's royal patron, this story was understood to stand in the distant past long before the monarchy.

At the outset of the story, Danil undertakes a series of ritual acts that dispose the god Baal to act on his behalf. The reason for Danil's prayer to the god goes unstated, but as the following actions make clear, he desires a son.[26] On the seventh day, Baal approaches El with favor *(ḥnt)*[27] for Danil. Perhaps Baal is Danil's family or personal god, or in biblical terms, "the god of the father" (see Exod. 15:2).[28] This scene (1.17 I 15-33) presents Baal before El as he describes Danil's lamentable situation, namely that he has no son like others[29] in his family. Up to this point, Danil has been making offerings to the gods. Baal's request for blessing gives voice to concern for Danil's lamentations undertaken in 1.17 I 1-15. Baal asks El to bless Danil with a son, who can perform the proper filial duties. Such a concern for blessing is common within the family context, and this concern frames the beginning and end of the entire story, as the daughter Pughat asks for her father's blessing in 1.19 IV 32-33.[30] Clothing, too, serves an important role from the beginning of the story to its end: clothing signals Danil's state in 1.17 I, just as it serves later to mark his lamentation (1.19 I 36-37, 46-48) as well as Pughat's later deception at the very end of the attested story (1.19 IV 43-46). From these passages, it seems that the use of clothing represents a recurring motif, not entirely unlike its well-known usage in the biblical story of Joseph (Genesis 37, 39, 41).[31]

The duties of the son, as spelled out initially by Baal to El, are sixfold (1.17 I 26-33, reiterated three times, in I 44-48; II 1-8; and 16-23):[32] (1) to establish in the sanctuary a symbol (evidently a standing stone or stele) in honor of the memory of the family ancestor, "the divine father" (lines 26-27);[33] (2) to undertake the proper rituals on behalf of the deceased ancestor (lines 27-28); (3) to protect the family from trouble (lines 28-29); (4) to take care of the living patriarch when he is drunk (lines 30-31); (5) to eat the sacrificial portion in the temples of Baal and El (lines 31-32); and (6) to maintain the roof of the family house during the rainy season and to wash clothing or gear when it gets dirty (lines 32-33). The list is important for the story, as it conjures up the world of the family household, its physical needs, and its piety. The son here is to help the patriarch with the performance of ritual duties, namely the erection of the stele and the maintenance of ritual meals on behalf of the family in the temples of two main gods, Baal and El. The son is also to aid the patriarch in his traditional duties to guard the family household from external threats in the larger social realm, and to take care of the household physical plant in its annual needs. In addition, the son is to take care of the patriarch when he gets drunk, a depiction seen also with the drunken Jerusalem who has no sons to take her hand (Isa. 51:17-18)[34] and with Noah and his sons (Gen. 9:20-27).[35] The god, El, similarly has sons who help him in his drunken condition in KTU 1.114.[36]

After Baal informs El of Danil's lamentable circumstances, El blesses him (1.17 I 34, 48-49).[37] El's blessing adds a crucial thematic detail, the wish that Danil may live (KTU 1.17 I 36-37). The line is difficult: *npš yḥ dn'il [mt rp'i]*, which seems to mean, "(with) life-force *(npš)*, may Danil, [the man of the Harnamite] live."[38] The blessing seems to suggest not that Danil is simply "a living person" (or "living being"; cf. biblical *nepeš ḥayyâ*, in Gen. 2:7).[39] Rather, without a son, socially he is truly not a living human being. Like the act of blessing and the motif of clothing noted above, this feature links this opening episode with the end of the story, where the same wish is made for Pughat (1.19 IV 36). The word *npš* seems to be a key word in the story. Its usage in the sense of "life-force" appears not only in the blessings that frame the story, but it also marks the death of Aqhat later in 1.18 IV 25, 36 and also in 1.17 II 14; 1.19 II 38. The same word in its meaning "appetite" occurs in 1.17 V 17, 23. Accordingly, the story of Aqhat in no small measure concerns the meaning of *npš* in both its literal, physical sense and in its metaphorical social meaning. This broad concern for what it means to be a living person broadly informs the filial duties noted above. The fulfillment of these duties on the part of the son makes the father continue his life as a social being, even after he has died.

In this connection, we may focus for a moment on the filial duty to erect a stele for the divine father. This feature of the stele may be compared with two Aramaic inscriptions from the Iron II period. One of Panamuwa's inscriptions (KAI 214:16-17, 21-22), from the site of Zinjirli, commands a royal son's offerings so that in the king's postmortem state his *nbš* may eat and drink with the god Hadad.[40] The difference between Aqhat and the Panamuwa inscription is that the latter envisions the feasting taking place "with Hadad." In the first millennium, the monarchy's special status before death perhaps generated a notion of the king's afterlife with the gods or at least a patron god, as seen in this text. In the case of the second Aramaic inscription, it states that it was erected for the *nbš* of a figure named KTMW (perhaps Kuttamuwa) who dedicates the stele.[41] There may be elite emulation involved in the case of the royal official, Kuttamuwa, who in his inscription calls himself "a servant of Panamuwa." The feasting that Kuttamuwa's stele commands is to take place at the stele, which seems to stand closer to the situation in Aqhat. I would add a further observation about the use of *nbš* in the Kuttamuwa inscription. In commanding the slaughter of animals *bnbšy*, lines 10-11 might suggest not that the *nbš* is "in my stele," but "in proximity to my stele," as Dennis Pardee understands the phrase.[42] If this action describes the slaughter in proximity to the stele, the same may apply to the usage of *nbš* in line 5: "a ram for my *nbš* that (will be in proximity) to this stele." If correct, the point is not that the *nbš* of Kuttamuwa resides in the stele, but it comes to the stele, which is the place where the ritual is to be performed on its behalf. In this case, the *nbš* of Kuttamuwa comes and performs what is represented visually on the stele, namely his eating and drinking.[43] In Aqhat, the filial duties of the son are to promote the *npš* of the family patriarch as well as the larger good of the family unit.

To achieve Danil's goal of gaining a son, El commands him to mount his bed[44] and to engage in sexual relations with his wife that will result in her pregnancy. As a result, El proclaims, Danil will have a son who will perform all of the filial duties. At this point, the text is missing about twenty lines. It is evident that this message is repeated by Baal or perhaps by a divine messenger to Danil, for when the legible part of the story resumes in the second column of the tablet (1.17 II), the message is being told to him (1.17

II 1-8). On receiving this news, Danil lights up with joy and laughter, and he proclaims that he can enjoy rest now that a son has been granted to him with divine aid (1.17 II 8-23).[45] Danil then is said to go home (1.17 II 24-25), and the Kotharat, the "skillful" goddesses,[46] are present; either they arrive at this point or they have already arrived (1.17 II 26-27).[47] Danil offers them traditional hospitality for seven days, and on the seventh day they depart (1.17 II 27-40). The text is broken at this point, but the goddesses' skill seems to be implied: Danil and his wife enjoy sexual relations and then he is counting the months of her pregnancy (1.17 II 41-46).[48]

The bottom of the column is missing about ten lines. It is clear from later in the story that Danil and his wife have a son as a result of this pregnancy. Two columns are also missing at this point (1.17 III-IV). If other passages concerning newly-born children in Ugaritic literature may offer any guidance, these columns might have included description of the son's birth (cf. 1.23.51-52), the announcement of the son's birth to the father who then rejoices (cf. 1.10 III 33-37; 1.23.52, 59), perhaps the naming of the new-born son (cf. 1.12 I 25-29), and perhaps the clothing of the infant son (cf. 1.5 V 23). The missing columns might have also included the birth of Aqhat's sister Pughat[49] and perhaps some initial material naming Danatayu, Danil's wife.[50] In addition, they could have described the manufacture of the bow by the craftsman-god, Kothar wa-Hasis (perhaps along the lines of the description for a bow provided in 1.17 VI 20-23),[51] as well as some mention of his abode in Egypt (cf. 1.3 VI).

When the preserved text resumes, it opens with a first person speech apparently given by Kothar wa-Hasis, who declares his intention to deliver the bow and arrows to Danil (1.17 V 2-3).[52] Presumably the prior material includes the rest of the scene in which the god makes this declaration. The formulaic opening of the next line, "then on the seventh day" (1.17 V 3-4), suggests that the preceding scene may have involved a larger six-day unit detailing the god's speech (perhaps preceded by some action on the god's part as well). The "seventh day" seems to switch the narrative focus to Danil,[53] presenting him among the leaders[54] adjudicating the cases of widow and orphan. There are two points of interest here. While earlier Danil is noted for his proper piety toward the gods (1.17 I-II), now his activity seems to be another marker of his proper social capacity as an elder engaged in judgment (1.17 V 4-8). Furthermore, this activity may be represented here as characteristic for him, since elsewhere in Ugaritic the representation of figures in an activity considered characteristic for them seems to be standard for scenes involving arrivals of other figures.[55] Danil's very name echoes his role in judging.[56]

As Danil undertakes justice on behalf of the widow and orphan, he perceives the god Kothar wa-Hasis coming in his direction with the bow and arrows (1.17 V 9-13). The formulary here is standard for sighting figures.[57] However, the mention of the bow and arrows is extra, and these constitute the major point of the scene. At this point, Danil orders his wife Danatayu to prepare food and wine for the god in fairly stereotypical fashion, and she executes his commands verbatim (1.17 VI 13-25).[58] In a rather rapid sequence, Kothar wa-Hasis arrives and gives the bow and arrows to Danil, Danatayu serves the god, and then the god departs (1.17 V 26-33). These events receive no elaboration: neither the god, nor his bow and arrows, nor the manner of the service of food and drink is given any particular attention.[59] It is also to be noted that the wife, Danatayu, appears nowhere else in the extant material of the story. It would appear that she is only a minor player in the story. Indeed, her very name seems to be derivative of Danil's.[60]

3. The Son's Gift of the Hunt to the Goddess and His Weapons Withheld

The next set of episodes revolves around Danil's hunt and the dialogue of the hero and the goddess Anat concerning his bow. With the departure of the god Kothar, the scene in 1.17 V turns to the father and son. Danil addresses Aqhat about the hunt (1.17 V 37-39):

prʿm ṣdk yb[n]	"The first/best[61] of your game, o so[n],
[ ]/prʿm ṣdk	[Set (?)][62] the first/best of your game,
hn[ ][63]*/ṣd bhk[lh]*	See, [set (?)] the game in [her][64] temp[le]."

The father seems to be giving his son instructions in the hunt, and these presuppose that Danil gives the weapons to his son, Aqhat. It is not clear whether any significance is to be attached to this "re-gifting" on the part of the father. In other words, the bow and arrows were gifts of the god for the father; the text shows no indication that these were intended for the son. Elsewhere, when we see the craftsman-god with such gifts, they seem to be intended for the use of the recipient.[65] Perhaps the audience is simply to assume that the weapons are to be transferred to the son,[66] but David Wright raises the possibility that something may not be quite right here: is Danil exercising misplaced judgment in transferring the gift to his son?[67] The question is reasonable, and the situation is not clear. Perhaps this scene is part of the larger ambiguity that seems to attend the weapons from this point onwards.

The context here involves the loss of about twenty lines at the bottom of this column of 1.17 V. It may be assumed that these lines include the narration of Aqhat's successful hunt, for the next column shows him at the feast that evidently serves the meat of the game animal that he has hunted. In the lost material, the hunt may have focused on the young hunter and his great capacities (cf. 1.12 I 34-41). The hunt may further entail possible danger facing the hunter from the hunted beasts (cf. 1.12 II 52-55?). Whatever happens in this gap of about twenty lines, Aqhat seems to be successful in his first hunt, for it appears that he offers "the first of the hunt," perhaps to the goddess, in the feast in the next scene.

The final column of the first tablet (1.17 VI) opens with a feasting scene (lines 3-9 [?]), perhaps preceded by an invitation to the feast (lines 1-2).[68] It might be thought that the lines missing from before line 1 included more material of this invitation. In lines 3-9, some of the lines include standard banqueting formulary (lines 4-6), but the rest of the context (lines 1-4 and 6-9) is unclear due to considerable gaps on the left-hand side of the column. Lines 6b-8 seem to continue with elements of feasting, with mention of cups *(krpn ʿl krpn)* and perhaps the service of new wine *(wtʿl trṯ),* as the recognized parallel with 1.5 IV 18-21 shows.[69] David Wright also sees lines 8b-9a as part of the feast and lines 9b-10a as a description of Aqhat loading an arrow and drawing his bow.[70] For lines 8b-9a there is no corresponding line in the parallel feasting in KTU 1.5 IV 11-14,[71] and so they may refer to a further matter. For lines 9b-10a, the crucial matter is the verb *yṣbt,* which might reflect the same root (**ṣby,* "to covet")[72] as *tṣb* in line 13. If the word refers to Anat's desire in line 13, it may do so here as well. In this case, lines 8b-10a may describe Anat's wish for a bow before her sighting of Aqhat in lines 10b-11a. Before proceeding to lines 11b and following, it is to be noted that to judge from lines 13-18[73] the feast is Anat's. The person(s) with whom she may be feasting appear unknown at first glance. The only other figure in her retinue is Yatpan, who appears only later in the story (1.18 IV). It may be surmised that she is feasting with Aqhat himself in her temple. He has brought "the first (or best) of his game," perhaps as ordered earlier by his father, and it might be presumed that the location is Anat's temple, since she is there when she lifts up her eyes and encounters Aqhat there.

That Aqhat is present there is evident from lines 10-11, that "when she raises her eyes, she catches sight of . . . its/his sinews like lightning." The sinews could refer either to Aqhat's anatomy (as in 1.3 III 33, 35//1.4 II 17,

19; 1.16 I 54, VI 50; and 1.19 II 46) or the bowstring of the bow (as in 1.3 II 16; 4.182.9, 26). In other words, Anat sees either Aqhat himself or the bow that Aqhat carries with him as he presents his offering to the goddess. The goddess's desire for the weapon may include Aqhat himself, as some scholars have suggested.[74] Given the particularly strong association of warriors with their weapons,[75] it is not unreasonable to see an association in this context. Indeed, "those objects that are in closest contact with their owners become, as it were, 'extra-somatic body parts.'"[76]

Accordingly, 1.17 VI 13-14 have been read as evidence of the goddess's perception of the weapon: "she longs *(tṣb)*[77] for the bow *(qšt)* . . . , her eyes/its [appe]arance like a serpent. . . ."[78] Despite the uncertainty of these lines, they may denote the goddess's desire for Aqhat's bow. This desire on the part of the goddess, it might be added, would end up as a curse for the young Aqhat, not unlike the sort of curse attributed to another warrior-goddess: "may Ishtar, the goddess of men, the lady of women, take away their bow, bring them to shame and make them bitterly weep."[79] Perhaps the story of Aqhat offers a narrative illustration of this sort of curse. The elements of the feast as seen in lines 4-7 resume in lines 15-16. These lines show a response on Anat's part: "[. . .] on the earth//Her cup she pours out [on the ground]."[80] She may be offering a libation in honor of Aqhat.[81]

At this point in 1.17 VI, the text becomes clearer.[82] The goddess offers Aqhat silver and gold[83] in exchange for the bow and arrows (1.17 VI 15-19). Aqhat does not refuse the goddess directly. He suggests instead that she gather the proper materials to give to Kothar wa-Hasis so that he can make a magnificent, composite bow for her (1.17 VI 20-25).[84] Although it was a Levantine import into Egypt beginning in the Second Intermediate Period, the composite bow became widespread during New Kingdom Egypt.[85] It is perhaps fitting then that it is the craftsman-god Kothar with his home in Egypt (KTU 1.3 VI 13, 15-16; 1.17 V 31) who makes such a superb bow.[86]

In making this suggestion, Aqhat is not being callous toward the goddess. Indeed, he appears diplomatic in this initial response. Aqhat may not wish to relinquish to the goddess what is properly not his to give away, even as he seems to be making an effort not to offend the warrior-goddess. At the same time, the response appears misguided: a mortal, a relatively young one at that, is hardly in a position to make suggestions to the goddess. At this point, the goddess takes no offense, yet she is not dissuaded from the object of her attention. She immediately makes a second offer for the bow: he may ask and she will give to him[87] "life"[88] and "nondeath," a condition that according to this context would place Aqhat in the class of deities like

Baal and El (1.17 VI 25-29). The comparison with the two gods here might suggest that this life is eternal, at least in some sense, yet it is somewhat ambiguous whether this involves literal immortality, life after death, or long life. This pair, "life"//"nondeath," as paralleled in the story of Kirta (1.16 I 14-15),[89] would seem to suggest the continuation of human life, and not life after death or immortality. We will discuss the significance of this parallel after we look at the rest of the goddess's speech to Aqhat.

Anat goes on to characterize this sort of "life" with an extended simile (1.17 VI 30-33):

> "Like Baal/*baal*, when he is made to live,[90]
> The one made to live is served;
> One serves and gives him drink,
> He chants and sings over him, does the goodly one,[91]
> And so I myself[92] would answer (?)[93] him,
> I would make Hero Aqhat live."[94]

While the vocabulary and syntax of this speech are generally understood, the overall meaning has been debated, due mostly to the ambiguity of the first and final lines of this speech. The first noun in question, *bʿl*, is taken commonly to be the god Baal[95] in his capacity as "a dying and rising god." The verb in this view means "to be made alive," in other words, "to revive (from death)." The implication, if this reading were correct, is that Aqhat is analogous to Baal: Anat will make Aqhat rise from the dead just as Baal rises as "a dying and rising god." Several scholars, most notably Johannes C. de Moor, Klaas Spronk, and more recently T. N. D. Mettinger, have championed this view, arguing that Anat is offering to Aqhat a human postmortem existence, as known elsewhere in the Ugaritic texts for dead kings and heroes *(rp'um)*.[96] As noted at the beginning of section 2 above, Danil is called *mt rp'i*, "the man of Rp'," and this figure is the divine eponymous ancestor of the Rp'um, attested in a number of Ugaritic and biblical texts. In Ugaritic these include divine ancestral heroes of old, sometimes known collectively as Rp'um and individually as Rp'. (KTU 1.161, studied in Chapter Five, attests to both the Rp'um collectively and individuals with the title of Rp'u.) In sum, it might seem that Anat is offering to Danil the sort of afterlife that such heroic figures were thought to have. If this is the case, Anat would be offering Aqhat something that she otherwise does not show an ability to achieve. The offer might then seem to be bogus, which at first glance seems to fit with Aqhat's negative response to the goddess's offer.

This approach is dependent on the view of Baal as a "dying and rising god," which came out of modern "myth and ritual" theory (often associated with the name of James George Fraser). This theory has incurred considerable criticism, and today it is largely discredited.[97] However, translators continue to presume the understanding that *bʿl* here refers to the god Baal as one who comes back to life.[98] This view has no particular basis in Ugaritic literature. An offer of life after death like one of the Rephaim seems not to cohere well with Aqhat's response that he must die the death of all (KTU 1.17 VI 38). Presumably, Aqhat's statement that he must die is an objection to an offer that would suggest that he does not have to die.

As a variation on this approach, *bʿl* in Anat's comparison might refer to a human figure rather than the god Baal. This possibility, disregarded by older commentators, is suggested by the human use of *bʿl* in the Ugaritic texts, including the story of King Kirta (1.15 IV 28; V 20), royal letters (such as 2.23.2, 4, 6, etc.; 2.33.22, 26, 31; 2.39.11, 13, 19), and a monarchic funerary text (1.161.20-21).[99] In these contexts, the reference is to a human king and not to the god Baal. If one were to follow this approach, *bʿl* in Anat's speech would be a human figure who is revived like the Rp'um. In this case, the goddess would be offering to Aqhat the kind of eternal afterlife enjoyed by glorious heroes and kings. As in the first scenario, here Anat would be offering to Danil the sort of afterlife that such heroic figures enjoy. Anat would again be claiming the ability to revive humans from the dead, a capacity that the goddess does not otherwise seem to possess, and it would be no wonder that Danil in his response expresses utter skepticism. Without the baggage of the theory of "dying and rising gods," this second variation on this approach would seem preferable. However, this one incurs the same problem raised by Aqhat's objection to Anat's offer that he must die (1.17 VI 38-39). As this objection indicates, Anat's offer would not seem to be a matter of postmortem existence, but of everlasting life without death.

There is another possibility that avoids this problem: Anat may be promising "immortality,"[100] more specifically long life for Aqhat and not life after death. This approach fits with Aqhat's objection that he will die. It also enjoys a greater number of specific parallels within Ugaritic. The only other passage in Ugaritic with "life" and "nondeath" in poetic parallelism appears in the text of King Kirta (KTU 1.16 I 24-25). In this context, "life" and "nondeath" refer to a lengthy lifetime before death. Here Kirta's son is lamenting the prospect of his father's death. After mentioning the joy taken by the king's subjects in his "life" and "nondeath," his son asks: "how can you die like a mortal?" (KTU 1.16 I 17-18; see also 1.16 I 24-25). Here Kirta's son is apparently expressing the notion in royal ideology that the king is considered to live forever.

Anat's offer of life to Aqhat also compares closely with Ugaritic royal blessings for the preservation of the life of the king (and not for his return from death). For example, the long duration of time associated here in 1.17 VI 28-29 with the gods, Baal and El, is similar to the time expressed in the blessing offered on behalf of the king at the end of KTU 1.108.26-27: "For the days of Shapshu and Yarih, for the goodly years of El."[101] The royal blessing for long life was well known, as suggested by its elaborate formulation in the scribal text in KTU 5.9 I 2-6: "May the gods preserve you, give you peace, strengthen you, for a thousand days and ten thousand years, forever." Long life for the king is also expressed: "may the king live *(yḥ mlk)*" (KTU 2.7.9; cf. 5.10.2; 5.11.4; 6.30.1).[102]

Later parallels for the blessing of long life also appear in royal contexts. The Phoenician inscriptional record shows the transitive *D*-stem usage of the verb **ḥwy* in royal blessings: "may the lady of Byblos bless Yehawmilk, king of Byblos; may she preserve his life *(tḥww)* and may she lengthen his days and years" (KAI 10:8-9).[103] A biblical royal psalm likewise attributes the request of long life to the king (Ps. 21:5[4]): "he asked for life *(ḥayyîm)* from you; you gave it to him *(nātattâ lô).*" The formulation here matches closely with the opening of Anat's second offer (1.17 VI 27): "request life *(ḥym)* and I will give (it) to you *('atnk).*" Moreover, it is to be noted that in Ps. 21:5(4), the life requested entails the preservation of the king's life, thanks to the god's help in battle (vv. 1, 5, 8, 12, 13).[104] Preservation of the king's life is a central theme also in Hezekiah's prayer in Isa. 38:16: "My life-force *(rûḥî)* is revived *(ḥayyê)* (?); you have restored me and made me live *(wĕhaḥăyēnî).*"[105] It is restoration of the king's health that is at stake in all these uses of **ḥyy,* not revivification from the dead.

In keeping with the blessing expressed in these texts, Anat's offer involves a blessing of Aqhat for a long life, a gift that the goddess can provide in the form of martial protection while he is living. Just as Anat says in KTU 1.17 VI 32 that she would help Aqhat live *('aḥwy),* later she withdraws her support of him first in ordering his execution (KTU 1.18 IV 21-26). She declares: "Thus I'll not let live *(l'aḥwy)!*" (KTU 1.18 IV 26-27).[106] After the execution, she states: "I struck him down for his bow, For his arrows him I did not let live *(l'aḥw)* (KTU 1.19 I 15-16). The verb forms in these passages match the verb in her original offer. Aqhat's long life and not a return to life is what is involved in the goddess's offer. In exchange for the bow, Anat would seem to be offering the ideal for a warrior, namely great success in conflict aided by the divine patron of human warriors issuing in a victory feast. This also fits with the feast and singing by the *nʿm* that de Moor rightly observed in both Anat's offer and Baal's victory feast in KTU 1.3 I.[107] This passage describes Baal being feted, however not after his revival from the dead as de Moor would have it,[108] but evidently after Baal's victory over Yamm in KTU 1.2 IV. The comparison would suggest that Anat is promising Aqhat the sort of preservation of life that Baal enjoys in 1.3 I: the victory feast following the mortal threat of battle. In this reading, *bʿl* in line 30 of 1.17 VI could refer to either the god Baal after battle or a human lord victorious in warfare.

This interpretation suggests the following (somewhat paraphrastic) translation for Anat's offer in 1.17 VI 30-33:

> "Like Baal/a *baal*, when he is kept alive (preserved in battle),
> The one whose life is preserved is served (in a victory feast);
> One serves and gives him drink,
> He chants and sings over him, does the goodly one *(nʿm)*,[109]
> Also I myself would answer (?) him (?),
> I would keep alive Hero Aqhat."

In this reading, Anat is offering what the monarchy understood to be an ideal of ancient heroes and kings in their lifetimes, and Aqhat should accept the offer. However, just as Gilgamesh rejects Ishtar's offer, so too Aqhat rejects Anat's. In a moment, we will see the reason why.

Before turning to Aqhat's response, it remains to be asked how the idioms of life in Anat's speech might have been heard in the monarchic context that provided the patronage for the extant text. The monarchy perhaps looked to Danil as well as Aqhat as anchors in ancient time and also as object lessons for heroic values and behavior. The story of Aqhat seems to have served as an act of commemoration of the monarchy's forebears. Danil as *mt rp'i* would become one of the Rp'um after his death. Within the story's imaginative world, this postmortem issue is not yet operative, but it is anticipated by the royal commemoration of Danil as a figure of old. The same applies to Aqhat. This line of discussion raises a further, related issue: since the parallels cited above suggest how the exchange between Anat and Aqhat is replete with expressions also attested in association with royalty, did the story of Aqhat serve as an argument for the need for kingship? This tale might have served to demonstrate the vulnerability of warrior leadership without kingship and its ideological supports. In sum, Anat's offer may be viewed as a matter of long life for Aqhat, an approach that also compares well with parallel expressions elsewhere in Ugaritic literature and other West Semitic texts. It also fits with Aqhat's response that follows, especially when he says that he must die.

Aqhat responds to the goddess's second offer with a two-part[110] answer (KTU 1.17 VI 33-41). Aqhat begins with the words (1.17 VI 34-35): "Do not be twisty[111] with me, O Maiden, for to a hero your twistiness is muck *(ḫḫ)*." The final noun in this colon, *ḫḫ*, is also used for the underworld (KTU 1.4 VIII 13; 1.5 II 16), which suggests "mire, muck."[112] It is tempting to suggest that Aqhat's speech is playing on this sense of the word, for in his statement that follows, he alludes to death (1.17 VI 35-36): "As for a man, in the end what does he get?[113] What does a man get in what comes after?" Furthermore, Aqhat states, it is inevitable that he will receive mortuary treatment (1.17 VI 36-37)[114] and "die the death of all" (1.17 VI 38),[115] an expression not too distant from the question posed by Kirta's son and daughter: "how can you die like mortals?" (1.16 I 17-18; II 40).[116] Aqhat seems to be suggesting that he is mortal like all humans, and thus death is what Anat cannot or will not prevent from happening. His response does not seem to indicate that the discussion involves revivification from death: he is mortal, and his death is inevitable. No postmortem existence is in view in Aqhat's words.

In any case, Aqhat believes that Anat is making an offer that she cannot or will not produce. In Marvin Pope's words, "it is . . . clear from Aqhat's reply (CTCA 17 VI 33-38 = *KTU* 1.17 VI 33-38) that even the goddess could not be trusted to make good the promise of immortality to a mortal."[117] If the offer involves her divine protection for a long life, it would appear that he does not believe that she will make good on it. This sounds like Gilgamesh's response to Ishtar, who invites him to be her spouse.[118] He refuses her offer and notes how badly she treats her lovers. Thus the offer is something that she might be capable of, but does or will not do. The same may be true of Anat: she is able but is not likely to preserve his life, as heroes commonly die without reaching long life, perhaps even with the goddess's patronage. The point is echoed in *Odyssey* 3:236-38: "But clearly death that is common to all not even the gods ward off even from a man they love, whenever the fell fate of pitiless death strikes him down."[119]

The second part of Aqhat's response (1.17 VI 39-41) is briefer by comparison. Here he states an objection more pertinent to the topic at hand, namely the bow. At this point Aqhat claims that bows are for warriors and questions whether females hunt. We will return to this response of Aqhat's part in the final section of this chapter, but at this point it is important to observe that

Aqhat is hardly displaying diplomatic skills. Compared to his response to Anat's first offer, Aqhat offers a rather offensive-sounding retort on his part.

Anat has the final word (1.17 VI 42-45). She laughs in response to Aqhat here (line 41) and in her later meeting with him (1.18 I 22). This nonverbal expression may be read as scorn not only in these passages, but also in KTU 1.3 II 25 (cf. Ps. 2:4; 59:8; Prov. 1:26).[120] In 1.17 VI 41, she is also said to "plot in her heart." The expression sounds like the similar idiom in Akkadian, *ikpudma libbašu lemutta*, "he plotted evil in his heart."[121] Anat's action here seems as if she may be thinking to herself.[122] On the face of it, this reading is undermined by the fact that she then addresses him openly. However, the content of the threat does not match what takes place later in the narrative. Rather than waiting until she meets him, she immediately takes the initiative to destroy him. Perhaps then she really does plot in her heart as she says something very different to Aqhat. If this is the case, then the expression "to plot in her heart" may signal that things will play out differently in the narrative from what she says here to Aqhat. And indeed, it does, because her threat that follows is not how the story goes: "If I meet you on the path of rebellion . . . on the path of pride, I will lay you low under [my feet]." The speech continues with a series of titles for Aqhat that we will address in the next section. The sense of the threat in the verb, literally, "to cause to fall," may perhaps be captured by the colloquial expression in English for violence taken against another party, that Anat will "lay low" or "take down" Aqhat.[123] In the context of the larger narrative, this verb in Anat's threat anticipates the curse later uttered four times (and realized in the fourth case) against the birds that may have consumed Aqhat's remains (1.19 III 1-38): "May Baal break the wings of bird-PN, may Baal break the pinions of his, so that he may fall beneath my feet."[124]

Anat's speech anticipates the next set of actions. Anat's plotting in her heart anticipates her vengeance on Aqhat, which takes place in 1.18 IV. Her threat also anticipates the mourning rites of Danil and Pughat over the loss of their male family member, with the similar curse expressed against the birds in 1.19 I 3-38. The final scene of the story, which involves Pughat's vengeance on behalf of her brother, perhaps goes without any allusion in Anat's speech here; Pughat's act of vengeance is itself a response to Anat's vengeful destruction of Aqhat via Yatpan. However, if Anat's speech is seen to anticipate what follows, Aqhat's own question about women wielding weapons in his second response to Anat perhaps foreshadows Pughat's girding of weapons secretly in the final part of the story. Indeed, within the larger context of the story, his question sounds deeply ironic, since his sister apparently succeeds later (see 1.19 IV) where he himself now fails. Moreover, Pughat, in her later act of revenge for her brother, acts with no less stealth (1.19 IV 43-46) than Anat in her action taken against Aqhat. All in all, the exchange between Anat and Aqhat issues in an undesirable outcome, what David P. Wright calls a "ritual failure,"[125] which drives the narrative from this point forward. In the final section of this chapter, we will return to this crucial passage when we consider some of its ideas about warriors.

4. The Hero's Death by the Goddess and the Rituals for the Hero

Following her threat to Aqhat (KTU 1.17 VI 43-45), Anat sets her plan in motion. The first step is her journey to El undertaken to gain his permission to let her do as she wishes (1.17 VI 46–1.18 I 19).[126] Anat's journey to El sounds stereotypical, as suggested by the largely parallel passage involving her journey to El in the Baal Cycle (1.17 VI 46-49//1.3 V 4-8; cf. Athirat's parallel journey to El in 1.4 IV 20-26).[127] The threat that Anat makes to El at the beginning of the story's second tablet, 1.18, is likewise stereotypical and paralleled in the Baal Cycle (1.18 I 7-11//1.3 V 19-25). El's initial response in 1.18 I 15-16 is similarly paralleled in 1.3 V 27-29. At this point in the exchange, however, 1.18 I and 1.3 V diverge. In 1.3 V 28-29 El asks Anat what she desires, but in 1.18 I 17-19 El tells her to depart, calls her "impious of heart,"[128] and then says to her: "you will seize upon whatever is in your innards, you will set on [what is in] your breast; the one who resists you will become soft!" (1.18 I 17-19).[129] The final line of this speech may be marked with a gendered expression, perhaps not unlike Erra IV:56: "whose manhood Ishtar changed to womanhood." Anat, like Ishtar, is a warrior-goddess who can turn manly warriors into cowardly women.

In El's speech here, concession seems to pass for permission. In the larger context of the narrative, Anat's exchange with El may also be read further as a foil to her earlier exchange with Aqhat. Anat threatens El just as she had threatened Aqhat, but this time when Anat requests what she wants, her male interlocutor simply concedes. El here gives in, where by contrast Aqhat resists Anat's requests. In addition, El's reference here to "in your innards" and "your breast" (cf. 1.19 I 34-35) may echo the earlier narrative referring to Anat plotting "in her heart." El is telling her to do what she wants, but the force of his response may be stronger: he is informing her that she may do what she has been plotting all along against Aqhat.

The next step in Anat's plan involves her return to Aqhat to set him up for his fall (1.18 I 20-34 [?]). The language for her journey (lines 20-22) and the formulary used for her address to Aqhat (in lines 22-23) is stereotypical. The remaining lines, largely lost in the left-hand side of the column, diverge from the common formulary, and the plot specific to Anat's plans seems to take over. Only a handful of expressions can be made out here. In line 24, the critical words *'at 'aḫ w'an* may be interpreted in two ways: "you are my brother and I am [your] br[other],"[130] or "Come, (my) brother, and I. . . ."[131] Whichever is correct, it is evident that the goddess addresses Aqhat as "my brother." In this manner Anat expresses a relationship with him, or at least the pretense of such a bond.[132] The ideal outcome of their earlier meeting would have been to issue in a relationship, here expressed as human "brother" and divine "sister"; this relationship would be realized as the human, male hunter who makes the offering of the hunt and the divine, female hunter who receives it. Based on the putative parallel with Gilgamesh involving his would-be relationship with Ishtar, it has been thought that Anat's address of Aqhat as "my brother" involves a bond analogous to a human couple, in other words a sort of "sacred marriage."[133] In this understanding, it would seem that the human hero is to engage in a relationship with the female divine warrior, apparently in a form of a "sacred marriage" analogous to or resonant with royal "sacred marriage."[134] Wright suggests Anat's words may represent "a more general attempt to seduce the boy, as Ishtar tried to do to Gilgamesh, but here with the goal of killing him."[135] It is not clear that this is the immediate goal at this point. Wright may be closer to the mark in his alternative view that "the line may be a pretense of reconciliation."[136] Anat seemingly proposes her divine mentorship to the hero, for in line 27 she tells him, "you will go on a hunt" *(tlk ṣd),* and in line 29 she says, "I will teach you" *('almdk).* Here she seems to be offering Aqhat instructions for his next hunt.[137] Lines 30-31 may provide the location where Aqhat should undertake this hunt, namely at or near "the town of 'Ablm."[138] For the place name, Shalom Spiegel drew attention to the root "to mourn,"[139] which perhaps as a matter of wordplay here would anticipate the family's mourning over Aqhat. The town is also said to be in the environs of "[the town of Prince Ya]rikh,"[140] perhaps with a tower as mentioned in the following line 32. This hunt represents the second in Aqhat's experience as a hunter; the first was undertaken earlier at the behest of his father, his human mentor, and now the second is proposed to him by Anat, his would-be divine mentor. This appears to be part of her ruse, as the later part of her plan indicates.

After the two lost columns in the story's second tablet, the extant text resumes in column IV,[141] with the same region of 'Abiluma invoked (1.18 IV

7-8, again somewhat broken). The next attested part of Anat's plan (1.18 IV 5-37) depicts her traveling in lines 5-6, once again in stereotypical fashion, this time to Yatpan, who is called *mhr št*. Arguably this phrase casts Yatpan as a "warrior of the lady" (e.g., Anat) or a "warrior of the Sutu," a title that, if correct, would be significant for the storyline, as will be noted below.[142] At this point, it is important to observe that the title would offer a contrast to the figure of Aqhat, who has completed only one round of hunting experience and has no experience at warfare. By contrast, Yatpan as a Sutu would be represented as an experienced warrior, and as the story later shows, he seems to be the head of a military camp.[143] While Aqhat is a warrior novice, Yatpan is a war veteran. Anat instructs Yatpan to go to 'Ablm, the very town to which she had directed Aqhat (1.18 IV 6-11). She then seems to be characterizing the time for this journey as the phase of the new moon: "How could Yariḫ/the moon not be new, . . . in his right horn, in the (?) . . . his head?"[144] While the expressions seem to point to the new moon's horns,[145] the context is not clear, and little weight should be placed on them beyond referring to the timing of Yatpan's journey to the place. Yatpan responds by informing Anat that she will (or should) kill him for his bow and arrows, and he tells her what Aqhat is presently up to, namely the preparation of a meal in his camp (1.18 IV 11-15). As an experienced warrior, Yatpan seems to have been doing reconnaissance (a military role that Sutu are known for),[146] and he has information ready for Anat. The timing of the meal may not be accidental for this plan, as it was also at a meal, namely the offering and banquet at the temple (1.17 VI), when Anat first encountered Aqhat. The new moon may be an occasion for Aqhat to be making offerings at 'Ablm and perhaps plays on the town's association with the moon god. All in all, Yatpan seems to propose that Anat seek out Aqhat at his encampment and kill him.

Anat has similar plans but a different strategy. She addresses Yatpan with the imperative *ṯb*, literally, "turn" (perhaps "pay attention"?), the same imperative used in her address to Aqhat in their conversation in 1.17 VI 42.[147] She reveals her plan to Yatpan to put him in the sheath of her belt and have him attack Aqhat from the air while Aqhat is sitting to eat (1.18 IV 17-27). According to the proposal, Anat will launch in flight like a bird and fly among the raptors (perhaps as camouflage).[148] Then she will launch Yatpan against Aqhat as what Pope used to call "an air-to-ground missile." Elsewhere Anat is characterized as a flyer: "Anat of the wing, the flyer, soaring [in the hea]vens on high" (1.108.8-9).[149] Her flight is also explicit elsewhere (1.10 II 10-12), and yet other texts seem to assume a picture of her taking off in flight (see 1.3 V 4-5//1.17 VI 46).[150] More pertinent to the context here is the simile about Anat in 1.22 I 9-10:[151] "As when Anat goes hunting,/Sets to flight the birds of heaven." Reading Anat's plan in light of this simile, she proposes to do what she customarily does when she goes flying, namely hunt. She hunts like predatory birds. Anat's plan may evoke the further trope of birds eating dead animals, as reflected in Ugaritic literature: "Birds eat his flesh, fowl devour his parts; flesh to flesh cries out" (1.6 II 35-37).[152] Anat in a sense hunts Aqhat, evidently an ironic twist on his earlier effort to offer to her the game of his hunt.

No less intriguing is the picture of Yatpan, otherwise a human warrior, here launched in flight. Yatpan is to be put in Anat's belt "like a raptor" (or "like a vulture," *km nšr*) (1.18 IV 17-18).[153] Anat will not kill Aqhat as Yatpan suggests; the goddess instead proposes that Yatpan will strike him dead. It is difficult to know why Anat uses Yatpan rather than just killing Aqhat herself as she threatens. Her plan allows the murder to be blamed on someone who can be killed in turn, as the narrative seems to require. In either case, if Yatpan is a "Sutean warrior" as suggested above, then this portrayal comports with the reputation of Suteans for killing and ambushes.[154] The possible background of "the Sutean" for the story of Aqhat may be clarified further by MB Emar fragment 2 of Gilgamesh (col. i, lines 28′-31′), which adds "the Sutean" to Ishtar's famous list of lovers: "You loved the [. . .] Sutean."[155] This passage also mentions a tent[156] as well as the field of battle. Despite this text's fragmentary state, it may offer a helpful parallel to the figure of Yatpan. This portrait would fit the description of this warrior as well as his relationship to the goddess. The mention of the Sutean's tent in this version of Gilgamesh also comports with the description of Yatpan with the troops and his tent in KTU 1.19 IV 46-61. We may suppose that this variation in the Gilgamesh list of the goddess's lovers coming from Emar might reflect a West Semitic background, as does the story of Aqhat. Yatpan as a Sutean warrior suits the situation of the goddess as well as the story's literary requirements.

Anat wastes little time in executing the final part of her plan (1.18 IV 27-37). The description here is a verbatim repetition of the proposal that Anat makes to Yatpan (1.18 IV 16-27). At the end of this successful attack on Aqhat, there is suddenly a different emotional expression on Anat's part (1.18 IV 37-42). The lines are very fragmentary, but what is evident is that "and she wept *(wtbk)*" (line 39). Anat also says that she took his life for his bow and arrows (lines 40-41). It is not clear how her statement in lines 40-41 should be read, but Anat seems to lament the situation. The words that she utters in lines 40-42 on one level echo Yatpan's advice in 1.18 IV 12-13, but in view of her weeping, these lines seem to gain additional force. The reason for the murder of Aqhat becomes part of Anat's lament over his demise, which she herself caused. Perhaps this scene provides a glimpse into the heart of her paradoxical character. Even after Anat has Aqhat executed, she mourns for him, her would-be "brother," just as his human sister Pughat will weep over him (1.19 I 34-35). For a moment, one side of Anat sounds like a tenderhearted sister, but the other side is no less in view: she is the one who ordered his execution.

The third and final tablet of the story, KTU 1.19 I, opens with the very broken lines 1-19.[157] After the superscription in line 1, the narrative refers to the bow (line 4) as well as the goddess (line 5). Perhaps the bow is lost, if it is the subject of the verb *tql,* "it falls," in line 3; it would be tempting to see the bow as having fallen "to the midst of the water," mentioned in line 2. If correct, it would not be difficult to see here Anat's failure to secure the bow once Aqhat has been killed. At the same time, it is important to remember that any reconstruction of this section remains highly tentative. Only with lines 13-16 does the text become clear. Here Anat repeats her earlier words (1.18 IV 40-41) that she killed Aqhat for his bow and arrows, but she now adds the further complaint in line 17 that "even so, his bow was not given to me." The result is "a lose-lose situation" for Anat: she has gone to considerable lengths to have Aqhat killed and she has also lost his bow, which she apparently presumed that she would gain.

The final part of this section opens a long narrative that illustrates the terrible situation of the family. The first indication of its cursed state appears in 1.19 I 18-19, which refers to the "firstfruit of summer,[158] the ear [in] its husk." From the later description of the desiccated condition of the ground in which "the ear" is supposed to grow (1.19 II 19-20), lines 18-19 evidently relate the desiccated condition of "the ear." This description may presuppose that Aqhat's death has taken its toll on nature.[159] Within the wider narrative, the characterization of this "ear" as "the first (fruit) of summer" perhaps echoes "the first" of Aqhat's game in 1.17 V 37. Anat's desire for the bow and the possibly corresponding rejection of his offer issue in her decision to bring a deadly attack on him, which in turn leads to the death of the first of the summer fruit. This cause-and-effect may not be immediately evident to the two family members who now reenter the narrative.

1.19 I 19-37 contain a series of observations made by Aqhat's father and sister.[160] The passage begins with Danil sitting as before (1.17 V 4-13) in the gate adjudicating the cases of the widow and orphan. In 1.19 I, he notes the situation on the threshing floor. The context at this point (lines 29-31) is very broken, but with the verbs "to be dried up" *(yḫrb)* and "to droop" *(yǵly),* as well as the noun "fruit" *('ib),*[161] it would appear that the narrative relates the summer fruit's poor condition.[162] Another ill omen in lines 32-33 describes the birds of prey soaring or circling over "the house of the father." The appearance of the birds is a bad portent to Pughat, which informs her weeping in lines 34-35. Perhaps like her father at this point in the story, Pughat does not know the reason for the birds' cursed appearance,[163] though she may suspect more. Hers is not public lamentation, as she weeps to herself in lines 34-35 ("in her heart . . . in the innards"), echoing Anat's earlier plotting in her heart (1.17 VI 42). Pughat's private weeping also anticipates her public weeping that will take place later, following the proper burial of Aqhat's remains (1.19 IV 9-17). From this point on, the narrative moves inexorably toward the father and daughter learning of the death of their beloved son and brother.

The appearance of the birds induces the family lament, as marked by the tearing of Danil's clothing (1.19 I 36-37). The words *tmzʿ kst* may be translated either "the clothing was torn" or "she," that is Pughat herself, "tore the clothing."[164] As Wright notes,[165] the act of mourning customarily issues in one's tearing one's own clothing, but he also suggests that Pughat possibly performs the act of tearing, as she is mentioned in the immediately preceding bicolon (1.19 I 34-35). H. L. Ginsberg long ago ascertained that "she realizes that the blight upon the land must be due to the murder of some innocent person. She has the gift of divination."[166] Natan-Yulzary suggests the following reasoning: "why does she tear Dana'il's garment? Again, we must construe our own interpretation of the character's state of mind: Dana'il is unaware of what happened, and is oblivious of the omens."[167] The description of lines 36-37 forms an inclusion[168] with lines 46-48 around the speech of Danil.

In this context, Danil gives his verbal response to the situation (1.19 I 38-48).[169] Two factors have played a significant role in interpreting this speech. The first was Ginsberg's brilliant comparison of lines 44-46 with 2 Sam. 1:21.[170] Ginsberg noted the two negative particles plus terms for precipitation, "dew" and "rain," in both this biblical verse and the story of Aqhat (KTU 1.19 I 44b-46a). Each term for precipitation is preceded by a negative particle: "no dew, no rain."[171] Ginsberg's comparison of lines 44b-46a with 2 Sam. 1:21a would make these Ugaritic lines seem quite fitting as a curse, just like the biblical parallel. Other texts contain a curse relevant to lines 45-46, *bl ṭb ql bʿl,* "no good voice of Baal." The Laws of Hammurabi close with a series of curses including one invoking the wish: "May the god Adad, lord of abundance, the canal-inspector of heaven and earth, my helper, deprive of the benefits of rain from heaven and flood from the spring."[172] The Aramaic Bukan inscription dated to about 700 B.C.E. offers a series of curses on "whoever will remove this stele," including "seven years may Hadad not give his voice (i.e., his thunder) in his country."[173] From these two examples in addition to the relevant biblical passages (2 Sam. 1:21; 1 Kgs. 17:1),[174] it may be surmised that Danil's speech entails traditional curse formulary.

The second major consideration in the discussion of Danil's speech has been the verb *yṣly* in 1.19 I 39. Commentators have discussed the semantics of the root, **ṣly:* the nominal form **ṣlt-* in KTU 1.119.34 refers to prayer, while the syllabic form of the noun, *ṣi-il-yv[ ],* in the *Ugaritica V* polyglot is given correspondences in Akkadian and Hurrian that mean "to curse."[175] As a result, scholars are divided over the precise meaning of *yṣly* in 1.19 I 39.[176] A curse might seem to imply that Danil already knows that his son is dead, but the narrative has provided no indication of this realization. The news does not come to him until 1.19 II 27-44, and Danil's wish expressed in 1.19 II 17-18 shows that he does not know yet that Aqhat is dead. If prayer were involved instead, it would explain better the motivation for Danil's speech at this point. Accordingly, "to pray,"[177] "to implore,"[178] or "to abjure"[179] might seem preferable to "to curse" and to alternatives that would obviate the problem of translating *yṣly* in 1.19 I 39 as "to curse" (such as "to utter a spell").[180] In 1.19 I 40-46 (or 42-46), the narrative may relate Danil's fear over the possible curse of drought that may be in effect, even though he does not know its ultimate cause. Given this understanding, lines 40-42 could represent a narrative continuation of lines 38-39: "Then Danil, the man of Rp'u, prayed for the clouds in the grievous heat, for the rain (that) the clouds make[181] in the summer, for the dew (that) makes dew for the grapes." Or, it might represent Danil's wish for rain in the face of the "grievous heat": "Let the rain of the clouds make rain in the summer, let the dew make dew on the grapes."[182] Either way, Danil would be expressing concern in the form of a declaration (or perhaps questions) reflecting his fear of a cursed situation, that "Baal will be lacking for seven years, the Cloudrider for eight:[183] no dew, no rain, no rush[184] of the deeps, no sweet voice of Baal." In this approach, the formulary as known in Danil's speech and in 2 Sam. 1:21 would be adaptations shaped by their contexts.[185] As Natan-Yulzary has observed,[186] the speech in Aqhat is not a curse, but a recognition that "the drought will continue for seven years." Similar content need not require the same form of verbal utterance; it need not be a curse in both instances. The context here, in contrast to the parallels of 2 Sam. 1:21 and Tell Bukan inscription, suggests fear of a cursed situation. The tearing of Danil's clothing in lines 36-37 and 46-48 shows that mourning ritual has come into play. So mourning the lack of rain would hardly be out of place,[187] even if the truth of the situation is not yet fully understood by Danil or Pughat. As noted above, the repetition of lines 36-37 in lines 46-48 closes this subunit.

The final line of 1.19 I introduces another speech by Danil that runs into the second column, 1.19 II 1-5. Here he commands Pughat to ready his riding animal. The language of the command is stereotypical, as seen in KTU 1.4 IV 2-7. The titles of Pughat in lines 1-3//5-7 suggest her domestic role ("shoulderer of water") as well as her ability to read signs provided by nature ("collector of dew from fleece" [?] and "knower of the courses of the stars").[188] The mention of her capacities at this point may be a reminder that she may discern a further threat from the omen of the raptors seen earlier in 1.19 I 32-33. She may sense more than what her father does. In complying in lines 8-10 with her father's command given in lines 3-5, three times she is said, apparently, to be weeping *(bkm)*.[189]

At 1.19 II 12, the narrative focuses on Danil by fronting his name at the head of the clause.[190] Line 12 opens a new subunit detailing his movement through the dessicated land, his embrace of the stalks, and his wish voiced both for their successful comeback and for Aqhat's harvest of the renewed stalks (lines 12-25). This final wish suggests that Danil still does not know that Aqhat is dead. This provides a transition for the arrival of messengers beginning in lines 26-27. The final words of his speech "had not left his mouth"[191] when Danil lifts up his head and sees the legation entering the picture. This manner of presentation echoes two earlier scenes in the story involving the perception of parties arriving (1.17 V 9; 1.19 I 28-29). What Danil sees exactly in lines 27-36 is unclear.[192] Line 28 refers to "young men" *(ǵlmm)*. H. L. Ginsberg entertained two possibilities for these "youths": "Somebody finds out what has happened to Aqhat: either because Paghat sees two supernatural beings act it out in dumb show, or because two attendants of Danil hear the tale from the dying boy."[193] Nick Wyatt thinks that these figures are hunting companions of Aqhat,[194] which would explain how they happen to witness Aqhat's demise as related in lines 29-30. These lines echo the description of Yatpan's attack on Aqhat back in 1.18 33-34. No such companions are known from the earlier narrative, and the narrative at this point may simply understand *ǵlmm* as messengers (as in KTU 1.2 I 19, 39; 1.3 II 8, IV 5; 1.4 V 43; see also 1.3 V 15), without reflecting any effort or concern to explain how they happen to know about Aqhat's death. Within this context, many cola remain unclear (lines 27-28, 28-29, 31-32, 34-36). Even lines 32-34, containing the motif of weeping in lamentation known elsewhere (1.14 I 28-30),[195] are unclear about their subject.[196] Line 37 seems to open a first person singular speech announcing the news (*ʾabšrkm,* "I will tell you [pl.?]").[197] The news emerges clearly in lines 38b-39 (lines 37b and 38a are a mess). The announcement here mirrors precisely the narrative description of Aqhat's death in 1.18 IV 36-37. However, it is unclear who the recipient of this initial announcement is in lines 37-39. It is not Danil, for line 40 begins a second announcement of Aqhat's death, this time clearly to Danil (lines 41-44). The first announcement might be made to Pughat, as Alan Cooper reasonably surmises,[198] but the identity of the person signaled by the first person form *ʾabšrkm,* "I will tell you," remains unclear. It would seem not to be the plural "youths" (unless one emends the verb to the plural form[199] or one messenger announces the news to the other). In sum, the announcement might be represented twice, but the circumstances of the first announcement remain unclear.

Lines 44-49 and presumably the six lines missing after line 49 in 1.19 II recount Danil's reaction to the news. The physical response of trembling in lines 44-47 is stereotypical for bad news (1.3 III 33-35; 1.4 II 16-20), but Danil's verbal response in line 48 and following cannot be made out. When the narrative resumes at the very end of column II (lines 56-57), another episode begins with Danil raising his eyes and seeing.[200] This time he looks at the clouds and sees something, which is lost in the lacuna in line 57a. Given his speech against the birds in the following lines in the opening of the next column, 1.19 III, it is reasonable to follow the common reconstruction of *nšrm* ("raptors") in the lacuna in line 57a. With his wishes expressed beginning in 1.19 I 1-6 to find his son's remains in the belly of the bird that ate his remains, Danil understands the significance of the birds that Pughat might have suspected earlier. Three times Danil expresses a curse against the raptors that would allow him to find Aqhat's "fat" and "bone" and then give them a proper burial. With his attempts undertaken against raptors in general and then the father of the raptors in particular (1.19 III 1-28), his effort is unsuccessful. So he prays for their "building" *(bn)* by Baal, and they are restored. However, in Danil's third curse, this time against the mother of the raptors, he is successful. He finally finds Aqhat's remains (1.19 III 28-39) and buries them (1.19 III 39-40). He weeps for him as he inters him (1.19 III 40-41) at *knrt,* perhaps the name of a town or region.[201] Danil then utters a curse against any raptors that would fly over his grave and deprive Aqhat of his sleep. This sort of curse against disturbing the dead is also known in burial inscriptions,[202] and the characterization of death as sleep is an old motif as well.[203] Danil also utters a curse against three places near the locale where Aqhat was slain (KTU 1.19 III 45-IV 7). Not all of the details involved in his curses are clear (for example, the precise nature of Danil's curse in 1.19 III 47[204] and his apparent gesture repeated three times, in 1.19 III 49, 56 and 1.19 IV 7).[205] However, they point to the notion of bloodguilt on a place near the site of an unresolved murder (scholars often compare the situation described in Deuteronomy 21). These curses also seem somewhat playful in their language, with *ʿnt* ("now") twice in line 48 evoking the name of the goddess, Anat, and the curse of lines 53-54 perhaps echoing the "drooping" (**ǵly*) condition in which Danil had found the vegetation in 1.19 I 29-30.

In 1.19 IV 8-17, Danil mourns in his house for his dead son. This lamentation is a socially recognized process, as he is assisted by "weepers"//"mourners" who are female (*⟨b⟩kyt//mšspdt;* cf. Jer. 9:17-19) and male "breakers of skin" (*pẓǵm ǵr;* cf. Amos 5:16-17).[206] The lamentation period of seven years is unusually long,[207] and it echoes the number of years that Danil had earlier voiced in his lament over nature (1.19 I 44-48). A seven-year drought would have been catastrophic; perhaps this circumstance is to be understood as running concurrently with Danil's seven years of lamentation. In the seventh year, Danil dismisses the weepers and closes this episode by making an offering to the gods in 1.19 IV 17-25.[208] The feast seems to be accompanied by musical instrumentation of cymbals and castanets of ivory, the same instruments that accompany the feast of Rp'u in 1.108.1-7.[209] The music may suggest celebration and thus would mark a break from the rituals of mourning over Aqhat. Danil is now finished with his ritual actions.

5. The Heroic Daughter's Revenge

With the completion of Danil's public lamentation in 1.19 IV 17-26,[210] the narrative shifts back to Pughat in 1.19 IV 28. The story largely focuses on her for the remainder of the extant text (1.19 IV 28-61). Pughat's speech in lines 29-31 repeats almost verbatim the narrative description of Danil's feast in lines 22-25. The major differences involve the verbs. When Pughat refers to the feast, she uses the suffix forms of the verbs, suggesting that her father's actions are now completed and she can make her request. Lines 29-35 may be heard as connected:[211]

> "My father has presented an offering to the gods,
> Has sent up his incense to the heavens,
> The incense of the Hrnmy[212] to the stars.
> You can surely bless me that I may go blessed,

You can strengthen[213] me that I may go strengthened.
I would slay the slayer of my brother,
I would finish off the o[ne] who finished off my brother."[214]

The request for blessing and strength echoes the opening of the story when Baal requests the blessing from El on behalf of Danil (1.17 I 23-24). It was supposed to be his son who would provide such blessing and strength for Danil in this early part of the story. Now the request for blessing[215] and strength,[216] as put by Pughat to her father, is to help achieve revenge for the death of this son, her brother (lines 34-35). The vocabulary used, here as elsewhere (1.4 II 24-26),[217] is language of family vengeance.

Danil responds, with an opening address to Pughat that perhaps encapsulates the issue of the text: "With life-breath, may Pughat, shoulderer of water, collector of dew from fleece (?), knower of the courses of the stars, live." His initial expression here, "(with) life-breath *(npš)* may Pugh[at], bearer of water, live,"[218] seems to be a simple opening formula in his direction to Pughat, but it is freighted with a further sensibility. It echoes Aqhat's loss of his *npš*, commanded in 1.18 IV 25, executed in 1.18 IV 36, and announced in 1.19 II 38, 42 (reconstructed). Danil's life now is bound with the death of his son and the death of his son's slayer. The death of one who caused death is the only recourse for Danil's *npš*.[219] As noted earlier in this chapter, the story of Aqhat offers a reflection on what constitutes the family's collective *npš* struggling through life and death.

In his blessing, Danil addresses Pughat by her common titles (lines 36-38), followed by an unclear line 39 and then an affirmation of her plan at vengeance, once again in the family idiom in lines 39-40. At this point, Danil drops from view, and the focus at this point falls entirely on Pughat. Lines 40-41 perhaps have her washing her clothing "in the sea" (the only words legible in lines 40-41; cf. 1.4 II 5-7). Then in lines 41-43 she applies cosmetics to herself (cf. the parallel in the story of a heroic female killing a foreign military leader, in Jdt. 12:15).[220] The language here is similar to what Anat does in 1.3 III 1-2 and III 45-46 after her battling, and what Kirta is commanded to do in 1.14 II 9-11 and performs in III 52-54 before making an offering and going to battle. Such washing may mark a transition to another state of preparation and perhaps purification (cf. Jdt. 12:5-9). In lines 43-46, Pughat ties a sword on her sheath beneath her "woman's outfit." The language for tying the weapon on herself echoes Anat putting Yatpan in her sheath in order to launch him for his attack on Aqhat (1.18 IV 17-18, 27-29). The irony of the echo is evident: Pughat seeks to kill in stealth mode much as Anat herself had hidden her own role in the execution of Aqhat.[221] More specifically, Pughat will now hide a knife tied on her person just as Anat had Yatpan tied on her person.

In the final scene in lines 46-61, Pughat goes to the camp of Yatpan.[222] Word is brought to him (lines 50-51; cf. 1.23.52, 59 for the wording): "the *ʾagrtn* has come into your camp, . . . has come to the ⟨te⟩nts"[223] (lines 51-52). The term *ʾagrtn* has been thought to designate Pughat as either "our hireling,"[224] or "our hirer," in other words, "our boss," namely Anat.[225] In the second view, Pughat would be disguising herself as Anat. Militating against this alternative, Anat is not elsewhere called *pǵt* as this figure is in line 55 (and as reconstructed by KTU, Parker, and Pardee in line 51); nor does it seem likely that the female would be misconstrued by Yatpan as the goddess or that Yatpan would give orders to Anat as he does in lines 53-54. As there is no apparent indication of Anat in this context,[226] it would seem preferable to understand that the men in this scene perceive the figure of Pughat as "our hireling," namely a prostitute working the army camp. In focusing on whether the figure in question is Anat or Pughat that is involved, the scholarly discussion may have missed a further point. The text seems to refer to a female hireling, and it is not surprising that KTU and many commentators reconstruct [*pǵt*] in the lacuna parallel to *ʾagrtn*, "our hireling," in line 51 (which would also fit with the attestation of *pǵt* in line 55). If correct, this hireling is referred to as "[the young female]" ([*pǵt*]), as the word commonly means.[227] Yatpan's camp does not realize that the female generically called [*pǵt*] in line 51 is in fact Pughat herself. The play of the use of the generic word on the specific name of Aqhat's sister may be crucial to the literary effect in this scene.

The ignorance of Yatpan and the rest of his camp does not end there. Yatpan does not know that Pughat is dressed to kill.[228] This reading would be closer to other stories with the motif of the woman who stealthily kills an enemy general or leader (see Judith 12-13; cf. Judg. 4:17-21; 5:24-27).[229] The narrative omits any introduction of Pughat to Yatpan, but moves immediately to his offer of drink to her in lines 52-54.[230] After she follows his offer, he declares to her: "I will prevail *(ʾilʾa)* . . ."[231] (line 57). Yatpan seems to be offering a toast to his own glory as a warrior, although the end of the first line and its relationship to the second line[232] are not quite clear. In lines 58-59, Yatpan exalts in his own power, with reference to the dead Aqhat: "my hand (that) slew Aqhat the Hero, may it slay the enemy by the thousands!"[233] As the final scene in the extant version nears the end, it is quite unfortunate that lines 59-61 are so unclear. Lines 59-60 might refer to the spells that Pughat herself puts in the tents.[234] Pughat seems to be in the process of seducing Yatpan, and perhaps then she casts spells on him. For a female who knows the courses of the stars, such an idea may not be far-fetched. Lines 60-61 may contain two similes, "[her/his . . .] like a ram (?)" and "her/his heart like a snake." These lines might refer to "his heart,"[235] suggesting Yatpan's desire for Pughat, but the two similes may convey the emboldening of "her heart" to act against him at this moment.

The final lines of the surviving text seem to show Pughat's turn at taking the initiative with the wine. Not once but "twice she gave him to drink *(tšqy)* mixed drink, to him she gave drink *(tšqy)*."[236] The extant text now comes to an end in the middle of this scene. As a result, most commentators surmise that a fourth tablet would have completed the scene here, which based on parallels[237] would have included Pughat removing the knife from underneath her clothing, as mentioned in lines 43-46, and killing Yatpan, in accordance with her stated goal in lines 34-35 and seconded by her father in lines 39-40. The picture of the heroic female giving the enemy a drink and then killing him occurs also in Judg. 4:19-21 (cf. 5:25-26) and Judith 12-13. Beyond this putative ending for the scene between Yatpan and Pughat, it is hard to say what, if anything, the further narrative may have recounted.[238] In any case, this section of the extant story focuses on the young woman Pughat's vengeance on the warrior who slew her brother, the young would-be warrior. In the end, the story of Aqhat embodies the very curse for such a warrior, as expressed in *Odyssey* 4.667-68: "may Zeus destroy his might before he ever reaches the measure of manhood."[239] Indeed, while the gods provide help at the beginning of the story, the appearance of Anat in 1.17 VI sets in motion a tale of a cursed family with no support from the gods.

6. The Heroic Code of Honor and the Gender of Human and Divine Warriors

Informed by the reading of the preceding sections, this final section of the chapter focuses on the representation of the story's warrior characters, along with associated cultural values and ideas. We begin with the story's key term for "hero." At the opening of the narrative (1.17 I 1), Danil is identified with a series of titles, including *ǵz[r]*, and *ǵzr* repeats often over the course of the story. The bulk of the word's Ugaritic occurrences are found in Aqhat. It is attested in Aqhat twenty-seven times (1.17 I 17, 35, 37; II 28; V 5, 14, 34; VI 20, 26, 33, 42, 51; 1.18 I 21; IV 14; 1.19 I 20, 37, 48; II 18, 42; III 47, 53; IV 4, 12, 16, 19), compared with its other twenty-one cases found elsewhere in the Ugaritic texts.[240] The usages of the word from the opening column in 1.17 I through 1.17 V involve the adult Danil, father of the young Aqhat. Danil's capacity as an adult hero comports with his role later sitting in the city-gate and giving judgment (1.19 I 19-25). Such adult heroes become members of the assembly of elders.[241] Outside of the literary context, the word *ǵzr* has a more generic meaning. In Ugaritic administrative texts, *ǵzrm* reflects a broad meaning of "young men," for example in KTU 4.102.3 (reconstructed), 16, 18, 19, 20, 23; 4.349.1. 4.102.16 lists *ǵzrm* between *ʾaṯt ʾadrt,*[242] perhaps "preeminent women," and *nʿrt,*[243] perhaps female retainers or assistants, all in the household of the official *(skn).*[244] In these cases, *ǵzrm* seem to be young, male retainers. Recent authors on these texts, including David Schloen and Kevin McGeough, see these as references to adolescent males.[245] In these contexts, the word seems to refer not to "heroes" as such, but to "young males." The two meanings for the word *ǵzrm* compare closely with Akkadian *eṭlūtu,* denoting "manliness" (implying bravery in battle), related to *eṭlu,* "manly, young man." The parallel usages in Akkadian and Ugaritic are suggestive of a semantic process of the word developing from "young man" to "hero."

The Ugaritic word is cognate with the BH root **ʿzr,* in particular in the nominal forms for "strength, might," according to Ginsberg, followed by Moshe Held and Patrick D. Miller.[246] Ginsberg noted in particular the word in 1 Chr. 12:1 and the juxtaposition of *gibbôrîm:* "this word is defined . . . as 'the *ʿzrym* — i.e., *ǵzrm* — of war.'"[247] Miller's review of the evidence suggests the association of *ʿzr* and *gibbôr,* evident in Judg. 5:23; Ps. 89:19; Ezek. 32:21; 1 Chr. 12:22.[248] To cite one of these examples, Ps. 89:19 reads: "You said: 'I have set[249] might *(ʿēzer)* upon a warrior *(gibbôr).*'"

In the story of Aqhat, a young male — it is hoped — would emerge as a "hero" *(ǵzr).*[250] As noted above, the word is used for young Aqhat. We may compare similar characterizations for heroes. Of Goliath, it is said in 1 Sam. 17:33: "he has been a warrior [literally, 'a man of war'] from his youth" *(wĕhûʾ ʾîš milḥāmâ minnĕʿūrāyw).*[251] Young men with fighting ability and hunting prowess[252] as well as other physical capabilities were favored for military forces and sometimes for leadership, for example, Jephthah (Judg. 11:1) and Saul (1 Sam. 9:1-2). Jephthah himself is said to be *gibbôr ḥayil.* Saul's father is also attributed this expression, and Saul himself stands out for his size.

In 1.17 VI 20 the narrative first applies this epithet to Aqhat when he initially encounters Anat. Anat addresses him as "Aqhat the Hero" in this same scene, both at the very opening of her speech and in the very last line of the speech (1.17 VI 26, 33). Here "Aqhat the Hero" marks who this figure is for the goddess. The goddess also identifies him in this way three more times in this column: in her offer to keep him alive (1.17 VI 33), in her final threat to him (1.17 VI 42), and then when she maligns him before El (1.17 VI 51). Anat's second meeting with Aqhat again identifies him according to this title (1.18 I 21; and possibly in line 24 as sometimes reconstructed).[253]

When the title occurs next in Aqhat, its use reverts to the father. At this point in the story, he does not know of his son's death; in this context the title occurs three times (1.19 I 20, 37, 48). It is at this point that the news of Aqhat's death is brought to Danil. The title reverts back to the son, with the messengers referring to the dead son as Aqhat the Hero (1.19 II 48). When Danil enters into the formal acts of mourning, Aqhat the Hero is the one he laments (1.19 IV 11-12, 15-16), and at this point, the father too is again called the Hero (1.19 IV 19). With the father mourning his son, the two are linked in this title: the elderly hero weeps for his son, the young slain hero. The final use of the title is deployed for neither father nor son, but for Danil's daughter, Aqhat's sister Pughat. In the final, extant scene of the text, it is this female figure who takes on the clothing of the hero (1.19 IV 43). Clothing marks her identity in this scene, to avenge the death of her brother, the Hero, and the honor of her father, the Hero.

In this see-saw of heroic identity, the story focuses on the family warriors. The narrative shows nothing of the cultural context of king or priest. These roles do not appear in this text. Moreover, apart from the brief subordinate appearance put in by Danatayu in 1.17 V, the human mother is hardly present in this family. Instead, the only female authority in our text is a divinity, the commanding figure of Anat. In contrast to the story of Kirta or the biblical patriarchs, the story does not focus on the wifely or maternal side of familial life. Unlike the story of Kirta and his wife Huray, or the family story of Jacob and Esau, with their parents Isaac and Rebecca and their concerns for blessing and inheritance, the story of Aqhat skews the family situation to the specific theme of family members as warriors.[254] In 1.17 V, the divine gift of the bow and arrows initiates the beginning of Aqhat's training as a warrior. Bows and arrows begin a trajectory of life toward warriorship, perhaps in the terms expressed by Gen. 49:23-24, to be one of the "archers," literally "lords of arrows," whose "bow remains taut" (see NJPS).

The end of the same column, 1.17 V, refers to a significant element in the heroic paradigm, namely the notion that the gift of the hunt is ultimately one given by the female divinity warrior to the male warrior, who is in turn to offer it back to her. With the weapons, Danil approaches his young son and addresses him about "the first/best of your game" to be delivered to a temple (1.17 V 37-39). In context, this seems to be Anat's temple, and it may also reflect her capacity as goddess of the hunt,[255] as well as its divine patroness. Up to this point in our story, hunting represents the beginning of the training and socialization of a young male as warrior.[256] Early on, this is largely a family matter between father and son, a preliminary stage before a young man reaches the status as a fighting man.[257] In this literary world of warriors, the human matriarch largely disappears, with the substantial attention given to the female divinity of warfare.

1.17 VI involves the famous encounter between goddess and warrior. Anat's offer of life to Aqhat in 1.17 VI is indeed a notorious scene, yet its warrior context and meanings have failed to garner as much scholarly attention. Lines 1-6 involve a feast of the goddess, cast perhaps in earthly terms; the goddess is in her temple. The clearest part of this opening passage in column VI involves clichés of feasting. According to line 10, Anat raises her eyes, and while the lines are broken here, it is evident that it is Aqhat that she sees and more specifically, his bow, first mentioned in the extant text in line 13. It would seem that the Hero is heeding his father's words from the previous column, namely that he should bring to the goddess in her temple the firstfruit of his hunt. Some sense of this scene is provided in the representation of a hunt's aftermath on a Hittite silver alloy cup, which includes two gods.[258] Worshippers are depicted as bringing wine and bread to the gods, and behind them lies a stag. We may imagine Aqhat similarly bringing the animal of his hunt to Anat in her temple. We might surmise that the setting of Anat's temple, as the initial meeting place between the goddess and the human male, marks the successful completion of the first phase of this human warrior's training; it is a successful hunt, accompanied by the appropriate religious ritual of offering to the divine patroness of the hunt. With this meeting, the narrative sets out the basic gender polarity of warrior culture, which focuses on the young male human warrior and the experienced female divine warrior. The narrative presents her temple as the setting for their meeting. The father and his household pass from view; the young would-be warrior now faces the exigencies of the hunt and its offering on his own.

It is at this point in the narrative that Anat offers Aqhat silver and gold in exchange for the weapons (1.17 VI 17-19).[259] At first glance, there is no apparent reason for her request. Perhaps either the narrative or Anat herself presupposes the notion that the successful warrior deposits weapons in the temple as dedicated to the patron deity. Natan-Yulzary has recently drawn attention to a cylinder-seal containing scenes bearing components analogous to the situation between Aqhat and Anat: "a figure of a winged goddess, an altar next to it, while another figure hands a bow over to her, and in another scene we see a bird above a seated figure, probably Aqhat."[260] Perhaps this scene provides the elements presupposed in the conversation between the goddess and the human, including a bow being handed over. This seal might not depict the Aqhat scene in particular, as Natan-Yulzary suggests, since in the story the bow is not handed over. Perhaps the seal represents what may be the goddess's expectation in the story of Aqhat, namely that she should receive the bow. The analogous practice of depositing weapons as trophies informs the report in 1 Sam. 22:10, that Goliath's sword had been given to the priests at Nob thanks to David's victory over him. 1 Sam. 31:10 describes how Saul's armor was placed in the temple of Ashtarot. We may also note the dedication of the shield of metal in KTU 1.123.2.[261] The axe in a deposit in the Tell Qasile temple may be viewed also along these lines.[262]

At the same time, it is not clear that in this context receiving the bow would be a normal expectation. Anat may simply desire the divinely-made weapon, as noted by David Wright.[263] The goddess of the hunt and warfare, Anat herself uses the bow and arrows, as evoked by the description of her driving off captives by means of a staff and bowstring in KTU 1.3 II 15-16.[264] As a divine patroness of the hunt, it is hardly surprising that Anat would be drawn to Aqhat's extraordinary, divinely-crafted bow and arrows. In turn, Aqhat seems to make matters worse. At this point in their conversation, Aqhat's answer points to a further aspect of warrior worldview. His response contains the one occurrence of *ǵzr* where it is not someone's title: "Do not be twisty with me, O Maiden, for to a hero your twistiness is muck." Here expressing this component of the code of honor risks conflict with the wishes of a deity, and in particular the deity that in this text embodies divine warrior identity. Instead of accepting her offer, Aqhat accepts the fate that all humans face, namely death (1.17 V 35-38). This answer thus shows a fundamental aspect of the warrior's code; it involves not simply honor at the risk of death, but also the warrior's recognition of death as the destiny of all mortals: "the death of all I shall die; I — I shall surely die" *(mt kl 'amt/w'an mtm 'amt).* Either way, the warrior risks death, itself a basic fact of heroic existence.

As poignant as Aqhat's response here is, his next statement is deadly; Aqhat here seems to make a misstep. He declares to the goddess what is well known about human women. He tells her in no uncertain terms: "Bows are [weapons of?] warriors; now shall womanhood go hunting?" This second line, *ht tṣdn t'inṯt,* may be understood not as a question but perhaps as a sarcastic claim: "now womenfolk hunt!" Either way, in this statement Aqhat asserts the common gendered understanding about human warrior life: it belongs to men and not to women. A similar viewpoint is expressed by Telemachus, the son of Odysseus, when he says to his mother Penelope:

"Go to your chamber. . . . The bow shall be for men" (*Odyssey* 21:350).[265] The world of human warriors is a male world. This male-female split in the warrior situation is largely correct, but in telling Anat that the hunt is not for womanfolk, Aqhat seems to make a category error. Indeed, as Kelly J. Murphy has noted, Anat is not a reflection of reality for human women in Late Bronze Age Ugarit.[266] Anat is presented as the opposite of reality for most human women. The hunt may not be for human women, but this does not apply to some goddesses.[267] Aqhat seems not to understand that the hunt is precisely the domain of warrior goddesses.[268] The son appears naïve (had his father not fully informed the son?), and he seems to be insulting her a second time. Perhaps it is for this reason that the son incurs her wrath. As Wright suggests,[269] both Anat and Aqhat seem culpable, and there appear to be flaws in both figures. Their meeting, with their failings all too apparent, leads to explosive and destructive results: Anat's wrath and Aqhat's death. Expressed in more abstract terms, being a human male warrior in relationship with a divine warrior like Anat offers possible benefits such as divine mentorship and bonds on the one hand; on the other hand, it may entail possible dangers, even to the point of engendering the goddess's fury. Perhaps there is not — or cannot be — the force of divine warriorship without the fury of the ideal warrior.[270]

There may be more to the picture if the bow and arrows carry sexual overtones, as suggested by Delbert Hillers.[271] In support of this view, it has been noted that the bow and arrows are more broadly symbols for masculinity,[272] while the spindle by contrast is thought to be a mark of femininity.[273] These sorts of objects reflect activities associated with each gender,[274] as illustrated by a Sumerian birth-incantation from Ebla: "If it is female, spindle (and) needle may she (the mid-wife) bring out. If it is male, throwing-stick (and) weapon may she bring out."[275] The surface meaning of the narrative hints in this direction of sexuality, yet it does not pursuit it, except with Anat's address to Aqhat as "brother" (1.18 I 24). The underlying sexual tensions have been underscored well by Jean-Marie Husser; here I quote his statement about Anat at some length:

> elle propose au jeune héros une relation où l'érotisme et la sexualité restent camouflés sous l'apparence virile d'un partenariat de chasse. Comme chasseresse et guerrière, Anat inverse les rôles assignés à l'homme et à la femme dans la société et, par cette double transgression — à l'égard de le féminité comme à l'égard de la pratique cynégétique — elle incarne pour le jeune homme une sorte d'absolu de la virilité guerrière à laquelle il ac-

> cède. It apparaît bien que le ressort de l'intrigue réside précisément dans l'incapacité d'Aqhat à déchiffrer cette situation et l'ambivalence de son rapport à la déesse. Son refus de lui donner son arc droit donc s'entendre comme une faute rituelle: il signifie sa méconnaissance d'un code symbolique propre à signifier et à structurer son passage à l'âge adulte et son agrégation au monde des hommes. De ce point de vue, l'épisode de la mort d'Aqhat est le récit paradigmatique de l'échec de ce passage pour quiconque refuse le code social définissant les rapports entre les sexes et l'autorité de la déesse en la matière. On l'a dit, la valeur symbolique de l'arc d'Aqhat se comprehend également dans un usage métaphorique du vocabulaire cynégétique pour signifier la quête sexuelle. L'exercise cynégétique sert ici tout à la fois d'épreuve initiatique et de métaphore au jeu érotique.[276]

As Husser understands, Aqhat's bow stands in for Aqhat himself. The bow of the warrior is an extension of himself; as the warrior's basic tool, it is his "extra-somatic body part."[277] In failing to give up his bow, Aqhat is, in a fundamental sense, refusing his relationship with the goddess. The would-be relationship between the young human male warrior and the young divine female warrior literally embodies the tensions in the underlying sexual inversions of warrior culture.

In the story of Aqhat, the roles of the divine and human warriors do not line up along gender lines. As Husser's remarks make clear, there is instead an inversion of gender roles[278] in the area of warriors and hunting: the goddess, rather than any god, is the prominent warrior in this text, and the young human male is the conventional human warrior. Yet more than gender inversion of roles is involved in the story. Unlike a god such as Baal,[279] Anat is not simply a model for Aqhat as a potential hunter-warrior. Anat is also to be his mentor, to be formalized in a bonding expressed in terms of sexuality. Gender inversion in divine and human warrior roles goes with the female-male warrior bonding between the female deity and the male human. (I will return to the importance of this point not only for Anat, but also for Athtart, in Chapter Seven.)

Anat's final response to Aqhat is no less telling for the values of warrior culture (1.17 VI 42-45). Scholars have mostly focused their attention on the fact that she threatens him, but the terms of the threat also deserve attention. She demands first that he pay attention to her (lines 42-43), specifically to her threat. The protasis of her threat mentions her chancing upon him on "the path of rebellion"//"the path of pride." The precise import of these parallel phrases is unclear. One may surmise that another aspect of the warrior code is asserted: just as falsehood is inappropriate to a warrior, so are rebellion and pride. At the same time, Anat is also warning him about their next encounter, that it will be fatal; as she says in lines 44-45, "I will make you fall beneath [my feet] *('ašqlk tḥt/[pʿny])*."

The titles that she uses here to address him are notable. As we noted above, Anat calls him "hero" when she first meets him in the story (KTU 1.17 VI 26 and probably to be reconstructed in 1.17 VI 17). Here he is also called *nʿmn*. This word has been rendered in a variety of ways in 1.17 VI 45; 1.18 IV 14: "finest" (later "fine");[280] "pretty-boy";[281] and "most handsome."[282] Arabic attests to the root **nʿm*, "to live in comfort, enjoy," and its noun, *nuʿm*, "favor, good will, grace."[283] BH **nʿm* in its various forms means "pleasant, delightful, lovely."[284] When applied in warrior contexts, it seems to evoke a warrior's "appeal" for others. It may reflect how others perceive him, specifically the magnetism of successful warriors or military leaders. Aqhat is also called *ʿmq nšm*, sometimes rendered as "cleverest of fellows,"[285] presumably assuming comparison with Akkadian *emqu*, "to be wise."[286] That word is generally applied to craftsmen, educated or wise persons, kings, but not to warriors. Thus the Ugaritic word may entail the sense suggested by Akkadian *emūqu*, "strength, force,"[287] as proposed by Jonas C. Greenfield.[288] As noted in Chapter Three, this term is used for the figure of Gilgamesh at several points in the Gilgamesh Epic,[289] beginning with SBV I.211 and 218: "Gilgamesh is perfect in strength."[290] As Shamhat puts the point to Enkidu about Gilgamesh (SBV I.238),[291] "he has a strength more mighty than you" *(dan-na e-mu-qa e-li-ka i-ši)*.[292] Elsewhere Gilgamesh's incomparability is tied to his physique (SBV I.29). Aqhat, too, seems to be *ʿmq nšm*, "strongest of men."[293] The syntax with *nšm* suggests a superlative: Aqhat stands out relative to other males.

After her response to Aqhat, Anat makes her way to El to get him to let her do as she wishes (1.17 VI 46–1.18 I 19),[294] which she then executes. She returns to Aqhat and addresses him (1.18 I 23-31). She tells him to go on a hunt (*tlk bṣd*, 1.18 I 27), and she evidently says that she will instruct him (*'almdk*, 1.18 I 29). The context is very broken, but this passage may suggest the notion that following the father's initial instruction in the hunt, perhaps the patron goddess instructs young Aqhat as well. The two sets of texts, with their parallel elements, point in this direction. With the father and the son, there are four basic components: (1) the father's approach to his son; (2) the paternal instruction to hunt and to present the game to the temple; (3) the human pursuit of the hunt in accordance with the instructions; and (4) the apparent presentation of the hunted game at a temple, evidently the goddess's. A similar pattern appears later in the story with Anat: (1) the goddess's invocation of her relationship to Aqhat as "my brother"; (2) the divine instruction to hunt; (3) the human pursuit of the hunt in accordance with the divine instructions (in terms of place, perhaps time, etc.); and (4) the apparent disposition of the game at a sanctuary, this time at the sanctuary of the moon god, Yariḫ. In providing instruction, the human father is succeeded by the divine "sister."

After two lost columns (1.18 II and III), the extant text resumes in column IV. It is perhaps not without significance that instead of Aqhat's name, only his title is used to refer to him as *nʿmn ǵzr* (1.18 IV 14), both perhaps echoing Anat's earlier speeches to him. At this point in the story, Anat is hovering among the birds above Aqhat. With this attack, the blood of Aqhat spills from his head, and his life-breath departs from his body (1.18 IV 33-37). The description is fairly brief and perhaps stereotypical-sounding.[295] We might think this is the end of the warrior's story, and yet there is a surprise. Having caused Aqhat's death, Anat weeps (*wtbk*, 1.18 IV 39) for him, this very same figure which the text now calls "her warrior" (*mhrh*, 1.18 IV 38). What I want to emphasize here is not only the word *mhr*, which refers here to an expert soldier,[296] but also the fact that passage calls Aqhat *"her mhr"* (my italics). Aqhat here seems in some sense hers. This possessive might convey her role as a divine patroness of warriors. Now she feels the loss that she has caused. In this context (1.18 IV 40), she adds *ʾabn ʾank*, which Pardee takes to mean that she would have built up his household,[297] and, I would add — perhaps in her capacity as patroness of warriors.

The lines that follow are broken; they include a reference to his arrows and probably his bow (1.18 IV 40-41) and then the word "to perish" (*ḫlq*, in 1.18 IV 42), the same word used for the fallen warrior, the god Baal, in 1.5 VI 8-10.[298] At this point, with Anat and Aqhat, we glimpse the goddess in mourning over the very warrior whom she has had executed. We might think this to be a contradiction or at least paradoxical, but both express values about the goddess. On the one hand, her own status as divine warrior and huntress is to be properly acknowledged. On the other hand, in what Marvin Pope called "the tender side of ʿAnat's nature,"[299] Anat's weeping is perhaps a double act of divine modeling, that warriors as well as their women weep for their fallen heroes.

The story of Aqhat portrays a family of heroes, father and son, not to mention the unexpectedly heroic daughter. The training of the male hero appears to take place in adolescence. With the instruction of his father, the young hero has not only learned the skills of the hunt, but also that it is an activity belonging to males and not to females, including his sister who will heroically seek to avenge his death. Honor is also a part of the code of behavior learned, whether that means avoiding deception or is a matter of defending the family, again as in Pughat's case. She violates the gender expectation, as represented by her clothing: she places the clothing of a woman over the clothing of a warrior along with weapons (1.19 IV 43-46). Here we may compare Deut. 22:5, forbidding a woman to put on the *kĕlî geber*. The first noun in this biblical verse means, literally, "implement." It is often taken to be "clothing," but it may be the "weapon" of a *geber*, possibly a "warrior" and not generically a "man."[300] In this reading, women are not to dress themselves as warriors, which would compare quite well with the description of Pughat clothing herself with warrior garments underneath her woman's clothing. As a figure, Pughat does not publicly represent her warrior role.[301] As a human female, her goal is executed with stealth. Insofar as martial conflict is disguised here, it reinforces the social code of the human world of male warriors. Her exceptional dress signals her exception to her gender and anticipates her exceptional execution.

With the story of Aqhat, readers have often focused on the seemingly inexplicable act of Anat's violence against the hero. Still, there is more to the story in what it expresses about warrior culture. Anat's violent nature is itself an expression of this warrior culture, and so is Aqhat's failure to learn, or at least to understand, the place of the goddess in the scheme of things, that she is a divine exception to the human rule. She is not merely the recipient of the firstfruit of the hunt. She may also be potentially dangerous in her capacity as a great warrior in her own right. Even human warriors, who otherwise observe the warrior code in making proper offerings to Anat, need to recognize her properly; Aqhat did not. Their conflict captures the deadly threat that warrior life entails: wherever Aqhat would turn, death may await. In Aqhat's case, he does not reach the next point in his development as a warrior. He does not become a fighting man, and he never enjoys the friendship of another beloved brother in arms. In this respect, Aqhat seems to represent an object lesson.[302]

The story of Aqhat is a cautionary tale that imagines Danil as a hero known in the distant past. It is also an act of recollection or memory on the part of the Ugaritic monarchy that patronized the writing and transmission of this story. Commemoration is a crucial element of both what we may call warrior and royal cultures, and at Ugarit it assumed a further expression through the figure named Rp'u and the group known as the Rp'um (biblical Rephaim). In the next chapter we will look at these figures and specifically how they embody the commemoration of dead warriors.

CHAPTER FIVE

The Commemoration of the Dead Rephaim Warriors

At the beginning of the extant text of Aqhat that we examined in the preceding chapter, there is a title given to Danil that gives expression to his socio-religious identity. He is called *mt rp'i*, "man of *rp'u*."[1] This title is no incidental matter in Aqhat: it is used for Danil often in conjunction with his title *ǵzr*, "hero" (KTU 1.17 I 1, 17, 35, 37, 42; II 28 V 5, 14, 34; 1.19 I 20, 37, 39, 47; II 41; IV 13, 17, 18, 36). As noted in the preceding chapter, these two epithets convey a good deal about Danil's identity. Danil is a hero, as well as a man *(mt)*[2] devoted to the figure known as *rp'u* (cf. biblical *(hā)rāpā'* in 1 Chr. 20:6, 8).[3]

With the name of *rp'u*, we enter the tradition of Ugarit's divine ancestral lore,[4] often centered around the *rp'um*. (Since this plural form is cognate with the biblical Rephaim, they are often called the Rephaim.) To anticipate the discussion below, *rp'um* were evidently viewed as heroes of old predating Ugarit's royal line. These *rp'um* enjoyed "divine" or "semi-divine status"[5] in their postmortem existence along with the royal line.[6] As both minor divinities and ancient heroes, the *rp'um* compare in some respects with the epic heroes of the *Iliad*. According to the classicist Hans van Wees, in Homer the epic hero of old was not only outstanding in terms of bravery or some other remarkable feature, but also held "semi-divine status after his death. . . . In historical times, then, heroes existed only in the shape of the spirits of the great dead. But evidently, the Greeks imagined that the Mycenaeans had been living heroes."[7] In this respect, the Greek *heros* has its West Semitic comparands in Ugaritic *rp'u*/*rp'um*, and in the biblical *(hā) rāpā'* in 1 Chr. 20:6, 8.

We begin this chapter with the figure of *rp'u* and the feast that he holds for other figures, possibly including the *rp'um* themselves (KTU 1.108). Then we will turn to the *rp'um* in a collection of texts (KTU 1.20–1.22), sometimes called "the Rephaim texts." We will end with a ritual (KTU 1.161) that reflects how the royal cult at Ugarit recalled the old *rp'um*. My central concern in this chapter is to understand the warrior values and notions in these Ugaritic representations of the figures designated by the root **rp'*.[8]

1. The Eponymous Ancestor of Heroic Rephaim Warriors

The figure called *Rp'u* appears in one passage[9] describing his banquet (KTU 1.108.1-5):[10]

1	[Her]e[11] Rp'u, the Eternal King,[12] drinks,[13]	*[hl]n.yšt.rp'u.mlk.ʿlm.*
1-2	Drinks/does [the god], mighty and noble,[14]	*wyšt/[ʾil] gṯr.wyqr*
	The god enthroned[15] in ʿthtrt,	*ʾil.yṯb.bʿṯtrt*
3	The god ruling in Hdrʿy,	*ʾil ṯpṭ.bhdrʿy*
	Who sings and makes music,	*dyšr.wydm̱r*
4	With[16] lyre and flute,	*bknr.wṯlb.*
	With drum and cymbals,	*btp.wmṣltm.*
4-5	With ca/stanets of ivory,[17]	*bm/rqdm.dšn.*
	With the good ones divined[18] by[19] Kothar.	*bḥbr.kṯr.ṭbm*

In this text, Rp'u[20] is presented as a royal figure, an "eternal king,"[21] befitting the head of the divinized deceased *rp'um*. This title, "eternal," as well as "king," is applied to the figure called *zbl mlk ʿllmy* in 1.22 I 10. While this phrase has often been taken as a plural reference to the Rephaim (as noted in the discussion of this text in the following section), it may be the title of their leader, in other words Rp'u himself. What is important to note is that whatever is the correct understanding of *zbl mlk ʿllmy* in 1.22 I 10, the phrase sounds suggestive of kingship (even if *mlk* is a name or title for a god). Rp'u here in KTU 1.108.1 is also called a "god" *(ʾil)*.

The kingship of Rp'u is said in this passage to be based in two towns in the region of the Transjordan, known also from the Bible, as first noted by Baruch Margolis (Margalit).[22] These places, ʿAshtarot (Tell ʿAshtara) and Edrei (modern Deraa), are mentioned in Deut. 1:4; 3:1, 10 as part of the domain held by the legendary King Og, himself said to be the last of the Rephaim (v. 11; see also 2:11, 20).[23] This is the same region associated with the memory of King Rp'u in 1.108.1-2. In this text, the topography of remembrance lies well outside of Ugarit, to its south. It would appear that the region's fame in this regard independently informed both Ugaritic and biblical texts.[24] Given the importance of the biblical evidence, we will devote more attention to this tradition in Part IV of this study, specifically in the final chapter of our story.

Beginning in line 3, Rp'u is also said to be a singer and musician, a role that suits heroes in the Baal Cycle (1.3 I 18-22), the *Iliad* (9:185-192), the Bible (2 Sam. 1:19-27), and elsewhere. Musical instrumentation appears on a very fragmentary side of KTU 1.113, in the form of *tp* (lines 1 and 5) and *ṯlbm* (lines 3 and 8).[25] This might merit little notice in this discussion, except that the other side of the tablet lists the kings of Ugarit, each preceded by *'il*, suggesting their divinized status. KTU 1.113 seems to show two of the same concerns as this passage about Rp'u in 1.108: musical instrumentation and divinized ancestors related to the royal line. The only other relevant Ugaritic passage, in the story of Aqhat (KTU 1.19 IV 26-27), mentions *mṣltm*, "cymbals" as in KTU 1.108.4, and then *mrqdm dšn*, the same phrase that appears in KTU 1.108.5. That phrase could be read as "dancers [anointed] with (literally, 'of') oil" (cf. Ps. 23:5), which would provide better parallelism with line 5, rendered "the goodly ones divined by Kothar" or "the goodly companions of Kothar" (as noted above); however, 1.19 IV 26-27 is in a broken context and its interpretation is uncertain.[26] It is possible that only musical instruments are meant by *mrqdm dšn*. A number of the musical instruments in 1.108 appear together in biblical contexts (e.g., "lyre," *kinnôr*, and "drum," *tôp*, in Isa. 5:12; see also Gen. 31:27; 1 Sam. 10:5; 2 Sam. 6:5; 1 Chr. 13:8; Isa. 30:32; Ps. 149:3; and Job 21:12). Other biblical contexts (e.g., Exod. 15:20; Isa. 24:8; Ps. 150:4) mention dance as well. The context is suggestive of celebration (see "joy," *simḥâ*, with the instruments in Gen. 31:27; see also 1 Sam. 18:6). In the next chapter, we will take a closer look at the unnamed "hero" *(ǵzr)* singing before Baal in his victory feast (1.3 I 18-22).

Rp'u is represented as both the exemplum of the ancient heroic line now deceased and a musical celebrant. In this passage, a further group in this feast comes into view in line 5. As noted above, this body is called "those divined by Kothar." This reference may be an allusion to the *rp'um*. The word taken here as "divined" *(ḥbr)* has often been read as "companions," but this sense of divination (or magic) by Kothar is attested at the end of the Baal Cycle with reference to the Rephaim (KTU 1.6 VI 45-47):

> Sun rules the Rephaim *(rp'im)*,
> Sun rules the divinities *('ilnym)*.

Your company are the gods *('ilm)*,
See, the dead *(mtm)* are your company.
Kothar is your diviner *(ḥbr)*,
Hasis, your expert *(d'tm)*.[27]

In view of this passage, the ones "divined by Kothar" in this banquet scene of KTU 1.108 seem to be an allusion to the Rephaim. The excerpt from the end of the Baal Cycle provides additional and fundamentally important information about the Rephaim. They are called "divinities" *('ilnym)* as well as "gods" *('ilm)* and "dead ones" *(mtm)*. Thus, they are divine in status, and they are comprised of deceased humans.

In KTU 1.108, subsequent lines mention the goddess Anat (lines 6-10), a number of lesser-known divinities (lines 11-14), and the god Rashpu (line 15). The preserved text on the back of the tablet includes three more references to *rp'u mlk 'lm* (lines 19, 21, 22) as well as a reference to Baal (line 18). When the words emerge more clearly in line 22b, it is evident that it involves a blessing for a party who goes unnamed in the extant text. The content in lines 23b-27 suggests a blessing invoked for the figure of the Ugaritic king:

"From (?) the Re[ph]aim of the underworld,
May your strength,
Your power, your might,
Your paternity, your splendor, be
In the midst of Ugarit,
For the days of Sun and Moon,
And the best of the years of El."[28]

This speech includes classic formulary of blessing for the long life of the king, as known from other sources.[29] From this text, it seems that both major deities and divinized dead belong within the same royal scope of divine feasting and blessing. It shows the monarchy's interest in the major gods, such as Baal and El, as well as Rp'u, the divinized eponymous ancestor of the Rephaim, and perhaps the Rephaim themselves. At Ugarit, the eponymous head of the deceased Rephaim and the major gods converge in the royal expression of concern for the kingdom's well-being and prosperity and also in the monarchy's concern for its place in the scheme of reality as mediator between the divine realms above and below and the human realm in between.[30]

2. The Journey and Late Summer Feast of the Rephaim

KTU 1.108 is hardly the only text that depicts the Rephaim feasting. This is a central theme in a group of Ugaritic texts often called "the Rephaim texts" (KTU 1.20–1.22). The surviving pieces of these texts have at least one column of writing on the front and another column on the back.[31] It is impossible to tell how long each column is, as either the top or the bottom of each one is broken off. Moreover, what does survive of each column is very badly damaged. Finally, while they have commonly been treated as three tablets (KTU 1.20–1.22), both the number of tablets and their order have been questioned.[32] These fragmentary and obscure pieces have sometimes been considered a sequel to the story of Aqhat, because both mention his father Danil (KTU 1.20 II 7). However, there is no clear indication of a connection between these two textual complexes.[33] At a minimum, Danil in the two textual complexes provides a human and perhaps heroic reference point: in Aqhat he is central in matters of human life and death; and in the Rephaim texts he plays a role in postmortem celebration.

In what follows, I will review the fragments for information that can be gleaned about the Rephaim. I hasten to add that given the poor condition of the fragments, I have tried to involve minimal reconstruction and conjecture, and I have not tried to sort out the vexing question of their order.[34] It is true that there is substantial repetition of specific motifs and idioms, providing a basis for some reconstruction. Despite advances in the epigraphic study of these tablets by Wayne Pitard and more recently by Dennis Pardee,[35] it remains difficult to trace exactly the progression of the three fragments, much less the order of their columns. For the purposes of convenience to readers, the numbering and ordering of the tablets found in the standard edition of KTU are used here.

Before proceeding, it may be helpful to mention the main figures that appear in the text. In addition to Danil (1.20 II 7), there appear to be references to at least three deities. The first seems to be El, who may invite the Rephaim to his house (1.21 II 8)[36] and who may be mentioned in descriptions (1.22 I 6-7, 20). On this score one may register some hesitation, since the word *ʾil* in these cases could mean "(the) god" or "(the) divine (one)." In 1.22 II 8 where it is used in narrative, *ʾil* might refer to either Rp'u or Baal. In view of the feast that Rp'u hosts for the Rephaim in KTU 1.108, Rp'u might be "the god" in 1.22 I 8 and 1.22 II 2 (as a possible reconstruction). The second deity is Baal, mentioned in the final tablet (1.22 II 7; 1.22 I 8-9, 26). The third is Anat, whose name occurs twice alongside Baal's in a characterization of the

Rephaim (1.22 II 8; 1.22 I 9). She herself does not appear as such in the text. There is a further unnamed figure in 1.22 II 17-18. According to these lines, he is a monarch who takes his royal throne. Perhaps this figure called *mlk* is *rp’u*, who otherwise makes no explicit appearance in the Rephaim texts.

First Fragment (KTU 1.20 I = RS 3.348): the front

About half of the left side of the first column on the front of this fragment (often called the “obverse”) has broken off, as have the bottom and back of the entire tablet. The right side of the first column has about ten fragmentary lines, which refer to a feast of the Rephaim.

1	[. . . The Repha]im will feast,	*[. . . rp]’um.tdbḥn*
2	[. . . Sev]en times the divinities,	*[. . . šb]‘d.’ilnym*
3	[. . .] like the dead.	*[. . .] kmtmtm*
4	[. . .] when the assembly approaches,	*[. . .]b.kqrb.sd*
5	[. . .]. on the summer day	*[. . .]n bym.qẓ*
6	[. . . the diviniti]es will eat,	*[. . . ’ilny]m.tlḥmn*
7	[. . .] . . . will drink.	*[. . .]m.tštyn*
8	[. . .] the god of the fragrant plants (?)[37]	[. . .]*[. . .]’il.d‘rgzm*
9	[. . .] who is over . . .	*[. . .]dt.‘l.lty*
10	[. . .] feasts (?) . . .	*[. . .]tdbḥ.’amr*
11	[. . .] . . .[. . .]	*[. . .]y[. . .]*

Overall, the setting of the feast may seem reminiscent of Rp’u’s feast in KTU 1.108, as seen in the preceding section. Feasting is, of course, a common motif involving deities. The feast is also the medium for the meeting of humans and deities, as we saw in the story of Aqhat in the last chapter. In the Rephaim texts, it is unclear when this feasting occurs, apart from the reference to summer. Without further temporal markers, the feasting could take place in the past, present, or future. Because the Rephaim move “near” in the next bicolon, Theodore J. Lewis sees the verb here as well as those that appear in the following lines as future.[38]

The opening two lines present the Rephaim feasting. The “seven times,” if correctly reconstructed, may refer to the number of days that the feasting takes place, as suggested by KTU 1.22 I 21-26 (see below). The comparison with "the dead" in line 3 is suggestive of a possible practice of the human dead eating offerings made to them, but this goes beyond the evidence here. In lines 4-5, the Rephaim are characterized as a collective body, here called an "assembly *(sd).*" In biblical material, this word may refer to the "assembly" of divinities.[39] According to line 4, the collectivity of the Rephaim shows movement toward a place, not yet named in the extant text. Both the mode of movement and the locale to which they go will be clearer in the next column. The feast is given here a specific temporal setting, "on the summer day" (*bym qẓ*, line 5). We may imagine that the celebration is to take place at the time of the harvest of summer fruit, which makes sense in light of the later references to an apple (1.20 II 11) and oil (1.22 II 15). Combined with the earlier mention of "seven times," we may imagine a seven-day celebration in the late summer, which perhaps corresponds to the seven-day fall celebration known in the Ugaritic ritual (1.41//1.87).[40] One version of this text, 1.41, contains an addendum referring to a further ritual action (lines 50-55) that includes "dwellings of branches" (line 50). For many commentators, this ritual suggests a parallel to the biblical autumn feast of Sukkot ("Booths").[41]

Lines 8-11 add little clear information to the overall picture. This fact should remind us that there is likely more to the feast than what we can presently recover from the words that do survive.

First Fragment (KTU 1.20 II = RS 3.348): the back

The back of the first tablet (often called the "reverse") has about eleven lines, which are better preserved. The first line of the preserved text seems to reflect the end of a speech inviting the Rephaim to the speaker's house for a seven-day feast. Danil, the father of Aqhat, is mentioned in line 7; he may be the speaker.

1	". . . eight in the midst of my palace."	*ṯmn.bqrb.hkly[. . .]*
1-2	The Re[phaim to the place[42]]/hastened, To the place the gods hastened.	*r[p'um.'aṯrh]/ndd*[43] *'aṯrh.ndd.'ilm*
2-3	They secured/[chariots], They hitched horses . . .	*[mrkbt.]/'asr* *sswm.tṣmd*

4	They mounted their chariots, They ca[me on their stallions[44]].	*tʿln.lmrkbthm* *tʾi[tyn.ʿrhm]*
5	They went for a day, and for a second; After sun[set on the third],	*tlkn.ym.wṯn* *ʾaḫr.š[pšm.bṯlṯ]*
6-7	The Rephaim arrived at the threshing floor, The di[vinities in the midst of]/the plantations.	*mǵy rpʾum.lgrnt* *ʾi[lnym[45].bqrb]/mṭʿt*
7-8	And Danil, [the man of Rpʾu,] spoke up, Said the Hero, the man of the Harnamite:	*wyʿn.dnʾil.[mt.rpʾi]* *yṯb.ǵzr.mt hrnmy*
8-9	"[The Rephaim] are/at the threshing floor, the gods in the midst of the plan[tations.]	*[rpʾum.]/bgrnt* *ʾilm.bqrb.m[ṭʿt]*
10	Those who have come, let them eat, feed . . ."	*dtʾit.yspʾi.* *spʾu.q[. . .]*
11	[. . .] apple	*[. . .]tpḥ.ṭṣr* *shr*

In line 1, we seem to have the end of a speech, given the first person suffix on the final word. Given the customary pattern of parallelism for the number eight, it has been surmised that the preceding line, now lost, contained the number seven. It is not clear who the speaker is, though based on his reading of later uses of "my palace" (1.21 II 3, 11, largely reconstructed; 1.22 II 20, reconstructed), Lewis surmises that it is El.

Lines 1-4 offer a description of the divine Rephaim mounting their horses and chariots and journeying to the threshing floor. Over forty years ago, William J. Horwitz offered an intriguing comparison with the spirits of the dead heroes in Iranian literature:

> Some interesting parallels are provided by the Iranian Fravashis. . . . Just as the *rpʾm* are warriors, in the Pahlavi books the Fravashis are likened to spear-carrying horsemen fighting on the side of good in the war against evil. They are particularly allied with Ahura Mazda in his creating and sustaining the universe. Furthermore, the maintenance of the entire cosmos depends on them. The Fravashis of the righteous dead and of ancestors

> are also invoked to provide protection for an individual. In addition, the Fravashis are concerned with fertility.
>
> One may theorize that the Canaanite *rp'm* and the Iranian Fravashis, which share many traits, underwent the following parallel historical development. Originally, the mythological concept symbolized an essential force over which death was not victorious. This force was expressed in two ways — fertility and ancestor spirits or shades. Fertility represents the essence of the living, and the shades represent the essence of the dead. The shades, as an eternal human power, continued to play a major role for the living by being considered indispensable helpers of the important gods. The fertility aspects of the *rp'm* were probably forgotten as early as the mid-second millennium B.C.E. Then the crucial roles that they played as ancestors-spirits were forgotten. By the first millennium B.C.E. the *rp'm* had lost their power and were no longer well understood; their status as shades no longer represented man's victory over death, but death's victory over man.[46]

Whatever one may think about some of the speculative aspects of this description, it captures four basic characteristics of the *rp'um* as seen in the Ugaritic Rephaim texts: (1) they are ancestral spirits; (2) they are understood as a military force with chariots; (3) they stand in relationship with, if not service to, major deities, such as Baal and Anat (and perhaps more loosely to El); and (4) they are tied to the celebration of natural fertility in the summer-fruit harvest, as seen in the journey in lines 5-7.

In these lines, the destination of the journey is the threshing floor in parallelism with what I have translated here as "plantations," in other words, "cultivated areas." (The translation "plantations" resonates with the verbal root "to plant.) Lines 8-11 present Danil first speaking. Lines 8-9 provide his formulary known also from Aqhat. In lines 10-11, Danil acknowledges (to whom?) the presence of the Rephaim at the threshing floor and plantations. He seems in line 10 to issue an invitation to them to eat.[47] Line 11 provides a single clear word, "apple," presumably something of the fare offered. After this line, the text is broken off. It is unclear from this context where Danil is relative to the Rephaim. He appears nowhere else in the extant text; so there is no parallel context that helps to clarify this question. Perhaps he is the host for the feast of the Rephaim at the threshing floor. The location here is a domestic site and not a temple as such.[48]

Second Fragment (KTU 1.21 = RS 2.[019])

One side of the tablet (KTU 1.21 I) contains only five letters *([. . .]d.lʾarṣ),* preserving only one intelligible phrase, "to the earth."

The other side of the tablet (KTU 1.21 II) is badly broken, with about twelve incomplete lines.

1-2	"[. . .] my [ma]rzeah,[49] Go to my house/. . .	*[. . . m]rzʿy.* *lk bty/[. . .]*
2-3	[Into] my [house] I summon you, I call/[you into the midst of] my [palace]."	*[bbt]y.ʾaṣḥkm* *ʾiqrʾa/[km.bqrb.hkl]y*
3-4	To the place, O Rephaim,/[hasten], [To the place], O divinities, hasten.	*ʾaṯrh.rpʾum/[ltdd]* *[ʾaṯrh].ltdd.ʾilnym*
5-6	[. . .] my [ma]rzeah So, I, O Reph[aim . . . [. . . like] a shepherd (?).	*[. . . m]rzʿy* *ʾap ʾank[50].yrp[ʾim . . .]* *[k]m.rʿy*
6-8	Now I will go/[for a day and a second], [On] the third I will arrive at/[my] house, [. . . in the midst] of my palace."	*ht.ʾalk/[ym.wṯn.]* *[b]ṯlṯt[51].ʾamǵy.lbt/[y]* *[. . . bqrb].hkly*
8	The god/El (?) speaks up:	*wyʿn.ʾil*
9	". . . Come to my house,[52] O Rephaim.	 *lk.bty.rpʾim*
10-11	[Into my house I su]mmon you, I call you/[into the midst of] my [palace].	*[bbty.ʾaṣ]ḥkm.* *ʾiqrʾakm/[bqrb.hkl]y.*
11-12	To the place may the Rephaim,/[indeed hasten], To [the place] may [the divi]ni[ties] indeed hasten."	*ʾaṯrh.rpʾum/[ltdd]* *[ʾaṯr]h.ltdd.[ʾil]n[ym]*
13	[. . .]	*[. . .]rn[. . .]*

Like the preceding tablet, this one describes an invitation to a feast issued to the divine Rephaim. The speaker of the first seven surviving lines might not be El (or "the god"), since that figure is also named in line 8. It is theoretically possible that the same figure speaks twice, though *wyʿn* does not usually function in this manner in Ugaritic literature.[53] The other figure mentioned in the Rephaim texts in a speaking capacity is Danil, but it is not clear that he is the speaker here. To my mind, the issue remains unresolved. In lines 3-4 and 11-12 (also 1.22 II 5 and 11), *ʾatrh* may be an accusative with locative *-h* ("to the place" as rendered here following Pardee)[54] or prepositional ("after him"), which would suggest a picture of the Rephaim following someone as they travel. That figure would logically be their leader, in other words, *rpʾu mlk ʿlm* as known from KTU 1.108.1.1-5.[55] In this case, the scene would understand Rpʾu as leading the Rephaim to the marzeah. The form *ʾaṯrh* may also involve a noun **ʾaṯr*, thus meaning literally, "his place"; more generally it could refer to a "shrine."[56] In this reading, some sort of domestic shrine may be intended.

This passage provides further information for the feast. It is to take place in "my marzeah" *(mrzʿy)*. El elsewhere is said to have a marzeah (KTU 1.114.15;[57] see also 1.1 IV 4[58]), and that certainly comports with line 9. However, the marzeah in the first speech may not be his. As an alternative, could it be that Danil has this marzeah? Outside of the literary texts, the location of the marzeah is a house in one clear instance.[59]

The further question involves the inclusion of the marzeah here in the Rephaim texts. The marzeah is a much-discussed social association for elite males (as in KTU 3.9).[60] While it is not a funerary association as such, it would appear to include a variety of drinking occasions, including times of lamentation for the dead (see Jer. 16:5-8). The summoning of the ancient deceased ancestors to feast would seem to fit within this notion of the marzeah. In response to strong claims about the funerary or mortuary character of the marzeah made by Marvin H. Pope,[61] it is now common for scholars to question or dismiss his emphasis on the funerary associations of the marzeah.[62] This debate may obscure a larger point. If the "funerary connection" is not the issue, it may be asked why the literary representation of the Rephaim here situates their feasting activity in the context of a marzeah. Just as the Rephaim traditions elsewhere mythologize the monarchy's heroic past (for example, in Kirta, in KTU 1.15 III 2-4, 13-15, discussed below), this passage may mythologize the upper-class marzeah. This may further reflect an effort at royal emulation, since, as we have seen, the Rephaim are involved in both royal ritual and the well-to-do male institution of the marzeah.

The prose texts point to the marzeah as a social association of upper-class men, and the inclusion of the marzeah in the mythic setting of the Rephaim texts suggests their identification with its traditional male, military ideal, although there is no indication from the marzeah prose texts that such men formed any sort of military group in reality. Moving from the poetic sources to the prose, the marzeah seems to shift from an old heroic, military ideal to an economic reality of its well-to-do patrons.[63] Like the king himself, the men of the marzeah were little involved directly in warfare as far as is known. Where the royal ritual of KTU 1.161 envisions the Rephaim as the distant antecedent to the dynastic line, the marzeah texts seem to suggest some sort of identification of upper-class males with the old traditions of the Rephaim. Furthermore, it is to be noted that both the royal ritual of KTU 1.161 and the marzeah associations at Ugarit were explicitly supported by the monarchy,[64] and in turn, such old ideals as expressed in both contexts likely suited the social and political goals of the Ugaritic dynasty.

Third Fragment (KTU 1.22 = RS 2.[024])

As noted above, the third fragment has two columns on one side.[65] The first column, when it becomes intelligible, shows a speech:

2-3	"Behold your son(s), behold . . .	*hn bnk.hn [. . .]*
	The grandson(s) (?)[66] after you.[67]	*[. . .] bnbn.ʾaṯrk.*
3-4	Behold . . ./your hand,	*hn [ ]r*[68]*/ydk*
	The young one will kiss your lips . . ."	*ṣǵr.tnšq.šptk*
4-6	There,/shoulder to shoulder,	*ṯm/ṯkm.bmṯkm*
	Brothers . . .[69]	*ʾaḫm*[70]*.qym.ʾil/blsmt*
6-7	There the dead[71] celebrate (?) the name of El,	*ṯm.yʿbš*[72]*.šm.ʾil.mtm*
	The heroes celebrate (?) in blessing the name of El.	*yʿbš.brkn.šm.ʾil.ǵzrm*
8-9	There the Rephaim of Baal . . .[73]	*ṯm.ṯmq.rpʾu.bʿl.*
	Warriors of Baal, warriors of Anat.	*mhr bʿl mhr.ʿnt*
9-10	There circled about the forc/es	*ṯm.yḥpn.ḥyl/y*[74]
	of Prince Mlk the Eternal.[75]	*zbl.mlk.ʿllmy*

10-11	As when Anat goes/hunting, Sets to flight the birds of heaven,	*km.tdd/ʿnt.ṣd.* *tštr.ʿpt.šmm*
12-13	They slaughtered oxen, sheep as well, They felled bulls,/fatling rams,	*ṭbḫ.ʾalpm.ʾap ṣʾin.* *šql.ṯrm/wmrʾi*[76] *ʾilm*
13-14	Year-old calves, Lambs of the flock, (with) kids.	*ʿglm.dt.šnt* *ʾimr.qmṣ.llʾim*
14-15	Like silver/for travelers, olive, (Like) gold for travelers, date (?).[77]	*kksp/lʿbrm.zt.* *ḫrṣ.lʿbrm.kš*
16-17	Indeed, a calf on the table with fruit,[78] With fruit/(fit) for kings.	*ʾu pr*[79]*.ṯlḥn.bqʿl.* *bqʿl/mlkm.*
17-18	Behold, for a day they poured wine,[80] There (?)[81]/must of wine for[82] rulers.	*hn.ym.yṣq.yn.* *ṯmk/mrṯ.yn.srnm*
18-19	Wine without (?)[83] the gleaning,[84] Wine of happiness[85] . . .	*yn.bld/ǵll* *yn.ʾišryt.ʿnq*
19-20	Blossoming vine[86]/of Lebanon,[87] Sack of must (that) El tills (?).[88]	*smd/lbnn.* *ṭl*[89]*.mrṯ.yḥrṯ.ʾil*
21-22	Behold, for a day, then a second, The Rephaim ate,/they drank.	*hn.ym.wṯn.* *tlḥm<n>*[90]*.rpʾum/tštyn*
22-24	A third, then a fourth; A fifth,/then a sixth, The Rephaim ate,/they drank.	*ṯlṯ.rbʿ.ym.* *ḫmš/ṯdṯ.ym* *tlḥmn.rpʾum/tštyn*
24-25	At the house of eating, on the summit, in the narrow (?),[91] in the heart[92] of the Lebanon.	*bt.ʾikl.bprʿ* *bṣq[.]bʾirt.lbnn.*
25-26	Then, on the seventh/[day], [The]n Mightiest Baal . . .	*mk.bšbʿ/[ymm.]* *[ʾapn]k.ʾalʾiyn.bʿl*
27-28	shepherd (?) my father (?) . . .	*[. . .].rʿh ʾaby[. . .]* *[. . .]*

The speech in lines 2-3 is without parallel in the Ugaritic texts, and its significance in this context is unclear. One can only speculate. It may be that some sort of intergenerational expression, perhaps at a domestic shrine, takes place. If *'aṯrk* here instead were to mean "after you" (and not "your place"), perhaps the Rephaim are arranged by generation, and perhaps it includes those who died young (for example, in battle). Who the speaker and addressee are remains unknown, and the significance of the words in this context is no less problematic. Pardee has very reasonably suggested that *bn* and *bn bn* are singular, here referring to the lineage of Danil.[93] As a less likely alternative, the speaker might be Rp'u, who arranges his Rephaim by generation, and he is addressing the lineage of Rephaim.

Lines 4-10 describe the ranks of the Rephaim "there," perhaps at "the banquet house" in Lebanon mentioned in lines 24-25. (Is this place to be identified with the domestic shrine to which they are earlier invited, or is this a further destination?) Lines 4-6 seem to present the forces of Rephaim standing "shoulder to shoulder," and lines 6-7 might present them offering their allegiance to El. The description of the Rephaim in lines 8-9 (see also in 1.22 II 7-8) links them to major deities; they are soldiers of the two warrior deities, Baal and Anat.[94] The Rephaim are called "warriors of Baal, warriors of Anat" (*mhr bʿl mhr ʿnt*, 1.22 I 8-9, II 7-8). Up to this point, the Rephaim have appeared as "heroes," but this is the first context where they are also called "warriors."[95] We may surmise from this double title that these two divine warriors are considered the patrons and/or models for the Rapi'uma who stand in the ranks of these two deities. The goddess Anat in Aqhat plays a role in the transition from adolescence to adulthood for a warrior, while the god Baal perhaps models the standard role of a warrior who has completed this transition. These two figures are well-known divine warriors, perhaps linked as brother and sister because of their martial character. In the first section of this chapter, we saw how KTU 1.108 juxtaposes Baal with Rp'u and the Rephaim in the royal expression of blessing for Ugarit. Here in the Rephaim texts, the deceased divine warriors are linked to Baal and Anat as the divine leaders of the deceased divinized warriors. In this respect, the horizons of the major deities are linked with the Rephaim, as together they play a role in the monarchic sense of Ugarit's well-being.

The military terms in lines 9-10, echoing 1.22 II 12, comport with their characterization as "warriors" in lines 8-9. Lines 10-14 show stereotypical language for the feast, as elsewhere for the major deities (for example, in 1.4 VI 40-43).[96] Lines 14-20, while not entirely clear, also mark a new level of description for the feast, one not found elsewhere in Ugaritic literature.

The description of wine is elaborated in lines 17-20 in terms otherwise little known.[97] The feasting table is set with fruit and wine, both products of the late summer harvest. The remaining lines describe the seven-day feast of the Rephaim in a newly-named location, the banquet house in the Lebanon, followed by the introduction of the god Baal. The tablet breaks off before it becomes known what Baal does or says.

This Rephaim text offers the most sustained glimpse into this group of deceased, divinized warriors. The texts offer a basic military vocabulary for the identity of this group not attested elsewhere. They are also depicted traveling military-style, with chariots and horses. The location, perhaps a shrine of Danil, is called a banquet-house in the Lebanon mountain range. In the preceding section of this chapter, we saw the home domain of Rp'u located in Ashtaroth and Edrei, in the region of Bashan. Here the Lebanon is the locus of the final feast in the Rephaim texts. The Lebanon, freighted with a reputation for great fertility, is an imagined sanctuary space known elsewhere.[98] It is not simply a place of the Rephaim. In Gilgamesh, the Lebanon is the home of the divine council.[99] Thus the Rephaim meet in a locale associated with the divine meeting-place. In this context, in death these heroic Rephaim enjoy a relationship with the major deities. They stand in the military ranks of Baal and Anat, and Baal himself makes an entry into the story of their feast in the Lebanon; it is unfortunate that the tablet breaks off just when Baal is introduced. El, too, seems to be an object of respect on the part of the Rephaim.

When it becomes intelligible, the second column reflects the end of a speech:

1-2	"[On the] thi[rd I will arrive at my house], [In the mids]/t of my palace."	*[. . . b]ṯl[ṯ.ʾamǵy.lbty.]* *[bqr]/b.hkly*
2	[And the god/El spoke up: (?)]	*[wyʿn.ʾil(?)]*[100]
2-3	["... to my marzeah] Go to my house, [O Rephaim].	*[. . . mrzʿy]* *lk bty.[rpʾim]*
3-4	[Into my house I call]/you, I cal[l you into the midst of my palace."]	*[bbty.ʾaṣḥ]/km.* *ʾiqr[ʾakm.bqrb.hkly]*
5-7	To the place the Re[phaim indeed hastened], [To the place]/the divi[nities] hastened, Warriors of Baal, [warriors of]/Anat.	*ʾaṯrh.r[pʾum.ltdd]* *[ʾaṯrh]/ltdd.ʾil[nym]* *mhr.bʿl [mhr.]/ʿnt*

8-10	“Come to my house, O Rephaim,	*lk b[ty.rpʾim.]*
	[Into my house]/I summon you,	*[bbty]/ʾaṣḥ.km.*
	[I call you to the midst]/of my palace.”	*[ʾiqrʾakm.bqrb]/hkly*
10-11	[To] the pla[ce the Rephaim hastened],	*ʾaṯ[rh.rpʾum.ltdd]*
	To the place [the divinities] indeed ha[stened].”	*ʾaṯrh.lt[dd.ʾilnym]*
12	Forces . . . circled about (?) . . .[101]	*yḥpn.ḥy[ly . . .]*
13-14	“Listen, you [Rephaim],	*šmʿ.ʾatm.[rpʾim]*
	[. . . divini]ties.	*[. . . ʾiln]/ym*
14	. . .	*lm.qd[. . .]*
15	oil. . .	*šmn.prs*[102] *[. . .]*
16	He vowed (?) . . .	*ydr.hm.y[. . .]*
17	Tree . . .	*ʿṣ.ʾamr.*
17-18	He to[ok the throne of his kingship],	*yʾu[ḫd.ksʾa.mlkh]*[103]
	The resting-place, the seat of his do[minion].	*nḫ*[104]*t.kḥṯ.d[rkth]*[105]
18-20	“[Into my house]/I summon the Rephaim,	*[bbty]/ʾasḥ.rpʾim[.]*
	[I call the divinities]/	*[ʾiqrʾa.ʾilnym]/*
	into the midst of [my] pa[lace].”	*bqrb.h[kly.]*
20-21	[To the place the Rephaim]/hastened,	*[ʾaṯrh.rpʾum]/tdd*
	[To] the place [the divinities hastened].	*ʾaṯr[h.tdd.ʾilnym]*
22	They secured ch[ariots],	*ʾasr.m[rkbtm]*
	[They hitched horses.]	*[sswm.tṣmd.]*
23-24	They mounted [their] c[hariots],	*tʿln.lm[kbthm.]*
	[They came]/on their stallions.	*[tʾityn.]/ʿrhm*
24-25	They we[nt for one day, and for a second],	*tl[kn.ym.wṯn.]*
	[After sunset],/on the third,	*[ʾaḫr.špšm]/bṯlṯ*

25-26	[The Rephaim] arrived [at the threshing floor], The di[vini]t[ies at the plantations].	*mǵy[.rp'um.lgrnt]* *'i[ln]y[m.mṭ't.]*

The first five lines are damaged, but they seem to contain an invitation to the Rephaim. Line 1 may duplicate 1.21 II 7-8, and lines 2-4 read like the invitation in 1.21 II 1-3. Lines 5-11 describe the travel of the Rephaim to the house of the speaker, whose invitation is then quoted. In lines 7-8, the Rephaim are once again called "warriors of Baal, warriors of Anat." This interesting piece of information occurs on the other side of this same tablet (1.22 I 8-9, presented and discussed above). Lines 12-17 are badly damaged. Line 12 seems to contain another military characterization of the Rephaim (see further below in 1.22 I 9-10, with the same military vocabulary). The mention of "oil" in line 15 is not insignificant, as we noted in the introductory comments; it is somewhat indicative of the late summer setting of the Rephaim texts.

The highly broken lines 17-18 repeat idioms known from other passages in the Ugaritic corpus (see 1.2 IV 12-13, 19-20; 1.3 IV 2-3; 1.6 VI 28; 1.16 VI 23-24). The rest of the lines in this column describe the journey of the Rephaim to the house. An important departure of this column relative to what we have seen thus far is the unnamed figure in lines 17-18. These lines describe a figure who takes up his throne and seems then to invite the Rephaim to his palace. The identity of this figure is very unclear. As I mention above in my introductory comments to these texts, I have entertained the notion that this enthroned figure might be Rp'u, who is otherwise unmentioned (in this group of texts, at least in the surviving material in these tablets). In 1.108.1-2, Rp'u is enthroned. Lines 18-20 repeat the invitation above in lines 3-4, 8-11 (also 1.21 II 3-4). Lines 20-26 repeat almost verbatim 1.20 II 1-7.

What we see of the Rephaim in these texts is a postmortem relationship with the deities perhaps modeled on religious devotion: devotion to El and military modeling after two great military deities, Baal and Anat. Even the central act of these texts, the feasting of the Rephaim, seems modeled on the high life of the feasting deities. Moreover, their role in the scheme of matters is linked to the important deities in offering a divine presence in both the domestic and extradomestic spheres on the terrestrial plane. The figure of Danil himself seems to provide a model of piety toward these figures. He is an ancient figure who shows proper behavior and piety in Aqhat, and in the context of the Rephaim texts, he shows the proper summoning of the deceased line of heroes. The Rephaim are also aligned with the Ugaritic dynasty in the very next text involving the Rephaim that we will examine, KTU 1.161.

3. Royal Commemoration: Calling on Dead Heroes and Kings

At various points in this chapter, as well as the preceding one, I have suggested that commemoration of ancient heroes is very much in the interests of the Ugaritic monarchy. The old heroes are represented as both cautionary tale and models, and they serve further to provide a sense of antiquity for the dynasty. One sizable funerary text, KTU 1.161, offers another use for the old Rephaim. The texts that we have examined thus far in this chapter as well as the preceding chapter show the monarchy's *interest in narratives about* old heroes, while KTU 1.161 shows the monarchy's *use in ritual of* old heroes along with their prior kings.[106] Here the old heroes are represented as the antecedents of the monarchy. In this ritual, they provide the monarchy with a sense of its own antiquity and antecedent identity as well as a certain powerful presence.

In order to show how KTU 1.161 achieves its ritual effect, I present its basic text and translation (with my added section headings), followed by a section-by-section discussion:[107]

Superscription

1	Document for the sacrifice(s) of the Protectors:	*spr.dbḥ.ẓlm*

Section I: Invocation of Predecessors

2	You are called,[108] O Rephaim of the un[derworld],[109]	*qr’itm[.]rp’i.’a[rṣ . . .]*
3	You are summoned,[110] O Council of Di[danu].	*qb’itm.qbṣ.d[dn . . .]*
4	Called is Ulkn, the Rp['u],	*qr’a.’ulkn.rp[’u . . .]*
5	Called is Trmn, the Rp['u].	*qr’a.trmn.rp[’u . . .]*
6	Called is Sdn-and-Rd[n],[111]	*qr’a.sdn.wrd[n . . .]*
7	Called is "Bull Eternal" (?),	*qr’a.ṯr.ʿllmn[. . .]*
8	They have called[112] the Ancient Rephaim.	*qr’u.rp’im.qdmym[. . .]*
9	You are called, O Rephaim of the Underworld,	*qr’itm.rp’i.’arṣ*
10	You are summoned, O Council of Didanu.	*qb’itm.qbṣ.dd[n]*
11	Summoned is King Ammithtamru,	*qr’a.ʿmṯtmr.mlk*
12	Summoned is King Niqmaddu as well.	*qr’a.’u.nqmd[.]mlk*

Section II: Ammurapi's Ritual Lamentation for King Niqmaddu

13	O throne of Niqmaddu, be wept for,[113]	*ks’i.nqmd[.]’ibky*

14	And may he (Ammurapi) shed tears at his (Niqmaddu's) footstool.	*w.ydm‘.hdm.p‘nh*
15	Before him (Niqmaddu) may he (Ammurapi) weep at[114] the roy[al] table,[115]	*lpnh.ybky.ṯlḥn.ml[k]*
16	Indeed, may he swallow his tears in misery[116]:	*w.ybl‘.ʾudm‘th/‘dmt.*
17	Indeed, in misery upon misery!	*w.‘dmt.‘dmt*

Section III: Ritual Descent of the Sun-Goddess and King Ammurapi

18	Be hot (go down),[117] O Sun,	*ʾišḫn.špš.*
19	Indeed, be hot (go down),/O Light, O Great One[118]!	*w.ʾišḫn/nyr.rbt.*
	Above Sun cries out:	*‘ln.špš.tṣḥ*
20	After your [lo]rd(s)[119] from[120] the throne,	*ʾaṯr.[b]‘lk.l.ksʾi[121].*
21	After/your lord(s) to the underworld descend,	*ʾaṯr/b‘lk.ʾarṣ.rd.*
22	To the underworld/descend and be low in the dust:	*ʾarṣ/rd.w.špl.‘pr.*
23	With[122]/Sdn-and-Rdn,	*tḥt/sdn.w.rdn.*
24	With "Bull/Eternal" (?),	*tḥt.ṯr/‘llmn.*
	With the Ancient Rephaim.	*tḥt.rpʾim.qdmym*
25	With King Ammithtamru,	*tḥt.‘mṯtmr.mlk*
26	With King Niq[maddu] as well.	*tḥt[123].ʾu.nq[md].mlk*

Section IV: Offering on Behalf of King Ammurapi

27	One (time) and an offe[ring],[124]	*‘šty.wṯ[‘y.]*
	[Two and] an offer[ing],	*[ṯn.]w.ṯ‘[y]*
28	Three [and] an offering,	*ṯlṯ.[w].ṯ‘y[.]*
	F[ou]r and an offer[ing],	*ʾa[rb]‘.w.ṯ‘[y]*
29	Five and an offering,	*ḫmš.w.ṯ‘y.*
	Six [and] an offering,	*ṯṯ[w.]ṯ‘y*
30	Seven and an offering.	*šb‘.w.ṯ‘y.*
	You shall present a bird.	*tqdm‘ṣr*

Section V: Blessing Formulary

31	May peace, peace be to ‘Ammur[api],	*šlm[125] šlm[126].‘mr[pʾi]*
32	And peace to his house;	*w.šlm.bth[127].*
	Peace to [Tha]riyelli,	*šlm.[ṯ]ryl[128]*

33	Peace to her house;	*šlm.bth.*
	Peace to U[ga]rit,	*šlm.ʾu[g]rt/*
34	Peace to its gates!	*šlm.ṯǵrh*

Line 1 is an extratextual rubric (superscription) introducing this sacrificial text. This title indicates that the text is a record or document indicating sacrifice, evidently for[129] the dead, assuming *ẓlm* means "shades" or "protectors."[130] Whether *dbḥ* is singular or plural cannot be determined on the basis of form. Superscriptions of ritual texts (1.148.1; 1.162.1)[131] perhaps use the singular form collectively even when the ritual involves multiple offerings as in 1.161.27-31.

Section I, consisting of lines 2-12, invokes two names for a group: the dead, ancient heroes (lines 4-7) framed by the designations Rapi'uma of the Underworld (cf. biblical Rephaim), and the Council of Didanu (lines 2-3, 8-10). Didanu is known from sources going back to the Middle Bronze Age. The variant form of the name, Ditanu, appears in Old Babylonian records, specifically in the Genealogy of the Hammurapi Dynasty, as one of the ancient heroes of the West Semitic royal line of Hammurapi.[132] At Ugarit, the tradition of Didanu is attested with the Rephaim in the story of King Kirta (KTU 1.15 III 2-4, 13-15):[133]

May Kirta be greatly exalted,	*mʾid rm krt*
In the midst of the Rephaim of the underworld,	*btk rpʾi ʾarṣ*
In the assembly of Ditanu's company.	*bpḫr qbṣ dtn*

This wedding blessing presupposes that Kirta will be a successful king destined to join the ranks of the line of deceased heroes. The Rephaim were the divine dead, and here they are also "powerful venerated ancestors."[134] In this context, Ditanu, an alternative spelling of Didanu, is recalled as one of the great old heroes of this line. In Ugaritic tradition, this Ditanu is also attested as a divinized figure, one whom even a representative of the great gods consults for an oracle (KTU 1.124).[135] Pardee regards this figure as the "head of the dynasty."[136] Both the Ugaritic and Babylonian dynasties evidently traced their lineages back to an ancient hero, Ditanu/Didanu.

Within the frame, lines 4-7 mention a number of specific figures otherwise unknown. The frame itself is suggestive of the view that the figures inside the frame constitute members of the grouping named there; *ʾulkn* and *trmn* in lines 4-5 are called *rp[ʾu]*. In this context, the participants in the royal context for this text would evidently have assumed that the figures named in lines 6-7 (mentioned later in lines 23-24 as well) were also considered to be *rp'u*. The designation *rp'u* here is important, for it suggests that particular Rephaim could be called by the same designation as the god Rp'u, whom we discussed in the first section of this chapter. It would appear that a given member of the Rephaim could be labeled with what seems to be the name of the eponymous head of the Rephaim. In other words, it would appear that a given member of the Rephaim could be the instantiation of the eponymous ancestor in their time within the remembered lineage of heroes. Of the other names here, only the name *trmn* occurs elsewhere in the Ugaritic texts in KTU, in the phrase *bn trmn* in KTU 4.612.6 and RS 99.1072.32.[137] The expression *ṯr ʿllmn* in line 7 looks like a title, with *ṯr* possibly designating high status[138] and *ʿllmn* as a possible qualifier.[139] These are suggestive of high status (cf. *zbl mlk ʿllmy* in 1.22 I 10, discussed above). To guess from these qualifiers as well as this figure's placement last in the sequence of named figures, he may have been considered the most important, perhaps even the leader in this context. No name as such seems to be given for this figure, and perhaps it was expected that the royal audience of this ritual would have known that he is none other than some other famous figure, perhaps *zbl mlk* of 1.22 I 10 or even Rp'u of 1.108.1, themselves possibly the same figure.

These Rephaim do not belong to the names of kings as known in the various king lists. The list of names is followed by a reference to *rp'im qdmym*, "the ancient Rephaim" (line 8). This designation is important, as it signals the antiquity of these figures from the perspective of the monarchy, whose more recent figures are mentioned by name in lines 11-12. As we saw in the preceding section, the Ugaritic dynasty recalled the Rephaim as warriors of great antiquity. These dead heroes come from an older time before the kings of Ugarit, who themselves were evidently viewed as divine upon their deaths.[140] In addition to the ancient heroes named in lines 4-7, the historical kings, Ammithtamru and Niqmaddu, are invoked in order to summon their presence in the ritual. From the perspective of the ritual participants, these figures are viewed as dwelling in the netherworld, as suggested by the phrase "Rephaim of the Underworld," as provided by the frame (lines 2 and 9).

The singular verbal forms in lines 4-7 and 11-12 could morphologically be imperatives or suffix indicatives, but the second person plural forms in lines 2-3, 8-10 would appear to preclude the first option.[141] The forms could be either active perfect forms in lines 2-3 and 9-10 and imperatives in lines 4-7,[142] or passive suffix indicative forms throughout.[143] On the theory that all four sections address participants in the ritual, the forms seem to be passive "performative perfects," a possibility since the *G*-passive is a regular form for Ugaritic.[144] In favor of this view, it is to be noted that the alternation between singular and plural verbal forms, if passives, would correspond to the number of the nouns in the same lines.

One question involves the shift in verb form in line 8, *qr'u,* which is notable and deserves some attention. Line 8 cannot be understood as the same as the preceding lines, since "the ancient Rephaim" stand in the oblique case (genitive or accusative plural), and thus the verb cannot be understood as a performative passive perfect. Instead, as Pierre Bordreuil and Dennis Pardee quite correctly translate, the verb is to be understood as an active form, whether as a perfect or an imperative; they favor the former.[145] They attempt to account for this shift with their rendering of line 8: "they (in turn) have called the Ancient *Rapa'ūma.*" This translation seems to presuppose that the subject of the verb is the preceding named figures and that they are the ones commanded to call the Ancient Rephaim here. This view (if correctly characterized) seems to ignore the force of the frame in lines 2-3 and 9-10, which would point to all the figures named in between as Ancient Rephaim. It seems better to understand line 8 as a transition line following the named figures and reintroducing the collective identified in the frame in lines 9-10. The question remains as to who the implied plural speaker is ritually imagined to be. To my mind, it may be the living royal figures (perhaps along with their royal "households") named later in lines 31-34.

Section II, lines 13-17, contains a number of debated matters. The subjects of the verbs may represent the biggest problem. Theodore J. Lewis, J. Glenn Taylor, and Manfried Dietrich and Oswald Loretz take the royal furniture as the second person subjects of the verbs in lines 13-16. For Pardee, the subject is impersonal. According to either view, the pieces of furniture are invoked to weep for their deceased lord, Niqmaddu,[146] the last named figure in the first section and predecessor of the living king, ʿAmmurapi, mentioned in the final section of the ritual. The point of the commands is mourning for the king to whom the furniture belongs.[147] In other words, King ʿAmmurapi is to lament for his predecessor on the royal furniture.[148] Accordingly, ʿAmmurapi is taken here as the subject of the verbs in lines 14-16.

Line 17's threefold mention of *ʿdmt,* "misery," is here divided, as suggested by *w-*. For the first two of the three usages of the noun here, the superlative is involved, comparable to BH *melek mĕlākîm,* "king of kings" (e.g., Ezek. 26:7), and *šîr haššîrîm,* "the song of songs" (Song 1:1). It is possible that a threefold superlative use is intended (cf. *qādôš* in Isa. 6:3, possibly signifying superlative degree[149]), but this view may seem less likely in view of the placement of the *w-* preceding the third occurrence of *ʿdmt.*

Section III, lines 18-26, begin by invoking the sun goddess either "to burn" (so Pardee) or "to bow down" (as adopted by Lewis). In lines 19b-26, Shapshu calls to the living king, ʿAmmurapi,[150] to descend to the underworld to be with his deceased predecessors. A biblical parallel for the picture of the living ritually descending to the dead has been noted in Jacob's speech referring to Joseph whom he presumes to be dead in Gen. 37:35: "I will descend to my son in mourning to Sheol." Other scholars prefer to see the recently deceased king Niqmaddu as the addressee.[151] The narrative rubric at the end of line 19 precisely matches 1.6 VI 22-23. At this point, the sun goddess appears as a participant in this ritual. She is commanded and in turn addresses the main ritual participant, argued to be the new king, ʿAmmurapi, to ritually descend to the Rephaim of lines 2-10 here presented in abbreviated fashion.

Section IV, lines 27-30, begins with a series of offerings. With the seven offerings in lines 27-30a, no verb may be involved, only a series of nouns.[152] Elsewhere such series function as temporal modifiers to verbs (CAT 1.4 VI 24-32; 1.14 III 2-4, 10-12, etc.),[153] and it is assumed here that the number plus *ṯʿy* essentially means "x-times as an offering." *Ṯʿy* could be an incense offering,[154] but the context in KTU 1.40 suggests a more generic sense.[155] If correct, then the bird might be the animal for the sacrifice, *ṯʿy* is a general word for offering, and *šlm* is the name of the sacrifice. In this case, only in lines 30b-31a is the command completed: these offerings are to be given as a peace offering in the form of a bird.

The goal of the intended ritual, as suggested by Section V, lines 31-34, is peace for the royal household and Ugarit. Given the royal background of the names listed in the third section, it may be supposed that the royal family is involved. The king and his house precede mention of the queen and her house. As suggested by Lauren Shedletsky (Monroe) and Baruch Levine,[156] this juxtaposition of royal houses in poetic parallelism may suggest that at the royal level, the notion of the "house of the mother" was embedded within the "house of the father."[157] Furthermore, since the final section is devoted to a blessing of peace for ʿAmmurapi, his household, and Ugarit more generally, King ʿAmmurapi is the ritual participant summoned to make the offering.

On the whole, this text shows the Rephaim in their individual and collective manifestations in the ritual life of Ugarit's monarchy. The names of individual, perhaps otherwise forgotten, Rephaim are named within the larger collective body of Rephaim to participate in the royal life-cycle event involving the death of one king and the accession of another. Not only dead kings, but also their forebears among the Rephaim are made present, providing a royal support-structure in a moment of transition. For this transition, the divinized dead heroes and kings form a single lineage present to welcome the newly-deceased monarch to join their ranks and also to support his successor, the royal household, and the kingdom of Ugarit.

The form that this royal ritual expression assumes is poetic. Pardee offers an important insight into this aspect of KTU 1.161: "The poetic form of the text appears, therefore, to reflect the perception at Ugarit that talk about the gods was to be poetic in form (as opposed to the essentially administrative talk about the care and feedings from the gods in their earthly structures that characterize the prose ritual texts)."[158] It is true that the literary texts involve talk about deities, and they, too, are poetic in form.[159] The only other poetic text with or within the ritual corpus involves the prayer in KTU 1.119.26-36.[160] Both this prayer and the ritual of 1.161 involve direct discourse. In short, poetic parallelism in the literary texts and in the ritual texts appears to reflect the perception among Ugarit's ritual-scribal specialists that talk *about* and *to* deities was to be poetic. In other words, poetry is a textual medium that bridges the world of the divine and the world of the monarchy. Royal commemoration not only of their monarchic predecessors, but also of their earlier heroic forebears is made here in poetic form. As we saw in the preceding chapter with the story of Aqhat and in the texts about Rp'u and the Rephaim in this chapter, poetry is the medium for talking about deities and talking to them. In other words, poetry is a means of evoking the ancient heroes in literary texts and for invoking them in ritual. In literature, poetry is what takes the human audience to the world of the ancient heroes and their time, and in ritual, poetry serves to bring the Rephaim to the world and time of the human audience. Poetry also serves to turn the audience into participants. It is poetry that links past and present and provides an imaginative movement between the two. The commemoration of ancient heroes, then, is essentially an act of poetry and poetic imagination that allows an audience to sense their present reality, as expressed in their literary and ritual lives, in terms of a past long gone.

In Chapter Four, we saw how the story of Aqhat acknowledges the fate of the hero in death; it is a destiny that the hero recognizes awaits all — and especially the young hero himself. At the same time, the arc of a hero's destiny does not end with his death, but begins when he dies, starting with his family's mourning (KTU 1.19 III 40–IV 17). The hero's fate then continues with the postmortem recollection that others maintain for him. For the Ugaritic monarchy, this postmortem recollection of what it considered its ancient heroes included a focus on the figures of Rp'u and the Rephaim, as seen in this chapter. These figures expressed the reality of what ultimately awaited heroes: while the memory of them or their specific acts may have faded in time, those heroes whom the monarchy recalled as its long-gone forebears remained valuable participants in the scheme of reality. The Rephaim ritual of KTU 1.161 invoked these ancient heroes to join in the ritual with the living, while the Rephaim narratives evoked these figures and their travels to the realm of the living. Together, these ritual and narrative materials allowed the Rephaim and their royal commemorators, not to mention their "literary executors" (their scribal transmitters), to participate together in celebrating these ancient heroes in and for the ongoing life of the monarchy.[161] The arc of the lives of these heroic figures continued in their royal recollection. In the end, with acts of textual commemoration, the past was all about the present.

CHAPTER SIX

Divine Warriors in the Baal Cycle

Central to the action of the Baal Cycle (KTU 1.1–1.6)[1] are several divine warriors. This chapter begins with two conflicts: Baal versus Yamm (1.1–1.2) and Baal versus Mot (1.4 VIII–1.6). The discussion focuses on two passages that detail the physical conflicts involving these gods (1.2 IV 7-27 and 1.6 VI 16-22). It will also entail a brief look at ʿAthtar, a warrior who largely serves as a foil (1.2 III; 1.6 I). Next we will turn to a particularly colorful figure in the Baal Cycle, one who also plays an important supporting role to Baal in his two major conflicts. This is Baal's ally and sister, Anat. As we saw in Chapter Four, this goddess is a divine warrior capable of considerable violence against humans. That role is vividly on display also in the Baal Cycle. Like ʿAthtar, she makes a major appearance in both the Baal-Yamm and Baal-Mot sections (1.3 II and 1.6 II). I save for the final section of this chapter one passage that portrays the central hero, Baal, in his victory feast (1.3 I). Often overshadowed in the extant text by Baal's battle against Yamm on one side (1.2 IV) and Anat's destructive warfare on the other (1.3 II), the feast of Baal offers a glimpse into many of the basic attitudes and practices of warrior culture. Before beginning, it is important to note that divine warfare in these texts involves individual combat, not collective leadership. To be sure, in some contexts, the texts provide an inkling of a divine retinue accompanying the deity into battle, but these depictions stand in the background of the action.[2]

1. Baal, Yamm, and Mot

Baal-Yamm

The central conflict in the first of the three parts of the cycle (KTU 1.1–1.2) pits Baal, the mighty storm god, against Yamm, the divine Sea (1.2 IV).[3] Toward the opening, Kothar, the craftsman god, predicts Baal's ultimate victory (lines 7-10). Then he pronounces the name of the first weapon with incantational force (lines 11-15).[4] It takes off on its own power and pounds Yamm on his torso, but to no avail (lines 15-18). Like the first weapon, the second receives an incantational pronouncement from Kothar (lines 18-23). Then it takes off and strikes Yamm on the head; this one is successful (lines 23-25). With this second attack, Yamm crumples to the ground (lines 25-26). Only at this point does Baal himself return to the action, where he is said to drag out Yamm and destroy him (line 27). This scene does not offer the classic picture of two warriors engaged in battle.[5] Instead, for most of the action, Baal recedes from the narrative, and the weapons made by Kothar take center stage.

The focus on the weapons is no small element of conflict in literary texts. The personified weapon, Sharur, plays a central role in Lugale-e.[6] As we saw in Chapter Four, the weapon of Aqhat has a crucial place in the unsuccessful relationship between the hero and the goddess Anat (KTU 1.17 VI). These passages may alert us to the central importance of the weapons in the Baal-Yamm conflict. Like the bow of Aqhat, the weapons of Baal are the divine creation of Kothar wa-Hasis, the craftsman god. Weapons may serve a range of literary functions for describing the exploits of the warrior. The weapons of Saul and Jonathan in 2 Samuel 1 draw the audience's attention to these figures in ways aimed to be evocative and poignant: the shields including Saul's "there" *(šām)* after battle in v. 21; and the bow of Jonathan and sword of Saul presented in parallel terms as fiercely engaged in battle in v. 22. The former "did not turn back" *(lōʾ nāśôg ʾāḥôr),* the latter "never returned empty" *(lōʾ tāšûb rêqām).*[7]

Before turning to Baal's struggle with Mot, there is a detail in the description of Yamm's messengers that conveys the martial atmosphere of the situation before Baal meets Yamm in conflict.[8] In the scene of the divine council in 1.2 I, the messengers of Yamm appear before the assembled deities:[9]

31-32	Standing, they s[peak] a speech,[10]/ [Reci]te their instructions.	*qmm.ʾa[mr].ʾamr/* *[ṯn]y.dʿthm.*

32-33	A flame, two flames they appear,/	*ʾišt.ʾištm.yʾitmr./*
	Their [ton]gue a sharp sword.	*ḥrb.lṭšt[lš]nhm.*

In this passage, the messengers of Yamm appear in a fierce manner. The description of their body parts is cast in terms of weaponry, "a sharp sword." The image is stock material for enemies. Jer. 9:8 refers to the wicked as enemies: "Their tongue is a sharpened arrow." Similarly, Ps. 57:4 states: "I lie down in the midst of lions that greedily devour the sons of men; their teeth are spears and arrows, their tongues sharp swords."[11] The lion is further associated with the sword at Ugarit: sometimes on weaponry a lion is represented with an open mouth.[12] For example, a ceremonial axe from Ugarit depicts a "figure of a wild boar and two lions' heads that appear to be spitting out the iron blade."[13] As evoked by the image of the sword in 1.2 I 32-33, the overall atmosphere of the Baal-Yamm section (KTU 1.1–1.2) involves warriors vying for power through fearful appearance and conflict.[14]

Baal-Mot

The Baal-Mot conflict (1.4 VIII–1.6 VI) is of a different character. Perhaps most notably, Mot unlike Yamm is called *ǵzr*, "hero" (1.4 VII 47; VIII 32; 1.5 I 8, 14; II 9; 1.6 VI 31).[15] The Baal-Mot section also shows another distinctive feature. There is no extant description of the first meeting of Baal and Mot. Instead, the audience learns of Baal's destruction from reports of their conflict. After Mot demands that Baal enter his realm of the underworld, Baal engages in sexual relations, and the text breaks off (1.5 V). The next extant part of the text (1.5 VI) contains the description of how El's messengers came across Baal (lines 5-10):

5-6	We came/to the pleasant land of the outback,	*mǵny. lnʿmy.ʾarṣ.dbr*
7	To the beautiful field of Death's realm.	*lysmt.šd.šḥlmmt*
8-9	We [c]ame upon Baal fallen to the ea/rth;	*mǵny.lbʿl.npl.lʾa/rṣ*
9	Dead is Mightiest Baal,	*mt.ʾalʾiyn.bʿl*
10	Perished the Prince, Lord of the Earth.	*ḫlq.zbl.bʿl.ʾarṣ.*

This announcement of Baal's death is in language of lamentation. Before addressing this feature, we will take a closer look at this speech.

The first two lines, a bicolon (lines 5-7), recount the messengers' arrival to the place of their discovery. It lies at the edge of the world (evident from the preceding lines 3-5), far from the center of human or divine society and near the realm of Death. The location is called *dbr* (like BH *midbār*), not so much a desert as a distant region. The translation "outback" captures not only the etymological sense of the word (cf. BH *dĕbîr* for the "holy of Holies," a designation for the room in the back of the temple).[16] "Outback" also conveys the distance in the periphery far away from the center of society. This is the realm where Death roves about. This area is also called "pleasant" *(nʿmy)* and "beautiful" *(ysmt)*, which may be euphemisms.[17] For the outback's lack of rain and human habitation, these expressions may signal the opposite of their common meanings. However, desert regions are starkly beautiful, and perhaps the realm is as well, despite its association with Death.[18] The prior lines 3-5 also describe the area as "watery," which may suggest a certain beauty. The place is also called *šḥlmmt*, which is very difficult. The consonants *mmt* seem to denote the place of death (if *mmt* is a *m*-preformative noun), or perhaps it contains a reference to "Death" himself (if *šḥlm mt* were read).[19] The element *šḥl(m)* is a bit of a mystery in Ugaritic studies. "Shore of Death"[20] seems to fit the spatial context, especially after the reference to this place being at the "edge of the water" (*ksm mhyt,* in line 5a).[21]

The next poetic unit, a tricolon (lines 8-10), announces Baal's death. The first line of this tricolon, *mǵny.lbʿl.npl.lʾarṣ,* echoes the first line of the preceding bicolon in lines 5-7, *mǵny. lnʿmy.ʾarṣ.dbr;* both describe how "we came . . . to . . . the earth." The tricolon has a description of Baal, while the prior bicolon has a description of the place. Here the mention of Baal precedes the two lines announcing his death, his perishing. While no battle has been described, Baal's death is announced in terms of a fallen, dead warrior. The opening statement of the discovery of Baal fallen to the earth is cleverly contrasted with the description of Baal: while other titles for the god might have been used, his epithet "Lord of the Earth" appears here, perhaps most ironically. For at this point, the god seems anything other than "Lord of the Earth." The verbs are no less poignant in context, for they report a "fallen" warrior[22] who is "dead *(mt)*" and "perished *(ḫlq)*."[23]

The lament for Baal echoes the classic formulary for fallen warriors. For the first line in the report of Baal's death, we may note another divinity fallen to the earth, namely Dagon in 1 Sam. 5:3, evidently defeated by Yahweh as symbolized by the ark (mentioned in the preceding v. 2). In 2 Sam. 3:34, David laments of Joab: "like one falling before treacherous men, you have fallen (*nāpaltā;* see also 2 Sam. 2:16). David also laments of Joab that this warrior is dead, a report that is weighty and definitive. In this connection, we may also mention the report about Goliath in 1 Sam. 17:51: *mēt gibbôrām*, "their warrior was dead." No less instructive about warrior lamentation is David's lament over the fallen Jonathan and Saul in 2 Sam. 1:19-27. This passage gives this poignant expression three times (vv. 19b, 25a, 27a): "how the mighty have fallen" *(ʾêk nāpĕlû gibbôrîm)*. This lament echoes Baal's own fall (**npl*) to the earth.[24]

Later Mot tells Anat the circumstances of Baal's death (1.6 II 15-23). Mot first relates how he was going hunting (*ʾaṣd* in line 15) throughout the earth (lines 15-17), because his appetite "lacks humans" (lines 17-19). In other words, he is ravenously hungry, and he likes to feed on humans. Mot's voracious appetite described earlier in 1.5 II 2-3 in terms of "[one lip to ea]rth,[25] one lip to heaven, [to]ngue to the stars"; it includes everything edible.[26] In 1.6 II 17-19 Mot has an appetite *(npš)*[27] for humans.[28] Mot then reports how he came to the very place (1.6 II 21-23) mentioned earlier by the messengers (1.5 VI 5-7). There,

21	I approached Mightiest Baal,	*ngš*[29]*.ʾank.ʾalʾiyn bʿl*
22	I set him like a lamb in my mouth,	*ʿdbnnʾank.*[30]*ʾimr.bpy*
23	Like a kid in the crush of my throat he was destroyed.	*kllʾi.bṯbrn.q⟨n⟩y.ḫtʾuhw*[31]

Here Mot's report includes no word of conflict. Did Baal struggle with Mot or surrender to him? The text offers no indication either way. Instead, this omission, as well as the simile used here, evokes Mot's overwhelming force.

The story is totally different with their encounter at the end of the Baal Cycle. In 1.6 VI 16-22, Baal and Mot fight in hand-to-hand combat ending in a draw:[32]

16-17	They eyed each other like fighters:	*ytʿn.kgmrm*
	Mot was fierce, Baal was fierce.	*mt.ʿz.bʿl.ʿz*
17-19	They gored each other/like wild bulls:	*ynghn/krʾumm*
	Mot was fierce, Baal was fierce.	*mt.ʿz.bʿl/ʿz*
19-20	They bit each other like serpents:	*ynṯkn.kbṯnm*
	Mot was fierce, Baal was fierce.	*mt.ʿz.bʿl.ʿz*
20-22	They dragged each other like runners:	*ymṣḫn/klsmm*
	Mot fell,/Baal fell.	*mt.ql/bʿl.ql*

The final meeting of Baal and Mot here is represented as a head-to-head conflict between warriors. The description of Mot as "fierce" is hardly unusual for Ugaritic. A letter laments the difficult situation, perhaps of a plague: "the hand of the gods, like Mot (Death), is exceedingly fierce" (KTU 2.10.11-13). The images from nature are stock material. For the four images of one-on-one force, we may compare: "They butt each other like young goats."[33] The scene of Baal and Mot combat also recalls Marduk and Tiamat in *Enuma Elish* (IV:86), especially in the final line of Marduk's address to Tiamat: *endīmma anāku u kâši ī nīprus šašma,* rendered somewhat literally, "come close to me, let us make battle, you and I."[34] Harry Hoffner compared texts describing two warriors facing off,[35] specifically the single combat of David and Goliath, the twelve sets of warriors facing off in 2 Sam. 2:12-17, and the Apology of Hattusili III's description of a tribal champion from north of the Halys River.[36] To these examples, Alan Millard added Sinuhe's fight with the champion of a hostile tribe, called "a hero of Retenu": "When he charged me, I shot him, my arrows sticking in his neck. He screamed; he fell on his nose. I slew him with his ax."[37] We see this sort of weaponry also in Mot's speech to Baal (KTU 1.5 VI 6-11), commanding him to bring with him to the underworld his meteorological weaponry of his clouds, winds, thunderbolts, and rains, along with his military force of seven/eight "youths," and Pidray and Tallay, his two meteorological females. Meteorological retinues are likewise stock material for epic conflict, not only in *Enuma Elish,* which is commonly compared. We may also compare the "seven gales" that Ninurta rides on in his meteorological retinue in Lugal-e.[38]

Titles in the Baal Cycle likewise highlight the warrior context of these conflicts. The title *ǵzr* is used for Mot in 1.4 VII 47; VIII 32; 1.5 I 8, 14; II 9; and 1.6 VI 31.[39] While treated as a warrior, Baal himself is not given the title *ǵzr.* Instead, he receives a superlative appellation, "Mightiest of Warriors" *(ʾalʾiy qrdm),* appearing five times in the Baal Cycle (1.3 III 14 = 1.3 IV 7-8; 1.4 VIII 34-35; 1.5 II 10-11, 18; reconstructed for a sixth occurrence in 1.3 VI 25).[40] This is his own title, shared with no other god.[41] It suggests a superlative capacity for warfare. This title occurs with his unique name of "Mightiest Baal" *(ʾalʾiyn bʿl),* which enjoys attestation no less than sixty-eight times.[42] Mot is *ǵzr,* but Baal is superlative in the company of warriors. Where Mot belongs to the category of divine heroes,[43] Baal is its superlative expression. In sum, a range of roles and titles celebrates the warrior abilities of three main males in the Baal Cycle. As warriors competing for kingship, they also embody the ideals of the king as warrior. All are competing for kingship, and they receive titles reflecting their royal aspirations and achievements. Baal, in particular, is heralded by Anat and Athirat as "our king" and "our leader, with none above him" (KTU 1.3 V 32-33; 1.4 IV 43-44).[44] This royal-warrior ideal is the case for other well-known figures, such as Gilgamesh and David.

2. ʿAthtar

Overshadowed by Baal, Yamm, and Mot is the figure of ʿAthtar. This god appears in each of the two major conflicts between Baal and his two archrivals, Yamm and Mot (1.2 III and 1.6 I). I will pass over the episode apparently involving ʿAthtar in KTU 1.2 III in view of the text's terribly fragmentary character.[45] Instead, the discussion here will focus on the second and clearer of the two episodes involving ʿAthtar in the Baal Cycle (1.6 I). Standing within the larger context of the Baal-Mot conflict, this passage describes two potential successors to Baal, who is dead at this point in the story.[46] The first son of Athirat nominated for kingship, the shadowy figure of Ydʿ-Ylḥn ("He knows, he understands"), is rejected as one so weak that "he cannot run like Baal, nor handle the lance like Dagan's son" (1.6 I 50-52). To judge from his name, he is a god of intelligence (perhaps on the model of the wise king, as exemplified by Solomon). Lacking in warrior brawn or prowess, he cannot run so well (cf. Ps. 19:5; Job 15:25-26; 16:14), nor can he handle a spear (cf. 1 Sam. 18:11; 2 Sam. 23:18; cf. Saul's capacity to wield the spear in 1 Sam. 20:33). This figure is not much of a warrior. Against such a rival, Baal remains the paradigmatic male divine warrior.

The second nominee to replace Baal, ʿAthtar, is not big enough. Size matters for warriors, and ʿAthtar is too small for his feet to reach the footstool or for his head to reach the headrest of the divine throne (1.6 I 53-61). In more colloquial terms, he cannot fill Baal's shoes. ʿAthtar himself admits to his physical insufficiency: "I cannot be king on the summit of Sapun" (1.6 I 62). As a result, ʿAthtar descends from the throne of Mightiest Baal, and he is said to rule in (or perhaps "over") "all the great earth" (1.6 I 63-65). It is unclear what realm exactly is covered by "earth" in this context, but it is clear that ʿAthtar cannot measure up to Baal. Physical capacity with weapons and size are marks of Baal. His size is reminiscent of Goliath's in 1 Sam. 17:4. Saul, too, shows considerable size (1 Sam. 9:2). Once it is clear that the two nominees are physically inadequate to replace Baal, the narrative moves toward his return as king over the heavens and earth with the aid of Anat (1.6 II) and with the support of El (1.6 VI 22-35).

This brief episode about 'Athtar seems to assume broader knowledge of this figure. This knowledge is in evidence in the earlier passage from the Baal Cycle involving 'Athtar (1.2 III 20). In this passage, he refers to himself using the metaphor of the lion: "As a lion, I will descend with my life *(lb'um. 'ard.bn[p]šy.)*."[47] The image of the lion in this passage, along with the god descending, conjures up a picture of a defeated warrior. This line seems to point to 'Athtar's sense of himself as a lion, in other words a warrior worthy of consideration in the struggle for kingship. Another passage with 'Athtar as a lion comes from a Ugaritic story about the arrangement of marriage made between two moon deities, the West Semitic god Yariḫ and the Mesopotamian goddess Nikkal (KTU 1.24). The suitor Yariḫ is given advice by the matchmaker who offers an alternative to Nikkal:[48]

28	'Athtar will be opposed (?);	*yǵtr.'ṯtr*
28-29	W/ed for yourself Ybrdmy the daugh[ter (?)];	*t/rḫ lk ybrdmy.b[t(?)*[49]*]*
29-30	Her [fath]er, the lion, will stir.	*['a]/bh lb'u y'rr*

It would seem that 'Athtar is represented here as the father of Nikkal, and the matchmaker believes that he will oppose her marriage to Yariḫ. In this context, 'Athtar may be the one characterized as "a lion" *(lb'u)*. Yariḫ goes on to insist on his marriage to Nikkal (lines 30-32), and he then pays the bride-price (lines 32-37). The characterization of 'Athtar as a lion would point to his reputation as a warrior. In the Baal Cycle, in KTU 1.6 I, he may not measure up to Baal. At the same time, he serves as a suitable foil there because he enjoys a reputation as a warrior, as suggested by his title, "lion."

As noted in section 1 above, the lion serves to mark a warrior-figure. In Chapter Seven, we examine the word "lioness" (as well as the word "panther"), applied to the goddess 'Athtart (Astarte), and in Chapter Ten we will see the image of lions used in a simile to describe the human warriors, Saul and Jonathan. In the case of 'Athtart, she seems to be the lioness, or in the terms of inscribed Iron Age arrowheads, "the lion lady" *(*lb't)*. Benjamin Mazar and Amihai Mazar suggest that this title in the arrowhead inscriptions may point to a class of professional bowmen.[50] In this connection, both Mazars note the image of the lions in Ps. 57:4 (quoted in the first section above), which would not be literal for the Mazars, but refer to warriors.[51] The image of 'Athtar as a "lion" suggests the sense of this god as a warrior god of some rank. This would fit with his significant status in texts outside of the Ugaritic corpus. Among the Arameans and Arabs, he is known as "'Attar of the heavens," and in Old South Arabic he is a leading god.[52]

3. Anat

The most dramatic divine warrior is Baal's sister and ally, Anat. In New Kingdom Egypt, she is described as "Anat the divine, she the victorious, a woman acting as a warrior, clad as men and girt as women."[53] Her best-known appearance as warrior takes place in the Baal Cycle.[54] If ʿAthtar is the foil to Baal standing in his shadow, the warrior goddess Anat is a dramatic force pursuing the god's well-being and projecting his dominion in the world.

Anat's battling with her slaughter of her captives in KTU 1.3 II 5-30 is a classic description in Ugaritic literature.[55]

5-7	And look! Anat fi/ghts in the valley, Battl[es] between/the two towns.	*whln.ʿnt.tm/tḫṣ.bʿmq.* *tḫtṣ[b].bn/qrytm*
7-8	She fought the people of the se[a]-shore,/ Struck the populace of the su[nr]ise.	*tmḫṣ.lʾim.ḫpy[m]/* *tṣmt.ʾadm.ṣʾat.š[p]š*
9-11	Under her, like balls, were hea[ds],/ Above her, like grasshoppers, hands, Like locusts,/heaps of warrior-hands.	*tḥth.kkdrt.rʾi[š]/* *ʿlh.kʾirbym.kp.* *k.qṣm/ǵrmn.kp.mhr*
11-13	She fixed/heads to her back, Fastened/hands on her waist.	*ʿtkt/rʾišt.lbmth.* *šnst/kpt.bḥbšh.*
13-15	Knee-deep she glea[n]ed/warrior-blood, Neck-deep in the gor[e] of soldiers.[56]	*brkm.tǵl[l]/bdm.ḏmr.* *ḥlqm.bmm[ʿ]/mhrm*
15-16	With a club she drove away/captives, With her bow-string, the foe.	*mṭm.tgrš/šbm.* *bksl.qšth.mdnt*
17-18	And look! Anat arrives at her house,/ The goddess takes herself to her palace.	*whln.ʿnt.lbth.tmǵyn/* *tštql.ʾilt.lhklh*
19-20	But she was not satisfied with her fighting in the valley,/ With battling between the two towns.	*wl.šbʿt.tmtḫṣh.bʿmqx/* *tḫtṣb.bn.qrtm.*
20-22	She arranged/chairs for the soldiery,	*tṯʿr/ksʾat.lmhr.*

	Arranged tables/for the hosts,	*ṯʿr.ṯlḥnt/lṣbʾim*
	Footstools for the heroes.	*hdmm.lǵzrm*
23-24	Hard she fought and looked about,/	*mʾid.tmtḫṣn.wtʿn/*
	Anat battled, and she surveyed.	*tḫtṣb.wtḥdy.ʿnt*
25-27	Her innards swelled with laughter,	*tǵdd.kbdh.bṣḥq.*
	Her heart filled/with joy,	*ymlʾu/lbh.bšmḫt.*
	Anat's innards/with victory.	*kbd.ʿnt/tšyt.*
27-28	Knee-deep she gleaned in warrior/blood,	*kbrkm.tǵllbdm/ḏmr*
	Neck-deep in the gore of soldiers,	*ḥlqm.bmmʿ.mhrm*
29-30	Until she was sated with fighting in the house,/	*ʿd.tšbʿ.tmtḫṣ.bbt/*
	With battling between the tables.	*tḫtṣb.bn.ṯlḥnm.*

The two major parts of this passage, lines 5-16 and 17-30, show several correspondences. First, both scenes dramatize the beginning of their action with the same clause-opening construction (lines 5 and 17): "and look! *(whln).*" Second, both involve the soldiers whom Anat opposes (see lines 13-15, 20-22, 27-28). Third, in both engagements, Anat is said to glean "knee-deep" and "neck-deep" in the blood and gore of her warrior enemies (lines 13-15, 27-28). Fourth, both sections end with a characterization about Anat's satisfaction (lines 19-20, 29-30).

This characterization serves to mark a dramatic contrast in the situation at the end of the two sections. In the first, Anat is unsatsified (lines 19-20), but at the end of the second, she is sated (lines 29-30). There are other notable differences between these two major parts of this passage. First, the battlefield is the setting for lines 5-16, while the action in lines 17-30 transpires in Anat's house with tables and chairs.[57] Second, in lines 5-16, the goddess wields weapons, a staff and a bowstring (the latter referring by synecdoche to a bow and arrows), while no weapons are manifest in lines 17-30. Third, destruction of the humans is incomplete in lines 5-16, while they seem decimated by the end of lines 17-30. The question is the nature of this destruction.

The interpretation of this second scene may take a cue from Anat's warfare in KTU 1.13.3-7.[58] This passage provides a text with some parallel expressions to what is found in 1.3 II. KTU 1.13.3-7 additionally uses the term *ḫrm* (cognate with biblical *ḥērem*) for Anat's activity:[59]

3-4	"]Make *ḫrm* for two days,	*]ḫrm.ṯn.ym/m.*
4	Po[ur blood (?) for three] days,	*šp[k.dm (?).ṯlṯ] ymm.*
4-5	Go kill for fo[ur] days.	*lk./hrg. ʾar[bʿ.] ymm.*
5-6	Harvest hand(s), pour out [blood?],	*bṣr.kp.šsk.[dm. (?)]*
6-7	To your waist attach heads."	*lḥbšk.ʿtk.rʾiš[t]*

Lines 5-7 rather strongly echo 1.3 II 11-13. From the two texts' shared picture of hands and heads taken by Anat, it would appear that they partake of the same conceptual world. Lines 3-5 in turn may suggest a backdrop for the feast that Anat hosts in her house in 1.3 II 17-30. Given the scene with tables and chairs in 1.3 II and the parallel language in 1.13, the feast in 1.3 II 17-30 seems to presuppose Anat's divine consumption of her captives at tables and chairs, leading to her satisfaction that she had not experienced in the earlier battle scene. If correct, Anat's feasting in her house provides a literary analogue for biblical representations of the victor that "feeds on the flesh" of captives (Deut. 32:42) and "drinks the blood of the slain" (Num. 23:24).[60] The "*ḥērem*-warfare" in ancient Israel may presuppose the notion of the deity receiving warfare captives as offerings for victory.[61] The parallel scenes of battle and celebration hardly constitute a dissonant analogue. Perhaps as we hear of Inanna, so too for Anat, "battle is a feast for her."[62] Or, as Lugal-e describes battle: "In a clash of weapons, the festival of manhood, Inanna's dance. . . ."[63]

One final passage in the Baal Cycle, KTU 1.6 I 15-29, may reflect a warrior sensibility. In this passage, Anat makes funerary offerings for her deceased brother, Baal:

15-18	She carried him to Sapan's summit,	*tšʿlynh/bṣrrt.ṣp⟨ʿ⟩n.*
	Bewailed him and buried him,	*tbkynh/wtqbrnh.*
	Set him in a divine pit in the Earth.	*tštnn.bḫrt/ʾilm.ʾarṣ.*
18-20	She slaughtered seventy water buffalo,	*tṭbḫ.šbʿm/rʾumm.*
	An offering (?) for Mightiest Baal.	*kgmn.ʾaliyn/bʿl*
20-21	She slaughtered seventy oxen,	*tṭbḫ.šbʿm.ʾalpm*
	[An off]ering (?) for] Mightiest Baal.	*[kg]mn.ʾalʾiyn.bʿl.*
22-23	[She sla]ughtered seventy sheep,	*[tṭ]bḫ.šbʿm.ṣʾin/*
	[An offeri]ng (?) for Mightiest Baal.	*[kgm]n.ʾalʾiyn.bʿl*

24-25	[She slaug]htered seventy deer, [An offering (?) for] Mightiest Baal.	*[tṭb]ḫ.šbʿm.ʾaylm/* *[kgmn.]ʾalʾiyn/bʿl*
26-27	[She slaughtered se]venty mountain-goats, [An offering (?) for Migh]tiest Baal.	*[tṭbḫ.š]bʿm.yʿlm/* *[kgmn.ʾal]ʾiyn.bʿl*
28-29	[She slaughtered seventy] asses (?), [An offer]ing (?) [for] Migh[ti]est B[aal].	*[tṭbḫ.šbʿm.(?)]ḥmrm/* *[kgm]n.ʾalʾiyn[.]b[ʿl]*

Here Anat concludes her ritual acts with a series of six animal sacrifices, each one seventy in number, the mark of completion or in this case fullness, signaling her pious duty to her brother. It is evident from the context that the sacrifices are funerary in character, intended on behalf of the dead.[64] The crux in the description of the six sacrifices is *kgmn*. The Ugaritic word is notoriously difficult,[65] and commentators offer widely varying views, with respect to both its form and meaning; no fully convincing etymology has been offered.[66] As a result, many scholars take the word generically as a term for offering.[67] Manfried Dietrich, Oswald Loretz, and Joacquín Sanmartín plausibly compare Akkadian *kukumnu/kikamunu*, a "three-year old" animal offering.[68] Still, the better part of wisdom for now may be to refrain from imputing anything more specific than "offering." The animals offered are generally clear: *rʾumm* in line 19, *ʾalpm* in line 20, *ṣʾin* in line 22, *ʾaylm* in line 24, and *yʿlm* in line 26. The first two sets belong to the larger animals, "(water) buffalo" and "oxen," while the others are the smaller animals, "sheep," "deer," and "(mountain) goats." The only particular difficulty is the sixth set, called *]ḥmrm*, on the face of it perhaps "asses."[69] Donkeys are themselves objects of burial in this period[70] as well as offering-animals, and so in theory they could be the offering.[71] Some of these species are known from the Ugaritic ritual texts, while others are not. Clearly some are domesticated, while others are not. The question is why there are both domesticated and undomesticated species in this context. It might be suggested that for warriors, hunting is a central activity,[72] and thus undomesticated species are fitting for Anat's offerings for her brother.

Anat stands out among the divine warriors on a number of scores. First, unlike warrior-gods, the warrior goddess Anat bears no titles denoting her activity as a warrior in the Baal Cycle. Thus far there is only one instance anywhere in the form of a warrior epithet: "Anat, the stron[g]" *(ʿnt gṯr⟨t⟩)* in KTU 1.108.6.[73] Second, Anat rarely, if ever, engages in military conflict with other divine warriors. Even her famous conflict with Mot is not cast as a conflict of warriors, but as an emotionally driven urge of the heart: "Like the heart of the cow for the calf,/like the heart of the ewe for her lamb,/So is the heart of Anat for Baal/She seizes Divine Mot . . ." (1.6 II 28-31).[74] Third, Anat's conflicts are often with human enemies on the terrestrial level. She fights in the valley in 1.3 II, and her conflict with Aqhat in 1.17 VI takes place in a terrestrial location, evidently at her sanctuary. This is not to ignore her claims of victory over divine enemies in the Baal Cycle (KTU 1.3 III 38-47). Still, the plot gives little attention to these victories, which lie in the past from the narrative perspective. It would appear that where Baal is a heavenly model of warriors, Anat is not only a heavenly model and not only an earthly model. She is also an earthly patron of human warriors and their mentor, as suggested in Chapter Four. Fourth and finally, Anat's gender demarcates her. In gender terms, the male human-human bonding of warrior pairs, such as David and Jonathan, perhaps emblemizes the exclusion of human females, as we saw in Chapters Two and Three. As we noted in Chapter Four, Aqhat's famous retort to Anat expresses a gender division (1.17 VI 39-41): "Bows are . . . warriors; now shall womanhood go hunting?" In this statement, Aqhat asserts the gender understanding that the world of human warriors is a male world.[75] The gender difference of Anat seems to express two aspects of warrior perception of reality. She is at once the sister of Baal; to put the point in terms of their shared character, they are sibling warriors. He is the paradigmatic divine warrior on the heavenly level, while she is his corresponding divine warrior on the earthly level. He battles little with human warriors (though KTU 1.4 VII 7-13 is one instance); by contrast, her interaction with human male warriors is central to her identity. The sibling relationship of Baal and Anat perhaps expresses their essential relatedness as warriors; it may also capture the correspondence and difference between their realms of military activity.

There may be more here to observe, especially when it comes to the gender roles of these deities. Of great importance for scholarly discussions of anthropomorphism are the characterizations of goddesses hunting and in combat. Anat and ʿAthtart appear as hunting in a number of texts, while it is equally clear that human females are expected not to hunt, as Aqhat's response to Anat shows. As we saw in Chapter Four, Aqhat says to the goddess (KTU 1.17 VI 40), either as a question, "now do womenfolk hunt?" or perhaps as a sarcastic claim, "now womenfolk hunt!" *(ht tṣdn tʾinṯt)*. However the line is to be rendered, it seems that human women on this matter are considered differently from the way that a number of texts present Anat as well as ʿAthtart, as we will see in the next chapter. Anthropomorphism may occasionally work in inverse terms rather than parallel terms. To be sure, in many instances, divine roles parallel the human roles: gods may be represented like human males in the arenas of patriarchy and kingship, and goddesses are like human females in the arena of marriage and domestic chores. However, a notable exception involves the goddesses' roles in hunting and battle.[76]

This observation calls for further explanation. Both gods and goddesses are hunters as well as warriors. Baal engages in hunting (KTU 1.10 II) and warfare (KTU 1.2 IV; 1.4 VII 7-14); Rashpu, too, may be considered a hunter (see KTU 4.262.2). While Baal clearly mirrors these male human preoccupations, in terms of gender ʿAthtart and Anat represent an inversion of this role relative to the societal attitude toward human women. How is the gender situation with deities in these roles to be explained? Why are both a god and goddess represented in these roles when there is a disparity in the representation of these roles for human males and females?[77] Peggy L. Day asks the right question with respect to Anat: "Why is Anat a hunter and a warrior?" Her answer focuses on Anat's liminal status as an adolescent unattached to male social structure via marriage and motherhood. Anat is, after all, *btlt,* a young woman of marriageable age who has not borne children.[78] This status of the goddess at the divine level seems inverse to her relationship with Aqhat. In other words, her relationship ("my brother") with the young would-be hunter in the story of Aqhat perhaps corresponds to her lack of spousal relationship to any god, at least in the Ugaritic texts.

We may take a further hint on this subject, again from the story of Aqhat, although this is a rather speculative deduction. As noted above, Anat gives instructions to Aqhat (KTU 1.18 I 24, 27, 29): "Come, my brother, and . . . you will go on a hunt . . . I will instruct you."[79] This passage, if correctly understood, suggests that the goddess has a relationship with the human addressee and represents herself as his instructor in hunting. Thus, while the god Baal and the goddesses Anat and ʿAthtart may manifest the human male hunting role, a goddess may not simply show an inverse mirroring, but also has an additional dimension: she is represented as both role model and mentor. In a sense, the goddess can bond with Aqhat in the matter of the hunt and thus address him in intimate terms ("my brother"). She — unlike the god — is represented as present and active in his development as a hunter. Thus gender lies at the heart of the conceptualization of human, male warriors and the different notions of their relations to Baal and Anat. Gender is key. At this point, we turn to a context in the Baal Cycle likewise informed by important gender contrasts.

4. The Warrior's Feast: Music, Gender, Sex

For the Baal Cycle's literary representation of warriors, I would like to turn to one scene in KTU 1.3 I 2-27 that has received relatively little attention. The passage stands between two very famous battles in the extant Baal Cycle that we have examined above, Baal's battle against Yamm in 1.2 IV and Anat's fight in 1.3 II. For all its relative obscurity, this scene shows significant features of the heroic worldview in its presentation of a victory celebration. The text and translation of 1.3 I 2-27 follow, with my added section headings.[80]

Baal's Victory Banquet: Food

2-4	He served Might[iest] Baal,	*ʿbd.ʾalʾi[yn]/bʿl.*
	Waited on the Prince, Lord of the Earth.	*sʾid.zbl.bʿl/ʾarṣ.*
4-8	He stood, arranged,[81] and offered him food,	*qm.yṯʿr/wyšlḥmnh/*
	Sliced a breast before him,	*ybrd.ṯd.lpnwh*
	With a salted knife, a cut of fatling.	*bḥrb.mlḥt/qṣ.mrʾi.*

Baal's Drink

8-11	He stood, served, and offered him drink,	*ndd/yʿšr.wyšqynh/*
	Put a cup in his hand,	*ytn.ks.bdh/*
	A goblet in both his hands:	*krpnm*[82]*.bklʾat.ydh*
12-13	A large, imposing vessel,	*bkrb.ʿẓm.*
	A rhyton for mighty men;	*rʾidn/mt.šmm.*
13-15	A holy cup women may not see,	*ks.qdš/ltphnh.ʾaṯt.*
	A goblet Athirat may not eye.	*krpn/ltʿn.ʾaṯrt.*
15-17	A thousand jars he drew of the wine,	*ʾalp/kd.yqḥ.bḫmr*
	A myriad he mixed in his mixture.	*rbt.ymsk.bmskh*

Music and Sex (?)

18-19	He stood, chanted, and sang,	*qm.ybd.wyšr/*
	Cymbals in the virtuoso's hands.	*mṣltm.bd.nʿm*
20-22	Sweet of voice, the hero sang	*yšr.ǵzr.ṭb.ql/*
	About Baal on the summit of Sapan.	*ʿl.bʿl.b.ṣrrt/ṣpn*

22-25	Baal gazed at his daughters, Eyed Pidray, Daughter of Light, Then Tallay, [Daughter] of Rain.	*ytmr.bʿl/bnth.* *yʿn.pdry/bt.ʾar.* *ʾapn.ṭly/[bt.] rb.*
25-27	Pidru knew . . . Indeed, the [No]ble [Brides] . . .	*pdr.ydʿ/[. . .]t* *hm.[k]lt./[knyt] . . .*

This scene initially presents its audience with two males. Baal here is served by one called *ǵzr,* either a young servant as befits the context, or perhaps "hero," as it appears elsewhere in the Baal Cycle, the story of Aqhat, and the Rephaim texts.[83] In either case, Baal is labeled at the outset as "Mightiest," suggesting his preeminence as a warrior. The following subsections of the feast begin by the unusual sequence of verbs (a suffix verb form followed by two prefix verb forms) in lines 4-5, 8-9, and 18. In the discussion of this passage, I will discuss first music, then drinking and gender, and finally, sexual behavior.

Music and Song (lines 18-22)

The server at the feast in 1.3 I, we are told, has a fine or good voice.[84] He sings over Baal with cymbals.[85] For the figures involved, we might compare the ritual instruction in KTU 1.106.15-17: "the singer shall sing the song, several times, before the king."[86] A more explicitly heroic context involves the singing role of David apparently with a lyre before King Saul, according to 1 Sam. 18:10: "David would play by hand day by day" *(wĕdāwîd mĕnaggēn bĕyādô kĕyôm bĕyôm).* We may also note the song of Achilles before Patroklos, in *Iliad* 9:185-92, witnessed in a feasting scene by the legation sent by Agamemnon and headed by Phoenix and Odysseus:

> Now they came beside the shelters and ships of the Myrmidons
> And they found Achilles delighting in his heart in a lyre,
> clear-sounding,
> Splendid and carefully wrought, with a bridge of silver upon it,
> Which he won out of the spoils when he ruined Eëtion's city.
> With this he was pleasuring his heart, and singing of men's fame,
> as Patroklos was sitting over against him, alone, in silence,
> watching Aiakides and the time he would leave off singing.[87]

Warriors at song are hardly peripheral to the representation of warrior culture. On the contrary: in these cases, we see song associated with great warrior figures.

Drink and Gender (lines 8-17)

The parallel of *Iliad* 9 with Baal's feast does not end with song, but includes the scale of drinking. The feasting of Baal places a decided emphasis on the drinking in lines 8-17, as opposed to any other activity, certainly compared with food service in lines 4-8 or the singing in lines 18-21. (It is difficult to judge how long the activity of lines 22-28 goes on, with twelve to fourteen lines missing from the bottom of the tablet; I will return to this matter shortly.) Drinking occupies a central place in this feast. A superhuman effort is involved in Baal's consumption. When Achilles and Patroklos welcome Odysseus and his legation into their tent, Achilles calls to Patroklos in these words (lines 202-4):

> "Son of Menoitios, set up a mixing-bowl that is bigger,
> and mix us stronger drink, and make ready a cup for each man,
> since these who have come beneath my roof are the men I love best."

Excessive drinking, even to the point of falling into drunken stupor, is a standard trope for warrior culture (cf. Ps. 78:65: "like a warrior shaking off wine," NJPS; cf. Jer. 23:9).

The descriptions of the drinking in KTU 1.3 I and *Iliad* 9 offer gender expressions that locate males at the center of the feast. In the Baal Cycle, the vessel for drinking is "a huge vessel," *bkrb* (line 12), one perhaps for "mighty men," *mt šmm* (line 13).[88] Clearly this vessel is not for women: it is called a "a holy cup (that) women may not see *(ks qdš ltphnh 'aṯt)*//a goblet (that) Athirat may not eye *(krpn lt'n 'aṯrt)*."[89] In other words, this drinking puts males at the center of activity and excludes women; not even the goddess Athirat is supposed to lay her eyes on it.[90] The mention of the goddess in this manner seems to be a sort of superlative, gendered delimitation: no female, human or divine, is to look upon this vessel of male drinking. In this context, this vessel marks the domain of males at the center of this drinking feast. The polarity of gendered expressions here evokes a boundary: men at the center, women at the periphery or in subservience.[91] For this picture, we may note the picture painted on limestone, perhaps from Tell el-Amarna.[92] A Syrian warrior named Tarura is seated, with his spear behind his seat and a dagger in his belt. He is drinking from a tube connected to a vessel holding a liquid. The tube is held by a second, smaller figure. Behind the server sits a female, identified as his wife *(nbt pr),* Arbura.[93]

Unlike these private or perhaps even domestic male-dominated scenes, women — as well as men — can celebrate in song in the public context when the warriors return from conflict. Ps. 68:25 and 1 Sam. 18:6-7 are emblematic of this female role (see also Exod. 15:20-21; Judg. 11:34). This sort of behavior is perhaps modeled by Anat, when she sings of the love of Mighty Baal (KTU 1.3 III 4-8 and its parallel in 1.101). This female role in the inverse situation of postbattle lamentation is given particular prominence in David's lament over Jonathan and Saul (2 Sam. 1:20, 24). The daughters of Israel are told to weep over Saul (v. 24), while Israel is also commanded in v. 20: "Tell it not in Gath, do not announce it in Ashkelon's streets, lest the daughters of the Philistines rejoice, lest the daughters of the uncircumcised exult."[94] Women likewise lament in the face of battle's defeat (cf. 1 Sam. 15:33). This is not to say that there is no joint male-female celebration of victory (see Exodus 15; Psalm 68, esp. vv. 24-27). At the same time, there is an important difference between male and female song with respect to martial engagements: female singing in many contexts is separate from the feast of the warriors. The song of women is a public function, while for the men's feast, song is represented in some instances as a private or domestic function in comparison; it also contrasts with a public feast, such as Baal's inauguration of his palace to which all the deities are invited (KTU 1.4 V).

Sex (lines 22-27)

In Baal's feast in KTU 1.3 I, the gendered expression about the drinking vessel is emblematic of the gendered nature of the entire scene. Females do not celebrate as colleagues of the males. Instead, Baal's female subordinates are the objects of Baal's attention, and only at the end of the scene (lines 22-27). It would seem that the girls are off to the side of the feast, and they would seem to be the objects of the last part of the feast for the males. Baal literally "eyes" (*ʿ*yn*) Pidray and Tallay.[95] They are his "daughters" *(bnth),* in this context probably Baal's girls or females. In view of their title *klt* elsewhere (often reconstructed for line 26), it has often been thought that they are Baal's "brides" or "fiancées."[96] The term "daughter" *(bt)* is not used simply literally, but expresses their affiliation[97] with meteorological phenomena associated with Baal's rain-making capacity. This aspect of the females is captured, for example, in the name of Tallay, which means "Dewy," and her title here, "daughter of rain." The term "daughter" may also express a lower rank (compared for example to the term "sister" for a lover, who would have been a social equal, as in Song 4:9 cited below). The presentation of Baal and his girls in 1.3 I casts in narrative form their meteorological relationship in terms of both affiliation and subordination. In the narrative world of the feast, these are Baal's "women." These females are affiliated with Baal, here more specifically as the objects of his visual attention.[98]

The nature of the gaze that Baal lavishes upon these two females is left unstated, and the context breaks off just when a clearer picture might have emerged. To unpack the scene here, we may briefly note the lexicon of visual activity here. Two verbs of perception in this passage are *'*mr*, "to look, appear" (1.3 I 22; cf. 1.2 I 32), and *‘*yn*, "to eye, notice" (1.3 I 22; cf. 1.10 II 14-15; 1.3 II 23). By contrast, Ugaritic uses the following verbs elsewhere: **phy*,[99] "to see, perceive" (1.2 I 22; 1.4 IV 27; 1.16 I 53; 1.17 V 9; 1.19 II 13), and by analogy, "to experience" (1.6 V 12, 14, 15 [reconstructed], 16, 17, 18); **ḥdy*, "to look" (1.127.32), "to examine" (1.19 III 33), and "to look about, survey" (1.3 II 24).[100] It is evident that these verbs involve visual activity, with different nuances that can sometimes be inferred from context. 1.3 I 22-25 uses the *t*-form of *ytmr*, which may suggest reflexive yet transitive action; perhaps it is Baal's prolonged vision, perhaps "to gaze" or "to stare." It is followed in parallelism by the verb *‘*yn*, literally, "to eye." For the two verbs, J. C. L. Gibson translates "caught sight" and "perceives."[101] Yet more may be involved.

Unlike Anat's travel and arrival in 1.3 IV 38-40, the entrance of the three women in 1.3 I is not mentioned; during Baal's feast, they may have been in attendance in the background. Their relationship with Baal may furnish a further clue about the meaning of Baal's visual attention given to them in this final section of 1.3 I. The description of Baal's love and his three women in 1.3 III 5-7 uses terms that may suggest a sexual aspect to their relationship, and Baal's interaction at the end of 1.3 I may involve more than visual recognition. Indeed, the approximately fourteen lines in the lacuna could accommodate a description of further action. Sexual relations following the god's visual gaze appear in divine stories (for example, the story of Enlil and Ninlil),[102] and perhaps this is the case here.[103] If Baal's gaze is only a prelude to sexual relations, then the visual nuance involves more than catching sight of his women; it is perhaps a gaze induced by and further inducing the god's sexual passion. Gazing or prolonged eye contact, also called "the 'copulatory' gaze," is a "labile psychophysiological response" that may involve the dilation of the pupils, "a sign of extreme interest."[104] One might suggest that Baal's case could involve this dilation of the pupils, a sign of visual intensity or gaze signaling his sexual intent. It is the "reflexive" use of one's eyes in the action that may dictate the use of infix *t*-stem form, as with other bodily actions,[105] but not for other verbs of vision.

This scene of Baal and his women is reminiscent of the "copulatory gaze," evoked by the female protagonist's mention of the intensity of her lover's visual attention in Song 6:5: "Turn your eyes away from me, For they overwhelm me!" *(hāsēbbî ʿênayik minnegdî šehēm hirhîbūnî).*[106] Her lover later describes the emotional intensity of her eyes (Song 4:9):

> "You have captured my heart, my sister, my bride
> *(libbabtīnî ʾăḥōtî kallâ),*
> You have captured my heart with one [glance] of your eyes
> *(libbabtînî bĕʾaḥad mēʿênayik).*"[107]

Visual interaction as a prelude to further sexual activity is apparently depicted on a copper pinhead from the second half of the third millennium from southwest Iran. In Gwendolyn Leick's characterization,[108] the pin depicts a couple in a house: "the woman on the right touches the man's shoulder while they gaze into each other's eyes."

A sexual interpretation of the end of the scene in KTU 1.3 I cannot be precluded, given what we know elsewhere of Pidray. This female figure is mentioned in what has been understood as a sexual context in KTU 1.132. Lines 1-3 open the text with the prescription: "on the nineteenth of the month you are to prepare the bed of Pidray with the king's bed-covers" *(btšʿ ʿšrh trbd ʿrš pdry bšt mlk).*[109] Following several sections of sacrifices, the ritual ends with the order: "before nightfall, you will remove the bed" *(pn ll tnʿr ʿrš).*[110] Some commentators interpret this text as a "sacred marriage" involving Pidray and the king, although the context affords little insight into the precise nature of this ritual.[111] It might be inferred that the end of 1.3 I similarly presupposes the idea of sexual relations between Baal and his women, including Pidray. The end of 1.3 I may have envisioned a pairing of Baal and Pidray,[112] possibly informed by the language of sacred marriage. If so, Baal may be the model of the divine king with whom Pidray was thought to enjoy sexual congress. Whether or not this particular speculation is right, the scene in 1.3 I seems to exclude women in general and the high goddess in particular (lines 13-15), with the lower status females set on the side (lines 22-27). In sum, the scene in 1.3 I expresses a number of central warrior values and attitudes.

Over the course of the Baal Cycle, many of its warrior themes are cast at various points as matters of divine kingship. In turn, human kingship constitutes the overarching sponsorship of the text in the colophon at the end of tablet VI (KTU 1.6 VI 54-59). Between the language of divine kingship and the colophon of human kingship, it would appear that the heroic poetry of the Baal Cycle offered models of warrior values in service to Ugarit's royal establishment. The Baal Cycle as a whole encodes several of the basic themes about warriors, in particular victory and song, gender and sex, focused on the figure of Baal along with other deities serving as enemies, foils, or aids to this divine warrior-king. Over the course of the text, the goddess Anat also figures prominently, supportive of Baal and central to his success.

There is yet another goddess who plays a small role in the extant text of the Baal Cycle (KTU 1.2 I and IV). She is sometimes paired with Anat and is no less important in some Ugaritic sources. This is the goddess ʿAthtart, the subject of the next chapter.

CHAPTER SEVEN

'Athtart among the Divine Warriors

1. Introduction

The preceding chapter discusses a number of divine warriors of the Baal Cycle, especially Baal and Anat, as well as 'Athtar. These deities have received their share of attention over the past two decades.[1] Besides these figures, divine warriors in the Ugaritic texts include the god Rashpu (sometimes called Resheph based on the spelling of his name in Hab. 3:5), who has likewise been discussed extensively.[2] There is yet a further divine warrior in the Baal Cycle who has not been examined sufficiently, namely the goddess 'Athtart. Until relatively recently, scholars could note the lack of sources about this goddess.[3] However, this situation has been changed by a recent discovery from Ugarit, along with the reedition of some relevant Ugaritic texts, as well as texts available from Late Bronze Age Emar.[4]

My main purpose in this chapter is to provide the basic information about this warrior goddess in the texts[5] from Ugarit and Emar. These two Syrian Late Bronze Age sites show significant overlap in information on this topic. At the same time, each corpus offers information about 'Athtart lacking in the other. Anat receives an emphasis in the texts at Ugarit, with 'Athtart not uncommonly paired with her.[6] By contrast, 'Ashtart is a major figure at Emar, with Anat virtually absent from sources there.[7] The genres attesting to the goddesses at Ugarit and Emar are considerably different as well. While Emar is richer in ritual texts, Ugarit is richer in literary texts.

Before proceeding, it is important to note four particular difficulties in studying this goddess. First, there is disagreement over the etymology of her name, variously given as 'Athtart at Ugarit, 'Ashtart at Emar, 'Ashtoret and *ʿAshtarah in the Bible, and Astarte in Greek sources.[8] As a result, the name offers little help for clarifying her character.[9] Second, ʿAthtart/ʿAshtart is difficult to track across regions in the different periods. As an old Syrian goddess known from the texts at Ebla,[10] she has a long history ranging from the third millennium down through the turn of the era. She is well attested also in Egypt.[11] Accordingly, this survey is provisional, in view of the number and distribution of the sources.[12]

Third, generalizations about the deity have arguably impeded progress. For example, it is assumed, with some reason, that ʿAthtart is identified as the evening star corresponding to ʿAthtar as the morning star. In William Foxwell Albright's words, "the name *ʿAthtart* was always connected with the evening star, just as ʿAthtar (the corresponding masculine name) was always connected with the morning star all over the West Semitic world from Syria to South Arabia. The ancients early on became aware of the fact that the evening and morning stars were simply manifestations of the same entity — since they saw that the two had the same magnitude and never appeared together, yet were always in related positions in the heavens."[13] Albright's reasoning proceeded from analogies with two other deities, both of whose names are etymologically related to the goddess's. One is with the masculine West Semitic astral god ʿAthtar,[14] while the other lies with Ishtar, the Mesopotamian goddess. In his view, Albright was hardly alone. The view is taken up by J. J. M. Roberts in his book *The Earliest Semitic Pantheon*,[15] and by Nicholas Wyatt in his contribution to the standard resource, *Dictionary of Deities and Demons*.[16] However, neither Albright nor other scholars cite any clear West Semitic astral evidence for ʿAthtart/ʿAshtart. Thus, Albright's generalization for an astral ʿAthtart "all over the West Semitic world" is disproportionate to the evidence.[17] At the same time, we cannot assume that the texts recovered are fully representative.[18]

For the representation of the goddess in the texts that we do have, any putative astral aspect was not particularly important. The sources do not emphasize this side of the goddess; in fact, the available sources do not mention or allude to this aspect of her as far as we can tell. So a description based on the presently attested texts may reflect the relative priorities about the goddess for those who produced and transmitted these attested texts. In other words, what we know of the goddess may constitute a statement about how she was thought to fit into the societies that produced the texts as presently attested. (Of course, the discovery of a new text or a few new texts could alter the understanding of the goddess.) In retrospect, the etymological and comparative approach informing Albright's treatment assumed an undemonstrated generalization as well as a somewhat static picture not particularly concerned with possible regional variation or temporal change. Such an approach runs a possible risk of adversely affecting the attested evidence at a single site, or in the case of this study, two sites.

Fourth and finally, another limitation concerns the intersection between the societies and the goddess. Generally, scholarly descriptions of deities tend to focus on the literary representations of the goddess and to generalize about her character or profile based on these representations. To some degree, this is a necessary and even useful procedure, but it suffers from the limitations of literary texts, which may not address a range of issues. For example, how was the goddess perceived in different social levels and segments? Did her profile or characteristics vary according to various religious and political settings? How did people relate to her? How (if at all) was she understood to be manifest to people? Most, if not all, of these questions cannot be answered (at least adequately), but as an initial inoculation against generalizing and abstracting some kind of nature of the goddess, it may be helpful to include information from nonliterary genres along with data from literary texts. Together, these suggest some importance of the goddess for the monarchy. The administrative and ritual texts were largely produced for and by the monarchy and thus reflect the goddess's place in the royal scheme of things. How she was understood in other sectors of society is unknown, although it might be argued that the monarchic version of the goddess reflects, at least in part, how she was understood more broadly.

With these initial considerations in mind, we will look at the goddess at Ugarit and Emar, with some attention to sources elsewhere. The discussion will proceed in three parts: (1) 'Athtart as a figure of hunting and warfare; (2) the goddess's relations to other deities; and (3) the goddess's attribute animal. Before beginning, it is important to note the goddess's relative importance for the monarchy. At Ugarit, she appears in several administrative and ritual texts. KTU 4.219.2 records a payment of silver collected for the house of 'Athtart immediately preceding payment for the house of Resheph-*gn* in line 3. David M. Clemens comments about this temple: "The recurrent emphasis upon 'Aṯtartu in a wide range of documents from PR [Palais Royal] indicates the significance of this deity to the Ug. Dynasty and its administration. This suggests (though by no means conclusively) that it [the temple] was situated in the vicinity of Ugarit if not within the palace complex itself."[19] She seems to have another sanctuary (RS 17.22 + 17.87.21-23),[20] and Ugaritic administrative material shows cultic personnel devoted to the goddess (KTU 4.168.3-4; RS 20.235.17-18).[21] Clothing for the goddess (that is, her statue) is attested in KTU 4.245 I 1 and 11. Her title in this text, ʿAthtart *šd,* attested also in the ritual texts (e.g., KTU 1.111.8-10; see also 1.91.10; 1.148.18),[22] seems to relate to Ishtar *ṣēri* (e.g., RS 17.352).[23] The epithet seems to mean "field" or "steppe-land," which may represent the location of a sanctuary from which the goddess comes in the royal entry ritual in KTU 1.91.10.[24]

Other ritual texts provide some further information about the goddess. KTU 1.50.1, 3, 4 provide evident references to ʿAthtart (all partially reconstructed and all with room following for possible epithets added). Might this text suggest acknowledgment of the different manifestations of ʿAthtart? KTU 1.81.18, 19 refer, respectively, to *ʿṯtrt ndrg* and *ʿṯtrt ʾabḏr,* but it is difficult to know the significance of these references. No less intriguing, the former is preceded by *qdšt,* "the Holy One" (feminine). The context with ʿAthtart in a ritual suggests that *qdšt* here is the title of a goddess;[25] it may be the closest West Semitic analogue for Egyptian Qedeshet. Other ritual contexts likewise mention the goddess. KTU 1.112.13 refers to an offering of a jar[26] of wine for ʿAthtart *ḫr,* a title to which we shall return below.

ʿAthtart is also known from three incantational texts. Two involve incantations against snakebites, KTU 1.100.20, 78 and 1.107.39 (discussed in the third section below). The deities-lists and letters give a different sense of the goddess's relative importance at Ugarit. On the one hand, the deities-lists seem to show her in a position of relative unimportance. In KTU 1.148.7, an offering list to deities, ʿAthtart appears in a group of goddesses, as she does in the deities-lists 1.47.25 and 1.118.24. In these groups, she appears last. If this order is any indication, the "ritual ʿAthtart" is not particularly important. On the other hand, the "political ʿAthtart," as attested in the letters, seems to be a different story. The list of deities in the Ugaritic letter 2.42.6-9 is suggestive:[27] "I do indeed speak to Baal Sapun (?),[28] . . . to the Eternal Sun, to ʿAthtart . . . , to Anat, to all the gods of Alishi[ya]. . . ." This letter was perhaps sent from Alashiya by a high-ranking official of Ugarit.[29] From the mention of the "ship(s)" *(ʾanyt)* in lines 24 and 26 and "merchant" *(mkr)* in line 25, it might be supposed that the letter concerns maritime commerce between Alishiya and Ugarit. Accordingly, the letter would represent a recognition of the deities of the two lands, with Baal in initial position and with ʿAthtart in the initial position for Ugaritic goddesses.[30] In any case, she appears before Anat. In sum, this text may furnish some sense of the political recognition of the goddess.

There is one final piece of evidence that arguably points to the relative importance of the goddess at Ugarit. ʿAthtart *šd,* "ʿAthtart of the field" (KTU 1.91.10; 1.148.18; 4.182.55, 58), which will be addressed further below, has a syllabic counterpart in the name *ištar ṣēru,* "Ishtar of the steppe-land" in RS

17.352.12,[31] as noted by Dennis Pardee.[32] This instance points to the goddess's importance at Ugarit, as the divine name appears in an international context involving the kings of Carchemish and Ugarit. The "oath" *(māmīta)* represented in this decree between the parties is "before Ishtar of the steppe-land." Here the goddess serves as the one divine witness to the decree and its terms. The goddess, it might be deduced, may be the divine patron of the queen Ahatmilku, who is named earlier in the text (line 7), but this would exceed the evidence. Whether or not this is the case, the international character of this text is suggestive of her importance within royal circles at Ugarit. The Akkadian milieu for this international dossier of materials also suggests that the goddess was recognized across the various lands involved in this decree, perhaps with little distinction being made in this context between 'Athtart/'Ashtar/Ishtar.

As at Ugarit, at Emar 'Ashtart was a significant goddess. She is the recipient of not only a major cult (e.g., Emar 370, 460),[33] but also a major temple on Emar's highest point (Emar 42, 43, 45, 52).[34] The importance of the goddess may be gauged further by Emar 43.1, with its reference to the treasure of 'Ashtart of the city (Emar 265.11, *^{d}Inanna uru.ki*).[35] To put the goddess in the larger context at Emar, we may note her association with Dagan.[36] Daniel E. Fleming deduces that the important pair of local deities would have been the storm god and the North Syrian Hurrian Hebat, which he calls "the nearer Aleppo pairing," in contrast to Baal and 'Ashtart, which he would understand as "a distinctively Levantine (perhaps 'Canaanite') combination."[37] For the pairing of Baal and 'Ashtart, Fleming notes that the two are the recipients of temples together.[38] Although there is no further evidence as such for their pairing from Emar, Fleming points to the popularity of the personal names Zū-Ba'la and Zū-Aštarti.[39] For example, Zu-Aš-tar-ti is the name of a king (Emar 17.1,12, 41; 32.21; 256.33, etc.),[40] as well as the name of a diviner (Emar 279.5) and a priest (Emar 336.105).[41] There are also a number of other 'Ashtart names at Emar.[42] The range of the goddess's attestation is further indicated in the following section.

2. Goddess of the Hunt and Warfare

In the texts from Ugarit and Emar, the goddess is best known in her hunting capacity, with her role of warfare attested less.[43] Accordingly, the review of the goddess's roles begins with the hunt. The Ugaritic material provides literary representations of hunting, while Emar supplies ritual recognition of the hunt.

ʿAthtart and the Hunt at Ugarit

For Ugarit, an important text for ʿAthtart hunting is KTU 1.92. It is one of the very rare texts with ʿAthtart as its chief protagonist. It is presented here based on the newer readings of Pardee,[44] along with headings indicating different parts:

Tranche supérieure

1	(the text) of Ṯb'il	*d ṯbʾil[. . .]*

Recto

The Hunt of the Goddess

2	ʿAthtart the huntress . . .	*ʿṯtrt ṣwd[. . .]*
3	She goes in the outback . . .	*tlk bmdb⸢r⸣[. . .]*
4	(Her) eye looks, and there . . .	*tḥd ʿn w hl[. . .]*
5	and the deep flows[45] . . .	*wtglṯ thmt . ⸢-⸣[. . .]*
6	goes out. Its thicket (?) she desires . . .	*yṣʾi.ǵlh tḥmd[. . .]*
7	her spear[46] at the vast (area?) she . . .	*mrḥh l ʾadr t⸢-⸣[. . .]*
8	ʿAthtart sits in her thicket (?) . . .	*tṯb ʿṯtrt bǵl⸢h⸣[. . .]*
9	. . .[47] she sets to the left . . .	*qrẓ tšt . l šmʾa⸢l⸣[. . .]*
10	. . . she lifts her eyes and . . .	*ʾarbḫ . ʿnh tšʾu w ⸢-⸣[. . .]*
11	a doe that is resting (?), a bull that . . .	*ʾaylt tǵpy ṯr . ṯ⸢r⸣[. . .]*
12	. . .[48] Her spear she ta[kes . . .],	*bqr . mrḥh . tʾi⸢ḫ⸣[d . . .]*
13	Her . . . in her right hand . . .	*š⸢ḫ⸣rh bm ymn . t⸢-⸣[. . .]*
14	She (?) makes low, lord (?) . . .	*⸢- š⸣pl bʿl . ʿb⸢-⸣[. . .]*

The Feast for El's Household

15	Bull, her father, El, she serves . . .	*ṯr ʾabh ʾil . tṯr⸢m⸣[. . .]*
16	She serves Yariḫ food[49] . . .	*tšlḥm yrḫ . ggn[. . .]*
17	. . . Wise[50] . . .	*k[-]⸢-⸣rš . ḫssm[. . .]*
18	. . . ʿAthtar[t] . . .	*⸢-⸣[— —]⸢-⸣m ʿṯt⸢r⸣[t]*
19	. . .	*[ ]ṯ⸢r⸣[. . .]*

ca. 4 lines missing

Verso

The Goddess Dresses (?)

20	. . . the guardian of the vineyard	*[. . .]⸢- ⸣t b nǵr krm*
21	. . . her father, the vineyard ʾAr[51]	*[. . .] ⸢-⸣ʾabh . krm ʾar*
22	. . . a cloth of linen	*[. . .]ʾi . mḥtrt . pṯṯm*
23	. . . a vestment, cypress[52]	*[. . .]⸢— -⸣ . ʾušpǵt tʾišr*

24	. . . she raises a gleam like the stars	*[. . .]⸢-⸣mh . nš'at ẓl k kbkbm*
25	. . . like a star she . . .	*[. . .]⸢-⸣b km kbkb tk⸢-⸣n*

The Desire of Baal for ʿAthtart

26	Baal desires her, he . . .[53]	*[. . .]⸢-⸣l'a bʿl yḥmdnh . yrṯy*
27	her beauty. Dimaranu before her descends	*[. . .]⸢n⸣ʿm⸢h⸣ dmrn . lpnh yrd*
28	Mightiest Baal . . .	*[. . .]⸢'a⸣l'iy⸢n⸣ bʿl . šm⸢-⸣ rgbt . y'u*[54]
29	. . . her/his horn(s) (?)	*[. . .]⸢-⸣mn[-] w srmy ⸢-(-)-⸣rnh*
30	. . . attack (?). Pidru answers (?) her: "may she/you attack (?)	*[. . .]⸢-⸣ǵr[-]⸢-⸣nyh pdr . ttǵr*
31	. . . do not give . . .	*[. . .]⸢-⸣[ ]šrk . 'al ttn . l n*
32	. . . give to the bed (?)	*[. . .]⸢ — - ⸣tn l rbd*
33	. . . you will desire her (?)	*[. . .]⸢- ⸣ʿlthwyn*
34	. . . cloud	*[. . .]⸢-⸣ ʿrpt*
35	. . . and . . .	*[. . .]⸢-⸣n . w mn'udg*
36	. . . Mightiest Baal	*[. . .]l 'al'iyn bʿl*
37	. . . Cloud-rider . . .	*[. . .]l rkb ʿrpt*

The opening of the text names ʿAthtart as a huntress who goes into the outback (lines 2-3). She lifts her eyes and sees something; what it is seems to fall in the lacuna at the end of line 4. According to line 5, the deeps surge with water; this line may refer to some sort of celestial sign or the watery condition in the landscape (a watery terrain?), where the goddess is hunting.

In lines 6-13, the goddess seems to be involved in hunting. She desires and takes cover in the low ground (?), while she holds her weapons (lines 6-13). At line 14, she seems to fell what may be an animal named only as *bʿl* of something, perhaps horns (?). This does not seem to be the name of the god (who seems to enter the picture only in lines 26-27). Instead, given what follows in lines 15-16, *bʿl* appears to be part of a designation that refers to the animal fed to El and Yariḫ by the goddess. El is the head of the divine household, Yariḫ, the moon god known elsewhere as a member of this household (see KTU 1.114.4, discussed below). The front of the text continues, but without a clear indication of the narrative line.

The back of the tablet shows a new scene after a gap. Several nouns in lines 20-25 are discernible. Line 20 mentions the guardian of the vineyard, a figure known from KTU 4.141 III 17; in that text, he is listed with the guardian of the sown (4.141 III 16), a figure known from KTU 1.23.68-69.[55] Both of these guardians in 4.141 III 16-17 belong to the royal workers (4.141 I 1). So line 20 may reflect a mythological counterpart to this administrative role. The goddess appears to be provided with clothing in lines 22-23, followed in lines 24-25 with an expression perhaps of her appealing appearance. According to the text, she literally "raises a shadow" (*ẓlm* in KTU 1.170.8; cf. 1.161.1; cf. *ẓl ḫmt*, the "shaded pavilion" in 1.14 IV 55), like the stars. In other words, it would seem, her appearance is brilliant (cf. *ẓl ksp*, "the gleam of silver," in 1.4 III 26-28).[56]

This scene moves to Baal's desire for her, specifically for her beauty or loveliness, in lines 26-27. His title *dmrn* is known also from KTU 1.4 VII 39 and also from Philo of Byblos.[57] He seems to approach her at the end of line 27. The verb **yrd*, "to go down, descend," is more than a verb of approach, however. It may denote his approach to her in a particular space. What transpires in the remainder of the text is difficult to discern. Line 28 mentions the god again, and lines 29-30 seem to involve a discussion about a topic that is unclear. It may be that the verb **gry*, "to attack," occurs twice in these lines, and this might work with the reconstruction of **qrnh* here, "her/his horn" (cf. 1.12 II 21-25, referring to the enemies of Baal and Anat with a reference to her horns). However, this remains speculative. The figure *pdr* seems to be attested in 1.3 I 22, possibly as an attendant of Baal or a title for Baal himself.[58] The precise role of the figure is unclear. Meindert Dijkstra speculates that this figure "warns Baal not to waste his vigor in fighting, destroying the vineyard of Ari, and convinces him to prepare himself for marriage rites."[59]

Lines 31-32 contain the verb "to give" plus a noun that might refer to a bed[60] (cf. *trbd* in 1.132.2; and *mrbd*, "cover, blanket," in KTU 4.127.7; 4.270.11; 4.275.4 [?]; 4.385.9; 9.432.34[61]), though it could be the name of a person (?). Apart from the name and titles of Baal and a mention of the word "cloud," lines 33-37 provide little clear information. What is clear in this text is 'Athtart's role as huntress without any other deities. The text then follows with a section presenting Baal's desire for the goddess, a matter that will be discussed below.

Hunting activity for 'Athtart is evident also in KTU 1.114, but in this case she is paired with Anat. The readings of the text, as established by Pardee,[62] are followed here, except for his partial brackets for readings (which are left aside in this case). Instead, only a basic text and translation according to the poetic lines, along with headings are provided:

Front of the Tablet

The Drinking Party

1	El slaughtered game[63] in his house,	*ʾil dbḥ.bbth.mṣd*
1-2	game in the midst/of his palace,	*ṣd.bqrb/hklh.*
2	invited the gods to the choice cuts.[64]	*ṣḥ.lqṣ.ʾilm*

2-3	The gods ate/and drank,	*tlḥmn/ʾilm.wtštn.*
	drank wi⟨ne⟩ till they[65] were loaded,	*tštn y⟨n⟩ ʿd šbʿ*
4	new wine[66] till they were drunk.	*ṯrt.ʿd škr*
4-5	Yariḫ set/his body[67] (down) like a d[o]g,	*yʿdb.yrḫ/gbh.km.k[l]b.*
5-6	he crawled[68]/beneath the tables.	*yqṯqṯ.tḥt/ṯlḥnt*
6	The god who did know him/	*ʾil d ydʿnn/*
7	prepared food of the game for him;	*yʿdb lḥm.d mṣd lh*
7	And the one who did not know him/	*w d lydʿnn/*
8	beat him with sticks on the . . . (?) beneath./ the table	*ylmnn.ḫṭm.bq[ ] tḥt.ṯlḥn/*
9	ʿAthtart and Anat he[69] approached;/	*ʿṯtrt.wʿnt.ymǵy/*
10	ʿAthtart prepared a steak for him,/	*ʿṯtrt.tʿdb.nšb lh/*
11	And Anat a tenderloin./	*wʿnt.ktp/*
11-12	The gatekeeper/of El's house rebuked them;	*bhm.ygʿr.ṯǵr/bt.ʾil.*
12-13	Still for a dog they prepare/a steak,	*pn[70] lm[71] klb[72]. tʿdbn/nšb.*
13	prepare a shoulder-cut for a hound.[73]	*lʾinr.tʿdbn.ktp/*
14	His father El he rebuked.[74]	*bʾil.ʾabh.gʿr*
14-15	El was seated in/. . .	*yṯb.ʾil.kr/ʾašk . . .*[75] (?)
15	El was seated in his drinking-party.[76]	*ʾil.yṯb.bmrzḥh*
16	He drank wine till he was loaded,	*yšt.yn.ʿd šbʿ*
	fine wine till he was drunk.	*ṯrt.ʿd škr*

El staggers home with the help of two of his sons

17	El went to (?)[77] his house,	*ʾil.hlk.lbth.*
17-18	He made his way/to his court;	*yštql./lḥẓrh.*
18-19	Thukamuna/and Shunama helped him along;	*yʿmsn.nn.ṯkmn/wšnm.*
	and he confronted him, did the hoofed(-god),[78]	*wngšnn.ḥby.*
20	lord of horns and a tail.[79]	*bʿl.qrnm.wḏnb.*
20-21	He smeared[80] him/with his crap and his piss;[81]	*ylšn/bḫrʾih.wṯnth.*
21	El collapsed like a corpse,	*ql.ʾil.km mt*
22	El, like those who descend to the underworld.	*ʾil.kyrdm.ʾarṣ.*

Two of El's daughters go in search of ingredients to cure his hangover

22-23	Anat/and ʿAthtart hunt . . .	*ʿnt/wʿṯtrt.tṣdn.*

(Lines 23b-28 are broken. They may include the ingredients described in lines 29-31.)

The back of the tablet (beginning in line 25) issuing in El's revival

26	ʿAthtart and Anat . . .	*ʿṯtrt.w ʿnt*
27	With them they brought back stuff for him[82];	*wbhm.tṯṯb.mdh*
28	As they heal, there — he awakened.[83]	*km.trpʾa.hn nʿr*

Instructions to cure the effects of drunkenness (with a scribal line separating this section from the preceding one)

29	What one should apply[84] to his forehead:	*dyšt.llṣbh.*
	"hair of dog";[85]	*šʿr klb*
30	and (as for) the head, *pqq*;[86] and (for) his navel (as well)	*wrʾiš.pqq.wšrh*
31	one should apply together with it the juice of fresh olive.	*yšt ʾaḥdh.dm zt.ḫrpnt*[87]

The narrative is set in El's household, with lines 1-16 focussed on drinking (with lines 2-3 and 16 framing the action), and lines 17-28 centered on taking care of the dead-drunk El.[88] The game that El prepares at the outset of the text (lines 1-2) is not given any background story. The text does not tell the audience how El came to have this game, but in view of the text's later description of Anat and ʿAthtart going out to hunt,[89] it might be surmised that the two goddesses were assumed to have hunted for the game mentioned at the outset. It would also be for this reason that the two goddesses are in a position to distribute meat in lines 9-11. Here we may recall KTU 1.92.15-16, which describes ʿAthtart serving El and Yariḫ:

15	Bull, her father, El, she serves . . .	*ṯr ʾabh ʾil . tṯr⌜m⌝[. . .]*
16	She serves Yariḫ food[90] . . .	*tšlḥm yrḫ . ggn[. . .]*

These lines seem to present the sort of food service from the hunt that informs KTU 1.114. The two goddesses ʿAthtart and Anat are also the figures that distribute the meat (in lines 9-11). Afterwards, they play no role in the text until the end of the narrative (in lines 23-28), when they go hunting for ingredients to cure El's drunkenness and apparently return with them. Notably 'Athtart appears before Anat,[91] unlike their pairings elsewhere. The text then follows with instructions for curing the effects of intoxification. Broadly speaking, the cure in the prose section following the scribal line corresponds to El's heavy drinking in the poetic, mythic material. More specifically, the words for the ingredients are connected with the narrative. The "hair of the dog" is probably a plant name of the sort known in Mesopotamian medicinal texts[92] and correlates with the discussion of the dog in the narrative. It seems quite plausible also that the other ingredients are the material for which Anat and 'Athtart are said to go hunting in lines 26-27, as these seem to refer to healing, more specifically provisions for a remedy[93] (*rp') and reviving (*'rr in the *N*-stem). Thus it appears that elements of the prescription inform the general topic of the narrative as well as many of its details.

For the purposes of understanding 'Athtart, several features are notable. First, she is referenced as hunting. This hunting is presented here as a matter of medicinal ingredients, but it may also be inferred, as noted above, that this "hunting" presumes her role of hunting for game as seen explicitly in KTU 1.92. Second, in her hunting activity here, she is paired with Anat. It is to be noted that 'Athtart stands before Anat in this text in lines 9 and 26 but not in lines 22-23. This difference of order contrasts with other texts where these two goddesses appear together; in those instances, Anat precedes 'Athtart. Third, 'Athtart is presented as a member of El's household. Fourth, the two goddesses seem to apply the medicinal components so as to effect the healing. The verbal form *trp'a* in line 28 has been understood as a dual feminine verbal form;[94] if correct, the two goddesses are credited with the activity of healing.

The cultural background for the divine hunt is difficult to get at. There are some hints in the Ugaritic corpus. In Chapter Four, we saw the father's instructions to his son (KTU 1.17 V 33-39), which he presumably is to follow and which culminate in the presentation of the game in the goddess's temple (see KTU 1.18 I). A similar pattern appears later in the story (KTU 1.18 I 24, 27, 29, 30-31). Aqhat follows her instructions, ending in an assumed presentation of the game at a sanctuary, this time at the sanctuary of the moon god Yariḫ (KTU 1.18 IV). It is difficult to know how representative such a picture was as a cultural practice. Such a background might lie ultimately behind the representations of the hunt in the Ugaritic texts described.

There is one further form of the goddess possibly relevant to 'Athtart as huntress, and that is her title, 'Athtart *šd*, "'Athtart of the field" (KTU 1.91.10; 1.148.18; 4.182.55, 58), which is noted above. The specification might refer to the outback where the hunt takes place. The association of this form of the goddess follows the syllable version of the name Ishtar *ṣēri* (e.g., RS 17.352.12),[95] the second element of which is *ṣēru*, "steppe-land," as noted by Pardee.[96] The Akkadian counterpart at Ugarit is of further importance as it appears in an international context involving the courts of Carchemish and Ugarit. In sum, the two Ugaritic narrative texts, KTU 1.92 and 1.114, suggest a profile for the goddess as huntress in Ugaritic literary tradition, while the title ʿAthtart *šd* and its Akkadian counterpart point to this feature of the goddess in a broader band of texts, specifically in ritual and administrative material as well as an international decree. At this point, we turn to the Emar evidence for the goddess hunting.

ʿAshtart and the Hunt at Emar

The hunt is attested for ʿAshtart at Emar in a ritual context. Emar 452:21 refers to "the hunt of ʿAthtart" *(ṣa-du ša* ^{d}*Iš*$_8$-tár) on day 16 of the month of Abi.[97] As Fleming notes, this ritual also mentions a procession to Ashtar-sarba, which Fleming regards as an "Old Syrian form" of Eshtar/Ashtart (meaning "The Poplar-Eshtar")."[98] The two rituals on the same day of the month are, according to Fleming, "two related activities: the procession from 'the storehouse' and the 'hunt' (or 'rounds'? *ṣâdu*), both for the goddess, Aštart, under two different names." The specific agricultural activity signaled by the "storehouse" is otherwise unknown in West Semitic sources, and it may represent a particular feature of this specific manifestation of the goddess.

By contrast, the activity of the hunt is more consistent with sources not only from Ugarit, but also from additional information from Emar. According to Emar 446.87-90, "the hunt of ʿAshtart" *(ṣa-du ša* ^{d}*Iš*$_8$-tár) takes place on the sixteenth day of the month of Mar-za-ḫa-ni,[99] followed by the hunt of Baal on the next day. Fleming notes that the object of this hunt is not clarified, and he raises a number of possibilities:[100] "She could be looking for game, provision in general, or even an agricultural god who has died."[101] Fleming notes, however, against the last of these options that the hunt of the god Baal is mentioned immediately (Emar 446.91-94) after the hunt of the goddess. The ritual hunts of the goddess and the god are represented together, as double scribal lines precede line 85 and follow line 94. This juxtaposition suggests two points. First, game or provision more generally is involved. Second, the goddess and god appear in tandem, perhaps under the influence of their pairing attested elsewhere.[102] The god is known in

Ugaritic as a hunter (for example, KTU 1.10 II), but never in tandem with the goddess. In sum, the role of 'Athtart/'Ashtart as huntress is clear in sources from both Ugarit and Emar.

It is important to note that the goddess hunting is attested more broadly. A late Aramaic text written in demotic is translated by Richard C. Steiner: "Hand of my father, hand of Baal, hand of Attar my mother! . . . Face of Baal! Cover, coat his wounds (with spittle)! Face of the Huntress (and) face of Baal!"[103] Steiner understands the reference to "Attar my mother" as "the huntress" named afterwards. This text is of further interest for four points. First, it seems to work well with the picture of 'Athtart as healer with Anat in KTU 1.114, mentioned above. The role of healing is attributed also to the goddess in the London Medical Papyrus containing Northwest Semitic incantations written in hieratic syllabic script. The attested name *ʾ-s-t-t-r* is somewhat ambiguous (it may be Ishtar), but given that it is accompanied with the name Eshmun, it would appear preferable to see the name of a West Semitic goddess.[104] Second, the pairing with Baal is suggestive of their relationship, as noted further below. Third, "face of Baal" is mentioned in association with the goddess, a feature that is well known in other contexts and that will also be discussed below. Fourth and finally, the late Aramaic text suggests an ongoing Levantine tradition of the goddess as huntress down through the latter part of the first millennium.[105]

War

'Athtart and warfare: Ugaritic evidence

The evidence for 'Athtart at Ugarit as a warrior is circumstantial. She is depicted in KTU 1.2 I 40 as helping to restrain the god Baal:

[His right hand (?)'An]at seized,	*[ymnh (?).ʿn]t.tʾuḫd*
His left hand 'Athtart seized.	*šmʾalh.tʾuḫd.ʿṯtrt*

As in the hunt in KTU 1.114, here in this description of physical confrontation, 'Athtart is paired with Anat, who is better attested as a warrior (the parade instance being KTU 1.3 II noted in the preceding chapter).

In connection with the goddess as a warrior, it is tempting to relate the reference to *ʿṯtrt* in KTU 1.86, "dream-book" *(s[p]r ḥlmm)*, as it is called in line 1. Mentioned in line 6 are horses of *ʿṯtrt*. While in theory this could be either a place name or goddess, the second option seems likelier in view of the mention of Baal in line 3.[106] Perhaps her horses suggest an assumption of the goddess as a warrior. In support for this notion may be ʿAthtart represented on horseback in Egyptian iconography.[107]

Ashtart and warfare: evidence from Emar

The Emar evidence points to the goddess as a warrior, for example, in her widespread title Ashtart *ša tāḫāzi*, "'Ashtart of combat" (Emar 370:20; 373:12; 379:1; 380.2; 381:11; 382.1, 6; 460.1, 6, 9; 495:3′; Westenholz[108] #30.1). Emar 460 mentions this Ashtart several times:

> Line 1: "This tablet is of the cry of Ashtart of combat"
> Line 6: "consecration of Ashtart of combat"
> Line 9: consecration of the priest of Ashtart of combat
> (cf. line 25: Ashtart du piétinement)

Joan Goodnick Westenholz comments: "The cult of ʿAštarte-of-Battle was probably the basis of the ʿAštarte cult in Emar; her priestess seems to have been the *maš'artu* and the principal participants in her night festival were known as 'men-of-battle.' "[109] Evidence for Ashtart as a martial figure also extends to the onomasticon: *Aštartu-qarrād*, "Ashtaru is a warrior" (PN *Aš-tar-ti*-ur.sag, 215.15);[110] and *Aštartu-lit*, "Ashtartu is power."[111]

The goddess as warrior is attested elsewhere. A Late Bronze seal from Bethel depicts the goddess as a warrior and includes the spelling of her name in hieroglyphs.[112] She is also famous as one of the West Semitic war goddesses in New Kingdom Egypt.[113] She is called "furious and tempestuous" in "Astarte and the Sea," a local Egyptian version of a West Semitic myth.[114] 1 Sam. 31:10 (cf. 1 Chr. 10:10) might reflect the idea of the goddess as a divinity of warfare, as the armor of Saul won in battle is put by the Philistines into her temple.[115] The curse in the treaty of Esarhaddon with Baal of Tyre invokes her: "May Astarte break your bow in the thick of battle, and have you crouch at the feet of your enemy."[116] This characterization comports closely with Ishtar's title as "lady of battle and war" from the same period.[117] In this connection, it is to be noted that in the Aramaic text noted above, the goddess ʿAthtart and the god Baal appear as divine aids against "our enemy," the scorpion that has bitten. This role is analogous to divine combat against cosmic or divine enemies in the Ugaritic texts.

3. 'Athtart's Relations with Other Deities

'Athtart's relationships with other deities are somewhat indicative of her warrior nature. A brief treatment of her relations with a number of other deities is provided, in order to flesh out this side of her character.[118]

Relationship to the Storm God

Pairing?

Circumstantial evidence for the pairing of Baal and 'Ashtart at Emar (especially in the rituals of the hunt in Emar 446) has been noted above. As Fleming observes, her temple appears to be paired with Baal's, and although there is no further evidence as such for their pairing from Emar, Fleming has noted the popularity of the personal names Zū-Baʿla and Zū-Aštarti.[119]

The Ugaritic evidence is scant at best. Above, KTU 1.92 is cited in full. If *rbd* in line 32 of this text were a bed, especially in the wake of Baʿl's desire (**ḥmd* in line 26 and perhaps **hwy* in line 33; cf. KTU 1.5 I 14; 1.133.4), this section might suggest a sexual relationship between Baʿl and a second party, perhaps 'Athtart. This is, of course, the very sort of speculation that scholars have criticized about older sexual interpretations of other Ugaritic texts naming Baal and Anat.[120] At the same time, such well-placed criticism does not answer the question about the figure with whom Baal is engaging in sexual relations, either in those texts or possibly here (assuming such relations are involved in this context). It may be suspected but can hardly be confirmed that Baʿl and 'Athtart were thought to engage in sexual relations in this passage. If this hypothetical reconstruction were correct, it would explain Baal's desire in this text. It might also help to understand 'Athtart as a recipient of sacrifice in 1.148.16, a text that may bear the heading in line 1, "for the family (?) of Baʿlu."[121] However, it must be reiterated that this is highly speculative.

In general, there is no particularly firm evidence for the god and goddess as consorts, as held by some scholars.[122] At the same time, this notion of Baal and 'Athtart as a couple would fit roughly contemporary as well as later evidence for Baʿl and the goddess. However, the data are scant at best. In the New Kingdom Egyptian text sometimes called "The Contest of Horus and Seth for the Rule," Anat and Astarte are regarded as divine daughters as well as would-be wives of Seth,[123] although the view has been debated by Egyptologists.[124]

There is also later evidence for the goddess as Ba'l's consort to be considered. A Neo-Punic dedicatory inscription from Mididi in Tunisia (12 km. west of Maktar) reads:

mqdš bn' l'štrt št b'l	Sanctuary built for 'Ashtart consort of Baal;
bn' b'l' hmyddm	the citizens of Mididi built (it).[125]

A similar picture seems to inform a description of the two deities in Philo of Byblos: "Greatest Astarte and Zeus, called both Demarous and Adodos, king of gods, were ruling over the land with the consent of Kronos."[126] Here Astarte appears with Zeus Demarous/Adodos, in other words, Ba'l. In sum, there is little explicit evidence of their pairing from early sources[127] or in later material. So it must be emphasized that there are few indications of their relationship thematized as a matter of consort relations. It is possible that what little evidence we have may point in the direction of the relationship as a particularly Levantine phenomenon. As noted above, Fleming sees this pairing as a coastal (possibly Canaanite) phenomenon, one not necessarily native to inland Emar. This situation would also serve to explain a better-known phenomenon regarding the two deities, namely the goddess as "the name" of the god attested also around the Mediterranean basin, as well as her adoption among the Philistines (1 Sam. 31:10/1 Chr. 10:10).

'Athtart as the "Name of Ba'l" and "Face of Ba'l"

The goddess as the "name of Ba'l" is well known from two parallel passages involving a curse, KTU 1.2 I 7-8 = 1.16 VI 55-57:

"May [Horan] bre[ak, O Yamm],	*yṯb[r.ḥrn.yymm]*
[May Horan break your head,	*[yṯbr.ḥrn/r'išk.*
'Athtart, Na[me of Ba'l, your skull.]"	*'ṯtrt.š[m.b'l.qdqdk]*
"May Horan break, my son,	*yṯbr/ḥrn.ybn.*
May Horan break your head,	*yṯbr.ḥrn r'išk.*
'Athtart, Name of Ba'l, your skull."	*'ṯtrt.šm.b'l.qdqdk*

As many commentators have noted, the goddess also bears the title "name of Baal," *šm b'l*, in a fifth-century Phoenician royal inscription from Sidon (KAI 14:18).[128]

There is some possible evidence that this notion was known in Egypt as well. According to James K. Hoffmeier and Kenneth A. Kitchen, *ʿstrt rn*, "Astarte name," on a private votive stele from Tell el-Borg is a reference to Astarte as the "name of Baal."[129] As noted above, a late Aramaic text written in demotic attests to the "face of Baal," but with some elaborations. As noted above, the relevant lines are translated: "Hand of my father, hand of Baal, hand of Attar my mother! . . . Face of Baal! Cover, coat his wounds (with spittle)! Face of the Huntress (and) face of Baal!"[130] It would seem that this text preserves an older usage of ʿAthtart as "the face of Baal," an expression famously attested in Phoenician-Punic texts predicated of Tnt as *pn bl* (KAI 78:2; 79:1, 10-11; 85:1; 86:1; 87:2; 88:1; 137:1) and *pʿn bʿl* in KAI 94:1; 97:1; 102:1; and 105:1 and in Greek transcriptions as *phanē bal* (KAI 175:2) and *phenē bal* (KAI 176:2-3).[131]

"Tnt, face of Bal" is also paired with the god Baal (KAI 78:2; 79:1-2), more commonly *bʿl ḥmn* (KAI 85:1-2; 86:1-2; 88:1-2; 94:1-2; 97:1-2; 102:1-2; 105:1; 137:1).[132] In view of the new evidence from Egypt provided by Steiner, it might be tempting to identify Tnt as Astarte, but the two are named as separate goddesses in KAI 81:1; thus they appear to be distinguished.[133] At the same time, in view of the ambiguities of the evidence, perhaps it is possible that if Tnt is a title (its meaning remains *sub iudice*), then perhaps it was enjoyed by more than one figure in different locales and times. James Pritchard published an inscription from Sarepta dedicating a statue "to Tnt-ʿAshtart" *(ltntʿštrt)*.[134] Pritchard suggested that Tnt and ʿAshtart here were identified in the form of a double name or "there is an implied conjunction between the two divine names . . . both of whom were served in the same shrine."[135] Choon-Leong Seow favors the first view suggested by Pritchard: "it is possible that role of ʿAthtart/ʿAštart in the Eastern Mediterranean world was replaced in North Africa by the goddess Tnt."[136] This conclusion would work well with the evidence noted by Steiner. The passage is unusual in mentioning the god and goddess together with this "face" and "hand." This text is expansive in its usage compared with the prior cases of "name of Baʿl" that scholars have observed.

The meaning of these expressions, "name of Baal," and "face of Baal," remains a matter of discussion.[137] P. Kyle McCarter refers to these sorts of expressions as "hypostases" and sees them as representing the "cultically available presence in the temple of the god."[138] It is true that the "name" of the deity is a cultically attested divine feature in Ps. 29:2 and is suggestive of McCarter's view, at least in some instances. For "the name of Baal," I have compared PNs that consist of the same formation, for example, *šmbʿl*

(KTU 4.116.7; 4.682.8).[139] This name seems to denote this person's identity, as "name" does elsewhere[140] in relationship to the god in a manner analogous to the goddess's designation as *šm bʿl*. Accordingly, this title denotes the goddess's identity marked in relation to the god. This view may be combined with McCarter's interpretation. It could also accommodate the notion of the goddess as "the face of Baal," given the use of "face" for presence (cf. Ps. 42:3[2]).[141]

In a recent survey of the evidence for the "name" in Ugaritic, Theodore J. Lewis understands KTU 1.2 IV 28 as "By/With the Name, ʿAthtartu hexed (Yammu)."[142] For Lewis, the "name" is a weapon magically wielded by the goddess, and accordingly he ties this usage with her title "name of Baal." As noted by Lewis, there are other understandings of 1.2 IV 28. In KTU 1.114.14, the verb in question *(gʿr)* takes the preposition *b-*, which if applicable in this instance would not work as well with Lewis's interpretation of KTU 1.2 IV 28. It is thus unclear that the "name" is a weapon in this case, although this interpretation is not to be excluded. In sum, "name" denotes identity, while "face" suggests presence. The question remains: in what manner does the goddess ʿAthtart express or participate in the identity of the god Baal?

Combination with Anat

There is relatively little evidence for Anat in the cult of Emar.[143] By contrast, Ugaritic evidence for Anat and ʿAthtart in combination together is widespread. In several instances, Anat precedes ʿAthtart; the major exception is 1.114, with its multiple references to ʿAthtart and Anat. The two goddesses appear linked by *w*, "and," in two incantational texts, KTU 1.100.20 and 1.107.20, as well as the narrative of 1.114.9, 22-23, and 26. For example, KTU 1.100.20 represents one listing among many for deities: *ʿnt w{.}[[x]]ṯtrt ʾinbbh*, "Anat and ʿAthtart at Inbb." What is special about ʿAthtart in this instance is that her name is combined with Anat's. Otherwise, this text only contains double-barreled names of deities, which is perhaps the reason why Pardee translates "Anatu-wa-ʿAthtartu," as if it were a single name.[144] The destination is Anat's home at Inbb and not ʿAthtart's. Not only a pairing of the two goddesses is involved, but relative to Anat, ʿAthtart here seems secondary to her. Is ʿAthtart here part of a fuller expression of the identity of Anat at Inbb, or is she added here to fit her into the larger scheme of the text?

In the same text, in KTU 1.100.77-79, her name appears in an instruction: "After Reshep, (add) ʿAthtart, (namely) 'to ʿAthtart at Mari, my incantation for a snake-bite.'" As this instruction indicates, these lines, written on the side of the tablet, were meant to be read with the full formulary as the other entries and would be read after line 34 and before line 35, which begins the next section.[145] It seems that ʿAthtart may have been a bit of an afterthought in lines 20 and 78. The first instance involves ʿAthtart of Ugarit, while in the second, ʿAthtart at Mari would seem to point in the direction of the figure of ʿAthtart as well known at Mari, namely Ishtar at Mari. We will return to this figure below.

The second of the two snakebite incantations also pairs Anat and ʿAthtart. In KTU 1.107.39, the wish is expressed: "May Anat and ʿAthtart gather the venom." This wish follows the same wish for [Baal?] and Dagan, and it precedes the same wish made of Yarih and Resheph. The wishes are all structured here in the form of pairs. While the reason for each pairing may not be obvious, it might not be surprising for Anat and ʿAthtart, in view of their involvement in healing in KTU 1.114. It is to be noted that once again Anat precedes ʿAthtart in the pairing. This is the usual order of the goddesses' names in the Ugaritic texts, as has been noted.

A few texts also show the two goddesses in poetic parallelism, for example, KTU 1.2 I 40: "[His right hand?] Anat seized,//His left hand ʿAthtart seized." Comparable poetic parallelism may be seen in KTU 1.14 III 41-42 = 1.14 VI 26-28, in its physical comparison of the human Huray with the two goddesses:

. . . whose loveliness is like the loveliness of Anat,	*dk nʿm ʿnt nʿmh*
whose beauty is like the beauty of ʿAthtart.[146]	*km tsm ʿṯtrt tsmh*

We may note at this point this feature of her beauty, which seems to be mentioned also in 1.92.27 according to Pardee's reading, *[. . .]⌜n⌝ʿm⌜h⌝*. Beauty is a hallmark of the young warrior goddesses. The parade example of the two goddesses together is KTU 1.114.10-11,[147] which connects them both syntactically and by parallelism:

ʿAthtart and Anat he approached;	*ʿṯtrt wʿnt ymǵy*
ʿAthtart had prepared a steak for him,	*ʿṯtrt tʿdb nšb lh*
And Anat a tenderloin.	*wʿnt ktp*

Overall, the pairing of the two goddesses seems to be based on their shared roles as beautiful, hunting warrior-goddesses.[148]

Combination with Rashpu (Resheph)

There is no evidence on this score for Emar, but Ugaritic contains some possible hints in this direction. ʿAthtart seems to be mentioned with Rashpu (possibly Rashapu), perhaps because of their shared capacity as deities of warfare.[149] At the same time, it is to be noted that the Ugaritic evidence is not terribly extensive. We begin with the administrative text KTU 4.219.2-3. Its first two listings of wine (*yn,* line 1), by jars (as suggested by *kdm* and *kd* in subsequent lines), are devoted to these deities:

> Eighteen [(jars) for] the house of ʿAthtart
> Thirteen (jars) [for the h]ouse of Rashpu-*gn*

KTU 1.91 lists wine (*yn,* line 1) apparently for various occasions.[150] Lines 10-11 give the occasion for ʿAthtart and for the Rashpus:

> (for) when ʿAthtart *šd* enters the house of the king.
> (for) when the Rashpus *(ršpm)* enter *(tʿrbn)* the house of the king.[151]

The Rashpus may either be the retinue of the god or the collectivity of the god's manifestations. It is unclear if there is any consistent reason for the listing in this text. We may also note the warrior gods, Baal in line 14 and Rashpu *ṣbʾi* in line 15. The pairing of Rashpu and ʿAthtart in Ugaritic also fits with their mention together in one of Amenhotep's inscriptions: "Rashap and Astarte were rejoicing in him for doing all that his heart desired."[152] A private votive stele from Tell el-Borg likewise mentions the two deities and depicts them as well.[153]

We may mention one final possible correspondence between the two deities, in this case one involving their attribute animals. Above we saw in RIH 98/02 evidence for the lion as the emblem animal for the goddess. In his study of Rashap,[154] Edward Lipiński mentions Rashap *gn* being attested on a clay rhyton in the form of "a face of a lion," as mentioned in the inscription on the object, KTU 6.62.[155] Yigael Yadin had suggested that the form of the lion was selected because this may have been the god's emblem animal.[156] This representation is perhaps analogous to the lioness as the emblem of a corresponding warrior-goddess, an issue that we will examine below. In sum, the amount of evidence for this pairing is not particularly great, yet it comports reasonably well with what is known of the two deities.

ʿAthtart in the Household of El

Relatively little has been made by scholars of ʿAthtart's place in the household of El. As noted earlier, KTU 1.114 pairs ʿAthtart with Anat within the scene of El's household.[157] KTU 1.92, it was also seen, shows ʿAthtart providing game for El and Yarih. Otherwise, neither text provides much sense of ʿAthtart within El's household. Thankfully, line 3 in the new hymn to ʿAthtart (RIH 98/02), which is presented more fully in the next section, provides further information on this score: *tṣpq lḥt d gr ʾil*, "May she shut the jaw of El's attackers."

This translation for the line requires some explanation. Pardee translates line 3: "She has banged shut the maw of the whelp of El." In his scenario, ʿAthtart is the opponent to El's "whelp," a figure that Pardee compares with the various divine enemies of Baal associated with El in KTU 1.3 III 43-46. Pardee also compares the filial duties in Aqhat (KTU 1.17 I 28-29; II 2-3, 18-19, and reconstructed for 1.17 I 47), which include to "shut the jaws *(lḥt)* of his (father's) detractors." In both this line from Aqhat and in RIH 98/02, the agent is to act against aggressors who would oppose the patriarchal household (in one case, Danil's, and in the other, El's). In both cases, the protection provided against such aggressors is cast in terms of either "shutting the jaws" or "striking the jaws" of such potentially threatening parties. This parallel from the story of Aqhat, as noted by Pardee, would suggest that the direct object represents El's enemies and not, as he suggests, his favored "whelp" (like the cosmic enemies named in 1.3 III 43-46). Accordingly, *gr* here would not be "whelp," namely one of El's beloveds, but instead an "attacker" (cf. *gr*, "to attack," in KTU 1.119.26; BH **gwr II/*grh*). In this interpretation, this text casts ʿAthtart in the role of filial defender of the patriarch and his household.

This role attributed to the goddess may be contrasted with the filial duties in Aqhat on one important score. In Aqhat this role is represented as a typically male role, namely a duty of the son. In the hymn to ʿAthtart, it is the goddess who defends the patriarchal household of El. What we see here may be another inversion of roles between the human and divine spheres. We noted in the preceding chapter that while most divine roles are maintained along gender lines as known in human society,[158] gender inversion is involved with the roles of hunting and warfare. In these capacities, human women are not expected to play a role, but here divine females excel.[159] The protection of the divine household here may reflect a comparable inversion between the divine and human levels.

4. The Warrior Attribute Animal of ʿAthtart

A related expression of the goddesses as warriors involves their emblem animals. There is one particularly important text about ʿAthtart on this score, one that includes a very rare indication of the goddess's attribute animal. The attribute animal[160] of ʿAthtart has been a longstanding issue. A number of scholars[161] have argued for this goddess as the lioness or "lion-lady" (an expression in Ugaritic and on inscribed arrowheads, to which we will return shortly). A recently published Ugaritic text offers a fresh contribution to the question. The text in question is RIH 98/02, lines 1-5, which contains a hymn to ʿAthtart:[162]

1	The name of ʿAthtart let[163] my voice sing,	*šm ʿṯtrt ql yšr*
2	I will praise the name of the lion.	*ʾiḏmr šm lbʾi.*
	O name, may you be victorious over . . .[164]	*šm tkšd l[. . .]*
3	May you/she shut the jaw of El's attackers.	*tṣpq*[165] *lḥt d gr ʾil*
4	A great[166] panther[167] is ʿAthtart,	*nmr ḥṯrt ʿṯtrt*
5	A great panther that pounces.	*nmr ḥṯrt trqṣ*

These lines contain three bicola in parallelism.[168] This observation has guided the translation for lines 1-2, which may contain a first person referent (cf. Pardee's rendering of line 1: "May the name of ʿAthtaru be sung"). In line 2a, it is important to note that *lbʾi* is masculine.[169] Here the word serves as a description for the goddess. It is unclear why **lbʾit* is not used instead (see below for forms with *-t*); perhaps it is metaphorical. The same question does not apply to the predication of the term *nmr* to the goddess in lines 4 and 5, since this noun is modified by a feminine adjective. Thus *nmr* there would appear to be unmarked with respect to gender; perhaps *lbʾi* is used similarly in line 2a. For line 2b, Pardee proposes: "by (her) name she is victorious over." Pardee's translation arguably involves two issues: the lack of "her" and a preposition corresponding to "by" (cf. *bšm* in KTU 1.2 IV 28), though Pardee's translation is hardly impossible. As an alternative, *šm* is taken as a vocative and the verb as second person singular.[170] This interpretation entails no grammatical difficulties. Line 3 has been discussed in the preceding section. The parallelism of lines 4-5 might suggest an asyndetic relative clause for the second line, although Pardee's rendering is possible: "(As) a mighty panther does she pounce."

Overall, lines 1-3 of RIH 98/02 emphasize the goddess and her name.

Lewis ties this use of "name" with her title as "the name of Baal," as noted above. It is comparable with the PN *šmlb'i* (KTU 4.63 IV 13). Given the Ugartic usage in RIH 98/02, this Ugaritic PN would appear to allude to 'Athtart as the lioness (cf. *šmlb'u* in KTU 4.366.13, 14; note also *šmb'l* in 4.116.7; 4.682.8; and Amorite *su-mu-la-ba*).[171] Line 2 also calls her "lioness," which fits with the metaphor in lines 4-5 comparing her with a "panther." Pardee nicely notes the comparative evidence for related goddesses as leonine figures.[172] This hymn to 'Athtart, RIH 98/02, provides the first clear evidence for the West Semitic goddess as a lioness. This hymn also uses additional leonine language *(nmr)* to describe 'Athtart. This evidence would tend to support claims of related imagery as belonging to this goddess (although other goddesses associated with conflict cannot be definitively excluded). 'Athtar seems to be called *lb'u* in KTU 1.24.30 (see also 1.2 III 20), which parallels possible evidence for 'Athtart as *lb'u*.[173]

This language may hold implications for other leonine imagery, in particular the PN "servant of the Lioness," *'bdlb't* in the old Canaanite arrowheads[174] and *'bdlb'it* in Ugaritic (KTU 4.63 III 38; RS 94.2290.11; RS 94.2275 II 7).[175] This type of name, **'bd* plus divine name or title, is common in West Semitic languages.[176] In the Amarna letters, this name type appears in the name of not only the famous figure Abdi-Ashirti, but also of the lesser-known Abdi-Ashtarti (EA 63:3; 64:3; 65:3). Given the structure of the name *'bdlb't*, it has long been thought that the element **lb't*, "lioness," is a title for a goddess.

The identification of the goddess associated with **lb't* on the arrowheads has been discussed at considerable length for over a half century. In 1954, Frank Moore Cross suggested that Athirat is the goddess in question, based largely on his assumption that Athirat is to be identified with Qudshu, since the Winchester plaque names Qudshu along with Astarte and Anat[177] and because Qudshu is represented as standing on a lion on Egyptian stelae dedicated to her at Deir el-Medinah.[178] Cross later entertained 'Athtart and Anat as possibilities. In 1959, Levy Yitzhaq Rahmani identified the element **lb't* in the arrowheads with Sekhmet-Astarte.[179] In 1983, Michael L. Barré also arrived at the identification with 'Ashtart. He reasons that since Ishtar is a lioness and Ishtar is identified with 'Ashtart, 'Ashtart is the best candidate for West Semitic lion-lady.[180]

The identification of specific goddesses with the lion has attracted criticism, in particular from Steve A. Wiggins.[181] As his survey indicated, the major problem in the claim was the weakness of the evidence. The situation is now rectified in part by the Ugaritic hymn to 'Athtart. She appears to be the female leonine figure in both this text and quite likely also **lb'it* ("lioness") in the PNs from Ugarit. In view of this evidence, she is perhaps then the referent also in the element **lb't* in PNs in the Iron I inscribed arrowheads.

The name of Anat also appears in several arrowheads, including one mid–eleventh century El-Khadr V arrowhead: "(arrow of) *'bd-lb't,* (son of) *bn-'nt.*"[182] The PN *bn 'nt* appears not only in arrowheads, but also in Judg. 3:31; 5:6.[183] Accordingly, it may be surmised that Anat was a divine patroness of warriors.[184] As this arrowhead might suggest, Anat may be named in distinction from the "lioness" *(lb't).* As there is no particular evidence for Anat as leonine and Asherah is not represented as a warrior, the best candidate for *lb'it* in the inscribed arrowheads is 'Ashtart. As suggested by the two names on El-Khadr V, it may be then that both of the two warrior-goddesses were divine patrons of warriors in the arrowheads.

The evidence of the Ugaritic hymn to 'Athtart may hold implications also for leonine iconography. Particularly notable in this regard are figurines with a leonine face and a female, human body.[185] The first example was discovered at Beth-Shean more than four decades ago. Rahmani thought that it might represent a woman with a cult-mask.[186] He also believed that this figurine was not the emblem of any goddess as such, but "represents a woman who wishes to have a child, and who, for that purpose, identifies herself with Hathor-Astarte, and with Sekhmet-Astarte."[187] Rahmani like others after him interpreted these figurines in terms of the Egyptian goddess, the lion-headed Sekhmet,[188] but he also considered the possibility of interpreting these lion-headed female figurines in terms of Ashtart (Astarte) in the form of a lioness.[189] (Rahmani also believed that Sekhmet and Astarte were identified and assimilated to one another.) He identified the "lion-lady" of the inscribed arrowheads with this goddess. Additional examples discovered afterwards are relevant. A Late Bronze IIA clay figurine from Tel Rehov (stratum D-9b) shows a lion face with a female, human body.[190] Another example was found in excavations from Iron I Jerusalem.[191] This figurine tradition continued into the Iron Age IIA/B, represented by an example from Tel el-Zira'a (located on the eastern side of the Jordan south of the Yarmuk River).[192]

Similar difficulties affect the interpretation of the iconography on a ceramic box from Tel Rehov, found in Area C, Building F, stratum IV, and dated to the ninth century.[193] Measuring 15 in. wide and 11 in. in height, the box on its top-front edge shows an animal figure lying in a prone position, with its front limbs outstretched. The end of each limb is represented with nails extended and set on a human head. The deeply cut, rendered paws and nails of the crouching animal of the Tel Rehov model shrine recall the "deeply cut, schematically rendered paws"[194] on the Taanach stand with the two series of crouching lions.[195] Although the head of the animal on the Tel Rehov model is unclear, the extended nails on the depiction of the crouching animal representation may point to a leonine figure. According to Amihai Mazar and Nava Panitz-Cohen, the open mouth and dangling tongue are also common leonine motifs.[196] The gender of the lion figuration is unclear. Under this figure, the box has a large opening, which suggests either the modeling of the entrance of a shrine or perhaps the opening for the placement of a divine image within the box.[197] Mazar and Panitz-Cohen suggest that the religious, artistic background is pre-Israelite and Syrian.[198] They conclude: "The entire creation seems to have been a local product, tailor-made for a specific local ritual. We cannot know if a mythological or some other narrative prompted this dramatic scene."[199]

Comparison with similar-looking representations does not clarify the nature or gender of the animal. One fragment (apparently of a cult stand) excavated in 1999 from Pella (Tell Husn), in Jordan, shows a somewhat similar figure (though standing), with an animal head and outstretched top limbs.[200] However, it might represent a human figure (in mask?) with hands raised up. Moreover, the context of this figure is unclear (a cult stand?). The style of the animal figure in prone position with front limbs extended appears also on the lip of a large chalice from Cyprus (perhaps Kition?), dating to the Archaic Period (ca. 750-475 B.C.E.).[201] Below the animal's right limb is a human pipe-player (a second pipe-player seems to have broken off the chalice under the animal's left front limb). In this case, the animal figure is not menacing toward the human figures; on the contrary, the pipe-players perhaps offer music on behalf of or even to the animal, if it reflects a deity.[202]

The Iron IIA ceramic box from Tel Rehov and its leonine representation are difficult to interpret. If the box was intended to symbolize a shrine model or a box for a divine image to be housed, then the leonine figure is perhaps to guard against inimical human intrusion. In this approach, the leonine figure would be exercising power against the human figures. A deity with a leonine emblem animal may be involved. The box may constitute a scene of the deity represented by her or his emblem animal threatening humans. The position of the nails set on the two human heads might constitute an iconographical analogue to RIH 98/02, line 3, noted above: "May you/she shut the jaw of El's attackers" *(tṣpq lḥt d gr ʾil)*. To be sure, the iconographic representation of nails positioned on human heads differs from the text referring to the jaws of human enemies. At the same time, both iconography and text would represent an aggressive posture assumed by the animal entity against potential enemies.

These Iron Age iconographic depictions bear little context that clarifies the constellation of their symbolic associations. By contrast, the Late Bronze Age context at Ugarit furnishes a rich environment for understanding the emblem animals associated with various deities. Moving from Ugarit's texts and iconography to the inscriptions on the Iron I arrowheads entails a major shift in the degree of information available, and yet a further difference is incurred by the iconography from Tel Rehov, Pella, and Cyprus. The same may be said of the female flanked by lions on the famous Taanach stand,[203] which in view of RIH 98/02.1-5 may be interpreted as ʿAthtart.[204] By comparison with the Ugaritic material, these pieces are lacking in a surrounding context that might provide insight into the constellation of symbolism informing their representations. In any case, any judgment about the leonine figures in the iconography involves a significant extrapolation. Still, it remains worthwhile to offer a provisional hypothesis: if any of these involves a female representation of a divinity and if the animal involved is leonine, then the best candidate seems to be ʿAthtart, especially in light of RIH 98/02. At this point, we have reached the end of our considerations of these issues.

From this chapter as well as Chapter Four, it is evident that Anat and ʿAthtart provided models of warfare as well as relationships with human male warriors. The story of Aqhat discussed in Chapter Four dramatizes his relationship with Anat. One aspect of this narrative involves Aqhat's father, whose title, "man of Rp'u," explicitly links him to the Rephaim tradition. In Chapter Five, the Rephaim texts associate the warrior Rephaim to the monarchy. They are represented as the antecedents to the royal line, and they embody its heroic ideals. In Chapter Six, we saw how in the Baal Cycle, the god Baal could provide a model for Ugarit's warriors in his defeat of his cosmic enemies and an ideal for the monarchy in his quest for kingship. Indeed, as these chapters in Part III suggest, most of the Ugaritic literary texts involve warriors. All of the heroic poems of ancient Ugarit are associated in one way or another with monarchy as well.[205] Part III of our study generally shows how heroic poetry served to express warrior ideals supportive of the monarchy.

In the context of Iron I Israel, aspects of warrior culture were no less important, yet they would play out rather differently, as we will see in Part IV. Where the Ugaritic texts show various components of warrior culture at home in the royal establishment at Ugarit, in earliest Israel its warrior culture was operative in a tribal context, as suggested by Judges 5. In this respect, the contexts of warrior culture at Ugarit and in early Israel could not be more different. This story of heroic poetry in early Israel down through the tenth century and beyond is the subject of Part IV of this study, to which we now turn.

PART IV

Israelite Warrior Poetry in the Early Iron Age

CHAPTER EIGHT

Introduction to Early Israelite Poetry: The Problem of Dating "Old Poetry" and the Poem of Judges 5

1. Introduction to "Old Poetry" and Its Dating

At the center of the Bible's witness to early Israel is a group of biblical poems that have often been dubbed "old poetry." Many of these poems thought to be old are embedded in the prose corpus of Genesis through Kings (the poems in Genesis 49; Exodus 15; Numbers 23–24; Deuteronomy 32–33; Judges 5; 1 Samuel 2; 2 Samuel 1 and 22–23), while others appear in other parts of the Bible (e.g., Psalms 29 and 68, as well as Habakkuk 3). The topic is an old one, addressed by a number of scholars including W. F. Albright.[1] His efforts go back to and reflect his response to his teacher, Paul Haupt.[2] A number of European scholars, such as Sigmund Mowinckel, also took up the subject with the Balaam oracles and other poems.[3] The subject, at least in the United States, gained considerable prominence, thanks to one of the two dissertations produced by Frank Moore Cross and David Noel Freedman.[4] At the same time, matters of old grammar were taken up by a number of scholars, such as H. L. Ginsberg and E. Y. Kutscher. In their hands, specific points of grammar and lexicon were used to support the agenda of detecting and establishing "old poetry."[5] Kutscher in particular developed a contrast between the grammatical features of old Hebrew (generally premonarchic in date) and standard biblical Hebrew (the monarchic period). This model fits with the approach of Cross and Freedman in understanding "old poetry" as the basic corpus exemplifying "old Hebrew." The method of Kutscher was taken up by a number of scholars, including Shlomo Morag[6] and Avi Hurvitz.[7]

The approach of Cross and Freedman was also consolidated in the 1966 Yale dissertation by David A. Robertson, directed by Marvin Pope and published in 1972 under the title *Linguistic Evidence in Dating Early Poetry.*[8] Several scholars, including Cross and his student Baruch Halpern,[9] heralded Robertson's results.[10] In North America and in Israel as well, the high date of the old poems came to be viewed as well established.[11] In addition, there has been a strain of European scholarship that has viewed the poems as old. This can be seen already for Judges 5 in the 1835 commentary of Gottlieb Ludwig Studer,[12] C. F. Burney's 1918 commentary on Judges,[13] and in the more recent publications of Johannes C. de Moor and Heinz-Dieter Neef.[14]

By contrast, a number of Continental scholars argue for a later dating for the so-called old poems, such as Judges 5. For example, Giovanni Garbini placed the date of Judges 5 between the Gezer Calendar in the tenth century and eighth-century Hebrew,[15] and in this Garbini was followed by J. Alberto Soggin.[16] Michael Waltisberg militates for a later dating, to the fifth to the third centuries, based on what he sees as Aramaisms in Judges 5.[17] Endorsing Waltisberg's findings, Christoph Levin follows suit with his literary-redactional approach to the poem.[18] Ernst Axel Knauf proposes a tenth-century date, based on what he calls the archaisms and "Gileadisms" (comparing the Balaam inscription, specifically the *-în* ending on *middîn* in v. 10[19] and **mḥq* in v. 26),[20] suggesting a provenience in the court of "a tribal king."[21] Knauf thinks Eshbaal or Jeroboam I could be that king. (I will argue at the end of this chapter that the final composition of Judges 5 fits this setting.) More recently, Ian Young has voiced questions about the *terminus ad quem* for grammatical archaism.[22] He also directed the now-published doctoral dissertation produced by Robyn Vern, which strongly criticizes the linguistic arguments for high dating of the so-called old poetry.[23]

2. Assessment of Criteria and Method

As the differences among these authors indicate, the problem of dating Judges 5 based on grammatical features is particularly acute.[24] We may note a number of specific features in the poem that have been claimed to be signs of antiquity. William L. Moran cites the divine title *zeh sînay* in v. 5.[25] However, this epithet lacks for comparanda that would fix its time frame. Indeed, like many commentators including Cross, Knauf compares Nabatean Dushara, and on that basis, he suggests a fifth-century date for *zeh sînay.*[26] Kutscher focused on the second feminine singular perfect in 5:7, *šaqqamtî,* to which I will return shortly; this feature, too, has parallels in later Hebrew.[27] Robertson was struck by the possible antiquity of the "energic indicative" in

5:29a,[28] despite its notable usages in later Hebrew, in Deut. 32:13; Prov. 18:14; Ps. 8:5; Mic. 6:6.[29] Halpern concluded that the "case for Judges 5 is especially strong," based on the locative sense of *ʾăšer* in v. 27.[30] Halpern thinks that this feature would raise the poem's date, despite the later locative sense for the word in Exod. 32:34; 1 Sam. 23:13; Jer. 1:7, and arguably elsewhere. Another grammatical feature suggesting an older date for this poem for Chaim Cohen is the lack of the direct object marker.[31]

As a further sign of the poem's antiquity, Robertson noted a number of **yaqtul* preterites in Judges 5: *yēlĕkû* in v. 6, *yāgûr* and *yiškôn* in v. 17, *tišlaḥnâ* in v. 26, and *taʿănênnâ* and *tāšîb* in v. 29.[32] Perhaps. Two of these verbal forms have final *nuns* that look like energic indicatives, while the others have been viewed as durative past forms. None of these is in a narrative sequence, which would help to affirm the criterion of a **yaqtul* preterite. This **yaqtul* preterite constituted one of Robertson's main criteria of antiquity[33] (the high date proposed for the poem of Exodus 15 being particularly dependent on this feature).[34]

There have been a number of responses to the **yaqtul* preterite as a diagnostic feature for dating old poetry. Alviero Niccacci prefers not to look diachronically at the **yaqtul* in BH poetry in terms of the old preterite prefix form, but to try to see the verbal forms in Hebrew poetry together as a synchronic system.[35] Yigal Bloch has reviewed the attestation of the **yaqtul* preterite in 2 Samuel 22/Psalm 18; Exodus 15; and Deuteronomy 32 and has reached the conclusion that these poems do show its use.[36] However, Bloch sees its use also in Isa. 41:1-5 and Psalm 44, casting doubt on its value as a diagnostic feature for "old poetry." As a result, Bloch would date these poems to the eighth–seventh centuries, or perhaps even to the ninth century. In any case, he argues that the **yaqtul* preterite does not provide justification for dating 2 Samuel 22/Psalm 18; Exodus 15; and Deuteronomy 32 to the thirteenth–tenth centuries. Vern has also questioned the **yaqtul* preterite as a feature of so-called "archaic Biblical Hebrew."[37] Finally, there is a more general concern, as voiced by Michael Patrick O'Connor: "The basic fact is clear: prefixed verb forms can have past tense reference in poetry; but the system is obscure. Robertson's exposition serves his scholarly purpose of crudely characterizing the time reference of some passages of verse, but since it relies crucially on reconstructions of relevant narrative sequences on the basis of sources outside the poems, it cannot help to characterize the system within the poems."[38] As suggested by O'Connor's comments, the verbal system for early BH narrative poetry remains rather unclear, given its relative paucity. By contrast to this trend, Jan Joosten has maintained the archaic **yaqtul* preterite, especially for Deuteronomy 32,[39] and Tania Notarius has defended the archaic nature of this verbal usage in Judges 5.[40] However, Joosten also notes preterite **yiqtol* in prose passages (Gen. 37:7; Deut. 2:12; Judg. 2:1; 1 Kgs. 7:8; 20:33; 21:6; 2 Kgs. 8:29 = 9:15), in which case the form would not be restricted to archaic Hebrew.[41] Notarius herself notes both the small sample of specifically archaic verbal usages as well as the diversity of verbal usage within archaic Biblical Hebrew. Such a situation hardly precludes genuine archaic usages. Indeed, Notarius's work represents the most recent serious effort in this regard. At the same time, the available data also constitute a meager basis for generalizing about a clear archaic verbal system. Indeed, it is also difficult to discern a verbal system in poetry as opposed to prose.

There has been another development in the scholarly literature complicating the matter of the so-called preterite past use of **yaqtul*. This involves the interpretation of Ugaritic verbal forms, which had been used to support the old **yaqtul* preterite in early Hebrew. Edward L. Greenstein has observed that **yaqtul* and **yaqtulu* in Ugaritic do not show correspondingly different usages. Greenstein observes that several **yaqtulu* forms appear in passages with parallel texts using **yaqtul* forms. Greenstein regards both as narrative indicative prefix forms to be viewed as historically present (in other words, the short form has assimilated to the longer form in terms of usage).[42] This view has been disputed by Holger Gzella: "this idea will presumably not find many followers, since a more sophisticated discourse-based approach can explain several of the allegedly interchangeable usages."[43] Gzella explains further that many instances of the distinctly long forms (**yaqtulu*) can be understood as circumstantial, especially in speech-opening formulas, which may tend to be imperfective.[44]

However this issue is resolved, the Ugaritic texts will need to be scrutinized further to support the **yaqtul* preterite in biblical poetry. To be sure, there are other resources for doing so, Arabic as well as Byblian Amarna, as described by Moran. Thus, the Ugaritic situation need not affect the overall reconstruction for Hebrew. It might be that on this score Hebrew is typologically prior to the situation in Ugaritic (as with other features such as *śîn* as an original consonant). However, it will be interesting to see if text-linguistic approaches to the verbal usage in the old poems will issue in a different sense of their use of the prefix to indicate verbal forms. Either way, it seems that O'Connor was right: Ugaritic poetry does not provide, as of now, a very clear picture about the **yaqtul* preterite. One may remain open to see it as lying in the background of both Ugaritic and biblical usage (with the *wāw*-consecutive).[45] However, the status of the freestanding **yaqtul* preterite requires more assessment at this stage of the discussion. To summarize the grammatical features in Judges 5 considered up to this point, they could fit an Iron I context, but none of them demonstrates or requires an Iron I date.

At this point, I want to turn to three other grammatical features in Judges 5 that have also played a role in this discussion: **tnh* in v. 11 (cf. Judg. 11:40[46]);[47] feminine singular *ḥakmôt* in v. 29;[48] and the relative *š*-.[49] Following Burney, Gary Rendsburg suggests that the features may be traced to northern Hebrew. Rendsburg also views these features as early Hebrew.[50] Here Rendsburg echoes the older view, found in the works of Studer and Burney, for an early date.[51] In contrast, the more critical tradition represented by Michael Waltisberg regards these features as Iron II Aramaisms.[52] Perhaps to be added to the group of features identified by Rendsburg is **mḥq* in v. 26,[53] perhaps a regional variant of **mḥṣ*, as scholars such as Halpern have argued. This is not much different from the view of Knauf proposing this verb as a regional Gileadite feature, along with the -*în* ending on *middîn* in v. 10.[54]

A good example illustrating the issues at hand here is the second feminine singular perfect form, embedded in *šaqqamtî* in v. 7.[55] As Kutscher knew, the form might be considered an Aramaism, and other such forms for the second feminine singular perfect are attested (several in Kethib forms) in Jer. 2:33; 3:4, 5; 4:19 (?); 31:21, Ezek. 16:18 (etc.); Mic. 4:13; Ruth 3:3, 4.[56] When one further considers the attestation of the form in 2 Kgs. 4:23, it may not date to the Iron I; instead, it reflects a northern dialect. Some of these passages are northern, while others represent direct discourse. In this regard, it is interesting to note also the second feminine independent pronoun *ʾattî* in 2 Kgs. 4:7, 16, 23; 8:1, regarded as a colloquial speech form by William Schniedewind and Daniel Sivan.[57] Rendsburg himself regards *šaqqamtî* in 5:7 as a feature of archaic Biblical Hebrew and/or northern Hebrew and, he says, "with a link to Aramaic."[58] In Rendsburg's case, the evidence that he cites in defense of the form's high antiquity is based on material that dates not only to the Late Bronze Age, but also to the Iron II period or later, which would hardly militate in favor of an Iron I date for the form in Judges 5. Indeed, it is to be noted how Rendsburg appeals to the same Aramaic features for his picture of northern Hebrew that Waltisberg and other critics use to support their view of Aramaic features in the poem.[59] For both sides, the comparative material under discussion often consists of Iron II texts and thus is a weak basis for an early dating in the Iron I period.

The particle *š*- as a relative particle ("which") embedded in the form *šaqqamtî* has also been claimed as a mark of archaic Hebrew.[60] Kutscher thought the particle in Judges 5 was a feature of archaic Hebrew generally.[61]

At the same time, commentators also note its later usage.[62] There is the additional matter of whether the form might reflect northern dialect, as opposed to a putatively southern *ʾăšer,* since the form *ʾš* occurs in Phoenician.[63] Baruch Levine notes the parallel developments of the Phoenician *ʾš* and Hebrew *ša-/še-*, and he considers seriously the regional usage behind the latter.[64]

In order to build an argument based on linguistic features, there needs to be some basis for comparison for suggesting a plausible *terminus ad quem.* In other words, an older date for such a feature should not necessarily be precluded. When trying to make a case, it must be built on what can be reasonably shown and thus depends on comparing the use of the feature elsewhere. For comparison within Hebrew, there is the notable usage of the particle in the narrative of the Gideon chapters of Judges 6-8. In Judges 6, *ʾăšer* occurs both in narrative (vv. 11, 21) and direct discourse (v. 13), while *ša-* is in direct discourse, in v. 17, and in narrative, in 7:12 and 8:26. In 8:26, *ʾăšer* and *ša-* occur together in narrative. Based on *miššellānû* in 2 Kgs. 6:11, Schniedewind and Sivan note the attestation of the Hebrew particle in direct discourse in northern texts.[65] Overall, the distribution of *ša-* versus *ʾăšer* would suggest at least a feature of northern Hebrew. But what would that suggest for its use in Judges 5? It might be early. However, even if scholars discovered many Iron I inscriptions with *ša-*, these would still not indicate where its use in Judges 5 would put the poem on a time line between Iron I usage and the northern Iron II uses in Judges 6-8 and elsewhere in the Bible. Beyond distribution, another possible way to argue the point would be to see if the attestation of the particle in Judges 5 shows some aspect or nuance that helps to single it out relative to its other occurrences; however, I see nothing particular to the use of the particle *ša-* in Judges 5 to warrant such a conclusion.

So where does this discussion lead thus far? At this point, we may step back and articulate some general points that can be taken from this discussion. Seven points may be addressed briefly in turn. First, there is the matter of the available sample. It is quite small. Relatively speaking, there is a lack of a critical density of biblical poetic tradition before the eighth century. If we can rely on Amos, Hosea, and Isaiah for eighth-century poetry, we have no comparable measure for any century before the eighth century, until we get back to the Ugaritic literary texts in the twelfth century. (These, however, are not directly antecedent to biblical tradition, although it is clear from the work of Cassuto, Cross, and many others that these two literary traditions have many linkages in terms of grammar, poetry, and literary content.)[66] There is little yardstick for the poetry between the Ugaritic texts and the eighth-century prophets. More specifically, there is neither enough linguistic material *in itself* nor enough specimens of this so-called "old poetry," nor understanding of their historical circumstances, to develop a sufficient linguistic basis for dating them to specific centuries prior to the eighth century. (This does not even include the problem of analyzing grammar according to different genres.) It is impossible to avoid the problem of insufficient material for making precise historical judgments.

Second, the dating of features said to be old is open to question. Robertson himself noted that every feature that he believes to be a sign of "old poetry" is found in later poetry. As a result, scholars have been forced to deploy other strategies for dating.

Third, the density of so-called old features as a criterion for dating a composition is problematic. In some of the older scholarly discussions, the judgment of antiquity relied on an implicit standard invoking density of the features considered to be old. For example, this standard was a centerpiece in Robertson's work.[67] He suggested that outside of "old poetry," only two other passages contain three old features. It was this perceived density that tilted the balance in judgment from a simple matter of a vestige or two (or possibly archaizing) and toward claims for a genuinely older poem. Morag made an analogous argument for the number of vocabulary items in the Balaam oracles.[68] However, it may be asked: Is relative density a sufficient means for demonstrating antiquity when the same features are attested later? The density argument does not seem terribly strong. While it may suggest a date prior to the eighth century, the criterion of density of features provides no clear help for pinpointing a date between the twelfth and ninth centuries.

Fourth, the types of features that are examined vary in the scholarly discussions. The debate has sometimes tended to focus on morphology, at the expense of the lexicon and perhaps syntax. (Robertson has no vocabulary in his discussion.)[69] As we will see, I will note one item of syntax that has played little or no role in the discussion.

Fifth, there is finally the matter of the methodology used in making judgments about grammatical features. In some instances, features appear in old poems and then are lost and unparalleled in either early or later literature. In other cases, many features that could be quite old could also be quite late. In still other cases, features that are late can also be quite old. Nuance and context are key. For example, it may be a matter of how features were combined. For example, Gen. 49:10 combines *šîlô*, either derived from or to be read as **šaylô* with the parallel term *yiqqĕhat* (cf. Ps. 68:30).[70] To be sure, *šay* is attested in Ps. 76:12 and Isa. 18:7 and **yqh* appears in Prov. 30:17 (cf. the root twice in KTU 1.2 I 34-35).[71] However, simple attestation later is not the end of the matter for understanding the antiquity of Gen. 49:10. Not only does this verse show the combination of the two words unparalleled elsewhere; the later usage of **yqh* in Prov. 30:17 has moved from the political realm to the familial "homage to a mother" *(yîqqăhat-'ēm)*. Generally with "old poetry," there are nuances of semantics to consider, and there are also the shifting combinations of terms to bear in mind. After all, "old poetry" is no different from any other texts; it, too, reflects language in transition. Uniformity in the rate of change of features is not to be expected.

Sixth, as will be clear from the discussion above, the features in question are not only linguistic, but also cultural. Some of these linguistic-cultural features do not occur later at all, while others occur in frozen form.

Seventh and perhaps most critically, all arguments in any direction turn on arguments from silence. This very fact indicates that claims either way are inherently suspect and possible at the same time. For better or worse, all arguments in this topic of "old poetry" cannot escape this problem. So the question of distribution as well as arguments based on distribution are to be handled very carefully, and necessarily in conjunction with other sorts of strategies of reasoning.

Because of these seven considerations, the approach taken by either side in their broad outlines is not acceptable. Let me explain. On the one side, I do not accept Young's approach in which he argues that there can be no dating by linguistic features and that such variation is to be attributed to different style.[72] But more fundamentally, Young's own claim that older features may be a matter of style and not date poses a false dichotomy, to my mind. It also relies on a claim that style can be shown to be the operative factor and not time frame, but Young has not shown this; and indeed, any given feature appears in texts themselves showing a variety of styles. Thus style might not be the operative factor in many, if not most, of the instances. It seems to me that Young's approach is no less vulnerable with respect to style than those whom he criticizes on dating.[73]

On the other hand, I do not accept the conclusions reached by Cross and Freedman, Robertson, and others. Indeed, I applaud some aspects of Young's critique because it should force defenders of early dates of "old poetry" to argue their case more rigorously. It is Cross himself who in recent years expressed some doubt as to the reliability of linguistic evidence for early dating: "I have become less certain of the results of our work, given the problem of the long transmission of the text of these poems, only partially overcome by modern text-critical methods, and perhaps more serious, our uncertain knowledge of the details of the Hebrew language in which the poems were composed."[74] Cross's cautionary sense here seems warranted. Finally, both approaches are overly circumscribed in terms of what features they consider or how the features are considered.

My view is that a case is to be built initially on a narrow base of evidence that combines three criteria. The first is what may be called the criterion of dissimilarity, in other words, language features attested early but not later. The second, taken from Hurvitz's work on SBH and LBH,[75] is to attempt to indicate any later term or feature replacing the corresponding earlier term or feature. Recognition of such pairs of corresponding older and later features helps to overcome the argument from silence inherent in the first criterion of distribution. I add the caveat that such a linguistic contrast in the first instance is helpful only within the most basic literary unit in which it appears (and not across whole biblical books or major parts of books, unless indicated by a sufficient number of features). The third entails features that combine linguistic and cultural information. In order to know the sense of the word, it is important to know its sense of the world, in other words what it is referring to, and that is often a matter of culture. While some language purists may have little interest in culture, language is indeed grounded in culture,[76] and in the case of "old poetry," it is this interface that provides significant help for dating a poem such as Judges 5. This is not to say that the recovery of cultural information does not entail its own challenges.[77] However, scholars who give up the linguistic features that show a cultural interface give up too much of the ground for earlier dating. "Not by language alone," to cite the title of an essay on the topic by Alexander Rofé,[78] can biblical texts be dated. Combined with the criterion of dissimilarity, features with a linguistic-cultural interface lie at the heart of the matter of dating Judges 5.

Finally, before proceeding to a list of old features for Judges 5, I would add a further caveat generally concerning the time frame for "old poetry." While we may make a case for some parts of Judges 5 in the Iron I, we have to note that a number of poems often included as "old poetry" may date down into the ninth century. Genesis 49 contains what appear to be some older sayings (Iron I-IIA), although the form of its present collection may be later.[79] Levine has argued for the first half of the ninth century as the date of Balaam oracles in Numbers 23-24.[80] With its reference to monarchy (v. 10), 1 Samuel 2 likewise shows the trending of "old poetry" down into the monarchy.[81] Like the poem in 1 Samuel 2, Habakkuk 3 refers to the monarchy (v. 13).[82] The introduction to the poem in v. 2 locates the speaker of this poem as later than the old-looking description of the deity that initially follows (vv. 3-7). I am hesitant about dating Exodus 15 to the Iron I or even to the tenth century.[83] This means that old-looking features could continue to be used in Iron II A (tenth-ninth centuries). So when I discuss "old poetry" as a general term, I refer to poetry possibly trending down into the ninth century. In the case of Judges 5, I will argue for some of its composition and/or tradition in the premonarchic period, and I will propose that its present composition dates to the early monarchic period. For the first point of my argument, I am echoing the conclusion of the most recent book-length work on the subject that I have seen on Judges 5, namely the 2008 work by Charles L. Echols.[84] For the second, I am concurring with Knauf.[85] In both instances, my reasons differ somewhat from what these two authors offer.

3. Features of Antiquity in Judges 5

At this point, I turn to features that I think suggest a fairly old date for some parts of Judges 5. Some of these features are purely linguistic; others show a significant linguistic-cultural interface; and still others involve entirely cultural matters. There is another set of features suggesting the antiquity of material. This involves prior material apparently borrowed from prior tradition and imported into the poem, which suggests earlier composition that can be seen in distinction from the later level of the poem. This differs from later secondary additions, such as v. 31 according to most commentators.

To anticipate the discussion below, I will argue that the evidence supports the conclusion that at least the tradition of the core of the poem of Judges 5 did not originate in the Iron II period; rather, its tradition, if not a significant portion of its composition, is to be dated in the Iron I. Before beginning, it is to be noted that no particular weight should be placed on any one of these features, as the interpretation offered for any one feature may be disputed.

Linguistic Features

There is one linguistic feature worth considering, yet it has played little role in the discussion. The feature involves the syntax of v. 8. This clause has been understood for a long time as a double-question, for example, in the King James Version and RSV. This understanding of the verse's syntax has also been accepted by modern critics, such as Moore, Burney, and *BDB*.[86] It may be translated:

Was a shield or *(ʾim)* even[87] a spear seen[88]
Among the forty thousand in Israel?

While the word order of this double-question is difficult, its force has been thought to be asseverative.[89] The question is to assert something that was surely not the case. For this reason, in his classic study of this construction Moshe Held called this sort of double-question a "rhetorical question."[90] The NJPS translation makes this point by using a negative formulation plus exclamation point: "No shield or spear was seen//Among forty thousand in Israel!"

Before looking more closely at the double-question in Judges 5:8, we should lay out the structures of the double-question as it appears in Ugaritic and in Hebrew, based on Held's study and extended recently by Edward Silver.[91] Held noted the standard understanding of the BH double-question, in which the first clause or element begins with interrogative *h-* and the second with *ʾim.*[92] We may begin with a couple of BH cases. In Judg. 11:25, Jephthah asks the king of the Ammonites whether Balak the king of Moab battled against Israel:

hărōb rāb ʿim-yiśrāʾēl	Did he really contend with Israel,
ʾim nilḥōm nilḥam bām	Or did he really fight against them?

A second example from biblical poetry comes from Isa. 10:15:

hăyitpāʾēr haggarzen	Does the axe glorify itself
ʿal haḥōṣēb bô	over the one who hews with it,
ʾim-yitgaddēl hammaśśôr	Or does the saw magnify itself
ʿal-mĕnîpô	above the one who wields it?

To this standard BH form of the double-question (see also 1 Kgs. 22:15; Gen. 37:32),[93] Held compared the structure of the double-question in Ugaritic, consisting of no interrogative element in the initial position in the first clause, plus *hm* in the initial position in the second clause.[94] A well-known example appears in the story of King Kirta, where El asks Kirta what he desires (KTU 1.14 I 41-43):

mlk kʾabh yʾarš	Is it kingship like his father's that he desires,
hm drk[t] k ʾab ʾadm	or domin[ion] like the Father of Humanity's?

There are two critical differences between the double-question in the two languages. Ugaritic lacks interrogative *hê* at the head of the first clause, which is standard for BH. A slightly different particle fronts the second clause in each language, *hm* in Ugaritic and *ʾim* in BH.

From the perspective of the standard Ugaritic and BH forms of the double-question, Judg. 5:8b stands typologically in between.[95] As in Ugaritic, the double-question in Judg. 5:8 lacks the interrogative *hê* before the first clause, but like BH it has the particle *ʾim* fronting the second clause. In addition, the double-question in Judg. 5:8 shows unusual word order, with the verb before the second noun with prefixed *wāw*. The word order seems to front the word "shield" in a conspicuous manner. Such fronting also marks the Ugaritic example from Kirta, and such fronting occurs in other Ugaritic instances of the double-question, for example, KTU 1.4 IV 59-62, with its two questions. El asks: "So am I a servant, a slave of Athirat? So am I a servant who handles a tool, or *(hm)* a servant-girl of Athirat who makes bricks?" The second question, like Judg. 5:8b, fronts the main nouns.[96]

The syntax of the double-question in Judg. 5:8 appears to stand typologically between Ugaritic and Standard Biblical Hebrew (SBH). Not only is this form of the double-question not attested later (as far as I know), the double-question in the form found in v. 8 is evidently replaced by what may be recognized as the standard form in BH. Is there any means available to get a fix on the time frame for when this replacement might have taken place? The two BH instances of the double-question cited from Judg. 11:25 and Isa. 10:15 may be dated to the eighth century. So by the eighth century, it would appear that the BH standard form was known. Is there any earlier case? An earlier-looking context for the standard form of the double-question is Hab. 3:8; it is actually a triple-question, also with fronting for emphasis:

hăbinhārîm ḥārâ yhwh	Was it at Rivers that you, O Yahweh, were angry,
ʾim bannĕhārîm ʾappekā	At Rivers, your wrath,
ʾim bayyām ʿebrātekā	Or at Sea, your fury . . . ?

While the poem in Habakkuk 3 in its entirety may not be archaic, this part of the text may be drawing on an older-looking Hebrew that may predate most, if not all, of the other passages with the double-question in Hebrew.[97] This feature of Judges 5 fits at least with a ninth-century dating; there is nothing to preclude an earlier date. In the following chapter, I will suggest that this verse belongs to a tenth-century composer's introduction to the poem.

One other feature that may be entertained as old is *bn mšptym* in v. 16. The expression used here for Reuben applies also to Issachar in Gen. 49:14,[98] and it may compare with *bên šĕpattāyim* in Ps. 68:14. The distribution is suggestive of an old feature. There is a further telling argument for its relative antiquity, and that is not simply its lack of attestation later, but also our basic ignorance of the meaning. This is not for any lack of guesses or fancy philological work.[99] The point is important: the basic lack of attestation and understanding may constitute a datum for considering an early dating for this feature.

Linguistic-Cultural Features

At this point, the discussion may move to another group of features, which combine linguistic and cultural material. To anticipate the discussion in the following chapter, I will suggest that as with the double-question in v. 8 addressed above, these belong to the tenth-century composer's introduction reflecting on conditions in the Iron I period before kings.

*Verse 2 *prʿ*

Various views have been proposed for the meaning of **prʿ*.[100] The one that seems best supported contextually involves the practice of leaving hair long (**prʿ*)[101] for battle. The line "when locks were long in Israel" suggests a picture of tribal militia at war. This root **prʿ* is doubly attested in this verse in both initial infinitive construct form (fronted by the preposition *b-*, "when") and the plural noun form. The nominal form is attested elsewhere only in Deut. 32:42, "from the head of the locks of the enemy" *(mērōʾš parʿôt ʾôyēb).*

Standing in a long line of commentary on this feature,[102] H. L. Ginsberg commented: "Occurring only in these two passages, the noun designates fighting men and would seem to mean literally 'longhairs' (cf. *péraʿ* 'untrimmed [hair],' Num 6:5; Ezek 44:20) because of a presumable custom of leaving the hair of the head unshorn for the duration of a military campaign."[103] The idiom of the longhair appears in the Iron II context in a clichéd manner in Deut. 32:42. It appears there as a standard or frozen expression used in that context for the enemy; thus it seems to show some literary development of the motif. (The battle sensibility with this word may be used ironically in Exod. 32:25.) The other Iron II contexts for the practice of leaving hair long can be seen in the specifically religious formulation of the Nazirite vow, as explained by Ginsberg's comments. The story of Samson, the warrior Nazirite, provides a legendary reading of the uncut hair, explained as the source of his power (see Judg. 13:5, 7; 16:17-20; 16:22 with 16:28-30; see also *nězîr* in Gen. 49:26).[104] The Iron II manifestations of the motif of the uncut hair show development compared with the usage in Judg. 5:2, and this dissimilarity in the treatments of the motif is suggestive of an older background embedded in this verse.[105] It is possible that this practice has a Late Bronze antecedent in the Ugaritic Baal Cycle, although the passage is difficult. Robert M. Good compared Ugaritic *rmt pr't* in KTU 1.4 VII 53-56/1.8 II 6-9:

'n gpn w'ugr	See, O Gapnu wa-Ugaru,
bn ǵlmt 'mmym	Sons of darkness (?), the forces (?),
bn ẓlmt rmt pr't	Sons of shadow (?), the high longhairs (?).

This passage may reflect the longhairs of Judg. 5:2, as well as the usage of *'mmyk* in v. 14. This example is admittedly difficult. It may also be useful to compare the Epic of Tikulti-Ninurta,[106] in referring to the practice of warriors tying up their hair before going into battle: "they have bound up their hair *(pirēti)*."[107] Treatment of hair in different manners signals the departure from routine life that entering battle represents.[108]

These passages are suggestive of an older background to this feature in Judg. 5:2. In addition, there is some discontinuity between the expression in this verse and the related expression in Deut. 32:42. In sum, the distribution works with an Iron I setting for the tradition of the practice in Judg. 5:2. It is not necessary to speculate on the demise of the older practice in later Israel in order to make the case for the early dating of this practice. This feature fits in a poem that does not mention the monarchy at a battle; instead, it is said to have involved multiple tribes.[109]

Verse 6 ntybwt

The word "routes" *(nětîbôt)* is cognate with Ugaritic *ntbt*,[110] and its usage there may be pertinent to v. 6.[111] This word in Judg. 5:6 may not be simply a general term for routes, but a reference to a more specific economic practice, as seen in a number of Ugaritic texts that use the same term. KTU 4.336 reads: "On the day of the new moon, in the month of *pgr*, Iwrpzn, Argdd, Ktkn (and) Ybrk took the route(s) for 220 total in gold." The phrase rendered literally "took the route(s)" has been generally understood to refer to the purchase of trading concessions for traveled routes.[112] The economic situation in this text seems to involve individuals who have bought the rights from the royal authority to exact tolls from traders or travelers. The same situation underlies KTU 4.266. This text uses the same formulary as KTU 4.336, except that instead of *ntbt* in the former, the sale of trading rights in the latter involves *ma'ḫd,* literally the harbor serving Ugarit.[113] These texts all concern financial arrangements for trade. Trade matters also underlie the similar, but broken text, 4.388. The letter KTU 2.36 involves Egypt's *ntbt* through the kingdom of Ugarit. It is quite feasible to understand the word, attested in lines 16 and 17, as "the caravans of Egypt."[114] It has been argued that it more specifically involves the "right of way" of Egypt.[115] The text is admittedly very broken and difficult.

That such a meaning may be seen in Judg. 5:6 may be supported by the other occurrence of the word in Biblical Hebrew. Prov. 8:2 mentions "a house of *ntybwt,*" which "may refer to a customs house or toll building."[116] Thus, the word has a later history, but it is the particular circumstances of the situation to which the word refers in Judg. 5:6 that arguably point to its high antiquity. The introduction to the poem at this point in v. 6 situates the cause of battle as Israel's loss of the use of the trade route or right of way through the Jezreel Valley.[117]

In sum, the Ugaritic texts point to concerns about trade routes by members of Ugarit's elite. In contrast, Judges 5 may concern a complaint over the lack of access to trade routes by Israelites. The Ugaritic texts, especially KTU 2.36, and Judges 5 may provide two sides of the picture of the conditions involving trade routes. The Ugaritic texts point to the financial management of trading routes and rights of ways, while Judges 5 suggests a complaint of the loss of such rights of use or rights of way on the part of local users of such routes. The verse characterizes the situation in the Iron I period rather than in the Iron II when the Israelites controlled the Jezreel Valley.[118] While the use of the word in v. 6 may point to an older background, it is also true that this usage need not be Iron I; it could well be early Iron II looking back on the situation in the Iron I.

Verses 7 and 11 pĕrāzôn

The word appears in both v. 7 and v. 11. V. 11, in proclaiming "the victories of the *pĕrāzôn* in Israel," shows that this is a term for people and not place.

This word has been taken as a term for hamlet population or the like: "rural population, rustics"[119] and "villages."[120] In line with this approach, Lawrence Stager compares *pĕrāzôt*, "unwalled villages" or "type of rural settlement,"[121] while Nadav Na'aman compares Amarna EA 137, *ālāni puruzi*, "rural unwalled settlements"[122] (although questions about Naaman's interpretation have been raised by Brendon C. Benz).[123] In this connection, the cognate *pĕrāzî* for "hamlet-dweller" in Deut. 3:5; 1 Sam. 6:18; Esth. 9:19 may be noted as well.

Rejecting the translation "villagers," Albright proposed "warriors" based on *prṯ* in "Craft of the Scribe," Papyrus Anastasi I, 23.4,[124] followed by Robert Boling, Michael Coogan, and Ronald Hendel.[125] Burney highlighted the reading *dynatoi*, "mighty ones,"[126] in LXX B, while Hendel notes Greek *dynatōn*, "mighty ones," for *pĕrāzā(y)w* (see Q/K) in Hab. 3:14, also a military context.[127] Albright's Egyptian cognate is problematic for his interpretation. He rightly saw *pĕrāzôn* as a "collective," but the cognate that he proposed is open to question. James Allen transliterates the Egyptian word as *pirtji* and translates it in context: "You will take the bow and make a *pirtji* on your left so that you might let the chiefs see."[128] Allen deduces: "the context suggests that this refers to the action of drawing the bow."[129] For a cognate, he cites the discussion of the word by James E. Hoch, who himself proposes "laceration" (?) and entertains a number of etymologies.[130] However, none of these approximates "soldiers" as proposed by Albright et al. Still, even as Albright's proposal for a cognate and the resulting semantics do not appear on target, his instincts about the *pĕrāzôn* as a collective seem right. The nominal form taking a plural verb seems to suggest a collective.[131] It is also evident that other nominal uses of the root point to a fighting force (e.g., Hab. 3:14).[132]

The cognate biblical terms would suggest some sort of collective population living in unwalled settlements (so Stager et al.). This population is prepared to fight (again, per Albright et al.). It is clear from v. 11 that this word does not denote the Israelites in general. In v. 7, this military collective is unable to meet the threat, while in v. 11 it experiences victory. In a sense, Stager and Albright each capture one side of the term: village warriors, operating in the form of militia, may be involved.[133] The underlying derivation may be relatively mundane, compared with Albright's proposed cognate: just as *ʿam* may denote both a population and its fighting force (see v. 11; cf. 2 Sam. 1:12; 1 Kgs. 20:10 for good examples), so perhaps may *pĕrāzôn*. In conclusion, the meanings of the cognates, *pĕrāzôt* and *pĕrāzî*, and its usage in this context suggest the meaning of *pĕrāzôn* as "village militia." This feature best fits an Iron I context prior to the sorts of standing armies described for Israelite kings.[134]

Verse 11 mḥṣṣym?

Proposals include "archers" (cf. BH *ḥēṣ*, "arrow"),[135] "singers,"[136] and "cymbals."[137] However, there is no particular etymological support for the translation "cymbals." Might *mḥṣṣym* refer to war divisions, celebrating spoils taken in battle (**ḥṣṣ*, "to divide spoils")? Burney discusses this idea,[138] but rightly questions it. The picture in the verse may entail a celebration of the victorious force, those who divide spoils (for such a celebration, see Isa. 9:2(3); see Num. 31:36, 43 for **meḥĕṣâ*, "half of spoils"). This approach would stay closer to the other attestations of the geminate root "to divide" (cf. Prov. 30:27 for locusts divided into companies or swarms).[139] If so, does the possible hint of dividing war-spoils here connect to this theme in v. 30? Perhaps the image involves despoilers celebrating. If so, those called to sing do so at the places where the victors celebrated their victory. Whatever it means, and one should not put much weight on this, the singularity of the usage (not to mention scholarly ignorance about it) is perhaps indicative of its antiquity.

Cultural and Literary Features

Parts of the poem have a number of other cultural features also suggestive of an early date for them: Seir and Edom in v. 4; Shamgar ben-ʿAnat in v. 6; the representation of the stars in v. 20; and the curse of Meroz in v. 23. In addition, variants in other old poems are suggestive of high antiquity for the background of such variants. I will address these in turn.

Both the specific names of Seir and Edom in v. 4a as well as their geographical variants elsewhere are suggestive of the high antiquity of this verse. The place names are two of the four references associated with the region southeast of Israel: Edom/Paran/Teiman/Seir/Sinai in Deut. 33:2; Judg. 5:4; Ps. 68:8-9, 18 (Eng. 7-8, 17); Hab. 3:3, 7.[140] The variations in other details in Judg. 5:4-5 I will discuss in Chapter Nine. At this point, I want to focus on Edom and Seir, which comport with an older setting. As a highland area,[141] Edom seems to represent a region and not necessarily a particular site.[142] This region appears in an Egyptian list of lands dating to Amenophis (and Ramesses II) that includes "the land of the Shasu, Yhw3" and "land of the Shasu, Sʿrr." The first has often been conjectured to be a reference to a place named after the god Yahweh, and the second would be Seir (see also Seir in the summary of the northern wars of Ramesses III,[143] and perhaps in EA

288:26; cf. Seir in Deut. 33:2 and parallel with Edom in Judg. 5:4). Both would be located southeast of Canaan.[144] In connection with these place names, it is to be noted that the place name of Edom is likewise attested with the Shasu, "the Shasu tribes of Edom," in "The Report of a Frontier Official," in Papyrus Anastasi VI.[145] Like Seir, Edom is mentioned in the old poetic references to Yahweh (Judg. 5:4). Concerning "the land of the Shasu, Yhw3," it might be named for a deity, though this is quite unclear.[146] Addressing this putative Egyptian reference to Yahweh, Anson Rainey remarks: "Is this a reference to Yahweh? No one knows."[147] Rainey then mentions Judg. 5:4 and comments: "Perhaps it is only a coincidence, but the most ancient literary tradition we have associated Yahweh with an area that can quite possibly be equated with a territory occupied by Shasu pastoralists." If the putative reference to Yahweh were correct, this god may have originated in the region of Seir and Edom and not within Israel, as known in the Mernepteh stele.[148] It would be for this reason that later biblical tradition, especially in the Pentateuch, remembered Sinai, a mountain in the distant south, as Yahweh's sanctuary mountain.[149] In the following chapter, I will address the parallel with Ps. 68:8-9, which would point to Judg. 5:4-5 being an old Iron I piece that was incorporated into its context by the Iron II composer of the poem's introduction.

Verse 6

The reference to Shamgar ben-ʿAnat in v. 6 is enigmatic. The figure is known also in Judg. 3:31, but that reference to him may have drawn on this reference in Judg. 5:6. Within biblical tradition, he is otherwise an unknown figure. The two attestations are notable both for their distribution and for their lack of information about him. These suggest that he was unknown in later Israelite tradition. It is rare that an Israelite hero would have a foreign name, and is suggestive of a figure no longer known to Israel.[150] He belonged to Israel's early history, but not later. In that sense, he belonged to the "lost world" of early Israel. A further clue to this figure is the second part of his name. This is well known in old Canaanite arrowheads. For example, El-Khadr V arrowhead reads: "(arrow of) *ʿbd-lbʾit,* (son of) *bn-ʿnt*"[151] In sum, Shamgar seems to have been a forgotten hero of early Israel's "lost world" in the Iron I context. In Judges 5, the figure seems to be used to signal the high antiquity of the poem's events.

Verse 14 ʿmlq

For the name of Amalek, MT is supported by LXX B and the Vulgate. LXX B has Ephraim uprooting (*exerrizōsen* ‹ *ekkeraizō*, "pillage, cut off root and branch") those in Amalek. Many commentators, such as Moore, Burney, *BDB*, and Raymond Tournay, read *ʿmq*, "valley," based on LXX A *koiladi.*[152] Tournay surmised that an anti-Samaritan scribe added the *lamed* in order to relate the Samaritans, under the name of Ephraim, to Amalek.[153] One question with the proposed rereading is that the context here is not negative, but positive: the tribal unit is one that does the right thing in the context of the poem. Adding *l* to create *ʿmlq* would read against the context; this is possible, but not preferable.

De Moor thinks it is hard to believe that Amalek would be presented as an ally in light of animosity elsewhere in Judges (3:13; 6:3, 33; 7:12; 10:12). It is precisely the difficulty that lends credence to this representation as early, prior to the historical conflict between Amalek and Israel. Indeed, J. David Schloen notes another neutral Ephraim reference to Amalek in Judg. 12:15.[154] As BH *šoršām* in this verse would suggest, Amalek seems to have had some sort of kin-based relationship with Ephraim.[155] The question is how this relationship might have developed; following Schloen's study, trade may be a possible avenue. It is possible that Ephraim enjoyed a trade relationship with Amalek that engendered ties or "root" (again, see also Judg. 12:15). It would seem that given the inimical references to Amalek that this relationship suffered with the rise of the northern tribal kingdom, such a neutral or positive relationship may have lasted until the times of the negative references of Amalek. It would be my sense that this dies out at least in the early ninth century, if not earlier.

Verse 20

The translation of the verse here reads the parallelism against MT, but with any number of modern scholars:[156]

> From heaven the stars fought,
> From their courses they fought with Sisera.

This reading shows not only parallelism of the same verb in the two lines, but also sonant-morphological parallelism between the initial terms in both lines, each consisting of the preposition "from" *(min)* plus their objects, which are not only syntactically parallel, but also sonantly parallel, each with the sequence initial *m* + sibilant + final *m*.

The one word requiring comment in v. 20 is *mslwtm*. Several commentators emend to *mazzĕlôtām*.[157] Cross and Freedman suggest that the "change *z* > *s* may be due to an error in oral transmission." However, as Burney remarks,[158] the change is unnecessary, and he suggests that MT may reflect the substitution of a common term for the more unusual word, given the attestation of **mazzālôt* in 2 Kgs. 23:5 and **mazzārôt* in Job 38:32. This term is evidently a loan, according to the standard work by Paul V. Mankowski, S.J. and the more recent study of Cory Ke Michael Peacock.[159] Scholars have compared the Ugaritic *hlk kbkbm* in KTU 1.19 II 3, 7.[160] Less certain in this regard is BH *hălîkôt* in Hab. 3:6, which is taken as "orbits" by *DCH*.[161] This may correspond to Akkadian *alaktu* as used for astral bodies.[162]

Scholars in recent years have interpreted the stars in Judges 5 in a variety of ways. Susan Ackerman regards the behavior of the stars in Judg. 5:20 as unusual: the very forces of nature are commanded by Yahweh to deviate from their unusual behavior "in order to wage war on Yahweh's and Israel's behalf."[163] Levine adds a mythological dimension to the picture. For Levine, the verse offers a picture of "theomachy, the war of creation, wherein the God of Israel subdued the forces of nature, represented as other gods, and subsequently ruled over them."[164] He further takes the verse as a veiled reference to astral religion, and in context the verse "alludes to YHWH's enlistment of the stars to do battle on Israel's behalf."[165] Moshe Weinfeld interprets the stars in v. 20 as coming "from their courses"; in other words, these are shooting or flashing stars perceived to be fighting on behalf of the victors.[166] For this view, he draws on Egyptian texts (Gebel Barkal stele of Thutmose III and also the poetic stele of the same king), as well as Greek passages involving battle (*Iliad* 4.75ff. and the Homeric Hymn to Apollo). He also understands Num. 24:17 in this way: "A star marches forth from Jacob, a meteor (comparing Akkadian *šibṭu*) comes forth from Israel." Leonid Kogan compares a description of stars fighting in an Old Babylonian epic of Sargon:

> Sargon had (barely) ventured into the land of Utu-rapashtim,
> (When) as if he were hostile, the forest waged war against him.
> It set darkness in place of the light of heavens.
> The sun dimmed, the stars sallied forth against the enemy.[167]

In view of this passage, Kogan accepts the old view of J. F. A. Sawyer that the biblical verse contains manifestations of "hostile nature," and he also notes Sawyer's surmise that this verse may reflect a solar eclipse "shortly after midday on 30th September 1131."[168] The point to be drawn from Kogan's discussion is that the references to the stars in Judg. 5:20 may not be Yahwistic and perhaps not theistic except in a general way.

It would be reasonable to understand Yahweh as the source of the astral power, if the verse is understood in terms of the overall poem. However, Yahweh appears very little in the battle narrative proper, indeed only once, in v. 23, itself a literary "isolate" (as we will note below). Thus read within the context of the poem's core, Yahweh's divine leadership of the stars may not be indicated here.[169] Viewed in its immediate context, the verse suggests only that the stars collectively (possibly the gods generally) were on the side of the tribal coalition.[170] Within Israelite tradition, the motif of the stars fighting is exceptional and seems quite old.

Verse 23

This verse has been considered to be a separate piece that was included in this context. Peter R. Ackroyd suggests the possibility that vv. 23-24, with their curse on Meroz and their blessing on Jael, form a "quotation" from earlier traditions of the battle utilized by the poet.[171] According to Cross, the curse holds important implications for understanding "this instance of league 'holy war.' "[172] For Cross, the verse presupposes such a league,[173] and it is Yahwistic in character given the reference to Yahweh here. Thus for this chunk of material, the tradition of battle was Yahwistic, but this is not nearly as evident in other parts of the poem's core, especially in the representation of battle in v. 20, which also interestingly stands at some distance from the curse. In the next chapter, we will examine the distributions of the names of Israel and Yahweh in Judges 5, which are hardly uniform.

At this point, we may draw some conclusions. Very few purely linguistic features in Judges 5 show a specifically Iron I date, although none militate against such a high date. The double-question in v. 8 may put the poem in at least the ninth century, if not earlier. The other two purely linguistic features that were mentioned also comport with this conclusion. It might be argued that purely linguistic criteria provide a sense of an "old poem" prior to the eighth century, but in themselves do not produce more precise results. The linguistic-cultural features are arguably more helpful. The following items fit an earlier time, perhaps a late (if not earlier) Iron I or tenth-century setting: **pr*ʿ in v. 2; *ntybwt* in v. 6; and *przwn* in vv. 7 and 11. In addition, the cultural references to Seir and Edom that shift to other names in later tradition, the "lost" figures of Shamgar ben-ʿAnat and Meroz, and the neutral reference to Amalek evoke an Iron I setting.

To anticipate the discussion in the following chapter, the traditional material in the poem suggests an early date (at least to the Iron IIA or early IIB). A maximal conclusion would put the poem in the Iron I period. It might be argued that there is little that precludes an Iron I date for the poem (not counting some possible additions). A minimal conclusion is that several traditions of the poem go back to the Iron I period, but that the poem belongs to the Iron II (perhaps early Iron IIB, though this may be too late). A view in between these alternatives may be entertained: most of the core of the poem's body (vv. 14-30), as well as the independent piece in vv. 4-5, goes back to the Iron I. The basic composition of the various pieces used by a tenth-century composer (e.g., the *topos* of the divine warrior and the tribal sayings) shows their prior literary history, and so these pieces at least seem to be at home in the Iron I period. The representation of the divine warrior, the battle itself, the tribes that did or did not come to fight, and the neutral reference to Amalek belong to the collective memory in the Iron I period that would be passed down to, received by, and modified by the tenth-century composer. (In view of this reconstruction, it seems plausible that other versions of this poem or at least of the battle would have circulated in Iron I Israel.) These early features could have been included in the tradition from the Iron I, but composed in its present version in the tenth century. Indeed, some of the old Iron I content may serve to evoke the old time from a tenth-century perspective. Both the tradition of much material and perhaps even the oral composition of some of this material may have been known already in the Iron I. However, it is not possible to demonstrate that the poem as a whole was composed in the Iron I period.

As we will see in the next chapter, the emphases on Israel and Yahweh in the poem's introduction in vv. 2-13 suggest an effort on the part of the composer to assert the reality of Israel as pantribal entity, with Yahweh as its divine patron. The older body of the poem, as well as some of its further components drawn into the poem's introduction (e.g., the march of the divine warrior in vv. 4-5), was refigured by the poem's introduction to serve a larger purpose of asserting national identity, a myth-making process that would serve the emerging northern kingdom in the tenth century. When the discussion gets to issues of what the composer drew on and how the composer shaped the material, the discussion is moving into literary judgments, which largely lie beyond the scope of this chapter. What the composer did with the older material is addressed in the following chapter.

CHAPTER NINE

Human and Divine Warriors of Israel in Judges 5

The poem of Judges 5 is a key text for the discussion of early Israel.[1] In the last chapter, an argument was made for the Iron I period as the background for many of the poem's traditions, if not also for much of its composition. In this chapter, I argue for an early Iron II dating for the reception of the older poetic tradition and material in the poem and for the poem's overall composition, as it is presently preserved (not including later additions, such as v. 31). To highlight the development of the traditions of the poem's Iron I materials as well as their tenth-century configuration, we will explore the literary features of the poem, first from a diachronic perspective and then from a synchronic point of view.

1. Traditional Material in Judges 5

To understand what the composer received and worked with, we return to a series of observations about traditional material in the poem made in the preceding chapter. There we noted several features that suit the Iron I period: the use of **pr*ʿ for military "long-hairs" in v. 2; the mention of Seir and Edom in vv. 4-5, the economic background of trade routes *(ntybwt),* as well as the reference to Shamgar ben-ʿAnat in v. 6; the "village militia" *(pĕrāzôn)* in vv. 7 and 11; the neutral reference to Amalek in v. 14; and the description of the stars as a heavenly army without Yahweh in v. 20. These features best fit an Iron I setting. There is more to the story of the old material within the poem of Judges 5. As Peter Ackroyd, Michael David Coogan, and other scholars have noted,[2] the poem works with traditional material, including a series of scenes. Such "moments" in the poem's sequence are crucial for its reading. In creating — or re-creating — scenes, the composer chose to include old motifs and to modify them. What did the composer receive and how did the composer use it? It is difficult to know precisely, but some inferences may be drawn on the basis of literary comparisons.

For many commentators, especially Coogan,[3] a number of pieces in the poem have stood out for their traditional character as "formulaic passages": the theophany in vv. 4-5, the negative sayings in vv. 15b-17, the curse of Meroz in v. 23, and the scene in vv. 24-27. I will comment on these in turn. In the preceding chapter, I noted these as possible vestiges of the Iron I period; here I focus attention on their modification. What we will see is that poetic commemoration of warriors involves the reuse of older pieces and their reconfiguration and reinterpretation by their author-arranger.

Verses 4-5

Some scholars have viewed the theophany of vv. 4-5 as an independent trope based on a comparison with Ps. 68:8-9 (Eng. 7-8).[4] Others see literary dependence between the two passages. For example, Michael Fishbane sees Judg. 5:4-5 as a quotation of Ps. 68:8-9,[5] while Herbert Niehr views Ps. 68:8-9 as the quotation of Judg. 5:4-5.[6] Perhaps militating in favor of Psalm 68 as the relatively older context is v. 18(17), with its reference to Sinai in the clause, *ʾădōnāy bām sînay baqqōdeš*. Thus *zeh sînay* fits the context in Ps. 68:9. However, Judg. 5:4-5 and Ps. 68:8-9 show enough differences that it seems that neither was copied from the other. A major difference involves the place names evoked: Sinai in Psalm 68 as opposed to Seir and Edom in Judges 5. The theory of copying does not provide sufficient explanation about the motivation for altering the place names. Since such significant differences exist between the two works, other scholars view the relationship in terms of "reworking." Thus Coogan posits Judg. 5:4-5 as the source for Ps. 68:8-9. Alexander Rofé similarly understands Ps. 68:8-9 as an "Elohistic" reworking of Judg. 5:4-5.[7] Following another line of scholarship, Israel Knohl has proposed seeing the influence working in the opposite direction, based mostly on the expansion in Judg. 5:4-5 relative to Ps. 68:8-9.[8] Like the theory of scribal copying, the theory of reworking in either direction suffers, as it provides little explanation for minor differences, apart from the place names in Judg. 5:4-5. For example, the second lines (ii) show the variation of *gm* and *ʾp*. These are semantic variants;[9] neither would have been copied from the other (unless the copying was from memory).[10] This case seems to fit Cross's theory of "ancient oral variants."[11]

The question of literary dependence has often focused on *zh syny* in these two passages. The phrase is often regarded as a secondary gloss, taken as identifying the mountain: "this is Sinai."[12] It is thought to have been introduced into Judg. 5:5 from Ps. 68:9. Some scholars take it as a gloss on the name of the deity ("the One of Sinai"), while others, such as Fishbane, argued for *zh syny* after the reference to the deity as a gloss meaning "this is Sinai," pertaining to the preceding reference to mountains *(hrym)*.[13] This approach assumed an imbalance in the lines of Judg. 5:5. It was thought that *hrym nzlw mpny yhwh zh syny* in Judg. 5:5 was too overloaded and thus the title *zh syny* must be glossed from Ps. 68:9. However, this approach requires a reading of the two poems in tandem that does not appear to be required. The poetic lines involved need to be seen in their contexts describing the effects of the divine march:[14]

	Judges 5:4b-5	**Psalm 68:8-9**
(i)	*ʾrṣ rʿšh*	*ʾrṣ rʿšh*
(ii)	*gm šmym nṭpw*	*ʾp šmym nṭpw*
(iii)	*gm ʿbym nṭpw mym*	
(iv)	*hrym nzlw*	
(v)	*mpny yhwh zh syny*	*mpny ʾlhym zh syny*
(vi)	*mpny yhwh ʾlhy yśrʾl*	*mpny ʾlhym ʾlhy yśrʾl*

The third line, (iii) in Judg. 5:4b-5, is without any parallel within Ps. 68:8-9, and so seems to be a secondary expansion within its own context. Cross suggests that *gm ʿbym nṭpw mym* may have been attracted by *šmym nṭpw* in Judg. 5:4. The theory that *zeh sînay* was an addition to Judg. 5:5 depended on taking line (iv) together with line (v). However, this view is not necessary. Line (iv) shows inner expansion in Judg. 5:4-5 in adding here a subject and a verb. Whether this expansion was made to smooth the addition of the third line (iii) is not clear. Relative to Ps. 68:8-9, it is not necessarily *zeh sînay* in Judg. 5:4-5 (here line v) that is secondary, but the additional noun and verb in the preceding line (iv). Furthermore, if one removes *zeh sînay* from Judg. 5:5, then it would create an imbalance of poetic lines, and it would remove the phrase parallel to *ʾlhy yśrʾl*. This observation undermines the theory that *zeh sînay* is a gloss derived from Ps. 68:9. In addition, the context would suggest that this phrase is best understood as a divine title, on analogy with the Nabatean divine name Dushara, "He-of-the Šara (mountain)."[15] In sum, the evidence for the phrase as a gloss is insufficient.[16]

In these verses, both Psalm 68 and Judges 5 drew on what was a traditional trope of the divine march with its meteorological theophany. By comparison, the composer of Judg. 5:4-5 expanded the trope. Later I will suggest that the poet who drew on the traditional material of Judg. 5:4-5 did so in order to create a correspondence with the received reference to heavens in v. 20 and to waters in the Wadi Kishon in v. 21. In other words, the composer of the poem's introduction may have been inspired to add traditionally-known elements under the influence of the thematically corresponding material used in the body of the poem. For the sake of our examination, perhaps such "additions" as vv. 4-5 drawn from traditional material may be considered among the choices made by the composer. If so, what does our composer add or change here compared to the trope of the divine warrior's march from the south in its attestations elsewhere?

First, in the use of the place names, the composer of Judges 5 uses Edom and Seir, which differs in the other exemplars of the trope. The citation of Edom and Seir in Judg. 5:4 contrasts with Psalm 68, which mentions Sinai in two different contexts, not only in the theophanic section in v. 8 but further in v. 18(17). Hab. 3:3 refers to Teiman and Paran. Teiman appears also in Kuntillet ʿAjrud inscriptions, and on this basis one might conclude that such references were known during the monarchy (cf. the reference to the king in Hab. 3:13). Deut. 33:2 attests to Sinai, Seir, and Paran. In its move from a standard pair to a threefold mention, this chapter elaborates vis-à-vis all of these passages, in particular in adding the figure of Moses and his teaching. Seir in this passage, as in Judg. 5:4, seems to have remained in the list. Of all these passages, only Judg. 5:4 has Edom. This is not say that Edom/Seir did not constitute a traditional poetic pair; it did (e.g., Num. 24:18), but in this example of the trope Edom seems to drop out. One might put some historical-cultural weight on this distinctive feature in Judg. 5:4. It might suggest its high antiquity, as Edom emerges later as the epitome of hostility, not a likely source later for Yahweh's point of his theophanic march.[17] Perhaps the composer reached back for an earlier-sounding place, for a time before such hostilities, in an effort at evoking a distant past.

A second difference involves *gm ʿbym nṭpw mym,* which according to Cross was attracted by *šmym nṭpw* in Judg. 5:4, since it is missing from Psalm 68. May this apparent addition be viewed as the composer's elaboration and not simply some sort of mistake? In the context, one might be inclined to see a poetic touch here. The subjects "earth," "heavens," "clouds," and "mountains" seem to suggest reading the lines as A: B :: B′: A′. If correct, then perhaps there is a poetic elaboration here. With the repetition of the verb, the poem of Judges 5 perhaps stresses the rain. This consideration depends on the matter of the etymology of **ntp*. Cross derived *nṭpw* from *ṭpp*, "shook," predicted of "heavens."[18] For this view, Cross cited William F. Albright, who posited the root based on Arabic *ṭaffa, ṭafṭafa*, "to flap the wings (bird)," and Aramaic *ṭpṭp*, "flicker."[19] This is not particularly strong support for *ṭpp* in Judg. 5:4. However, there is good evidence for *nṭp*, "to stream" or the like, e.g., Amos 9:13, *wĕhiṭṭîpû hehārîm ʿāsîs*, and Deir Alla, combination II, line 36, *nṭp* used of dew: *tṭpn šr*, "they will drip with heavy rain," and *tṭpn ṭl*, "they will drip with dew."[20] So one may see some stress on water here.[21] As I will argue further below, the composer may have expanded on the theme of the heavens dripping with water (**nṭp*) in lines (ii) and (iii), as it resonates with the water theme in the core of his poem in the battle later in v. 21. This particular emphasis was made by both Judg. 5:5 and Ps. 68:9.[22] This idea also seems comparable with the Ugaritic motif in El's vision in anticipation of Baal's return to life, specifically that "heavens rain oil, wadis run with honey . . ." (*šmm šmn tmṭrn//nḫlm tlk nbtm*, KTU 1.6 III 6-7, 12-13).

Before considering another unit with traditional formulas, it is to be noted that the tradition of the theophany considered here explicitly stresses the deity as Yahweh, in counterdistinction from other materials in vv. 14-30 (except for v. 23, which constitutes an isolated piece to be discussed further below). It may be that it was the emphasis on Yahweh in Judg. 5:4-5 that motivated the poet-composer to bring it into the poem. By drawing on the old trope of vv. 4-5, the poem becomes more oriented to this deity. If a further speculation may be entertained, the purpose of adding a traditional trope so heavily laden with the name of Yahweh in connection with a storm theophany might have been to clarify that it was Yahweh who was responsible for the victory in the storm theophany and not some other god well known for this function, in other words, Baal.[23] In sum, the older material of vv. 4-5 was drawn upon by the composer as a building block in the introduction (vv. 2-13), fronted to the body of the poem (vv. 14-30). We will return to this view after examining a few other traditional pieces in the poem.

Verses 14-18

As commentators have long noted, the sayings in vv. 14-18 have formulaic parallels.[24] They regularly note the citation of the war cry in v. 14, "after you, O Benjamin," as found in Hos. 5:8. For Coogan,[25] the shared wording suggests a formula known in the tradition, and we would add more specifically, in the tradition of the northern kingdom.

Also notable are the parallels between these verses and the tribal sayings elsewhere, especially in Genesis 49. For example, the saying about dwelling by the sea is said of Zebulun in Gen. 49:13, but it is applied to Asher in Judg. 5:17. Similarly, in Gen. 49:14, it is Issachar who is at the "sheepfolds" (?), but in Judg. 5:16 this saying is used of Reuben. Cross regards these as reflecting a tradition of oral sayings used and adapted in each context, what he calls "stock oral formula."[26] These would seem to predate their use in Judg. 5:14-18.

Both Hans-Jürgen Zobel and Coogan have noted how the nuance of the sayings in Judg. 5:14-18 seems to have slightly shifted relative to their usages elsewhere.[27] The original setting of the saying as seen in Gen. 49:14 would be a characterization of the tribe as one who lives or dwells (cf. *rōbēṣ* there). However, in its usage in Judg. 5:16, it expresses the point that Reuben "stayed" (**yšb*) away from the battle. This sense of the word in Hebrew is common.[28] For example, Gen. 25:27 contrasts Jacob with Esau in these terms: Jacob "stayed in camp *(ʾōhālîm)*," while Esau was "a man of the field." Num. 22:19 likewise uses the root in this meaning: "stay here tonight."[29] Judg. 6:18 shows the deity promising to Gideon "to remain until you come back." Similarly, 2 Sam. 11:1: "It was at the turn of the year, the time when kings go out [to battle], that David sent Joab and his servants with him and all Israel, and they devastated the Ammonites and they besieged Rabbah, but David remained *(yôšēb)* in Jerusalem."[30] There may be only a slight shift in sense from residence to remaining, represented by the sayings in Gen. 49:15 and Judg. 5:16. In this context, the shift is telling.

Similarly, the root **škn* in the original setting of the saying would be a characterization of the tribe as one who dwells in Transjordan, as seen in the same root in the saying for Benjamin in Deut. 33:12.[31] However, in Judg. 5:17, **škn* serves to explain that Gilead remained away from the battle; the verse also applies the root to Asher. This sense, "to stay, remain," appears in Gen. 26:2: "Yahweh appeared to him and said: 'Do not go down to Egypt; stay (**škn*) in the land that I tell (indicate to) you.'" The use of these two roots in Judg. 5:14-18 plays on their semantics in order to state the failure of certain tribes to come to the battle.

As a further matter of possible composition, Cross regards the Reuben saying in vv. 15b and 16b as two variants:[32]

Among the divisions of Reuben
Great were (its) considered decrees.
16Why did you stay among the sheepfolds (?),
Listening to the whistlings of the flocks?

As to the divisions of Reuben,
Great were (its) considered searchings.

If vv. 15b and 16b were included purposefully, it would appear that the composer pauses with Reuben. No other tribe, positive or negative, receives the same number of lines, and perhaps there was a message about Reuben being made here by the composer.[33]

Finally for the composition in vv. 14-18, there is the question of the names of what have been generally regarded as "tribes." (Parenthetically, one might put "tribes" in quotation marks for Judges 5, since the word for tribe does not appear in this section, and in fact not in the poem as such.) The composer evidently drew on a known repertoire of tribal names, though it was hardly uniform.[34] Compared with Genesis 49 or Deuteronomy 33, Judg. 5:14-18 is interesting for several reasons. First, vv. 14-18 constitute a compact series compared with the other poems broadly structured around the names of the tribes involved. By comparison, Judg. 5:14-18 seem to have drawn on the traditional repertoire compared with what is attested of tribal sayings elsewhere; and as we have seen with the nuance of the verbs involved, this part of Judges 5 additionally modified the sense of the sayings to suit the context here. Second, Judges 5 is interesting not simply for Judah missing; so are Simeon and Levi. It does seem that the poem shows an old northern sense of the tribes, one without a Judah[35] and Simeon and prior to claims for Levi. Third, the list also shows a slightly different sense from what will become more common in the tribal names. There is Gilead (cf. Gad in Deut. 33:20-21; Gad and Gilead in 1 Sam. 13:7; 2 Sam. 24:5-6; Gad apart from Israel in the Mesha stele, KAI 181:7-8). There are also Ephraim and Machir for Joseph (cf. Gen. 50:23 for a narrative rationalization), not even Ephraim and Manasseh, as in the saying of Joseph in Deut. 33:17 (cf. Gen. 48:5, 13-14). With Judg. 5:14-18, we may sense that we are in a slightly different world, perhaps an old northern one. In sum, the sayings of vv. 14-18 seem to partake of an older tribal environment, perhaps dating to the time of the tenth-century composer or earlier.

Verse 23

This has been considered to be a further separate piece included here. Ackroyd suggests the possibility that v. 23 with the curse on Meroz forms a "quotation" from earlier traditions of the battle utilized by the poet.[36] Indeed, v. 23

is the only material in the poem marked as quotation. According to Cross, the curse holds important implications for understanding "this instance of league 'holy war.'"[37] For Cross, the verse presupposes such a league, and it is presumably Yahwistic in character, given the reference to Yahweh here. For this piece of material, the tradition of battle was Yahwistic, a point that is not nearly as evident in other parts of the poem, especially in the representation of battle in v. 20, which also interestingly stands at some distance from the curse. Indeed, it may be noted how little the name of Yahweh appears in the body of the poem (following the double-introduction of vv. 2-13). On this score, v. 23 is an isolated piece, highlighting the lack of the divine name in the rest of the poem's body. Thus, this one verse may signal a Yahwistic identity for this one isolated subunit, but not for the traditions of the other portions of the poem's body. I will return to this point below.

Verses 24-27

These verses combine traditional *topoi* of praise, hospitality to strangers, and attack. The blessing formula of v. 24, if it may be read as a bicolon,[38] works beautifully, with the repetition of the verb, *tĕbōrak,* the first heading the first line and the second ending the second line, and the repetition of the superlative *minnāšîm.* In addition, the lines show the near "sound pair" of the otherwise disparate *yāʿēl* and *ʾōhel.* The closest parallel to a blessed woman who slays an enemy warrior occurs in the story of Aqhat. Pughat requests a blessing before she goes to avenge the death of her brother: "bless me *(ltbrkn)* that I may go blessed (*brktm* [?]), empower me that I may go empowered" (KTU 1.19 IV 32-33).[39] Perhaps this Ugaritic passage suggests that blessing is tied to the martial purpose in Judg. 5:24-27.

Judg. 5:25 shows the theme of hospitality, with its sequence of water *(mym),* milk *(ḥlb),* and curd *(ḥmʾh).* The combination of water and milk appears in a recollection of hospitality in the story of Sinuhe: "One of their leaders, who had been in Egypt, recognized me. He gave me water and boiled milk for me. I went with him to his tribe. What they did for me was good."[40] The combination of *ḥlb* and *ḥmʾh* has also been noted in the hospitality scene in Gen. 18:8 (cf. KTU 1.23.14).[41] All these instances show some variation. The visit in Genesis 18 includes meat, unlike the initial contact in Sinuhe and Judg. 5:25. Jael's service is for an initial meeting; service of meat takes place in settings for a whole meal.

The scene of hospitality in Judges 5 also refers to the vessel involved as *spl.* From context, this is a vessel that can bear a liquid for drinking. The word "bowl" is used in many translations, but perhaps a very large vessel is what Judg. 5:25 is presenting,[42] perhaps to indicate the largesse of Jael's hospitality. This would fit with its qualification by *'addîrîm.* The term modifying *spl* is *'dryrm,* which perhaps further connects this scene to the earlier scene with this term (v. 13; cf. *'abbîrāyw* in v. 22).[43] Connections can be impressionistic or associative, evoked through verbal links. So **šlḥ* in the next verse compares with v. 15, and **hlm* of v. 22 is picked up in the next verse (note **rgl* in vv. 15 and 27 [2x]). The use, or better reuse, of terms is one means that the composer used to evoke connections between what otherwise might seem rather disparate sections of the poem.

For vv. 26-27, commentators have long noted the closest literary parallel to v. 26b in Baal's smashing of Yamm's head in KTU 1.2 IV 18-26, with the resulting slumping of the defeated figure.[44] Both passages mention **r'š,* but use a different parallel term, *bn ʿnm* in the Baal conflict (1.2 IV 22, 25) and *raqqātô* in Judg. 5:26. The two passages share the verb *hlm* as well as **mḥṣ* here and in 1.2 IV 9, perhaps suggesting a shared West Semitic traditional vocabulary for this type-scene. By comparison, Judg. 5:26 adds *mḥqh,* perhaps a variant of **mḥṣ* as Baruch Halpern argues,[45] and another verb, **ḥlp.* Judg. 5:26 also develops the picture of the physical damage. If Halpern is correct, then the composer seems to have drawn on a regional variant in his poetic oral diction. We will return to this question.

One final observation about the comparison with KTU 1.2 IV: Judg. 5:26 stresses Jael as the agent compared with Baal, who recedes to the background, as the weapon seems to work almost on its own, at least in terms of presentation.[46] It is to be noted that Jael's action is compact by comparison with the scene of Baal's weapon elaborated in discernibly more detail. The figure of Sisera in v. 27 likewise recalls Yamm's slumping at the end of the beating that he takes from Baal's weapon. In view of the comparison, the biblical verses seem to be drawing on an older literary *topos* involving enemy combatants. This may not demonstrate its antiquity, but it fits with such a theory. These comparisons also suggest that the literary tradition engaged in substitutions of particular terms and phrases as well as expansions.

2. The Composition of Judges 5 in Diachronic Perspective

As we noted, the composer of the poem drew on older traditions. The poet worked them in keeping with a particular purpose, to which I would now like to turn.[47] Michael D. Coogan and others have noted a double-introduction in vv. 2-13.[48] The poem of Judges 5 does not begin with a simple introduction compared with other passages, such as the beginning of Exodus 15 ("Let me sing . . ."), or Deuteronomy 32 (with its opening call, "Pay attention, O Heavens, that I may speak//May the Earth hear the words of my mouth"), or Genesis 49 (with its imperative, "Assemble and listen, O Sons of Jacob"), or Num. 23:18 (with its command, "Rise, Balak, and listen"). In all these cases, the declaration to speak or the command to listen occupy the opening of the poem, but this is not the case in Judges 5. It partakes of some of these elements in v. 3, but includes them in a much longer and complex introduction that in the poem's present form runs from v. 2 arguably to v. 13.[49] It is to be observed at the outset that the recognition of the double-introduction itself suggests two stages in the development of this introduction.

The nature of the introduction of Judg. 5:2-13 (or rather, its double-introductions in vv. 2-9 and 10-13) and its relationship to 5:14-30 call for comment. To anticipate, Judg. 5:2-13, along with v. 31,[50] show some distinctive features relative to 5:14-30. We have already seen how this introduction draws on one traditional *topos* in vv. 4-5 and mentions some older features. Otherwise, we see the composer at work introducing the subject matter. The composer does not generate a brief generic introduction, but a rather elaborate one, one that signals the divine role (vv. 2-5), as well as human leadership (vv. 6-9), and it also issues a call to praise on the part of both this human leadership and those for whom the battle is won (vv. 10-14).

In this respect, my approach is somewhat similar to a contribution made by Volkmar Fritz.[51] Fritz favored a diachronic approach with the original song, beginning in v. 12. He also viewed the material in vv. 2-13 as secondary interpretive material. (It seems to me that in view of what we have already seen with vv. 4-5, this need not be quite the case for all of vv. 2-13.) Fritz saw some secondary material embedded in vv. 14-30, such as the second line of v. 15 (which he sees as "an annotation") and v. 21b (which he takes to be dissonant in terms of its meter), but he does not sift through vv. 14-30 to see what the composer may have inherited and altered. In short, Fritz sees the original song as vv. 12-22 and 24-30, with various additions and a new interpretation in vv. 2-11.

Fritz's diachronic approach belongs to a long line of interpretation.[52] Hans Peter Müller had posited an old core of vv. 6-8, 12-17 (18), 19-22, 23, 24-27, 28-30.[53] Heinz-Dieter Neef sees newer additions of vv. 2-3, 9-11a, 31a + 4-5 and an older prestate piece of vv. 6-8, 11b, 12-23 (without *ml'k*), 24-30.[54] Henrik Pfeiffer goes further, positing five layers of redaction added to an old core, not including various minor additions.[55] The *Grund* text for him consists of vv. 12-13a, 18-21b, 22, 24-30 (deleting some minor items such as 24b). A first hymnic redaction by the author of the prose narrative in Judges 4 comprises vv. 1-2, 10-11, and the second hymnic redaction involves vv. 3-5. The next addition, vv. 6-9, orients the composition to the *Richterbuch*. Finally, there is the *Ausbau* of v. 18 to the *Stämmenliste* in vv. 14-17. While Pfeiffer's effort to nail down each piece of the poem is admirable, it seems to lie beyond discernible means of confirmation.

I would approach the poem in a manner that draws on both the diachronic approach of Fritz and the synchronic approach of Coogan.[56] Unlike Coogan, and with Fritz, I would see evidence for diachronic development reflected in the poem's first person references (discussed below) and in the handling of older material (as noted above). Unlike Fritz and with Coogan, I am inclined to see vv. 2-13 in its present arrangement as constituting a double-introduction to vv. 14-30. I would also see the composer dynamically handling older material, which I will explain momentarily; and later I will argue for a synchronic arrangement somewhat following Coogan's lead. I should pause at this point and say that Fritz may be right that v. 12 was the original beginning of an older poem, and interestingly, this seems to be implicitly underscored by the prose introduction of v. 1. As commentators have noted, Judg. 5:1 relates that it was Deborah and Baraq who sang, while 5:12 in the poem seems to suggest that it was Deborah who was called to sing. The prose author of 5:1, in adding Baraq, was a sensitive interpreter of v. 12 in its parallelism. For v. 12a and 12c call Deborah and Baraq: *ʿûrî ʿûrî dĕbôrâ//qûm bārāq*. Then with a nice play of the verb on her name, in v. 12b Deborah is called to sing: *ʿûrî ʿûrî dabbĕrî-šîr*. V. 12d by comparison, and in its implicit parallelism given the parallelism of v. 12a and 12c, calls on Baraq to take captives: *ûšăbēh šebyĕkā ben-ʾăbînōʿam*. There may be a female/male division of labor with v. 12b and 12d, but v. 1 presents both figures as singing. As an aside, it is to be noted that the prose author of v. 1 probably understood the old second person feminine ending of the verb in v. 7, "until you arose *(šaqqamtî)*," in terms of the later standard classical Hebrew grammar, namely as a first person singular verb. Accordingly, the author of v. 1 interpreted Deborah as speaking about herself in v. 7, in keeping with the prose author's notion that hers was the "I-voice" of the poem. We will return to the question of the poem's "I-voice" below.

If the Song of Deborah in its present form is not to be seen as commencing until v. 13, then the following questions may be posed: How are these verses constituted? Whose voice is represented by these verses? How are these verses to be construed in connection to vv. 14-30? I would like to explore the possibility that considerably more is involved in the double-introduction represented by vv. 2-13 in relation to the scenes in the rest of the poem. It seems that the composer not only offers two introductions with these verses, but also generates material in them that correlates with the scenes in vv. 14-30, and in doing so, the composer provides in the introduction of vv. 2-13 an interpretation or statement about the meaning of the scenes in vv. 14-30. In other words, vv. 2-13 anticipate elements attested in vv. 14-30 and provide an interpretive lens for them. Building on the work of Fritz and others, it is possible to suggest six ways in which vv. 2-13 provide interpretive parameters for vv. 14-30.

First, the reading of the battle shifts, as we move from the introduction to the battle proper. What represents a truly dramatic difference involves the word Israel. It appears in vv. 2, 3, 5, 7, 8, 9 and 11 (2x) within vv. 2-13, but there is no Israel in vv. 14-30.[57] The net effect is to transform this conflict from a coalition of local units into a battle involving Israel.[58] The use of the term *ʿam* arguably reflects this shift as well. In the introduction, *ʿam* occurs four times (vv. 2,[59] 9, 11, 13), where it functions to name the whole or the collective involved in the battle.[60] In contrast, the word occurs only once in the description of battle or postbattle, in v. 18, where it is used of Zebulun and not of Israel (cf. Gen. 49:16 for Dan and "his *ʿam*"). In the battle, it denotes one unit within the larger coalition. In short, the dominant use of Israel and *ʿam* in the introduction in vv. 2-13 may mask an older picture of the battle of a coalition of groups that may not have fully constituted Israel or a single *ʿam*, but were viewed as such by the time of the composer.

Second, as commentators note,[61] Yahweh plays a prominent role in vv. 2-13 compared with the rest of the poem. Yahweh is mentioned seven times in vv. 2-13 (vv. 2, 3, 4, 5, 9, 11, 13), in contrast to the single attestation of this divine name, in v. 23, within vv. 14-30.[62] (As we noted above, v. 23 is a literary subunit or "isolate.") The net effect of the occurrences of the divine name is to increase the sense of this battle as divine war and specifically as Yahweh's. V. 11 in particular relates that this victory is one of the *ṣidqôt yhwh*.[63] In this context, the battle is not only attributed to Yahweh, but it is also located within a string of divine acts.[64] From the relative absence of the name of Yahweh in vv. 12-30, Fritz concludes: "Thus, the veneration of Yahweh and the association of the tribes constitute independent dimensions that should be differentiated from one another."[65] One might compare the single reference to Yahweh in Genesis 49, in v. 18, likewise found in a first person declaration (cf. the series of terms for El in 49:24-26); by comparison,

Deuteronomy 33 contains many occurrences of the name of Yahweh (vv. 2, 7, 11, 12, 13, 21, 23, 29).

Third, vv. 2-13 address leadership that is manifest in the battle proper. This is clearest with the references to Deborah and Baraq in the introduction in vv. 7 and 12 and the battle proper in v. 15. Vv. 7b-8 also raise the issue of leadership. V. 7b clearly gives preeminence of Deborah over Baraq, in contrast to both v. 12 and v. 15, where the two leaders stand in parallelism (cf. the parallelism of Saul and David in 1 Sam. 18:7 = 21:11 = 29:5).[66] Stressing Deborah as a mother in Israel raises her leadership profile, even as it provides for a foil to Sisera's mother in v. 28.[67] As noted above, the leadership term, with *ḥqq, in v. 9 anticipates the use of the same root in vv. 14 and 15. The descent of the force to the gates in v. 11d[68] anticipates v. 14.

Fourth, the invocation of kings in v. 3 anticipates the kings of v. 19. Fifth, vv. 4-5, as we may have seen, constitute one of the older traditional pieces incorporated into the poem. It is not integrated into the battle proper. In view of its attestation with variations elsewhere as noted above,[69] it seems to constitute an older traditional *topos* that was brought into this context,[70] perhaps to anticipate the military action of the stars in vv. 20-21 and also to indicate that the battle of the stars in these verses represents this deity's theophanic battle. I have already mentioned the water of this theophany, which may link to the waters of the Kishon in v. 21. Sixth and finally, the reference to Jael in v. 6 anticipates her role in vv. 24-27, as commentators have noted.[71]

If this way of reading the introduction of vv. 2-13 is advisable, then what are the larger implications for the composition as a whole, especially for questions of its literary coherence or aesthetics? First, Judges 5 does not partake of the sort of literary coherence in the sense prevalent in the study of Hebrew poems through the end of the twentieth century. The coherence in part operates within sections, but it equally involves a horizontal aesthetic across sections, one that coordinates different components in different sections, sometimes evoked by as little as repeated words or roots. Second, the compositional technique coordinates pieces, which in some cases predate their use in the poem. As Coogan and Ackroyd's discussions suggest, the poem contains older chunks of material or set lists that were added to further the thematic purposes of the composition. Third, the composer provides a set of interpretive materials in the introduction that anticipate various elements in the battle and postbattle descriptions. There is a coordination of introductory material and materials in the battle/postbattle scenes. In addition, the introductory material generates information that serves as the interpretive horizons for the presentation of the battle and postbattle material.

If the horizontal reading of Judg. 5:2-13 vis-à-vis Judg. 5:14-30 is correct, then "commentary" in a limited or implicit sense is part and parcel of the composition of Judges 5. It lies within the poem itself. The composer has provided in the introduction an interpretive lens or "commentary" on the battle and postbattle scenes. With particular emphasis on deity, people, and Israel in vv. 2-13, the composer has indicated what the scenes in vv. 14-30 mean: they are all about "promoting group identity"[72] under the banner of deity, people, and country. In this sense, the composer has provided "commentary" evidently important to the composer and to the audience served by the poem in his time. Retelling, performing, and interpretation are operative as an early, implicit form of commentary in what seems to be among our earliest biblical compositions. One might say that retelling, performing, and interpretation constitute a single constellation of features bundled together in oral composition, which anticipates the constellation of reading, writing, and interpretation that marks much of the development of Israel's later literature.

Finally, let us turn to the implications that this reading of Judges 5 holds for the larger historical questions about early Israel and the question of ethnicity. In a great deal of biblical scholarship, Judges 5 is perhaps the text most often cited to anchor discussions about Israel during the Iron I period. This approach assumes that the poem is relatively old, that is to say, Iron I. It is possible to hold a somewhat later date for the poem's present composition and still maintain the importance of the poem for anchoring historical discussions for Israel in the Iron I period. In other words, the poem in its current written form was an early Iron II composition, and at the same time the pieces in vv. 4-5 and 14-30 as well as some other usages in vv. 2-13 originated orally in the Iron I period (as noted at the outset of this chapter and discussed in the preceding one). As noted above, Fritz sees the original song in vv. 12-22 and 24-30 as "pre-state."[73] This is essentially the view of the most recent literary study of this poem by Pfeiffer despite the multiple levels of subsequent redaction.[74] My own sense is this: the poem's old material is largely concentrated in vv. 14-30 and in select, older pieces embedded in the introduction in vv. 2-13, such as vv. 4-5; these may be Iron I. However, the material of the composer concentrated in the Introduction otherwise contains little or no such older material and thus may well be Iron II, perhaps tenth century and even possibly the ninth century (but arguably older-looking than eighth-century poetry).

No less important are the multiple levels of tradition in the different sections of the poem. This issue of multiple levels in the poem specifically bears on the matter of positing and describing early Israel. The view of the poem offered here would locate the entity of Israel within the interpretive lens of the composer and not as part of the battle/postbattle description. The composer interprets as Israel the list of units in vv. 14-18, which constitutes a list of social units not labeled Israel in this context. With Israel limited to the introduction, in vv. 2-13, it is unclear to what degree, if at all, the notion of Israel or a collective of Israel informs traditions behind scenes in vv. 14-30. The upshot of the new formation of the introductory material is to make a new statement about the national patron god and the emergent kingdom of Israel. In other words, the older tradition that largely lacked references to Yahweh or to Israel as a whole was reformed into a vision befitting the emergent Israel in the tenth century. The early Israelite monarchy could look back to an older battle and its various traditions as a way to express its own identity. Unlike the older situation in which tribes might or might not participate in regional conflicts,[75] a whole Israel under the northern monarchy would overcome such limitations.[76] The past represented by the Iron I traditions and material embedded in Judges 5 could, in the tenth-century context, serve the new emerging nation[77] of Israel to proclaim "God and country."[78]

To my mind, the poem embodies various processes involved in collective memory and amnesia over this issue.[79] It arguably recalls the past in light of the composer's present: the various social units named are interpreted as a people called Israel. Moreover, the characterization of the victory as religious warfare is heightened and the Israelite national god is moved to center stage. This victory is not regarded as an isolated event, but is represented as part of an oral tradition celebrating a series of divine acts (v. 11). The oral retelling referenced in this verse suggests a site of collective memory, an oral memory that was malleable.[80] The introduction itself may belong to or was even produced by this site of memory. This site not only recalls the past, but also represents its social location for the reception of this past and perhaps molds the past event in light of its own horizons. The introduction, and perhaps even the poem as a whole, was, in Coogan's words, "composed some time after the events it relates, a conclusion confirmed by the repeated use of *'az* and by the reference to the 'days of Jael' (v 6)."[81] Thus the poetic composer works with composite material and adds as it seems appropriate. It would be possible to accept this sort of depth of tradition and still date much of the basic composition to the Iron I period.

The world of early Israel that some modern scholars think of when they read the poem is thus arguably one largely created by the composer of vv. 2-13 and perhaps not the poem as a whole. For example, many commentators favor a notion of an early collective Israel as the *ʿam yhwh.* This is the world of the composer's introduction (v. 13), but it may not be the older world of the battle or its postbattle context. A similar issue involves the maximal number of tribes claimed in the battle. In taking *l-* (on *lmh* in vv. 16-17) as an asseverative particle, Cross included all the tribes explicitly named as participants in the battle.[82] Cross stated: "this has important consequences for our understanding of this instance of league 'holy war.'" This is indeed true. The question is whether Cross and other commentators who maximize the number of tribes are influenced by the perspective of the introduction. If so, they have perhaps followed the lead of the introduction in positing an Israelite league as such. The poem may in fact both express and repress the problem of social-political identity in early Israel.[83]

The "changing character" of Israel in Judges 5 has been keenly noted by Yairah Amit. In connection with the representation of what she calls "the six tribes" in Judg. 5:14-18, Amit comments on the phrase "the men of Israel" from Naphtali, Asher, and Manasseh in 7:23: "It is precisely the changing and flexible meaning attached to this term that brings out one of the central problems of the period of the judges: an unstable reality, in which there is no centrality, fixity or unity."[84] In his consideration of the tribes in the poem, Fritz suggests that the original victory belonged not to Israel, but to Zebulun and Naphtali, only to be later enshrined as the victory of Israel more generally. He comments: "The victory of one member of the association was therefore the occasion for calling together its participant tribes. . . . It is precisely the differentiation that must be made between the events of the war and the gathering of the association that provides an insight into the constitution of pre-state Israel, even though the theory of the amphictyony of the 12 tribes should be abandoned."[85] Many commentators have worked with the notion that it is the association that makes the battle possible, but here Fritz poses the relationship in reverse terms, with the original battle prior to the confederation. The battle as remembered and celebrated in the original song is the source for the prestate tribal association. Fritz concludes that the song can still be taken as evidence for the worship of Yahweh by the tribes in the prestate period, yet Fritz is also saying that this worship was not part of or the source for the original battle but that the original battle as celebrated helped to generate this religious identity in the prestate period. Put in terms of the distribution of *ʿam* in the poem noted above, the *ʿam* led victoriously by Zebulun and its compatriots became celebrated as the *ʿam* of Israel more broadly.

Finally, the very nature of the battle, seen as Israelites versus Canaanites, depends on reading and matching up the Canaanite kings of v. 19 against

Israel of vv. 4 and 11.[86] However, one might bracket Israel as such out of the immediate context of v. 19, and instead view the battle as a conflict between a coalition of various units (which the poem never called "tribes" as such) and an alliance of Canaanite kings. In other words, the poem arguably presents a political-military conflict, which takes on a specifically Israelite cast only when vv. 14-19 are read through the lens of vv. 2-13.

In this discussion, I have attributed the tradition of battle and much of its material to a late prestate tradition in the Iron I, with the overall formation seeming to belong to the tenth century. Ackroyd summarized his overall sense of the composition: "the resulting poem gives no detailed account of the battle, but impressions of the circumstances and of the events which — in the development of the tradition — had come to appear significant."[87] As we have noted, some pieces in the poem reflect selection from the tradition received about the battle. Ackroyd commented in this vein: "it is a common feature of popular poetry to select the significant points in an event rather than to explain the whole course of the action."[88] In other words, the composer and the audience share knowledge about the tradition of the battle. For example, the names of Shamgar and Meroz seem to be enough for the older composition; evidently, little else needed to be said of these names for the composer. Or, if the names were only barely known and largely forgotten, even this quality about them could have served a later poet's purpose in evoking this event precisely because of their antiquity. In either case, the composer-singer provides the briefest of allusions with these two names. In the case of the name of Deborah, the composer moves in the opposite direction, in dramatizing and elaborating her role beyond the received invocation of v. 12. It is evident from v. 12 that the older tradition knew her place in this poem. In the tradition of the composer, she was particularly championed, as seen in vv. 6-7. Perhaps equally important is the very fact that the composer can choose. The implication is that the poet culled from a larger-known tradition about the battle received by the time of the late prestate period. Perhaps it would be more accurate to say that the composer-arranger selected materials from various traditions associated with the battle and harmonized them in culling and recomposing them. Some of these older traditions were evidently more Yahwistic (vv. 4-5, 23). In the poem's introduction, the composer extended the Yahwistic traditions to generalize the claim of Yahweh's place in Israel's oldest memory, thereby masking the traditions that seemed to have lacked the figure of Yahweh. The same process of choice and composition likewise overwrote the lack of an original *'am yhwh* in some of the earliest traditions.

In closing this diachronic reading of the poem, the reading proposed here would continue to offer important information for Iron I Israel, as argued in the preceding chapter. However, contrary to the common scholarly use made of Judges 5, the older tradition of the poem arguably does not offer a picture of a collective early Israel with a sense of a single peoplehood or a single patron god. Indeed, the lack of an original or "primary" literary unity,[89] suggested by Judges 5's compositional process and composite nature, may parallel the lack of a clear, original picture of social coherence about Israel that many scholars have assumed based on this poem.

3. The Synchronic Structure of the Poem

The standard commentaries provide relatively little guidance on the matter of the poem's overall structure or unity. Based mostly on content, Gottlieb Ludwig Studer in his 1835 commentary favored seeing seven units: 1-6, 9-12, 12-15, 15-19, 19-23, 23-27, 28-31.[90] C. F. Burney focused on the parallelism, specifically the poem's climactic parallelism.[91] His division of the poem was based on a mix of content and number of *stichoi* (between six and eleven in a strophe): vv. 3-5, 6-8, 12, 9-11, 13-15a, 15b-18, 19-21, 22-23, 24-27, 28-30, 31.[92] Robert Boling divided the poem into nine parts without providing a rationale: vv. 2-9, 10-13, 14-16, 17-20, 21-22, 23, 24-27, 28-30, 31.[93] J. Alberto Soggin has some pertinent observations, but offers little overall sense of the poem's organization. Walter Gross's great commentary on Judges notes the issue of structure, but offers little guidance of its own on the question.[94]

Most specific studies on the poem are not much more helpful on the question of its organization. Shortly after the turn of the twentieth century, Vincenz Zapletal divided the poem along content lines: 3-4-2-5, 6-8, 9-11, 12-18, 19-22, 23-27, 28-30.[95] More than fifty years ago, in 1961, Joseph Blenkinsopp noted the problem of the poem's unity: "the unity of the poem is not literary, but theological."[96] The question of structure was raised in 1963 by Wolfgang Richter,[97] in 1978 by Michael David Coogan,[98] and again in 1989 by Ulrike Bechmann.[99] In response to Blenkinsopp, Coogan identified salient features in Judges 5 that he believes contribute to "the unity of the poem on a literary level."[100] Coogan's treatment is in many respects the most substantive proposal, and so we may begin with his account.

For vv. 2-13, two stanzas were claimed by Coogan: vv. 2-8 and 9-13. Both begin with *yiśrāʾēl* and *ʿām,* along with the command to bless Yahweh (vv. 2, 9). Each of these is followed with a second person plural address (vv. 3,

10), with a further address in the second singular (vv. 4-5, resumed in 7, 12), ending with what Coogan calls a "historical statement" (vv. 6-8, 12). Coogan comments: "This parallel structure is admittedly not entirely symmetrical, but it does suggest a division into two distinct units with the same pattern."

Coogan lists the overall schema for the poem according to content:[101]

I. vv. 2-8	Preliminary to battle with an emphasis on Yahweh
II. vv. 9-13	Second preliminary to battle
III. vv. 14-18	Response of the tribes
IV. vv. 19-23	The battle
V. vv. 24-30	Sequel to battle: Jael (positive); Sisera's mother (negative)

Coogan proceeds to chart the verbal repetitions (as indicative of verbal and thematic relationships between stanzas).[102] He then offers a metrical analysis.[103] In this connection, he discusses poetic techniques such as alliteration, paronomasia, repetitive parallelism, and chiasm.[104] Coogan also references what he calls "formulaic passages," namely the theophany of vv. 4-5 and the tribal list of vv. 14-18.[105] (In this context, we note Ackroyd's similar comment concerning the curse of Meroz in vv. 23-24.[106])

This overall approach to the poem does not exhaust the features worth noting. Indeed, in the vein of Coogan's observations, specific elements suggest some level of coherence within units. As noted above, Coogan points to the features contributing to coherence in vv. 2-13. For the postbattle scenes of vv. 24-30, this section is marked in particular by terms of speech, specifically curse and blessing, namely the curse of Meroz, v. 23 and **brk* twice in v. 24. This is not to mention other terms of sound, especially the repetition of **hlm* in the two different scenes, in vv. 22 and 26, but also other words for speech (**'mr*, v. 23; **š'l*, v. 25). We hear the speech of Sisera's mother, and we are told in v. 29 the verbal answer. Speech is a recurring feature of vv. 23-31, which dramatizes for the audience the implications of the battle. Additionally, the curse and blessing in vv. 23-31 may hold further significance for reading the poem. Indeed, it might be entertained whether the curse and blessing in vv. 23-31 are designed to echo or balance the opening blessings in the prebattle scenes, in vv. 2 and 9.

In the heart of the poem, in the battle discussion proper, other sorts of terms dominate, which show verbal connection to the prebattle and postbattle scenes. First, the poem contains a series of leadership terms: *ḥôqĕqê* in v. 9, *mĕḥōqĕqîm* in v. 14, and *ḥiqĕqê-lēb* in v. 15; *gibbôrîm* in vv. 13, 23 and cf. 30; *ʾaddîrîm* in vv. 13, 25 (cf. *ʿădārîm* in v. 16); **sār* vv. 15 (masc.) and 29 (fem. pl.); *ʾabbîrîm* in v. 22. The terms of battle are no less prominent in the poem: **lḥm* in vv. 8 (apparently), 19, 20; **ʿam* in vv. 2, 9, 11, 13, 14, 18; *rōkĕbê* in v. 10, *rekeb* in v. 28; *markĕbôt* in v. 28; cf. the possible verbal echoing of *beṣaʿ* in v. 19 and *ṣebaʿ* in v. 30. Nicely complementing the terms of battle is the use of body parts to describe matters: **prʿ* in v. 2; **lēb* in vv. 9, 15, 16; **rgl* in vv. 15, 27; **rōʾš* in vv. 26, 30; **yād* in v. 26; *paʿămê* in v. 28; *nišqĕpâ* in v. 28; *ṣawwĕ(ʾ)rê* in v. 30. The human bodies in the drama are evoked further with terms of movement and stasis: **qwm* in vv. 7, 12; **yšb* in vv. 10, 16, 17, 23; **drk* in vv. 10, 21; **yrd (rdh)* in vv. 11, 13, 14 (cf. *hayyardēn* in v. 17); **ʾaḥr* in vv. 14, 28; **šlḥ* in vv. 15, 26; **škn* and **gwr* in v. 17; **bwʾ* in vv. 19, 23, 28; **krʿ*, **npl*, **škb* in v. 27; and **bōšeš* in v. 28.

The poem is intensely verbal and physical, and it is this quality of the poem that helps to explain its dramatic quality. Still, observations such as these do not explain the compositional nature of vv. 2-13. These verses do not really constitute a scene or series of scenes as such, in comparison with the rest of the poem. As Blenkinsopp and Soggin noted,[107] the model of literary coherence that has been used to judge the poem's literary merits seems inadequate for assessing Judges 5 in general and vv. 2-13 in particular. Still Coogan, I think, was very much on the right track in speaking of the composer's "selective use and modification of traditional material."[108] In particular, the overall content of vv. 2-13, what Coogan called two preliminaries to battle, suggests a composer's introduction to the various scenes, what Studer long ago called the singer's "Proömium."[109] (This point is particularly evident when the very brief introductions to other poems are compared, as noted above.)

Coogan's article is important, especially for its observations about the poem's literary features. Indeed, to my mind, Coogan's efforts constitute the single greatest advance on this matter.[110] It may be said that subsequent treatments of the poem draw on Coogan's discussion (e.g., de Moor, Halpern, Stager, Schloen), but they do not much advance the literary understanding of the poem. (An exception is Jan P. Fokkelman.[111]) At the same time, Blenkinsopp's claim about the poem's lack of literary coherence remains poignant. Coogan's study, impressive and important as it is on several details, amounts to a series of observations rather than a picture of coherence as such, apart from the first and last units. This is an important finding, not a problem. To my mind, Coogan's analysis in a sense mirrors the poem's own heterogeneity. The aesthetic sensibility of late-twentieth-century interpreters rested on a notion of literary coherence,[112] which Blenkinsopp disputed for Judges 5 and Coogan sought to counter. However, it may be the notion of literary coherence that is lacking. Perhaps the nature of literary coherence in this case has not been properly fathomed.

The tenth-century composer set out the materials that were available from the known tradition in a series of thematic diptychs. (The first and last of these were suggested by Coogan, among others, as discussed above.) To illustrate this structure, I provide a translation[113] at this point, with headings that mark the synchronic structure of diptychs:

PROSE INTRODUCTION

1 And Deborah, along with Baraq, son of Abinoam, sang on that day (saying):

POETIC INTRODUCTION: LEADERSHIP	*Word Count/ Syllable Count*
Focus on the divine leader	
2 When locks were long in Israel,	3/10
When the people committed itself, bless Yahweh!	4/10
3 Hear, O kings, Listen, O rulers,	4/12
I, to Yahweh may I sing,	4/12
May I intone to Yahweh, the God of Israel:	4/12
4 O Yahweh, when you departed from Seir,	3/9
When you marched from the highland of Edom,	3/9
The earth shook,	2/5
Heavens streamed, too,	3/7
Clouds, too, streamed with water,	4/8
5 Mountains shook	2/5
Before Yahweh, the One of Sinai,	4/8
Before Yahweh, the God of Israel.	4/11
Focus on human leaders	
6 In the days of Shamgar ben Anat, in the days of Yael,	6/11
Routes and wayfarers ceased,	4/13
They went on roundabout routes.	3/10
7 The village militia ceased in Israel,	3/10
They ceased until you, Deborah, arose,	4/10
Until you arose, O Mother, in Israel.	3/8
8 It (Israel) chose new leaders/gods (?);	3/8

Then it fought at the gates (?). 3/6
Was a shield or even a spear seen 3/9
Among the forty thousand in Israel? 3/10
9 My heart is for the leaders of Israel, 3/9
Those committed among the people, bless Yahweh! 4/12

CALL TO SONG: CONTRAST IN PERSONNEL

People called to sing

10 O riders on tawny asses, 3/9
Sitting on cloths, 2/6
And walkers on the road, sing! 3/9
11 At the sound of divisions at the water-holes, 4/10
There they may recount the victories of Yahweh, 4/8
The victories of his village-militia in Israel, 3/9
(How) then they went down to the gates,
did the "people" of Yahweh. 5/11

Leadership called to sing

12 Stir, stir Deborah, 3/7
Stir, stir, strike up the song! 4/8
Arise, Baraq, 2/3
And take your captives, Son of Abinoam! 4/11
13 Then may the surviving rule over the mighty, 5/10
May the people of Yahweh rule for me over the warriors! 4/9

PREBATTLE MUSTER: TRIBES IN CONTRAST

Tribes that fight

14 From Ephraim those whose root is in Amalek, 4/11
After you, Benjamin, with your forces, 3/12
From Machir, leaders[114] came down, 4/11
And from Zebulun those who wield the bronze scepter.[115] 4/13
15 And my princes of Issachar were with Deborah, 4/11
And Issachar so (too) with Baraq, 3/7
Sent under his command into the valley. 3/8

Tribes that do not fight

Among the divisions of Reuben 2/6
Great were (its) considered decrees. 3/7

16 Why did you stay among the sheepfolds (?), 4/11
Listening to the whistlings of the flocks? 3/9
As to the divisions of Reuben, 2/6
Great were (its) considered searchings. 3/6
17 Gilead in Transjordan remained, 4/10
And Dan, why did he sojourn on ships? 4/9
Asher stayed at the seashore, 4/8
And remained at its inlets. 3/7

BATTLE AND ITS IMMEDIATE AFTERMATH

Battle Engaged

18 Zebulun was a force that mortally scorned its own life. 5/10
And Naphtali was up on the highlands. 4/10
19 Kings came, they fought, 3/8
Then the kings of Canaan fought, 4/9
At Taanach, by the waters of Megiddo, 4/8
Spoil of silver they did not take. 4/8
20 From heaven the stars fought, 4/11
From their courses they fought with Sisera. 4/12

Battle's Aftermath

21 The wadi Kishon swept them away, 3/7
The ancient wadi, the wadi Kishon. 4/9
March on, O my soul, in strength! 3/6
22 Then the horses' hoofs pounded, 4/8
From his steeds galloping, galloping. 3/10
23 "Curse Meroz," said Yahweh⟨'s messenger(?)⟩. 5/10(⟨4/8⟩?)
"Curse harshly[116] its inhabitants, 3/8
For they did not come to Yahweh's aid, 5/9
To Yahweh's aid among the warriors." 3/9

POSTBATTLE: TWO WOMEN IN POSTBATTLE CONTRAST

Jael

24 May Jael be most blessed of women, 3/8
⟨Wife of Heber the Qenite⟩[117] ⟨3/7⟩
Most among women in tents may she be blessed: 3/9
25 Water he requested, milk she served, 4/9
In a vessel of warriors she brought curd. 4/11

26 Her hand to the peg she put, 3/8
Her right to the workers' hammer. 3/9
She pounded Sisera, smashed his head, 4/11
She smashed, she pierced his temple. 3/11
27 Between her feet, he slumped, he fell, he lay; 5/10
Between her feet, he slumped, he fell, 4/8
Where he slumped, there he fell destroyed. 5/10

Sisera's Mother

28 Through the window, she peers, she cries, 4/12
The mother of Sisera through the lattice: 4/9
"Why is his chariot slow in coming? 4/9
Why do the hooves of his chariot-horses delay?" 4/13
29 The wisest of her princesses answered her, 3/10
She, indeed, answered her with her words: 5/9
30 "Surely they have come upon spoil, splitting 4/11
A maiden, two for the head warrior, 4/11
Spoil of dyed clothes for Sisera, 3/9
Spoil of woven dyed clothes, 3/7
Two woven dyed clothes, 2/6
On the neck of the despoiler." 2/6

Poetic Coda to the War Poem

31 Thus may all your enemies perish, O Yahweh, 5/11
And may those who love you be like the rising of the sun
in its strength. 4/13

Prose Frame

And the land was quiet for forty years.

With this translation in view, some brief comments on the construction of each diptych may be offered. We begin with the first one, which consists of vv. 2-9. Scholars have long noted the wording shared by vv. 2 and 9:[118]

> 2 When locks were long in Israel,
> When the people committed itself, bless Yahweh!
>
> 9 My heart is for the leaders of Israel,
> Those committed among the people, bless Yahweh!

There is no missing the similarities between these two verses. They frame the whole in calling on both Israel as a whole and its leaders specifically to bless Yahweh. The slight differences are perhaps indicative of the thrusts of their immediate contexts. The first initially begins with Israel to recognize its divine leader, while the second centers on its human leadership.

The second diptych of the call to sing involves vv. 10-13. The two parts of this unit are parallel, with their final lines concerning the "people of Yahweh" *(ʿam yhwh)*. In each part, there is a call to sing: the people are called to sing in vv. 10-11, while the leadership is called to sing in vv. 12-13.

The third diptych comprises vv. 14-17. It is clearly divided into the tribes that join the battle and those that do not come.

The fourth diptych involves vv. 18-23. V. 18 is often thought to belong to the muster of tribes, but it seems instead to put the two tribes at the head of the battle account.[119] This placement honors the memory of their role in battle.

Long observed by commentators, the fifth and final diptych, vv. 24-30, is quite clear in contrasting the two women, Yael (vv. 24-27) and the mother of Sisera (vv. 28-30). The contrast between their situations relative to the combatants could perhaps not be stronger. Yael the Kenite, an outsider to the combatants, offers refuge to Sisera on the run, only to assassinate him. Sisera's mother, apparently a queen, awaits a son who will never return home. As noted above, the description of Yael draws on very traditional material. The scene of Sisera's mother appears stereotypical, with her royal ladies surrounding her as she awaits her son's victorious return. The two sections share little in common, but stand largely in contrastive terms. Even the references to body parts in both sections point to their difference: Sisera lying at the feet of Jael and Sisera's mother hoping for spoil that may go on the neck of despoilers. Sisera is the central term that ties the two women together.

This reading offers a synchronic whole that has taken a panoply of traditional materials and arranged them with a certain literary coherence. This poem seems to show a "secondary unity," as espoused by Luis Alonso Schökel: "A later writer could take already completed pieces and bring them together skillfully to form a new and complex unity."[120] The analysis offered thus far and extended below does not confirm Coogan's implicit argument for primary unity; at the same time, it hardly supports Blenkinsopp's claim that "the unity of the poem is not literary, but theological."[121] In its present form, the poem shows considerable coherence, both in the sorts of details noted by Coogan and also in its structure, which was imposed upon the inherited tradition selected by the composer.

4. The Poem and Its Performance: The First Person Voice

Performance and production are key considerations in thinking about texts and their aesthetics. It seems to me that the literary coherence in this text is intertwined with the poem's representation of its performance and production. To further understand the whole and its parts, I would like to address the composer's own mode of representation and what this composer had to work with and, I hope, a sense of the difference between the two. For the composer's handling of material, one feature appears particularly conspicuous.[122]

This feature concerns the poem's first person references.[123] The first person lines tend to be treated cursorily by some commentators, but in theory they should be taken seriously, as they ostensibly constitute the composer's first person self-representation. The first person references in particular are to be regarded as one of the composer's major contributions to the poem. There are five first person references, in vv. 3, 9a, 13b, 15, 21b. This poem is hardly alone in having such first person references (cf. the first person references in Gen. 49:3, 6-7, 9, 18;[124] Exod. 15:1-2), but of all the so-called old poetry rendered in the third person (cf. the first person poems of Numbers 23-24), Judges 5 contains more than any other than I am aware of. In this instance, its first person references would appear to correspond thematically to division-units, with each of the first person references dramatizing the theme in each of these subunits. The poem's initial first person reference, in v. 3, declares the wish to sing to Yahweh, and vv. 2-5 concern Yahweh's power. The wish expressed informs the whole poem, and it stresses Yahweh as the party ultimately responsible for the battle's positive outcomes. The next first person reference, in v. 9a, states the first person concern ("my heart"[125]) for the leaders of Israel, and vv. 6-9 discuss human leadership. The third, in v. 13b, if textually not suspect, anticipates battle in the calls to song in vv. 10-13. The fourth, in v. 15, shows the speaker referring to "my princes" (or "chiefs," so NJPS), as they go into battle. In the fifth and final first person reference in v. 21b, again if not textually suspect,[126] the speaker offers a command addressed to the speaker's "self" to march imaginatively at the battle:[127] "My very self marches in power."[128] What was the point of the first person references?

This first person voice continues the singer voice announced first in v. 3. The poet moves on from this verse, purporting to be with the human leaders in v. 9, acknowledging their victory in v. 13, referring to the heads as "mine" in v. 15, and calling on the first person self to participate in the battle victory in v. 21. This is a kind of participation in the narrated past. The first person lines provide a rhetorical foregrounding that represents a personal excitement for the past events, arguably designed to similarly move the audience. What the first person references accomplish is to express the imaginative participation of the composer in the battle and, by implication, to invite the audience to do likewise.[129] The second person addresses (in vv. 4, 7, 12, 14, 16)[130] likewise contribute to this imagined relationship between the "singer-I" and the divine and human figures addressed in the poem. In view of the command to Deborah to sing in v. 12, the first person "I-voice" was likely not hers, but belonged to an unnamed singer who seeks to imitate what it recalls as her role as a singer in battle as marked in v. 12. The participation of the "I-voice" extends not only to being with the leaders and participating imaginatively in the events of battle, but also in imitating Deborah's role as singer.[131]

In this reading, the singer of the poem as presently constructed identifies her or his anonymous singing role in the persona of Deborah. In a sense, she is represented somewhat like the Muse of the *Odyssey,* as characterized by Ralph Hexter, as the "repository of the community's memory and the acknowledged source of the bard's song, the guarantee that *The Odyssey* draws on and transmits communal truth. The Muse represents sung tradition itself and guides the epic singer in the right paths as he chooses elements from the vast ocean of memory and song."[132] Deborah, too, is a model for the unnamed composer of Judges 5: she is the model of communal memory about this primordial, foundational conflict, and her example inspires the composer in his choice of the varied elements of Judges 5. Like Deborah, the Muse is addressed in the second person by an explicit first person voice (*Odyssey* 1.1).[133]

The first person voice in Judges 5 might be called the represented "singer 'I,'" as this singing is the stated intent of v. 3. Initially, in v. 3 this "I" sings or at least represents the self as a singer. This is the "I" of what Peter Machinist calls the "epic poet-reciter" of archaic Greek and ancient Near Eastern cultures or what Susan Niditch calls "the epic-bardic voice."[134] What may be called the epic "I" voice of the *Iliad* (for example, in 2.484-93, 761; 11.218; 12.176), noted by Gregory Nagy,[135] is a first person voice compared to what we see in Judg. 5:3, 9, 13 (if not to be emended), 15, 21.[136] Similarly, examples of second person address appear in Judg. 5:10, 12, 16, and in *Iliad* 4.127, 146; 7.104; 13.603; 17.679, 702; 23.600 (addressed to Menelaus), and in 16.20, 584, 692-93, 744, 754, 787, 812, 843 (addressed to Patroklos).[137] In addition, rhetorical questions (e.g., Judg. 5:8b, 16-17; cf. *Iliad* 8.273-74) seem pertinent to the sort of voice in these texts. The general thrust of these observations may suggest the poet-reciter as a represented voice that is not so much masking another identity[138] as "adding" one.

With this broad sense of the first person voice in the older poetic tradition, we may turn to its attestations in Judges 5 and ask what the representations of the "I-voice" "sound like" in this poem. At its most expansive, the "I-voice" in v. 3 relates specifically to an imagined royal audience:

> Hear, O kings, Listen, O rulers,
> I, to Yahweh may I sing,
> May I intone to Yahweh, the God of Israel.

This verse expresses a devotion to a vision of Yahweh as the national god of Israel addressed to the kings and rulers. As possibly suggested by this verse as well as other features of the poem, the "singer-I" is a representation by a tenth-century composer-singer creatively participating in the Iron I event of the battle. Such a creative voice is operating in a context where an address to kings and rulers might make sense. Such an address appears, for example, in Ps. 2:10. This royal psalm represents its praise of god and king as putative instruction for foreign rulers. Perhaps the voice of Judg. 5:3 is like the "I-voice" of the royal court in Ps. 45:1-2 or like the poet of Habakkuk 3 sitting in a royal court fondly evoking ancient great acts of God. Like Psalm 2, Judges 5 may offer instruction to kings and rulers to know of the mighty victory of Yahweh. At the same time, Judges 5 uses the recalled past (perhaps even reconstructed past) for its instruction about God and country. It would seem that the "I-voice" of the poem is at home in the royal court, and in view of the poem's contents, it may be located in the court of the early, northern monarchy.[139]

The court seems to be the final reception-point for the wide variety of traditions in Judges 5 that enjoyed oral circulation, which in turn suggests oral performance and production from the Iron I period. What the text seems to perform is nothing less than the transformation of "the unscripted activities of war into ritualized spectacles."[140] The text also shows multiple levels of tradition and composition, serving as an example of what Nagy calls "recomposition-in-performance."[141] In short, the written form of Judges 5, with its different pieces and traditions, may point to various oral forms of the poetic tradition recalling the battle; and with so little of the battle recalled in Judges 5, what we have in the poem's current form may be nothing less than an excerpt[142] (or excerpts) of a broader oral tradition about the battle that may have circulated in a variety of forms. Some of these may have been crafted together by the composer of the present form of the poem and recontextualized for an early Iron II audience.

5. Divine and Human Warriors in Judges 5

At this point, it is time to turn to the representation of the divine and human warriors in the poem. In view of the discussion over the course of this chapter and the preceding one, it seems necessary to delineate between what seem to be the poem's Iron I traditions about the warriors, on the one hand, and, on the other hand, their further arrangement and representation by the tenth-century composer. Thus we read about warriors in the poem with "bifocal lenses" that see both Iron I traditions and material and an early Iron II arrangement and material.

The Iron I Traditions of the Divine and Human Warriors

We may begin with the representation of the divine warrior in the earlier traditions in the poem. First and foremost, some of the early materials include Yahweh. The deity is drawn into the poem in the old trope of vv. 4-5 and in the mention of the curse of Meroz in v. 23. Vv. 4-5 do not belong to the battle narrative as such, but derive from an independent tradition that was brought into its present context in the poem by the composer. Here Yahweh is indeed the divine warrior, a figure who battles without any reference to any human fighting force. In context, it became part of the atmospherics of battle, but in its original setting it is hardly a part of this battle memory in the body of the poem in Judges 5.

V. 23 is the opposite of vv. 4-5 in two respects. First, it is represented in reference to the battle of the poem. Second, the representation of the deity as a warrior is rather different. As a postbattle divine sanction uttered by either Yahweh or a divine messenger, this verse does not represent Yahweh exactly as missing in action. This verse needs to be scrutinized, as it suggests a complex view of Yahweh's role:

> "Curse Meroz," said Yahweh⟨'s messenger (?)⟩.
> "Curse harshly its inhabitants,
> For they did not come to Yahweh's aid,
> To Yahweh's aid among the warriors."

Whether or not the word "messenger" is bracketed, the wording of this verse points to the involvement of Yahweh in the battle. The verse speaks of Meroz's failing to "come to Yahweh's aid . . . among the warriors." In other words, Yahweh was in the battle according to this piece of tradition. At the same time, that specific divine presence is not otherwise presented in the poem. The nature of that presence as presented in the verse is worth noting. The verse does not give a role as such to Yahweh in the battle. The parallelism of the last two lines suggests a picture quite at odds with the prominent role given to Yahweh in vv. 4-5. In v. 23, "the aid of Yahweh" of the first line of the bicolon is further explained in the second line as "the aid of Yahweh among the warriors." While the expression "to Yahweh's aid" might suggest "dass die Aktivität der Israelitisichen reduziert auf ein Zuhilfekommen zu Jahwes Machttat,"[143] the final line is not so "reductive"; it further suggests a picture of Yahweh's power manifest "among the warriors." There is no separate manifestation assigned to Yahweh in v. 23, and the human role is marked in the battle as well.

V. 23 also intimates some reflection on the relationship between the divine warrior and the human warriors. It is most intriguing that this verse refers to the inhabitants of Meroz in terms of the "help (or assistance) of Yahweh" *('ezrat yhwh)* that they could provide to Yahweh. The Hebrew word does not seem to denote some sort of notion that Yahweh needs help. At most, the deity receives human assistance. As a further possibility, the word's meaning here is closer to "strength, might,"[144] although the resulting translation is not quite clear. In this case, it may be that the phrase refers to the warriors as Yahweh's (indeed, as the dedicated of Yahweh as in v. 2), not that Yahweh was involved as such in the battle. At most, the divine role is synergistic with human efforts. It may be closer to the wording of vv. 20 and 23 to regard human efforts there as manifesting divine efforts.[145] Vv. 20 and 23 hardly offer a picture of the sort of divine battle that the Israelites only witness but do not participate in (in contrast to a poem such as Exodus 15 and perhaps Psalm 68). The synergy conveyed here is remarkable.

We may surmise further from this verse and from the other older pieces in the poem that the battle could be referenced both with and without Yahweh. Except for v. 23, Yahweh is absent from the older traditions about the battle. Thus we may be reckoning with multiple versions of the poem having circulated orally. Indeed, apart from the two brief pieces, vv. 4-5 and 23, the poem of Judges 5 is remarkably free of any focus on this divine warrior. Instead, the only possibly divine help that is otherwise mentioned in the older, traditional material comes from the divine army represented by the stars in v. 20:

From heaven the stars fought,
From their courses they fought with Sisera.

These stars are, in other words, the heavenly host, the divine army. The perception is not only a heavenly one; these stars are said to fight with Sisera. V. 21 relates how the river Kishon swept "them" away (the kings of Canaan of v. 19). Arguably important for understanding Israelite polytheism in the Iron I context, these stars are a collective divine force described here without any reference to Yahweh. Thus the one divine source of help described at the battle itself is represented without reference to Yahweh. One might wish to read vv. 20 and 23 in tandem and thus import Yahweh more fully into the picture of the battle, but this would arguably represent a conflation of two rather different divine portraits. Indeed, it is the stars in v. 20 that are helping the human warriors, while in v. 23 the curse concerns those human warriors who did not come to the "aid" of Yahweh.

Otherwise, the focus on warriors in the battle falls decidedly on the human side of the enterprise. At the same time, this representation of the Iron I tradition is not about Israel, but about the leaders and forces that managed to come together in a rather local conflict. The older tradition of the poem invests the human warriors with rich details that exude a palpable sensibility about their condition on the occasion of this battle: the warrior "longhairs" (v. 2) that meet the crisis prompting the occasion of battle (v. 6) are "village militia" (vv. 7, 11), lacking proper equipment to take on the conflict against superior forces (v. 8). Despite the range of units that came and did not come (vv. 14-17), the forces headed up by Zebulun and Naphtali engage battle (v. 18), aided by the divine astral militia (v. 20). The postwar scenes shift dramatically to women engaged in the destiny of the enemy general (vv. 24-30). In short, the older story of the poem tells a story of battle unlike any other in the Bible, and it is unlike any other biblical representation of the divine forces engaged in battle.

The Tenth-Century Composition's Vision of the Divine and Human Warriors

When we move to the composition of the whole poem, a rather different story emerges. First of all, Yahweh and Israel become the central, twin foci emphasized in the new double-introduction through which the rest of the poem is to be read. Accordingly, Yahweh is the divine hero for the whole text. The composer loaded Yahweh into the new introduction to the poem (vv. 2, 3 [2x], 4, 5 [2x], 9, 11, 13), which included the older tradition of Yahweh in vv. 4-5. At the same time, the composer's own voice, for example in v. 3, puts Yahweh at the center of the poem's expressed theme:

> Hear, O kings, Listen, O rulers,
> I, to Yahweh may I sing,
> May I intone to Yahweh, the God of Israel.

Here we hear the composer's own represented voice, with its focus on Yahweh. As a result of the composer's devoted attention to Yahweh in the introduction, the body of the poem is read through the lens of this Yahweh-packed introduction, aided by the inclusion of the old tradition about Meroz in v. 23, with its threefold mention of Yahweh. As a result, Yahweh emerges as divine warrior for the whole poem and its events and not only in the limited, older pieces of vv. 4-5 and 23.

As we have noted, the original context of the divine march in vv. 4-5 has little to do with either the geography or martial situation at hand in the poem's body. However, placed in the introduction, these verses present Yahweh as Israel's military god in the central hill-country in the premonarchic period. (In terms of the coordination between the representation of Yahweh in the introduction and in the body, we might say that the tradition of the southern sanctuary in v. 4 has come north.) The emphasis on Yahweh in the poem's introduction also provides an interpretive reading for v. 20, namely that the divine aid received via the stars in v. 20 was thanks to the divine leadership of Yahweh. Indeed, the "I-voice" of v. 11 further includes this battle in a line of "victories of Yahweh."

At the end of this study of Judges 5, we recognize the rather long path in its development. The early, older traditions seem to show a rather diverse set of materials, which often differed thematically from the later composition that preserved and arranged them in their present form. The older tradition told a story of battle that focused on the basic and somewhat poor condition of a diverse group of village militia "longhairs" prepared to face a stronger enemy and aided by divine forces of astral bodies. The stars were with them, along with the apparently supernaturally-inspired force of the Wadi Kishon.[146] The later composer put the god Yahweh at the head of the poem and at the heart of the identity of the human forces. These human militia forces become in this reading of the poem "the people of Yahweh," and in turn Yahweh emerges as "the god of Israel."

This mutual reinforcing identity of the national god with the national people in the early Iron II composition transformed and reshaped the older story, as told in the Iron I traditions and material. This long path behind the composition of Judges 5 shows how the poetic commemoration of warriors reuses older pieces and also reconfigures them, giving them a new integration and a new reinterpretation by their author-arranger. The older pieces perhaps evoked the time of the poem for later audiences, while their new arrangement provided a vision of Israelite heroism as well as the challenges faced within Israel that warfare brought. The poetic commemoration of Israel's ancient heroes was hardly limited to a descriptive task. It could also perform a prescriptive function for ongoing audiences. In hearing, reciting, or reading this great song, later generations could acknowledge the indispensable role of their God, and thus understand themselves as grateful beneficiaries of the divine help that had begun so long ago.[147]

CHAPTER TEN

The Lamentation over Fallen Warriors in 2 Samuel 1:19-27

The discussion up to this point in Part IV has centered on the representation of warriors and their activities, as well as aspects of the warrior worldview and values, as they appear in Judges 5. The poem of 2 Sam. 1:19-27 also holds a prominent place in the consideration of warriors, their military activities and values. In the nine verses of this lament, the conceptual world of traditional warrior attitudes and sensibilities comes to the fore. The first section of this chapter provides a translation of this poem with notes. The second part situates the poem's warrior features within the larger context of ancient Near Eastern literature, especially the Ugaritic texts of the Baal Cycle and Aqhat, discussed earlier in Part III. The third and final part of this chapter takes up the matter of the poem's structure and its representation of David's "voices." The discussion closes with some observations about what these "voices" in the poem may suggest about the production of heroic poetry in early Israel.

1. Translation of 2 Samuel 1:19-27 with Notes[1]

Below I have laid out the translation in order to highlight the poem's structure. The headings (along with the letters A, B, C, B′, A′) point to the opening and closing invocations of the two heroes (A and A′), framing the two sets of instructions about proclaiming the battle (B and B′), themselves framing the poem's central section (C).[2] This larger chiastic construction, as marked by these symmetrical components, is followed by a final expression, distinguished by its rather different "voice."

A: Opening invocation to Saul (parallel to v. 25)

19 The[3] Gazelle,[4] O Israel, is slain[5] upon your heights![6]
How[7] the warriors fell!

B: Instructions about Philistine women rejoicing (inverse to v. 24)

20 Make no proclamation[8] in Gath,[9]
No announcement in Ashkelon's streets,[10]
Lest the daughters[11] of the Philistines rejoice,
Lest the daughters of the uncircumcised[12] exult:[13]

C: Central section of lament

21 O mountains[14] in the[15] Gilboa, no dew,[16]
No rain upon you, O lofty[17] fields![18]
For[19] there begrimed was the shield[20] of warriors,
The shield of Saul ungreased[21] with oil.[22]
22 From the blood[23] of the slain,
From the fat of warriors,
The bow[24] of Jonathan was not turned back,[25]
And the sword of Saul never withdrew[26] empty.[27]
23 Saul and Jonathan, beloved and desirable,[28]
In life and in death[29] inseparable[30] —
They were swifter[31] than eagles,[32]
They were stronger[33] than lions![34]

B′: Instructions to Israelite women to weep (inverse to v. 20)

24 O daughters of Israel, weep for Saul,
Who[35] clothed you in crimson[36] along with fineries,[37]
Who put[38] gold ornament upon your clothing.

A′: Closing evocation of Jonathan (parallel to v. 19)

25 How the warriors fell in the midst of battle!
Jonathan slain upon your heights!

A first person reprise[39] invoking Jonathan

26 I am in pain over you, my brother;
O Jonathan, you were so desirable to me.
Wondrous[40] was your love for me,
Greater than the love of women.
27 How the warriors fell,
The weapons of war[41] perished!

Before proceeding to the details of warrior culture embedded in this poem, it may be helpful to sketch out the narrative of the poem as a whole. As the layout of the poem above suggests, it invokes the first of the father-son team lamented in the main part of the poem. In the opening v. 19, the poem announces the subject of the lament with the image of the dead hero slain. Though not stated explicitly, this is assumed to be the father, anticipating his naming in v. 21; this is balanced by the naming of the son later in v. 25 (with the two names balanced together in between, in v. 22). The second line of the opening verse adds an expression that reverberates twice later in the poem (vv. 25 and 27). The poem in v. 20 widens the scene by turning from the king's body and the announcement of fallen heroes to a command that the news is not to be announced in two cities of Philistia so that the defeat unknown to Israel's enemies there would not be celebrated by their "daughters." V. 21a moves to yet another address, this time to the hills and fields of the site of battle. The verse expresses the wish — or perhaps the cursed reality — that no rain or dew is upon them, signaling the massive importance and impact of the royal death: no king, no rain. The lament names not only a human loss; it is also one that affects all of life. V. 21b finally introduces the cause of the loss.

Vv. 21b-23 take the audience to the battle scene. The language hints at the decimation of the heroes via the description of the weapons strewn on the field, there without their wielders. Only hinted at in death, in life they are resurrected in verbal form, with the inspiring description here of son and father inseparably linked and locked in battle, fighting at each other's side. This beautiful evocation of the son-father warrior pair may hint at the poet's preference for Jonathan; the expected order of father-son resumes in v. 23. With v. 24, the poem directs the audience's way back from the battle to the present. The evocation of the two warriors gives way in v. 24 to an address again to "daughters" (as in v. 20), this time to Israel's daughters telling them to weep for Saul. V. 25 returns to the earlier announcement, "how the warriors fell," and here names Jonathan as the slain on the heights, like his father in v. 19. Thus the poem opens in v. 19 with the father and comes full circle with the same language for the son in v. 25.

At v. 26, the poem shifts from an evocation of the two figures to an invocation of only one of them, the son. This invocation links to the preceding verse, yet focuses on the son without reference to the father, and does so in an emotional tenor not seen before in the poem. The personal cry of v. 26 magnifies the facts of loss stated already in vv. 19-25 and gives to them a deeply personal cast. Where vv. 19-25 speak to all Israel, as named in v. 19, in v. 26 the poem with its "I-voice" becomes much more individual. The audience is invited, for a moment, into the intimacy expressed by the "I" who laments the fallen, beloved Jonathan.

V. 27a literally repeats the line, "how the warriors fell," as seen in vv. 19b and 25a. The poem ends with a final echo of the warriors' demise expressed via their weapons, "the weapons of war" now perished. With the shift at v. 26a, vv. 26-27 echo a number of expressions in vv. 19-25. At the same time, it transforms them and raises the rhetorical force and tenor, setting the rather traditional sounding vv. 19-25 into a new and highly charged key. Because of their echoes of what precedes, vv. 26-27 serve as a reprise,[42] issuing in a heightened transformation of the poetic expression. At this point, we may explore the individual warrior features in the poem before returning to the poem as a whole.

2. Traditional Warrior Motifs in the Lament

The initial noun in v. 19, "gazelle," while debated, seems best understood as a title for Saul,[43] used to signal at once his martial prowess and his leadership. Patrick D. Miller notes this word as a term of leadership in the Ugaritic story of King Kirta (KTU 1.15 IV 7, 18).[44] This particular term elsewhere evokes the image of the warrior as a gazelle. According to 1 Chr. 12:8, the Gadites who withdrew with David to the wilderness were "valiant men, armed with shield and spear, and they had the appearance of lions and gazelles upon the mountains."[45] In 2 Sam. 2:18, the warrior Asahel is praised for being "swift of foot" *(qal bĕraglāyw),*[46] like a gazelle that is in the (open) field."[47] "Swift of foot" is also a standard title of Achilles (*Iliad* 1.84, 148, 215, 489, etc.).[48]

In v. 19, the evocation of Saul in this context sets up a poignant wordplay. With Saul said to be fallen in this verse, an audience may hear in the words "upon your heights" *(bāmôtêkā)* a further echoing of the hero's death, as this phrase may have suggested the expression "in your death" (**bĕmôtĕkā*). It also anticipates the very similar expression in v. 23a, "in their death" (**bĕmôtām*). The association of the "fallen" and "dead" warrior appears also in the report of El's messengers finding Baal (KTU 1.5 VI 8-10; see also 1.5 VI 30-31):[49]

We came upon Baal *fallen* to the earth:	*mǵny lbʿl npl lʾarṣ*
Dead is Mightiest Baal,	*mt ʾalʾiyn bʿl*
Perished the Prince, Lord of the Earth.[50]	*ḫlq zbl bʿl ʾarṣ*

As I have italicized in this translation, the combination of "fallen" and "dead" is traditional. So it might be thought that "upon your heights" is used very cleverly to evoke both the fact of the warrior's death and the site of his demise. The verbs are no less poignant in context, for they report a "fallen" warrior[51] who is "dead" and "perished." The divinity Dagon is said to be fallen to the earth in 1 Sam. 5:3, evidently defeated by Yahweh as symbolized by the ark mentioned in the preceding verse. In 2 Sam. 3:34, David laments of Abner: "like one falling before treacherous men, you fell" (*nāpaltā;* see also 2 Sam. 2:16).[52] David also laments that Abner is dead, a report for a warrior that is weighty, definitive. In this connection, we may also note the report about Goliath in 1 Sam. 17:51, *mēt gibbôrām,* "their warrior was dead."

Vv. 20 and 24 show the role of singing women in the public context in the aftermath of battle.[53] The picture of the Philistine women in v. 20 fits the paradigm of women singing of victory, as known from other sources. 1 Sam. 18:6-7 is emblematic of this female role of song.[54] The inverse role of women in postbattle lamentation[55] is given particular prominence in v. 24. There the daughters of Israel are told to weep over Saul in v. 24, while in v. 20 Israel is commanded to refrain from publicizing the defeat so that Philistine women not rejoice (cf. Mic. 1:10). Elsewhere women lament in the face of military defeat (cf. 1 Sam. 15:33; Jer. 9:17-20). Possibly pertinent as well is Anat weeping for Aqhat.[56] V. 24 expresses not only the women's traditional role to weep; it also describes these same women in terms of the spoils of war, namely the wonderful clothing that Saul had provided them. Thus the single verse contrasts with a particular sharpness the present role of women in lamentation and their earlier celebration, both owing to the same figure of Saul.

Mourning and rejoicing are, according to Gary A. Anderson,[57] ritual states consisting of sets of discrete behaviors and fixed literary formulas. Anderson further characterizes them as related "symbolic antitypes,"[58] with one potentially leading to the other. V. 24 evokes prior occasions of rejoicing, here turned to mourning. Thomas M. Greene emphasizes the community formed by the performance of epic lament: "In the common field of performance, . . . the grief of the poet merges with the performer's, and the character's, and the audience's."[59] Viewed in light of Green's observations, David's postbattle lament may be understood as a ritualized behavior that serves "to create a community of shared mourners."[60] The poem as a whole serves to generate a communal identity for a post-Saulide "Israel" invoked in v. 19, while it strives in v. 24 to deny such an identity-building opportunity to the Philistines.

The curse of the site of the hero's demise is likewise a traditional motif. A commonly cited instance is the series of curses uttered by Danil on behalf of his dead son Aqhat in 1.19 III 45-IV 6.[61] It has been common to compare this passage from Aqhat with the ruling in Deut. 21:1-9 concerning the discovery of someone *ḥālāl . . . nōpēl baśśādeh,* "slain . . . fallen in the (open) field." In this case, a ritual of resolving the bloodguilt incurred is undertaken in the place located closest to where the corpse is discovered. It is to be noted that the two descriptors for the corpse in Deut. 21:1 are *ḥālāl* and *nōpēl,* which likewise inform our poem.

The lament addressed to nature in v. 21a received its classic formulation from H. L. Ginsberg in 1938, thanks to the parallel usage of negatives with terms for precipitation, "dew" and "rain," that he noted in the story of Aqhat (KTU 1.19 I 44-46).[62] In that context, each term for precipitation is preceded by a negative particle: "no dew, no rain *(bl ṭl bl rbb).*"[63] These terms for dew and rain occur together also in Elijah's words to Ahab in 1 Kgs. 17:1: "(by) the life of Yahweh, the God of Israel whom I serve, (may such and such happen to me if) there is *dew* or *rain* except at my bidding" (my italics).[64] Here we have a prosaic linkage of the pair. The terms also appear together in Deut. 32:2; Job 38:28 (cf. Dan. 4:33; 5:21).

Somewhat difficult in 2 Sam. 1:21a is the next phrase, *śĕdê tĕrûmōt,* which Ginsberg proposed to emend to *šrʿ thmtm,* "the upsurging of the deeps," following the third term for precipitation in the Aqhat passage.[65] The emendation has been called "gratuitous."[66] Lawrence E. Stager views the expression as a reference to "built fields" that "were probably artificial agricultural terraces constructed on the mountain slopes."[67] As a further alternative, the phrase *śĕdê tĕrûmōt* might be read literally as "fields of offerings." While the meanings for each of the two nouns are well attested, the combination of the two nouns in these meanings would be unusual.[68] In this case, the unusual expression would be playing off the more traditional *topos* as identified by Ginsberg. Here the lines would balance the topographical terms of "mountains" and "fields," but the resulting parallelism is unimpressive. If it were correct, the announcement of "no rain, no dew" would signal the loss of precipitation needed for the crops used as offerings. In other words: no rain, no offerings; with the king dead, the land languishes.[69] This reading could fit with the parallel in Aqhat where the crops wither as a result of the hero's death. The semantic parallelism in this proposal remains problematic. A further alternative retains a comparable sense of the verse's context without losing its poetic parallelism. It seems feasible to understand *śĕdê tĕrûmōt* as "lofty highlands,"[70] reflecting an Israelite adaptation[71] to the older *topos,*[72] as originally recognized by Ginsberg. In this case, the phrase would be a second topographical expression corresponding to *hārê baggilbōaʿ*. This approach is adopted in the translation in the preceding section.

The weapons and their condition in vv. 21-22 come to the fore at this point in the poem. In some respects, they recall the Ugaritic Baal Cycle's presentation of Baal and Yamm as two warriors.[73] In KTU 1.2 IV, the two gods are hardly at the forefront of battle, as the weapons made by Kothar take center stage.[74] Here we might also compare the personified weapon, Sharur, in Lugale-e[75] and perhaps the central role that weapons play in the story of Aqhat. Weapons may play a range of literary roles in highlighting the exploits of warriors. In the *Iliad*, Achilles encourages Patroklos to use his armor (*Iliad* 16.129), leading the Trojans to believe that Achilles has returned to the field of battle (16.278-83). Hector seizes the armor after he slays Patroklos with Apollo's aid (cf. 16.818-28; cf. 16.798-99). Moreover, Thetis tells Achilles that Hector is said to exult in his armor, but he will face Achilles himself, the original owner (18.130-33). In due course, Achilles slays the slayer of his beloved friend (22.326-30) by thrusting a spear through the one point unprotected by the armor (22.324). Achilles' armor captures the story of Patroklos' end and Hector's as well, thus bringing the conflict of the *Iliad* to its climax.[76]

The weapons of Saul and Jonathan in 2 Samuel 1 poignantly draw the audience's attention to these figures: the shields including Saul's "there" *(šām)* after battle in v. 21 and the bow of Jonathan and sword of Saul presented in parallel terms as fiercely engaged in battle in v. 22. Stanley Gevirtz, I think, got the point right in suggesting that "Saul and Jonathan are themselves the perished instruments of war."[77] The notion likewise informs the warning to the addressee in the New Kingdom Papyrus Anastasi I, "The Craft of the Scribe": "Your leather armor has fallen on the ground: it is buried in the sand and has become part of the barren land."[78] Insofar as the weapons in v. 21 reflect the situation of their wielders, "those objects that are in closest contact with their owners become, as it were, 'extra-somatic body parts.'"[79] For warriors, weapons are the "extra-somatic" markers of their identity.

This sense of the weapons is expressed further by the wordplay in v. 21: the shield ungreased with oil *(bĕlî māšîaḥ baššāmen)* evokes Saul's status as "anointed," the traditional title for the monarch.[80] King Saul, like his weapon, is anointed no more: the weapon is "ungreased"; by implication the king is "un-anointed." These shields of defeat, strewn upon the battlefield, contrast with shields of victory that would hang in public view as testimony of great victory. Shields hanging on tower walls are a sign of Tyre's military strength in Ezek. 27:11 (see also v. 10). Similarly, a thousand shields adorning the tower of David serve as analogy for the woman's beauty in Song 4:4. Small shields are said to decorate the front of the rededicated temple in 1 Macc. 4:57.[81]

The description of the warriors in v. 23 captures not only the affective effect of the slain on those who lament. The term "beloved" conveys something of the attractiveness of the warriors. The word **nʿm,* usually rendered "lovely" or the like, but rendered here "desirable," conveys something of the leader's appeal.[82] While a variety of translations have been suggested, the use of Akkadian *damqu* as applied to Enkidu in Gilgamesh SB I.207 seems to capture the leader's magnetic appeal: "You are handsome, Enkidu, you are just like a god" *([dam]-⸢qa-ta* ᵈ*en⸣-ki-dù ki-i ili*(dinger) *ta-ba-áš-ši).*[83] One could translate "handsome" here as well for **nʿm* in v. 23. The sense of attraction might seem flat, say by comparison with a more colloquial translation (such as "beefy, buff, cut; hot, sexy").[84] Or, since the preceding substantive, the *N*-stem participle of **ʾahb,* conveys the perspective of those who perceive the warriors, the translation for **nʿm* should perhaps follow suit; a word such as "desirable" may be fitting. This translation conveys physical attractiveness in the eyes of the beholders, which may include both men and women. The Hebrew term here perhaps expresses the physical attractiveness and magnetism of "alpha male" warriors.

The same word is applied in an image of the warrior in the Egyptian Satirical letter: "You slay like a lion, O wondrous warrior" *(abata kama ir mahir neʿam).*[85] This line also uses the image of the lion for the warrior, just as we find in v. 23. The image of the lion occurs also in *Iliad* 7.256; there it is applied to two opposing warriors. Indeed, the image of warriors as lions is a common motif in the *Iliad* (e.g., 5.299; 10.297; 11.129, 173; 12.42, 292-93).[86] 1 Chr. 12:8 is particularly germane to v. 23, as it combines the image of the lion with the swiftness of the gazelle for the Gadite warriors. The Gadites that withdrew with David to the wilderness are said to be "valiant men, armed with shield and spear, and they had the appearance of lions and gazelles upon the mountains."[87]

The aspect of the poem that has perhaps garnered the most attention involves the relationship of David and Jonathan as expressed in v. 26. As Saul Olyan has stressed,[88] David's invocation of Jonathan in this verse seems to convey considerably more than traditional covenantal language (for example, as in 1 Sam. 23:18), especially given the reference to "love of women" here.[89] Olyan is quite right, as noted in Chapter Three; we will also return to this expression in the next section. For now, we may note that the male bonding of David and Jonathan may in part emblemize the exclusion of females, reflected in Aqhat's famous retort to Anat (KTU 1.17 VI 39-41): "Bows are

. . . warriors; now shall womanhood go hunting?" In this statement, Aqhat asserts the gendered understanding of warrior culture.[90] So does Hector when he refers to "a woman who knows not the deeds of war" (*Iliad* 7.236). The world of human warriors is considered a male world, and as we saw in Chapter Three, for warriors within that world their bond may be experienced as stronger than the sexual love between a man and a woman.[91] The expression in v. 26 is thus not a common or traditional one, by comparison with the warrior idioms noted for vv. 19-25. The difference is also telling for the poem's composition, as we will see in the next section.

3. The Poetic Voice(s) of David

In the prose tradition that precedes the poem in 2 Sam. 1:19-27, this lament is represented as David's response to the news of the fall of the king and his son, David's beloved friend. This representation of the lament as David's own has been accepted by a number of critics, such as P. Kyle McCarter:

> The composition of an elegy for Saul and Jonathan generations after their death would be pointless. It is difficult, then, to think of the origin of the present poem at a date long after the events described in the surrounding narrative. But is the attribution to David spurious? Again, probably not. The sentiments expressed in the lament correspond to those that David held. . . . The highly personal declaration of grief over Jonathan's death in vv. 25-26, moreover, would be out of place on any lips but David's.[92]

Since the time of McCarter's Samuel commentary, there has been considerable skepticism about biblical representations of the past in general, and this extends to the poem.[93] Indeed, many modern commentators would — and arguably should — see ideological reasons for finding such a poem on David's lips, while other scholars are — and arguably should be — suspicious of David's motives, that he is responding to the expectation of the context.[94] In any case, a public expression on the part of a major leader such as a David might well be expected to reflect concern about how he is perceived as being "heard" and "overheard," to echo the phrases from a rather brilliant essay by Tod Linafelt.[95] Some scholars hear the expression of genuine loss, while others hear in this voice a larger public motive. For Steven Weitzman, it is a public relations effort to demonstrate David's heartfelt emotion over the loss of Saul as evidence against his involvement in the king's death,[96] while for Linafelt it is an implicit critique of Saul as king. In this approach, David's lament is a cold-blooded self-promotion cast in hot emotion. Finally, it is to be noted that a composition of an elegy generations after the death of Saul and Jonathan might not be as pointless as McCarter suggests, as it may have served to bolster claims of the Davidic line to the northern kingdom. At the same time, the poem fits a tenth-century dating either in David's time or shortly thereafter. Whether or not David produced the poem, it may be said to constitute a representation of David or, we might say, a representation of the heroic voice of this king. I will return to this matter below.

Like Weitzman, Mark W. Hamilton recognizes the concerns of David's own status in uttering this poem. Hamilton also highlights the differences between the poetry and the prose contexts, and he further suggests different purposes behind the poetic and prose accounts of Saul's demise as well as the circles that produced them.[97] For Hamilton, the poem's description of Saul's death is at odds with the description of Saul's taking his own life in 1 Samuel 31. Accordingly, the literary traditions that preserve the poetic and prose accounts were originally independent of one another; the poem's purpose is not a continuation of the prose's or vice-versa.[98] In Hamilton's view, David's "royal self-display"[99] in the poem offers praise of the dead king's valor, and in doing so, the lament releases social anxiety over his death.[100] While claims about social anxiety might seem speculative, both goals would serve David well in consolidating his kingship[101] and in grounding his claim for his own line, especially over and against Saul's royal descendants.[102]

The studies of these scholars as well as other analyses assume that the poem of 2 Sam. 1:19-27 constitutes a literary unity, despite occasional voicing of objections.[103] At first glance, the poem overall might seem to represent the emotional expression of David. In its use of warrior motifs, the poem presents David as a warrior poet. In this understanding, the text would attest to David's poetic elegy over Saul and Jonathan and its reception into its prose context. Such a picture of David might recall his singing with a lyre before King Saul (1 Sam. 18:10): "David would play by hand day by day" *(wĕdāwîd mĕnaggēn bĕyādô kĕyôm bĕyôm).* This is hardly incongruous for a warrior. For example, we may note the song of Achilles before Patroklos in *Iliad* 9.185-92, witnessed by the legation sent by Agamemnon and headed by Phoenix and Odysseus:

> Now they came beside the shelters and ships of the Myrmidons
> and they found Achilleus delighting his heart in a lyre, clear-sounding,
> splendid and carefully wrought, with a bridge of silver upon it,

> which he won out of the spoils when he ruined Eëtion's city.
> With this he was pleasuring his heart, and singing of men's fame,
> as Patroklos was sitting over against him, alone, in silence,
> watching Aiakides and the time he would leave off singing.[104]

Warriors at song were hardly peripheral to warrior interaction. On the contrary: in these cases, song is associated with two of the greatest of warrior figures, David and Achilles. At the same time, this is a persona for David that belongs to the prose context, and it is one that may misread or overread the poem.

The poem's structure, as well as its shift at v. 26a, arguably points to two voices: one is a public voice in vv. 19-25 and the other a reprise with a private voice in vv. 26-27. On the one hand, vv. 19-25 read as a neatly composed elegy with a tight chiastic structure, as seen in the following diagram:

- A: Opening invocation of Saul and the "warriors fallen" (v. 19, parallel to v. 25)
  - B: Instructions about Philistine women rejoicing (v. 20, inverse to v. 24)
    - C: Central section of lament (vv. 21-23)
  - B′: Instructions to Israelite women to weep (v. 24, inverse to v. 20)
- A′: Closing invocation of Jonathan and the "warriors fallen" (v. 25, parallel to v. 19)

In the reading of 2 Sam. 1:19-27 that I am entertaining, the public voice of vv. 19-25 would begin and end with the units containing "how the warriors fell" *('êk nāpĕlû gibbôrîm)* in vv. 19 and 25. Inside of vv. 19 and 25, vv. 20 and 24 are balanced by the address to "daughters" *(bĕnôt)*. This noun, *bĕnôt,* is echoed in sound in the outside frame by the word "heights," **bāmôt* (vv. 19, 25), and perhaps in the central lament section by "lofty," *tĕrûmōt* (v. 21), and "in death," **bĕmôt* (v. 23). It is this highly marked paronomasia in the heart of the poem that points to its oral character, according to a recent study by Robert D. Miller II.[105]

The poem of vv. 19-25 offers a breathtaking progression. Perhaps like the effect of a modern movie, it takes the audience through events backwards in time, back to the site of battle, and then moves forward back to the audience's present. It begins with the final state of the heroes' death (v. 19) and the instructions not to relate this news (v. 20), back to the site of battle in the Gilboa (v. 21), to the battlefield itself strewn with the ruined weapons remaining from the conflict (v. 22) and the heroes praised for their fighting prowess (v. 23). The weapons (vv. 21-23), themselves representing their wielders, Saul and Jonathan, evoke the scene of battle. At the center is a picture of father and son, "inseparable" in life and death. The shield (v. 21), together with the bow and the sword (v. 22), conjure up a picture of twin heroes, there at the front lines, there in the midst of the battle now silent, perhaps there at what Song 6:13(7:1) calls "dance of the two camps." The shield and the sword in particular evoke the dramatic moment of the two warrior heroes fighting and fallen at the front lines. After this point, at the end of v. 23, the audience is led back to the present, through instructions to the women (v. 24) and another invocation of the fallen warriors (v. 25). The two instances of the line "how the warriors fell" in vv. 19 and 25 form an inclusion showing what Shemaryahu Talmon calls "distant inverted parallelism."[106] They frame the beautiful chiastic construction of vv. 19-25. In this reading, these verses enshrine a lament addressed in a public manner to Israel and the daughters of Israel. This is a voice projected publicly, one that describes both Saul and Jonathan.

V. 26 shows a marked shift in voice. It does not offer an evocative description as in vv. 19-25, and it is not addressed to a public. Rather, v. 26 is an invocation, a very personal one, addressed specifically to Jonathan. At this point in the poem, a distinctive first person voice comes to the fore, with the phrase "to me" *(lî)* used three times along with the first person suffix on "brother."[107] It is a personal lamenting voice (cf. *ṣar lî* in 2 Sam. 24:14/1 Chr. 21:13; Pss. 31:9; 59:16; 69:17; 102:2; Lam. 1:20; cf. Ps. 66:14). It is reminiscent of Gilgamesh's first person voice in his lament for Enkidu in SBV X.132-33/233-34 (cf. SBV X.245-46): "my friend, whom I love so deeply, who with me went through every danger." The address to Jonathan is quite pronounced, with the second person singular forms of various sorts used four times in v. 26. This is a first person singular voice locked in lament over a second person singular intimate. Such singular devotion to Jonathan is what an audience might expect of David.

The personal voice in this poem also includes the famous gender-marked line of v. 26: "O Jonathan, you were so desirable to me./Wondrous *(npl'th)* was your love for me,/Greater than the love of women." For this expression, I have already noted Olyan's insights. I would also mention the analysis of Gilgamesh and Enkidu by Tikva Frymer-Kensky: "The gods' solution to Gilgamesh's arrogance indicates a cultural sense that the truest bonding possible is between two members of the same gender. The true equality that leads to great bonding is between male and male. The closeness of same-sex bonding holds true for females."[108] Susan Ackerman comments on the verse in similar terms: "I would interpret David's words in 2 Sam 1:26 to mean that David perceived Jonathan to have loved him in a way analogous to the sexual-emotional way in which a woman (Michal, say) would love a man and to imply that David returned that love, finding it to be something 'wonderful.'"[109]

Somewhat like Achilles lamenting the dead Patroklos in *Iliad* 19 or Gilgamesh mourning Enkidu in SB tablet VIII, the represented words of David build here on traditional formulary for his personal voice, now vibrant with emotion for his fallen beloved.[110] This reuse may be seen in how the reprise with its "I-voice" in vv. 26-27 echoes the lament of vv. 19-25, with some rather brilliant turns. Perhaps most cleverly and certainly with powerful affective force, the term used for the comparison of "love," namely "wonderful" *(npl'th),* brilliantly echoes the recurring expression of the heroes as "fallen" (**npl*). The roots **nʿm* (translated "desirable" in the first section above) and **'hb* (rendered "love") in v. 26 echo their use in v. 23 ("desirable" and "beloved"). The voice here personalizes what this lovely and beloved of v. 26 means to the speaker, "to me." While the "Davidic" voice celebrates the love of the other for him, it in effect laments the one who has fallen as the one most wonderful to the speaker. David's voice in v. 27 echoes the inclusion element, "how the warriors fell," in vv. 19 and 25. V. 27 closes the poem by recalling the perishing of the weapons that had been named in vv. 21 and 22. The picture of the single man lamenting over Jonathan in v. 26-27 offers a rhetorical counterpart to the collective of women who would weep over Saul in v. 24. It also seems to offer a counterclaim to the representation of Saul and Jonathan in vv. 19-25: where these verses represent the father and son as inseparable in life and death, vv. 26-27 represent David as the figure no less — and arguably more — deeply tied to Jonathan.

These differences between vv. 19-25 and vv. 26-27 are striking. An economical explanation for this shift would be that vv. 19-25 provide a formal or public lament of David directed to the wider community, as suggested by the addressees in vv. 20 and 24. With v. 26, the poetic David in a sense turns aside (cf. Gen. 42:24) and offers his own personal expression addressing the particular one of the two royals whom he loves. Thus the poem would represent the public elegy of David along with his private moment of grief.[111] Both are voices that the figure permits, perhaps even desires, to have "heard" and "overheard."

There is another possibility that I would like to consider. It is speculative, but it is one that I think also deserves a hearing: it is only after an anonymous lament of vv. 19-25 that we see the beginning of the Davidic voice as represented in this poem.[112] V. 26 shows a powerful shift in voice addressed to Jonathan alone, unlike the vv. 19-25 devoted to both Saul and Jonathan. While this could represent a shift from a public voice to a private one, as I have entertained above, it is also possible that vv. 19-25 were not originally attributed to David, while 26-27 may be the represented David's own reprise.[113] In other words, David's voice, as represented in vv. 26-27, was added to the poem of vv. 19-25, as it was produced in the aftermath of the battle by those of Saul's circle who had fought in it, survived it, and sung about it.[114] Vv. 19-25 may have been a traditional lamentation pronounced earlier (cf. the lament at the burial of fallen leaders in 2 Sam. 3:32-34). The additional reprise that I am entertaining for a "represented David" in vv. 26-27 perhaps compares with Achilles' lament for Patroklos in *Iliad* 19.315-37, he also not present when his comrade fell.[115] David was not there, while to my ear, the voice of vv. 19-25 sounds like someone who was.

This approach would solve a long-standing crux, and that is the distribution of the line "how the warriors fell," which many scholars have regarded as a refrain.[116] As the poem stands, this alleged "refrain" appears at vv. 19, 25, and 27. Commentators have noted that refrains usually take place after sections, which are regularly rather well balanced in length (e.g., Psalms 42-43, with its refrain at 42:5, 11, and 43:5). While there is some variation in the use of refrains,[117] they exhibit "a highly developed sense of symmetry."[118] Such refrains show nothing that approaches the alleged "refrain" at the opening of the poem in v. 19 or with the difference of length involving what would be stanzas in vv. 20-24 and in v. 26. With the so-called "refrain" appearing in the opening verse and with the lack of balance in the units that the alleged "refrain" would govern, the line "how the warriors fell" seems to be no refrain. Instead, in the reading that I am entertaining here, the instances in vv. 19 and 25 would not be a "refrain," but an envelope or inclusion around the older lament, while the further use of the line in v. 27 served to tie the highly personal reprise to Jonathan in vv. 26-27 to the earlier poem of vv. 19-25. Diana Vikander Edelman puts the point about v. 27 in this way: "In its present placement, it serves as an *inclusio* framing the expansion introduced in v. 26."[119] In this reading, Jonathan is evoked in v. 25c in a manner parallel to Saul in v. 19, providing a transition for David's first person invocation of Jonathan in the following v. 26.

To summarize, David's voice, as represented in vv. 26-27 of this poem, may echo a traditional feature of warrior culture, namely the circulation of songs for its fallen warriors, to which oral alterations or additions might have been made as they circulated. The reprise may have been David's response (or its representation) in receiving the news of the heroes' deaths as expressed in 2 Sam. 1:19-25. His own voice is added, perhaps as a claim for both his poetic talent[120] and his great attachment to one of the fallen heroes, not to mention the implicit claim to their succession. This reading of the poem and its context could work with a theory of different stages in its production and transmission: the poem produced in the aftermath of battle by an anonymous elegist; the poem's circulation more broadly; and its reception and expansion in the voice of David, whether on David's part or on the part of later Davidic propaganda.[121] In theory, I could entertain the possibility that this poem is David's political propaganda, one that could include some of his own feelings. The political heart is complex, and even calculating political intention may be freighted with deep emotion. However, it is also possible that the "historical David" had nothing to do with this poem and that he never had the level of relationship with Jonathan, as represented in this poem and in some of the prose passages in 1 Samuel. All of this could well be understood as largely the creation of monarchic political propaganda, whether during David's own reign or during the reigns of the immediately subsequent Davidic dynasts.

In any case, the tenth century would seem to be a fitting setting for the poem, by comparison with some later period, given the usage of "gazelle" in v. 19a as a leadership term, as well as the currency of the lament tradition over nature in v. 21a,[122] as noted above. A grammatical feature suggesting an older date for this poem to Chaim Cohen is the lack of the direct object marker.[123] The syntax of the opening phrase in v. 19 is also a bit unusual, and the past (perhaps past progressive or frequentative) use of the two participles in v. 24 is perhaps to be noted in this connection.[124] In short, the tenth century remains a viable setting for the poem, which, as we have seen, draws on traditional warrior features going back to the Iron I period.

The poem's larger prose context provides further information about the lament's circulation. First of all, the purpose named in the prose context is teaching. In contrast to the poetic emphasis on Israel, the prose notice in 2 Sam. 1:18 reports that this poem was taught to Judeans.[125] In contrast with the oral instructions in the poem directed to the women, the prose piece further relates how it was written in the document here called "the document[126] of Hayyashar." This alleged document is mentioned also in Josh. 10:12b-13a. A further reference to the work may underlie 1 Kgs. 8:13, the Greek version of which (3 Kgdms. 8:53) refers to *bibliom tēs ōdēs,* "the Book of the Song" (evidently reading **sēper haššîr* rather than *sēper hayyāšār*).[127] It has been supposed that this work represents "a collection of heroic poems,"[128] known in both Josh. 10:13 and 2 Sam. 1:18. Accordingly, it has been tempting to scholars to see an early "record of the upright/the valiant" (MT of Josh. 10:13 and 2 Sam. 1:18),[129] or "the record of the song" (so 1 Kgs. 8:13 LXX, perhaps as a reinterpretation?), or perhaps even an abbreviation for "the record of the (martial) power of Israel."[130] Whatever the nature of this putative document was (much less its name), the prose context provided by 2 Sam. 1:18 suggests how this poem was thought to have circulated in oral and written forms and perhaps in a written collection.[131] In other words, a process of transfer of oral poetry to a written collection seemed reasonable to the prose writer. Whether or not this particular reconstruction of the progression of 1 Sam. 1:19-27 is correct, both the poem and its prose context reconstruct oral song as a significant factor in its textual production and circulation.

Finally, it is to be noted that the poem may have exerted an effect on the prose context. It is notable that the narrative seems to delay the lament. Prior to David's lament, the prose account omits mention of lamenting over Saul, over his corpse at his burial in 1 Sam. 31:11-13. The prose context provides a convenient context for David to be the one who expresses the lament for the fallen king. Indeed, one may wonder whether the phrases of the prose report in 2 Sam. 1:4-5 were drawn at least in part from the poem. For example, did the prose writer derive the location of battle (at 1 Sam. 31:8) from the poem?

What this discussion may suggest is a series of stages in the poem's development. Poetic commemoration in the case of this poem shows the use of traditional tropes, along with a number of departures from such conventional material. The emotional expression directed to the memory of Jonathan, especially in v. 26, builds on the traditional elements otherwise seen in the poem. This mode of poetic commemoration seems also to be an effective means for reaching audiences in the wider Israelite society. The poem begins with well-known elements that would have resonated for an Israelite audience, and then the poem moves into the internal emotional world of the heroic speaker. Poetic commemoration serves not only to recall the past event and to make the audience feel its emotionally laden force. It also brings the audience into a new understanding of this past event: it offers a revelation of the heart of its great hero. Within the larger narrative, the poem's act of commemoration marks a watershed in the larger representation of David: he has developed from a successful warrior into a military leader who knows and feels devastating loss for himself and for Israel.

The battle story of 2 Sam. 1:19-27 is a song preserved not by hard historical memory. That such a heroic poem as this sounds legendary is not a flaw of history, but a fact of ancient cultural reality. It should not be taken as a sign of historical absence or lack, but as a signal of the societal setting of old textual production. This heroic song may detail battle, yet in this case it focuses on legends of the warriors' fall; the effect is to dramatize loss, not simply to report facts. The poem's commemorative purpose is not limited to evoking and invoking fallen heroes. It also serves to locate David in the larger tradition of early Israelite warrior poetry. David's lament in 2 Samuel 1 provides him with his place in the lineage of early Israelite heroes. We might say that this lament speaks over and against an earlier tradition of heroic poems such as Judges 5. On the literary level, an "epic struggle" is waged by the poem of 2 Samuel 1. The lament tells Israel that David is not simply some sort of latecomer to this heroic tradition. Its implicit claim is that he is much more: its best exemplar as well as the founder of the royal "Davidic" age. David in this poem is more a "person" than any other figure represented in early Israelite poetry, and he is the most important person to emerge from the early era of Israel. Just as the final form of Judges 5 prepares its audiences for royal governance across tribal lines, the poem of 2 Samuel 1 summons up a new communal identity for a post-Saulide "Israel," specifically with David and his line as its head. "David's" lament is an instrument of public speech that serves to constitute its audience(s) as political subjects[132] as Israel and specifically as David's Israel. This consideration of the lament is suggestive for the production and circulation of early heroic poetry in Israel, the issue addressed in the next chapter.

CHAPTER ELEVEN

The Cultural Settings for Warrior Poetry in Early Israel

In this chapter, we leave the central concern of the preceding chapters of Part IV, namely analysis of heroic poems and their representation of warriors. At this point, we turn our attention toward understanding the cultural contexts of warrior poetry in early Israel down through the tenth century. Despite the grave difficulties and the many limitations involving the available evidence,[1] I wish to consider the contexts for the production and transmission of warrior poetry as represented by biblical literature.[2] What does the available information suggest about the settings for the performance, production, and transmission of warrior poetry in early Israel? Before turning to the literary representation of these settings, a word is in order regarding oral and scribal composition in early Israel.

While the evidence suggests that oral composition was the basic mode of production for early heroic poetry, it is also the case that writing was part of the Iron I cultural landscape. As we will see in section 2 below, various inscriptions from the Iron I period show that writing was operative in this period, for example, the Izbet Sartah abecedary as well as inscribed arrowheads.[3] Indeed, it has been thought by a number of scholars, such as David M. Carr, that Judg. 5:14 refers to early scribalism in its reference to Zebulonites who "bear the staff of the scribe *(spr)*."[4] At the same time, while he is open to seeing scribal activity in earliest Israel,[5] Carr finds the monarchy to be the initial period for the writing down of oral compositions such as Judges 5.[6] Similarly, William Schniedewind assigns Judges 5 and 2 Sam. 1:19-27 to "the earliest biblical literature," which he also identifies as "oral literature."[7] That the two poems were originally oral is axiomatic for Terry Giles and William Doan.[8] According to a recent study of orality in ancient Israel by Robert D. Miller II,[9] the two poems would appear to be oral in origin. To judge from these scholarly discussions, there seems to be some consensus among scholars who have weighed in recently on the oral background of early heroic poetry.

It is not evident that scribal practice played a role in the initial composition of the heroic poetry under discussion, namely the older core within Judges 5 (as discussed in Chapter Nine) or the basic form of 2 Sam. 1:19-27, and especially vv. 19-25 (as discussed in Chapter Ten). I agree generally with Susan Niditch's claim that writing in Iron I Israel takes place in an "oral world,"[10] while the degree of literacy in this period remains unclear.[11] It is this largely "oral world" that seems to be the setting for heroic poetry in early Israel. As suggested in the preceding chapters, the activity of writing could have played a central role in the current versions of Judges 5 and 2 Sam. 1:19-27 in the tenth century, when there is further inscriptional evidence.[12]

1. The Represented Oral Settings of Warrior Poetry

Scholars working on early poems in ancient Israel point to a handful of biblical representations of their settings.[13] The most important is arguably Judg. 5:11, with its command to sing of victories. The allusion to women's song in 2 Sam. 1:20 is no less suggestive. In terms of their present literary contexts, these texts provide representations of settings for warrior poetry down through the time of David. Each one provides potential clues about the production and circulation of warrior poetry. These passages do not offer a single picture or setting for the production of heroic poetry, and they do not show a single sort of group involved in it. In other words, the passages offer a variety of perspectives about the practice of warrior poetry. The following discussion attempts to tease out information about the who, what, where, when, and how of early warrior poetry. Moreover, an effort is made to probe possible additional settings that are not explicitly mentioned in these contexts. As we proceed through this textual material, it remains important to emphasize the provisional character of this discussion of early Israel. In view of the difficulty of dating the specific verses addressed in this section, this discussion is offered as an effort at sketching possible contexts for the production and transmission of heroic poetry.

Judges 5:11

Judges 5:11 has played a major role in efforts to sketch an oral background for early Israelite literature. Ronald S. Hendel sees this passage as "the oldest reference in the Hebrew Bible to the performance of oral narrative in early Israel."[14] The verse is difficult, and so I provide a translation before proceeding to a detailed discussion of each line and then a broader consideration of its significance for the early setting of war poetry:

> At (or, louder than?) the sound[15] of divisions (?)[16] at the water-holes,
> There they recount[17] the victories of Yahweh,
> The victories of his village-militia in Israel:
> Then they went down to the gates, did the people of Yahweh.

The first two phrases of the first line are difficult. By contrast, the end of the first line seems to provide the settings for the rest of the verse. The location for activity is said to be *mšʾbym*. This *m*- preformative noun following the preposition *bên* and before *šām*, "there," may suggest a place rather than persons, thus "watering places."[18] The same West Semitic *m*- preformative noun is attested as a loanword, **mašʾaba*, "watering place," in Egyptian texts, according to James E. Hoch.[19]

The crucial term in this context for recitation is the verb **tny*. The setting for the other occurrence of this root, in Judg. 11:40, suggests northern Hebrew, according to a number of scholars.[20] (The comparable southern form seems to be **šny*.[21]) In this passage, Jephthah's home is said to be Mizpah (Judg. 11:34; see v. 11), usually identified with Tell en-Naṣbeh lying between Bethel and Gibeah (north of Jerusalem). According to Judg. 11:1-3, Jephthah is said to be a Gileadite who returns to Mizpah after settling secondarily in the land of Tob.[22] These areas would comport with a northern setting. This passage uses the root **tny* to refer to the chanting of laments for the unnamed daughter of Jephthah.[23] In this context, the root **tny* refers to oral recitation in her memory.[24] This view would fit with the Ugaritic verb **ṯny*,[25] used for recounting a message, especially by messengers (KTU 1.2 I 16; 1.3 III 12; VI 12; 1.4 VIII 31; 1.5 II 9; 1.16 VI 28; cf. PN in 4.339.14).[26] Oral delivery of messages is a characteristic use for this root in Ugaritic. What is evident in the biblical and Ugaritic cases is that oral recitation is what is imagined. It may be thought that the context of Judg. 5:11 predates its use in the northern prose context in 11:40. At least Judg. 5:11, and possibly 11:40, would predate the fall of the northern kingdom. Indeed, the story containing Judg. 11:40

may come from a core tradition of Judges stories from the north prior to its fall. The poem with 5:11 is recognized as being of greater antiquity (not only because of its older features).[27] There is no reason why the tradition of Judg. 5:11 could not date sometime prior to the ninth century.[28] The Ugaritic usages of **ṯny* indicate that this supposition is reasonable. Moreover, there is no reason not to think that for the composer of Judg. 5:11, **tny* entails oral recitation.

This is not quite the end of our consideration of Judg. 5:11. In Chapter Nine, I argued that the introduction to the poem, which includes v. 11, is the work of a compiler-composer that drew on earlier material. V. 11 is not part of the earlier material, and would therefore seem to date to the time of the composer rather than the time of the poem's sources (much less the time of the putative events recounted in the poem). In other words, v. 11 stands sometime after the events of the poem or even their recollection in the sources to the poem, but before the prose enshrinement of the poem and its events in Judges 4 (and prior to the larger narrative work that enshrined both Judges 4 and 5). With the composer's added emphasis on Israel as a collective and on Yahweh as its patron-god, the tenth century seems to be a reasonable *terminus ad quem* for the present composition of the poem, including its Judg. 5:11. In other words, this verse seems to represent what a tenth-century composer believed to be the case about oral recitation in earlier times.

With the tenth century as the time of Judg. 5:11, we may turn to what this verse says about the content of such recitations. The object of the verb "to recite" is *ṣdqwt yhwh,* literally, Yahweh's "righteous acts,"[29] which are often taken to mean "triumphs"[30] or the like.[31] The *ṣidqôt yhwh* in Mic. 6:5 are recalled as the events involving Balak and Balaam in Numbers 22-24 and the crossing of the Jordan in Joshua 3–4. In this prophetic passage, the audience is asked to remember (**zkr*) these events of old, a process that is to serve to induce a proper attitude toward the deity (see Mic. 6:6). Samuel's recitation of the *ṣidqôt yhwh* in 1 Sam. 12:7-12 involves military conflict beginning with the exodus from Egypt and continuing with the victories over Sisera, the Philistines, and the Moabites (v. 9).[32] It further recalls Israel's great leaders from this era, from well before the putative time of the speaker, Samuel. Considered in light of these later passages, Judges 5 may be an early representative of a commemorative tradition. Whether in the earlier poetic text of Judg. 5:11, the later poem of Mic. 6:5, or the later prose historiography of 1 Sam. 12:7, the *ṣidqôt yhwh* are part of Israel's collective memory of the deity's ancient efforts on its behalf. The term does not seem to be used for events regarded as contemporary or near past. In 1 Samuel 12, this older expression for the ancient acts of divine deliverance, the *ṣidqôt yhwh,* corresponds to a rather prosaic phrase in the prose account for the divine act that is about to unfold in the story. In vv. 16-17, Samuel announces "this great deed" *(haddābār haggādôl)* that Yahweh is about to perform on Israel's behalf.[33]

The context of Judg. 5:11 commemorates these victories as *ṣidqôt pirzōnô,* which I would translate as "the victories of his village-militia."[34] It is clear that the divine victories are qualified by the participation of Yahweh's human devotees. In other words, the vision of divine battle is synergistic; it is not Yahweh's task alone, but one in which the human forces of the deity also take part. Moreover, and quite importantly, it is to be noted that these victories in both the second and third lines of Judg. 5:11 are cast in the plural, not in the singular. The imagined speaker, apparently the represented "I-voice" in vv. 3, 9, 13, and 21,[35] refers in v. 11 to a practice of oral recitation not only for this one victory, but for multiple victories, which to judge from other uses of the expression of *ṣidqôt yhwh* in Mic. 6:5 and 1 Sam. 12:7-12, would not refer only to the victory over Sisera's army. In other words, we seem to have in Judg. 5:11 two occurrences of *ṣidqôt* that would include, but are not limited to, the victory narrated in the rest of the poem. What I hear behind the plural use in this context (that would otherwise seem to call for a singular if it were referring only to what is narrated in the rest of the poem) is an oral, poetic call to recall such victories. This call to remember seems to be an old poetic theme that may predate the usage in Mic. 6:5 and 1 Sam. 12:7, but would probably postdate the victory here and perhaps other victories that were remembered as following this one. In other words, this plural expression in the poetic context of Judg. 5:11 suggests a time postdating the construction of collective memory about Israel's putatively ancient battles.

The fourth line of Judges 5:11 seems to recount the beginning of victory: "Then they went down to the gates, did the people (army) of Yahweh." C. F. Burney viewed this line as a marginal note (as well as its apparent variant in v. 13).[36] Johannes C. de Moor suggests taking the last line as the title of a song as recalled at the watering places.[37] This is very clever; it also obviates the contextual problem: if this line were part of the narrative, then the army could not descend before Deborah and Baraq arise (as stated in v. 12). Perhaps the fourth line of v. 11 represents a reference to the battle that is to unfold.

The broader setting of v. 11 provides a clue about the setting imagined for this poem (and perhaps others of its like). V. 10 provides an addressee to whom v. 11 is addressed:

O riders on tawny[38] asses,[39]
Sitting on cloths,[40]
And walkers on the road, sing![41]

In this verse, travelers, both well-off riders and commoners with no access to riding animals,[42] are called to sing or chant the victory (perhaps to join the "I-voice" in singing the song of victories). In its address, Judg. 5:11 seems to imagine an audience that is "on the way" *('al derek)* to its destination.

J. David Schloen suggests watering places for caravan animals, which makes sense if v. 11 is taken with v. 10.[43] In the larger context of the poem's events, the watering holes of this site may connect with the recollection of the battle area "by the waters of Megiddo" in v. 19. The mention of watering places in the context of battle might also recall the motif of washing blood off in the aftermath of battle.[44] It seems that the setting for such a recollection at watering places would be sites on travel routes. Thus, one possible scenario for an invocation of both the well-to-do and the less well-to-do to sing at such places would be in the context of pilgrimage feasts possibly with animals in tow.[45] An alternative scenario would entail military forces en route.

Frank Moore Cross placed the tribal blessings in Genesis 49; Deuteronomy 33; and Judges 5 within the context of such early pilgrimage festivals.[46] While one may prescind from Cross's further suggestion that these blessings were part of "the reenactment of the epic victory of Yahweh" (which he labels also as the "ritual conquest"),[47] his suggestion would make sense for the reference to "watering places" in Judg. 5:11. In a later discussion, Cross entertained two possibilities: "in pilgrimage festivals or in assemblies for holy war, i.e., in ritual enactments of the wars of Yahweh, or actual rituals in battle camps."[48] The second scenario is a military one analogous to the content of the poem of Judges 5. In this scenario, the poem recalled a past victory in order to inspire a new victory. It would have been designed to inspire those who had managed to join in the battle forces and not have been concerned about those that did not join. While this might have been the function for vv. 14-18, it is not clear that it is also the setting for the later v. 11.

At first glance, v. 11 does not seem to imagine a singer belonging to a professional class of bards. Deborah is imagined as a singer in ancient Israel in v. 12, yet her professional activity is broader based than a bard's. Perhaps such victories were the subjects of known songs sung widely.[49] It is possible that the practice of such recitation was particularly prized when sung by specialists, as suggested by Num. 21:27. After the victory over Heshbon mentioned in the preceding verse, the narrative of Num. 21:27 introduces the victory poem of vv. 27-30 with the prose notice: "Therefore the *māšāl*-sayers[50] *(mōšělîm)* would say." Without more evidence, it is hard to say whether such oral specialists were known in early Israel before the ninth century[51] (although there is no reason that this could not have been an earlier, traditional practice). The prose verse, Num. 21:27, reflects the monarchic era,[52] and perhaps the "sayers" of the northern kingdom[53] do as well (known later as well in the south; cf. Ezek. 17:2; 18:2; 20:49[21:5]).[54] Apart from this passage, there is no evidence for this level of specialization in the older poetic sources of Israel; and indeed, it is notable that no such *mōšělîm* appear in association with any other older poetry. Support for such "professionals" might be sought in the Ugaritic literary representation of the singer of the god in KTU 1.3 I 18-22, discussed in Chapter Six,[55] or in the poetry with the "I-voice" in Judg. 5:3, 9, 13, 21 (cf. Exod. 15:1), discussed in Chapter Nine. While the degree of professional singers or bards in early Israel remains *sub iudice,* oral poetic activity likely ranged from specialists at one end to more common singing at the other end. Another part of this spectrum may be represented in the next example.

2 Samuel 1:20

If Judges 5:11 points to the oral recitation of war-poetry in travel outside of population centers, 2 Sam. 1:20 acknowledges this practice within such a center. According to this poem, the unnamed addressees are instructed in v. 20:

> Make no proclamation in Gath,
> No announcement in Ashkelon's streets,
> Lest[56] the daughters of the Philistines rejoice,
> Lest the daughters of the uncircumcised exult.

This verse represents "oral proclamation" in central, communal space, as Alan Millard has emphasized.[57] As imagined in this verse, the news of victory would be proclaimed in a specific sort of "outside" space *(ḥûṣôt).*[58] The association of this term with *rĕḥōbôt,* "broad places, squares," in later texts (e.g., Prov. 1:20; 7:12;[59] 22:13; Jer. 5:1; 9:20[21])[60] is likewise suggestive of public space for *ḥûṣôt* (often translated as "streets").[61] Prov. 1:20 mentions these two terms, along with the wall and the gate, specifically as communal spaces where Wisdom personified speaks out.[62] Punic attests to the term (in the singular), in connection with a town square located at a town gate: "this street (leading) to the square of the new gate" *(hḥṣ z lmqm šʿr hḥdš).*[63]

These are communal spaces that may also function as market sites. According to 1 Kgs. 20:34, *ḥûṣôt* in Damascus, as in Samaria, serve as space granted for sales of goods, due to a royal agreement that provided trading concessions to another polity. Jer. 37:21 refers to the "*ḥûṣôt* of the bakers." Ezek. 26:11-12 may also associate *ḥûṣôt* with commercial activity. Such verses are perhaps suggestive of different streets or areas devoted to different sorts of products for sale. It has also been suggested that *ḥûṣôt* used for commercial markets may have been public buildings in Iron Age Israelite towns.[64] It is also claimed from archaeological study that open space between houses was used for craft-activities.[65] Any of these might serve as *ḥûṣôt.* In any case, commercial activity is one function of outside, communal space. Communal, religious activity taking place in the streets of Jerusalem is imagined in Jer. 7:17.

According to 2 Sam. 1:20, it is in communal spaces of the town where news of battle may be announced. This verse indicates that more than an announcement is made; the news is also celebrated communally. As imagined in this verse, warrior poetry may lie at the heart of public celebration in the center of towns.[66] The opposite of this type of public celebration is public lamentation, and this, too, may transpire in this public setting, according to later texts (Amos 5:16; Isa. 15:3; 24:11).[67] This shared space of the town, used not only for public passage and commerce, functions as the location for public performance of celebration and lamentation, activities that affirm and shape shared identity over and against the identities of enemies. These are locations of reinforced difference vis-à-vis others and reinforced communality internally. In turn, such locations served as one of the places of communal reception of such news and the site of such news' initial social interpretation. Such expressions not only reflect the setting; the setting served as the spatial vessels for communicating such events. The communal space shaped the form of verbal communications. What is expressed in such a public context about the army, whether victory or defeat, is a matter of life and death for the people gathered there.

1 Samuel 18:7; 21:12(11); 29:5

Oral, poetic transmission is represented in an act of postbattle commemoration of victory three times, in 1 Sam. 18:7; 21:12(11); 29:5:

"Saul has slain his thousands,	*hikkâ šā'ûl ba'ălāpā(y)w*[68]
David, his ten-thousands."	*wĕdāwīd bĕribĕbōtā(y)w*[69]

Before discussing the oral contexts that the narrative provides for this couplet, we may note its poetic features and content.[70] The personal names, Saul and David, stand in parallelism. I will return to the importance of this parallelism. The verb mentioned in the first line ("has slain") carries over to and governs the second line as well. This gapping, here involving the ellipsis of the verb in the second line, is a hallmark of what scholars have long called "synonymous parallelism," by which they mean that the structure of the second line and often its meaning largely follow the first line. Stated differently, the second line is essentially "synonymous" in meaning and structure with the first, and may even be syntactically dependent on an element in this first line, in this case its verb. The numbers in the final phrase in the two lines show complex morphological and sonant parallelism (or matching). Both numbers belong to prepositional phrases beginning with the preposition *b-*, and both end with the same pronominal suffix, resulting in end-rhyme between the two words. In addition, the two numerals share consonants in the same phonological classes: the nasal consonants, /l/ in *ba'ălāpā(y)w* and /r/ in *bĕribĕbōtā(y)w;* and the bilabial consonants, /p/ in *ba'ălāpā(y)w* and /b/ in *bĕribĕbōtā(y)w,* further reinforced by the preposition *b-* preceding the numbers in both cases.

As commentators have noted for decades, the poetic parallelism of numbers is not to indicate a difference of scale between them. Rather, it is common in parallelism of numbers that the second line adds to the first (e.g., "three" parallel with "four," as in Prov. 30:15,[71] 18, 29; Amos 1:3, 6, 9, 11, 13; 2:1, 4, 6). When the scale of numbers goes beyond the hundreds, "thousands" and "ten thousands" (or "myriads") are poetic synonyms in Biblical Hebrew poetry (Deut. 33:17; Mic. 6:7; Ps. 91:7; Ps. 68:17, in reverse order) and in Biblical Aramaic poetry (Dan. 7:10); it is a traditional formulation known also in Ugaritic poetry.[72] The case in Psalm 68 may suggest the antiquity of its usage in ancient Israel, and the Ugaritic examples reinforce this impression. It is also to be noted that the numbers may involve wordplay. As Michael Patrick O'Connor observed,[73] the number **'ălāpîm,* "thousands," may also connote in this context the same term as used for military units. The couplet would capture magnitude with the military. All in all, the synonymous parallelism in this couplet is impressive.

At this point, we may return to the proper names of Saul and David standing in parallelism. The personal names constitute the couplet's only major departure from the standard poetic repertoire.[74] Fokkelien van Dijk-Hemmes and John T. Noble have emphasized that it is not common for the names of two different persons to stand in this sort of poetic parallelism.[75] On the face of it, the parallel names serve together as synonyms of heroic accomplishment, that Saul and David have gained this victory together. However, the parallelism of names is not to suggest that Saul's accomplishment is less; it is parallel and thus of the same order. However, the parallelism of the names implies more than the relative parity of status of the two warriors; since such parallelism of two subjects is exceptional in such passages, the addition of David is conspicuous. As noted by Athalya Brenner and van Dijk-Hemmes, the women's song in this couplet may imply a preference for David by including him in such high company as the king himself.[76] In short, while the contexts for the couplet in 1 Samuel are later, the tradition of warrior poetry as sung by women seems quite old.[77]

The prose representations provided for the setting and circulation of the couplet are important for understanding the oral context of warrior poetry as remembered later. More precisely, the prose settings for the couplet provide an Iron II (or later) representation of Israelite cultural memory for the oral contexts of older warrior poetry. The first time this rhyming couplet is pronounced in 1 Sam. 18:7 it is represented as the victory song that greets the victorious warriors immediately after battle.[78] David is returning from battle against the Philistines with the troops, and he is greeted by "the women of all the towns of Israel singing and dancing to meet Saul" with musical instruments (1 Sam. 18:6).[79] Women sing and dance as they voice the couplet (1 Sam. 18:7). This context is interesting: it is musical; the couplet is sung; and it belongs to a celebration. The song is imagined not as the work of professionals, but as the activity of women "from all the towns of Israel."

The further prose context of the poetic couplet in 1 Sam. 18:8 is also interesting, as it signals its impact as a potentially pointed statement. Saul is said to be distressed at the singing of this couplet, since it is represented as sounding to Saul as if David is given greater credit. The interpretation of the couplet attributed to Saul in v. 8, that David had slain ten times more than Saul, reflects a literal — and perhaps intentionally ironic — understanding of the well-known synonymous parallelism of "thousands"/"ten thousands." As noted above, these numbers in their poetic context are part of the couplet's "synonymous poetry." As such, they do not denote different accomplishments of the two men. Nonetheless, as David Noel Freedman noted, perhaps the monarch would not have been so pleased to have one of his leading warriors praised in parallel and thus comparable terms.[80] Indeed, for v. 8b, it might have suggested that as a great warrior, David was no less fit for kingship than Saul. The couplet's second occurrence in 1 Sam. 21:12(11), as well as its third occurrence in 1 Sam. 29:5, represent the poem as indicator of the circulation of David's military reputation among the Philistines. 1 Sam. 21:12(11) and 29:5 also show that this couplet was imagined as sung in tandem with dance.

These instances taken together suggest an ancient historical imagination about how women sang such a song in the context of celebration and how they circulated it orally.[81] Its enshrinement within the larger context of 1 Sam. 18:7; 21:12(11); 29:5 further suggests the wider circulation of David's reputation, which later royal chroniclers would enhance. Taking these occurrences together, we may trace the path of the heroic couplet, from its initial use in celebrating victory, to further circles of Israelites learning orally of David's reputation in battle, and finally into the national narrative of David's rise. While the textual representation is ideologically charged in advancing David's reputation, the point for this discussion is that the couplet's repetition was thought to be a reasonable representation of how such oral poetry could circulate and enshrine the reputation of the royal warrior, Saul, and his young protégé, David.

At this point, we may turn from these passages to the broader question of oral performance in early Israel. It might seem that Judges 5 and 2 Sam. 1:19-27, as well as the later prose contexts for the couplet about Saul and David, provide indicators of poetic orality in early Israel. However, it could be argued that it is a circular argument to base a picture for orality on the sources that represent such a picture of orality. In addition, it would be quite possible to see the representation of orality within the poetry as an ideologically charged claim from the tenth century (and possibly later) about earlier times. As long as there are scholars inclined to see later dates for poems such as Judges 5 and 2 Sam. 1:19-27, it may seem that not too much weight can be put on the poetic representations of orality. Indeed, according to my own dating of both poems in their present forms to the tenth century, these representations of performance provide little direct guidance for Iron I Israel.

Still there remains reason to suppose that both women's song and men's song contributed to the fund of early Israelite heroic poetry surviving in the Hebrew Bible. Apart from the arguments made thus far for dating these poems to what I have called early Israel (Iron I down into the ninth century), persuasive evidence for the actual oral background of these poems or their parts lies in the fact that these parts have formulaic counterparts elsewhere. In this regard, Judges 5 is quite productive. Apart from this poem's traditional language, the lack of unity among tribes as well as the absence of the name of Israel from what seems to be the poem's older core[82] is suggestive of an older context: "disputes between tribal groups or within the tribe are carried exclusively in poetry."[83] The lament of 2 Sam. 1:19-27 also shows a traditional formulary suggestive of an older tradition, even if one were inclined to a later date for this poem. The same may be said of parts of other poems, such as Genesis 49 and Psalm 68.[84] The setting represented of women's song, as noted in this section, may go back to Iron I Israel as well. The same may be thought of the setting represented in Judg. 5:11, though this seems less clear.

2. Inscribing the Warrior Songs

To relate this information about oral production and circulation in the context of the Iron I period, we may turn to the inscriptional evidence.[85] Known for Israel as early as the late eleventh century (Izbet Sartah[86]), abecedaries[87] are the beginning of the scribal craft,[88] and the production of lists would not follow far behind. The production of the inscribed arrowheads known from this period[89] involves an additional skill, namely incising in metal, not a traditional scribal medium.[90] Inscribing arrowheads may represent a scribal subspecialty. Thus, early scribal activity varied in genres of texts as well as their media.

Ryan Byrne suggests a social setting for this scribal activity: "Unlike the Late Bronze and Iron II epigraphic corpora, which reflects the dimensions of state interests, the Iron I evidence suggests a culture of scribalism that survived largely through circumstantial appeal to elite patronage."[91] Inscriptions on bowls (e.g., the Lachish Bowl Fragment,[92] the Qubur 'el-Walaydah Bowl Fragment)[93] point to the owners of the bowls as clientele of inscription and bowl producers. The Khirbet Raddana handle[94] and the Revadim seal[95] suggest their owners as the patrons of these objects along with their inscriptions. The same point applies to the inscribed arrowheads. As Byrne's discussion highlights, the patrons of these sorts of items would have been local well-to-do personages who not only could afford the items themselves, but also could bear the cost of having them inscribed. Byrne concludes: "The Iron I corpus of applied alphabetic writing consists of two basic categories: prestige objects (possessive, martial, votive, funerary) commissioned by elites, and curricular instruments used to preserve the very profession of scribalism during an era in which it existed on the margins of dominant exchange patterns."[96]

Byrne's comments provide a sense of the social horizons for writing in early Israel. His categories of possessive, martial, votive, and funerary point to the purposes of writing in Iron I Israel and at the same time also to the sorts of persons interested in such writing. The picture of writing in this period is not entirely clear. Miller notes the lack of inscriptions from sites where elites would be expected to support the production of inscriptions.[97] Miller's response to Byrne is understandable, yet it focuses on the absence of evidence,[98] and it does not sufficiently scrutinize Byrne's evidence. At the same time, I think Miller's cautionary notes are helpful. Given the unknown provenience of many inscribed arrowheads (not to mention doubts about the authenticity raised about some of the inscribed arrowheads that have emerged more recently[99]), these artifacts offer only provisional data — and perhaps very little for ancient Israel as such. Indeed, any number of the inscribed arrowheads may have originated in Lebanon, and thus would not constitute evidence for Iron I Israel. As a result, the Iron I inscribed arrowheads by themselves cannot serve as evidence about early Israel as such. In the following discussion, the evidence of inscribed arrowheads discovered in early decades is combined with provenanced Iron I inscriptions to serve as a heuristic means for suggesting a possible Iron I Israel context for the traditions of heroic poetry in early Israel.

Despite limitations of evidence, the four sorts of writing mentioned by Byrne suggest a certain level of income and social position capable of ownership of such objects along with their inscriptions. Of the four categories, it is the martial that is of particular interest for this study. At the most basic level of information, the arrowheads point to a social context consisting of warriors and their patrons. On the one hand, the arrowheads point to their owners as warriors. The very name of one owner of an arrowhead is *mhry*, "warrior."[100] We may suspect that some families were traditionally warriors and enjoyed a tradition of producing warriors. J. T. Milik and Cross theorized that the arrowheads pointed to hereditary guilds of warriors,[101] while Benjamin Mazar associated the arrowheads with professional archers.[102] At the same time, powerful patrons are also indicated by the arrowheads. Christopher A. Rollston thinks that the arrowheads are inscribed prestige objects.[103] This view would fit with McCarter's observation that some arrowheads bear the name of high-status individuals, for example, "king of Amurru":[104] "the arrows fired by the archers in a nobleman's personal retinue would bear their lord's name, thus claiming a portion of the spoils for him."[105] Another arrowhead owner has a father referred to as *špṭ*,[106] traditionally translated as "judge," but more likely the "ruler" or the like.[107] A formal structure is evident in other cases. For example, one arrowhead refers to *bny'*, the owner of one arrowhead, as *rb 'lp*, "leader of the contingent."[108] The arrowheads may thus be indicative not only of individuals, but also of military structure or organization under the leadership of regional military leaders. From these brief glimpses, it would appear that the arrowheads partake of a decentralized political world with local kings or rulers, a picture of early Israel that Miller has described from his examination of archaeological data.[109] The situation largely involves militias or fighting forces led by a particular leader,[110] with village elders serving as further social support.[111] Thus, various sorts of military leaders, all the way up to minor kings, may directly patronize or indirectly support the users of arrowheads and the production of the arrowheads for them. Byrne puts the point in this way: "The unprovenanced Iron I arrowheads indicate that they belonged not only to powerful men, but also to their retainers, whose inscribed equipment in turn enhanced the patrons' stature."[112] In addition, the social world of the arrowheads is not entirely confined to the warriors and their patrons. One arrowhead refers to its owner as the son of "the scribe" *(hspr)*.[113] A number of occupations often worked in a hereditary fashion (monarchy, priesthood, scribes, and more broadly based, agriculture); perhaps some tendency toward accomplishment in hunting and warfare also ran in families.

Taken together, the arrowheads point to a larger social world of warriors in a military context along with human patrons, as well as their warrior goddesses who were perhaps their divine patrons.[114] What mediated between this world of the arrowheads and their production were the scribes that produced the inscriptions, perhaps signaled by the title "the scribe," as noted above. The fact of martial patronage and martial writing in the inscriptional record may suggest a social concern for the maintenance of this arena of activity, not to mention the range of its practices that we have seen in this study.[115] "Warlordism," Byrne suggests, "ranks far below the ideal form of intellectual patronage, but it does afford survival."[116] It would seem that social leaders, operating in a relatively local context of political conflict, sometimes conveyed their status through scribal production.

For the purposes of this study, it is particularly notable that writing is at home both in the production of the inscriptions on the arrowheads and in the traditions of warrior poetry, as we have it in Judges 5 and 2 Sam. 1:19-27. This may be one of the only instances in which the arenas of Iron I-IIA activity referenced in both early biblical and extrabiblical written sources correspond.[117] Judg. 5:10 suggests an audience of both those who walk on the way, in other words, relative "commoners," and those who ride on she-asses, in other words, relatively speaking, "the tribal elite."[118] Indeed, such an elite would organize such performance for its people in order to celebrate the victories of deity and people and to affirm the elite's place in these victories. (There is no particular egalitarianism represented here, as has been suggested for early Israel.[119]) The evidence of orality noted above in section 1 suggests a place for oral performances of heroic poetry, at any number of points following battle, yet this is not the whole picture.

As we have seen, the textual enshrinement of warrior poetry is more complex not only by way of genre. With the two poems that we examined in Chapters Eight through Ten, there seem to be multiple levels of composition; thus we may speak of the recompositional process when it comes to the written artifacts as we have them. It is precisely the lack of unity in the two heroic poems examined in Chapters Eight through Ten that suggests their existence in multiple oral and written forms over the course of their history, perhaps exhibiting what Gregory Nagy calls "recomposition-in-performance."[120] At some point, oral and written forms could have existed together. While we have no access to either oral or written forms prior to the tenth century, oral forms are evident from the circumstantial evidence noted in section 1. The same might be said for some written forms of heroic poetry, based on the inscriptional evidence noted in section 2. In other words, information in some of the inscriptions points to the sort of social context that could have supported heroic poetry. The very fact of writing in the Iron I context also makes it possible that written forms of heroic poems could have existed this early. In sum, the inscriptional evidence for the Iron I period indicates the social support, the social interest, and the social means for the written production of heroic poetry. Thus, the question of heroic poetry in written forms during the Iron I remains open, despite the lack of evidence for its written production in this period.[121]

Given the present state of the evidence, the tenth century seems to be a more promising context for situating the written composition of heroic poetry, at least for the two poems that this study has examined in Chapters Eight through Ten. Still, in its earlier form, Judges 5 suggests social collectivity as an issue for northern warrior elites in the Iron I period.[122] The older core of Judges 5 shows the stresses of social cohesion and its evident lack, increasing in particular around the periphery of the northern highlands. 2 Sam. 1:19-27 points to concerns about warrior leadership ostensibly by the southern figure, David.[123] By contrast, the secondary introduction of the poem of Judges 5 represents an effort at assertion (or agency) of the notion of an "Israel" as "the people of Yahweh" consisting of the various social entities named in the poem's body. In Chapter Nine, I suggested that this newly formulated poetic introduction reflects early monarchic concerns over tribal cohesion. 2 Sam. 1:19-27 also reflects a moment of warrior agency: just as the fall of the great leader and his son would seem to crush their followers, a competitor figure is represented as asserting his own inheritance to the warrior mantle. In their current forms, the two poems signal elite concerns of emergent royal polities.[124]

Up to this point, the discussion has suggested a picture of the concerns of warrior poetry as it was circulated orally, instructed orally, and perhaps recomposed orally from the Iron I through the tenth century. We have not addressed how these warrior songs were inscribed in writing. With Judges 5, we seem to be talking about a traditional song or even group of songs, perhaps telescoped or rearranged in its present written form. Its current written form may have taken shape quite some time after the events that it recalled. By comparison, with 2 Sam. 1:19-27 the oral circulation of the poem in the immediate aftermath of war was perhaps not as long in becoming an inscribed song. One could imagine a scribal copy made in the wake of the announcement of such news, as Alan Millard has suggested.[125] Both poetic compositions as written matters seem to date to the tenth century, and as such we may imagine a reception into early royal circles, the older one, Judges 5, in the northern court[126] and the later, 2 Sam. 1:19-27, perhaps in the southern court.[127] Judges 5 shows some signs of the concerns of the royal court into which its traditions were received and reshaped in its present form. As for 2 Sam. 1:19-27, we need not rely on the prose report's historical veracity that the poem belonged to a collection of heroic poetry, as attractive as such a hypothesis might be for this study (and even possibly true). Royal scribalism seems to be a reasonable setting for the written production of the poems. Just as a king would give oral instructions for scribes to write in the form of letters,[128] so, too, scribes might receive texts in oral form as well as written forms to copy. The text was arguably written down to serve as a learning record and tool for oral perfor!mance.[129] Given the evidence of both Judges 5 and 2 Sam. 1:19-27 as analyzed in this work, the tenth century appears to be significant for the written enshrinement of Israelite heroic poetry. Yet, as we will see in the last chapter of our story, this is also the period when the oral production of heroic poetry seems to draw to a close. Before we turn to that final chapter, it is necessary to address the question of why such inscription of the songs would be patronized by monarchies.

3. The Iron II Written Reception of Warrior Poetry

Heroic poetry from the "lost world" of early Israel, both in the Iron I context of tribal Israel and the courts of the tenth century, was very useful for the later Israelite and Judean monarchies. This poetry became instruments of teaching, in other words, objects with agency in forming proper attitudes and ideas about the past in order to promote "nation-building." The use of the past within such poems served the monarchy: it rooted the monarchic "present" in a represented past, provided a sense of connection with it, and offered rationales for the monarchies. For Judges 5, the past of the poem not only celebrates "God and country"; it also shows the need for monarchy in the face of tribal disunity. The poem of 2 Samuel 1 heralds the place of David in the wake of Saul and his would-be successor, Jonathan. Perhaps no better political textbook could have been produced; the emotional appeal within this poem would have engendered an analogous emotional appeal on the part of its audience, that it should love David and his dynasty no less than Jonathan is said to have loved David.

The texts hardly represent the process by which these oral poems took written form. This matter of their textual production is no less interesting than the matter of their historical veracity, the matter often of greater concern among modern interpreters. In the case of Judges 5, there is no account of how it became a written text. For 2 Sam. 1:18, an old written work is said to be the collection point for oral poetry. There is no description of the actual process in this case; there is no mention of a scribe in this context writing down the words from an oral source (even if this is what was presupposed). Indeed, oral dictation to a scribe is better known from later texts,[130] for example, Jeremiah's dictation to the scribe Baruch.[131] This could have been the model involved for old poetry. However, the prose account of the reception of old poetry in 2 Sam. 1:18 adds a stage in appealing to the little known "Book of Yashar" (or better, "document of Yashar").[132] This detail may suggest oral dictation into a written composition and collection, and then the transmission of this collection. At first glance, this account serves to overcome the problem of how old poems survived through the centuries between their oral circulation, their written composition, and their later reception into the time of the great literary cycles of Israel (Genesis-Samuel). However, this very representation dovetails perhaps all too well with how later generations understood the process of how oral poetry was collected and written in collections transmitted and thus known later to the prose authors of the great historical works of Joshua, Judges, and Samuel.

It is interesting that no mention is made of this "Book of Yashar" elsewhere in the Bible, apart from the passages that mention the poems said to be included in this work. Elsewhere it is not said to be possible to consult (like the records of kings) or that it was otherwise known to anyone between the inclusion of poems into the collection and the later incorporation of the poems into the large literary cycles. It does not mention either the scribes involved in its production or the further context for its collection. Because of these gaps, making a strong assumption about historical veracity of the "Book of Yashar" (or lack thereof) arguably achieves little. Whether or not this collection of heroic poems was known to the scribes of the later Iron IIB (and following), it would seem that this represented their theory about heroic poetry: that it belonged to an old world now lost to them; that the poems received written form in a collection that mediated between this old "lost world" of early Israel (Iron I and tenth century) and the time of the collections of Joshua, Judges and Samuel (later Iron IIB and afterwards). In other words, the later prose writers that gave context to these works perhaps understood the history of transmission in the image and likeness of their own works and times, specifically that they had some written sources available to them that they used, and so the old heroic poetry came to them in similar fashion. Thus, the prose context may preserve the ancient writers' own theory about textual tradition. Still, one cannot demonstrate that work was a fiction, nor can one adopt an attitude of belief in it and use it to build a historical case about the transmission of old heroic poetry. As a piece of "evidence," it remains in limbo for modern scholarship.

This is not the end of the problems for trying to understand how the ancient writers thought of the transmission process for old heroic poetry. For the "Book of Yashar" is not said to include some old heroic poetry, such as the poem of Judges 5. In the case of the poem of Judges 5, the prose historiographers seem to have presupposed that it was composed at the time of the events mentioned in it. We have no indication from the context of Judges 5 how the prose historiographers of Judges 4 thought that they had received the poem in the context of the Iron IIB (or later). By implication, these later writers may have had little or no idea about how the process worked in the Iron I period. While their own model might have been operative in their time, they did not necessarily know about such processes in the earlier period; nor do we. We guess in our way about royal courts (as I have above), just as the ancient prose historiographers may have ventured their own views on the matter.

We might add that these monarchic contexts are, in a sense, royal courts in the making; these are not yet the full-fledged monarchies of the time of the Omrides in the north or later in the south. And so the poems themselves are part of the process of making these monarchies into what they became or hoped to become. We may see then a further purpose of the poems. They are not simply reflections of ideas about monarchs or monarchies. They are also tools for expressing what these monarchies and monarchs are for their people and how these dynasties in the making are continuous with the older, glorious past as represented in the poems. The agency of these poems, as monarchic tools of instruction, is echoed in the prose introduction for 2 Sam. 1:18. In short, the poems are textual monuments to a great past, with a potent formative function: the past as instructional literature for monarchies and their continuity with the great, earlier past of Israel as perceived in the poems.

In order to try to trace the transmission process for old heroic poetry, it seems necessary to return to the apparent settings within the poems' composition as we have them. In the case of Judges 5, a royal setting is discernible, arguably to be situated in the tenth century in the northern kingdom. To my mind, the imagined recitation at the watering-places is not the setting that provided for the poem's transmission and reception into the biblical tradition as we have it. Instead, the royal references in v. 3 suggest a royal setting for its reception and use (here I would consider contrasting the liturgical reception given to Psalm 68 as suggested by its threefold use of *selah*). The "I-voice" of the poem seems at home in the royal court, and in view of the poem's contents, it may be located in the court of the early northern monarchy.[133]

The passage that is most suggestive in this regard is not a historical text, and it is not one that shows any sort of process for our poems. However, it does suggest the sort of royal world in which such poems might be operative. This is the opening image of Psalm 45. For the majority of commentators,[134] this poem represents a wedding song of the northern court, relating the marriage of a royal scion of the northern kingdom to a Tyrian princess. We do not know the date of this text, although a date prior to the fall of the northern kingdom in the late eighth century seems advisable. Thus, the poem, even if it has additions, seems to offer a representation of the northern court in the Iron II period. Indeed, the royal praise in this poem is related without any negative judgment and suggests the atmosphere of a royal court. Praise of the royal male is announced in flowery detail with monarchic ideals of might, justice, and good looks. The corresponding praise of the princess focuses on her attractiveness. The poem opens in v. 1 with a self-representation of the "I-voice," which expresses the desire to do a good job with his praise of the bride and groom. This voice announces: "May my tongue be the implement[135] of a skilled[136] scribe." There are many details about this line to be noted. I will address three in turn: the context of the line; the image in the line; and the "I-voice" of the line.

First, there is the matter of context. Here we have a royal celebration, and this is the opportunity for an oral performance in the royal court. We may imagine various royal occasions when the recitation of heroic poetry might be performed for royal courts on special occasions. The content of Psalm 45 corresponds to the wedding setting suggested for it. We might see something analogous for the setting of heroic poetry. Might a poem such as Judges 5 be recited on the occasion of royal victory in the northern kingdom? And might a poem such as 2 Sam. 1:19-27 be fitting for the occasion of defeat of the royal army of Judah? Such poems in their recitation could have a performative purpose. The analogy may be not only between the poems' contents and their occasions, but also the audience of the occasions. The victory song of Judges 5 as performed in the northern royal court could further affirm that a northern victory, too, was yet another of the "victories of Yahweh." By the same token, the lament of David as performed either in the Jerusalem court or among Judeans more broadly (see 2 Sam. 1:18) provides a totemic sense of textual contact with the dynasty's putative founder; it may also affirm that losses of comrades so close in arms was a loss that had always been fathomed by the dynasty back to the time of its founding figure. Such lament over the fallen, it could be sensed in this dramatic poem, had always been thus. Just as a victory might be perceived as standing in the line of victories of its deity, a defeat could be felt to stand in line with the defeat lamented by its founder.

In a manner analogous to the royal court, temples may have served as potential sites of heroic memory. Temples may not have been the sites of oral recitation of heroics, but they may have exercised a complementary role in commemorating them. As Abraham Malamat noted,[137] the deposition of weapons in a temple served the purpose of communal memory of martial exploits. As we noted in Chapter One, weaponry may be dedicatory objects and trophies given to temples, for example, the dedication of the shield of metal in KTU 1.123.2.[138] While neither Ugaritic literature nor early Israelite poetry mentions this practice, later BH texts would suggest that it was traditional. Saul's armor is said to have been placed in the temple of Ashtarot (1 Sam. 31:10), and Goliath's sword is said to have been given by David to the priests at Nob (1 Sam. 22:10).[139] Perhaps to be noted in this connection is the axe found at a temple at Tell Qasile; it is thought to have been an offering.[140] The presentation of weapons in temples serves as a reminder of victory.

Temples may not be sites of recitation of such victories, yet they remain sites of recollection of military victory.

Second, the image itself in Ps. 45:1 is critical. The verse shows the mention of the oral, "the tongue," and the written, "a skilled scribe." There is an analogy being drawn here.[141] The oral performer expresses the hope of being able to use his tongue as well as a skillful scribe may use a writing implement. The hope expressed is literally to "make an impression," especially if Ps. 45:1 evokes the image of the scribe engraving an inscription on a stone surface with a metal instrument (as in Jer. 17:1; Job 19:24). André Caquot put the point of the verse this way: "l'auteur veut dire que son poème a pour son roi une fonction semblable à cette des inscriptions royales gravées sur la pierre en d'autres pays."[142] Heroic poetry, too, is to be understood in these terms, as textual monuments maintained by royal tradition.

More may be involved in Ps. 45:1 with this analogy. William C. Propp asks: "Is the poet boasting that his tongue is as good as a pen, or that his pen is his tongue? Perhaps he is reading the work from a scroll."[143] While there is no indication of reading in the performance here, Propp's question is not misplaced. The purpose may not be simply to evoke a comparison of oral performance and scribal practice. The first person voice locates his speech in the royal court that would include royal scribes and their well-known skill. By the time of the poem (if not earlier), the verse suggests the prestige of the scribal craft of writing. Indeed, while most of Israel was an "oral world" and writing largely functioned as "written word in oral world" (to evoke the name of Niditch's book by this name[144]), perhaps in the royal court by the time of this poem oral performance was functioning in what is increasingly becoming a writing context. The oral practitioner as represented by the first person voice in this poem shows no social disassociation from the scribal craft and may not simply be an oral bardic figure.[145] An oral performer of this sort may have had colleagues among the scribes. Examples are known from ancient Mesopotamia, and these may be suggested as possible analogues: "the elder (scholar) should repeat it to the younger."[146] In this connection, I might add the scribal case (cast in terms of father and son): "let the father repeat (the poem of Enuma Elish) and make his son learn (it) by heart."[147] Another case comes from Enuma Elish (VII:147), and it is of further interest as it involves recitation of a poem. I wonder if the nod to the skill of the scribe at the outset of Psalm 45 might suggest that this oral voice is recognized as one mastered by the skilled scribe.

Third, whatever the exact nature of the situation, the use of the "I-voice" in Psalm 45 is perhaps to be compared with the "I-voice" in both Judges 5 and

2 Samuel 1. The composition of these heroic poems with their "I-voice" set in the early courts of Israel and Judah corresponds to the "I-voice" of the same royal courts manifest in other royal poetry, such as Psalm 45. As a home to the commemoration of victory, the palace is one end point for receiving older traditions. The "I-voice" in Judg. 5:3 relates the poem's Yahweh-centric composition specifically to a royal audience:

> Hear, O kings, Listen, O rulers,
> I, to Yahweh may I sing,
> May I intone to Yahweh, the God of Israel.

This verse expresses a devotion to a vision of Yahweh as the national god of Israel addressed to the kings and rulers. This creative voice may be operating in a context where an address to king and rulers would make sense. Such an address appears, for example, in Ps. 2:10. This royal psalm represents its praise of god and king as putative instruction for foreign rulers. Perhaps he is like the "I-voice" of the royal court in Ps. 45:1-2, or like the poet of Habakkuk 3 sitting in a royal court fondly evoking ancient great acts of God. Like Psalm 2, Judges 5 may offer instruction to kings and rulers about the mighty victory of Yahweh. At the same time, Judges 5 uses the recalled past (perhaps even a reconstructed past) for its instruction about god and country. It would seem that the "I-voice" of the poem feels most at home in the royal court. Taken together, the various levels of Judges 5 may correspond to the course of poetic production in early Israel. Initially, the poem in its earliest traditions and pieces represents diverse backgrounds — some surrounding the battle and others not, and some Yahwistic and others not. These seem to be known and circulating apparently in oral form (mostly?), sometimes in the forms of variants adapted to context. Some of these include commemoration of the battle traditions on a broad level (perhaps the recollection said to be at watering places in v. 11). Finally, these traditions reach their present formulation in the context of the northern royal court, as given voice in v. 3.

For some sense of the context of Iron II textual practice, we may turn to another text that connects the scribal with oral recitation, found in a late-sixth-century letter from the site of Lachish in Judah (designated "Lachish Letter 3" by scholars). I provide a translation of part of the letter here with line numbers in parentheses:

> (4) Now open (5) please the eyes of (i.e., explain for) your servant about the letter that (6) my lord sent to your servant yesterday, for the heart

> (7) of your servant has been sick ever since you sent (it) to (8) your servant. My lord said: "You don't know how (9) to read a letter." As the Lord lives, no one has tried (10) to read me a letter. Moreover, (11) as for any letter that comes to me, if I have read it, (12) [the]n I can recite it, (down) to any pa[rt].[148]

The text is a draft of a text written from the perspective of a royal official in Lachish. It is addressed to "my lord" (line 6) and the speaker refers to himself as "your servant" (lines 5 and 7). Thus there is an acknowledged hierarchy of administrative offices. Lines 9-10 stress the claim that the speaker has the ability to read documents sent to him. Lines 11-12 go on to illustrate the practice of reading as well as verbal recitation. It is important to note at this point that this passage in the letter assumes a kind of middle ground in regard to memorization. Otherwise, the claim to recitation would simply be an assertion of being able to read, and the letter has already made that point. My emphasizing the letter's implicit acknowledgement of memorization as a piece of the scribal practice might seem to put too much weight on a point made only in passing. After all, this passage from Lachish Letter 3 generally stresses the administrator's ability to read, not to recite by heart. Yet what is only a passing reference may betray what was generally taken for granted in scribal practice: memorization of oral as well as written text may be a part of the process of learning texts.[149] The letter may be all the more revealing for what it assumed.

Other Lachish letters also mention the scribal aspect of the administrator's job. On Lachish Letter 4 (lines 3-4), Dennis Pardee comments: "the most likely interpretation is that the author of Lachish 4 was required to keep a running record of his official activities on a papyrus scroll with a column (*dlt* — Jer 36:23) devoted to each set of orders."[150] Lachish Letter 5 (lines 3-7) adds a mention of the circulation of texts. These letters taken together suggest the scribal practice of reading, writing, memorization, and transmission at a regional administrative site.[151] All of these tasks presuppose that a competent administrator is able not only to read texts, but also to recite them by heart. If this skill set could be expected of an official at the royal administration at Lachish, then the same skill set is likely to have been operative at the royal capitals.

Ps. 45:1 (Iron IIB) and Lachish Letter 3 (Iron IIC) attest to royal scribal contexts in the northern and southern kingdoms, where writing and recitation were valued skills. This situation corresponds to the recitation and transmission of heroic poetry that would require an oral and written skill set in the Iron II (from the tenth century onwards). Ps. 45:2 and Lachish Letter 3 arguably date to the period when heroic poetry would become attached to their contexts in the great literary works of Genesis-Samuel. Between their composition in the tenth century and their enshrinement in their biblical contexts, the poems of Judges 5 and 2 Samuel 1 may have circulated in both oral and written form in the royal scribal establishment (perhaps unlike Psalm 68, which shows signs of liturgical transmission).[152] When the poems of Judges and 2 Samuel 1 were incorporated into Genesis-Samuel, they took on a broader significance. They were then not only part of the story of Yahweh's victories in the case of Judges 5 or of national lament in the situation of 2 Samuel 1. As pieces within the larger narrative of Genesis-Kings, they further became part of Israel's story of the world and its place in it.

The production and transmission of heroic poetry from its oral composition to its written enshrinement in what is now the Bible point to an important aspect of the history of cultural memory in ancient Israel. In terms of the production and transmission of Israel's literature, there would be little preservation of the oral settings of family[153] or clan, or of oral literature that might be told at sites such as "the watering places" or by women in song. The settings of palace and temple would overtake and overwrite other settings that would diminish in social importance.[154] This entailed the social dislocation of the production of heroic poetry, the final chapter in our story.

CHAPTER TWELVE

The Passing of Warrior Poetry in the Era of Prosaic Heroes

The preceding chapter discusses some possible contexts for the performance of Israelite warrior poetry in the Iron I period (ca. 1200-1000 B.C.E.) through the tenth century. The focus in this chapter falls on the aftermath of heroic poetry, especially in the Iron IIB-C period (ca. 925-586). The first section discusses the heightened production of heroic poetry in the Ugaritic monarchic context, compared with its evident displacement under Israel's dynasties. This difference between Ugarit and Israel can be seen on two related fronts. In contrast to the Ugaritic Rephaim texts (discussed in Chapter Five), the diminished and fractured reception that traditions about the Rephaim received in the Bible is the topic of this chapter's second section. The third section returns to the goddesses, Anat and Astarte, well attested in the Ugaritic texts (discussed in Chapters Four, Six, and Seven), and traces their meager attestation in Iron IIB Israel, with a possible resurgence of the latter goddess under Assyrian influence in the Iron IIC. An overall trend for these three phenomena can be observed: heroic poetry, as well as the Rephaim and the two goddesses, is well attested in Late Bronze Age Ugarit; there is some indication of them in early Israel, and they seem to face their demise in Iron IIB Israel.

The further question is how to understand this pattern of development for these three phenomena, most especially heroic poetry. The final section of this chapter raises a number of observations and hypotheses about the diminishing production of heroic poetry in ancient Israel in the Iron IIB context and afterwards. At a minimum, it can be observed from the available evidence that while the *transmission* of older heroic poetry would continue (in part through its *recontextualization* in various genres), there seems to have been a *displacement* of the *production* of heroic poetry from Israel's circles of textual composition. At a maximum, there may have been a demise of warrior poetry from ancient Israel's elites and perhaps from its society more broadly. To ascertain this situation, we turn first to the contrast in heroic poetry from Ugarit and Israel.

1. The Biblical Record and the Ugaritic Classics in Counterpoint

As we saw in Chapter Ten, the figure of David is represented in 2 Sam. 1:19-27 in accord with the traditions of heroic poetry. However, this poetry does not become an enduring feature of the literature sponsored by the monarchies of Israel and Judah. Heroic poetry evidently flourished in premonarchic and early monarchic Israel. Indeed, it remains quite a notable feature of heroic poetry that it represents a significant portion of the early literature of Israel down into the tenth century. Afterwards, the ongoing production of heroic poetry and its social support are unclear. The known exemplars of older heroic poetry were preserved later within larger textual amalgamations, in the prose collections of Genesis through Samuel, in the poetic collections of Psalms (see Psalm 68), and occasionally in a prophetic context (such as Habakkuk 3).[1] However, there seems to be little new production of heroic poetry in the Iron IIB period onwards. In short, the tenth century seems to be a particularly important divide in the production of warrior poetry in ancient Israel.

There is an interesting literary correspondence to this observation, when we look at heroic poetry in Genesis–Kings. In the literary corpus, David appears as a watershed figure. There is heroic poetry represented before David (for example, in Judges 5), and there is heroic poetry represented in the life of David (in 2 Samuel 1; 22–23). However, after David there are no exemplars of warrior poetry recalled in the textual memory of Israel's history in Genesis–Kings. In biblical narrative, there are no heroic poems after David. The figure of David seems emblematic of a transition in the production and/or preservation of Israelite warrior poetry, when viewed from a literary vantage point. David's son Solomon may be further emblematic of the situation of heroic poetry. While his father was himself a lauded warrior to whom warrior poetry is attributed, Solomon is no warrior, but a monarch associated with wisdom (1 Kgs. 4:30; 5:12); the only poetry associated with him in Israel's great prose historiography concerns the temple (1 Kgs. 8:12-13).[2] In the books of Kings, no king after David is celebrated as a warrior, nor is David celebrated as a warrior in later prose passages.[3] In sum, what heroic poetry was being produced in the Iron IIB and later (an issue that we will return to below) was apparently achieved apart from the monarchic establishment; the monarchy's involvement in the production of heroic poetry appears to be limited.

This situation stands in stark contrast to the representation of warriors in Ugaritic literature. The classics of Ugaritic literature — the Baal Cycle, Kirta, and Aqhat — all bear themes of warriors or warfare, and they all contain colophons[4] that mark their royal-priestly production. We have little, if any, indicator of a tribal or clan setting for the heroic poetry represented by these three classics. Even in the Ugaritic Rephaim texts, the monarchy lays claim to the heroic lineage represented by the Rephaim, as seen explicitly in the one ritual text involving the Rephaim (KTU 1.161).[5] Whatever these traditions might have looked like elsewhere (as suggested by references in the Rephaim texts in Lebanon in KTU 1.22 I 20 or Transjordan in 1.108.2-3),[6] in their present form they serve to ground royal identity.[7]

The Ugaritic poetic material discussed in Part III of this study suggests mature productions. These are well-developed narratives, and they often offer sophisticated pictures of the human predicament. They belong to the end of the literary tradition at Ugarit. We unfortunately do not know about the oral form of any of these Ugaritic literary texts. As a corollary, we have no access to the sort of settings that might have given rise to the traditions of Aqhat or Kirta. It is possible to hypothesize about some aspects of the composition of literary texts. The Ugaritic Baal Cycle, for example, shows signs of both oral and written mistakes that may point to earlier versions, and further guesses can be made on the basis of literary comparisons and analysis, though these remain quite hypothetical.[8] The difficulties point to the lack of access that we have to older written versions, much less to any oral composition possibly lying behind written composition either in whole or part.

This is not to say that the texts lack any oral dimension. On the contrary, it is evident that written versions served to aid oral recitations. Scribal comments inserted at various points in the Ugaritic Baal Cycle and Aqhat (albeit rarely) tell the reciter to fill in certain standard parts of the plotline.[9] These compositions were both records of such texts and aids for their performance. Despite some ability to peer into the oral performance of these texts, we cannot peer very far into their earlier literary history that might betray something of their earlier composition (whether written or oral), much less the older settings underlying this process. In short, Ugaritic literary composition took place in a relatively brief compass of time and setting. Indeed, it has been argued in recent years that several of the Ugaritic literary texts date to the very end of the Late Bronze Age.[10] If so, the Ugaritic classics show a relatively short literary *floruit,* standing at the very end of a long royal history.[11] In any case, warrior poetry at Ugarit is, in effect, royal poetry.

When it comes to heroic poetry in the Bible, we note some major differences. Heroic poetry stands largely at the head of the Bible's literary tradition, one that by contrast with Ugaritic literature can be traced over a long period of time (arguably over a thousand years). When it comes to heroic poetry, the biblical literary tradition, by comparison to Ugarit's major classics, consists of shorter poetic pieces.[12] This difference is particularly notable when it comes to warrior poetry. Ugarit's literary classics include long pieces consisting of multiple tablets, commonly with six or eight columns.[13] No heroic poem in the Bible exceeds thirty-some verses.[14] In addition, the Bible's literary tradition includes lengthy prose compositions. If length is a consideration, some of these biblical prose compositions, in particular the story of David, might be considered in some respects to resemble their Ugaritic counterparts more closely than the heroic poetry of the Bible.[15] More conspicuously, biblical prose narrative is the literary context of most heroic poetry in the Bible, in contrast to the situation with Ugaritic poetry.[16] In short, we meet a good deal of the Bible's heroic poetry in secondary contexts. Still, these exemplars of Israelite warrior poetry are preserved in poetic contradistinction from their prose contexts; they are marked as different. No such distinction is readily apparent with Ugaritic heroic poetry, apart from scribal insertions, superscriptions, and colophons (often separated by scribal lines).

Why is there this fundamental difference with heroic poetry in the Ugaritic corpus compared with the Hebrew Bible? While heroic poetry is a fundamental feature of the Ugaritic literary corpus, it has been noted by critics, such as Robert S. Kawashima and F. W. Dobbs-Allsopp, that such poetry seems to fade in time as we move from the old poetry of early Israel (in the Iron I period down to the ninth century) and into the great era of prose (in the Iron IIB period and later).[17] I agree. Yet there may be more to the story of heroic poetry in ancient Israel. It looks as if the situation in ancient Israel involves a shift in the setting of warrior poetry. As I noted above, after David there are no older poems devoted to the topic of warriors or war within the Bible's great prose historiographical works in Genesis through Kings. It may be asked if any importance for the literary history of warrior poetry is to be discerned from this distribution. At the outset, I recognize that any discussion of these interrelated literary and cultural matters remains largely hypothetical and potentially circular. Still, the observation that there are no more old poems preserved in the great prose works seems to be an important datum, and it may point to a larger cultural issue involved in the setting of the production of warrior poetry. From what can be described from the literary remains in the Bible and the present epigraphic record, it appears that Israelite production of warrior poetry was situated within the tribal practices and traditions of early Israel and received into the early monarchies (down into the tenth or perhaps early ninth century). It was displaced from the centers of textual production responsible for the production and transmission of later literature in the Iron IIB period, from at least the eighth century onwards.[18]

In the first moment, the following investigation in this chapter remains primarily a study of literary matters. It is largely an issue involving the disposition of literary evidence: there is a gap between the old poetry and the prose historiographers. So for these historiographers what was old poetry for? These poems seemed to interest these historiographers because they appeared to be old, and more precisely because they appeared to be old witnesses to the events that they were narrating.[19] At a second level (and methodologically an even more precarious one), the apparent displacement or diminishment of heroic poetry in ancient Israel appears to be also a cultural and historical matter. At the outset, it is to be noted that while it is possible to offer some plausible speculations in this direction, the data available hardly "prove" the picture that I will sketch out.

To anticipate the basic point on this score, the setting for the production of warrior poetry may have undergone changes in the early monarchy. The leadership in the premonarchic period constituted the subjects of such poetry, and the structure of society supported this production. With the development of the monarchy, especially as it moved through the ninth century,[20] the setting for this type of production was apparently shifting; such traditional warrior poetry was no longer of the same interest to or supported by its leadership.

Heroic poetry is not an arena or topic of ongoing poetic enshrinement in Israel's traditions (as far as we know), as we move through the Iron II period. As at Ugarit, the monarchy is the home for the reception and transmission of such poetry. However, at Ugarit, this poetry receives major elaboration, and, as far as we know, it stands as the centerpiece of the literary corpus for the monarchy.[21] In the Bible, the scribal arm of the monarchy receives this older poetry, but it does not elaborate it or celebrate it. In the case of 2 Samuel 22/Psalm 18, the older poetry embedded in this composition appears to be sublimated by the monarchy, as Frank Moore Cross brilliantly observed.[22] Cross surmised that vv. 8-16(7-15) were an "ancient fragment" that has been incorporated into this royal psalm of thanksgiving.[23] If 2 Samuel 22/Psalm 18 is any indication, the monarchy recontextualized such poetry and overwrote it in other modes. Other traditions likewise preserve pieces of old poetry as witnesses to a distant past, but there is no ongoing tradition preserved for the production of warrior poetry. In short, this sort of literature was received and revised in cult (Pss. 18:8-16; 68), prophecy (Habakkuk 3),[24] and historiography (Judges 5 and 2 Samuel 22/Psalm 18:8-16), but heroic poetry in itself along with its production appears to have been displaced.[25] The heroes of the prosaic age receive prosaic notices (as we will note below), but whatever poetry might have celebrated their martial exploits, these were not included in the poetry of Israel's literary traditions.

As the monarchy moves through the Iron IIB-C context, there seems to be little or no ongoing tradition stream for the production of this poetry. Heroic poetry was generally not the specialty of priests or prophets, and arguably not even of the monarchy from the Iron IIB on. By the sixth century, it does not belong to the taxonomy of textual production in ancient Israel, delineated, for example, in the three major elite sectors noted by Jer. 18:18: "for instruction shall not fail from the priest, nor counsel from the wise, nor oracle from the prophet" (NJPS; cf. Jer. 2:8; 8:8).[26] To be sure, in this period there is recognition of warriors (so Jer. 9:23, with its parallelism of the warrior with the wise and the rich), but there is no allusion to heroic poetry. In this later context, older heroic poems may have been known in oral form for purposes of royal performance, and also in written form for instruction of a scribal, royal elite responsible for their written transmission.[27] With older, heroic poetry making its way into other genres, there seems to have been some interest or concern for the preservation of the past heroic poetry; it remained "useful" in other contexts, in particular for later prose historiography. Still, there was no corresponding interest for the ongoing production of warrior poetry in the Iron II period. Instead, what new production is seen later in the Iron II and beyond involved prosaic legends of warriors. The heroic model, while diminished in its older martial form, came to be applied to heroes or heroines of other sorts.[28] To note only two late instances, the book of Esther, it has been argued, evokes old heroic ideals in the Persian period,[29] and the story of Judith, with its echoes of Judges 4–5, would mark a strong evocation of the warrior model in the Hellenistic era.

2. Legendary Warriors and Rephaim in the Era of the Philistine Wars

When we look for heroic poetry after the figure of David, we find none through the end of the books of Kings. Nor is poetry about warriors a part of late biblical historiography in Ezra-Nehemiah or the books of Chronicles. The story is different with biblical prose. Biblical historiography surrounding warriors following David's ascent appears in prose notices that appear at the end of 2 Samuel, beginning in 21:14. That this verse marks the end of David's prose story can be seen by the thematic frame that it forms with the beginning of David's story following the death of Saul and Jonathan in 1 Samuel 31: where that chapter relates how the bones of these two warriors were given a proper respect, 2 Samuel 21 describes how David brought the bones of the two heroes and had them interred in Saul's family tomb in the territory of Benjamin. Thus, the story comes full circle. Accordingly, it would appear that what follows 2 Sam. 21:14 constitutes a series of additions.[30]

2 Sam. 21:15-22 and 23:8-39 largely consist of warriors' names with brief accounts of their associated exploits. These two sections frame two poems associated with the figure of David in 2 Sam. 22:2-51 and 2 Sam. 23:1-7. It is tempting to view 2 Sam. 21:15-22 and 23:8-39 as two sets of vignettes enveloping the two poems of 2 Samuel 22 and 2 Sam. 23:1-7.[31] However, the material in the vignettes about David's warriors varies considerably. From a literary perspective, 2 Sam. 21:15-22 and 23:8-39 have the feel of a variegated series of recollections about the great warriors of David.[32] The four incidents of 2 Sam. 21:15-22 focus on David and his warriors against a series of Rapah-figures from Gath. The listing in 2 Sam. 23:8-39 is provided with a heading: "these are the names . . ." (cf. Gen. 25:13; 36:10, 40; Exod. 1:1; 6:16; Num. 1:5; 3:2, 3, 18; 13:4, 16; 27:1; 34:17, 19, etc.). This section also focuses on groups of David's warriors, called "the three" (2 Sam. 23:9, 16-17, 18-19, 23; see also 1 Chr. 11:12, 15, 19, 20-21, 24, 25) and "the thirty" (2 Sam. 23:23, 24; see also 1 Chr. 11:15, 25).[33] The comparable material about David's warriors in 2 Samuel 23 shows an important contrast: 2 Sam. 21:15-22 gives more emphasis to the enemy warriors specifically associated with Gath, while 2 Sam. 23:8-39 focuses its attention on the Davidic heroes over enemies that are largely Philistine, but also include Moabites (v. 20) and an Egyptian (v. 21).[34] In addition, there is no reference to the Rapah as in 2 Sam. 21:15-22. Nonetheless, what may be noted about all of this material is its prosaic quality. Not simply cast in prose, the pieces of information appear to constitute a prose listing, often with bare details of the victories involved.

In the poems and prose of 2 Sam. 21:15–23:39, there seems to be a world of difference between the poetic David and the prosaic men of David. In this juxtaposition, the end of 2 Samuel gives witness to the passing of warrior poetry in the era of prosaic heroes. David's heroes here receive no heroic poetry, but little more than prose taglines. These brief episodes concerning minor heroic figures in 2 Samuel 21 and 23 suggest condensed notices of what may have once been longer oral tales about these figures.[35] Unlike the poems, these examples of prose "heroic legend,"[36] in Alexander Rofé's words, "seem to have been recounted by the warriors of the king (compare their mention in 2 Sam. 16:6; 20:7; 23:8; 1 Kgs. 1:8, 10), or, more generally, by courtiers."[37] Unlike the heroic poetry at various points over the course of Genesis–2 Samuel, such prose notices are buried in the prose appendix of 2 Samuel. This seems to reflect the literary fate of later heroes in the era of the kings.

This is another aspect of the prose listings that provides a further perspective on this transition, one that can be discerned from the first of these prose sections, 2 Sam. 21:15-22. The structure of this passage is identifiable by the repetition of the expression "there was again war" involving the Philistines (vv. 15, 18, 19, 20).[38] That these constitute separate incidents might be divined by the omission of the first one from the parallel material in 1 Chronicles (cf. 20:4-8), but the version in 2 Sam. 21:18-22 seems to reflect the view that all four recollections belong together, providing a final coda in v. 22 that all "four were descended from the Raphah in Gath, and they fell by the hands of David and his men" (NJPS). By contrast, 2 Sam. 23:8-9 draws in part on a different repetition, "and *after him*" (v. 9 = 1 Chr. 11:12; and v. 11),[39] a way of listing that partially informs two sets of formulas used also for so-called "minor judges": "and there arose *after him*" in Judg. 10:1, 3; and "and he ruled *after him* . . ." in Judg. 12:8, 11, 13.[40] These brief episodes concerning minor heroic figures in 2 Samuel 23 resemble Judges 10 and 12; these, too, look like condensed notices of what would presumably have once been longer oral tales about these figures.

The first episode (vv. 15-17) centers on David himself, who confronts an otherwise unknown warrior, identified as Ishi (or, Ishi-Benob) in the MT Qere.[41] Whoever the figure is here, he was born of (or perhaps dedicated to) the Rapah, according to the passage.[42] We will return to this detail momentarily, but for now we may note the legendary connotations in this context, with the mention of the bronze spear[43] weighing three hundred shekels. The second episode (v. 18) relates the great victory of Sibbecai over Saph, also said to have been born of the Rapah. No further information is provided in this context, but the parallel passage in 1 Chr. 20:4 says that this enemy was born of the Rephaim.

Before commenting on this difference, we may note the other incidents in this section of 2 Samuel 21. In v. 19, the famous parallel to the story of David and Goliath (in 1 Samuel 17),[44] Elhanan defeats Goliath. Like Ishi and Saph, this Goliath is considered to have been born to the Rapah. The weapon of Goliath is no less legendary here, as it is in 1 Sam. 17:7; in both passages, his spear is to have "a shaft like a weaver's bar" (NJPS). That 1 Samuel 17 represents an elaboration of the tradition of 2 Sam. 21:19 has long been recognized. That this literary relationship was apparent in antiquity may be surmised from 1 Chr. 20:5, the parallel passage to 2 Sam. 21:19, which names the Philistine enemy, Lahmi, as the brother of Goliath. Following this scholarly line,[45] commentators such as Sara Japhet and Ralph Klein suggest that in 1 Chr. 20:5 Lahmi, the name of Goliath's brother, derived from the name of Bethlehem as given in 2 Sam. 21:19.[46]

In the fourth and final incident from 2 Sam. 21:20-21, an unnamed Philistine is described in legendary terms: he has six digits on each hand and foot.[47] Like the other Philistine warriors in this passage, he is said to have descended from the Rapah. The same figure bears a similar description in the parallel verse, in 1 Chr. 20:6, except that Rapah is once again spelled as Rapa' with final *'ālep.*[48] The summary in 2 Sam. 21:22 recalls all four enemies as Rapah of the vicinity of Gath. The parallel verse in 1 Chr. 20:8 differs only in spelling Rapah as Rapa'.

Two notable differences between the parallel accounts in Samuel and Chronicles involve the spelling of Rapa' (cf. Rapah in 2 Sam. 21:18-22) and the one plural form of the Rephaim in 1 Chr. 20:4-8. The difference in spelling could be explained in any number of ways. Given the prominence of Rephaim elsewhere in the Bible (not to mention the older Ugaritic texts),[49] the spelling with *'ālep* in 1 Chronicles 20 might constitute an older spelling, or it might reflect a harmonization of the tradition with the Rephaim as elsewhere known to the author of this passage in 1 Chronicles 20. Most critics seem to favor the former.[50] Klein, for example, understands the forms with final *-h* in 2 Samuel 21 as possibly polemical, suggesting the weakness (**rph*) of the figures named.[51] It is understandable why scribes would alter the spelling of Rapa' to Rapah in order to demean this tradition; the opposite direction from Rapah to Rapa' would seem to be more difficult to explain. This approach would also suit other passages where Chronicles seems to preserve an older spelling where the parallel passages in Samuel appear polemical in their spellings. Conrad L'Heureux[52] compares the well-known cases involving **bōšet,* "shame" in the books of Samuel apparently substituted for the divine element **ba'al,* as attested in Chronicles (Eshbaal in 1 Chr. 8:33;

9:39,[53] versus Ish-boshet in 2 Sam. 2:8; and Meribbaal in 1 Chr. 8:34 versus Mephiboshet in 2 Sam. 4:4; 21:8).[54] Like the case of Rapa'/Rapâ, it seems easier to explain a scribal change from the spellings of **baʿal* in Eshbaal and Meribbaal to spellings with **bōšet* rather than the other way around.[55] While there well may be more to the development of the spelling tradition of Rapa'/Rapah than can be ascertained at present, it seems preferable at this point to view the spelling with *'ālep* as older, especially in view of the unusual character of the passage's material. A further question involves the meaning of the usage in this context.

L'Heureux argues for **yld* as a term not for actual birth or lineage but for "votary" status, in this case of a military nature (as in Num. 13:22, 28).[56] Following a longstanding scholarly view,[57] L'Heureux noted parallels with the Rephaim elsewhere in the Bible as well as the Ugaritic texts. What is missing from the discussion is a stronger parallel in usage. Perhaps more helpful as a parallel to the combination of **yld* with "the Rapah," or "the Rapa'," as it is found in the parallel passage in 1 Chronicles 20, is Ugaritic *mt rp'i*, "man of Rp'i."[58] This title for Danil is prominent in the story of Aqhat (KTU 1.17 I 2, 17, 18, 35, 36, 37, 42; II 28; V 4-5, 14, 33-34; VI 52; 1.19 I 20, 36-37, 38-39, 47; II 41; IV 13, 17, 18, 36). This appellation represents Danil as a devotee[59] of the divinity, Rp'u, himself the head of the long line of deceased, divinized ancestors named *rp'um*. The figures, as named by this moniker, conjure an older world of warriors that apparently were legendary already in the time of the Ugaritic texts.[60]

It also seems that 2 Sam. 21:15-22 and 1 Chr. 20:5-8 reflect a specific geographical tradition about these *rp'*-warriors. The four figures are understood to be Philistine, more specifically from Gath. According to P. Kyle McCarter, the reference to the summary verse in 2 Sam. 21:22 should be taken more specifically as "Rapha-in-Gath."[61] To this usage McCarter compares the divine names (DN) with the preposition "in" *(b-)* plus a specific geographical name (GN) in 2 Sam. 15:7; 21:6.[62] This usage of DN in GN has been recognized by McCarter and others as related in meaning to DN of GN (as a construct phrase), DN at GN (indicated by locative *-h*) and DN "dwelling/enthroned in" GN. Particularly germane to this discussion is a series of related usages all associated with Ashtaroth in Ugaritic: *mlk bʿṯtrt* (KTU 1.107.42); *mlk ʿṯtrth* (KTU 1.100.41); *rp'u mlk ʿlm . . . 'il yṯb bʿṯtrt* (KTU 1.108.1-2). In Chapter Five I rendered the third as "Rp'u Eternal Mlk . . . the god-dwelling/enthroned-in-Ashtaroth."[63] Given the use of construction for Rp'u, this example seems particularly analogous to McCarter's proposal to see "Rapha-in-Gath." In other words, like "Rapa'-in-Gath," as surmised by

McCarter, there is "Rpu'-in-Ashtaroth." McCarter deduces from the biblical usage that Rp'u was known to have a cultic center in Gath. Whether this particular conclusion is correct, there is little doubt that the narrative focuses on a specific regional tradition about the Rapa' and what 1 Chr. 20:4 identifies as the Rephaim.[64] In view of the traditional West Semitic background of Rp'u and the Rephaim, it would appear that the Philistines in the area of Gath were known to have the local West Semitic warrior tradition associated with these figures, much as Philistines in Ashdod (1 Sam. 5:1-7; 1 Macc. 10:83-84) and elsewhere (Judg. 16:23; 1 Sam. 31:10) had adopted West Semitic deities, such as Dagan.[65] Indeed, the same formulation of DN-in-GN appears in the expression *dgwn b'šdwd*, "Dagon-in-Ashdod" (1 Sam. 5:5).

From Judah's western flank in Philistia, we may turn to the Rephaim tradition in Transjordan.[66] This tradition appears not only in the Bible, but as noted above,[67] also in the Ugaritic texts. In Chapter Five the figure of Rp'u at Ashtaroth in KTU 1.108 (mentioned just above) was presented in some detail. Rp'u is said in this passage to be based in two locales in the region of the Transjordan. These places, ʿAshtarot (Tell ʿAshtara) and Edrei (modern Deraa),[68] are mentioned in Deut. 3:1, 10 as part of the domain held by the legendary King Og, himself said to be the last of the Rephaim (v. 11; see also 2:11, 20; Num. 21:33).[69] John Day would also include in this discussion Uzziah the Ashterathite (1 Chr. 11:44), one of David's warriors, as he hails from the region of Ashtaroth.[70] It would appear that the region's fame in this regard informed both Ugaritic and biblical texts independently.

At this point, we may note the speculation that these Rephaim traditions in these sources mentioning the Transjordanian region are to be associated with the local dolmens there,[71] and perhaps even with their subterranean tunnels.[72] The ancient, massive monuments might have been linked to old, heroic legends of the Rephaim, known independently in Ugaritic and biblical sources.[73] The association has been criticized by John F. Healey.[74] However, the biblical lack of knowledge of the Rephaim noted by Healey may be attributed to the distance at which the biblical literature stands relative to earlier evidence.[75] There is little, if any, evidence for the notion of the Rephaites as "a Canaanite tribe," as Healey instead suggests.[76] Edwin C. Hostetter considers polydactylism as a possible factor in the legends about warriors of excessive size,[77] following Richard D. Barnett.[78] Barnett compared this feature on winged bronze figures with human or animal heads and on Deir el-Balah sarcophagi as well as some carved tridachna shells. Barnett views these winged six-fingered figures as representations of the Rephaim invited to a funeral feast. In the Ugaritic texts, the Rephaim, however, are not described with wings or polydactylism, which itself is never attributed to the biblical Rephaim and relatively rarely attributed to any specific *rāpāh/rāpā'* in the Bible (see 2 Sam. 21:20). Whether or not Barnett is correct, it is the size of the Rephaim and not only polydactylism that the biblical material stresses about these warrior figures. If any stock is to be put in this possibility for understanding the Rephaim tradition, it may have been presumed in Late Bronze Age Ugarit that these Middle Bronze I burial dolmens were understood as pointing to the ancient, deceased warriors. This would provide an answer to the question rightly raised by Cross, as to why at Ugarit there might be interest in this region: this feature of the region was literally legendary.[79]

In the case of the biblical tradition, it also was legendary. The bed of King Og,[80] "last of the Rephaim," is said in Deut. 3:11 to be nine cubits in length and four cubits wide.[81] The same verse gives this tradition a further specificity about its tradition, as the bed is said to be in Rabbat of the Ammonites. Thus this passage seems to presuppose that this tradition of the Rephaim in Ashtarot and Edrei came to Israel via the Ammonites. The biblical tradition also understood this line of legendary Rephaim to be pre-Ammonite, but not pre-Israelite or part of Israelite tradition, even though the Transjordanian half-tribe of Manasseh is said to have taken over this region (Deut. 3:12-13). However, "the Rephaim" is represented as the Israelite term for this ancient line, while the Ammonites are said to have a different name for them (see Deut. 2:20). In other words, the Israelites, unlike the Ammonite tradition that is reported in Deuteronomy, have the same name for these Rephaim as the Ugaritic texts, suggesting that whatever ancient Israel attributed to the Ammonites in Deuteronomy, it is the Israelites who seem to have at least one element of the Rephaim tradition lacking in what they know of Ammonite tradition about the matter. Even as Israel is claiming that this is an Ammonite tradition, Israel may stand no less close to this tradition. The tradition of the Rephaim is also known in Phoenician and Punic.[82] In short, given the Ugaritic attestation to this tradition in the Late Bronze Age and the traditions enshrined in biblical and Phoenician sources, the complex of Rephaim associations predated the Iron Age kingdoms and was received by them in various manners and locales.[83] It is also explicitly recognized to be an ancient tradition; Og is only the last of the Rephaim that is known by name (cf. the names of the figures given in the list of Rephaim in KTU 1.161.4-7).[84] In contrast to the Homeric tradition of ancient heroes, the warrior achievements of these figures are little commemorated in either Ugaritic or biblical tradition.

What is different at Ugarit is how its monarchy embraces the tradition of the Rephaim, unlike the Israelite traditions, monarchic and premonarchic alike. Where Ugarit shows identification between the present monarchy and the ancient Rephaim, the biblical material shows a political and social "disidentification" between Israelites and the ancient Rephaim.[85] Another important difference lies in the form of their literary commemoration. The relatively coherent constellation of features associated with Rp'u and the Rephaim in the Ugaritic texts as the divine, deceased ancestors celebrated by the royal line as their predecessors seems by comparison fractured in the biblical traditions.[86] The biblical Rephaim appear in a series of rather different portraits. They are represented as constituting a legendary people grouped with other old peoples such as the Canaanites and the Amorites (Gen. 15:20; Josh. 15:8). Echoing the Transjordanian tradition of the Rephaim, they appear as an old people based in Ashtaroth-qarnaim, according to Gen. 14:5. Paralleling their royal and deceased status as attested in the Ugaritic texts, the Rephaim were also recalled in biblical poetic sources as kings in the underworld (Isa. 14:9) or simply as the dead in general (Ps. 88:10; Prov. 2:18; 9:18; 21:16; Job 26:5; Isa. 26:14). The warrior traditions of the Rephaim were only distant memories for Israel in the Iron IIB and afterwards. These traditions had long passed. Indeed, they may never have taken hold as an element of Israelite identity. Instead, the Rephaim became one of Israel's ways of talking about others, whether in this world or the next.

The literary commemoration of warriors in the Hebrew Bible, whether in the heroic poetry or the prose accounts, has little or no correspondence in the material record.[87] Given the discussion of Achilles and Patroklos in Part I of this study, we may pause here to compare the situation of the Rephaim in the biblical corpus with Homeric traditions in relation to the commemoration of famous warriors in Greek hero cults.[88] Homeric heroes seem to be prior to the hero cults. According to Seth L. Schein,[89] Homer makes little or no reference to the hero cults. Schein suggests that Homer resists hero cult,[90] as it is a local phenomenon, and Homer is aiming for a panhellenic picture. For Robert Parker, it is a literary problem that is involved: "Homer's characters cannot pay cult to the heroes if they themselves are those heroes."[91] In any case, the age of these heroes lies decidedly in a distant past relative to the hero cults dedicated to them. Heroic memory in Greece has been viewed as a matter of secondary recovery beginning in the Iron IIB. Gregory Nagy correlates the emergence of the Homeric epos with the upsurge of hero cults in the eighth century.[92] According to J. N. Coldstream,[93] hero cults, as they emerged in the eighth century and continued later, seemed to embrace Homeric heroes as part of a larger trend:

> During the second half of the eighth century, the Greeks became increasingly aware of a vanished heroic age — an age which, on archaeological grounds, we have learned to equate with the Mycenaean world shortly before its collapse. The princes of that remote age had become heroes of epic poetry; a new respect for them, and a new interest in establishing links with them, appears in three kinds of material evidence. First, there is the rapid growth of hero-cults in several regions, as shown by the new practice of leaving votive offerings in Mycenaean tombs. Secondly, some rich burials of our period seem to have been influenced in various ways by accounts of heroic funerals in epic poetry. Thirdly, in some LG [Late Geometric] figured scenes there are reminiscences of the heroic age, whether through reference to a specific story, or in details added to lend heroic colouring to a generic theme.[94]

Coldstream adds that the "chief cause" of the hero cults was "the great flowering of epic poetry which culminated in the work of Homer."[95]

The date of Greek hero cults has been debated, and the nature of their connection to Homeric tradition complicates the matter.[96] In part, this is due to variation in the character and dating of hero cults. For example, a considerably low date has been advocated by James Whitley, who argues that the heroes of epics did not become objects of cult much before the sixth century, itself seen in Attica as a major period of reorganization and centralization of state cults.[97] The identification of Mycenaean tombs later as those of heroes is particularly notable, for example, on a fifth-century shard inscription found in the region of Grave Circle A at Mycenae; it reads, "I belong to a hero."[98] In any case, the hero cults constitute a recollection of an earlier era of heroes, including figures from Homer. In the larger picture, hero cults represent in part a connection with the literary tradition of Homer. Indeed, it has even been suggested that "the great war celebrated by singers became precisely a war between Troy and Greeks under Mycenaean leadership for no other reason than that the giant ruins of Troy and Mycenae were the most magnificent remains of a heroic age for which only Homer's recent ancestors had developed a fascination."[99]

By contrast, the archaeological record in Israel and Judah shows no such hero cult, as far as we know. Still, the broader Levantine situation may parallel what can be seen in the Greek context: just as part of Greek hero cults involved older Mycenaean tombs serving later as sites for the memory of heroes, so too Transjordanian dolmens became associated with the old Rephaim traditions, as seen in both Ugaritic tradition (KTU 1.108) and biblical material (Deuteronomy 2–3).[100] The biblical traditions on this score themselves may be connected further, though perhaps only distantly, with the biblical *rapa'*-warriors of David discussed above. Although the biblical record shows a rejection of this constellation as non-Israelite, this tradition also suggests some sort of older Israelite knowledge of a tradition of old heroes.[101]

At the same time, there is a feature of the Greek hero cults and their use of Homeric heroic tradition that perhaps provides an analogy for the situation found in biblical literature. That is their commemorative function. Both the prose recontextualization of heroic poetry in biblical narrative and the material phenomenon of Greek hero cults in association with Homeric heroes served to commemorate what had passed away long ago. The preservation of heroic poetry in written form allowed the preservation of this early Israelite world that oral transmission perhaps did not meet.[102] Greek hero cults additionally provided physical sites in memory of epic heroes.[103] The heroic poetry of Homer and early Israel served to commemorate their warriors and to locate these figures in ancient time for later audiences. Put differently, both Greek and Israelite cultures created their own sites of memory. Greece managed to create remains for their heroes in both material and verbal forms, whereas Israel retextualized its older heroic memory. In both parts of the eastern Mediterranean basin, a textual bridge was built over the gap between the time recalled as a heroic age of old and its later commemorations.

3. The Fading of the Warrior Goddesses and the Rise of the National God

Part III of this study presents Late Bronze evidence for the warrior goddesses Anat and ʿAthtart. When it comes to Israel, these goddesses are poorly attested. To anticipate the discussion below, their apparent demise may correspond in some respects with shifts in cultural perception in Iron IIB and afterwards concerning the older traditions about warriors. In the case of Anat, the early evidence is confined to her name on Iron I arrowheads and two brief biblical references, as we noted in Chapter Seven. On the arrowheads her name occasionally appears in the patronymic *bn ʿnt*, "son of Anat." The two biblical mentions of the goddess's name as such likewise appear only in this patronymic for Shamgar ben ʿAnat (Judg. 3:31; 5:6). A maximal view has taken this name for the goddess as indicating her patronage of warriors who would have taken her name. In any case, apart from these most minimal of references there is little evidence[104] of Anat as a deity in ancient Israel. Accordingly, it would seem that her cult fades from Israel over the course of the twelfth to ninth centuries.

The Iron Age situation with ʿAshtart in Israel is more complicated. In surveys of ʿAshtart, scholars point to her general demise within Israelite circles, based on the lack of clear evidence. In Chapter Seven we noted Ugaritic evidence for the lion as ʿAthtart's attribute animal, which in turn points to this goddess as underlying the PNs with "servant of the lion" in arrowheads. Accordingly, one might posit the presence of the goddess at the end of the Late Bronze Age and into the Iron I period, though the evidence is not particularly clear. Earlier we also noted a Late Bronze Age seal from Bethel with the name of the goddess in hieroglyphic writing. Otherwise, the record for the goddess is quite weak, and thus several scholars posit a trend toward the goddess's demise.

Some support for this picture might be seen in the use of the goddess's name as a generic term for goddesses and for fertility. The first usage is well known from Judg. 2:13; 10:6; there are also extrabiblical references along these lines. For example, the second term in Akkadian *ilānu u ištarātu,* "gods and goddesses,"[105] has often been compared.[106] In addition, Othmar Keel and Christoph Uehlinger have pointed to an extraordinary example of this usage in an eighth-century Akkadian inscription from ʿAna on the middle Euphrates that describes Anat as "the strongest of the astartes" (goddesses).[107] ʿAshtart's name designating goddesses more generally is also known later, for example in Aramaic incantations.[108] The use of the goddess's name to refer to fertility (Deut. 7:13; 28:4, 18, 51)[109] is in keeping with the genericization of names of other deities (e.g., Resheph as "flame" and Deber as "pestilence").[110] In reference to the iconography of female deities, Keel and Uehlinger deduce that by "the tenth century these deities would not have been conceptualized as being equal to and independent of Yahweh, but would have been viewed as entities and powers of blessing under his control."[111] This overall trend seems to match the lack of attestation of the goddess in the Transjordanian kingdoms. The one clear example of the goddess in Ammonite identifies her as Phoenician: *ʿšt⟨rt⟩ bṣdn,* "ʿAshta⟨rt⟩ in Sidon."[112] Otherwise, she seems as foreign to the Transjordanian kingdoms as she is to ancient Israel. In short, ʿAshtart seems to be largely a coastal figure in the Iron Age.[113]

Within the context of this picture, biblical texts represent two imports of the goddess into Israel. The first is traced in the biblical context to Phoenicia. 1 Kgs. 11:5 says that Solomon "followed" ("worshipped" in 1 Kgs. 11:33)

'Ashtoreth, god[114] of the Sidonians, as well as a number of other national gods (see also 2 Kgs. 23:13). The name 'Ashtoreth seems to reflect Phoenician 'Ashtart, perhaps with the /o/ vowel shift characteristic of Phoenician[115] (in contrast to the reduced vowel in BH plural *'aštārôt,* in Judg. 2:13; 10:6; 1 Sam. 7:3, 4; 12:10).[116] As noted by Alan Cooper,[117] this shift vowel would not have taken place in BH, and so the Hebrew spelling in this case points to a Phoenician import (unless the vocalization were a secondary development under the polemical influence of the BH *bōšet,* "shame").[118] Phoenician evidence for this goddess is known in the inscriptional record,[119] as well as other sources.[120] Whether or not this representation of Solomon's practice derives from any historical kernel (perhaps Solomon's accommodation of the Phoenician cult of a consort) or is a secondary retrojection (perhaps under the later inspiration of Israelite reaction against Phoenician worship), the critique of the practice in 1 Kings 11 shows an awareness of a royal effort to provide a local accommodation for the cult of the Phoenician 'Ashtart. The goddess appears to be known to the biblical author, like the other national deities mentioned in this story.

The second apparent import involves the "Queen of Heaven," as known from Jer. 7:18; 44:15-30.[121] This title in this context has been understood as 'Ashtart,[122] Ishtar, or a fusion (or a cross-cultural identification) of Ishtar and Astarte,[123] and least likely Asherah.[124] Saul M. Olyan sees the best case being for 'Ashtart and a possible though lesser case for Ishtar.[125] Susan Ackerman has argued that the Queen of Heaven was a combination of elements of West Semitic 'Ashtart and East Semitic Ishtar.[126] The influence of Ishtar is suggested by BH *kawwānîm* as a loan from Akkadian *kamānu* in Jer. 7:18; 44:19,[127] not to mention Ishtar's iconography attested in the region during this period.[128] The basis for West Semitic 'Ashtart in the late Iron II is not entirely clear, although Olyan notes suggestive comparative evidence. Ackerman presupposes the continuation of the West Semitic 'Ashtart within Israel, perhaps as a matter of popular or local cult.[129]

This view might be supported by reference to the polemical attacks on the *'aštārôt,* in Judg. 2:13; 10:6; 1 Sam. 7:3, 4; 12:10, as noted above. These biblical references belong to the later tradents of these books, yet may reflect rejection of Astarte. These *'aštārôt* are not represented as a matter of Phoenician importation, which would suggest the vestige of an older West Semitic cult, one that could be indigenous to early Israel. It may have been a popular practice rather than a particularly royal one (apart from Solomon's reported adoption of 'Ashtoreth). It may also have been relatively minor, until the Iron II period when Neo-Assyrian influence of Ishtar may have increased its impact within Israelite religion, perhaps under the rubric of the Queen of Heaven. (Parenthetically, it may be noted that the name of Asherah, perhaps by this time more a matter of the symbol as Yahweh's asherah than a discrete symbol representing the goddess as such, may have been conflated with the similar-sounding name of the goddess ʿAshtart,[130] perhaps identified with the Queen of Heaven, who was evidently more a threat in this period than the goddess Asherah. This is all very speculative.[131]) If a general trend of the demise of ʿAshtart's cult may be seen despite what may be vestiges of her name (at least), the question remains: what was the reason for this demise?

It is difficult, if not impossible, to answer such questions. I would offer a few speculations about developments that may correlate with the demise of Anat and ʿAshtart in ancient Israel. The first is the demise of hunting as an activity associated with the sacred. The warrior-goddess is largely a coastal phenomenon in this period, while she seems to be fading in Israel and further inland. Her role of hunting is one that is represented rarely, if at all, in Israel for the national god. This situation may be reflected (or perhaps refracted) in the literary description of hunting in Genesis 27. This passage represents this activity as proper to Esau, but not Jacob. The text may reflect an Iron II "culture map" of Israel as a society little involved in hunting; there was a perception within Israel's Iron II elite that hunting is not a particularly Israelite activity.[132] Might an elite perception about the lack of Israelite hunting possibly reflected in this passage be correlated with the lack of witness to ʿAshtart in biblical texts?

As noted in Chapter One, the archaeological evidence for hunted animals shows up at various sanctuaries: in the Iron I site of Mount Ebal, the tenth-century cultic structure at Taanach, the Dan sacred precinct, and later at Iron II Lachish. Despite problems in interpretation, it is apparent that sacrificial cult included undomesticated species at some Israelite shrines. Following Oded Borowski,[133] it seems quite plausible that the meat of the hunt was sacrificed, thanks especially to the (albeit limited) archaeological evidence from Israelite shrines. Moreover, it may be suspected that hunted game was perhaps sacralized with prayers or blessings within the family or clan context. Deuteronomy 14 permits slaughter of such undomesticated animals[134] outside of the temple sacrificial system, which may have included religious treatment of such slaughter within family or clan circles. The cases of bones of hunted animals noted in Chapter One are hardly exhaustive, but they are sufficient to suggest a situation on the ground that the Bible says very little about. It is arguable from various lines of evidence that animals of the hunt served for sacrificial purposes both in the family orbit and at shrines, despite the lack of biblical evidence supporting this reconstruction.[135] This may point to families and local shrines as the religious home for conceptualization of the divine in terms of the hunt, as opposed to Israel's national temple and the royal and priestly elite that supported the production of biblical texts, which say very little about this sort of divine conceptualization.

This reconstruction would correlate with the loss of hunting as a divine role in Israel's national literature, but it would also support the reconstruction of a divine role for hunting at a local level, perhaps in popular cult as Susan Ackerman and John Day envision. At the national level, the goddesses' role in warfare as well as the gods' warfare role seem to have been conflated earlier with the role of the national god in Iron Age Israel. Indeed, the imagery of Anat's bloody warfare that is not attested for classic warrior-gods in Ugaritic literature is attributed in biblical descriptions to Yahweh.[136] Thus, it would seem that the traditional language of bloody, terrestrial divine warfare known earlier for Anat had become part of the repertoire of descriptions for Israel's national god. In general, the warrior roles seem to be attributed to the Israel's national god, with other warrior divinities reduced to a secondary role[137] or eliminated. Where a goddess such as Anat could "teach" or "train" (**lmd*)[138] the young warrior Aqhat for the hunt (*ʾalmdk*, KTU 1.18 I 29), Yahweh trains the king for war (*mĕlammēd*, 2 Sam. 22/Ps. 18:35). Warfare and not the hunt[139] remains an important role, and the Israelite god shows the roles that the goddesses exhibit in the Late Bronze and Iron I contexts. Broader matters may be involved as well. Perceptions about "foreignness" of some religious practices, for example in the case of the "Queen of Heaven," may have played a role in the new religious-political expression of later "reforms." In any case, in the emerging royal worldview, reductions of levels of religious praxis perhaps corresponded to reductions of levels in various divine powers, leaving Yahweh as virtually Judah's one and only.[140] The goddess's place in the Israelite pantheon at the national level might have diminished under this development.

4. The Social Dislocation of Heroic Poetry in Ancient Israel

The figure of David in Israel's historiography of Genesis–Kings is arguably emblematic of a shift from the lost world of heroic poetry in the Iron I–tenth century period to the prose cycles of the later Iron IIB-C and afterwards. In the representation of ancient Israel's great historiographical works, David was the last of such "poetic heroes." After David, there is no more "old poetry" in the great narrative work of Genesis–Kings. His poems in 2 Samuel 22–23 are the last ones in this work. By contrast, his military chiefs and elite soldiers are not the subjects of heroic poems. As we saw above in section 2, David's legendary warriors receive only bare prose notices (see 2 Sam. 21:18-22; 23:8-39) where they are not elaborated in prose sources (cf. Uriah the Hittite in 2 Samuel 11). Neither David's heroic warriors nor other warriors that may have followed are the subjects of warrior poetry attested in the Bible.[141]

This is not to say that the tenth century necessarily marked the end of poetry about warfare. Indeed, it is to be highlighted that poetry about war broadly speaking did continue in later biblical literature. The monarchy deployed the imagery of warriors and warfare.[142] The oracles against the nations constitute a body of warfare poetry from later Israel,[143] and warfare imagery for the deity continues in compositions such as Deuteronomy 32. In addition, many idioms found in heroic poetry continue in later literature. Moreover, prophetic parodies using warrior language (perhaps such as Ezekiel 19, with its lion imagery in vv. 2-3, 5-6) might suggest a general familiarity with an ongoing tradition of heroic poetry[144] that may have been displaced, not making its way into the surviving biblical corpus. However, there is a difference between the older heroic poetry and later poetry about warriors and warfare. Compared with heroic poetry of the early era, the prophetic war oracles or a later poem such as Deuteronomy 32 mark a significant change in the history of warfare poetry in ancient Israel. No longer focused on heroic men, later warfare poetry contrasts strongly with the earlier heroic poetry. Poetry about warfare was continuing in some ways in the Iron IIB-C, but it does not look (or, more importantly, sound) like heroic poetry. The exemplars of warfare poetry from the Iron IIB-C are suggestive of the cultural "distance" between the older heroic poetry and later warfare poems.

The question is why there was this apparent change. It seems unlikely that the absence of heroic poetry in later Israelite literature is to be attributed simply to a shift in types of textual production, say from the oral to the written.[145] In this theory, oral poetry simply would have died out in the ninth century or so. However, given the oral culture that Susan Niditch and David M. Carr have identified for ancient Israel throughout the Iron Age,[146] the loss of oral poetry as a cultural practice seems to be unsupported by the evidence. It would appear that ancient Israel continued in the Iron II B-C period to be an "oral world" (to use Niditch's expression) as much it was a "written world." The absence of heroic poetry from the Iron IIB period and following cannot be attributed simply to a putative shift from the oral to the written. The factors involved would seem to be more complex.

As studied in Chapter Ten, the tenth century seems to be a significant time for the written composition of Judges 5 and 2 Sam. 1:19-27 as presently attested. Thus, the emergent monarchies are an important factor in the history of heroic poetry. The later monarchies of the Iron IIB-C had experiences of royal warfare, victories and defeats alike. Such royal victories could have been celebrated in heroic poetry. Kings might have been remembered for their great victories, but these are remembered in prose (cf. the Mesha stele). It is true that the Bible preserves little royal poetry compared with other types of poetic literature (priestly, prophetic), and so such poems might have been lost. Where is the heroic poetry celebrating the exploits of Omri? Where are the songs singing the victories of Josiah? Where are the laments over his death, as remembered in 2 Chr. 35:25?[147] It remains a possibility that there were later heroic poems celebrating the victories of later kings. Thus, the issue might be in part a matter of textual preservation, and indeed, it may be said that the Bible as we presently have it is hardly a royal production. While the Bible contains many discussions of kings, relatively little biblical literature[148] shows an unalloyed monarchic perspective (royal psalms and Isaianic reflections on the king in Isaiah 7, 9, 11 would be exceptions).[149] In other words, biblical literature is hardly monarchic. However, it would not seem that the lack of monarchic texts is itself the reason for the lack of heroic poetry after David. If earlier heroic poetry could be preserved, then later heroic poetry could be preserved as well. Thus there seems to be more to the story.

Perhaps we should look to the social settings of textual production in the Iron I, Iron IIA, and Iron IIB-C for further clues. There were differences in the social settings of textual production in these phases of the Iron Age. A shift in the social settings for textual production might lie behind the diminished attestation of heroic poetry. Heroic poetry was not the product simply of oral culture; it was more specifically an oral culture that was clan and tribally based. It was produced in the aftermath of the premonarchic militias battling and coming home from war, where the postbattle practice involved oral song. David's poetry would perhaps be the last expression for this older militia world. The problem with this theory is that there is no reason to suppose that in the oral world of the Iron IIB-C, the victories of armies should stop being celebrated in song. Thus, there seems to be yet still more to the story. There may well have been oral composition celebrating Israel's victories and losses, but as we move through the Iron IIB period, these oral compositions that might have been produced did not transfer into the scribal apparatus of the monarchy. I would not necessarily attribute this situation to a shift of royal self-perception more toward the image of national leader and builder. (In this regard, one might think of Solomon as opposed to David as emblematic.) Indeed, the warrior remained a standard model of royal self-imaging (e.g., Ps. 45:3-5). However, for some reason the Israelite poetry of the Iron IIB-C did not issue in new heroic poetry centered on the king. Instead, such older heroic poetry would be adapted for royal use on occasion (e.g., the cases of 2 Sam. 22/Ps. 18:8-16 and perhaps Habbakuk 3, both discussed above).

The monarchy itself was perhaps not the crucial factor in the failure to record heroic poetry. As we have noted, royal poetry is attested albeit poorly in the biblical corpus, and so it is possible that there was royal, heroic poetry in the Iron IIB-C but it did not survive. Accordingly, the issue may hinge on the text-producing sectors related in different ways to the monarchies of Israel and Judah. It would appear that groups involved in textual production (e.g., priests, prophets, sages) in this period[150] do not seem to have held a particular regard for heroic poetry. The later biblical corpus shows little interest in heroic poetry. With the priestly tradition, human warfare does not seem to be a particularly central concern. The divine warrior of Israelite tradition, for example, becomes transmuted in Genesis 1 as the power beyond martial conflict or military prowess.[151] The "deuteronomistic" traditions seem to take issue with the value of warfare as a means for advancing Israel's service to God.[152] Warfare is mentioned as divine punishment of Israel, not as a matter of Israel's celebration. Prophetic and wisdom circles do not evidence any particular interest in the heroic tradition. Warfare, the setting that gave rise to heroic poetry in early Israel, was no less a concern in later Israel, but Israel's later text-producing venues seem not to have chosen heroic poetry as a significant mode of expression. It would appear that a shift in cultural and perhaps religious sensibility in Israel's leadership toward heroic poetry is involved: the later centers of written texts especially in Iron IIB-C Israel did not take over heroic poetry from either the monarchy (as and if such texts existed) or from the older clan- and tribal-based oral tradition, except for purposes of preservation (e.g., Judges 5; 2 Sam. 1:19-27) or recontextualization (e.g., 2 Samuel 22/Psalm 18). While such militia-based oral poetry might have persisted among armies of Judah and Israel in the Iron IIB-C, it did not translate into the royal and priestly scribal establishments, as far as we can tell from the extent evidence.

There was a pronounced gap between the period of the old heroic poetry and the textual production under the monarchies of the eighth century and following. While significantly fewer early Israelite texts are known from outside the Bible or alluded to within it, the massive appearance of written material both inside the Bible and in the extrabiblical record from Israel beginning in the eighth century may mark a watershed in the shifting roles of oral culture and writing in the collations of Israel's collective memories. Various works across the surviving biblical corpus would point to the eighth and seventh centuries[153] as a significant period in the rise of writing as a culturally prestigious form of cultural memory; these would include the production of the pre-P/pre-D pentateuchal material (commonly called in older source theory "the Yahwist" and "the Elohist" sources); the Neo-Assyrian context claimed for Deuteronomy 12–26; the evolving collections claimed for Joshua through Kings during the reign of Hezekiah, then later Josiah, and still later in the exilic and postexilic contexts; the first separate prophetic works in the eighth century onwards; a seventh-century redaction claimed for Isaiah; and the transmission[154] of Proverbs 25–29 effected by the "men of Hezekiah" (Prov. 25:1).

The importance of writing from the eighth century onwards in ancient Israel may signal a rupture between a traditional past and an awareness of its demise. Indeed, it may be noted that many biblical references to collective memory generally date to the eighth century or later. However, it would seem that some traditional contexts of (and societal anchoring for) oral memory did not retain their cultural prestige in the face of monarchic and priestly support for written forms of cultural memory. By the time of the massive appearance of writing in eighth-century sources, the shift in the relative power of the contexts that supported and generated oral and written forms of cultural memory was largely complete. It is tempting to relate this apparent gap between older poetic traditions and late prose amalgamations in terms of a divide perceived by the classicist Albert B. Lord, when it came to the writing down of the *Iliad* and the *Odyssey*. Lord suggested that the *Iliad* and the *Odyssey* came into writing under the influence of written traditions coming to the Aegean world in the ninth and eighth centuries. "I should like to suggest," Lord wrote, "that it would be normal for them [the Greeks] to look to the East during these centuries; for it was in the East that the cultural center was then located."[155] While this "Homeric question" is not the one before us, Lord's observations about the situation in the Levant in the ninth and eighth centuries are perhaps relevant to the problem of the absence of the ongoing production of heroic poetry in Israel from the ninth or eighth century onward. Lord's instincts about the massive amount of writing in the ancient Near East at this time may be germane. This does seem to be a watershed period separating the production of heroic poetry in ancient Israel from monarchic textual production.

The change in textual production may correspond to wider developments in ancient Israelite society and religion in the Iron IIB-C. This more general trend may have entailed the loss of the warrior-goddesses. While they are evident in the Iron I period, they fade by comparison in the Iron IIB-C, as far as we can see. The new situation perhaps involved a new understanding of both "god and king." In other words, the warrior-goddesses may have diminished, in part due to the increasing emergence of the national god. Perhaps the configuration of the Rephaim traditions, as attested in the Bible, suffered a similar fate in ancient Israel. There may be a broader pattern of diminishment of "warrior culture" represented by heroic poetry, the warrior goddesses, and the Rephaim in the Iron IIB-C context in ancient Israel.

An important book by Danièle Hervieu-Léger, *La religion pour mémoire*,[156] may help to put these developments into perspective. Building on several predecessors in the *Annales* tradition of historical research,[157] Hervieu-Léger discusses several important aspects of social memory that appear applicable to the fate of heroic poetry in ancient Israel: the destruction of traditional memory restructured and provided with new explanatory links; the conflictual nature of collective memory; the conflicting efforts on the part of shifting hierarchies to homogenize collective memory; and the role of what she calls "elective fraternity" in the reappropriation of reinvented memory. These are all features that biblical scholars would recognize in the accounts of Israel's past in priestly traditions in the Torah (Pentateuch) and in Deuteronomy as well as the historical books influenced by it, namely, Joshua through Kings. The past is provided with new connections to the present, and there are differences over such presentations of the past and evidently conflicts over such competing accounts. Hervieu-Léger is interested in how traditional religion in France recedes first in the face of the emerging nation-state, then is challenged by an increasing loss of traditional locus and practice of religion due to the modern forces of society, only to reappear in various forms of "elective fraternity." Hervieu-Léger's general perspective may be applied to Israelite religion. Traditional religion (and here read for Israel traditional religion of clans, with local "high-places" and shrines) is submerged first in the face of the rising nation-state, with its royal sanctuaries (here read the rise of the Judean and Israelite monarchies). It then recedes further due to an increasing loss of traditional locus and practice of religion (here read the loss of local patrimonies and lineages and nonroyal sanctuaries, especially from the eighth through the sixth centuries). There is a corresponding appearance of new forms of "elective fraternity" (read prophetic and perhaps priestly and "Deuteronomic" movements, gathering social force in reaction to the limitations of family and monarchic religion in the eighth through the sixth centuries). Here we see at work a rule of memory surviving in inverse proportion to historical order and power of social location: families and clans, with their memories generated largely through oral means, are socially weaker, relative to the priestly forces behind the textual formation and transmission of texts in regional shrines. As a result, family memory is submerged beneath the weight of priestly lines working in sanctuaries and then filtered through royal shrines, and ultimately through the royal shrine with a single priestly hierarchy in Jerusalem. Homogenization of societal narratives went only so far. Just as collective memory in France could maintain a variety of versions of national history, so within the Jerusalemite context several narratives, priestly and deuteronomic/deuteronomistic alike, could be maintained and modified, at once rejecting and responding to one another.

It would appear that the warrior setting for the composition of heroic poetry from Israel's "prehistory" (in the Iron I–tenth century) was dislocated by the time of the creation of the great prose narrative cycles in the IIB-C period and later. While the older poetry was elaborated and transmitted into later periods,[158] the older setting for composing this sort of warrior poetry seems to have suffered its demise. The creators of the later prose cycles may have been well aware that the poetic compositions that they incorporated came from a "lost world" of early Israel (Iron I–tenth century). Indeed, they may have used such poems precisely because they felt old to them and their audiences.[159] Including old poetry in the prose narrative works served the literary function of bringing their audiences closer to the time described by the poems. In some cases, they were joined deliberately with the prose accounts of such putatively old events (for example, in Exodus 14–15; Numbers 23–24; Judges 4–5). The early era of heroic poetry perhaps was a lost world already by the time of the final compositions of these heroic poems in the tenth century; it was all the more a lost world for the ancient Israelite prose historiographers in the Iron IIB-C period and later. As time passed, the heroic poems increasingly evoked an older world, a world that had vanished before Israel encountered the empires of Assyria, then Babylon and Persia, and later the Greeks and Romans. As enshrined in old warrior poetry, this lost world managed to outlast all of these empires. With their evocations of great acts and famous personas of old, these poems could continue to signal to later audiences great achievements of the past and to express no less great hopes for the future.

Notes

Notes to the Preface

1. Hedges, *War Is a Force That Gives Us Meaning* (New York: Public Affairs, 2002) 83. Note also his statement (p. 21): ". . . in mythic war we imbue events with meanings they do not have." This book first came to my attention by accident: Chris Hedges happened to be attending a dinner at New York University and we were sitting together. He recognized me from our time at Harvard Divinity School over three decades ago. Our conversation dramatized for me the distance between his understanding of war and my own, as known only through reading; and that sense of distance, captured also in his book, led me to question what I read in ancient heroic poetry. I wish to thank my friend Howie Stanger for lending me a copy of Hedges's book and for discussing it with me.

2. As I revise today (16 December 2011), the United States has declared its withdrawal from its nine-year war in Iraq.

3. For a critical discussion of the idea of war as sacrifice, see Ivan Strenski, *Contesting Sacrifice: Religion, Nationalism, and Social Thought in France* (Chicago: University of Chicago Press, 2002).

4. Seth Benardete, *Achilles and Hector: The Homeric Hero* (South Bend: St. Augustine's Press, 2005) 80.

5. Hedges, *War Is a Force That Gives Us Meaning,* 173.

6. Niditch, *War in the Hebrew Bible: A Study of the Ethics of Violence* (New York: Oxford University Press, 1993).

7. Corrine Carvalho, "The Beauty of the Bloody God: The Divine Warrior in Prophetic Literature," in *The Aesthetics of Violence in the Prophets,* ed. Julia M. O'Brien and Chris Franke (LHB/OTS 517; New York: T. & T. Clark, 2010) 131-52.

8. On the end-times in American culture, see Claudia Setzer and David A. Shefferman, eds., *The Bible and American Culture: A Sourcebook* (London: Routledge, 2011) 6, 201, 221-42.

9. See the survey of Jon R. Stone, "A Fire in the Sky: 'Apocalyptic' Themes on the Sil-

ver Screen," in *God in the Details: American Religion in Popular Culture*, ed. Eric Michael Mazur and Kate McCarthy (2nd ed.; London: Routledge, 2011) 62-79.

10. Dan W. Clanton, "Movies, TV and The Bible," in http://gbgm-umc.org/Response/articles/movies.html (accessed on 25 January 2012).

11. Coetzee, *Waiting for the Barbarians* (New York: Penguin, 1980) 143.

12. Other studies of ancient warrior poetry with an eye to present concerns include Caroline Alexander, *The War That Killed Achilles: The True Story of Homer's Iliad and the Trojan War* (New York: Viking, 2009).

13. See Andrew R. George, *The Babylonian Gilgamesh Epic: Introduction, Critical Edition, and Cuneiform Texts* (2 vols.; Oxford: Oxford University Press, 2003) 1:248, 250-51. In this connection, one might also mention Enkidu's desire to be declared "the mightiest," given as his motivation for seeking to confront Gilgamesh in Uruk (SBV I.221; see also SBV I.240).

14. See Katherine Callen King, *Achilles: Paradigms of the War Hero from Homer to the Middle Ages* (Berkeley: University of California Press, 1987).

15. For this text as well as its later echoes, see King, *Achilles*, 110 and 263 n. 1, and 149-52, 158; and Timothy D. Barnes, *Early Christian Hagiography and Roman History* (Tria corda 5; Tübingen: Mohr Siebeck, 2010) 186.

16. See King, *Achilles*, 28-37. Note also Dale Launderville, *Celibacy in the Ancient World: Its Ideal and Practice in Pre-Hellenistic Israel, Mesopotamia, and Greece* (Collegeville: Liturgical, 2010) xxii-xxiii.

17. John Roberts, ed., *The Oxford Dictionary of the Classical World* (New York: Oxford University Press, 2005), 3. Cf. Benardete, *Achilles and Hector*, 57: "Homer does not glorify war. As we become involved in the destiny of his heroes, he whispers more and more insistently, 'there is a world elsewhere.'"

18. For a critical discussion informed by a feminist perspective, see Carol Cohn, "Sex and Death in the Rational World of Defense Intellectuals," *Signs* 12 (1988) 687-718. She claims that "a highly masculinised culture within the defense establishment contributes to the divorcing of war from human emotion." See also J. Ann Tickner, *Gender in International Relations: Feminist Perspectives on Achieving Global Security* (New York: Columbia University Press, 1992).

Notes to the Acknowledgments

1. David R. Slavitt, trans., *Ausonius: Three Amusements* (Philadelphia: University of Pennsylvania Press, 1998) 3.

Notes to the Introduction

1. Baruch A. Levine, "The Triumphs of the Lord," *ErIsr* 20 (Yigael Yadin Memorial Volume; 1989) 202-14 (Heb.), 201* (Eng. summary); and Susan Niditch, "The Challenge of Israelite Epic," in *A Companion to Ancient Epic*, ed. John Miles Foley (Oxford: Blackwell,

2005) 279-80. Note also John Pairman Brown, "Peace Symbolism in Ancient Military Vocabulary," *VT* 21 (1971) 1-23. For a broad survey of the subject of heroes in the Hebrew Bible, see Gregory Mobley, *The Empty Men: The Heroic Tradition of Ancient Israel* (ABRL; New York: Doubleday, 2005). See also Philip F. Esler, *Sex, Wives, and Warriors: Reading Biblical Narrative with Its Ancient Audience* (Eugene: Cascade, 2011). See also note 4 below, which offers some distinctions between epic poetry and heroic poetry. Note also the broader use of "heroic literature" in Stanley Isser, *The Sword of Goliath: David in Heroic Literature* (Studies in Biblical Literature 6, Atlanta: Society of Biblical Literature, 2003). Reference courtesy of Julie Deluty.

2. Among many works, see Jean-Marie Durand, Thomas Römer, and Michael Langlois, ed., *Le jeune héros: Recherches sur la formation et la diffusion d'un thème littéraire au Proche-Orient ancien. Actes du colloque organisé par les chaires d'Assyriologie et des milieux bibliques du Collège de France, Paris, les 6 et 7 avril 2009* (OBO 250; Fribourg: Academic; Göttingen: Vandenhoeck & Ruprecht, 2011). For an indigenous term for heroic song, see Akkadian *qurdu,* in *CAD* Q:318, no. 3. I regret that this study has not benefitted from the Zimrī-Lim Epic to be published by Michael Guichard. See for now the summary and excerpts by Daniel Bodi, "Akkadian and Aramaic Terms for a 'Favorable Time' (*ḫidānu, adānu,* and *'iddānu*): Semitic Precursors of Greek *kairos*?" in *Time and History in the Ancient Near East: Proceedings of the 56th Recontre Assyriologique Internationale, Barcelona, July 26-30, 2010,* ed. Lluis Feliu et al. (Winona Lake: Eisenbrauns, 2010) 49-52.

3. The topic of heroic poetry is an old one in classical studies, e.g., C. M. Bowra, *Heroic Poetry* (London: Macmillan; New York: St Martin's Press, 1961). For only one of many appraisals of heroic poetry of Homer, see Seth L. Schein, *The Mortal Hero: An Introduction to Homer's* Iliad (Berkeley: University of California Press, 1984). In this connection, note Schein's comment (p. 96): "In the long run, however, for Homer to preserve Achilles or any warrior from death would be to deny him heroic life, that is, immortality through celebration in heroic poetry." A superb summary of heroes in classical tradition is to be found in Emily Vermeule, *Aspects of Death in Early Greek Art and Poetry* (Berkeley: University of California, 1979) 83-116. See also the studies discussed in Chapters Two and Three below.

4. Sometimes heroic poetry and epic poetry are treated as virtual synonyms, e.g., A. T. Hatto, "Introduction to Volume One," in *Traditions of Heroic and Epic Poetry,* Vol. 1: *The Traditions* (London: Modern Humanities Research Association, 1980) 10. While most, if not all, ancient Near Eastern epic poetry is heroic, it might be said that a good deal of ancient Near Eastern heroic poetry is not epic, if this term includes some sense of the poetic length as well as the scale of its characters and/or landscapes. These sorts of criteria are highly contested; see Niditch, "The Challenge of Israelite Epic," 277-80; and further in Chapter One below. Warfare poetry, too, overlaps with heroic poetry. The former would include various sorts of poetry bearing on war, such as war oracles, oracles against the nations, and military psalms. For these types of warfare poetry as they appear in the Hebrew Bible, see Duane L. Christensen, *Transformations of the War Oracle in Old Testament Prophecy: Studies in the Oracles Against the Nations* (Harvard Dissertations in Religion 3; Missoula: Scholars for Harvard Theological Review, 1975; repr. as *Prophecy and War in Ancient Israel: Studies in the Oracles Against the Nations in Old Testament*

Prophecy (Berkeley: BIBAL, 1989). In contrast to warfare poetry, heroic poetry also includes instances of figures not involved in warfare, e.g., Gilgamesh and Enkidu. For these figures, see Chapters Two and Three.

5. This title is taken from the name of the first chapter of Christopher P. Jones, *New Heroes in Antiquity: From Achilles to Antinoos* (Revealing Antiquity 18; Cambridge, MA: Harvard University Press, 2010).

6. The hymn is known from Ebla and Abu Salabikh; see Manfred Krebernik, "Mesopotamian Myths at Ebla: ARET 5, 6 and ARET 5, 7," in *Literature and Literary Language at Ebla* (ed. Pelio Fronzaroli; Quaderni di Semitistica 18; Florence: Dipartimento di Linguistica, Università di Firenze, 1992) 73, 82.

7. The Indo-European word for hero is old, thought to be attested already in Linear B *tiriseroe*, "thrice-hero." See Jones, *New Heroes in Antiquity*, 3-4. The thrust of "thrice" here is unclear; see John Chadwick, *The Decipherment of Linear B* (2nd ed.; Cambridge: Cambridge University Press, 1967) 126. Jones comments (*New Heroes in Antiquity*, 4): "the 'thrice' may suggest a being triply strong or valiant, a heroicized hero three generations back, or something else not yet understood." For questions about the word, see Jorge J. Bravo III, "Recovering the Past: The Origins of Greek Heroes and Hero Cult," in *Heroes: Mortals and Myths in Ancient Greece*, ed. Sabine Albersmeier (Baltimore: Walters Art Museum, 2009) 11 (with further references).

In the *Iliad*, *hērōs* primarily applies to the combatants at Troy. In the *Odyssey*, the usage includes figures that are hardly warriors. Thus Jones considers the Greek word in Homer to mean "lord" as much as "hero." For discussion of the view of *hērōs* as "lord," see also Hans van Wees, *Status Warriors: War, Violence, and Society in Homer and History* (Dutch Monographs on Ancient History and Archaeology 9; Amsterdam: Gieben, 1992) 8. According to M. L. West, "In Homeric epic the word *hērōs* is applied rather freely to living men . . . in several places the most suitable meaning is 'warrior.' . . . Nowhere in epic is there any hint of religious significance." See West, ed., *Hesiod's Works and Days* (Oxford: Clarendon, 1978) 370; cf. Schein, *The Mortal Hero*, 69-70. For criticism of this view that the term in Homer lacks religious significance, see van Wees, *Status Warriors*, 8. Van Wees (7) suggests that the epic hero of old was not only outstanding in terms of bravery or some other remarkable feature, but also held "semi-divine status after his death." See also Robert Parker, *On Greek Religion* (Ithaca: Cornell University Press, 2011) 103-4. In this respect, the Greek *hērōs* has its closest West Semitic comparand in the Ugaritic *rp'um*, often called the Rephaim after the biblical cognate (to which perhaps biblical *(hā)rāp̱ā'* in 1 Chr. 20:4-8 may be compared as well; see Chapter Twelve, section 2). It is evident from the parallelism of *rp'im* with *'ilnym*, "divine" in KTU 1.6 VI 46-47 that they were considered "divine" or in van Wees' terms, "semi-divine" (see Chapter Five, section 1).

8. The noun conveys "might"; note also BH verb **gbr*, "to be strong, mighty, to prevail" (over enemies), in 1 Sam. 2:9, etc. (BDB, 149; cf. Arabic *jabbar*, Akkadian *gabru*, and Aramaic *gibbārā'*, Dan. 3:20). The nominal forms with the middle radical doubled suggest a general condition or character of a person. For more on *gibbôr*, see Hans Kosmala, "*gāḇar*," *TDOT*, 2:367-82, esp. 373-74; and Chapter Eight below. See also *gibbôr(ê) ḥayil*, "hero(es) of strength" (Josh. 1:14; 6:2; 8:3; 10:7; Judg. 6:12; 11:1; 1 Sam. 9:1; 16:18; 1 Kgs. 11:28; 2 Kgs. 5:1; 15:20; 24:14; BDB, 298; Kosmala, *TDOT*, 2:374). Note also PNs

gbrn in KTU 4.141 II 19; 4.730.6 and *bn gbrn* in 4.309.17 (*DULAT* 293). See further Isac Leo Seeligmann, "Menschliches Heldentum und göttliche Hilfe: Die doppelte Kausalität im alttestamentlichen Geschichtsdenken," *TZ* 19 (1963) 385-411; republ. in *Gesammelte Studien zur Hebräischen Bibel,* ed. Erhard Blum (FAT 41; Tübingen: Mohr Siebeck, 2004) 137-59; and Mobley, *The Empty Men,* 35. The phrase "man of war," *'îš milḥāmâ,* occurs for the deity in Exod. 15:3, and also for David in 1 Sam. 16:18 and for Goliath in 1 Sam. 17:33 (see also Josh. 17:1; Judg. 20:17; 2 Sam. 17:8; Isa. 3:2; Ezek. 39:20; for the variations on this expression, see BDB, 536).

9. See Chapter Four on *ġzr* in Aqhat and elsewhere in Ugaritic for the meanings "noble, hero" as well as "champion, warrior" (so *DULAT,* 329). Its further meaning, "young man, youth," may also imply a male on the path to warriorhood. See also Ugaritic *qrd,* used for heroic warriors ("hero, powerful one," in *DULAT,* 709-10) and in particular as an epithet for the god Baal, *'al'iy qrdm,* "mightiest of warriors." For these titles, see Aicha Rahmouni, *Divine Epithets in the Ugaritic Alphabetic Texts,* trans. J. N. Ford (HO 1/93; Leiden: Brill, 2008) 49-52; for an argument for an Egyptian "translation" of *'al'iy qrdm* as *'ḥ3wtj nfr,* "perfect fighter," in the "Tale of the Two Brothers," see Thomas Schneider, "Innovation in Literature on Behalf of Politics: The Tale of the Two Brothers, Ugarit and 19th Dynasty History," *Ägypten und Levante/Egypt and the Levant* 18 (2008) 315-26, here 318. For *qrd,* see Joseph Martin Pagan, *A Morphological and Lexical Study of Personal Names in the Ebla Texts* (ARES 3; Roma: Missione Archeologica Italiana in Siria, 1998) 158, and also the etymologically related forms in Akkadian in note 10 below. Note also Ugaritic *ḏmr,* "brave, mighty," as used for soldiers; see Patrick L. Miller, "Ugaritic *ġzr* and Hebrew *'zr* II," *UF* 2 (1970) 161; and Michael L. Barré, "'My Strength and My Song' in Exodus 15:2," *CBQ* 54 (1992) 623-37, esp. 624-25.

10. *CAD Q*:140. Note also the adjective *qardu,* "heroic, valiant" (*CAD Q*:129), and the abstract form *qarradūtu,* "heroism, valor, bravery" (*CAD Q*:144), e.g. in Gilgamesh's question posed to Enkidu: "what has become of your great valor *(qarradūtika)?*" (OB Gilgamesh Yale tablet, iv 145, in *CAD Q*:144). See also *ilū qardūti,* "heroic gods," in Esarhaddon 96:10 (brought to my attention by Elizabeth Bloch-Smith), as cited in *CAD S*:230. Among other related forms, note also the factitive *qurrudu,* "to make into a hero," in *CAD Q*:320.

11. The expression is widely used. Mobley (*The Empty Men,* 5) employs the expressions "warrior culture" and "heroic culture." It is applied to Greek hoplites in W. G. Runciman, "Greek Hoplites, Warrior Culture, and Indirect Bias," *Journal of the Royal Anthropological Institute* 4 (1998) 731-51. It is used of samurai by Robert Ellwood, *Introducing Japanese Religion* (New York: Routledge, 2008) 105. See also the book by the military historian Martin van Creveld, *The Culture of War* (New York: Ballantine, 2008). To be sure, "culture" itself is a highly contested term (see note 13).

12. For tools in theories of culture, see the summary in Alessandro Duranti, *Linguistic Anthropology* (Cambridge: Cambridge University Press, 1997) 39-43. On the anthropology of "things," see Fernando Santos-Granero, ed., *The Occult Life of Things: Native Amazonian Theories of Materiality and Personhood* (Tucson: University of Arizona Press, 2009). Note also Arjun Appadurai, ed., *The Social Life of Things: Commodities in Cultural Perspective* (Cambridge: Cambridge University Press, 1988); Bill Brown, ed., *Things* (Chi-

cago: University of Chicago, 2004); and Annette B. Weiner and Jane Schneider, eds., *Cloth and Human Experience* (Washington: Smithsonian Institution Press, 1989).

13. Within the massive literature on theories of culture, I have found helpful the survey in Duranti, *Linguistic Anthropology*, 23-50. For a telling reflection on anthropological theorizing about culture, see Clifford Geertz, "A Life of Learning" (American Council of Learned Societies Occasional Paper 45; Charles Homer Haskins Lecture for 1999; available at: www.acls.org/publications/op/haskins/1999_cliffordgeertz.pdf). For a critique of the construction of cultures as stable and discrete groups that downplays change as well as internal tensions and conflicts, see Bruce Lincoln, *Gods and Demons, Priests and Scholars: Critical Explorations in the History of Religions* (Chicago: University of Chicago Press, 2012) 2-3. For issues of "culture" in the context of Iron I Israel, see Robert D. Miller II, "A 'New Cultural History' of Early Israel," in *Israel in Transition: From Late Bronze II to Iron IIA (c. 1250-850 BCE)*, vol. 2, ed. Lester L. Grabbe (European Seminar in Historical Methodology 8; New York: T. & T. Clark, 2010) 167-98. See further below.

14. See Pierre Bourdieu, *Outline of a Theory of Practice* (Cambridge Studies in Social and Cultural Anthropology 16; Cambridge: Cambridge University Press, 1977) 72, on the need to construct "the theory of the mode of generation of practices" (see also the discussion of "practice" on pp. 17, 77-79, 96-99). See further Duranti, *Linguistic Anthropology*, 43-45.

15. For the agency of texts, see Nathaniel B. Levtow, "Text Production and Destruction in Ancient Israel: Ritual and Political Dimensions," in *Social Theory and the Study of Israelite Religion: Essays in Retrospect and Prospect*, ed. Saul M. Olyan (SBLRBS 71; Atlanta: Society of Biblical Literature, 2012) 137. Citing Catherine Bell, Levtow suggests: "Texts in ancient Israel ought therefore to be viewed 'not simply as expressions or reflections of changing social situations but as dynamic *agents of change*'" (137).

16. A major matter of definition concerns the very word "war." See Frank Ritchel Ames, "The Meaning of War: Definitions for the Study of War in Ancient Israelite Literature," in *Writing and Reading War: Rhetoric, Gender, and Ethics in Biblical and Modern Contexts*, ed. Brad E. Kelle and Ames (SBLSymS 42; Atlanta: Society of Biblical Literature, 2008) 19-31. Cf. the issue in the modern context, discussed in Mary Ellen O'Connell, ed., *What Is War? An Investigation in the Wake of 9/11* (International Humanitarian Law 37; Leiden: Nijhoff, 2012).

17. An older classic on this subject is Dick Hebdige, *Subculture: The Meaning of Style* (London: Methuen, 1979). Since the 1990s, subcultures have become the subject of intense discussion focused on contemporary society. See Ken Gelder and Sarah Thornton, eds., *The Subcultures Reader* (New York: Routledge, 1997; 2nd ed., Gelder, 2005). See also Gelder, *Subcultures: Cultural Histories and Social Practice* (New York: Routledge, 2007); Sarah Thornton, *Club Cultures: Music, Media, and Subcultural Capital* (Hanover: University Press of New England, 1996); and Ross Haenfler, *Subcultures: The Basics* (London: Routledge, 2014). This is not a new subject; e.g., see the 1947 essay, "The Concept of the Sub-Culture and Its Application," by Milton M. Gordon, repr. in *The Subcultures Reader*. Ancient studies have also drawn on the concept of subcultures for analyzing various aspects of society. See, e.g., Rabun Taylor, "Two Pathic Subcultures in Ancient Rome," *Journal of the History of Sexuality* 7 (1997) 319-71. It has also been deployed for the study of

ancient Mayan culture by Robert J. Sharer, *The Ancient Maya* (5th ed.; Stanford: Stanford University Press, 1994) 66-67.

18. *CAD M*/1:281-82. For discussion, see Eva von Dassow, *State and Society in the Late Bronze Age: Alalaḫ under the Mitanni Empire* (Studies on the Civilization and Culture of Nuzi and the Hurrians 17; Bethesda: CDL, 2008).

19. This monarchic support is indicated by the surviving colophons on these texts. This is not to deny the oral background of the Ugaritic literary texts, as argued for many years (see *UBC* 1:29-35) and reaffirmed recently by Dennis Pardee, *The Ugaritic Texts and the Origins of West-Semitic Literary Composition* (Schweich Lectures 2007; Oxford: Oxford University Press, 2012) 26-28. It is only to note the royal patronage of the written forms in which these literary texts are currently known. Pardee (72 n. 64) suggests that the Ugaritic literary works reflect the royal ideology of the Ugaritic monarchy.

20. For the reflections on Homeric epic in this vein, see Egbert Bakker, "Storytelling in the Future: Truth, Time, and Tense in Homeric Epic," in *Written Voices, Spoken Signs: Tradition, Performance, and the Epic Text,* ed. Bakker and Ahuvia Kahane; Cambridge, MA: Harvard University Press, 1997) 11-36, esp. 13-17. The first person voice of old heroic poetry in the Bible brings the audience(s) into the description of the past (relative to this voice) mediated through its present expression, as will be discussed in Chapter Nine. Similarly, the old heroic poems examined in Chapters Eight through Ten point to multiple levels of tradition and composition, thus serving as examples of what Gregory Nagy calls "recomposition-in-performance." See Nagy, "Ellipsis in Homer," in Bakker and Kahane, *Written Voices, Spoken Signs,* 177.

21. See Vermeule, *Aspects of Death,* 99.

22. For a study relating the consequences of killing in biblical texts with the effects of warfare on combatants in modern literature, see David Bosworth, "'You Have Shed Much Blood and Waged Great Wars': Killing, Bloodguilt and Combat Stress," *Journal of Religion, Disability and Health* 12 (2008) 236-50.

23. For graphic descriptions of modern warfare practices that rarely make an appearance in heroic poetry, see Chris Hedges, *War Is a Force That Gives Us Meaning* (New York: Public Affairs, 2002).

24. The enslavement of women is named in Judg. 5:30, as is Achilles' enslavement of Lykaon in *Iliad* 21.34-96. See also the laments of Andromache and Hecabe (*Iliad* 24.725-45 and 748-59); for these speeches, see Deborah Beck, *Homeric Conversation* (Hellenic Studies 14; Washington: Center for Hellenic Studies, 2005) 245-51, 257. Note the *Odyssey* 8.523-53, which compares Odysseus' weeping with a slain husband's wife who is beaten and led into captivity. For the topic more broadly, see Vermeule, *Aspects of Death,* 112-15. For heuristic purposes, contrast the brutal experience of women in wartime, detailed by Miriam S. Chaiken, *Women Warriors and Kidnapped Kids: Girl Soldier/Brides in Sierra Leone* (Ithaca: Cornell University Press, 2009).

25. Cf. Seth Benardete, *Achilles and Hector: The Homeric Hero* (South Bend: St. Augustine's Press, 2005) 61: "Heroes are not much given to poetry: they rarely see their enemies as anything other than men to be killed. They leave to Homer the beautifying of their world." For the art of depicting battle conflict in the *Iliad,* see Vermeule, *Aspects of Death,* 84-94.

26. See Georges Bataille's reflections on murder, hunting, and war, in *Erotism: Death and Sensuality,* trans. Mary Dalwood (San Francisco: City Light, 1986; originally published as *L'Erotisme* in 1957) 71-80.

27. For this point more generally for epic, see Margaret Beissinger, Jane Tylus, and Susanne Wofford, "Introduction," in *Epic Traditions in the Contemporary World* (Berkeley: University of California Press, 1999) 12.

28. To be sure, warfare is regarded as an esteemed path of life for heroes. See Vermeule, *Aspects of Death,* 84.

29. This work for Homer was largely undertaken by Hans van Wees, *Status Warriors.*

30. On the Near Eastern side, see, e.g., Jack M. Sasson, "Some Literary Motifs in the Composition of the Gilgamesh Epic," *Studies in Philology* 69 (1972) 277; my thanks go to Professor Esther J. Hamori for this reference. Sasson entertains possible influence of Gilgamesh and Enkidu on Achilles and Patroklos. Cf. Hamori, "Echoes of Gilgamesh in the Jacob Story," *JBL* 130 (2011) 625-42. This proposal has found some reception among classicists (see, e.g., Schein, *The Mortal Hero,* 16-17). For resistance to this approach, see the discussion in Schein, *The Mortal Hero,* 41 n. 38. The view that the story of David and Jonathan has been influenced by Gilgamesh and Enkidu has been taken by Thomas Römer and Loyse Bonjour, *L'homosexualité dans le Proche-Orient ancien et la Bible* (Essais bibliques 37; Geneva: Labor et Fides, 2005) 100-101. It is to be noted that Gilgamesh is known in the Dead Sea Scrolls. As seen originally by J. T. Milik, the name of Gilgamesh is the name of one of the fallen angels in the Book of Giants, 4Q530 2:2 and 4Q531 17.12; the text may echo Huwawa as well in the form of the name Hobabish in 4Q203 3:2; see A. R. George, *The Babylonian Gilgamesh Epic* (Oxford: Oxford University Press, 2003) 1:60, as well as Loren T. Stuckenbruck, *The Book of Giants from Qumran: Texts, Translation, and Commentary* (TSAJ 63; Tübingen: Mohr Siebeck, 1997) 22-23, 72-73, 104-9, 164-67; D. R. Jackson, "Demonising Gilgameš," in *Gilgameš and the World of Assyria: Proceedings of the Conference Held at the Mandelbaum House, The University of Sydney, 21-23 July 2004,* ed. Joseph Azize and Noel Weeks (Ancient Near Eastern Studies Supplement 21; Leuven: Peeters, 2007) 107-14; and Matthew Goff, "Gilgamesh the Giant: The Qumran *Book of Giants'* Appropriation of Gilgamesh Motifs," *DSD* 16 (2009) 221-53 (the last reference courtesy of Joseph Angel). 4Q531 17 narrates a dream of Gilgamesh about strong adversaries, perhaps a resonance of his dream about Enkidu in Gilgamesh, OB II i 1-35 and SBV I.245-93. Given these attestations in the Dead Sea Scrolls, it is possible that this story was known earlier in Israel. For Gilgamesh iconography in the Levant down into the seventh century, see Hans Ulrich Steymans, "Gilgameš im Westen," in *Gilgamesch — Ikonographie eines Helden/Gilgamesh: Epic and Iconography* (OBO 245; Fribourg: Academic; Göttingen: Vandenhoeck & Ruprecht, 2010) 287-345.

31. While I prescind in this study from larger claims regarding literary contacts between the Aegean and the wider ancient Near East, it is to be noted that for over half a century intercultural engagement has been a major area of scholarly exploration, especially in the study of myth and literature. For the state of the question, see Carolina López-Ruiz, *When the Gods Were Born: Greek Cosmogonies and the Near East* (Cambridge, MA: Harvard University Press, 2010) 1-47. For Ugarit and Mycenae in particular, see Fr. Rougemont and J.-P. Vita, "Les enregistrements de chars à Ougarit et dans le monde

mycénien: approche comparative sur l'administration au Bronze Récent," in *Society and Administration in Ancient Ugarit: Papers Read at a Symposium in Leiden, 13-14 December 2007*, ed. W. H. van Soldt (Leiden: Nederlands Instituut voor het Nabije Oosten, 2010) 123-50. See also Eric H. Cline, *1177 B.C.: The Year Civilization Collapsed* (Princeton: Princeton University Press, 2014). This question of intercultural contact as reflected in literature was explored from the biblical side by Cyrus H. Gordon over fifty years ago; see Gordon, "Homer and the Bible: The Origin and Character of East Mediterranean Literature," *HUCA* 26 (1955) 43-108. Gordon was followed by his student, Michael C. Astour, *Hellenosemitica: An Ethnic and Cultural Study in West Semitic Impact on Mycenaean Greece* (Leiden: Brill, 1965). Note also Baruch Halpern's sophisticated consideration of biblical evidence within the context of Iron Age intercultural transfer between Mesopotamia and the Aegean. See Halpern, *From Gods to God: The Dynamics of Iron Age Cosmologies*, ed. Matthew J. Adams (FAT 63; Tübingen: Mohr Siebeck, 2009) 425-78.

From the side of the Aegean world, note John Pairman Brown, *Israel and Hellas* (3 vols.; BZAW 231, 276, 299; Berlin: de Gruyter, 1995-2001); Martin Litchfield West, *The East Face of Helicon: West Asiatic Elements in Greek Poetry and Myth* (Oxford: Clarendon, 1997); and Sarah Morris, "Homer and the Near East," in *A New Companion to Homer*, ed. Ian Morris and Barry Powell (Mnemosyne Sup 163; Leiden: Brill, 1997) 599-623. See also the older studies by C. Beye, "The Epic of Gilgamesh, the Bible, and Homer: Some Narrative Parallels," in Mnemai: *Classical Studies in Memory of Karl K. Hulley*, ed. Harold D. Evjen (Chico: Scholars, 1984) 1-19; and J. Wilson, "The *Gilgamesh Epic* and the *Iliad*," *Echos du Monde Classique/Classical Views* 30 (1986) 25-41. (Some of these references come courtesy of Sarah Morris.) From the Mesopotamian side, see Tzvi Abusch, "The Epic of Gilgamesh and the Homeric Epics," in *Mythology and Mythologies: Methodological Approaches to Intercultural Influences. Proceedings of the Second Annual Symposium of the Assyrian and Babylonian Intellectual Heritage Project. Held in Paris, France, Oct. 4-7, 1999*, ed. Robert M. Whiting (Helsinki: Neo-Assyrian Text Corpus Project, 2001) 1-6; and in the same volume Robert Rollinger, "The Ancient Greeks and the Impact of the Ancient Near East: Textual Evidence and Historical Perspective (ca. 750-650 BC)," 233-64.

For archaeological and literary evidence of trade and exchange, see the survey of Alexander Zukerman, "On Aegean Involvement in Trade with the Near East during the Late Bronze Age," *UF* 42 (2010) 887-901. As Ugarit is a particular focus on this study, I want to add that the question of trade and cultural relations between the Levant and the Aegean has been informed by textual evidence at Ugarit, e.g. in one letter in Akkadian (RS 16.238, lines 10-13), which refers to a "ship from Kapturu (Crete)." See Sylvie Lackenbacher, *Textes akkadiens d'Ugarit. Textes provenant des vingt-cinq premières campagnes* (Littératures anciennes du Proche-Orient 20; Paris: Cerf, 2002) 310-11; and Christopher Mountfort Monroe, *Scales of Fate: Trade, Tradition, and Transformation in the Eastern Mediterranean ca. 1350-1175 BCE* (AOAT 357; Münster: Ugarit-Verlag, 2009) 165-66. Kaphtor is also given as one of the homes of the craftsman god, Kothar wa-Hasis in Ugaritic literature (KTU 1.3 VI 14, in *UNP* 119 [and reconstructed in 1.1 III 1 and 18, in *UNP* 90, 91]; 1.100.46, in *UNP* 221 and *RCU* 177); note also the bibliog. in *DULAT* 453. Broader indicators are the Cypro-Minoan inscriptions discovered in the Levant; see Frank Moore Cross and Lawrence E. Stager, "Cypro-Minoan Inscriptions Found in Ashkelon," *IEJ* 56

(2006) 129-59. Inscriptions such as these contribute to the picture of trade relations with the Levant and complement what is known thanks to Minoan and Mycenaean pottery found at Ugarit and down the Levantine coast; see Marguerite Yon, *The City of Ugarit at Tell Ras Shamra* (Winona Lake: Eisenbrauns, 2006) 64, 127, 143, 145, 151, 155; Gert Jan van Wijngaarden, *Use and Appreciation of Mycenaean Pottery in the Levant, Cyprus and Italy (ca. 1600-1200 BC)* (Amsterdam Archaeological Studies; Amsterdam: Amsterdam University Press, 2003); and Caroline Sauvage, *Routes maritimes et systèmes d'échanges internationaux au Bronze Récent en Méditerranée orientale* (Lyon: Maison de l'Orient et de la Méditerranée, 2012).

In addition to well-known evidence mentioned by López-Ruiz (cited above), other discoveries from the Greek mainland are arguably relevant to this study, in particular Joseph Maran, "The Spreading of Objects and Ideas in the Late Bronze Age Eastern Mediterranean: Two Case Examples from the Argolid of the 13th and 12th Centuries B.C.," *BASOR* 336 (2004) 11-30. The armor scales found in the Argolid (discussed by Maran) are perhaps suggestive of intercultural exchange in the area of warrior culture. To be noted in connection with this evidence, the discovery of an ivory rod inscribed with logographic writing (perhaps Ugaritic), found at the Mycenaean site of Tiryns. See the radically different interpretations of Chaim Cohen, Joseph Maran, and Melissa Vetters, "An Ivory Rod with a Cuneiform Inscription, Most Probably Ugaritic, from a Final Palatial Workshop in the Lower Citadel of Tiryns," *Archäologischer Anzeiger* 2. Halbband (2010) 1-22; and Manfried Dietrich and Oswald Loretz, "Rhabdomantie im mykenischen Palast von Tiryns: Das Fragment eines kurz-keilalphabetisch beschrifteten Elfenbeinstabs (Ti 02 LXIII 34/91 VI d12.80 = KTU^3 6.104)," *UF* 42 (2010) 141-59. The evidence for westward intercultural contact continues to grow. A piece of agate with cuneiform writing was recently found at the sanctuary of Tas-Silg on the island of Malta, according to *Popular Archaeology* (December 2011); see http://popular-archaeology.com/issue/december-2011/article/rare-cuneiform-script-found-on-island-of-malta. I thank Walter Aufrecht for drawing my attention to this article. It is also reported that according to Werner Mayer, the tablet dates to the thirteenth century and came from Nippur; see http://www.culturaitalia.it/pico/modules/focus/en/focus_1072.html?print=true.

32. Susan Ackerman, *When Heroes Love: The Ambiguity of Eros in the Stories of Gilgamesh and David* (New York: Columbia University Press, 2005); Römer and Bonjour, *L'homosexualité dans le Proche-Orient*, 61-102; and Jean-Fabrice Nardelli, *Homosexuality and Liminality in the Gilgameš and Samuel* (Classical and Byzantine Monographs 64; Amsterdam: Hakkert, 2007). See also Anthony Heacock, *Jonathan Loved David: Manly Love and the Hermeneutics of Sex* (Bible in the Modern World 22; Sheffield: Sheffield Phoenix Press, 2011). For further bibliography, see Chapter Three.

33. Van Wees, *Status Warriors*.

34. For wealth and gift exchange in the *Iliad*, see van Wees, *Status Warriors*, 103-8, 228-37.

35. See Niditch, *War in the Hebrew Bible: A Study in the Ethics of Violence* (New York: Oxford University Press, 1993).

36. A partial exception is Baruch Margalit, *The Ugaritic Poem of Aqhat* (BZAW 182;

Berlin: de Gruyter, 1989). This work contains many speculations. Nonetheless, it is to be recognized for its observations about warriors in the story.

37. For the Ugaritic monarchy's interest in texts about warrior heroes, see Gregorio del Olmo Lete, "Littérature et pouvoir royal à Ougarit: Sens politique de la littérature d'Ougarit," in *Études ougaritiques II*, ed. Valérie Matoïan, Michel Al-Maqdissi, and Yves Calvet (RSO 20; Leuven: Peeters, 2012) 241-50.

38. See Isser, *The Sword of Goliath;* Niditch, *War in the Hebrew Bible,* and her fine essay, "The Challenge of Israelite Epic," in *A Companion to Ancient Epic,* ed. John Miles Foley (Oxford: Blackwell, 2005) 277-87; Mobley, *The Empty Men;* and Jacob L. Wright, "The Commemoration of Defeat and the Formation of a Nation in the Hebrew Bible," *Prooftexts* 29 (2009) 433-73; "Making a Name for Oneself: Martial Valor, Heroic Death, and Procreation in the Hebrew Bible," *JSOT* 36 (2011) 131-62; the author informs me that he has also has a book in progress on the topic: *A People-in-Arms: Military Organization and Peoplehood in Ancient Israel* (New York: Oxford University Press, in press). See also the essays in Kelle and Ames, *Writing and Reading War,* and in *Writing and Reading War,* vol. 2, ed. Jacob L. Wright, Brad E. Kelle, and Frank Ritchel Ames (Atlanta: Society of Biblical Literature, forthcoming). Note also C. L. Crouch, *War and Ethics in the Ancient Near East: Military Violence in Light of Cosmology and History* (BZAW 407; Berlin: de Gruyter, 2009).

39. The conventional dates used here for the Iron I and II periods have recently been subject to considerable controversy. The data for the tenth century are themselves a matter of significant debate. Some scholars would take the Iron IIA period (conventionally 1000-925) down into the ninth century. See Gabriel Barkay, "The Iron Age II-III," in *The Archaeology of Ancient Israel,* ed. Amnon Ben-Tor (New Haven: Yale University Press, 1992) 302-73. For further discussion, see Megan Bishop Moore and Brad E. Kelle, *Biblical History and Israel's Past: The Changing Study of the Bible and History* (Grand Rapids: Eerdmans, 2011) 236-37. The issue is taken up in Chapter One below.

40. Alexander Rofé, *Introduction to the Literature of the Hebrew Bible* (Jerusalem Bible Studies 9; Jerusalem: Simor, 2009) 293, 413.

41. David M. Carr, *The Formation of the Hebrew Bible: A New Reconstruction* (Oxford: Oxford University Press, 2011).

42. This is Carr's term, in *The Formation of the Hebrew Bible,* 8, 491.

43. See Carr's reflections, in *The Formation of the Hebrew Bible,* 8-9 and 488-90.

44. Carr, *The Formation of the Hebrew Bible,* 489.

45. See Konrad Schmid, *The Old Testament: A Literary History,* trans. Linda M. Maloney (Minneapolis: Fortress, 2012) 51.

46. Perhaps best exemplified by the joint 1950 dissertation of Frank Moore Cross, Jr. and David Noel Freedman, most recently published as *Studies in Ancient Yahwistic Poetry* (2nd ed.; BRS; Grand Rapids: Eerdmans; Livonia: Dove, 1997). See further the discussion of literature in Chapter Eight.

47. Cross, in his preface to the second edition of Cross and Freedman, *Studies in Ancient Yahwistic Poetry,* viii.

48. Johannes C. de Moor, *The Rise of Yahwism: The Roots of Israelite Monotheism* (BETL 91; Leuven: University Press/Peeters, 1990; rev. ed. 1997).

49. Freedman, "Early Israelite History in the Light of Early Israelite Poetry," in *Unity and Diversity*, ed. Hans Goedicke and J. J. M. Roberts (Baltimore: Johns Hopkins University Press, 1975) 3-35, repr. in Freedman, *Pottery, Poetry and Prophecy: Collected Essays on Hebrew Poetry* (Winona Lake: Eisenbrauns, 1980) 131-66; and "Early Israelite Poetry and Historical Reconstructions," in *Symposia Celebrating the Seventy-Fifth Anniversary of the Founding of the American Schools of Oriental Research (1900-1975)*, ed. Frank Moore Cross (Cambridge: American Schools of Oriental Research, 1979) 85-96, repr. in Freedman, *Pottery, Poetry and Prophecy*, 167-78.

50. See, e.g., Wilfred G. E. Watson, *Classical Hebrew Poetry: A Guide to Its Techniques* (JSOTSup 26; Sheffield: JSOT, 1984); Simon B. Parker, *The Pre-Biblical Narrative Tradition: Essays on the Ugaritic Poems* Keret *and* Aqhat (SBLRBS 24; Atlanta: Scholars, 1989); and Pardee, *The Ugaritic Texts*.

51. For different formulations of this view, see Michael D. Coogan and Mark S. Smith, *Stories From Ancient Canaan* (2nd rev. ed.; Louisville: Westminster John Knox, 2012) 3; Edward L. Greenstein, "Texts from Ugarit Solve Biblical Puzzles," *BAR* 36/6 (2010) 48-53; Pardee, *The Ugaritic Texts*, 79-80; Parker, *The Pre-Biblical Narrative Tradition*, 3-4; and Mark S. Smith, "Biblical Narrative between Ugaritic and Akkadian Literature: Part I: Ugarit and the Hebrew Bible: Consideration of Recent Comparative Research," *RB* 114 (2007) 5-29.

52. For a survey of the issues involved, see Smith, "Biblical Narrative between Ugaritic and Akkadian Literature: Part I"; "Biblical Narrative between Ugaritic and Akkadian Literature: Part II: Mesopotamian Impact on Biblical Narrative," *RB* 114 (2007) 189-207.

53. For more details about the issues under discussion here, see Chapter One (Introduction), section 3.

54. See below, esp. in Chapters Eleven and Twelve.

55. For a broad consideration of women's roles in support of battle, see Martin van Creveld, *Men, Women, and War* (London: Cassell, 2001).

56. For balance in other spheres of life in the Iron I period, see Carol L. Meyers, "Procreation, Production and Protection: Male-Female Balance in Early Israel," *JAAR* 51 (1983) 569-94.

57. For the archaeology of women's song, see Carol L. Meyers, "Of Drums and Damsels: Women's Performance in Ancient Israel," *BA* 54/1 (1991) 16-27.

58. Note generally the serious challenges to reconstructing the past via biblical sources, as outlined by Moore and Kelle, *Biblical History and Israel's Past*.

59. For a survey and discussion, see Georg G. Iggers, *Historiography in the Twentieth Century: From Scientific Objectivity to the Postmodern Challenge* (Middletown: Wesleyan University Press, 1997), esp. 118-47; and Laura Lee Downs, *Writing Gender History* (New York: Oxford Universitiy Press, 1994). Cf. Joyce Appleby, Lynn Hunt, and Margaret Jacob, *Telling the Truth About History* (New York: Norton, 1994). For responses to the "linguistic turn" and deconstructionism, see also Appleby, *A Restless Past: History and the American Public* (Lanham: Rowman & Littlefield, 2004) 123-31; and Todd Estes, "Searching for Synthesis: The Fragmentation of Early American History and the Prospects for Reunification — A Review Essay," *Register of the Kentucky Historical Society* 104 (2006) 95-126.

60. Iggers, *Historiography in the Twentieth Century*, 118.

61. On this score, see the unpacking of the deconstructionist approach in Appleby, *A Restless Past*, 127-31.

62. Van Wees, *Status Warriors*, 2.

63. An effort at establishing a sequence of events based on "old poetry" was undertaken by de Moor, *The Rise of Yahwism*.

64. Fernand Braudel, *On History*, trans. Sarah Matthews (Chicago: University of Chicago Press, 1980) 3. For a survey and critique of the *Annales* constellation of approaches, see Iggers, *Historiography in the Twentieth Century*, 51-64; cf. the reductionist and cynical assessment of John Vincent, *An Intelligent Person's Guide to History* (London: Duckworth Overlook, 2006) 160-67.

65. Braudel's approach was pioneered in biblical studies by Lawrence E. Stager, "The Archaeology of the Family in Ancient Israel," *BASOR* 260 (1985) 1-35; see also Philip J. King and Lawrence E. Stager, *Life in Biblical Israel* (Library of Ancient Israel; Louisville: Westminster John Knox, 2001) 7; and J. David Schloen, "Lawrence Stager and Biblical Archaeology," in *Exploring the* Longue Durée: *Essays in Honor of Lawrence E. Stager*, ed. Schloen (Winona Lake: Eisenbrauns, 2009) 1-3.

66. For a survey of *Annales* historians on social memory (in particular, Maurice Halbwachs, Jacques Le Goff, Pierre Nora, and Danièle Hervieu-Léger), see Mark S. Smith, *The Memoirs of God: History, Memory, and the Experience of the Divine in Ancient Israel* (Minneapolis: Fortress, 2004) 127-31; for an effort to apply this approach to ancient Israelite religion, see pp. 131-58.

67. Iggers (*Historiography in the Twentieth Century*, 77) notes Wierling's 1987 study that combines German Historical Social Science with the examination of the experience of housemaids in middle-class households.

68. See Iggers, *Historiography in the Twentieth Century*, 74-77 and 102-3.

69. For a useful survey of this approach, see Iggers, *Historiography in the Twentieth Century*, 101-17.

70. See the recent effort of William G. Dever, *The Lives of Ordinary People in Ancient Israel* (Grand Rapids: Eerdmans, 2012).

71. See the imaginative description by Karel van der Toorn, "Nine Months among the Peasants in the Palestinian Highlands: An Anthropological Perspective on Local Religion in the Early Iron Age," in *Symbiosis, Symbolism, and the Power of the Past: Canaan, Ancient Israel, and Their Neighbors — From the Late Bronze Age through Roman Palaestina*, ed. William G. Dever and Seymour Gitin (AIAR Anniversary Volume; Winona Lake: Eisenbrauns, 2003) 393-10; and the response of Dever, in "Discussions" in this volume, 556-57. For another act of "historical imagination" utilizing archaeological data, see Stager's illustrations of ancient life and household in King and Stager, *Life in Biblical Israel*, 18 (III.10), 29 (III.15).

72. E.g., in biblical studies, see J. Cheryl Exum, ed., *Virtual History and the Bible* (Leiden: Brill, 2000).

73. Here I am drawing on Stephen Greenblatt's "Toward a Poetics of Culture," in *The New Historicism*, ed. H. Aram Veeser (New York: Routledge, 1989) 1-14. This is his alternative descriptor for "New Historicism." New Historicism is valuable for thinking about the "historical" as evoked in ancient poetry, but as an essentially literary approach

it meshes less well with the textual and archaeological data of ancient societies, compared with either the *Annales* approach (noted above) or the interpretive approach undertaken by anthropologists such as Clifford Geertz; see his classic piece, "Thick Description: Toward an Interpretive Theory of Culture" in Geertz, *The Interpretation of Cultures: Selected Essays* (New York: Basic Books, 2000) 3-30; see also his lesser known essay, "A Life of Learning" (Charles Homer Haskins Lecture 1999; American Council of Learned Societies Occasional Paper 45).

74. Cf. "The Poetics and Politics of Culture," the addendum of Louis A. Montrose to Greenblatt's expression (see the preceding note). See Montrose, "Professing the Renaissance: The Poetics and Politics of Culture," in Veeser, *The New Historicism*, 15-36.

75. See Chapter Nine for the discussion of Deuteronomy 33 and its elaboration of the old trope of the march of the divine warrior in vv. 2-4.

76. Deuteronomy 32 incorporates an older trope in vv. 7-9. Poetic passages acknowledge that material embedded within them is older (see Deut. 32:7 and Hab. 3:2).

77. See, e.g., the discussion of 2 Sam. 22/Ps. 18:8-16 in Chapter Twelve.

Notes to Chapter One

1. A number of these matters are mentioned by Gregory Mobley, *The Empty Men: The Heroic Tradition of Ancient Israel* (ABRL; New York: Doubleday, 2005). A good deal of what occupies Mobley's study belongs to the Iron II period, which largely constitutes the aftermath to the story that this book tells (see Chapter Twelve).

2. The old classic on biblical and ancient Near East warfare is Yigael Yadin, *The Art of Warfare in Biblical Lands in Light of Archaeological Study*, trans. M. Pearlman (2 vols.; New York: McGraw-Hill, 1963). See also the important studies of Israel Eph'al, "The Assyrian Siege Ramp at Lachish: Military and Lexical Aspects," *TA* 11 (1984) 60-70; "On Warfare and Military Control in the Ancient Near Eastern Empires: A Research Outline," in *History, Historiography, and Interpretation*, ed. Hayim Tadmor and Moshe Weinfeld (Jerusalem: Magnes, 1983) 88-106; and *The City Besieged: Siege and Its Manifestations in the Ancient Near East* (Culture and History of the Ancient Near East 36; Leiden: Brill, 2009). Note also T. R. Hobbs, *A Time for War: A Study of Warfare in the Old Testament* (Old Testament Studies 3; Wilmington: Glazier, 1989); Philip J. King, "Warfare in the Ancient Near East," in *The Archaeology of Jordan and Beyond: Essays in Honor of James A. Sauer*, ed. Lawrence E. Stager, Joseph A. Greene, and Michael D. Coogan (Winona Lake: Eisenbrauns, 2000) 266-76; Nili Wazana, "Are Trees of the Field Human? A Biblical War Law (Deut. 20:19-20) and Neo-Assyrian Propaganda," in *Treasures on Camels' Humps: Historical and Literary Studies from the Ancient Near East Presented to Israel Eph'al*, ed. Mordechai Cogan and Dan'el Kahn (Jerusalem: Magnes, 2008) 274-95; Boyd Seevers, *Warfare in the Old Testament: The Organization, Weapons, and Tactics of Ancient Near Eastern Armies* (Grand Rapids: Kregel, 2013); and the other works cited in the Introduction, p. 343 note 38 above.

For chariotry, see Deborah O'Daniel Cantrell, *The Horsemen of Israel: Horses and Chariotry in Monarchic Israel (Ninth-Eighth Centuries* B.C.E.*)* (Winona Lake: Eisenbrauns,

2011); and Jacob L. Wright, "Chariots: Technological Developments from the 3rd Millennium BCE to the Hellenistic Period," in *Material Culture in the Biblical World,* ed. A. Berlegung, M. Daviau, M. Kamlah, and G. Lehman (Tübingen: Mohr Siebeck, 2012). To be noted in this regard is a recent find at Tel Motza of figurines of men and horses dating to the Iron IIA period. See http://www.israelnationalnews.com/News/News.aspx/163586, and http://www.haaretz.co.il/news/science/1.1894177.

For study of weapons in this region, roughly by period: Graham Philip, *Metal Weapons of the Early and Middle Bronze Ages in Syria-Palestine* (2 vols.; B.A.R. International Series 526; Oxford: B.A.R., 1989); Eli Miron, *Axes and Adzes from Canaan* (Prähistorische Bronzefunden Abteilung 9/19; Stuttgart: Steiner, 1992); Sariel Shalev, *Swords and Daggers in Late Bronze Age Canaan* (Prähistorische Bronzefunden Abteilung 4/13; Stuttgart: Steiner, 2004); and Allan Comstock Emery III, "Weapons of the Israelite Monarchy: A Catalogue with Its Linguistic and Cross-Cultural Implications" (Ph.D. diss., Harvard, 1998). See also Mark J. Fretz, "Weapons and Implements of Warfare," *ABD* 6:893-95; and Aaron J. Koller, *The Ancient Hebrew Semantic Field of Cutting Tools: A Philological, Archaeological, and Semantic Study* (CBQMS 49; Washington: Catholic Biblical Association of America, 2012).

For military terminology, see Israel Eph'al, "Lexical Notes on Some Ancient Military Terms," *ErIsr* 20 (Yigael Yadin Memorial Volume; 1989) 115-19 (Heb.).

For warfare in the ancient Near East, see also P. Abrahami, "Bibliographie sur les armées et les militaires au Proche-orient," *Revue des études militaires anciennes* 2 (2005) 3-19. Several studies have since appeared: Michael G. Hasel, *Military Practice and Polemic: Israel's Laws of Warfare in Near Eastern Perspective* (Berrien Springs: Andrews University Press, 2005); William J. Hamblin, *Warfare in the Ancient Near East to 1600 BC: Holy Warriors at the Dawn of History* (New York: Routledge, 2006); Fabrice De Backer, "Some Basic Tactics of Neo-Assyrian Warfare," *UF* 39 (2007) 69-99; Zainab Bahrani, *Rituals of War: The Body and Violence in Mesopotamia* (New York: Zone, 2008); and Jordi Vidal, "The Use of Military Standards by Old Babylonian Armies," *Akkadica* 130 (2009) 43-51. See also two collections of essays: Philippe Abrahami and Laura Battini, eds., *Les armées du Proche Orient ancien (IIIe-Ier mill. Av. J. C.): Actes du colloque international organisé à Lyon les 1er et 2 décembre 2006, Maison de l'Orient et de la Méditerranée* (B.A.R. International Series 1855; Oxford: Hedges, 2008); Jordi Vidal, ed., *Studies on War in the Ancient Near East: Collected Essays on Military History* (AOAT 372; Münster: Ugarit-Verlag, 2010), with considerable prior bibliog. in Vidal's "Introduction"; and also *Directions in the Military History of the Ancient World,* ed. Lee L. Brice and Jennifer T. Roberts (Association of Ancient Historians 10; Claremont: Regina, 2011). Valuable information on sieges, as well as the equipment, processes of siege, diplomacy in siege, and starving out people under siege is provided by Wilfred G. Lambert, *Babylonian Oracle Questions* (Winona Lake: Eisenbrauns, 2007) 144-47, 156.

For a survey of secondary literature on warfare in the ancient world, including for the Hittites and Greeks, see Barry Strauss, *The Trojan War: A New History* (New York: Simon & Schuster, 2006) 234-39. For classical Greece, see Hans van Wees, *Greek Warfare: Myths and Realities* (London: Duckworth, 2004); J. E. Lendon, *Soldiers and Ghosts: A History of Battle in Classical Antiquity* (New Haven: Yale University Press, 2005); and

Everett L. Wheeler, ed., *The Armies of Classical Greece* (Aldershot: Ashgate, 2007). For the Hellenistic period, see Angelos Chaniotis, *War in the Hellenistic World: A Social and Cultural History* (Malden: Blackwell, 2005).

3. On these matters, see the survey of Victor H. Matthews, "Introduction," in *Writing and Reading War: Rhetoric, Gender, and Ethics in Biblical and Modern Contexts,* ed. Brad E. Kelle and Frank Ritchel Ames (SBLSymS 42; Atlanta: Society of Biblical Literature, 2008) 2-4.

4. It would be possible to supplement this discussion with comparable material from the *Iliad* and Mesopotamian literature, but these lie beyond the scope of this chapter.

5. Cf. the comparable schema in Martin van Creveld, *The Culture of War* (New York: Ballantine, 2008).

6. The so-called "old poetry" in Biblical Hebrew trends down into at least the ninth century. See Chapter Eight for discussion. My sense of the timeframe of biblical prose historiography is mostly ninth-eighth century and later. The ninth century onward correlates with the emergence of monarchic apparatus for such historiography, which would comport with the theory that the Hebrew national script emerged in the ninth century, as suggested by Christopher A. Rollston, *Writing and Literacy in the World of Ancient Israel* (Archaeology and Biblical Studies 11; Atlanta: Society of Biblical Literature, 2010) 42-46; and "An Old Hebrew Stone Inscription from the City of David: A Trained Hand and a Remedial Hand on the Same Inscription," in *Puzzling Out the Past: Studies in the Northwest Semitic Languages and Literatures in Honor of Bruce Zuckerman,* ed. Marilyn J. Lundberg, Steven Fine, and Wayne T. Pitard (CHANE 55; Leiden: Brill, 2012) 189-96. Rollston notes that there is no Hebrew evidence for this ninth-century date (the evidence offered is Moabite). He suggests that the national script is a deliberate development; by contrast, other scholars see no such deliberate development, but simply an evolutionary one (see A. R. Millard, "The ABCs of Early Israel" [review of Rollston, *Writing and Literacy*], *BAR* 38/4 [2012] 59-60). The ninth century onward would work with a number of West Semitic inscribed stelae. For reflections on the attestation of stelae, see John A. Emerton, "The Kingdoms of Judah and Israel and Ancient Hebrew History Writing," in *Biblical Hebrew in Its Northwest Semitic Setting: Typological and Historical Perspectives,* ed. Steven E. Fassberg and Avi Hurvitz (Jerusalem: Magnes; Winona Lake: Eerdmans, 2006) 48. To be sure, writing is attested earlier (see Chapter Eleven for more on Iron I inscriptions). The Iron IIA inscription at Khirbet Qeiyafa has been claimed to point to early monarchic scribalism, according to Emile Puech, "L'ostracon de Khirbet Qeyafa et les débuts de la royauté en Israël," *RB* 117 (2010) 162-84; for the inscription, see also Yosef Garfinkel and Saar Ganor, *Khirbet Qeiyafa,* Vol. 1: *Excavation Report 2007-2008* (Jerusalem: Israel Exploration Society/Institute of Archaeology, Hebrew University, 2009) 243-70; for proposals about the site's identification, see the survey in Yigal Levin, "The Identification of Khirbet Qeiyafa: A New Suggestion," *BASOR* 367 (2012) 73-86. At the same time, doubts have been expressed about whether the Qeiyafa inscription's script or its language is Hebrew. See Christopher A. Rollston, "The Khirbet Qeiyafa Ostracon: Methodological Musings and Caveats," *TA* 38 (2011) 67-82; and "What's the Oldest Hebrew Inscription?" *BAR* 38/3 (2012) 32-40, 66-67. Such doubts are reasonable, yet these do not preclude the possibility that the inscription is Hebrew; the location of the site would arguably mili-

tate in favor of this view. For this issue, as well as other matters, see Aaron Demsky, "An Iron Age IIA Alphabetic Writing Exercise from Kirbet Qeiyafa," *IEJ* 62 (2012) 186-99. In general, the repertoire of tenth-ninth century inscriptions in Israel is, at present, fairly meager; for this corpus, see Amihai Mazar, "Three 10th-9th Century B.C.E. Inscriptions from Tēl Reḥōv," in *Saxa Loquentur: Studien zur Archäologie Palästinas/Israels: Festschrift für Volkmar Fritz zum 65. Geburtstag,* ed. Cornelis G. den Hertzog, Ulrich Hübner, and Stefan Münger; AOAT 302; Münster: Ugarit-Verlag, 2003) 171-84; Amihai Mazar and Shmuel Aḥituv, "The Inscriptions from Tel Rehov and Their Contribution to Research on Script and Writing in the Iron Age IIA Period," *ErIsr* 30 (Amnon Ben-Tor Volume; 2011) 300-16 (Heb.); and André Lemaire, "West Semitic Epigraphy and the History of the Levant during the 12th-10th Centuries BCE," in *The Ancient Near East in the 12th-10th Centuries BCE: Culture and History. Proceedings of the International Conference, Held at the University of Haifa, 2-5 May, 2010,* ed. Gershon Galil, Ayelet Gilboa, Aren M. Maeir, and Dan'el Kahn (AOAT 392; Münster: Ugarit-Verlag, 2012) 291-307.

Connected to the issue of national writing is the nature of Jerusalem as a capital in the Iron II period. The issues are complex and highly contentious. See Amihai Mazar, "Jerusalem in the 10th Century B.C.E.: The Glass Half Full," in *Essays on Ancient Israel in Its Ancient Near Eastern Context,* ed. Yairah Amit (Winona Lake: Eisenbrauns, 2006) 255-72; Joe Uziel and Itzhaq Shai, "Iron Age Jerusalem: Temple-Palace, Capital City," *JAOS* 127 (2007) 161-70; and F. González de Canales, L. Serrano and J. Llompart, "Tarshish and the United Monarchy of Israel," *Ancient Near Eastern Studies* 47 (2010) 137-64; cf. Nadav Na'aman, "The Growth and Development of Judah and Jerusalem in the Eighth Century BCE: A Rejoinder," *RB* 116 (2009) 321-35. See also Margreet Steiner, "Propaganda in Jerusalem: State Formation in Iron Age Judah," in *Israel in Transition: From Late Bronze II to Iron IIa (c. 1250-850 B.C.E.),* Vol. 1: *The Archaeology,* ed. Lester L. Grabbe (LHB/OTS 491; New York: Continuum, 2008) 193-202. Steiner sees Iron IIA Judah as an early state and Iron IIB as a mature state. For Steiner, Iron IIA Jerusalem involved a territory with loose boundaries, a military leader as ruler, a monopoly of force, two social classes, small administrative apparatus, a traveling ruler without a fixed court but with a capital with monumental architecture, and a demand for prestige goods. Iron IIA Jerusalem did not have mature state characteristics of craft specializations, standing army, money, regular tax levies, or a large bureaucracy. The recent archaeological work of Eilat Mazar (*The Palace of King David: Excavations at the Summit of the City of David* [Jerusalem: Hotsa'at Shoham, 2009]) has been the subject of considerable debate; see the recent discussion of Avraham Faust, "The Large Stone Structure in the City of David: A Reexamination," *ZDPV* 126 (2010) 117-22.

A related problem involves the chronology of the tribal kingdoms of Israel and Judah, much debated since the 1990s, e.g., Israel Finkelstein, "The Archaeology of the United Monarchy: An Alternative View," *Levant* 28 (1996) 177-87; Amihai Mazar, "Iron Age Chronology: A Reply to I. Finkelstein," *Levant* 29 (1997) 157-67; Israel Finkelstein, "Bible Archaeology or Archaeology of Palestine in the Iron Age? A Rejoinder," *Levant* 30 (1998) 167-73; and Finkelstein, "The Beginning of the State in Israel and Judah," *ErIsr* 26 (Frank Moore Cross Volume; 1999) *132-41. See more recently Israel Finkelstein and Amihai Mazar, eds., *The Quest for the Historical Israel: Debating Archaeology and the*

History of Early Israel (Atlanta: Society of Biblical Literature, 2007); Finkelstein and Eli Piasetzky, "The Iron Age Chronology Debate: Is the Gap Narrowing?" *NEA* 74 (2011) 50-54; and Amihai Mazar, "The Iron Age Chronology Debate: Is the Gap Narrowing? Another Viewpoint," *NEA* 74 (2011) 105-11.

7. What is Israelite in this period is a major question. See Elizabeth M. Bloch-Smith, "Israelite Ethnicity in Iron I: Archaeology Preserves What Is Remembered and What Is Forgotten in Israel's History," *JBL* 122 (2003) 401-25; cf. Robert D. Miller II, "Identifying Earliest Israel," *BASOR* 333 (2004) 55-68. This issue will be a particular challenge in trying to situate Israelite heroic poetry in conjunction with Iron I extrabiblical evidence, a matter taken up in Chapter Eleven.

8. The methodological underpinnings of this point are taken up below in section 3.

9. The passage also uses *'ḥz, "to learn" (according to NJPS 1731 n. c).

10. See also 1 Chr. 5:18; cf. Hos. 7:15. Note also that Artemis taught Menelaus to hunt, according to *Iliad* 5.51. For some remarks on the training of warriors in classical tradition, see Vermeule, *Aspects of Death in Early Greek Art and Poetry* (Berkeley: University of California, 1979) 99.

11. See Chapter Four for discussion. Cf. the famous hunting scenes on gold bowls from Ugarit; for photographs, see Joan Aruz, Kim Benzel, and Jean M. Evans, eds., *Beyond Babylon: Art, Trade, and Diplomacy in the Second Millennium* B.C. (New York: Metropolitan Museum of Art; New Haven: Yale University Press, 2008) 240-41, #146, and 242-43, #147.

12. The use of **lmd* in KTU 1.18 I 29 and 2 Sam. 22/Ps. 18:35 is noted by Simon B. Parker, *The Pre-Biblical Narrative Tradition: Essays on the Ugaritic Poems* Keret *and* Aqhat (SBLRBS 24; Atlanta: Scholars, 1989) 116.

13. Cf. the negative formulation in Mic. 4:3 = Isa. 2:4: "and no longer shall they learn (**lmd*) war." This follows a description of getting rid of weapons and not taking up arms.

14. See Chapter Four for discussion.

15. Cf. "hunters" in Akkadian *(bā'irtu)* as a military term, e.g., Lambert, *Babylonian Oracle Questions,* 24-25, line 38, and 144.

16. For a comparison of epic heroes becoming warriors and the passage through male adolescence in "preurban societies," see Hope Nash Wolff, *A Study in the Narrative Structure of Three Epic Poems:* Gilgamesh, *The* Odyssey, Beowulf (New York: Garland, 1987) 82-86. She comments (p. 88): "The stories in the epic myth, founded as they are in the life-cycles of heroes who are models for men, refer to this period of life so much because it is a crucial time for teaching the values, practices and relationships that man in culture needs to know."

17. Cf. Ugaritic *nʿr,* for both a "boy, youth" and "assistant, page," in *DULAT* 616, translated as "retainer" in J. David Schloen, *The House of the Father as Fact and Symbol: Patrimonialism in Ugarit and the Ancient Near East* (Studies in the Archaeology and History of the Levant 2; Winona Lake: Eisenbrauns, 2001) 324-25. See Judg. 9:54; 1 Sam. 14:1; 2 Sam. 18:15 and 19:18 for *naʿar/nĕʿārîm* also said to be arms-bearers; cf. the West Semitic loanword, **naʿarūna,* used for "soldiers, special detachment," in James E. Hoch, *Semitic Words in Egyptian Texts of the New Kingdom and Third Intermediate Period* (Princeton: Princeton University Press, 1994) 182-83 #24; and *ANET,* 256 n. 12 and 476 and 478. Hoch

(p. 183) suggests that the final *-n* on the Egyptian word points to "a derivation from a dialect/language such as Moabite or Aramaic." Add also three attestations in the Deir 'Alla inscription; see W. Randall Garr, *Dialectic Geography of Syria-Palestine, 1000-586 B.C.E.* (Philadelphia: University of Pennsylvania Press, 1985) 89-91. There are also some instances attested in Ugaritic; perhaps these are dialectic variant forms (see *UG,* 294, #53.313). For the BH masculine plural forms ending in *-în,* including in Judg. 5:10, see GKC 87e, which regards the forms as late; and Joüon-Muraoka, par. 90c, which takes the forms as Aramaic. The example in Judg. 5:10 may reflect a regional form, given the variants in Ugaritic, Moabite, and the Deir 'Alla inscription. See Chapter Eight for the language of the poem in Judges 5.

18. For archaeological evidence for bird hunting, see Hermann Genz, "Stunning Bolts: Late Bronze Age Hunting Weapons in the Ancient Near East," *Levant* 39 (2007) 47-69. For hunting iconography, see M. C. Loulloupos, "Hunting Scenes on Cypriot Vases of the Geometric Period," in *Early Society in Cyprus,* ed. Edgar Peltenburg (Edinburgh: Edinburgh University Press in association with the National Museums of Scotland and the A. G. Leventis Foundation, 1989) 171-79. For further discussion about hunting, see the following section.

19. See Victor Avigdor Hurowitz, "The Biblical Arms Bearer (נושא כלים)," in *"Up to the Gates of Ekron": Essays on the Archaeology and History of the Eastern Mediterranean in Honor of Seymour Gitin,* ed. Sidnie White Crawford (Jerusalem: W. F. Albright Institute of Archaeological Research/Israel Exploration Society, 2007) 344-49.

20. E.g., see "The Hunter," in Benjamin R. Foster, *Before the Muses: An Anthology of Akkadian Literature* (3rd ed.; Bethesda: CDL, 2005) 336-37. Note the iconography of the hunt on a Syrian dagger hilt, in Henri Frankfort, *The Art and Architecture of the Ancient Orient* (New York: Penguin, 1970) 245, #282. For hunting following battle, see A. Kirk Grayson, *Assyrian Rulers of the Early First Millennium BC,* Vol. 2: *(858-745 BC)* (Royal Inscriptions of Mesopotamia: Assyrian Periods 3; Toronto: University of Toronto Press, 1996) 54 (iii, lines 37b-45a), 55 (iv lines 15b-22a), etc.

21. For these cases, see Cyrus H. Gordon, "Indo-European and Hebrew Epic," *ErIsr* 5 (Benjamin Mazar Volume; 1958) 11*. To this theme, Gordon would add as an example the bow of Ishmael in Gen. 21:12-21. For more on the bow, see Chapter Four.

22. See Chapter Four for discussion.

23. The use of the bow is attested for several deities: Anat (see KTU 1.3 II 15-16); Baal (1.10 II 6); and Yahweh (Hab. 3:9, 11). Note also *rišpê-qāšet* in Ps. 76:4, usually understood as fiery arrows or the like (cf. Song 8:6), perhaps echoing Rashpu as a warrior god. Weaponry is known in iconography from a number of sources, including the Lachish reliefs and on a bulla recovered from Jerusalem, published by Nahman Avigad, "The 'Governor of the City' Bulla," in *Ancient Jerusalem Revealed,* ed. Hillel Geva (Jerusalem: Israel Exploration Society, 1994) 138; Gabriel Barkay, "A Second Governor of the City' Bulla," in Geva, *Ancient Jerusalem Revealed,* 141; and Aaron J. Koller, *The Semantic Field of Cutting Tools in Biblical Hebrew: The Interface of Philological, Semantic, and Archaeological Evidence* (CBQMS 49; Washington: Catholic Biblical Association of America, 2012) 189-90. See also the archer in the iconography of Kuntillet Ajrud (Pithos B), presented by Pirhiya Beck, in Ze'ev Meshel, *Kuntillet 'Ajrud (Ḥorvat Teman): An Iron Age II Religious Site on*

the Judah-Sinai Border (Jerusalem: Israel Exploration Society, 2012) 144-45, 177-78. It is to be noted that an Assyrian-style depiction of a warrior shooting an arrow with a bow with a Hebrew inscription (*lhgb*, "(belonging) to Hagab") has been discovered recently in archaeological excavations in the western wall plaza in Jerusalem (http://antiquities.org.il/article_Item_eng.asp?sec_id=25&subj_id=240&id=1442&module_id=#as; accessed 2 March 2012). The context is said to be a seventh-century building. The seal is also claimed to be unique, as it is the first known example with a Hebrew PN decorated in Assyrian style. I thank Elizabeth Bloch-Smith for drawing my attention to this information. The rod *(mṭh)* is also attested in the prose sources, e.g., Jonathan's in 1 Sam. 14:27, 43. Note also Anat's *mṭ* (KTU 1.3 II 15, perhaps "rod"; cf. "club," in *UNP* 107) and Yahweh's (rod or arrows in Hab. 3:9).

24. See Chapter Six for discussion.

25. ʿAthtart wields a spear (*rmḥ* in KTU 1.92. 7, 12), as does Yahweh (**ḥnyt* in Hab. 3:11).

26. BH *ḥereb* may be a short sword or dagger; "sword" would be misleading in many cases (see esp. Judg. 3:16, 21). For swords, see King, "Warfare in the Ancient Near East," 268-69. King believes that *ḥereb* may refer to either the straight sword or the curved sickle sword, which he suggests is indicated in the BH expression "with the edge of the sword" (e.g., Josh. 10:28-39). See also the extensive discussion of Koller, "The Ancient Hebrew Semantic Field of Cutting Tools," 172-226. See the following section for the long swords in Iron II Israel.

27. Fernando Santos-Granero, "Introduction," in *The Occult Life of Things: Native Amazonian Theories of Materiality and Personhood* (Tucson: University of Arizona Press, 2009) 14.

28. See Chapter Six for discussion.

29. Cf. Gen. 49:21?

30. See pp. 336-37 note 8 above.

31. Note also the physical strength and size of David's opponents in 2 Sam. 21:16, 19, 20.

32. Ehud is said to make his dagger (Judg. 3:16), the one that he straps on under his clothing (v. 16) and later uses to kill Eglon (v. 21). Cf. Papyrus Amherst 63, col. xx, lines 15-18, in *COS* 1:325.

33. This passage is discussed in Chapter Six.

34. See Udo Rüterswörden, "Der Bogen in Genesis 9," *UF* 20 (1988) 247-63, here 257; and J. A. Emerton, "Treading the Bow," *VT* 53 (2003) 465-86.

35. Cf. the deficit of shield and spear in Judg. 5:8; see also 1 Sam. 13:19-22.

36. See the discussion of these texts in Chapter Four. That this notion evidently appears in legal material seems to suggest a cultural practice and not only a literary description.

37. The vow in KTU 1.22 II 16 (*UNP* 202; see Chapter Five for reference to the passage) is unclear, due to its broken context. Cf. sacrifices before battle, in Kirta, in KTU 1.14 II 13-26 (*UNP* 14)//III 55-IV 8 (*UNP* 18); cf. Grayson, *Assyrian Rulers of the Early First Millennium* BC, 2:30 (iv line 2). Oaths taken before battle are also attested, in EA 74.30-32 and ARM 26:24; see Karel van der Toorn, *Family Religion in Babylonia, Syria,*

and Israel: Continuity and Changes in the Forms of Religious Life (Studies in the History and Culture of the Ancient Near East 7; Leiden: Brill, 1996) 89; and Daniel E. Fleming, *Democracy's Ancient Ancestors* (Cambridge: Cambridge University Press, 2004) 200. I am grateful to Brendon Benz for drawing my attention to these references concerning oaths before battle.

38. See lines 5-6: "bless Baal on a day of war [. . .], the name of El on the day of wa[r . . .]. Shmuel Aḥituv, Esther Eshel, and Ze'ev Meshel, in Meshel, *Kuntillet 'Ajrud,* 110 and 133. See also Aḥituv, *Echoes from the Past* (Jerusalem: Carta, 2008), 324-25.

39. Frank Moore Cross and David Noel Freedman, *Studies in Ancient Yahwistic Poetry* (2nd ed.; BRS; Grand Rapids: Eerdmans; Livonia: Dove, 1997) 3: "The Oracles of Balaam belong to the category of oracles delivered by a seer before battle."

40. For prebiblical West Semitic examples, see the Mari evidence adduced by Jack M. Sasson, "Oracle Inquiries in Judges," *Birkat Shalom: Studies in the Bible, Ancient Near Eastern Literature, and Postbiblical Judaism Presented to Shalom M. Paul on the Occasion of His Seventieth Birthday,* ed. Chaim Cohen et al. (Winona Lake: Eisenbrauns, 2008) 1:149-68. See also the older study of James S. Ackerman, "Prophecy and Warfare in Early Israel: A Study of the Deborah-Barak Story," *BASOR* 220 (1976) 5-13. Duane L. Christensen situates Deborah within a tradition of oracular divination delivered on the occasion of battle. As he observes, Deborah makes a prediction in Judg. 4:9 that comes to pass in v. 21. The arc of the story would bear out her profile as a prophet. Under this interpretation in 4:5b, *mišpaṭ* would be a specific divine response to the situation at hand. See Christensen, *Prophecy and War in Ancient Israel: Studies in the Oracles Against the Nations in Old Testament Prophecy* (Berkeley: BIBAL, 1989) 29. Other biblical examples of a war oracle victory pronounced by an intermediary include Num. 24:17; 2 Kgs. 3:18-19; 6:9-10, according to Christensen, *Prophecy and War,* 24, 35. See also the role of Samuel in 1 Sam. 7:7-11. Deut. 33:20 might be explained against this background, given its larger military context. A most explicit biblical example involves 1 Kings 22. See also the oracle given on the occasion of a military siege in the Zakkur inscription (KAI 202, conveniently presented by C. L. Seow, in *Prophets and Prophecy in the Ancient Near East,* ed. Martti Nissinen (SBLWAW 12; Atlanta: Society of Biblical Literature, 2003) 204, 206). For Akkadian examples of divination in the context of a military campaign, see Abraham Malamat, *Mari and the Early Israelite Experience* (Schweich Lectures 1984; Oxford: Oxford University Press, 1989) 90-92; Tikva Frymer-Kensky, *Reading the Women of the Bible* (New York: Schocken, 2002) 48; and Nissinen, *Prophets and Prophecy,* 39-40, 144-45, 146-48. See also the Epic of Zimri-Lim: "The hero of the land saw his sign, the prophet" (quoted in Nissinen, *Prophets and Prophecy,* 90). Divine inquiry is known in biblical prose sources (Deut. 1:27; Josh. 6:2; 7:7; Judg. 1:2; 13:1; 1 Kgs. 22:6, 15; 2 Kgs. 18:30; 19:10).

Another approach to Deborah has been taken by Klaas Spronk following J. C. de Moor, who compared KTU 1.124.3 and 12, where divination of the divine eponymous ancestor Didanu is to issue in a "judgment" or "ruling" *(mṯpṭ).* See de Moor, "Studies in the New Alphabetic Texts from Ras Shamra II," *UF* 2 (1970) 304. Spronk uses this Ugaritic evidence to suggest that Deborah is a necromancer like the woman of Endor in 1 Samuel 28. See Spronk, "Deborah, a Prophetess: The Meaning and Background of Judges 4:4-5," in *The Elusive Prophet: The Prophet as a Historical Person, Literary Character, and Anon-*

ymous Artist. Papers Read at the Eleventh Joint Meeting of the Society for Old Testament Study and het Oudtestamentisch Werkgezelschap in Nederland en België, held at Soesterberg 2000, ed. J. C. de Moor (OtSt 45; Leiden: Brill, 2001) 232-42. Noting the work of de Moor, *HALOT* 2:651 adds Zeph. 2:3; Mal. 2:17 and compares Ps. 50:6 and Isa. 58:2.

41. For this verse, see below in note 59.

42. See Susan Niditch, *"My Brother Esau Is a Hairy Man": Hair and Identity in Ancient Israel* (Oxford: Oxford University Press, 2008) 77-78. For prebattle hair ritual as the ancient background of the nazirite vow, see Chapter Eight; and the mythological "long-haired heroes" in *COS* 2:312; cf. the hair-do of certain priests in *COS* 1:532 (compared in n. 11). Corresponding to this practice is abstention from sexual relations with women, attested at least in later biblical sources (1 Sam. 21:4, 5; 2 Sam. 11:11), as part of the maintenance of ritual purity (1 Sam. 21:5).

43. Similarly, a practice known from Ugaritic sources is the self-marking of the warrior with red (evidently suggesting the blood of battle) in KTU 1.19 IV 41-43 (*UNP* 77); cf. KTU 1.14 II 9-11 (*UNP* 14) and III 52-54 (*UNP* 18) and KTU 1.3 II 2-3 (*UNP* 107). For discussion, see Chapter Three, section 3.

44. Perhaps Lamech's poem in Gen. 4:23-24 should be understood as a song of the sort voiced by warriors before heading into battle. See Stanley Gevirtz, *Patterns in the Early Poetry of Israel* (SAOC 32; Chicago: University of Chicago, 1963) 25-34.

45. The motif is known in royal inscriptions as well, e.g., Grayson, *Assyrian Rulers of the Early First Millennium* BC, 2:9 (line 34), 15 (line 26), 21 (line 59), 29 (ii line 4), 34 (lines 39 and 43), 39 (line 42), etc. See the washing of the weapons in the Mediterranean along with sacrifices (p. 51, lines 24-26).

46. Baruch A. Levine (*Numbers 21–36* [AB 4A; New York: Doubleday, 2000] 186) suggests that this line does not apply to "the lion" but to the combatants, as "lions would not drink the blood of stabbed enemy warriors." Cf. Psalm 58:11(10): "his feet he will wash in the blood of the wicked." Note also Psalm 68:24(23). For further discussion, see Mark S. Smith, *The Early History of God* (2nd ed.; BRS; Grand Rapids: Eerdmans and Livonia: Dove, 2002) 105.

47. Cf. Numbers 23:24; 24:8.

48. For presentation of this text with discussion of this imagery, see Chapter Six, section 3.

49. For these points, see Levine, *Numbers 21–36*, 186.

50. See James K. Hoffmeier, "David Triumph's Over Goliath: 1 Samuel 17:54 and Ancient Near Eastern Analogues," in *Egypt, Canaan and Israel: History, Imperialism, Ideology and Literature: Proceedings of a Conference at the University of Haifa, 3-7 May 2009*, ed. S. Bar, D. Kahn, and J. J. Shirley (CHANE 52; Leiden: Brill, 2011) 87-114.

51. See Pardee, *RCU*, 84-85; and Steven W. Holloway, "KTU 1.162 and the Offering of a Shield," *UF* 30 (1998) 353-61. For other proposed Mesopotamian examples, see Jordi Vidal, "Prestige Weapons in an Amorite Context," *JNES* 70 (2011) 247-52, here 248. For the function of weapons to witness and make judgments in OB texts, see Kathryn E. Slanski, "Representations of the Divine on the Babyonian Entitlement Monuments *(kudurrus). Part 1: Divine Symbols,*" *AfO* 50 (2003/4) 318-21.

52. To mention only two examples, note the dedication of weapons by Gudea of

Lagash and by Zimri-Lim of Mari. For the former, see Zainab Bahrani, *Rituals of War,* 189; for the latter, see Abraham Malamat, "Weapons Deposited in a Sanctuary by Zimri-Lim of Mari and David and Saul of Israel," in *Ex Mesopotamia et Syria Lux: Festschrift für Manfried Dietrich zu seinem 65. Geburtstag,* ed. Oswald Loretz, Kai A. Metzler, and Hanspeter Schaudig (AOAT 281; Münster: Ugarit-Verlag, 2002) 325-27. See also Vidal, "Prestige Weapons," 248. The practice of giving names to weapons found in Ugaritic (KTU 1.2 IV; *UNP* 103-4) and in Mesopotamian texts (Bahrani, *Rituals of War,* 189-92) is likewise of interest.

53. For details, see Amihai Mazar, *Excavations at Tell Qasile.* Part 2: *The Philistine Sanctuary: Various Finds, the Pottery, Conclusions, Appendixes* (Qedem 20; Jerusalem: Institute of Archaeology, Hebrew University, 1985) 3-4. See also *NEAEHL* 4:1210.

54. See Malamat, "Weapons Deposited in a Sanctuary," 327.

55. Vidal, "Prestige Weapons," 250.

56. Primary evidence for West Semitic "*ḥērem*-warfare" includes the Mesha stele (KAI 181:15-18), as well as many biblical passages (see BDB, 355-56). For the possible reading of the word in line 5 of the Tel Qeiyafa inscription, see Ada Yardeni, "Further Observations on the Ostracon," in Garfinkel and Ganor, *Khirbet Qeiyafa,* 1:259-60; and Puech, "L'ostracon de Khirbet Qeyafa," 171. For a possible reference to the practice, see also the Incirli Phoenician inscription, lines 11-15, as read by Stephen A. Kaufman, "The Phoenician Inscription of the Incirli Trilingual: A Tentative Reconstruction and Translation," *Maarav* 14/2 (2007) 12, 15, 23. For secondary literature of "*ḥērem*-warfare," see *UBC* 2:178-85; Lauren Monroe, "Israelite, Moabite and Sabaean War–*ḥērem* Traditions and the Forging of National Identity: Reconsidering the Sabaean Text RES 3945 in Light of Biblical and Moabite Evidence," *VT* 57 (2007) 318-41; Rüdiger Schmitt, *Der "Heilige Krieg" im Pentateuch und im deuteronomistischen Geschichtswerk: Studien zur Forschungs-, Rezeptions- und Religionsgeschichte von Krieg und Bann im Alten Testament* (AOAT 381; Münster: Ugarit-Verlag, 2011), esp. 56-61, 101-2, 212-13; Reinhard G. Kratz, "Chemosh's Wrath and Yahweh's No: Ideas of Divine Wrath in Moab and Israel," in *Divine Wrath and Divine Mercy in the World of Antiquity,* ed. Kratz and Hermann Spieckermann (FAT 2/33; Tübingen: Mohr Siebeck, 2008) 92-121, translated as "Der Zorn Kamoschs und das Nein JHWHs Vorstellungen von Zorn Gottes in Moab und Israel," in Kratz, *Prophetenstudien: Kleine Schriften II* (FAT 74; Tübingen: Mohr Siebeck, 2011) 71-98; Reinhard Achenbach, "Divine Warfare and YHWH's Wars: Religious Ideologies of War in the Ancient Near East and in the Old Testament," in Galil, et al., *The Ancient Near East in the 12th-10th Centuries BCE,* 1-26, here 16-21; and Ziony Zevit, "Mesha's *Ryt* in the Context of Moabite and Israelite Bloodletting," in Lundberg, Fine, and Pitard, *Puzzling Out the Past,* 235-38. Several of these treatments overlook the Ugaritic evidence; see Mark S. Smith, "Anat's Warfare Cannibalism and the West Semitic Ban," in *The Pitcher Is Broken: Memorial Essays in Honor of Gösta W. Ahlström,* ed. Lowell K. Handy and Stephen Holloway (JSOT-Sup 190; Sheffield: JSOT, 1995) 368-86. The Hebrew term *ḥērem,* usually translated as "ritual destruction, ban," describes a type of warfare in which enemies and living things connected with them are consecrated to the deity by killing them following battle. For further explication of "*ḥērem*-warfare," see the discussion of Anat in Chapter Six. For the destruction of humans captured in battle, note also Grayson, *Assyrian Rulers of the Early*

First Millennium BC, 2:14, lines 16-17: "(I) burned their adolescent boys (and girls)." Such *ḥērem*-warfare may presuppose the use of altars for sacrifice; this is known from prose sources such as 1 Sam. 14:35, which relates that the altar for postbattle sacrifice was the beginning of Saul's practice of "building" altars; cf. the literary-theological appreciation of this altar by L. Daniel Hawk, "Saul's Altar," *CBQ* 72 (2010) 678-87. Compare the report in Diodorus Siculus (20.65) that the Carthaginian army has "a sacred tent *(tēn hieran skēnēn)* . . . near the altar *(plēsion ousan tou bōmou)*"; see John Pairman Brown, "Peace Symbolism in Ancient Military Vocabulary," *VT* 21 (1971) 1-23, here 22.

57. For bird and dogs as preying on the corpses of warriors in classical texts (e.g., *Iliad* 11.454, 16.255 and 22.42, 66), see Vermeule, *Aspects of Death in Early Greek Art and Poetry*, 104-6. Vermeule also notes an Assyrian relief dating to Sennacherib depicting birds attacking a corpse.

58. See also the alternative tradition presented in 2 Sam. 21:10-14.

59. E.g., see Exod. 32:17-18 reflecting military song in the army camp, discussed in Levine, *Numbers 21–36*, 96. For other correlations in Exodus 32 with notions of the warrior camp in 1 Samuel 29, see "battle" in v. 4; *ʿnh* in v. 18 (cf. 1 Sam. 29:5); dance in v. 19 (cf. 1 Sam. 29:5). Note also *ṣḥq*, "to sport" in Exod. 32:6 (translated "to dance," by NJPS, and "to revel" by NRSV and NABRE), the same root in 2 Sam. 2:14 for warriors "sporting," by engaging in man-to-man combat. For these observations, see J. Gerald Janzen, "The Character of the Calf and Its Cult in Exodus 32," CBQ 52 (1990) 597-607; and Stephen C. Russell, *Images of Egypt in Early Biblical Literature: Cisjordan-Israelite, Transjordan-Israelite, and Judahite Portrayals* (BZAW 403; Berlin: de Gruyter, 2009) 51-54. Russell also notes the possible relationship of **prʿ* in Exod. 32:25 for the hair practice in Judg. 5:2 and Deut. 32:42 noted above. For man-to-man combat elsewhere in heroic literature, see Roland de Vaux, "Single Combat in the Old Testament," in *The Bible and the Ancient Near East*, trans. Damian McHugh (Garden City: Doubleday, 1971) 122-35; Harry Hoffner, "A Hittite Analogue to the David and Goliath Contest of Champions?" *CBQ* 30 (1968) 220-25; Mobley, *The Empty Men*, 51-55; David A. Bosworth, *The Story Within a Story in Biblical Hebrew Narrative* (CBQMS 45; Washington: Catholic Biblical Association of America, 2008) 88; and Alan Millard, "The Armor of Goliath," in *Exploring the Longue Durée: Essays in Honor of Lawrence E. Stager*, ed. J. David Schloen (Winona Lake: Eisenbrauns, 2009) 337-43, here 339-40. Note also iconographic evidence, e.g., two pairs of warriors in combat on a Syrian cylinder seal dated ca. 1850-1620 B.C.E., in Beatrice Teissier, *Ancient Near Eastern Cylinder Seals from the Marcopolic Collection* (Berkeley: University of California Press; Beverly Hills: Summa, 1984) 87-88 and 272 #547. See Chapter Six below for further discussion.

60. Cf. 1 Sam. 30:16.

61. See the final section of Chapter Six for text, translation, and discussion.

62. See Chapter Eleven for the case of David, in 1 Sam. 18:7; 21:11, and 29:5.

63. For the massive drinking in lines 8-17 and the passage as a whole, see Chapter Six.

64. *ANEP*, #332. Cf. the description of naked men paraded, due to their defeat at the hands of Erra, in Erra and Ishum III:20-21, in Foster, *Before the Muses*, 897.

65. For taking spoils, see also KTU 2.61, esp. line 6; Deut. 33:21; Isa. 9:2(3). Cf. the failure to take spoils in Judg. 5:19. Perhaps 2 Sam. 1:24 is to be heard in light of the failure

to win battle and thus to take spoils. For a discussion of evidence from later biblical sources in light of Mari, see Malamat, *Mari and the Early Israelite Experience,* 75-79; see the response of Moshe Greenberg, "Is There a Parallel in the Mari Tablets to the Biblical Herem?" *Er-Isr* 24 (Abraham Malamat Volume; 1993) 49-53 (Heb.). Note also the division of spoils of war, with some given to the deity, in Gen. 14:20; Num. 31:25-54; 1 Chr. 18:11 (references courtesy of K. Lawson Younger).

66. See Chapter Ten for a detailed discussion of 2 Sam. 1:19-27, where it is suggested that vv. 26-27 may have a different setting.

67. Gordon, "Indo-European and Hebrew Epic," 12*.

68. Greene, "The Natural Tears of Epic," in *Epic Traditions in the Contemporary World,* ed. Margaret Beissinger, Jane Tylus, and Susanne Wofford (Berkeley: University of California Press, 1999) 195.

69. Greene, "The Natural Tears of Epic," 189.

70. See Eunice B. Poethig, "The Victory Song Tradition of the Women of Israel" (Ph.D. diss., Union Theological Seminary, 1985); and Carol Meyers, "Mother to Muse: An Archaeomusicological Study of Women's Performance in Ancient Israel," in *Recycling Biblical Figures: Papers Read at a NOSTER Colloquium in Amsterdam, 12-13 May 1997,* ed. Athalya Brenner and Jan Willem van Henten (Studies in Religion and Theology 1; Leiden: Deo, 1999) 50-77. Both works are cited and discussed by Susan Ackerman, "Otherworldly Music and the Other Sex," in *The "Other" in Second Temple Judaism: Essays in Honor of John J. Collins,* ed. Daniel C. Harlow, Karina Martin Hogan, Matthew Goff, and Joel S. Kaminsky (Grand Rapids: Eerdmans, 2011) 86-100, here 87-90. See also the discussion over whether Miriam's song in Exod. 15:21 reflects an older tradition of women's song in victory. See Frank Moore Cross and David Noel Freedman, "The Song of Miriam," *JNES* 14 (1955) 237-50; Rita J. Burns, *Has the Lord Indeed Spoken Only Through Moses? A Study of the Biblical Portrait of Miriam* (SBLDS 84; Atlanta: Scholars, 1987) 11-40; Phyllis Trible, "Bringing Miriam Out of the Shadows," *BRev* 5 (1989) 14-25, 34; J. Gerald Janzen, "Song of Moses, Song of Miriam: Who Is Seconding Whom?" *CBQ* 54 (1992) 211-20; Athalya Brenner and Fokkelien van Dijk-Hemmes, *On Gendering Texts: Female and Male Voices in the Hebrew Bible* (Biblical Interpretation 1; Leiden: Brill, 1996) 38-42; and Carol Meyers, "Miriam, Music, and Miracles," in *Mariam, the Magdalen, and the Mother,* ed. Deirdre Good (Bloomington: Indiana University Press: 2005) 27-48. For the further issue of musical instrumentation associated with women, see Carol L. Meyers, "Of Drums and Damsels: Women's Performance in Ancient Israel," *BA* 54/1 (1991) 16-27, esp. 24; Sarit Paz, *Drums, Women, and Goddesses: Drumming and Gender in Iron Age II Israel* (OBO 232; Fribourg: Academic; Göttingen: Vandenhoeck & Ruprecht, 2007); and Raz Kletter and Katri Saarelainen, "Judean Drummers," *ZDPV* 127 (2011) 11-28. I am grateful to Seth Chalmer for drawing my attention to this issue. As Chalmer suggests, the Ugaritic literary evidence (see KTU 1.3 III 4-8 and 1.101.15-18; 1.16 I 31-45 as well as I 3-5, 17-19, II 40-42) arguably suggests a background for early biblical material such as Ps. 68:26 (cf. Exod. 15:20-21; Judg. 11:34; 1 Sam. 18:6). Note also the argument made for Prov. 31:10-31 as a woman's "heroic" poem by Albert M. Wolters, "Proverbs XXXI 30-31 as Heroic Hymn: A Form-Critical Analysis," *VT* 38 (1988) 452-53; and Richard J. Clifford, *Proverbs* (OTL; Louisville: Westminster John Knox, 1999) 273. In this reading, **ḥayil* in Proverbs 31:10

would echo its usage to denote a warrior (my thanks to Dick Clifford for drawing my attention to this reading).

71. Cf. Samuel A. Meier, "Women and Communication in the Ancient Near East," *JAOS* 111/3 (1991) 540-47.

72. See the probing discussion on this score by Brenner and van Dijk-Hemmes, *On Gendering Texts*, 1-42; and the discussion below for further suggestions in this vein. Such women poets may be analogous to what Jeremy M. Downes has called "the female Homer." See Downes, *The Female Homer: An Exploration of Women's Epic Poetry* (Newark: University of Delaware Press, 2010). Note also his emphasis (pp. 102-19) on the production of oral epic by women; cf. the comparative study of Yiqun Zhou, *Festivals, Feasts, and Gender Relations in Ancient China and Greece* (Cambridge: Cambridge University Press, 2010) 267-320, on "What Women Sang of." Women singers later in Israel are also known. 2 Chr. 35:25 mentions Jeremiah's laments for Josiah and those of the male and female singers. Neo-Assyrian records include women singers sent from Judah by Hezekiah as part of his tribute. See Sherry Lou Macgregor, *Beyond Hearth and Home: Women in the Public Sphere in Neo-Assyrian Society* (State Archives of Assyria Studies 21; Publications of the Finnish Assyriological Research 5; Helsinki: Neo-Assyrian Text Corpus Project, 2012) 29-54, esp. 30.

73. E.g., see the scenes from Ebla palace G and on the Megiddo ivory, both discussed in the next section on iconography.

74. See Chapter Three.

75. The case here is complicated; see Chapters Eight and Nine for discussion.

76. See Chapters Nine and Ten.

77. See Chapters Five and Twelve.

78. For warrior nicknames, including what he calls the "colorful Runyonesque names" of some of David's soldiers in 2 Samuel 23, see Mobley, *The Empty Men*, 1 and 33.

79. The common BH word, *bārāq*, is used to describe the sword (Deut. 32:41), spear (Nah. 2:4; Hab. 3:11), and arrowhead (Job 20:25; cf. Ezek. 21:15, 20, 33); BDB, 140. Note also Aqhat's weapon, which may be compared with *brq* (KTU 1.17 VI 11), but the context is unclear (see Chapter Four for discussion). The homology between weapon and warrior informs Baal as storm and warrior god; his weapons are meteorological, and these include *brqm* (see KTU 1.4 V 9; *UNP* 129; see also KTU 1.101.3-4); compare the same root used for Erra's weapon in Erra and Ishum I:5 and III:168 (*CAD, B*:104). In view of these references, the name of Baraq is perhaps a name denoting a flashing weapon. The word is evidently attested in Punic as Barcas, the surname of the leader Hamilcar. This, too, might be a warrior nickname, though Baraq could also simply be a name (cf. cuneiform examples cited by Richard Hess, "Israelite Identity and Personal Names from the Book of Judges," *HS* 44 [2003] 26-27). This question of name versus moniker might help to explain the textual picture in 1 Sam. 12:11. The figure, there called Bedan in the MT, is taken by LXX as Baraq (though oddly he appears after Jerubbaal here, while in Judges Baraq appears before Jerubbaal). See John Day, "Bedan, Abdon or Barak in 1 Samuel XII 11?" *VT* 43 (1993) 261-64; cf. Serge Frolov, "Bedan: A Riddle in Context," *JBL* 126 (2007) 164-67. Day would accept an emendation of Bedan to Baraq, while P. Kyle McCarter is critical of the emendation, which looks like a harmonization. See McCarter, *1 Samuel* (AB 8; Garden

City: Doubleday, 1980) 211. Does the LXX of 1 Sam. 12:11 substitute the name as known from Judges 4-5 for the obscure Bedan of the MT, and might the MT Bedan reflect his older name, while Baraq is his honorific title (assuming that Bedan and Baraq are to be associated)? For a different sort of nickname, see the discussion of Joseph Naveh, "Hebrew Graffiti from the First Temple Period," *IEJ* 51 (2001) 204-5.

80. Cf. Isa. 7:18 for bees as an image of divine warfare. According to Robert Kawashima, the original narrative roles of Baraq and Deborah ("Bee") were not humans but "aspects of God's theophanic terror," relating to the battle imagery of Yahweh's meteorological retinue (cf. Judg. 5:20; cf. 5:4-5). See Kawashima, "From Song to Story: The Genesis of Narrative in Judges 4 and 5," *Prooftexts* 21 (2001) 160-63 (p. 161 for the quote). It seems to me that an older narrative background such as this is unnecessary for the picture of Baraq and Deborah as partaking of the theophanic terror as expressed in Judg. 5:20. For a comparison of Deborah's name with Greek Melissa, see Daniel Vainstub, "Some Points of Contact between the Deborah War Traditions and Some Greek Mythologies," *VT* 61 (2011) 324-34.

81. For Zeeb, compare the martial image of Benjamin as a wolf in Gen. 49:27. See also the animal-name Eglon for the leader of the Moabites in Judg. 3:12, 14. Elizabeth Bloch-Smith has noted that several of these figures are Transjordanian.

82. See Gen. 49:17 for Dan as a serpent (*nāḥāš*//*šĕpîpōn*).

83. Other names with "lion" may also denote such a sensibility, which may be related to lion and lioness as emblem animals for a number of warrior deities, discussed in Chapter Seven. Perhaps pertinent is the Hebrew PN *šḥly* ("the one of the lion"), inscribed on a store jar from Tel Rehov (thought to be ninth century); see Mazar and Aḥituv, "The Inscriptions from Tel Rehov," 304-5 (Heb.).

84. See Chapter Four for Aqhat and Chapters Two and Three for Achilles and Enkidu. Note also the attitude attributed to David in 2 Sam. 23:17.

85. Perhaps such risk for warriors informs Aqhat's statement that death will be his fate (KTU 1.17 VI 38; *UNP* 61; see Chapter Four for discussion). Cf. the passages from the book of Judges where *npš*, one's "life-force," is used with **mwt*, "to die" (or other expressions) denoting mortal risk or mortality:

1. Zebulun's mortal risk on the battlefield is described in Judg. 5:18 (rendered rather literally): "Zebulun was a force that scorned its life to die." In other words, Zebulun was a military force willing to risk its life even to the point of death. Cf. NJPS: "that mocked at death" and p. 521 note b-b: "Lit. 'belittled its life to die.'"
2. In Judg. 9:17, Jotham is represented as claiming that Jerubbaal "cast forth (**šlk*) his life" in fighting for others.
3. Referring to battle, Jephthah says that he "set (**śym*) my life in my hand," in Judg. 12:3 (for the idiom, see also 1 Sam. 28:21; cf. colloquial English, "took his life in his hands").
4. Judg. 16:30 uses the expression of Samson: "may my life die" (cf. Judg. 16:16 describing Samson worn down by Delilah's words, *wattiqṣar napšô lāmût*). See Pnina Galpaz-Feller, "'Let My Soul Die with the Philistines' (Judges 16.30)," *JSOT* 30 (2006) 315-25.

86. The final section of Chapter Six is devoted to this passage.

87. See Chapter Four for Aqhat, and see Chapters Two and Three for Gilgamesh.

88. See the long list of male participants in battle in KTU 1.14 II 39-50 (Greenstein, *UNP* 15)//IV 21-28 (Greenstein, *UNP* 19). In this passage, the widow and the bride are also mentioned; these types of women are affected by the military deployment of the men, and they are to seek accommodations while the males that support them are engaged in the military campaign.

89. *UNP* 62; see Chapter Four. Cf. the speech of Erra's personified weapons (Erra and Ishum I:49-51): "Shall we eat woman food, like non-combatants? Have we turned timorous and trembling, as if we can't fight? Going to the field for the young and vigorous is like to a very feast" (Foster, *Before the Muses,* 883). For this sort of gendered language, see further below, and also Chapter Three.

90. E.g., in KTU 1.103 + 1.145, an Ugaritic text of omens (based on features of deformed fetuses, in the tradition of Akkadian *šumma izbu* series), the archers are characterized as *ṯnn ʿz,* lit., "archers of might" (line 17); see *RCU* 136, 139.

91. Note also *kōaḥ,* as in Ps. 103:20; cf. Ps. 33:16.

92. Cf. Akkadian *ezēzu* and its cognate forms, e.g., "with the fierceness of his bravery" (*ina mēzez qarradūtišu, CAD,* Q:144). Cf. the description of the king as "bold-hearted like Baal," in a stele of Seti I; see Keiko Tazawa, *Syro-Palestinian Deities in New Kingdom Egypt: The Hermeneutics of Their Existence* (B.A.R. 1965; Oxford: Archaeopress, 2009) 27, document 60. Note also Akkadian *šamru,* said of kings, warriors, and men, in *CAD,* Š/1:331, c. The anger of Erra is a notable example of battle-rage, e.g., Erra and Ishum V:19: "At a time you are angry, where is he who can face you?" (Foster, *Before the Muses,* 909).

93. This passage is discussed in Chapter Six. See also Yamm in KTU 1.2 IV 17. Note also Mot (or "death") in KTU 2.10.11-13: "and the hand of the gods [= pestilence] is here, for death/Death is very fierce *(ʿz).* Marvin H. Pope compared this line to Song 8:6 ("love is as strong as death"); *Song of Songs* (AB 7C; Garden City: Doubleday, 1977) 668; and Dennis Pardee, " 'As Strong as Death,' " in *Love and Death in the Ancient Near East: Essays in Honor of Marvin H. Pope,* ed. John H. Marks and Robert M. Good (Guilford: Four Quarters, 1987) 65-69. For *ʿ*zz* in PNs, see Joseph Martin Pagan, *A Morphological and Lexical Study of Personal Names in the Ebla Texts* (ARES 3; Rome: Missione Archeologica Italiana in Siria, 1998) 98-99. BH *ʿaz* is also used in Yahweh's battle in Hab. 3:4; and for the enemy in 2 Sam. 22/Ps. 18:18. See also the verbal usage in battle contexts with *yād* as the subject, e.g., Judg. 3:10; 6:2; cf. Ps. 89:14(13).

94. For further discussion, see Mark S. Smith, "The Heart and Innards in Israelite Emotional Expressions: Notes from Anthropology and Psychobiology," *JBL* 117 (1998) 427-36.

95. For anger in the Hebrew Bible, see Smith, "Heart and Innards"; Paul A. Kruger, "A Cognitive Interpretation of the Emotion of Anger in the Hebrew Bible," *JNSL* 26 (2000) 181-93; Zacharias Kotzé, "A Cognitive Linguistic Methodology for the Study of Metaphor in the Hebrew Bible," *JNSL* 31 (2005) 101-17; Ellen van Wolde, "Sentiments as Culturally Constructed Emotions: Anger and Love in the Hebrew Bible," *Biblical Interpretation* 16 (2008) 1-24; Reinhard G. Kratz and Hermann Spieckermann, eds., *Divine Wrath and Divine Mercy;* Deena Grant, "Wrath of God," in *NIDB,* 5:932-37, and *Divine Anger in the*

Hebrew Bible (CBQMS 52; Washington: Catholic Biblical Association of America, 2014); and Matthew R. Schlimm, *From Fratricide to Forgiveness: The Language and Ethics of Anger in Genesis* (Siphrut. Literature and Theology of the Old Testament 7; Winona Lake: Eisenbrauns, 2011).

96. Smith, "Heart and Innards."

97. So *DULAT* 83, on *'nš. See also P. Kyle McCarter, "When the Gods Lose Their Temper: Divine Rage and the Hypostasis of Anger in Iron Age Religion," in Kratz and Spieckermann, *Divine Wrath and Divine Mercy,* 78-91, here 81 ("Baal had lost his temper"). Note also "fury of Baal" in Tazawa, *Syro-Palestinian Deities in New Kingdom Egypt,* 36 document 99 (magical spell in the Leiden papyrus I); cf. the comparison of Ramesses III with Baal: "he is like Baal at the time of his raging" (Tazawa, *Syro-Palestinian Deities in New Kingdom Egypt,* 33 document 79). Tiamat in Enuma Elish Tablet II, lines 16-17 (also in Tablet III, lines 16-17, 74-75, 79-80) is likewise characterized in terms of warfare, anger and rage. See Foster, *Before the Muses,* 446, 452, 454.

98. See *DULAT* 88; *UNP* 161. It is claimed that Mot becomes angry *(kr)* in KTU 1.6 V 9; see Josef Tropper, "'Im Siebten Jahr wurde Mot wütend auf Baal': Zur Interpretation von KTU 1.6.V:8-10," *SEL* 16 (1999) 35-37; and W. G. E. Watson, "Jotting on Some Ugaritic Words," *SEL* 26 (2009) 15-21, here 17.

99. For recent studies, see the listing in n. 56.

100. Cf. divine *rûaḥ* in Isa. 30:28, with *'ap* and *za'am* in v. 27.

101. According to Baruch A. Levine, infusion of *rûaḥ* "ultimately originated in the heroic tradition, where we read that the divine spirit infuses the hero (Judg 3:10, 11:29, 13:25)." See Levine, *Numbers 21–36,* 354; for further discussion, see pp. 191, 350. The infusion of divine spirit into Gideon (Judg. 6:34) is related by Robert R. Wilson to "spirit possession," attested also for some prophets (Num. 11:25-26; 1 Kgs. 18:46; 2 Kgs. 3:15; Jer. 15:17). See Wilson, *Prophecy and Society in Ancient Israel* (Philadelphia: Fortress, 1980) 144-45. The usage for prophets may derive from the notion of infusion of divine spirit into warriors. The application of this idea to Elijah and Elisha may be part of the tradition's representation of them as mighty "holy men" and not only as prophetic spokesmen. For this point about Elijah and Elisha, see Mark S. Smith, "Recent Study of Israelite Religion in Light of the Ugaritic Texts," in *Ugarit at Seventy-Five,* ed. K. Lawson Younger, Jr. (Winona Lake: Eisenbrauns, 2007) 1-25. The story of the corpse thrown into Elisha's tomb and then miraculously reviving (2 Kgs. 13:20-21) may draw on a tradition of people traveling to the tombs of such prophets to seek help in health and other popular concerns. Edward B. Reeves's study of the cult of the dead saints in modern Egyptian society, their popular following, and the pilgrimage feasts centered on their burial sites may provide some helpful analogues to the phenomenon of biblical holy men Elijah and Elisha, their bands of disciples, and the cultic devotion paid to them after their deaths. See Reeves, *The Hidden Government: Ritual, Clientelism, and Legitimation in Northern Egypt* (Salt Lake City: University of Utah Press, 1990).

102. For this view and others, see Schlimm, *From Fratricide to Forgiveness,* 79 n. 19.

103. Cf. the characterization of Phinehas in Num. 25:13, with his wielding the spear in Num. 25:7-8. Gordon ("Indo-European and Hebrew Epic," 14*) compared what he regarded as the "wrath of Samson" (though there is no such term for Samson). (Cf. the

later transformation of this value from the martial to the intellectual in *b. B. Bat.* 21a: *qn't swprym trbh ḥkmh,* "the jealousy of scholars multiples wisdom [learning].")

104. This verse is of further interest, as it represents divine fury in the context of the fury of human warriors; in addition, the following v. 11 mentions the practice of repaying military vows. The vows made seem to concern the divine gift of battle fury given to human warriors. It seems similar to the *rûaḥ* that the deity gives to warriors. For some distinctions between human and divine *ḥēmâ,* see Deena Grant, "A Brief Discussion of the Difference between Human and Divine חמה," *Bib* 91 (2010) 418-24.

105. For Achilles' anger or wrath *(mēnin),* see Leonard Muellner, *The Anger of Achilles: Mênis in Greek Epic* (Ithaca: Cornell University Press, 1996). See Chapter Two (especially p. 395 note 74) for discussion of Achilles' fury.

106. Here I draw on the expression as used by Hans van Wees, *Status Warriors: War, Violence, and Society in Homer and History* (Dutch Monographs on Ancient History and Archaeology 9; Amsterdam: Gieben, 1992) 61, 153; it is applied to Achilles in van Wees, *Status Warriors,* 111, 122, 129, 133, 135.

107. For the semantics of the Hebrew terms, see Kruger, "A Cognitive Interpretation of the Emotion of Anger"; and Kotzé, "A Cognitive Linguistic Methodology for the Study of Metaphor."

108. See above in n. 85.

109. See Chapter Six, section 3, for this text.

110. The Egyptian phrase is also given as a name over one of the horses depicted in a war scene on the wall of Karnak dating to Seti I; see Tazawa, *Syro-Palestinian Deities in New Kingdom Egypt,* 81, document #30.

111. Ancient Near Eastern analogies for fury in warfare as a positive value can be seen in an Old Babylonian letter of Shibtu to Zimri-Lim of Mari. The letter reports a prophecy from the deity proclaiming: "I will rage and stand in victory" *(kinnekêm ara'ub u ina lītim azzaz).* For text and translation, see Nissinen, *Prophets and Prophecy,* 46. The goddess Astarte is addressed as "angry and raging goddess," in the "Tale of Two Brothers" (*COS* 1:35).

112. The imagery has been noted by many scholars, including Nili Wazana, "A Case of the Evil Eye: Qohelet 4:4-8," *JBL* 126 (2007) 685-702, here 699. For discussion, see below in Chapter Six, section 1.

113. Note the inverse image, that dreadful warriors may be compared in some respect with death, e.g., the seven weapons of Erra presented as warriors (Erra and Ishum I:26): "The breath is death" (Foster, *Before the Muses,* 882).

114. According to P. Kyle McCarter, Anat's battle is one of "rage" although the term is not present here. See McCarter, "When the Gods Lose Their Temper," 85.

115. See Wazana, "A Case of the Evil Eye," 697-99. Wazana cites this motif in the Tell Fekherye inscription and its parallels in the Sefire stele as well as the annals of Ashurbanipal, in Jonas C. Greenfield and Aaron Shaffer, "Notes on the Curse Formulae of the Tell Fekherye Inscription," *RB* 92 (1985) 54-55.

116. The further question is whether or not she consumes them as well. See Chapter Six, section 3. This would be similar to the situation in the Egyptian story of "The Destruction of Mankind" described here.

117. See Miriam Lichtheim, "The Destruction of Mankind," in *COS,* 1:36-37.

118. In this connection, also note the idea that the human eye in its great desire (sometimes cast in terms of the "evil eye") is insatiable; see Wazana, "A Case of the Evil Eye."

119. Lichtheim, "The Destruction of Mankind," 1:37.

120. NJPS: "Unstable (*$p\d{h}z$) as water." Cf. "the worthless scoundrels" hired by Abimelekh in Judg. 9:4, as well as Akkadian *puḫḫuzû*, "scoundrel" (*CAD*, P:33) and *paḫāzu*, "to be arrogant, high-handed" (*CAD*, P:32). Note also *wypḥz* in 4QSam[b] (4Q52, fragments 6-7) on 1 Sam. 20:34, considered the superior reading to MT *wyqm* ("and he rose") by Frank Moore Cross, *From Epic to Canon: History and Literature in Ancient Israel* (Baltimore: Johns Hopkins University Press, 1998) 134-35 n. 4; Cross, Donald W. Parry, Richard J. Saley, and Eugene Ulrich, *Qumran Cave 4: XII, 1-2 Samuel* (DJD 17; Oxford: Clarendon, 2005) 233 ("to be excited, to act in excitement"); and Jo Ann Hackett, *The Balaam Text from Deir 'Allā* (HSM 31; Chico: Scholars, 1980) 63. See the analogous application of the root to the realm of prophecy in Jer. 23:32 and Zeph. 3:4; see William McKane, *A Critical and Exegetical Commentary on Jeremiah*, Vol. 1: *I–XXV* (repr. with corrections; ICC; Edinburgh: T. & T. Clark, 1999) 594-95. For **pḥz* instead as matter of lewdness, see Jonas C. Greenfield, "The Meaning of פחז," in Greenfield, *'Al Kanfei Yonah*, ed. Shalom M. Paul, Michael E. Stone, and Avital Pinnick (Jerusalem: Magnes, 2001), 729-30 (note also BDB, 808). While the connotation of lewdness that Greenfield detects could be present in Gen. 49:4, Cross (*From Epic to Canon*, 136 n. 4) regards the meaning of "lewdness" to be later. Cf. Aaron D. Rubin, "Genesis 49:4 in Light of Arabic and Modern South Arabian," *VT* 59 (2009) 499-502. The meaning of **pḥz* in Gen. 49:4 should also suit the phrase's comparison with water; accordingly, "lewdness" seems less fitting. For further discussion of this term as well as **rêq*, "empty," in the larger social context, see Mobley, *The Empty Men*, 31-38; and Brian R. Doak, "'Some Worthless and Reckless Fellows': Landlessness and Parasocial Leadership in Judges," *JHS* 11 (2011), article 2.

121. Cf. the **rûaḥ* in Judg. 8:3 for the postbattle animus of the Ephraimites who felt left out of the fight.

122. Note also the figure of Erra in the story of Erra and Ishum, discussed by Peter Machinist, "Order and Disorder: Some Mesopotamian Reflections," in *Genesis and Regeneration*, ed. Shaul Shaked (Jerusalem: Israel Academy of Sciences and Humanities, 2005) 31-61. See also Bahrani, *Rituals of War*, 207-12. Cf. the incisive remarks of Diana Edelman, "Saul Ben Kish, King of Israel, as a 'Young Hero'?" in *Le jeune héros: Recherches sur la formation et la diffusion d'un thème littéraire au Proche-Orient ancien. Actes du colloque organisé par les chaires d'Assyriologie et des Milieux bibliques du Collège de France, Paris, les 6 et 7 avril 2009*, ed. Jean-Marie Durand, Thomas Römer, and Michael Langlois (OBO 250; Fribourg: Academic; Göttingen: Vandenhoeck & Ruprecht, 2011) 171: "warriors exemplify the thin line between the legitimatized use of force to maintain social order and the abuse of power for personal gain."

123. For this point, I am grateful for a discussion with Ilan Sharon.

124. In light of this usage, I have wondered about instances of warrior goddesses said to be the "name" of a warrior god. For discussion of this phenomenon, see Chapter Seven.

125. See Carol Meyers, "Of Seasons and Soldiers: A Topological Appraisal of the Premonarchic Tribes of Galilee," *BASOR* 252 (1983) 47-59, esp. 54-57; and Philip J. King

and Lawrence E. Stager, *Life in Biblical Israel* (Library of Ancient Israel; Louisville: Westminster John Knox, 2001) 239, 241.

126. For study of weapons in this region, by period: Graham Philip, *Metal Weapons of the Early and Middle Bronze Ages; Eli Miron, Axes and Adzes from Canaan* (Prähistorische Bronzefunden Abteilung 9/19; Stuttgart: Steiner, 1992); Sariel Shalev, *Swords and Daggers in Late Bronze Age Canaan* (Prähistorische Bronzefunden Abteilung 4/13; Stuttgart: Steiner, 2004); and Allan Comstock Emery III, "Weapons of the Israelite Monarchy: A Catalogue with Its Linguistic and Cross-Cultural Implications" (Ph.D. diss., Harvard, 1998).

127. Tamar Schick at al., *The Cave of the Warrior: A Fourth Millennium Burial in the Judean Desert* (IAA Reports 5; Jerusalem: Israel Antiquities Authority, 1998).

128. See esp. Aviram Oshri and Tamar Schick, "The Lithics," in Schick, *The Cave of the Warrior*, 59-62.

129. Rowan, "Prismatic Blades and Periodization: The Case of the Fourth Millennium BCE 'Cave of the Warrior,'" *ZDPV* 117 (2001) 1-4.

130. The information here derives from Hestrin, "A Hoard of Tools and Weapons from Kfar Monash," *IEJ* 13 (1963) 265-88. For a picture of some of the spearheads, see also *ANEP*, #783c.

131. Hestrin, "A Hoard of Tools and Weapons," 284. She notes that identical copper scales were found at Tell Gath.

132. For Middle Bronze I-II warrior burials, see Graham Philip, "Warrior Burials in the Ancient Near Eastern Bronze Age: The Evidence from Mesopotamia, Western Iran, and Syria-Palestine," in *The Archaeology of Death in the Ancient Near East*, ed. Stuart Campbell and Anthony Green (Oxford: Oxbow, 1995) 140-54 (with prior literature). The southern Levantine sites include Beth Shean, Tel Rehov, Megiddo, Jericho, Lachish, and Tell el-Ajjul. Northern Levantine sites include Ras Shamra, Amrith, Byblos, and Sidon. Philip also notes warrior burials at Tell el-Dab'a and Tell el-Maskhuta, which are "virtually indistinguishable from those found in Palestine" (p. 144). Several of these burials yielded not only daggers and axes but also metal belts (metal sheet sewn onto a leather backing). Note also the "warrior burial" at MB I Arqa and Sidon (Lebanon); see Jean-Paul Thalmann, "Tell Arqa: A Prosperous City during the Bronze Age," *NEA* 73/2-3 (2010) 98; and Claude Doumet-Serhal, "Sidon during the Bronze Age: Burials, Rituals and Feasting Grounds at the 'College Site,'" *NEA* 73/2-3 (2010) 118.

For Middle Bronze IIA warrior burials, see also Yosef Garfinkel, "Warrior Burial Customs in the Levant during the Early Second Millennium B.C.," in *Studies in the Archaeology of Israel and Neighboring Lands in Memory of Douglas L. Esse*, ed. Samuel R. Wolff (SAOC 59; Chicago: Oriental Institute of the University of Chicago; Atlanta: American Schools of Oriental Research, 2001) 143-61; and Garfinkel and Susan Cohen, eds., *The Middle Bronze Age IIA Cemetery at Gesher: Final Report* (AASOR 62; Boston: American Schools of Oriental Research, 2007). The following four Middle Bronze sites are discussed by Garfinkel:

(i) Gesher (central Jordan Valley, about 14 km. south of the Sea of Galilee): Graves 2, 12, 13, 14, identified as warrior burials by the bronze duck-bill axe placed next to the head;

(ii) Tel Rehov, central Jordan Valley south of Beth Shean: one tomb (#2), with dagger, two spearheads, and one duck-bill axe-head;
(iii) Kabri, in western Galilee, one warrior burial with duck-bill axe; and
(iv) Baghouz, 10 km. south of Mari, nine warrior burials, again with duck-bill axes.
Thirteen of the tombs had spearheads and axes.

For more on Gesher, see Yosef Garfinkel and Ruhama Bonfil, "Graves and Burial Customs of the MBIIA Period in Gesher," *ErIsr* 21 (Ruth Amiran Volume; 1990) 132-47 (Heb.); and Susan L. Cohen, "The Spearheads from the 2002-2004 Excavations from Gesher," *IEJ* 55 (2005) 129-42.

For the Middle Bronze IIA burials with weapons at Tell el-Dab'a (Egypt), see Irene Forstner-Müller, "Tombs and Burial Customs at Tell el-Dab'a in Area A/II at the End of the MBIIA Period (Stratum F)," in *The Middle Bronze Age in the Levant: Proceedings of an International Conference on MB IIA Ceramic Material. Vienna, 24th-26th of January 2001*, ed. Manfred Bietak (Vienna: Österreichischen Akademie der Wissenschaften, 2002) 165-66.

133. Philip, "Warrior Burials in the Ancient Near East Bronze Age," 140. The definition of warrior burials has been the subject of some discussion, since the identification of specific burials as "warrior burials" as such is arguably difficult. A tomb with only weapons and perhaps with armor arguably belongs to a warrior, but most tombs contain other household and/or daily-life items as well. A duckbill axe, dagger, and any other metal implement had multiple functions, only one of which would have been as a weapon. They all served household and subsistence functions (slaughtering animals, cutting down trees, etc.) and so should not necessarily be categorized as weapons. On the other hand, such weapons remain somewhat notable compared to other grave or tomb goods.

In her study of Middle and Late Bronze Age burials at Ashkelon, Jill Baker posits a basic "burial kit" quite common to burials of this period; weapons are not among the kit items. Indeed, of the burials that she studied, only one tomb contained a weapon (a dagger in Burial 158 dating to the Late Bronze I). See Baker, "The Funeral Kit: A Newly Defined Canaanite Mortuary Practice Based on the Middle and Late Bronze Age Tomb Complex at Ashkelon," *Levant* 38 (2006) 1-33, esp. 17.

134. John C. Barrett, "The Living, the Dead, and the Ancestors: Neolithic and Early Bronze Mortuary Practices," in *Contemporary Archaeology in Theory*, ed. Robert W. Preucel and Ian Hodder (Oxford: Blackwell, 1996) 394.

135. Philip, "Warrior Burials in the Ancient Near East Bronze Age," 144. Cf. Mike Parker Pearson, *The Archaeology of Death and Burial* (College Station: Texas A&M University Press, 2000) 85.

136. Garfinkel, "Warrior Burial Customs in the Levant," 155.

137. Philip, "Warrior Burials in the Ancient Near East Bronze Age," 145.

138. According to Hermann Genz, stunning bolts (used in bird hunting) have been found in a number of Late Bronze tombs. See Genz, "Stunning Bolts: Late Bronze Age Hunting Weapons in the Ancient Near East," *Levant* 39 (2007) 47-69.

139. Yon, *The City of Ugarit at Tell Ras Shamra*, 14, citing Sophie Marchegay, "La tombe no. 1008 de Minet el-Bheida," in *Le royaume d'Ougarit: Aux origins de l'alphabet*, ed. Genevieve Galliano and Yves Calvet (Lyon: Musée des Beaux Arts; Paris: Somogy,

2004) 246-55 (no. 273-302). I have been unable to obtain access to Marchegay's article or to her thesis, "Les tombes d'Ougarit: architecture, localization et relation avec l'habitat" (thèse, Lyon-2, 1999).

140. See James B. Pritchard, *The Cemetery at Tell es-Sa'idiyeh, Jordan* (University Museum Monograph 41; Philadelphia: University Museum, University of Pennsylvania, 1980); see, e.g., Tomb 101, on pp. 10-16, with the weaponry described on p. 16, and pp. 84-87, figs. 47-50. See also the summary in Jonathan N. Tubb, "Sa'idiyeh, Tell es," in *NEAEHL* 4:1299-1300; and Elizabeth M. Bloch-Smith, *Judahite Burials and Beliefs about the Dead* (JSOTSup 123; ASOR Monograph Series 7; Sheffield: JSOT, 1992) 155-56. It has been thought that Jer. 15:12 might reflect knowledge of the site's reputation for metalwork; see Dan Leven and Beno Rothenberg, "Early Evidence for Steelmaking in the Judaic Sources," *JQR* 92 (2001) 105-27, here 113. Cf. the group of eleven Late Bronze II tombs at Pella (Tel Husn), which included a burial of a large male wearing heavy bronze manacles; see Stephen J. Bourke, "Pre-Classical Pella in Jordan: A Conspectus of Ten Years' Work (1985-1995)," *PEQ* 129 (1997) 108.

141. Information courtesy of Samuel Wolff, based on a paper with Gershon Eidelstein, "Double Pithos Burials in the Levant: Some New Evidence and Thoughts," delivered at the meeting of the American Schools of Oriental Research in 2005 (cited with permission).

142. So Wolff in his unpublished presentation at ASOR 2005, and mentioned to me on 8 February 2011; cited here with his permission.

143. Discovered in the so-called "broad room" (Room B3); see Larry G. Herr, "Jordan in the Iron I Period," *Studies in the History and Archaeology of Jordan* 10 (2009) 549-61, here 552. Note also an Iron I bronze-smith's workshop at Deir 'Alla. See G. van der Kooij and M. M. Ibrahim, eds., *Picking Up the Threads . . . A Continuing Review of Excavations at Deir Alla, Jordan* (Leiden: University of Leiden Archaeological Centre, 1989) 80-81 and 93-94, no. 22; see also H. J. Franken and J. Kalsbeek, *Excavations at Tell Deir 'Alla I* (DMOA 16; Leiden: Brill, 1969).

144. Bloch-Smith, *Judahite Burials and Beliefs about the Dead*, 91-92.

145. Paice, "The Small Finds," in Timothy P. Harrison, *Megiddo 3: Final Report on the Stratum Excavations* (OIP 127; Chicago: Oriental Institute, University of Chicago, 2004): tomb 39 with bronze arrowheads and blade-knife (p. 86, #19-20; p. 87, #9-10) and an iron blade/knife (p. 88, #6); tomb 1101B Upper with iron blade/dagger (p. 88).

146. Bloch-Smith, *Judahite Burials and Beliefs about the Dead*, 91.

147. The Achzib sword was excavated by Eilat Mazar, *The Phoenician Family Tomb N. 1 at the Northern Cemetery of Achziv (10th-6th Centuries BCE)* (Cuadernos de arquelogía mediterránea 10; Barcelona: Bellaterra, 2004) 121, fig. 29 and 163, photo 119; and Mazar, "Achziv Cemeteries: Buried Treasure from Israel's Phoenician Neighbor," *BAR* 36/5 (2010) 34-47, here 39 (with a fine picture on p. 40). The long sword there belonged to a large group of weapons from the first phase of the tomb, namely in the tenth/early ninth century.

148. For the Vered Jericho sword, see Avraham Eitan, "A Rare Sword of the Israelite Period Found at Vered Jericho," *Israel Museum Journal* 12 (1994) 61-62; the site in which

the sword was found (a small single-period fortress or farmstead) is dated to the late seventh–early sixth century. Information courtesy of Ilan Sharon.

149. Information courtesy of Amihai Mazar, who is to publish the Rehov sword. For the iconographic evidence for Israelite swords, see *inter alia* the reliefs of Sennacherib in Nineveh; Aren Maeir, "The 'Judahite' Swords from the 'Lachish' Reliefs of Sennacherib," *ErIsr* 25 (Joseph Aviram Volume; 1996) 210-14 (Heb.).

150. Mazar, *The Phoenician Family Tomb N. 1,* 21-22 for general description, and 118-25 for the listing of weaponry with drawings; see also Mazar, *The Palace of King David,* 52-53. I have been aided in this discussion by Ilan Sharon, whom I thank.

151. Mazar, *The Phoenician Family Tomb N. 1,* 21.

152. See the comments on Iron I mortuary evidence by Robert D. Miller II, "'A New Cultural History' of Early Israel," in *Israel in Transition,* 2:188 ("the early Israelites had no mythos of a 'great warrior'"), 190 ("The early Israelites encoded no ideal of martial prowess in their burials"). Miller is right to note the lack of evidence. However, he does not discuss weaponry in tombs noted by Bloch-Smith mentioned above. For the problem of "warrior burials" in Greek sources, see Hans van Wees, "Greeks Bearing Arms: The State, the Leisure Class, and the Display of Weapons in Archaic Greece," in *Archaic Greece: New Approaches and New Evidence,* ed. N. Fisher and H. van Wees (London: Duckworth, 1998) 333-78, esp. 339. Van Wees (p. 340) endorses the old view of Wolfgang Helbig: "Dark Ages graves with weapons normally held not 'warriors', in the sense of men equipped as they would have been for battle, but men 'in peace-time costume,' yet with spears and swords."

153. See J. C. L. Gibson, *Textbook of Syrian Semitic Inscriptions,* Vol. 3: *Phoenician Inscriptions* (Oxford: Clarendon, 1982) 1-8; Frank Moore Cross, *Leaves from an Epigrapher's Notebook: Collected Papers in Hebrew and West Semitic Palaeography and Epigraphy* (HSS 51; Winona Lake: Eisenbrauns, 2003) 200-202, 217-18, 304; Émile Puech, "Les pointes de flèches inscrites de la fin du IIe millénaire en Phénicie et Canaan," in *Actas del IV Congreso Internacional de Estudios Fenicios y Púnicos: Cádiz, 2 a 6 de Octubre de 1995,* ed. María Eugenia Aubet Semmler and Manuela Barthélemy (4 vols.; Cádiz: Publicaciones Universidad de Cádiz, 2000) 1:251-69; Richard S. Hess, "Arrowheads from Iron Age: Personal Names and Authenticity," in Younger, *Ugarit at Seventy-Five,* 113-29; and Josette Elayi, "Four New Inscribed Phoenician Arrowheads," *SEL* 22 (2005) 35-45. See also the references to the literature below, and in Chapter Eleven.

154. See Cross, *Leaves from an Epigrapher's Notebook,* 200; Ryan Byrne, "The Refuge of Scribalism in Iron I Palestine," *BASOR* 345 (2007) 19; and Rollston, *Writing and Literacy,* 65. For the problem of forged inscriptions more generally, see Rollston, *Writing and Literacy,* 137-44; and Andrew G. Vaughan and Rollston, "The Antiquities Market, Sensationalized Textual Data, and Modern Forgeries," *NEA* 68 (2005) 61-68.

155. See the listing of fifty-one arrowhead inscriptions in Robert Deutsch and Michael Heltzer, *West Semitic Epigraphic News of the 1st Millennium* BCE (with a contribution by Gabriel Barkay; Tel Aviv: Archaeological Center, 1999) 13-19. Byrne ("The Refuge of Scribalism," 19) has characterized the work in these terms: it "doubtless contains authentic and dubious items alike." Information on provenienced inscribed arrowheads is hard to come by. For one case, see the Ruweiseh arrowhead discovered in a burial cave; M. P.-E. Guigues, "Pointe de flèche en bronze à inscription phénicienne," *MUSJ* 11 (1926) 325-28;

and Sébastien Ronzevalle, "Pointe de flèche en bronze à inscription phénicienne: Note sur le texte phénicien de la flèche publiée par M. P.-E. Guiges," *MUSJ* 11 (1926) 326-58. See Benjamin Sass, *The Genesis of the Alphabet and Its Development in the Second Millennium B.C.* (Ägypten und Altes Testament 13; Wiesbaden: Harrassowitz, 1988) 82; and P. Kyle McCarter, *Ancient Inscriptions: Voices from the Biblical World* (Washington: Biblical Archaeology Society, 1996) 78.

156. See Benjamin Sass, "Inscribed Babylonian Arrowheads of the Turn of the Second Millennium BC and their Phoenician Counterparts," *UF* 21 (1989) 349-56.

157. Peter Magee, "The Chronology and Regional Context of Late Prehistoric Incised Arrowheads in Southeastern Arabia," *Arabian Archaeology and Epigraphy* 9 (1998) 1-12.

158. See J. T. Milik and F. M. Cross in Cross, *Leaves from an Epigrapher's Notebook,* 303-8; Rollston, *Writing and Literacy,* 66.

159. McCarter, *Ancient Inscriptions,* 79; cited in Rollston, *Writing and Literacy,* 66.

160. Puech, "Les pointes de flèches inscrites," 260.

161. Rollston, *Writing and Literacy,* 66.

162. McCarter, *Ancient Inscriptions,* 79.

163. For this question, see Chapter Seven. Note also the inscribed bronze dagger from Lachish; see Rollston, *Writing and Literacy,* 15-16.

164. To the list of Transjordanian arrowheads may be added twenty-two iron arrowheads from Tall Abū al-Karaz in the Jordan Valley; see C. Wenger, "Appendix 3: A Note on the Arrowheads," in Peter M. Fischer and Rainer Fledbacher, "Swedish Jordan Expedition: Preliminary Report on the Eleventh Season of Excavation at Tall Abū Al-Kharaz, 2008," *ADAJ* 53 (2009) 149-50.

165. A wild bull surrounded by hunters and dancers dressed in animal skins appears on the north wall mural of room V 1 in a house in Neolithic Çatalhöyük. See James Mellaart, "Excavations at Çatal Hüyük, 1965: Fourth Preliminary Report," *AnSt* 14 (1966) pls. LIV, LVIIb, LVIII, and *Çatal Hüyük: A Neolithic Town in Anatolia* (London: Thames and Hudson; New York: McGraw-Hill, 1967), fig. 171; cited in Piotr Taracha, *Religions of Second Millennium Anatolia* (Dresdner Beiträge zur Hethitologie 27; Wiesbaden: Harrassowitz, 2009) 15.

166. Cf. "like an antelope in a net" *(kĕtô' mikmār)* in the Persian period passage Isa. 51:20; cf. SB *kamāru* A, in Enuma Elish IV:112 (*CAD,* K:111). There is considerable metaphorical use of BH **yqš,* but little if any clear literal usage in any period for deer or gazelle. See Amos 3:5; Ps. 124:7 for the use of this root in regard to fowling. The expression, *paḥ yāqûš,* in Hos. 9:8; Ps. 91:3 is unclear, but the comparable phrase in Ps.124:7 suggests fowling and not deer or gazelle. See also Ugaritic *yqšm,* "fowlers," in KTU 4.99.6; 4.126.25; *yqš,* game bird (?), in 1.48.7 (*DULAT,* 976). BH *rešet,* "net," is also used for birds in Hos. 7:12; Prov. 1:17 (cf. its Ugaritic cognate, *rṯt,* for fish, in KTU 1.4 II 32, *DULAT,* 750). Rabbinic texts attest to the practice of trapping deer (references courtesy of Stephen Pfann); see *m. Šabb.* 7:2, 13:6; *b. Ketub.* 103b.

167. For references, see the entry for Akkadian *šētu,* "net," in *CAD,* Š 2:340. Cf. Erra IV 94 (*CAD,* Š 2:341): "his people are wild animals, their god is their hunter, and the mesh of his net is very fine." Note also Akkadian *saparru,* "net, throw-net," also used for catching caprids, birds and fish (see *CAD,* S:161).

168. For the literary issues, see Baruch Schwartz, "'Profane' Slaughter and the Integrity of the Priestly Code," *HUCA* 67 (1996) 15-42.

169. For these two passages, see Naphtali S. Meshel, "Food for Thought: Systems for Categorization in Leviticus 11," *HTR* 101 (2008) 203-29.

170. Hesse and Wapnish, "An Archaeozoological Perspective on the Cultural Use of Mammals in the Levant," in *A History of the Animal World in the Ancient Near East*, ed. Billie Jean Collins (HO 1/64, Leiden: Brill, 2002) 483-91.

171. Rosen, "Subsistence Economy in Iron Age I," in *From Nomadism to Monarchy*, ed. Israel Finkelstein and Nadav Na'aman; Washington: Biblical Archaeology Society, 1994) 340.

172. Liora Kolska Horwitz, "Faunal Remains from the Early Iron Age Site on Mount Ebal," *TA* 13-14 (1986-87) 174. My thanks go to Jonathan Greer for this reference.

173. Zertal, "An Early Iron Age Cultic Site on Mount Ebal: Excavation Seasons 1982-1987," *TA* 13-14 (1986-87) 105-65. See also the convenient summary in Zertal, "Ebal, Mount," *ABD*, 2.254-58 (with earlier references).

174. See Rainey and R. S. Notley, "Zertal's Altar — A Blatant Phoney," *BAR* 4/1 (1986) 4; Rainey, "Notes on Two Archaeological Sites," *ErIsr* 29 (2009) 186*; and Kempinsky, "Joshua's Altar — An Iron Age I Watchtower," *BAR* 12/1 (1986) 42-49. For Zertal's criticism of their interpretation, see Zertal, "An Early Iron Age Cultic Site on Mount Ebal," 153-54. See also Klaus Koenen, "Zum Stierbild von *Ḍahret eṭ-Tawīle* und zum Schlangen des Hörneraltars von *Tell es-Seba'*," *BN* 121 (2004) 39-52.

175. Mazar, "The Iron Age I," in *The Archaeology of Ancient Israel*, ed. Amnon Ben-Tor; trans. Raphael Greenberg (New Haven; Yale University Press/Open University of Israel, 1992) 294.

176. For more detail, see Horwitz, "Faunal Remains from the Early Iron Age Site on Mount Ebal," 173-89.

177. Yosef Garfinkel, personal communication. The bone material is to be published in *Khirbet Qeiyafa* Vol. 2 (in preparation).

178. See Guy Bar-Oz, "Paleozoology and Animal Consumption at Iron I Kinrot," *NEA* 74 (2011) 86; and Justin S. E. Lev-Tov, Benjamin W. Porter, and Bruce E. Routledge, "Measuring Local Diversity in Early Iron Age Animal Economies: A View from Khirbet al-Mudayna al-'Aliya (Jordan)," *BASOR* 361 (2011) 67-93, here 80. Kinrot, according to Bar-Oz, also yielded bones of Mesopotamian fallow deer and mountain gazelle.

179. Frank S. Frick, *Tell Taannek 1963-1968 IV: Miscellaneous 2: The Iron Age Cultic Structure* (Bir Zeit: Palestinian Institute of Archaeology, Bir Zeit University, 2000) 65-66.

180. Frick, *Tell Taannek 1963-1968*, 66, citing Brian Hesse, "Pig Lovers and Pig Haters: Patterns of Palestinian Pork Production," *Journal of Ethnobiology* 1 (1990) 214-15; and "Husbandry, Dietary Taboos and the Bones of the Ancient Near East: Zooarchaeology in the Post-Processual World," in *Methods in the Mediterranean*, ed. David B. Small (Mnemosyne Sup 135; Leiden: Brill, 1995) 224. I have noted an announcement for the following, relevant volume: Muhammed M. Al-Zawahra, "The Animal Bones," in *Tell Taannek 1963-1968 IV: Miscellaneous 1* (Bir Zeit: Palestinian Institute of Archaeology, Bir Zeit University, in press).

181. Paula Wapnish and Brian Hesse, "Faunal Remains from Tel Dan: Perspectives on

Animal Production at a Village, Urban and Ritual Center," *Archaeozoologica* 4/2 (1991) 12-14, 18-19 (three gazelles associated with the ninth-eighth century "altar complex"), 29 ("in all periods with a high degree of urbanism at Tel Dan, deer are frequent as an alternate meat source"). See also Oded Borowski, "Animals in the Religion of Syria-Palestine," in Collins, *A History of the Animal World,* 412; Jacob Milgrom, *Leviticus 17–22* (AB 3A; New York: Doubleday, 2000) 1480; and Ziony Zevit, *The Religions of Ancient Israel: A Synthesis of Parallactic Approaches* (London: Continuum, 2001) 181.

182. Wapnish and Hesse, "Faunal Remains from Tel Dan," 36. See the detailed discussion of Jonathan Greer, "Dinner at Dan: A Biblical and Archaeological Exploration of Sacred Feasting at Iron Age II Tel Dan" (Ph.D. diss., Pennsylvania State, 2011).

183. Wapnish and Hesse, "Faunal Remains from Tel Dan," 36.

184. Liora Kolska Horwitz, "Animal Exploitation — Archeozoological Analysis," in Zvi Gal and Yardenna Alexandre, *Ḥorbat Rosh Zayit: An Iron Age Storage Fort and Village* (IAA Reports 8; Jerusalem: Israel Antiquities Authority, 2000) 221-32, esp. 227-28.

185. See Paul Croft, "Archaeozoological Studies," in *The Renewed Archaeological Excavations at Lachish (1973-1994),* ed. David Ussishkin (5 vols.; Tel Aviv University Sonia and Marco Nadler Institute of Archaeology Monograph 22; Tel Aviv: Emery and Claire Yass Publications in Archaeology, Institute of Archaeology, Tel Aviv University, 2004) 5:2344, 2259, 2261, 2291-94; and Borowski, "Animals in the Religion of Syria-Palestine," 412.

186. Deer and gazelle are reported for Iron Age Heshban. See Angela von den Driesch and Joachim Boessneck, "Final Report on the Zooarchaeological Investigation of Animal Bone Finds from Tell Hesban, Jordan" in *Faunal Remains: Taphonomical and Zooarchaeological Studies of the Animal Remains from Tell Hesban and Vicinity,* ed. Øystein Sakala LaBianca and von den Driesch (Hesban 13; Berrien Springs: Andrews University Press, 1995) 71, 85-90 (reference courtesy of Elizabeth M. Bloch-Smith). See also the essay in the same volume by the same authors, "Evidence of Deer in the Early Historical Period of Tell-Hesban, Jordan," 109-19. According to the first essay, wild animal bones in the Iron Age finds tally to thirty (cf. 2,495 for domestic animals).

187. Peter M. Fischer, "The Iron Age at Tall Abū al-Kharaz, Jordan Valley: The Third Major Period of Occupation. A Preliminary Synthesis," *Studies in the History and Archaeology of Jordan* 7 (2001) 312 (his article was brought to my attention by Elizabeth M. Bloch-Smith). See also Herr, "Jordan in the Iron I Period."

188. Lev-Tov, Porter, and Routledge, "Measuring Local Diversity," 75.

189. Approximately twenty-five thousand bones have been discovered at the Late Bronze–Iron I site of ʿUmayri; see Herr, "Jordan in the Iron I Period," 552. These include gazelle; see Joris Peters, Nadja Pöllath, and Angela von den Driesch, "Early and Late Bronze Age Traditional Subsistence at Tall al-ʿUmayri," in *Madaba Plains Project: The 1994 Season at Tall al-ʿUmayri and Subsequent Studies,* 5, ed. Larry G. Herr et al. (Berrien Springs: Andrews University Press, 2002) 311. See also Lev-Tov, Porter, and Routledge, "Measuring Local Diversity," 78, 79, 83.

190. Croft, "Archaeozoological Studies," 5:2344.

191. Lev-Tov, Porter, and Routledge, "Measuring Local Diversity," 83.

192. A correlation between decrease in population and the increase in hunting has

been proposed for Tel Batash by Baruch Halpern, based on the research of Paula Wapnish and Brian Hesse; see Halpern, *From Gods to God: The Dynamics of Iron Age Cosmologies*, ed. Matthew J. Adams (FAT 63; Tübingen: Mohr Siebeck, 2009) 377 (brought to my attention by Jonathan Greer).

193. There is also evidence for hunting lions; see, e.g., Deborah Sweeney, "A Lion-Hunt Scarab and Other Egyptian Objects from the Late Bronze Fortress at Jaffa," *TA* 30 (2003) 54-63.

194. See Pritchard, *The Cemetery at Tell es-Sa'idiyeh*, 22 and 63, figs. 24, 30. Note also antelope depicted on Late Bronze seals from the Levant, in Teissier, *Ancient Near Eastern Cylinder Seals*, 300, #664, 302, #665, #667, #669; and ibexes on the Late Bronze Age sherd from Jerusalem; see Mazar, *The Palace of King David*, 33.

195. See W. F. Albright, "An Incised Representation of a Stag from Tell El-'Oreimeh," *JPOS* 6 (1926) 167-68.

196. Menakhem Shuval, "A Catalogue of Early Iron Stamp Seals from Israel," in Othmar Keel, Shuval, and Christoph Uehlinger, *Studien zu den Stempelsiegeln aus Palästina/ Israel*, Vol. 3: *Die Frühe Eisenzeit: Ein Workshop* (OBO 100; Freiburg: Universitätsverlag; Göttingen: Vandenhoeck & Ruprecht, 1990) 100, 105-10. In many cases, the animal involved cannot be properly identified (see also pp. 280-84).

197. See Othmar Keel, "Bildträger aus Palästina/Israel und die besondere Bedeutung der Miniaturkunst," in Keel and Silvia Schroer, *Studien zu den Stempelsiegeln aus Palästina/Israel* (OBO 67; Freiburg: Universitätsverlag; Göttingen: Vandenhoeck & Ruprecht, 1985) 1:35-37.

198. See Nahman Avigad, Michael Heltzer, and André Lemaire, *West Semitic Seals: Eighth-Sixth Centuries* BCE (Haifa: University of Haifa, 2000) #46, 65 (a grazing gazelle), 76, 79; see also a reclining ibex on a Moabite seal, #129; note also #134. Note also ibex scaraboid in Othmar Keel, *Corpus der Stempelsiegel-Amulette aus Palästina/Israel: Von den Anfängen bis zur Perserzeit: Einleitung* (OBO 10; Freiburg: Universitätsverlag; Göttingen: Vandenhoeck & Ruprecht, 1995) 67.

199. The iconography of hunting and warfare in Egypt and the Ancient Near East is discussed in the older work of William Stevenson Smith, *Interconnections in the Ancient Near-East: A Study of the Relationships between the Arts of Egypt, the Aegean, and Western Asia* (New Haven: Yale University Press, 1965) 147-54. For the broader context of iconography of warfare in Mesopotamia, see Ruth Mayer-Opificius, "War and Warfare on Cylinder Seals in the Ancient Near East," in *The Iconography of Cylinder Seals*, ed. Paul Taylor (Warburg Institute Colloquia 9; London: Warburg Institute; Turin: Nino Aragno Editore, 2006) 51-61.

200. For easily accessible examples, see the smiting 'Astart form on a seal from Bethel (*ANEP*, #468), the god with weapon and shield from Megiddo (*ANEP* #495-496), as well as the many depictions of the warrior deities from Ras Shamra (*ANEP*, #481-484). For important studies with more evidence, see Ora Negbi, *Canaanite Gods in Metal* (Publications of the Institute of Archaeology 5; Tel Aviv: Tel Aviv University Institute of Archaeology, 1976); and Helga Seeden, *The Standing Armed Figurines of the Levant* (Prähistorische Bronzefunde I/1; Munich, 1980). Note also the many depictions of West Semitic warrior deities from New Kingdom Egypt. For these, see Izak Cornelius, *The Iconography*

of the Canaanite Gods Reshef and Baʿal: Late Bronze and Iron Age I Periods (c 1500-1000 BCE) (OBO 140; Fribourg: University Press; Göttingen: Vandenhoeck & Ruprecht, 1994); and *The Many Faces of the Goddess: The Iconography of the Syro-Palestinian Goddesses Anat, Astarte, Qedeshet, and Asherah, c. 1500-1000 BCE* (OBO 204; Göttingen: Vandenhoeck & Ruprecht & Fribourg: Academic Press, 2004). Many depictions of warrior-deities are included in Othmar Keel and Christoph Uehlinger, *Gods, Goddesses, and Images of God*, trans. Thomas H. Trapp (Minneapolis: Fortress, 1998).

201. See Paolo Matthiae, "Masterpieces of Early and Old Syrian Art: Discoveries of the 1988 Ebla Excavations in a Historical Perspective," *Proceedings of the British Art Academy* 75 (1989) 25-56, and pls. I-XII, esp. 34-38 and pl. IV. Matthiae discussed this material in his essay "Figurative Themes and Literary Texts" in *Literature and Literary Language at Ebla*, ed. Pelio Fronzaroli (Quaderni di Semitistica 18; Florence: Universita di Firenze, 1992) 219-41, esp. 228.

202. See Davida Eisenberg Degen, "A Hunting Scene from the Negev: The Depiction of a Desert Kite and Throwing Weapon," *IEJ* 60 (2010) 146-65.

203. Hamilton, *The Origins of the West Semitic Alphabet in Egyptian Scripts* (CBQMS 40; Washington: Catholic Biblical Association of America, 2006) 314. As Hamilton explains on p. 315, two consonants inform the sign for **ṯann*.

204. As pointed out to me by Christopher Rollston (personal communication).

205. **yōd-*, "hand (and wrist or arm)"; **kapp-*, "palm (and wrist)"; **ʿayn-/*ʿên-*, "eye"; **raʾš-/*ri(ʾ)š-*, "head (in profile)." See Hamilton, *The Origins of the West Semitic Alphabet*, 108, 116, 180, 221.

206. For listing and discussion of up to perhaps six letters in this domain, see Hamilton, *The Origins of the West Semitic Alphabet*, 312-14.

207. **mêm-*, "water." See Hamilton, *The Origins of the West Semitic Alphabet*, 138.

208. See **ʾalp-*, "ox" or "bull"; **lamd-*, "coil of rope." See Hamilton, *The Origins of the West Semitic Alphabet*, 29, 126.

209. For this topic, see Izak Cornelius, "The Iconography of Weapons and Warfare in Palestine/Israel c. 1500-1200 BCE," *JNSL* 25 (1999) 263-75.

210. See Aruz, Benzel, and Evans, *Beyond Babylon*, 309, fig. 101.

211. *ANEP*, #157; Aruz, Benzel, and Evans, *Beyond Babylon*, 264-65, #165.

212. Aruz, Benzel, and Evans, *Beyond Babylon*, 265.

213. Aruz, Benzel, and Evans, *Beyond Babylon*, 264.

214. As pointed out to me by Trude Dothan.

215. Teissier, *Ancient Near Eastern Cylinder Seals*, 300, #656. In this connection, there is also the representation of a hunt's aftermath on a fourteenth-thirteenth century Hittite silver alloy cup, which includes two gods. Worshippers are depicted as bringing wine and bread before an enthroned god; behind him lies a dead stag. See Hans Güterbock, "A Note on the Friezes of the Stag Rhyton in the Schimmel Collection," *Anadolu* 22 (1981-83) 1-5; Oscar White Muscarella, "Vessel in the Form of a Stag," in *Metropolitan Museum of Art Bulletin* n.s. 49/4 (1992) 6-7; and Aruz, Benzel, and Evans, *Beyond Babylon*, 181, #107 and fig. 57.

216. Teissier, *Ancient Near Eastern Cylinder Seals from the Marcopoli Collection*, 300, #659.

217. RS 16.056 + 28.031, in Yon, *The City of Ugarit at Tell Ras Shamra*, 136.

218. RS 24.627, in Yon, *The City of Ugarit at Tell Ras Shamra*, 153, #40.

219. Yon, *The City of Ugarit at Tell Ras Shamra*, 164.

220. RS 5.031, *ANEP*, 56 and 270, #183; Yon, *The City of Ugarit at Tell Ras Shamra*, 165; see also the photograph in Aruz, Benzel, and Evans, *Beyond Babylon*, 242, item #147.

221. For another hunting scene, see the depiction of hounds pursuing wild goats on a tripod in Vassos Karageorghis, *Ancient Art from Cyprus: The Cesnola Collection in the Metropolitan Museum of Art* (New York: Metropolitan Museum of Art, 2000) 61.

222. See Gordon Loud, *The Megiddo Ivories* (OIP 52; Chicago: Oriental Institute, University of Chicago, 1939) 13, pl. 4, no. 2a (photograph) and pl. 4, no. 2b (drawing). Both are reproduced in *ANEP*, #332. The measurement for thickness is provided by Loud; the figure for the length is given in *ANEP* (288), which also provides a longer description.

223. The latter information was brought to my attention by Elizabeth Bloch-Smith.

224. Loud, *The Megiddo Ivories*, 17 and pl. 32, no. 159.

225. Loud, *The Megiddo Ivories*, 17 and pl. 33, no. 161.

226. See Tallay Ornan, "The Mesopotamian Influence on West Semitic Inscribed Seals: A Preference for the Depiction of Mortals," in *Studies in the Iconography of Northwest Semitic Inscribed Seals*, ed. Benjamin Sass and Christoph Uehlinger (OBO 125; Freiburg: Universitätsverlag; Göttingen: Vandenhoeck & Ruprecht, 1993) 54-55; and in the same volume, Eric Gubel, "The Iconography of Inscribed Phoenician Glyptic," 106-8.

227. For a useful discussion and depiction, see Othmar Keel, *Goddesses and Trees, New Moon and Yahweh: Ancient Near Eastern Art and the Hebrew Bible* (JSOTSup 261; Sheffield: Sheffield Academic, 1998) 114-20 and figs. 106 and 107; and *Chronicles of the Land: Archaeology in the Israel Museum, Jerusalem*, ed. Michal Dayagi-Mendels and Silvia Rozenberg (Jerusalem: Israel Museum, 2010) 86, #26. Many commentators accept the depiction in rather "straightforward" terms as the image of a god combining his bovine and anthropomorphic representations, e.g., "Baal-Hadad" in King and Stager, *Life in Biblical Israel*, 321. Keel argues against this view and suggests that the horns suggest lunar iconography and thus a symbol of the moon god. In the end, though, Keel hedges; speaking of the Bethsaida and Hauran stelae, he comments: "the stelae show a moon god interpreted as a weather god or a lunarized weather god." If I understand Keel correctly, he acknowledges the influence of the weather god's iconography. In short, we are back to the influence of a bovine weather god, at least to some degree. See also Tallay Ornan, "The Bull and Its Two Masters: Moon and Storm Deities in Relation to the Bull in Ancient Near Eastern Art," *IEJ* 51 (2001) 1-26. For my sense of the calf iconography in this case, see Mark S. Smith, "Counting Calves at Bethel," in White Crawford, *"Up to the Gates of Ekron,"* 382-94.

228. Shuval, "A Catalogue of Iron Age Stamp Seals from Israel," 77-87 and 88-91.

229. In addition to what follows, see the evidence discussed by Pirhiya Beck, in Meshel, *Kuntillet ʿAjrud (Ḥorvat Teman)*, 177.

230. *ANEP*, #791 and #790.

231. J. David Schloen and Amir Fink, "Searching for Ancient Samʾal: New Excavations at Zinjirli in Turkey," *NEA* 72 (2009) 205.

232. So Oded Borowski and Seung Ho Bang, "Cult Objects in Field V at Tell Halif,"

paper delivered at the 2011 meeting of the American Schools of Oriental Research. I am grateful to Seung Ho Bang for bringing this object to my attenton.

233. The representation of mourning women may apply to other areas besides warrior death, but would include it. For such representations, see Trude Dothan, "Another Mourning-Woman Figurine from the Lachish Area," *ErIsr* 11 (I. Dunayevsky Memorial Volume; 1973) 120-21 (Heb.).

234. For discussion of the comparable problem in Archaic and Classical Greece, see van Wees, *Status Warriors,* 153-65.

235. See *UBC* 2:725-30; and Dennis Pardee, *The Ugaritic Texts and the Origins of West-Semitic Literary Composition* (Schweich Lectures 2007; Oxford: Oxford University Press, 2012) 42-45.

236. These passages contain instructions for returning to a certain point in the story. A somewhat comparable instruction appears in a ritual text (KTU 1.40.35); see *UBC* 2:576.

237. For the issue, see *UBC* 2:574-75.

238. Cf. the similarly cautious judgment of Pardee, *The Ugaritic Texts,* 74-75.

239. Pardee (*The Ugaritic Texts,* 72 n. 64) suggests that the scribe's literary works reflect the royal ideology of the Ugaritic monarchy.

240. This text is the subject of the final section of Chapter Five.

241. See Chapter Five, section 3, for the ritual.

242. This is not to say that the administrative texts do not reflect military personnel; on the contrary.

243. The quotation comes from Smend, *Yahweh War and Tribal Confederation: Reflections upon Israel's Earliest History,* trans. from the 2nd ed. by Max Gray Rogers (Nashville: Abingdon, 1970) 12.

244. For this quotation, see Smend, *From Astruc to Zimmerli: Old Testament Scholarship in Three Centuries,* trans. Margaret Kohl (Tübingen: Mohr Siebeck, 2007) 214.

245. Cross, *Canaanite Myth and Hebrew Epic* (Cambridge, MA: Harvard University Press, 1973).

246. See Cross, *Canaanite Myth and Hebrew Epic,* viii, 82-90, 343-46. For a later effort to shore up the category of epic in early Israel, see his book, *From Epic to Canon,* 22-52.

247. For criticism along these lines, see Charles Conroy, "Hebrew Epic: Historical Notes and Critical Reflections," *Bib* 61 (1980) 2-14; Simon B. Parker, "Some Methodological Principles in Ugaritic Philology," *Maarav* 2 (1979) 32-33; Delbert Hillers, "Analyzing the Abominable: Our Understanding of Canaanite Religion," *JQR* 75 (1985) 253-69; and Mark S. Smith, "Biblical Narrative between Ugaritic and Akkadian Literature: Part II," *RB* 114 (2007) 189-207. Susan Niditch offers a sympathetic view of Cross's understanding of Israelite epic; "The Challenge of Israelite Epic," in *A Companion to Ancient Epic,* ed. John Miles Foley (Oxford: Blackwell, 2005) 277-87.

248. Cross's articulation of this part of his theory is best seen in *From Epic to Canon,* 22-52.

249. Cf. the methodological remarks of John Bright (*Early Israel in Recent History Writing: A Study in Method* [SBT 19; London: SCM; Chicago: Allenson, 1956] 11-16), despite the optimistic evaluation of biblical traditions, not to mention the use of archaeological data for claiming their high antiquity.

250. Lord, *The Singer of Tales* (2nd ed., Stephen Mitchell and Gregory Nagy; Harvard Studies in Comparative Literature 24; Cambridge, MA: Harvard University Press, 2000) 156.

251. An exception is Robert S. Kawashima, *Biblical Narrative and the Death of the Rhapsode* (Bloomington: Indiana University Press, 2004) 7, 214. Kawashima (pp. 9, 20) also accepts Cross's application of the theory of Milman Parry and Albert Lord (see Lord, *The Singer of Tales*) to Israelite epic poetry. Despite the problematic issues with this view, Kawashima makes a critically important observation concerning the distance between the older poetry and later biblical narrative. See Chapter Twelve for discussion. In Kawashima's defense, his interest lies in what he perceives to be novel about biblical narrative, with his discussions of older epic poetry largely serving as background to, and foil for, later biblical narrative.

252. See the overview of David M. Carr, *The Formation of the Hebrew Bible: A New Reconstruction* (Oxford: Oxford University Press, 2011) 358-60; cf. Alexander Rofé, *Introduction to the Literature of the Hebrew Bible* (Jerusalem Bible Studies 9; Jerusalem: Simor, 2009) 260-91. Many scholars now dispute a Yahwist source altogether. See the debate in the essays in *A Farewell to the Yahwist? The Composition of the Pentateuch in Recent European Interpretation*, ed. Thomas B. Dozeman and Konrad Schmidt (SBLSymS 34; Atlanta: Society of Biblical Literature, 2006). See the German forerunner to this volume (with no question mark in the title), *Abschied vom Jahwisten: Die Komposition des Hexateuch in der jüngsten Diskussion*, ed. Jan Christian Geertz, Konrad Schmid, and Markus Witte (BZAW 315; Berlin: de Gruyter, 2002); cf. the response by Christoph Levin, "Abschied vom Jahwisten?" *Theologische Rundschau* 69 (2004) 329-44. Some scholars who accept a Yahwist source J date it to the exile: see John Van Seters, *Prologue to History: The Yahwist as Historian: Genesis* (Louisville: Westminster/John Knox, 1992) 332; and *The Life of Moses: The Yahwist as Historian in Exodus-Numbers* (Louisville: Westminster John Knox, 1994). See the early diaspora setting proposed by Christoph Levin, *Der Jahwist* (FRLANT 157; Göttingen: Vandenhoeck & Ruprecht, 1993) 433-34; and "The Yahwist: The Earliest Editor in the Pentateuch," *JBL* 126 (2007) 209-30. For defense of the "Elohist," see the authors noted by Carr, *The Formation of the Hebrew Bible*, 358 n. 7; and Robert K. Gnuse, "Redefining the Elohist?" *JBL* 119 (2000) 201-20.

253. See Frank H. Polak, "Linguistic and Stylistic Aspects of Epic Formulae in Ancient Semitic Poetry and Biblical Narrative," in *Biblical Hebrew in Its Northwest Semitic Setting*, ed. Steven E. Fassberg and Avi Hurvitz (Jerusalem: Magnes; Winona Lake: Eisenbrauns, 2006) 285-304; "Book, Scribe, and Bard: Oral Discourse and Written Text in Recent Biblical Scholarship," *Prooftexts* 31 (2011) 134; and "Language Variation, Discourse Typology, and the Sociocultural Background of Biblical Narrative," in *Diachrony in Biblical Hebrew*, ed. Cynthia L. Miller-Naudé and Ziony Zevit (Winona Lake: Eisenbrauns, 2012) 301-38, esp. 303, 310-12, 317. Efforts in this vein continue; see, e.g., Alexander Rofé, "Clan Sagas as a Source in Settlement Traditions," in *"A Wise and Discerning Mind": Essays in Honor of Burke O. Long*, ed. Saul M. Olyan and Robert C. Culley (BJS 325; Providence: Brown Judaic Studies, 2000) 191-203, esp. p. 199. See more on this point below.

254. The results of Jeffrey H. Tigay's comparative project on the documentary hypothesis are remarkably minimal for positing any older epic source and lend little support

to Cross's approach. See Tigay, "The Stylistic Criterion of Source Criticism in the Light of Ancient Near Eastern and Postbiblical Literature," in *Empirical Models for Biblical Criticism* (Philadelphia: University of Pennsylvania Press, 1985), esp. 172-73.

255. On this score, see the critique of Delbert R. Hillers and Marsh H. McCall, Jr., "Homeric Dictated Texts: A Reexamination of Some Near Eastern Evidence," *Harvard Studies in Classical Philology* 80 (1976) 19-23. Note also the various sorts of scribal errors in the Ugaritic literary texts that might be suggestive of copying from a prior written text (see *UBC* 1:35). Recently, the view that the scribe knew texts via oral means has been defended by Dennis Pardee (*The Ugaritic Texts*, 47-50), based on the recently published RS 92.2016.40-43, esp. the claim apparently made by Ilimilku (as Pardee translates) that *'ind ylmdnn*, "no one ever taught him (it)/taught it (to him)." Pardee (*The Ugaritic Texts*, 47) surmises from this statement that Ilimilku "was an oral poet, that he learned the stories, not from someone whose duties were primarily scribal or more broadly administrative, but by listening to other oral poets until he was able to recite the poems on his own." Pardee (*The Ugaritic Texts*, 47-48 n. 19) notes other views. Given the exceptional information provided in the colophon of RS 92.2016.42b, perhaps no one ever taught this specific text to Ilimilku, in contrast to other texts, whose colophons lack this information. See also Johannes C. de Moor, "How Ilimilku Lost his Master (RS 92.2016)," *UF* 40 (2008) 185. In any case, oral dictation, as imagined by Cross, is not what Pardee envisions as the process for the production of the Ugaritic classics.

256. A number of classicists have been strongly critical of the Parry-Lord theory. For discussion, see Richard Janko, "The *Iliad* and Its Editors: Dictation and Redaction," *Classical Antiquity* 9 (1990) 326-34; and Martin L. West, *The Making of the Iliad: Disquisition and Analytical Commentary* (Oxford: Oxford University Press, 2011) 8-10. For these problems, see also Robert D. Miller II, SFO, *Oral Tradition in Ancient Israel* (Eugene: Wipf and Stock, 2011). Note also the comments on this issue in the review of this book by Raymond F. Person, Jr., *Review of Biblical Literature* [http://www.bookreviews.org] (2012).

257. Yair Zakovitch, "Yes, There Was an Israelite Epic in the Biblical Period," *International Folklore Review* 8 (1991) 18-25.

258. In *Proceedings of the Seventh World Congress of Jewish Studies*, Vol. 2: *Studies in the Bible and the Ancient Near East* (Jerusalem: World Union of Jewish Studies, 1981) 57.

259. Fritz, "The Complex of Traditions in Judges 4 and 5 and the Religion of Prestate Israel," in *"I Will Speak the Riddles of Ancient Times": Archaeological and Historical Studies in Honor of Amihai Mazar on the Occasion of His Sixtieth Birthday*, ed. Aren M. Maier and Pierre de Miroschedji (Winona Lake: Eisenbrauns, 2006) 2:695: "there was no development of epic verse, as occurred, for example, in ancient Greece."

260. Parker, "Some Methodological Principles in Ugaritic Philology," 32-33. See also Conroy, "Hebrew Epic," 13-14. Cross has offered a renewed defense of his use of the term "epic," in *From Epic to Canon*, 22-52. Though without some of the historical particulars in Cross's reconstruction, his usage of epic has been defended by Kawashima, *Biblical Narrative and the Death of the Rhapsode*, 7. See the further discussion above.

261. Smith, "Biblical Narrative between Ugaritic and Akkadian Literature: Part I: Ugarit and the Hebrew Bible: Consideration of Recent Comparative Research," *RB* 114 (2007) 5-29.

262. This is a standard view. See *The New Princeton Encyclopedia of Poetry and Poetics,* ed. Alex Preminger and T. V. F. Brogan (Princeton: Princeton University Press, 1993) 361; M. H. Abrams, *A Glossary of Literary Terms* (6th ed.; Fort Worth: Harcourt Brace, 1993) 53; Margaret Beissinger, Jane Tylus, and Susanne Wofford, "Introduction," in *Epic Traditions in the Contemporary World,* 2; and any number of the essays in Foley, *A Companion to Ancient Epic.*

263. Cross, *From Epic to Canon,* 32 n. 26.

264. Coogan, "A Structural and Literary Analysis of the Song of Deborah," *CBQ* 40 (1978) 165.

265. Piquer Otero, *Estudios de sintaxis verbal en textos ugaríticos: El* Ciclo de Baal *y la "poesía bíblica arcaica"* (Estella: Verbo Divino, 2007) 759.

266. The secondary literature treating definitions of epic in classical studies and comparative literature is voluminous. For a valuable interdisciplinary collection on the topic, see the essays in Beissinger, Tylus, and Wolford, *Epic Traditions in the Contemporary World.* The discussion of epic for the Late Bronze and Iron Age context in this work shows a problem with the term; its vagueness highlights a fundamental problem in using it, esp. in the reconstruction of the cultural context for this literature.

267. See Fokkelien van Dijk-Hemmes in Brenner and van Dijk-Hemmes, *On Gendering Texts,* 29. If so, the elements of the two domains of usage may influence one another.

268. The issues are complicated for the Song of Deborah, since she is called to sing in Judg. 5:12. This would suggest that her being the singer of the song is the imaginative act of the unnamed singer and less an indication of her "authorship." Given the selection of content mentioned by van Dijk-Hemmes, the poem as a whole may well reflect the creation of a poem out of older pieces as a woman's song. In other words, Deborah being held up by the poem as the singer may still be an indicator of Judges 5 as a women's song. For discussion, see Chapter Nine.

269. See Chapter Eleven for discussion of this couplet.

270. See Chapter Ten.

271. I owe this observation to my student, Ella Metuqi. It is to be noted that the comparison of Enuma Elish and the Baal Cycle has been overdrawn, resulting in a number of misperceptions about the Baal Cycle. See *UBC* 1:79-87, 103-5; *UBC* 2:16-18; and Aaron Tugendhaft, "Baal and the Problem of Politics in the Bronze Age" (Ph.D. diss., New York University, 2012) 40-62.

272. See Gordon, "Indo-European and Hebrew Epic," 10*-15*. For Gordon, the epic tradition of ancient Israel belonged to an eastern Mediterranean tradition that was influenced by Indo-European immigrants. There is unfortunately little evidence for this theory. Still, a number of Gordon's specific comparisons are worth noting (see the preceding section).

273. See Cassuto, "The Israelite Epic," *Knesset* 8 (1943) 121-43 (Heb.); trans. in *Biblical and Oriental Studies,* Vol. 2: *Bible and Ancient Oriental Texts,* trans. Israel Abrahams (Jerusalem: Magnes, 1975) 69-109. See also Jonas C. Greenfield, "The Hebrew Bible and Canaanite Literature," in *The Literary Guide to the Bible,* ed. Robert Alter and Frank Kermode (Cambridge, MA: Belknap, 1987) 545-60.

274. See also Zakovitch, "Yes, There Was an Israelite Epic."

275. Cross, *Canaanite Myth and Hebrew Epic,* viii. Cross's disagreement with Cassuto seems to have stemmed from the former's unstated genre considerations. In a letter to me dated 27 November 1998, Cross wrote: "I draw a distinction between epic (placed in space and time with some, but not exclusively, human actors) and (raw) myth where only the gods are actors. Cassuto's 'epic' comes closer to my 'myth' — though this is an oversimplification. Keret is an epic, the Baʿl cycle a mythic cycle."

276. The point has been reaffirmed in more recent discussions: Smith, "Biblical Narrative between Ugaritic and Akkadian Literature: Part I"; Edward L. Greenstein, "Texts from Ugarit Solve Biblical Puzzles," *BAR* 36/6 (2010) 48-53; and Pardee, *The Ugaritic Texts,* 79-80. Greenstein ("Texts from Ugarit," 53) holds a particularly strong view of this relationship: "The ancient Hebrew authors were apparently trained in the conventions of ancient Canaanite literature, and in the course of their training they learned the classics of that tradition." While the first claim is evident from the multitudinous parallel uses of poetic conventions, the second claim is not nearly as well founded. Otherwise, I essentially agree with Greenstein's view.

277. See Polak, "Linguistic and Stylistic Aspects"; see further *UBC* 2:449. Note the older effort to see epic poetry in the prose of Samuel-Kings by D. Arvid Bruno, *Das hebräische Epos: Eine rhythmische und textkritische Untersuchung der Bücher Samuelis und Könige* (Uppsala: Almqvist & Wiksells, 1935). This effort also informs the perspective of Niditch, "The Challenge of Israelite Epic," 285.

278. Cross, *Canaanite Myth and Hebrew Epic,* ix.

279. See Parker, *The Pre-Biblical Narrative Tradition.*

280. In addition to his works mentioned above, see also Cross, "Telltale Remnants of Oral Epic in the Older Sources of the Tetrateuch: Double and Triple Proper Names in Early Hebrew sources, and in Homeric and Ugaritic Epic Poetry," in Schloen, *Exploring the Longue Durée,* 83-88. On this point, note also Holger Gzella, "Linguistic Variation in the Ugaritic Letters and Some Implications Thereof," in *Society and Administration in Ancient Ugarit,* ed. Wilfred H. van Soldt (Leiden: Brill, 2010) 59.

281. For the notion of Genesis through Kings as Israel's "anti-epic," see Smith, "Biblical Narrative between Ugaritic and Akkadian Literature: Part I" and "Part II."

282. For some recent discussions, see Mark S. Smith, *God in Translation: Deities in Cross-Cultural Discourse in the Biblical World* (FAT 57; Tübingen: Mohr Siebeck, 2008; Grand Rapids: Eerdmans, 2010) 139-43, 195-212; and Ronnie Goldstein, "A New Look at Deuteronomy 32:8-9 and 43 in Light of Akkadian Sources," *Tarbiz* 79 (2010-11) 5-21 (Heb.).

283. In this regard, note the argument for early Saul traditions written down in his reign (and later rewritten), as made by Marsha White, "'The History of Saul's Rise': Saulide State Propaganda in 1 Samuel 1–14," in Olyan and Culley, *"A Wise and Discerning Mind,"* 271-92; and Mark Leuchter, "'Now There Was a [Certain] Man': Compositional Chronology in Judges–1 Samuel," *CBQ* 69 (2007) 429-39, esp. 432-34. Evidence as such remains a difficulty for the view. See also the discussion below in the treatment of Avi Faust's work.

284. See the discussion and secondary literature in Lawson Stone, *From Tribal Confederation to Monarchic State: The Editorial Perspective of the Book of Judges* (Dissertations in Biblical Studies 50; Piscataway: Gorgias, 2009).

285. Faust, *Israel's Ethnogenesis* (London: Equinox, 2007). I wish to thank Avi Faust for his helpful response in an e-mail (10 September 2012), made to the discussion that follows. Based on his remarks, I have added some clarifications and modifications.

286. At the same time, note the criticisms of Bunimovitz and Faust on this score by Israel Finkelstein, "Chronology Rejoinders," *PEQ* 134 (2002) 118-29.

287. A further issue about Faust's book concerns whether or not biblical historiography and its claims about early Israel inform the horizons of his intellectual project of reconstructing early Israel. In fairness, few if any intellectual projects about early Israel (including my own here, and here note the admission of Cross, *Canaanite Myth and Hebrew Epic,* ix) can escape the influence of later Israelite historiography about the Iron I situation (and down into the tenth or ninth century), which from the perspective of Israel's prose historiography constitutes what I would (and do below) call Israel's "lost world." I leave it to readers to decide about the effort made here to rely primarily on earlier sources in or closer to the Iron I period. See further below.

288. See Faust, *Israel's Ethnogenesis,* 24-26, 83 n. 12, 178.

289. Faust, *Israel's Ethnogenesis,* 58.

290. See Faust, *Israel's Ethnogenesis,* 59-60, 80, and 82.

291. Faust, *Israel's Ethnogenesis,* 91.

292. Again, see White, " 'The History of Saul's Rise' "; and Leuchter, " 'Now There Was a [Certain] Man,' " esp. 432-34. Whether or not these traditions go back to Saul's own reign, as Leuchter would have it, is not demonstrated, but it is not entirely implausible. A tenth-century date is suggested by Baruch Halpern, *David's Secret Demons: Messiah, Murderer, Traitor, King* (BIW; Grand Rapids: Eerdmans, 2001) 57-72. For a critical assessment, see Edelman, "Saul ben Kish in History and Tradition."

293. See Faust, *Israel's Ethnogenesis,* 218, esp. n. 40.

294. The issue is discussed at considerable length in Chapters Eight and Nine below.

295. See Chapter Nine for this issue.

296. Faust's discussion of circumcision is a more complex case of using biblical texts. See Faust, *Israel's Ethnogenesis,* 86-90. Based almost exclusively on biblical prose texts, Faust (p. 88) concludes: "while there is agreement that the discussed texts are later than the Iron Age I, there is an interesting dichotomy: texts that refer to the Iron I use the term 'uncircumcised' to describe the Philistines, in contrast to texts that refer to the Iron II, which do not use the term for such purposes." However, it is arguable that the prose passages should be used as historical sources for the attitude about such matters in their time of composition (in the Iron II or later) rather than for the time to which they refer (Iron I) unless some further basis is provided; however, none is provided. Without further argumentation, such biblical passages cannot serve for drawing conclusions for the Iron I. Thus, the presupposition of cultural accuracy for such a negative attitude about Philistines as "uncircumcised" in the Iron I period based on texts known to be considerably later remains in the realm of speculation. To be sure, the older poetic source, 2 Sam. 1:20, which is also mentioned, would be a more promising starting point for grounding any cultural attitude about the Philistines by the end of the Iron I. Note also the broad generalization about the Philistines in the Bible, in Faust, *Israel's Ethnogenesis,* 146.

297. See also Faust, *Israel's Ethnogenesis,* 132 esp. n. 24, 187 n. 22, 230 n. 8. Note also his reflections on p. 230 on the use of biblical texts.

298. See the reflections of Frederic Brandfon, "The Limits of Evidence: Archaeology and Objectivity," *Maarav* 4 (1987) 5-43. For some brief considerations of the study of archaeological and biblical evidence, see also the critical comments by Anson F. Rainey, "The Identification of Philistine Gath: A Problem in Source Analysis for Historical Geography," *ErIsr* 12 (Nelson Glueck Memorial Volume; 1975) 75*-76*. For an effort to address the relationship between inscriptional texts and archaeology, see Seymour Gitin, "Israelite and Philistine Cult and the Archaeological Record in Iron Age II: The 'Smoking Gun' Phenomenon," in *Symbiosis, Symbolism, and the Power of the Past: Canaan, Ancient Israel, and Their Neighbors — From the Late Bronze Age through Roman Palaestina,* ed. William G. Dever and Gitin (AIAR Anniversary Volume; Winona Lake: Eisenbrauns, 2003) 279-95. This piece does not address the issues involving the use of biblical texts per se. William G. Dever has often addressed the roles of texts and archaeology in the reconstruction of history. See, e.g., the listing of Dever's articles on the subject in Dever, "Archaeology and the Current Crisis in Israelite Historiography," *ErIsr* 25 (Joseph Aviram Volume; 1996) 26*. At the same time, Dever's discussions do not focus on the methodological issues involving the use of biblical texts in tandem with archaeological research in producing a synthetic result. Mostly Dever refers to convergences between the two, but does not explore these matters in any depth. Cf. the survey of broader philosophical issues by J. David Schloen, *The House of the Father as Fact and Symbol: Patrimonialism in Ugarit and the Ancient Near East* (Studies in the Archaeology and History of the Levant 2; Winona Lake: Eisenbrauns, 2001) 7-48. Schloen's discussion does not address the use of biblical texts in historical synthesis with archaeological data.

299. For discussion and secondary literature, see Hamilton, *The Origins of the West Semitic Alphabet;* and Seth L. Sanders, *The Invention of Hebrew* (Urbana: University of Illinois Press , 2009). See also Sanders, "Writing and Early Iron Age Israel: Before National Scripts, Beyond Nations and States" in *Literate Culture and Tenth-Century Canaan: The Tel Zayit Abecedary in Context,* ed. Ron E. Tappy and P. Kyle McCarter (Winona Lake: Eisenbrauns, 2008) 97-112.

300. See Wayne Horowitz and Takayoshi Oshima, with Seth L. Sanders, *Cuneiform in Canaan: Cuneiform Sources from the Land of Israel in Ancient Times* (Jerusalem: Israel Exploration Society/Hebrew University, 2006).

301. See Part III of this study for resources for the Ugaritic texts.

302. The iconographic studies for the Late Bronze and Iron I periods in the southern Levant are numerous and highly involved. For a basic survey, see Keel and Uehlinger, *Gods, Goddesses, and Images of God.*

303. The standard translation at present is William L. Moran, ed., *The Amarna Letters* (Baltimore: Johns Hopkins University, 1992). A new edition was undertaken by the late Anson Rainey; it is hoped that it may yet appear.

304. A helpful summary can be found in Donald Redford, *Egypt, Canaan, and Israel in Ancient Times* (Princeton: Princeton University Press, 1992).

305. If the implicit defense for not citing such texts (readily available in translation, as suggested by the preceding citations) is that the book is a work of archaeological re-

search, this is understandable, but in that case then biblical texts on other topics should not be cited.

306. Shlomo Bunimovitz and Avi Faust, "Reconstructing Biblical Archaeology: Toward an Integration of Archaeology and the Bible," in *Historical Biblical Archaeology and the Future: The New Pragmatism,* ed. Thomas E. Levy (London: Equinox, 2011) 43-54. See also Faust's piece in the same volume, "Future Directions in the Study of Ethnicity in Ancient Israel," 55-68.

307. For a critical discussion of the older biblical archaeology, as practiced e.g. by William Foxwell Albright and G. Ernest Wright, see Thomas W. Davis, *Shifting Sands: The Rise and Fall of Biblical Archaeology* (Oxford: Oxford University Press, 2004).

308. In all fairness, I should at least mention an example of what I have in mind. Bunimovitz and Faust ("Reconstructing Biblical Archaeology," 48-49) offer the following:

> The common Biblical Hebrew word for east is *qedma* (forward), while the west is *ahora* (backward) (e.g. Drinkard 1992a, 1992b). As Malamat (1989: 67) phrased it: 'The early Israelite ego faced east'. Moreover, additional words for those directions indicate that the east had a good connotation while the west had a bad one. The common word for west in Biblical Hebrew is *yam,* literally 'Sea', which is the most conspicuous element in this direction. But the word *yam,* beside designating a large body of water and westerly orientation, had some other meanings as well, and in many cases it represents the forces of chaos, sometimes personified in the *Leviathan* or other legendary creatures (Lewis 1993: 335; see also Ahlström 1986: 49; Stoltz 1995: 1397-98; Keel 1978: 23, 35, 49, 50, 55, 73-75).
>
> The matching of the archaeological pattern, human tendency to prefer the east, and the evidence that the Israelites not only oriented themselves to the east but had even attributed positive and negative meaning to the various directions, seem to be sufficient to conclude that the Israelites viewed the east as a hospitable place (and the west as an inhospitable one), and this is the reason for the eastward orientation of structures and settlements.

This would-be "explanation" is given without basis for the Iron I period. No evidence is provided for an actual connection between the various meanings of this word (i.e., west and sea as the place where cosmic enemies dwell) and some of its putative cultural associations in ancient Israel (i.e., east as good and west or sea as "bad," or east as hospitable and west as inhospitable). In view of these issues, it seems that the quoted material weaves various bits of biblical information into a kind of imaginative midrash connecting real meanings and putative associations of *yām.*

309. Bunimovitz and Faust, "Reconstructing Biblical Archaeology," 49. Bunimovitz and Faust also note exceptions to the eastern orientation of structures and settlements in the first place as well, suggesting that the feature of the prevalent eastern orientation of houses and settlements may itself be in some doubt. It would be interesting to examine the picture of Israel more fully against corresponding remains in the Iron I Transjordan. See Herr, "Jordan in the Iron I Period."

310. For archaeological surveys of the Iron I period that appear to be more descriptive and less ideologically driven, see Elizabeth Bloch-Smith and Beth Alpert Nakhai,

"A Landscape Comes to Life: The Iron Age I," *NEA* 62 (1999) 72-102, 111-44; and Amihai Mazar, "Remarks on Biblical Traditions and Archaeological Evidence concerning Early Israel," in Dever and Gitin, *Symbiosis, Symbolism, and the Power of the Past,* 85-98. See also the essays in Grabbe, *Israel in Transition* 1.

311. A model of restraint in the use of the biblical text in an archaeologist's discussion of early Israel is Mazar, "Remarks on Biblical Traditions."

312. Knauf, "Deborah's Language: Judges Ch. 5 in Its Hebrew and Semitic Context," in *Studia Semitica et Semito-hamitica: Festschrift für Rainer Voigt anlässlich seines 60 Geburtstages am 17. Januar 2004,* ed. Burtea Bogdan, Josef Tropper, and Helen Younansardaroud (AOAT 317; Münster: Ugarit-Verlag, 2005) 170.

313. See Chapters Eight through Ten for the arguments for the dating of the biblical poems used. It is my view that the traditions of Judges 5 or at least parts of it date to the Iron I period and that in the main 2 Sam. 1:19-27 dates to the tenth century. The issues are complex, as Chapters Eight through Ten indicate.

314. See David A. Robertson, *Linguistic Evidence in Dating Early Poetry* (SBLDS 3; Missoula: Society of Biblical Literature, 1972) 3.

315. E.g., in v. 10, the combination of *šîlōh,* understood as **šaylô* with the parallel term, *yiqqĕhat.* See William L. Moran, "Genesis 49,10 and Its Use in Ez 21,32," *Bib* 39 (1958) 405-25; and Richard Steiner, "Poetic Forms in the Masoretic Vocalization and Three Difficult Phrases in Jacob's Blessing," *JBL* 129 (2010) 209-35, here 219-26; see also Steiner, "Four Inner-Biblical Interpretations of Genesis 49:10: On the Lexical and Syntactic Ambiguities of עַד as Reflected in the Prophecies of Nathan, Ahijah, Ezekiel, and Zechariah," *JBL* 132 (2013) 33-60. Cf. Ps. 68:30. I am aware of the attestation of the former in Ps. 76:12 and Isa. 18:7 and of the latter in Prov. 30:17 (cf. the root twice in KTU 1.2 I 34-35; *UBC* 1:290-91).

316. This seems to be Asherah, given the parallelism of "your father," which appears to be El (cf. the juxtaposition with El and Shadday earlier in the verse).

317. See the negative conclusion about the high date of Genesis 49 reached by Robertson, *Linguistic Evidence in Dating Early Poetry,* 138. However, Robertson does not consider matters of lexicon or culture.

318. The oldest — and most optimistic — dating for Psalm 68 of which I am aware is given in two on-line articles by Israel Knohl, "Pharaoh's War with the Israelites: The Untold Story," *Azureonline* 41 (2010) on-line journal: http://www.azure.org.il/article.php?id=543; and Knohl, "Psalm 68: Structure, Composition and Geography," *JHS* 12/5 (2012) http://www.jhsonline.org/JHS/Articles/article_177.pdf. According to Knohl, Psalm 68 (except vv. 1-4 and some other secondary additions) is a victory hymn over Merneptah in the Transjordan following the geographical progression of the place names in the Merneptah stele (Ashkelon, Gezer, and Yanoam) following the lead of Anson Rainey, "Whence Came the Israelites and Their Language?" *IEJ* 57 (2007) 41-64; "Redefining Hebrew — a Transjordanian Language," *Maarav* 14 (2007) 67-81; and "Inside, Outside: Where Did the Early Israelites Come From?" *BAR* 34/6 (2008) 45-50. The body of the psalm, for Knohl, would have been composed shortly after the battle ca. 1210. The geographical progression may indicate a location to the north or east of Gezer; a location in Transjordan, while possible, is not required by the Merneptah stele. For strong criticism of the linguistic component of Rainey's argument, see Jo Ann Hackett and Na'ama Pat-El,

"On Canaanite and Historical Linguistics: A Rejoinder to Anson Rainey," *Maarav* 17 (2010) 173-88. It is to be noted that an earlier reference to Israel in an Egyptian inscription said to date to the reign of Ramesses II has been claimed by Peter van der Veen, Christoffer Theis, and Manfred Görg, "Israel in Canaan (Long) Before Pharaoh Merneptah? A Fresh Look at Berlin Statue Pedestal Relief 21687," *Journal of Ancient Egyptian Interconnections* 2/4 (2010) 15-25 (http://jaei.library.arizona.edu).

319. I do not say "final form," because from a text-critical point of view, "final form" is arguably a very late matter (dating to the turn of the era), if not a mirage (given the ongoing changes of the text for many centuries subsequently). For some of the issues, see John Barton, "Intertextuality and the 'Final Form' of the Text," in *Congress Volume: Oslo 1998*, ed. André Lemaire and Saebø Magne (VTSup 80; Leiden: Brill, 2000) 33-37; cf. Georg Steins, *Kanonisch-intertextuelle Studien zum Alten Testament* (Stuttgarter Biblische Aufsatzbände 48; Stuttgart: Katholisches Bibelwerk, 2009).

320. I am aware of criticism of the linguistic dating of old poetry. See Ian Young, "Biblical Texts Cannot Be Dated Linguistically," *HS* 46 (2005) 342-43; see also his earlier essay, "The Style of the Gezer Calendar and Some 'Archaic Biblical Hebrew' Passages," *VT* 42 (1992) 362-75; and Robyn C. Vern, *Dating Archaic Biblical Hebrew Poetry: A Critique of the Linguistic Arguments* (Perspectives on Hebrew Scriptures and Its Contexts 10; Piscataway: Gorgias, 2011). Cf. Avi Hurvitz, "The Historical Quest for 'Ancient Israel' and the Linguistic Evidence of the Hebrew Bible: Some Methodological Observations," *VT* 47 (1997) 301-15. See also the two-volume work of Young with Robert Rezetko, *Biblical Hebrew: Studies in Chronology and Typology* (New York: T. & T. Clark, 2003). For critical responses, see Hurvitz, "The Recent Debate on Late Biblical Hebrew: Solid Data, Experts' Opinions, and Inconclusive Arguments," *HS* 47 (2006) 191-210; Jan Joosten, "Diachronic Aspects of Narrative *wayhi* in Biblical Hebrew," *JNSL* 35/2 (2009) 43-61, esp. 58-59; and Jacobus A. Naudé, "Linguistic Dating of Biblical Hebrew Texts: The Chronology and Typology Debate," *JNSL* 36/2 (2010) 1-22, esp. 15-18; Joosten, Review of Ian Young and Robert Rezetko, with the assistance of Martin Ehrensvärd, *Linguistic Dating of Biblical Texts*, Vol. 1: *An Introduction to Approaches and Problems*, in *Babel und Bibel 2011* (in press). See also Robert Holmstedt and John Cook, http://ancienthebrewgrammar.wordpress.com/. See the discussion in Chapter Eight.

321. Levine, *Numbers 21–36*, 232.

322. By contrast, an older-looking piece consisting of vv. 8-16 has perhaps been incorporated into the royal psalm of thanksgiving of 2 Samuel 22//Psalm 18; see Cross, *Canaanite Myth and Hebrew Epic*, 158-59. In their older study, Cross and Freedman proposed a ninth-eighth century date for Psalm 18//2 Samuel 22, based on the orthographic evidence. See Cross and Freedman, *Studies in Ancient Yahwistic Poetry*, 7. The verbal discrepancies between these two versions show additional updating of vocabulary. See Georg Schmuttermayr, *Psalm 18 und 2 Samuel 22: Studien zu einem Doppeltext. Probleme der Textkritik und Ubersetzung und das Psalterium Pianum* (SANT 25; Munich: Kösel, 1971); and Cross, *Canaanite Myth and Hebrew Epic*, 158-59.

323. For a late-twelfth-century or early-eleventh-century dating based on linguistic and other criteria, see Cross, *Canaanite Myth and Hebrew Epic*, 124; Cross and Freedman, *Studies in Ancient Yahwistic Poetry*, 33; Robertson, *Linguistic Evidence in Dating Early*

Hebrew Poetry, 147-56; and more recently, Brian D. Russell, *The Song of the Sea: The Date of Composition and Influence of Exodus 15:1-21* (Studies in Biblical Literature 101; New York: Lang, 2007). A high date is also entertained by Aloysius Fitzgerald, F.S.C., *The Lord of the East Wind* (CBQMS 34; Washington: Catholic Biblical Association of America, 2002) 70 n. 14. However, he also comments that the "linguistic evidence is not that easy to control," and he allows for the possibility of a ninth-century dating for Exodus 15. For a critique of higher datings as well as late datings, see Stephen C. Russell, *Images of Egypt in Early Biblical Literature: Cisjordan-Israelite, Transjordan-Israelite and Judahite Portrayals* (BZAW 403; Berlin: de Gruyter, 2009) 133-48. I would comment on one of the alleged grammatical criteria. The high date of Exodus 15 has been been based in part on its poem's use of the so-called old **yaqtul* preterite. However, this view is arguably complicated by the **yaqtulu* form in the poem (*yirgāzûn* in v. 14, along with two **qatal* forms), as well as the number of **qatala* forms to set the past timeframe for the poem. As a result, the so-called **yaqtul* preterite as claimed may be neither correct nor significant for a high date. See the discussion of this feature in Chapter Eight.

324. See esp. Chapter Eleven, as well as Chapter Seven.

325. For comparable issues in Homeric scholarship, see van Wees, *Status Warriors,* 15-23.

326. The classic statement was Lawrence E. Stager, "The Archaeology of the Family in Ancient Israel," *BASOR* 260 (1985) 1-35.

327. See Abraham Malamat, "Premonarchical Social Institutions in Israel in the Light of Mari," in *Congress Volume: Jerusalem 1986,* ed. John A. Emerton (VTSup 40; Leiden: Brill, 1988) 165-76; and "A Recently Discovered Word for 'Clan' in Mari and Its Hebrew Cognate," in *Solving Riddles and Untying Knots: Biblical, Epigraphic, and Semitic Studies in Honor of Jonas C. Greenfield,* ed. Ziony Zevit, Seymour Gitin and Michael Sokoloff (Winona Lake: Eisenbrauns, 1995) 177-79.

328. See Jonas C. Greenfield, "The 'Cluster' in Biblical Poetry," in *Sopher Mahir: Northwest Semitic Studies Presented to Stanislav Segert,* ed. Edward M. Cook (Santa Monica: Western Academic) = *Maarav* 5-6 (1990) 159-68; repr. in Greenfield, *'Al Kanfei Yonah,* 789-98. Ezekiel 14 and 28 show knowledge of the figure of Danil, and many biblical passages contain other information prominent in Ugaritic literature. For a stronger view of the relationship, namely, that biblical authors learned the classic texts known at Ugarit, see Greenstein, "Texts from Ugarit Solve Biblical Puzzles," 53.

329. This point was demonstrated with a number of vocabulary items found in Ugaritic and in later Hebrew. See, e.g., Baruch A. Levine, "*Mulugu/Melûg:* The Origins of a Talmudic Legal Institution," *JAOS* 88 (Essays in Memory of E. A. Speiser; 1968) 271-84. Levine's dissertation was dedicated to this topic: "Survivals of Ancient Canaanite in the Mishnah" (Ph.D. diss., Brandeis, 1962).

330. For this question, see Chapter Twelve. My dates for the early poetry are discussed in Chapters Eight and Ten (namely Judges 5 and 2 Sam. 1:19-27).

331. For further discussion, see Mark S. Smith, "Why Was 'Old Poetry' Used in Hebrew Narrative? Historical and Cultural Considerations about Judges 5," in Lundberg, Fine, and Pitard, *Puzzling Out the Past,* 197-212. See also Levine, *Numbers 21–36,* 92: "an epic citation confirms the narrative, and is quoted for that purpose. Quite possibly, this

is the function of such epic poems as Exodus 15, the Song of the Sea, and Judges 5, the Song of Deborah, both of which are preceded by narratives covering the events celebrated in the poems."

332. Faust, *Israel's Ethnogenesis*, 114-19. Whether or not this is truly a matter of interplay between rural and urban dynamics, Faust's observation is important.

333. Nor do I assume or seek to apply specific social-science models to early Israel. On this question, compare the older discussions of Jack W. Sasson, "On Choosing Models for Recreating Israelite Premonarchical Israel," *JSOT* 21 (1981) 3-24; Abraham Malamat, "Die Frühgeschichte Israels: eine methodologische Studie," *TZ* 39 (1983) 1-16; and the essays on Iron I Israel in David Chalcraft, ed., *Social Scientific Old Testament Criticism* (Biblical Seminar 47; Sheffield: Sheffield Academic, 1997). Note also Carol Meyers, "The Family in Early Israel," in Leo G. Perdue, Joseph Blenkinsopp, John J. Collins, and Meyers, *Families in Ancient Israel* (Louisville: Westminster John Knox, 1997) 1-47; and "Early Israel and the Rise of the Israelite Monarchy," in *The Blackwell Companion to the Hebrew Bible*, ed. Leo G. Perdue (Oxford: Blackwell, 2001) 61-86. For more recent discussions, see Emanuel Pfoh, ed., *Anthropology and the Bible* (Biblical Intersections 3; Piscataway: Gorgias, 2010); and Saul M. Olyan, ed., *Social Theory and the Study of Israelite Religion: Essays in Retrospect and Prospect* (SBLRBS 71; Atlanta: Society of Biblical Literature, 2012).

Notes to Chapter Two

1. For the background of Thetis' marriage to Peleus, see David R. West, "The Lion and the Serpent: Two Semitic Themes of the Goddess Thetis," *UF* 35 (2003) 709-11.

2. Gregory Nagy, *The Best of the Achaeans: Concepts of the Hero in Archaic Greek Poetry* (rev. ed.; Baltimore: Johns Hopkins University Press, 1999) 26: "It is an overall Iliadic theme that Achilles is 'best of the Achaeans.'" For consideration of this theme, see section two below in the discussion of Achilles and Patroklos.

3. For these pairs of warriors, see Susan Ackerman, *When Heroes Love: The Ambiguity of Eros in the Stories of Gilgamesh and David* (New York: Columbia University Press, 2005); and Jean-Fabrice Nardelli, *Homosexuality and Liminality in the Gilgameš and Samuel* (Classical and Byzantine Monographs 64; Amsterdam: Hakkert, 2007). Note also Thomas Römer and Loyse Bonjour, *L'homosexualité dans le Proche-Orient ancien et la Bible* (Essais bibliques 37; Geneva: Labor et Fides, 2005) 61-102. For further discussion of the sexual nature of these male-male relationships, see the next chapter.

4. By the way, this epic feature corresponds to the epic importance of the enemy faced by the hero: the hero is only as great as the enemy that he defeats: the more fierce and terrifying the enemy, the greater the hero. Thus, the enemy is particularly important for elevating the epic hero. Such enemies include not only Humbaba (Huwawa) in the Gilgamesh tradition, or Goliath for David, but also Tiamat in *Enuma Elish* and Yamm and Mot in the Ugaritic Baal Cycle, as well as Leviathan (Litan). An analogous issue involves the differing relationships among the deities hovering over the destinies of the heroic pairs. This matter lies beyond the scope of this discussion, but I would mention one comparative discussion of divine and human causality of events in the *Iliad*, the Bible,

and Mesopotamian texts: Isac Leo Seeligmann, "Menschliches Heldentum und göttliche Hilfe: Die doppelte Kausalität im alttestamentlichen Geschichtsdenken," *TZ* 19 (1963) 385-411, republished in *Gesammelte Studien zur Hebräischen Bibel,* ed. Erhard Blum (FAT 41; Tübingen: Mohr Siebeck, 2004) 137-59.

5. Unless otherwise indicated, the text and translation as well as references reflect the magisterial work of Andrew R. George, *The Babylonian Gilgamesh Epic: Introduction, Critical Edition, and Cuneiform Texts* (2 vols.; Oxford: Oxford University Press, 2003). See also George's transliteration of the text on-line at http://www.etana.org/abzu (reference courtesy of Peter Machinist). I have standardized the English spellings of some of the personal names in the translations, e.g., Gilgamesh and Huwawa.

6. Tigay, *The Evolution of the Gilgamesh Epic* (Philadelphia: University of Pennsylvania Press, 1982; repr. Wauconda: Bolchazy-Carducci, 2002). See also Tigay, "The Evolution of the Pentateuchal Narratives in the Light of the Evolution of the Gilgamesh Epic," in *Empirical Models for Biblical Criticism* (Philadelphia: University of Pennsylvania Press, 1985; repr. Eugene: Wipf & Stock, 2005) 21-52.

7. George, *The Babylonian Gilgamesh Epic,* 1:3-70. See also Thorkild Jacobsen, *The Treasures of Darkness: A History of Mesopotamian Religion* (New Haven: Yale University Press, 1976) 208-15; "The Gilgamesh Epic: Romantic and Tragic Vision," in *Lingering Over Words: Studies in Ancient Near Eastern Literature in Honor of William L. Moran,* ed. Tzvi Abusch, John Huehnergard, and Piotr Steinkeller (HSS 37; Atlanta: Scholars, 1990) 231-49. See also William L. Moran, "The Gilgamesh Epic: A Masterpiece from Ancient Mesopotamia," in *CANE,* 4:2327-36; repr. in *The Epic of Gilgamesh: A New Translation, Analogues, Criticism,* trans. and ed. Benjamin R. Foster (New York: Norton, 2001) 171-83; and Moran's essay, "The Epic of Gilgamesh: A Document of Ancient Humanism," *Bulletin of the Canadian Society for Mesopotamian Studies* 22 (1991) 15-22; repr. in Moran, *The Most Magic Word,* ed. Ronald S. Hendel (CBQMS 35; Washington: Catholic Biblical Association of America, 2002) 5-20. Note also the diachronic remarks in Walther Sallaberger, *Das Gilgamesh-Epos: Mythos, Werk und Tradition* (Munich: Beck, 2008); and in the older study of Jerrold S. Cooper, "Gilgamesh Dreams of Enkidu: The Evolution and Dilution of Narrative," in *Essays on the Ancient Near East in Memory of Jacob Joel Finkelstein,* ed. Maria de Jong Ellis (Memoirs of the Connecticut Academy of Arts & Sciences 19; Hamden: Archon, 1977) 39-44. For a recent discussion esp. of the OB material, see Daniel E. Fleming and Sara J. Milstein, *The Buried Foundation of the Gilgamesh Epic: The Akkadian Huwawa Narrative* (Cuneiform Monographs 39; Leiden: Brill, 2010). See also Sara J. Milstein, "Reworking Ancient Texts: Revision through Introduction in Biblical and Mesopotamian Literature" (Ph.D. diss., New York University, 2010) 89-123.

8. Daniel Arnaud, *Corpus des texts de bibliothèque de Ras Shamra-Ougarit (1936-2000) en sumérien, babylonien et assyrien* (AuOrSup 23; Barcelona: Editorial AUSA, 2007). See also Andrew R. George, "The Gilgamesh Epic at Ugarit," *AuOr* 25 (2007) 237-54; Milstein, "Reworking Ancient Texts," 89-100; and Catherine Mittermayer, "Gilgameš im Wandel der Zeit," in *Gilgamesch — Ikonographie eines Helden/Gilgamesh: Epic and Iconography,* ed. Hans Ulrich Steymans (OBO 245; Fribourg: Academic; Göttingen: Vandenhoeck & Ruprecht, 2010) 135-64.

9. Steymans, *Gilgamesch — Ikonographie eines Helden/Gilgamesh.* The essay by W. G.

Lambert in this volume appeared earlier in *Gilgamesh: A Reader,* ed. John Maier (Wauconda: Bolchazy-Carducci, 1997) 50-62; originally published in *Monsters and Demons in the Ancient and Medieval Worlds,* ed. Ann E. Farkas, Prudence O. Harper and Evelyn B. Harrison (Mainz: von Zabern, 1987). For the issue of early representations, see Anthony Green, "Myths in Mesopotamian Art," in *Sumerian Gods and Their Representations,* ed. Irving L. Finkel and Markham J. Geller (Cuneiform Monographs 7; Groningen: Styx, 1997) 137-39; and Douglas Frayne, "Gilgameš in Old Akkadian Glyptic," in Steymans, *Gilgamesch,* 165-208. For the iconography of the scenes of the slaying of Humbaba and the Bull of Heaven, see Tallay Ornan, "Picture and Legend: The Case of Humbaba and the Bull of Heaven," *ErIsr* 27 (Hayim and Miriam Tadmor Volume; 2003) 18-32; "Humbaba, the Bull of Heaven and the Contribution of Images to the Reconstruction of the Gilgameš Epic," in Steymans, *Gilgamesch,* 229-60; Dominique Collon, "The Depiction of Giants," in *Gilgamesch,* 113-33; and Mehmet-Ali Atacç, "Representations and Resonances of Gilgamesh in Neo-Assyrian Art," in *Gilgamesch,* 261-87. For an effort to relate the Bull of Heaven episode to bull-leaping, see Collon, "Bull-Leaping in Syria," *Ägypten und Levante/International Journal for Egyptian Archaeology and Related Disciplines* 4 (1994) 81-88, here 84.

10. For a structural approach to the story's trajectory, see Jacobsen, *The Treasures of Darkness,* 215-19, and esp. the chart on p. 216. For a recent proposal for the massive chiastic structure of the SBV of Gilgamesh, see Michael S. Moore, *WealthWatch: A Study of Socioeconomic Conflict in the Bible* (Eugene: Pickwick, 2011) 30-73. Moore's chiastic structure is notable; no less notable is the bulk of attention devoted to each chiastic element. The last takes up a great deal of the epic, especially relative to its corresponding first term.

11. Sensitively seen by Moran, *The Most Magic Word,* 13-20; and Foster, "Gilgamesh: Sex, Love and the Ascent of Knowledge," in Maier, *Gilgamesh: A Reader,* 63-78. Foster's essay was originally published in *Love and Death in the Ancient Near East: Essays in Honor of Marvin H. Pope,* ed. John H. Marks and Robert M. Good (Guilford: Four Quarters, 1987) 21-42.

12. See esp. Piotr Michalowski, "Sailing to Babylon, Reading the Dark Side of the Moon," in *The Study of the Ancient Near East in the Twenty-First Century: The William Foxwell Albright Centennial Conference,* ed. Jerrold S. Cooper and Glenn M. Schwartz (Winona Lake: Eisenbrauns, 1996) 188; and the elaboration in his essay, "Commemoration, Writing, and Genre in Ancient Mesopotamia," in *The Limits of Historiography: Genre and Narrative in Ancient Historical Texts,* ed. Christina Shuttleworth Kraus (MnemsoyneSup 191; Leiden: Brill, 1999) 69-90, esp. 77, 88. Michalowski ("Sailing to Babylon," 188) reads SBV Gilgamesh as "an elaborate *narû,* a gigantic royal inscription." He continues: "Here the commemorative nature of first-millennium Babylonian narrative, whose authority is rooted in antiquity but that now seeks authors and authorities, reaches its highest level. It is a matter that we will have to rethink in the future, since our own notions of hero, author, and redactor are simply inadequate to handle such a situation. The Gilgamesh text is narrated in third person, is ascribed to an author named Sinleqe-unnini, but is actually treated as a third-person autobiography of Gilgamesh." For further thoughts on genre matters in Gilgamesh (with some response to Michalowski), see A. R. George, "The Epic of Gilgameš: Thoughts on Genre and Meaning," in *Gilgameš*

and the World of Assyria: Proceedings of the Conference Held at the Mandelbaum House, The University of Sydney, 21-23 July 2004, ed. Joseph Azize and Noel Weeks (Ancient Near Eastern Studies Supplement 21; Leuven: Peeters, 2007) 37-65.

13. On this score, OB Gilgamesh might be read against the exploits of a king as represented in a royal text such as the Old Assyrian Sargon Legend, which emphasizes the monarch as hunter and athlete, provider and resister of darkness, and conquering hero. For a convenient translation with some comparisons with Gilgamesh, see Benjamin R. Foster, *Before the Muses: An Anthology of Akkadian Literature* (3rd ed.; Bethesda: CDL, 2005) 71-75; Foster views the text as a parody. I thank Beate Pongratz-Leisten for drawing my attention to this text, which is included in her forthcoming book.

14. For references, see the preceding note; and note also below in the discussion. For a good summary of Gilgamesh's attributes as a hero, see Nele Ziegler, "Gilgameš: le roi héroïque et son ami," in *Le jeune héros: Recherches sur la formation et la diffusion d'un thème littéraire au Proche-Orient ancien. Actes du colloque organisé par les chaires d'Assyriologie et des Milieux bibliques du Collège de France, Paris, les 6 et 7 avril 2009*, ed. Jean-Marie Durand, Thomas Römer, and Michael Langlois (OBO 250; Fribourg: Academic; Göttingen: Vandenhoeck & Ruprecht, 2011) 289-305.

15. George, *The Babylonian Gilgamesh Epic*, 1:141. For the iconography showing this difference in status, see Ursula Seidl, "Gilgameš: Der Zug zum Zedernwald," in Steymans, *Gilgamesch*, 209-28.

16. George, *The Babylonian Gilgamesh Epic*, 1:71. See also Ziegler, "Gilgameš," 292-93 and Gonzalo Rubio, "Reading Sumerian Names, II: Gilgameš," *JCS* 64 (2012) 3-16.

17. George, *The Babylonian Gilgamesh Epic*, 1:141.

18. For the tradition of Gilgamesh's parentage by Lugalbanda and Ninsun, see SBV I.35-36; for discussion see also George, *The Babylonian Gilgamesh Epic*, 1:106-9. For Lugalbanda as his father in OB Nippur, obv., line 8, see George, *The Babylonian Gilgamesh Epic*, 1:241, 242-43; and as his personal god, see OB Harmal-1, rev., line 15, and SBV VI.165, in George, *The Babylonian Gilgamesh Epic*, 1:250-51 and 628-29). For a discussion of Gilgamesh's devotion to his deceased father Lugalbanda in SBV VI, see Karel van der Toorn, *Family Religion in Babylonia, Syria, and Israel: Continuity and Changes in the Forms of Religious Life* (Studies in the History and Culture of the Ancient Near East 7; Leiden: Brill, 1996) 48, 58-59, 100-1. Cf. the dedication in a building inscription of Sin-kashid of Uruk: "For the god Lugalbanda, his personal god, (and) for the goddess Ninsun, his mother." For text and translation, see Douglas Frayne, *Old Babylonian Period (2003-1595)* (Royal Inscriptions of Mesopotamia. Early Periods Vol. 4; Toronto: University of Toronto Press, 1990) 454 no. 8.

19. See also OB II, col. ii, line 43: "so that I shall make him your equal." This sentiment of Ninsun is expressed in SBV I.258, 266, 285, 290. For discussion, see Cooper, "Gilgamesh Dreams of Enkidu," 40-41.

20. E.g., OB III, col. iii, lines 106, 119, 129, 140, 161; OB Schøyen 1, obv., line 6′; OB Schøyen 2, obv., lines 4, 33, 84; OB Nippur, obv., lines 1, 9; OB Harmel 1, obv., line 3, rev., line 10; OB Harmel 2, obv., line 48; OB Ishchali obv., lines 11′, 15′.

21. George (*The Babylonian Gilgamesh Epic*, 1:140) understands *ibru* as "bosom friend and companion," but Fleming and Milstein (*The Buried Foundation of the Gilgamesh Epic*,

33 n. 36) cite the *CAD*'s view that "*ibru* was originally devoid of emotional connotation." *CAD*, I/J:5 lists "comrade, fellow, colleague, friend," as meanings of the word.

22. George, *The Babylonian Gilgamesh Epic*, 1:141. George also notes the tradition (represented in the Sumerian version) characterizing Enkidu as Gilgamesh's servant.

23. So *AHw*, 364. It may be worth asking if Akkadian *ibru* and *ibrūtu* might also be related to BH *bĕrît*, although this possibility is not customarily considered in discussions of the word. See below note 25.

24. *CAD*, I/J:7.

25. For a survey of etymological proposals of BH *bĕrît*, see Moshe Weinfeld, "b^{e}rîṯ," in *TDOT*, 2:253-55; and the monumental work of Kenneth A. Kitchen and Paul J. N. Lawrence, *Treaty, Law and Covenant in the Ancient Near East* (3 vols.; Wiesbaden: Harrassowitz, 2012) 2:235, 237-38. BH *bĕrît* is commonly compared with Akkadian *birītu*, "clasp, fetter; contract," and/or with the Semitic loan into Egyptian, **birīta*, "treaty." For these views, see Frank Moore Cross, *Canaanite Myth and Hebrew Epic* (Cambridge, MA: Harvard University Press, 1973) 267; and Kenneth A. Kitchen, "Egypt, Ugarit, Qatna and Covenant," *UF* 11 (C. F. A. Schaeffer Festschrift; 1979) 453-64. For the Akkadian evidence, see also *CAD*, B:254; for the Egyptian evidence, see also James E. Hoch, *Semitic Words in Egyptian Texts of the New Kingdom and Third Intermediate Period* (Princeton: Princeton University Press, 1994) 108-9. Another major alternative has been to compare Akkadian *birīt*, "between" (see Kitchen and Lawrence, *Treaty, Law and Covenant*, 2:237). This view has been criticized by Hayim Tadmor, since a preposition would not seem to provide a fitting comparison for a noun in another language; see Tadmor, "Treaty and Oath in the Ancient Near East: A Historian's Approach," in *Humanizing America's Iconic Book*, ed. Gene M. Tucker and Douglas A. Knight (SBLCP 6; Chico: Scholars, 1982) 138. It is not entirely clear why the Akkadian noun *birītu* might not have developed as an ellipsis for *māmītu birīt*, "sworn agreement with (each other)" (e.g., EA 149:60 and RS 19.68, cited in *CAD*, M/1:191) or *riksu birīt* (*CAD*, R:353), which occur rather commonly for relations between two parties. Or, to paraphrase one Mari text, it is "a good *(dam-q[a-tim])* between" two parties; see M.5653 + M.11012, line 4′, in Jean-Marie Durand, *AEM*, 1/1, p. 312; Wolfgang Heimpel, *Letters to the Kings of Mari: A New Translation, with Historical Introduction, Notes, and Commentary* (Mesopotamian Civilizations 12; Winona Lake: Eisenbrauns, 2003) 232. For the possibly analogous relationship between the preposition *birīt* and the noun *birītu* (as applied to land), see the comments of J. J. Finkelstein, " 'Mesopotamia,' " *JNES* 21 (1962) 88. Yet another proposal for BH *bĕrît* is to derive it from **br'/brh*, "to cut"; so Tadmor, "Treaty and Oath in the Ancient Near East," 137-38 (following a suggestion given privately by Moshe Held, himself citing Ibn Janah). For a sympathetic response, see Frank Moore Cross, *From Epic to Canon: History and Literature in Ancient Israel* (Baltimore: Johns Hopkins University Press, 1998) 17 n. 48; in this case, Cross would see the original root as **brw*, as in Old South Arabic (e.g., Sabaean **brw*, "to cut off, slaughter; contend with, attack," according to Joan Copeland Biella, *Dictionary of Old South Arabic: Sabaean Dialect* [HSS 25; Chico: Scholars, 1982] 55). Parenthetically, it is to be noted that Sabaean also attests to *brt*, "pledge, oath" (Biella, *Dictionary of Old South Arabic*, 59, taking the noun as a geminate).

26. George (*The Babylonian Gilgamesh Epic*, 1:1.78) translates the word here as "rival."

27. For discussion, see Ackerman, *When Heroes Love,* 78.

28. Cooper, "Gilgamesh Dreams of Enkidu," 40.

29. For royal bull hunts as well as later resonances of Gilgamesh's slaying of the Bull of Heaven, see Chikako E. Watanabe, *Animal Symbolism in Mesopotamia: A Contextual Approach* (Wiener Offene Orientalistik 1; Vienna: Institut für Orientalistik, Universität Wien, 2002) 72-75.

30. Stephanie Dalley, *Myths from Mesopotamia: Creation, the Flood, Gilgamesh, and Others* (rev. ed.; Oxford: Oxford University Press, 2000) 83. Cf. *CAD,* A/1:203 (under *aḫu,* "brother"): "the two friends sat down"; and George (*The Babylonian Gilgamesh Epic,* 1:629): "both of them (then) sat down together." George (*The Babylonian Gilgamesh Epic,* 1:629 n. 35) also offers an alternative translation, "both the brothers sat down." See also Ziegler, "Gilgameš," 301.

31. George (*The Babylonian Gilgamesh Epic,* 2:848, note to 139) notes that the phrase is a construct plus genitive (lit., "friend of your brother"). For discussion, note also Ziegler, "Gilgameš," 302.

32. *CAD,* T:96. See further George, *The Babylonian Gilgamesh Epic,* 2:848, note to 139.

33. See Gary Beckman, "Hittite Gilgamesh," in Foster, *The Epic of Gilgamesh,* 163, tablet III, par. 3.

34. See Beckman, "Hittite Gilgamesh," 158, tablet I, par. 2. Cf. the two(-thirds) of the divine spirit given to Elisha in 2 Kgs. 2:9 (so NJPS, with reference to Zech. 13:8).

35. George, *The Babylonian Gilgamesh Epic,* 1:560-61.

36. George, *The Babylonian Gilgamesh Epic,* 1:74-75, 310-13.

37. George, *The Babylonian Gilgamesh Epic,* 1:167.

38. Lambert, "Gilgamesh in Literature and Art," in Maier, *Gilgamesh: A Reader,* 52 and 55, fig. 1. Lambert reads the scene as a reflection of the Sumerian version in which Enkidu's subordinate status is highly marked.

39. See Foster, "Gilgamesh: Sex, Love and the Ascent of Knowledge," 65, 66-68.

40. So George, *The Babylonian Gilgamesh Epic,* 628-29, in his translation of the word in SBV VI.158. Or, her name denotes a type of prostitute; see *CAD,* Š/2:311, 312. See the plural usage in the Descent of Ishtar, line 130 (partially reconstructed), recently treated by Pirjo Lapinkivi, *The Neo-Assyrian Myth of Ištar's Descent and Resurrection* (SAA Cuneiform Texts 6; Helsinki: Neo-Assyrian Text Corpus, 2010) 22, 28, 32. The word derives from *šamāḫu* A, "to grow thickly, abundantly; to flourish, to attain beauty or stature" (*CAD,* Š/2:289); in other words, she is sexually appealing. For further discussion, see V. A. B. Hurowitz, "Finding New Life in Old Words: Word Play in the Gilgameš Epic," in Azize and Weeks, *Gilgameš and the World of Assyria,* 68-69.

41. Foster, "Gilgamesh: Sex, Love and the Ascent of Knowledge," 65. Foster notes in the SBV "the emphasis on knowledge and on love and sex as intermediary states to perfect knowledge." However, sex and love play little role in Foster's description of some of the episodes, as he understands them.

42. See Foster, "Gilgamesh: Sex, Love and the Ascent of Knowledge," 65, 66-68.

43. Fleming and Milstein, *The Buried Foundation of the Gilgamesh Epic,* 36. For essentially this view of Enkidu, see also Aage Westenholz and Ula Koch-Westenholz, "Enkidu — the Noble Savage?" in *Wisdom, Gods and Literature: Studies in Assyriology*

in Honour of W. G. Lambert, ed. Andrew R. George and Irving L. Finkel (Winona Lake: Eisenbrauns, 2000) 437-51.

44. On the meaning of *lullû*, see Moran, *The Most Magic Word*, 14; Julia M. Asher Greve, "Decisive Sex, Essential Gender," in *Sex and Gender in the Ancient Near East: Proceedings of the XLVII*ᵉ Rencontre Assyriologique International, Helsinki, July 2-6, 2001, Part I, ed. Simo Parpola and Robert M. Whiting (CRRAI 47/1; Helsinki: Neo-Assyrian Text Corpus Project, 2002) 11, 14; George, *The Babylonian Gilgamesh Epic*, 2:795-96 n. 178. See also George's comparison with the Babylonian understanding of the earliest humans as expressed in the literary dispute between Ewe and Grain (1:450):

> the humans of far-off days
> did not know the eating of bread,
> did not know the wearing of clothes.
> The people went naked-limbed,
> eating grass with their mouths like sheep,
> drinking water from ditches.

45. Fleming and Milstein, *The Buried Foundation of the Gilgamesh Epic*, 19-42. See also Milstein, "Reworking Ancient Texts," 104-23, here 108. While the approach taken to the Yale tablet with reference to Enkidu appears to be persuasive, still this tablet refers to him as having been born and grown up in the steppe (III, col. iv, line 151).

46. In addition to the term *lullû*, see also Gilgamesh's characterization of Enkidu as "a mule on the run, donkey of the uplands, panther of the wild" (SBV X.227). Cf. the conditions Zimrī-Lim and his men endured according to lines 112-23 of the Epic of Zimrī-Lim, in Pierre Marello, "La vie nomade," in *Recueil d'études en l'honneur de Michel Fleury*, ed. Jean-Marie Durand (Memoires de Nabu 1; Florilegium Marianum 1; Paris: SEPOA, 1992) 115-25, esp. 122 n. 9.

47. Note the reversal in Aristophanes, *Lysistrata*, lines 781-96, with its gender marked expression:

> "I wish to tell you a tale once I heard
> when but a lad:
> In olden times lived a young man named Melanion,
> In flight from marriage he went off to the wilderness
> and lived in the mountains
> and kept a dog
> and wove traps
> and hunted rabbits;
> but he never went home again because of his hatred.
> That's how much he loathed women.
> And, being wise, we loathe them just
> As much as Melanion did."

Jeffrey Henderson, *Aristophanes: Birds, Lysistrata, Women at the Thesmophoria* (LCL 179; Cambridge, MA: Harvard University Press, 2000) 374-75; noted in Robert A. Segal, *Myth: A Very Short Introduction* (Oxford: Oxford University Press, 2004) 135.

48. Harris, "Images of Women in the Gilgamesh Epic," in Abusch, Huehnergard, and Steinkeller, *Lingering Over Words,* 224-25; repr. in Foster, *The Epic of Gilgamesh,* 207-18; and in Maier, *Gilgamesh: A Reader,* 79-94.

49. Harris, "Images of Women in the Gilgamesh Epic," 225.

50. To the sexual relations between Shamhat and Enkidu, Jerrold S. Cooper compares an Akkadian mythological fragment (CT 15 5 ii), in which Ereshkigal seduces Nergal. Like Enkidu, Ereshkigal has not according to this text had sexual relations, and those relations change her; she "can no longer interact as before with the Netherworld gods." See Cooper, "Virginity in Ancient Mesopotamia," in Parpola and Whiting, *Sex and Gender in the Ancient Near East,* 98 n. 52.

51. Moran, *The Most Magic Word,* 13-15. For this point, Moran acknowledges and builds on the study of Hope Nash Wolff, "Gilgamesh, Enkidu, and the Heroic Life," *JAOS* 89 (1969) 392 n. 2. Note also her book: *A Study in the Narrative Structures of Three Epic Poems:* Gilgamesh, *The* Odyssey, Beowulf (New York: Garland, 1987). See also George, *The Babylonian Gilgamesh Epic,* 2:194-95; and Fleming and Milstein, *The Buried Foundation of the Gilgamesh Epic,* 47-48, 103.

52. By comparison, in the OB, its two occurrences stand on either side of the Huwawa episode, as emphasized by Fleming and Milstein, *The Buried Foundation of the Gilgamesh Epic,* 48.

53. This initial socialization of Enkidu involves not only sexual relations, but also partaking of bread and "strong drink," as noted by Susan Niditch, *"My Brother Esau Is a Hairy Man": Hair and Identity in Ancient Israel* (Oxford: Oxford University Press, 2008) 72. Niditch uses this episode to illustrate the point that "to abstain from wine is to be removed from the social and the cultural."

54. See the classic work of A. Leo Oppenheim, *The Interpretation of Dreams in the Ancient Near East: with a Translation of an Assyrian Dream Book* (Transactions of the American Philosophical Society 46/3; Philadelphia: American Philosophical Society, 1956) 215-17. For further discussion of the dreams, see below.

55. For Gilgamesh's travels in SBV IX-X, see Wayne Horowitz, *Mesopotamian Cosmic Geography* (Mesopotamian Civilizations 8; Winona Lake: Eisenbrauns, 2011) 96-106; for the topography of Gilgamesh's descent into the Apsu in SBV XI, see Horowitz, p. 132.

56. Moran, *The Most Magic Word,* 13.

57. Moran, *The Most Magic Word,* 15.

58. For further references and discussion, see Ackerman, *When Heroes Love,* 78-80.

59. Thorkild Jacobsen notes the hospitality offered both to Enkidu by the shepherds and to Gilgamesh by Ut-napishti. See Jacobsen, *Toward the Image of Tammuz and Other Essays on Mesopotamian History and Culture,* ed. William L. Moran (HSS 21; Cambridge, MA: Harvard University Press, 1970) 49. Thus the meals in these instances may likewise mark a certain parallelism in the progression of the two heroes.

60. For the problem of *šam-mu ni-kit-ti,* see George, *The Babylonian Gilgamesh Epic,* 2:895-86; and Hurowitz, "Finding New Life in Old Words," 76.

61. It has been customary to see the initial section of the SBV as a secondary introduction added to an older version. According to the colophon to the OB Pennsylvania tablet, the series was known as *šutur eli šarri;* see George, *The Babylonian Gilgamesh*

Epic, 1:180-81. The phrase occurs in SBV 1.29, thus suggesting that lines 1-28 constitute a secondary prologue prefixed with the SBV version. As a result, most scholars have considered lines 1-28 as an SBV addition to the older version. So see Moran, "The Gilgamesh Epic," in Foster, *The Epic of Gilgamesh,* 175; and Moran, *The Most Magic Word,* 6-10; George, *The Babylonian Gilgamesh Epic,* 1:23 n. 63; and Hurowitz, "Finding New Life in Old Words," 77 n. 24. This assumption has been overturned by the discovery of a Middle Babylonian (MB) fragment of Gilgamesh at Ugarit, which shows that the prologue of SBV I.1-28 was not a SBV invention, but that some version of it goes back considerably earlier. For this MB Ugarit of Gilgamesh, see Arnaud, *Corpus des texts,* 130-34. For discussion, see George, "The Gilgamesh Epic at Ugarit"; and Milstein, "Reworking Ancient Texts," 89-104.

62. Moran, *The Most Magic Word,* 15; and the discussion further below. See also Wolff, *A Study in the Narrative Structures,* 60-62; and Agustinus Gianto, "Grief, Joy, and Anger in Ugaritic Literary Texts," in *Society and Administration in Ancient Ugarit,* ed. W. H. van Soldt (Leiden: Nederlands Instituut voor het Nabije Oosten, 2010) 55.

63. For the relation of this instruction to "The Dialogue of Pessimism," line 76, see W. G. Lambert, *Babylonian Wisdom Literature* (Oxford: Clarendon, 1960) 140-41. Lambert suggests that it may be a stock phrase.

64. For the motif of examining the foundation in these passages, see Hanspeter Schaudig, "The Restoration of Temples in the Neo- and Late-Babylonian Periods," in *From the Foundations to the Crenellations: Essays on Temple Building in the Ancient Near East and Hebrew Bible,* ed. Mark J. Boda and Jamie Novotny (AOAT 366; Münster: Ugarit-Verlag, 2010) 148. According to Schaudig, this is a variant form of "exposing the foundation to daylight" *(temenna nuwwuru)* as found in an inscription of Marduk-apla-iddina II dating to 703.

65. Gilgamesh's postmortem fame and devotion to his memory are particularly notable, as reflected in his elevation to the status of a demigod and as remembered in the Sumerian King List. For Gilgamesh in god-lists as a divine name, see George, *The Babylonian Gilgamesh Epic,* 1:119-20; and Jeremiah Peterson, *Godlists from Old Babylonian Nippur in the University Museum, Philadelphia* (AOAT 362; Münster: Ugarit-Verlag, 2009) 71. His name appears also in the omen series *šumma ālu:* "If a man repairs a figure of Gilgamesh, the anger of the gods will be released." See Sally M. Freedman, *If a City Is Set on a Height: The Akkadian Omen Series Šumma ālu ina melê sakin* (Philadelphia: University of Pennsylvania Museum, 1998) 161. Note also Bilgamesh as a place name in Old Akkadian and Ur III texts; see M. Such-Gutiérrez, "Untersuchungen zum Pantheon von Adab im 3. Jt." *AfO* 51 (2005/6) 9.

The wall as commemoration of Gilgamesh as well as an act of devotion to him is reflected in a building inscription of Anam of Uruk. Anam says that he "restored the wall of Uruk, the ancient work of divine Gilgamesh, constructed it (the wall) for him (divine Gilgamesh) in baked bricks in order that water might roar in its (the wall's) surrounding (moat)." For the text and translation, see Frayne, *Old Babylonian Period (2003-1595),* 474-75, no. 4, cited in Schaudig, "The Restoration of Temples," 161; see also Jacobsen, *Toward the Image of Tammuz,* 144 and 379 n. 48.

For later mentions of the name of Gilgamesh and other figures of the story, see

George, *The Babylonian Gilgamesh Epic*, 1:60-69; Dalley, *Myths from Mesopotamia*, 47-48; and André Lemaire, "Nabonide et Gilgamesh: L'araméen en Mésopotamie et à Qoumrân" (with response by Jonathan Ben-Dov and Discussion), in *Aramaica Qumranica: Proceedings of the Conference on the Aramaic Texts from Qumran in Aix-en-Province 30 June–2 July 2008*, ed. Katell Berthelot and Daniel Stökl Ben Ezra (STDJ 94; Leiden: Brill, 2010) 125-44. For Gilgamesh iconography in the Levant down into the seventh century, see Hans Ulrich Steymans, "Gilgames im Westen," in Steymans, *Gilgamesch*, 287-345.

Enkidu, too, is recalled in later Mesopotamian tradition. E.g., an incantation regards Enkidu as able to put a crying baby to sleep. See Cynthia Jean, "Male and Supernatural Assistants in Mesopotamia Magic," in Parpola and Whiting, *Sex and Gender in the Ancient Near East*, 256.

66. Moran, *The Most Magic Word*, 20.

67. For the wisdom mentioned in this line and its association with building, see Raymond C. Van Leeuwen, "Cosmos, Temple, House: Building and Wisdom in Ancient Mesopotamia and Israel," in Boda and Novotny, *From the Foundations to the Crenellations*, 405-6.

68. Foster, "Gilgamesh: Sex, Love and the Ascent of Knowledge," 188. See also George, "The Epic of Gilgameš," 57-58.

69. In Homeric terms, "the destiny of a hero is his tradition," according to Egbert J. Bakker, "Storytelling in the Future: Truth, Time, and Tense in the Homeric Epic," in *Written Voices, Spoken Signs: Tradition, Performance, and the Epic Text*, ed. Bakker and Ahuvia Kahane (Cambridge, MA: Harvard University Press, 1997) 32.

70. RS 25.130, lines 4′-5′ in Arnaud, *Corpus des texts*, 142. This text is quite similar to Emar 767, in Arnaud, *Recherches au pays d'Aštata*. Emar 6/4: *Textes de la bibliothèque, transcriptions et traductions* (Paris: Editions Recherche sur les Civilisations, 1987) 360, cited below in this chapter. For a critical edition of the texts, see Bendt Alster, *Wisdom of Ancient Sumer* (Bethesda: CDL, 2005) 288-322.

71. Emar 767, in Arnaud, *Recherches au pays d'Aštata*, 360. For the version from Ugarit, see RS 25.130, lines 4′-5′ in Arnaud, *Corpus des texts*, 142.

72. For a selective survey of modern views about Homer, see Hugh Lloyd-Jones, "Becoming Homer," in *The Further Academic Papers of Sir Hugh Lloyd-Jones* (Oxford: Oxford University Press, 2005) 3-17. The common ascription of the *Iliad* and *Odyssey* to Homer has come under critical scrutiny and even denial on the part of a number of scholars, e.g., Martin L. West, *The Making of the Iliad: Disquisition and Analytical Commentary* (Oxford: Oxford University Press, 2011) 8-10. To be sure, this remains the major, if not, general view of the field. West (*The Making of the Iliad*, 9) prefers the alternative name known in the tradition, namely "Melesigenes (or Meles, or Melesagoras, or Melesianix)." For West, "Homer" may have been an imaginary eponym of the guild of rhapsodes known as the Homeridai. In addition, it is to be noted that West (*The Making of the Iliad*, 11-14, 21) rejects the Parry-Lord oral approach to the *Iliad* and the *Odyssey*, and he supposes that the author was a singer-poet who wrote out the lengthy poem and that the same poet later made insertions and alterations. For this question, see also Richard Janko, "The *Iliad* and Its Editors: Dictation and Redaction," *Classical Antiquity* 9 (1990) 326-34. For a review of the traditions about Homer with some response to West and other scholars on the

issues, see Maarit Kivilo, "The Early Biographical Tradition of Homer," in *Identities and Societies in the Ancient East-Mediterranean Religions: Comparative Approaches. Henning Graf Reventlow Memorial Volume,* ed. Thomas R. Kammerer (AOAT 390/1; Acta Antiqua Mediterranea et Orientalia 1; Münster: Ugarit-Verlag, 2011) 85-104. These questions do not affect this study. The later date for the *Iliad,* to "probably between 680 and 640," as suggested by West (*The Making of the Iliad,* 19), suggests caution in using Homer for high historical claims or reconstructions. Note also observations by various scholars about later datings, e.g., in an area pertinent to this study, namely the lack of depiction of weapons in Homer compared with sources prior to the eighth century and the lack of artistic depiction of the *Iliad*'s heroes until the seventh-sixth centuries. For the former, see Hans van Wees, "Greeks Bearing Arms: The State, the Leisure Class, and the Display of Weapons in Archaic Greece," in *Archaic Greece: New Approaches and New Evidence,* ed. Nick Fisher and van Wees (London: Duckworth, 1998) 333-78, esp. 341, 343; for the latter, see K. Friis Johansen, *The Iliad in Early Greek Art* (Copenhagen: Munksgaard, 1967) 25-26. For the historical background of the *Iliad* possibly only a matter of generations before Homer, see Kurt A. Raaflaub, "Epic and History," in *A Companion to Ancient Epic,* ed. John Miles Foley (Oxford: Blackwell, 2005) 55-70, esp. 58-60.

73. For the opening of the *Iliad,* see James Redfield, "The Proem of the Iliad: Homer's Art," *Classical Philology* 74 (1979) 95-110.

74. Achilles is the only human in the Iliad attributed *mēnis,* according to Seth Benardete, *Achilles and Hector: The Homeric Hero* (South Bend: St. Augustine's Press, 2005) 120 n. 50; see also p. 133: "Homer began his *Iliad* by asking the Muse to sing the wrath of Achilles; he asked her to describe not Achilles, but Achilles' wrath." See also Seth L. Schein, *The Mortal Hero: An Introduction to Homer's* Iliad (Berkeley: University of California Press, 1984) 91; and Hans van Wees, *Status Warriors: War, Violence, and Society in Homer and History* (Dutch Monographs on Ancient History and Archaeology 9; Amsterdam: Gieben, 1992) 61-165, 345-78.

Note the detailed discussion of Leonard Muellner, *The Anger of Achilles: Mēnis in Greek Epic* (Ithaca: Cornell University Press, 1996). According to Muellner, *mēnis* means more than an individual's emotional response; it denotes behavior that violates the most basic rules of human society. On *kotos* as long-term anger outside of the immediate battle context and *cholos* as short-term battle-fury in Homer, see Thomas R. Walsh, *Fighting Words and Feuding Words: Anger and the Homeric Poems* (Lanham: Rowman and Littlefield, 2005) 28-29. On Achilles' *kotos* in *Iliad* 1.178-81 and his *cholos* in *Iliad* 18.107-11, see Walsh, *Fighting Words and Feuding Words,* 85 and 218.

For Achilles' character more broadly, see also Gregory Nagy, "The Epic Hero," in Foley, *A Companion to Ancient Epic,* 87-88. Nagy stress that Achilles is (a) unseasonal; (b) extreme, mostly in a positive sense; and (c) antagonistic to the god Apollo, "to whom he bears an uncanny resemblance." For a comparative perspective, see Patrick Considine, "The Theme of Divine Wrath in Ancient East Mediterranean Literature," *SMEA* 8 (1969) 85-159. For a helpful sketch of Achilles' many sides, see Katherine Callen King, *Achilles: Paradigms of the War Hero from Homer to the Middle Ages* (Berkeley: University of California Press, 1987) 1-49.

Gianto ("Grief, Joy, and Anger," 56) compares the vengeful wrath of Achilles with

"Pughat's vengeful anger upon learning the death of his brother Aqhat." Pughat may well be angry as Gianto suggests; if so, her anger remains implicit, expressed through her father's actions and her carrying forth her vengeance. This muted literary representation stands in interesting contrast with the explicit presentation of Achilles. The difference may point to a difference of gender treatments: the male hero is explicit in his emotional expression, the female who is not supposed to be a hero barely intimates her emotion and perhaps does so through the male character of her father.

75. In *Iliad* 9.302, Achilles is addressed: "as though you were a god"; and in 9.603, "the Achaians will honor you like a god." Several other figures are also called "godlike" (in varying expressions), e.g., Priam (24.483); Aias (10.112); Odysseus (10.243; 11.140); Patroklos (11.644); and Sarpedon (12.307). Aeneas is "honored by the people like a god" (11.58). For Achilles as "godlike," see Benardete, *Achilles and Hector*, 14-15. For King (*Achilles*, 18-28), Achilles is godlike and bestial. See further below.

76. Ancient Near Eastern analogies for fury in warfare as a positive value can be seen in an Old Babylonian letter of Shibtu to Zimri-Lim of Mari. The letter reports a prophecy from the deity proclaiming: "I will rage and stand in victory" *(kinnekêm ara'ub u ina lītim azzaz)*. For text and translation, see Martti Nissinen, *Prophets and Prophecy in the Ancient Near East* (SBLWAW 12; Atlanta: Society of Biblical Literature, 2003) 46. The goddess Astarte is addressed as "angry and raging goddess," in the "Tale of Two Brothers" (*COS*, 1:35). In a Ugaritic hymn to Astarte ('Athtart), she is called a "fierce panther," see RIH 98/02.4-5, in Dennis Pardee, "A New Ugaritic Song to 'Athartu (RIH 98/02)," in *Ugarit at Seventy-Five*, ed. K. Lawson Younger, Jr. (Winona Lake: Eisenbrauns, 2007); and "Deux tablettes ougaritiques de la main d'un même scribe, trouvées sur deux sites distincts: RS 19.039 et RIH 98/02," *Semitica et Classica* 1 (2008) 9-38, esp. 11-13. For this text, see Chapter Seven. The goddess Anat is likewise a model of martial insatiety in KTU 1.3 II 19-20 and 29-30, although this text does not use a term for fury or wrath (see Chapter Six, section 3, for the text with translation and discussion); still, it does refer to her exulting in victory over the enemy (see lines 25-26; cf. Achilles over Hector in *Iliad* 22.330).

77. So Benardete, *Achilles and Hector*, 51. Benardete translates the word as "merciless."

78. Benardete, *Achilles and Hector*, 133.

79. For these images and this point, see King, *Achilles*, 15-28.

80. See the close attention to the character of Achilles in Schein, *The Mortal Hero*, 89-167.

81. See Schein, *The Mortal Hero*, 93, 95-96, 100-101, 132, 149-50.

82. For the larger background of this story with critical discussion, see Pierre Brulé, *Women of Ancient Greece*, trans. Antonia Nevill (Edinburgh: Edinburgh University Press, 2003) 44-54. See also Jonathan Gottschall, *The Rape of Troy: Evolution, Violence, and the World of Homer* (Cambridge: Cambridge University Press, 2008) 59-63.

83. The description has later echoes (e.g., 7.113-14; 18.104, 248; 19.46) that make this portrait of Achilles bear a certain force until he returns to the field of battle.

84. According to *Iliad* 11.785, his father was Menoetius, who was himself son of Actor, king of Opus. The name of Patroklos' mother varies considerably.

85. On this point with further reference to *Iliad* 21.189, see Benardete, *Achilles and Hector*, 28.

86. See Nagy, *The Best of the Achaeans*, 33, who further characterizes Patroklos as the "ritual substitute" of Achilles. He also remarks: "The death of Patroklos inside the *Iliad* foreshadows the death of Achilles outside the *Iliad*."

87. Contrast David's refusal to wear Saul's gear for battle against Goliath (1 Sam. 17:38-40). For this biblical story, see the discussions cited in Chapter Twelve.

88. For Achilles' laments over Patroklos, see Deborah Beck, *Homeric Conversation* (Hellenic Studies 14; Washington: Center for Hellenic Studies, 2005) 257-69.

89. Gottschall, *The Rape of Troy*, 63. See also Schein, *The Mortal Hero*, 89.

90. Benardete, *Achilles and Hector*, 81, noting *Iliad* 21.99-106; 21.95; 23.746-47.

91. Benardete, *Achilles and Hector*, 108.

92. Hector in his dying words to Achilles likewise warns him (*Iliad* 22.355-60). See also 1.504-5.

93. I do not understand Benardete's view that Achilles now has "a softened heart." See *Achilles and Hector*, 110, 115. To be sure, Achilles sets aside his rage against Agamemnon and so curbs his heart (18.111-13; 19.35-36, 75). I sense little "soft-hearted" in Achilles when he returns to the field of battle, as seen in the references that follow. Schein (*The Mortal Hero*, 98-99) seems closer to the mark when he stresses Achilles' warfare savagery after the death of Patroklos: "At this point, for Achilles, love and hate are one and the same" (p. 99).

94. John Roberts, ed., *The Oxford Dictionary of the Classical World* (Oxford: Oxford University Press, 2005) 3. For an expression of this excess, see Achilles' abuse of Hector's corpse at the tomb of Patroklos in *Iliad* 24.15-17, summarized in 24.22: "Thus Achilles in his fury attempted to disfigure noble Hector." For the public function of corpse mutilation to demoralize enemies in the *Iliad*, see Hans van Wees, "Heroes, Knights, and Nutters: Warrior Mentality in Homer," in *Battle in Antiquity*, ed. Alan B. Lloyd (Swansea: Classical Press of Wales, 2009) 52-53; note also Lawrence A. Tritle, "Hector's Body: Mutilation of the Dead in Ancient Greece and Vietnam," *Ancient History Bulletin* 11 (1997) 123-36. Cf. Joab's treatment of Amasa's corpse after he kills him in 2 Sam. 20:10-12.

95. Roberts, ed., *The Oxford Dictionary of the Classical World*, 3.

96. For other examples of such vengeance in the *Iliad*, see van Wees, "Heroes, Knights, and Nutters," 16.

97. For this view, see among many scholars King, *Achilles*, 37-38; and Donald G. Kyle, *Sport and Spectacle in the Ancient World* (Oxford: Blackwell, 2007) 55. For a discussion of the scenes and speeches at the games, see Beck, *Homeric Conversation*, 232-44.

98. So Benardete, *Achilles and Hector*, 127.

99. See Johansen, *The Iliad in Early Greek Art*, 49-51, 246; for other depictions, see pp. 127-38. See also Jane Henle, *Greek Myths: A Vase Painter's Notebook* (Bloomington: Indiana University Press, 1973) 137 fig. 64, and 138 fig. 65.

100. Beck, *Homeric Conversation*, 127; for a superb, critical discussion of this conversation, see pp. 135-44. For further observations on the scene, see also King, *Achilles*, 41-45.

101. See the analysis of Beck, *Homeric Conversation*, 139, 141-44.

102. Thomas M. Greene has drawn attention to the central importance of the hero shedding tears at the end of both the *Iliad* (24.507-16) and the *Odyssey* (23.259-62, 271-73). See Greene, "The Natural Tears of Epic," in *Epic Traditions in the Contemporary World*, ed. Margaret Beissinger, Jane Tylus, and Susanne Wofford (Berkeley: University of California

Press, 1999) 189-202, here 190-91. He suggests a similar point for OB Gilgamesh, as well as Beowulf and a number of other epics.

103. Cf. Benardete, *Achilles and Hector,* 132.

104. Murray, *Homer: Iliad II, Books 13-24,* rev. William Wyatt (LCL 171; Cambridge, MA: Harvard University Press, 1999) 605.

105. For heroes as lions, see Emily Vermeule, *Aspects of Death in Early Greek Art and Poetry* (Berkeley: University of California Press, 1979) 85-91.

106. Vermeule, *Aspects of Death in Early Greek Art and Poetry,* 112.

107. Morris, *Daidalos and the Origins of Greek Art* (Princeton: Princeton University Press, 1992) 18. See also Schein, *The Mortal Hero,* 160.

108. Lattimore, *The Iliad of Homer: Translated with an Introduction* (Chicago: University of Chicago Press, 1951) 490. Cf. "his dear comrade" in LCL.

109. See Nagy, *The Best of the Achaeans,* 104-5. The term has been traced to Linear B *heqetas* at Pylos and Knossos. See http://projectsx.dartmouth.edu/classics/history/bronze_age/lessons/les/25.html.

110. For the varied use of this expression in the *Iliad,* see Nagy, *The Best of the Achaeans,* 26-41; and Bruce Louden, *The Iliad: Structure, Myth, and Meaning* (Baltimore: Johns Hopkins University Press, 2006) 2-3, 25-46. On the one hand, it is a term expressing the contention between Agamemnon and Achilles (1.91; 2.82); see Nagy, *The Best of the Achaeans,* 26. On the other hand, uses of the expression serve to contribute to the ultimate picture of Achilles as "best of the Achaeans"; so Louden, *The Iliad,* 2-3. There are also a number of related expressions. Hector calls Agamemnon "the best of the men" (11.288), and Achilles is "the best of the Myrmidons" (18.10). There are also a number of comparable expressions: "the best of the Trojans" (17.80; see also 24.384); "best of the Aetolians" (5.843; 15.282); "best of the Phocians" (17.307); and "best among the Thracians" (6.7).

111. Demodocus is represented as singing the story of the Trojan horse in *Odyssey* 8:499-520. For Paris' role in Achilles' death, see the post-Homeric epic cycle of the *Aethiopis;* Jeffrey Henderson, *Hesiod, Homeric Hymns, Homerica* (LCL 57; Cambridge, MA: Harvard University Press, 1936) 507-8. Note also the remarks of Aristonicus on the *Iliad,* reflecting the problem of the interpretation of Achilles' death: "(The critical sign is) because from this passage [*Iliad* 17.719] post-Homeric writers have derived Achilles being carried by Ajax with Odysseus defending him. But if Homer had been describing the death of Achilles, he would not have had the body carried by Ajax, as the later writers do." For this translation, see Martin L. West, *Greek Epic Fragments from the Seventh to the Fifth Centuries BC* (LCL 497; Cambridge, MA: Harvard University Press, 2003) 115. The motif of Achilles' heel is a late addition; see Roberts, *The Oxford Dictionary of the Classical World,* 3. Note the depiction of the sack of Troy already in the seventh-century Mykonos pithos, discussed in Johansen, *The Iliad in Early Greek Art,* 26-28.

112. See also *Iliad* 23.83-84, 243-44; see Nagy, *The Best of the Achaeans,* 21.

113. Cf. *Iliad* 7.89-91: "'This is the mound of a man who died long ago, whom once in his prowess glorious Hector slew.' So someone will say, and my glory will never die."

114. For the cultural sensibility of the *Iliad* as "recollections of a heroic past," see the section of the book by this title in J. N. Coldstream, *Geometric Greece: 900-700 BC* (2nd

ed.; London: Routledge, 2003) 341-57. See also Ian Morris, "The Use and Abuse of Homer," *Classical Antiquity* 5/1 (1986) 81-138.

115. For the prose traditions about the biblical pair, see Römer and Bonjour, *L'homosexualité dans le Proche-Orient ancien et la Bible,* 68-76; Jacques Vermeylen, *La loi du plus fort: Histoire de la rédaction des récits davidiques de 1 Samuel à 1 Rois 2* (BETL 154; Leuven: Leuven University Press, 2000); Klaus-Peter Adam, *Saul und David in der judäischen Geschichtsschreibung: Studien zu 1 Samuel 16–2 Samuel 5* (FAT 51; Tübingen: Mohr Siebeck, 2007); A. Graeham Auld and Erik Eynikel, eds., *For and Against David: Story and History in the Books of Samuel* (BETL 232; Leuven: Peeters, 2010); and Christophe Nihan, "David et Jonathan: une 'amitié héroïque? Enquête littéraire et historique à travers les récits de 1-2 Samuel (1-2 Règnes)," in Durand, Römer, and Langlois, *Le jeune héros,* 306-30. For the historiography of Samuel, see also Rachelle Gilmour, *Representing the Past: A Literary Analysis of Narrative Historiography in the Book of Samuel* (VTSup 143; Leiden: Brill, 2011). Daniel E. Fleming has attempted to identify older northern traditions associated with David separate from the later southern traditions associated with him; see *The Legacy of Israel in Judah's Bible: History, Politics, and the Reinscribing of Tradition* (Cambridge: Cambridge University, 2012) 98-109. At the later end of textual development, Nihan observes that scholarly description of David and Jonathan must contend with issues of the text's longer and shorter recensions — the former represented by the MT and a group of Greek manuscripts (Acx), and the latter represented by Vaticanus and some minuscules (group Bya^2), which corresponds to the prehexaplaric recension and is corroborated in its antiquity by 4QSam^c (nine times against the MT). See the discussion of Frank Moore Cross, in Cross, Donald W. Parry, Richard J. Saley, and Eugene Ulrich, *Qumran Cave 4; XII, 1-2 Samuel* (DJD 17; Oxford: Clarendon, 2005) 252-54. In the following discussion, I do not offer a stratigraphic analysis of the material according to these textual recensions, but mention some of the more seminal matters noted by Nihan. In any case, it is apparent that the differing recensions reflect an ongoing tradition of reflection on the relationship between David and Jonathan.

116. Mark V. Hamilton, *The Body Royal: The Social Poetics of Kingship in Ancient Israel* (Biblical Interpretation 78; Leiden: Brill, 2005) 156. For the complexity of the prose traditions, see the discussion above. A particularly helpful treatment is Nihan, "David et Jonathan," 306-30.

117. Even as biblical prose material seems distant from the manner of epic as found in Homer or *Gilgamesh,* I would note Cross's conviction that biblical prose works such as the book of Samuel were "interpreting the later history of Israel in Epic patterns" (*Canaanite Myth and Hebrew Epic,* ix). For the problem of epic in biblical prose, see Chapter One above.

118. See Römer and Bonjour, *L'homosexualité dans le Proche-Orient ancien et la Bible,* 101-2; and Nihan, "David et Jonathan," 327-29, following in the vein of Nardelli, *Homosexuality and Liminality in the Gilgameš and Samuel.*

119. To be sure, the account of David's anointing in 1 Sam. 16:12-13 (see also v. 6) suggests a second tradition of David's coming to kingship, compared with his southern and northern anointings after Saul's death (2 Sam. 2:4, 7 and 5:3). This feature suggests some harmonization of at least two narrative arcs for David's story.

120. For efforts to discern the historicity of the accounts of David, see Baruch Halpern, *David's Secret Demons: Messiah, Murderer, Traitor, King* (BIW; Grand Rapids: Eerdmans, 2001); and Steven L. McKenzie, *King David: A Biography* (Oxford: Oxford University Press, 2000). For a critical assessment, see David A. Bosworth, "Evaluating King David: Old Problems and Recent Scholarship," *CBQ* 68 (2006) 191-210; and "Faith and Resilience: King David's Reaction to the Death of Bathsheba's Firstborn," *CBQ* 73 (2011) 691-707, esp. 696 and 706-7. For a lengthy review with strong and often well-placed criticism of these efforts, see J. Randall Short, *The Surprising Election and Confirmation of King David* (HTS 63; Cambridge, MA: Harvard University Press, 2010). However, it is to be noted that the features isolated by Short (pp. 78-84) are precisely those that might lead to the sorts of readings that he otherwise contests. Moreover, while the criticisms marshaled by Short may be correct on formal grounds, they hardly disprove the readings of Halpern and McKenzie. Cf. also Joel Baden, *The Historical David: The Real Life of an Invented Hero* (San Francisco: HarperOne, 2013); and Jacob L. Wright, *King David and His Reign Revisited* (Aldina Media, 2013). For other efforts at a literary reading of the narrative, see Robert Pinsky, *The Life of David* (New York: Schocken, 2005); and Paul Borgman, *David, Saul, and God: Rediscovering an Ancient Story* (Oxford: Oxford University Press, 2008). The same skepticism may apply as well to Saul's so-called "madness." Among the many discussions, note Siam Bhayro, "The Madness of King Saul," *AfO* 50/51 (2003/4) 285-92.

121. For the following passages, see Martti Nissinen, *Homoeroticism in the Biblical World: A Historical Perspective,* trans. Kirsi Stejerna (Minneapolis: Fortress, 1998) 54-55; Ackerman, *When Heroes Love,* 165-89.

122. Nihan, "David et Jonathan," 308, 318. Nihan would date this piece to the Neo-Assyrian period.

123. For the "friend like himself," see Deut. 13:6. For the prepositional phrase, see the famous formulation of Lev. 19:18 and also 19:34, in connection with Esarhaddon's loyalty oath commanding that "you will love Assurbanipal as yourselves," discussed by William L. Moran, "The Ancient Near Eastern Background of the Love of God in Deuteronomy," *CBQ* 25 (1963) 77-87; repr. in Moran, *The Most Magic Word,* 170-81; note also Akkadian *kīma napšati,* e.g., *CAD,* R:141, #2′: "I love their (the gods') beautiful forms as (I do my own) precious life." Note also Abraham Malamat, "'You Shall Love Your Neighbor as Yourself': A Case of Misinterpretation?" in *Die hebräische Bibel und ihre zweifache Nachgeschichte: Festschrift für Rolf Rendtorff zum 65. Geburtstag,* ed. Erhard Blum, Christian Macholz, and Ekkehard W. Stegemann (Neukirchen-Vluyn: Neukirchener, 1990) 111-15; and "'Love Your Neighbor as Yourself' — What It Really Means," *BAR* 16/4 (2000) 50-51. Based on the idiom **'hb l-* in 2 Chr. 19:2, Malamat takes the expression in Lev. 19:18 to mean "to be useful or beneficial to" someone.

124. Nihan, "David et Jonathan," 308. Nihan contrasts the picture of Glaucos and Diomedes in *Iliad* 6.230-35: "and let us make an exchange of armor with each other, so that these men too may know that we declare ourselves to be friends from our fathers' days" (*Homer: Iliad, Books 1-12,* trans. A. T. Murray, rev. William F. Wyatt [LCL 170; Cambridge, MA: Harvard University Press, 1999] 291).

125. See Nihan, "David et Jonathan," 310-11.

126. See BDB, 152, which suggests that the infinitive construct is implied from the preceding main verb, "to weep" (**bky*). The conjunction *'ad* may take a perfect verb though it seems rare (e.g., 1 Sam. 14:9). The verb *higdîl* may be taken as David expressing himself greatly, relative to the preceding verbs. In putting the point in this manner, the text is focusing on David's increase in emotional expression, perhaps compared with Jonathan's. A number of scholars would instead emend the text. See the discussion in P. Kyle McCarter, *1 Samuel* (AB 8; Garden City: Doubleday, 1980) 334, where he leaves the phrase untranslated, and p. 341, where he discusses the text-critical issues. He does not see sufficient support for emendation.

127. See Peggy L. Day, "Abishai the *śāṭān* in 2 Samuel 19:17-24," *CBQ* 49 (1987) 543-47.

Notes to Chapter Three

1. For book-length studies of gender and sexuality in the Mesopotamian and biblical material discussed below, see Martti Nissinen, *Homoeroticism in the Biblical World: A Historical Perspective,* trans. Kirsi Stejerna (Minneapolis: Fortress, 1998); Susan Ackerman, *When Heroes Love: The Ambiguity of Eros in the Stories of Gilgamesh and David* (New York: Columbia University Press, 2005); Thomas Römer and Loyse Bonjour, *L'homosexualité dans le Proche-Orient ancien et la Bible* (Essais bibliques 37; Geneva: Labor et Fides, 2005); Innocent Himbaza, Adrien Schenker, and Jean-Baptiste Edart, *Clarifications sur l'homosexualité dans le Bible* (Paris: Cerf, 2007), trans. as *The Bible on the Question of Homosexuality,* trans. Benedict M. Guevin (Washington: Catholic University of America Press, 2011); Jean-Fabrice Nardelli, *Homosexuality and Liminality in the Gilgameš and Samuel* (Classical and Byzantine Monographs 64; Amsterdam: Hakkert, 2007); and Anthony Heacock, *Jonathan Loved David: Manly Love in the Bible and the Hermeneutics of Sex* (Bible in the Modern World 22; Sheffield: Sheffield Phoenix, 2011).

For David and Jonathan, see also the following articles: Silvia Schroer and Thomas Staubli, "Saul, David und Jonathan — eine Dreiecksgeschichte?" *BK* 51 (1996) 15-22, trans. as "Saul, David and Jonathan — The Story of a Triangle? A Contribution to the Issue of Homosexuality in the First Testament," in *A Feminist Companion to Samuel and Kings,* ed. Athalya Brenner (2nd ser.; Sheffield: Sheffield Academic, 2000) 22-36; the response by Markus Zehnder, "Exegetische Beobachtungen zu den David-Jonathan-Geschichten," *Bib* 79 (1998) 153-79; Saul M. Olyan, "'Surpassing the Love of Women': Another Look at 2 Samuel 1:26 and the Relationship of David and Jonathan," in *Authorizing Marriage? Canon, Tradition, and Critique in the Blessing of Same-Sex Unions,* ed. Mark D. Jordan, with Mehan T. Sweeney and David M. Mellott (Princeton: Princeton University Press, 2006) 7-16, 165-70 (I wish to thank Saul Olyan for providing me with a copy of this essay), repr. in Olyan, *Social Inequality in the World of the Text: The Significance of Ritual and Social Distinctions in the Hebrew Bible* (Journal of Ancient Judaism Sup 4; Göttingen: Vandenhoeck & Ruprecht, 2011) 85-99; Anthony Heaton, "Wrongly Framed? The 'David and Jonathan Narrative' and the Writing of Biblical Homosexuality," *Bible and Critical Theory* 3 (2007), available at www.epress.monash.edu/bc); Markus Zehnder, "Observations on the Relationship between David and Jonathan and the Debate on Homosexuality," *WTJ* 69 (2007) 127-74; and the 2009 survey by Bruce L. Gerig, "Jonathan and David: The Debate Continues," on-line at http://epistle.us/hbarticles/jondave11.html. See also the summaries offered by Richard M. Davidson, *Flame of Yahweh: Sexuality in the Old Testament* (Peabody: Hendrickson, 2007) 165-67; and Ovidiu Creangă, "Variations on the Theme of Masculinity: Joshua's Gender In/stability in the Conquest Narrative (Josh. 1–12)," in Creangă, ed., *Men and Masculinity in the Hebrew Bible and Beyond* (Bible in the Modern World 53; Sheffield: Sheffield Phoenix, 2010) 98-99. See also Theodore W. Jennings, Jr., "YHWH as Erastes," in *Queer Commentary and the Hebrew Bible*, ed. Ken Stone (JSOTSup 334; London: Sheffield Academic; Cleveland: Pilgrim, 2001) 36-74.

For a good deal of the Greek material cited below, see Hans van Wees, "Heroes, Knights, and Nutters: Warrior Mentality in Homer," in *Battle in Antiquity*, ed. Alan B. Lloyd (Swansea: Classical Press of Wales, 2009) 1-86; and Angelos Chaniotis, *War in the Hellenistic World: A Social and Cultural History* (Oxford: Blackwell, 2005). For methodological matters, see also David M. Halperin, *One Hundred Years of Homosexuality* (New York: Routledge, 1990); Halperin, John J. Winkler, and Froma I. Zeitlin, eds., *Before Sexuality: The Construction of Erotic Experience in the Ancient Greek World* (Princeton: Princeton University Press, 1990); Sandra Boehringer, *L'homosexualité féminine dans l'Antiquité grecque et romaine* (Collection d'Etudes Anciennes, 135; Série grecque; Paris: Belles Lettres, 2007); Daniel Ogden, "Homosexuality and Warfare in Ancient Greece," in Lloyd, *Battle in Antiquity*, 107-68; Steven M. Oberhelman, "Hierarchies of Gender, Ideology, and Power in Ancient and Medieval Greek and Arabic Dream Literature," in *Homoeroticism in Classical Arabic Literature*, ed. J. W. Wright Jr. and Everett K. Rowson (New York: Columbia University Press, 1997) 55-93; and Dale Launderville, *Celibacy in the Ancient World: Its Ideal and Practice in Pre-Hellenistic Israel, Mesopotamia, and Greece* (Collegeville: Liturgical, 2010).

2. I would use the term "nemesis" here in its general sense as an opponent, but I do not wish to suggest its more specific etymological meaning as an inflictor of retribution or agent of downfall. For the background of the Greek word, see H. A. Shapiro, "Helen: Heroine of Cult, Heroine in Art," in *Heroes: Mortals and Myths in Ancient Greece*, ed. Sabine Albersmeier (Baltimore: Walters Art Museum, 2009) 50.

3. Cf. the "epic triangle" of three deities surrounding the hero in *Gilgamesh* and the *Iliad* as well as Aqhat, as suggested by Bruce Louden, "The Gods in Epic, or the Divine Economy," in *A Companion to Ancient Epic*, ed. John Miles Foley (Oxford: Blackwell, 2005) 90-104; and *The Iliad: Structure, Myth, and Meaning* (Baltimore: Johns Hopkins University Press, 2006) 240-45.

4. Cf. Ackerman, *When Heroes Love*, 150: "these women function simultaneously as mirrors of the liminal imagery that predominates in the Epic's text and as crucial linchpins that facilitate the narrative's movement through the phases of the rites-of-passage model." On liminality in Gilgamesh, see the extensive discussion in Ackerman, *When Heroes Love*, 88-150, and the discussion below.

5. See Seth L. Schein, *The Mortal Hero: An Introduction to Homer's* Iliad (Berkeley: University of California Press, 1984) 91-93; and Laura M. Slatkin, *The Power of Thetis: Allusion and Interpretation in the Iliad* (Berkeley: University of California Press, 1991). For

a proposed Semitic background to Thetis, see David R. West, "The Lion and the Serpent: Two Semitic Themes of the Goddess Thetis," *UF* 35 (2003) 709-15.

6. To be sure, Diomedes wounds Aphrodite (*Iliad* 5.330-51); and Achilles does fight Scamander until Hera and Hephaestus stop him (see 21.324-82).

7. See Pierre Brulé, *Women of Ancient Greece*, trans. Antonia Nevill (Edinburgh: Edinburgh University Press, 2003) 44-54. Note also Seth Benardete, *Achilles and Hector: The Homeric Hero* (South Bend: St. Augustine's Press, 2005) 32-39, 86-87, 96; and Jonathan Gottschall, *The Rape of Troy: Evolution, Violence, and the World of Homer* (Cambridge: Cambridge University Press, 2008) 59-63. Benardete captures something of the thematic symmetry between Helen and Briseis when he refers to Briseis as "the equal of Helen" (*Achilles and Hector*, 96). Cf. the intertextual approach of Christos C. Tsagalis that the *Iliad* "is using *female figures* not only as plot agents but also as intertextual pathways leading to the retrieval of necessary information." Tsagalis, *The Oral Palimpsest: Exploring Intertexuality in the Homeric Epics* (Hellenic Studies 29; Washington, DC: Center for Hellenic Studies, 2008) xv (Tsagalis's italics). For example, "Iliadic Helen is used as a vehicle for intertextual rivalry and subsequently as a metaphor for the supremacy of the Iliadic tradition" for Tsagalis (*The Oral Palimpsest*, xvi). This highly suggestive approach lies beyond the scope of this study. Seizure of another man's concubine is a traditional source of conflict in biblical material (e.g., Gen. 49:4; 2 Sam. 3:7).

8. According to Deborah Beck, the narrative draws Agamemnon's character in a way that makes him "an effective foil for Achilles." See Beck, *Homeric Conversation* (Hellenic Studies 14; Washington: Center for Hellenic Studies, 2005) 205.

9. For Helen as the original cause of war, see *Iliad* 2.161, 177, 589-90; 3.84-94, 154-60; 4.19, 174; 9.339. When the idea of ransom for Helen is rejected as a way to end the war in Book 7 (see 7.399-411; cf. 7.350-51), she is little more than the pretext for war, now more a matter of fame (*kleos*, 4.197, 207; 5.3, 273; 9.413, 415; 10.212; 17.16, 131, 232; 18.121; cf. 7.451-53) and glory (*kudos*, 4.415-16; 8.236-37; 16.84; 17.251, 285-87, 321-22; 22.111-30; see also 15.610-14; on the theme of personal and collective glory, see van Wees, "Heroes, Knights, and Nutters," 23-25). Still Helen remains represented as the ostensible reason for battle (19.325). For Benardete (*Achilles and Hector*, 86-87), Helen is the original *casus belli*, but she is then "discarded, and becomes merely a theme for heroic exploits. . . . She is the plaything of the future (of her own renown) and no longer manages her own destiny. She is caught up in a larger issue and concedes her own significance." For Benardete (p. 90; see also his comments in this vein on pp. 122, 129), Helen is the first cause of war, fame the second, and Patroklos the third and last. The causes, it may be said, are cumulative. According to 21.297, the story is still about Achilles' "glory" in the LCL translation of *euchos* (better "boast" or "pride"); see also 21.542-43. The entire picture is arguably more complex according to van Wees ("Heroes, Knights, and Nutters," 58): "The pursuit of glory in Homer is but one combat drive among many, and its effect on combat etiquette is limited." Interestingly, the war is not, in the end, for Troy itself for which the work is named; its demise lies beyond its scope.

10. For references for this expression and discussion, see section 2 in Chapter Two.

11. For the relationship of Yahweh to the heroic figure of David as homoerotic, see Jennings, "YHWH as Erastes." Jennings does not offer explicit biblical statements along

these lines, compared with what we see for pairs of heroes noted below in this chapter (e.g., 2 Sam. 1:26 discussed below and in Chapter Ten). Jennings's treatment of the language used does not differentiate between classic expressions of covenant ("steadfast love" and "servant," in his translations on p. 65) and homoerotic expression. Contrast the nuanced discussion of the language involved by Olyan, " 'Surpassing the Love of Women,' " 7-16, 165-70. Jennings's discussion (p. 74) assumes that since YHWH is male without a divine consort, "the erotic finds expression not in relation to a consort but in relation to the humans he has chosen as companions, friends and lovers." While this is explicit in images of Israel or Jerusalem as God's spouse in prophetic literature, comparable, explicit language is absent for Yahweh's relationship with David.

12. For this point, see further in Chapter Twelve.

13. For the importance of this difference in the biblical story, see Römer and Bonjour, *L'homosexualité dans le Proche-Orient ancien et la Bible,* 93-94. Römer and Bonjour elsewhere emphasize the reduced sexual representation of Yahweh in priestly literature; it might be wondered if this development may have played any role in the reduced sexual representation of the relationship of David and Jonathan. To be sure, a goddess could well be the divine patron of the ruling dynasty in other ancient Near Eastern contexts, e.g., Ishtar's patronage of Neo-Assyrian kings. Similarly, goddesses seem to be the divine patron of the dynasty in some Phoenician texts (a situation perhaps also reflected in the Ekron inscription). However, this does not seem to be the approach in ancient Israel or Judah or in the Transjordanian states where a national god seems to be the norm.

14. Cf. the fine observations in Louden, "The Gods in Epic," 90-99.

15. This point is not to discount the importance of Shamhat in *Gilgamesh,* a human female who drives part of the narrative about Enkidu; and certainly the heroes engage in sexual relationships in all three narratives. See below for discussion.

16. See below for discussion.

17. See a critical discussion about Homeric warriors generally as kings and princes by Hans van Wees, *Status Warriors: War, Violence, and Society in Homer and History* (Dutch Monographs on Ancient History and Archaeology 9; Amsterdam: Gieben, 1992) 281-98.

18. Thorkild Jacobsen, *The Treasures of Darkness: A History of Mesopotamian Religion* (New Haven: Yale University Press, 1976) compares how the introductions to both *Gilgamesh* and the *Odyssey* evoke their "strange and stirring experiences" in "far-off regions." As Jacobsen suggests, the landscapes experienced in the heroes' long journeys are comparable in the two epics. Tzvi Abusch would add a comparison of Siduri in *Gilgamesh* with Calypso in the *Odyssey;* "Mourning the Death of a Friend: Some Assyriological Notes," in *Gilgamesh: A Reader,* ed. John Maier (Wauconda: Bolchazy-Carducci, 1997) 109-21. For comparisons of the plots of *Gilgamesh* and the *Odyssey,* see Hope Nash Wolff, *A Study in the Narrative Structures of Three Epic Poems:* Gilgamesh, *The* Odyssey, Beowulf (New York: Garland, 1987). Jacobsen also notes a crucial difference in the introductions, in particular the place of the city of Uruk in *Gilgamesh.* With their different trajectories, the *Odyssey* and *Gilgamesh* are opposites in several crucial respects. The nature of the heroes and their journeys differs, as does the nature of their losses. Gilgamesh is haunted by the loss of his one comrade, while the memory of his home and the Trojan War generally hangs over Odysseus. The one loss that Odysseus has in mind is one that can

be regained; it is not another comrade in arms but his comrade in family, his beloved Penelope. Moreover, the force of their journeys is correspondingly opposite: the memory of Enkidu compels Gilgamesh out to far-away places, while it is the hope of regaining Penelope that drives Odysseus homeward. The endings likewise differ. Odysseus finds home and hearth with his beloved Penelope; while failing in his quest for immortality Gilgamesh returns home to the city, as Jacobsen noted. Gilgamesh remains to the end more akin to Achilles, with each changed forever by his friend's death.

19. For the term, see the discussion in Chapter One, section 3.

20. By one count, 243 named figures are killed in the *Iliad.* See Emily Vermeule, *Aspects of Death in Early Greek Art and Poetry* (Berkeley: University of California Press, 1979) 97.

21. Beck, *Homeric Conversation,* 1.

22. Benardete, *Achilles and Hector,* 3.

23. See Benardete, *Achilles and Hector,* 26.

24. See Chapter Twelve for further discussion of these verses.

25. See Chapter Ten for a detailed discussion of this poem.

26. The complex issue of epic in ancient Israel has been under discussion for a long time. For discussion, see section 3 of Chapter One.

27. It was Rivkah Harris's treatment of Ishtar that pushed my thinking and observations in this direction, although her points are somewhat different from what I am emphasizing. She examines how goddesses within themselves embody gender inversions; I am stressing the inversion of gender in the roles of goddesses relative to the roles of human females. See Harris, "Inanna-Ishtar as Paradox and a Coincidence of Opposites," *HR* 30 (1991) 261-78; I wish to thank Corri Carvalho for originally bringing this article to my attention. I have also found helpful the critical reflections on the social construction of gender and gender roles in cross-cultural perspective by Serena Nanda, *Neither Man nor Woman: The Hijras of India* (Belmont: Wadsworth, 1990).

28. Tikva Frymer-Kensky, *In the Wake of the Goddesses: Women, Culture, and the Biblical Transformation of Pagan Myth* (New York: Free Press, 1992) 14: "When goddesses portray and represent women in society, they are women writ large, with the same positions in the god-world that women have in the human world."

29. As seen for Anat by Jean-Marie Husser, "La mort d'Aqhat: chasse et rites de passage à Ugarit," *RHR* 225 (2008) 323-45, here 343. Contrast the situation with the West Semitic gods, who are warriors, e.g., Baal and Yahweh.

30. My thanks to Saul Olyan for this suggestion.

31. The warrior goddesses involved, Athena in the *Iliad* and Ishtar in Mesopotamian literature, are more famously daughters and not mothers. Athena is particular has no divine mother and is clearly an anomaly in terms of family structure; the same may be said for Ugaritic Anat. This Ugaritic goddess is preeminently a sister (to Baal) and daughter (to El, apparently); see Chapter Seven for discussion. These goddesses have no spouses. Susan Ackerman (personal communication) has suggested that these figures thus reflect a gender inversion with regard to their familial relationships. For Anat on this score, see Neal H. Walls, *The Goddess Anat in Ugaritic Myth* (SBLDS 135; Atlanta: Scholars, 1992) 13-75, 217-24.

32. See Chapter Four.

33. See also Artemis, discussed in Launderville, *Celibacy in the Ancient World,* 280.

34. So also Louden, "The Gods in Epic," 96-97.

35. For the importance of the former, see Rikva Harris, "Images of Women in the Gilgamesh Epic," in *Lingering Over Words: Studies in Ancient Near Eastern Literature in Honor of William L. Moran,* ed. Tzvi Abusch, John Huehnergard, and Piotr Steinkeller (HSS 37; Atlanta: Scholars, 1990) 221-22; repr. in *The Epic of Gilgamesh: A New Translation, Analogues, Criticism,* trans. and ed. Benjamin R. Foster (New York: Norton, 2001); and in Maier, *Gilgamesh: A Reader.*

36. Note also the intercessory role attributed by Ninsun to Aya, the wife of Shamash, in SBV III.56-58, 74-79. On this point, see Karel van der Toorn, *Family Religion in Babylonia, Syria, and Israel: Continuity and Changes in the Forms of Religious Life* (Studies in the History and Culture of the Ancient Near East 7; Leiden: Brill, 1996) 138; and Andrew R. George, *The Babylonian Gilgamesh Epic: Introduction, Critical Edition, and Cuneiform Texts* (2 vols.; Oxford: Oxford University Press, 2003) 1:459-61.

37. Harris, "Inanna-Ishtar as Paradox," 268 and 270.

Foster notes about Ishtar's offer to Gilgamesh: "The poet's intention is clear: Gilgamesh is first urged to be a lover, then her husband. By this device the poet undermines the legitimacy of her proposal, as not only is a woman here proposing to a man, but she is proposing intercourse before marriage"; "Gilgamesh: Sex, Love and the Ascent of Knowledge," in Maier, *Gilgamesh: A Reader,* 70. Foster sees in this episode the beginning of Gilgamesh's self-knowledge, specifically in the form of "antithesis and rejection."

Tikva Frymer-Kensky sees in Gilgamesh's refusal of Ishtar a rejection of the entire philosophy of kingship in the Akkadian and Ur III periods; "The Marginalization of the Goddesses," in Maier, *Gilgamesh: A Reader,* 102-3.

Nissinen (*Homoeroticism in the Biblical World,* 23) comments: "Ištar's proposal . . . appears as an alternative to Gilgameš's relationship with Enkidu. Gilgameš does not refuse this honor because of his sexual orientation; it is not a matter of homosexuality or heterosexuality. The issues lie deeper in the ideological structure of the epic. Ištar represents the world that Gilgameš is leaving behind — the lavish and sex-hungry city culture, the world fostered by his own excessive life." See the association of Ishtar's sexual activity and the city in the hymn called "Ishtar Will Not Tire," in Benjamin R. Foster, *Before the Muses: An Anthology of Akkadian Literature* (3rd ed.; Bethesda: CDL, 2005) 678. See also Victor Avigdor Hurowitz, "An Old Babylonian Bawdy Ballad," in *Solving Riddles and Untying Knots: Biblical, Epigraphic, and Semitic Studies in Honor of Jonas C. Greenfield,* ed. Ziony Zevit, Seymour Gitin, and Michael Sokoloff (Winona Lake: Eisenbrauns, 1995) 543-58 (Hurowitz questions whether the figure Ishtar named in the "bawdy ballad" is in fact the goddess by the same name, but the text provides no reason to suppose otherwise). Accordingly, at the head of the story of Gilgamesh, Gilgamesh is quite like Ishtar being in the city and highly sexually involved.

Similarly, Brigitte Groneberg quite interestingly reads the exchange between Gilgamesh and Ishtar in connection with the Old Babylonian dialogue between two lovers; " 'The Faithful Lover' Reconsidered: Towards Establishing a New Genre," in *Sex and Gender in the Ancient Near East: Proceedings of the XLVIIe Rencontre Assyriologique In-*

ternational, Helsinki, July 2-6, 2001, Part I, ed. Simo Parpola and Robert M. Whiting (CRRAI 47/1; Helsinki: Neo-Assyrian Text Corpus Project, 2002) 165-83, esp. 169-70, 174.

Tzvi Abusch sees Ishtar's offer to Gilgamesh as an invitation to rule in the Netherworld. He detects in her offer veiled allusions to death, entombment and descent to the Underworld; "Ishtar's Proposal and Gilgamesh's Refusal: An Interpretation of *The Gilgamesh Epic* Tablet 6, Lines 1-79," *HR* 26 (1986) 143-87.

For further discussion, see Neal H. Walls, *Desire, Discord, and Death: Approaches to Ancient Near Eastern Myth* (ASOR Books 8; Boston: American Schools of Oriental Research, 2001) 34-50; and Tracy Davenport, "An Anti-Imperialist Twist to the Gilgameš Epic?" in *Gilgameš and the World of Assyria: Proceedings of the Conference Held at the Mandelbaum House, The University of Sydney, 21-23 July 2004,* ed. Joseph Azize and Noel Weeks (Ancient Near Eastern Studies Supplement 21; Leuven: Peeters, 2007) 14-16.

38. The point has been characterized in this manner by Hugh R. Harcourt: "the power of love that Ishtar represents . . . is the bond of comradeship, social solidarity and unbreakable loyalty. . . . The implacable fury of this same Ishtar is the force that destroys the bond that united the heroes, leaving the survivor desolate and inconsolable." See Harcourt, "An Odyssey of Love and Hate," in *Archaeology, History, and Culture in Palestine and the Near East: Essays in Honor of Albert E. Glock,* ed. Tomis Kapitan (ASOR Books 3; Atlanta: Scholars, 1999) 240.

39. See Chapter Two, section 1, for discussion.

40. For the warrior goddesses Anat and Athtart, see Chapters Four, Six, and Seven. For the issue of their "disappearance" from Israelite warrior culture, see Chapter Twelve. For this scenario, see also Mark S. Smith, *The Early History of God: Yahweh and the Other Deities in Ancient Israel* (2nd ed.; BRS; Grand Rapids: Eerdmans; Dearborn: Dove, 2002) 101-7. I see in the biblical tradition a convergence of the cosmic warrior god with the motifs of terrestrial conflict associated with the warrior goddess.

41. See Chapter Twelve for a fuller description.

42. This case is laid out in detail for the Rephaim, also warrior figures, in Chapter Five, and Chapter Twelve returns to the issue.

43. For this notion of social roles performed in warfare, see van Wees, "Heroes, Knights, and Nutters," 30.

44. For this point in the Greek world, see Chaniotis, *War in the Hellenistic World,* 103. See, e.g., the women set in huts (away from battle) in *Iliad* 19.280.

45. For Gilgamesh's taking of Uruk's women in SBV I.90-93, see Davenport, "An Anti-Imperialist Twist to the Gilgameš Epic?" 3-7.

46. Harris, "Images of Women in the Gilgamesh Epic," 224-25. The essay was republished in Foster, *The Epic of Gilgamesh,* 207-18, and in Maier, *Gilgamesh: A Reader,* 79-94.

47. The Instructions of Amen-em-het, *ANET,* 419, col. ii, lines 4-5.

48. For translation and prior treatments, see Miriam Lichtheim, *COS* 1:85-89, here 87.

49. Erra, Tablet I 46, 50; see Foster, *Before the Muses,* 883.

50. *Enuma Elish,* Tablet II, lines 92 and 116; see Foster, *Before the Muses,* 449. Cf. Tablet II, lines 143-144 (*Before the Muses,* 451), where Marduk refers negatively to Tiamat as "a woman" after he asks his grandfather Anshar: "What man is it who has sent forth his battle against you?"

51. Chapman, *The Gendered Language of Warfare in the Israelite-Assyrian Encounter* (HSM 62; Winona Lake: Eisenbrauns, 2004) 33-58. See, e.g., the "Treaty Between Ashurnirari V of Assyria and Mati'ilu of Arpad," in *ANET,* 533 in (v) 8-9.

52. *CAD,* Ṣ:51; Chapman, *The Gendered Language of Warfare,* 49.

53. For the verse as well as its association of women with spindles, see *UBC* 2:440-41.

54. Chapman, *The Gendered Language of Warfare,* 12, 33-58. See also Tarja Philip, "Woman in Travail as a Simile to Men in Distress in the Hebrew Bible," in Parpola and Whiting, *Sex and Gender in the Ancient Near East,* 499-505; Claudia D. Bergmann, *Childbirth as a Metaphor for Crisis: Evidence from the Ancient Near East, the Hebrew Bible, and 1QH XI, 1-18* (BZAW 382; Berlin: de Gruyter, 2008) 96-98; and Launderville, *Celibacy in the Ancient World,* 304.

55. Benardete, *Achilles and Hector,* 11-12, noting also 7.96, 235-36; 22.389; and 23.409. See also van Wees, "Heroes, Knights, and Nutters," 21-23.

56. Vermeule, *Aspects of Death in Early Greek Art and Poetry,* 101; and van Wees, "Heroes, Knights, and Nutters," 67 n. 59. He notes how *Iliad* 8.163 and 20.252-55 also use the figure of women for the cowardice of men. Van Wees also mentions 11.389-90, which combines the negative figures of a boy and a woman.

57. Benardete, *Achilles and Hector,* 42. See also *Iliad* 20.251-52.

58. See further Vermeule, *Aspects of Death in Early Greek Art and Poetry,* 101-3.

59. Cited in Chaniotis, *War in the Hellenistic World,* 102.

60. W. Kendrick Pritchett, *The Greek State at War* (Berkeley: University of California Press, 1991) 5:46, cited in Chaniotis, *War in the Hellenistic World,* 102.

61. Launderville, *Celibacy in the Ancient World,* 304. Philip ("Woman in Travail as a Simile," 503) cites Isa. 42:13-14 as well as a Middle Assyrian medical text: "like a warrior in her fray, she is cast in her blood" (for this text, see W. G. Lambert, "A Middle Assyrian Medical Text," *Iraq* 31 [1969] 28-39).

62. This is not to detract from the force of her appearances elsewhere, e.g., her lament over the slain Patroklos in *Iliad* 19.282-301.

63. Chaniotis, *War in the Hellenistic World,* 112-13.

64. For an extensive survey in classical sources about human war plunder, including females, see Kathy L. Caca, "The Andrapodizing of War Captives in Greek Historical Memory," *Transactions of the American Philological Association* 140 (2010) 117-61.

65. Chaniotis, *War in the Hellenistic World,* 103. Phylarchos is cited in Plutarch, *Pyrrhos* 28.4-5.

66. See Brulé, *Women of Ancient Greece,* 51. Thomas M. Greene emphasizes the community formed by the performance of epic lament: "In the common field of performance, . . . the grief of the poet merges with the performer's, and the character's, and the audience's"; "The Natural Tears of Epic," in *Epic Traditions in the Contemporary World,* ed. Margaret Beissinger, Jane Tylus, and Susanne Wofford (Berkeley: University of California Press, 1999) 189-202, here 195. Greene (pp. 190-91) also notes that the lament of men often involves the tears of the central hero, including Achilles, Odysseus, and Gilgamesh.

67. Goitein, "Women as Creators of Biblical Genres," *Prooftexts* 8 (1988) 1-33, here 3. This is an English translation of a much earlier article in Hebrew, "Nashim k'yotsrot Sugey Sifrut Bammiqra'," in *Iyyunim Bammiqra* (Tel Aviv: Yahneh, 1957) 248-317.

68. Fokkelien van Dijk-Hemmes in Athalya Brenner and van Dijk-Hemmes, *On Gendering Texts: Female and Male Voices in the Hebrew Bible* (Bible Interpretation 1; Leiden: Brill, 1996) 30-31.

69. Brenner and van Dijk-Hemmes, *On Gendering Texts,* 10-11 (Brenner), 34-37 (van Dijk-Hemmes). See Chapter Eleven for discussion of this couplet.

70. Cf. the negative response of Michal to David when he celebrates his victory in 2 Sam. 6:16, 20.

71. Chaniotis, *War in the Hellenistic World,* 107.

72. This ideal appeal is a trope of the warrior-king at his wedding in Ps. 45:2-3(1-2) (see also v. 9). Compare Solomon with his warriors in Song 3:7-11. This passage, like Psalm 45, associates this language with the context of the royal wedding. Cf. the love of the young women for the male in Song 1:3. The inversion of this discourse is to compare the beauty of women in terms of the emblems of male warfare, as in Song 4:4. The famous similes of Song 8:6, "love is as strong as death, passion as fierce as Sheol," have been compared with the strength of death in KTU 1.6 VI 16-20, where this figure fights Baal; see Marvin H. Pope, *Song of Songs* (AB 7C; Garden City: Doubleday, 1977) 668. The biblical verse goes on to state that the arrows of love are arrows of fire. The language of weaponry here is clearly military, suggesting that the similes suggest the romantic love of the man and the women in the Song is stronger than the fierceness of warriors engaged in a life-and-death struggle.

73. Phylarchos is cited in Plutarch, *Pyrrhos* 28.5, quoted in Chaniotis, *War in the Hellenistic World,* 192.

74. Chaniotis, *War in the Hellenistic World,* 192.

75. Pughat, too, rouges herself before her conflict in KTU 1.19 IV 42. For discussion of these passages and the cosmetics of war, see *UBC* 2:144-45. Cf. the victorious wading in blood following the divine victory in Ps. 68:23. The notion is applied to the moral realm in Ps. 58:10: the righteous when he avenges himself against the wicked will bathe his feet in their blood. Cf. 1 Kgs. 22:38. This sort of representation is applied also to the deity in Isa. 63:1-6. For further discussion, see Chapter Six, section 3.

76. For Hellenistic depiction of blood in battle, see Chaniotis, *War in the Hellenistic World,* 199-200.

77. See Thomas K. Hubbard, ed., *Homosexuality in Greece and Rome: A Sourcebook of Basic Documents* (Berkeley: University of California Press, 2003) 182-83.

78. See Hubbard, *Homosexuality in Greece and Rome,* 76 and 183. See also Christopher Gill, trans., *Plato: The Symposium* (New York: Penguin, 1999) 69 n. 35.

79. See Hubbard, ed., *Homosexuality in Greece and Rome,* 218. See further Bernard Sergent, *Homosexuality in Greek Myth,* trans. Arthur Goldhammer (Boston: Beacon, 1986).

80. For the question as it involves Achilles and Patroklos, see the discussion in Hubbard, *Homosexuality in Greece and Rome,* 14-15. Representatives of the view of Gilgamesh and Enkidu as sexual lovers include: Ann Kilmer, "A Note on an Overlooked Word-play in the Akkadian Gilgamesh," in *Zikir Šumim: Assyriological Studies Presented to F. R. Kraus on the Occasion of His Seventieth Birthday,* ed. G. van Driel, T. J. H. Krispijn, M. Stol, and K. R. Veenhof (Leiden: Brill, 1982) 128-32; George, *The Babylonian Gilgamesh Epic,* 1:732-

33; 2:902-3 n. to lines 96-99; and Nardelli, *Homosexuality and Liminality,* 8. For David and Jonathan as possible lovers, see Olyan, "'Surpassing the Love of Women,'" 7-16. See also Schroer and Staubli, "Saul, David und Jonathan," trans. in Brenner, *A Feminist Companion to Samuel and Kings,* with response by Zehnder, "Exegetische Beobachtungen." See further below for those who dispute this view or prescind from a strong view either way.

81. The issue for these biblical texts does not come up in the most recent and quite comprehensive survey of Launderville, *Celibacy in the Ancient World.* By comparison, the case of Gilgamesh and Enkidu occupies a considerable discussion (pp. 193-96).

82. See van Wees, "Heroes, Knights, and Nutters," 19.

83. See Ogden, "Homosexuality and Warfare in Ancient Greece," 124-25. As for what he calls "evidence," Ogden points specifically to three items: (i) Achilles' wish that all Trojans and Greek should perish and that Patroklos and he should take the city (*Iliad* 16.97-100); (ii) Achilles weeping for "the manliness and goodly might of Patroclus" (24.6-9); and (iii) his mother's advice to relieve his grief for Patroklos by having sexual relations with a woman (24.128-32). Ogden puts a particular emphasis on the particle *de* in 24.130: "it is a good thing to copulate in love even *(de)* with a woman," implying as opposed to a man. Ogden also places some weight on the fact that Patroklos serves Achilles like a woman. This observation militates against Ogden's conclusion about the lack of hierarchy in their alleged homosexual relationship (p. 125): "it is 'military' homosexuality" (see note 152 below).

84. Olyan, "'Surpassing the Love of Women,'" 10-16. See also the discussion in Ellen van Wolde, *Reframing Biblical Studies: When Language and Text Meet Culture, Cognition, and Content* (Winona Lake: Eisenbrauns, 2009) 49-50; and Römer and Bonjour, *L'homosexualité dans le Proche-Orient ancien et la Bible,* 67-73, 77-79. The classic treatment of love as a treaty term is William L. Moran, "The Ancient Near Eastern Background of the Love of God in Deuteronomy," *CBQ* 25 (1963) 77-87; repr. in Moran, *The Most Magic Word,* ed. Ronald S. Hendel (CBQMS 35; Washington: Catholic Biblical Association of America, 2002) 170-81. See also Susan Ackerman, "The Personal Is Political: Covenantal and Affectionate Love *('ĀHĒB, 'AHĂBÂ)* in the Hebrew Bible," *VT* 52 (2002) 437-58; and Jacqueline E. Lapsley, "Feeling Our Way: Love for God in Deuteronomy," *CBQ* 65 (2003) 350-69. The corpus of "love" expressions continues to grow. See the use of "love" in a legal document in RS 94.2168, lines 11-12: "the one whom 'Abdimilki will love (*'ihb,* i.e., 'prefer') among his sons." See Pierre Bordreuil and Dennis Pardee, *A Manual of Ugaritic* (Winona Lake: Eisenbrauns, 2009) 258-59; and Bordreuil and Pardee, *BSV* 135, 136.

85. To be sure, the prose and poetry constitute very different sources with different presuppositions. See Chapter Ten for further discussion on this score.

86. Römer and Bonjour, *L'homosexualité dans le Proche-Orient ancien et la Bible,* 78.

87. See also Nele Ziegler, "Gilgameš: le roi héroïque et son ami," in *Le jeune héros: Recherches sur la formation et la diffusion d'un thème littéraire au Proche-Orient ancien. Actes du colloque organisé par les chaires d'Assyriologie et des Milieux bibliques du Collège de France, Paris, les 6 et 7 avril 2009,* ed. Jean-Marie Durand, Thomas Römer, and Michael Langlois (OBO 250; Fribourg: Academic; Göttingen: Vandenhoeck & Ruprecht, 2011) 300-301.

88. Winter compares the descriptions of Gilgamesh with the representation of

Naram-Sin on his stele found at Susa. See Winter, "Sex, Rhetoric, and the Public Monument: The Alluring Body of Naram-Sîn of Agade," in *Sexuality in Ancient Art,* ed. Natalie Boymel Kampen (Cambridge: Cambridge University Press, 1996) 11-26; repr. in Winter, *On Art in the Ancient Near East,* Vol. 2: *From the Third Millennium* B.C.E. (CHANE 34.1; Leiden: Brill, 2010) 2:85-107; "The Eyes Have It: Votive Statuary, Gilgamesh's Axe, and Cathected Viewing in the Ancient Near East," in *On Art in the Ancient Near East,* 2:431-60, here 436-38.

89. George, *The Babylonian Gilgamesh Epic,* 1:552-53; see also *CAD,* K:614.

90. See also the discussion in Walls, *Desire, Discord, and Death,* 17. As Walls notes, the same noun is not applied to Ishtar. In the *Epic of Gilgamesh,* one might think that Ishtar would represent another magnetic pole of sexual attraction in the story, but Foster, followed by Walls, observes that the text omits her own sexual allure, in contrast to other texts about the goddess. See Foster, "Gilgamesh: Sex, Love and the Ascent of Knowledge," 40, 45. To be sure, Ishtar is sexually aggressive, but she holds little or no allure for Gilgamesh.

91. For Achilles on this score, see Benardete, *Achilles and Hector,* 44-46. For David, see Saul M. Olyan, *Disability in the Hebrew Bible: Interpreting Mental and Physical Differences* (Cambridge: Cambridge University Press, 2008) 15-16; and further Chapter Ten. Note also the description of Absalom in 2 Sam. 14:25 and of Adonijah in 1 Kgs. 1:6. David's magnetism is also conveyed through his success, characterized as divine support in 1 Sam. 18:14 (cf. Joseph in Gen. 39:2, 23); accordingly, v. 16 says, "all Israel and Judah loved David."

92. For the royal model for Gilgamesh, himself a king, note Winter's comparison with Naram-Sin and further in Mesopotamian royal tradition (see above n. 88). For the royal ideal in ancient Israel, see Ps. 45:3-10(2-9), introduced by the specific ideal of the king's beauty (see above n. 72).

93. In addition to scholarly interest in the "public" male body in Mesopotamian studies, the representation of the male body and masculinity has become a major topic in biblical and classical studies. See Creangă, *Men and Masculinity in the Hebrew Bible and Beyond;* Meriel Jones, *Playing the Man: Performing Masculinities in the Ancient Greek Novel* (Oxford: Oxford University Press, 2012), esp. Chapter Three on "Masculinity and Sexual Ideology"; and Maud W. Gleason, *Making Men: Sophists and Self-Presentation in Ancient Rome* (Princeton: Princeton University Press, 1995) esp. 70-81 and 159-68.

94. Moran, *The Most Magic Word,* 21, rendering OB Meissner = Sippar (VA+BM), col. ii, lines 0′-5′; cf. SBV X.55-57, 132-34, 232-34. For the passage, see Tzvi Abusch, "Gilgamesh's Request and Siduri's Denial. Part II: An Analysis and Interpretation of an Old Babylonian Fragment about Mourning and Celebration," *JANES* 22 (Comparative Studies in Honor of Yochanan Muffs; 1993) 3-17; and George, *The Babylonian Gilgamesh Epic,* 1:277-78.

95. Nissinen, *Homoeroticism in the Biblical World,* 1-17, 56; Walls, *Desire, Discord, and Death,* 11-17; and Ackerman, *When Heroes Love,* 1-30. For the issue in Hittite sources, see Ilan Peled, "Expelling the Demon of Effeminacy: Anniwiyani's Ritual and the Question of Homosexuality in Hittite Thought," *Journal of Ancient Near Eastern Religions* 10 (2010) 69-81. Note also the later Arabic sources in Wright and Rowson, *Homoeroticism in Classical Arabic Literature.*

96. Ackerman (*When Heroes Love,* 45) rightly warns that approaching the issue as a matter of whether the two heroes are represented as homosexual "quickly falls into the trap . . . to assume that the categories of heterosexual and homosexual that we use today can be used to discuss opposite-sex and same-sex erotic and sexual interactions in the ancient Mesopotamian world." Römer and Bonjour (*L'homosexualité dans le Proche-Orient ancien et la Bible,* 9; see also 79, 100-101) stress the anachronism involved with the term "homosexual," a word that they note was not invented until 1869. It is to be noted that the fact of the word being an anachronism is not sufficient in itself to remove it from scholarly discourse. On this point about anachronism, see Jonathan Z. Smith, *Relating Religion: Essays in the Study of Religion* (Chicago: University of Chicago Press, 2004) 193-94 and 207-8. For the issue of anachronism as it applies specifically to sexuality and sexual relations, see David M. Halperin, *One Hundred Years of Homosexuality* (New York: Routledge, 1990). At the same time, the modern assumptions that inform such a term are not to be imputed to the ancient cultures and the artifacts that they produced, including the texts under study here.

97. See Jean Bottéro and H. Petschow, "Homosexualität," in *Reallexikon der Assyriologie und vorderasiatischen Archäologie,* ed. Erich Ebeling and Bruno Meissner (Berlin: de Gruyter, 1975) 4:459-68.

98. See, e.g., Römer and Bonjour, *L'homosexualité dans le Proche-Orient ancien et la Bible,* 7-10; Nissinen, *Homoeroticism in the Biblical World,* 56; and Jerrold S. Cooper, "Buddies in Babylonia: Gilgamesh, Enkidu and Mesopotamian Homosexuality," in *Riches Hidden in Secret Places: Ancient Near Eastern Studies in Memory of Thorkild Jacobsen,* ed. Tzvi Abusch (Winona Lake: Eisenbrauns, 2002) 76-77.

99. For a helpful survey of the distance in understanding between the ancient and modern contexts, see Nissinen, *Homoeroticism in the Biblical World,* 1-17, and for the possible influence of the modern cultural context on the issue, see p. 56; note also Ackerman, *When Heroes Love,* 1-30.

100. Römer and Bonjour, *L'homosexualité dans le Proche-Orient ancien et la Bible,* 101.

101. My discussion combines a number of features discussed in considerably more detail by others, e.g., Walls, *Desire, Discord, and Death,* 9-92; and Ackerman, *When Heroes Love,* 47-87. See also further bibliog. below.

102. For Mesopotamian dream literature, see the surveys of A. Leo Oppenheim, *The Interpretation of Dreams in the Ancient Near East: with a Translation of an Assyrian Dream Book* (Transactions of the American Philosophical Society 46/3; Philadelphia: American Philosophical Society, 1956) 215-21; and S. A. L. Butler, *Mesopotamian Conceptions of Dreams and Dream Rituals* (AOAT 258; Münster: Ugarit-Verlag, 1998). See further below.

103. Jacobsen, "How Did Gilgameš Oppress Uruk?" *AcOr* 8 (1929-30) 62-74, esp. 70.

104. Oppenheim, *The Interpretation of Dreams,* 215.

105. George, *The Babylonian Gilgamesh Epic,* 1:454.

106. Ackerman, *When Heroes Love,* 55.

107. Oppenheim, *The Interpretation of Dreams,* 215.

108. Rochberg, *The Heavenly Writing: Divination, Horoscopy, and Astronomy in Mesopotamian Culture* (Cambridge: Cambridge University Press, 2004) 82.

109. For a description of such practices, see Oppenheim, *The Interpretation of Dreams,* 237-45. However, as Oppenheim (p. 237) says, "only a few and very specific dreams can dispense with all interpretive process."

110. Oppenheim, *The Interpretation of Dreams,* 217-20; *CAD,* P:241, #8. Oppenheim (p. 218) also reconstructed this verb at the end of Ninsun's speech to Gilgamesh in SBV I.273: "your dream is [so]lved." However, this reconstruction is not accepted by George, *The Babylonian Gilgamesh Epic,* 1:554.

111. Oppenheim, *The Interpretation of Dreams,* 221.

112. *CAD,* K:441.

113. For this point, George (*The Babylonian Gilgamesh Epic,* 1:793) cites the Sumerian poem of Lugalbanda and other sources.

114. For analogy and analogical thinking in signs, see Rochberg, *The Heavenly Writing,* 56-58, 173, 259.

115. Oppenheim, *The Interpretation of Dreams,* 215.

116. Walls, *Desire, Discord, and Death,* 64; and Ackerman, *When Heroes Love,* 61, 65.

117. See Daniel E. Fleming and Sara J. Milstein, *The Buried Foundation of the Gilgamesh Epic: The Akkadian Huwawa Narrative* (Cuneiform Monographs 39; Leiden: Brill, 2010) 46.

118. See Esther J. Hamori, "A Note on ki-ma LI-i-im (Gilgamesh P 218, 224)," *JAOS* 127 (2007) 67-72.

119. For the veil as a marker of bridal status in Mesopotamia, see Karel van der Toorn, "The Significance of the Veil in the Ancient Near East," in *Pomegranates and Golden Bells: Studies in Biblical, Jewish, and Near Eastern Ritual, Law, and Literature in Honor of Jacob Milgrom,* ed. David P. Wright, David Noel Freedman, and Avi Hurvitz (Winona Lake: Eisenbrauns, 1995) 327-39, esp. 330-34. Van der Toorn notes the use of the veil with the expression "like a bride" not only in the Gilgamesh passage, but also in Emar 369, lines 63-64. For this text, see Daniel E. Fleming, *The Installation of Baal's High Priestess at Emar: A Window on Ancient Syrian Religion* (HSS 42; Atlanta: Scholars, 1992) 187-88. For the veil, see also Launderville, *Celibacy in the Ancient World,* 106-7, 257; for the Greek bridal veil, see pp. 275-76, 473; for Tamar and her veil, see pp. 473-74. Note the "red robe" put on Dumuzi at the end of "The Descent of Ishtar," line 129; see Pirjo Lapinkivi, *The Neo-Assyrian Myth of Ištar's Descent and Resurrection* (SAA Cuneiform Texts 6; Helsinki: The Neo-Assyrian Text Corpus, 2010) 13, 22, 32, 90. Lapinkivi (p. 90) cites the view of Stephanie Dalley relating this line to the practices of corpses wrapped in red cloth for burial; see Dalley, *Myths from Mesopotamia: Creation, the Flood, Gilgamesh, and Others* (rev. ed.; Oxford: Oxford University Press, 2000) 162 n. 21. Read against this background, the burial cloth informs the image of the bridal veil here. Contrast the images of a bereft husband and father used of Achilles at the funeral of Patroklos in *Iliad* 23.222-25.

120. Note also the analogy in SBV VIII.44-45: "I shall mourn, Enkidu, my friend,/ like a professional mourning woman I shall lament bitterly."

121. George, *The Babylonian Gilgamesh Epic,* 1:172-73, 196-97, and 141, respectively.

122. George, *The Babylonian Gilgamesh Epic,* 1:733 (George's italics).

123. George, *The Babylonian Gilgamesh Epic,* 1:732.

124. George, *The Babylonian Gilgamesh Epic,* 2:902-3 n. to lines 96-99.

125. Dalley, *Myths from Mesopotamia*, 123: "[Your wife (?),] whom you touched, and your heart was glad."

126. So *CAD*, N/2:2:57.

127. Cited in *CAD*, N/2:59, 60, respectively.

128. For this matter, see Ackerman, *When Heroes Love*, 67. On this score, compare *Sports Illustrated* (19 July 2010, p. 50) on the Argentinian soccer star, Diego Maradona, turned coach of the national team, for his response to his journalistic critics after his team "got off to a rousing start." Maradona asked the journalists to apologize: "I'm not suggesting that you drop your trousers, but it would be honest and great so we all get along better." The report continues: "Asked about his penchant for hugging and kissing his men, Maradona, 49, flashed a look of mock horror and insisted, 'I am dating Veronica, who is blonde and 31 years old.'" Cf. the older essay by Alan Dundes, "Into the Endzone for a Touchdown: A Psychoanalytic Consideration of American Football," *Western Folklore* 37/2 (1978) 75-88.

129. George, *The Babylonian Gilgamesh Epic*, 2:641.

130. *CAD*, D:70.

131. So Jeremy Black, Andrew George, and Nicholas Postgate, *A Concise Dictionary of Akkadian* (2nd, corrected printing; Wiesbaden: Harrassowitz, 2000) 176, sub *lalû*.

132. See further Walls, *Desire, Discord, and Death*, 17-18.

133. Kilmer, "A Note on an Overlooked Word-play," 66-67.

134. See the further remarks on this pair in Cooper, "Buddies in Babylonia," 77-80.

135. Cf. P. S. Vermaak, "A New Interpretation of the Playing Objects in the Gilgamesh Epic," *JSem* 20 (2011) 109-38.

136. Kilmer, "The Investiture of Enkidu in The Epic of Gilgamesh Tablet III," in Parpola and Whiting, *Sex and Gender in the Ancient Near East*, 283-88.

137. See, e.g., Ackerman, *When Heroes Love*, 59-60; and V. A. B. Hurowitz, "Finding New Life in Old Words: Word Play in the Gilgameš Epic," in Azize and Weeks, *Gilgameš and the World of Assyria*, 71 n. 16.

138. Nissinen, *Homoeroticism in the Biblical World*, 33-34. Note also the discussion of Kilmer's proposals by George, *The Babylonian Gilgamesh Epic*, 1:452-54. Nissinen (pp. 28-33) in particular notes the association of these figures with Ishtar. For this side of Ishtar, see also Harris, "Inanna-Ishtar as Paradox," 276-77.

139. Nissinen, *Homoeroticism in the Biblical World*, 34.

140. See *CAD*, K:437.

141. See Foster, "Gilgamesh: Sex, Love and the Ascent of Knowledge," 18-34. For the numerical "six days and seven nights" here, see George, *The Babylonian Gilgamesh Epic*, 2:194-95; cf. the more explicit numerical narration of Baal's sexual coupling in KTU 1.5 V 19-22.

142. See also the Hittite version on this score, in Gary Beckman, "Hittite Gilgamesh," in Foster, *The Epic of Gilgamesh*, 159, tablet I, par. 10.

143. Might the absence of such from the *Iliad* stem partially from the narrative fact that the soldiers are at battle? Cf. 2 Sam. 11:11-13. For two very different approaches to the larger context of 2 Samuel 11-12, see Jacques Vermeylen, *La loi du plus fort: Histoire de la rédaction des récits davidiques de 1 Samuel à 1 Rois 2* (BETL 154; Leuven: Leuven Univer-

sity Press, 2000); and Daniel Bodi, *The Demise of the Warlord: A New Look at the David Story* (Hebrew Bible Monographs 26; Sheffield: Sheffield Phoenix, 2010).

144. Ackerman, *When Heroes Love,* 120-21; Cooper, "Buddies in Babylonia," 73-85; and Launderville, *Celibacy in the Ancient World,* 194.

145. See Cooper's discussion of Jacobsen's studies on the issue as well as his own psychological interpretation; "Buddies in Babylonia," 73-85. Note also Ackerman, *When Heroes Love,* 47-51.

146. Jacobsen, *The Treasures of Darkness,* 218; and "The Gilgamesh Epic: Romantic and Tragic Vision," in Abusch, Huehnergard, and Steinkeller, *Lingering Over Words,* 245.

147. As noted also by Ackerman, *When Heroes Love,* 35.

148. Lambert, "Prostitution," in *Aussenseiter und Randgruppen: Beiträge zu einer Sozialgeschichte des Alten Orients,* ed. Volkert Haas (Das Konstanzer Altorientalische Symposium 3; Xenia 32; Konstanz: Universitätverlag Konstanz, 1992) 156-57 n. 31.

149. Foster, "Gilgamesh: Sex, Love and the Ascent of Knowledge," 65-66.

150. Foster, "Gilgamesh: Sex, Love and the Ascent of Knowledge," 66.

151. Harris, "Images of Women in the Gilgamesh Epic," 229.

152. Ackerman, *When Heroes Love,* 77, 120-21. Ackerman explores the relationship of Gilgamesh and Enkidu in terms of the categories of the active partner (*erastēs,* "lover") and the passive one (*erōmenos,* "beloved") in Greek homosexual practice, which she views also as the Mesopotamian cultural construction. In the classical model, the passive partner was typically between ages twelve and eighteen, although examples of older men functioning in this sexual role are known and cases of homosexual relations are attested in Greek armies. See Ogden, "Homosexuality and Warfare in Ancient Greece," 107-68, esp. 125. Ogden (p. 125) suggests a rather different model for Achilles and Patroklos: "We should simply accept that the sexual relationship between Achilles and Patroclus is an unhierarchised one between men who are to all intents and purposes peers: it is 'military' homosexuality."

153. Harris, "Images of Women in the Gilgamesh Epic," 228. Davenport ("An Anti-Imperialist Twist to the Gilgameš Epic?" 1-19) proposes seeing a political critique behind the representation of Gilgamesh as "an unjust ruler who abuses his royal authority" (p. 19).

154. For the following texts, see Nissinen, *Homoeroticism in the Biblical World,* 25, 27, 35. See also his further examination of the question in his essay, "Are There Homosexuals in Mesopotamian Literature?" *JAOS* 130 (2010) 73-77.

155. Ann Kessler Guinan, "Auguries of Hegemony: The Sex Omens of Mesopotamia," *Gender and History* 9 (1997) 462-79, esp. 468, cited by Nissinen (see preceding note). For discussion of this omen, see also Lapinkivi, *The Neo-Assyrian Myth of Ištar's Descent and Resurrection,* 75. Cf. Greek dream interpretation in Oberhelman, "Hierarchies of Gender, Ideology, and Power," 73 (e.g., Dreambook of Astrampschus: "To dream of performing intercourse on a male whom you like is a profitable sign").

156. Cf. Arabic dream literature on the subject discussed by Oberhelman: "the dream is a good sign if the dreamer is the penetrator. Submissive partners are males of a lower social class, eunuchs, young boys, or slaves. Sex between males of equal social rank is not even mentioned" (Oberhelman, "Hierarchies of Gender, Ideology, and Power," 70).

157. For the issue in Hittite sources, see Peled, "Expelling the Demon of Effeminacy."

158. Nissinen, *Homoeroticism in the Biblical World,* 23.

159. Nissinen, *Homoeroticism in the Biblical World,* 24.

160. Nissinen, *Homoeroticism in the Biblical World,* 24 (see also p. 56). Nissinen (p. 24) suggests further: "They experience unity and share each other's worlds — unlike a man and a woman, who lived in separate worlds. This exemplifies less a homoerotic than a homosocial type of bonding, which is often strong in societies in which men's and women's worlds are segregated."

There is little evidence for the "archaic" practice of "initiatory homoerotic relations" mentioned by Chaniotis for Boiotia; see Chaniotis, *War in the Hellenistic World,* 48. At the same time, it would not be difficult to see such as the background for pairs of warriors. The omen cited above from *šumma ālu* is perhaps suggestive in this direction.

161. Bahrani, "Sex as Symbolic Form: Eroticism and the Body in Mesopotamian Art," in Parpola and Whiting, *Sex and Gender in the Ancient Near East,* 56. For remarks also along these lines, see also Anna Maria G. Capomacchia, "Eros in Heroic Times," in Parpola and Whiting, 82. Note also the comments of Nissinen (*Homoeroticism in the Biblical World,* 23): "Ištar represents the world that Gilgameš is leaving behind — the lavish and sex-hungry city culture, the world fostered by his own excessive life."

162. For recent discussion, see Ackerman, *When Heroes Love,* 88-123; and the review of Jean-Fabrice Nardelli in *Bryn Mawr Classical Review* 2007.10.46 (http:///ccat.sas.upenn.edu/bmcr/2007/2007-10-46.html. Nardelli has written his own book on the subject, *Homosexuality and Liminality in Gilgamesh and Samuel.* In her study of epic heroes, Hope Nash Wolff considers them liminal figures by definition; see Wolff, *A Study in the Narrative Structures,* 88-89. These scholars draw on Van Gennep's notion of liminality to characterize these relationships; the two books differ in several respects, as suggested by Nardelli's review. Warriors engaged in conflict would typically stand in a liminal state, as marked by leaving their hair uncut (this is to my mind the best interpretation of Judg. 5:2 and Deut. 32:42, relative to Num. 6:5), as noted by H. Louis Ginsberg, *The Israelian Heritage of Judaism* (Texts and Studies of the Jewish Theological Seminary of America 24; New York: Jewish Theological Seminary of America, 1982) 101 n. 131. See Chapters One and Eight for further discussion.

163. Ackerman, *When Heroes Love,* 121 (Ackerman's italics).

164. Walls, *Desire, Discord, and Death,* 67, 80. Ackerman, *When Heroes Love,* xiv (Ackerman's italics): "the use of the erotic and sexual ambiguity in both the stories of Gilgamesh and David is ultimately not an impediment but a key — perhaps even *the* key — to the interpretation of these texts."

165. Løland, *Silent or Salient Gender? The Interpretation of Gendered God-Language in the Hebrew Bible, Exemplified in Isaiah 42, 46 and 49* (FAT 2/32; Tübingen: Mohr Siebeck, 2008).

166. Walls, *Desire, Discord, and Death,* 56-57.

167. See Fleming and Milstein, *The Buried Foundation,* 46.

168. Foster, "Gilgamesh: Sex, Love and the Ascent of Knowledge," in Maier, *Gilgamesh: A Reader,* 63-78.

169. It might be asked why such a relationship is constructed in this manner. Theoretically, the intimacy of this relationship might have been expressed in terms primarily

of brotherly relations. Clearly the texts go beyond brotherly terms or affection. Such brotherly relations involve elements of competition (so the initial meeting of Gilgamesh and Enkidu), yet this element of brotherly competition seems to be further sublimated as a sort of love that transcends the usual relationships of society, whether of brothers or of husband and wife. The relationships of these warrior pairs partake of both, and in a sense transcend both.

170. Walls, *Desire, Discord, and Death,* 58. See also Ackerman, *When Heroes Love,* 68-70.

171. Niditch compares warfare defeat with rape: "the Israelite war tradition . . . equates death on the battlefield with sex . . . the defeated warrior metaphorically is the woman who has been raped." See Niditch, "The Challenge of Israelite Epic," in Foley, *A Companion to Ancient Epic,* 284. Ackerman (personal communication) has suggested further that both combat and sexual relations are understood hierarchically: the victor in battle over the slain; and in male-female sexual intercourse, the male over the woman; and in the case of male-male sexual copulation, the penetrator over the penetrated.

172. Robert D. Biggs, *ŠÀ-ZI.GA: Ancient Mesopotamian Potency Incantations* (Texts from Cuneiform Sources 2; Locust Valley: Augustin, 1976) 37, no. 18, line 4′, cited in *CAD,* T:46 (under *tāḫazu*).

173. See Pope, *Song of Songs,* 605. Cf. the image of the two armies as two lines of reapers in *Iliad* 11.67-71.

174. John H. Oakley and Rebecca H. Sinos, *The Wedding in Ancient Athens* (Madison: University of Wisconsin Press, 1993) 20; cited in Chaniotis, *War in the Hellenistic World,* 102.

175. Van Wees, "Heroes, Knights, and Nutters," 29.

176. Vermeule, *Aspects of Death in Early Greek Art and Poetry,* 101.

177. See *CAD,* H:40. See also W. F. Albright, "Archaic Survivals in the Text of Canticles," in *Hebrew and Semitic Studies Presented to Godfrey Rolles Driver in Celebration of His Seventieth Birthday,* ed. D. Winton Thomas and W. D. McHardy (Oxford: Clarendon, 1963) 1-7, esp. 5; and Pope, *Song of Songs,* 605.

178. For the following passages, see *CAD,* I/J:197; Harris, "Inanna-Ishtar as Paradox," 269 n. 42. For the second passage, see also *CAD,* Q:15, #1c. See also under *CAD,* M/2:15, 17, and Harris, "Inanna-Ishtar as Paradox," 274. See also the discussion of Frymer-Kensky, *In the Wake of the Goddesses,* 66.

179. See also *CAD,* A/1:314a, 346b.

180. See Mark S. Smith, "Anat's Warfare Cannibalism and the West Semitic Ban," in *The Pitcher Is Broken: Memorial Essays in Honor of Gösta W. Ahlström,* ed. Lowell K. Handy and Stephen Holloway (JSOTSup 190; Sheffield: JSOT, 1995) 368-86. For a critical discussion, see *UBC* 2:159-64, 174-85, esp. 182. See also Chapter Six for the text and discussion.

181. See Fleming and Milstein, *The Buried Foundation,* 46.

182. Walls, *Desire, Discord, and Desire,* 63.

Notes to Chapter Four

1. Major studies of Aqhat include: Simon B. Parker, *The Pre-Biblical Narrative Tradition: Essays on the Ugaritic Poems* Keret *and* Aqhat (SBLRBS 24; Atlanta: Scholars, 1989) 99-144; Baruch Margalit, *The Ugaritic Poem of Aqhat* (BZAW 182; Berlin: de Gruyter, 1989); Kenneth T. Aitken, *The Aqhat Narrative: A Study in the Narrative Structure and Composition of an Ugaritic Tale* (JSS Monograph 13; Manchester: University of Manchester Press, 1990); David P. Wright, *Ritual in Narrative: The Dynamics of Feasting, Mourning, and Retaliation Rites in the Ugaritic Tale of Aqhat* (Winona Lake: Eisenbrauns, 2001); Chloe Sun, *The Ethics of Violence in the Story of Aqhat* (Gorgias Dissertations 34; Near Eastern Studies 9; Piscataway: Gorgias, 2008); and Shirly Natan-Yulzary, "Narration and Characterization in the Epic of Aqhat from Ugarit" (Ph.D. diss., Tel-Aviv University 2010 [Heb.]), to appear in English as *Narration and Characterization in the Epic of Aqhat from Ugarit* (Piscataway: Georgias, in preparation).

Key articles over the history of scholarship include: H. L. Ginsberg, "The North-Canaanite Myth of Anath and Aqhat," *BASOR* 97 (1945) 3-10; Andrée Herdner, "La légende cananéenne d'Aqhat d'après les travaux récents," *Syria* 26 (1949) 1-16; "Les cananéens: La légende de Kéret, la légende d'Aqhat, fils de Danel," in *L'Orient ancien* (Paris: Éditions d'Art, Mazenod, 1961) 141-51; Meindert Dijkstra and Johannes C. de Moor, "Problematical Passages in the Legend of Aqhâtu," *UF* 7 (1975) 171-215; W. G. E. Watson, "Puzzling Passages in the Tale of Aqhat," *UF* 8 (1976) 371-78; Manfried Dietrich and Oswald Loretz, "Bemerkungen zum Aqhat-Text: Zur ugaritischen Lexikographie (XIV)," *UF* 10 (1978) 65-71; Meindert Dijkstra, "Some Reflections on the Legend of Aqhat," *UF* 11 (C. F. A. Schaeffer Festschrift; 1979) 199-210; André Caquot, "Notes philologiques sur la légende ougaritique de Danel et d'Aqhat, I," *Sem* 37 (1987) 5-16 and "II (sur KTU 1 18 IV 9-11)," *Sem* 38 (1990) 73-79; Kenneth T. Aitken, "Oral Formulaic Composition and Theme in the Aqhat Narrative," *UF* 21 (1989) 1-16; David P. Wright, "The Play of Ritual in the 'Aqhat Narrative," in *Crossing Boundaries and Linking Horizons: Studies in Honor of Michael C. Astour on His 80th Birthday*, ed. Gordon Douglas Young, Mark W. Chavalas, Richard E. Averbeck, and Kevin L. Danti (Bethesda: CDL, 1997) 577-98; J. Aboud, "Abschnitte vom Aqhat-Epos neu übersetzt und analysiert," in *"Und Mose schrieb dieses Lieb auf. . . ." Studien zum Alten Testament und zum Alten Orient: Festschrift für Oswald Loretz zur Vollendung seines 70. Lebenjahres mit Beiträgen von Freunden, Schülern und Kollegen*, ed. Manfried Dietrich and Ingo Kottsieper; Münster: Ugarit-Verlag, 1998) 1-14; Jean-Marie Husser, "La mort d'Aqhat: chasse et rites de passage à Ugarit," *RHR* 225 (2008) 323-46; Kelly J. Murphy, "Myth, Reality, and the Goddess Anat: Anat's Violence and Independence in the Ba'al Cycle," *UF* 41 (2009) 525-41; and Shirly Natan-Yulzary, "Divine Justice or Poetic Justice? The Transgression and Punishment of the Goddess 'Anat in the 'Aqhat Story: A Literary Perspective," *UF* 41 (2009) 581-99 (a Hebrew version by the same title appears in *Moed* 20 [2010] 1-20); "Contrast and Meaning in the 'Aqhat Story," *VT* 62 (2012) 433-49.

My reading in this chapter is informed by these studies, esp. those by Parker, Wright and Natan-Yulzary, as well as the translations in *ANET, COS* 1, *MuE, TO* 1, *MLC, RTU,* and *UNP;* I do not rehearse many of their fine observations. I would also note two rather literate translations: Michael D. Coogan and Mark S. Smith, *Stories From Ancient Canaan*

(2nd ed.; Louisville: Westminster John Knox, 2012); and Francis Landy, *The Tale of Aqhat* (London: Menard, 1981).

2. Elsewhere epic poetry attests to the theme of the older father-hero who has accomplished his social status standing at odds with the son who has not done so but is supposed to be destined to replace him. Hope Nash Wolff considers them liminal figures by definition. See Wolff, *A Study in the Narrative Structures of Three Epic Poems:* Gilgamesh, *The* Odyssey, Beowulf (New York: Garland, 1987) 90-91.

3. The vowels for this name are unknown. See Dennis Pardee, *COS*, 1:249 n. 63 (which leaves the name unvocalized). Some scholars spell the name Yatipan or Yatupan. For the latter, see Wright, *Ritual in Narrative*, 128 n. 4. The etymology of the name is no less debated.

4. Natan-Yulzary, "Narration and Characterization in the Epic of Aqhat"; and "Contrast and Meaning." I wish to thank the author for providing me with a prepublication copy of the latter essay and for her generous permission to use it. Natan-Yulzary ("Contrast and Meaning") additionally sees the Anat-Pughat contrast as one of "bad daughter — good daughter."

5. See Parker, *The Pre-Biblical Narrative Tradition*, 142-44; *UNP* 50.

6. Wright, *Ritual in Narrative*.

7. In this respect, I am in some agreement with Margalit, *The Ugaritic Poem of AQHT*. However, Margalit (pp. 253, 336, 428) views the poem as a critique of the norms and values of a "warrior-aristocratic" society. I would agree that there is a reflection involved, one that illustrates some dangers and difficulties. However, I am not sure that there is enough evidence to sustain the notion of the text broadly as a social critique. For a different approach, see the discussion below.

8. Sun (*The Ethics of Violence*) assumes (1) that El is sympathetic to Aqhat in this matter and silently disapproves of Anat's action and (2) that Baal desists from responding; he is also regarded as having limited power in this situation. This interpretation compares with what Hans van Wees says of the gods in Homer: "the gods try to do two things at once: they do seek to punish mortals who act unjustly or improperly, but they also wish to support their kin and friends. When it is not possible to do both, *obligations to kin and friends have priority over the demands of justice*"; van Wees, *Status Warriors: War, Violence, and Society in Homer and History* (Dutch Monographs on Ancient History and Archaeology 9; Amsterdam: Gieben, 1992) 146 (van Wees's italics). Sun's argument assumes that the attention of the deities is directed generally to this problem. The characterization of Baal as desisting is not in the text, but is imputed. Given this absence, the view might be slightly modified: when responding to the death of Aqhat, the deities act at times not only in terms of their personal ties or sympathies, but also in modes characteristic for them elsewhere in the Ugaritic texts: El's compassion early on and later his efforts at accommodating Anat; Baal's intercession of El; the Kotharat's role in aiding human childbirth; Kothar's weapon-making; and Anat's violence. In some of these cases (El, Yatpan), there are some divine responses to the specific issue of Anat's slaying of Aqhat; and in other instances, there are not (Baal, Kotharat). Sun takes a similar tack to matters on the human level. As family relatives of Aqhat, his father Danil and sister Pughat feel that the act is unjust; they are also seen as not knowing the full story of Aqhat's behavior

toward Anat. According to Sun, the text does not resolve the issue of the ethics of Anat's violence, instead expressing both views that Aqhat's death is unjust and that his death is justified by his arrogance and rebellion against the goddess's wish to have his weapons. See the discussion further below.

9. As correctly noted by Pardee, *COS*, 1:354 n. 115; and *The Ugaritic Texts and the Origins of West-Semitic Literary Composition* (Schweich Lectures 2007; Oxford: Oxford University Press, 2012) 103. See also the list of critics provided by Parker, *The Pre-Biblical Narrative Tradition*, 142. Nick Wyatt (*RTU*, 250-312) defends the view that Aqhat's is a royal family. There are three major problems with this view. First, great weight has been placed on reading *mlk* as "king" in 1.19 III 46. For this view, see also Wright, *Ritual in Narrative*, 185. However, the first letter may belong to the end of the name *qr-mym* in 1.19 III 46 (so *UNP*, 74), which leaves *lk*, quite possibly a prepositional phrase, "to you." Or *mlk* here may mean, "what is yours" (Pardee, *COS*, 1:354 n. 115). Either way, the putative word **mlk*, "king," would be a mirage. Second, as Pardee observes, Danil is otherwise not called king; contrast the use of the title "king" *(mlk)* for Kirta (1.14 VI 14-15; 1.16 I 59-60), as well as the root elsewhere in the story of Kirta (see 1.14 I 7, 41; 1.15 V 20; 1.16 VI 23, 37, 53). Third, most, if not all, of the roles in the story singled out by Wyatt as royal are exercised by patriarchs, elders, and judges. Nothing in the story of Aqhat calls clearly for the royal character of its human characters. For discussion, see also Parker, *The Pre-Biblical Narrative Tradition*, 143.

10. The famous places mentioned in Aqhat are the Egyptian home of Kothar wa-Hasis (1.17 V 20, 31) and the Lebanon (1.17 VI 21). The places otherwise named in the story are three towns (1.18 I 30-31; IV 8-9; 1.19 III 45-46, 50, 51-52; IV 1-2); these, by the way, may be largely emblematic in their literary usage.

11. See *UNP*, 52-56; Pardee, *COS*, 1:344-45. See the following section for details.

12. This colophon appears on the left-hand side of KTU 1.17, which reads: "[scribe (is) Ilimilku, the Shubbanite, student of Attenu, the di]viner." See *UNP*, 63. The square brackets indicate how almost all of this colophon is reconstructed. Its ending with the letters *rln* does, however, match the end of the series of titles for this same scribe named in the colophon at the end of the Ugaritic Baal Cycle (KTU 1.6 VI 54-55). See *UNP*, 164; *UBC*, 2:725-26. In that colophon, the patronage by the monarchy and its priesthood is spelled out in detail, in lines 55-58. For a recent detailed discussion of Ilimilku, his colophons, and his practice of oral recitation (RS 92.2016.40-43), see Pardee, *The Ugaritic Texts*, 41-49.

13. For this issue as it applies to Aqhat, see Gregorio del Olmo Lete, "Littérature et pouvoir royal à Ougarit: Sens politique de la littérature d'Ougarit," in *Études ougaritiques II*, ed. Valérie Matoïan, Michel Al-Maqdissi, and Yves Calvet (RSO 20; Leuven: Peeters, 2012) 241-50, here 243-44.

14. E.g., *UNP*, 49. The narrative of the murder of Yatpan might have required only a single column (if the narrative pace does not slow down relative to the end of the third, extant tablet). In this hypothesis, the fourth tablet might have had approximately three more columns for further episodes. What those three columns might have included has been the subject of considerable speculation in the history of Ugaritic studies. It is tempting to suggest some sort of material that would connect to the appearance of Danil in the Rephaim texts (KTU 1.20–1.22), as these include both the figure of the patriarch

and dead heroes, a theme that might work somehow with the death of Aqhat (see *ANET*, 155). An alternative view to the idea of a fourth tablet might be inferred from the direction written on the left edge of the tablet, *whndt yṯb lmspr* (see KTU 1.19 IV 62). Parker (*UNP*, 78) suggested that this instruction is written on "the side of the tablet where the plot resumes after the interruption caused by Daniel's rituals following Aqhat's death." Pardee (*COS*, 1:356) translates, "Here is where to resume the story," and comments (1:356 n. 140): "The form of the colophon here is . . . an indication of how the story is to be taken up on the next tablet." As this sort of instruction elsewhere refers to including material that is not written but is to be supplied orally (e.g., KTU 1.4 V 42-43, in *UNP*, 131), perhaps this instruction also involves oral material, perhaps even the oral completion of the story involving Pughat's assassination of Yatpan. Where KTU 1.4 V 42-43 tells the reciter the point in the story to turn to (see *UBC*, 2:575-76), the instruction inscribed on the left hand side of KTU 1.19 IV 23-24 does not. So might this instruction refer to oral recitation of the rest of the story that comes after 1.19 IV? If so, it might have entailed only the conclusion of this scene; see Coogan and Smith, *Stories from Ancient Canaan*, 55.

15. Parker (*The Pre-Biblical Narrative Tradition*, 143) regards the story as possibly a source of amusement for Ugaritic society, but even more as a classic of Ugaritic literature that "may have been enjoyed as a satisfying portrayal of life in an idealized past era, a life with its own tragedies, but also with its own orderly and beautiful institutions that in the end prevailed."

16. The surviving prose label (or superscription), namely to the third of the three tablets (KTU 1.19 I 1), preserves *[l]'aq[ht]*, "[(belonging) to (the tablet series called)/about] Aq[hat]"; the other two tablets (1.17 and 1.18) do not preserve the very top of their initial columns where the superscription would have been written.

17. For the epigraphy of lines 1-24, see Pierre Bordreuil and Dennis Pardee, *A Manual of Ugaritic* (Linguistic Studies in Ancient West Semitic 3; Winona Lake: Eisenbrauns, 2009) 172-77; Manfried Dietrich and Oswald Loretz, "Baal bittet El um Kindersegen für den Inkubanten Danil (KTU 1.17 I 1-24)," *UF* 40 (2009) 191-204; and Dennis Pardee, "Illustrated Epigraphic Remarks to the First Tablet of the *'Aqhatu* Text, Lines 1-24," *UF* 42 (2010) 903-18. For the interpretation of lines 1-24, see Wright, *Ritual in Narrative*, 20-47. For a recent study of the two initial columns, see Koowon Kim, *Incubation as a Type-Scene in the 'Aqhatu, Kirta, and Hannah Stories: A Form-Critical and Narratological Study of KTU 1.14 I–1.15 III, 1.17 I-II, and 1 Samuel 1:1–2:11* (VTSup 145; Leiden: Brill, 2011) 89-162. This work refutes the view of Baruch Margalit and Jean-Marie Husser that denies seeing the passage as an incubation scene; see Margalit, *The Ugartic Poem of Aqht*, 260-66; Husser, *Le songe et la parole: Étude sur le rêve et sa fonction dans l'ancien Israël* (BZAW 210; Berlin: de Gruyter, 1994) 29-62; *Dreams and Dream Narratives in the Biblical World*, trans. Jill M. Munro (Biblical Seminar 63; Sheffield: Sheffield Acdemic, 1999) 77-78; "The Birth of a Hero: Form and Meaning of KTU 1.17 i-ii," in *Ugarit, Religion and Culture: Essays Presented in Honour of Professor John C. L. Gibson*, ed. Nicholas Wyatt, Wilfred G. E. Watson, and Jeffrey B. Lloyd (Ugaritisch-biblische Literatur 12; Münster: Ugarit-Verlag, 1996) 85-98. Kim notes that the criteria for the incubation used by Husser and Margalit are too narrowly tied to the specifics of Greek tradition and that incubation ritual varies from culture to culture. For incubation in Mesopotamia with reference to Aqhat, see

S. A. L. Butler, *Mesopotamian Conceptions of Dreams and Dream Rituals* (AOAT 258; Münster: Ugarit-Verlag, 1998) 217-39.

18. Later the text relates how Danil goes home (1.17 II 24-25), suggesting that he is not at home at the opening of the narrative.

19. KTU 47 n. 2; Pardee, *COS*, 1:343.

20. So Parker, *The Pre-Biblical Narrative Tradition*, 20.

21. For this view, see John F. Healey, "The Rephaites of Ancient Palestine and Ugarit," in *Studies in the History and Archaeology of Palestine II*, ed. Shawqi Shaath (Proceedings of the First International Symposium on Palestine Antiquities; Damascus: Aleppo University/Palestine Archaeological Centre, 1986) 159-63, here 161. The connection has long been made by commentators, e.g., H. L. Ginsberg, *ANET*, 149 n. 2.

22. For this meaning, see PNs such as *mtbʿl* in KTU 4.75 V 21; 4.130.10; 4.310.4 (cf. *bn mt* in 4.335.15; 4.785.12; *DULAT*, 599; and RS 94.2064.50, in Bordreuil and Pardee, *BSV*, 66. For a listing of Akkadian PNs with the element **mutu-*, see *CAD*, M/2:316, suggesting "man of DN," as devotee of that deity. Ugaritic *mt* is thought to signify "hero" as well (*DULAT*, 598). In view of Ugaritic *mt* and Akkadian *mutu* used for warriors, Ugaritic *mt* in Danil's title might also enjoy a martial sensibility. Accordingly, *DULAT* (598) renders *mt rpʾi*, "the Raphaite hero."

23. See Ginsberg, *ANET*, 149, comparing Harnaim in Syria, in "A Satirical Letter," in *ANET*, 477 (see "Hermon," in *COS*, 3:12); for bibliographical references, see *DULAT*, 346. For further views, see Marvin H. Pope, *Probative Pontificating in Ugaritic and Biblical Literature: Collected Essays*, ed. Mark S. Smith (Ugaritisch-biblische Literatur 10; Münster: Ugarit-Verlag, 1994) 238; and Aboud, "Abschnitte vom Aqhat-Epos neu übersetzt und analysiert," 1-2.

24. For wordplay as key to relations among realities, note the comments of Helen Vendler, *The Art of Shakespeare's Sonnets* (Cambridge, MA: Belknap, 1997) 361: "Language, and especially self-conscious rhyme, is thus seen as an access route to paradoxical but true relations among entities."

25. The point has long been made by many scholars, e.g., Ginsberg, *ANET*, 149. See Michael Patrick O'Connor, "The Human Characters' Names in the Ugaritic Poems: Onomastic Eccentricity in Bronze-Age Semitic and the Name Daniel in Particular," in *Biblical Hebrew in its Northwest Semitic Setting: Typological and Historical Perspectives*, ed. Steven E. Fassberg and Avi Hurvitz (Jerusalem: Magnes; Winona Lake: Eisenbrauns, 2006) 280-82. Ezek. 28:3 stresses Daniel's singular wisdom, while 14:14 and 20 emphasize his righteousness.

26. For the oracular question put to the god about getting a son, see Wilfred G. Lambert, *Babylonian Oracle Questions* (Mesopotamian Civilizations 13; Winona Lake: Eisenbrauns, 2007) 94-95 (K 8156 + 10942, line 14).

27. For **ḥnt* in line 16, Ginsberg (*ANET*, 150) translates "plea," while Parker (*The Pre-Biblical Narrative Tradition*, 101) entertains both "compassion" and "supplication." See also James W. Watts, "*Ḥnt*: An Ugaritic Formula of Intercession," *UF* 21 (1989) 443-49. Echoing Ginsberg's approach, Watts compares the use of the root in KTU 2.15.3: "intercede *(ḥnny)* for me before the king." For Watts (p. 447), the word not only "describes Baal's disposition ('favor') toward Danel"; it also "represents the notion of intercession." Cf. the nighttime

prayer carried out over a week's time by David in 2 Sam. 12:16-18 (cf. KTU 1.17 I 1-15), followed by the expression concerning the divine compassion (**ḥnn*) in 2 Sam. 12:22 (cf. **ḥnt* in KTU 1.17 I 16). The situation before the two leaders is directly inverse: Aqhat's lament before his god for a son that he does not have, versus David's lament for the loss of his son that his god is taking away from him.

28. See Karel van der Toorn, *Family Religion in Babylonia, Syria, and Israel: Continuity and Changes in the Forms of Religious Life* (Studies in the History and Culture of the Ancient Near East 7; Leiden: Brill, 1996) 264.

29. For a listing of parallel iterations of this lament in this story, see Kim, *Incubation as a Type-Scene*, 102.

30. For resonances between the opening incubation scene (1.17 I-II) and the third tablet (1.19), see Wright, *Ritual in Narrative*, 204; and Kim, *Incubation as a Type-Scene*, 156-61.

31. Note also Tamar's garb in Genesis 38. It is to be noted that the usages in both Aqhat and Genesis include tearing of clothing to express lament (1.19 I 36-37, 46-48 and Gen. 37:34). Although sleep is not explicitly mentioned in this context, Kim (*Incubation as a Type-Scene*, 116) would see it as another motif here that recurs later in the story.

32. On the duties, see Wright, *Ritual in Narrative*, 48-69. See also earlier discussions in Theodore J. Lewis, *Cults of the Dead in Ancient Israel and Ugarit* (HSM 39; Atlanta: Scholars, 1989) 53-71; and Marvin H. Pope, "Notes on the Rephaim Texts from Ugarit," in *Essays on the Ancient Near East in Memory of Jacob Joel Finkelstein*, ed. Maria de Jong Ellis (Memoirs of the Connecticut Academy of Arts and Sciences 19; Hamden: Archon, 1977) 163-82. For further discussion of the social setting, see also the older discussions of Klaus Koch, "Die Sohnesverheissung an den ugaritischen Daniel," *ZA* 24 (1967) 211-21; and Claus Westermann, *The Promises to the Fathers: Studies on the Patriarchal Narratives.* trans. David E. Green (Philadelphia: Fortress, 1980). The greatest divergence in interpretation involves lines 28-29. See below.

33. For discussion of this passage and esp. for *'il'ib* as the divine ancestor, see van der Toorn, *Family Religion in Babylonia, Syria, and Israel*, 154-68. The term *ztr* remains unclear, but its referencing as some sort of object is suggested by its parallelism with *skn*. Commentators generally posit comparison with Hittite *sittar(i)*, "votive (sun) disk"; others prefer to see a term for "thyme" or the like; see *DULAT*, 1001-2.

34. See Ginsberg, *ANET*, 150 n. 8.

35. See the cautionary comments of David M. Goldenberg, "What Did Ham Do to Noah?" in *"The Words of a Wise Man's Mouth Are Gracious" (Qoh 10,12): Festschrift for Günter Stemberger on the Occasion of His 65th Birthday*, ed. Mauro Perani (Studia Judaica 32; Berlin: de Gruyter, 2005) 257-65.

36. For this text, see Chapter Seven. For the duties, van der Toorn (*Family Religion in Babylonia, Syria, and Israel*, 154) suggests: "The tasks listed, in other words, are those a son is expected to fulfill when his father has grown old and the effective leadership has been passed on to him. . . . The acts of filial piety suppose a situation in which the father has become too weak to take care of himself."

37. See Wright, *Ritual in Narrative*, 70-80; and Kim, *Incubation as a Type-Scene*, 134-42.

38. This reading essentially follows Ginsberg, *ANET,* 150. The noun cannot be either in construct or the subject of the verb, as the gender of the verb is feminine in the parallel in KTU 1.19 IV 36 (see below); thus Danil is subject here, while Pughat is the subject there. Note also the opposite word order for the oath formulary, as in RS 94.2284.12 (*BSV,* 182, 185): *ḥy npšk.* Pardee (*COS,* 1:344 n. 13) renders the term literally as "throat" (parallel with *brlt* as "gullet"), but notes that the two terms "here denote metonymically the life forces." A more literal usage would fit the context of the word-pair in 1.17 V, but even there it is hardly required; "life-force" and "desire" (in the sense of appetite) would work in that context as well. To be sure, the word could refer to appetite (see Prov. 13:25) in 1.17 V 17-19, but not in 1.17 I 37-38. See the usage of *npš* also in RS 94.2284.32b (*BSV,* 181, 182).

39. For animals as living beings in Gen. 1:20, 24, 30; 2:19; Lev. 11:10, 46; Ezek. 47:9. Cf. *npš* plus the root **ḥyy* in the *D*-stem, "to preserve oneself alive," in Ps. 22:30 (?); Ezek. 18:27; "to preserve persons alive," in Ezek. 13:18-19; and "to preserve life" in 1 Kgs. 20:31. See *BDB,* 311. See the discussion of 1.17 VI below.

40. For this insight, see Jonas Greenfield, "Un rite religieux araméen et ses parallèles," *RB* 80 (1973) 46-52, republished in *'Al Kanfei Yonah: Collected Studies of Jonas C. Greenfield on Semitic Philology,* ed. Shalom M. Paul, Michael E. Stone, and Avital Pinnick (2 vols.; Leiden: Brill; Jerusalem: Magnes, 2001) 1:104-10. See also Mark S. Smith and Elizabeth M. Bloch-Smith, "Death and Afterlife in Ugarit and Israel," *JAOS* 108 (1988) 277-84. Cf. CIS I 6000bis.4: "because his spirit *(rḥ)* is rejoicing with holy ones." See Philip C. Schmitz, *The Phoenician Diaspora: Epigraphic and Historical Studies* (Winona Lake: Eisenbrauns, 2012) 87, 89-90, 95. Schmitz (p. 95) compares the wording of Isa. 24:19.

41. For the inscription, see Dennis Pardee, "A New Aramaic Inscription from Zinjirli," *BASOR* 356 (2009) 51-71; "Une nouvelle inscription araméenne de Zincirli," *Comptes rendus des séances de l'année 2009: Académie des Inscriptions et des Belles-Lettres* (2009) 799-806; and Seth L. Sanders, "The Appetites of the Dead: West Semitic Linguistic and Ritual Aspects of the Katumuwa Stele," *BASOR* 369 (2013) 35-55. For the stele's context and iconography, see J. David Schloen and Amir S. Fink, "New Excavations at Zincirli Höyük in Turkey (Ancient Sam'al) and the Discovery of an Inscribed Mortuary Stele," *BASOR* 356 (2009) 1-13; Eudora J. Struble and Virginia Rimmer Herrmann, "An Eternal Feast at Sam'al: The New Iron Age Mortuary Stele from Zinjirli in Context," *BASOR* 356 (2009) 15-49.

42. Pardee, "A New Aramaic Inscription from Zinjirli," 54.

43. See Sanders, "The Appetites of the Dead," 87, 93-94, 100-101. Note the later Aramaic use of *npš* in the context of grave inscriptions discussed by Pope, *Probative Pontificating in Ugaritic and Biblical Literature,* 148-50; and Ziony Zevit, "Phoenician *nbš/npš* and Its Hebrew Semantic Equivalents," *Maarav* 5-6 = *Sopher Mahir: Northwest Semitic Studies Presented to Stanislav Segert,* ed. Edward M. Cook (Winona Lake: Eisenbrauns, 1990) 337-44, here 342. See further R. Ḥachlili, "The *Nefeš:* The Jericho Column-Pyramid in Jewish Art," *PEQ* 113 (1981) 33-38; Joseph Patrich, *The Formation of Nabatean Art* (Jerusalem: Magnes; Leiden: Brill, 1990) 122-23.

44. Cf. Gen. 49:4 for the expression.

45. For Danil's joy here, see H. L. Ginsberg, "The North-Canaanite Myth of Anath and Aqhat II," *BASOR* 98 (1945) 15 n. 20; and *ANET,* 150; Greenfield, "Lexicographical

Notes II," in *'Al Kanfei Yonah,* 2:682, 685; Mayer I. Gruber, *Aspects of Nonverbal Communication in the Ancient Near East* (Studia Pohl 12; Rome: Bibical Institute, 1980) 2:568; Kim, *Incubation as a Type-Scene,* 144-49. Ugaritic narrative may describe body language of joy, lament, or fear preceding the oral expression for these emotions, e.g., KTU 1.3 III 32-IV 4; 1.4 II 16-26; 1.5 VI 11-25; 1.19 II 44-49.

46. For an extensive discussion of the root, see Mark S. Smith, "Kothar wa-Hasis, the Ugaritic Craftsman God" (Ph.D. diss., Yale, 1985) 51-84; for the Kotharat, see Smith, "Kothar wa-Hasis," Appendix I, 466-72. Note also Pardee, *DDD,* 491-92. For these figures in the story, see Wright, *Ritual in Narrative,* 81-86; and Kim, *Incubation as a Type-Scene,* 149-53.

47. The former view applies if *'rb* is an infinitive absolute, the latter if the form is a suffix verb. For the narrative infinitive, see Amikam Gai, "The Reduction of Tenses (and Other Categories) of the Consequent Verb in North-West Semitic," *Or* 51 (1982) 254-56. The suffix form of the verb to depart *(tb')* occurs also in line 39 used with the same descriptive formulary about the goddesses (for this verb, see Kim, *Incubation as a Type-Scene,* 153). It would seem that lines 26-27 and 39-40 mark the beginning and the end of the goddesses in the scene, and perhaps the two bicola of these lines mark a unit. If so, it may militate in favor of viewing *'rb* as a suffix verbal form.

48. So David Tsumura, "Ritual Rubric or Mythological Narrative? — CTA 23 (UT 52):56-57 Reconsidered," in *Proceedings of the Seventh World Congress of Jewish Studies: Studies in the Bible and the Ancient Near East Held at the Hebrew University of Jerusalem 7-14 August 1977* (Jerusalem: World Union of Jewish Studies, 1981) 9-16, followed by Kim, *Incubation as a Type-Scene,* 153-54; cf. Baruch Margalit, "New Readings in Aqhat," *AuOr* 17-18 (1999-2000) 105-12, here 105-6.

49. Since Pughat is one of the three most important human characters in the story and appears without any introduction in the extant text at 1.19 I 34, I have wondered if some part of the missing text in either of the first two tablets might have included her birth (and conception?). Since 1.18 I and IV are both concerned with Anat's plot to kill Aqhat, the missing columns 1.18 II and III might seem a less likely setting for the introduction of the figure of Pughat. By comparison, since 1.17 I-II deals with the conception and birth of young Aqhat and 1.17 V moves on to Aqhat as a young man, the conception and birth of his sister Pughat might have been a suitable subject for the missing material following the birth of Aqhat. Her name is the common Ugaritic noun meaning "female young one" (see *DULAT,* 666; O'Connor, "The Human Characters' Names," 278). This might hint at the birth order here, that she is perhaps younger than Aqhat, in which case her birth would follow his in the narrative. Her titles attested later (see 1.19 II 1-3/5-7; IV 36-38) might be suggestive of a possible earlier discussion of her character. Theoretically, she could be Aqhat's older sister, in which case she might have been introduced in some unknown tablet that preceded KTU 1.17. This seems less likely both because of her name and because of the lack of evidence for such a putative tablet. For Aqhat's name (evidently an elative of **qht*), see *DULAT,* 93, noting the alternative elative proposal from **wqy,* "Most Obedient"; see also Margalit, *The Ugaritic Poem of AQHT,* 6-7; and Stefan Schorch, "Der hebräische Wurzel *QHT,*" *ZAH* 10 (1997) 76-84, here 81-82.

50. Danil's wife receives no narrative introduction when she first appears. She is

called by name first when Danil addresses her in direct discourse in KTU 1.17 V 16. Though she plays no role in the extant text beyond this episode in 1.17 V, perhaps she would have been introduced earlier in the narrative, again perhaps somewhere in 1.17 III or IV or in the ten lines missing from the bottom of 1.17 II.

51. So Parker, *UNP,* 57.

52. See Wright, *Ritual in Narrative,* 87-96.

53. For further examples of a switch in subject with the expression, "then on the seventh day," see KTU 1.6 V 8; 1.17 I 15-16; 1.22 I 25; cf. 1.14 V 6. In other cases, there is no switch in subject, e.g., in 1.4 VI 31-33; 1.14 III 3-4. (The same point applies to the analogous expression "then in the seventh year": there is a switch of subject in 1.6 V 8, but not in 1.19 IV 17-18.) Note the case of 1.17 II 39 where the new subject is the direct object in the preceding clauses marked by days one through six.

54. Lit., "among the powerful ones (chiefs)" *(tḥt 'adrm).* Cf. *taḫtamu/ta'tamu,* "assembly" at Mari (*CAD,* T:299).

55. E.g., KTU 1.4 II 3-16.

56. For his name as "'Ilu is one judging" (with either suffix verbal form or participle), see O'Connor, "The Human Characters' Names," 277. In the context of the story, his name also suggests his own role as adjudicator.

57. For an example, see KTU 1.4 II 12-16.

58. For this hospitality scene in comparison with Genesis 18, see Paolo Xella, "L'épisode de Dnil et Kothar (KTU 1.17 [= CTA 17] v 1-31 et Gen. xviii 1-16," *VT* 28 (1978) 483-88; and Parker, *The Pre-Biblical Narrative Tradition,* 109-11.

59. See the hieratic inscription *pḏ.t* from Late Bronze Age Beth-Shean, which was connected to the bow in the story of Aqhat by Stefan J. Wimmer, "Chapter 13B: A Hieratic Inscription: The 'Bow of Anat'?" in *Excavations at Tell Beth-Shean 1989-1996,* Vol. 3: *The 13th-11th Century BCE Strata in Areas N and S,* ed. Nava Panitz-Cohen and Amihai Mazar (Jerusalem: Israel Exploration Society and Institute of Archaeology, Hebrew University, 2009) 696-99 (a revision and translation of Wimmer, "'Ber Bogen der Anat' in Bet-Schean?" *BN* 73 [1994] 36-41). According to Wimmer, the reading of the hieratic word (partially reconstructed) is to be seen as Anat's bow. Without any particular evidence, Wimmer speculates that Anat did not lose the bow in the story, and he further sees the motif of the bow in the story as an etiology for her weapon.

60. The *-y* ending on the PN *dnty* is the rare feminine ending alternative to final *-t;* cf. the *-y* ending on the name of the wifely figure *ḥry* in 1.14 III 39 (etc.) (see O'Connor, "The Human Characters' Names," 277) as well as PNs *ṭly, 'arṣy,* and *pdry* (cf. BH *śāray* versus *śārâ* in Gen. 17:15). There is also the example of the noun *brky* in 1.5 I 16 (versus the more common feminine *-t* ending on *brkt* in the parallel text, 1.133.6).

61. See Pardee, *COS,* 1:346 n. 34; *DULAT,* 679. Cf. *rē'šît kol-pĕrî* in Deut. 26:2.

62. From the perspective of poetic structure, a verb might be expected here (cf. the slightly different syntax in KTU 1.2 IV 8-9). Perhaps to be reconstructed is a verb in the semantic field of depositing. Accordingly, KTU reconstructs *[bln]* in the second line of the tricolon, while Wyatt (*RTU,* 270) and Wright (*Ritual in Narrative,* 94) reconstruct a verb ("you should place") at the end of what is taken here as the third line. Some sort of verb seems indicated, perhaps "bringing" (cf. *tṯṯb* in KTU 1.114.27 for the results of

the goddesses hunting for ingredients for El's drunkenness; cf. Exod. 23:19; 34:26; Deut. 26:4, 10; Neh. 10:38), "setting down" (cf. Deut. 26:2, 4), or "giving" (cf. Num. 18:12). See *DCH*, 8:381, #2.

63. KTU reads *p[rʿm]*, while Parker (*UNP*, 59) reads no letter before the break. If Parker is correct, perhaps the verb to be reconstructed in the second line might be read in the lacuna in the third line as well.

64. The suffix is in some doubt. KTU reads *hkly*, with a first person suffix (so too Wright, *Ritual in Narrative*, 94). CTA reads a third person suffix, and Pardee (*COS*, 1:346) and Wyatt (*RTU*, 270) translate with a third person suffix, "his temple/palace." Parker (*UNP*, 59) reads *hk[lh]*, which is followed here. The practice of "firstfruits" might suggest the temple of a deity. It is to be noted that the lines shared by 1.5 IV 19-22 and 1.17 VI 7-8, as nicely shown by Wright (*Ritual in Narrative*, 106), would point in the direction of a deity's temple, since that is the locale for 1.5 IV 19-22 (*bt ʾil*, in line 21). Wyatt suggests Kothar's as a thank-offering for the gift, but a temple of his is nowhere in view in this text. The preserved text of the next column might take place in Anat's temple or in Danil's palace (so Wright, *Ritual in Narrative*, 106, 107).

65. Cf. the weapons given to Baal by Kothar in 1.2 IV, the gifts made by Kothar for Athirat in 1.4 III, or the temple made by Kothar for Baal in 1.4 VI.

66. For this reasonable view, see also Wright, *Ritual in Narrative*, 96.

67. Wright, *Ritual in Narrative*, 95.

68. For this very difficult section, see Wright, *Ritual in Narrative*, 100-107. For lines 1-2, Wright compares the invitation to the feast in KTU 1.23.6.

69. Wright, *Ritual in Narrative*, 100, 105, and esp. 106.

70. Wright, *Ritual in Narrative*, 100 and esp. n. 1.

71. Wright, *Ritual in Narrative*, 106.

72. Margalit, *The Ugaritic Poem of Aqhat*, 180, 301, 324. Cf. *DULAT*, 986.

73. For this quite difficult section, see Wright, *Ritual in Narrative*, 108.

74. See Delbert R. Hillers, "The Bow of Aqhat: The Meaning of a Mythological Theme," in *Orient and Occident: Essays Presented to Cyrus H. Gordon*, ed. Harry A. Hoffner (AOAT 22; Neukirchen-Vluyn: Neukirchener, 1973) 71-80. Cf. H. H. P. Dressler, "Is the Bow of Aqht a Symbol of Virility?" *UF* 7 (1975) 217-20.

75. For discussion of weapons as symbolic for the warriors that wield them, see the Introduction as well as the discussion of 2 Sam. 1:21b in Chapter Ten.

76. Fernando Santos-Granero, "Introduction," in *The Occult Life of Things: Native Amazonian Theories of Materiality and Personhood* (Tucson: University of Arizona Press, 2009) 14

77. The putative root would be third weak (for this interpretation, see *DULAT*, 986). If correct, it may also be seen in *yṣbt* in line 9. In turn, the sentence in line 10, "when she lifts her eyes, she catches sight of . . . ," might bear an overtone of "coveting." Cf. Akkadian *našû ina* for "covet" in the Code of Hammurabi, par. 25, in *ANET*, 167; Martha T. Roth, *Law Collections from Mesopotamia and Asia Minor*, ed. Piotr Michalowski (SBLWAW 6; Atlanta: Scholars, 1995) 85; *CAD*, N/2:104b. To be sure, the language of line 10 is the customary expression for an initial sighting of someone.

78. Cf. Margalit, "New Readings in *Aqhat*," 106-7. Ugaritic similes involving serpents

seem a common enough trope (KTU 1.6 VI 19; 1.19 IV 61; 1.170.3), but none of these instances provides help here.

79. Treaty of Ashur-nerari V with Mati'ilu of Arpad, V, lines 12-14 in Simo Parpola and Kazuko Watanabe, *Neo-Assyrian Treaties and Loyalty Oaths* (SAA 2; Helsinki: Helsinki University Press, 1988) 12. For further usages along these lines, see *CAD,* Q:149.

80. So Parker, *UNP,* 60.

81. Cf. the idiom in Isa. 57:6: "also to them you poured out (**špk*) a libation." For the practice with the verb **nsk,* see also Gen. 35:14; Exod. 30:9b; Num. 28:7; 2 Kgs. 16:13; Hos. 9:4; cf. Jer. 7:18; 19:13; 32:29; 44:17-25; Ezek. 20:28; Ps. 16:4 (*BDB,* 650). For the noun *nesek,* see *BDB,* 651.

82. See Wright, *Ritual in Narrative,* 109-22.

83. For the idioms of request and giving, KTU 1.108.20; 5.9 I 7-16; cf. EA 34:21-22, 35, 49; 44:25-29. See *UBC,* 2.121 n. 35. Cf. **'rš* in royal correspondence, in 2.41.16; 2.45.24. Cf. Akkadian *erištu* in EA 158:17: "write me what you wish and see, I shall grant (the object of) of your wish," in *CAD,* E:298.

84. William Foxwell Albright and George E. Mendenhall, "The Creation of the Composite Bow in Canaanite Mythology," *JNES* 1 (1942) 227-29. Watson ("Puzzling Passages in the Tale of Aqhat," 372-73) compares the bow here with the one that Marduk makes for himself in *Enuma Elish* V and with the bow in Anzu.

85. Alan Gardiner, *Egyptian Grammar* (3rd ed.; London: Oxford University Press, 1957) 511 n. 1; I. Shaw, "Egyptians, Hyksos and Military Technology: Cause, Effects or Catalysts?" in *The Social Context of Technological Change: Egypt and the Near East, 1650-1550 BC,* ed. Andrew J. Shortland (Oxford: Oxbow, 2001) 60; Lawrence E. Stager, "Chariot Fittings from Philistine Ashkelon," in *Confronting the Past: Archaeological and Historical Essays on Ancient Israel in Honor of William G. Dever,* ed. Seymour Gitin, J. Edward Wright, and J. P. Dessel (Winona Lake: Eisenbrauns, 2006) 169; Hermann Genz, "Stunning Bolts: Late Bronze Age Hunting Weapons in the Ancient Near East," *Levant* 39 (2007) 49 (with further documentation). For composite bows in Egypt, see W. McLeod, "An Unpublished Egyptian Composite Bow in the Brooklyn Museum," *AJA* 62 (1958) 397-401; *Composite Bows from the Tomb of Tut'ankhamun* (Oxford: Oxford University Press, 1970). For iconography of bows (including a depiction on a platter from Ugarit), see Richard H. Wilkinson, "The Representation of the Bow in the Art of Egypt and the Ancient Near East," *JANES* 20 (1991) 83-99. The iconography of the bow extends symbolically to the West Semitic letter **ṯann,* "bow," which derives from two Egyptian signs for bow (the "archaic bow" sign, what is called J32/J32A, and the "composite bow" sign, what is called T10), according to Gordon J. Hamilton. See Hamilton, *The Origins of the West Semitic Alphabet in Egyptian Scripts* (CBQMS 40; Washington: Catholic Biblical Association of America, 2006) 314-15. For Mesopotamian evidence for the composite bow, see W. W. Hallo, "More on Bows," *ErIsr* 20 (Yigael Yadin Memorial Volume; 1989) 68*-*71. For earlier bows, see Edward McEwen, "The Bow," in *The Cave of the Warrior: A Fourth Millennium Burial in the Judean Desert,* ed. Tamar Schick (Israel Antiquities Authority Reports 5; Jerusalem: Israel Antiquities Authority, 1998) 45-53. See further Shelley Wachsman, "On Drawing the Bow," *ErIsr* 29 (Ephraim Stern Volume; 2009) 238*-257*.

86. According to Wilkinson ("The Representation of the Bow," 83-99), it takes years

for the composite bow to cure. In the Late Bronze Age Taanach letter No. 2, the speaker asks "if the bow is finished being made, then send it in the charge of Purdaya. . . . Furthermore, if there are arrows, let them be given." See Anson Rainey, "Taanach Letters," *ErIsr* 26 (Frank Moore Cross Volume; 1999) 157*. For bows, see also EA 22:36, 45-46; for arrows, see EA 22:31, 47-48.

87. For this formula for divine gift, cf. Ps. 2:7; 1 Kgs. 3:6.

88. Cf. the idiom "to give life" in KTU 5.10.2 and 5.11.4, noted in *DULAT,* 381.

89. Cf. Henri Frankfort, *Cylinder Seals: A Documentary Essay on the Art and Religion of the Ancient Near East* (London: Macmillan, 1939) 135-36, referring to a speech of Gilgamesh: "the gods in their first creation of mortals allotted Death to man, but life they retained in their keeping." "It is also clear from this opposition, that 'life,' in its opposition to 'death,' means everlasting life." For the parallelism of this pair, "life," *ḥayyîm*//"non-death," *'l mwt* in Prov. 12:28, see Bruce K. Waltke, *The Book of Proverbs: Chapters 1–15* (NICOT; Grand Rapids: Eerdmans, 2004) 518 n. 38; cf. the critical evaluations of Pope, *Probative Pontificating in Ugaritic and Biblical Literature,* 345; and Richard J. Clifford, *Proverbs* (OTL; Louisville: Westminster John Knox, 1999) 129.

90. Ginsberg (*ANET,* 151) renders "gives life." Given his translation of the verb forms as transitive, Ginsberg evidently understood the verb form as *D*-stem. David Marcus has demonstrated that generally forms of the verb with **ḥwy* are *D*-stem (as in this instance) while forms with **ḥy(y)* are *G*-stem. See Marcus, "The Verb 'To Live' in Ugaritic," *JSS* 17 (1972) 76-82. T. N. D. Mettinger follows Marcus on this point; *The Riddle of Resurrection: "Dying and Rising Gods" in the Ancient Near East* (ConBOT 50; Stockholm: Almqvist & Wiksell, 2001). So do I. We also agree on the translation: "So I will make Hero Aqhat live." If correct, the first instance of the verb would be passive: "like *b'l,* when he is made to live." Moreover, there is no evidence elsewhere for the notion of Baal giving life. In translating the first usage as a *G*-stem form and the second as a *D*-stem form, Johannes C. de Moor (*An Anthology of Religious Texts from Ugarit* [Nisaba 16; Leiden: Brill, 1987] 238), Parker (*UNP,* 61) and Pardee (*COS,* 1:347) disregard the distinction made by Marcus. See below for a possible resolution to the grammatical issues.

91. I like Pardee's rendering of the prepositional phrase here, "in his honor" (*COS,* 1:347).

92. For *'ap 'ank,* see also KTU 2.11.13; 2.33.15; 2.41.19.

93. The reading of]*'nynn* is clear (my thanks to Dennis Pardee for checking the reading, 15 April 2012, personal communication). There is space on the tablet for at least part of the horizontal wedge of *q,* thus precluding *[.w'a]qnyn,* "and I will establish him." KTU reads: *n'm[n.w.y]'nynn.* Most commentators favor seeing **'ny* here, but as Pardee notes, the sense is unclear (*COS,* 1:347 n. 43). As Pardee suggests, for what Anat has asked him to request in line 26, in line 32 she would answer his request. Anat seems to be referring to the Hero Aqhat at this point in the third person (so Pardee, *COS,* 1:347); the suffix on the verb may refer to him. Mettinger (*The Riddle of Resurrection,* 69 n. 62) suggests **'ny,* "to sing," hence, ". . . [and on]e celebrates him with song." Apart from the question of the attestation of this meaning in Ugaritic, the syntax remains problematic.

94. For this translation and the basis for some of the choices, see *UBC,* 2:121-22.

95. So Parker, *UNP,* 61; and Pardee, *COS,* 1:347 n. 44. De Moor comments: "It is ab-

solutely clear that the goddess is referring here to Baal"; *An Anthology of Religious Texts,* 239 n. 102. For a more recent expression of support for the theory of Baal as "a dying and rising god" here, see Mettinger, *The Riddle of Resurrection,* 68-71.

96. De Moor, *New Year with Canaanites and Israelites* (2 vols; Kamper Cahiers 21-22; Kampen: Kok, 1972) 1.6, 7 n. 24, and 2.11, and *An Anthology of Religious Texts,* 238 n. 101; Spronk, *Beatific Afterlife in Ancient Israel and in the Ancient Near East* (AOAT 219; Kevelaer: Butzon & Bercker; Neukirchen-Vluyn: Neukirchener, 1986) 151-53; Mettinger, *The Riddle of Resurrection,* 68-71.

97. See Jonathan Z. Smith, "Dying and Rising Gods," *Encyclopedia of Religion* 4 (1987) 521-27; "The Glory, Jest and Riddle: James George Frazer and *The Golden Bough,*" (Ph.D. diss., Yale, 1969); and Mark S. Smith, "The Death of 'Dying and Rising Gods' in the Biblical World: An Update, with Special Reference to Baal in the Baal Cycle," *SJOT* 12 (1998) 257-313. For a response, see Mettinger, *The Riddle of Resurrection.* It is impossible to fully address Mettinger's book, but it may be said that it does not answer sufficiently some of the fundamental problems of the putative category, namely that some of these gods do not die, some do not rise, and some are also mortals. In order to defend the category of dying and rising gods, the book stresses how the figures overlap, and it glosses over their fundamental differences; it also reconfigures the definition of the category of "dying and rising gods" so that the ritual dimension so central for older theorists is dismantled.

98. Pardee, *COS,* 1:347; Parker, *UNP,* 61; Wyatt, *RTU,* 273; Mettinger, *The Riddle of Resurrection,* 69.

99. For the text and translation, see below in Chapter Five, section 3. For the discussion of this point, see *UBC* 2.121-24, with reference to prior discussions.

100. See Pope, *Probative Pontificating in Ugaritic and Biblical Literature,* 345.

101. For this example and the ones following, see Greenfield, "Notes on the Curse Formulae of the Tell Fekherye Inscription," in *'Al Kanfei Yonah,* 265-68; Michael L. Barré, "An Analysis of the Royal Blessing in the Karatepe Inscription," *Maarav* 3 (1982) 177-94. Cf. "long life" that Solomon did not request, in 1 Kgs. 3:11. The royal wish for long life is a standard ancient Near Eastern trope, e.g., the prayer for the king: "Grant me life, let me live a long time," in Benjamin R. Foster, *Before the Muses: An Anthology of Akkadian Literature* (3rd ed.; Bethesda: CDL, 2005) 643; and Christopher G. Frechette, *Mesopotamian Ritual-prayers of "Hand-lifting" (Akkadian Šuillas)* (AOAT 379; Münster: Ugarit-Verlag, 2012) 7. For further examples, see *CAD,* B:55. For royal blessing more broadly, see Martin Leuenberger, *Segen und Segenstheologien im alten Israel: Untersuchungen zu ihren religions- und theologiegeschichtlichen Konstellationen und Transformationen* (ATANT 90; Zurich: Theologischer Verlag Zürich, 2008).

102. *DULAT,* 379. Cf. the request of God made on the king's behalf in a royal psalm: "let him live" (Ps. 72:15). The formulary in this royal psalm for royal "eternity "(vv. 5 and 17) is addressed by Greenfield, *'Al Kanfei Yonah,* 267 (cf. Ps. 89:19-37).

103. In this connection, Barré ("An Analysis of the Royal Blessing," 185 n. 28) cites Ps. 41:2: "May Yahweh guard him and keep him alive *(wyḥyhw).*"

104. Cf. the same formulary of the divine offer of asking and giving in the royal psalm Psa. 2:7-8, also in the context of enemies. In Psalm 45, the eternity of the king's throne (v. 6) follows on his military victory (vv. 3-5). For a narrative representation of

the king requesting and receiving life from his enemies, see Psalm 18/2 Samuel 22, esp. vv. 7, 18-19.

105. The verse is very difficult. See Michael L. Barré, S.S., *The Lord Has Saved Me: A Study of the Psalm of Hezekiah (Isaiah 38:9-20)* (CBQMS 39; Washington: Catholic Biblical Association of America, 2005) 153-68.

106. See *COS*, 1:350 n. 75 (reading *mhrh* for *mprh*): "And moreover I'll not allow his soldiership (i.e., the abstract expression of the qualities making him a soldier) to continue living." For discussion, see Manfried Dietrich and Oswald Loretz, *Orbis Ugariticus: Ausgewählte Beiträge von Manfried Dietrich und Oswald Loretz zu Fest- und Gedenkschriften. Anlässlich des 80. Geburtstag von Oswald Loretz*, ed. Dietrich (AOAT 343; Münster: Ugarit-Verlag, 2008) 296-301.

107. De Moor, *The Seasonal Pattern in the Ugaritic Myth of Baʿlu* (AOAT 16; Kevelaer: Butzon & Bercker, 1971) 42-43, 56-57. For discussion and critique, see *UBC*, 2:121-25. For KTU 1.3 I, see *UNP*, 106; for details see Chapter Six, section 4.

108. De Moor, *The Seasonal Pattern in the Ugaritic Myth of Baʿlu*, 42-43, 56-57. For discussion and critique, see *UBC*, 2:121-25.

109. As shown by the parallel attestation of *nʿm* in KTU 1.3 I 19 (see below), *nʿm* in this line is not Baal (cf. Frank Moore Cross, *Canaanite Myth and Hebrew Epic: Essays in the History of the Religion of Israel* [Cambridge, MA: Harvard University Press, 1973] 185 n. 169).

110. As marked in 1.17 VI 39 by the formula: "[Also an]other word I would speak" *([ʾap m]ṯn rgmm ʾargm)*. For other examples, see 1.3 IV 31-32; 1.4 I 19-20.

111. Ugaritic **šrg*, "to twist, tangle up" > "to deceive, delude, entangle" (*DULAT*, 844); cf. BH *śrg*, "to intertwine"; and *śarig*, "tendril, twig" (*BDB*, 974). *DULAT*, 844 notes the possible relationship to Arabic *saraga*, "lie" (see Lane, 1343-44), following Fred Renfroe, (*Arabic-Ugaritic Lexical Studies* [ALASP 5; Münster: Ugarit-Verlag, 1992] 147), who sees it as a possible by-form of *šrg*.

112. See Pope, *Probative Pontificating*, 140-42; *DULAT*, 389; for the etymological possibilities, see Pardee, *COS*, 1:347 n. 45.

113. For the idiom here, cf. Num. 23:10: "May my *nepeš* die the death of the upright, May my end *(ʾaḥărîtî)* be like theirs." See also Prov. 5:11; 23:32; Job 8:7; 42:12. Cf. *Odyssey* 15.299: "ah me, wretch that I am! What in the end will befall me?" (A. T. Murray, *Homer: Odyssey, Books 1-12* [LCL 104; New York: Putnam, 1919] 205). See also line 312. "My end" has been interpreted, however, as "posterity," by Menahem Kister, "Some Blessing and Curse Formulae in the Bible, Northwest Semitic Inscriptions, Post-Biblical Literature and Late Antiquity," in *Hamlet on a Hill: Semitic and Greek Studies Presented to Professor T. Muraoka on the Occasion of His Sixty-Fifth Birthday*, ed. M. F. J. Baasten and W. Th. van Peursen (OLA 118; Leuven: Peeters, 2003) 317-25. This solution, while philologically supported by the Neirab inscriptions cited, does not address the poetic parallelism of Num. 23:10, nor does it acknowledge the Ugaritic usage. It is possible that the apparent equivalence of *wyhʾbdw zrʿk* in Neirab I with *wʾḥrth tʾbd* in Neirab II (thus *zrʿk*, "your seed," as the sense of *ʾḥrth*, "his future/end"), as insightfully surmised by Kister, could reflect a further development of the latter, compared to the word's usages in 1.17 VI 35-36 or in Num. 23:10.

114. The proposal that the "glaze"//"plaster, quicklime" to be poured on the human head is to be compared with skulls excavated at Neolithic Jericho goes back at least to Edwin M. Good, "Two Notes on Aqhat," *JBL* 77 (1958) 73-74. The theory has been repeated since Good. See Margalit, *The Ugaritic Poem of Aqhat,* 309-10, 336, with a critical evaluation and listing of prior critics provided by Wright, *Ritual in Narrative,* 147-48 and esp. n. 52; see also Pardee, *COS,* 1:347 n. 46; Renfroe, *Arabic-Ugaritic Lexical Studies,* 118-20. The theory depends on Ugaritic *sgsg* here meaning, "plaster," "glaze," or the like, which is not entirely clear, as noted by Renfroe and Wright.

115. Aqhat's response here is compared by Baruch A. Levine with the final words of the warrior, Samson: "let my *nepesh* die with the Philistines" (Judges 16:30); *Numbers 21–36* (AB 4A; New York: Doubleday, 2000) 178-79.

116. Cf. the Hittite Prayer of Kantuzzili (CTH 373): "Life is bound up with death and death is bound up with life. A human does not live forever. The days of his life are counted." See Itamar Singer, *Hittite Prayers* (SBLWAW 11; Atlanta: Society of Biblical Literature, 2002) 32, par. 5, in obverse 20′-23′. The lines seem to be stock material; cf. Prayer of a Mortal (CTH 372), in Singer, *Hittite Prayers,* 38, par. 11, ii 40-50; Num. 16:29: "if these (men) die like the death of all humanity. . . ."

117. Pope, *Probative Pontificating,* 345.

118. Her offer is in SB VI 6-21, his response in SB VI 22-79. See Andrew R. George, *The Babylonian Gilgamesh Epic: Introduction, Critical Edition, and Cuneiform Texts* (2 vols.; Oxford: Oxford University Press, 2003) 618-23.

119. Murray, *Homer: Odyssey, Books 1-12,* 97.

120. On the motif of divine laughter as scorn, see R. J. Clifford, "Proverbs IX: A Suggested Ugaritic Parallel," *VT* 25 (1975) 298-306. For the text and discussion of Anat's laughter in KTU 1.3 II 25, see section 3 in Chapter Six.

121. See *CAD,* K:173. So also Watson, "Puzzling Passages in the Tale of Aqhat," 376, citing Isa. 32:6.

122. For Akkadian idioms denoting "speaking in the heart," see A. Kirk Grayson, "Murmuring in Mesopotamia," in *Wisdom, Gods and Literature: Studies in Assyriology in Honour of W. G. Lambert,* ed. A. R. George and I. L. Finkel (Winona Lake: Eisenbrauns, 2000) 304-6. The image of speaking in one's heart is a common biblical idiom (e.g. Ps. 14:1 = Ps. 53:1); cf. Hannah "praying in her heart" (with only her lips moving) in 1 Sam. 1:13.

123. Anat's threat might also bear an overtone of "felling" (the C-stem of middle weak **ql*) Aqhat like an animal for the sacrifice. The verb attested here in 1.17 VI 44b is used for animals in literary contexts, e.g., in 1.4 VI 41; 1.22 I 12; for examples also in ritual texts, see 1.46.11; 1.109.4. (KTU 1.23.10 uses the form in a viticultural image: "he fells . . . like a vine, *km gpn.*) However, no such overtone need be detected in this verb in Anat's speech in line 44b, since not every use of this form involves a sacrificial usage. E.g., the case in 1.16 VI 32, 44 bears no such connotation.

124. As noted by Natan-Yulzary, "Divine Justice or Poetic Justice?" 592. The indicative sense is also possible for the final clause: "and he will fall beneath my feet." See the discussion in Watson, "Puzzling Passages in the Tale of Aqhat," 371-72. For the motif "under my feet" for subjugation, see KAI 26A I 16-17; *DNWSI,* 928. The motif of "under my feet" in 2 Sam. 22/Ps. 18:39 is compared by Natan-Yulzary, "Divine Justice or Poetic

Justice?" 583 n. 10. For the combination of the two motifs, "breaking the wings" and enemies "beneath the feet," see the prophetic message to Esarhaddon; see K 4310, I, lines 6′-16′, in Simo Parpola, *Assyrian Prophecies* (SAA 9; Helsinki: Helsinki University Press, 1997) 4; cf. Jacob L. Wright, "The Commemoration of Defeat and the Formation of a Nation in the Hebrew Bible," *Prooftexts* 29 (2009) 449.

125. Wright, *Ritual in Narrative*, 112.

126. See Wright, *Ritual in Narrative*, 123-26.

127. For these parallels, see Parker, *The Pre-Biblical Narrative Tradition*, 115-16; *UBC*, 2:335-36, 337-38, 339-40, 349-50.

128. So Natan-Yulzary, "Divine Justice or Poetic Justice?" 584-85; see also *DULAT*, 399. Parker (*UNP*, 64) renders "haughty of heart." For the root with "heart," see Job 36:13, where "the impious (or haughty) of heart" are worse than the disobedient. The translation of Pardee (*COS*, 1:348) does not construe *ḫnp* with *lb*, "heart": "(So) let anger (against me) depart (from) [your heart]." It is questionable whether **ḫnp* denotes "anger," or whether the verb is volitive (rather than an imperative), or whether the sense "from" is to be imputed with *lb*, "heart," without a preposition. Without incurring any of these difficulties, Natan-Yulzary nicely emphasizes the use of the root **ḫnp* to indicate Anat's offense against El. She also compares EA 162:74-75 and 288:7-8 where the root "signifies an evil act against a ruler or person of high rank." For the root, *CAD*, Ḫ:76 and Anson F. Rainey (*Canaanite in the Amarna Tablets* [4 vols.; Atlanta: Society of Biblical Literature, 2010] 2:199; 3:47) translate "villainy." William L. Moran (*The Amarna Letters* [Baltimore: Johns Hopkins University Press, 1992] 250, 331) renders as "sacrilege" for the root in EA 162 and as "impious" in EA 288. For this letter, Rainey (*Canaanite in the Amarna Tablets*, 2:276; 3:170) also renders "audacity."

129. See *DULAT*, 283 for **dwṯ*, "to soften, become soft," as in Arabic (Lane, 941). Cf. "will be beaten" or the like, as understood by Ginsberg, *ANET*, 152; Cross, *Canaanite Myth and Hebrew Epic*, 185; *TO* 1:436 n. f; *COS*, 1:348. This approach to the final main verb assumes cognates with BH **dwš*, Akkadian *dâšu*, *diāšu* (*CAD*, D:121), and Arabic *dāsa* (see *DULAT*, 283; cf. the verb read as a geminate in Daniel Sivan, *A Grammar of the Ugaritic Language* [2nd impression with corrections; HO 1/128; Leiden: Brill, 2001] 174). In this second proposal, the permutation of sibilants between the Ugaritic word and the putative Arabic cognate would be irregular.

130. *COS*, 1:348: "You are (my) brother and I am [your] sister." KTU reads: *'a[ḫtk]*.

131. *UNP*, 64.

132. For other literary examples of sustained deception, see Enlil and Ninlil, in Thorkild Jacobsen, *The Harps That Once . . . : Sumerian Poetry in Translation* (New Haven: Yale University Press, 1987) 175-79; and The Descent of Ishtar to the Netherworld, lines 40-75, in Foster, *Before the Muses*, 500-501). My thanks to Stephen Russell for these comparisons.

133. Scholars often compare this scene with Ishtar's proposal to Gilgamesh in tablet VI (*ANET*, 84). For a good discussion of the parallels between the scenes, see Parker, *The Pre-Biblical Narrative Tradition*, 113-16; see also Wright, *Ritual in Narrative*, 130. For a detailed study of the scene in Gilgamesh, see Tzvi Abusch, "Ishtar's Proposal and Gilgamesh's Refusal: An Interpretation of *The Gilgamesh Epic* Tablet 6, Lines 1-79," *HR* 26

(1986) 143-87. Contrast the positive relationship between Gilgamesh and Inanna in the Sumerian Gilgamesh episodes, as noted by Samuel N. Kramer, *From the Poetry of Sumer* (Berkeley: University of California Press, 1979) 74, cited by Rivkah Harris, "Inanna-Ishtar as Paradox and a Coincidence of Opposites," *HR* 30 (1991) 264 n. 16. The complexity of Mesopotamian sources suggests a general comparison of type-scene with the Ugaritic scene and not with the specific reasons and motivations of the figures in the scene. For further discussion, see Margalit, "New Readings in *Aqhat*," 107-8.

134. For this topic, see *Sacred Marriages: The Divine-Human Sexual Metaphor from Sumer to Early Christianity*, ed. Martti Nissinen and Risto Uro (Winona Lake: Eisenbrauns, 2008). The ritual expressions of "sacred marriage" seem more conceptual than literal. The conceptual expression may underlie KTU 1.23, as noted in Mark S. Smith, *Rituals and Myths of the Feast of the Goodly Gods of KTU/CAT 1.23* (SBLRBS 51; Atlanta: Society of Biblical Literature, 2006) 10-11, 127-28, 132-33.

135. Wright, *Ritual in Narrative*, 130.

136. Wright, *Ritual in Narrative*, 130-31.

137. For the divine teacher role (**lmd*), compare Yahweh as the trainer for war in 2 Sam. 22/Ps. 18:35, as noted by Parker, *The Pre-Biblical Narrative Tradition*, 116. See also Ps. 144:1; cf. Judg. 3:2. For **lmd* for warrior training, see Song 3:8; cf. Isa. 2:4 = Mic. 4:3.

138. The word means "meadow" or "grasslands." For further discussion with a proposal, see Wilfred G. E. Watson, *Lexical Studies in Ugaritic* (AuOr Sup 19; Barcelona: Editorial AUSA, 2007) 195.

139. Spiegel proposed that the Aqhat tradition about 'Ablm is echoed in the notion of mourning in Abeline (spelled variously as Abelsya'el, Abelsya'il, Lesya'el) in 1 En. 13:9 (see these variant readings of the name in *OTP*, 1:20 n. l). See Spiegel, "Noah, Daniel, and Job," in *Louis Ginzberg Jubilee Volume* (New York: American Academy for Jewish Research, 1945) 336-41; see also Greenfield, *'Al Kanfei Yonah*, 355; Aaron Demsky, "On Reading Ancient Inscriptions: The Monumental Aramaic Stele Fragment from Tel Dan," *JANES* 23 (1995) 33 n. 16. For the wordplay on the place name and mourning, note also *COS*, 1:349 n. 61. The word and its multiple associations might be used for any number of places. The two other places cursed by Danil may also bear symbolic meanings of lamentation: *qr mym* may suggest weeping (cf. 1.16 I 26-27: "Do not waste, O son, the fountain of your eyes, *'al tkl bn qr 'nk*); and *mrrt tǵll bnr* might mean "bitterness gleans in the fallow ground (cf. **ǵll* in 1.3 II 13, 27, discussed in *UBC*, 2:155-56; and BH *nîr* in Jer. 4:3; Hos. 10:12; Prov. 13:23, in *BDB*, 644).

140. The reconstruction is supported by 1.19 IV 1-2.

141. See Wright, *Ritual in Narrative*, 127-35.

142. These and other alternatives are discussed in Pardee, *COS*, 1:349 n. 64; *DULAT*, 851; Wright, *Ritual in Narrative*, 213. The translation "Sutean" (so Parker, *UNP*, 65; Margalit, *The Ugaritic Poem of AQHT*, 337-40, among others) fits with other details in the Aqhat story noted below. It has been objected that the word lacks the gentilic.

143. In 1.19 IV 51, a message to Yatpan refers to "your camp" *(ḏdk)*.

144. For various interpretations, see Dietrich and Loretz, *Orbis Ugariticus*, 71-74. See also Marvin H. Pope, in M. S. Smith, "A Potpourri of Popery: Marginalia from the Life and Notes of Marvin H. Pope," *UF* 30 (1998) 661.

145. Dietrich and Loretz, *Orbis Ugariticus,* 74.

146. According to Jordi Vidal, Sutean warriors would be suitable not for regular military engagement, but *inter alia* for reconnaissance and ambushes; "Sutean Warfare in the Amarna Letters," in *Studies on War in the Ancient Near East: Collected Essays on Military History* (AOAT 372; Münster: Ugarit-Verlag, 2010) 95-103, here 97, 101-2.

147. To be sure, the expression in 1.17 VI 42 is *ṯb ly* and not just *ṯb* as it is 1.18 IV 16; so the nuance presumably differs somewhat.

148. See Parker, *The Pre-Biblical Narrative Tradition,* 141.

149. This translation largely follows Pardee, *RCU,* 194; note also the discussion of this root by Ellen van Wolde, *Reframing Biblical Studies: When Language and Text Meet Culture, Cognition, and Context* (Winona Lake: Eisenbrauns, 2009) 160-61. For the translation "soar," see Cross, *Canaanite Myth and Hebrew Epic,* 323.

150. For this issue, see *UBC,* 2:335-37.

151. See the second section of the next chapter for the context of this passage.

152. The trope is common in the Hebrew Bible, e.g., "anyone belonging to him [Baasha] who dies in the open country shall be devoured by the birds of the sky" (1 Kgs. 16:4). See also Deut. 28:26; 1 Sam. 17:44, 46; 2 Sam. 21:1-4, 10; 1 Kgs. 14:11; Jer. 15:3; Ezek. 29:5. See also *Iliad* 1:4-5; *Odyssey* 14:133-34; 22:30. See further below.

153. See W. G. E. Watson, "The Falcon Episode in the Aqhat Tale," *JNSL* 5 (1977) 69-75.

154. See Vidal, "Sutean Warfare in the Amarna Letters." Note the Suteans sent to kill in EA 122:31-39, in Moran, *The Amarna Letters,* 202 n. 3. For further information about the Suteans, see Wolfgang Heimpel, *Letters to the King of Mari: A New Translation, with Historical Introduction, Notes, and Commentary* (Mesopotamian Civilizations 12; Winona Lake: Eisenbrauns, 2003) 13, 597, 634-36; Dominique Charpin, "The Desert Routes around the Djebel Bishri and the Sutean Nomads according to the Mari Archives," *Al-Rafidan* Special issue (2010) 239-45. See also the older work by Michael Heltzer, *The Suteans* (with a contribution by Shoshana Arbeli-Raveh; Istituto universitario orientale, Seminario di studi asiatici, Series minor 13; Naples: Istituto universitario orientale, 1981).

155. George, *The Babylonian Gilgamesh Epic,* 1:333-34.

156. This is a fairly common representation of the Sutu, e.g., in the inscriptions of Esarhaddon: "the Sutû, who live in tents" in Erle Leichty, *The Royal Inscriptions of Esarhaddon, King of Assyria (680-669 BC)* (Royal Inscriptions of the Neo-Assyrian Period 4; Winona Lake: Eisenbrauns, 2011) 22; cf. Lambert, *Babylonian Oracle Questions,* 69 (line 5): "the [Sutû] and Aḫlamû, tent-dwelling warriors."

157. For highly divergent attempts at interpreting lines 1-19, see Alan Cooper, "Two Exegetical Notes on Aqhat," *UF* 20 (1988) 19-23 (as the narrative of Anat's dismemberment of Aqhat's body to feed her birds); Pardee, *COS,* 1:350-51 (as Anat's speech about what happened); and Wright, *Ritual in Narrative,* 134-56 (as a description of Anat losing the bow while cleansing herself in water followed by her lament over his death).

158. Cf. KTU 4.279.1, "on the day of the first fruit." The word has been read in this manner also in 1.22 I 24, but there the word has also been understood as "summit" (see *DULAT,* 679). See Chapter Five, section 2, for this passage.

159. Cf. the famine resulting from Saulide bloodguilt over the death of Gibeonites

and its resolution through the execution of two of Saul's sons in 2 Samuel 21. See Arvid S. Kapelrud, *God and His Friends in the Old Testament* (Oslo: Universitetsforlaget, 1979) 41-50.

160. See Wright, *Ritual in Narrative*, 157-60.

161. See *DULAT*, 5, comparing Akkadian *inbu* (*AHw*, 381; *CAD*, I/J:144). The Ugaritic word also informs the second element in the divine name, *nkl w-ʾib* in KTU 1.24 and apparently the divine name *ʾib* in 1.111.20.

162. Some commentators translate the verb *tphn* in line 29 as masculine (e.g., Parker, in *UNP*, 68), but the verb may be feminine in form, hence Wright, *Ritual in Narrative*, 157. For the lacuna that follows in line 29, Wright (*Ritual in Narrative*, 159-60) reconstructs *šʿr* ("wool" or "fleece") and compares Judg. 6:36-40. The larger context of the attested text might seem to point to fruit or crops and not to animals or their products.

163. Cf. the curse in Esarhaddon's Succession Treaty, lines 425-26 (par. 41), in Parpola and Watanabe, *Neo-Assyrian Treaties and Loyalty Oaths*, 46: "may Ninurta . . . feed your flesh to the eagle and the vulture." See also line 519 (p. 51).

164. Ginsberg, *ANET*, 153.

165. Wright, *Ritual in Narrative*, 162.

166. *ANET*, 153 n. 32.

167. Natan-Yulzary, "Contrast and Meaning," 438.

168. Wright, *Ritual in Narrative*, 162. Wright also suggests the possibility of the second occurrence as being "a resumptive repetition to introduce the other ritual responses in 1.19 I 46–II 25."

169. E.g., Ginsberg, *ANET*, 153; Watson, "Puzzling Passages in the Tale of Aqhat," 377. See the survey of discussions in Wright, *Ritual in Narrative*, 161-66.

170. Ginsberg, "A Ugaritic Parallel to 2 Sam 1 21," *JBL* 57 (1938) 212 n. 14; and *ANET*, 153 n. 34, following T. H. Gaster, "The Story of Aqhat," *SMSR* 13 (1937) 49; see also *UT* 19.2488; and NJPS n. d-d. For the issues with the etymology for the Ugaritic word proposed by Gaster and followed by Ginsberg, see Renfroe, *Arabic-Ugaritic Lexical Studies*, 146-47. Renfroe suggests that the Ugaritic word in this context may instead refer to a storm or tempest (cognate with BH *sʿr*). It is to be noted that Ugaritic also attests a word with the same spelling that appears in a list of goods in KTU 1.148.21.

171. Translation of Ginsberg, *ANET*, 153; cf. "no dew, no downpour," by Parker, *UNP*, 69. For *ṭl* and *rbb* together, see also KTU 1.3 II 39 (also reconstructed for 1.3 II 40-41); 1.3 IV 43-44; Mic. 5:7 and 1QM 12:9-10. Terms for dew and rain occur together, also in biblical literature (Deut. 32:2; 1 Kgs. 17:1; Job 38:28; cf. Dan. 4:33; 5:21). For further discussion, see Chapter Ten.

172. Martha Roth, in *COS*, 2:352; and in *Law Collections from Mesopotamia and Asia Minor*, 138.

173. See K. Lawson Younger, in *COS*, 3:219.

174. See the discussion in Chapter Ten, section 2.

175. For this entry, see John Huehnergard, *Ugaritic Vocabulary in Syllabic Transcription* (HSS 32; Atlanta: Scholars, 1987) 57, 63, 170, 260, 287-88, 306 ("v" here in Huehnergard's reconstructed spelling represents an unspecified vowel). Huehnergard gives *ṣ*ilyatu*

as one of the two possible realizations of the syllabic form. This reading would conform to the alphabetic form of the noun.

176. For discussion, see Parker, *The Pre-Biblical Narrative Tradition,* 123. Wyatt (*RTU,* 296 n. 207) suggests "curse," as Danil's reaction to Pughat's tearing of the garment (reading Pughat as the subject of *tmzʿ*).

177. Wright, *Ritual in Narrative,* 161. The broadly attested cognates likewise fit with this meaning. See Greenfield, *ʿAl Kanfei Yonah,* 252.

178. *DULAT,* 784.

179. So Parker, *UNP,* 68.

180. Pardee, *COS,* 1:351.

181. For the nuances of the terms for rain in this line, see Mark Futato, "Sense Relations in the 'Rain' Domain of the Old Testament," in *Imagery and Imagination in Biblical Literature: Essays in Honor of Aloysius Fitzgerald, F.S.C.,* ed. Lawrence Boadt and Mark S. Smith (CBQMS 32; Washington: Catholic Biblical Association of America, 2001) 81-94.

182. See Parker, *UNP,* 69; Wright, *Ritual in Narrative,* 161. Cf. Isa. 5:6: "and the clouds I will command not to rain rain upon it."

183. For the parallelism of "seven years" and "eight," see KTU 1.12 II 44-45; 1.23.66-67. For a period of seven years, see also later in Aqhat, in 1.19 IV 17-18, as well as 1.6 V 8-9. Seven years is also the lengthy period after which Athirat remembers the vow that Kirta made to her (1.15 III 22). It represents a round number for a considerable number of years. Seven years also constitutes "a ritual period" in the expansion of the *zukru*-ritual in Emar 373, according to Daniel E. Fleming, *Time at Emar: The Cultic Calendar and the Rituals from the Diviner's Archive* (Mesopotamian Civilizations 11; Winona Lake: Eisenbrauns, 2000) 54, 56, 63-68. In Danil's prayer it refers to a lengthy period of agricultural disaster, one that is potentially insurmountable (cf. Genesis 41).

184. For the issues with the etymology for the Ugaritic word, see *DULAT,* 843; and Renfroe, *Arabic-Ugaritic Lexical Studies,* 146-47. Renfroe suggests that the Ugaritic word in this context may instead refer to a storm or tempest (cognate with BH *sʿr*); cf. **šaʿr* in Ebla personal names, discussed by Joseph Martin Pagan, *A Morphological and Lexical Study of Personal Names in the Ebla Texts* (ARES 3; Rome: Missione Archeologica Italiana in Siria, 1998) 234. However, a storm or tempest is perhaps not an ideal characterization for *ththm* (cf. Hab. 3:10; Ps. 42:7). Another possibility is "flow" (see *DULAT,* 843).

185. See also Elijah's words in 1 Kgs. 17:1: "As Yahweh lives, the God of Israel whom I serve, there will be no *dew* or *rain* except at my bidding" (my italics).

186. Natan-Yulzary, "Contrast and Meaning," 436-37.

187. It is to be noted that in mourning ritual, ritual action regularly precedes ritual words. See the acts followed the words of mourning by both El and Anat in KTU 1.5 VI and 1.6 I, respectively; see Smith, *UNP,* 148-52. Cf. the bodily action followed by words in 1.4 II; see *UNP,* 122-23.

188. For a modern analogue to traditional astral knowledge, Harriet Nash and Dionisius A. Agius, "The Use of Stars in Agriculture in Oman," *JSS* 56 (2011) 167-82.

189. So Parker, *UNP,* 69. If the form is a verb, it would be an infinitive absolute, as noted by Sivan (*A Grammar of the Ugaritic Language,* 125). Sivan (p. 179) understands the final *-m* on *bkm* as adverbial. The participle would bear the feminine ending *-t* (*bkyt*

as often read in 1.16 VI 4 is taken this way by *DULAT*, 221, but the context does not seem to accord with this meaning of the form). That the infinitive may be used in this construction with a feminine subject is clear from *bky* in 1.16 II 35-36: "she raises her voice as she cries *(ttn gh bky).*" For the same construction with a masculine subject, see 1.16 I 13-14. The same construction with a feminine subject for *bkm* would also fit 1.16 II 50: "As she weeps she enters . . . *(bkm tʿrb).*" Cf. the masculine subject with *bkm* with this construction in 1.107.12 (note also the form *bkyh* in 1.14 I 31). See Wright, *Ritual in Narrative,* 166-67. The alternative proposed is to take *bkm* as an adverbial particle, "then" or the like. This meaning appears with *bkm* in 1.4 VII 42, and it might underlie the case of *bkm* in 1.10 III 29 (see *DULAT*, 220 for alternatives for this instance). The word *bkm* in 1.19 II 8-10 is translated "straightaway," in *DULAT*, 219 (taking the verb *tlmdn* as masculine singular [!]). The threefold use of this word as an adverbial particle here would seem unusual, unless it is used for the kind of particular emphasis as suggested by the *DULAT* translation. Such temporal particles more commonly occur once at the head of a subunit.

190. Wright, *Ritual in Narrative,* 173-75.

191. See 1.2 IV 6 for the same construction (*UBC*, 1:334); cf. RS 94.2406.39 (in *BSV*, 156, 157).

192. Wright, *Ritual in Narrative,* 167-72.

193. Ginsberg, *ANET*, 154.

194. Wyatt, *RTU*, 300 n. 221.

195. The lads may be lamenting as they come to Danil. The possible reference to hair in lines 31-34 might compare with the acts of lamentation for Enkidu in SBV VIII:39, 62-64 (George, *The Babylonian Gilgamesh Epic*, 1:652-53, 656-57).

196. Margalit, "New Readings in *Aqhat,*" 109-10.

197. Some read the first person plural. See Wright, *Ritual in Narrative,* 174 n. 9.

198. Cooper, "Two Exegetical Notes on Aqhat," 24.

199. See Wright, *Ritual in Narrative,* 174.

200. See Wright, *Ritual in Narrative,* 175-81.

201. Opinions over the place of burial, *bmdgt.bknrt* (as well as the reading of the words), have been split. See Wayne Pitard, "The Reading of *KTU* 1.19:III:41: The Burial of Aqhat," *BASOR* 293 (1994) 31-38. For the theory that this is the lake of the Kinneret, see Margalit, "New Readings in *Aqhat,*" 110-11; cf. Pardee, *COS*, 1:353 n. 114.

202. See KAI 13, trans. in *ANET*, 662; Wyatt, *RTU*, 307.

203. For a general consideration of sleep as death, see Thomas H. McAlpine, *Sleep, Divine and Human, in the Old Testament* (JSOTSup 38; Sheffield: JSOT, 1987).

204. See Delbert R. Hillers, "A Difficult Curse in Aqhat (19 [1 Aqht] 3.152-154)," in *Biblical and Related Studies Presented to Samuel Iwry*, ed. Ann Kort and Scott Morschauer (Winona Lake: Eisenbrauns, 1985) 105-7; Fred Renfroe, "QR-MYM's Comeuppance," *UF* 18 (1986) 455-57; Wright, *Ritual in Narrative,* 182-90.

205. Some scholars see an expression of "destiny" here, but this line may refer simply to the fact that "he set the end of his staff" to get walking to the next place in the narrative. So see with slight variations in *RTU*, 307; *COS*, 1:354.

206. See Parker, *The Pre-Biblical Narrative Tradition*, 126.

207. That the mourning transpires over seven years rather than the customary seven

days "heightens the connections between Danel's son and the powers of fertility," according to Coogan and Smith, *Stories from Ancient Canaan*, 12.

208. See Parker, *The Pre-Biblical Narrative Tradition*, 126-27; Wright, *Ritual in Narrative*, 195-97, for discussion and parallels.

209. For text, translation, and notes for this passage, see Chapter Five, section 1.

210. See Wright, *Narrative in Ritual*, 200-203.

211. Parker (*The Pre-Biblical Narrative Tradition*, 132) connects her incense offering and the female revenge with Judith's prayer and the time of the incense offering in Jdt. 9:1. For other passages, see Parker, *The Pre-Biblical Narrative Tradition*, 130, 33, as well as further below.

212. See above note 23.

213. See Wright, *Narrative in Ritual*, 39 n. 79.

214. See Wright, *Narrative in Ritual*, 203-5.

215. Cf. Gilgamesh, SB II, line 5. See Stephanie Dalley, *Myths from Mesopotamia: Creation, the Flood, Gilgamesh, and Others* (rev. ed.; Oxford: Oxford University Press, 2000) 62.

216. Cf. Judith's prayer for strength before she kills Holofernes in Jdt. 13:7. Note also the divine commission of strength (**kōaḥ*) to Gideon to go and defeat the army of the Midianites (Judg. 6:14)

217. See *UBC*, 2:450.

218. Most commentators understand Danil here to be referring to his own *npš*, hence "my life-breath" (or the like); cf. Ginsberg, *ANET*, 150: "With life-breath shall be quickened. . . ." If so, since there is no first person suffix *-y* on the noun, the noun should be in the nominative case and thus the subject of the verb and not part of a prepositional phrase (such as "by my life," as in *UNP*, 77; cf. *COS*, 1:344 n. 13). Cf. 1.17 I 36-37.

219. Cf. 1.6 II-III, where the death of Death by the hands of the divine sister Anat makes possible the return to life of Baal, her brother.

220. For this passage, with parallels in Ugaritic literature, see Wright, *Ritual in Narrative*, 206-9. For iconographic and archaeological evidence for cosmetics, see Michal Dayagi-Mendels, *Perfumes and Cosmetics in the Ancient World* (Jerusalem: Israel Museum, 1989) 36-58. Dayagi-Mendels (p. 51) notes the discovery of a duck-shaped cosmetic box at Ugarit as well as several other sites in the Levant. Note also the treatment of the woman's face on a relief from Tel Dan; see Dalia Pakman, "'Mask-Like' Face Reliefs on a Painted Stand from the Sacred Precinct at Tel Dan," *ErIsr* 27 (Hayim and Miriam Tadmor Volume; 2003) 196-203.

221. Wright, *Ritual in Narrative*, 210.

222. Wright, *Ritual in Narrative*, 209-20.

223. See Cross, *Canaanite Myth and Hebrew Epic*, 55 n. 43. See also *l'ahlm* in line 50. Pope (*Probative Pontificating*, 51-52) rejected the emendation and read *bhlm* as an adverb, "here," parallel to the noun *ḏdk*, "your abode." Adverbs, however, are not commonly parallel with nouns. The particle *hlm* usually opens a clause (KTU 1.2 I 21; 1.3 II 5; 1.4 IV 27; 1.16 I 53; 1.100.6, in *DULAT*, 337); and I am not aware of another instance where it is combined with *b-* as an adverb.

224. Pardee, *COS*, 1:355. See also Parker, *The Pre-Biblical Narrative Tradition*, 130-31.

225. So de Moor, Margalit, and Wright as well as Landy; see Wright, *Ritual in Narrative,* 209, 211; Landy, *The Tale of Aqhat,* 13, 57.

226. There seems to be little or no basis for the view that Yatpan mistakes Pughat here for Anat simply because of the parallels for the washing of Pughat and Anat. See Watson, "Puzzling Passages in the Tale of Aqhat," 376. Kirta too acts similarly in washing and rouging himself. Moreover, it seems dubious that someone who works for Anat would mistake a human female for this goddess. (I am unaware of any cases of mistaken identity between a human and a deity in this corpus.) More to the point is the broader thematic analogy between Pughat and Anat as sisters avenging their brothers; see Julie Faith Parker, "Women Warriors and Devoted Daughters: The Powerful Young Woman in Ugaritic Narrative Poetry," *UF* 38 (2006) 562-66, esp. 564-66.

227. See *DULAT,* 666, citing examples from 4.102.2, 19; 4.349.4. Cf. *hē paidiskē hē kalē,* "this pretty girl" (NRSV), in Jdt. 12:13.

228. Watson, "Puzzling Passages in the Tale of Aqhat," 375.

229. The comparisons are noted by Parker, *The Pre-Biblical Narrative Tradition,* 132-33. Note also Sidnie Ann White Crawford, "In the Steps of Jael and Deborah: Judith as Heroine," in *"No One Spoke Ill of Her": Essays on Judith,* ed. James C. VanderKam (SBLEJL 2; Atlanta: Scholars, 1992) 5-16. Note also the stealthy role played by Jael in Judges 4-5.

230. The action in lines 54-56 seems to be represented as taking wine, and not as one party giving it to another (as in KTU 5.9 I 9-15). If correct, the scene has her drinking in these lines, while lines 60-61 emphasize the amount that Yatpan drinks. Cf. Jdt. 12:17-20.

231. Wright, *Ritual in Narrative,* 210. Cf. "I'll defeat the god," in *UNP,* 78. But what god is unclear. Or, might it be a term of divinity for a human?

232. Cf. Cross, *Canaanite Myth and Hebrew Epic,* 69 and n. 97.

233. Parker (*UNP,* 78) instead takes the two clauses as asyndetic relative clauses.

234. *DULAT,* 371; Wright, *Ritual in Narrative,* 210. Parker (*UNP,* 78) translates: ". . . enchanters to the tents." This rendering introduces new figures whose role would otherwise go unexplained.

235. So Parker, *UNP* 78. See further Margalit, "New Readings in *Aqht,*" 111-12.

236. The direct object *hwt* shows that the verb here is transitive.

237. See Jael in Judges 4–5 and Judith 12–13 (see Parker, *The Pre-Biblical Narrative,* 131-33). Cf. a male parallel of a man hiding a sword under his garment and then pulling it out to make the kill; see Judges 3, especially verses 16 and 21.

238. For the issue, see note 14 above.

239. Murray, *Homer: Odyssey, Books 1-12,* 167.

240. Manfried Dietrich and Oswald Loretz, *Word-List of the Cuneiform Alphabetic Texts from Ugarit, Ras Ibn Hani and Other Places* (KTU: 2nd ed.; ALASP 12; Münster: Ugarit-Verlag, 1996) 166. According to the index in *BSV,* the word does not occur in the texts published in that volume.

241. For Akkadian *eṭlum* for a hero who is also a member of the assembly, see Thorkild Jacobsen, *Toward the Image of Tammuz and Other Essays on Mesopotamian History and Culture,* ed. William L. Moran (HSS 21; Cambridge, MA: Harvard University Press, 1970) 403-4 n. 44. For cross-cultural consideration of how elders deliberate, see Richard P. Martin, "The Seven Sages as Performers of Wisdom," in *Cultural Poetics in Archaic*

Greece: Cult, Performance, Politics, ed. Carol Dougherty and Leslie Kurke (Oxford: Oxford University Press, 1998) 119-20.

242. Kevin M. McGeough, *Exchange Relationships at Ugarit* (Ancient Near Eastern Studies Sup 26; Leuven: Peeters, 2007) 98.

243. McGeough, *Exchange Relationships at Ugarit,* 97-98.

244. See McGeough, *Exchange Relationships at Ugarit,* 101.

245. See McGeough, *Exchange Relationships at Ugarit,* 100.

246. Ginsberg, "A Ugaritic Parallel to 2 Sam 1:21," 210-11 n. 5; Held, "The Action-Result (Factitive-Passive) Sequence of Identical Verbs in Biblical Hebrew and Ugaritic," *JBL* 84 (1965) 278-79 n. 31; and Miller, "Ugaritic *ǵzr* and Hebrew *ʿzr* II," *UF* 2 (1970) 159-75, who lays out the two roots as follows: Hebrew **ʿzr* I + PS **ʿḏr,* "to help" = Ugaritic *ʿḏr* = Aramaic *ʿdr* and Arabic and OSA *ʿḏr;* Hebrew **ʿzr* II = PS **ǵzr,* "to be strong, mighty, valiant" = Ugaritic *ǵzr* = Arabic *ǵzr* (?). For Ugaritic *ʿḏr* written in the syllabic transcription as *i-zi-ir,* see Sivan, *A Grammar of the Ugaritic Language,* 46, 84. See also Aicha Rahmouni, *Divine Epithets in the Ugaritic Alphabetic Texts,* trans. J. N. Ford (HO 1 93; Leiden: Brill, 2008) 195. Cf. *DULAT,* 329.

247. Ginsberg, "A Ugaritic Parallel to 2 Sam 1:21," 211 n. 5.

248. Miller, "Ugaritic *ǵzr* and Hebrew *ʿzr* II," esp. 165-69; cf. B. Q. Baises, "Ugaritic *ʿḏr* and Hebrew *ʿzr,*" *UF* 5 (1973) 41-52. Line 3 of the smaller Ketef Hinnom amulet (late preexilic in date) may also show the meaning of "warrior" for **ʿzr,* given its collocation with the verb "to rebuke": "Blessed be he/she by Yahweh the warrior/the helper *(hʿwzr)* and the one who rebukes [e]vil/[E]vil." See Gabriel Barkay, Andrew G. Vaughn, Marilyn J. Lundberg, and Bruce Zuckerman, "The Amulets from Ketef Hinnom: A New Edition and Evaluation," *BASOR* 334 (2004) 41-71, here 64-65 and 69 (I depart from their translation in not taking the final phrase as construct).

249. For the construction for the verb **šwh* II, "set, place" (*D*-stem), *BDB,* 1001 compares Ps. 21:6, also in reference to the king: "Splendor and majesty You have set upon him" *(hôd wĕhādār tĕšawweh ʿālāyw).*

250. This sense would fit also with the occurrence of the singular form at the head of KTU 1.169.1: "To cast out the tormenters of a young man *(ǵzr).*" See Pardee, *RCU,* 160-61. This incantation is aimed against sexual impotency, a threat to masculinity. This incantational context involving potency fits the use of *ǵzr* rather than the biological relation *bn* (cf. 4.102.1, 5) or *nʿr,* the nonbiological lesser in either age or rank (4.102.8; for young age for *nʿr,* see 1.107.40, *km nʿr//km ṣǵr*). Cf. terms such as Ugaritic *yld* and BH *yeled/yaldâ,* which may refer to a newborn as well as a young child; Ugaritic *ǵlm/ǵlmt* and BH *ʿelem/ʿalmâ.* For further biblical terms and discussion, see Joseph Fleishman, "The Age of Legal Maturity in Biblical Law," *JANES* 21 (1992) 35-43; Mayer I. Gruber, "Breast-Feeding Practices in Biblical Israel and in Old Babylonian Mesopotamia," *JANES* 19 (Semitic Studies in Memory of Moshe Held; 1989) 69 n. 45. Gruber would include BH *zĕʿêr* in Isa. 28:10 as cognate with Akkadian *ṣeḫrum,* "child." See also Nadav Na'aman, "The *ṣuḫāru* in Second Millennium BCE Letters from Canaan," *IEJ* 54 (2004) 92-99.

251. Given the attestation of *naʿar* for "youth" but also for warriors, the usage in the context here sounds like wordplay. For BH *naʿar,* see *HALOT,* 2:707-8. For these senses in Ugaritic, see Sivan, *A Grammar of the Ugaritic Language,* 77; cf. *DULAT,* 616. For the mil-

itary usage, see also James E. Hoch, *Semitic Words in Egyptian Texts of the New Kingdom and Third Intermediate Period* (Princeton: Princeton University Press, 1994) 182-83, #245.

252. To be clear, I do not assume hunting as training for warfare in some formal sense, but as part of male upbringing.

253. E.g., Parker, *UNP*, 64.

254. Putting the comparisons with these other stories a bit differently, the Aqhat story is taken up only with the concerns of the subplot of the father, Isaac, and his son, Esau, the "skilful hunter, a man of the field" in contrast to his brother, Jacob, who "remained indoors," in Gen. 25:27. The sequence of action in this scene was compared to the figure of Ishmael and his bowmanship in Genesis 21, by Good, "Two Notes on Aqhat," 72-73.

255. In 1.114.23, she is paired with the goddess ʿAthtart. For this text with translation and discussion, see Chapter Seven.

256. Cf. hunting in the training of Greek warriors; see Alain Schnapp, "Images of Young People in the Greek City State," in *A History of Young People in the West*, Vol. 1: *Ancient and Medieval Rites of Passage*, ed. Giovanni Levi and Jean-Claude Schmitt; trans. Camille Naish (Cambridge, MA: Belknap, 1997) 50; and Angelos Chaniotis, *War in the Hellenistic World: A Social and Cultural History* (Oxford: Blackwell, 2005) 24, 48, 61. For hunting in Greek art, see Jerome J. Pollitt, *Art in the Hellenistic Age* (Cambridge: Cambridge University Press, 1986) 41-42 figs. 34-35, 130 fig. 136, 201 fig. 214. For warfare represented as a hunting scene in Polybios, see Chaniotis, *War in the Hellenistic World*, 195.

257. See Akkadian *etlūṭu* in this sense in SBV II.260; see George, *The Babylonian Gilgamesh Epic*, 1:457.

258. For a good picture and discussion, see Joan Aruz, Kim Benzel, and Jean M. Evans, eds., *Beyond Babylon: Art, Trade, and Diplomacy in the Second Millennium* B.C. (New York: Metropolitan Museum of Art; New Haven: Yale University Press, 2008) 181, #107 and fig. 57.

259. For a depiction of a Syrian carrying a bow and arrows, see Aruz, Benzel, and Evans, *Beyond Babylon*, 309, fig. 101, from a wall painting in the tomb of Rehkmire (TT109), dynasty 18, reigns of Thutmose III–Amenhotep II.

260. Natan-Yulzary, "Divine Justice or Poetic Justice?" 591. The seal appears in Elizabeth Williams-Forte, *Ancient Near Eastern Seals: A Selection of Stamp and Cylinder Seals from the Collection of Mrs. William H. Moore* (New York: Metropolitan Museum of Art, 1976) no. 63.

261. See Pardee, *RCU*, 84-85; and Steven W. Holloway, "KTU 1.162 and the Offering of a Shield," *UF* 30 (1998) 353-61.

262. Amihai Mazar, *Excavations at Tell Qasile*. Part 2: *The Philistine Sanctuary: Various Finds, the Pottery, Conclusions, Appendixes* (Qedem 20; Jerusalem: Institute of Archaeology, Hebrew University, 1985) 3-4. See also *NEAEHL*, 4:1210.

263. See Wright, *Ritual in Narrative*, 117.

264. Cf. Ishtar's bow and arrows, e.g., in Esarhaddon's inscriptions; see Leichty, *The Royal Inscriptions of Esarhaddon*, 15.

265. A. T. Murray and George E. Dimock, *Homer: Odyssey, Books 13-24* (rev. ed.; LCL 105; London: Heinemann; Cambridge, MA: Harvard University Press, 1966) 329.

266. Murphy, "Myth, Reality, and the Goddess Anat," 538-40.

267. Iconography of female warriors with bows can be seen in Izak Cornelius, *The Many Faces of the Goddess: The Iconography of the Syro-Palestinian Goddesses Anat, Astarte, Qedeshet, and Asherah c. 1500-1000 BCE* (OBO 204; Fribourg: Academic; Göttingen: Vandenhoeck & Ruprecht, 2004) 118, no. 4.4 and 118-19, no. 4.5. See Wilkinson, "The Representation of the Bow." The vast majority of scenes depict the king as the ideal warrior-hunter.

268. According to Sun (*The Ethics of Violence*, 96-97), Aqhat is killed because Aqhat refuses Anat's request for his weapons and because he insults "Anat's gender role."

269. See Wright, *Ritual in Narrative*, 117-18.

270. Cf. how the goddess Astarte is addressed as an "angry and raging goddess," in "The Tale of Two Brothers" (*COS*, 1:35). Ancient Near Eastern analogies for fury in warfare as a positive value can be seen in an Old Babylonian letter of Shibtu to Zimri-Lim of Mari. The letter reports a prophecy from the deity proclaiming: "I will rage and stand in victory" *(kinnekêm ara'ub u ina lītim azzaz)*. For text and translation, see Martti Nissinen, *Prophets and Prophecy in the Ancient Near East* (SBLWAW 12; Atlanta: Society of Biblical Literature, 2003) 46. Recall from Chapter Two the characteristic fury of Achilles, "the best of the Achaeans."

271. Hillers, "The Bow of Aqhat." Cf. H. H. P. Dressler, "Is the Bow of Aqhat a Symbol of Virility?" *UF* 7 (1975) 217-20. See also Walls, *The Goddess Anat*, 186-206; and Wright, *Ritual in Narrative*, 116.

272. 2 Sam. 1:22; 22:35; 2 Kgs. 13:15-19; Hos. 1:5; and Ps. 127:4-5 are cited to this effect by Harold Torger Vedeler, "Reconstructing Meaning in Deuteronomy 22:5: Gender, Society, and Transvestitism in Israel and the Ancient Near East," *JBL* 127/3 (2008) 470.

273. Harry A. Hoffner, "Symbols for Masculinity and Femininity: Their Use in Ancient Near Eastern Sympathetic Magic Rituals," *JBL* 85 (1966), 326-34, esp. 328-29, cited and followed by Vedeler ("Reconstructing Meaning in Deuteronomy 22:5," 470), who cites Prov. 31:19; 2 Sam. 3:29. According to the former, weaving and its tool, the spindle, belong within the domain of women's labor (see also v. 13). The latter considers it a curse that a man be one who "handles the spindle" *(maḥăzîq bappelek)*. Women are attributed the role of spinning in Exod. 35:25-26. Tobit 2:11 calls weaving cloth "the kind of work women do" (NAB). Upon birth, girls in Mesopotamian culture would be consecrated by placing beside them a spindle and a hairclasp; so Karel van der Toorn, *From Her Cradle to Her Grave*, trans. Sara J. Denning-Bolle (Biblical Seminar 23; Sheffield: JSOT, 1994) 20; for further discussion, see M. Malul, "David's Curse of Joab (2 Sam 3:29) and the Social Significance of *mḥzyq bplk*," *AuOr* 10 (1992) 52-56. For this evidence as well as further Ugaritic information, see *UBC*, 2:440-41 (with reference to older works). See also the following note.

274. The spindle was regularly associated with women (see *UBC*, 2:441). Cf. the curse in the Succession Treaty of Esarhaddon, par. 91: "May all the gods who are called by name in this treaty spin you around like a spindle-whorl, may they make you like a woman before your enemy" (Parpola and Watanabe, *Neo-Assyrian Treaties and Loyalty Oaths*, 56). It is also a trope of royal boasting, e.g.: *ʾšt tk* (perhaps, *t<l>k?*) *lḥdy dl plkm*, "a woman walks along (?) with (her) spindles" (KAI 26 A II 5-6). For older instances of the

royal boast in Ur III texts, see Piotr Michalowski, *The Correspondence of the Kings of Ur: An Epistolary History of an Ancient Mesopotamian Kingdom* (Mesopotamian Civilizations 15; Winona Lake: Eisenbrauns, 2011) 294-95, Part B, line 6′; and 373-74, lines 10-11: "their men go wherever they wish and their women hold spindles and needles, wandering on whatever roads they wish."

275. Graham Cunningham, *"Deliver Me from Evil": Mesopotamian Incantations, 2500-1500 BC* (Studia Pohl: Ser. Maior 17; Rome: Pontificio Istituto Biblico, 1997) 33. For the motif, see also a Neo-Sumerian period incantation, lines 46-48 in Cunningham, pp. 69-72.

276. Husser, "La mort d'Aqhat: chasse et rites de passage à Ugarit," *RHR* 225 (2008) 323-45, here 343-44. See also "Chasse et érotisme dans les mythes ougaritiques," *Ktema* 33 (2008) 235-44.

277. Santos-Granero, "Introduction," 14.

278. For this point more generally, see Ilona Zsolnay, "Do Divine Structures of Gender Mirror Mortal Structures of Gender?" in *In the Wake of Tikva Frymer-Kensky*, ed. Steven Holloway, JoAnn Scurlock, and Richard Beal (Piscataway: Gorgias, 2009) 103-20. My inspiration for this point came from Harris, "Inanna-Ishtar as Paradox," 261-78. See also the comments of Murphy, "Myth, Reality, and the Goddess Anat," 538-40; and further below.

279. In contrast to Anat or Athtart, Baal is the model of the king-warrior. See the rhetoric of the god Baal as model for the king in El Amarna letter 147: "who gives forth his cry in the sky like Baal" (Moran, *The Amarna Letters*, 233). Cf. the boast of king Shalmaneser, in A. Kirk Grayson, *Assyrian Rulers of the Early First Millennium BC*, Vol. 2: *(858-745 BC)* (Royal Inscriptions of Mesopotamia: Assyrian Periods 3; Toronto: University of Toronto Press, 1996) 29: "I slaughtered the extensive Guti like the god Erra. I thundered like the god Adad. . . . My soldiers flew up against them like the *anzû*-bird."

280. Parker, *UNP*, 62 and 65.

281. Coogan and Smith, *Stories from Ancient Canaan*, 39.

282. Rahmouni, *Divine Epithets in the Ugaritic Alphabetic Texts*, 247. As noted by Rahmouni (pp. 246-47), the Ugaritic word signifies both "good, pleasant" and "beautiful, lovely." Cf. Pardee (*COS*, 1:276 n. 5), according to whom Ugaritic *nʿm* is "the primary adjective for expressing goodness, *ṭb* the secondary one, that is, the distribution is just the opposite of the one in biblical Heb." See also Hoch, *Semitic Words in Egyptian Texts*, 181 #244. Perhaps cf. Akkadian *damqu* as applied to Enkidu in Gilgamesh SB I:207: "You are handsome, Enkidu, you are just like a god" *([dam]- qa-ta ^{d}en -ki-dù-ki-i ili*(dinger) *ta-ba-áš-ši)*; so George, *The Babylonian Gilgamesh Epic*, 550, 551; and for the evidence for the reconstruction based on the parallel text from Boghazköy MB $Bogh_1$ Fragment a, 1, so George, *The Babylonian Gilgamesh Epic*, 799 note to 207.

283. Wehr, 980.

284. BDB, 653.

285. *UNP*, 62; see also Holger Gzella, "Some Pencilled Notes on Ugaritic Lexicography," *BO* 64 (2007) 535.

286. *CAD*, E:151-52.

287. *CAD*, E:157-61.

288. So Greenfield, *'Al Kanfei Yonah,* 855-56; see also *DULAT,* 165.

289. See the listing at *CAD,* E:158a.

290. George, *The Babylonian Gilgamesh Epic,* 550-51.

291. George, *The Babylonian Gilgamesh Epic,* 552-53.

292. *CAD,* E:158b. Cf. Dalley, *Myths from Mesopotamia,* 57: "He is more powerful in strength of arms than you."

293. Cf. Hebrew *'mq* II? as given in *HALOT,* 2:848-49, suggested as a possibility for the root in Jer. 21:13; 47:5; 49:4.

294. This may not be a divine council scene as such, but El delivers what Cross calls a decree (*Canaanite Myth and Hebrew Epic,* 185). For the idea, see the following omen, with an apodosis that shows the gods issuing a negative result for humans: "the gods will gather together and give a piece of advice (which is) not good"; see Ulla Jeyes, *Old Babylonian Extispicy: Omen Texts in the British Museum* (Uitgaven van het Nederlands Historisch-Archaeologisch Instituut te Istanbul 64; Istanbul: Nederlands Instituut voor het Nabije Oosten, 1989) 183.

295. For lines 33-34, cf. 1.2 IV 24-25; Judg. 5:26. Cf. the more developed and graphic images of violence in some Greek sources; see Chaniotis, *War in the Hellenistic World,* 189-213.

296. For the word, see Jeffrey Zorn, "LU.*PA-MA-ḪA-A* in EA 162:74 and the Role of the *Mhr* in Egypt and Ugarit," *JNES* 50 (1991) 129-38. For the semantic development of "quick, agile" to "warrior," see Shelomo Morag, *Studies in Biblical Hebrew* (Jerusalem: Magnes, 1995) 158-60 (Heb.), noted in Rahmouni, *Divine Epithets in the Ugaritic Alphabetic Texts,* 220 n. 5.

297. Pardee, *COS,* 1:350 n. 77.

298. Cf. the image in OB extispicy: "my heroes and those of the enemy will fall" (**maqāṭu*); "the heroes (and) the bodyguard will fall"; and "two heroes will die." See Jeyes, *Old Babylonian Extispicy,* 28.

299. Pope, in Smith, "A Potpourri of Popery," 661. See also Wright, *Ritual in Narrative,* 134.

300. See Jeffrey H. Tigay, *Deuteronomy* (JPS Torah Commentary; Philadelphia: Jewish Publication Society, 1996) 200 and 383 n. 13; and Vedeler, "Reconstructing Meaning in Deuteronomy 22:5." Vedeler arrives at the idea of *geber* in this passage as a warrior, yet his translation, "superior man," does not quite capture his interpretation that *geber* refers to a warrior.

301. Agustinus Gianto compares the vengeful wrath of Achilles with "Pughat's vengeful anger upon learning of the death of her brother Aqhat"; "Grief, Joy, and Anger in Ugaritic Literary Texts," in *Society and Administration in Ancient Ugarit,* ed. W. H. van Soldt (Leiden: Nederlands Instituut voor het Nabije Oosten, 2010) 56. Pughat may be angry as Gianto suggests, but if so, her anger remains implicit, expressed through her father's actions and her carrying forth her act of vengeance. This muted literary representation stands in contrast with the explicit presentation of Achilles. The difference may point to a difference of gender treatments: the text represents the male hero explicitly in his emotional expression, while the text represents the female as one who is not supposed to be a hero and largely keeps her emotional expression to herself (see above for the

discussion of 1.19 I 34-35: "Pughat wept in the heart, she shed tears in the innards," in other words, to herself).

302. See Wolff, *A Study in the Narrative Structures,* 88: "The stories in epic myth, founded as they are in the life-cycles of heroes who are models for men, refer to this period of life so much because it is a crucial time for teaching the values, practices and relationships that man in culture needs to know."

Notes to Chapter Five

1. Ugaritic has three different cuneiform signs for the consonant *'aleph,* and its spelling in this word (in both the singular and plural forms) varies according to case ending. I use the nominative in the discussion below.

2. Cf. PNs consisting of *mt* plus DN, such as *mtb'l,* "man of Baal" (KTU 4.75 V 21; 4.130.10). Note also biblical Methuselah (Gen. 5:21-22).

3. See section 1 for the figure of *rp'u* and Chapter Twelve for the biblical evidence, including the parallel *(hā)rāpâ* in 2 Sam. 21:20, 22, as well as the same title in 2 Sam. 21:16, 18.

4. As put by *DULAT,* 742.

5. The parallelism of *rp'im* with *'ilnym,* "divinities," has long been noted in KTU 1.20 I 1-2; II 1-2, 6-7, 8-9; 1.21 II 3-4, 11-12, and 1.22 II 5-6, 10-11, 13-14, 18-20, 20-21, 25-26 (with several of these instances reconstructed in part or whole; see below for texts and translations); cf. the fuller description below in 1.22 I 6-10. The parallelism was noted by Frank Moore Cross, *Canaanite Myth and Hebrew Epic* (Cambridge, MA: Harvard University Press, 1973) 20. Note also KTU 1.6 VI 46-47 (*UNP,* 164), translated below. The parallelism suggests that the *rp'um* were considered "divine" in some sense. See Matthew J. Suriano, *The Politics of Dead Kings: Dynastic Ancestors in the Book of Kings and Ancient Israel* (FAT 2/48; Tübingen: Mohr Siebeck, 2010) 152; and Christopher B. Hays, *Death in the Iron Age II and in First Isaiah* (FAT 79; Tübingen: Mohr Siebeck, 2011) 107-8, 111-12. Note also that in the first text analyzed below the figure *rp'u* is explicitly called *'il,* "god." There is little evidence of the "democratization" of divinity for the dead more broadly entertained by Hays (*Death in the Iron Age II,* 115), but as he observes, KTU 1.6 VI 46-47 might be suggestive in this vein; in context, it could also be understood in the more restricted sense of the old military Rephaim.

6. For a judicious survey of the Ugaritic Rephaim, see James N. Ford, "The 'Living Rephaim' of Ugarit: Quick or Defunct?" *UF* 24 (1992) 73-101.

7. Van Wees, *Status Warriors: War, Violence, and Society in Homer and History* (Dutch Monographs on Ancient History and Archaeology 9; Amsterdam: Gieben, 1992) 7. See also Robert Parker, *On Greek Religion* (Ithaca: Cornell University Press, 2011) 103-4, 287-92. Note also the important study of Brian R. Doak, *The Last of the Rephaim: Conquest and Cataclysm in the Heroic Ages of Ancient Israel* (Boston: Ilex Foundation; Washington: Center for Hellenic Studies, 2012).

8. It is generally acknowledged (*DULAT,* 742) that the Ugaritic root means "to heal" in KTU 1.114.28 (presented in Chapter Seven). The precise meaning of the nominal forms *rp'u* and *rp'u/'im* remains unclear. Pardee (*RCU,* 282) entertains a stative sense ("healthy

one(s)") and an active sense ("healers") as alternatives. See Pierre Bordreuil and Dennis Pardee, *A Manual of Ugaritic* (Linguistic Studies in Ancient West Semitic 3; Winona Lake: Eisenbrauns, 2009) 350, where they suggest a semantic development of "healthy one" to "shade" (ancestor)." By contrast, J. F. Healey believes that their name is to be tied to Safaitic *rp'*, "to safeguard, protect"; "Ugarit and Arabia: A Balance Sheet," *Proceedings of the Seminar for Arabian Studies* 21 (1991) 69-78. For further discussion, see P. J. Williams, "Are the Biblical Rephaim and the Ugaritic RPUM Healers?" in *The Old Testament in Its World*, ed. Robert P. Gordon and Johannes C. de Moor (OtSt 52; Leiden: Brill, 2005) 266-75. In support of this sense for the word, one might appeal to *ẓlm* in KTU 1.161.1 (see below), with the possible connotation of "protection."

9. Another possible text with this figure could be KTU 1.166, but the context is unclear. Line 13 of this text contains the reading *rp'i yqr*, but the form of the first word may be plural construct. The text also seems to involve the gods Dagan and Baal (line 9).

10. The readings are based on *RCU*, 193-94. The siglum "/" marks line breaks. For the text, see also the important work of Dennis Pardee, *Les textes para-mythologiques de la 24e campagne (1961)* (RSO 4; Paris: Editions Recherche sur les Civilisations, 1988) 75-97.

11. Ugaritic *hln* is a presentative particle, conveying attention drawn to the content designated by the rest of the clause (e.g., 1.3 II 5, 17; cf. 2.36.12). It is sometimes translated "behold," "look," or "see" or the like, and sometimes with an exclamation point (*DULAT*, 337; Daniel Sivan, *A Grammar of the Ugaritic Language* [2nd impression with corrections; HO 1/128; Leiden: Brill, 2001] 185, 186). The question is whether *hl, hln*, etc. are presentation particles with a spatial sense ("there — " or the like; see KTU 1.17 V 12-13), in contrast with other presentative particles such as *ht*, with a temporal sense ("now," as in its threefold use in KTU 1.2 IV 8-9). Pardee (*RCU*, 193) translates *hln*, "now," but Bordreuil and Pardee (*A Manual of Ugaritic*, 312) consider *hln* an "extended form" of *hl*, which they translate "here (is), look, behold."

12. As suggested by Pardee (*RCU*, 204-5 n. 6), the title *mlk 'lm* may evoke the name of the god Mlk, with whom Rp'u seems to have been identified, as suggested by the shared address of *rp'u mlk 'lm* here in line 2 with *mlk 'ṯtrth* (KTU 1.100.41), *mlk b'ṯtrt* (KTU 1.107.42), and *mlk 'ṯtrt* (4.790.16); Pardee also compares the Phoenician-Punic deity *mlk'štrt*. To be sure, more than one deity can inhabit a single location, but it is the combination of the same place with the apparent title *mlk* in KTU 1.108.1-2 that militates in this direction. See further Manfried Dietrich and Oswald Loretz, "Rapi'u und Milku aus Ugarit: Neuere historisch-geographische Thesen zu *rpu mlk 'lm* (KTU 1.108: 1) und *mt rpi* (KTU 1.17 I 1)," *UF* 21 (1989) 123-31; see also their older study, "Baal *rpu* in KTU 1.108; 1.113 und nach 1.17 VI 25-33," *UF* 12 (1980) 171-82. Pardee holds that Rp'u is a title of Mlk. One might entertain the further possibility that *rp'u mlk 'lm* in KTU 1.108.1 might not be "Rapi'u the eternal king," as the phrase is generally taken, but "the Rapiu, Milku, the eternal one." In this case, one might think that the order would appear in reverse as **mlk rp'u* on the pattern of the names plus *rp['u]* in KTU 1.161.4-5 (see section 3 below for treatment of this text).

Mlk does appear to be attested as a deity name (e.g., KTU 4.790.16). According to Alfonso Archi, the listing of Milku after Nergal in the Anatolian rituals in Emar 472.62 and 473.15 points to this god "as a god of similar qualities, whom they [the Hittites] had acquired from Syria." Mlk is known also at Emar ("the seven ^{d}Im-li-ku of the seven gates" in Emar 373.124; 378.41). Milku is also an Amurrite god as attested in the Hittite treaty of Murshili II with Tuppi-Teshub of Amurru listing ^{d}*Mi-il*$_5$-ku [KUR ^{uru}*A-mur]-ri,* either Milku of Amurru or the Milkus of Amurru. See Archi, "Kizzuwatna amid Anatolian and Syrian Cults," in *Anatolia Antica: Studi in memoria di Fiorella Imparati,* ed. Stefano de Martino and Franca Pecchioli Daddi (Florence: LoGisma, 2002) 50.

13. *RCU,* 193-94 takes the verbs as volitive, which is possible. This would work well with the request for blessing on the reverse of this tablet. Perhaps in accord with this approach, Wayne T. Pitard suggests understanding KTU 1.108 as an incantation: "As each deity was given the offering, a part of the incantation was spoken. The final lines (18-27) indicate that the function of the ritual and incantation was to encourage Rapi'u and Baal to strengthen the king"; "Canaanite Literature," in *From an Antique Land: An Introduction to Ancient Near Eastern Literature,* ed. Carl S. Ehrlich (Lanham: Rowman & Littlefield, 2009) 296. On other hand, the volitive form does not seem to fit with the presentative particle, *[hl]n,* which heads the clause in line 1. This particle typically opens a description, not an expression of a wish. Pardee's translation "Now" (see note 11 above) for the particle seems to be an effort to obviate the difficulty.

14. Cf. *rp'i yqr* in KTU 1.166.13, but the context is unclear, and the right-hand side of the tablet is lost.

15. Following the treatment of the verbal construction by Marvin H. Pope, *Probative Pontificating in Ugaritic and Biblical Literature: Collected Essays,* ed. Mark S. Smith (Ugaritisch-biblische Literatur 10; Münster: Ugarit-Verlag, 1994) 198, 239, this view is generally accepted. Cf. the ungrammatical interpretation of Cross, *Canaanite Myth and Hebrew Epic,* 20-21; *From Epic to Canon: History and Literature in Ancient Israel* (Baltimore: Johns Hopkins University Press, 1998) 76-77 n. 14; for the grammatical issues, see Saul M. Olyan, *Asherah and the Cult of Yahweh in Israel* (SBLMS 34; Atlanta: Scholars, 1988) 48-49. The verbal construction may denote either residence or enthronement. Parallelism here favors enthronement.

For this verbal denoting divine residence, note "the mountain that God desired for his dwelling (**yšb*)"//indeed, (where) Yahweh resides *(škn)* forever," Ps. 68:16; "Jerusalem your established dwelling-place (**yšb*)," Sir. 36:13. See also KAI 26A ii 18-19/26C iii 15-16; 214:19, "I made this/my god dwell (**yšb*) in it" (see *DNWSI,* 475). For this meaning with Akkadian *ašābu,* see *CAD,* A/1:396. See also the eight instances **yṯb b- GN* for residence in KTU 4.382.23-34 (*DULAT,* 995).

For enthronement for Ugaritic **yṯb,* see KTU 1.23.8. Ugaritic **yṯb l ks'/kḥṯ* ("seat, throne") in KTU 1.10 III 13-14; 1.16 VI 22-25 could mean "to return to his royal throne." The usage in 1.101.1 probably means "to sit" ("Baal sits like the sitting of the mountain"), but enthronement may be connoted. For BH **yšb* for sitting on a throne or enthronement, see Amos 1:5, 8; Exod. 15:15, so Cross, *Canaanite Myth and Hebrew Epic,* 130 n. 65. The meaning is also evident in Phoenician, in KAI 24.9 *(yšb 'l ks');* see Charles R. Krahmalkov, *Phoenician-Punic Dictionary* (OLA 90; Studia Phoenicia 15; Leuven: Peeters and Department Oosterse Studies, 2000) 216. See also Akkadian *ašābu ina* with respect to enthronement; *CAD,* A/1:390-92; *CAD,* Š/3:135, #2'c'.

16. The *b-* of instrument. Still one might translate "on the lyre and flute. . . ."

17. This view is supported by comparison with KTU 1.19 IV 26-27. See *DULAT,* 576-77. Note also the musical scene with cymbals in 1.3 I 18-22, presented in the final section of the following chapter.

18. Support for this view was adduced by Mark S. Smith, "The Magic of Kothar wa-Hasis, the Ugaritic Craftsman God, in KTU 1.6 VI 49-50," *RB* 91 (1984) 377-80, based largely on similar language in the magical context of the incantation KTU 1.169.9-11. See also Theodore J. Lewis, *Cults of the Dead in Ancient Israel and Ugarit* (HSM 39; Atlanta: Scholars, 1989) 36-37 n. 158; James N. Ford, "The Ugaritic Incantation against Sorcery RIH 78/20 (KTU^2 1.169)," *UF* 34 (2002) 182-84. The same proposal is made (without reference to prior literature) by Oswald Loretz, "'Schwarze Magie' des Tages in Hi 3,8 und KTU 1.6 VI 45b-53; 1.14 I 19-20; 1.4 VII 54-56," *UF* 32 (In memoriam Cyrus H. Gordon; 2000) 272. See further note 27 below.

19. Lit., "of."

20. Cf. *rp'* on inscribed arrowheads; see J. C. L. Gibson, *Textbook of Syrian Semitic Inscriptions,* Vol. 3: *Phoenician Inscriptions* (Oxford: Clarendon, 1982) 5-6, fig. 2; Benjamin Sass, *The Genesis of the Alphabet and Its Development in the Second Millennium* B.C. (Ägypten und Altes Testament 13; Wiesbaden: Harrassowitz, 1988) 79. Cf. the form of the first personal name on an authentic (?) Hebrew seal inscription, *rp' bn bn 'nt,* "Rapa', son of Ben-'Anat," published by Nahman Avigad, Michael Heltzer, and André Lemaire, *West Semitic Seals: Eighth-Sixth Centuries* BCE (Haifa: University of Haifa, 2000) 97, #76. The second name is suggestive of a warrior father, and perhaps a warrior son as well (see Chapters Seven and Eleven). The name *rp'* is just as likely a hypocoristicon (e.g., in Repa'yahu, "Yahu has healed," as attested on p. 99, #77, or Repa'el, "El/God has healed"), as noted by the authors.

21. Based largely on his understanding of *nmry mlk 'lm* in KTU 2.42.9, Alan Cooper prefers to read this phrase as "king of eternity." See Cooper, "MLK 'LM: 'Eternal King' or 'King of Eternity'?" in *Love and Death in the Ancient Near East: Essays in Honor of Marvin H. Pope,* ed. John H. Marks and Robert M. Good (Guilford: Four Quarters, 1987) 2. For different views of *nmry mlk 'lm* (which follows the mention of deities), see *DULAT,* 632; Itamar Singer, "A Political History of Ugarit," in *Handbook of Ugaritic Studies,* ed. Wilfred G. E. Watson and Nicolas Wyatt (HO 1/39; Leiden: Brill, 1999) 678. For the context of KTU 2.42, see A. Bernard Knapp, "An Alashiysan Merchant at Ugarit," *TA* 10 (1983) 38-45.

22. The comparison of the Ugaritic evidence here with the biblical place names was first made by Baruch Margulis (Margalit), "A Ugaritic Psalm (RŠ 24.252)," *JBL* 89 (1970) 292-304, here 293-94; cf. Manfred Görg, "Noch einmal: Edrei in Ugarit?" *UF* 6 (1974) 474-75. For Edrei in Egyptian sources, see Görg, "Edrei in ägyptischer Nebenüberlieferung," *BN* 84 (1996) 36-40. For the difference in the spelling of the initial consonant in the Ugaritic and Hebrew forms of the place name, see Edward L. Greenstein, "Another Attestation of Initial *h* > ' in West Semitic," *JANES* 5 (T. H. Gaster Festschrift; 1973) 157-64, esp. 162 n. 31; Aicha Rahmouni, *Divine Epithets in the Ugaritic Alphabetic Texts,* trans. J. N. Ford (HO 1 93; Leiden: Brill, 2008) 48 n. 13.

23. For the relationship of the biblical evidence to the Ugaritic material about the Rephaim, see Chapter Twelve, section 2.

24. See Chapter Twelve, section 2.

25. For KTU 1.113, see *RCU,* 201-4. Note that the latter instrument has a final *-m* in this text, suggesting possibly a dual "double-flute" (so *RCU,* 208 n. 33)

26. In Ps. 22:30, the phrase *kol-dišnê-'ereṣ,* lit., "all the fat ones of the earth (or, underworld)," may refer to the dead, given its proximity to *kol-yôrĕdê-'āpār,* "all descending to dust," a fairly standard expression for the deceased. For discussion, see Nicholas J. Tromp, *Primitive Conceptions of Death and the Nether World in the Old Testament* (BibOr 21; Rome: Pontifical Biblical Institute, 1969) 32-35; and Mark S. Smith, "The Invocation of Deceased Ancestors in Ps 49:12c," *JBL* 112 (1993) 105-7.

27. This interpretation likewise fits these terms, *ḥbr* and *d'tm,* in KTU 1.169.10. See Smith, "The Magic of Kothar wa-Hasis." The associated terms in KTU 1.169.10 are rendered similarly by James N. Ford as "spellcaster"/"the expert (in divination)." See Ford, "The New Ugaritic Incantation against Sorcery RS 1992.2014," *UF* 34 (2002) 137; and "The Ugaritic Incantation against Sorcery." Ford ("The Ugaritic Incantation against Sorcery," 183 n. 157) does not apply this understanding of the same terms to their appearance together in 1.6 VI 49-50.

28. See Ford, "The 'Living Rephaim' of Ugarit," 77-80.

29. E.g., KAI 10:8-10, 26 A III 2-7; Pss. 21:5; 72:15. See Michael L. Barré, "An Analysis of the Royal Blessing in the Karatepe Inscription," *Maarav* 3 (1982) 177-94; Jonas C. Greenfield, "Scripture and Inscription," in *'Al Kanfei Yonah: Collected Studies of Jonas C. Greenfield on Semitic Philology,* ed. Shalom M. Paul, Michael E. Stone, and Avital Pinnick (2 vols.; Leiden: Brill; Jerusalem: Magnes, 2001) 2:716-19; *UBC,* 2:354. See also the discussion in the preceding chapter.

30. For this issue as it applies to the Rephaim texts, see Gregorio del Olmo Lete, "Littérature et pouvoir royal à Ougarit: Sens politique de la littérature d'Ougarit," in *Études ougaritiques II,* ed. Valérie Matoïan, Michel Al-Maqdissi, and Yves Calvet (RSO 20; Leuven: Peeters, 2012) 241-50, here 247-48.

31. The discussion here is heavily dependent on the following resources. For editions of these tablets with readings, see Wayne Pitard, "A New Edition of the 'Rāpi'ūma' Texts: KTU 1.20-22," *BASOR* 285 (1992) 33-77; Theodore J. Lewis, "Toward a Literary Translation of the Rapiuma Texts," in *Ugarit: Religion and Culture. Proceedings of the International Colloquium on Ugarit, Religion and Culture, Edinburgh, July 1994. Essays Presented in Honour of John C. L. Gibson* (Ugaritisch-Biblische Literatur 12, ed. N. Wyatt, W. G. E. Watson, and J. B. Lloyd; Münster: Ugarit-Verlag, 1996) 115-49; Dennis Pardee, "Nouvelle étude épigraphique et littéraire des textes fragmentaires en langue ougaritique dits "Les Rephaïm" (*CTA* 20-22)," *Or* 80 (2011) 1-65 (I wish to thank Professor Pardee for providing me with a prepublication copy of this article and for his permission to use it). Readings follow Pardee, but without the half-brackets as provided by Pardee. As a result, the presentation here simplifies the actual epigraphic situation. For these details, interested readers are encouraged to consult Pardee's important study.

For an introduction, transliteration, and translation, see in addition Lewis, *UNP,* 196-205. The translation below draws also from Michael D. Coogan and Mark S. Smith, *Stories From Ancient Canaan* (2nd ed.; Louisville: Westminster John Knox, 2012) 61-67.

For expansive discussions, cf. the older studies of Marvin H. Pope, "Notes on the Rephaim Texts from Ugarit," in *Essays on the Ancient Near East in Memory of Jacob Joel*

Finkelstein, ed. Maria de Jong Ellis (Memoirs of the Connecticut Academy of Arts and Sciences 19; Hamden: Archon, 1977) 165-77; repr. in Pope, *Probative Pontificating,* 185-224; and Johannes C. de Moor, *New Year with Canaanites and Israelites* (2 vols.; Kampen: Kok, 1972). While these works contain a good deal of speculation, they also contain much of value.

32. De Moor suggested that only one tablet was involved, and Pardee has entertained this possibility. See de Moor, *An Anthology of Religious Texts from Ugarit* (Nisaba 16; Leiden: Brill, 1987) 265-73; and Pardee, "Nouvelle étude épigraphique et littéraire," 2-11.

33. Simon B. Parker, *The Pre-Biblical Narrative Tradition: Essays on the Ugaritic Poems* Keret *and* Aqhat (SBLRBS 24; Atlanta: Scholars, 1989) 134-35.

34. See the review of prior views and the fresh proposal of Pardee, "Nouvelle étude épigraphique et littéraire," 2-10.

35. Pitard, "A New Edition of the 'Rāpi'ūma' Texts," 33-77; and Pardee, "Nouvelle étude épigraphique et littéraire," 1-65.

36. As Lewis (*UNP,* 205 n. 4) notes, many scholars emend *'il* here to ⟨*dn*⟩*'il,* but he cautions against this emendation without further evidence.

37. See *DULAT,* 182; W. G. E. Watson suggests possible comparison with Akkadian *margūṣu(m),* "an aromatic" (*CAD,* M/1:279) or "a resinous bush" (*CDA,* 197). See Watson, "Akkadian Cognates to Some Ugaritic Words," *SEL* 25 (2008) 58.

38. Lewis, *UNP,* 197.

39. Cf. BH *sôd* for a divine sort of "council" or "assembly" in Jer. 23:18, 22; Ps. 89:8; it is not, however, applied to the biblical Rephaim. For discussion of the word, see Abraham Malamat, "The Secret Council and Prophetic Involvement in Mari and Israel," in *Mari and the Bible* (Studies in the History and Culture of the Ancient Near East 12; Leiden: Brill, 1998) 134-41.

40. See *RCU,* 56-62.

41. See *RCU,* 57 for a good assessment of the question.

42. Or "to/toward it" or "to his place" or "to the place" (so Pardee), namely the "palace." Pardee understands this bicolon here and elsewhere as a continuation of the preceding speech. For further discussion see note 56 below.

43. Pardee's two readings of *ndd* for *tdd* are new, adding to the discussion over whether suffix verbal forms are used "to indicate a change of actor, speaker, or scene" in Ugaritic narrative, as proposed by Edward L. Greenstein, "Forms and Functions of the Finite Verb in Ugaritic Narrative Verse," in *Biblical Hebrew in Its Northwest Semitic Setting: Typological and Historical Perspectives,* ed. Steven E. Fassberg and Avi Hurvitz (Jerusalem: Magnes, 2006) 75-102, here 96, with discussion on 96-98. See also *UBC,* 2:26-27 and 28.

44. One might render "asses," but the chariots mentioned here as well as the horses suggest a synonym such as "stallions" (Lewis, *UNP,* 198).

45. Or possibly *'ilm.* See Lewis, *UNP,* 198.

46. Horwitz, "The Significance of the Rephaim: *rm.aby.btk.rpim,*" *JNSL* 12 (1979) 37-43, here 42-43.

47. Cf. the invitation to eat and drink in KTU 1.23.6 (note also the approach of a party in 1.23.71-76 with references to food and wine). See also the biblical invitation in Isa. 55:1. For this theme, see Richard J. Clifford, "Isaiah 55: Invitation to a Feast," in *The Word of the*

Lord Shall Go Forth: Essays in Honor of David Noel Freedman in Celebration of His Sixtieth Birthday, ed. Carol L. Meyers and M. O'Connor (Winona Lake: Eisenbrauns, 1983) 27-35.

48. As the Rephaim seem to constitute a positive force in the context of the late summer (cf. the blessing discussed for KTU 1.108 in the preceding section), they may contrast with the voracious, destructive "Goodly Gods" in 1.23, another text that evokes a feast in the late summer. For this text, see Mark S. Smith, *The Rituals and Myths of the Feast of the Goodly Gods, KTU/CAT 1.23: Royal Constructions of Opposition, Intersection, Integration, and Domination* (SBLRBS 51; Atlanta: Society of Biblical Literature; Leiden: Brill, 2006).

49. For this English translation marzeah, I have adopted the conventional spelling based on the biblical spelling of the word. See further below. The other spelling of this word in Ugaritic is *mrzḥ* (KTU 1.1 IV 4; 1.114.15; 3.9.1, 13; 4.399.8; 4.642.4-7). For the two Ugaritic spellings *mrzʿ/mrzḥ* as variants, see John Huehnergard, *Ugaritic Vocabulary in Syllabic Transcription* (rev. ed.; HSS 32; Winona Lake: Eisenbrauns, 2008) 178, 272. Huehnergard regards the form with *ʿayin* in both the Ugaritic alphabetic spelling *mrzʿ* and in the Ras Shamra Akkadian spellings *mar-za-i* and *mar-zi-i* to reflect "intervocalic voicing of /ḥ/ to [ʿ].

50. This is a new reading of Pardee, "Nouvelle étude épigraphique et littéraire," 23.

51. Usually written in this formulary for multiple days without final *-t,* does the numeral here involve a dittography (with the first wedge of the following *'aleph*)?

52. For the construction (without preposition), see Richard C. Steiner, *Early Northwest Semitic Serpent Spells in the Pyramid Texts* (HSS 61; Winona Lake: Eisenbrauns, 2011) 36. See note 42 above.

53. According to Lewis (*UNP,* 200), El is the speaker of the speech in lines 1-7 as well as the speech in lines 9-12. He translates the narrative rubric introducing the second speech in line 8, *wyʿn 'il,* as "Again El spoke." However, as far as I know, the particle *w-* in *wyʿn* does not otherwise convey this sense, "again," in Ugaritic narrative; see 1.1 III 17; IV 13; 1.2 III 18; 1.4 IV 58; V 58, 63; VI 1; VI 14; VII 14, 37; 1.5 I 11; 1.6 I 49, 61; V 23; 1.17 VI 20, 33; 1.18 I 15; IV 11; 1.19 IV 35, 52, 56; 1.20 II 7. These cases all involve a speaker speaking following either a speech by another party or a piece of narrative. (I have not included reconstructions; perhaps emend *kyʿn* in 1.16 IV 9 to *wyʿn.*) The only possible exception that I have found is in 1.2 III 24, but the context is very broken. I grant that the context in 1.22 II 8 is not easy and that El could be the speaker of both speeches, but still it seems more likely to me that a party other than El may be involved in speaking in lines 1-7. Horwitz ("The Significance of the Rephaim," 41) might be correct in suggesting that "El, as titular head of the pantheon, may have been considered the major patron of the *rp'm ex officio.*"

54. Pardee, "Nouvelle étude épigraphique et littéraire," 23.

55. For this passage, see the first section of this chapter.

56. Many commentators compare *'aṯrh* here with BH *māqôm,* lit., "place," sometimes used for shrine; e.g., Lewis, *UNP,* 198, 199, 200, 201, 202, 203. It is also possible to translate *'aṯrh,* "after him" (so *DULAT,* 127). Other instances of this word with verbs of motion are prepositional, "after" (e.g., 1.43.24, with **hlk;* 1.5 VI 24 and 1.161.20, with **yrd*). Arguably one problem with seeing this approach here is the lack of an antecedent for the suffix on *'aṯrh.* Setting aside the rather different case of 1.22 I 3, Ugaritic narrative poetry includes a named antecedent for the only other occurrences of the form *'aṯrh* apart from the

cliché of travel in the Rephaim texts, namely the two instances attested in KTU 1.17 I 28 and 46 (whatever its meaning there). This data base is hardly definitive for the question, and it also remains possible that either the antecedent might be in the lost lines of the Rephaim texts and/or that the referent was known enough in context that it did not need mentioning in some, if not all, of the occurrences. See note 42 above.

57. See Chapter Seven for this text.

58. For discussion, see *UBC*, 1:140-44.

59. KTU 3.9.1 41 "the marzeah that Shamumanu established in his house," *mrzḥ dqny šmmn b btw*. The form of the suffix *-w* is anomalous; for discussion, see *UG*, 221. Note also RS 15.70, lines 3-18, discussed in John L. McLaughlin, *The Marzēaḥ in the Prophetic Literature: References and Allusions in Light of the Extra-Biblical Evidence* (VTSup 86; Leiden: Brill, 2001) 15-17.

60. See McLaughlin, *The Marzēaḥ in the Prophetic Literature;* Lorena Miralles Maciá, *Marzeah y thíasos: una institución convival en el Oriente Próximo Antiguo y el Mediterráneo* ('Ilu. Revista de Ciencas de las Religiones. Anejos. Series de monografías 20; Madrid: Universidad Complutense, 2007). See also Stefan Schorch, "Die Propheten und der Karneval: Marzeach–Maioumas–Maimuna," *VT* 53 (2003) 397-415; José-Angel Zamora, "L'ébriété à Ougarit et la Bible: un heritage discuté," in *La Bible et l'héritage d'Ougarit*, ed. Jean-Marc Michaud (Proche-Orient et Littérature Ougaritique; Québec: GGC, 2005) 183-207; Marina Tryfonidou, "The Origins of Feasting in the Eastern Mediterranean Basin of the 8th Cenury B.C.," *Polish Journal of Biblical Research* 7 (2008) 33-45.

61. Pope, "The Cult of the Dead at Ugarit," in *Ugarit in Retrospect: Fifty Years of Ugarit and Ugaritic*, ed. Gordon Douglas Young (Winona Lake: Eisenbrauns, 1981) 159-79; repr. in Pope, *Probative Pontificating*, 225-50.

62. E.g., see the critical remarks of Lewis, *Cults of the Dead*, 84-86; and Dennis Pardee, "*Marziḫu, Kispu*, and the Ugaritic Funerary Cult: A Minimalist View," in Wyatt, Watson, and Lloyd, *Ugarit, Religion and Culture*, 273-87, and *RCU*, 184-85.

63. For a comparable shift reflected in the Greek symposion, see Oswyn Murray, "The Symposion between East and West," given at the American Schools of Oriental Research 2012 meeting; this paper was originally presented in Italian to the 2009 Magna Grecia conference in Taranto on the theme "La Vigna di Dioniso: vite vino e culti in Magna Grecia." Murray also posits influence of the marzeah on the symposion.

64. For the pertinent texts showing Ugaritic royal patronage of the marzeah, see RS 15.70 and 15.88 as well as the king of Siyannu's support in RS 18.01; see McLaughlin, *The Marzēaḥ in the Prophetic Literature*, 14-18.

65. The other column on this side is too fragmentary to read (one letter, *b*, in line 5), and it is left out of consideration here. See Pardee, "Nouvelle étude épigraphique et littéraire," 30-31.

66. Cf. BH *bĕnê bānîm for grandsons, e.g., in Judg. 12:14; Jer. 2:9; 27:7; note also "son and grandson," in the Sefire inscription, KAI 222 C 3, 8 (*SSI*, 2:32-33) and KAI 224:12, 15 (*SSI*, 2.48-49). Some of these cases involve issues of lineage, as may be the import here.

67. Temporal use of *'aṯr*, "after," according to *DULAT*, 1127. Cf. Lewis, *UNP*, 203, "your shrine," putatively in keeping with the prior occurrences of the word in the Rephaim texts (although the meaning "after him" might apply to those instances; see note 56 above).

The translation "of your place" is also theoretically possible; in this case the preceding noun could be plural.

68. Pardee offers a reading of *ǵzr*, with the first two letters in partial brackets.

69. The views on the remainder of this line vary widely; see *DULAT*, 505 ("those who assist DN with alacrity," taking *blsmt* as *b-* plus **lsmt*, comparing Akkadian *lismu*).

70. For the morphology of the word, see Huehnergard, *Ugaritic Vocabulary in Syllabic Transcription*, 273.

71. It is possible that *mtm* here refers to living figures who celebrate (?) El (so Pardee, "Nouvelle étude épigraphique et littéraire," 52-53), but the overall context arguably may have Rephaim in view.

72. There is no consensus on the etymology; see *DULAT*, 146. The BH root **ʿbš* is *hapax*, attested in Joel 1:17, where it is thought to mean "to shrivel" (BDB, 721, citing Arabic **ʿbs*, "to contract, frown [of faces]"). This sense does not seem to fit the verb in 1.22 I 6-7. The second occurrence of the form *yʿbš* in 1.22 I 6-7 might be a dittography (esp. if *brkn* were to turn out to be a parallel semantic term). The translation here follows Pardee, "Nouvelle étude épigraphique et littéraire," 44, inferred from context.

73. *DULAT*, 917 takes *ṯmq* as a personal name. The syntactical slot may suggest a verb.

74. Despite the near consensus about the meaning (*DULAT*, 381), the final *-y* remains a question.

75. The line is often translated "the eternal royal princes" (so *UNP*, 203) or the like. This translation is feasible from a philological perspective. However, three contextual considerations make the translation offered here also worthy of consideration: (1) elsewhere *zbl* is a term for one figure (e.g., Baal in 1.2 I 38, 43; IV 8; 1.3 I 3; 1.5 VI 10; 1.6 I 42; III 3, 9, 21; IV 5, 16; 1.9.17; Yamm in 1.2 III 8, 16, 21; IV 7, 14, 22, 24, 29; Yariḫ in 1.15 II 4, 19; IV 2; Rashpu in 1.15 II 6; cf. *zbl ṣr* in 5.22.9); (2) KTU 1.108.1 (discussed in the first section of this chapter) contains *rp'u mlk ʿlm*, "Rp'u, the eternal king," possibly with overtones of the divine name Mlk (see note 12 above); and (3) the title *ʿllmy* is used for an individual *rp'u* in 1.161.7. In terms of lexicon, the closest parallel to 1.22 I 9-10 may be 1.13.26-27, with *zbl mlk šmm* and *ḥl ʾamr* (the context is very difficult).

76. Since this is the construct form (the absolute form would be **mrʾim*), the following word belongs to this line. Cf. *UNP*, 203-4. For the morphology, see Huehnergard, *Ugaritic Vocabulary in Syllabic Transcription*, 300 n. 17, who views the form here as a scribal error (by comparison with *mrʾiʾa* elsewhere); thus one might expect (again, by comparison) **mrʾiʾi* for the genitive plural form. For the verbal root **mrʾ*, "to fatten," see Hayim ben Yosef Tawil, *An Akkadian Lexical Companion for Biblical Hebrew: Etymological-Semantic and Idiomatic Equivalents with Supplement on Biblical Aramaic* (Jersey City: Ktav, 2009) 222-23; see also Jastrow, 842; for the noun, see *UBC*, 1:70; Tawil, *An Akkadian Lexical Companion*, 222.

77. For this meaning, see *DULAT*, 466, comparing Arabic *kušš*, *kasīs* (citing J. G. Hava, *Arabic-English Dictionary for the Use of Students* [Beirut: Catholic, 1921] 655).

78. Or perhaps "vine blossom," so *TO*, 1:475-76 n. I; see Huehnergard, *Ugaritic Vocabulary in Syllabic Transcription*, 85, 175.

79. This is the reading of Pardee ("Nouvelle étude épigraphique et littéraire," 29),

which picks up the flow of lines 13-14 above. This had been read as *dpr*, "to exude a strong smell" (*DULAT*, 277), which would fit the overall context, but it would be a *hapax*.

80. The division of the line has been an issue (cf. *DULAT*, 914).

81. In view of difficulties at understanding *ṯmk*, the word may be a proper name. It is also attested in RS 92.2016.2; see André Caquot and Anne-Sophie Dalix, "Un texte mythico-magique," in *Études ougaritiques*, Vol. 1: *Travaux, 1985-1995*, ed. Marguerite Yon and Daniel Arnaud (RSO 14; Paris: Editions Recherche sur les Civilisations, 2001) 393-405. Based on the attestation of the word *ṯmk* in KTU 1.22 I 17, Johannes de Moor surmises that "Ṯamuka was a region renowned for its excellent wine which was libated in the ancestral cult"; "How Ilimilku Lost His Master (RS 92.2016)," *UF* 40 (2008) 180 n. 5. As an alternative, Pope ("Notes on the Rephaim Texts from Ugarit," 168, 176) suggests "spill" as a verb parallel to **yṣq* and cognate with Arabic **ṯbq*.

82. Lit., "of."

83. *bl + d-?* See the following note.

84. For this meaning for **ǵll* in 1.3 II 13 and 27, see *UBC*, 2:155-56, based on Robert M. Good, "Metaphorical Gleanings from Ugarit," *JJS* 33 (Essays in Honour of Yigael Yadin; 1982) 55-59. The meaning fits the context of wine. KTU 2.34.32-33 has been compared by Wilfred G. E. Watson (*Lexical Studies in Ugaritic* [AuOr Sup 19; Barcelona: Editorial AUSA, 2007] 20), which one might consider translating with some modification of Watson's rendering: "See *(hn)*, the must-wine *(mrṯ)* that I have set I shall send out in your containers *(ldtk)*."

85. The root is **'šr*, "to be happy." For this usage, cf. **śmḥ*, "to give joy" (in the D-stem), used to describe the effects of alcohol in Judg. 9:13; Ps. 104:15. For specifics concerning this usage of **śmḥ*, see H. L. Ginsberg, "The North-Canaanite Myth of Anath and Aqhat II," *BASOR* 98 (1945) 15 n. 20; and *ANET*, 150; Jonas C. Greenfield, "Lexicographical Notes II,"in *'Al Kanfei Jonah*, 2:682, 685; Gruber, *Aspects*, 2:568.

86. Cf. *DULAT*, 763, comparing BH *sĕmādar* as in Song 2:13.

87. See *DULAT*, 763 for this difficult line.

88. The verb here followed by a nominal form may suggest an asyndetic clause. For the verb, see *DULAT*, 371. See Lewis, *UNP*, 204. Note the rendering of the Lebanon mountain region in 1.22 I 19-20, according to Wilfred G. E. Watson, "Wonderful Wine (KTU 1.22 I 17-20)," *UF* 31 (1999) 778: "wine of happiness/the gem of Lebanon's necklace *(smd)*/dew of the must cultivated by El." If correct, the produce of Lebanon is figured as its necklace, and it has a particular association here with El. However, the interpretation of the lines and specifically *smd* are highly disputed.

89. Reading for *ṭṣ* (*UNP*, 205 n. 6). Pope compared Arabic *ṭalla*, "delicious," applied to wine and perfume. He also noted the proposal of David Wortman (oral communication to Pope) relating the Ugaritic word to Aramaic *ṭîlā*, referring to a very strong wine. Either would work in this context. See Pope, "Notes on the Rephaim Texts from Ugarit," in Ellis, *Essays on the Ancient Near East*, 177.

90. See *UNP*, 205 n. 7, suggesting possible haplography and noting the form with final *-n* in line 22.

91. Cf. *DULAT*, 110, 241; Manfried Dietrich, "Der Brief des Kommandeurs Šumiyanu an den ugaritischen König Niqmepaʿ (RS 20.33): Ein Bericht über Aktivitäten nach der

Schlacht bei Qadeš 1275 v. Chr.," *UF* 33 (2001) 145. The parallelism may suggest a place (cf. the four terms beginning in such poetic parallelism in KTU 1.3 III 30-31; cf. 1.3 IV 20).

92. The expression in 1.22 I 25 *b'irt lbnn* = *i-na i-ir-ti* ḫuršan*li-ib-la-ni* in *Ugaritica V*, p. 71, RS 20.033.19. See Dietrich, "Der Brief des Kommandeurs Šumiyanu," 128, 145. *DULAT*, 110, 241 suggests "slope." As *DULAT* notes, the same word is used in the bodily idiom in KTU 1.6 III 19 = 1.17 II 13. The word refers also to the body in 1.3 III 5/1.101.17; 1.4 V 5; 1.18 I 19. Cf. the unclear instance in 1.5 V 25. "Slope" may represent an overly specific sense.

93. Pardee, "Nouvelle étude épigraphique et littéraire," 44, 49-51.

94. Horwitz ("The Significance of the Rephaim," 39) comments: "I think that the *rp'm* were the soldiers of Baal and Anat. The soldiers were not thought by the ancients to be part of the *rp'm;* the *rp'm* were thought to be soldiers. There were no *rp'm* who were not considered soldiers."

95. It is a common term for "warrior" in the Ugaritic texts. The preceding chapter discusses its usage in the story of Aqhat for Yatpan. For another military usage, see KTU 1.3 II 13-15, 20-22. For the word in this passage, see *UBC*, 2:155. For the word, see also Zorn, "LU.*PA-MA-ḪA-A*." For the semantic development of, "quick, agile" to "warrior," see Shelomo Morag, *Studies in Biblical Hebrew* (Jerusalem: Magnes, 1995) 158-60 (Heb.), noted in Rahmouni, *Divine Epithets in the Ugaritic Alphabetic Texts*, 220 n. 5.

96. *UBC*, 2:628 for further discussion.

97. For these lines, see Watson, *Lexical Studies in Ugaritic*, 18-21. For an emphasis on drinking at a feast compared with the eating, see also the drink in KTU 1.3 I 8-17 compared with the food service in lines 4-8 of the same column (*UNP*, 106).

98. I am grateful to P. Kyle McCarter for drawing my attention to this point in an unpublished paper presented to the Colloquium for Biblical Research.

99. Gilgamesh OB IM (Baghdad) 17-18/OB Ishchali rev. 38′, and SBV V:6. See Andrew R. George, *The Babylonian Gilgamesh Epic: Introduction, Critical Edition, and Cuneiform Texts* (2 vols.; Oxford: Oxford University Press, 2003) 1:264-65, 268-69, 602-3, and 2.822 n. 6.

100. So Lewis, *UNP*, 201.

101. The same line appears in a fuller form below at the third tablet, back, lines 9-10 (= KTU 1.22 I 9-10). See the discussion there.

102. Cf. Pardee's reading of *prsǵ* (with the last letter in partial brackets). The word *prs* is thought to refer to a measure. See Huehnergard, *Ugaritic Vocabulary in Syllabic Transcription*, 62, 169. The instances of the root listed in *DULAT*, 682 are regarded as signifying "dry measure." If the word more generally refers to "measure," then perhaps the context involves some expression for "measure" with respect to a description of the "oil" here.

103. For the reconstruction, see the parallels in KTU 1.2 III 18 (*UNP*, 96) and 1.6 VI 28 (*UNP*, 163).

104. The letter is emended from *z* to *ḫ* based on parallels.

105. For the reconstruction, see the parallels in KTU 1.2 IV 13 (*UNP*, 103) and 20 (*UNP*, 104).

106. For the archaeological evidence for this type of ritual at Ugarit as well as other Syrian sites, see Herbert Niehr, "The Royal Funeral in Ancient Syria: A Comparative View on the Tombs in the Palaces of Qatna, Kumidi and Ugarit," *JNSL* 32 (2006) 1-24.

107. This presentation of the text relies on the following works. Readings are based on Bordreuil and Pardee, *A Manual of Ugaritic,* 215-18, which also provides a vocalization and notes. The volume also comes with a CD with images of the tablet. The readings with partial brackets by Bordreuil and Pardee are not included here. For the text with translation, see also Pardee, *RCU,* 85-88; "Poetry in Ugaritic Ritual Texts," in *Verse in Ancient Near Eastern Prose,* ed. Johannes C. de Moor and Wilfred G. E. Watson (AOAT 42; Kevelaer: Butzon & Bercker; Neukirchen-Vluyn: Neukirchener, 1993) 208-10. For the poetic divisions, see also Pardee, "Poetry in Ugaritic Ritual Texts," 208-10. Issues of interpretation have been reviewed in some detail in Lewis, *Cults of the Dead,* 5-46; Pierre Bordreuil and Dennis Pardee, "Les textes en cunéiformes alphabétiques," in Bordreuil, *Une bibliothèque au sud de la ville: Les textes de la 34e campagne (1973)* (RSO 7; Paris: Éditions Recherche sur les Civilisations, 1991) 151-63; David T. Tsumura, "The Interpretation of the Ugaritic Funerary Text KTU 1.161," in *Official Cult and Popular Religion in the Ancient Near East: Papers of the First Colloquium on the Ancient Near East — The City and Its Life, Held at the Middle Eastern Culture Center in Japan (Mitaka, Tokyo) March 20-22 1992,* ed. Eiko Matsushima (Heidelberg: Winter, 1993) 40-55. Cf. Brian B. Schmidt, *Israel's Beneficent Dead: Ancestor Cult and Necromancy in Ancient Israelite Religion and Tradition* (FAT 11; Tübingen: Mohr [Siebeck], 1994) 100-20; and the review of Mark S. Smith in *CBQ* 58 (1996) 724-25. For bibliog., see also Bordreuil and Pardee, "Les textes en cunéiformes alphabétiques," 152; Pardee, "Poetry in Ugaritic Ritual Texts," 208-10; Schmidt, *Israel's Beneficent Dead,* 100-20; Matthew Suriano, "Dynasty Building at Ugarit: The Ritual and Political Context of KTU 1.161/Construcción de la Dinastía en Ugarit: El contexto ritual y político de KTU 1.161," *AuOr* 27 (2009) 105-23; Hays, *Death in the Iron Age II,* 108-10.

108. For the use of the root for the dead, see 1 Sam. 28:15. These prefix indicative verb forms as "performative perfects" (see Lewis, *Cults of the Dead,* 13; *RCU,* 113 n. 124; and see below) make good sense for ritual performance. For the verbs, see Bordreuil and Pardee, *A Manual of Ugaritic,* 215; cf. Baruch A. Levine and Jean-Michel de Tarragon, "Dead Kings and Rephaim: The Patrons of the Ugaritic Dynasty," *JAOS* 104 (1984) 652 (and n. 12). It is important to emphasize the performative character of these passive verb forms (excepting line 8), which themselves enact the ritual performance of what they communicate, as noted by Lewis, *Cults of the Dead,* 13. Thus they are to be rendered not so much as past progressive ("X have/has been called" and the like in Bordreuil and Pardee), but in the present.

109. According to Bordreuil and Pardee (*A Manual of Ugaritic,* 29), "there is no separate case for the vocative." The form *rp'i* in this line suggests that whatever case ending is used, it is not the nominative. The vocative in Ugaritic perhaps could take the accusative as in Arabic. One form that poses problems for reconstructing the accusative as the ending for the vocative is *ks'i* in line 13, which also has been thought to reflect loss of final ending (hence **ks'i'a*); see *UG,* 306-7, par. 54.121.2, and 313-17, and par. 54.21; J. G. Taylor, "A Long-Awaited Vocative Singular Noun with Final Aleph in Ugaritic (KTU 1.161.13)?" *UF* 17 (1986) 315-18; E. L. Greenstein, Review of D. Sivan, *A Grammar of the Ugaritic Languge, IOS* 18 (1998) 397-420, esp. 414.

110. For the meaning "summon," see *DULAT,* 690 with respect to *qb'at* in 1.6 VI 40. *DULAT* translates the verb here by "invoke," which works well in this context. Cf.

Akkadian *qabû*, "to tell, say" (*CAD*, Q:23, #1), but also "to mention the name" (*CAD*, Q:26, #1d, 2′, *šuma qabû*); cf. the epistolary use of *qabû* common in the Akkadian letters of Ugarit. Note the discussion in Lewis, *Cults of the Dead*, 14-15, who draws attention to the connotation of mourning for the Akkadian word.

111. The singular verbal ending suggests a double name here (see Lewis, *Cults of the Dead*, 18). Is this pairing here due to the similarity of the names?

112. Bordreuil and Pardee (*A Manual of Ugarit*, 215) translate "(they) in turn have called . . . ," which sounds as if they understand the prior named Rephaim as in turn calling the Ancient Rephaim. However, since they seem to belong to the Ancient Rephaim, the verbal form may be an impersonal third person plural.

113. For this transitive sense in the *G*-stem, see Gen. 37:35. The translations of Lewis (*Cults of the Dead*, 8) and Levine and de Tarragon ("Dead Kings and Rephaim," 650) have the furniture weeping and shedding tears in lines 13-16.

114. Bordreuil and Pardee (*A Manual of Ugarit*, 215) translate "over," but some sort of preposition would be required, as opposed to the adverbial accusative, as translated here.

115. See the intelligent consideration of the syntax in Holger Gzella, "Some Pencilled Notes on Ugaritic Lexicography," *BO* 64 (2007) 559. Lines 13 and 15 are parallel here, as are lines 14 and 16, and they are amplified by line 17.

116. So a number of writers comparing Arabic *ʿadima*, "to be wanting, lacking, needy, destitute." W. W. Hallo (personal communication) has suggested the possibility of a threefold repetition of *ʿdmt*, "how long?" Hallo compares BH *ʿad-mātay* and Akkadian *adi mati*, used in lament literature (for the Akkadian expression, see *CAD*, A/1:119a).

117. For the problem of the verbal root involved, see Lewis, *Cults of the Dead*, 22-23. The second sense, "go down" (Lewis, p. 8), seems to stretch the semantic field of the word compared with its putative cognates. For the root, see Moshe Held, "Pits and Pitfalls in Akkadian and Biblical Hebrew," *JANES* 5 (T. H. Gaster Festschrift; 1973) 173-90.

118. The expression may be appositional given the different gender of the two words, as translated here following Bordreuil and Pardee, *A Manual of Ugaritic*, 217; and Rahmouni, *Divine Epithets in the Ugaritic Alphabetic Texts*, 242-45 (noting the usage also in 1.16 I 37-38). For discussion of the sun's title in Gen. 1:14, see Mark S. Smith, *The Priestly Vision of Genesis 1* (Minneapolis: Fortress, 2009) 94 and 256 n. 44.

119. A singular may be involved; if so, it would refer, in my mind, to Niqmaddu.

120. Grammatically, "to" is another feasible interpretation, but the funerary ritual calls for descent from the throne and probably not to a throne located in the underworld, nor is the throne invoked here. See Lewis, *Cults of the Dead*, 13; J. G. Taylor, "A First and Last Thing to Do in Mourning: *KTU* 1.161 and Some Parallels," in *Ascribe to the Lord: Biblical & Other Essays in Memory of Peter C. Craigie*, ed. Lyle Eslinger and Glen Taylor (JSOTSup 67; Sheffield: JSOT, 1988) 153; Manfried Dietrich and Oswald Loretz, "Grabbeigaben für verstorbenen König: Bemerkungen zur Neuausgabe von RS 34.126 = KTU 1.161," *UF* 23 (1991) 106.

121. Pardee ("Poetry in Ugaritic Ritual Texts," 209) reads *ksh* and suggests that the reading should be *ksʾi*. Or is the reading perhaps *ks⟨ʾi⟩h* if **bʿl* here is singular? One can read that the figures named in the following lines point to a plural here, but I am more

inclined to see a distinction being made between the one recently deceased king after whom the new king is to descend and the other figures.

122. The preposition could mean "among" (cf. *tḥt 'adrm*, "among the chiefs," in 1.17 V 6-7; *UNP*, 58), and in that sense, "with." Dietrich and Loretz ("Grabbeigaben für verstorbenen König," 106): "zusammen mit." Lewis (*Cults of the Dead*, 9) suggests "down to." Pardee argues instead that "beneath" may be literally the case: the dead king may have been ritually lowered seven times into the deep shaft located between the two large tombs in the royal palace. Thus the dead king would be "beneath" his deceased ancestors. See Pardee, "*Marziḥu, Kispu,* and the Ugaritic Funerary Cult," 274. Even in this explanation, it is unclear that the deceased king would be "beneath" his ancestors as such. In this archaeological reconstruction, they would go "down to," as suggested by Lewis's translation.

123. Reading with Pardee ("Poetry in Ugaritic Ritual Texts," 209) for *tḥm*.

124. I have rendered the lines in this section rather literally. Bordreuil and Pardee (*A Manual of Ugarit*, 216) translate what I have taken as a noun as verbs, which is possible as well and which is certainly the point. The syntax appears to conform to what Joshua Blau regards as a "sentence adverbial" demarcated from the rest of the clause that it modifies by the particle *w*. See Blau, *An Adverbial Construction in Hebrew and Arabic: Sentence Adverbials in Frontal Position Separated from the Rest of the Sentence* (Israel Academy of Sciences and Humanities Proceedings 6/1; Jerusalem: Israel Academy of Sciences and Humanities, 1977).

125. It would be possible to take the first instance of *šlm* here with the previous line in the meaning of "peace-offering" (in which case the word for "bird" could be singular or plural). However, the word with the meaning "peace-offering" is usually spelled *šlmm*. So it seems preferable to take the first word here with this line. Given the structure of lines 32-34, however, one might suspect a dittography. It is true that if both instances of the word in line 32 are to be read, and if the first were to be read with the preceding line as suggested by Bordreuil and Pardee, the lines would be more balanced in terms of length.

126. The use of *šlm* here may be understood as a wish for blessing in the form of a nominal clause. Cf. *šlm* in 1.123.1-3, taken as "Hail" plus DN in the vocative (so Gregorio del Olmo Lete, *Canaanite Religion according to the Liturgical Texts of Ugarit*, trans. Wilfred G. E. Watson [Bethesda: CDL, 1999] 343; cf. *RCU*, 151, "give well-being").

127. For *b'at*, Pardee ("Poetry in Ugaritic Ritual Texts," 210) reads as another possibility *bnh*, "her/his sons." See also Bordreuil and Pardee, *A Manual of Ugaritic*, 217. Parallelism favors Pardee's rendering here.

128. Others are less confident as to the reading of the final letter, which Pardee marks with partial brackets. As a result, Lewis (*Cults of the Dead*, 10) offers this possibility as well as an alternative, *['a]ry[h]*, "his kinsmen."

129. The genitive here expresses, according to Bordreuil and Pardee (*A Manual of Ugaritic*, 217), "for" the shades.

130. The various options are listed in Tsumura, "The Interpretation of the Ugaritic Funerary Text," 53-54. For the common translation "shades," see Lewis, *Cult of the Dead*, 11. The sense of shades for this word may not include the English usage of "shades" for the dead. For the further sense often proposed, "protectors," see Wayne T. Pitard, "The Ugaritic Funerary Text RS 34.126," *BASOR* 232 (1978) 65-75, here 68; Levine and de Tarragon,

"Dead Kings and Rephaim," 651; and Hays, *Death in the Iron Age II*, 109 n. 86. Lewis objects that if this were the meaning, then the Ugaritic form would be *ẓllm*. However, some geminate plurals do not show the final radical, e.g., *hrm*, "mountains," in KTU 1.107.32, 44 (*DULAT*, 345); for further examples, see Sivan, *A Grammar of the Ugaritic Language*, 65, 66. For the word in Akkadian PNs, see Joseph Martin Pagan, *A Morphological and Lexical Study of Personal Names in the Ebla Texts* (ARES 3; Rome: Missione Archeologica Italiana in Siria, 1998) 200.

131. Cf. the plural construct form presumably in 1.91.2, assuming that lines 3-20 of this text involve a list of sacrificial rituals (e.g., del Olmo Lete, *Canaanite Religion*, 257).

132. For the text, see J. J. Finkelstein, "The Genealogy of the Hammurapi Dynasty," *JCS* 20 (1966) 95-118. For discussion, see Lewis, *Cult of the Dead*, 16; Hays, *Death in the Iron Age II*, 109. As noted generally by scholars, the noun evidently means "bison, auroch" (related to Akkadian *tidānu*; see *CAD*, D:164-65). See Franz A. M. Wiggerman, *Babylonian Prophylactic Figures: The Ritual Texts* (Amsterdam: Free University Press, 1986) 303; Piotr Steinkeller, "Early Semitic Literature and Third Millennium Seals with Mythological Motifs," in *Literature and Literary Language at Ebla*, ed. Pelio Fronzaroli (Quaderni di Semitistica 18; Florence: Dipartimento di Linguistica, Università di Firenze, 1992) 261-63.

133. The text here is based on the two occurrences of the tricolon, each of which is missing some material that is extant in the other.

134. John F. Healey, "The Rephaites of Ancient Palestine and Ugarit," in *Studies in the History and Archaeology of Palestine II*, ed. Shawqi Sha'ath, Proceedings of the First International Symposium on Palestine Antiquities (Damascus: Aleppo University/Palestine Archaeological Centre, 1986) 159-63, here 161.

135. For a convenient presentation, see *RCU*, 170-72. Cf.]*ddn* in KTU 1.170.2. See also the PN *bn ddn* in KTU 4.760.5 and the PN *bn dtn* in KTU 4.69 II 9 (?); VI 29, and RS 94.2090.35′ in Bordreuil and Pardee, *BSV*, 72.

136. *RCU*, 171. See also Frank Moore Cross, "Inscriptions in Phoenician and Other Scripts," in *Ashkelon 1: Introduction and Overview (1985-2006)*, ed. Lawrence E. Stager, J. David Schloen, and Daniel M. Master (Final reports of the Leon Levy Expedition to Ashkelon 1; Winona Lake: Eisenbrauns, 2008) 357. To the evidence, Cross adds a fifth-century–early fourth-century inscription of *dtyn* attested on an Attic black-glaced kylix from Ashkelon.

137. Bordreuil and Pardee, *BSV*, 103.

138. The title is used not only for the god El in the literary texts, but also for a human in an administrative text, in KTU 4.360.3. See J. David Schloen, *The House of the Father as Fact and Symbol: Patrimonialism in Ugarit and the Ancient Near East* (Studies in the Archaeology and History of the Levant 2; Winona Lake: Eisenbrauns, 2001) 327; and Mark S. Smith, *The Origins of Biblical Monotheism: Israel's Polytheistic Background and the Ugaritic Texts* (Oxford: Oxford University Press, 2001) 58-59. See also the PN *'ilṯr* in KTU 4.607.32 and RS 94.5002 + 94.5018 + 96.2018 + 96.2020.27 and RS 94.2050 + RS 94.2092.45 (Bordreuil and Pardee, *BSV*, 24, 45).

139. Note the same form in KTU 1.1 IV 5. It is perhaps a title of El: "El sits in [his] ma[rzeah (?)] . . ./The shame of the Eternal One (?). . . ."

140. For the evidence for divinized kings, see Pardee, *RCU*, 195-204. The *mlkm* in the

deities lists (slot 33 in *RCU,* 15 and 16) also comport with the divinized, deceased kings. Note Huehnergard, *Ugaritic Vocabulary in Syllabic Transcription,* 147.

141. See Pope, "Notes on the Rephaim Texts from Ugarit," 177.

142. Wayne Pitard, "RS 34.126: Notes on the Text," *Maarav* 4 (1987) 75-86; Levine and de Tarragon, "Dead Kings and Rephaim," 652; Sivan, *A Grammar of the Ugaritic Language,* 114, 120.

143. Lewis, *Cults of the Dead,* 7-8; Pardee, "Poetry in Ugaritic Ritual Texts," 208-9.

144. See *UT,* 9.31; David Marcus, "The Qal Passive in Ugaritic," *JANES* 3 (1970) 102-11; Sivan, *A Grammar of the Ugaritic Language,* 126-28. For the G-stem passive in West Semitic languages, see also Ronald J. Williams, "The Passive *qal* Theme in Hebrew," in *Essays on the Ancient Semitic World,* ed. John W. Wevers and Donald B. Redford; Toronto: University of Toronto Press, 1970) 43-50.

145. Bordreuil and Pardee, *A Manual of Ugaritic,* 215. See also Sivan, *A Grammar of the Ugaritic Language,* 111.

146. According to Bordreuil and Pardee (*A Manual of Ugaritic,* 217), the Niqmaddu named in lines 12 and 26 is one of the ancestors of the king who has just died, also named Niqmaddu. It seems to make as much sense (and enjoys more economy) to regard the Niqmaddu named in lines 12, 13, 26 as the recently deceased monarch and not to distinguish two Niqmaddus here.

147. As many of the scholars who have worked on this text have observed, Isa. 14:9 preserves another reflex of the Rephaim as the dead kings of old; these have furniture in the underworld: "Sheol beneath is stirred up/To meet you when you come; it rouses the Rephaim to greet you,/all who were leaders of the earth. It raises from their thrones/all who were kings of the nations." Thrones are, in a sense, the tools or "extra-somatic body parts" for monarchs. For this notion, see Fernando Santos-Granero, "Introduction," in *The Occult Life of Things: Native Amazonian Theories of Materiality and Personhood* (Tucson: University of Arizona Press, 2009) 14.

148. Pardee, "Epigraphic and Philological Notes," *UF* 19 (1987) 211-16.

149. Levine and de Tarragon call the three words "a rare triplication"; "Dead Kings and Rephaim," 652. On this possibility for Isa. 6:3, I am indebted to Professor Levine. See also threefold repetitions in Jer. 7:4; 22:29.

150. So Lewis, *Cults of the Dead,* 43. Given the implicit command to ʿAmmurapi in the preceding section, that he is to lament for the dead king, I am inclined to see ʿAmmurapi as the addressee in this section as well. The parallel wording with other texts noted below also militates in favor of this view. A third possibility, namely the royal furniture, is contextually plausible, but the parallel wording noted below would militate against this view. For a thorough, critical review, see Tsumura, "The Interpretation of the Ugaritic Funerary Text," esp. 45-52. As this discussion indicates, no view is without difficulty.

151. So Bordreuil and Pardee, "Les textes en cunéiformes alphabétiques," 158.

152. Unless the forms are taken as denominative verbs, with Lewis, *Cults of the Dead,* 9, 26-27; and apparently Pardee, "Poetry in Ugaritic Ritual Texts," 209.

153. See R. David Freedman, "Counting Formulas in Akkadian Epics," *JANES* 3 (1970-71) 65-81.

154. So Lewis, *Cults of the Dead,* 27.

155. *UT* 19.2715; Jean-Michel de Tarragon, *Le culte à Ugarit d'après les textes de la pratique en cunéiformes alphabétiques* (CahRB 19; Paris: Gabalda, 1980) 58, 75 n. 11.

156. Shedletsky (Monroe) and Levine, "The *mšr* of the Sons and Daughters of Ugarit," *RB* 106 (1999) 334-35.

157. The queen here has been understood to be the king's mother, since some documents involving this queen predate ʿAmmurapi. See Jacques Freu, "La fin d'Ugarit et l'empire hittite: Données nouvelles et chronologie," *Sem* 48 (1999) 27; and Singer, "A Political History of Ugarit," 690-91, 696-700 (as noted in *RCU*, 113 n. 122). The importance of queen mothers and their roles have been emphasized in the secondary literature. See Niels-Eric A. Andreasen, "The Role of the Queen Mother in Israelite Society," *CBQ* 45 (1983) 179-94; Cyrus H. Gordon, "Ugaritic *rbt/rabītu*," in Eslinger and Taylor, *Ascribe to the Lord*, 127-32; Susan Ackerman, "The Queen Mother and the Cult in Ancient Israel," *JBL* 112 (1993) 385-401; Hennie J. Marsman, *Women at Ugarit and Israel: Their Social and Religious Position in the Context of the Ancient Near East* (OtSt 49; Leiden: Brill, 2003) 345-70. See the cautions for the biblical evidence made by Zafrira Ben-Barak, "The Status and Right of the *Gĕbîrâ*," *JBL* 110 (1991) 23-34. To be sure, the reference to mothers of kings in Judah, esp. in the formulary notices about kings in 1-2 Kings, is suggestive of queen mothers.

Ugaritic literature shows the role of the mother who is queen (and not queen mother) in the royal family structure. This gender distinction underlies the social terms named in the extant opening lines of Kirta: "The house of a king perished,/one with seven brothers,/the eight sons of a mother" (KTU 1.14 I 7-9, *UNP*, 12). The same distinction appears in the mythic usage in KTU 1.6 VI 11, 15 (*UNP*, 162). The role of the so-called queen who is mother (not queen mother) also informs KTU 1.6 I (*UNP*, 153-54). In this passage, Athirat selects two possible successors among sons within her household, but they fail to become king. These passages suggest the importance of the gender-marked households that the royal mothers head. The prominence of the queen's household may also inform the many letters between royal son and mother: KTU 2.11.1; 2.13.2, 5, 6, 11; 2.16.2, 6, 18; 2.30.1, 4, 5, 9, 21; 2.34.2, 6, 8; 2.72.1, 2, 5, 15, 31, 33; 2.80.1; see Singer, "A Political History of Ugarit," 696-700. This *topos* of epistolary usage is apparently so common that it appears in a scribal practice text, KTU 5.10.3. In short, the household of the queen (not queen mother) is attested. The "house(hold) of the queen" would also fit the importance accorded royal wives in Akkadian political texts from Ugarit, presently the subject of a Harvard University dissertation in preparation by Christine Thomas Freedberg, who made a presentation at the 2011 meeting of the American Schools of Oriental Research under the title "Women on the Verge of the Hittite Empire: Circulating Imperial Subjects at Ugarit." As a possibly related feature, Caroline Sauvage drew attention to queens exchanging gifts in EA 48 and RS 34.154, in her lecture at the 2011 meeting of the American Schools of Oriental Research, entitled "Ugarit and Crete in the 13th c. B.C.E.: Exploring the Possibilities of Direct Diplomatic Relationships." The house of Queen Addu-dûri of Mari is known from a number of texts (see ARM XXI 112 12; XXIV 6 38′, 40′; XII 141 and 146 as 242; cf. XXV 382; and XII 141 15, 146 4-5, 242 3; XI 68 6-7; references courtesy of Julie Deluty).

This broader context seems to suggest the importance of the royal mother (whether queen or queen mother), within the larger context of the royal establishment as headed by the king. In this context, the queen may be understood as heading a household within the king's household, whether she is the queen or queen mother. In this context, we may note the biblical expression "house of (the/my) mother"; see Gen. 24:28; Ruth 1:8; Song 3:4; 8:2. Commentators have suggested that the phrase "house of the mother" points to the mother's household or quarters (presumably within the larger household of the father). See Dom Calmet, cited in Marvin H. Pope, *Song of Songs* (AB 7C; Garden City: Doubleday, 1977) 421. For this approach studied in considerable depth (and with recent bibliog.), see Cynthia Ruth Chapman, "The House of the Mother and the Brokering of Marriage in the Bible: Economic Reciprocity Among Natal Siblings," in *In the Wake of Tikva Frymer-Kensky*, ed. Steven Holloway, JoAnn Scurlock, and Richard Beal (Piscataway: Gorgias, 2009) 143-70. I thank Professor Chapman for sharing her work with me on this subject, which has been an immense help to me in thinking about the gender expression in KTU 1.161.31-33.

The gender distinction in 1.161.31-33 has been discussed in relation to the marked gender-division in the collective ritual of KTU 1.40 and its parallel texts by Shedletsky (Monroe) and Levine, "The *mšr* of the Sons and Daughters of Ugarit"; see also *RCU*, 77-83, esp. 78. It contains six sections, the first, third, and fifth of which are addressed collectively to males ("son") and the second, fourth, and sixth addressed collectively to females ("daughter"). While such a representation of "sons" has good parallels (e.g., RS 17.238; PRU IV, 107-8), it has been noted that there is no such parallel referencing for "daughters," according to Shedletsky (Monroe) and Levine, p. 335. That these singular family terms in KTU 1.40 serve as collectives for "sons" and "daughters" is evident from the plural pronouns *-km* (lines 30, 31, 32) and *-kn* (lines 21, 22, and lines 38, 39, 40), respectively. In the extant text, sections 3-4 and 5-6 involve a different animal: *š* for sections 3 and 4 in lines 17 and 25 and *ʿr* for sections 5 and 6 in lines 34 and 43; a third animal would be expected for the missing corresponding lines in sections 1-2. The correspondence between each of the three pairs of sections may be signaled bv *wṯb lmspr*, as seen at the head of section 6 in line 35 (with the same perhaps having headed the now missing beginnings of sections 2 and 4), to mark a return to the beginning of the ritual as paralleled by the sections addressed to males in sections 1, 3, and 5. Considering together the final section of KTU 1.161 and the ritual of 1.40, it might be thought that the house of the king and the house of the queen in 1.161 align with the collective gender division in 1.40. In other words, the households of the king and queen in 1.161 are the national symbolic embodiments of the social gender divide as marked in 1.40. The further question of whether the verb forms in 1.40 with prefixed *n-* are *N*-stem (third masculine sg.) or first person plural *G*-stem remains *sub iudice*. The latter is hardly impossible; note the comparison of these Ugaritic verbal forms with first person plural in ritual from Ebla by Pelio Franzaroli, "The Ritual Texts of Ebla," in *Literature and Literary Language at Ebla* (Quaderni di Semitistica 18; Florence: Dipartimento di Linguistica, Università di Firenze, 1992) 185. At the same time, it is to be noted that Ugaritic ritual lacks first person plural forms (that are not in quoted speech such as prayer; see KTU 1.119.28-34; *RCU*, 53). If they are first person plural forms, an overarching collective identity linking both sets of collective genders would be expressed in all sections.

It is not clear that the gender-marked expression "a woman/women may eat of it" *(wtlḥm 'aṯt)* in 1.115.8 (*RCU*, 66) refers to the queen in contrast to the king named in 1.115.1, as argued by Shedletsky and Levine, "The *mšr* of the Sons and Daughters of Ugarit," 334; and Levine, *In the Presence of the Lord: A Study of Cult and Some Cultic Terms in Ancient Israel* (SJLA 5; Leiden: Brill, 1974) 10 n. 21. In context, this interpretation makes sense, but that statement in 1.115.8 would appear to compare with the statement two lines later, *kl l ylḥm bh*, taken by them as "He (= the king) partakes of it fully." However, this latter line may be understood as "all may eat of it" (so *RCU*, 66), in accordance with *kl ykly*, "all will (or may) eat," in KTU 1.127.8 (*RCU*, 130).

158. *RCU*, 86.

159. Cf. *RCU* 1: "It can be said in general that texts prescribing or describing the rituals that are performed in honor of the divine are in prose, while those that deal primarily or entirely with the acts of the gods are in poetry."

160. See *RCU*, 50-53, 149-50. See also Pardee's comment on 1.119.26-36 (*RCU*, 149): "This is one of the rare examples of a text formally addressed to humans that is in poetry, apparently because the long embedded text, the prayer itself, is addressed to a deity."

161. For reflections on Homeric epic in this vein, see Egbert J. Bakker, "Storytelling in the Future: Truth, Time, and Tense in the Homeric Epic," in *Written Voices, Spoken Signs: Tradition, Performance, and the Epic Text*, ed. Bakker and Ahuvia Kahane (Cambridge, MA: Harvard University Press, 1997) 11-36, esp. 13-17. I will suggest a similar point for the biblical material examined in Part IV. The first person voice of old heroic poetry in the Bible brings the audience(s) into the description of the past (relative to this voice) mediated through its present expression, as will be seen in Chapters Nine and Ten. Similarly, the old heroic poems examined in these chapters point to multiple levels of tradition and composition, thus serving as examples of what Gregory Nagy calls "recomposition-in-performance"; "Ellipsis in Homer," in Bakker and Kahane, *Written Voices, Spoken Signs*, 177.

Notes to Chapter Six

1. For the first four tablets of the Baal Cycle, see the commentaries *UBC* 1 and *UBC* 2 (the third volume covering the fifth and sixth tablets is in process); cf. Baruch Margalit, *A Matter of "Life" and "Death": A Study of the Baal-Mot Epic (CAT 4-5-6)* (AOAT 206; Kevelaer: Butzon & Bercker; Neukirchen-Vluyn: Neukirchener 1980). See also the recent discussions of the Baal Cycle in Dennis Pardee, *The Ugaritic Texts and the Origins of West-Semitic Literary Composition* (Schweich Lectures 2007; Oxford: Oxford University Press, 2012) 50-77; and Aaron Tugendhaft, "Baal and the Problem of Politics in the Bronze Age" (Ph.D. diss., New York University, 2012) 122-246. Note also the older studies: J. C. de Moor, *The Seasonal Pattern in the Ugaritic Myth of Baʿlu: According to the Version of Ilimilku* (AOAT 16; Kevelaer: Butzon & Bercker; Neukirchen-Vluyn: Neukirchener, 1971); Petrus J. van Zijl, *Baal: A Study of Texts in Connexion with Baal in the Ugaritic Epics* (AOAT 10; Kevelaer: Verlag Butzon & Bercker; Neukirchen-Vluyn: Neukirchener, 1972). See further below.

2. See, e.g., the attendants of Baal in KTU 1.5 V 6-9, in *UNP,* 147. For discussion, see Mark S. Smith, *The Origins of Biblical Monotheism: Israel's Polytheistic Background and the Ugaritic Texts* (Oxford: Oxford University Press, 2001) 67-68.

3. For the text, translation, and discussion of this passage with photographs, see *UBC,* 1:318-61 and pls. 42-47.

4. This incantational view of Kothar's words here goes back to Julius Obermann, "How Baal Destroyed a Rival: A Magical Incantation Scene," *JAOS* 67 (1947) 195-208; see *UBC,* 1:341-42. For further discussion and evidence, see *UBC,* 1:341-42. This passage calls to mind the *Kultmittelgebete,* Mesopotamian ritual incantations that are intended to pass onto the person or object being praised those powers needed for effective functioning. These incantations seek to summon a certain power in the object and to transmit that efficacy to the object of the spell. See Tzvi Abusch, "Blessing and Praise in Ancient Mesopotamian Incantations," in *Literatur, Politik und Recht in Mesopotamien: Festschrift für Claus Wilcke* (ed. Walther Sallaberger, Konrad Volk and Annette Zgoll; Orientalia Biblica et Christiana 14; Wiesbaden: Harrassowitz, 2003) 1-14. For this information on the *Kultmittelgebete,* I wish to thank my student, Julie Deluty.

5. See below for discussion.

6. See Thorkild Jacobsen, *The Harps That Once . . . : Sumerian Poetry in Translation* (New Haven: Yale University Press, 1987) 242-44.

7. For more details, see the treatment of this passage in Chapter Nine.

8. The order of KTU 1.2 I before 1.2 IV has been questioned by Dennis Pardee, "RS 3.367, Colonne 'IV': étude épigraphique suivie de quelques remarques philologiques," in *"He unfurrowed his brow and laughed": Essays in Honour of Professor Nicolas Wyatt,* ed. Wilfred G. E. Watson (AOAT 299; Münster: Ugarit-Verlag, 2007) 227 n. 1; the argument is based on the tablet's curvature. See also the discussion of the question in Tugendhaft, "Baal and the Problem of Politics," 135-38. The issue does not affect the discussion here.

9. See *UBC,* 1:259-316 for this passage.

10. Following KTU, *DULAT,* 126 reads *qmm 'aṯr 'amr* and translates "standing they transmitted (their) demand." See also Pardee, *The Ugaritic Texts,* 54. *DULAT* takes **'ṯr* here as *D*-stem. Apart from the question of this reading (see *UBC,* 1:288-89), the *D*-stem of this root is otherwise unattested, and it seems questionable whether the *G*-stem "to be behind" in the *D*-stem would have the meaning "to transmit" (from "to cause to be behind").

11. See below for further discussion of the possible warrior background of this passage.

12. Joshua Berman, "The 'Sword of Mouths' (Jud. III 16; Ps. CXLIX 6; Prov. V 4): A Metaphor and Its Ancient Near Eastern Context," *VT* 52 (192) 291-303. Berman cites C. F. A. Schaeffer, *Ugaritica 1* (MRS 3; Paris: Geuthner, 1939) 111, fig. 102 and 118, fig. 107.

13. Marguerite Yon, *The City of Ugarit at Tell Ras Shamra* (Winona Lake: Eisenbrauns, 2006) 167, #60.

14. For further discussion, see Aldina Da Silva, "A Comparison between the Avenging Angel of 1 Ch 21 and Analogous 'Angel-like' figures in the Ugaritic Ba'al Cycle," *Journal for Semitics/Tydskrif vir Semitistiek* 6 (1994) 154-69.

15. See *UBC*, 2:687-89, with discussion of recent literature on the subject. See Chapter Four for a discussion of the term.

16. So BDB, 184, comparing Arabic *dabar*, "back," and *dabr*, "part behind."

17. The view is a longstanding one in Ugaritic studies; see J. C. L. Gibson, *Canaanite Myths and Legends* (2nd ed.; Edinburgh: T. & T. Clark, 1978) 73 n. 4.

18. Pardee (*COS*, 1:267 n. 234) sees no antiphrastic sense here.

19. Marvin H. Pope, *Song of Songs* (AB 7C; Garden City: Doubleday, 1977) 425.

20. *DULAT*, 812, "Mortality shore," citing Arab, *sāḥilu mamātin;* Lane, 1320 and 2741.

21. Cf. the same words in 1.16 II 3-4.

22. See also the description of Baal's "fall" (**npl*) in 1.12 II 53-55. The context is unclear.

23. The root **ḫlq* appears also in Aqhat (1.18 IV 42), but the usage is unclear; it may refer to the birds mentioned in the preceding, clear lines. Less likely it could refer to Aqhat.

24. See the discussion of usage of **npl* in the lament of 2 Sam. 1:19, 25, 27 in Chapter Ten. Cf. Ps. 20:9(8).

25. For the same formula, see 1.23.61-62. See *COS*, 1:266 for a proposal to reconstruct a verb in the lacuna here.

26. See the image of the *npš* of Sheol in Isa. 5:14 (cf. the image of bones being scattered at the mouth of Sheol in Ps. 141:7).

27. See also Mot's *npš* described in KTU 1.5 I 14-16: "Is my appetite the appetite of the lion in the wild, or the desire of the dolphin in the sea?" (Smith, *UNP*, 142). The double-question here is rhetorical, to state that Mot's appetite surely is. For a different view of *thw* here, see Edward L. Greenstein, "Another Attestation of Initial *h* > ʾ in West Semitic," *JANES* 5 (T. H. Gaster Festschrift; 1973) 158-60. It is unclear how Greenstein's translation of *thw* as "live prey" relates to his claim that the root meaning is "desire, craving." In addition, the gloss "prey" seems to be a semantic stretch.

28. Note the mouth of the "earth" (underworld?) swallowing people alive in Num. 16:30-33; 26:10; Deut. 11:6. See also "the mouth of the Pit" in Ps. 69:15.

29. The form is the narrative infinitive. The larger sequence of verbs in this speech relating the past is interesting: a first person focus plus durative past prefix forms *('an ʾitlk wʾaṣd)* governing lines 15-17; a subject with first person suffix plus stative verb *(ḫsrt)* describing general conditions at the time in lines 17-19; a line-initial simple past action suffix verb *(mǵt)* governing lines 19-20; and a predicative infinitive with first person focus *(ngš ʾank)*, followed by an energic indicative *(ʿdbnn ʾank)* describing the dramatic final action of Mot's destruction of Baal in lines 21-23.

It is my view that the energic form here provides a dramatic quality (like the energic indicatives in 1.16 II 30-35), set off from a simple sequence of past actions marked commonly by **yqtl* indicative forms in initial position. For *ʿdbnn.ʾank* as first person (for *ʾʿ*dbnn*), see the older discussions of H. L. Ginsberg, "Baʿl and ʿAnat," *Or* 7 (1938) 8 n. to lines 32-33; and *UT*, 5.38. Cf. *ʿdbk* (evidently first person) in KTU 1.18 IV 22. See also Ronald J. Williams, "Energic Verbal Forms in Hebrew," in *Studies on the Ancient Palestinian World: Presented to Professor F. V. Winnett on the Occasion of His Retirement 1 July 1971*, ed. John W. Wevers and Donald B. Redford (Toronto: University of Toronto

Press, 1972) 75-85; Edward L. Greenstein, "On the Prefixed Preterite in Biblical Hebrew," *HS* 29 (1988) 12 n. 15; and Juliane Kutter, *nūr ilī: Die Sonnengottheiten in den nordwestsemitischen Religionen von der Spätbronzezeit bis zur vorrömischen Zeit* (AOAT 346; Münster: Ugarit-Verlag, 2008) 93 and 147-55. The alternative possibility is to see another predicative infinitive with energic suffix (by analogy with the prefix energic indicative).

30. The comparative particle *k*- is often reconstructed here in accordance with its attestation in 1.4 VIII 17 (Smith, *UNP,* 156); in the case of line 6 here, perhaps *k*- with *ll'i* in line 7 does duty also for *'imr* in this line.

31. The form of the pronoun marks it as the subject of the verb, not its object (which would require *hwt*). The verb form is a problem. *DULAT,* 413 would read an *N*-infinitive ⟨*n*⟩*ḫt'u* for *ḫt'u* here. Cf. *DULAT,* 413 on the parallel in 1.4 VIII 20: *k ll'i b ṯbrn qnh tḫt'an,* "like a sucking lamb in the opening of his esophagus you shall remain ground up." As this parallel line indicates, a form of **ḫt'* is to be read in KTU 1.6 II 23.

32. Cf. Smith, *UNP,* 162.

33. Martti Nissinen, *Prophets and Prophecy in the Ancient Near East* (SBLWAW 12; Atlanta: Society of Biblical Literature, 2003) 139.

34. For *endimma,* "come close to me," see *CAD,* E:139a, 3′, under *emēdu.* With Marduk addressing Tiamat, the verb is feminine, so the fem. sg. is *imdī* (the standard form of the G-imperative being *imid*), which here takes the simple *-m* for the ventive (direction toward the speaker). The *en-* writing seems to be some sort of accommodation to the following dental, when one might expect *iddī-*. The two volitive forms connected with *-ma* express purpose/result. The verb is interesting in that it envisions direct physical contact at the outset: "Lean on me so we can fight, I against you!" The pronouns are also odd. For *anāku u kâši,* see *CAD,* K:288: "emphatic use (as one of a pair of coordinated subjects and to stress suffixes, both dat. and acc., on verbs)." For the translation of most of the line, see *CAD,* Š/II:173, under *šašmu* ("battle, warfare"), rendering the line: "let us engage in battle, you and I." Benjamin Foster renders the line: "Come within range, let us duel, you and I"; *Before the Muses: An Anthology of Akkadian Literature* (3rd ed.; Bethesda: CDL, 2005) 460. Stephanie Dalley translates "Stand forth, and you and I shall do single combat"; *Myths from Mesopotamia: Creation, the Flood, Gilgamesh, and Others* (rev. ed.; Oxford: Oxford University Press, 2000) 253. See also David A. Bosworth, *The Story Within a Story in Biblical Hebrew Narrative* (CBQMS 45; Washington: Catholic Biblical Association of America, 2008) 88.

35. Hoffner, "A Hittite Analogue to the David and Goliath Contest of Champions?" *CBQ* 30 (1968) 220-25. For the topic, see also Roland de Vaux, "Single Combat in the Old Testament," in *The Bible and the Ancient Near East,* trans. Damian McHugh (Garden City: Doubleday, 1966) 122-35.

36. William F. Albright compared *'îš habbēnayim* in 1 Sam. 17:4, 23 as an "agent, representative, champion" with Ugaritic *bnš bnny* in KTU 2.33.34 as "a middleman, intermediary, agent"; "Specimens of Late Ugaritic Prose," *BASOR* 150 (1958) 38 n. 12. This reference was brought to my attention by Jeffrey Zorn, who has published his own study on the subject, "Reconsidering Goliath: An Iron Age I Philistine Chariot Warrior," *BASOR* 360 (2010) 1-22, esp. 16-17. Zorn takes the phrase in 1 Sam. 17:4, 23 to refer to the man "in between" in the chariot.

Ugaritic *bnny* is a hapax (J.-L. Cunchillos, J.-P. Vita, and J.-Á. Zamora, *A Concordance of Ugaritic Words* [Piscataway: Gorgias, 2003] 463). *DULAT*, 229 lists *bnny* and notes the meaning: "intermediary, neutral person." Following Albright, *DULAT* cites Mishnaic Hebrew *bynwny* (Jastrow, 163) and takes it from the preposition *bn*. See also Dennis Pardee, "Further Studies in Ugaritic Epistolography," *AfO* 31 (1984) 216 and 220 n. 32, where he mentions 1 Sam. 17:4, 23 and notes Jean Carmignac, "Précisions apportées au vocabulaire de l'hébreu biblique par la Guerre des fils de lumière contre le fils de ténèbres," *VT* 5 (1955) 354-57 for "Qumran attestations." Pardee translates lines 34-36: "may the king send an intermediary (?) to me with this messenger-party of mine." The speaker may be requesting a champion to be sent back with the speaker's messengers, which would fit the problem of the enemy at hand.

37. Millard, "The Armor of Goliath," in *Exploring the Longue Durée: Essays in Honor of Lawrence E. Stager*, ed. J. David Schloen (Winona Lake: Eisenbrauns, 2009) 339, citing the translation of Miriam Lichtheim, "Sinuhe," in *COS*, 1:79. For several of these comparisons of man-to-man combat, see also Serge Frolov and Allen Wright, "Homeric and Ancient Near Eastern Intertextuality in 1 Samuel 17," *JBL* 130 (2011) 451-71.

38. Jacobsen, *The Harps That Once . . .*, 240.

39. Aicha Rahmouni takes the word as part of a longer title for Mot, *ydd 'il ǵzr*, "beloved of Ilu, the hero"; *Divine Epithets in the Ugaritic Alphabetic Texts*, trans. J. N. Ford (HO 1 93; Leiden: Brill, 2008) 195.

40. Rahmouni, *Divine Epithets in the Ugaritic Alphabetic Texts*, 49.

41. See Rahmouni, *Divine Epithets in the Ugaritic Alphabetic Texts*, 49-52.

42. According to Cunchillos, Vita, and Zamora, *A Concordance of Ugaritic Words*, 70-72; see also Rahmouni, *Divine Epithets in the Ugaritic Alphabetic Texts*, 53-63. Cf. the superlative title in Linear B, "thrice-hero" *(ti-ri-se-ro-e)*, where it appears in a list of offerings to deities, e.g., in Michael Ventris and John Chadwick, *Documents in Mycenaean Greek: Three Hundred Selected Tablets from Knossos, Pylos, and Mycenae with Commentary and Vocabulary* (2nd ed.; Cambridge: Cambridge University Press, 1973) 287 #172 (Kn02 = TN316), reverse line 3, with comment on p. 289. The word may be an expression of superlative degree, as Christopher P. Jones notes: "the 'thrice' may suggest being strong or valiant, a heroicized ancestor three generations back, or something else not yet understood"; *New Heroes in Antiquity: From Achilles to Antinoos* (Revealing Antiquity 18; Cambridge, MA: Harvard University Press, 2010) 4. For further discussion, see above Introduction, note 2.

43. The only one of the male combatants lacking an explicit warrior title is Yamm. He is called "lord" (*'adn;* e.g., 1.12 I 17) and "prince" (*zbl;* e.g., 1.2 III 8, 16, 21; IV 7, 14, 22, 24, 29). It is to be noted that Greek *hērōs* denotes "lord" (see Jones, *New Heroes in Antiquity*, 4). Yamm's titles might in context carry comparable semantic freight. A title arguably expressive of warrior character is his epithet of *ṯpṭ nhr*, "Judge River." Applied to Yamm, it occurs no less than ten times in a single column (1.2 I 7, 17, 22, 26, 28, 30, 34, 41, 44, 45), not to mention twelve other times for this god (1.2 III 7, 9, 16, 21, 22, 23; IV 15, 16, 22, 25, 27, 30). The title is often translated "judge," but it seems to refer to a broader sense, "leader" or "ruler." Mari *šāpiṭum* is always an appointed governor subordinate to a ruler. It does not apply to tribes, but to districts of a kingdom. Mari *šāpiṭum* does not lead in battle

or the like. For this information, see Daniel E. Fleming, *Democracy's Ancient Ancestors: Mari and Early Collective Governance* (Cambridge: Cambridge University Press, 2004) 54, 66, 86, and 87. At first glance, then, we should perhaps be more circumspect in how we situate this term in a warrior context. Indeed, its Ugaritic attestation, for both the verb and the noun, may mean "to judge a case" (1.17 V 8; 1.16 VI 34; *DULAT*, 926). At the same time, it does refer to the role of a leader or ruler, not only for Baal (see also the PN *ṯpṭbʿl*) but also for Rp'u in 1.108.3 (see below). In this sort of context, the word might be understood as leader, whose expected roles include making judgments and decrees. Cf. Temba L. J. Mafico, *Yahweh's Emergence as "Judge" among the Gods: A Study of the Hebrew Root* špt (Lewiston: Mellen, 2007).

44. This use of *ʿl* was compared with the similar expression in Ps. 16:4 by Mitchell J. Dahood, *Psalms I: 1–50* (AB 16; Garden City: Doubleday, 1965) 87. Note also the personal name "ʿAshtart is above" *(ʿštrtʿl)*, inscribed on an unprovenienced Phoenician electrum pendant thought to date to the eighth-seventh centuries. See Robert Deutsch and André Lemaire, *The Adoniram Collection of West Semitic Inscriptions* (Geneva: Archaeological Center Publication, 2003) 40. Cf. the relief inscription at Beit el-Wali, a temple of Ramesses III, which in commemorating a victory of this king over the Syrians reports a speech of a Syrian chief: "(I) believed (that) there was none like Baal." See Keiko Tazawa, *Syro-Palestinian Deities in New Kingdom Egypt* (B.A.R. International Series 1965; Oxford: Archaeopress, 2009) 28, doc. #63.

45. The reading of the god's name in this very difficult column has come under some doubt in recent years. In one case (KTU 1.2 III 18), the name is partially reconstructed, and in the other (1.2 III 12), the reading is open to question (Dennis Pardee, oral communication via Aaron Tugendhaft).

46. For this episode in KTU 1.6 I, see Jonas C. Greenfield, "Baʿal's Throne and Isa. 6:1," in *ʿAl Kanfei Yonah: Collected Studies of Jonas C. Greenfield on Semitic Philology*, ed. Shalom M. Paul, Michael E. Stone, and Avital Pinnick (Leiden: Brill; Jerusalem: Magnes, 2001) 2:892-97. For transliteration and translation, see *UNP*, 153-54.

47. For text, translation, and discussion of this line with photographs, see *UBC*, 1:211, 217, 219, 223, 254, and pls. 34-36. As noted above, the reading of the god's name in this column is open to discussion.

48. For these lines, see *UNP*, 217, with transliteration and a translation, which mine follows in part. The reconstruction for the third line comes from KTU and makes good sense contextually.

49. KTU reads *bt*.

50. Benjamin Mazar, *The Early Biblical Period: Historical Studies*, ed. Shmuel Ahituv and Baruch A. Levine; trans. Ruth and Elisheva Rigbi (Jerusalem: Israel Exploration Society, 1986) 87. Mazar comments on such warriors behind the literary description in Ps. 57:5: "mercenaries called *l*^{e}*bāʾim*, 'lions', apparently referring to members of a military unit whose emblem was a lion-goddess." Amihai Mazar, "The Iron Age I," in *The Archaeology of Ancient Israel*, ed. Amnon Ben-Tor; trans. R. Greenberg (New Haven: Yale University Press; Tel Aviv: Open University, 1992) 300. See also Frank Moore Cross, *Canaanite Myth and Hebrew Epic: Essays in the History of the Religion of Israel* (Cambridge, MA: Harvard University Press, 1973) 33.

51. For this context, see J. A. Emerton, "Treading the Bow," *VT* 53 (2003) 465-86, here 480.

52. For a survey, see *UBC*, 1:240-50; and Mark S. Smith, "The God Athtar in the Ancient Near East and His Place in KTU 1.6 I," in *Solving Riddles and Untying Knots: Biblical, Epigraphic, and Semitic Studies in Honor of Jonas C. Greenfield*, ed. Ziony Zevit, Seymour Gitin, and Michael Sokoloff (Winona Lake: Eisenbrauns, 1995) 627-40.

53. The narrative with this description of Anat appears in a magical spell (p. Chester Beatty VII verso), addressed recently by Tazawa, *Syro-Palestinian Deities in New Kingdom Egypt*, 78; see also *ANET*, 250. Since the context entails her making a request before "her father" (here named as Pre), the passage in which this description occurs seems to be parallel to her audience before El making her requests in KTU 1.3 V; 1.17 VI. See further Thomas Schneider, "Texte über den syrischen Wettergott aus Ägypten," *UF* 35 (2003) 619-22. This magical text bears on the claim of Tazawa (pp. 78, 145) that KTU 1.10-1.11 show Baal and Anat engaging in sexual relations. This interpretation has been disputed by Neal H. Walls (*The Goddess Anat in Ugaritic Myth* [SBLDS 135; Atlanta: Scholars, 1992] 122-44) and Peggy L. Day (who summarizes the problem and references to their work in her article, "Anat," *DDD*, 37). Tazawa cites Walls and Day, but does not mention their view on this matter. Tazawa suggests that this Egyptian magical spell involving the rape of Anat by Seth reflects sexual intercourse of Anat and Baal in the Ugaritic texts (KTU 1.10–1.11), but Walls and Day dispute the comparison. Walls and Day demonstrate the problems with the evidence, but they do not demonstrate as such that Baal and Anat do not engage in sexual relations. The issue arguably remains *sub iudice*.

54. For discussion of Anat in the Baal Cycle, see Kelly J. Murphy, "Myth, Reality, and the Goddess Anat: Anat's Violence and Independence in the Baʿal Cycle," *UF* 41 (2009) 525-41.

55. For the text, philology, and issues of interpretation, see the detailed discussion in *UBC*, 2:127-94 and images 04-07. This layout in poetic lines with translation as well as vocalization appears on pp. 132-37. See also Manfried Dietrich and Oswald Loretz, *Orbis Ugariticus: Ausgewählte Beiträge von Manfried Dietrich und Oswald Loretz zu Fest- und Gedenkschriften. Anlässlich des 80. Geburtstag von Oswald Loretz*, ed. Dietrich (AOAT 343; Münster: Ugarit-Verlag, 2008) 302-4.

56. For a possible resonance of this word in the administrative texts, see Dietrich and Loretz, *Orbis Ugariticus*, 295-96.

57. H. L. Ginsberg (*ANET*, 136; his italics) surmised that the references to tables and chairs in lines 20-22 involves her imagination: "She *pictures* the chairs as heroes/ *Pretending* a table is warriors,/and that the footstools are troops." See also P. Kyle McCarter, "When the Gods Lose Their Temper: Divine Rage and the Hypostasis of Anger in Iron Age Religion," in *Divine Wrath and Divine Mercy in the World of Antiquity*, ed. Reinhard G. Kratz and Hermann Spieckermann (FAT 2/33; Tübingen: Mohr Siebeck, 2008) 78-91, here 84-85. McCarter, following Ginsberg's approach, suggests that Anat has entered "the realm of hallucination" (p. 84) and has reached "the point that her confused mental state and bizarre behavior approaches the psychotic" (p. 85). The problem with this view is primarily philological; there is no basis for viewing the verbs with the meanings suggested by Ginsberg, and McCarter's effort to have both Ginsberg's inter-

pretation and the correct rendering of the verbs "("she arranged") works poorly, as does the rendering of the preposition *l-* as "as" ("she arranged the chairs as warriors, arranged the tables as troops, the footstools as heroes"). Cf. *UBC,* 2:161-63, 174-82.

58. Smith, "Anat's Warfare Cannibalism and the West Semitic Ban," in *The Pitcher Is Broken: Memorial Essays for Gösta W. Ahlström,* ed. Stephen W. Holloway and Lowell K. Handy (JSOTSup 190; Sheffield: Sheffield Academic, 1995) 368-86; and *UBC,* 2:178-85. For discussions of *ḥērem* in Moabite and biblical material, see Lauren Monroe, "Israelite, Moabite and Sabaean War-*ḥērem* Traditions and the Forging of National Identity: Reconsidering the Sabaean Text RES 3945 in Light of Biblical and Moabite Evidence," *VT* 57 (2007) 318-341; Reinhard G. Kratz, "Chemosh's Wrath and Yahweh's No: Ideas of Divine Wrath in Moab and Israel," in Kratz and Spieckermann, *Divine Wrath and Divine Mercy,* 92-121, publ. also as "Der Zorn Kamoschs und das Nein JHWHs Vorstellungen von Zorn Gottes in Moab und Israel," in Kratz, *Prophetenstudien: Kleine Schriften II* (FAT 74; Tübingen: Mohr Siebeck, 2011) 71-98; Rüdiger Schmitt, *Der "Heilige Krieg" im Pentateuch und im deuteronomistischen Geschichtswerk: Studien zur Forschungs-, Rezeptions- und Religionsgeschichte von Krieg und Bann im Alten Testament* (AOAT 381; Münster: Ugarit-Verlag, 2011), esp. 56-61, 101-2, 212-13; Reinhard Achenbach, "Divine Warfare and Yhwh's Wars: Religious Ideologies of War in the Ancient Near East and in the Old Testament," in *The Ancient Near East in the 12th-10th Centuries* BCE: *Culture and History: Proceedings of the International Conference Held at the University of Haifa, 2-5 May, 2010,* ed. Gershon Galil, Ayelet Gilboa, Aren M. Maeir, and Dan'el Kahn (AOAT 392; Münster: Ugarit-Verlag, 2012) 1-26, here 16-21; and Ziony Zevit, "Mesha's *Ryt* in the Context of Moabite and Israelite Bloodletting," in *Puzzling Out the Past: Studies in the Northwest Semitic Languages and Literatures in Honor of Bruce Zuckerman,* ed. Marilyn J. Lundberg, Steven Fine, and Wayne T. Pitard (CHANE 55; Leiden: Brill, 2012) 235-38.

59. This layout in poetic lines with translation as well as vocalization appears in *UBC,* 2:178-80 and images 91-92.

60. Cf. Ps. 58:10: "his feet he will wash in the blood of the wicked." See also Ps. 68:23. See Mark S. Smith, *The Early History of God* (2nd ed.; BRS; Grand Rapids: Eerdmans and Livonia: Dove, 2002) 105. See also the image of the deity in Isa. 63:1-6.

61. For references, see pp. 355-56 note 56 above.

62. Rivkah Harris, "Inanna-Ishtar as Paradox and a Coincidence of Opposites," *HR* 30 (1991) 269, citing *CAD,* I/J:197.

63. Jacobsen, *The Harps That Once . . . ,* 243. Note Song 6:13's comparison for the dance of the Shulammit "like the dance of the two army-camps" *(kimḥōlat hammaḥănāyim).* See Pope, *Song of Songs,* 601-12.

64. Cf. Margalit, *A Matter of "Life" and "Death,"* 140.

65. See Margalit, *A Matter of "Life" and "Death,"* 142 n. 1; Wilfred G. E. Watson, "What Does Ugaritic *gmn* mean?" *AuOr* 7 (1989) 129-31; *DULAT,* 300. Cf. Pardee, "The New Canaanite Myths and Legends," *BO* 37 (1980) 269-91; *COS,* 1:268-69 n. 242.

66. See *ANET,* 139; T. H. Gaster, *Thespis: Ritual, Myth, and Drama in the Ancient Near East* (New York: Norton, 1977) 215-16; Peter J. van Zijl, *Baal: A Study of Texts in Connexion with Baal in the Ugaritic Epics* (AOAT 10; Kevelaer: Verlag Butzon & Bercker; Neukirchen-Vluyn: Neukirchener, 1972) 184; Gregorio del Olmo Lete, *MLC,* 24; Margalit,

A Matter of "Life" and "Death," 141. Some relate *gmn to BH and Aram *gml, as a "kind of benefit." To this John Gray (*The Legacy of Canaan* [2nd ed.; VTSup 5; Leiden: Brill, 1965] 64 n. 5) adds that *ḥesed gĕmal* is "to show pious duty to the dead" (cf. van Zijl, *Baal,* 186). The difference in the final consonant of the putative cognate does not inspire confidence in this approach.

67. Taking the word as a funerary offering, *DULAT,* 300 compares Akkadian *kamānu,* a type of cake (*CAD,* K:110; *AHw,* 430), unlikely given the animal offerings named in this passage.

68. Dietrich, Loretz, and Sanmartín, "Ug. *kgmn* oder *k gmn* (CTA 6 I 19-29)," *UF* 8 (1976) 432. See *CAD,* K:501. For these authors, the word is thought to be Hurrian.

69. See de Moor, *The Seasonal Pattern in the Ugaritic Myth of Baʿlu,* 200; van Zijl, *Baal,* 184-85. H. L. Ginsberg reconstructs and identifies *[y]ḥmrm* (cf. BH *yaḥmûr*) as the fallow deer, *Cervus dama mesopotamica,* and *ʾayl* (BH *ʾayyāl*) as the goat-sized *Cervus capreolus.* He comments that recent writers have doubted the existence of roebuck in Israel, thereby questioning the identification of this species with BH *yaḥmûr.* See Ginsberg, "The Rebellion and Death of Baʿlu," *Or* 5 (1936) 194; *ANET,* 131-32; "Ugaritico-Phoenicia," *JANES* 5 (T. H. Gaster Festschrift; 1973) 131 n. 3. Ginsberg (*ANET,* 132) argued that *ḥmr* for "ass" would be a late Ugaritic form for the older words *ʿr/pḥl* (see KTU 1.4 IV 7, 12), not to be expected of the oldest Ugaritic myth but attested in Ugaritic ritual (1.40.18, 26, 35). Ginsberg also argued that the other sacrifices in this context consist of horned ruminants and therefore the last sacrifice would also consist of one. In this case, "asses" would be out of place, while "fallow deer" would be fitting (cf. Gibson, *Canaanite Myths and Legends,* 75; Margalit, *A Matter,* 141). CTA (115 n. 2; cf. KTU) disputed Ginsberg's reconstruction on epigraphic grounds, but Ginsberg rejected the argument that there may not be enough room for the extra letter. Ginsberg's view is attractive, but the translation above retains what the extant text actually offers rather than the reconstruction; this, though, is no guarantee of correctness.

Based on her research of animal bones, Paula Wapnish ("Selected Animal Identifications in Cuneiform Sources: An Interdisciplinary Approach Based on Folk Taxonomy" [Ph.D. diss., Columbia University, 1984] 71-72, esp. 72 n. 1) notes the presence of a roebuck, *Capreolus capreolus,* at Late Bronze Age Ta'anach as well as Aphek, Gush Halav, and Miron. Therefore the identification is open. Wapnish (personal communication in a letter dated 10 December 1986) has noted the presence of four types of deer in the Levant, which raises further possibilities for particular identifications. Based on her further research at Tel Dan, now known are the roe deer *(Capreolus capreolus),* the red deer *(Cervus elpahus),* and two forms of fallow deer *(Dama dama mesopotamica* and *Dama dama dama).* As a result, it is not presently possible to specify the identifications to the degree that Ginsberg proposes.

70. Kenneth C. Way, "Assessing Sacred Asses: Bronze Age Donkey Burials in the Near East," *Levant* 42 (2010) 210-25.

71. See, e.g., Vera Müller, "Offering Practices in the Temple Courts of Tell el-Dabʿa and the Levant," in *The Middle Bronze Age in the Levant: Proceedings of an International Conference on MB IIA Ceramic Material. Vienna, 24th-26th of January 2001,* ed. Manfred

Bietak (Vienna: Verlag der Österreichischen Akademie der Wissenschaften, 2002) 271, 275.

72. See Chapter Four for discussion of Anat as a hunter. See also Chapter Seven.

73. Rahmouni, *Divine Epithets in the Ugaritic Alphabetic Texts,* 260-62, 383.

74. It has been common to compare the description of Mot's destruction by Anat with the destruction of the calf in Exodus 32. For an older, standard discussion of this comparison, see S. E. Loewenstamm, "The Making and Destruction of the Golden Calf," *Bib* 48 (1967) 481-90; repr. in Loewenstamm, *Comparative Studies in Biblical and Ancient Oriental Literatures* (AOAT 204; Kevelaer: Butzon & Bercker; Neukirchen-Vluyn: Neukirchener, 1980) 236-45. Note also the response of Leo Perdue, "The Making and Destruction of the Golden Calf — A Reply," *Bib* 54 (1973) 237-46, with the reaction of Loewenstemm, "The Making and Destruction of the Golden Calf — A Rejoinder," *Bib* 56 (1975) 30-43, also in Loewenstamm, *Comparative Studies,* 503-16. A no less proximate literary parallel is provided by Ninurta's destruction of his defeated enemy, Azag, in Lugale-e: "like ripe grain he shook Azag, made its seed (cones) drop off it, piled them up together like broken mud brick, its capable 'hands,' as were they but ashes, he strewed like flour; like clay pulled out of a terre pisée wall, he heaped them together" (Jacobsen, *The Harps That Once . . . ,* 250).

75. For the point that Anat's violence in the Baal Cycle does not correspond to human women (as warriors or the like), see Murphy, "Myth, Reality, and the Goddess Anat," 533.

76. Cf. "to go to war is a festival for young men" and "battle is a feast for her [Inanna]," cited from *CAD,* I/J:197 by Harris, "Inanna-Ishtar as Paradox," 269.

77. Day, "Why is Anat a Hunter and Warrior?" in *The Bible and the Politics of Exegesis: Essays in Honor of Norman K. Gottwald on His Sixty-Fifth Birthday,* ed. David Jobling, Day, and Gerald T. Sheppard (Cleveland: Pilgrim, 1991) 141-46, 329-32.

78. And not a virgin, as has been long noted by commentators. Cf. a magical spell in the Harris Magical Papyrus: "the womb of Anat and Astarte was closed, the two great goddesses, when they were pregnant, but could not give birth," in Tazawa, *Syro-Palestinian Deities in New Kingdom Egypt,* 79, doc. 22.

79. See *UNP,* 64.

80. For the text, philology, and issues of interpretation, see the detailed discussions in Dennis Pardee, *Ugaritic and Hebrew Poetic Parallelism: A Trial Cut ('nt I and Proverbs 2)* (VTSup 39; Leiden: Brill, 1988) 1-67; and *UBC,* 2:91-125 and images 02-03. This layout in poetic lines with translation as well as vocalization appears on pp. 94-97.

81. In addition to the discussion in *UBC,* 2:95 n. 4, 105-6, 160-61, 190, see Kenneth L. Barker, "Proverbs 23:7 — 'To Think' or 'To Serve Food'?" *JANES* 19 (Semitic Studies in Memory of Moshe Held; 1989) 3-8.

82. Note that the reading is *krpn[m]m.* See *UBC,* 2:92 for discussion.

83. For discussion of the word, see the beginning of Chapter Four.

84. For song in this passage and a broader discussion of the topic, see Matahisa Koitabashi, "Music in the Texts from Ugarit," *UF* 30 (1998) 363-96.

85. For the cymbals discovered at Megiddo and Akko, see Joachim Braun, *Music in*

Ancient Israel/Palestine: Archaeological, Written, and Comparative Sources, trans. Douglas W. Stott (BIW; Grand Rapids: Eerdmans, 2002) 109-10; see 44-45, 71, 107.

86. *RCU,* 54-55. RS 94.2519.5, 17 confirms the meaning "singers" for Ugaritic *šrm* in the administrative texts, provided the parallel listing of LÚ.MEŠ.NAR; see Bordreuil and Pardee, *BSV* 44, 46. Cf. the very extensive study of singers in the cult and court of Mari provided by Nele Ziegler, *Les Musiciens et la musique d'après les archives de Mari* (Mémoires de N.A.B.U. 10; Paris: Sepoa, 2007).

87. Richmond Lattimore, trans., *The Iliad* (Chicago: University of Chicago Press, 1951) 203. Cf. Odysseus' description of the feast in *Odyssey* 9.2-10.

88. Smith, *UNP,* 106. For different views, see *UBC,* 2:109.

89. For *ks* here, see Aaron Koller, "The *Kos* in the Levant: Thoughts on Its Distribution, Function, and Spread from the Late Bronze to the Iron Age II," in Galil et al., *The Ancient Near East in the 12th-10th Centuries* BCE, 270-71.

90. Cf. the instruction about the sacrifice in KTU 1.115.6-8 that "a woman may eat (of it) *(wtlḥm 'aṯt)*" only after the priest is to "desacralize (?) the hands in the sanctuary of the god of the palace."

91. Cf. Wilfred G. E. Watson, "An Antecedent to Aṯirat and 'Anat?" in *Ugarit, Religion and Culture: Essays Presented in Honour of Professor John C. L. Gibson,* ed. Nick Wyatt, Watson, and Jeffrey B. Lloyd (Proceedings of the International Colloquium on Ugarit, Religion and Culture, Edinburgh, July 1994; Münster: Ugarit-Verlag, 1996) 315. Watson sees something of a contradiction between this cup and the one that in 1.4 IV 40-47 Athirat says she will bear to Baal. The two vessels seem to show different purposes: the cup of 1.3 I is one that is not to be seen in Baal's feast, while the cup of 1.4 IV 40-47 marks the goddess's acceptance of Baal's kingship.

92. *ANEP,* #157; Joan Aruz, Kim Benzel, and Jean M. Evans, eds., *Beyond Babylon: Art, Trade, and Diplomacy in the Second Millennium B.C.* (New York: Metropolitan Museum of Art, 2008) 264-65, item #165.

93. Both Tarura and Arbura are foreign names (see Aruz, Benzel, and Evans, *Beyond Babylon,* 265). In this connection, I would mention also one of the scenes on a bronze bowl (ca. 675-625) from Cyprus. The third scene of the bowl involves men reclining in banquet, with standing figures, possibly musicians. So Vassos Karageorghis, *Ancient Art from Cyprus: The Cesnola Collection in the Metropolitan Museum of Art* (New York: Metropolitan Museum of Art, 2000) 181, #298.

94. For 2 Sam. 1:20, 24, see Chapter Ten.

95. It is to be noted that elsewhere Baal's three females, Pidray, Arsay, and Tallay, are named in tandem (1.3 IV 48-52; V 3-4, 35-44; 1.4 I 4-18; IV 47-57; IV 62–V 1). Here Arsay is not mentioned.

96. See Steve A. Wiggins, "Pidray, Tallay and Arsay in the Baal Cycle," *JNSL* 29 (2003) 83-101, here 86-87. Wiggins understands them to be Baal's unmarried daughters. In 1.24.25-26, the husband involved is the moon god Yariḫ, who is presented as their potential spouse, but in the context of the Baal Cycle, no alternative figure is named. Wiggins's hypothesis makes sense of the idea that not only Baal but also his "females" lack for a house according to his lament (in the passages listed above); in other words, this father cannot provide a home for his family. Despite the advantages to Wiggins's theory,

it remains possible that the Baal Cycle may offer an alternative mythology that casts Baal himself as their husband, prospective or otherwise. It is unclear that the more literal interpretation of *bnth* here is in fact the case (for more generalized usages, see *DULAT*, 245). Despite unanswered questions, Wiggins has drawn attention to an important lacuna in our knowledge; his reconstruction is plausible, and it makes sense of a number of details.

97. The construction **bn* + PN produced by way of analogy **bn* + common noun to denote belonging to a category named by the noun. E.g., BH *ben ḥayil*, lit., "son of strength," is a strong person.

98. Contrast 2 Sam. 6:22, with David's response to Michal's complaint about his dance: "among the slave-girls of whom you speak I will be honored" *(wĕʿim-hāʾămāhôt ʾăšer ʾāmart ʿimmām ʾikkabēdâ)*. Baal complains about a feast with slave-girls for some unknown reason (KTU 1.4 III 18-21).

99. The root is spelled fully in 3.1.15 and in *ynphy* in 1.163.5; cf. *phy* in 7.75.1 and the royal PN *ʿmph* in 1.113.15.

100. Perhaps also **rʾy*, "to see," in *rʾidn* in 1.3 I 12, as suggested by some commentators, but it seems unlikely. If correct, it would be the only occurrence of the root in Ugaritic, which also makes it less likely than the accepted alternative for *rʾidn*, namely "rhyton." For a review, see *UBC*, 2:108-9.

101. Gibson, *Canaanite Myths and Legends*, 46.

102. See Jacobsen, *The Harps That Once . . .*, 171-72. My thanks go to Stephen Russell for drawing my attention to this example.

103. See Pope, *Song of Songs*, 293.

104. Helen E. Fisher, *Anatomy of Love: The Natural History of Monogamy, Adultery, and Divorce* (New York: Norton, 1992) 21; see also pp. 21-24, 29, 30, 129-30; and "Lust, Attraction, and Attachment in Mammalian Reproduction," *Human Nature* 9 (1998) 23-52, esp. 32. For attraction and its other psychophysiological responses with some discussion of their chemical bases, see Fisher, "Lust, Attraction, and Attachment," 30-39; for arousal and its effects on the brain more generally, see Joseph LeDoux, *The Emotional Brain: The Mysterious Underpinnings of Emotional Life* (New York: Simon and Schuster, 1996) 288-90.

105. See the *Gt*-stems of **rḥṣ* for washing, of **šql* for locomotion, **ḫṣb* and **mḫṣ* for battling, of **wpy* for beautifying oneself. For discussion, see *UBC*, 2:117-18.

106. H. L. Ginsberg, *The Five Megilloth and Jonah* (2nd ed.; Philadelphia: Jewish Publication Society of America, 1974) 13.

107. Ginsberg, *The Five Megilloth and Jonah*, 10.

108. Leick, *Sex and Eroticism in Mesopotamian Literature* (London: Routledge, 1994) pl. 3.

109. Pardee, *RCU*, 98. See also William L. Moran, *The Amarna Letters* (Baltimore: Johns Hopkins University Press, 1992) 199 n. 11; cf. EA 84:13; and texts 54 and 55 in Simo Parpola, ed., *The Correspondence of Sargon II*. Part I: *Letters from Assyria and the West* (SAA 1; Helsinki: Helsinki University Press, 1987) 50-52.

110. Pardee, *RCU*, 98-99.

111. Pardee, *RCU*, 96. For a summary of the pertinent Emar evidence, see *UBC*, 2:118. For recent reassessments of "sacred marriage," see the essays in Martti Nissinen and Risto

Uro, eds., *Sacred Marriages: The Divine-Human Sexual Metaphor from Sumer to Early Christianity* (Winona Lake: Eisenbrauns, 2008).

112. This pairing may underlie two references to them in a late Aramaic text written in Demotic, Papyrus Amherst Egyptian 63: "May Baal from Zephon bless you; Pidra[i]/⟨i⟩ from Raphia — she should bless you." See Richard C. Steiner, "The Aramaic Text in Demotic Script," in *COS*, 1:313. See also in the same text (*COS*, 1:320): [Pid]rai is your sturdy beam. Great Baal! Tip a pitcher of must and drink me." The final sentence, like the scene in 1.3 I, involves Baal and a vessel of great drinking.

Notes to Chapter Seven

1. See the listings for these deities in *DDD*; note also the survey of John Day, *Yahweh and the Gods and Goddesses of Canaan* (JSOTSup 265; Sheffield: Sheffield Academic, 2000). For the god Baal, see Daniel Schwemer, *Die Wettergottgestalten Mesopotamien und Nordsyriens im Zeitalter der Keilschriftkulturen: Materialen und Studien nach den schriftlichen Quellen* (Wiesbaden: Harrassowitz, 2001); Alberto R. W. Green, *The Storm-God in the Ancient Near East* (Biblical and Judaic Studies 8; Winona Lake: Eisenbrauns, 2003). For Baal iconography, see Izak Cornelius, *Iconography of the Canaanite Gods Reshef and Ba'al: Late Bronze and Iron I Periods (c 1500-1000 BCE)* (OBO 140; Fribourg: University; Göttingen: Vandenhoeck & Ruprecht, 1994). For the Egyptian evidence, see also Keiko Tazawa, *Syro-Palestinian Deities in New Kingdom Egypt: The Hermeneutics of Their Existence* (B.A.R. International Series 1965; Oxford: Archaeopress, 2009) 13-37, 114-16. For Anat in the Ugaritic texts, see Neal H. Walls, *The Goddess Anat in Ugaritic Myth* (SBLDS 135; Atlanta: Scholars, 1992); Peggy L. Day, "Why Is Anat a Hunter and Warrior?" in *The Bible and the Politics of Exegesis: Essays in Honor of Norman K. Gottwald on His Sixty-Fifth Birthday*, ed. David Jobling, Day, and Gerald T. Sheppard (Cleveland: Pilgrim, 1991) 141-46, 329-32. For her iconography, see Izak Cornelius, *The Many Faces of the Goddess: The Iconography of the Syro-Palestinian Goddesses Anat, Astarte, Qedeshet, and Asherah c. 1500-1000* (OBO 24; Fribourg: Academic; Göttingen: Vandenhoeck & Ruprecht, 2004). See also Tazawa, *Syro-Palestinian Deities in New Kingdom Egypt*, 72-83, 119-20. For a survey of 'Athtar, see Mark S. Smith, "The God Athtar in the Ancient Near East and His Place in KTU 1.6 I," in *Solving Riddles and Untying Knots: Biblical, Epigraphic, and Semitic Studies in Honor of Jonas C. Greenfield*, ed. Ziony Zevit, Seymour Gitin, and Michael Sokoloff (Winona Lake: Eisenbrauns, 1995) 627-40. Study of this god remains a desideratum.

2. Edward Lipiński, *Resheph: A Syro-Canaanite Deity* (OLA 181; Studia Phoenicia 19; Leuven: Peeters, 2009); and Maciej M. Münnich, *The God Resheph in the Ancient Near East* (ORA 11; Tübingen: Mohr Siebeck, 2013). See also Tazawa, *Syro-Palestinian Deities in New Kingdom Egypt*, 83-95, 116-19.

3. See John Gray, *The Legacy of Canaan: The Ras Shamra Texts and Their Relevance to the Old Testament* (2nd rev. ed.; VTSup 5; Leiden: Brill, 1965) 176: "Beyond isolated references, however, the goddess stands definitely in the background in the Ras Shamra myths."

4. The Emar material does not appear in the 1999 article on the goddess by Nicholas

Wyatt, "Astarte," in *DDD*, 109-14. For Emar material, I have relied heavily on the work of my colleague Daniel E. Fleming, as will be clear below in the citations of his published research. The material from earlier Bronze Age Syrian sites, such as Mari, is not addressed, except in passing.

5. There are some remarks on the iconography thought to be associated with the goddess, but this material is treated only in brief. For a survey, see Izak Cornelius, "'Re-visiting' Astarte in the Iconography of Bronze Age Period Canaan/Syro-Palestine," in "'Athtart in Late Bronze Age Syria," *International Conference on Ishtar/Astarte/Aphrodite: Transformations of a Goddess, Keio University, Tokyo, 25-26 August 2011*, ed. David Sugimoto (in preparation).

6. The idea of the two goddesses as a pair is fairly standard. For an example, see Johannes C. de Moor, *An Anthology of Religious Texts* (Nisaba 16; Leiden: Brill, 1987) 188 n. 5. He also refers to Anat as the double of 'Athtart and vice-versa (30 n. 132; 33 n. 147; 43; 148 n. 10). See below for further discussion of this pairing.

7. The early survey of deities in the Emar texts by Gary Beckman does not include Anat. See Beckman, "The Pantheon of Emar," in *Silva Anatolica: Anatolian Studies Presented to Maciej Popko on the Occasion of His 65th Birthday*, ed. Piotr Taracha (Warsaw: Agade, 2002) 39-54. The GN of Anat has been read in Emar 26.7 and 14 by S. Basetti, "Anat in a Text from Emar," in *Richard F. S. Starr Memorial Volume*, ed. David L. Owen and Gernot Wilhelm (Studies on the Civilization and Culture of Nuzi and the Hurrians 8; Bethesda: CDL, 1996) 245-46.

8. The goddess's name is attested in an Emar PN, *aštarti-'ila;* see Regine Pruzsinszky, *Die Personennamen der Text aus Emar*, ed. David L. Owen and Gernot Wilhelm (Studies on the Civilization and Culture of Nuzi and the Hurrians 13; Bethesda: CDL, 2003) 192. As recognized by Alan Cooper, the form of the name **'aštartu* is reflected also in the Alalakh PN **aštartu* (D. J. Wiseman, *The Alalakh Tablets* [London: British Institute of Archaeology at Ankara, 1953] 130, #235.4) and in Akkadian spellings of the place **ashtartu* in EA 197:10; 256:21. See Cooper, "A Note on the Vocalization of *'ashtoret [Hebrew],*" *ZAW* 102 (1990) 98. According to Cooper, the /o/ vowel in the first BH spelling (1 Kgs. 11:5, 33; 2 Kgs. 23:13) points to the Phoenician vowel shift of *a > o and thus to a Phoenician loanform of the goddess's name, as opposed to the second BH spelling, as known from the plural form (Judg. 2:13; 10:6; 1 Sam. 7:4; cf. 1 Sam. 31:10).

9. Proposals for the etymology of the masculine form, 'Athtar, include: Arabic *'attâr,* "to be strong" (Albert Jamme); Tigre *'astär,* "heaven"; Ge'ez *'astar,* "sky"; Amharic *astär,* "star" (from Ge'ez); and Bilin *astär,* "sky" (Leslau); *'tr,* "to be rich" (Gonzague Ryckmans); Arabic *'attarî,* "soil artificially irrigated" (Robertson Smith, Theodore Gaster, Ryckmans, and Johannes C. de Moor). For these views, see Smith, "The God Athtar in the Ancient Near East," 636-38. The first two proposals would theoretically fit both the god and the goddess with the corresponding name. For an alternative view, see Ignace J. Gelb, "The Language of Ebla in the Light of the Sources from Ebla, Mari, and Babylonia," in *Ebla 1975-1985: Dieci anni di studi linguistici e filologici. Atti del convegno internazionale (Napoli, 9-11 ottobre 1985)*, ed. Luigi Cagni (Naples: Istituto universitario orientale, 1987) 55, noted in Joseph Martin Pagan, *A Morphological and Lexical Study of Personal Names in the Ebla Texts* (ARES 3; Rome: Missione Archeologica Italiana in Siria, 1998) 205. Gelb

suggested relating the DN to "*šittar*/*sitar*/ or /*star*/ in cuneiform Hittite (Nesite) and other Indo-European languages."

10. For the goddess in the Ebla documents, see Alfonso Archi, "Divinités sémitiques et divinités de subtrat: les cas d'Išḫara et d'Ištar à Ebla," *MARI* 7 (1993) 71-78; Francesco Pomponio and Paolo Xella, *Les dieux d'Ebla: Étude analytique des divinités éblaïtes à l'époque des archives royales du IIIe millénaire* (AOAT 245; Münster: Ugarit-Verlag, 1997) 63-67. Her name there is spelled ^{d}*aš-dar*, without the final feminine *-t* characteristic of her name in later texts known from Ugarit and Emar. For iconographic evidence of the goddess's cult at Middle Bronze Ebla, see Frances Pinnock, "The Doves of the Goddess: Elements of the Cult of Ishtar at Ebla in the Middle Bronze Age," *Levant* 32 (2000) 121-28.

11. For the Egyptian evidence, see Tazawa, *Syro-Palestinian Deities in New Kingdom Egypt*, 83-95, 120-21.

12. This issue is raised in a critical way by Noga Ayali-Darshan, " 'The Bride of the Sea': The Traditions about Astarte and Yamm in the Ancient Near East," in *A Woman of Valor: Jerusalem Ancient Near Eastern Studies in Honor of Joan Goodnick Westenholz*, ed. Wayne Horowitz, Uri Gabbay, and Filip Vukosavovic (Bibliotheca del Proximo Oriente Antiguo 8; Madrid: C.S.I.C., 2010) 19-33.

13. Albright, *Yahweh and the Gods of Canaan: A Historical Analysis of Two Contrasting Faiths* (1968; repr. ed. Winona Lake: Eisenbrauns, 1990) 134.

14. For the god as astral, see ^{d}*Aš-tar* mul in Emar 378.39′, noted in Smith, "The God Athtar in the Ancient Near East," 629. Note also KTU 1.111.15-22. In this text, a bride-price is paid to the lunar deity 'Ib, as Dennis Pardee comments, "apparently in view of her marriage to ʿAṯtaru Šadî, probably an astral-deity on the pattern of other manifestations of ʿAṯtar(t)u"; see *RCU*, 90. For ʿAthtar as an astral god in South Arabian sources, see Albert Jamme, "La religion arabe pré-islamique," *Histoire des religions* (Paris: Bloud et Gay, 1956) 4:265-65, 276-78. The etymology of the name is highly debated; see Jamme, "La religion arabe pré-islamique," 265; and Smith, "The God Athtar in the Ancient Near East," 636-38. See also Jamme's earlier and copiously documented study, "Le pantheon sud-arabe préislamiques d'après les sources épigraphiques," *Mus* 60 (1947) 57-147, esp. 88 and 100. For an accessible example of Athtar in Sabean sources, see *ANET*, 663 and n. 5 (where Jamme calls Athtar "a star-god"), and in Minaean sources, see *ANET*, 666 and n. 5 (where his name appears with Sharqân, an "epithet characterizing the star-god as 'the eastern' "). For some doubts about this view of the god, see Jacques Ryckmans, "South Arabia, Religion of," *ABD*, 6:172; and Alexander Sima, "Religion," in *Queen of Sheba: Treasures from Ancient Yemen*, ed. St John Simpson (London: British Museum Press, 2002) 163. The evidence cited for Athtar's astral character is based largely on the title *ʿṯtr šrqn*. The noun **šrq* refers to the rising of a star or sunrise (based on Arabic *šaraqa* with these meanings). The Sabaean noun also means "east, eastern land." For this information, see Joan Copeland Biella, *Dictionary of Old South Arabic: Sabaean Dialect* (HSS 25; Chico: Scholars, 1982) 528.

15. Roberts, *The Earliest Semitic Pantheon: A Study of Semitic Deities Attested in Mesopotamia before Ur III* (Baltimore: Johns Hopkins University Press, 1972) 37-40 and 101 n. 285.

16. See Wyatt, "Astarte," *DDD*, 110, citing W. Heimpel, "A Catalogue of Near Eastern

Venus Deities," *Syro-Mesopotamian Studies* 4 (1982) 13-14. Note the response to Heimpel by Brigitte Groneberg, "Die sumerische-akkadische Inanna-Ištar: Hermaphroditos?" *WO* 17 (1986) 25-46. Note also Michael L. Barré, *The God-List in the Treaty between Hannibal and Philip V of Macedonia: A Study in Light of the Ancient Near Eastern Treaty Tradition* (Baltimore: Johns Hopkins University Press, 1983) 54 and 167 n. 131, citing D. O. Edzard, in *WdM,* 84.

17. The astral assumption was questioned in some older studies. See Roberts, *The Earliest Semitic Pantheon,* 101 n. 285. The title "Queen of Heaven," known for ʿAthtart in Egyptian sources, need not denote a specifically astral aspect, though it may. For this Egyptian information, see W. Herrmann, "Aštart," *MIO* 15 (1969) 51, noted by Roberts, *The Earliest Semitic Pantheon,* 101 n. 285.

18. RS 92.2016 contains several instances of *kbkb* plus DN, none of which are ʿAthtar or ʿAthtart (but see the lacuna in line 12). For the text, see André Caquot and Anne-Sophie Dalix, "Un texte mythico-magique," in *Études ougaritiques,* Vol. 1: *Travaux, 1985-1995,* ed. Marguerite Yon and Daniel Arnaud (RSO 14; Paris: Editions Recherche sur les Civilisations, 2001) 393-405, esp. 393, 400; *UBC,* 2:232-33; cf. Johannes C. de Moor, "How Ilimilku Lost His Master (RS 92.2016)," *UF* 40 (2008) 179-89.

19. Clemens, *Sources for Ugaritic Ritual and Sacrifice* (AOAT 284; Münster: Ugarit-Verlag, 2001) 1:380-81, cited in Theodore J. Lewis, "ʿAthtartu's Incantations and the Use of Divine Names as Weapons," *JNES* 70 (2011) 225 n. 99.

20. *Ugaritica V,* 9; John Huehnergard, *Ugaritic Vocabulary in Syllabic Transcription* (rev. ed.; HSS 32; Winona Lake: Eisenbrauns, 2008) 145; Silvie Lackenbacher, *Textes akkadiens d'Ugarit: Textes provenant des vingt-cinq premières campagnes* (LAPO 20; Paris: Cerf, 2002) 254 (largely followed here).

21. *Ugaritica V,* 178-79; Lackenbacher, *Textes akkadiens d'Ugarit,* 279.

22. KTU 1.48.17 mentions another offering to ʿAthtart *šd* (line 16 in *RCU* 118).

23. *PRU IV,* 121. See discussion of Nougayrol, *Ugaritica V,* 56; Lackenbacher, *Textes akkadiens d'Ugarit,* 107 n. 330. For ʿAthtar *šd* in 1.111.18-10, see *RCU,* 92-93.

24. See the discussion of this possibility in *RCU,* 70; on the entry ritual, see also Gregorio del Olmo Lete, *Canaanite Religion according to the Liturgical Texts of Ugarit,* trans. Wilfred G. E. Watson (Bethesda: CDL, 1999) 136, 291.

25. *DULAT,* 697.

26. *RCU,* 37, reading *kd;* cf. KTU *k{b}d.*

27. For text and translation, see Dennis Pardee, "Epigraphic and Philological Notes," *UF* 19 (1987) 204-9, esp. 205; and in *COS,* 3:104.

28. There is a question about the reading. KTU reads: *bʿl ṣp[n].* A. Bernard Knapp has *bʿly x* and translates "Baʿal"; "An Alashiysan Merchant at Ugarit," *TA* 10 (1983) 39, 40. Following Mario Liverani, Pardee ("Epigraphic and Philological Notes," 206-7) would see Baal Ṣpn here.

29. Following one of the suggestions made by Virolleaud in the *editio princeps,* Pardee reasonably suggests reconstructing *rb mʾi[ḫd],* "Chief of Maʾ[ḫadu]," the port town of the kingdom of Ugarit, today Minet el-Bheida. See Pardee, *COS,* 3:104 n. 125.

30. The older generation of deities, such as El and Athirat, do not receive this sort of acknowledgement in the corpus of Ugaritic letters.

31. *PRU IV,* 121.

32. *RCU,* 275; and see also above. In this connection, one might compare possible male corresponding figures in Ugaritic: Athtar *šd* (1.111.19-20, as read by *RCU,* 92-93; cf. KTU Athtar *šb*) and perhaps the very difficult line *ʾil šdy ṣd mlk* in 1.108.12. Pardee (*RCU,* 205-6 n. 13) also discusses the possible relationship of this line with BH *ʾēl šadday.*

33. See Fleming, *The Installation of Baal's High Priestess at Emar* (HSS 42; Atlanta: Scholars, 1992) 99: "*Aštartu tāḫāzi* is one of the major gods of the Emar cult."

34. Fleming, *The Installation of Baal's High Priestess at Emar,* 216-21.

35. Note also, Westenholz #25.8-18 lists the "Ornamentation of 'Aštar(t)-*ḫaši,*" the divine name found also in the colophon in Emar 767.26; see Joan Goodnick Westenholz, *Cuneiform Inscriptions in the Collection of the Bible Lands Museum Jerusalem: The Emar Tablets* (Cuneiform Monographs 13; Groningen: Styx, 2000) 64-65. On this form of the goddess, see Westenholz's comments on p. 65. For the colophon, see Daniel Arnaud, *Recherches au pays d'Aštata. Emar VI.4: Textes de la bibliothèque, transcriptions et traductions* (Paris: Editions Recherche sur les Civilisations, 1987) 362. Westenholz suggests geographical candidates for *ḫaši.*

36. See Fleming, *The Installation of Baal's High Priestess at Emar,* 240-47, and *Time at Emar: The Cultic Calendar and the Rituals from the Diviner's Archive* (Mesopotamian Civilizations 11; Winona Lake: Eisenbrauns, 2000) 49, 98. See also Lluis Feliu, *The God Dagan in Bronze Age Syria,* trans. Wilfred G. E. Watson (CHANE 19; Leiden: Brill, 2003); and A. Otto, "Das Oberhaupt des westsemitischen Pantheons ohne Abbild? Überlegungen zur Darstellung des Gottes Dagan," *ZA* 96 (2006) 242-68.

37. Fleming, "'The Storm God of Canaan' at Emar," *UF* 26 (1994) 130; see also *The Installation of Baal's High Priestess at Emar,* 76, 222-25 (on the storm god and Hebat) and *Time at Emar,* 169-71. As Fleming notes, in Emar 446 the primary storm god of Emar is also mentioned along with the storm god of Canaan, and the two are equated. The relative chronological priority of the two sets of deities at Emar remains *sub iudice.* The Hittite arrival at Emar, despite the lack of Hittite culture there, may have advanced the place of Hebat there. If so, it may be that the older pairing at Emar was Baal and 'Ashtart. This line of reasoning was suggested to me by Fleming.

38. See Fleming, *The Installation of Baal's High Priestess at Emar,* 216-20; Fleming, *Time at Emar,* 35.

39. Fleming, *The Installation of Baal's High Priestess at Emar,* 216.

40. See also Gary Beckman, *Texts from the Vicinity of Emar in the Collection of Jonathan Rosen* (History of the Ancient Near East 11; Padova: Sargon srl, 1996) 15, 138. For this king, see Yoram Cohen and Lorenzo d'Alfonso, "The Duration of the Emar Archives and the Relative and Absolute Chronology of the City," in *The City of Emar among the Late Bronze Age Empires: History, Landscape, and Society: Proceedings of the Konstanz Emar Conference 25.-26.04.2006,* ed. d'Alfonso, Cohen, and Dietrich Sürenhagen (AOAT 349; Münster: Ugarit-Verlag, 2008) 3-25, esp. 7-8; and in the same volume, Daniel E. Fleming, "Reading Emar's Scribal Traditions Against the Chronology of Late Bronze History," 27-43, esp. 39-40. For the name, see Pruzsinszky, *Die Personennamen der Text aus Emar,* 285-86 and n. 366.

41. See also Emar 36.4, 8; 37.6, 20; 64.12; 65.8, 17, 18, 28, 39; 66.9; 80.6, 34; 81.2, 7, 11;

86.14, 19; 91.19, 35; 102.4?; 128.20; 132.5; 167.7?; 171.11; 176.33; 202.5, 8, 19, 21; 251.6; 285.9; 319.2; 343.4; 344.7?; 347.2?. See the full listing in Beckman, *Texts from the Vicinity of Emar,* 138.

42. Other ʿAshtart PNs include Ashtar-ummī (Emar 178.2; Pruzsinszky, *Die Personennamen der Text aus Emar,* 117; see also Ugaritic *ʿṯtrʾum,* KTU 4.426.1; 4.410.31; 4.504.2; cf. *eš₄-dar-um-mi* in Ignace J. Gelb, *Computer-Aided Analysis of Amorite* (AS 21; Chicago: University of Chicago Press, 1980) 73, 97). The Ugaritic and Amorite corpus shows no specifically marked feminine form. See also Greek *astharumos,* attested in Josephus, *Contra Apionem,* I 123, cited in Charles R. Krahmalkov, *Phoenician-Punic Dictionary* (OLA 90; Studia Phoenicia 15; Leuven: Peeters and Department Oosterse Studies, 2000) 390, as the brother and successor of Methonastartos, king of Tyre. Cf. Anat-ummī (Emar 216.6, 8, 13, 15, 19). For other ʿAshtart names, see also Emar 36.14; 78.17, 19; 120.12; see Pruzsinszky, *Die Personennamen der Text aus Emar,* 192.

43. See the older survey of Herrmann, "Aštart," *MIO* 15 (1969) 6-55.

44. Dennis Pardee, "Deux tablettes ougaritiques de la main d'un meme scribe, trouvées sur deux sites distincts: RS 19.039 et RIH 98/02," *Semitica et Classica* 1 (2008) 9-38. Note also the older studies of Johannes de Moor, "'Athtartu the Huntress (KTU 1.92)," *UF* 17 (1986) 225-30; and Meindert Dijkstra, "The Myth of Astarte, the Huntress (KTU 1.92)," *UF* 26 (1994) 113-26. The translation here includes few reconstructions (see line 12; cf. Dijkstra's rather full reconstruction of lines).

45. See the root also in KTU 1.4 V 9; 1.101.7-8. In both cases, it refers to the motion of water. For discussions, see Marvin H. Pope, *Song of Songs* (AB 7C; Garden City: Doubleday, 1977) 459-60; Steven Tuell, "A Riddle Resolved by an Enigma: Hebrew GLŠ and Ugaritic GLṮ," *JBL* 112 (1993) 99-104; *UBC,* 2:560.

46. W. G. E. Watson, "Tools of the Trade (KTU 4.127 and 4.385)," *UF* 34 (2002) 924.

47. For proposals for *qrẓ* and *ʾarbḫ,* see Wilfred G. E. Watson, *Lexical Studies in Ugaritic* (AuOr Sup 19; Barcelona: Editorial AUSA, 2007) 126 and 132.

48. Pardee translates ("Deux tablettes ougaritiques," 19): "à la fontaine," while Dijkstra ("The Myth of Astarte, the Huntress," 117) renders "the cow," with the preceding words.

49. This line might continue: "to [his] innards" (?) *(ggn[h]).* See esp. KTU 1.4 VII 49, discussed in *UBC,* 2:689-90. For the word, see Fred Renfroe, *Arabic-Ugaritic Lexical Studies* (ALASP 5; Münster: Ugarit-Verlag, 1992) 105; and Watson, *Lexical Studies in Ugaritic,* 48. The possible other instance of this form appears in 1.16 VI 26. Edward L. Greenstein (*UNP,* 47 n. 162) emends to *g⟨n⟩gnh,* which he takes to mean "windpipe" and hence "spirit" or "soul" or the like (see pp. 40 and 47 n. 163).

50. Given the other deities in the immediate context, it might be tempting to reconstruct Kothar wa-Hasis, but the space and readings available for the beginning of the line do not seem to militate in this direction.

51. For proposals for *ʾar* as "storehouse," see Watson, *Lexical Studies in Ugaritic,* 196.

52. For the word, see Watson, *Lexical Studies in Ugaritic,* 123. It is unclear that there is a syntactical relationship between this noun and the preceding as assumed sometimes: "a coat of cypress-wooden mail." This often-cited suggestion may be traced to Johannes C. de Moor, "Studies in the New Alphabetic Texts from Ras Shamra II," *UF* 2 (1970) 311.

53. It is common for the verb to be taken in the sense of "possess" or "obtain," based on Akkadian *rašû;* see *DULAT,* 750; Watson, *Lexical Studies in Ugaritic,* 103.

54. The **y'u-* imperfect prefix of first aleph verb pertains in Ugaritic to three roots: **'hb,* "to love"; **'ḫd,* "to take hold of"; and **'kl,* "to eat." Given Baal's desire in line 26, context might point in the direction of the first root.

55. Mark S. Smith, *The Rituals and Myths of the Feast of the Goodly Gods, KTU/CAT 1.23: Royal Constructions of Opposition, Intersection, Integration, and Domination* (SBLRBS 51; Atlanta: Society of Biblical Literature; Leiden: Brill, 2006) 122.

56. Smith, *UNP,* 123.

57. For Philo of Byblos, see Eusebius, *Praeparatio evangelica* 1.10.19, 28, 31 in Harold W. Attridge and Robert A. Oden, Jr., *Philo of Byblos: The Phoenician History* (CBQMS 9; Washington: Catholic Biblical Association of America, 1981) 50-55. For discussion, see *UBC,* 2:679.

58. Dijkstra, "The Myth of Astarte, the Huntress," 121: "certainly not another name of Baal."

59. Dijkstra, "The Myth of Astarte, the Huntress," 121.

60. *DULAT,* 731.

61. Watson, "Tools of the Trade," 925.

62. Pardee, *RCU* 168-70; *Les textes para-mythologiques de la 24e campagne (1961)* (RSO 4; Mémoire 77; Paris: Editions Recherche sur les Civilisations, 1988) 13-74. See also his translation and notes in *COS,* 1:302-5. The following translation and discussion has benefitted also from Theodore J. Lewis, *UNP,* 193-96; Kevin Cathcart, "Ilu, Yarihu and the One with the Two Horns and a Tail," in *Ugarit, Religion and Culture: Essays Presented in Honour of Professor John C. L. Gibson,* ed. Nick Wyatt, Watson, and Jeffrey B. Lloyd (Proceedings of the International Colloquium on Ugarit, Religion and Culture, Edinburgh, July 1994; Münster: Ugarit-Verlag, 1996) 1-7; Manfried Dietrich and Oswald Loretz, *Studien zu den ugaritischen Texten,* Vol. 1: *Mythos und Ritual in KTU 1.12, 1.24, 1.96, 1.100 und 1.114* (AOAT 269/1; Münster: Ugarit-Verlag, 2000) 403-523; Dietrich, "Heilkraft der rituellen Magie nach Aussage altorientalischer Texte," in *Identities and Societies in the Ancient East–Mediterranean Religions: Comparative Approaches. Henning Graf Reventlow Memorial Volume,* ed. Thomas R. Kammerer (AOAT 390/1; Acta Antiqua Mediterranea et Orientalia 1; Münster: Ugarit-Verlag, 2011) 31-45, here 33-37; and James Ford, "Ugaritic *pqq* 'dung pellet' in the Ugaritic Magico-Medical Text RS 24.258 (KTU2 1.114)," paper presented at the 218th Meeting of the American Oriental Society, Ancient Near East IV: Ugarit (Chicago, 15 March 2008); used with the gracious permission of the author.

63. See Pardee, *Les textes para-mythologiques,* 22 and 23-34. Given the sequence of type-elements of the feast consisting of preparations, invitation, service of food and drink, as noted by Murray H. Lichtenstein, the first line would appear to present preparations. See Lichtenstein, "The Banquet Motifs in Keret and Proverbs 9," *JANES* 1 (1968) 25; "Episodic Structure in the Ugaritic Keret Legend: Comparative Studies in Compositional Technique" (Ph.D. diss., Columbia, 1977) 25-30. Accordingly, the bicolon would not seem to present a general statement about El holding a feast; cf. the translation along these lines in Dietrich and Loretz, *Studien zu den ugaritischen Texten,* 411.

64. Elsewhere Ugaritic *mr'i* refers to the animals cut for the feast (e.g., KTU 1.4 VI

42-43). The word *qṣ* here refers to the cutting of the game named in the first two lines of this triplet (tricolon); cf. 1.4 III 42, VI 58.

65. The final words in the two lines may be rendered as nouns; cf. BH *lĕśōbaʿ*.

66. *DULAT,* 880 notes BH *tîrôš,* Phoenician *trš* (*DNWSI,* 1234), and Ebla *tí-ri-su.* See also W. G. E. Watson, "Akkadian Cognates to Some Ugaritic Words," *SEL* 25 (2008) 61-62. Watson compares Akkadian *turšummu,* "a type of wine" (*CAD,* T:489) and some putative Indo-European cognates, e.g., Hieroglyphic Hittiite *tuwarsa* and Greek *thyrsos.*

67. Ugaritic *gb* occurs in KTU 1.169.5-6 in parallelism to *tmnt*; both refer to the human body.

68. The verb occurs elsewhere only in 1.2 IV 27; there it is not reduplicated. The meaning "draws" or "drags" fits both contexts. In 1.2 IV 27 the verb is transitive, while in this context it seems to refer back to the subject; for this reason it is translated reflexively.

69. Or possibly, "they (the two of them) approached."

70. Ugaritic *pn* here is generally taken as "lest" (here, "that . . . not"), based largely on BH *pen.* It is to be noted that *pn* occurs very rarely in Ugaritic (this is the only example listed in *DULAT,* 674). Another possible understanding is "rather" or "still." As noted by *DULAT,* Kjell Aartun has taken *pn* instead as *p-* plus *-n* ("Dann"); see Aartun, *Die Partikeln des Ugaritischen* (AOAT 21/1-2; 2 vols.; Kevelaer: Butzon & Bercker; Neukirchener-Vluyn: Neukirchener, 1974, 1978) 2:87-88. Aartun analyzes the form as *p-* plus *-n,* perhaps analogous to other particles attested with and without *-n:*

> Ugaritic *wn* as *w-* plus *-n* (Aartun, *Die Partikeln des Ugaritischen,* 2:63, 86; *DULAT,* 940)
> Ugaritic and BH *kn* as *k-* plus *-n* (see *DULAT,* 448, *kn* III: KTU 1.12 II 53)
> Ugaritic and BH *hn* as *h-* plus *-n?* (see *DULAT,* 342-43).

In this approach, *p-* in *pn* would be an adverbial formed with *-n,* which according to *DULAT,* 656 is "adversative, contrastive" meaning "rather, but, although." For Arabic *fa,* Wehr (691) lists "and, then; and then; and so, thus, hence, therefore; but then, then, however; for, because" (see also Lane, 2321). By comparison, BH *pn* as "lest" would seem to represent an inner-Hebrew semantic development comparable to the adversative or contrastive sense seen with Ugaritic *p-* and *pn* and with Arabic *fa.* (The matter of the final *-n* is itself complicated and lies beyond the scope of this footnote.) As an Ugaritic example of *p-*, *DULAT,* 657 cites *p d ʾin b bty tt,* "rather, what is not in my house, give," in KTU 1.14 III 38; for this example, see also Wilfred G. E. Watson, "The Particle *P* in Ugaritic," *SEL* 7 (1990) 75-86, here 77-78. Perhaps the most persuasive BH instance of *p-* is to be seen at the end of Ps. 50:10 *(hrry ʾlp;* cf. Ps. 36:7, *hrry ʾl),* which is to be read with the following verb in v. 11. For this particle in this biblical verse, see Kjell Aartun, "Textüberlieferung und vermeintliche Belege der Konjunktion *pV* im Alten Testament," *UF* 10 (1978) 1-13, here 5-7. For the particle, see also Mats Eskhult, "h^akaf in Jdc 8,6.15," *Orientalia Suecana* 33-34 (1984-85) 117-21; Giovanni Garbini, "La congiunzione semitica **pa-*," *Bib* 38 (1957) 419-27; Norbert Nebes, "Zur Syntax der Partikel *f-* im Sabäischen," in *Proceedings of the Fifth International Hamito-Semitic Congress 1987,* ed. Hans G. Mukarovsky (2 vols.; Veröffentlichungen der Institute für Afrikanistik und Ägyptologie der Universität Wien 56; Beiträge zur Afrikanistik 40-41; Vienna: Afro-Pub, 1991) 2.259-75; and Watson, "Ugaritic *P* Again," *UF* 26 (1994) 493-95. For a derivation of BH *pen* instead from **pny,* see Fabrizio A. Pennacchietti, "La congiunzione ebraica *'pen',*" *AuOr* 29 (2011) 89-98.

71. Enclitic *mem* on *l-* (otherwise unattested in published material). See BH *lĕmô* as alternative form of *l-* in Job 38:40; 40:4; and perhaps 29:21 (*DCH,* 4:552). Cf. BH *kĕmô* like *k-* before a noun (e.g., *kĕmô-'āben* in Exod. 15:5).

72. Reading for *rlb* (Pardee, *RCU,* 185 n. 7). For **gʿr b-* introducing direct discourse, see 1.2 IV 28.

73. Ford takes the two lines as direct discourse and understands *pn* as a particle: "Now to a dog you give a *nšb*-cut (of meat)!/To a pup you give a shoulder-cut!?" See Ford, "Ugaritic *pqq* 'dung pellet.'"

74. The **yqtl/*qtl* parallelism of the same root, **gʿr b-,* in the first and fourth lines might suggest a four-line unit here. It might be thought that the gatekeeper rebukes El for allowing such a feeding or for his excessive drinking (although this is not really clear until the following lines). Or, did he rebuke the two goddesses by El or the name of El? As a further alternative, Dietrich and Loretz (*Studien,* 412) take lines 11-12 as the speech-opening formula for the following line. Ford takes line 14 as a rebuke of El, with El's response **ṯwb*) in lines 14-15.

75. Pardee (*RCU* 169) suggests, "his drinking group" (**'aškrh*). Cf. Dietrich and Loretz (*Studien zu den ugaritischen Texten,* 412): "und zwar wahrlich volltrunken."

76. Cf. KTU 1.1 IV 4-5: "El sits in [his] dr[inking-party]."

77. The usual idiom is "to" (Lewis, *UNP,* 195). From the initial line it might appear that El is already at his house. It would be possible to take *l-* as "from," but the text does not indicate why El would leave his house in his drunken condition. For an effort to resolve the problem, see Pardee, *Les textes para-mythologiques,* 57-59; *RCU,* 168; and *COS,* 1:302. Pardee locates the slaughter at the courtyard at El's temple followed by a banquet in a temple hall; then his drinking party takes place in a special room at the temple, which is followed by his going to his house, i.e., the inner sanctuary. If this is correct, it is to be noted that no movement from the first site ("courtyard") to the second site ("temple hall") is indicated. Pardee's reconstruction is based on a comparison with the Baalshamin sanctuary at Palmyra; he notes that no such banqueting hall is known for the Ugaritic royal palace. Whether or not this reconstruction is what is involved, Pardee does seem to be right in thinking that El is in two parts of his palace or house in lines 1 and 17.

78. In keeping with the description that follows. Note Ford's comparison with the rare Akkadian word *ḫabûm,* some sort of goat or the like; "Ugaritic *pqq* 'dung pellet.'" *CAD,* Ḫ:20 lists the word as *ḫābu* B and understands the word as middle weak, not final weak; see similarly in *AHw,* 306. The word has only one attestation in these dictionaries.

79. As demons may have horns and a tail, that may be what is involved here. An alternative speculation would involve Resheph, who has these traits in Egyptian iconography. See Izak Cornelius, *The Iconography of the Canaanite Gods Reshef and Baʿal: Late Bronze and Iron Age I Periods (c. 1500-1000 BCE)* (OBO 140; Fribourg: University Press; Göttingen: Vandenhoeck & Ruprecht, 1994). The cases include inscriptions with identifications of the figure as Resheph: he has a bull's tail (e.g., pp. 35 and 36); and his crown has the emblem of a gazelle (see pp. 32, 41, and 42). Cornelius informs me that the gazelle also occurs on the brow of the deity on the Horus cippi (see A. Strandberg,

The Gazelle in Ancient Egyptian Art: Image and Meaning [Uppsala: Uppsala Universitet, 2009] 140ff. fig. 70); the god Shed also has a gazelle. In the case of Resheph, the gazelle on the crown is thought to reflect "the military aspect or the fertility aspect" of the god's character, according to John H. Choi, "Resheph and YHWH ṢEBA'OT," *VT* 54 (2004) 17-28, here 23. Perhaps it is an emblem animal for Resheph.

80. For this hapax, see *DULAT,* 505, "soil, plaster." Ford translates "slimes him" and cites an Aramaic incantation, *wl' tlwšyn,* "do not besmear."

81. See Ford, "Ugaritic *pqq* 'dung pellet.' "

82. Dative suffix.

83. *N*-stem of *'wr,* "to wake up" (*DULAT,* 178; Pardee, *RCU,* 169), perhaps "sobered up," i.e., getting over the effects of the hangover; cf. the root in Isa. 51:17. For awakening from a drunken sleep (**yqṣ/*qwṣ*), see Gen. 9:24; Joel 1:5; Ps. 78:65; Prov. 23:35. My thanks go to Shalom Paul on this point.

84. The form is ambiguous. Theoretically, *yšt* here might derive from **šty,* "to drink," instead of **šyt,* as rendered here, but the object "forehead" seems to point in the direction of **šyt.* In addition, line 31 uses *'aḥdh* (see *UG,* 320; Watson, *Lexical Studies in Ugaritic,* 71 on this form as a loan translation/calque of Akkadian *ištēniš*), and so the content of that line should also be applied and not ingested. The verb may be passive or an impersonal active, as translated here (for the prescriptive use of the prefix verb in a medicinal context, compare KTU 4.767: "PN has collected henna plant; the sick man *(dw)* must eat *(y'kl).*" Otherwise, the translation here largely follows Ford.

85. Perhaps the name of a plant and not literally dog-hair. Cf. the plants called "dog flesh, dog's tooth, dog's bone, hound's tongue"; see *CAD,* Š/3:51; see also *CAD,* L:209; *AHw,* 425; R. Campbell Thompson, *A Dictionary of Assyrian Botany* (London: British Academy, 1949) 21, 23, 26, 68, 257, 347; cf. "dog of Gula" as a plant name, in Thompson, p. 151. Note also "shoot of dog" *(CAD,* P:273 sub *per'u).*

86. Often thought to be another plant name (so Pardee, *Les textes para-mythologiques,* 71; Lewis, *UNP,* 196). See also other views cited in *DULAT,* 677-78. Cf. Ford, "Ugaritic *pqq* 'dung pellet,' " citing Akkadian *piqannu* (*CAD,* P:385) and noting the use of dung in medical prescriptions elsewhere.

87. Emending from the reading *ḫrp'at* (Pardee, *RCU,* 170)/*ḫr[p]'at* Lewis, *UNP,* 196).

88. That line 17 begins the new section can be seen by the syntactical disjunction with the preceding section, with *'il* in initial position followed by the suffix indicative verb, *hlk.* Moreover, the openings of the two sections are parallel, with El in his house in both lines 1 and 17.

89. For further evidence of Anat as huntress, see KTU 1.22 I 10-11: "As when Anat hastens to hunt/sets to flight birds of the heavens" (*UNP,* 203).

90. As previously noted, this line might continue: "to [his] innards" (?) *(ggn[h]).* See esp. KTU 1.4 VII 49, discussed in *UBC,* 2:689-90. For the word, see Renfroe, *Arabic-Ugaritic Lexical Studies,* p. 48. The other possible instance of this form appears in 1.16 VI 26. Greenstein (*UNP,* 47 n. 162) emends to *g⟨n⟩gnh,* which he takes to mean "windpipe" and hence "spirit" or "soul" or the like (see pp. 40 and 47 n. 163).

91. Against the broad "law of decreasing members," the shorter term (here Anat) ap-

pears after the longer term ('Athtart). Thus the position of the name of 'Athtart is further notable. I wish to thank Steve Fassberg for making this observation.

92. See note 85 above.

93. For a possible West Semitic nominal form **harpê*, "remedy," in an Egyptian context, see James E. Hoch, *Semitic Words in Egyptian Texts of the New Kingdom and Third Intermediate Period* (Princeton: Princeton University Press, 1994) 215.

94. See the commentators in favor of this view cited by Pardee, *Les textes paramythologiques*, 67 n. 314. Pardee, while open to this view, prefers to see a singular form here, in which case it would refer to Anat in his reconstruction. Cf. Lewis, *UNP*, 195, where he reads the names of both goddesses in line 26.

95. *PRU IV*, 121.

96. See note 32 above.

97. For this point, see Fleming, *Time at Emar*, 166, 179, 182.

98. Fleming, *Time at Emar*, 182.

99. If the month name bears any significance, one might be inclined to the possible association with *marzaḫu* and 'Aštart. Cf. RS 18.01, in *PRU IV*, 230; Lackenbacher, *Textes Akkadiens d'Ugarit*, p. 141; John L. McLaughlin, *The Marzēaḥ in the Prophetic Literature: References and Allusions in Light of the Extra-Biblical Evidence* (VTSup 86; Leiden: Brill, 2001) 17 (adapted): "From this day, concerning the vineyards of the Hurrian Ishtar (^{il}*ištar ḫur-*ri) which is in Shuksu, the vineyard of the Hurrian (?) Ishtar (is) between the men of the marzeah of Aru (in Ugarit) and between the men of the marzeah of Siyannu; man against man will not transgress. Seal of Padiya king of Siyannu." For Ishtar *ḫur-ri*, see below p. 572 n. 123.

100. Fleming, *Time at Emar*, 183. For discussion, see Fleming, pp. 149, 151, 165-67; and treatment of the text on pp. 268-80.

101. Fleming, *Time at Emar*, 183.

102. For this point, see Fleming, *Time at Emar*, 165.

103. Steiner, "The Scorpion Spell from Wadi Ḥammamat: Another Aramaic Text in Demotic Script," *JNES* 60 (2001) 260, 264. The Aramaic spelling *'tr* rather than **'štr* is notable; see Steiner, p. 267. Perhaps the name derived from a Phoenician context "subsequently borrowed and adapted by Arameans being borrowed by the Egyptians for their use" (I borrow this formulation from Steiner's discussion of the West Semitic incantations in the London Medical Papyrus in his essay, "Northwest Semitic Incantations in an Egyptian Medical Papyrus of the Fourteenth Century B.C.E.," *JNES* 51 [1992] 199, discussed below).

104. See Steiner, "Northwest Semitic Incantations," 194.

105. For another example of game and slaughter of the ritual hunt, this one involving the god 'Athtar in Old South Arabian inscriptions, see "when he sacrificed to 'Athtar," *ywm ḏbḥ 'ṯtr*, basically following Biella, *Dictionary of Old South Arabic*, 91; see Maria Höfner, *Sabäische Inschriften (Letze Folge)* (Sitzungsberichte der Österreichischen Akademie der Wissenschaften 378; Vienna: Österreichischen Akademie der Wissenschaften, 1981) 32; and "the day he hunted the ritual hunt of 'Athtar *(ywm ṣd ṣyd 'ṯtr)* and the *krw*-hunt/feast" in RES 4177:3-4, cited in Biella, *Dictionary of Old South Arabic*, 421; on this passage, see also R. B. Serjeant, *South Arabian Hunt* (London: Luzac, 1976) 72 and 111 n. 376. Note

also a sixth-century B.C.E. inscription from Marib, referring to the "[hu]nt of ʿAthtar," in A. G. Lundin and S. A. Frantsouzoff, "An Inscribed Sabaean Bronze Altar from the British Museum," *St. Petersburg Journal of Oriental Studies* 9 (1997) 384-91; Sima, "Religion," 168. For older studies of the ritual hunt in South Arabian sources, note A. F. L. Beeston, "The Ritual Hunt: A Study in Old South Arabian Religious Practice," *Mus* 61 (1948) 183-96; J. Pirenne, in *Corpus des inscriptions et antiquités sud-arabes* (Louvain: Peeters, 1977) 1:165-67; and Jacques Ryckmans, "La chasse rituelle dans l'Arabie du Sud ancienne," in *Al-Baḥīṯ: Festschrift Joseph Henninger* (St. Augustin: Anthropos-Instituts, 1976) 259-308. See more recently Joy McCorriston, *Pilgrimage and Household in the Ancient Near East* (Cambridge: Cambridge University, 2011) 68. Marvin H. Pope drew my attention to this material in the early 1980s.

106. So translated in *RCU*, 146.

107. J. Leclant, "Astarté à cheval d'après les représentations égyptiennes," *Syria* 37 (1960) 1-67; and Cornelius, *The Iconography of Gods Reshef and Baʿal*, 81.

108. Westenholz, *Cuneiform Inscriptions*, 74-75. Texts from this volume are henceforth cited as Westenholz.

109. Westenholz, *Cuneiform Inscriptions*, 75. It is to be noted that the motif of the hunt for the goddess in Emar 446 is probably older according to Fleming (personal communication), and thus part of the basis for the goddess's cult at Emar. To my mind, the features of the hunt and combat for the goddess seem to cohere.

110. For the name, see Pruzsinszky, *Die Personennamen der Text aus Emar*, 117.

111. For the name, see Pruzsinszky, *Die Personennamen der Text aus Emar*, 117.

112. See Othmar Keel and Christoph Uehlinger, *Gods, Goddesses, and Images of God in Ancient Israel*, trans. Thomas H. Trapp (Minneapolis: Fortress, 1998) 88, esp. n. 28; for an illustration, see p. 87, #109 (reference courtesy of Elizabeth M. Bloch-Smith). According to Keel and Uehlinger (p. 88 n. 28), the two deities depicted on the seal, Baal-Seth and the goddess *ʿstrt*, "guard the name of Astarte (as one would at the entrance to a shrine)." For further discussion of this evidence, see Cornelius, "'Revisiting' Astarte in the Iconography."

113. *ANET*, 250; Leclant, "Astarté à cheval," 1-67; Rainer Stadelmann, *Syrisch-Palästinensische Gottheiten in Ägypten* (Probleme der Ägyptologie 5; Leiden: Brill, 1967) 101-12; Charles C. Van Siclen III, "A Memphite Lintel with Astarte," *Varia Egyptica* 7 (1991) 131-34; Donald B. Redford, *Egypt, Canaan, and Israel in Ancient Times* (Princeton: Princeton University Press, 1992) 232-35; Linda Carless Hulin, "The Worshippers of Asiatic Gods in Egypt," in *Papers for Discussion: Presented by the Department of Egyptology, The Hebrew University. Jerusalem*, Vol. 1: *1981-1982*, comp. and ed. Sarah Groll and H. Emily Stein (Jerusalem: Hebrew University, 1982) 270-77.

114. *ANET*, 17.

115. Day, "Ashtoreth," *ABD*, 1:492. To be sure, the spelling is not the normal singular form.

116. *ANET*, 534.

117. E.g., the vassal treaties of Esarhaddon, col. vi, line 453, in Donald J. Wiseman, *The Vassal-Treaties of Esarhaddon* (London: British School of Archaeology in Iraq, 1958) 63-64; Simo Parpola and Kazuko Watanabe, *Neo-Assyrian Treaties and Loyalty Oaths*

(SAA 2; Helsinki: Helsinki University Press, 1988) 48. See also the Esarhaddon text in Martti Nissinen, *Prophets and Prophecy in the Ancient Near East* (SBLWAW 12; Atlanta: Society of Biblical Literature, 2003) 140, #97, line 74.

118. Noga Ayali-Darshan has proposed that a number of sources, most prominently the Egyptian text sometimes known as "Astarte and the Sea," suggest a tradition of Yamm and Astarte in which the goddess attempts to seduce the god through physical allurement. More specifically, Astarte in some traditions is the consort of Sea, according to Ayali-Darshan, "'The Bride of the Sea': The Traditions about Astarte and Yamm in the Ancient Near East," in Horowitz, Gabbay, and Vukosavović, *A Woman of Valor*, 19-33. The evidence is not clear.

119. Fleming, *The Installation of Baal's High Priestess at Emar*, 216.

120. See Walls, *The Goddess Anat in Ugaritic Myth;* and Day, "Why Is Anat a Hunter and a Warrior?"; also "Anat," *DDD*, 36-43. Walls's discussion is quite detailed and addresses many specific Ugaritic texts, while Day's treatment is more general in scope. Both studies show considerable precision and proper probing of the Ugaritic evidence. Walls in particular parses out the evidence and offers qualified conclusions in such a manner so as to quarantine data that are suggestive of the goddess as Baal's consort. E.g., Walls (*The Goddess Anat in Ugaritic Myth*, 146 n. 65) assumes that "The Contest of Horus and Seth for the Rule" (mentioned shortly below) involves a misunderstanding, a position for which he provides no evidence. There is also evidence from a later Aramaic stele from Egypt with the reading *bʿl bʿl ʿnwt*, "Baal, husband of Anat," as read by *DNWSI*, 183, based on André Dupont-Sommer, "Une stèle araméene d'un prêtre de Baʿal trouvée en Égypte," *Syria* 33 (1956) 79-87, here 81, line 3. In her criticism of Dupont-Sommer, Day ("Anat," *DDD*, 41) offers her doubts not on epigraphic grounds, but "largely based on his understanding that Anat is represented as Baal's wife at Ugarit and thus proceeds from a debatable reading of the Ugaritic evidence with which I do not agree." While Walls and Day have provided a much-needed corrective to prior studies, the issue is not entirely settled, as the data mentioned below may suggest. At the same time, it should be said in support of their approach that Late Bronze sources that we have show no particular picture of either goddess as the consort of the god.

121. So *RCU*, 118, with irregular correspondence of the third consonant in *ṯpḥ bʿl;* cf. "the assembly of Baʿlu," in KTU 1.39.7.

122. See, e.g., John Day, "Ashtoreth," *ABD*, 1:491, 492.

123. *ANET*, 15.

124. For discussion, see Walls, *The Goddess Anat in Ugaritic Myth*, 144-52. Concerning the interpretation of the text, see further Edward F. Wente, "Response to Robert A. Oden's 'The Contendings of Horus and Seth' (Chester Beatty Papyrus No. 1): A Structural Interpretation," *HR* 18 (1979) 370-72.

125. See the publication by M'hamed Hassine Fantar, "L'archéologie Punique en Tunisie 1991-1995," *Revue des Études Phéniciennes-Puniques et des Antiquités Libyques* 11 (1999) 49-61, esp. 58. Note also Corinne Bonnet, *Astarté: Dossier documentaire et perspectives historiques* (Contributi alla storia della Religione Fenicio-Punica 2; Collezione di Studi Fenici 37; Rome: Consiglio Nazionale delle Ricerche, 1996) 106-7; and Karel

Jongeling, *Handbook of Neo-Punic Inscriptions* (Tübingen: Mohr Siebeck, 2008) 154. The inscription dates to the first century C.E., according to Bonnet, *Astarté*, 166.

126. Eusebius, *Praeparatio evangelica* 1.10.31, in Attridge and Oden, *Philo of Byblos*, 54, 55. The passage further locates this Astarte in Tyre; if so, then this Baal here may be Baal Shamem. Cf. pairing of Astarte and Rhea with Kronos (El), in 1.10.24, in Attridge and Oden, 52-53 (cf. the model of KTU 1.23, with its pairing of two unnamed females with El).

127. Keel and Uehlinger (*Gods, Goddesses, and Images of God*, 88 n. 28) see a pairing of the two deities in the Late Bronze seal from Bethel (noted above).

128. See *ANET*, 662. Pardee also notes KAI 49:3; "Preliminary Presentation of a New Ugaritic Song to *ʿAṯtartu* (RIH 98/02)," in *Ugarit at Seventy-Five*, ed. K. Lawson Younger, Jr. (Winona Lake: Eisenbrauns, 2007) 32.

129. Hoffmeier and Kitchen, "Resheph and Astarte in North Sinai: A Recently Discovered Stela from Tel el-Borg," *Ägypyten und Levante/Egypt and the Levant* 17 (2007) 127-36, here 132. See also Tazawa, *Syro-Palestinian Deities in New Kingdom Egypt*, 39 doc. 1 and n. 194.

130. Steiner, "The Scorpion Spell from Wadi Ḥammamat," 260, 264.

131. For this listing, see Choon-Leong Seow, "Face," in *DDD*, 322. Sergio Ribichini ("Gad," in *DDD*, 340) cites a Phoenician dedicatory text from Nora: "For the Lady, for Tanit, Face-of-Baal and Fortune" (RES 1222). Note also the Greek translation of the Neo-Punic formulary in an inscription from El-Hofra: "(to) Kronos ⟨and?⟩ Thenith, face of Bal" *(kronōi ⟨kai⟩ theneith phenē bal)*; see James Noel Adams, *Bilingualism and the Latin Language* (Cambridge: Cambridge University Press, 2003) 241-42; Robert M. Kerr, "Latino-Punic and Its Linguistic Environment" (Ph.D. diss., Leiden, 2007) 166 (I wish to thank the author for providing me with his work).

132. Note also the theory about Phoenician female masks as Tannit, in her form as the "face of Baal." For discussion, see Michal Dayagi-Mendels, *The Akhziv Cemeteries: The Ben-Dor Excavations, 1941-1944* (IAA Reports 15; Jerusalem: Israel Antiquities Authority, 2002) 160.

133. See KAI 2.98; Frank Moore Cross, *Canaanite Myth and Hebrew Epic: Essays in the History of the Religion of Israel* (Cambridge, MA: Harvard University Press, 1973) 30. As Cross notes, the text also goes on to mention their temples in the plural. For the problems of the identification of Tnt, see Cross, pp. 28-35; Robert A. Oden, *Studies in Lucian's* De Syria Dea (HSM 15; Missoula: Scholars, 1977).

134. Pritchard, *Recovering Sarepta, A Phoenician City: Excavations at Sarafand, Lebanon, 1969-1974, by the University Museum of the University of Pennsylvania* (Princeton: Princeton University Press, 1978) 104-5. Pritchard notes many divine double names (what he calls "compounds").

135. Pritchard, *Recovering Sarepta*, 107.

136. Seow, "Face," 322. So already Cross, *Canaanite Myth and Hebrew Epic*, 29.

137. Note the older discussions by Michael D. Coogan, *Stories from Ancient Canaan* (Philadelphia: Westminster, 1978), 74; Saul M. Olyan, *Asherah and the Cult of Yahweh in Israel* (SBLMS 34; Atlanta: Scholars, 1988) 48; Mark S. Smith, *The Origins of Biblical Monotheism: Israel's Polytheistic Background and the Ugaritic Texts* (Oxford: Oxford University Press, 2001) 74-76, 238-41.

138. McCarter, "Aspects of the Religion of the Israelite Monarchy," in *Ancient Israelite Religion: Essays in Honor of Frank Moore Cross*, ed. Patrick D. Miller, Jr., Paul D. Hanson, and S. Dean McBride (Philadelphia: Fortress, 1987) 147. On the "name" as "hypostasis," McCarter stands in a long line of tradition; see Smith, *The Origins of Biblical Monotheism*, 74 and 239 nn. 59-62.

139. Smith, *The Origins of Biblical Monotheism*, 74-76. Add (assuming its authenticity) the same PN in an inscribed arrowhead published by P. Kyle McCarter, Jr., "Two Bronze Arrowheads with Archaic Alphabetic Inscriptions," *ErIsr* 26 (Frank Moore Cross Volume; 1999) 123*-28*; and note McCarter's discussion of the name on p. 127* n. 13.

140. Cf. the opponents who wish to know the name of their antagonist, in the Sumerian fable "The Lion and the She-Goat," in Bendt Alster, *Wisdom of Ancient Sumer* (Bethesda: CDL, 2005) 362; and in Gen. 32:27.

141. See the comprehensive study of Friedhelm Hartenstein, *Das Angesicht JHWHs: Studien zu seinem höfischen und kultichen Bedeutungshintergrund in den Psalmen und in Exodus 32–34* (FAT 55; Tübingen: Mohr Siebeck, 2008). Note also Simeon Chavel, "The Face of God and the Etiquette of Eye-Contact: Visitation, Pilgrimage, and Prophetic Vision in Ancient Israelite and Early Jewish Imagination," *JSQ* 19 (2012) 1-55, as well as the older study of Mark S. Smith, "'Seeing God' in the Psalms: The Background to the Beatific Vision in the Hebrew Scriptures," *CBQ* 50 (1988) 171-83.

142. Lewis, "'Athtartu's Incantations," 207, 212, 216, 217, 218, 219. For another survey focusing on "name" in Deuteronomy, see Michael Hundley, "To Be or Not to Be: A Reexamination of Name Language in Deuteronomy and the Deuteronomistic History," *VT* 59 (2009) 533-55.

143. See above, note 8.

144. Pardee, *RCU*, 175.

145. See Pardee, *RCU*, 188 n. 40. Note also the observation of William W. Hallo, "Haplographic Marginalia," in *Essays on the Ancient Near East in Memory of Jacob Joel Finkelstein*, ed. Maria de Jong Ellis (Memoirs of the Connecticut Academy of Arts & Sciences 19; Hamden: Archon, 1977) 101-3: "A minor difficulty with this interpretation (from the point of view of Mesopotamian scribal usage) is only that the insertion seems to be placed physically *before* the stanza on Resheph!" (Hallo's italics).

146. See *UNP*, 17, 23.

147. For the full context of this passage, see above.

148. In Egyptian texts the two West Semitic goddesses are mentioned together. Tazawa, *Syro-Palestinian Deities in New Kingdom Egypt*, 76, doc. 11; 77, doc. 14; 79, doc. 23; 95, doc. 46; see also 128, 133-34, 163. Contrary to the claim on p. 128, Astarte is not named as a wife of El in the Ugaritic texts. Contrary to p. 133, Astarte is not called "a consort of Baal" in KTU 1.2 and 1.16, but "the name of Baal" (see above). See also *ANET*, 15 and 250.

149. This idea of pairing with Rashpu appears in Anja Herold, "Piramesses — The Northern Capital: Chariots, Horses and Foreign Gods," in *Capital Cities: Urban Planning and Spiritual Dimensions. Proceedings of the Symposium Held on May 27-29, 1996, Jerusalem, Israel*, ed. Joan Goodnick Westenholz (Jerusalem: Bible Lands Museum, 1998) 140.

150. As noted above, del Olmo Lete (*Canaanite Religion*, 261) understands KTU 1.91 as part of a list of rituals, with line 10 referring to 1.148.18-22.

151. The long form of the verb with *-n* plural ending indicates that the *-m* on the subject is not a singular with enclitic. For Reshephs in Egyptian and Phoenician sources, see Smith, *The Origins of Biblical Monotheism,* 67-68.

152. *ANET,* 244; Tazawa, *Syro-Palestinian Deities in New Kingdom Egypt,* 56, doc. 52.

153. Hoffmeier and Kitchen, "Resheph and Astarte in North Sinai," 127-86; see also Lipiński, *Resheph,* 170-71; and Tazawa, *Syro-Palestinian Deities in New Kingdom Egypt,* 38-39, doc. 1.

154. Lipiński, *Resheph,* 104.

155. Pardee, *RCU,* 126.

156. Yadin, "New Gleanings on Resheph from Ugarit," in *Biblical and Related Studies Presented to Samuel Iwry,* ed. Ann Kort and Scott Morschauer (Winona Lake: Eisenbrauns, 1985) 266-68, 271. Yadin preferred to associate the leonine iconography with Athirat. See the following section for further discussion.

157. In the understanding presupposed in this text, the two goddesses would then be daughters of El. For the phenomenon of the "daughters of 'Il" in Nabatean and ancient South Arabian, see Christian Robin, "À propos des 'filles de Dieu': Complément à l'article publié dans *Semitica* 50, 2001, pp. 113-192," *Sem* 52-53 (2002-7) 139-48.

158. Tikva Frymer-Kensky, *In the Wake of the Goddesses: Women, Culture, and the Biblical Transformation of Pagan Myth* (New York: Free Press, 1992) 14: "When goddesses portray and represent women in society, they are women writ large, with the same positions in the god-world that women have in the human world."

159. Cf. Ilona Zsolnay, "Do Divine Structures of Gender Mirror Mortal Structures of Gender?" in *In the Wake of Tikva Frymer-Kensky,* ed. Steven Holloway, JoAnn Scurlock, and Richard Beal (Piscataway: Gorgias, 2009) 103-20.

160. "Attribute animal" is common in the work of Pierre Amiet, *Sceaux-cylindres en hématite et pierres diverses* (Corpus des cylindres de Ras Shamra-Ougarit 2: RSO 9; Paris: Éditions Recherche sur les Civilisations, 1992) 68; *Art of the Ancient Near East,* trans. J. Shepley and C. Choquet (New York: Abrams, 1980) 440 n. 787. For this phenomenon, there is the indigenous Akkadian word *simtu,* "characteristic, insignia" (something considered suitable), used to describe what the lioness is in relation to Ishtar: "he harnessed for her (Ishtar) the seven lions, symbol of her divinity" (*CAD,* L:24). For other examples of *simtu* in this usage, see *CAD,* S:279, #1b.

161. See below for Frank M. Cross and Michael L. Barré in support of this identification.

162. The fundamental treatments are Dennis Pardee, "Preliminary Presentation of a New Ugaritic Song," 27-39; "Deux tablettes ougaritiques," esp. 11-13. A photograph and drawing of this tablet have been provided by Pierre Bordreuil, Robert Hawley, and Dennis Pardee, "Données nouvelles sur le déchiffrement de l'alphabet et sur les scribes d'Ougarit," *Comptes Rendus de l'Académie des Inscriptions et Belles-Lettres* 2010, 4:1628-35. Pardee's transcription and translation of lines 1-5 have been closely followed by Lewis, "'Athtartu's Incantations," 226-27. My translation, while differing in some details (noted below), is based on Pardee's rendering of lines 1-5. Lines 33-35, which Pardee has published, are not relevant to the discussion here.

163. First person jussive, or possibly indicative ("my voice will sing"), but not cohor-

tative, which would show *-h* on the verb. For another example of the first person without *-h,* in the opening of a hymn, see *'ašr* in KTU 1.24.1 (see also line 40).

164. This clause and the next could also be asyndetic (unmarked or "headless") relative clauses (like line 5) that continue from the preceding bicolon: "The name that is victorious over . . ./that shuts the jaws of El's attackers." I thank Tania Notarius for this suggestion.

165. The word is new for the Ugaritic lexicon; Pardee compares Arabic *ṣafaqa,* "to strike," etc. (Wehr, 518: "slap, smack"; "shut, slam, bang").

166. This is another new word for the Ugaritic lexicon. It is rendered "mighty," according to Pardee ("Preliminary Presentation of a New Ugaritic Song," 35, 37), based on Arabic *ḫaṭira,* "be thick, hard; be or become large or great." Alternatively, it is taken as "fierce" by Wilfred G. E. Watson, "Non-Semitic Words in the Ugaritic Lexicon (7)," *UF* 40 (2008) 551-52; Watson's meaning is based on putative Egyptian cognates.

167. Pardee's translation. BH *nāmēr* is taken as "panther" in *BDB,* 649, but it also may refer to a leopard in Jer. 13:23, where it is said to have spots. Akkadian *nimru* denotes panther or leopard; so *AHw,* 790; Simo Parpola and Robert M. Whiting, eds., *Assyrian-English-Assyrian Dictionary* (Helsinki: Neo-Assyrian Text Corpus Project, 2007) 76 sub *nemru. CAD,* N/II:234-35 lists the meaning "panther," although one of the examples is said to be spotted. See also the comparison of this passage with Jer. 13:23 by Hayim ben Yosef Tawil, *An Akkadian Lexical Companion for Biblical Hebrew: Etymological-Semantic and Idiomatic Equivalents with Supplement on Biblical Hebrew* (New York: Ktav, 2009) 241, which renders "panther." For Aramaic *nmr',* "panther," see *DNWSI,* 733 (e.g., KAI 222A 31; 223A 9, Ahiqar lines 118-19). See Arabic *namir,* "leopard, tiger," in Wehr, 1000; and Ethiopic *namr,* "leopard," according to Leslau, 398, with cognates. Cf. Arabic *nimir/nimr,* "leopard," used for bravery, according to R. B. Serjeant, *South Arabian Hunt* (London: Luzac, 1976) 38, citing the Arabic expression *anā anmar minnak,* "I am more courageous than you are." The word may denote panther or leopard in Sabean; see Biella, *Dictionary of Old South Arabic,* 307; and Albert Jamme, *Sabaean Inscriptions from Maḥram Bilqîs (Mârib)* (Baltimore: Johns Hopkins University Press, 1962) 339. Jamme also discusses whether or not the word is used as military terminology. For the question of whether the word is used for "adversary" or the like, see J. Ryckmans, "Himaritica, IV," *Mus* 87 (1974) 507-8; and Biella, p. 307. For ancient Mediterranean and Near Eastern iconography of the leopard, see Nadine Nys and Joachim Bretschneider, "Research on the Iconography of the Leopard," *UF* 39 (2007) 555-615.

168. Pardee, "Deux tablettes ougaritiques," 12: "Malgré l'état délabré des deux textes, on y trouve des elements de parallélisme, surtout dans les cinq premières lignes de RIH 98/02, conservées presque intégralement."

169. For the word in the Semitic languages, see Edward Lipiński, "'Lion' and 'Lioness' in Northwest Semitic," in *Michael: Historical, Epigraphical and Biblical Studies in Honor of Prof. Michael Heltzer,* ed. Yitzhak Avishur and Robert Deutsch (Tel Aviv: Archaeological Center, 1999) 213-20. For the words for lion in Hebrew, see Hans Rechenmacher, "Kognitive Linguistik und althebräische Lexikographie," *JNSL* 30 (2004) 43-59 (reference courtesy of Aaron Koller).

170. I wish to thank Steve Fassberg for offering this suggestion. The other possibility is that "name" is feminine.

171. Herbert B. Huffmon, *Amorite Personal Names in the Mari Texts: A Structural and Lexical Study* (Baltimore: Johns Hopkins University Press, 1965) 225, 248; Ignace J. Gelb, *Computer-Aided Analysis of Amorite* (Assyriological Studies 21; Chicago: Oriental Institute, University of Chicago, 1980) 354.

172. Pardee, "Preliminary Presentation of a New Ugaritic Song," 33-35. Note also the discussion of Silvie Blétry, "Le lion, symbole du pouvoir féminin en Orient (et en Grèce?)," in *Images et représentations du pouvoir et de l'ordre social dans l'antiquité,* ed. Michel Molin (Paris: de Boccard, 2001) 121-28.

173. So Frauke Gröndahl, *Die Personennamen der Texte aus Ugarit* (Studia Pohl 1; Rome: Päpstliches Bibelinstitut, 1967) 154. To be sure, any number of strong gods might be called lion; cf. Emar PN La'bu-Dagan, said to be in the Akkadian onomasticon, in Regine Pruzsinszky, *Die Personennamen der Texte aus Emar* (Studies on the Civilization and Culture of Nuzi and the Hurrians 13; Bethesda: CDL, 2003) 196 and n. 460. In addition, a Late Bronze male figurine with the leg of a lion was discovered at Tell Abu-al Kharaz; Peter M. Fischer, "Tell Abu al-Kharaz: A Bead in the Jordan Valley," *NEA* 71 (2008) 196-309, here 209-10. For some human-leonine figurine composites of a female sort, see the discussion below.

174. See Frank Moore Cross, *Leaves from an Epigrapher's Notebook: Collected Papers in Hebrew and West Semitic Palaeography and Epigraphy* (HSS 51; Winona Lake: Eisenbrauns, 2003) 200-202, 217-18, 304; Richard S. Hess, "Arrowheads from Iron Age I: Personal Names and Authenticity," in Younger, *Ugarit at Seventy-Five,* 113-129, esp. 119-20; and Hess, "Israelite Identity and Personal Names from the Book of Judges," *HS* 44 (2003) 38. See also the listing in Émile Puech, "Les pointes de flèches inscrites de la fin du IIe millénaire en Phénicie et Canaan," in *Actas del IV Congreso International de Estudios Fenicios y Púnicos: Cádiz, 2 a 6 de Octubre de 1995,* ed. María Eugenia Aubet Semmler and Manuela Barthélemy (4 vols.; Cádiz: Universidad de Cádiz, 2000) 1:251-69, 32, 3, 4, 11, 12 (all from the early El-Khadr group). Note also the listing of fifty-one arrowhead inscriptions in Robert Deutsch and Michael Heltzer, *West Semitic Epigraphic News of the 1st Millennium* BCE (with a contribution by Gabriel Barkay; Tel Aviv: Archaeological Center, 1999) 13-19.

175. For the latter two references, see Bordreuil and Pardee, *BSV,* 98, 101. Cf. Huffmon, *Amorite Personal Names,* 225.

176. For Ugaritic, see Gröndahl, *Die Personennamen der Texte aus Ugarit,* 104-6.

177. The approach assumes that a third goddess stands behind the word Qudshu. See also Ziony Zevit, *The Religions of Ancient Israel* (London: Continuum, 2001) 323-24 n. 133. For an entirely different approach, Wolfgang Helck, followed by Eduard Lipiński, took Qud(a)shu to be originally an amulet or "holy object" that secondarily became a goddess. See Lipiński, *Resheph,* 181, 198-203. The date for the evidence that Lipiński cites for this word in referring to an amulet (eighth century and later) is very late compared with the older Egyptian evidence for the female figure marked with the word. See further Zevit, p. 323 n. 131.

178. See Cross, *Leaves from an Epigrapher's Notebook,* 305, and *Canaanite Myth and*

Hebrew Epic, 33-35. Earlier J. T. Milik and Cross pointed to the ambiguous identification of *lb't* ("the lioness") on the 'El-Hadr arrowheads as 'Athirat/'Asherah, 'Athtart/Ishtar/'Ashtart/Astarte, or Anat; "Inscribed Javelin-Heads from the Period of the Judges: A Recent Discovery in Palestine," *BASOR* 134 (1954) 5-15, esp. 6-9; cf. Cross, *Canaanite Myth and Hebrew Epic,* 33-34, where he favors an identification with 'Athirat/'Asherah. See also Anthony J. Frendo, "A New Punic Inscription from Żejtun (Malta) and the Goddess Anat-Astarte," *PEQ* 131 (1999) 24-35; Oden, *Studies in Lucian's* De Syria Dea, 58-107.

179. Rahmani, "A Lion-Faced Figurine from Bet She'an," *'Atiqot* Eng. ser. 2 (1959) 185.

180. Barré, *The God-List in the Treaty,* 69.

181. Wiggins, "The Myth of Asherah: Lion Lady and Serpent Goddess," *UF* 23 (1991) 383-94, repr. in *A Reassessment of Asherah: With Further Considerations of the Goddess* (Gorgias Ugaritic Studies 2; Piscataway: Gorgias, 2007) 223-37; see also *A Reassessment of Asherah,* 131, 280, in which he notes Judith M. Hadley's view for Asherah's association with the lions on the Pella stand. See Hadley, *The Cult of Asherah in Ancient Israel and Judah* (University of Cambridge Oriental Publications 57; Cambridge: Cambridge University Press, 2000) 169.

182. Note also the late-eleventh-century inscription, with "arrow of Zakar-ba'l, son of *bn 'nt.*" For these two inscriptions, see Frank Moore Cross, "The Arrow of Suwar, Retainer of 'Abdy," *ErIsr* 25 (Joseph Aviram Volume; 1996) 9*-17*, here 14*. The datings are Cross's. For a listing of examples of *bn 'nt* in the arrowheads, see also Puech, "Les pointes de flèches," 252, #5; 253, #12. The tradition of this name continues into the late Iron Age. Note the Hebrew seal inscription: *rp' bn bn 'nt,* "Rapa', son of Ben-Anat," published by Nahman Avigad, Michael Heltzer, and André Lemaire, *West Semitic Seals: Eighth-Sixth Centuries* BCE (Haifa: University of Haifa, 2000) 97, #76. The name *bn'nt* also appears on an incised inscription from Ekron said to reflect a seventh-sixth century cursive script; see Seymour Gitin, Trude Dothan, and Joseph Naveh, "A Royal Dedicatory Inscription from Ekron," *IEJ* 47 (1997) 14.

183. See the old study of Benjamin Mazar, "Shamgar Ben Anat," *PEFQS* 66 (1934) 192-94. See also the name in Ugaritic, e.g. KTU 4.307.6; 4.320.4; RS 94.2382.11' (Bordreuil and Pardee, *BSV,* 39). Cf. the name in Akkadian texts from Ugarit, in *DULAT,* 229; and a Late Bronze Akkadian court record from Hazor reading ^{m}DUMU-ḫa-nu-ta; for the text from Hazor, see W. W. Hallo and H. Tadmor, "A Lawsuit from Hazor," *IEJ* 27 (1977) 2-5; Wayne Horowitz and Takayoshi Oshima, *Cuneiform in Canaan* (Jerusalem: Israel Exploration Society, 2006) 70-71. Egyptian sources from the time of Ramses II witness to *bint Anat;* see Cross, *Leaves from an Epigrapher's Notebook,* 218-19. See further T. C. Mitchell, "Another Palestinian Inscribed Arrowhead," in *Palestine in the Bronze and Iron Ages: Papers in Honor of Olga Tufnell,* ed. Jonathan N. Tubb (Occasional publication 11; London: Institute of Archaeology, 1985) 137, no. 5; Robert Deutsch and Michael Heltzer, *Forty New Ancient West Semitic Inscriptions* (Tel Aviv-Jaffa: Archaeological Center, 1994) 15-16, 17. Note also a seal inscription dated to the eighth-seventh centuries, "belonging to Rafa' son of BenAnat." See Nahman Avigad, *Corpus of West Semitic Stamp Seals,* rev. and completed by Benjamin Sass (Jerusalem: Israel Academy of Sciences and Humanities/Israel Exploration Society/Institute of Archaeology, Hebrew University of Jerusalem, 1997) 150, 488.

184. John C. L. Gibson, *Textbook of Syrian Semitic Inscriptions,* Vol. 3: *Phoenician Inscriptions* (Oxford: Clarendon, 1982) 7-8: "perhaps she was the patroness of the archers' guild."

185. I thank Ami Mazar for suggesting that I discuss this material and for alerting me to the sites where this type of figurine is attested.

186. Rahmani, "A Lion-Faced Figurine from Bet She'an," 184-85 and pl. XXIV, no. 1-3.

187. Rahmani, "A Lion-Faced Figurine from Bet She'an," 185.

188. Rahmani, "A Lion-Faced Figurine from Bet She'an," 185; Dieter Vieweger and Jutta Häser, "Tall Zira'a: Five Thousand Years of Palestinian History on a Single-Settlement Mound," *NEA* 70/3 (2007) 147-67, here 162-63; Eilat Mazar, *The Palace of King David: Excavations at the Summit of the City of David. Preliminary Report of Seasons 2005-2007* (Jerusalem: Shoham Academic Research, 2009) 40.

189. Rahmani, "A Lion-Faced Figurine from Bet She'an," 185.

190. Amihai Mazar, *NEAEHLSup,* 2014.

191. Mazar, *The Palace of King David,* 39-40, with photograph.

192. Vieweger and Häser, "Tall Zira'a," 162-63; Zieweger, *NEAEHLSup,* 1843. See also Peter M. Fischer, "The Iron Age at Tall Abū al-Kharaz, Jordan Valley: The Third Major Period of Occupation. A Preliminary Synthesis," *Studies in the History and Archaeology of Jordan* 7 (Amman: Department of Antiquities, 2001) 305-16, esp. 312, 315. While the appearance is said to resemble Egyptian Sekhmet, the figure seems to be "a local male copy of the Egyptian female original" (p. 312). My thanks to Elizabeth Bloch-Smith for drawing my attention to this bronze figurine.

193. Photographs for the shrine and the animal figure on it appear in Amihai Mazar and Nava Panitz-Cohen, "A Few Artistic and Ritual Artifacts from the Iron Age at Tel Rehov," *Qad* 40/134 (2007) 96-102, here 101. See also Mazar and Panitz-Cohen, "To What God? Altars and a House Shrine from Tel Rehov Puzzle Archaeologists," *BAR* 34/4 (2008) 40-47, esp. 40-41, 45-46. For another picture with a brief discussion, see Amihai Mazar, "Reḥov, Tel," in *NEAEHLSup,* 2015-16, and pl. VII for a color photograph. The figure has a lump on its back, which has not been explained. The stand is currently on exhibit in the Israel Museum.

194. Pirhiya Beck, *Imagery and Representation: Studies in the Art and Iconography of Ancient Palestine* (Occasional Publications 3; Tel Aviv: Institute of Archaeology, 2002) 399.

195. According to Elizabeth M. Bloch-Smith, one set is to be associated with Astarte and the other with Asherah; "Acculturating Gender Roles: Goddess Images as Conveyors of Culture in Ancient Israel," in *Image, Text, Exegesis: Iconographic Interpretation and the Hebrew Bible,* ed. Izaak J. de Hulster, Joel M. LeMon, and Rüdiger Schmitt (LHB/OTS; Bloomsbury: T. & T. Clark, in press).

196. Mazar and Panitz-Cohen, "To What God?" 45.

197. Mazar and Panitz-Cohen ("To What God?" 46) compare the Middle Bronze shrine from Ashkelon that contained a statue of a calf.

198. Mazar and Panitz-Cohen, "To What God?" 41.

199. Mazar and Panitz-Cohen, "To What God?" 45-46.

200. http://www.astarte.com.au/html/pella_s_canaanite_temple.html. This was

brought to my attention by Elizabeth Bloch-Smith. Stephen Bourkes (personal communication) informs me that the piece is to be published shortly in the *Annual of the Department of Antiquities of Jordan.*

201. For a picture of the chalice, see Pavlos Flourentzos, *A Guide to the Larnaka District Museum* (Nicosia: Department of Antiquities, 1996) 50. The piece was brought to my attention by Elizabeth Bloch-Smith.

202. Another figure with extended limbs appears on a ceramic box discovered in a pit at Yahneh Yam (dated ca. 750-650). See Raz Kletter, Irit Ziffer, and Wolfgang Zwickel, *Yavneh I: The Excavation of the 'Temple Hill' Repository Pit and the Cult Stands* (OBO 30; Fribourg: Academic; Göttingen: Vandenhoeck & Ruprecht, 2010) pl. 67, #3; pl. 68, #1 and 2 (CAT 27). This piece was brought to my attention by Elizabeth Bloch-Smith. Ziffer (*Yavneh I*, 77) understands the figure as a schematic winged head with appendages. The head is unclear.

203. A fine photograph of this stand appears in *Encyclopedia of Archaeological Excavations in the Holy Land*, ed. Michael Avi Yonah and Ephraim Stern (Jerusalem: Massada; Englewood Cliffs; Prentice-Hall, 1978) 4:1142. For a good discussion, see Pirhiya Beck, "The Cult-Stands from Ta'anach: Aspects of the Iconographic Tradition of Early Iron Age Cult Objects in Palestine," in *From Nomadism to Monarchy: Archaeological and Historical Aspects of Early Israel*, ed. Israel Finkelstein and Nadav Na'aman (Jerusalem: Yad Izhak Ben-Zvi/Israel Exploration Society; Washington: Biblical Archaeological Society, 1994) 352-81; repr. in Beck, *Imagery and Representation*, 392-422, esp. 394-95. Beck locates this iconography at the end of a long tradition going back to Middle Bronze Anatolia. See also the discussions of Ruth Hestrin, "The Cult Stand from Ta'anach and Its Religious Background," in *Phoenicia and the East Mediterranean in the First Millennium* B.C., ed. Edward Lipiński (OLA 22; Studia Phoenicia 5; Leuven: Peeters, 1987) 61-77, esp. 73 n. 23; Frank S. Frick, *Tell Taannek 1963-1968*, Vol. 4: *Miscellaneous 2: The Iron Age Cultic Structure* (Palestinian Institute of Archaeology Excavations and Surveys; Bir Zeit: Palestinian Institute of Archaeology, Bir Zeit University, 2000) 120-29; and Hadley, *The Cult of Asherah*, 169-76.

204. Smith, *The Early History of God: Yahweh and the Other Deities in Ancient Israel* (San Francisco: HarperSanFrancisco, 1990) 20, with earlier bibliog.

205. See Gregorio del Olmo Lete, "Littérature et pouvoir royal à Ougarit: Sens politique de la littérature d'Ougarit," in *Études ougaritiques 2*, ed. Valérie Matoïan, Michel Al-Maqdissi, and Yves Calvet (RSO 20; Leuven: Peeters, 2012) 241-50.

Notes to Chapter Eight

1. Albright, "The Song of Deborah in the Light of Archaeology," *BASOR* 62 (1936) 26-31; "Some Additional Notes on the Song of Deborah," *JPOS* 2 (1922) 284-85. Note also the early study of Samuel Rolles Driver, "The Book of Judges: III. Deborah and Barak," *Expositor* 8/3 (1912) 24-38; and later Israel W. Slotki, "The Song of Deborah," *JTS* 33 (1932) 341-54. Cf. Robert M. Engberg, "Historical Analysis of Archaeological Evidence: Megiddo and the Song of Deborah," *BASOR* 78 (1940) 4-9.

2. See Haupt, "Zum Deborahliede," *ZAW* 34 (1914) 229-31. Note also Haupt, "Moses' Song of Triumph," *AJSL* 20 (1904) 149-72.

3. Mowinckel, "Der Ursprung der Bilʿamsage," *ZAW* 48 (1930) 233-71; see also "Zum Psalm des Habakkuk," *TZ* 9 (1953) 1-23.

4. Cross and Freedman, *Studies in Ancient Yahwistic Poetry* (2nd ed.; BRS; Grand Rapids: Eerdmans; Livonia: Dove, 1997; orig. 1975, based on their 1950 Johns Hopkins University dissertation).

5. Kutscher, *A History of the Hebrew Language*, ed. Raphael Kutscher (Jerusalem: Magnes, 1982) 12, 38, and 79-80. For an example from Ginsberg's work, see "Ugaritico-Phoenicia," *JANES* 5 (Gaster Festschrift; 1973) 134 n. 19, discussed further below.

6. Morag, "'Layers of Antiquity' — Some Linguistic Observations on the Oracles of Balaam," *Tarbiz* 50 (1980-81) 1-24. See also Tania Notarius, "Poetic Discourse and the Problem of Verbal Tenses in the Oracles of Balaam," *HS* 49 (2008) 55-86, esp. 85. According to Notarius, the imperfect **yqtl* is used in some archaic functions: for the simple present, for the immediate future, and perhaps for a background circumstantial event or the historical present (in contrast to the participle in later Hebrew). She also views the use of the jussive for the subjunctive mood as relatively archaic. See also Notarius, *The Verb in Archaic Biblical Poetry: A Discursive, Typological, and Historical Investigation of the Tense System* (Studies in Semitic Languages and Linguistics 68; Leiden: Brill, 2013).

7. See below for the important work of Hurvitz.

8. (SBLDS 3; Missoula: Society of Biblical Literature, 1972).

9. Cross, *Canaanite Myth and Hebrew Epic: Essays in the History of the Religion of Israel* (Cambridge, MA: Harvard University Press, 1973) 103 n. 43, 121 n. 32; Halpern, *The Emergence of Israel in Canaan* (SBLMS 29; Chico: Scholars, 1983) 32 n. 48.

10. See also Michael P. O'Connor, *Hebrew Verse Structure* (Winona Lake: Eisenbrauns, 1980) 164-65.

11. For the high antiquity of the "old poetry" more broadly, see Cross and Freedman, *Studies in Ancient Yahwistic Poetry;* Douglas K. Stuart, *Studies in Early Hebrew Meter* (HSM 13; Missoula: Scholars, 1976); Stephen A. Geller, *Parallelism in Early Biblical Poetry* (HSM 20; Missoula: Scholars, 1979); Halpern, *The Emergence of Israel in Canaan*, 32; Ronald S. Hendel, *Remembering Abraham: Culture, Memory, and History in the Hebrew Bible* (Oxford: Oxford University Press, 2005) 100, 124 n. 2. The twelfth-century date for Judges 5 is regarded as the consensus view by Jeffrey C. Geoghagen, *The Time, Place, and Purpose of the Deuteronomistic History: The Evidence of "Until This Day"* (BJS 347; Providence: Brown Judaic Studies, 2006) 150. That this is not quite so is indicated by the discussion below and the views mentioned by Christoph Levin, "Das Alter des Deborahlieds," in *Fortschreibungen: Gesammelte Studien zum Alten Testament* (BZAW 316; Berlin: de Gruyter, 2003) 126 n. 13.

12. Studer, *Das Buch der Richter grammatisch und historisch erklärt* (Bern: Dalp, 1835) 113. I thank Christoph Levin for providing me with access to a copy of Studer's commentary.

13. Burney, *The Book of Judges* (London: Rivingtons, 1918).

14. De Moor, *The Rise of Yahwism: The Roots of Israelite Monotheism* (BETL 91; Leuven: University Press; Peeters, 1990) 110, 154 n. 237, 173, 198; (2nd ed., 1997) 124, 267; "The

Twelve Tribes in the Song of Deborah," *VT* 43 (1993) 483-94, here p. 484. See also Neef, *Deboraerzählung und Deboralied: Studien zu Jdc 4,1–5,31* (Biblisch-theologische Studien 49; Neukirchen-Vluyn: Neukirchener, 2002); "Deboraerzähling und Deborahlied: Beobachtungen zum Verhältnis von Jdc. IV und V," *VT* 44 (1994) 47-59.

15. Garbini, "Il cantico di Debora," *La Parola des Passato* 33 (1978) 5-31. To date, I have been unable to gain access to this article; my summary is drawn from Soggin (see the following note).

16. Soggin, *Judges,* trans. John Bowden (OTL; 2nd ed.; Philadelphia: Westminster, 1987; orig. Italian, 1981) 80-81, 93-94.

17. Waltisberg, "Zum Alter der Sprache des Deboraliedes R. 5," *ZAH* 12 (1999) 218-32.

18. Levin, "Das Alter des Deboralieds," 124-41. To be clear, Levin does not address matters of language, but relies generally on the study of Waltisberg. Most of these features were noted by Studer (*Das Buch der Richter,* 128-29), who characterized them as "dies Eigentümlichkeiten des nord-hebräischen Dialekts" (p. 129).

19. For this feature and its distribution in the Iron II inscriptional record, see W. Randall Garr, *Dialect Geography of Syria-Palestine, 1000-586* B.C.E. (Philadelphia: University of Pennsylvania Press, 1985) 89-91. There are also some instances attested in Ugaritic; perhaps these are dialectic variant forms (see *UG,* 294, #53.313). For the BH masculine plural forms ending in *-în,* including in Judg. 5:10, see also GKC 87e, which regards the forms as late; and Joüon-Muraoka, par. 90c, which takes the forms to be Aramaic. The form in Judg. 5:10 may reflect a regional form in view of the forms in Ugaritic, Moabite, and the Deir ʿAlla inscription.

20. For this feature, see below.

21. Knauf, "Deborah's Language: Judges Ch. 5 in Its Hebrew and Semitic Context," in *Studia Semitica et Semito-hamitica: Festschrift für Rainer Voigt anlässlich seines 60 Geburtstages am 17. Januar 2004,* ed. Bogdan Burtea, Josef Tropper, and Helen Younansardaroud (AOAT 317; Münster: Ugarit-Verlag, 2005) 167-82, here 174-75, 180.

22. Young, "Biblical Texts Cannot Be Dated Linguistically," *HS* 46 (2005) 342-43. He claims that feminine singular final *-â* would be *-ati* in any text prior to 1000 and that the so-called old poems do not show such a form. However, the form is attested sometimes in "old poetry." See *zimrat* in Exod. 15:2 (reused in Ps. 118:14; Isa. 12:2); the apparently "double" feminine form, *ʾêmātâ* in Exod. 15:16 (the form otherwise being *ʾêmâ*); and *ḥakmôt* in Judg. 5:29; see Ginsberg, "Ugaritico-Phoenicia," 134 n. 19; Gary A. Rendsburg, "Northern Hebrew Through Time," in *Diachrony in Biblical Hebrew,* ed. Cynthia L. Miller-Naudé and Ziony Zevit (Linguistic Studies in Ancient West Semitic 8; Winona Lake: Eisenbrauns, 2012) 343. In both Exodus 15 and Judges 5, there are also a few cases of feminine singular nouns ending in *-â;* these could show the transition to the standard BH form for the feminine singular ending (or could they be the result of grammatical updating such as seen in Psalm 18 = 2 Samuel 22?). Young does not mention this possibility in this context, but he does elsewhere, e.g., in Ziony Zevit, "Symposium Discussion Session: An Edited Transcription," *HS* 46 (2005) 375. See also Young, "The Style of the Gezer Calendar and Some 'Archaic Biblical Hebrew' Passages," *VT* 42 (1992) 368-74; *Diversity in Pre-Exilic Hebrew* (FAT 5; Tübingen: Mohr Siebeck, 1993) 122-25; "The 'Archaic' Poetry of the Pentateuch in the MT, Samaritan Pentateuch and 4QExod^{c}," *AbrN* 35 (1998) 74-75.

23. Vern, *Dating Archaic Biblical Hebrew Poetry: A Critique of the Linguistic Arguments* (Perspectives on Hebrew Scriptures and Its Contexts 10; Piscataway: Gorgias, 2011). See also Ian Young, Robert Rezetko, and Martin Ehrensvärd, *Linguistic Dating of Biblical Texts,* Vol. 1: *An Introduction to Approaches and Problems* (London: Equinox, 2008). This work is addressed below.

24. For works addressing the grammar of Judges 5 in addition to the preceding, see Charles L. Echols, *"Tell me, o Muse": The Song of Deborah (Judges 5) in the Light of Heroic Poetry* (LHB/OTS 407, London: T. & T. Clark, 2008); Andrés Piquer Otero, *Estudios de sintaxis verbal en textos ugaríticos: El Ciclo de Baal y la "poesía bíblica arcaica"* (Instituto Biblico y Oriental, ser. minor; Estella: Verbo Divino, 2007); Walter Gross, *Richter* (HTKAT; Freiburg: Herder, 2009) 295-302.

25. Moran, "The Hebrew Language in Its Northwest Semitic Background," in *The Bible and the Ancient Near East: Essays in Honor of William Foxwell Albright,* ed. G. Ernest Wright (Garden City: Doubleday, 1961) 61.

26. Knauf, "Deborah's Language," 176.

27. So Kutscher, *A History of the Hebrew Language,* 37-38.

28. See Robertson, *Linguistic Evidence in Dating Early Poetry,* 62-65, 116-17; also Gary A. Rendsburg, "Hurvitz Redux: On the Continued Scholarly Inattention to a Simple Principle of Hebrew Philology," in *Biblical Hebrew: Studies in Chronology and Typology,* ed. Ian Young (JSOTSup 369; London: T. & T. Clark, 2003) 104-28, here 126.

29. See Anson F. Rainey, "The Ancient Hebrew Prefix Conjugation in the Light of Amarnah Canaanite," *HS* 27 (1986) 4-19; "The Energic in Northwest Semitic," *Or* 77 (2008) 79-83. In response to Rainey's distinction, see Josef Tropper, "Kanaanäisches in den Amarnabriefen," *AfO* 44/45 (1997/1998) 136: "Hier zwischen 'injunktivischem' und 'indicativischem' Energikus unterscheiden zu wollen, ist sinnlos. . . . Es gibt nicht einen 'indicativischen Energikus' und einen 'injunktivischen Energikus,' sondern vielmehr indikativische und nicht-indikativische Verbalformen mit einen und demselben Energikusmorphem -(a)nnV." See also Tamar Zewi, *A Syntactical Study of Verbal Forms Affixed by -n(n) Endings in Classical Arabic, Biblical Hebrew, El-Amarna Akkadian and Ugaritic* (AOAT 260; Münster: Ugarit-Verlag, 1999) 105-9, esp. 108. In Ugaritic, the "energic indicative" is also evident in cases of verbs in the singular and without a suffix, e.g., "Danil went *(ymǵyn)* to his palace" (KTU 1.17 II 24; *UNP,* 56). See also the two forms in parallelism in KTU 1.5 II 6-7 (*UNP,* 143). KTU 2.15.7, 10 is a *tour de force* for the energic indicative, as the same first person singular verb has the energic ending in line 7 yet lacks it in line 10. The vast majority of Ugaritic cases of energic indicatives do not appear in prose contexts, but see the energic indicative forms in KTU 2.82.20; 4.182.59.

30. Halpern, *The Emergence of Israel in Canaan,* 32 n. 48. See also Moran, "The Hebrew Language in Its Northwest Semitic Background," 61. This older locative relative is thought to have developed from the noun **'aṯr,* "place" (Ugaritic *'atr;* cf. Akkadian *asru;* Aramaic *'atra)* into a relative, as attested in KTU 2.39.33b-35: *'adm 'aṯr 'it bqṯ w št̃n ly,* "As for the person, wherever he is, find (him) and send him/it (word of him, in a letter) to me." For the general understanding, see Dennis Pardee, "A Further Note on PRU V, No. 60," *UF* 13 (1981) 152, esp. his comment (p. 156): "If these readings are correct, it becomes clear that *'aṯr* is not functioning as a relative pronoun, though the syntactic function of

the word here is the very one that led to its becoming a relative pronoun (accusative of a noun meaning 'place' = 'in whatever place' → 'wherever' → 'which')." For comparisons of this passage with EA 143:13-17 and its parallel use of Akkadian *ašar,* see Anson Rainey, "Observations on Ugaritic Grammar," *UF* 3 (1971) 162; *UG,* 798. For further discussions, see *UT,* 19.422; *UG,* 558, 595, 819, 884, 905, 909; *DULAT,* 1:127. For the forms of *'ăšer/ ba'ăšer* as relatives ("wherever"), see, e.g., 1 Sam. 23:13; Ruth 1:16; *BDB,* 82, #4b; John Huehnergard, "On the Etymology of the Hebrew Relative *š*-," in *Biblical Hebrew in Its Northwest Semitic Setting: Typological and Historical Perspectives,* ed. Steven E. Fassberg and Avi Hurvitz (Jerusalem: Magnes; Winona Lake: Eisenbrauns, 2006) 103-25, esp. 104-5, 107-10, 123-25. The construction *bimqôm 'ăšer* also may reflect a typologically middle stage in the development of *'ăšer* as a relative particle of place (see Gen. 35:13, 14; 39:20; Deut. 1:31; 8:15; so, too, *'ăšer* following a noun of place or space, as in Num. 13:27) and thus might suggest locative *'ăšer* as an early grammatical feature. Still, some passages with the locative usage, such as Exod. 32:34; 1 Sam. 23:13, hardly guarantee its antiquity.

31. See Cohen, "Diachrony in Biblical Hebrew Lexicography and Its Ramifications for Textual Analysis," in Miller and Zevit, *Diachrony in Biblical Hebrew,* 365.

32. Robertson (*Linguistic Evidence in Dating Early Poetry,* 32), in contrast, regards this verbal syntax as "standard poetic Hebrew." Halpern also sees two preterite **yaqtul* forms in MT *wattĕyabbēb* in v. 28 and in *ta'ănênnâ* in v. 29.

33. Cited for particular notice by Cross, *Canaanite Myth and Hebrew Epic,* 103 n. 43.

34. For his treatment of the verbs in Exodus 15, see Alvieri Niccacci, "Esodo 15: Esame letterario, composizione, interpretazione," *Liber Annuus* 59 (2009) 9-26, esp. 23-24 n. 37. Cf. Robert Shreckhise, "The Problem of Finite Verb Translation in Exodus 15.1-8," *JSOT* 32 (2008) 287-310. For a critique of the **yaqtul* preterite for the high antiquity of Exodus 15, see also Vern, *Dating Archaic Biblical Hebrew Poetry,* 452-54.

35. Niccacci, "The Biblical Hebrew Verbal System in Poetry," in Fassberg and Hurvitz, *Biblical Hebrew in Its Northwest Semitic Setting,* 247-68.

36. Bloch, "The Prefixed Perfective and the Dating of Early Hebrew Poetry — A Re-evaluation," *VT* 59 (2009) 34-70.

37. Vern, *Dating Archaic Biblical Hebrew Poetry,* 45-55.

38. O'Connor, *Hebrew Verse Structure,* 145.

39. Joosten, *The Verbal System of Biblical Hebrew: A New Synthesis Elaborated on the Basis of Classical Prose* (Jerusalem Biblical Studies 10; Jerusalem: Simor, 2012) 417-19; see also pp. 14-15. The use in this poem may be archaic as Joosten suggests; if so, perhaps this archaic style has perdured into the Iron II period.

40. See Notarius, *The Verb in Archaic Biblical Poetry;* "The Archaic System of Verbal Tenses in 'Archaic' Biblical Poetry,'" in Miller-Naudé and Zevit, *Diachrony in Biblical Hebrew,* 193-207.

41. Joosten, *The Verbal System of Biblical Hebrew,* 287. Most of the examples appear in direct discourse. In the cases of Judg. 2:1; 1 Kgs. 7:8, the long form of the third-*hê* verb is used for past.

42. Greenstein, "Forms and Functions of the Finite Verb in Ugaritic Narrative Verse," in Fassberg and Hurvitz, *Biblical Hebrew in Its Northwest Semitic Setting,* 75-102. In favor

of the argument would also be the **yaqtul* form when used for the future (e.g., *w'aḥd*, "and I will look," in 1.19 III 19; *UNP*, 73).

43. Gzella, "Some Pencilled Notes on Ugaritic Lexicography," *BO* 64 (2007) 547. See also Piquer Otero, *Estudios de sintaxis verbal en textos ugaríticos*. This research is built on his text-linguistic study of the verbal usage in the Ugaritic Baal Cycle: "Estudios de Sintaxis Verbal en Textos Ugaríticos Poéticos" (Diss., Universidad Complutense de Madrid, 2003).

44. Gzella, Review of Pierre Bordreuil and Dennis Pardee, *A Manual of Ugaritic*, *BO* 67 (2010) 369-70.

45. See Ola Wikander, "The Hebrew Consecutive *Wâw* as a North West Semitic 'Augment': A Typological Comparison with Indo-European," *VT* 60 (2010) 260-70; and with special attention to Epigraphic South Arabic, see Yaakov Gruntfest, "The Consecutive Imperfect in Semitic Epigraphy," in *Michael: Historical, Epigraphical and Biblical Studies in Honor of Prof. Michael Heltzer*, ed. Yitzhak Avishur and Robert Deutsch (Tel Aviv: Archaeological Center, 1999) 171-80. For the issue of the form in Aramaic, see the debate discussed in Takamitsu Muraoka and Max Rogland, "The *waw* Consecutive in Old Aramaic? A Rejoinder to Victor Sasson," *VT* 48 (1998) 99-101. Note also the summary in Jo Ann Hackett and Na'ama Pat-El, "On Canaanite and Historical Linguistics: A Rejoinder to Anson Rainey," *Maarav* 17 (2010) 184-86. For an older discussion, see Mark S. Smith, *The Origins and Development of the Waw-Consecutive: Northwest Semitic Evidence from Ugarit to Qumran* (HSS 39; Atlanta: Scholars, 1991; repr. Winona Lake: Eisenbrauns, 2009) 12, 65-67.

46. Judg. 11:40 suggests northern Hebrew, according to Burney, *The Book of Judges*, 129, 172-73, 176; Baruch Halpern, "Dialect Distribution in Canaan and the Deir Alla Inscriptions," in *"Working with No Data": Semitic and Egyptian Studies Presented to Thomas O. Lambdin*, ed. David M. Golomb (Winona Lake: Eisenbrauns, 1987) 124; note also the possible use of *tny* in one blessing from Kuntillet 'Ajrud plaster fragments; see Shmuel Aḥituv, *Echoes from the Past: Hebrew and Cognate Inscriptions from the Biblical Period*, trans. Anson F. Rainey (Jerusalem: Carta, 2008) 322; Aḥituv, Esther Eshel, and Ze'ev Meshel, in Meshel, *Kuntillet 'Ajrud (Ḥorvat Teman): An Iron Age II Religious Site on the Judah-Sinai Border* (Jerusalem: Israel Exploration Society, 2012) 105, 107. The southern form of the verb with *šîn* appears in an inscription on an ostracon from Horvat 'Uzza (see Aḥituv, *Echoes from the Past*, 173-76). Perhaps a northern usage in the meaning "to recount" (**tny*) has been developed semantically in distinction from southern **šny*, "to repeat." The northern usage of **tny* would fit with the verb **ṯny*, used for recounting a message in Ugaritic, especially by messengers (KTU 1.2 I 16; 1.3 III 12; VI 12; 1.4 VIII 31; 1.5 II 9; 1.16 VI 28; cf. PN in 4.339.14). By contrast, **tny* in Judg. 5:11 is taken as reflecting Aramaic influence; e.g., see Philippe Guillaume, *Waiting for Josiah: The Judges* (JSOTSup 385; London: T. & T. Clark, 2004) 150 n. 20 (although it is not clear how 11:40 is "a direct quote of Judg. 5:11"). It may be a matter of Aramaic influence on northern Hebrew. Yigal Bloch has noted cases of Proto-Semitic **t* realized in Canaanite dialects as *š* and not as *t*; thus **tny* would be a matter of Aramaic influence; "On Some Alleged Developments of the Proto-Semitic Phoneme /t/ in Iron Age Dialects," *JSS* 53 (2008) 1-28, esp. 21-22. Bloch's evidence is derived mostly from cuneiform spellings of West Semitic proper names in

Neo-Assyrian documents. Bloch himself raises questions about the use of proper names for linguistic generalizations; given the limits of the sample, Aramaic influence on **tnh* remains questionable. See also p. 545 note 21 below.

47. The root may also underlie *tĕnû* in Prov. 31:31; so Al Wolters, "Proverbs XXXI 30-31 as Heroic Hymn: A Form-Critical Analysis," *VT* 38 (1988) 449, 451, 453; R. J. Clifford, *Proverbs* (OTL; Louisville: Westminster John Knox, 1999) 277; Victor Avigdor Hurowitz, "The Seventh Pillar — Reconsidering the Literary Structure and Unity of Proverbs 31," *ZAW* 113 (2001) 215 (also noting Ps. 8:2; Prov. 9:4 following G. R. Driver).

48. For the singular *ḥakmôt* in Ugaritic, Phoenician, and Biblical Hebrew (Prov. 1:20; 9:1, and probably 14:1), see Ginsberg, "Ugaritico-Phoenicia," 134 n. 19. As Ginsberg's discussion indicates, the northern provenience of such a feature does not guarantee an early date for it.

49. So Kutscher, *A History of the Hebrew Language*, 32, based on its distribution in the Song of Deborah, three times in the story of Gideon (Judges 6-8: 6:17; 7:12; 8:26), and once in the Israelite (northern) section of 2 Kgs. 6:11. It appears in LBH more broadly (e.g., Ecclesiastes). See also William Schniedewind and Daniel Sivan, "The Elijah-Elisha Narratives: A Test-Case for the Northern Dialect of Hebrew," *JQR* 87 (1997) 303-37, here 328-30. Robert G. Boling characterizes it as archaic; *Judges* (AB 6A; Garden City: Doubleday, 1975) 109, 115. See, too, Huehnergard, "On the Etymology of the Hebrew Relative *še-*," esp. 104.

50. Rendsburg, "Hurvitz Redux"; "Northern Hebrew Through Time."

51. See Burney, *The Book of Judges*, 171-76. Even in regarding the poem as very old ("hohen Alters," p. 113), Studer (*Das Buch der Richter*, 128-29) saw these features as Aramaic, yet also as "dies Eigenthümlichkeiten des nord-hebräischen Dialekts" (p. 129).

52. Waltisberg, "Zum Alter der Sprache des Deborahliedes R. 5"; Levin, "Das Alter des Deboralieds."

53. Halpern, "Dialect Distribution in Canaan and the Deir Alla Inscriptions," 125-26.

54. Knauf, "Deborah's Language," 174-75, 180.

55. So Kutscher, *A History of the Hebrew Language*, 37-38.

56. So GKC, #44h; Kutscher, *A History of the Hebrew Language*, 37.

57. Schniedewind and Sivan, "The Elijah-Elisha Narratives," 333. Cf. Rendsburg, "Northern Hebrew Through Time," 345.

58. Rendsburg, "Hurvitz Redux," 123.

59. See generally Waltisberg, "Zum Alter der Sprache des Deborahliedes R. 5." See also Levin, "Das Alter des Deboralieds," 127, specifically regarding **tnh*.

60. Boling, *Judges*, 132. Cf. Knauf, who takes the form as a *shaphel* form; "Deborah's Language," 171; his translation for the verb on p. 181 reads "you rose a rising."

61. Kutscher, *A History of the Hebrew Language*, 32.

62. Soggin, *Judges*, 116.

63. See Gotthelf Bergsträsser, "Das hebräische Präfix שׁ," *ZAW* 29 (1909) 40-56; Stanley Gevirtz, "On the Etymology of the Phoenician Particle ša," *JNES* 16 (1957) 124-27.

64. Baruch A. Levine, "The Pronoun שׁ in Biblical Hebrew in the Light of Ancient Epigraphy," *ErIsr* 18 (Avigad Volume; 1985) 147-52 (Heb.). For more recent information for

the Transjordanian West Semitic languages, see Robert Holmstedt, "The Relative Clause in Canaanite Epigraphic Texts," *JNSL* 34 (2008) 8-10.

65. Schniedewind and Sivan, "The Elijah-Elisha Narratives."

66. See the discussion in Chapter One, section 3. The point has been reaffirmed in more recent discussions: Mark S. Smith, "Biblical Narrative between Ugaritic and Akkadian Literature: Part I: Ugarit and the Hebrew Bible: Consideration of Recent Comparative Research," *RB* 114 (2007) 5-29; Edward L. Greenstein, "Texts from Ugarit Solve Biblical Puzzles," *BAR* 36/6 (2010) 48-53; Dennis Pardee, *The Ugaritic Texts and the Origins of West-Semitic Literary Composition* (Schweich Lectures 2007; Oxford: Oxford University Press, 2012) 79-80.

67. Robertson, *Linguistic Evidence in Dating Early Poetry*, 135.

68. Morag, "'Layers of Antiquity.'" It is to be noted that the ancients could well be aware of "antiquated words," as it is put in a Neo-Assyrian letter; see Simo Parpola, *Letters from Assyrian Scholars to the Kings Esarhaddon and Assurbanipal* (repr. Winona Lake: Eisenbrauns, 2007) 1:82-83, letter #116 (*ABL*, 722).

69. Note Simcha Kogut, "The Importance of Syntax for Determination of Historical Periods of the Hebrew Language," *Leš* 42 (1991) 95-100 (Heb.).

70. William L. Moran, "Genesis 49,10 and Its Use in Ez 21,32," *Bib* 39 (1958) 405-25; Richard Steiner, "Poetic Forms in the Masoretic Vocalization and Three Difficult Phrases in Jacob's Blessing," *JBL* 129 (2010) 209-35, here 219-26. Cf. Serge Frolov, "Judah Comes to Shiloh: Genesis 49:10ba, One More Time," *JBL* 131 (2012) 417-22; apart from the problems that Frolov himself notes in his approach, it provides for no poetic parallelism for the bicolon of Gen. 49:10b. For the reading in the Samaritan Pentateuch, see Stefan Schorch, "Der hebräische Wurzel *QHT*," *ZAH* 10 (1997) 76-84, here 77-80.

71. *UBC*, 1:290-91. See Joseph Martin Pagan, *A Morphological and Lexical Study of Personal Names in the Ebla Texts* (ARES 3; Rome: Missione Archeologica Italiana in Siria, 1998) 190.

72. For substantial efforts to relate style and relative chronology of language, Frank H. Polak, "Linguistic and Stylistic Aspects of Epic Formulae in Ancient Semitic Poetry and Biblical Narrative," in Fassberg and Hurvitz, *Biblical Hebrew in Its Northwest Semitic Setting*, 285-304; "Book, Scribe, and Bard: Oral Discourse and Written Text in Recent Biblical Scholarship," *Prooftexts* 31 (2011) 134; "Language Variation, Discourse Typology, and the Sociocultural Background of Biblical Narrative," in Miller-Naudé and Zevit, *Diachrony in Biblical Hebrew*, 301-38.

73. For substantial criticisms, see Avi Hurvitz, "The Recent Debate on Late Biblical Hebrew: Solid Data, Experts' Opinions, and Inconclusive Arguments," *HS* 47 (2006) 191-210; Jan Joosten, "Diachronic Aspects of Narrative *wayhi* in Biblical Hebrew," *JNSL* 35 (2009) 43-61, esp. 58-59; Jacobus A. Naudé, "Linguistic Dating of Biblical Hebrew Texts: The Chronology and Typology Debate," *JNSL* 36 (2010) 1-22, esp. 15-18; Joosten, Review of Ian Young and Robert Rezetko, with the assistance of Martin Ehrensvärd, *An Introduction to Approaches and Problems, Babel und Bibel* (in press). See also Robert Holmstedt and John Cook, at http://ancienthebrewgrammar.wordpress.com/; Ronald Hendel, "Unhistorical Hebrew Linguistics: A Cautionary Tale," at http://www.bibleinterp.com/opeds/hen358022.shtml. See the rejoinder by Rezetko, Young, and Ehrensvärd, "A

Very Tall 'Cautionary Tale': A Response to Ron Hendel," at http://www.bibleinterp.com/articles/rez358028.shtml. On the verbal system in LBH, see also Joosten, *The Verbal System of Biblical Hebrew*, 377-410; Steven E. Fassberg, "The Shift from *qal* to *piel* in the Book of Qoheleth," in Ἐν πάσῃ γραμματικῇ καὶ σοφίᾳ: *Saggi di linguistica ebraica in onore di Alviero Niccacci, OFM*, ed. Gregor Geiger, in collaboration with Massimo Pazzini (Milan: Terra Santa, 2011) 123-27.

74. Cross, in his preface to the second edition of Cross and Freedman, *Studies in Ancient Yahwistic Poetry*, viii.

75. See among Hurvitz's many publications, "Linguistic Criteria for Dating Problematic Biblical Texts," *Hebrew Abstracts* 14 (1973) 74-79; "Continuity and Innovation in Biblical Hebrew — the Case of 'Semantic Change' in Post-Exilic Writings," in *Studies in Ancient Hebrew Semantics*, ed. T. Muraoka (AbrNSup 4; Louvain: Peeters, 1995) 1-10; "The Historical Quest for 'Ancient Israel' and the Linguistic Evidence of the Hebrew Bible: Some Methodological Observations," *VT* 47 (1997) 301-15 (review article of P. R. Davies, *In Search of 'Ancient Israel'* [JSOTSup 148; Sheffield: JSOT, 1992]); "The Relevance of Biblical Hebrew Linguistics for the Historical Study of Ancient Israel," in *Proceedings of the Twelfth World Congress of Jewish Studies. Division A: The Bible and Its World* (Jerusalem: World Union of Jewish Studies, 1999) 21*-33*; "Can Biblical Texts be Dated Linguistically? Chronological Perspectives in the Historical Study of Biblical Hebrew," *Congress Volume: Oslo 1998*, ed. André Lemaire (VTSup 80; Leiden: Brill, 2000) 143-60. For a recent survey of responses to Hurvitz's work, see Dong-Hyuk Kim, *Early Biblical Hebrew, Late Biblical Hebrew, and Linguistic Variability: A Sociolinguistic Evaluation of the Linguistic Dating of Biblical Texts* (VTSup 156; Leiden: Brill, 2013) 1-44.

76. For the topic of lexicography on this score, see Richard C. Steiner, *Stockmen from Tekoa, Sycomores from Sheba: A Study of Amos' Occupations* (CBQMS 36; Washington: Catholic Biblical Association of America, 2003); Aaron J. Koller, *The Semantic Field of Cutting Tools in Biblical Hebrew: The Interface of Philological, Semantic, and Archaeological Evidence* (CBQMS 49; Washington: Catholic Biblical Association of America, 2012). Cf. Ellen Van Wolde, *Reframing Biblical Studies: When Language and Text Meet Culture, Cognition, and Context* (Winona Lake: Eisenbrauns, 2009).

77. For consideration of this issue within the study of linguistic information, see James N. Pohlig, "Cognition and Biblical Documents: Towards Overcoming Theoretical and Methodological Obstacles to Recovering Cultural Worldviews," *JNSL* 29 (2003) 21-35.

78. Rofé, "Not by Language Alone: The Dating of Biblical Sources," in *Houses Full of All Good Things: Essays in Memory of Timo Veijola*, ed. Juha Pakkala and Martti Nissinen (Publications of the Finnish Exegetical Society 95; Helsinki: Finnish Exegetical Society; Göttingen: Vandenhoeck & Ruprecht, 2008) 656-65. On this point, see also Peter C. Craigie, "The Song of Deborah and the Epic of Tukulti-Ninurta," *JBL* 88 (1969) 254.

79. See Jean-Daniel Macchi, *Israël et ses tribus selon Génèse 49* (OBO 171; Fribourg: Academic; Göttingen: Vandenhoeck & Ruprecht, 1999); Raymond de Hoop, *Genesis 49 in Its Literary and Historical Context* (OtSt 39; Leiden: Brill, 1999).

80. Levine, *Numbers 21–36* (AB 4A; New York: Doubleday, 2000) 232.

81. By contrast, it has been thought that an older-looking piece of vv. 8-16 has been incorporated into the royal psalm of thanksgiving of 2 Samuel 22/Psalm 18; see Cross, *Ca-*

naanite Myth and Hebrew Epic, 158-59. In their older study, Cross and Freedman proposed a ninth- or eighth-century date for Psalm 18//2 Samuel 22, based on the orthographic evidence. See Cross and Freedman, *Studies in Ancient Yahwistic Poetry*, 4. The verbal discrepancies between these two versions show additional updating of vocabulary. See Georg Schmuttermayr, *Psalm 18 und 2 Samuel 22: Studien zu einem Doppeltext. Probleme der Textkritik und Übersetzung und das Psalterium Pianum* (SANT 25; Munich: Kösel, 1971); and Cross, *Canaanite Myth and Hebrew Epic*, 158-59.

82. See Shmuel Aḥituv, "The Sinai Theophany in the Psalm of Habakkuk," in *Birkat Shalom: Studies in the Bible, Ancient Near Eastern Literature, and Postbiblical Judaism Presented to Shalom M. Paul*, ed. Chaim Cohen et al. (Winona Lake: Eisenbrauns, 2008) 1:225-32. For a rather different approach, see Steven Cook, "Habakkuk 3, Gender and War," *lectio difficilior* (2009) Ausgabe 1.

83. See also Yigal Bloch, "The Third-Person Masculine Plural Suffixed Pronoun *-mw* and Its Implications for the Dating of Hebrew Poetry," in Miller-Naudé and Zevit, *Diachrony in Biblical Hebrew*, 147-70.

84. Echols, *"Tell me, o Muse,"* 61-63.

85. Knauf, "Deborah's Language," 174-75 and 180.

86. George Foot Moore, *A Critical and Exegetical Commentary on Judges* (ICC 7; Edinburgh: T. & T. Clark, 1895) 147; Burney, *The Book of Judges*, 103, 120; *BDB*, 50.

87. This may to be a case of the pleonastic *wāw* before a noun. See Marvin H. Pope, " 'Pleonastic' *waw* before Nouns in Ugaritic and Hebrew," *JAOS* 73 (1953) 95-98, repr. in *Probative Pontificating in Ugaritic and Biblical Literature: Collected Essays*, ed. Mark S. Smith (Ugaritisch-biblisch Literatur 10; Münster: Ugarit-Verlag, 1994) 311-16. For this reason, I have rendered it "right" (cf. *št ʾalp qdmh//mrʾa wtk pnh*, "He set an ox before him,/A fatling *right* in his face," in KTU 1.4 V 45-46).

88. The verb seems to be positioned before the second term for emphasis. The first part of the question might be taken as a nominal question, with the verb operative in the second half: "was there a shield, or was even a spear seen . . . ?" Blane Conklin renders the clause as an oath formula: "If any shield or was lance seen, [may I be cursed]"; *Oath Formulas in Biblical Hebrew* (Linguistic Studies in Ancient West Semitic 5; Winona Lake: Eisenbrauns, 2011) 39. Conklin omits the remainder of the clause ("among the forty thousand") and does not discuss how such an oath works in the clause's larger context. Simcha Kogut (personal communication) has suggested rendering *ʾim* as "or" and viewing the verse as a double-assertion and not as a double-question: "Shield and spear will not be seen . . ." (his suggested translation). However, I have not been able to find another instance of BH *ʾim* by itself in this meaning (cf. *ʾim . . . ʾim* clauses in Exod. 19:13; Lev. 3:1; 27:26; Deut. 18:3; 2 Sam. 15:21; Ezek. 14:20). Instead, it is *ʾô* that shows this usage; see Anne Garber Kompaoré, "The *qatal* Verb Form and the Conjunction [ʾô] in Biblical Hebrew," *JNSL* 33 (2007) 33-53. I agree that the force in the clause is a negative assertion, but in order to be negative in force, such a double-assertion as opposed to a double-rhetorical question would also have a negative particle. In addition, the lack of *ʾim* by itself, as Kogut suggests, remains an impediment to his interpretation; I thank Professor Kogut for our discussion of this matter.

89. *GKC*, 149e.

90. Held, "Rhetorical Questions in Ugaritic and Biblical Hebrew," *ErIsr* 9 (W. F. Albright Festschrift; 1969) 71-79. For further discussion and BH examples, see also Joüon-Muraoka, par. 161e. Some texts contain interrogative *hê* in the first clause and *ʾô* fronting the second, including Judg. 18:19; 2 Kgs. 6:27; Job 16:3; 38:28, 31; Mal. 1:8, noted in Joüon-Muraoka, 161e. The case in Job 38:28 with this sort of double-question stands near the double-question with *ʾim* in 38:33, and note the double-question of *mî* . . . *ʾô* in 38:36 (cf. Eccl. 2:19). It is noted by Edward Silver that in some cases the double-question seems to request information and is not "rhetorical"; "The Prophet and the Lying Pen: Jeremiah's Poetic Challenge to the Deuteronomic School" (Ph.D. diss., Chicago, 2009) 188-89. For this reason, it may be better to prescind from characterizing the double-question (or triple-question) as a "rhetorical question."

91. Silver, "The Prophet and the Lying Pen," 182-93.

92. Silver ("The Prophet and the Lying Pen," 188) notes that the double- and triple-question in Ugaritic and Hebrew are not entirely continuous, by pointing to elaborations in both traditions. However, this claim obscures the basic continuity that is laid out here and is otherwise accepted by Silver himself.

93. So Daniel Sivan, *A Grammar of the Ugaritic Language* (2nd impression with corrections; HO 1/28; Leiden: Brill, 2001) 216, following Held, "Rhetorical Questions in Ugaritic and Biblical Hebrew," 71-79.

94. For the spellings of Ugaritic *hm*/BH *ʾim*, see E. L. Greenstein, "Another Attestation of Initial *h* > *ʾ* in West Semitic," *JANES* 5 (T. H. Gaster Festschrift; 1973) 157-64. Note also instances of Ugaritic *ʾim*, "if," rather than the more common *hm* (e.g., KTU 2.15.8; 2.72.20). See *UG*, 800.

95. Ps. 68:13b-14a might be read also in this manner, with nothing (zero element) at the head of the first clause and *ʾim* fronting the following clause:

ûnwat bayit tĕḥalleq šālāl	Does the pasturing household divide the spoil,
ʾim-tiškĕbûn bên šĕpattāyim	Or would it remain among the sheepfolds?

96. There is the further possibility that the verb in the double-question represents an asyndetic relative clause of a double-question that is essentially a nominal clause. However, unlike the examples in Ugaritic, under this interpretation as a double-nominal question ("was there a shield or spear that was seen . . . ?"), there would be no proper predicate. Accordingly, the double-question in Judg. 5:8 seems to be a verbal sentence with the verb predicated of both nouns; the verb would be applied to the first noun as a matter of regressive ellipsis. I thank Tania Notarius for suggesting this possibility.

97. For the triple rhetorical question, see Silver, "The Prophet and the Lying Pen," 174-298.

98. Frank Moore Cross, *From Epic to Canon* (Baltimore: Johns Hopkins University Press, 1998) 55 n. 7.

99. "Pens" or the like has been the leading guess for a long time (see Moore, *Judges*, 157). See also "sheepfold" (NJPS) or "folds" (Burney, *The Book of Judges*, 141). The etymological support is lacking, as noted by Studer and Moore. Moore (*Judges*, 157) translates "fireplace." For support, Moore pointed to the noun *ʾašpōt* ("ash-heap [?], refuse-heap, dung-hill," *BDB*, 1046) as well as the verb in 2 Kgs. 4:38; Ezek. 24:3. A similar proposal,

"hearths," made by Albright ("A Catalogue of Early Hebrew Lyric Poems [Psalm 68]," *HUCA* 33, Part One [1950-51] 22), was followed by Boling (*Judges*, 112) and Cross (*From Epic to Canon*, 54), as well as Lawrence E. Stager ("Archaeology, Ecology, and Social History: Background Themes to the Song of Deborah," in *Congress Volume: Jerusalem 1986*, ed. John A. Emerton [VTSup 40; Leiden: Brill, 1988] 227-28). Boling cites Albright's suggestion based on its defense by Paul Haupt, who Albright claimed "was certainly correct." The root **ṯpd* "became **ṯpt* "by partial assimilation," according to Albright; "The North-Canaanite Epic of ʾAlʾêyân Baʿal and Môt," *JPOS* 12 (1932) 202 n. 83. Albright ("A Catalogue of Early Hebrew Lyric Poems," 22) adds that the Hebrew verb means to "set (a cauldron) on the hearth," "which is obviously denominative." Albright in turn related the word to Ugaritic *mṯpdm*, which he also took to mean "hearths." This meaning is hardly clear for Ugaritic *mṯpdm* and its parallel term, *mtḥ*. For *mṯpdm* several scholars have cited Arabic **ṯfd*, "one thing set upon another" (see Fred Renfroe, *Arabic-Ugaritic Lexical Studies* [ALASP 5; Münster: Ugarit-Verlag, 1992] 154; *UBC*, 1:183; *DULAT*, 605-6). The meaning of the word is unclear. However, for the second Ugaritic term, *mtḥ*, Emar has provided a precise cognate, *mataḫu*, specifically used as a measurement of length, e.g., in a legal contract for the sale of a field; Gary A. Beckman, *Texts from the Vicinity of Emar in the Collection of Jonathan Rosen* (History of the Ancient Near East/Monographs 2; Padova: Sargon srl, 1996) 84; Lucia Mori, *Reconstructing the Emar Landscape* (Quaderni de Geografia Storica 6; Rome: Università degli Studi di Roma "La Sapienza," 2002) 105; see also Emar 168:14′ and Daniel Arnaud, *Textes syriens de l'âge du Bronze récent* (Aula orientalis Sup 1; Barcelona: Sabadell, 1991) 11. The Akkadian term from Emar suits the Ugaritic term both etymologically and semantically (so Eugene J. Pentiuc, *West Semitic Vocabulary in the Akkadian Texts from Emar* [HSS 49; Winona Lake: Eisenbrauns, 2001] 123). The word is also attested at Ekalte and Tell Hadidi (for references, see Mori, *Reconstructing the Emar Landscape*, 105 n. 19). The second term, *mtḥ*, entails some sort of length, and given its parallelism with the term *mṯpdm* it too should involve some length. So given that lengths are involved in the Ugaritic terms, Albright's etymology for *mṯpdm* seems problematic. Working with the putative relationship between the Ugaritic and BH words, one might have guessed "hollows"; perhaps these are geological depressions where flocks might take refuge. Cf. Johannes de Moor, "Donkey-Packs and Geology," *UF* 13 (1982) 303-4. However, "hollows" is a guess.

J. David Schloen cites an old suggestion by Aapeli Saarisalo, rendering the word "two panniers," i.e., "the double-harness in which the loads of the donkey are placed"; Saarisalo, *The Boundary Between Issachar and Naphtali: An Archaeological and Literary Study of Israel's Settlement in Canaan* (Helsinki: Suomalaisen kirjallisuuden seura, 1927) 92; Schloen, "Caravans, Kenites, and *Casus Belli*: Enmity and Alliance in the Song of Deborah," *CBQ* 55 (1993) 28 n. 38. The view goes back at least to John Skinner, *A Critical and Exegetical Commentary on the Book of Genesis* (ICC 1; New York: Scribner, 1910) 526. This proposal would work with the observation of Stager ("Archaeology, Ecology, and Social History," 227-28) that Reuben and Gad are noted for flocks in Num. 32:1 ("specialized pastoral economy"). In reference to the word's attestation in Gen. 49:14, Schloen suggests: "the men are symbolized by the animal that they handle." Schloen would derive the root from BH **špt*, "to set, place." The same expression applies to Issachar in Gen. 49:14; Michael David Coogan, "A Structural and Literary Analysis of the Song of Deborah," *CBQ* 40 (1978) 143-66; Cross, *From Epic to Canon,* 55 n. 7. For criticisms of Saarisalo's view as it applies to that context, see Stanley Gevirtz, "The Issachar Oracle in the Testament of Jacob," *ErIsr* 12 (Nelson Glueck Memorial Volume; 1975) 104*-12*, esp. 106*. The proposal is somewhat attractive, but not fully convincing. The verbal root is attested in 2 Kgs. 4:38; Isa. 26:12; Ezek. 24:3; Ps. 22:16 (*BDB,* 1046). Yet, it would be helpful for this proposal if the verb were used even once in a context involving harnesses or donkeys.

100. See Barnabas Lindars, S.S.F., *Judges 1–5,* ed. A. D. H. Mayes (Edinburgh: T. & T. Clark, 1995) 225-27; Menaḥem Zevi Kaddari, "Homonymy and Polysemy in the New Modern Hebrew Lexicon of the Hebrew Bible," in Fassberg and Hurvitz, *Biblical Hebrew in Its Northwest Semitic Setting,* 153; *A Dictionary of Biblical Hebrew* (Ramat-Gan: Bar-Ilan University, 2006) 882; Robert D. Miller II, "When Pharaohs Ruled: On the Translation of Judges 5:2," *JTS* 59 (2008) 650-54.

101. Cf. Arabic *farʿ* and Akkadian *pirtu,* so Burney followed by Peter C. Craigie, "A Note on Judges V 2," *VT* 18 (1968) 398 n. 2.

102. See similarly Burney, *The Book of Judges,* 107-8; Arthur Weiser, "Das Deborahlied," *ZAW* 71 (1959) 67-97; John Gray, "Israel in the Song of Deborah," in *Ascribe to the Lord: Biblical and Other Essays in Memory of Peter C. Craigie,* ed. Lyle Eslinger and Glen Taylor (JSOTSup 67; Sheffield: JSOT, 1988) 421-22.

103. Ginsberg, *The Israelian Heritage of Judaism* (Texts and Studies of the Jewish Theological Seminary of America 24; New York: Jewish Theological Seminary of America, 1982) 101 n. 131. For this reading in Judges 5, see also Cross and Freedman, *Studies in Ancient Yahwistic Poetry,* 9; Schloen, "Caravans, Kenites, and *Casus Belli,*" 21-22; Susan Ackerman, *Warrior, Dancer, Seductress, Queen: Women in Judges and Biblical Israel* (ABRL; New York: Doubleday, 1998) 32-34; Baruch A. Levine, "Scripture's Account: The Nazirite," in *Torah Revealed, Torah Fulfilled: Scriptural Laws in Formative Judaism and Earliest Christianity,* ed. Jacob Neusner, Bruce D. Chilton, and Baruch A. Levine (New York: T. & T. Clark, 2008) 49. The issues with later biblical expressions lie beyond the scope of this discussion. The proposed meaning of "leaders" for the word in Judg. 5:2 is supported by LXX. At the same time, the LXX may represent a guess and there may be a different nuance in v. 9. The root for "leaders" does not have this meaning clearly in West Semitic languages. The appeal to Ugaritic *prʿt* in this specific meaning is dubious, given its single occurrence in a very difficult passage (see the rendering "lofty peaks," *DULAT,* 679; see the discussion below of the one attestation, in KTU 1.8 II 9, where it may refer to "longhairs"); and the appeal to Egyptian *pr-ʿ* in Papyrus Anastasi in itself seems at best weak; see the discussion below, and James E. Hoch, *Semitic Words in Egyptian Texts of the New Kingdom and Third Intermediate Period* (Princeton: Princeton University Press, 1994) 121-22, #153; 122-23, #155. Robert D. Miller's criticism on the semantics of **prʿ* does not address the cultural background involved ("When Pharaohs Ruled," 650-54). His proposal to see the plural of Pharaoh here, "when the Pharaohs pharaohed," is clever and might suit a broader reading of the poem's background (see Mark Leuchter, "'Why Tarry the Wheels of His Chariot?' (Judg 5,28)," *Bib* 91 [2010] 267 n. 31). However, Miller's suggestion is not supported by the parallelism or by the parallel with Deut. 32:42.

104. See Christophe Lemardèle, "Samson le nazir: une mythe du jeune guerrier,"

RHR 222 (2005) 259-86; Jean-Marie Husser, "La mort d'Aqhat: chasse et rites de passage à Ugarit," *RHR* 225 (2008) 323-46, here 330.

105. See Robert McClive Good, *The Sheep of His Pasture: A Study of the Hebrew Noun ʿAm(m) and Its Semitic Cognates* (HSM 29; Chico: Scholars, 1983) 22. It is hard to know whether *ʿmmym* and *prʿt* in this passage bear the military significance that they do in Judg. 5:2. See *UBC,* 2:365, 371-74, 694-95.

106. Craigie, "A Note on Judges V 2," 397-99. Cf. Chaim Rabin, "Judges V, 2 and the 'Ideology' of Deborah's War," *JJS* 6 (1955) 125-34.

107. *CAD,* K:259; *CAD,* P:415.

108. See Susan Niditch, *"My Brother Esau Is a Hairy Man": Hair and Identity in Ancient Israel* (Oxford: Oxford University Press, 2008) 75-77. Note also the discussion of Richard L. Goerwitz, "Long Hair or Short Hair in Ezekiel 44:20," *JAOS* 123 (2003) 371-76.

109. It was supposed by Gösta W. Ahlström that the poem might have been expected to mention Judah as well in the Iron II period; "Judges 5:20f. and History," *JNES* 36 (1977) 288. However, a purely northern event in the early divided monarchy might not be expected to have made reference to Judah.

110. See *DULAT,* 651.

111. See David A. Dorsey, *The Roads and Highways of Ancient Israel* (Baltimore: Johns Hopkins University Press, 1991) 45-46; Kevin McGeough, *Exchange Relationships at Ugarit* (Ancient Near Eastern Studies Sup 26; Leuven: Peeters, 2007) 132 n. 302. The majority view is to take the phrase as "crossroads." See Richard J. Clifford, *Proverbs* (OTL; Louisville: Westminster John Knox, 1999) 90, 94; Michael V. Fox, *Proverbs 1–9* (AB 18A: New York: Doubleday, 2000) 265-66; Bruce Waltke, *The Book of Proverbs: Chapters 1–15* (NICOT; Grand Rapids: Eerdmans, 2004) 386, 394. See also Dennis Pardee, *The Ugaritic Texts and the Origins of West-Semitic Literary Composition* (Schweich Lectures 2007; Oxford: Oxford University Press, 2012) 95.

112. See Jack M. Sasson, "Canaanite Maritime Involvement in the Second Millennium B.C." *JAOS* 86 (1966) 136, followed by Michael C. Astour, "Maʾḫadu, the Harbor of Ugarit," *Journal of the Economic and Social History of the Orient* 13 (1970) 120; Meindert Dijkstra, "Ugaritic Stylistics. 1 Ugaritic Prose," in *Handbook of Ugaritic Studies,* ed. Wilfred G. E. Watson and Nicolas Wyatt (HO 1; Leiden: Brill, 1999) 146; David M. Clements, *Sources for Ugaritic Ritual and Sacrifice,* Vol. 1: *Ugaritic and Ugarit Akkadian Texts* (AOAT 284; Münster: Ugarit-Verlag, 2001) 352; *DULAT,* 651; McGeough, *Exchange Relationships at Ugarit,* 132. Sasson compared Akkadian *ḫarrānu* and Sumerian KASKAL, which mean both "road" and "business venture." For a different view, see Mario Liverani, "La dotazione dei mercanti di Ugarit," *UF* 11 (C. F. A. Schaeffer Festschrift; 1979) 495-503. Liverani takes *ntbt* as "donations," but the putative cognate with Akkadian *nadānu,* "to give," would involve an irregular correspondence of consonants.

113. See E. Y. Kutscher, "מחוז = Harbour in the DSS," *IEJ* 25 (1961) 160-61. For options, see Manfred Dietrich and Oswald Loretz, "Ugaritisch *mi/aḫd* 'Hafen' und *m(i/a) ḫdy* 'Hafenbewohner,'" *UF* 32 (2000) 195-201. Since other uses of the word attested in this manner as a synonym for *ntbt* are rare (see *DULAT,* 514, citing 4.172.6; 4.266.5), the second option would appear to be less likely.

114. See Cunchillos, *TO* 2, 404-6. Cf. the Akkadian text RS 16.386 (*PRU III,* pp. 165-

66), discussed by Ignacio Márquez Rowe, "'How Can Someone Sell His Own Fellow to the Egyptians?'" *VT* 54 (2004) 342 n. 17. As noted by Rowe, this text exempts an individual from doing work for the king concerning caravans of Egypt and Hatti ("they do not have to do any service for the palace or the overseer of the palace"; *CAD,* Š/3:82).

115. Dietrich and Loretz, "Ugaritisch *mi/aḫd* 'Hafen' und *m(i/a)ḫdy* 'Hafenbewohner,'" 195-96; and the discussion in *DULAT,* 651.

116. McGeough, *Exchange Relationships at Ugarit,* 132 n. 302.

117. See Schloen, "Caravans, Kenites, and *Casus Belli,*" 18-38. For related topography, Dale W. Manor, "The Topography and Geography of the Jezreel Valley as They Contribute to the Battles of Deborah and Gideon," *Near Eastern Archaeological Society Bulletin* N.S. 28 (1987) 25-33. For a broader consideration of trade in this region from an archaeological perspective, see Jack S. Holladay, Jr., "Toward a New Paradigmatic Understanding of Long-Distance Trade in the Ancient Near East: From the Middle Bronze II to Early Iron II — A Sketch," in *The World of the Arameans,* Vol. 2: *Studies in History and Archaeology in Honour of Paul-Eugène Dion,* ed. P. M. Michèle Daviau, John W. Wevers, and Michael Weigl (JSOTSup 325; Sheffield: Sheffield Academic, 2001) 136-73.

118. Such control would be a major goal of the monarchy in the north, as reflected in the description of Solomon's activity there. Even if 1 Kgs. 9:15, with its reference to Hazor, does not prove to be historical, this would be a goal for the early northern monarchy. For this point, see Israel Finkelstein and Nadav Na'aman, "Shechem of the Amarna Period and the Rise of the Northern Kingdom of Israel," *IEJ* 55 (2005) 182.

119. *BDB,* 826.

120. Burney, *The Book of Judges,* 115.

121. Stager, "Archaeology, Ecology, and Social History," 224-25.

122. Na'aman, *Canaan in the Second Millennium* B.C.E. (Winona Lake: Eisenbrauns, 2005) 280-83.

123. Because of its occurrence only once and its marking with the determinative for city (URU), this view has been criticized by Benz, "The Varieties of Sociopolitical Experience in the Late Bronze Age Levant and the Rise of Early Israel" (Ph.D. diss., New York University, 2012) 479. Benz prefers to understand the word as the place name Burusilim, following William L. Moran, *The Amarna Letters* (Baltimore: Johns Hopkins University Press, 1992) 219.

124. Albright, *Yahweh and the Gods of Canaan: A Historical Analysis of Two Contrasting Faiths* (Jordan Lectures 1965; Garden City: Doubleday, 1968) 49 n. 101.

125. Boling, *Judges,* 109; Coogan, "A Structural and Literary Analysis," 147; Hendel, *The Epic of the Patriarch: The Jacob Cycle and the Narrative Traditions of Canaan and Israel* (HSM 42; Atlanta: Scholars, 1987) 164.

126. Burney, *The Book of Judges,* 115.

127. Hendel, *The Epic of the Patriarch,* 164 n. 70.

128. Allen, *COS,* 3:13.

129. Allen, *COS,* 3:13 n. 46.

130. Hoch, *Semitic Words in Egyptian Texts,* 122-23 #155. Another educated guess, "feint," was made by John A. Wilson, in *ANET,* 477.

131. A third approach based on the sense of context, e.g., "deliverance," appears in NJPS. This approach does not address the singular noun governing a plural verb.

132. See Robert D. Haak, *Habakkuk* (VTSup 44; Leiden: Brill, 1992) 99-100.

133. See Gösta Ahlström, "Where Did the Israelites Live?" *JNES* 41 (1982) 136.

134. This may explain how the collective noun loses its association with village militia in a passage such as Hab. 3:14.

135. *BDB*, 346.

136. Burney, *The Book of Judges*, 127 citing LXX *anakrouomenon*, "singers" < *anakrouō*, "thrust back," used to "strike musical strings, make a prelude."

137. Albright, *Yahweh and the Gods of Canaan*, 50, followed, e.g., by Boling, *Judges*, 110; Hendel, *The Epic of the Patriarch*, 164.

138. Burney, *The Book of Judges*, 126.

139. *BDB*, 346. For South Semitic cognates for the geminate root, see Wolf Leslau, *Ethiopic and South Arabic Contributions to the Hebrew Lexicon* (Berkeley: University of California Press, 1958) 21, under **ḥṣh.*

140. See Moore, *Judges*, 139-40; Burney, *The Book of Judges*, 109-11; Cross, *Canaanite Myth and Hebrew Epic*, 100-102; Lars Eric Axelsson, *The Lord Rose Up from Seir* (ConBOT 25; Lund: Almqvist and Wiksell, 1987); John Day, *Yahweh and the Gods and Goddesses of Canaan* (JSOTSup 265; Sheffield: Sheffield Academic, 2000) 15-16; André Lemaire, *The Birth of Monotheism: The Rise and Disappearance of Yahwism* (Washington: Biblical Archaeology Society, 2007) 21-23; Mark S. Smith, *The Early History of God: Yahweh and the Other Deities in Ancient Israel* (2nd ed.; Grand Rapids: Eerdmans; Dearborn: Dove, 2002) 25, 32-33, 81; *The Origins of Biblical Monotheism: Israel's Polytheistic Background and the Ugaritic Texts* (Oxford: Oxford University Press, 2001) 143-46; Klaus Koch, *Der Gott Israels und die Götter des Orients: Religionsgeschichtliche Studien II. Zum 80. Geburtstag von Klaus Koch*, ed. Friedhelm Hartenstein und Martin Rösel (FRLANT 216; Göttingen: Vandenhoeck & Ruprecht, 2007) 174-75. By contrast, Christoph Levin ("Das Alter des Deboralieds," in *Fortschreibungen: Gesammelte Studien zum Alten Testament* [BZAW 316; Berlin: de Gruyter, 2003] 132-35) views these as late insertions. See also Konrad Schmid, Review of André Lemaire, *The Birth of Monotheism, Die Welt des Orients* 38 (2008) 257-60. For discussion, see Henrik Pfeiffer, *Jahwes Kommen von Süden: Jdc 5, Hab 3, Dtn 33, und Ps 68 in ihrem literatur- und theologiegeschichtlichen Umfeld* (FRLANT 211; Göttingen: Vandenhoeck und Ruprecht, 2005) 19-116. See also Manfred Görg, *Richter* (KAT; Würzburg: Echter, 1993) 31-32; and the older discussion of Studer, *Das Buch der Richter*, 118-25.

141. For "highland," see Cross, *Canaanite Myth and Hebrew Epic*, 101; William Propp, "On Hebrew *śāde(h)*, 'Highland,'" *VT* 37 (1987) 230-36, comparing Akkadian *šadû* A (*CAD*, Š/1: 49-59).

142. For early Edom, see Thomas E. Levy, Mohammad Najjar, and Thomas Higham, "Iron Age Complex Societies, Radiocarbon Dates and Edom: Working with Data and Debates," *Antiguo Oriente* 5 (2007) 13-34; Levy, "Ethnic Identity in Biblical Edom, Israel, and Midian: Some Insights from Mortuary Contexts in the Lowlands of Edom," in *Exploring the Longue Durée: Essays in Honor of Lawrence E. Stager*, ed. J. David Schloen (Winona Lake: Eisenbrauns, 2009) 251-61; André Lemaire, "Edom and the Edomites," in *The Books*

of Kings: Sources, Composition, Historiography and Reception, ed. Lemaire and Baruch Halpern (VTSup 129; Leiden: Brill, 2010) 225-43.

143. *ANET,* 262.

144. Representative of this view are Manfred Weippert, "Semitische Nomaden des zweiten Jahrtausends," *Bib* 55 (1974) 271 (for the historical reconstruction), and 427 and 430 (for the readings of the Egyptian inscriptions); Karel van der Toorn, "Yahweh," *DDD,* 911-12; Lawrence E. Stager, "Forging an Identity: The Emergence of Ancient Israel," in *The Oxford History of the Biblical World,* ed. Michael D. Coogan (Oxford: Oxford University Press, 1998) 145. See also Shmuel Aḥituv, *Canaanite Toponyms in Ancient Egyptian Documents* (Jerusalem: Magnes; Leiden: Brill, 1984) 121-22; Axelsson, *The Lord Rose Up from Seir,* 48-59; Jean Leclant, "Le 'Tétragramme' à l'époque d'Aménophis III," in *Near Eastern Studies Dedicated to H. I. H. Prince Takahito Mikasa on the Occasion of His Seventy-Fifth Birthday,* ed. Masao Mori, Hideo Ogawa, and Mamoru Yoshikawa (Wiesbaden: Harrassowitz, 1991) 215-19; Manfred Görg, "Jahwe," in *Neues Bibel-Lexikon,* ed. Görg and Bernhard Land (Zurich: Benzinger, 1992) 2:265; "YHWH — ein Toponym? — Weitere Perspektiven," *BN* 101 (2000) 10-14; Donald B. Redford, *Egypt, Canaan, and Israel in Ancient Times* (Princeton: Princeton University Press, 1992) 272-73; Manfred Weippert, *Jahwe und die anderen Götter: Studien zur Religionsgeschichte des antiken Israel in ihrem syrisch-palästinischen Kontext* (FAT 18; Tübingen: Mohr Siebeck, 1997) 40, 97; Cross, *From Epic to Canon,* 67 n. 51. For further discussion with the relevant hieroglyphs represented and transliterated, see Raphael Giveon, *Les bédouines Shosou des documents egyptiens* (DMOA 18; Leiden: Brill, 1971) 26-28, no. 6a; and 74-77 no. 16a, with reading corrected by Weippert, "Semitische Nomaden des zweiten Jahrtausends," *Bib* 55 (1974) 265-80, 427-33, here 427, 430. See also http://www.divinename.no/archaeology.htm. Cf. Irfan Shahid, "The Ethnic Origin of the Edomites," *Studies in the History and Archaeology of Jordan* 10 (2009) 133-36.

145. *ANET,* 258.

146. See *ANET,* 250 n. 28; Ernest Axel Knauf, "Edom," *DDD,* 273-74.

147. See Rainey, "Amarna and Later: Aspects of Social History," *in Symbiosis, Symbolism, and the Power of the Past: Canaan, Ancient Israel, and Their Neighbors — From the Late Bronze Age through Roman Palaestina,* ed. William G. Dever and Seymour Gitin (AIAR Anniversary Volume; Winona Lake: Eisenbrauns, 2003) 180.

148. See van der Toorn, "Yahweh," 912; Smith, *The Early History of God,* 32-33 n. 45; see also Day, *Yahweh and the Gods and Goddesses of Canaan,* 15-16; Lemaire, *The Birth of Monotheism,* 21-23.

149. I provide a more detailed consideration of this tradition and its development within the BH poetic passages in the next chapter. See also Smith, "God in Israel's Bible: Divinity between the World and Israel, between the Old and the New," *CBQ* 74 (2012) 5-22.

150. The non-Hebrew nature of the name has been a longstanding view. See Benjamin Mazar, "Shamgar Ben 'Anat," *PEFQS* 66 (1934) 192-94. This remains the standard view, although which language the name derives from is disputed. See Richard S. Hess, "Israelite Identity and Personal Names from the Book of Judges," *HS* 44 (2003) 27-29.

151. Frank Moore Cross, "The Arrow of Suwar, Retainer of 'Abdy," *ErIsr* 25 (Jo-

seph Aviram Volume; 1996) 9*-17*, here 14*. Cross dates this arrowhead to the eleventh century. See also *'bdlb'it* in Ugaritic (KTU 4.63 III 38; RS 94.2290.11; RS 94.2275 II 7, in Bordreuil and Pardee, *BSV*, 98 and 101). See further the end of Chapter Seven.

152. Moore, *Judges*, 152; Burney, *The Book of Judges*, 132-33; *BDB*, 771; and Tournay, "Quelques rélectures bibliques antisamaritaines," *RB* 71 (1964) 504-36.

153. See the favorable evaluation of this proposal in de Moor, "The Twelve Tribes in the Song of Deborah," 485; Steve Weitzman, "Reopening the Case of the Suspiciously Suspended Nun in Judges 18:30," *CBQ* 61 (1999) 454. For the text-critical issues involved, see Emanuel Tov, "The Textual History of the Song of Deborah in the A Text of the LXX," *VT* 28 (1978) 225; Robert H. O'Connell, *The Rhetoric of the Book of Judges* (VTSup 63; Leiden: Brill, 1996) 464-65.

154. Schloen, "Caravans, Kenites, and *Casus Belli*," 27.

155. Perhaps the Ephraim-Amalekite relationship involved some exogamous marriage alliance following in the wake of trade. For a consideration of this sort of marriage alliances in the Iron I period, see Gunnar Lehmann, "Reconstructing the Social Landscape of Early Israel: Rural Marriage Alliances in the Central Hill Country," *TA* 31 (2004) 141-75.

156. E.g., Burney, *The Book of Judges*, 146; NJPS.

157. Cross and Freedman, *Studies in Ancient Yahwistic Poetry*, 12 note g (following Winckler and others) cite *mzl* in Kirta, KRT A:99, 188 = KTU 1.14 II 46, IV 25. It is to be noted *mzl* in Kirta does not concern stars and their courses, but the blind man who stumbles along. See John A. Emerton, "The Meaning of the Root 'MZL' in Ugaritic," *JSS* 14 (1969) 22-33.

158. Burney, *The Book of Judges*, 146.

159. Mankowski, *Akkadian Loanwords in Biblical Hebrew* (HSS 47; Winona Lake: Eisenbrauns, 2000) 86-88; Peacock, "Akkadian Loanwords in the Hebrew Bible: Social and Historical Implications" (Ph.D. diss., New York University, 2012) 90-91.

160. Coogan, "A Structural and Literary Analysis," 150 n. 47.

161. *DCH*, 2:544 (so also **hlk* in 3:11 (?), so *DCH*, 2:556).

162. *CAD*, A/1:298b, #3a, and the verb *alāku* in *CAD*, A/1:309, #3a; *CAD*, K:47a.

163. Ackerman, *Warrior, Dancer, Seductress, Queen*, 46.

164. Levine, *Numbers 21–36*, 92.

165. Levine, *Numbers 21–36*, 93.

166. Weinfeld, "Divine Intervention in War in Ancient Israel and in the Ancient Near East," in *History, Historiography and Interpretation: Studies in Biblical and Cuneiform Literatures*, ed. Hayim Tadmor and Moshe Weinfeld (Jerusalem: Magnes, 1986) 121-47, esp. 124-31. Add also SAA 9 3.3, lines ii 14-17, in Martti Nissinen, *Prophets and Prophecy in the Ancient Near East* (SBLWAW 12; Atlanta: Scholars, 2003) 120. Note also the divinatory omens involving stars and warfare in Nissinen, *Prophets and Prophecy*, 155-56. Cf. the omen of Adad's prosperity in Enuma Anu Enlil, tablet 46: "If Adad thunders in the middle of the Sebettu . . . and if (thereby) their seven stars are showered upon the earth. . . ." For this text, see Erlend Gehlken, *Weather Omens of Enūma Anu Enlil: Thunderstorms, Wind and Rain (Tablets 44-49)* (Cuneiform Monographs 43; Leiden: Brill, 2012) 81. For a consideration of Josh. 10:9-14 along these lines, see Hennie Kruger, "Sun and Moon as

Marking Time: A Cursory Survey of Exegetical Possibilities in Joshua 10:9-14," *JNSL* 26 (2000) 137-52.

167. Kogan, "Comparative Notes in the Old Testament (I)," *Memoriae Igor M. Diakonoff* (Babel und Bibel 2; Winona Lake: Eisenbrauns, 2005) 735-36, citing Joan Goodnick Westenholz, *Legends of the Kings of Akkade* (Mesopotamian Civilizations 7; Winona Lake: Eisenbrauns, 1997) 59-60.

168. Sawyer, "'From Heaven Fought the Stars' (Judges v 20)," *VT* 31 (1981) 87-89.

169. For this point, see below, and Chapter Nine.

170. Cf. Rebecca H. Sinos's comment on epiphanies in Greek literature: "divine assistance should be a sign not of human weakness and need but of the privilege of divine favoritism"; "Divine Selection: Epiphany and Politics in Archaic Greece," in *Cultural Poetics in Archaic Greece: Cult, Performance, Politics*, ed. Carol Dougherty and Leslie Kurke (Oxford: Oxford University Press, 1998) 79.

171. Ackroyd, "The Composition of the Song of Deborah," *VT* 2 (1952) 161.

172. Cross, *Canaanite Myth and Hebrew Epic*, 235 n. 74.

173. The sociopolitical organization reflected by Meroz in this verse has been recently studied by Benz ("Varieties of Sociopolitical Experience," 481, 486), which in effect recasts Cross's notion of the "league" in Judges 5. Like Cross, Benz suggests that Meroz was expected to join the coalition in battle because it was one of the sociopolitical units that belonged to the land of Israel. By the latter, Benz is referring to what he calls "multipolity decentralized *mātus*" (the Akkadian word for land). These political entities, such as the land of Amurru and the land of Shechem in the Amarna letters, comprise a form of political organization among various groups and towns (as opposed to city-states, also attested in the Amarna letters), usually with a single figure at the head of political authority (e.g., Labaya of Shechem in the Amarna letters or Saul in 2 Sam. 2:8-9); for Benz, Meroz would be a town that would have belonged to the emergent decentralized multipolity land of Israel consisting mostly of tribal entities.

Notes to Chapter Nine

1. On the poem's composition and structure, see the following (listed in alphabetical order): Susan Ackerman, *Warrior, Dancer, Seductress, Queen: Women in Judges and Biblical Israel* (ABRL; New York: Doubleday, 1998) 27-180; Peter R. Ackroyd, "The Composition of the Song of Deborah," *VT* 2 (1952) 160-62; Ulricke Bechmann, *Das Deborahlied zwischen Geschichte und Fiktion: eine exegetische Untersuchung zu Richter 5* (Dissertationem Theologische Reihe 33; St. Ottilien: EOS, 1989); Joseph Blenkinsopp, "Ballad Style and Psalm Style in the Song of Deborah: A Discussion," *Bib* 42 (1961) 61-76; André Caquot, "Les tribus d'Israël dans le cantique de Débora (Juges 5,13-17)," *Sem* 36 (1986) 47-70; Michael David Coogan, "A Structural and Literary Analysis of the Song of Deborah," *CBQ* 40 (1978) 143-66; Peter C. Craigie, "The Song of Deborah and the Epic of Tukulti-Ninurta," *JBL* 88 (1969) 253-65; Frank Moore Cross and David Noel Freedman, *Studies in Ancient Yahwistic Poetry* (2nd ed.; BRS; Grand Rapids: Eerdmans; Livonia: Dove, 1997; orig. 1975, based on their 1950 Johns Hopkins University dissertation) 9-14; Charles L.

Echols, *"Tell me, o Muse": The Song of Deborah (Judges 5) in the Light of Heroic Poetry* (LHB/OTS 487; London: T. & T. Clark, 2008); Jan P. Fokkelman, "The Song of Deborah and Barak: Its Prosodic Levels and Structures," in *Pomegranates and Golden Bells: Studies in Biblical, Jewish, and Near Eastern Ritual, Law, and Literature in Honor of Jacob Milgrom*, ed. David P. Wright, David Noel Freedman, and Avi Hurvitz (Winona Lake: Eisenbrauns, 1995) 595-628; Volkmar Fritz, "The Complex of Traditions in Judges 4 and 5 and the Religion of Pre-state Israel," in *"I Will Speak the Riddles of Ancient Times": Archaeological and Historical Studies in Honor of Amihai Mazar on the Occasion of His Sixtieth Birthday*, ed. Aren M. Maier and Pierre de Miroschedji (Winona Lake: Eisenbrauns, 2006) 2:689-98; Giovanni Garbini, "Il cantico di Debora," *La Parola des Passato* 33 (1978) 5-31; Gillis Gerleman, "The Song of Deborah in the Light of Stylistics," *VT* 1 (1951) 168-80; Terry Giles and William J. Doan, *Twice Used Songs: Performance Criticism of the Songs of Ancient Israel* (Peabody: Hendrickson, 2009) 67-84; Alexander Globe, "The Literary Structure and Unity of the Song of Deborah," *JBL* 93 (1974) 493-512; John Gray, "Israel in the Song of Deborah," in *Ascribe to the Lord: Biblical and Other Essays in Memory of Peter C. Craigie*, ed. Lyle Eslinger and Glen Taylor (JSOTSup 67; Sheffield: JSOT, 1988) 421-55; Oscar Grether, *Das Deboralied: Eine metrische Reconstruktion* (BFCT 43/2; Gütersloh: Bertelsmann, 1941); Baruch Halpern, "Doctrine by Misadventure: Between the Israelite Source and the Biblical Historian," in *The Poet and the Historian*, ed. Richard Eliot Friedman (HSS 26; Chico: Scholars, 1983) 41-73; "The Resourceful Israelite Historian," *HTR* 76 (1983) 379-401; *The First Historians: The Hebrew Bible and History* (San Francisco: Harper & Row, 1988); Alan Hauser, "Two Songs of Victory: A Comparison of Exodus 15 and Judges 5," in *Directions in Biblical Hebrew Poetry*, ed. Elaine R. Follis (JSOTSup 40; Sheffield: Sheffield Academic, 1987) 265-84; Yutaka Ikeda, "The Song of Deborah and the Tribes of Israel," in *Studies in the Bible and the Hebrew Language Offered to Meir Wallenstein on the Occasion of His Seventy-fifth Birthday*, ed. Chaim Rabin, David Patterson, B. Z. Luria, and Yishaq Avishur (Jerusalem: Kiryat Sefer, 1979) 65-79 (Heb.); Robert S. Kawashima, *Biblical Narrative and the Depth of the Rhapsode* (Bloomington: Indiana University Press, 2004); Cesare Lepre, *Il Canto di Debhorah* (Storia e testi 6; Naples: D'Auria, 1987); Mark Leuchter, "'Why Tarry the Wheels of His Chariot?' (Judg 5,28)," *Bib* 91 (2010) 256-67; Christoph Levin, "Das Alter des Deborahlieds," in *Fortschreibungen: Gesammelte Studien zum Alten Testament* (BZAW 316; Berlin: de Gruyter, 2003) 124-41; Nadav Na'aman, "Literary and Topographical Notes on the Battle of Kishon (Judges 4-5)," in *Canaan in the Second Millennium B.C.E.: Collected Essays* (Winona Lake: Eisenbrauns, 2005) 2:303-16; Heinz-Dieter Neef, "Deboraerzähling und Deborahlied: Beobachtungen zum Verhältnis von Jdc. IV und V," *VT* 44 (1994) 47-59; *Deboraerzählung und Deboralied: Studien zu Jdc 4,1–5,31* (Biblisch-theologische Studien 49; Neukirchen-Vluyn: Neukirchener, 2002); Robert H. O'Connell, *The Rhetoric of the Book of Judges* (VTSup 63; Leiden: Brill, 1996); Henrik Pfeiffer, *Jahwes Kommen von Süden: Jdc 5, Hab 3, Dtn 33, und Ps 68 in ihrem literatur- und theologiegeschichtlichen Umfeld* (FRLANT 211; Göttingen: Vandenhoeck und Ruprecht, 2005); J. David Schloen, "Caravans, Kenites, and *Casus Belli*: Enmity and Alliance in the Song of Deborah," *CBQ* 55 (1993) 18-38; Jane Shaw, "Constructions of Woman in Readings of the Story of Deborah," in *Anti-Covenant: Counter-Reading Women's Lives in the Hebrew Bible*, ed. Mieke Bal (Bible and Literature 22; JSOTSup 81; Sheffield: Almond, 1989) 113-32;

Rudolf Smend, *Yahweh War and Tribal Confederation: Reflections upon Israel's Earliest History*, trans. Max Gray Rogers (Nashville: Abingdon, 1970); Kenton Sparks, *Ethnicity and Identity in Ancient Israel: Prolegomena to the Study of Ethnic Sentiments and Their Expression in the Hebrew Bible* (Winona Lake: Eisenbrauns, 1998) 94-124; Lawrence E. Stager, "Archaeology, Ecology, and Social History: Background Themes to the Song of Deborah," in *Congress Volume: Jerusalem 1986*, ed. John A. Emerton (VTSup 40; Leiden: Brill, 1988) 221-34; Mark A. Vincent, "The Song of Deborah: A Structural and Literary Consideration," *JSOT* 91 (2000) 61-82; Arthur Weiser, "Das Deborahlied," *ZAW* 71 (1959) 67-97; Gregory T. K. Wong, "Song of Deborah as Polemic," *Bib* 88 (2007) 1-22; Vincenz Zapletal, *Das Deborahlied* (Freiburg: Universitäts-Buchhandlung, 1905); Hans-Jürgen Zobel, *Stammesspruch und Geschichte: Die Angaben der Stammessprüche von Gen 49, Dtn 33 und Jdc 5 über die politischen und kultischen Zustande im damaligen "Israel"* (BZAW 95; Berlin, Topelmann, 1965).

2. Ackroyd, "The Composition of the Song of Deborah," 160-62; and Coogan, "A Structural and Literary Analysis," 165. See further O'Connell, *The Rhetoric of the Book of Judges*, 105-6, 113-26. There are many valuable observations in this latter treatment, though sometimes its judgments of satire and criticism in the poem seem to entail psychologizing assessments that are less than explicit in the text.

3. Coogan, "A Structural and Literary Analysis," 160-64.

4. Coogan, "A Structural and Literary Analysis," 161-62. See in particular the list of common elements on p. 162. Coogan suggests a theory of direct literary relationship "quite possibly in written form." Coogan posits Judg. 5:4-5 as the source for Ps. 68:8-9.

5. See Fishbane, *Biblical Interpretation in Ancient Israel* (Oxford: Clarendon, 1985) 54-55, 75 n. 30.

6. Niehr, "He-of-the-Sinai," *DDD*, 387.

7. Rofé, *Introduction to the Literature of the Hebrew Bible* (Jerusalem Bible Studies 9; Jerusalem: Simor, 2009) 445.

8. Knohl, "Pharaoh's War with the Israelites: The Untold Story," *AZURE* 41 (Summer 2010) http://www.azure.org.il/article.php?id=543. See also Knohl, "Psalm 68: Structure, Composition and Geography," *Journal of Hebrew Scriptures* 12/5 (2012) http://www.jhsonline.org/JHS/Articles/article_177.pdf.

9. See Christo H. J. van der Merwe, "The Biblical Hebrew Particle *'aph*," *VT* 59 (2009) 266-83.

10. See Alexander Rofé, "The Text-Criticism of Psalm 80 — Revisited," *VT* 61 (2011) 298-309.

11. Frank Moore Cross, *Canaanite Myth and Hebrew Epic: Essays in the History of the Religion of Israel* (Cambridge, MA: Harvard University Press, 1973) 101 n. 35.

12. See George Foot Moore, *A Critical and Exegetical Commentary on Judges* (ICC 7; Edinburgh: T. & T. Clark, 1895) 142; Wilhelm Nowack, *Richter, Ruth und Bücher Samuelis übersetzt und erklärt* (HKAT 1/4; Göttingen: Vandenhoeck and Ruprecht, 1902) 43-44; C. F. Burney, *The Book of Judges* (London: Rivingtons, 1918) 113; *GKC*, 137d note 2; Manfred Görg, *Richter* (KAT; Würzburg: Echter, 1993) 31; Levin, "Das Alter des Deboralieds," 132-35, with older references.

13. Fishbane, *Biblical Interpretation in Ancient Israel*, 54-55 and 75 n. 30. Problem-

atic for Fishbane's view, the gloss identifies a singular, while the word putatively glossed "mountains" is plural; so, too, is the verb. To obviate these problems, Fishbane reads the gloss as "this (refers to the event at) Mount Sinai." This effort at explanation is not persuasive.

14. See also the layout and discussion of the two passages by Walter Gross, *Richter: Übersetzt und ausgelegt* (HTKAT; Freiburg: Herder, 2009) 306. For the march in Judg. 5:4a, see also Aloysius Fitzgerald, *The Lord of the East Wind* (CBQMS 34; Washington: Catholic Biblical Association of America, 2002) 86 n. 31.

15. The view was originally proposed by Hubert Grimme, according to William F. Albright, who endorses it in his essay "A Catalogue of Early Hebrew Lyric Poems (Psalm 68)," *HUCA* 33, Part One (1950-51) 20. See also among many scholars, Cross, *Canaanite Myth and Hebrew Epic,* 101; Niehr, "He-of-the-Sinai," 387-88.

16. According to Cross, the "gloss approach" seems to excise what is inconvenient; *Canaanite Myth and Hebrew Epic,* 101.

17. It is for this reason that it has also been supposed that Ps. 68:9, with its omission of Edom, is a paraphrase of Judg. 5:4. See Rofé, *Introduction to the Literature of the Hebrew Bible,* 445; see also 419.

18. Cross, *Canaanite Myth and Hebrew Epic,* 101.

19. Albright, "A Catalogue of Early Hebrew Lyric Poems," 20.

20. See *DNWSI,* 2.729; Jo Ann Hackett, *The Balaam Text from Deir 'Allā* (HSM 31; Chico: Scholars, 1984) 74, 80.

21. See the critique of Cross here by Fitzgerald, *The Lord of the East Wind,* 91 n. 47, in particular that Cross "revocalizes rain out of the text."

22. See Fitzgerald, *The Lord of the East Wind,* 91 n. 47.

23. I owe this suggestion to Susan Ackerman.

24. Zobel, *Stammesspruch und Geschichte,* 50-51; Coogan, "A Structural and Literary Analysis," 164.

25. Coogan, "A Structural and Literary Analysis," 164.

26. Frank Moore Cross, *From Epic to Canon: History and Literature in Ancient Israel* (Baltimore: Johns Hopkins University Press, 1998) 140.

27. Coogan, "A Structural and Literary Analysis," 160-64. Contrast the comments of Cross (*From Epic to Canon,* 55 n. 7): "The question I find difficult to resolve is this: does the list of tribal sayings in the Song of Deborah simply give typical sayings — often with martial flavor — or does the bard borrow and modify such sayings to reprimand those who fail to show up for muster? I am inclined to the former view, and hence suggest an archaic usage of *lm(h).*" Against Cross, Zobel and Coogan are inclined to the latter view, as am I. For a recent refutation of the view of Cross on this score, see Jacob Wright, "War Commemoration and the Interpretation of Judges 5:15b-17," *VT* 61 (2011) 505-21.

28. The usage is quite common, as indicated by the listing for the root in *BDB,* 442, #2a. 29. Note the contextual parallel with Num. 22:8, "spend the night here." For discussion, see Richard C. Steiner, "Does the Biblical Hebrew Conjunction -ו Have Many Meanings, One Meaning, or No Meaning at All?" *JBL* 119 (2000) 249-67, here 258-59.

30. Reference courtesy of William Brown. The clause is both circumstantial as the

participial usage suggests and adversative in keeping with the semantic contrast of the verbs.

31. *BDB*, 1014-15 gives this sense as the common one for the root.

32. Cross, *From Epic to Canon*, 54 n. 7. For a sophisticated studies of variants within biblical verses, see Shemaryahu Talmon, "Double Readings in the Massoretic Text," *Textus* 1 (1960) 144-84; Rofé, "The Text-Criticism of Psalm 80" (with further bibliog.).

33. See the historical sketch of early Reuben by Cross, *From Epic to Canon*, 53-70, esp. 54-55.

34. One need not follow Johannes C. de Moor's dexterous textual surgery getting all twelve tribes into the poem; "The Twelve Tribes in the Song of Deborah," *VT* 43 (1993) 483-94.

35. For historical reasons for the absence of Judah, see Cross, *From Epic to Canon*, 55 n. 8.

36. Ackroyd, "The Composition of the Song of Deborah," 161.

37. Cross, *Canaanite Myth and Hebrew Epic*, 235 n. 74.

38. The middle line may be secondary, imported from the prose version, specifically from Judg. 4:17.

39. Cf. Parker in *UNP*, 77. For discussion of these lines, see Chapter Four, section 5.

40. *COS*, 1:78, with n. a, citing Judg. 4:19; 5:25. See also Anson F. Rainey, "Sinuhe's World," in Maier and de Miroschedji, *"I Will Speak the Riddles of Ancient Times,"* 1:284.

41. For discussion of these elements in these meals, see Mark S. Smith, *The Rituals and Myths of the Feast of the Goodly Gods of KTU/CAT 1.23: Royal Constructions of Opposition, Intersection, Integration, and Domination* (SBLRBS 51; Atlanta: Society of Biblical Literature; Leiden: Brill, 2006) 52-57.

42. Cognates for *spl* also fit with large size:

1. Ugaritic *spl*. The word is taken to be "platter, tray," according to *DULAT*, 766. The contexts (1.104.8; 4.123.17; cf. 4.385.3) do not clarify. Gordon (*UT*, 19.1791) comments on the word in its Akkadian form at Ras Shamra: "The bronze *sà-ap-lu* in Queen Aḫâtmilk's trousseau weighs 2 talents and 1,500 shekels (PRU III, p. 185). It is therefore a huge metal vessel. Of the 2 O.T. occurrences of סֵפֶל, Jud. 5:25 requires a huge (metal) vessel and Jud. 6:38 strongly favors it. There is thus no basis for the current definition 'a (small) dish'. (The bronze *sà-ap-lu* in PRU III, p. 81, weighs 200 shekels). Cf. Minoan *su-pà-la*."
2. West Semitic **sipla?* for a "large drinking bowl, crater" in Egyptian texts; see James E. Hoch, *Semitic Words in Egyptian Texts of the New Kingdom and Third Intermediate Period* (Princeton: Princeton University Press, 1994) 364, #541.
3. Akkadian *saplu*, "bowl" (*CAD*, S:165, citing EA 22 iv 21; and MRS 12 49:12; also listed among bronze cups).

For the claim that the word is northern Hebrew, see Gary A. Rendsburg, "Notes on Israelian Hebrew (I)," in *Michael: Historical, Epigraphical and Biblical Studies in Honor of Prof. Michael Heltzer*, ed. Yitzhak Avishur and Robert Deutsch (Tel Aviv: Archaeological Center, 1999) 257-58.

43. See the use of this noun in KTU 1.17 V 7 (*UNP*, 58).

44. This parallel militates against the comparison of Jael here with Anat. E.g., see J. Glen Taylor, "The Song of Deborah and Two Canaanite Goddesses," *JSOT* 23 (1982) 99-108; Ackerman, *Warrior, Dancer, Seductress, Queen,* 63, 64. Note also Peter C. Craigie, "Deborah and Anat: A Study of Poetic Imagery (Judges 5)," *ZAW* 90 (1978) 374-81. The closer comparison with Yael in this scene is Baal. Still, the overall point about the fund of literary representation in this area seems right.

45. Halpern, "Dialect Distribution in Canaan and the Deir Alla Inscriptions," in *"Working with No Data": Semitic and Egyptian Studies Presented to Thomas O. Lambdin,* ed. David M. Golomb (Winona Lake: Eisenbrauns, 1987) 125. See also Shmuel Aḥituv, *Echoes from the Past: Hebrew and Cognate Inscriptions from the Biblical Period,* trans. Anson F. Rainey (Jerusalem: Carta, 2008) 434.

46. See *UBC,* 1:330, 338, 342, 351.

47. For this proposal of this section, see Mark S. Smith, "What Is Prologue Is Past: Composing Israelite Identity in Judges 5," in *Thus Says the Lord: Essays on the Former and Latter Prophets in Honor of Robert R. Wilson,* ed. John J. Ahn and Stephen L. Cook (LHB/OTS 502; London: T. & T. Clark, 2009) 43-58.

48. Coogan, "A Structural and Literary Analysis," 153.

49. Below I will defend the division of vv. 2-9 and 10-13 in the present arrangement of the poem, but the double-introduction arguably has a more complex history behind it that may have shown an evolving structure. E.g., v. 12 might have been the introduction to an older version of the poem. On this point, see further below.

50. Regarding v. 31 as secondary, see many commentators, e.g., Robert G. Boling, *Judges* (AB 6A; Garden City: Doubleday, 1975) 105; Christoph Levin, "Das Alte des Deboralieds," in *Fortschreibungen: Gesammelte Studien zum Alten Testament* (BZAW 316; Berlin: de Gruyter, 2003) 130, comparing Pss. 37:20; 68:3-4(2-3); 73:27; 92:10(9). It is theoretically possible, though not likely, that the verse belongs to the work of the composer of vv. 2-13 (see below). In any case, the issue is moot for the discussion below.

51. Fritz, "The Complex of Traditions in Judges 4 and 5 and the Religion of Pre-state Israel," in Maier and Pierre de Miroschedji, *"I Will Speak the Riddles of Ancient Times,"* 692-93.

52. See the survey of Gross, *Richter,* 337-41.

53. Müller, "Der Aufbau des Deboraliedes," *VT* 16 (1966) 446-59.

54. Neef, *Deboraerzählung und Deborahlied: Studien zu Jdc 4,1–5,31* (Biblische-Theologische Studien 49; Neukirchen-Vluyn: Neukirchener, 2002) 59-69.

55. Pfeiffer, *Jahwes Kommen von Süden,* 31-34 for a translation and 58-69 for discussion.

56. For a different manner of reading the poem's parts and their integration, see Jacob L. Wright, "Deborah's War Memorial: The Composition of Judges 4-5 and the Politics of War Commemoration," *ZAW* 123 (2011) 519: "Within the Song it is relatively easy to distinguish two strands: one that is symbolic and mythical, and another that is concrete and realistic. The first strand (vv. 2-5, 8-11, 13-14, 16-18, 19-23, 31) is comparable to the style of Exodus 15 and Psalm 68. . . . Conversely, the other thread of the Song (vv. 6-7, 12, 15, 24-30) is much more concrete. The former is graphically realistic or even 'naturalistic' in the technical sense, while the latter employs highly rarified, mythical symbols." The

thematic basis for this separation seems vague and seems to be based, at least in part, on a modern division between the natural and supernatural.

57. I wish to thank Daniel E. Fleming (personal communication) for bringing this point to my attention. See also Fleming, *The Legacy of Israel in Judah's Bible: History, Politics, and the Reinscribing of Tradition* (Cambridge: Cambridge University Press, 2012) 64-66. Cf. Gray, "Israel in the Song of Deborah."

58. So a number of commentators. See Gösta W. Ahlström, *The History of Ancient Palestine* (Minneapolis: Fortress, 1993) 40-41, 379-81.

59. Could v. 2 involve the break-up of stereotyped expression (***ʿ*am yiśrāʾēl*) in parallelism? So it would presume this older phrase (see Num. 11:29; 2 Sam. 1:12; cf. ʿ*am kĕmôš* in Num. 21:29; Jer. 48:46), as noted by commentators, e.g., Cross, *From Epic to Canon,* 12.

60. For BH ʿ*am* as militia, see Rudolf Smend, *Yahweh War and Tribal Confederation* (Nashville: Abingdon, 1970), cited and discussed by Robert McClive Good, *The Sheep of His Pasture: A Study of the Hebrew Noun* ʿAm(m) *and Its Semitic Cognates* (HSM 29; Chico: Scholars, 1983) 124. See also Lawrence Kutler, "A Structural Semantic Approach to Israelite Communal Terminology," *JANES* 14 (1982) 71-72; Klaus Koch, *Der Gott Israels und die Götter des Orients: Religionsgeschichtliche Studien II. Zum 80. Geburtstag von Klaus Koch,* ed. Friedhelm Hartenstein and Martin Rösel (FRLANT 216; Göttingen: Vandenhoeck & Ruprecht, 2007) 190-92.

61. J. Alberto Soggin, *Judges,* trans. John Bowden (OTL; Philadelphia: Westminster, 1981) 97; Alan Hauser, "Two Songs of Victory: A Comparison of Exodus 15 and Judges 5," in *Directions in Biblical Hebrew Poetry,* ed. Elaine R. Follis (JSOTSup 40; Sheffield: Sheffield Academic, 1987) 266, 268; Yairah Amit, *The Book of Judges: The Art of Editing,* trans. Jonathan Chipman (Biblical Interpretation 38; Leiden: Brill, 1999) 213 n. 57.

62. See the chart of Coogan, "A Structural and Literary Analysis," 155.

63. See also Deut. 33:21; 1 Sam. 12:7; Mic. 6:5, noted often by commentators, e.g., Gottlieb Ludwig Studer, *Das Buch der Richter grammatisch und historisch erklärt* (Bern: Dalp, 1835) 138; Levin, "Das Alter des Deboralieds," 128 n. 24; Koch, *Der Gott Israels und die Götter des Orients,* 228.

64. Fritz ("The Complex," 692, 694) sees the achievement in battle by Yahweh generally as a later interpretation, but views v. 13 as part of the original song.

65. Fritz, "The Complex of Traditions," 697.

66. For discussion of the bicolon in 1 Sam. 18:7 = 21:11 = 29:5, see Chapter Eleven.

67. As Boling noted in his commentary, *Judges,* 109.

68. De Moor took this line as a song title; "The Twelve Tribes in the Song of Deborah," 487.

69. For the literary context of this tradition, see Pfeiffer, *Jahwes Kommen von Süden,* 19-116. For its background, see Cross, *Canaanite Myth and Hebrew Epic,* 100-2; Smith, *The Origins of Biblical Monotheism,* 143-46. Exodus 15 is arguably not "the best example" of the march from the southern mountains, as Cross maintains.

70. The literary connection has been noted by Ackerman, *Warrior, Dancer, Seductress, Queen,* 46: "The dichotomies introduced in vv. 4-5 and 6-7 again manifest themselves, as Yahweh's divine soldiers from the heavens (vv 20-21) fight together with Deborah's human recruits on earth (vv 14-18) to ensure the defeat of Sisera's Canaanite army

(v 19)." As this comment illustrates, Ackerman addresses the matter on a descriptive and synchronic level and does not probe it as part of the first person singer's performance. See below.

71. Boling, *Judges*, 109.

72. This phrase is drawn from the discussion of the poem by Terry Giles and William J. Doan, *Twice Used Songs: Performance Criticism of the Songs of Ancient Israel* (Peabody: Hendrickson, 2009) 78. To be clear, Giles and Doan do not propose a diachronic reading of the poem itself. While no analysis of the poem is offered in this work, its notions of performance are certainly to the point. See further below about the voice or voices of the poem, in particular what I call the "I-voice" that invokes Deborah in v. 12 and situates the performance of the poem in her name; she herself is not the "I-voice" as shown by the delay of the invocation to v. 12; rather, the "I-voice" is represented as the voice that sings the Song of Deborah in the tradition of the figure of Deborah when she sings in battle, as represented in v. 12. It is the prose context (Judg. 5:1) that conflated the invocation of Deborah in v. 12 with the "I-voice" represented at various moments in the poem as we have it.

73. Fritz, "The Complex of Traditions," 696.

74. Pfeiffer, *Jahwes Kommen von Süden*, 19-116.

75. This aspect of the poem is particularly emphasized by Wong, "Song of Deborah as Polemic," 1-22.

76. Wong ("Song of Deborah as Polemic," 15) assumes that a monarchic date would not work for the poem since it devotes attention to nonparticipation in battle. However, the issue does not simply entail a lack of participation, but specifically tribal nonparticipation. This specific quality of the lack of partipation would have been suitable to a monarchic audience that sees its standing army as central to royal purpose and national well-being. For a monarchic audience, the poem could show the unreliability of tribal militia and thus the rationale for a royal standing army.

77. I borrow the phrase from the title of the article by Larry G. Herr, "Emerging Nations," *BA* 60 (1997) 114-51, 154-83.

78. Chris Hedges, *War Is a Force That Gives Us Meaning* (New York: Public Affairs, 2002) 46: "national myths ignite collective amnesia in war. . . . Almost every group, and especially every nation, has such myths."

79. A number of biblical scholars have reflected on these issues. See Marc Zvi Brettler, "Memory in Ancient Israel," in *Memory and History in Christianity and Judaism*, ed. Michael Signer (Notre Dame: University of Notre Dame Press, 2001) 1-17; Ronald S. Hendel, "The Exodus in Biblical Memory," *JBL* 120 (2001) 601-22; "Exodus: A Book of Memories," *BRev* 18/4 (2002) 38-45, 52-53; *Remembering Abraham: Culture, Memory, and History in the Hebrew Bible* (Oxford: Oxford University Press, 2005); "Cultural Memory," in *Reading Genesis: Ten Methods* (Cambridge: Cambridge University Press, 2010) 28-46; Edward L. Greenstein, "Mixing Memory and Design: Reading Psalm 78," *Prooftexts* 10 (1990) 197-218; Mark S. Smith, "Remembering God: Collective Memory in Israelite Religion," *CBQ* 64 (2002) 631-51; *The Memoirs of God: History, Memory, and the Experience of the Divine in Ancient Israel* (Minneapolis: Fortress, 2004). See also Daniel Fleming, "Mari and the Possibilities of Biblical Memory," *RA* 92 (1998) 41-78.

80. See Chapter Eleven for discussion.

81. Coogan, "A Structural and Literary Analysis," 145 n. 11.

82. Cross, *Canaanite Myth and Hebrew Epic,* 235 n. 74. De Moor goes further, finding all twelve tribes in the poem; "The Twelve Tribes in the Song of Deborah."

83. For such textual "repression" of early Israelite tradition in biblical literature, see Hendel, "Cultural Memory," 45.

84. Amit, *The Book of Judges,* 70. Note also her comment (p. 335): "relations of intertribal alienation and estrangement are alluded to throughout the book (5:15c, 16, 17, 23; 8:1-21; 12:1-6)."

85. Fritz, "The Complex of Traditions," 697.

86. See Boling, *Judges,* 113.

87. Ackroyd, "The Composition of the Song of Deborah," 161.

88. Ackroyd, "The Composition of the Song of Deborah," 160.

89. I draw here on Luis Alonso Schökel's notion of primary and secondary unity in *A Manual of Hebrew Poetics* (Subsidia biblica 11; Rome: Pontificio Istituto Biblico, 1988) 190. Cf. Wong, "Song of Deborah as Polemic," esp. p. 4. Wong works with "the unity of the poem in its current form."

90. Studer, *Das Buch der Richter,* 113-14.

91. Burney, *The Book of Judges,* 158-71.

92. Burney, *The Book of Judges,* 101.

93. Boling, *Judges,* 101-5.

94. Gross, *Richter,* 294, with further lit.

95. Zapletal, *Das Deborahlied,* 1-2.

96. Blenkinsopp, "Ballad Style and Psalm Style," 67-68.

97. Richter, *Traditionsgeschichtliche Untersuchungen zum Richterbuch* (BBB 18; Bonn: Hanstein, 1963) 65-110.

98. Coogan, "A Structural and Literary Analysis."

99. Bechmann, *Das Deborahlied zwischen Geschichte und Fiktion,* 184-89.

100. Coogan, "A Structural and Literary Analysis," 154.

101. Coogan, "A Structural and Literary Analysis," 153.

102. Coogan, "A Structural and Literary Analysis," 154-57.

103. Coogan, "A Structural and Literary Analysis," 157-58.

104. Coogan, "A Structural and Literary Analysis," 158-60.

105. Coogan, "A Structural and Literary Analysis," 161-65. Other scholars see vv. 14-17 as interpolated, e.g., Caquot, "Les tribus d'Israël," esp. 54-55; see also Na'aman, "Literary and Topographical Notes on the Battle of Kishon," 305.

106. Ackroyd, "The Composition of the Song of Deborah," 161.

107. Blenkinsopp, "Ballad Style and Psalm Style," 67-68; Soggin, *Judges,* 97. I take up Soggin's observation below.

108. Coogan, "A Structural and Literary Analysis of the Song of Deborah," 165.

109. Studer, *Das Buch der Richter,* 113; see also p. 139. To be clear, this was his characterization of vv. 2-12, not 2-13.

110. The synchronic approach taken by Wong ("Song of Deborah as Polemic," 1-22) does not eventuate in an overall sense of the whole.

111. Fokkelman, "The Song of Deborah and Barak," 595-628. See below.

112. Discussions of unity often focused on specific formal features marking coherence over the length of a poem, e.g., alphabetic acrostics, refrains, inclusion and chiasm, keyword/root and other sorts of patterns (which may be viewed as reflecting on the macrolevel of the poem the sorts of features used on the microlevel of the colon). For better discussions of these features with examples, see Meir Weiss, *The Bible From Within: The Method of Total Interpretation* (Jerusalem: Magnes, 1984); Alonso Schökel, *A Manual of Hebrew Poetics,* 189-200; Paul E. Dion, *Hebrew Poetics* (2nd ed.; Mississauga: Benben, 1992) 37-44. It may be argued that this phase of study was influenced by New Criticism and related approaches (e.g., *Werkinterpretation*); see Weiss, *The Bible From Within,* 1-46. While such features are clearly important for interpreting biblical poetry, there have been complaints of a certain formalism issuing from analysis that overemphasizes these. Greenstein has commented on the two-dimensional formalism of much poetic analysis in this vein with its focus on poetic features and techniques; "Mixing Memory and Design." To his credit, Alonso Schökel shows an appreciation for poetic dynamism well beyond such formalism. He also reckons with various sorts of unity, including primary and secondary unity. As discussed below, it is the latter that seems to obtain in the poem in Judges 5.

113. Many prosodic analyses assume rather short lines, e.g., Cross and Freedman, and Michael Coogan; see Cross and Freedman, *Studies in Ancient Yahwistic Poetry,* 9-14; Coogan, "A Structural and Literary Analysis," 145-51. Where these scholars see shorter lines, Burney and Na'aman read longer lines; see Burney, *The Book of Judges,* 161-65; Na'aman, *Canaan in the Second Millennium* B.C.E., 305. In a number of instances, Burney's division into longer lines creates more semantic and syntactical parallelism (e.g., vv. 7a, 25, 26, 28). With Burney, some of the putative short lines (e.g., vv. 3a, 6a, 19a, 25a) may be construed as longer lines with internal parallelism. Such a division is not to disregard the staccato effect of some lines, especially those with internal parallelism.

114. For the semantics, see Baruch A. Levine, *Numbers 21–36* (AB 4A; New York: Doubleday, 2000) 97-98. Levine prefers the juridical sense, "magistrates."

115. For weapons used as scepters at Mari, see Jordi Vidal, "Prestige Weapons in an Amorite Context," *JNES* 70 (2011) 249-50.

116. For this usage of the infinitive absolute, see Yoo-Ki Kim, *The Function of the Tautological Infinitive in Classical Biblical Hebrew* (HSS 60; Winona Lake: Eisenbrauns, 2009); and the review by Holger Gzella, "Emphasis or Assertion? Remarks on the Paronomastic Infinitive in Hebrew," *BO* 67 (2010) 487-98. Perhaps "focus (i.e., the most salient information in a communicative setting)" but probably not "factuality (i.e., concerning the truth-value of the proposition)" applies in this case.

117. Often thought to be inserted from Judg. 4:17. The parallelism of the first and third line would certainly comport with this view.

118. See Coogan, "A Structural and Literary Analysis," 152; Vincent, "The Song of Deborah," 69-70; Wong, "Song of Deborah as Polemic," 5-6. For the semantics of the root **ndb,* see also Levine, *Numbers 21–36,* 96-97.

119. So too Wong, "Song of Deborah as Polemic," 13-14.

120. Alonso Schökel, *A Manual of Hebrew Poetics,* 189.

121. Blenkinsopp, "Ballad Style and Psalm Style," 67-68.

122. The particle *'āz,* which appears in a number of scenes (vv. 8a, 11d, 13a, 19, 22). According to Na'aman, *Canaan in the Second Millennium* B.C.E., 304, this particle marks five stages of battle. The five uses move the action along at some points, but they do not seem to constitute specific structural markers for five stages. E.g., it is not clear that v. 8 commences battle at the gates as Na'aman maintains; it arguably conveys the conditions of new leadership to be met when battle could begin. Even v. 11d, not an easy line to understand in context, does not seem to mark a stage in battle as such, but seems to stand for the context of the song to be sung, the victories of Yahweh as put in v. 11c, one of which is about to unfold. Still I think Na'aman has put his finger on a significant matter. The particle may not signal stages of battle per se, but focuses on various aspects of battle. The particle works to anticipate and dramatize its coming in vv. 8a, 11d, 13a; to signal its engagement in v. 19; and to signal retreat in v. 22. The use of this particle draws the audience's attention to the battle before it has begun and helps to keep it there, right up to its opening and finally into its end.

123. See Fokkelman, "The Song of Deborah and Barak," 596-97.

124. These first person usages are not uniform. While the first person representations in Gen. 49:3 and 9 ("my son") sound like the voice of Jacob, the first person usage in v. 7 sounds like a divine judgment against Simeon and Levi, and v. 6 sounds to me like a human declaration of separation from these two tribes. If so, vv. 6-7 may be taken as a human pronouncement against the two tribes with an addition of a divine (prophetic?) judgment against them. If such an intuition is correct, it implies different settings for the pronouncements about the different tribes. The short tribal sayings of vv. 13-22 and 27 are entirely lacking first person usage, except for the unusual expression of v. 18, which could be associated with the prophetic voice that I have suggested for vv. 6-7. (V. 22 could be added in this interpretation, if one were to suppose that vv. 23-26 represent an expansion on v. 22.)

125. For a defense of the MT against emendations, see O'Connell, *The Rhetoric of the Book of Judges,* 464.

126. V. 21b is difficult. Levin ("Das Alter des Deboralieds," 129 n. 30) regards it as "unverständlich" and emends the root of the verb from **drk* to **brk*. This would work with the two occurrences of **brk* in v. 24. esp. if the composer builds his first person expressions from the material that he then recounts. At the same time, such "building" might still work with **drk* if we may regard the proximity of the two roots as "sonant parallelism" (see the account by Adele Berlin, *The Dynamics of Biblical Parallelism* [rev. ed.; BRS; Grand Rapids: Eerdmans; Livonia: Dove, 2008]). Moreover, there is no particular text-critical support for this emendation. The Greek versions favor "may you my strong soul trample" or the like. For the Greek versions, see Paul Harlé (with the collaboration of Thérèse Roqueplo), *La Bible d'Alexandrie: Les Juges* (Paris: Cerf, 1999) 126. It is the syntax of the final noun that may seem problematic, and it may be adverbial, a feature that the Greek versions might not represent. In either case, one may retain the root as is and translate, "may you, my soul, march in strength" or the like. For this language of strength, perhaps cf. Job 41:14a: "Strength *('ōz)* dwells *(yālîn)* on his neck." For discussion of the verse, see Frank M. Cross, "Ugaritic DB'AT and Hebrew Cognates," *VT* 2 (1952) 162-63.

127. Cf. the view of Peter C. Craigie that this line is a war-cry; "The Song of Deborah and the Epic of Tukulti-Ninurta," 257. The question is, in context, whose cry would this be?

128. This essentially follows Levine's translation (*Numbers 21–36,* 200): "My body marches powerfully." For *ʿz* in conflict, see the Introduction (Chapter One), section 1. Cf. the use of the word also in the conflict of Baal and Mot in KTU 1.6 VI 16-20, discussed in Chapter Six, section 1.

129. Some of these usages as well as their representation as "spontaneous response to the victory" are noted by Amit, *The Book of Judges,* 219.

130. Cf. the second person addresses made in the *Iliad,* e.g., to Patroklos in 16.843, discussed by Deborah Beck, *Homeric Conversation* (Hellenic Studies 14; Washington: Center for Hellenic Studies, 2005) 181-82.

131. For this notion, see the comments of Guy Debord, *The Society of the Spectacle* (New York: Zone, 1994) no. 61, cited in Adam T. Smith, "Representational Aesthetics and Political Subjectivity: The Spectacular in Urartian Images of Performance," in *Archaeology of Performance: Theaters of Power, Community, and Politics,* ed. Takeshi Inomata and Lawrence S. Coben (Lanham: AltaMira, 2006) 111 (reference courtesy of Daniel Fleming). It is often assumed that Deborah is the singer of the song as a whole. Furthermore, it is viewed as an example of a woman's victory song, expressing a number of women's concerns and perspective. For this approach, see Fokkelien van Dijk-Hemmes in Athalya Brenner and van Dijk-Hemmes, *On Gendering Texts: Female and Male Voices in the Hebrew Bible* (Bible Interpretation 1; Leiden: Brill, 1996) 32-34.

132. Hexter, *A Guide to the Odyssey: A Commentary on the English Translation of Robert Fitzgerald* (New York: Vintage, 1993) lxvii.

133. For this aspect of *Iliad* 1.1, see Gregory Nagy, "Ellipsis in Homer," in *Written Voices, Spoken Signs: Tradition, Performance, and the Epic Text,* ed. Egbert Bakker and Ahuvia Kahan (Cambridge, MA: Harvard University Press, 1997) 188.

134. Machinist, "The Voice of the Historian in the Ancient Near Eastern and Mediterranean World," *Int* 57 (2003) 117-37, esp. 120-21, 126, 131-36; Niditch, *Judges* (OTL; Louisville: Westminster John Knox, 2008) 9-10, 77-78. Note also Niditch, *War in the Hebrew Bible: A Study of the Ethics of Violence* (Oxford: Oxford University Press, 1993) 90-105.

135. Nagy, "Ellipsis in Homer," 186-89.

136. For this commonly overlooked "I"-voice in Judges 5, see Smith, "What Is Prologue Is Past."

137. Noted by Seth Benardete, *Achilles and Hector: The Homeric Hero* (South Bend: St. Augustine's Press, 2005) 80, 108-9. Is second person address showing a particular sympathy for the tragedy of these two figures?

138. See Machinist, "The Voice of the Historian."

139. So Ernest Axel Knauf, "Deborah's Language: Judges Ch. 5 in Its Hebrew and Semitic Context," in *Studia Semitica et Semito-hamitica: Festschrift für Rainer Voigt anlässlich seines 60 Geburtstages am 17. Januar 2004,* ed. Bogdan Burtea, Josef Tropper, and Helen Younansardaroud (AOAT 317; Münster: Ugarit-Verlag, 2005) 167-82. Cf. the dating of the poem to the tenth or ninth century by Gross, *Richter,* 349. See Chapter Eight for discussion.

140. Here I am echoing Smith, "Representational Aesthetics and Political Subjectivity," 109 (reference courtesy of Daniel Fleming).

141. Nagy, "Ellipsis in Homer," 177. This characterization would apply whether or not it was of a purely literary sort unrelated to court recitation.

142. This view was suggested to me by Alan Cooper, whom I thank.

143. See Rüdiger Schmitt, *Der "Heilige Krieg" im Pentateuch und im deuteronomistischen Geschichtswerk: Studien zur Forschungs-, Rezeptions- und Religionsgeschichte von Krieg und Bann im Alten Testament* (AOAT 381; Münster: Ugarit-Verlag, 2011) 116.

144. In this instance, Patrick D. Miller entertains the further nuance of "strength, might"; "Ugaritic *ǵzr* and Hebrew *ʿzr* II," *UF* 2 (1970) 159-75, here 168. In this approach, Miller was following H. L. Ginsberg, "A Ugaritic Parallel to 2 Sam 1:21," *JBL* 57 (1938) 210-11 n. 5; and Moshe Held, "The Action-Result (Factitive-Passive) Sequence of Identical Verbs in Biblical Hebrew and Ugaritic," *JBL* 84 (1965) 278-79 n. 31. For the usage in Ugaritic, see Miller, pp. 162-64; and the discussion in the final section of Chapter Four.

145. This discussion takes some cues from comments made about the relationship between human and divine efforts in battle in later biblical texts made by Isac Leo Seeligmann, "Menschliches Heldentum und göttliche Hilfe: Die doppelte Kausalität im alttestamentlichen Geschichtsdenken," *TZ* 19 (1963) 385-411; repr. *Gesammelte Studien zur Hebräischen Bibel*, ed. Erhard Blum (FAT 41; Tübingen: Mohr Siebeck, 2004) 137-59.

146. For this piece of mythopoesis, see Leuchter, "'Why Tarry the Wheels of His Chariot?'" 259.

147. In his discussion of how the formation of Israel was produced out of its experience of defeat, Jacob L. Wright has offered important observations concerning the historical experience of Israel in the Iron II period and later; "The Commemoration of Defeat and the Formation of a Nation in the Hebrew Bible," *Prooftexts* 29 (2009) 433-72, reiterated in "A Nation Conceived in Defeat," *Azure* 42 (2010) 83-101; and "Hare'shit ha'agumah shel ha'am hayehudah," *Techelet* 42 (2011) 60-74. Wright's observations are not intended to address early Israel, as represented in Judges 5. It may also be suggested that the era of the Philistine wars produced victories that helped to make Israel into a kingdom. For this line of approach, see Ronald Cohen, "Warfare and State Formation: Wars Make States and States Make War," in *Warfare, Culture, and Environment*, ed. R. Brian Ferguson (Studies in Anthropology; Orlando: Academic, 1984) 329-58. These issues lie beyond the scope of this discussion; see Chapter Twelve.

Notes to Chapter Ten

1. For the text critical issues, see Richard W. Nysse, "An Analysis of the Greek Witnesses to the Text of the Lament of David," in *The Hebrew and Greek Texts of Samuel*, ed. Emanuel Tov (Jerusalem: Academon, 1980) 69-104. For studies of the poem, see Alfred Guillaume, "David's Lament over Saul and Jonathan," *JTS* 16 (1915) 491-94; Frank Moore Cross and David Noel Freedman, *Studies in Ancient Yahwistic Poetry* (2nd ed.; BRS; Grand Rapids: Eerdmans; Livonia: Dove, 1997; orig. 1975, based on their 1950 Johns Hopkins University diss.) 15-18; Stanley Gevirtz, *Patterns in the Early Poetry of Israel* (SAOC

32; Chicago: University of Chicago Press, 1963) 81; William L. Holladay, "Form and Word-Play in David's Lament over Saul and Jonathan," *VT* 20 (1970) 153-89; William H. Shea, "David's Lament," *BASOR* 221 (1976) 141-44; David Noel Freedman, *Pottery, Poetry, and Prophecy: Studies in Early Hebrew Poetry* (Winona Lake: Eisenbrauns, 1980) 263-74; Michael Patrick O'Connor, *Hebrew Verse Structure* (Winona Lake: Eisenbrauns, 1980) 230-33, 468-71; Francis Landy, "Irony and Catharsis in Biblical Poetry: David's Lament over Saul and Jonathan," *European Judaism* 15 (1981) 3-12; J. P. Fokkelman, *Narrative Art and Poetry in the Books of Samuel,* Vol. 2: *The Crossing Fates (I Sam. 13-23 & II Sam. 1)* (SSN 23; Assen: Van Gorcum, 1986) 654-56; Shemaryahu Talmon, "Emendation of Biblical Texts on the Basis of Ugaritic Parallels," in *Studies in Bible,* ed. Sara Japhet (ScrHier 31; Jerusalem: Magnes, 1986) 279-300; orig. Hebrew in *ErIsr* 14 (H. L. Ginsberg Volume; 1978) 117-24; repr. in *Text and Canon of the Hebrew Bible: Collected Studies* (Winona Lake: Eisenbrauns, 2010) 273-94; Diana Vikander Edelman, "The Authenticity of 2 Sam 1,26 in the Lament over Saul and Jonathan," *SJOT* 2 (1988) 66-75; Gale A. Yee, "The Anatomy of Biblical Parody: The Dirge Form in 2 Samuel 1 and Isaiah 14," *CBQ* 50 (1988) 565-86; Steven P. Weitzman, "David's Lament and the Poetics of Grief in 2 Samuel," *JQR* 85 (1995) 341-60; W. Boyd Barrick, "Saul's Demise, David's Lament, and Custer's Last Stand," *JSOT* 73 (1997) 25-41; Mark George, "Assuming the Body of the Heir Apparent: David's Lament," in *Reading Bibles, Writing Bodies,* ed. Timothy K. Beal and David M. Gunn (London: Routledge, 1997) 164-74; Zvi Mozan, "Praise or Surprise (2 Samuel 1:19): הצבי ישראל על במותיך חלל. Another Explanation for David's Lament," *Beit Mikra* 52 (2007) 21-40 (Heb.); Tod Linafelt, "Private Poetry and Public Eloquence in 2 Samuel 1:17-27: Hearing and Overhearing David's Lament for Jonathan and Saul," *JR* 88 (2008) 497-526; Terry Giles and William J. Doan, *Twice Used Songs: Performance Criticism of the Songs of Ancient Israel* (Peabody: Hendrickson, 2009) 41-44; Nissim Amzallag and Mikhal Avriel, "Complex Antiphony in David's Lament and Its Literary Significance," *VT* 60 (2010) 1-14.

2. This approach to vv. 19-25 is anticipated in Shemaryahu Talmon, "The Textual Study of the Bible — A New Outlook," in *Qumran and the History of the Biblical Text,* ed. Frank M. Cross and Talmon (Cambridge, MA: Harvard University Press, 1975) 365; and Edelman, "The Authenticity of 2 Sam 1,26," 72. See further below for discussion.

3. There are four proposals:

1. It seems simplest to see here the definite article perhaps with a demonstrative force, which would emphasize *the* warrior lying slain "upon your heights." Joüon-Muraoka (par. 137f) refers to the article as originally a demonstrative that retains a weak demonstrative value. Thus one might read *hṣby* in 2 Sam. 1:19 as *h-* (or *hn*) with weak demonstrative force plus *ṣby:* "Behold the Gazelle, O Israel, upon your heights lies slain!" In this connection, it is to be noted that Ugaritic occasionally uses *hn* and *h-* to express definiteness; see *hbt* in KTU 2.70.16, rendered "this house," by Pierre Bordreuil and Dennis Pardee, *A Manual of Ugaritic* (Linguistic Studies in Ancient West Semitic 3; Winona Lake: Eisenbrauns, 2008) 310. See also *hn bnš hw,* "behold, that servant," in RS 96.2039 in *COS* 3:103 n. 118, with Pardee's comment: "the use of *hn* here before a noun that is further modified by the demonstrative *hw,* a function that must have been paralleled in proto-Hebrew and led to the adoption of

the particle *hn* there as a true definite article." For considerable discussions by Holger Gzella, see his articles: "Die Entstehung des bestimmten Artikels im Semitischen," *JSS* 51 (2006) 1-18; "Some Pencilled Notes on Ugaritic Lexicography," *BO* 64 (2007) 543-44; "Linguistic Variation in the Ugaritic Letters and Some Implications Thereof," in *Society and Administration in Ancient Ugarit: Papers Read at a Symposium in Leiden, 13-14 December 2007*, ed. W. H. van Soldt (Leiden: Nederlands Instituut voor het Nabije Oosten, 2010) 66-67. Note also *h-* in *hspr,* "the scribe," on an inscribed Iron I arrowhead; see Émile Puech, "Les pointes de flèches inscrites de la fin du IIe millénaire en Phénicie et Canaan," in *Actas del IV Congreso International de Estudios Fenicios y Púnicos: Cádiz, 2 a 6 de Octubre de 1995*, ed. María Eugenia Aubet Semmler and Manuela Barthélemy (Cádiz: Servicio de Publicaciones Universidad de Cádiz, 2000) 1:254, #18.

2. *h-* has been read as a particle of lament, which would be very suitable at the head of the poem. So Frank Moore Cross, *From Epic to Canon: History and Literature in Ancient Israel* (Baltimore: Johns Hopkins University Press, 1998) 145. Similarly, P. Kyle McCarter (*II Samuel* [AB 9; Garden City: Doubleday, 1984] 74) reads *h-* as *hō,* "alas," as in Amos 5:16 and for the MT interrogative *h-* in 2 Sam. 3:33. The MT word is written in Amos 5:16 as *hô* (with final *wāw*). McCarter posits *h-* as the archaic spelling (i.e., without *wāw* as a *mater lectionis*). More broadly, note also Akkadian *ū'i,* "woe," cited in connection with Amos 5:16 by Shalom M. Paul, *Amos* (Hermeneia; Minneapolis: Fortress, 1991) 179 n. 196, and Hebrew *hāh* in Ezek. 30:2, said to be cognate with Arabic *'āh,* "alas" (see *HALOT,* 4th ed., 240). See also *hî* in Ezek. 2:10 and **'i* in Eccl. 4:10. Attestation of such a particle in either Ugaritic or Amarna Akkadian would bolster the case, but there is no such particle. In this interpretation, the two nouns are sometimes read as a construct phrase, "prince of Israel," by William F. Albright, "The Earliest Forms of Hebrew Verse," *JPOS* 2 (1922) 85 n. 3, followed by Patrick D. Miller, "Animal Names as Designations in Ugaritic and Hebrew," *UF* 2 (1970) 177-86, here 185. There is a problem here: if Israel is not vocative (as in these translations), then there is no antecedent for the second person suffix on "your heights."
3. The particle *h-* here might be understood as the definite article serving as a vocative particle. Joüon-Muraoka (par. 137g) notes *h-* in vocative usage, e.g., in Judg. 3:19 (" I have a secret word [to deliver] to you, O King") and 2 Kgs. 9:5 ("I have a word [to deliver] to you, O Commander," v. 5a; also "To you, O Commander," v. 5b); see also Jer. 2:31. For more on this usage, see the helpful treatment of Cynthia L. Miller, "Definiteness and the Vocative in Biblical Hebrew," *JNSL* 36 (2010) 43-64. The syntax assumed in this approach does not work well. V. 19a-b would end up being translated: "O Gazelle of Israel, Upon your heights lies slain." In this case, the pronominal suffix would refer to the addressed leader himself, which seems awkward.
4. The interpretation of the particle as the interrogative *h-* reads against the MT:

see James L. Kugel, *The Great Poems of the Bible: A Reader's Companion with New Translations* (New York: Free Press, 1999) 98.

4. Usually translated "glory" or the like (NJPS; *BDB*, 840; Linafelt). For this noun as a title for a military leader, see KTU 1.15 IV 7, 18, discussed by Miller, "Animal Names as Designations," 185. See further below.

5. Lit., a noun, "a slain one." The series of *l*'s in my translation here is intended to reflect *l*'s in -*'el . . . ʿal . . . ḥālāl.*

6. V. 21 suggests "heights" here also; see below for the wordplay involved. Cf. Gevirtz, *Patterns in the Early Poetry of Israel*, 81, reading the word as back or body of the slain; he also makes *hṣby* into a verb.

7. *'êk* for lament in Jer. 2:21; 9:18; Mic. 2:4; Eccl. 2:16 (*BDB*, 32). According to Joüon-Muraoka, par. 162, this is an exclamatory particle; also cite in this regard Ps. 73:19 ("how [*'êk*] quickly they have come to ruin") as well as Lam. 1:1; Isa. 1:21.

8. This form of translation avoids adding any expressed direct object ("e.g., "Tell *it* not . . . ,//Do not proclaim *it* . . ." (NJPS; my italics). The implied object of these verbs in v. 20 is the death of Saul and Jonathan; the form it might have taken might be vv. 21-23. If so, this may affect also the understanding of the corresponding v. 24. V. 24 would in turn suggest a possible picture of the women weeping and lamenting with the words of vv. 21-23. For the verbal expression, cf. *pen-yaggîdû* ("lest they tell") in 1 Sam. 27:11, which also involves communication about conflict with the Philistines. There any man or woman is thought to be able to pass on the news, which may be the case here as well.

9. Gevirtz, *Patterns in the Early Poetry of Israel*, 83 comments on the imbalance of these first two lines in this verse. He would emend to *brḥbwt gt*, since *rḥbwt* and *ḥwṣwt* are paired nine times elsewhere. Gevirtz especially notes Amos 5:16, with its lament context. It is true that the first line of the couplet is quite short relative to the parallel line following it. See the comments of Baruch A. Levine on the mention of places in laments (Isaiah 15-16; Jeremiah 48); *Numbers 21-36* (AB 4A; New York: Doubleday, 2000) 102, in his comment on Num. 21:30.

10. For *ḥwṣwt* as "streets" (perhaps "plazas"), see the discussion in Chapter Ten. For streets in Ashkelon in the Iron II, see *Ashkelon 1: Introduction and Overview (1985-2006)*, ed. Lawrence E. Stager, J. David Schloen, and Daniel M. Master (Leon Levy Expedition to Ashkelon; Winona Lake: Eisenbrauns, 2008) 284, 288, 307, 310. For city planning in other Philistine sites, see Ze'ev Herzog, *Archaeology of the City: Urban Planning in Ancient Israel and Its Social Implications* (Sonia and Marco Nadler Institute of Archaeology Monograph 13; Tel Aviv: Emery and Claire Yass Archaeology, 1997) 201-4.

11. There is no easy way to capture in English the alliteration of *pen bĕnôt.*

12. For *plštym//ʿrlym*, see 1 Sam. 14:1, 6; cf. Judg. 14:3; 15:18, 20; 1 Sam. 17:26, 36; 31:4; 2 Sam. 1:20. Note also the issue of circumcision in Jer. 9:25-26; *ANEP*, 332 (Megiddo ivory) and *ANET*, 326, 629, as well as circumcised divine figurines; see also Ora Negbi, *Canaanite Gods in Metal: An Archaeological Study of Ancient Syro-Palestinian Figurines* (Tel Aviv: Institute of Archaeology, 1976) 14, 108, and pl. 17; reference courtesy of Saul Olyan). See Philip J. King, "Circumcision — Who Did It, Who Didn't and Why," *BAR* 32/4 (2006) 49-55; Richard Steiner, "Incomplete Circumcision in Egypt and Edom: Jeremiah (9:24-25) in the Light of Josephus and Jonckheere," *JBL* 118 (1999) 497-505. See also William C. Propp,

"The Origins of Infant Circumcision in Ancient Israel," *HAR* 11 (1987) 355-70; Saul M. Olyan, *Rites and Rank: Hierarchy in Biblical Representations of Cult* (Princeton: Princeton University Press, 2000) 64-90, 153-54 n. 18 (reference courtesy of Olyan); Avraham Faust, *Israel's Ethnogenesis: Settlement, Interaction, Expansion and Resistance* (Approaches to Anthropological Archaeology; London: Equinox, 2006) 85-91; David A. Bernat, *Sign of the Covenant: Circumcision in the Priestly Tradition* (Ancient Israel and Its Literature 3; Atlanta: Society of Biblical Literature, 2009).

13. Might the following Israelite lament be used as just such a taunt? For the utterance of a lament by others, see Mic. 2:4. *GKC*, 148b characterizes it as "a mocking imitation of lament."

14. For construct plus prepositional phrase, see *GKC*, 130a; Gevirtz, *Patterns in the Early Poetry of Israel*, 85 n. 40; McCarter, *II Samuel*, 75. My translation here is quite close to O'Connor, *Hebrew Verse Structure*, 230.

15. Translation commonly omits the definite article as attested in the MT. The definite article occurs six times with Gilboa (1 Sam. 28:4; 31:1, 8; 2 Sam. 1:6, 21; 21:12) and twice without (1 Chr. 10:1, 8). So S. Noah Lee, "The Use of the Definite Article in the Development of Some Biblical Toponyms," *VT* 52 (2002) 334-49, here 338. Note also the definite article on *tmn* once in the Kuntillet 'Ajrud inscriptions; otherwise, they lack the definite article on this name. See Shmuel Aḥituv, Esther Eshel, and Ze'ev Meshel, in Meshel, *Kuntillet 'Ajrud (Ḥorvat Teman): An Iron Age II Religious Site on the Judah-Sinai Border* (Jerusalem: Israel Exploration Society, 2012) 100.

16. The force of the clause may be volitive: "let there be no dew . . . let there be no rain" (so Joüon-Muraoka, par. 160a, citing also Isa. 62:6; Ps. 83:2[1]). Or, it may express the fear of such a cursed situation. See further below.

17. It is more common for the word to be taken with respect to offerings ("fields yielding sacred imposts," *BDB*, 929, under *tĕrûmâ*, "contribution, offering, for sacred uses") or fertility ("bountiful fields," so NJPS). The parallelism with *hārê baggilbōa'* may suggest another term for height as in the translation here. For such a use for *trwmt*, McCarter (*II Samuel*, 69) compares *mĕrômê śādeh* in Judg. 5:18; so also Freedman, *Pottery, Poetry, and Prophecy*, 270; cf. the metaphorical sense of *trmwt* for "height" (of heart) in Jer. 14:14. The parallel is also discussed by Shemaryahu Talmon, *Text and Canon of the Hebrew Bible*, 280-87. Talmon suggests that the phrase was originally **wtrwmt śdy*, having been inverted to the present reading of *wśdy trwmt*. See the discussion below.

18. For this sense of the word, see William H. C. Propp, "On Hebrew *śāde(h)*, 'Highland,'" *VT* 37 (1987) 230-36.

19. The opening *kî* here nicely balances with *bĕlî*, if one construes these two lines as four short lines. Note also *kî šām*, which forms sonant parallelism with *māšîaḥ*, *šām*, and **šemen* and thus frames *māgēn* in the second and third lines.

20. Freedman (*Pottery, Poetry, and Prophecy*, 270) wants to take *māgēn* here as a term of leader (comparing Punic *māgon*). In this case, the fourth line would refer to the leader as the anointed one. See further McCarter, *II Samuel*, 71.

21. MT *bĕlî* is generally a negative modifier, mostly in poetry (cf. Gen. 31:20). See Joüon-Muraoka, par. 160m. I am reading the image as a statement of the weapon's condition reflecting its owner's condition, in effect parallel to "there was begrimed." Cf.

Freedman, *Pottery, Poetry, and Prophecy,* 271, who would take *bly* as asseverative, since Saul was the anointed king; this seems, however, to miss the point about the weapon's condition, not to mention the clever wordplay between the anointing of the weapon and the royal status (rather than a literal statement about Saul as Freedman would have it). The form *mašîaḥ* is not the common *G*-stem passive participle (e.g., 2 Sam. 3:39) and thus might be understood as a substantive. For the semantics of the word, see further below.

22. For parallels, see Alan R. Millard, "Saul's Shield Not Anointed With Oil," *BASOR* 230 (1978) 70. Millard follows Driver's citation of Isa. 21:5, *mišḥû magen,* lit., "grease the shield." Millard additionally cites Akkadian evidence for "oil to rub shield(s)" in *CAD,* K:1, under *kabābu,* "shield." Cf. the description of Gilgamesh cleaning his equipment of battle as well as himself in SB Gilgamesh 6:1-3, as rendered by Andrew R. George (*The Babylonian Gilgamesh Epic: Introduction, Critical Edition, and Cuneiform Texts* [Oxford: Oxford University Press, 2003] 1:619): "He washed his matted hair, he cleaned his equipment, he shook his locks down over his back, He cast aside his dirty things, he clothed himself with his clean things. . . ."

23. For blood and fat in battle, Gevirtz, *Patterns in the Early Poetry of Israel,* 88, citing Isa. 34:6.

24. According to Greenstein (personal communication), the poem takes its name in v. 18 from *qešet* here in v. 22. Gevirtz reads v. 18 as the opening colon of the poem.

25. The idiom denotes victory (cf. defeat in Ps. 44:18; Jer. 38:22; 46:5 and shame in Isa. 42:17). For the enemies of Yahweh driven back, see Isa. 42:17; Jer. 46:5; Pss. 35:4; 40:14 = 70:2 (*BDB,* 690). McCarter (*II Samuel,* 71) compares Ps. 129:5.

26. Contrast the picture in Judg. 3:21-22.

27. For the idiom also in Jer. 50:9, see S. David Sperling, "Late Hebrew *ḥzr* and Akkadian *saḫāru,*" *JANES* 5 (Gaster Festschrift; 1973) 403. Mark W. Hamilton renders: "Saul's sword did not retract clean"; *The Body Royal: The Social Poetics of Kingship in Ancient Israel* (Bible Interpretation 78; Leiden: Brill, 2005) 155 and commenting in n. 32: "literally, 'empty,' but here in the sense of 'without blood and gore on it,' hence 'clean.'"

28. The word is often translated "lovely." The Hebrew root here denotes physical appeal, both for women and for men. From the perspective of men and specifically for warriors, "lovely" as a translation seems less fitting for the physical attractiveness of men to both men and women, and "lovely" seems misplaced for men, especially warriors. So oral communication, Leslie Hoppe; the translations "desirable" and "beefy" (cf. "hunk") were suggested by Corrine Carvalho. The former translation has the further advantage of end-rhyme with the following line as well as alliteration with the preceding word in the same line. See below for further discussion.

29. The phrase here puns on **bāmôt,* "heights," in v. 19 (see also v. 25c)

30. Or, "never parted" (NJPS). Given the use of the root for social units, the usage might suggest that the two are represented here as belonging to the same fictive social unit, e.g., that they are understood, in effect, as brothers. An analogous thrust may be seen in Ruth's declaration that God not part (**prd*) Naomi and her in Ruth 1:17; for this social sense of Ruth's speech here, see Mark S. Smith, "'Your People Shall Be My People': Family and Covenant in Ruth 1:16-17," *CBQ* 69 (2007) 242-58. This sense of the BH root **prd* may be seen also in its use to denote families separating (Gen. 13:9, 11, 14), the

branching out of social entities (Gen. 10:5, 32), socially "separate" units (Gen. 25:23; cf. Deut. 32:8) or social "disaffiliating" (Judg. 4:11); see *DCH,* 6:754-55. A speculation about a further, possible nuance: Akkadian **parādu* (often when used with "heart," *libbu* as the subject) refers to being afraid or troubled (*CAD,* P:142), which might fit the context here; if so, it would refer to their never being afraid and thus their bravery together in battle.

31. For **gbr//*qll,* see Amos 2:14-16; Jer. 46:6; Eccl. 9:11, etc. For the stative verbs in v. 23b, see Jan Joosten, *The Verbal System of Biblical Hebrew: A New Synthesis on the Basis of Classical Prose* (Jerusalem Biblical Studies 10; Jerusalem: Simor, 2012) 89.

32. For the eagle image here, see Jer. 4:13; Lam. 4:19 (so Gevirtz, *Patterns in the Early Poetry of Israel,* 92). See also the combination with the lion, discussed in the following note.

33. For *gbwr* applied also to the lion, see Prov. 30:30, as noted by Brent A. Strawn, *What Is Stronger Than a Lion? Leonine Image and Metaphor in the Hebrew Bible and the Ancient Near East* (OBO 212; Fribourg: Academic; Göttingen: Vandenhoeck & Ruprecht, 2005) 352.

34. For the image of the warrior "with the heart of a lion," see 2 Sam. 17:10. Strawn (*What Is Stronger Than a Lion?* 334) notes the combination of the explicit eagle comparison and the implicit lion imagery in Lam. 4:19, and he further notes the appearance of the two animals together in Ezek. 10:14 (p. 354). For the image in 2 Sam. 1:23, see also his comments on pp. 55, 236-37. For a wide variety of lion imagery applied to warriors in the *Iliad,* see, e.g., 11.113, 383; 12.40-50, 293, 299-308 (Seth Benardete, *Achilles and Hector: The Homeric Hero* [South Bend: St. Augustine's Press, 2005]); 16.752, 756; 17.20-23 (Benardete, 123). For the king as lion in ancient Near Eastern material, see Strawn, 174-84 and 236-48; to be added is the ancient Near Eastern proverbial material, e.g., the Sumerian proverb: "The palace is forest, the king is a lion," in Bendt Alster, *Sumerian Proverbs in the Schøyen Collection* (Cornell University Studies in Assyriology and Sumerian 2; Bethesda: CDL, 2007) 94. Strawn (p. 236) draws a contrast between the imagery in ancient Near Eastern literature and the biblical corpus; the lack of evidence of the biblical material is interpreted as ideologically meaningful. However, there are far more royal texts attested from Egypt and Assyria than from ancient Israel, raising a question about this thematic contrast. Even if they do not appear with the specific qualifications made by Strawn, there are biblical comparisons of the king to a lion, e.g., Prov. 19:12; 20:2; see also 22:13; 30:30-31 as well as Gen. 49:9 (cf. Zeph. 3:3); see Bruce K. Waltke, *The Book of Proverbs Chapters 15–31* (NICOT; Grand Rapids: Eerdmans, 2005) 106-7. These are perhaps suggestive of a broader fund of Israelite imagery comparing the king to a lion. See further Chapter Seven for lion imagery. For further studies, see also Izak Cornelius, "The Lion in the Art of the Ancient Near East: A Study of Selected Motifs," *JNSL* 15 (1989) 53-85; H.-G. Buchholz, "Beobachtungen zur nahöstlichen, zyprischen und frühgriechischen Löwenikonographie," *UF* 37 (Stanislav Segert *in memoriam;* 2005) 27-215; Sharon Zuckerman, "Fit for a (not-quite-so-great) King: A Faience Lion-Headed Cup from Hazor," *Levant* 40 (2007) 115-25; David S. Reese, "On Incised Scapulae and Tridacna," *ErIsr* 29 (Ephraim Stern Volume; 2009) 190*-91*, for an incised Tridacna with a lion's head from Byblos. For matters of method, see J. O. Gransard-Desmond, "Le lion dans la Syrie antique: confrontation des textes au matériel archéologique," *Orient Express* 1/4 (2001) 16-18.

35. The definite article as relative pronoun (Joüon-Muraoka, par. 145) is attested in Ps. 18:32 = 2 Sam. 22:33 (might this be one of the older uses of the definite article?).

36. See Prov. 31:21.

37. The word *ʿădānîm* in the first line resonates with *ʿădî* in the second line. The former is a problem here; see McCarter, *II Samuel*, 72-73. For the other terms, see Gevirtz, *Patterns in the Early Poetry of Israel*, 93-95, citing fine parallels of Jer. 4:30; Job 40:10.

38. For the verbal usage, cf. 1 Kgs. 10:16, 17; note also Amos 8:10.

39. For this term, see the discussion in note 42 below.

40. The form is anomalous; it is understood as a third-ʾ root formed on analogy with third-*h* verbs (see Joüon-Muraoka, par. 78g; McCarter, *II Samuel*, 73). GKC, 75oo translates as a third feminine singular: "it was wonderful" (see also LXX; NJPS, etc.). By contrast, Cross and Freedman (*Studies in Ancient Yahwistic Poetry*, 18; see O'Connor, *Hebrew Verse Structure*, 233) reconstruct נפלא〈א〉ת, "surpassing wast thou." O'Connor renders the lines: "You were a wonder./Your love was mine *(ʾhbtk ly)*./What is the love of women? *(mʾhbt-nšym)*." My reservation for the reconstruction of *nplʾ* 〈ʾ〉*t*, apart from the unnecessary emendation, involves the time frame of the verbal form. If it is a participle in direct discourse, it might be expected to be translated in the present tense. However, given that the figure evoked is dead, a past time frame verb would seem more fitting. For BH participles for present time frame (in many instances, in direct discourse), see Joüon-Muraoka, par. 121d; Mark S. Smith, "Grammatically Speaking: The Participle as a Main Verb of Clauses (Predicative Participle) in Direct Discourse and Narrative in Pre-Mishnaic Hebrew," in *Sirach, Scrolls, and Sages: Proceedings of a Second International Symposium on the Hebrew of the Dead Sea Scrolls, Ben Sira and the Mishnah, Held at Leiden University, 15-17 December 1997*, ed. Takamitsu Muraoka and John F. Elwolde (STDJ 33; Leiden: Brill, 1999) 278-332.

41. O'Connor, *Hebrew Verse Structure*, 233 cites a suggestion of David Noel Freedman that the last line should be understood that they perished "along with/by means of" the weapons of war. Apart from reading against the plain (-looking) sense of the line, it misses the weapons as standing for Saul and Jonathan. See further below.

42. Given that vv. 26-27 constitute part of a song and they reprise many of the themes and expressions of vv. 19-25, it does not seem inappropriate to use this musical term to characterize this section. In music, the term refers to an end piece that repeats a phrase or verse or returns to an earlier theme; a reprise may also modify and heighten the earlier part. Both are operative in the case of 2 Sam. 1:26-27 relative to what precedes in the poem. My thanks go to Corrine Carvalho for this suggestion. Earlier I had used the term "coda": "A coda (Italian: tail) is the ending of a piece of music. This may be very short, but in a composition on a large scale may be extended" (http://www.naxos.com/education/glossary). The word "coda" seems insufficient for the further heightening effects that vv. 26-27 generate.

43. I have taken the title to refer to Saul (so Cross) rather than Jonathan (so Freedman and O'Connor); see O'Connor, *Hebrew Verse Structure*, 470. I also see the reference to Saul here balancing the reference to Jonathan in v. 25.

44. Miller, "Animal Names as Designations," 185; *DULAT*, 1003. For the question of

the use of animal names for military terminology, see also Albert Jamme, *Sabaean Inscriptions from Maḥram Bilqîs (Mârib)* (Baltimore: Johns Hopkins University Press, 1962) 339.

45. See Strawn, *What Is Stronger Than a Lion?* 48, noting also 2 Sam. 17:10. Cf. Song 2:8-9, with the physical movement of the beloved, compared also with a gazelle (brought to my attention by Saul Olyan).

46. Lit., "light on his feet." Note also the inverse expression for Abner, that his hands were unbound and his feet not in fetters, in 2 Sam. 3:34. Cf. the English nickname "lightfoot" (e.g., Francis Lightfoot Lee, 1734-1797, signatory to the Declaration of Independence).

47. To be sure, in context the description seems ironic, since Asahel's capacity to run after Abner leads to his death at the hands of this enemy (2 Sam. 2:19-23), as pointed out to me by Leslie Hoppe.

48. According to Benardete (*Achilles and Hector,* 47), "Achilles' most frequent epithet" is " 'swift-footed,' which seems to occur in such reckless profusion throughout the *Iliad,* but Homer manages its use more finely than many suppose." For this epithet, see further Benardete, 127.

49. As noted by many commentators, e.g., Weitzman, "David's Lament and the Poetics of Grief," 349-50. Cf. Robert D. Miller II, SFO, *Oral Tradition in Ancient Israel* (Eugene: Wipf and Stock, 2011) 93, citing an oral presentation of mine on this section.

50. This statement cleverly captures the contrast with Baal: while other titles for the god might have been used, his epithet "Lord of the Earth" appears here, perhaps most ironically, for at this point in the story, the god seems anything other than "Lord of the Earth."

51. See also the description of Baal's "fall" *(npl)* in KTU 1.12 II 53-55. The context is unclear.

52. See David Noel Freedman, "On the Death of Abiner," in *Love and Death in the Ancient Near East: Essays in Honor of Marvin H. Pope,* ed. John H. Marks and Robert M. Good (Guilford: Four Quarters, 1987) 125-27, repr. in *Divine Commitment and Human Obligation: Selected Writings of David Noel Freedman,* Vol. 2: *Poetry and Orthography,* ed. John R. Huddleston (Grand Rapids: Eerdmans, 1997) 227-31; Elisha Qimron, "The Lament of David over Abner," in *Birkat Shalom: Studies in the Bible, Ancient Near Eastern Literature, and Post-Biblical Judaism Presented to Shalom M. Paul on the Occasion of His Seventieth Birthday,* ed. Chaim Cohen et al. (Winona Lake: Eisenbrauns, 2008) 143-47.

53. See Athalya Brenner and Fokkelien van Dijk-Hemmes, *On Gendering Texts: Female and Male Voices in the Hebrew Bible* (Bible Interpretation 1; Leiden: Brill, 1996) 44, 83-84.

54. See Chapter Eleven for discussion of this verse and its importance for pointing to the role of women in heroic poetry in early Israel.

55. Note also the analogy in SBV VIII.44-45: "I shall mourn, Enkidu, my friend,/like a professional mourning woman I shall lament bitterly." For mourning women in classical tradition, see Emily Vermeule, *Aspects of Death in Early Greek Art and Poetry* (Berkeley: University of California Press, 1979) 15-16.

56. See Chapter Four, section 4, for discussion of this lament, apparently ironic in view of the fact that Anat arranged his execution.

57. Anderson, *A Time to Mourn, A Time to Dance: The Expression of Grief and Joy in Israelite Religion* (University Park: Pennsylvania State University Press, 1991) 73.

58. Anderson, *A Time to Mourn, A Time to Dance*, 60, 95-97.

59. Greene, "The Natural Tears of Epic," in *Epic Traditions in the Contemporary World*, ed. Margaret Beissinger, Jane Tylus, and Susanne Wofford (Berkeley: University of California Press, 1999) 195.

60. Greene, "The Natural Tears of Epic," 189.

61. See Chapter Four, section 4, for discussion.

62. See Chapter Four, section 4, for discussion.

63. Translation of Ginsberg, *ANET*, 153. Cf. "no dew, no downpour," by Parker, *UNP*, 69. For *ṭl* and *rbb* together, see also KTU 1.3 II 39 (also reconstructed for 1.3 II 40-41); 1.3 IV 43-44; Mic. 5:7; 1QM 12:9-10. For discussion of the passage from Aqhat, see Chapter Four. Hamilton (*The Body Royal*, 156) views the association of nature here with kingship in terms of Neo-Assyrian expressions.

64. I have added the assumed syntax in order to indicate that the negative is not expressed before the words "dew" or "rain," as in the poetic version of 2 Sam. 1:21. For the grammar of the oath here, see Blane Conklin, *Oath Formulas in Biblical Hebrew* (Linguistic Studies in Ancient West Semitic 5; Winona Lake: Eisenbrauns, 2011) 39. For the first part of this oath, note the same wording in 2 Kgs. 5:16.

65. Ginsberg, "A Ugaritic Parallel to 2 Sam 1 21," *JBL* 57 (1938) 212 n. 14; *ANET*, 153 n. 34. Note T. H. Gaster, "The Story of Aqhat," *SMSR* 13 (1937) 49; see also *UT* 19.2488; NJPS, p. 644 n. d-d; Edward L. Greenstein, "Texts from Ugarit Solve Biblical Puzzles," *BAR* 36/6 (2010) 52: "This verse was taken almost directly from Danel's exclamation of grief over the death of his son in the Epic of Aqhat." For the issues with the etymology for the Ugaritic word proposed by Gaster and followed by Ginsberg, see Fred Renfroe, *Arabic-Ugaritic Lexical Studies* (ALASP 5; Münster: Ugarit-Verlag, 1992) 146-47. Renfroe suggests that the Ugaritic word in this context may instead refer to a storm or tempest (cognate with BH *sʿr*). It is to be noted that Ugaritic also attests a word with the same spelling that appears in a list of goods in KTU 1.148.21.

66. Lawrence E. Stager, "The Archaeology of the Family in Ancient Israel," *BASOR* 260 (1985) 6.

67. Stager, "The Archaeology of the Family," 6.

68. Greenstein ("Texts from Ugarit," 70 n. 2) disputes the translation "steppes of offerings" for the last line of the verse based on the Hebrew: "This makes no sense."

69. This approach to the verse was suggested by Thomas McCreesh.

70. McCarter, *II Samuel*, 69, compares *mĕrômê śādeh* in Judg. 5:18; so also Freedman, *Pottery, Poetry, and Prophecy*, 270; see also Stager, "The Archaeology of the Family," 6. Note also *sdh wmrm h[* in one Kuntillet Ajrud inscription, in Aḥituv, Eshel, and Meshel, 115.

71. My view here is close to Freedman, *Pottery, Poetry, and Prophecy*, 270. See also the famous discussion of Talmon, most recently in his collected essays, *Text and Canon of the Hebrew Bible*, 280-87. That some change or adaptation is evident in the version in 2 Sam. 1:21 can also be seen from the lack of one line found in the Aqhat version of the lament, namely "no benefit of Baal's voice," *bl ṭbn ql bʿl* (KTU 1.19 I 44-45, in *UNP*, 69).

72. In view of the difference in the Hebrew, it is arguable that 2 Sam. 1:21a here reflects a modification of a known *topos* of the curse of precipitation, known, e.g., in the laws of Hammurapi and the Tell Bukan inscription (as well as 1 Kgs. 17:1). For the former, see Martha T. Roth, in *COS*, 2:352, and in *Law Collections from Mesopotamia and Asia Minor*, ed. Piotr Michalowski (SBLWAW 6; Atlanta: Scholars, 1995) 138; for the latter, see K. Lawson Younger, in *COS*, 3:219. Cf. omens of Adad's prosperity in Enuma Anu Enlil, tablet 44, e.g., in line 24: "If Adad thunders four times, Adad will set up abundance in the land." See Erlend Gehlken, *Weather Omens of Enūma Anu Enlil: Thunderstorms, Wind and Rain (Tablets 44-49)* (Cuneiform Monographs 43; Leiden: Brill, 2012) 19. In Chapter Four, I have suggested following Shirly Natan-Yulzary that the story of Aqhat in KTU 1.19 I 44b-46a draws on this *topos* without it being a curse as such. I would regard *rkb bʿrbt* in Ps. 68:5 as another possible instance of a modification of an older phrasing, in this instance of *bʿl ʿrpt* as in KTU 1.2 IV 8 rather than a corruption or mistake for it, as is commonly assumed.

73. For discussion of this passage, see Chapter Six, section 1.

74. *UBC*, 1:345. It may be argued that Baal is nothing without his weapons charged by Kothar in KTU 1.2 IV, in *UNP*, 103-4. Does this picture correspond to the image of weapons provided by the gods to the king, which "rise up and kill my enemies" (*The Royal Inscriptions of Esarhaddon, King of Assyria [680-669* BC], ed. Erle Leichty [RINAP 4; Winona Lake: Eisenbrauns, 2011] 209 and 215)?

75. See Thorkild Jacobsen, *The Harps That Once . . . : Sumerian Poetry in Translation* (New Haven/London: Yale University Press, 1987) 242-44.

76. See also the reflections on Achilles' armor by Jeffrey R. Asher, "An Unworthy Foe: Heroic Ἔθη, Trickery, and an Insult in Ephesians 6:11," *JBL* 130 (2011) 734. For further discussion of weapons identified with their warrior owners in classical texts, see Hans van Wees, "Heroes, Knights, and Nutters: Warrior Mentality in Homer," in *Battle in Antiquity*, ed. Alan B. Lloyd (Swansea: Classical Press of Wales, 2009) 32-33.

77. Gevirtz, *Patterns in the Early Poetry of Israel*, 95. Cf. the image of the warrior king as a weapon, in Esarhaddon Monument A: "the merciless weapon that makes the enemy land tremble, am I"; see Leichty, *The Royal Inscriptions of Esarhaddon*, 185.

78. *COS*, 3:12. The notion has been noted for warriors in the *Iliad*, e.g., Diomedes (5.181-83; see Benardete, *Achilles and Hector*, 42-43).

79. Fernando Santos-Granero, "Introduction," in *The Occult Life of Things: Native Amazonian Theories of Materiality and Personhood* (Tucson: University of Arizona Press, 2009) 14.

80. For a recent survey, see Adela Yarbro Collins and John J. Collins, *King and Messiah as Son of God: Divine, Human, and Angelic Messianic Figures in Biblical and Related Literature* (Grand Rapids: Eerdmans, 2008). See also the earlier discussion of John J. Collins, *The Scepter and the Star: The Messiahs of the Dead Sea Scrolls and Other Ancient Literature* (ABRL; New York: Doubleday, 1995) 11-48.

81. For this information, see Marvin H. Pope, *Song of Songs* (AB 7C; Garden City: Doubleday, 1977) 468. Note also the dedication of the shield of metal in KTU 1.123.2; cf. the dedication of the armor in the shrine of Apollo in *Iliad* 7.83.

82. See the discussion of the root in Chapter Four.

83. So Andrew R. George, *The Babylonian Gilgamesh Epic: Introduction, Critical Edition, and Cuneiform Texts* (Oxford: Oxford University Press, 2003) 1:550, 551; for the evidence for the reconstruction based on the parallel text from Boghazköy MB $Bogh_1$ Fragment a, 1, see George, 2:799 note to 207.

84. These translations were raised in the discussion of this chapter at the Old Testament Colloquium in 2012. I wish to thank the participants for the discussion. See note 28 above.

85. *ANET,* 477 and n. 41. For *n-ʿ-mu* here, see James E. Hoch, *Semitic Words in Egyptian Texts of the New Kingdom and Third Intermediate Period* (Princeton: Princeton University Press, 1994) 181, #244. For *ma-ha-r* here, see Hoch, 147 #190; Jeffrey Zorn, "LU.*PA-MA-ḪA-A* in EA 162:74 and the Role of the *Mhr* in Egypt and Ugarit," *JNES* 50 (1991) 129-38. The first part of the phrase is more problematic. For the context of the passage, see Adam Zertal, "The Arunah Pass," in *Egypt, Canaan and Israel: History, Imperialism, Ideology and Literature: Proceedings of a Conference at the University of Haifa, 3-7 May 2009,* ed. Shay Bar, Dan'el Kahn, and J. J. Shirley (CHANE 52; Leiden: Brill, 2011) 348-49.

86. See the discussion of the motif by Christos Tsagalis, *The Oral Palimpsest: Exploring Intertextuality in the Homeric Epics* (Hellenic Studies 29; Washington: Center for Hellenic Studies, 2008) 155-61.

87. Cf. the images of warriors as lions in *Iliad* 5.299; 10.297; 11.129, 239. For other lion imagery, see *Iliad* 11.173; 12.42, 293.

88. Olyan, " 'Surpassing the Love of Women': Another Look at 2 Samuel 1:26 and the Relationship of David and Jonathan," in *Authorizing Marriage? Canon, Tradition, and Critique in the Blessing of Same-Sex Unions,* ed. Mark D. Jordan (Princeton: Princeton University Press, 2006) 7-16, 165-70, here 10-16; repr. in Olyan, *Social Inequality in the World of the Text: The Significance of Ritual and Social Distinctions in the Hebrew Bible* (Journal of Ancient Judaism Sup 4; Göttingen: Vandenhoeck & Ruprecht, 2011) 85-99. See also Christophe Nihan, "David et Jonathan: une amitié héroïque? Enquête littéraire et historique à travers les récits de 1-2 Samuel (1-2 Règnes)," in *Le jeune héros: Recherches sur la formation et la diffusion d'un thème littéraire au Proche-Orient ancien. Actes du colloque organisé par les chaires d'Assyriologie et des Milieux bibliques du Collège de France, Paris, les 6 et 7 avril 2009,* ed. Jean-Marie Durand, Thomas Römer, and Michael Langlois (OBO 250; Fribourg: Academic; Göttingen: Vandenhoeck & Ruprecht, 2011) 328. The classic treatment of political "love" is William L. Moran, "The Ancient Near Eastern Background of the Love of God in Deuteronomy," *CBQ* 25 (1963) 77-87. See also Susan Ackerman, "The Personal Is Political: Covenantal and Affectionate Love (*'ĀHĒB, 'AHĂBÂ*) in the Hebrew Bible," *VT* 52 (2002) 437-58; Jacqueline E. Lapsley, "Feeling Our Way: Love for God in Deuteronomy," *CBQ* 65 (2003) 350-69. The corpus of expressions of love keeps growing. See the use of "love" in a legal document in RS 94.2168, lines 11-12: "the one whom ʿAbdimilki will love (*'ihb,* i.e., 'prefer') among his sons." See Pierre Bordreuil and Dennis Pardee, *A Manual of Ugaritic* (Winona Lake: Eisenbrauns, 2009) 258-59 and *BSV,* 135, 136.

89. One might compare Saul's calling David "my son" also a treaty-covenant usage, but one that also carries considerable emotional freight in context (1 Sam. 24:16).

90. For discussion of this passage, see Chapter Four, section 6.

91. For reflections on love in modern warfare, see Chris Hedges, *War Is a Force That Gives Us Meaning* (New York: PublicAffairs, 2002) 158-59: "a sense of purpose, of calling . . . is a quality war shares with love . . . this is what war often looks and feels like, at its inception, love. The ancient Greeks understood this strange relationship between love and death in wartime." And I would add to "the Greeks" other cultures as well.

92. McCarter, *II Samuel*, 78-79.

93. For skepticism about the poem's date, see Nihan, "David et Jonathan," 328. See further below.

94. See Steven L. McKenzie, *King David: A Biography* (New York: Oxford University Press, 2000); Baruch Halpern, *David's Secret Demons: Messiah, Murderer, Traitor, King* (BIW; Grand Rapids: Eerdmans, 2001). For an assessment, see David A. Bosworth, "Evaluating King David: Old Problems and Recent Scholarship," *CBQ* 68 (2006) 191-210. Note also the strong rejection of the negative reconstruction of David in J. Randall Short, *The Surprising Election and Confirmation of King David* (HTS 63; Cambridge, MA: Harvard University Press, 2010). Cf. also Joel Baden, *The Historical David: The Real Life of an Invented Hero* (San Francisco: HarperOne, 2013); and Jacob L. Wright, *King David and His Reign Revisited* (Aldina Media, 2013). For literary-critical treatments, see Jacques Vermeylen, *La loi du plus fort: Histoire de la rédaction des récits davidiques de 1 Samuel à 1 Rois 2* (BETL 154; Leuven: Leuven University Press, 2000); Klaus-Peter Adam, *Saul und David in der judäischen Geschichtsschreibung: Studien zu 1 Samuel 16–2 Samuel 5* (FAT 51; Tübingen: Mohr Siebeck, 2007); A. Graeme Auld and Erik Eynikel, eds., *For and Against David: Story and History in the Books of Samuel* (BETL 232; Leuven: Peeters, 2010). For the historiography of Samuel, see Rachelle Gilmour, *Representing the Past: A Literary Analysis of Narrative Historiography in the Book of Samuel* (VTSup 143; Leiden: Brill, 2011). Daniel E. Fleming has attempted to identify older northern traditions associated with David separate from the later southern traditions associated with him; *The Legacy of Israel in Judah's Bible: History, Politics, and the Reinscribing of Tradition* (Cambridge: Cambridge University Press, 2012) 98-109.

95. Linafelt, "Private Poetry and Public Eloquence in 2 Samuel 1:17-27: Hearing and Overhearing David's Lament for Jonathan and Saul," *JR* 88 (2008) 497-526. See also Weitzman, "David's Lament and the Poetics of Grief," 341-60; Paul Borgman, *David, Saul, and God: Rediscovering an Ancient Story* (Oxford: Oxford University Press, 2008) 154-57.

96. Weitzman, "David's Lament and the Poetics of Grief," 354-55. Weitzman also sees a larger literary function for the lament within 2 Samuel.

97. Hamilton, *The Body Royal*, 153-59.

98. Hamilton, *The Body Royal*, 156. For the complexity of the prose traditions, see the discussion above in Chapter Two. A particularly helpful treatment is Nihan, "David et Jonathan," 306-30.

99. Hamilton, *The Body Royal*, 157.

100. Hamilton, *The Body Royal*, 158.

101. See Nihan, "David et Jonathan," 328.

102. Perhaps some consideration is to be given to David's situation as a regional leader pressed on either side by the two great powers of the Israelites and the Philistines. This geopolitical situation suggests an effort at self-preservation as much as anything else.

103. E.g., O'Connor, *Hebrew Verse Structure,* 470-71; Edelman, "The Authenticity of 2 Sam 1,26," 66-75.

104. Richard Lattimore, trans., *The Iliad of Homer* (Chicago: University of Chicago Press, 1951) 203. For cases in the *Odyssey,* see Charles Segal, *Singers, Heroes, and Gods in the Odyssey* (Ithaca: Cornell University Press, 1994). Note also the older study of Robert P. Creed, "The Singer Looks at His Sources," *Comparative Literature* 14 (Studies in Old English Literature in Honor of Arthur G. Brodeur; 1962) 44-52, here 48-49.

105. Miller, *Oral Tradition in Ancient Israel,* 93. Cf. the oral song in praise of the king in a Neo-Assyrian letter; see Simo Parpola, comp., *Letters from Assyrian Scholars to the Kings Esarhaddon and Assurbanipal* (1970; repr. Winona Lake: Eisenbrauns, 2007) 1:97, 98, letter #124 (*ABL,* 435), lines 10-14.

106. Talmon, "The Textual Study of the Bible," 365; repr. *Text and Canon of the Hebrew Bible,* 63-64 (see also pp. 283-84).

107. Cf. Prov. 18:24: "there is a friend [lit., one who loves] who is closer [lit., clings more] than a brother." See Richard J. Clifford, *Proverbs* (OTL; Louisville: Westminster John Knox, 1999) 169.

108. Frymer-Kensky, *In the Wake of the Goddesses: Women, Culture, and the Biblical Transformation of Pagan Myth* (New York: Free Press, 1992) 30. As evidence of the latter, Frymer-Kensky goes on to cite the figure of Saltu, a double of Ishtar, created to battle her and to curb her ferocity. For this text, see Benjamin R. Foster, "Ea and Saltu," in *Essays on the Ancient Near East in Memory of J. J. Finkelstein,* ed. Maria de Jong Ellis (Hamden: Academy of Arts and Sciences, 1977) 79-84. For discussion, see also Rivkah Harris, "Inanna-Ishtar as Paradox and a Coincidence of Opposites," *HR* 30 (1991) 266-67.

109. Ackerman, *When Heroes Love: The Ambiguity of Eros in the Stories of Gilgamesh and David* (New York: Columbia University Press, 2005), 192. In the case of David and Jonathan, Ackerman goes on to suggest "David and Jonathan were in fact imagined to be same-sex partners by the Samuel narratives" (p. 194). While this could be so, the broader question about the sexual relations among these male pairings lies largely beyond reach. Her characterization of this relationship as "sexual-emotional" is arguably enhanced by comparisons with Gilgamesh and Enkidu; see Chapter Three for discussion. Here Ackerman is drawing on Olyan, " 'Surpassing the Love of Women,' " 7-16.

110. See Ackerman, *When Heroes Love,* 189. Note also the acts of lamentation, including weeping, upon receiving the news, in 2 Sam. 1:11-12. Cf. the figure of Odysseus weeping in *Odyssey* 8:499-534 as he hears the song of Demodocus recounting the story of the fall of Odysseus' comrades at Troy.

111. This approach was suggested to me by Susan Niditch, in conjunction with other members of the Colloquium for Biblical Research, at the meeting held on 15 August 2010 at Princeton Theological Seminary. I am grateful to Professor Niditch.

112. Cf. Edelman, "The Authenticity of 2 Sam 1,26," 73: "I would suggest that v. 26, and possibly also v. 27, represents a secondary expansion of the original lament over Saul and Jonathan that was quoted in the Book of Jashar." Edelman takes v. 26 "probably to be a literary creation by the biblical writer responsible for shaping the Saulide narratives." At the same time, Edelman concedes: "it is not impossible that David could have written the lament himself." It is evident that the matter of authorship of v. 26, much less the entirety

of vv. 19-27, remains rather speculative, but it does not eviscerate the literary observations that Edelman has noted.

113. This view is close to that of Hans J. Stoebe, *Das zweite Buch Samuelis* (KAT 8; Gütersloh: Gütersloher, 1994) 96, discussed by Olyan, "'Surpassing the Love of Women,'" 168 n. 15.

114. Fleming, *The Legacy of Israel in Judah's Bible*, 151: "it could be read as a celebration of Saul from his own circle."

115. See Andrew Dalby, *Rediscovering Homer: Inside the Origins of the Epic* (New York: Norton, 2006) 12. See also Achilles' speeches in *Iliad* 23.19-23, 43-53. Note also the poignant *Iliad* 23.54-107. Cf. *Iliad* 23:391 for the idea of the victorious warriors singing their victories as they return from battle.

116. The problem was noted by Cross and Freedman, *Studies in Ancient Yahwistic Poetry*, 15; Freedman, *Pottery, Poetry, and Prophecy*, 263.

117. See Paul R. Raabe, *Psalm Structures: A Study of Psalms with Refrains* (JSOTSup 104; Sheffield: Sheffield Academic, 1990) 164-66.

118. Raabe, *Psalms Structures*, 165, commenting on the refrains found in Psalms 39, 42-43, 46, 49, 56, 57, 59, 67, 80.

119. Edelman, "The Authenticity of 2 Sam 1,26," 74.

120. In this connection, I have been struck by male poetic competitions reported in some cultures. See the discussion of Heikki Palva, Review of Nadia G. Yaqub, *Pens, Swords, and the Springs of Art* (Leiden: Brill, 2007), in *ZDPV* 160 (2010) 185-88.

121. Cf. "Let the first one hear and te[ll it] to the later ones!"; "The Hunter," in Benjamin R. Foster, *Before the Muses: An Anthology of Akkadian Literature* (3rd ed.; Bethesda: CDL, 2005) 337.

122. These features might fit less well with a substantially later dating for the poem, even if one could find reasons for such a composition at a later period (whether it was composed later or simply received later). It is possible to argue that the reference to Philistines could have been made later, based on knowledge from the prose sources, but it also fits the tenth-century era of the Philistine wars.

123. See Cohen, "Diachrony in Biblical Hebrew Lexicography and Its Ramifications for Textual Analysis," in *Diachrony in Biblical Hebrew*, ed. Cynthia L. Miller-Naudé and Ziony Zevit (Linguistic Studies in Ancient West Semitic 8; Winona Lake: Eisenbrauns, 2012) 365.

124. See the past progressive use of the attributive participle in Ps. 18/2 Sam. 22:13. However, I do not put much weight on this feature, in view of 1 Samuel 1:26. See Joüon-Muraoka, par. 121i.

125. Gevirtz reads v. 18 as the opening colon of the poem. According to Greenstein (personal communication), the poem takes its name in v. 18 from *qešet* here in v. 22. For further suggestions, see the works noted by Weitzman, "David's Lament and the Poetics of Grief," 342-43. Greenstein's suggestion lacks for evidence, yet in this connection may be compared the oral warrior song called "The Bow," found in the Sunjata epic narrative that celebrates the founder of the thirteenth-century Mali empire. See Stephen Paterson Belcher IV, "Stability and Change: Praise-Poetry and Narrative Traditions in the Epics of Mali" (Ph.D. diss., Brown, 1985) 283-94; Ivor Wilks, "The History of the *Sunjata* Epic: A

Review of the Evidence," in *In Search of Sunjata: The Mande Oral Epic as History, Literature, and Performance,* ed. Ralph A. Austen; Bloomington: Indiana University Press, 1998) 29-30, 38-39. As Wilks notes, the Song called "the Bow" is used by oral singers (called "griots") at different points in the performance of the Sunjata epic. The remaining issue is the relative date of this prose notice in 2 Sam. 1:18. In the recent study of Daniel E. Fleming, such a reference to Judeans would be relatively secondary within the prose traditions of 2 Samuel; *The Legacy of Israel in Judah's Bible,* 98-109, esp. 108 n. 56.

126. BH *sēper* is often translated here as "book," but there were no books in this period. The word *sēper* refers to a record or document and not the medium in which it is written (cf. Ugaritic *spr* for documents written on tablets, including ritual texts such as KTU 1.161.1).

127. "The Book of Yashar," as this work has been called, has been the subject of considerable speculation as well as skepticism. For the information here, see Isac Leo Seeligmann, *Gesammelte Studien zur Hebräischen Bibel,* ed. Erhard Blum (FAT 41; Tübingen: Mohr Siebeck, 2004) 147. See also the discussions in Duane L. Christensen, "Jashar, Book of," *ABD,* 3:646-47; William Schniedewind, *How the Bible Became a Book: The Textualization of Ancient Israel* (Cambridge: Cambridge University Press, 2004) 53-54. For an optimistic yet plausible reconstruction informed by performance theory, see Terry Giles and William J. Doan, *Twice Used Songs: Performance Criticism of the Songs of Ancient Israel* (Peabody: Hendrickson, 2009) 25-47.

128. Levine, *Numbers 21–36,* 177. See also the uncharacteristic confidence expressed in the historicity of this work by Seeligmann, *Gesammelte Studien zur Hebräischen Bibel,* 361 n. 25.

129. For the latter, see Levine, *Numbers 21–36,* 177, comparing the root in Num. 23:10 and in Ps 112:2 where it is parallel with *gibbôr.* See also Levine, "The Triumphs of the Lord," *ErIsr* 20 (Yigael Yadin Memorial Volume; 1989) 202-14, here 207 (Heb.).

130. Seeligmann, *Gesammelte Studien zur Hebräischen Bibel,* 147 n. 23.

131. For these processes in this passage, see Susan Niditch, *Oral World and Written Word: Ancient Israelite Literature* (Louisville: Westminster John Knox, 1996) 94.

132. For performed texts as political vehicles of public spectacle, see Lawrence S. Coben and Takeshi Inomata, "Behind the Scenes: Producing the Performance," in *Archaeology of Performance: Theaters of Power, Community, and Politics,* ed. Inomata and Coben (Lanham: AltaMira, 2006) 5. To be sure, there is no archaeological evidence for this spectacle in David's case.

Notes to Chapter Eleven

1. See Chapter One, esp. section 3, for discussion.

2. Note the call for consideration that "orality, and in particular the oral performance, is" to be "accorded its due place in culture and society," by Frank H. Polak, "Book, Scribe, and Bard: Oral Discourse and Written Text in Recent Biblical Scholarship," *Prooftexts* 31 (2011) 133. See also the older studies of Burke Long, "Recent Field Studies in Oral Literature and the Question of *Sitz im Leben,*" *Semeia* 5 (1976) 35-49; Robert C. Culley,

"Oral Tradition and Biblical Studies," *Oral Tradition* 1 (1986) 30-65, esp. 58-59 for some well-placed cautions. For the following discussion, cf. Stanley Isser, *The Sword of Goliath: David in Heroic Literature* (Studies in Biblical Literature 6; Atlanta: Society of Biblical Literature, 2003).

3. See the final section of Chapter Seven and further below. On this matter, see Ryan Byrne, "The Refuge of Scribalism in Iron I Palestine," *BASOR* 345 (2007) 1-31; Seth L. Sanders, *The Invention of Hebrew* (Urbana: University of Illinois Press, 2009); Christopher A. Rollston, *Writing and Literacy in the World of Ancient Israel* (Archaeology and Biblical Studies 11; Atlanta: Society of Biblical Literature, 2010) 27-35. Note also the remarks on the tenth- or ninth-century Tel Zayit abecedary in Richard S. Hess, "Writing about Writing: Abecedaries and Evidence for Literacy in Ancient Israel," *VT* 56 (2006) 342-46.

4. Carr, *Writing on the Tablet of the Heart: Origins of Scripture and Literature* (Oxford: Oxford University Press, 2005) 118. It is to be noted that *spr* has been understood in this context in other ways (e.g., comparisons made instead with Akkadian *siparru*, "bronze"). Some would appeal the representation of scribal practice in Judg. 5:14, even though its reliability as a historical witness to writing in Iron I Israel lies beyond confirmation; cf. the scribal practice in Isa. 10:19b. See the discussion in David W. Jamieson-Drake, *Scribes and Schools in Monarchic Judah: A Socio-Archeological Approach* (JSOTSup 109; Social World of Biblical Antiquity 9; Sheffield: Almond, 1991) 13.

5. Carr, *Writing on the Tablet of the Heart,* 115 n. 11, responding to William M. Schniedewind, *How the Bible Became a Book: The Textualization of Ancient Israel* (Cambridge: Cambridge University Press, 2004) 63 (see also p. 48).

6. Carr, *Writing on the Tablet of the Heart,* 163-64.

7. Schniedewind, *How the Bible Became a Book,* 52-54. Note also the comments on David's lament over Saul and Jonathan (2 Sam. 1:19-27) made by Susan Niditch, *Oral World and Written Word: Ancient Israelite Literature* (Louisville: Westminster John Knox, 1996) 94.

8. Giles and Doan, *Twice Used Songs: Performance Criticism of the Songs of Ancient Israel* (Peabody: Hendrickson, 2009) 41-44, 67-84. I use the word "axiomatic," since no argument vis-à-vis the cultural context of ancient Israel is made for their position. The argument made is a formal one involving a perceived fit between the ancient poems and different observations drawn from performance theory.

9. Miller, *Oral Tradition in Ancient Israel* (Eugene: Wipf and Stock, 2011) 90-93. For recent discussion in classical studies, see Elizabeth Minchin, ed., *Orality, Literacy and Performance in the Ancient World* (Orality and Literacy in the Ancient World 9; Mnemosyne Sup 35; Leiden: Brill, 2012).

10. For this view, see Niditch, *Oral World and Written Word,* 1, 4. Note also Schniedewind (*How the Bible Became a Book,* 48): "Early Israel was an oral society. . . . The 'literature' of the early Israelites was an oral literature." See also Mark S. Smith, *The Memoirs of God: History, Memory, and the Experience of the Divine in Ancient Israel* (Minneapolis: Fortress, 2004) 23: "ancient Israel in this period [Iron I] was not 'a people of the Book,' but a society largely working in oral modes of religious memory and communal celebration." Joachim Schaper comments: "Never in its entire history was Israel entirely without

writing, as becomes clear from the existence of scribes in its midst from the earliest times onwards"; "Exilic and Post-Exilic Prophecy and the Orality/Literacy Problem," *VT* 55 (2005) 324-42, here 337. Note also Dominique Charpin's remarks on the cultural priority of the oral in early Mesopotamia: "The oral — who can be surprised? — came first: Mesopotamia was fundamentally a civilization based on giving one's spoken word" and Charpin's broader generalization that "the large volume of cuneiform texts that have come down to us (more than 500,000 inventoried) must not conceal the truth from us: the transmission of information and knowledge in Mesopotamian civilization was for a long time primarily an oral affair"; *Reading and Writing in Babylon,* trans. Jane Marie Todd (Cambridge, MA: Harvard University Press, 2010) 176, 247. There are relatively few reflections on illiteracy in West Semitic sources; see Isa. 29:11-12, discussed by Jonas C. Greenfield, "'Because He/She Did Not Know Letters': Remarks on a First Millennium C.E. Legal Expression," *JANES* 22 (Comparative Studies in Honor of Yochanan Muffs; 1993) 39-44.

11. The degree of literacy in early Israel remains *sub iudice.* The evidence presently available is not particularly compelling for a substantial degree of literacy, despite assumptions made in this direction. For a circumscribed assessment, see Rollston, *Writing and Literacy;* "The Phoenician Script of the Tel Zayit Abecedary and Putative Evidence for Israelite Literacy," in *Literate Culture and Tenth-Century Canaan: The Tel Zayit Abecedary in Context,* ed. Ron E. Tappy and P. Kyle McCarter (Winona Lake: Eisenbrauns, 2008) 61-96. Note also the qualified appraisal by Carr, *Writing on the Tablet of the Heart,* 115-16, 165-66. See also the useful two-part survey of Ian Young, "Israelite Literacy: Interpreting the Evidence," *VT* 48 (1998) 239-53, 408-22. For more optimistic appraisals, see Richard S. Hess, "Writing about Writing"; "Literacy in Iron Age Israel," in *Windows into Old Testament History: Evidence, Argument, and the Crisis of "Biblical Israel,"* ed. V. Philips Long, David Weston Baker, and Gordon J. Wenham (Grand Rapids: Eerdmans, 2002) 82-102; cf. the response of Ian Young, "Israelite Literacy and Inscriptions: A Response to Richard Hess," *VT* 55 (2005) 565-68. Note also Miller, *Oral Tradition in Ancient Israel,* xiv, 43-44, 109; Aaron Demsky, *Literacy in Ancient Israel* (Jerusalem: Mosad Bialik, 2012) (Heb.). An optimistic view for literacy has also been argued for Mesopotamia by Charpin, *Reading and Writing in Babylon,* 53-67, 113, 125, 236-38.

12. The Tel Qeiyafa and Tel Zayit inscriptions may be mentioned in this connection. For the former, see Yosef Garfinkel and Saar Ganor, *Khirbet Qeiyafa,* Vol. 1: *Excavation Report 2007-2008* (Jerusalem: Israel Exploration Society/Institute of Archaeology, Hebrew University, 2009) 243-70; Émile Puech, "L'ostracon de Khirbet Qeyafa et les débuts de la royauté en Israël," *RB* 117 (2010) 162-84; Christopher Rollston, "The Khirbet Qeiyafa Ostracon: Methodological Musings and Caveats," *TA* 38 (2011) 67-82; cf. Gershon Galil, "The Hebrew Inscription from Khirbet Qeiyafa/Neṭaʿim: Script, Language, Literature and History," *UF* 41 (2009 [2011]) 193-242; Aaron Demsky, "An Iron Age IIA Alphabetic Writing Exercise from Kirbet Qeiyafa," *IEJ* 62 (2012) 186-99. For the latter, see Tappy and McCarter, *Literate Culture and Tenth-Century Canaan;* André Lemaire, "West Semitic Epigraphy and the History of the Levant during the 12th-10th Centuries BCE," in *The Ancient Near East in the 12th-10th Centuries BCE. Culture and History: Proceedings of the International Conference Held at the University of Haifa, 2-5 May, 2010,* ed. Gershon Galil,

Ayelet Gilboa, Aren M. Maeir, and Dan'el Kahn (AOAT 392; Münster: Ugarit-Verlag, 2012) 300.

13. Cf. the reported setting for the recitation of victory song following battle in Beowulf discussed by Robert P. Creed, "The Singer Looks at His Sources," *Comparative Literature* 14 (Studies in Old English Literature in Honor of Arthur G. Brodeur; 1962) 44-52. For the oral background of Beowulf, see John D. Niles, "Understanding Beowulf: Oral Poetry Acts," *Journal of American Folklore* 106 (1993) 131-55.

14. Hendel, *The Epic of the Patriarch: The Jacob Cycle and the Narrative Traditions of Canaan and Israel* (HSM 42; Atlanta: Scholars, 1987) 164.

15. For five possibilities for the initial *m-*, see C. F. Burney, *The Book of Judges* (London: Rivingtons, 1918) 125. One includes this initial *min* as comparative: "Louder than the sound of archers" (so NJPS; cf. p. 525 note h-h or "thunderpeals"). Robert G. Boling takes this initial line of v. 11 with the last line of v. 10, as suggested orally to him by David Noel Freedman; *Judges* (AB 6A; Garden City: Doubleday, 1975) 110. In Boling's view, the *m-* before *qôl* is to be taken as enclitic with the preceding imperative. The rendering that I am proposing involves less textual surgery; for this construction, see Pss. 44:17; 55:4.

16. Proposals include "archers" (cf. **ḥṣṣ*, "to divide spoils," or *ḥēṣ*, "arrow"; so *BDB*, 346); or "singers" (Burney, *The Book of Judges*, 127, citing LXX *anakrouomenōn*, "singers" < *anakrouō*, "thrust back," used to strike musical strings, make a prelude); cf. "cymbals" (William F. Albright, *Yahweh and the Gods of Canaan* [Garden City: Doubleday, 1968] 50, followed, e.g., by Boling, *Judges*, 110; Hendel, *The Epic of the Patriarch*, 164). However, no particular etymological support is given for the translation "cymbals." Might *mḥṣṣym* refer to war divisions celebrating spoils taken in battle? Burney (*The Book of Judges*, 126) discusses this idea. One might see a celebration of the victorious force, those who divide spoils (for such a celebration, see Isa. 9:3). This approach would stay closer to the other attestations of the geminate root "to divide" (cf. Prov. 30:27 for locusts divided into companies or swarms; *BDB*, 346). For South Semitic cognates for the geminate root, see Wolf Leslau, *Ethiopic and South Arabic Contributions to the Hebrew Lexicon* (Berkeley: University of California, 1958) 21, under **ḥṣh*. If so, does the possible hint of dividing war spoils here connect to this theme in v. 30?

17. The verbal form may be jussive; see Boling, *Judges*, 102, 111.

18. Albright, *Yahweh and the Gods of Canaan*, 50. With these *m-* preformative forms, contrast BH *G*-active participle, in Deut. 29:10; Josh. 9:21, 23, 27 for men, and for women, in Gen. 24:11. Cf. Ugaritic *š'ab* in *spr š'ab mq[dšt]*, "record of water-carriers of the sanc[tuary]," in KTU 6.25.2; *š'bt* for women who draw water, 1.14 III 9, V 1; see also 1.12 II 59 (see *DULAT*, 795); see Hoch, *Semitic Words in Egyptian Texts of the New Kingdom and Third Intermediate Period* (Princeton: Princeton University Press, 1994) 275, #392 for **sō'ibta* ?, "vessel."

19. Hoch, *Semitic Words in Egyptian Texts*, 156, #205.

20. Burney, *The Book of Judges*, 129, 172-73, 176. See also Baruch Halpern, "Dialect Distribution in Canaan and the Deir Alla Inscriptions," in *"Working with No Data": Semitic and Egyptian Studies Presented to Thomas O. Lambdin*, ed. David M. Golomb (Winona Lake: Eisenbrauns, 1987) 124. Note also the possible use of *tny* in one blessing from Kuntillet 'Ajrud plaster fragments; see Shmuel Aḥituv, *Echoes from the Past: Hebrew and*

Cognate Inscriptions from the Biblical Period, trans. Anson F. Rainey (Jerusalem: Carta, 2008) 322; Shmuel Aḥituv, Esther Eshel, and Ze'ev Meshel, in Meshel, *Kuntillet ʿAjrud (Ḥorvat Teman): An Iron Age II Religious Site on the Judah-Sinai Border* (Jerusalem: Israel Exploration Society, 2012) 105, 107.

21. The southern form of the verb with *šîn* is attested on an inscription on an ostracon from Horvat ʿUzza, according to Ahituv, *Echoes from the Past*, 173-76. There may be also some semantic differentiation between *šny*, "to repeat, do again," and **tny*, "to recite." Cf. Akkadian *šanû*, "repeat, relate." See above, pp. 501-2, notes 46 and 47.

22. For Tob, see also 2 Sam. 10:6. It is a principality south of Hermon east of Upper Galilee; see Paul-Eugéne Dion, *Les Araméens à l'âge du fer: Histoire politique et structures sociales* (EBib N.S. 34; Paris: Gabalda, 1997) 80-81.

23. For the setting of this passage, see Peggy L. Day, "From the Child Is Born the Woman: The Story of Jephthah's Daughter," in *Gender and Difference in Ancient Israel* (Minneapolis: Fortress, 1989) 58-74. See also Michaela Bauks, *Jephtas Tochter: Traditions-, religions- und rezeptionsgeschichte Studien zu Richter 11,29-40* (FAT 71; Tübingen: Mohr Siebeck, 2010). Cf. David Janzen, "Why the Deuteronomist Told about the Sacrifice of Jephthah's Daughter," *JSOT* 29 (2005) 339-57.

24. This is the root's apparent function, but not its meaning (which is "to chant"), *contra* the ascription of this view to an oral presentation of mine made by Miller, *Oral Tradition in Ancient Israel*, 112.

25. *DULAT*, 924-25.

26. The BH form is assumed to be Aramaic by several commentators, e.g., Philippe Guillaume, *Waiting for Josiah: The Judges* (JSOTSup 385; London: T. & T. Clark, 2004) 150 n. 20 (although it is not clear how 11:40 is "a direct quote of Judg. 5:11," as is claimed). This approach to several linguistic features in the poem enjoys some scholarly support. See Michael Waltisberg, "Zum Alter der Sprache des Deborahliedes Ri 5," *ZAH* 12 (1999) 218-32. It is unfortunate that little or no effort is made to show Aramaic influence otherwise in Judges 11 or in the regions that Judges 5 and 11 represent. To my mind, this alternative view (which I do not share) does not affect the points made here beyond the matter of the BH root's derivation.

27. For discussion, see Chapter Eight.

28. For a fuller discussion of the issues in the rest of the poem in Judges 5, see Chapters Eight and Nine.

29. *BDB*, 842.

30. Albright, *Yahweh and the Gods of Canaan*, 50.

31. For discussion, see Isac Leo Seeligmann, *Gesammelte Studien zur Hebräischen Bibel*, ed. Erhard Blum (FAT 41; Tübingen: Mohr Siebeck, 2004) 171-72 n. 28, 358, 442 n. 62.

32. Cf. the recitation of enemies in the prayer in Ps. 83:9-11.

33. The notion seems to be enshrined in later prose historiography in the characterization of divine action as "the deed" *(hammaʿăśeh)* in Judg. 2:7, 10 and "his wonders" *(niplĕʾōtāyw)* in Judg. 6:13. Note also the later poetic *ḥasdê yhwh*/*tĕhillôt yhwh* in Isa. 63:7, also in a context of oral recounting of divine military victory.

34. See the discussion of the second word in Chapter Eight, section 3.

35. For discussion of this "I"-voice in Judges 5, see Chapter Nine, section 4.

36. Burney, *The Book of Judges*, 131.

37. De Moor, "The Twelve Tribes in the Song of Deborah," *VT* 43 (1993) 483-94, here 487.

38. Burney, *The Book of Judges*, 124: Arabic "light reddish gray" or "white flea-speckled with red" (with references). Cf. Ugaritic *ṣḥrrt* in *nrt 'ilm špš ṣḥrrt/l'a šmm byd bn 'ilm mt* (KTU 1.3 V 17-18; 1.4 VIII 21-24; 1.6 II 24-25). For a recent study, see John E. Hartley, *The Semantics of Ancient Hebrew Colour Lexemes* (Ancient Near Eastern Studies Sup 33; Louvain: Peeters, 2010) 162-64. Hartley concludes that the asses are shiny light grey, possibly with a tint of red. Hartley also notes, following Athalya Brenner, that the term here may denote luminosity rather than hue (Symmachus *stilbousōn*, "gleaming, glittering"; Peshitta *ḥewwār*, "white"). The notion of a lighter grey or white is based largely on the versions, but it seems to have little support from Arabic lexical evidence cited. There is, *contra* Hartley, no particular evidence that Ugaritic *ṣḥrrt* means "white" (he also cites no works after 1976 concerning Ugaritic lexicography). See Johannes C. de Moor, *The Seasonal Pattern in the Ugaritic Myth of Ba'u* (AOAT 16; Kevelaer: Butzon & Bercker, 1979) 227, "dust-colored, brownish"; *DULAT*, 782-83, "to roast"; cf. the discussion in *UBC*, 2:346.

39. BH *'ātôn* appears to mean "donkey." The Bible includes examples of both men (Num. 22:21-33) and women (2 Kgs. 4:21-24) using them for riding. Athirat has her animal prepared for her riding on *'r/pḥl/'atnt* in KTU 1.4 III 4-7, 9-12. Akkadian *atānu* regularly refers to a female horse, but may also refer to a female donkey (for references, see *UBC*, 2:504-5). Officials of the king are often described as *rākib imêrim*, "rider of an ass," in Mari letters (see *UBC*, 2:504-5). While the "rider of an ass" is certainly at a lower social level than the king, the term is an honorific title and thus does not bear a pejorative sense with regard to donkey riding. The relative status of riding a horse as opposed to a donkey is seen in EA 88:46-48, where Rib-Adda of Byblos complains that "the messenger of the king of Akko is honored more than my messenger, for they gave him a horse to ride." On the other hand, the donkey appears in BH as the animal upon which the king rides in Zech. 9:9. Yet for Israel, equally relevant is the use of the mule *(pirdâ)* as the royal animal in 1 Kgs. 1:33, 38, 44, where David orders Solomon to be placed on David's own mule to indicate that Solomon is David's choice for successor and has become the legitimate king (cf. also 2 Sam. 18:9). Cf. *rekeb ḥămôr* in Isa. 21:7. It is to be noted that caravan trade with camels is absent from this context.

40. *BDB*, 551: "cloth, carpet (for sitting on); *HALOT*, 3:546: "gown, robe." See also *md* (with suffix) in 1.3 II 6. Before saddles, cloths were tied on riding animals. One might gloss as "riding cloths." Following LXX^{B} *kriteriou* (means for judging; court of judgment), Robert McClive Good (*The Sheep of His Pasture: A Study of the Hebrew Noun* 'Am(m) *and Its Semitic Cognates* [HSM 29; Chico: Scholars, 1983] 135) and Freedman (apud Boling, *Judges*, 110), citing Prov. 20:8, instead read the root **dyn* with *m*- preformative as "on the judgment seat." Albright (*Yahweh and the Gods of Canaan*, 49-50 n. 102) takes the noun as a dissimilated form of *mdl*, "caparison," in the sense of "lead," citing an oral suggestion from Delbert Hillers drawing on a study of *mdl* by Jonas Greenfield, "Ugaritic *mdl* and Its Cognates," *Bib* 45 (1964) 527-34; repr. *'Al Kanfei Yonah: Collected Studies of Jonas C. Greenfield on Semitic Philology*, ed. Shalom M. Paul, Michael E. Stone, and Avital Pinnick

(Leiden: Brill; Jerusalem: Magnes, 2001) 847-54. While such a lead rider is evident in 1.4 IV, this proposal messes up the poetic parallelism for Judg. 5:10; note that to restore the parallelism, Albright renders: "Ye who sit on caparisoned ⟨male donkeys⟩ (?)." J. David Schloen reads Midian here, but the resulting syntax is not strong ("you who sit over Midian"); "Caravans, Kenites, and *Casus Belli:* Enmity and Alliance in the Song of Deborah," *CBQ* 55 (1993) 25-27. Schloen concedes the difficulty in a footnote (p. 26 n. 30): "It is true that there are no other examples of the phrase *yōšĕbê ʿal* (with this preposition) followed by the name of a people or place, but such a construction is not impossible (e.g., Isaiah 40:22)." Perhaps, instead, wordplay with Midian is to be seen here. For the construct before a preposition, see GKC, 130a for other examples; the construct plural form also serves for morphological parallelism.

41. LXX[A] consists of two lines: *epibebēkotes epi hypozygiōn, kathēmenoi epi lampēnōn.* LXX[B] has three lines, with a paraphrasing expansion in the third line *(kai poreuomenoi epi hodous synedrōn ephʾ hodō).*

42. T. H. Gaster (*Myth, Legend, and Custom in the Old Testament* [New York: Harper & Row, 1969] 418-19) sees the first two lines as referring to the wealthy (riders) (cf. Judg. 10:4; so George F. Moore, *A Critical and Exegetical Commentary on Judges* [ICC; New York: Scribner's, 1901] 148), and the third line as the lowly (walkers) and thus an inclusion for the entire population (so Burney, *The Book of Judges,* 123). Boling (*Judges,* 110) adds that the former are the caravan owners with their chief clients, the latter the groomsmen. This characterization may be too specific for the terms used here. Gaster's proposal has the virtue of reading the initial *wāw* of the third line as demarcating; in contrast, the first two lines lack any such *wāw* between them and are in apposition.

43. Schloen, "Caravans, Kenites, and *Casus Belli,*" 25.

44. Cf. Ps. 58:7-10 (note the blood on the soldiers' feet in 1 Kgs. 2:5; see also Ps. 68:23; cf. KTU 1.3 II 30-35).

45. For this approach, cf. the cattle shrine at Kheshiya in early Arabian pilgrimage society, discussed in Joy McCorriston, *Pilgrimage and Household in the Ancient Near East* (Cambridge: Cambridge University Press, 2011) 85-134.

46. Cross, *From Epic to Canon: History and Literature in Ancient Israel* (Baltimore: Johns Hopkins University Press, 1998) 20; see also p. 55 n. 7.

47. For the problem of Cross's theory of early epic, see Chapter One, section 3.

48. Cross, *From Epic to Canon,* 55 n. 7.

49. In view of the poem of Num. 21:27-30, it would be tempting to add to the old tradition of warfare poetry those old poetic pieces said to belong to the "Book of the Wars of Yahweh" (Num. 21:14). See Baruch A. Levine, "The Triumphs of the Lord," *ErIsr* 20 (Yigael Yadin Volume; 1989) 202-14 (Heb.), Eng. summary 201*.

50. Often translated "bards" (NJPS) or the like from context. For discussions of the word, see Baruch A. Levine, *Numbers 21–36* (AB 4A; New York: Doubleday, 2000) 102-3; A. Yadin, "Samson's *Ḥîdâ,*" *VT* 42 (2002) 407-26. Following one line of interpretation, Levine (pp. 102-3) believes that "composers of *mĕšālîm*" in Num. 21:27 refer to producers of poetry consisting of sets of two-line units that are of "similar length or valence." If correct, this category would be disassociated from early Israelite heroic poetry, which includes tricolas (e.g., Judg. 5:3, 10, 11, 24 [unless the second line is bracketed as a prosaic

intrusion from 4:17], 27; 2 Sam. 1:24; cf. the later Exod. 15:8, 11, 15). Cf. the monocolon of Exod. 15:18. The other line of interpretation for *měšālîm* is that they involve content that compares similar concepts and phenomena. Heroic poetry also does not comport with this notion. Thus, whichever view one might accept, heroic poetry would not belong to *měšālîm*.

51. Cf. Mic. 2:4 for a later representation of such an oral composition *(māšāl)* of lament. See also Isa. 14:4; Hab. 2:6 for oral *māšāl*.

52. See Levine, *Numbers 21–36*, 132.

53. The Balaam poems point to religious pronouncement by a seer (called *māšāl*'s by the prose introductions in Num. 23:7, 18; 24:3, 15).

54. Cf. oral knowledge emblemized in the figure of Solomon in 1 Kgs. 4:32(5:12). What songs would have been included in the figure of 1,005 there?

55. *UNP*, 106, discussed in Chapter Six; cf. Anat herself in 1.3 III 4-8 (*UNP*, 109); the lamenting women in KTU 1.16 I 43; Judg. 11:40. Here I am not including temple singers (e.g., KTU 1.106.16; Pardee, *RCU*, 54, 55; Ps. 68:26). Cf. classical professional singers, such as Demodocus who is represented as singing the story of the Trojan horse in *Odyssey* 8:499-520.

56. For the particle *pen*, see p. 483 note 70 above.

57. Millard, "Oral Proclamation and Written Record: Spreading and Preserving Information in Ancient Israel," in *Michael: Historical, Epigraphical and Biblical Studies in Honor of Prof. Michael Heltzer*, ed. Yitzhak Avishur and Robert Deutsch (Tel Aviv: Archaeological Center, 1999) 237-41.

58. Lit., "outsides," presumed to be outside of houses or other habitations in space shared by persons of multiple houses or habitations. See *BDB*, 299.

59. Cf. Inanna and her lover in the square in "Love by the Light of the Moon," in *COS*, 1:542-43.

60. See William P. Brown and John T. Carroll, "The Garden and the Plaza: Biblical Images of the City," *Int* 54 (2000) 3-11.

61. Cf. *BDB*, 300; see also Punic evidence noted in *DNWSI*, 398. For streets and plazas for Iron Age Israel, see Yigal Shiloh, "Elements in the Development of Town Planning in the Israelite City," *IEJ* 28 (1978) 36-51; Ze'ev Herzog, *Archaeology of the City: Urban Planning in Ancient Israel and Its Social Implications* (Sonia and Marco Nadler Monograph 13; Tel Aviv: Tel Aviv University, 1997). Herzog pp. 216, 232-33, 245) mentions streets in the city design of tenth-century Tell el-Far'ah (North), ninth/eighth-century Tell es-Sa'idiyeh, and eighth-century Beersheba.

62. Millard, "Oral Proclamation and Written Record," 237. Millard compares Wisdom to "hawkers" of wares. See below for the business side of such communal spaces. Cf. Akkadian *maḫīru*, "market place," in *CAD*, M/1:93.

63. As rendered by *DNWSI*, 398, 550, 680.

64. Larry G. Herr, "Tripartite Pillared Buildings and the Market Place in Iron Age Palestine," *BASOR* 272 (1988) 47-67, esp. 57-58. However, these buildings have been interpreted also as storehouses, stables, or barracks; see Ze'ev Herzog, "Administrative Structures in the Iron Age," in *The Architecture of Ancient Israel from the Prehistoric to the Persian Periods: In Memory of Immanuel (Munya) Dunayevsky*, ed. Aharon Kem-

pinski and Ronny Reich (Jerusalem: Israel Exploration Society, 1992) 225-28. See further Avraham Biran, "Two Bronze Plaques and the *Huṣṣot* of Dan," *IEJ* 49 (1999) 43-54, esp. 50. Note also Herzog, *Archaeology of the City,* 228.

65. E.g., Iron I Beth Shemesh; see Herzog, *Archaeology of the City,* 205.

66. The mention of the bones of Saul and Jonathan in the plaza *(rĕḥōb)* of Beth-shean in 2 Sam. 21:12 suggests a celebration of military victory on the part of the Philistines there.

67. Note *rĕḥôb* in Deut. 13:17(16); Judg. 19:15. Cf. the reading of the Torah in the *rĕḥôb* at the Water Gate in Neh. 8:3 and the rabbinic evidence for prayer in the town square; see Sidney B. Hoenig, "Historical Inquiries: I. Heber Ir II. City-Square," *JQR* 48 (1957) 123-39.

68. No *yôd* in 1 Sam. 18:7; 21:12(11).

69. No *yôd* in 1 Sam. 21:12(11); 29:5.

70. For discussion of the couplet, see Michael Patrick O'Connor, "War and Rebel Chants in the Former Prophets," in *Fortunate the Eyes That See: Essays in Honor of David Noel Freedman in Celebration of His Seventieth Birthday,* ed. Astrid B. Beck, Andrew H. Bartelt, Paul R. Raabe, and Chris A. Franke (Grand Rapids: Eerdmans, 1995) 327-30.

71. This example has two, three, and four in a triplet in parallelism.

72. E.g., KTU 1.4 I 26-28: "He casts silver by the thousands,/Gold he casts by the ten-thousands" (*UNP,* 121). See also KTU 1.3 I 15-17 (*UNP,* 106; presented in Chapter Six); the internal parallelism in 1.3 IV 38 (*UNP,* 114) and 1.3 VI 17-18 (*UNP,* 119); 1.14 I 39-40 (*UNP,* 15); 1.14 IV 17-18 (*UNP,* 19); 5.9.5. See *DULAT,* 730-31. Note also Keiko Tazawa, *Syro-Palestinian Deities in New Kingdom Egypt: The Hermeneutics of Their Existence* (B.A.R. 1965; Oxford: Archaeopress, 2009) 34, doc. #85: "A thousand men cannot stand before him [Ramesses III]; hundred-thousands quail at the sight of him."

73. O'Connor, "War and Rebel Chants in the Former Prophets," 327.

74. The names are slotted into the grammatical framework of the couplet, as noted by O'Connor, "War and Rebel Chants in the Former Prophets," 334. For a different sort of slotting in tribal sayings, cf. the shared line between Zebulun in Gen. 49:13a and Asher in Judg. 5:17b, and the shared line between Issachar in Gen. 49:14b and Reuben in Judg. 5:16a. On these comparsions, see further below.

75. Van Dijk-Hemmes in Athalya Brenner and van Dijk-Hemmes, *On Gendering Texts: Female and Male Voices in the Hebrew Bible* (Biblical Interpretation 1; Leiden: Brill, 1993) 36; Noble, "Another Demand for a King," in *In the Wake of Tikva Frymer Kensky,* ed. Steven Holloway, JoAnn Scurlock, and Richard Beal (Gorgias Précis Portfolios 4; Piscataway: Gorgias, 2009) 183.

76. Brenner and van Dijk-Hemmes, *On Gendering Texts,* 36.

77. For this role for women, see p. 357 note 70 above and Chapter Three, section 3. Note also the archaeology of women's song in Carol L. Meyers, "Of Drums and Damsels: Women's Performance in Ancient Israel," *BA* 54/1 (1991) 16-27.

78. Cf. the boast about Gilgamesh in SBV VI.174-175, which Thorkild Jacobsen (*The Treasures of Darkness: A History of Mesopotamian Religion* [New Haven: Yale University Press, 1976] 202) reconstructs with the name of Enkidu after the name of Gilgamesh: "Gilgamesh is noblest of youths!/Enkidu most renowned of swains!" In contrast, other scholars reconstruct the second line with the name of Gilgamesh, removing any reference

to Enkidu. See Andrew R. George, *The Babylonian Gilgamesh Epic: Introduction, Critical Edition, and Cuneiform Texts* (Oxford: Oxford University Press, 2003) 1:629; *The Epic of Gilgamesh: A New Translation, Analogues, Criticism,* trans. and ed. Benjamin R. Foster (New York: Norton, 2001) 51.

79. Cf. Judg. 11:34. Note also Amihai Mazar, "Ritual Dancing in the Iron Age," *NEA* 66 (2003) 126-32.

80. Freedman, Review of Stanley Gevirtz, *Patterns in the Early Poetry of Israel* (SAOC 32; Chicago: University of Chicago Press, 1963), *JBL* 83 (1964) 201, cited in O'Connor, "War and Rebel Chants in the Former Prophets," 329.

81. This picture also conforms to the prose representation of such potential publicity in 1 Sam. 27:11, which also involves communication about conflict with the Philistines. Cf. 2 Chr. 35:25 with its narrative about the laments of Jeremiah for the slain Josiah augmented by the laments of male and female singers. For the point of different possible oral settings for a text, see Burke O. Long, "Recent Field Studies in Oral Literature and the Question of Sitz im Leben," *Semeia* 5 (1976) 35-49.

82. See the extensive discussion in Chapter Nine.

83. George E. Mendenhall, "Prophecy and Poetry in Modern Yemen," in *The Archaeology of Jordan and Beyond: Essays in Honor of James A. Sauer,* ed. Lawrence E. Stager, Joseph A. Greene, and Michael D. Coogan (Winona Lake: Eisenbrauns, 2000) 342.

84. See the discussion in Chapter One.

85. Note Dennis Pardee, *The Ugaritic Texts and the Origins of West-Semitic Literary Composition* (Schweich Lectures 2007; Oxford: Oxford University Press, 2012) 35-36.

86. Aaron Demsky, "A Proto-Canaanite Abecedary Dating from the Period of the Judges and Its Implications for the History of the Alphabet," *TA* 4 (1977) 14-27; "The ʿIzbet Ṣarṭah Ostracon Ten Years Later," in *ʿIzbet Ṣarṭah: An Early Iron Age Site near Rosh Haʿayin, Israel,* ed. Israel Finkelstein (B.A.R. 299; Oxford: B.A.R., 1986) 186-92; Frank Moore Cross, "Newly Found Inscriptions in Old Canaanite and Early Phoenician Scripts," *BASOR* 238 (1980) 8-15. For a convenient presentation, Aḥituv, *Echoes from the Past,* 249-52; see also Benjamin Sass, *The Genesis of the Alphabet and Its Development in the Second Millennium* B.C. (Ägypten und Altes Testament 13; Wiesbaden: Harrassowitz, 1988) 65-69. Note also the more recent discovery of the Tel Zayit abecedary; see Tappy and McCarter, *Literate Culture and Tenth-Century Canaan;* Hess, "Writing about Writing."

87. For abecedaries (in addition to the works cited in the preceding note), see Christopher A. Rollston, "Scribal Education in Ancient Israel," *BASOR* 344 (2006) 67; *Writing and Literacy,* 111. See also the listing in Gordon J. Hamilton, *The Origins of the West Semitic Alphabet in Egyptian Scripts* (CBQMS 40; Washington: Catholic Biblical Association of America, 2006) 28 n. 53. I am not assuming the existence of scribal "schools" in early Israel. For this matter, see Byrne, "The Refuge of Scribalism," 5-6; Rollston, "Scribal Education in Ancient Israel," 49-50, *Writing and Literacy,* 91-125; Millard, "Scripts and Their Uses in the 12th-10th Centuries BCE," in *The Ancient Near East in the 12th-10th Centuries* BCE. *Culture and History: Proceedings of the International Conference Held at the University of Haifa, 2-5 May, 2010,* ed. Gershon Galil, Ayelet Gilboa, Aren M. Maeir, and Dan'el Kahn (AOAT 392; Münster: Ugarit-Verlag, 2012) 405-12.

88. For the "learning curve" involved in learning the alphabet, see Rollston, "Scribal Education in Ancient Israel," 48-49; cf. Millard, "Scripts and Their Uses," 412.

89. For the arrowheads, see Frank Moore Cross, *Leaves from an Epigrapher's Notebook: Collected Papers in Hebrew and West Semitic Palaeography and Epigraphy* (HSS 51; Winona Lake: Eisenbrauns, 2003) 200-18, 304; Sass, *The Genesis of the Alphabet*, 72-79; P. Kyle McCarter, *Ancient Inscriptions: Voices from the Biblical World* (Washington: Biblical Archaeology Society, 1996) 79; Émile Puech, "Les pointes de flèches inscrites de la fin du IIe millénaire en Phénicie et Canaan," in *Actas del IV Congresso International de Estudios Fenicios y Púnicos: Cádiz, 2 a 6 de Octubre de 1995*, ed. María Eugenia Aubet Semmler and Manuela Barthélemy (4 vols.; Cádiz: Universidad de Cádiz, 2000) 1:251-69; and in the same volume, Hélène Sader, "Une pointe de flèche phénicienne inédite du Musée National de Beyrouth," 1:271-79; Richard S. Hess, "Arrowheads from Iron Age I: Personal Names and Authenticity," in *Ugarit at Seventy-Five*, ed. K. Lawson Younger (Winona Lake: Eisenbrauns, 2007) 113-29; Byrne, "The Refuge of Scribalism," *BASOR* 345 (2007) 19; Millard, "Scripts and Their Uses," 408, 410-11. See the listing of fifty-one arrowhead inscriptions in Robert Deutsch and Michael Heltzer, *West Semitic Epigraphic News of the 1st Millennium BCE* (with a contribution by Gabriel Barkay; Tel Aviv: Archaeological Center, 1999) 13-19. Byrne has characterized the work: it "doubtless contains authentic and dubious items alike." Any result premised on the arrowheads entails the problem of their authenticity.

90. On this matter, see John C. L. Gibson, *Textbook of Syrian Semitic Inscriptions*, Vol. 3: *Phoenician Inscriptions* (Oxford: Clarendon, 1982) 1-2.

91. Byrne, "The Refuge of Scribalism," 3.

92. Sass, *The Genesis of the Alphabet*, 62-63; Byrne, "The Refuge of Scribalism," 18.

93. Cross, "Newly Found Inscriptions," 1-4; Sass, *The Genesis of the Alphabet*, 70-71 (with further bibliog.); Byrne, "The Refuge of Scribalism," 18.

94. Sass, *The Genesis of the Alphabet*, 58-60 (with prior bibliography); and Byrne, "The Refuge of Scribalism," 18.

95. Cross, *Leaves from an Epigrapher's Notebook*, 299-302; Byrne, "The Refuge of Scribalism," 18-19.

96. Byrne, "The Refuge of Scribalism," 22. See also the comments on Byrne's reconstruction by Millard, "Scripts and Their Uses," 409-10. Millard believes that the existence of the inscribed arrowheads "point to a wider use of writing."

97. Miller comments: "This probably underplays cases where writing was reserved for a ritual function. . . and bypasses the trend in similar societies for literature to be oral even among the literate. . . . The most curious factor is the restriction of written texts to small, obscure sites: Izbet Sartah, Khirbet Tannin, and Manahat. Why no inscriptions from Shechem, Dothan, Shiloh, Tell el-Farah North, Ai, Bethel, Gibeon, Gibeah — if scribalism was, indeed, an indulgence of the elite?"; "A 'New Cultural History' of Early Israel," in *Israel in Transition 2*, Vol. 2: *From Late Bronze II to Iron IIA (c. 1250–c. 850 B.C.E.): The Texts*, ed. Lester L. Grabbe (LHB/OTS 521; New York: T. & T. Clark, 2010) 184. Miller (p. 190) comments further: "Writing was also known, although not widely used. It may have served a ritual function. It is questionable whether writing was the object of elite patronage, private instruction, and a luxury commodity, given the restriction of

surviving written texts to small, obscure sites, for which I have no explanation." While providing no basis for the ritual usage of writing in the Iron I context, Miller provides no evidence against writing as a matter of elite patronage, etc. Miller forgoes, arguably not without reason, information from inscribed arrowheads. For Miller's views, see also his book, *Oral Tradition in Ancient Israel,* 43-44.

98. It is to be noted that the so-called minor judges in Judg. 10:1-5; 12:8-15 (assuming that they would provide any indication of verisimilitude for leaders in the early period) also do not come from major centers.

99. See Cross, *Leaves from an Epigrapher's Notebook,* 200; Byrne, "The Refuge of Scribalism," 19; and Rollston, *Writing and Literacy,* 65. For the problem of forged inscriptions more generally, see Rollston, *Writing and Literacy,* 137-44; Andrew G. Vaughan and Rollston, "The Antiquities Market, Sensationalized Textual Data, and Modern Forgeries," *NEA* 68 (2005) 61-68.

100. Puech, "Les pointes de flèches," 253, #16, 261.

101. See Cross, *Leaves from an Epigrapher's Notebook,* 200. Note also the older theory of Samuel Iwry that arrows were used for bellomancy; "New Evidence for Bellomancy in Ancient Palestine and Phoenicia," *JAOS* 81 (1961) 27-34. Of the material cited by Iwry, Ezek. 21:21(26) is perhaps the best biblical evidence for this practice.

102. Mazar, *The Early Biblical Period: Historical Studies,* ed. Shmuel Aḥituv and Baruch A. Levine (Jerusalem: Israel Exploration Society, 1986) 87. Mazar further sees such warriors behind the literary description in Ps. 57:4, "mercenaries called *l^{e}ba'im,* 'lions,'" apparently referring to members of a military unit whose emblem was a lion-goddess.

103. Rollston, *Writing and Literacy,* 66. See Wayne T. Pitard, "Canaanite Literature," in *From an Antique Land: An Introduction to Ancient Near Eastern Literature,* ed. Carl S. Ehrlich (Lanham: Rowman & Littlefield, 2009) 305. Pitard suggests about the arrowheads: "they seem too fine for ordinary hunting and, thus, might have been votive offerings to a god or made to be used in a religious or divinatory ritual."

104. Puech, "Les pointes de flèches," 253, #13, and 261.

105. McCarter, *Ancient Inscriptions,* 79.

106. Puech, "Les pointes de flèches," 256, #26. See also 255, #21.

107. For the meaning "ruler," see Herbert Niehr, *Herrschen und Richten: Die Wurzel špṭ im Alten Orient und im Alten Testament* (FB 54; Würzburg: Echter, 1986); see also Holger Gzella, "Some Pencilled Notes on Ugaritic Lexicography," *BO* 64 (2007) 560. The root meaning seems to be "to exercise authority"; see Joseph Martin Pagan, *A Morphological and Lexical Study of Personal Names in the Ebla Texts* (ARES 3; Rome: Missione Archeologica Italiana in Siria, 1998) 184. The meaning fits with its use for district governors in Mari texts, as noted by Daniel E. Fleming, *Democracy's Ancient Ancestors: Mari and Early Collective Governance* (Cambridge: Cambridge University Press, 2004) 54, 67-68, 76, 78, 86-87, 144. The roots **mlk* and **špṭ* are attested also in the Tel Qeiyafa inscription believed to date to the late eleventh-tenth century. See Garfinkel and Ganor, *Khirbet Qeiyafa,* 1:243-70; Puech, "L'ostracon de Khirbet Qeyafa"; Galil, "The Hebrew Inscription from Khirbet Qeiyafa/Neṭa'im."

108. See Frank Moore Cross, "Newly Discovered Inscribed Arrowheads of the Elev-

enth Century BCE," *Israel Museum Journal* 10 (1992) 57-62; Puech, "Les pointes de flèches," 256, #24.

109. Miller, *Chieftains of the Highland Clans: A History of Israel in the 12th and 11th Centuries* B.C. (BIW; Grand Rapids: Eerdmans, 2005). See also Mario Liverani, *Israel's History and the History of Israel*, trans. Chiara Peri and Philip R. Davies (London: Equinox, 2005) 83-85; Megan Bishop Moore and Brad E. Kelle, *Biblical History and Israel's Past. The Changing Study of the Bible and History* (Grand Rapids: Eerdmans, 2011) 221-24.

110. See Carol Meyers, "Of Seasons and Soldiers: A Topological Appraisal of the Premonarchic Tribes of Galilee," *BASOR* 252 (1983) 47-59, esp. 54-57.

111. For elders in ancient Israel, see Volker Wagner, "Beobachtungen am Amt der Ältesten im alttestamentlichen Israel," *ZAW* 114 (2002) 391-411, 560-76. For the importance of elders in the Iron I, see the comments based on archaeological evidence from Tell 'Ein Zippori made by the excavator, J. P. Dessel, "In Search of Biblical Elders: Public Space and Rural Elites in Pre-Monarchic Israel," in *The Culture of Jewish Objects* (Ann Arbor: Frankel Institute for Advanced Judaic Studies, 2010) 50-52. For the role of elders as agents of collective governance in the northern monarchy, see Daniel E. Fleming, *The Legacy of Israel in Judah's Bible: History, Politics, and the Reinscribing of Tradition* (Cambridge: Cambridge University Press, 2012) 101-6, 109, 111, 140, 179-92, 215, 232; he sometimes discusses the governance power of elders in terms of "collective Israel." Whatever larger influences may lie behind it, the Covenant Code (Exod. 20:19 [NRSV 20:22]–23:33) may have been produced in its present form in a nonroyal background. The social world of this material includes the well-to-do (Exod. 21:2-6; 22:7; 23:2) as well as a *nāśî'* (Exod. 22:27), but not kings. The date for the Covenant Code is highly debated; see, e.g., the tenth-ninth century date proposed by David M. Carr, *The Formation of the Hebrew Bible: A New Reconstruction* (Oxford: Oxford University Press, 2001) 470-72 (the Covenant Code assuming a weaker monarchic apparatus); the seventh-century date suggested by David Wright, *Inventing God's Law: How the Covenant Code of the Bible Used and Revised the Laws of Hammurabi* (New York: Oxford University Press, 2009) (presupposing Mesopotamian contact between the Assyrian conquest of the north and the late monarchic production of the basic law in Deuteronomy that draws on the Covenant Code); and the postexilic dating of Reinhard G. Kratz, *The Composition of the Narrative Books of the Old Testament*, trans. John Bowden (London: T. & T. Clark, 2005) 142 (assuming a particular internal development that for Kratz fits the later situation). See Raymond Westbrook, "What Is the Covenant Code?" in *Law from the Tigris to the Tiber: The Writings of Raymond Westbrook*, Vol. 1: *The Shared Tradition*, ed. Bruce Wells and Rachel Magdalene (Winona Lake: Eisenbrauns, 2009) 97-118; Bernard M. Levinson, "The Case for Revision and Interpolation within the Biblical Legal Corpora," in *"The Right Chorale": Studies in Biblical Law and Interpretation* (FAT 54; Tübingen: Mohr Siebeck, 2008) 201-23; and the forthcoming survey by William Morrow, "Legal Interactions: The *mišpāṭîm* and the Laws of Hammurabi." A basic legal corpus such as the Covenant Code could have absorbed traditional legal materials from Mesopotamia and developed them within a royal polity but not necessarily under its aegis or its scribal apparatus. See Douglas A. Knight, "Village Law and the Book of the Covenant," in *"A Wise and Discerning Mind": Essays in Honor of Burke A. Long*, ed. Saul M. Olyan and Robert C. Culley (BJS 325; Providence: Brown

Judaic Studies, 2000) 163-79. Fleming has drawn attention to elders acting independently of royal establishments in a number of texts from Ekalte and Emar; "Textual Evidence for a Palace at Late Bronze Emar," in *Organization, Representation, and Symbols of Power in the Ancient Near East: Proceedings of the 54th Rencontre Assyriologique Internationale at Würzburg, 20-25 July 2008*, ed. Gernot Wilhelm (Winona Lake: Eisenbrauns, 2002) 101-10, here 102-3, 106; and in the same volume, Lena Fijałkowska, "Power Transition and Law: The Case of Emar," 543-50. E.g., the legal authority of elders is evident in a number of land sale documents from Emar in the so-called "Syro-hittite" tablet format as opposed to the so-called "Syrian" tablet format, which does reference the king as a witness in land sales (for these tablet terms, see "conventional" Middle Euphrates style as opposed to "free format," proposed by Fleming and Sophie Démare-Lafont, "Tablet Terminology at Emar: 'Conventional' and 'Free Format,'" *AuOr* 27 [2009] 19-26). Both sources of legal authority were operative at Emar; the authority of elders is also evident in the land sales from Ekalte. For these texts, see Daniel Oden, "Grapes from a Distant Vineyard: Power over Land in Ancient Syrian Legal Documents and Its Characterization in 1 Kings 21:1-16" (Ph.D. diss., New York University, 2012) chs. 7 and 9. It is to be noted that Ugaritic legal texts (such as KTU 3.9), even in a polity as dominated by the monarchy as Ugarit was, could be produced independently of it. KTU 3.9 as well as the letter KTU 2.70 "show no ties with the official administration of the kingdom of Ugarit," according to Pardee, *The Ugaritic Texts*, 33. It is to be noted that despite their significant differences, cuneiform land sales from Emar and Ekalte (not to mention KTU 3.9) and a good deal of the Covenant Code are legal texts involving property. Like town elders, Elijah and Elisha may also be reflective of rural religious authority over and against temple and palace that might be productive of at least oral texts. Edward B. Reeves's study of the cult of the dead saints in modern Egyptian society, their popular following and the pilgrimage feasts centered on their burial sites may provide some helpful analogues to the phenomenon of biblical holy men Elijah and Elisha, their bands of disciples, and the cultic devotion paid to them after their deaths; *The Hidden Government: Ritual, Clientelism, and Legitimation in Northern Egypt* (Salt Lake City: University of Utah Press, 1990). See also p. 560 note 20 below.

112. Byrne, "The Refuge of Scribalism," 23.

113. Puech, "Les pointes de flèches," 254, #18, and 261.

114. For discussion of the goddesses in the arrowheads, see Chapter Seven, section 4.

115. See the survey of battle practices and attitudes in particular in the first section in Chapter One.

116. Byrne, "The Refuge of Scribalism," 22.

117. One might also compare the scribal activity of the Izbet Sartah abecedary and the reference to the unnamed scribe in Judg. 8:14 who draws up a list of names, another typical scribal activity. At the same time, the biblical passage is unnecessary for the discussion here.

118. Ernst Axel Knauf, "Deborah's Language: Judges Ch. 5 in Its Hebrew and Semitic Context," in *Studia Semitica et Semitohamitica: Festschrift für Rainer Voigt anlässlich seines 60 Geburtstages am 17. Januar 2004*, ed. Bogdan Burtea, Josef Tropper, and Helen Younansardaroud (AOAT 317; Münster: Ugarit-Verlag, 2005) 176 n. 46. Knauf suggests a tenth-century date, however. See Chapter Eight for an argument for an Iron I date for

the older material in the poem, as well as an argument for a tenth-century date for its final composition.

119. See the discussion of the work of Avi Faust in Chapter One, section 3.

120. Nagy, "Ellipsis in Homer," in *Written Voices, Spoken Signs: Tradition, Performance, and the Epic Text,* ed. Egbert Bakker and Ahuvia Kahane (Cambridge, MA: Harvard University Press, 1997) 177. For oral and written forms of heroic tradition associated with David, see further Isser, *The Sword of Goliath,* 72-99.

121. So see Millard, "Scripts and Their Uses," 405-12.

122. See Fleming, *The Legacy of Israel,* 287-88.

123. In the prose of 2 Samuel (esp. chs. 15-19), Daniel E. Fleming has identified northern traditions of Israel as a political unit associated with David as the older material relative to the southern traditions of Judah as a polity associated with him: "all the references to Judah in 2 Samuel are influenced by later consciousness of the separate kingdom by that name"; *The Legacy of Israel,* 98-109, here 108. Fleming (pp. 107-8) acknowledges Hebron as David's political base, but Judah as a polity plays no role in the older literary traditions in 2 Samuel.

124. It is not my intention to address in this context the larger issues of state formation or its chronology. See Chapter One for discussion.

125. Millard also suggests that oral texts for business deals were announced in communal spaces of towns and then written down afterwards; "Oral Proclamation and Written Record," 237-41, citing a Nuzi text: "the deed was written down in Nuzi at the town gate after the announcement" (HSS 5 17:30, cited in *CAD,* M/1:93).

126. I am unable to think of another royal poem belonging to the northern court in the tenth century (Psalm 29 is a candidate for being an Iron I northern poem, but it is not evidently a royal psalm celebrating the human king). For an Iron II northern royal psalm, see Psalm 45; Carr (*The Formation of the Hebrew Bible,* 390-91), noting its northern background, dates it to the "early monarchal period." Another possible candidate would be Psalm 20; see Carr, pp. 395-97. On these northern psalms, see Gary A. Rendsburg, *Linguistic Evidence for the Northern Origin of Selected Poems* (SBLMS 43; Atlanta: Scholars, 1990). Cf. the northern or Israelite royal themes in Num. 24:15-19, which has been situated in the first half of the ninth century by Levine, *Numbers 21–36,* 232. Even if this poem was composed in the Transjordan as Levine understands it, it was received into the royal court of Israel before its demise; the poem would suit the northern court.

127. The reception of the poem in the south is suggested by the reference to the Judeans in 2 Sam. 1:18. However, this may be relatively late (see also above note 123). Gen. 49:8-12, however one views its various parts, may also be situated in the southern court in the Iron IIA or IIB period. See the remarks in this vein made by Frank Moore Cross and David Noel Freedman, *Studies in Ancient Yahwistic Poetry* (2nd ed.; BRS; Grand Rapids: Eerdmans; Livonia: Dove, 1997; orig. 1975, based on their 1950 Johns Hopkins University dissertation) 47. Raymond de Hoop offers a comparison of Gen. 49:8-10 and Psalm 72 that suggests a southern royal context; *Genesis 49 in Its Literary and Historical Context* (OtSt 39; Leiden, 1999) 137-38; for interpretational and literary critical issues, see de Hoop, pp. 114-48, 289-94. For v. 10b, see the more recent discussion of Richard Steiner, "Poetic Forms in the Masoretic Vocalization and Three Difficult Phrases in Jacob's Blessing," *JBL*

129 (2010) 209-35, here 219-26. Other candidates for early royal psalms in the southern court would include the early cores of Ps. 18/2 Sam. 22:8-16 (Cross and Freedman, *Studies in Ancient Yahwistic Poetry,* 85; cf. the cautions of Carr, *The Formation of the Hebrew Bible,* 398); and perhaps 2 Sam. 23:1-7, although the core of the latter could also be northern in origin and arguably shows some late features; see Carr, *The Formation of the Hebrew Bible,* 397; Steven L. McKenzie, "The Typology of the Davidic Covenant," in *The Land That I Will Show You: Essays on the History and Archaeology of the Ancient Near East in Honor of J. Maxwell Miller,* ed. J. Andrew Dearman and M. Pattrick Graham (JSOTSup 343; Sheffield: Sheffield Academic, 2001) 152-78.

128. To mention only one instance, "let them write me whatever the king, my lord, says" (*ABL* 21 r. 5, cited in *CAD Š/1*:446).

129. This is true of another royal sponsored text, namely the Ugaritic Baal Cycle, in which the reciter is occasionally provided instructions about the recitation of the text; in one case, the instructions are demarcated by scribal lines. See KTU 1.4 V 42-43 in *UNP,* 131; *UBC,* 2:574-76.

130. Niditch, *Oral World and Written Word,* 94-95, 117-20, for "the writing down of oral compositions." If Niditch's discussion is any indication, the biblical evidence for this process is remarkably meager. See also Karel van der Toorn, *Scribal Culture and the Making of the Hebrew Bible* (Cambridge, MA: Harvard University Press, 2007) 115.

131. The example is discussed by many authors, esp. in recent years. See Niditch, *Oral World and Written Word,* 95, 104, 133; Carr, *Writing on the Tablet of the Heart,* 118, 147, 151; van der Toorn, *Scribal Culture,* 82-84, 110-11, 184-87. In this connection, see also the older treatment of Gösta W. Ahlström, "Oral and Written Transmission: Some Considerations," *HTR* 59 (1966) 69-81.

132. See the discussion of this putative collection in Chapter Ten, section 3.

133. So Knauf, "Deborah's Language," 167-82. Cf. the dating of the poem to the tenth or ninth century by Walter Gross, *Richter* (HTKAT; Freiburg: Herder, 2009) 349. See Chapter Eight for discussion.

134. The view has represented something of a consensus for over a half-century. See T. H. Gaster, "Psalm 45," *JBL* 74 (1955) 239-51; more recently, Christoph Schroeder, "'A Love Song': Psalm 45 in the Light of Ancient Near Eastern Marriage Texts," *CBQ* 58 (1996) 417-32; Nancy R. Bowen, "A Fairy Tale Wedding? A Feminist Intertextual Reading of Psalm 45," in *A God So Near: Essays on Old Testament Theology in Honor of Patrick D. Miller,* ed. Brent A. Strawn and Bowen (Winona Lake: Eisenbrauns, 2003) 53-71; William H. C. Propp, "Is Psalm 45 an Erotic Poem?" *BRev* 20/2 (2004) 33-37, 42. It has been read instead as a coronation text by James M. Trotter, "The Genre and Setting of Psalm 45," *ABR* 57 (2009) 34-46. This reading depends on the claim that the closest parallels are in coronation texts (Psalms 2, 72, 110) and "enthronement of Yahweh hymns" (Psalms 47, 93, 95–99). By contrast, Schroeder (p. 417) notes: "Psalm 45 is unique." Trotter (pp. 44-45) himself says that for the obeisance expressed in v. 12, the wedding ceremony, particularly a royal wedding, provides a most likely setting.

135. The picture evoked by the common modern translation "pen" is quite distant from the Iron Age reality. Note the word used for an iron stylus in Jer. 17:1; Job 19:24. See André Caquot, "Cinq observations sur le Psaume 45," in *Ascribe to the Lord: Biblical &*

Other Studies in Memory of Peter C. Craigie, ed. Lyle Eslinger and Glen Taylor (JSOTSup 67; Sheffield: JSOT, 1988) 253-64, here 255-56.

136. Caquot ("Cinq observations sur le Psaume 45," 256 n. 11) notes **mhr* in 1 Esdr. 7:6 and Ahiqar, in addition to Isa. 16:5; Prov. 22:29. Note also the word in the discussion of Jeffrey Zorn, "LU.*PA-MA-ḪA-A* in EA 162:74 and the Role of the *Mhr* in Egypt and Ugarit," *JNES* 50 (1992) 129-38.

137. Malamat, "Weapons Deposited in a Sanctuary by Zimri-Lim of Mari and David and Saul of Israel," in *Ex Mesopotamia et Syria Lux*, ed. Manfried Dietrich (AOAT 281; Münster: UGARIT-Verlag, 2002) 325-27, here 327.

138. Pardee, *RCU*, 84-85; see also Steven W. Holloway, "KTU 1.162 and the Offering of a Shield," *UF* 30 (1998) 353-61.

139. Malamat, "Weapons Deposited in a Sanctuary," 325-27.

140. For details, see Amihai Mazar, *Excavations at Tell Qasile. Part 2: The Philistine Sanctuary — Various Finds, the Pottery, Conclusions, Appendixes* (Qedem 20; Jerusalem: Institute of Archaeology, Hebrew University, 1985) 3-4. See also *NEAEHL*, 4:1210.

141. See Caquot, "Cinq observations sur le Psaume 45," 255-56.

142. Caquot, "Cinq observations sur le Psaume 45," 256.

143. Propp, "Is Psalm 45 an Erotic Poem?" 34.

144. Niditch, *Oral World and Written Word*.

145. There seems to be little basis for the idea of a "cultic prophet" here (see Schroeder, "'A Love Song,'" 432 n. 37). The voice here is represented as the poet's, and evidently not as divine words.

146. *CAD*, M/1:109, citing LKA 62 rev. 9.

147. Enuma Elish VII:147, cited in *CAD*, Š/1:401.

148. Readings and discussion are based on Dennis Pardee, in Pardee et al., *Handbook of Ancient Hebrew Letters: A Study Edition* (SBLSBS 15; Chico: Scholars, 1982), 84-89. I have not included the partial brackets in Pardee's reconstruction. See also Johannes Renz, *Handbuch der althebräischen Epigraphik*, Vol. 1: *Die althebräischen Inschriften*. Pt. 1: *Text und Kommentar* (Darmstadt: Wissenschaftliche Buchgesellschaft, 1995) 412-19; Sandra Landis Gogel, *A Grammar of Epigraphic Hebrew* (SBLRBS 23; Atlanta: Scholars, 1998) 416-18. The discussion here is based on Mark S. Smith, *The Priestly Vision of Genesis 1* (Minneapolis: Fortress, 2009) 111-12. This letter is discussed by many scholars who have worked on orality and writing in ancient Israel, e.g., Niditch, *Oral World and Written Word*, 53.

149. Cf. the following: "this omen is not from the (canonical) series *ša pi-i ummâni šû*, it is from the oral tradition of the scholars." For ABL 519 r. 2, see Parpola, SAA 10 8, cited in *CAD*, P:466. Cf. *CAD*, P:465: *taklum ša awâtim na pí-i-im iṣabbatu*, "a reliable person who is able to retain an oral message" (ARM 1 76: 27).

150. Pardee, in *Handbook of Ancient Hebrew Letters*, 92.

151. Another sort of royal recitation may serve as a contrast for this discussion of textual transmission in early Israel. I refer to the representation of the oral report to the king made about one of Elisha's miracles in 2 Kgs. 8:4-5. See Alexander Rofé, *The Prophetical Stories: The Narratives about the Prophets in the Hebrew Bible, Their Literary Types and History* (Jerusalem: Magnes, 1988) 26. The account presents the story of this miracle only in passing. The story is said to be told; it is neither sung nor is it communal.

It is represented as no more than a prosaic report simply made to the king. In this case, there is relatively little "performance" represented as such, compared with Judges 5. See p. 563 note 35 below.

152. For Psalm 68, note its use of *selāh* (vv. 8, 20, 33). Exodus 15 (if early) presents military song (Ex. 15:2) that is rather religious as well. Perhaps, like Psalm 68, the recitation of military song of Exodus 15 was adopted and adapted for liturgical usage (as suggested by its prose context in 15:1, 20-21; see p. 357 note 70 above and Chapter Three, section 3).

153. Cf. the representation of what "fathers tell" (**spr*, e.g., in Deut. 32:7; Judg. 6:13; cf. Hab. 3:2a.

154. For such "tectonic shifts" in institutions and their collective memory in ancient Israel, see Smith, *The Memoirs of God*, 124-40. This discussion draws extensively from work on collective memory relative to the changing instituitional settings, as studied by a number of social historians associated with the *Annales* school, specifically Maurice Halbwachs, Jacques Le Goff and Pierre Nora, and Danièle Hervieu-Léger. See also the following chapter.

Notes to Chapter Twelve

1. See further below for discussion.

2. For a recent study with bibliog. and extensive comparative material, see Meik Gerhards, "'Die Sonne lässt am Himmel erkennen Jahwe . . .': Text- und religionsgeschichtliche Überlegungen zum Tempelweihspruch aus I Reg 8,12f. (M) (III Reg, 53a [LXX]," *UF* 42 (2010) 191-260. Gerhards views the tradition of the solar deity in the poetic piece as pre-Davidic.

3. For ancient Israel, it might be thought that warrior poetry in the time of Solomon and later perhaps would pose a challenge to royal authority, one based less on the king's own military leadership, which was delegated to a formal structure headed by generals. However, this way of looking at the question would not explain the same division of labor at Ugarit. Two different royal strategies may have been at work in Israel and Ugarit: while the Israelite monarchies do not continue the practice of heroic poetry, the Ugaritic monarchy embraced it, perhaps to express royal authority, as discussed below in this section.

4. For examples from the Baal Cycle, see the left-hand side of KTU 1.4 VIII, in *UNP*, 141; and 1.6 VI 54-58, in *UNP*, 164. For Kirta, see 1.16 VI, left-hand edge, in *UNP*, 42. For Aqhat, see the left-hand side of KTU 1.17 VI, in *UNP*, 63. For a recent discussion of these colophons, see Dennis Pardee, *The Ugaritic Texts and the Origins of West-Semitic Literary Composition* (Schweich Lectures 2007; Oxford: Oxford University Press, 2012) 41-49.

5. See the discussion in Chapter Five, section 3.

6. These passages are discussed in Chapter Five, in sections 2 and 1, respectively. See further the discussion below.

7. For the Ugaritic monarchy's interest in texts about heroes, see Gregorio del Olmo Lete, "Littérature et pouvoir royal à Ougarit: Sens politique de la littérature d'Ougarit," in *Études ougaritiques II*, ed. Valérie Matoïan, Michel Al-Maqdissi, and Yves Calvet (RSO 20; Leuven: Peeters, 2012) 241-50.

8. For these questions with reviews of the secondary literature, see *UBC*, 1:29-36; 2:10-16. Note also Pardee, *The Ugaritic Texts*, 50-77.

9. For a scribal insertion in the Baal Cycle, see KTU 1.4 V 42-43, in *UNP*, 131. For Aqhat, see the scribal instruction on the left-hand side of the third tablet, 1.19 IV 23, in *UNP*, 78. Such inserted scribal instructions occur in nonliterary texts as well, e.g., in one of the incantations for snakebites, KTU 1.100.78, in *UNP*, 221.

10. See Pardee, *The Ugaritic Texts*, 41-49, esp. 45.

11. See RS 94.2518, the Ugaritic king list in *RCU*, 203-4, as well as the king lists published by Daniel Arnaud, "Prolégomènes à la rédaction d'une histoire d'Ougarit II: Les bordereaux de rois divinisés," *Studi Micenei ed Egeo-Anatolici* 41 (1998) 153-73. These lists are suggestive of a long royal history at Ugarit. For a historical survey, see Itamar Singer, "A Political History of Ugarit," in *Handbook of Ugaritic Studies*, ed. Wilfred G. E. Watson and Nicolas Wyatt (HO 1/39; Leiden: Brill, 1999) 603-733.

12. To be sure, there are several shorter poetic pieces in Ugaritic. See KTU 1.114.1-24, in *UNP*, 194-95, treated in Chapter Seven, section 2.

13. The Rephaim texts of KTU 1.20–1.22 have long been thought to involve three tablets, each with two columns. However, as noted in Chapter Five, this view has been recently challenged. See Dennis Pardee, "Nouvelle étude épigraphique et littéraire des textes fragmentaires en langue ougaritique dits "Les Rephaïm" (*CTA* 20-22)," *Or* 80 (2011) 1-65.

14. Psalm 68 has thirty-six verses; Judges 5 has thirty-one verses; 2 Samuel 1:19-27 consists of nine verses. Exodus 15, if it is to be included, has eighteen verses. To be sure, Psalm 18/2 Samuel 22 has fifty-one verses, but it is only vv. 8-16 that are counted as "old poetry" by Frank Moore Cross, *Canaanite Myth and Hebrew Epic: Essays in the History of the Religion of Israel* (Cambridge, MA: Harvard University Press, 1973) 158-59. Cross calls vv. 8-16 an "ancient fragment" and says that its current context "appears not to be original."

15. Note the remarks by Erhard Blum, "Historiography or Poetry? The Nature of the Bible Prose Traditions," in *Memory in the Bible and Antiquity*, ed. Loren T. Stuckenbruck, Stephen C. Barton, and Benjamin G. Wold (WUNT 212; Tübingen: Mohr Siebeck, 2012) 25-45.

16. The same point might be said of the poetic composition of KTU 1.114.1-28, tied as it is to the prose medical prescription in 1.114.29-31. See Chapter Seven, section 2. For convenient reference, see also *UNP*, 194-96.

17. For the watershed between the older poetic tradition and biblical narrative, see Kawashima, *Biblical Narrative and the Death of the Rhapsode* (Bloomington: Indiana University Press, 2004) 14-15; Dobbs-Allsopp, "Space, Line, and the Written Biblical Poem in Texts from the Judean Desert," in *Puzzling Out the Past: Studies in Northwest Semitic Languages and Literatures in Honor of Bruce Zuckerman*, ed. Marilyn J. Lundberg, Steven Fine, and Wayne T. Pitard (CHANE 55; Leiden: Brill, 2012) 52. To account for this shift, both scholars emphasize what Kawashima calls "a shift from the medium of the spoken to the written word." This may help to situate Kawashima's primary concern, namely what he perceives to be novel about biblical narrative; it is less clear that this approach addresses sufficiently the apparent demise of older poetry. Cf. the comparative comments of John

Pairman Brown, "Peace Symbolism in Ancient Military Vocabulary," *VT* 21 (1971) 1-23, here 1, 11. For further discussion, see section 4 below.

18. Cf. the remarks of Frank H. Polak, "Book, Scribe, and Bard: Oral Discourse and Written Text in Recent Biblical Scholarship," *Prooftexts* 31 (2011) 121-22. Note his comments also on p. 133: "Ample justification exists for the inference that by the second half of the ninth century (roughly the period in which the Mesha stele was chiseled), ancient Israelite narrative already formed a distinct literary entity."

19. For this question, as well as circumstantial evidence for the ancient awareness of early Hebrew poetry as old relative to later biblical Hebrew prose, see Mark S. Smith, "Why Was 'Old Poetry' Used in Hebrew Narrative? Historical and Cultural Considerations about Judges 5," in Lundberg, Fine, and Pitard, *Puzzling Out the Past*, 197-212.

20. There may be some transfer of heroic notions to prophetic figures in the ninth-eighth-century context. According to Baruch A. Levine, infusion of *rûaḥ* "ultimately originated in the heroic tradition, where we read that the divine spirit infuses the hero (Judg 3:10, 11:29, 13:25)"; *Numbers 21–36* (AB 4A; New York: Doubleday, 2000) 354; for further discussion, see pp. 191, 350. The infusion of divine spirit into Gideon (Judg. 6:34) is attested also for some prophets (Num. 11:25-26; 1 Kgs. 18:46; 2 Kgs. 3:15; Jer. 15:17). See Robert R. Wilson, *Prophecy and Society in Ancient Israel* (Philadelphia: Fortress, 1980) 144-45. The application of this warrior ideal to Elijah and Elisha may be part of the tradition's representation of them as mighty "holy men" and not only as prophetic spokesmen. For this point about Elijah and Elisha, see Mark S. Smith, "Recent Study of Israelite Religion in Light of the Ugaritic Texts," in *Ugarit at Seventy-Five*, ed. K. Lawson Younger Jr. (Winona Lake: Eisenbrauns, 2007) 1-25, esp. 12-13; and pp. 553-53 note 111 above.

21. Cf. the reception of the *Iliad* and *Odyssey* at Athens and other locales in the sixth century, discussed by H. A. Shapiro, "Hipparcos and the Rhapsodes," in *Cultural Poetics in Archaic Greece: Cult, Performance, Politics*, ed. Carol Dougherty and Leslie Kurke (Oxford: Oxford University Press, 1998) 92-107. Shapiro mentions Walter Burkert's theory that rhapsodes of this period were "desperately trying to turn the Homeric poems into 'classics' in order to compete with the newer and more appealing musical genres of choral and monodic lyre" (p. 104). This issue of the status and development of ancient texts as "classics" is intriguing for other ancient literary corpora, such as biblical works, but this matter lies beyond the scope of the present work.

22. Cross, *Canaanite Myth and Hebrew Epic*, 158-59.

23. For the Neo-Assyrian period for the psalm as a whole, see Eckart Otto, "Politische Theologie in den Königspsalmen zwischen Ägypten und Assyrien: Die Herrscherlegitimation in den Psalmen 2 und 18 in ihren altorientalischen Kontexten," in *"Mein Sohn bist du" (Ps 2,7): Studien zu den Königspsalmen*, ed. Otto and Erich Zenger (Stuttgart: Katholisches Bibelwerk, 2002) 45-50, cited and discussed by David M. Carr, *The Formation of the Hebrew Bible: A New Reconstruction* (Oxford: Oxford University Press, 2001) 315.

24. For this poem, see Theodore Hiebert, *The God of My Victory: The Ancient Hymn in Habakkuk 3* (HSM 38; Atlanta: Scholars, 1986); Robert D. Haak, *Habakkuk* (VTSup 44; Leiden: Brill, 1992) 78-106; Shmuel Aḥituv, "The Sinai Theophany in the Psalm of Hababkkuk," in *Birkat Shalom: Studies in the Bible, Ancient Near Eastern Literature, and*

Post-Biblical Judaism Presented to Shalom M. Paul on the Occasion of His Seventieth, ed. Chaim Cohen et al. (Winona Lake: Eisenbrauns, 2008) 1:225-32; John E. Anderson, "Awaiting an Answered Prayer: The Development and Reinterpretation of Habakkuk 3 in its Contexts," *ZAW* 123 (2011) 57-71. For the poem's meteorological imagery, see Aloysius Fitzgerald, F.S.C., *The Lord of the East Wind* (CBQMS 34; Washington: Catholic Biblical Association of America, 2002) 82-97. The use of *selâ* three times in Hab. 3:3, 9, 13 appears to be a liturgical marker, which if correct might suggest that this poem existed in a liturgical context when it was incorporated into Habakkuk 3. To be sure, the use of *selâ* has been thought to represent a considerably later addition to the poem; H. St. John Thackeray, *The Septuagint and Jewish Worship: A Study in Origins* (Schweich Lectures 1920; 2nd ed.; London: Oxford University Press, 1923) 51. That the poem of Habakkuk 3 belonged to a collection sponsored by the monarchy might be inferred from the reference to the anointed in v. 13. The royal background might be suspected also from v. 19, esp. when it is compared with the very similar line in the royal psalm of thanksgiving, Ps. 18/2 Sam. 22:33(34); *wayyāśem* in the former would appear to be an updating or at least more common verb used by comparison with *měšawweh* in the latter. For this difference, see Francis I. Andersen, *Habakkuk* (AB 25; New York: Doubleday, 2001) 348-49. For royal psalms of the tenth-ninth centuries, see Carr, *The Formation of the Hebrew Bible*, 386-402. Thus, in the case of the poem of Habakkuk 3, it is possible to entertain a scenario by which this piece of heroic poetry went through two shifts in setting, from its earliest form as a piece of heroic poetry in vv. 3-15, to its inclusion into a (royal?) liturgical collection, as marked by the addition of vv. 1-2, 16a, 18-19, and finally to its inclusion within the prophetic context of Habakkuk 3, with the addition of v. 1. For this analysis, note Anderson, "Awaiting an Answered Prayer."

25. In this group of poems might be included the preserved six-line poem from Kuntillet Ajrud; Shmuel Aḥituv, Esther Eshel, and Ze'ev Meshel, in Meshel, *Kuntillet ʿAjrud (Ḥorvat Teman): An Iron Age II Religious Site on the Judah-Sinai Border* (Jerusalem: Israel Exploration Society, 2012) 110. This poem describes a theophany in the context of warfare (with *ʾl* and *[y]hw[h]* in line 2, "the Holy One *[q{š}dš]* over the gods" in line 4, *bʿl* in line 5, and *ʾl* in line 6). This piece may be an older preservation analogous to what survives in Hab. 3:3-8; Deut. 33:2-5.

26. For Jer. 2:8; 18:18 as late preexilic witnesses to social segments responsible for textual production, see also Carr, *The Formation of the Hebrew Bible*, 405-6. For discussion of the settings of scribal production in the Iron IIB-C, see Carr, *Writing on the Tablet of the Heart: Origins of Scripture and Literature* (Oxford: Oxford University Press, 2005) 119-20, 141, 146, 152; Karel van der Toorn, *Scribal Culture and the Making of the Hebrew Bible* (Cambridge, MA: Harvard University Press, 2005) 85-96, 122, 183. For inscriptional evidence for a formal standardized scribal education in Iron II Israel, see Christopher Rollston, "Scribal Education in Ancient Israel: The Old Hebrew Epigraphic Evidence," *BASOR* 344 (2006) 47-74; "An Old Hebrew Stone Inscription from the City of David: A Trained Hand and a Remedial Hand on the Same Inscription," in Lundberg, Fine, and Pitard, *Puzzling Out the Past*, 189-96.

27. The sort of model being considered here does not belong to any of the four models for writing discussed by Susan Niditch, *Oral World and Written Word: Ancient Israelite*

Literature (Louisville: Westminster John Knox, 1996) 117-29, as the discussion there does not reckon much with the royal setting of oral literature, nor with evidence from outside of Israel that might have pointed in this direction. At the same time, it is to be said that the model being entertained here builds on Niditch's central point about the importance of orality in the scribal culture of ancient Israel, applied here to the royal scribal context. This approach also dovetails with studies of Mesopotamian scribal culture; on this score, see Carr, *Writing on the Tablet of the Heart;* van der Toorn, *Scribal Culture and the Making of the Hebrew Bible.* Cf. the five phases of Homeric epic from the second millennium to the second century as sketched out by Gregory Nagy, "Ellipsis in Homer," in *Written Voices, Spoken Signs: Tradition, Performance, and the Epic Text,* ed. Egbert Bakker and Ahuvia Kahane (Cambridge, MA: Harvard University Press, 1997) 180-81.

28. For prophetic "spirit" as possibly influenced by the divine "spirit" given to heroes, see above note 20.

29. Kevin McGeough, "Esther the Hero: Going beyond 'Wisdom' in Heroic Narratives," *CBQ* 70 (2008) 44-65. Note also the evocation of Saul for Mordecai as hero in the book of Esther; see the discussion of Aaron Koller, *Queen of Politics: Esther in the Context of Ancient Jewish Intellectual History* (Cambridge: Cambridge University Press, 2014) ch. 4. Daniel in the lion's den (Daniel 6) may echo the exploit of the warrior, Benaiah, in 2 Sam. 23:20.

30. These materials may constitute a series of additions spliced between 2 Sam. 21:14 and the resumption of David stories in 2 Samuel 24–1 Kings 2 (although the latter seem to provide a proper transition to the figure of Solomon). For the view that 2 Samuel 21–24 are arranged chiastically, see Alexander Rofé, *Introduction to the Literature of the Hebrew Bible* (Jerusalem Biblical Studies 9; Jerusalem: Simor, 2009) 67. In their present position these chapters serve as an appendix to 1-2 Samuel, according to Rofé, p. 69. More widely within the complex of 1-2 Samuel, it seems that the poems of 2 Samuel 22 and 23 offer a "royal" frame of "warrior poetry" with Hannah's song in 1 Samuel 2, surrounding the Samuel-Saul-David complex: both 2 Samuel 23 (v. 1) and 1 Samuel 2 (v. 10) refer to the king. The literary issues involved here lie beyond the scope of this discussion.

31. Since David himself figures in 2 Sam. 21:15-22 and not in 2 Sam. 23:8-39, it may seem fitting for the poems attributed to him to appear after the former, but not after the latter. On a very different level of connection between the end of the poetry and the resumption of the prose, there is perhaps a verbal link between *baššābet* in the final line of the poem in 2 Sam. 23:7 and *baššebet* in the first line of the prose in 2 Sam. 23:8.

32. See also the warriors of David, mentioned in the succession narrative in 1 Kgs. 1:8, 10; 1 Chr. 29:24; see Hans Kosmala, "gābar," *TDOT* 2:367-82, esp. 374-75.

33. See also 1 Chr. 11:42; 27:6; cf. Jer. 38:10. For thirty as a social unit, see also the "thirty sons" in Judg. 10:4; 12:9. For the number of thirty persons for a feast as in 1 Sam. 9:22, cf. the comment of Carol Meyers: "The number of participants typically transcends the number of people in an individual household; that is, a feast may involve several households or lineages, a larger group (such as a clan) connected by kinship or proximity, or even an entire community"; "The Function of Feasts: An Anthropological Perspective on Israelite Religious Festivals," in *Social Theory and the Study of Israelite Religion: Essays*

in Retrospect and Prospect, ed. Saul M. Olyan (SBLRBS 71; Atlanta: Society of Biblical Literature, 2012) 153.

34. See Benjamin Mazar, "The Military Elite of King David," in *The Early Biblical Period: Historical Studies,* ed. Shmuel Aḥituv and Baruch A. Levine (Jerusalem: Israel Exploration Society, 1986) 83-103; and Sara Japhet, *I & II Chronicles* (OTL; Louisville: Westminster John Knox, 1993) 367.

35. These compare in length to what Alexander Rofé sees as the condensation of six oral folk tales about Elisha in 2 Kgs. 2:19-22, 23-24; 4:1-7, 38-41, 42-44; 6:1-7; *The Prophetical Stories: The Narratives about the Prophets in the Hebrew Bible, Their Literary Types and History* (Jerusalem: Magnes, 1988) 13-18. Rofé opines: "That these stories were handed down by word of mouth is also attested by the king's request of Gehazi to relate to him 'all the wonderful things that Elisha has done' (2 Kgs 8:4-6). . . . The longest of these takes about seventy-five seconds to read. It is unconceivable that the ancient Israelite storyteller could not have held his audience's attention for longer than this." See also pp. 557-58 note 151 above. Cf. the report of the story of the Trojan horse in *Odyssey* 8:499-520.

36. See Rofé, *Introduction to the Literature of the Hebrew Bible,* 16-17. Note also Gregory Mobley, *The Empty Men: The Heroic Tradition of Ancient Israel* (ABRL; New York: Doubleday, 2005) 1, 31-34, 48.

37. Rofé, *Introduction to the Literature of the Hebrew Bible,* 17. In his discussion of 2 Sam. 21:15-22; 23:11-12, Rofé (p. 17) notes how the section ends: "YHWH effected a great deliverance," the same words used of an act of David (1 Sam. 19:5). Rofé (pp. 17-18) comments further: "It seems clear that acts of deliverance were originally attributed to the hero himself; and it is only later the divine element of deliverance came to be emphasized, and the specific name of YHWH added. These short summaries of heroic legends undoubtedly included elements which were true."

38. See Ralph W. Klein, *1 Chronicles,* ed. Thomas Krüger (Hermeneia; Minneapolis: Fortress, 2006) 410. See also Moshe Garsiel, "David's Elite Warriors and Their Exploits in the Books of Samuel and Chronicles," *JHS* 11 (2011) 150-64, which includes an elaboration of his essay, "The Four Sons of Rephaim who Fell in Combats with David and His Heroes," *Beit Mikra* 54 (2009) 39-61 (Heb.; Eng. summary 7*).

39. Shammah in v. 11 is absent from the text of 1 Chronicles 11; instead, the presentation of Eleazar in 1 Chr. 11:12-14 contains some of the details that appear in the story of Shammah in 2 Sam. 23:11-12, specifically 2 Sam. 23:12 = 1 Chr. 11:14. In other words, 1 Chr. 11:12-14 presents one figure with the details associated with two figures in 2 Sam. 23:9-12. For the literary issues, see Klein, *1 Chronicles,* 293 n. 26 and 303; Carr, *The Formation of the Hebrew Bible,* 76.

40. See also Neh. 11:8.

41. It is sometimes thought that this figure as named in the MT Qere is to be identified with Ithay in 1 Chr. 11:31; see Donald G. Schley, "Ithai," *ABD,* 3:579. However, the significant textual problems cast some doubt on the name. "Benob" has been understood as a prepositional phrase (cf. Garsiel, "David's Elite Warriors," 6), with the preceding word taken with the Kethib *(wyšbw)* as a verb read as either "and they stayed" or "and he captured him." With this understanding, the name of Ishi disappears. It is unclear how the following prepositional phrase would work. See S. R. Driver, *Notes on the Hebrew*

Text and the Topography of the Books of Samuel (2nd ed.; Oxford: Clarendon, 1913) 353; Edouard Dhorme, *Les livres de Samuel* (EBib; Paris: Gabalda, 1910) 422-23. This problem has engendered more textual surgery, e.g., by P. Kyle McCarter, *II Samuel* (AB 9; Garden City: Doubleday, 1984) 447, 448: "and Dodo son of Joash, one of the votaries of Rapha, captured him."

42. Conrad E. L'Heureux understands **yld* to denote not birth, but "votary" status; "The *yĕlîdê hārāpā'* — a Cultic Association of Warriors," *BASOR* 221 (1976) 83-85; "The Ugaritic and Biblical Rephaim," *HTR* 67 (1974) 265-74. The view, as it applies to the references in 2 Samuel, is accepted by McCarter, *II Samuel,* 449-50; and Klein, *1 Chronicles,* 411; Klein would see a literalizing reading of **yld* for the usage in the Chronicles parallel. See the discussion below.

43. For the problem, see McCarter, *II Samuel,* 448.

44. 1 Samuel 17 lies beyond the scope of this study. For the textual development of this passage, see Dominique Barthélemy, David W. Gooding, Johan Lust, and Emanuel Tov, *The Story of David and Goliath, Textual and Literary Criticism: Papers of a Joint Research Venture* (OBO 73; Fribourg: Éditions universitaires; Göttingen: Vandenhoeck & Ruprecht, 1986); Alexander Rofé, "The Battle of David and Goliath," in *Judaic Perspectives on Ancient Israel,* ed. Jacob Neusner, Baruch Levine, and Ernest S. Frerichs (Philadelphia: Fortress, 1987) 117-51; see also Rofé, "An Enquiry into the Betrothal of Rebekah," in *Die Hebräische Bibel und ihre zweifache Nachgeschichte: Festschrift für Rolf Rendtorff zum 65. Geburtstag,* ed. Erhard Blum, Christian Macholz, and Ekkehard Stegemannn (Neukirchen: Neukirchener, 1990) 27-39, here 34-35; and Benjamin J. M. Johnson, "Reconsidering 4QSam[a] and the Textual Support for the Long and Short Versions of the David and Goliath Story," *VT* 62 (2012) 534-49. For the story as an Israelite response to sixth-century Greeks in Philistia, see Azzan Yadin, "Goliath's Armor and Israelite Collective Memory," *VT* 54 (2004) 373-95. For criticism of this proposal, see Serge Frolov and Allen Wright, "Homeric and Ancient Near Eastern Intertextuality in 1 Samuel 17," *JBL* 130 (2011) 451-71. For a comparison of the biblical description of Goliath's armor with the armor of heroes in the *Iliad,* see Brown, "Peace Symbolism in Ancient Military Vocabulary," 2-7. For the Indo-European etymologies proposed for the name of Goliath, see Aren Maeir, Stefan J. Wimmer, Alexander Zukerman, and Aaron Demsky, "A Late Iron Age I/Early Iron Age II Old Canaanite Inscription from Tell eṣ-Ṣâfi/Gath, Israel: Paleography, Dating, and Historical-Cultural Significance," *BASOR* 351 (2008) 39-71, esp. 57-58. For arguments for the high antiquity of the story's descriptions, see Alan Millard, "The Armor of Goliath," in *Exploring the Longue Durée: Essays in Honor of Lawrence E. Stager,* ed. J. David Schloen (Winona Lake: Eisenbrauns, 2009) 337-43; Philip J. King, "David Defeats Goliath," in *"Up to the Gates of Ekron": Essays on the Archaeology and History of the Eastern Mediterranean in Honor of Seymour Gitin,* ed. Sidnie White Crawford (Jerusalem: W. F. Albright Institute of Archaeological Research/Israel Exploration Society, 2007) 350-57; Jeffrey R. Zorn, "Reconsidering Goliath: An Iron Age I Philistine Chariot Warrior," *BASOR* 360 (2010) 1-22; James K. Hoffmeier, "The Aftermath of David's Triumph Over Goliath: 1 Samuel 17:54 and Ancient Near Eastern Analogues," in *Egypt, Canaan and Israel: History, Imperialism, Ideology and Literature: Proceedings of a Conference at the University of Haifa, 3-7 May 2009,* ed. Shay Bar, Dan'el Kahn, and J. J. Shirley (CHANE 52; Leiden: Brill, 2011) 87-114. For the weapons, see also

Aaron J. Koller, *The Semantic Field of Cutting Tools in Biblical Hebrew: The Interface of Philological, Semantic, and Archaeological Evidence* (CBQMS 49; Washington: Catholic Biblical Association of America, 2012) 193-97.

45. E.g., Driver, *Notes on the Hebrew Text,* 354-55.

46. Japhet, *I & II Chronicles,* 368-69; Klein, *1 Chronicles,* 411.

47. For the polydactylism attributed to Goliath, see Richard D. Barnett, "Sirens and Rephaim," in *Ancient Anatolia: Aspects of Change and Cultural Development: Essays in Honor of Machteld J. Mellink,* ed. Jeanny Vorys Canby, Edith Porada, Brunilde Sismondo Ridgeway, and Tamara Stech (Madison: University of Wisconsin Press, 1986) 112-20. Barnett noted this feature on winged bronze figures. See also Barnett, "Polydactylism in the Ancient World," *BAR* 16/3 (1990) 47.

48. Cf. **rp'* without final *'ālep* in Jer. 8:11 (cf. the same expression using **rp'* with final *'ālep* in Jer. 6:14).

49. For Rp'u and the Rephaim in the Ugaritic texts, see Chapter Five.

50. See among others, McCarter, *II Samuel,* 451.

51. Klein, *1 Chronicles,* 411 n. 9.

52. L'Heureux, "The *yělîdê hārāpā',*" 85 n. 18.

53. See also Ugaritic *'išb'l* in KTU 4.617.35; 4.785.18 and RS 94.2050 + RS 94.2092.23, in Bordreuil and Pardee, *BSV,* 59; cf. KTU 4.623.8.

54. This interpretation, though widely accepted, has been disputed. See Matitiahu Tsevat, "Ishbosheth and Congeners: The Names and Their Study," *HUCA* 34 (1975) 71-87; Gordon J. Hamilton, "New Evidence for the Authenticity of *bšt* in Hebrew Personal Names and for Its Use as a Divine Epithet in Biblical Texts," *CBQ* 60 (1998) 228-50. Note also Hannes D. Galter, "Bashtu," *DDD,* 163-64; and the recent proposal of Michael Avioz, "The Names of Mephibosheth and Ishbosheth Reconsidered," *JANES* 32 (2011) 11-20.

55. Note also the two words together in MT Jer. 11:13b (cf. Jer. 3:24). For the textual and interpretational issues in Jer. 11:13b, see William McKane, *Jeremiah,* Vol. 1: *Introduction and Commentary on Jeremiah I–XXV* (ICC; Edinburgh: T. & T. Clark, 2001) 240. LXX is missing "altars for the Shame" *(mizběḥôt labbōšet),* suggesting that the MT represents a possible addition. If correct, the usage of **bōšet* here and in the PNs of Saul's line may postdate Chronicles. For this approach to the Saulide PNs with this element, see Reinhard Müller, "Wiping Out the Memory of Baal: Post-Chronistic Changes in the Proto-Masoretic Text of Samuel," in *Rereading the Relecture? International Symposium on the Question of (Post)chronistic Influence in the Latest Redactions of the Books of Samuel,* ed. Hannes Bezzel and Reinhard Müller (FAT; Tübingen: Mohr Siebeck, in press). Note also Jerubeshet in 2 Sam. 11:21 for Jerubbaal in Judg. 6:32. This preservation in Judg. 6:32 would suggest that the alleged process of substitution is not a general one of works that scholars have grouped under the rubric of the so-called "Deuteronomistic History." These works would appear to have had variegated scribal transmissions.

56. The comparison with Num. 13:22, 28 is well known, e.g., Driver, *Notes on the Hebrew Text,* 354.

57. E.g., see Ginsberg, *ANET,* 149 n. 2; Pardee, *COS,* 1:343 n. 1.

58. For this view, see among commentators, John F. Healey, "The Rephaites of Ancient Palestine and Ugarit," in *Studies in the History and Archaeology of Palestine II,* ed.

Shawqi Shaath (Proceedings of the First International Symposium on Palestine Antiquities; Damascus: Aleppo University/Palestine Archaeological Centre, 1986) 159-63, here 161.

59. For this meaning, see PNs such as *mtbʿl* in KTU 4.75 V 21; 4.130.10; 4.310.4 (cf. *bn mt* in 4.335:15; 4.785.12; *DULAT,* 599). For a listing of Akkadian PNs with the element **mutu-*, see *CAD,* M/2:316, suggesting "man of DN," as devotee of that deity. Ugaritic *mt* is also thought to signify "hero" as well (*DULAT,* 598). In view of Ugaritic *mt* and Akkadian *mutu* used for warriors, Ugaritic *mt* in Danil's title might also enjoy a martial sensibility. Accordingly, *DULAT* (598) renders *mt rp'i,* "the Raphaite hero."

60. Their high antiquity from the Ugaritic perspective is also reflected in the blessing to Kirta in KTU 1.15 III 2-4/13-15, in *UNP,* 25, 26. The phrase *rp'i 'arṣ* is parallel with *qbṣ dtn,* the second element of which has been noted in the genealogy of the Hammurabi dynasty (see *UBC,* 1:112-13). The figure of *dtn* (also spelled *ddn*) has been thought to date to the third millennium.

61. McCarter, *II Samuel,* 448, 451.

62. For more on this phenomenon of DN in GN, see P. Kyle McCarter, Jr., "Aspects of the Religion of the Israelite Monarchy: Biblical and Epigraphic Data," in *Ancient Israelite Religion: Essays in Honor of Frank Moore Cross,* ed. Patrick D. Miller, Jr., Paul D. Hanson, and S. Dean McBride (Philadelphia: Fortress, 1987) 137-55, drawing on Michael L. Barré, *The God-List in the Treaty between Hannibal and Philip V of Macedonia: A Study in Light of the Ancient Near Eastern Treaty Tradition* (Baltimore: Johns Hopkins University Press, 1983) 186 n. 472. Note also Paul Dion, cited as a personal communication, in Walter E. Aufrecht, *A Corpus of Ammonite Inscriptions* (Ancient Near Eastern Texts & Studies 4; Lewiston: Mellen, 1989) 147. The subject has been studied more recently by Spencer L. Allen, "The Splintered Divine: A Study of Ištar, Baal, and Yahweh Divine Names and Divine Multiplicity in the Ancient Near East" (Ph.D. diss., Pennsylvania, 2011; publically accessible Penn Dissertations Paper 309; http:/repository.upenn.edu/edissertations/309); Adam L. Bean, "'Deity Name of Geographical Name' Formulations in Ancient Near Eastern Epigraphs and the Phenomenon of Local Manifestations of Deities," a paper given at the 2011 meeting of the Society of Biblical Literature; Mark S. Smith, "The Problem of the God and His Manifestations: The Case of the Baals at Ugarit, with Implications for Yahweh of Various Locales," in *Die Stadt im Zwölfprophetenbuch,* ed. Aaron Schart and Jutta Krispenz (BZAW 428; Berlin: de Gruyter, 2012) 205-50.

63. This view is generally accepted, following the treatment of the verbal construction by Marvin H. Pope (*Probative Pontificating in Ugaritic and Biblical Studies: Collected Essays,* ed. Mark S. Smith [Ugaritisch-Biblische Literatur 10; Münster: Ugarit-Verlag, 1994] 198, 239). See also the authors cited in note 69 below. The initial name and title are more generally rendered by scholars as "Rp'u, the eternal king" or the like. My rendering of *mlk* as a name or title rather than the generic noun meaning "king" here is perhaps suggested by the shared address of *rp'u mlk ʿlm* with Mlk at Ashtaroth in *mlk ʿṯtrth* (KTU 1.100.41) and *mlk bʿṯtrt* (KTU 1.107.42). To be sure, more than one deity can inhabit a single location, but it is the combination of the same place with the apparent title *mlk* in 1.108.1-2 that has pushed my thinking in this direction.

64. Not far from this area is another regional tradition underlying the place name Valley of Rephaim (2 Sam. 23:13), located to the southwest of Jerusalem.

65. See John F. Healey, "Dagon," *DDD*, 218.

66. The matter has been treated by many scholars. For a recent discussion with citation of secondary literature, see Francesca Stavrakopoulou, *Land of Our Fathers: The Roles of Ancestor Veneration in Biblical Land Claims* (LHB/OTS 473; New York: T. & T. Clark, 2010) 68-70.

67. See also Chapter Five, section 1.

68. The comparison of the Ugaritic evidence here with the biblical place names was first made by Baruch Margulis (Margalit), "A Ugaritic Psalm (RŠ 24.252)," *JBL* 89 (1970) 292-304, here 293-94; cf. Manfred Görg, "Noch einmal: Edrei in Ugarit?" *UF* 6 (1974) 474-75. For the difference in the spelling of the initial consonant in the Ugaritic and Hebrew forms of the place name, see E. L. Greenstein, "Another Attestation of Initial *h* > ' in West Semitic," *JANES* 5 (T. H. Gaster Festschrift; 1973) 157-64, esp. 162 n. 31; Aicha Rahmouni, *Divine Epithets in the Ugaritic Alphabetic Texts,* trans. J. N. Ford (HO 1/93; Leiden: Brill, 2008) 48 n. 13. For Edrei in Egyptian sources, see Görg, "Edrei in ägyptischer Nebenüberlieferung," *BN* 84 (1996) 36-40. For further references, see Mark S. Smith, *The Early History of God: Yahweh and the Other Deities in Ancient Israel* (2nd ed.; BRS; Grand Rapids: Eerdmans; Dearborn: Dove, 2002) 178-79 n. 69. For biblical sources, see Burton MacDonald, *"East of the Jordan": Territories and Sites of the Hebrew Scriptures* (Boston: American Schools of Oriental Research, 2000) 108, 126-29. For Edrei, see also Erich Kettenhofen, "Zur Geschichte der Stadt *Der'ā* in Syrien," *ZDPV* 107 (1991) 77-91. Note also Claude Reignier Condor, "The Inscriptions of Edrei," *PEFQS* 22 (1890) 188-89.

69. For the relationship of the biblical evidence to the Ugaritic material about the Rephaim, see the surveys of Manfried Dietrich, Oswald Loretz, and Joaquín Ascaso Sanmartín, "Die ugaritischen Totengeister *rpu(m)* und die biblischen Rephaim," *UF* 8 (1976) 45-52; Shemaryahu Talmon, "Biblical Repa'îm and Ugaritic *rpu/i(m)*," *HAR* 7 (1983) 235-49; James N. Ford, "The 'Living Rephaim' of Ugarit: Quick or Defunct?" *UF* 24 (1992) 73-101; Mark S. Smith, "Rephaim," in *ABD*, 5:674-76; Oswald Loretz, "Ugaritic and Biblical Literature": Das Paradigma des Mythos von den *rpum* — Rephaim," in *Ugarit and the Bible,* ed. George J. Brooke (Münster: Ugarit-Verlag, 1994) 175-22; Hedwige Rouillard-Bonraisin, "L'énigme des refa'îm bibliques résolue grâce aux rapa'uma d'Ougarit?" in *La Bible et l'héritage d'Ougarit,* ed. Jean-Marc Michaud (Proche-Orient et Littérature Ougaritique; Sherbrooke: GGC, 2005) 145-82; Nicholas Wyatt, "A la Recherche des Rephaïm Perdus," in *Le royaume d'Ougarit de la Crète à l'Euphrate,* ed. Jean-Marc Michaud (Sherbrooke: GGC, 2007) 567-78. For a broad comparative study, see Brian R. Doak, *The Last of the Rephaim: Conquest and Cataclysm in the Heroic Ages of Ancient Israel* (Boston: Ilex Foundation; Washington: Center for Hellenic Studies, 2012).

70. John Day, "Ashtaroth," *ABD*, 1:491.

71. The association of the biblical Rephaim in the Bashan region with the Middle Bronze I dolmens (built as tombs) goes back to Paul Karge, *Rephaim: Die vorgeschichtliche Kultur Palästinas und Phöniziens: Archaeologische und religionsgeschictliche Studien* (Collectanea Hierosolymitana 1; Paderborn: Schoeningh, 1925); see *HALOT*, 2:795. The literature on dolmens is massive. See Claire Epstein, "The Dolmen Problem in the Light

of Recent Excavations," *ErIsr* 12 (Nelson Glueck Memorial Volume; 1975) 1-8 (Heb.). In her 1971-72 excavation of twenty-five dolmens in the Golan, Epstein noted that the weapons recovered include spearheads similar to some found at Ugarit. See also the survey of Mattanyah Zohar, "Dolmens," *NEAEHL*, 1:352-56. More recent studies include: Stephen H. Savage, "Jordan's Stonehenge," *NEA* 73 (2010) 32-45; Abdulla al-Shorman, "Testing the Function of Early Bronze Age I Dolmens," *NEA* 73 (2010) 46-49; James A. Fraser et al., "The Megalithic Landscape at Tall ar-Ras in Wadi ar-Rayyan: The 2007 Season of the North Jordan," *ADAJ* 53 (2009) 45-61. As noted by Zohar, while dolmen fields mark the narrow strip of land on both sides of the so-called "Syro-African Rift Valley," there are a number of concentrations.

72. For critical comments on this matter, see Dennis Pardee, *Les textes paramythologiques de la 24e campagne (1961)* (RSO 4; Paris: Recherche sur les Civilisations, 1988) 97.

73. Cf. the heroic legends of giants associated with the massive megaliths in northern Laos. See Madeleine Colani, *Mégalithes du Haut-Laos* (2 vols.; Paris: Éditions d'art et d'histoire, 1935) 1:27: "Ces ancêtres des temps héroïques, grand, forts, barbus au teint bronzé et aux traits accentués, auraient été les premiers occupants du pays." See also Colani, *Mégalithes*, 1:94, 120, 122; 2:233, 267. Other legends associating giants with megaliths are hardly uncommon; see, e.g., Jan Albert Bakker, "Chronicle of Megalith Research in the Netherlands 1547-1900: From Giants and a Devil's Cunt to Accurate Recording," in *Antiquarians at the Megaliths*, ed. Magdalena S. Midgley (B.A.R. International Series 1956; Oxford: Archaeopress, 2009) 7-8.

74. Healey, "The Rephaites of Ancient Palestine and Ugarit," 160. Healey's discussion largely reprises his earlier treatment of these matters in "The Last of the Rephaim," in *Back to the Sources: Biblical and Near Eastern Studies In Honour of Dermot Ryan*, ed. Kevin J. Cathcart and Healey (Dublin: Glendale, 1989) 33-44.

75. Chronological distance as a factor is noted by Ford, "The 'Living Rephaim,'" 98.

76. Healey, "The Rephaites of Ancient Palestine and Ugarit," 162.

77. Hostetter, *Nations Mightier and More Numerous: The Biblical View of Palestine's Pre-Israelite Peoples* (Bibal Dissertation Series 3; North Richmond Hills: Bibal, 1995) 96-101.

78. Barnett, "Sirens and Rephaim."

79. Frank Moore Cross, *From Epic to Canon: History and Literature in Ancient Israel* (Baltimore: Johns Hopkins University Press, 1998) 76 n. 14.

80. For the name, see Chaim Rabin, "Og," *ErIsr* 8 (E. L. Sukenik Memorial Volume; 1967) 251-54 (Heb.). Rabin related the name to modern South Arabian *ghaig*/Soqotri *'ag*, "man." See also *HALOT*, 2:794. The inscriptional evidence from fifth-century Byblos claimed for Og (as listed in *HALOT*, 2:794) has been read differently by Frank Moore Cross, "A Recently Published Phoenician Inscription of the Persian Period from Byblos," IEJ 29 (1979) 40-44; repr. with an addendum in Cross, *Leaves from an Epigrapher's Notebook: Collected Papers in Hebrew and West Semitic Palaeography and Epigraphy* (HSS 51; Winona Lake: Eisenbrauns, 2003) 282-85.

81. In recent years, commentators have come to view the length of Og's bed as influenced by the same length given for the bed of Marduk in the Esagila temple. See Maria

Lindquist, "King Og's Iron Bed," *CBQ* 73 (2011) 477-92. At the same time, such a connection may have been possible thanks to the older tradition of the great size of the old Rephaim. Cf. the Bedu in Canaan characterized in the Egyptian "Satirical Letter": "The narrow valley is dangerous with Bedouin, hidden under the bushes. Some of them are of four or five cubits *(from) their noses to the heel,* and fierce of face." *ANET,* 477 (*ANET* italics). Like the Bedu in this passage, the Rephaim are considered legendary giants. Deut. 2:10-11, 20-21 connects the Rephaim with the Anakim that biblical historiography locates in the land long before Israel took it. Besides the references in the Introduction to Deuteronomy, see Num. 13:29, 33. For Deut. 2:20-21, the Rephaim is the rubric under which other gigantic lines are subsumed, and for Num. 13:33, these various lines of ancient legendary heroes were traced back to the Nephilim (see Gen. 6:4). Cf. Doak, *The Last of the Rephaim,* 81-95, 177-79, 186-87. For later Jewish tradition about Og, see Admiel Kosman, "The Story of a Giant Story: The Winding Way of Og King of Bashan in the Jewish Haggadic Tradition," *HUCA* 73 (2002) 157-90.

82. KAI 13:8; 14:8; cf. KAI 117:1; see Hedwige Rouillard-Bonraisin, "Rephaim," *DDD,* 695; Matthew J. Suriano, *The Politics of Dead Kings: Dynastic Ancestors in the Book of Kings and Ancient Israel* (FAT 2/48; Tübingen: Mohr Siebeck, 2010) 154-58. A Phoenician text formerly thought to refer to Og is now read differently; see *DNWSI,* 1:824; cf. Gregorio del Olmo Lete, "Og," *DDD,* 639 (with older references); Cross, "A Recently Published Phoenician Inscription."

83. See the helpful reflections of Nili Wazana, "Natives, Immigrants and the Biblical Perception of Origins in Historical Times," *TA* 32 (2005) 220-44, esp. 238 n. 25, and note the king lists from Ras Shamra; see Daniel Arnaud, "Prolégomènes à la rédaction d'une histoire d'Ougarit II: Les bordereaux de rois divinisés," *Studi micenei ed egeo-anatolici* 41 (1999) 153-73.

84. For this text, see Chapter Five, section 2.

85. For this point, see Smith, "Recent Study of Israelite Religion," 18-19.

86. Smith, "Rephaim," *ABD,* 5:675. See the important study of Doak, *The Last of the Rephaim,* 164-99.

87. This is a different matter from what is discussed by Jacob Wright, "The Commemoration of Defeat and the Formation of a Nation in the Hebrew Bible," *Prooftexts* 29 (2009) 433-72.

88. See the recent surveys with secondary literature in Carla M. Antonaccio, *An Archaeology of Ancestors: Tomb Cult and Hero Cult in Early Greece* (Lanham: Rowman and Littlefield, 1995); "Tomb and Hero Cult in Early Greece: The Archaeology of Ancestors," in *Cultural Poetics in Archaic Greece: Cult, Performance, Politics,* ed. Carol Dougherty and Leslie Kurke (Oxford: Oxford University Press, 1998) 46-70; Robert Parker, *On Greek Religion* (Ithaca: Cornell University Press, 2011) 287-92, with a listing of theories on pp. 290-92; see also the further references in Hostetter, *Nations Mightier and More Numerous,* 96-101.

89. Schein, *The Mortal Hero: An Introduction to Homer's* Iliad (Berkeley: University of California Press, 1984) 47-49.

90. For Homer's knowledge of hero cult, see Bruno Currie, *Pindar and the Cult of Heroes* (Oxford: Oxford University Press, 2005) 48-59.

91. Parker, *On Greek Religion*, 288.

92. Nagy, *The Best of the Achaeans: Concepts of the Hero in Archaic Greek Poetry* (rev. ed.; Baltimore: Johns Hopkins University Press, 1999) 114-16. Cf. the turn in the seventh-sixth centuries to heroes as subjects of vase painting. See K. Friis Johansen, *The Iliad in Early Greek Art* (Copenhagen: Munksgaard, 1967) 25-26.

93. Coldstream, *Geometric Greece: 900-700* (2nd ed.; London: Routledge, 2003) 341-57, 409-10.

94. Coldstream, *Geometric Greece*, 341.

95. Coldstream, *Geometric Greece*, 341.

96. For different discussions of the relationship of Greek hero cults and Homeric epics, see Hans van Wees, "Greeks Bearing Arms: The State, the Leisure Class, and the Display of Weapons in Archaic Greece," in *Archaic Greece: New Approaches and New Evidence*, ed. N. Fisher and H. van Wees (London: Duckworth, 1998) 333-78; Antonaccio, *An Archaeology of Ancestors;* Maria Deoudi, *Heroenkulte in homerischer Zeit* (B. A. R. International Series 806; Oxford: Archaeopress, 1999). My thanks go to Sarah Morris for help on these matters.

97. Whitley, "The Monuments That Stood before Marathon: Tomb Cult and Hero Cult in Archaic Attica," *AJA* 98 (1994) 213-30, here 226.

98. Parker, *On Greek Religion*, 291.

99. Kurt A. Raaflaub, "Epic and History," in *A Companion to Ancient Epic*, ed. John Miles Foley (Oxford: Blackwell, 2005) 60.

100. See Chapter Five, section 1.

101. Little along these lines can be surmised from the mention of the burial places of the heroes in Judg. 8:32; 16:31; cf. 2 Sam. 2:32: some of these are simply a matter of burial on family land. Others receive only a notice about the locale of burial, in Judg. 10:2, 5; 12:7, 10, 12, 15. See Elizabeth M. Bloch-Smith, *Judahite Burial Practices and Beliefs About the Dead* (JSOTSup 123; ASOR Monograph 7; Sheffield: JSOT, 1992) 115-16. The attention paid to the bones of Samuel and Jonathan (1 Sam. 31:8-13; 2 Sam. 21:11-14) might also be fit into such a hypothesis. However, it is notable that neither Deborah nor Baraq receive any such notice, in contrast to the burials of patriarchs or matriarchs or Moses or kings or even occasional prophets; Bloch-Smith, 114-21. For a more recent discussion, see Stavrakopoulou, *Land of Our Fathers*.

102. See Dominique Charpin, *Reading and Writing in Babylon*, trans. Jane Marie Todd (Cambridge, MA: Harvard University Press, 2010): "the written text allows communication not only across space but also across time" (114); "written communication was made necessary by the limits of oral transmission" (115). Note the citation of Shulgi Hymn E by Charpin, 23: "let no one neglect the songs about me . . . so that they never pass out of memory." See further Charpin, 250.

103. Coldstream, *Geometric Greece*, 346-52.

104. I am not including the problematic evidence of place names (e.g., Beth-ʿAnat in Judg. 1:33; ʿAnatoth, in Isa. 10:30, etc.; see *BDB*, 779, as well as the gentilic formed off this place name, Jer. 29:27, etc.). See Peggy L. Day, "Anat," *DDD*, 39-40, 42-43. Cf. Anat mentioned in Papyrus Amherst 63, col. vii (Richard Steiner, *COS*, 1:314)

105. E.g., Enuma Elish VI:116: "let their gods and goddesses *(ištaršina)* bring offer-

ings." For this passage and other instances, see *CAD,* I:97, #1c. For this meaning of *ištartu,* see *CAD,* I:271b, 273-74.

106. See Nicholas Wyatt, "Astarte," *DDD,* 114.

107. Keel and Uehlinger, *Gods, Goddesses, and Images of God in Ancient Israel,* trans. Thomas H. Trapp (Minneapolis: Fortress, 1992), 105, citing Antoine Cavignaux and Bahija Khalil Ismail, "Die Statthalter von Suḫu und Mari im 8. Jh. V. Chr. Anhand neuer Texte aus den irakischen Grabungen im Staugebiet des Qadissiya-Damms," *Baghdader Mitteilungen* 21 (1990) 321-456, here 380-81, no. 17, lines 1 and 3-4.

108. For this later genericization of *ʾ/ʿystrtʾ nqbt* for "female goddesses" (as opposed to *ʾlhy dkry* for "male gods" in Aramaic incantations, see Joseph Naveh, *Studies in West-Semitic Epigraphy: Selected Papers* (Jerusalem: Magnes, 2009) 212, 214, 346. Naveh also cites a Nabatean text that uses *ʾʿtry* (or ʾ + *ʿtry*ʾ) for "gods." Note also Dan Levene and Gideon Bohak, "A Babylonian Jewish Aramaic Incantation Bowl with a List of Deities and Toponyms," *JSQ* 19 (2012) 56-72

109. According to KTU 1.111.17-18, "seven ew<es>" are characterized as "perfect ones of ʿAthtar of the field *(ʿṯtr šd)*" (see *RCU,* 92, 93). There may be here an association of the flock to the deity in a manner that recalls the expression in Deut. 7:13; 28:4, 18, 51. The connection would be even closer if the name of ʿAthtar in 1.111.18 were emended to ʿAthtart, not an entirely unreasonable suggestion given that the further designation *šd* is only elsewhere used for the goddess (KTU 1.91.10; 1.148.18; 4.182.55, 58, as discussed above) and not the god. To explain the loss of the final *-t,* one might appeal to a haplography of this letter (consisting of a single horizontal wedge) in the goddess's name in 1.111.18 that might have taken place following the writing of the final single horizontal wedge of the letter *r* in the same divine name.

110. For a survey of this phenomenon, see Judit M. Blair, *De-Demonising the Old Testament: An Investigation of Azazel, Lilith, Deber, Qeteb and Reshef in the Hebrew Bible* (FAT 2/37; Tübingen: Mohr Siebeck, 2009).

111. Keel and Uehlinger, *Gods, Goddesses, and Images of God,* 149.

112. See Aufrecht, *A Corpus of Ammonite Inscriptions,* 147.

113. This situation stands in contrast to that of ʿAshtar in the first millennium, who is attested at inland locales. See Mark S. Smith, "The God Athtar in the Ancient Near East and His Place in KTU 1.6 I," in *Solving Riddles and Untying Knots: Biblical, Epigraphic, and Semitic Studies in Honor of Jonas C. Greenfield,* ed. Ziony Zevit, Seymour Gitin, and Michael Sokoloff (Winona Lake: Eisenbrauns, 1995) 627-40. It would be tempting to suggest for the Iron Age situation a western emphasis for the goddess and an eastern one for the god with the corresponding name. In this connection, it may also be recalled that ʿAthtart has been thought to have connected with the evening star, just as ʿAthtar was connected with the morning star. For this issue, see Chapter Seven, section 1.

114. Or, perhaps generically, "deity"; cf. Phoenician *ʾlm* in reference to ʿAshtart (and also Isis) in KAI 48:2. See Charles R. Krahmalkov, *A Phoenician-Punic Dictionary* (OLA 90; Leuven: Peeters, Department Oosterse Studies, 2000) 52.

115. For this Phoenician vowel shift, see W. Randall Garr, *Dialect Geography of Syria-Palestine, 1000-586 B.C.E.* (Philadelphia: University of Pennsylvania Press, 1985) 33-35.

116. There is some confusion with respect to the name in the LXX.

117. Cooper, "A Note on the Vocalization of עַשְׁתֹּרֶת," *ZAW* 102 (1990) 98-100.

118. So see John Day, "Ashtoreth," *ABD*, 1:492.

119. E.g., *lrbt lʿštrt wltnt blbnn* (KAI 81.1), "to the Ladies, to ʿAshtart and to Tannit in Lebanon." P. Kyle McCarter Jr. takes Tannit as the only referent for *blbnn* ("Aspects of the Religion of the Israelite Monarchy," 141), while Krahmalkov, *A Phoenician-Punic Dictionary*, 391, sees this attribution to both "ladies." See also *ʿšt⟨rt⟩ bṣdn*, "ʿAshta⟨rt⟩ in Sidon," preserved on an Ammonite seal. See Aufrecht, *A Corpus of Ammonite Inscriptions*, 147.

120. Josephus records an account derived from Menander of Ephesus in *Ant.* 8.5.3, par. 146 (cf. *C. Ap.* 1.119). See H. St. J. Thackeray and Ralph Marcus, *Josephus V: Jewish Antiquities, Books V-VIII* (LCL; London: Heinemann; Cambridge, MA: Harvard University Press, 1934) 649-51. For *Contra Apion*, see Thackeray, *Josephus I: The Life/Against Apion* (LCL; Cambridge, MA: Harvard University Press; London: Heineman, 1926) 209-11.

121. For the MT reading *meleket*, see Jan Joosten, "A Note on the Anomalous Jussive in Exodus 22:4," *Textus* 25 (2010) 12.

122. See John Day, "Ashtoreth," 492.

123. For these points, see Frank Moore Cross, "Inscriptions in Phoenician and Other Scripts," in *Ashkelon 1: Introduction and Overview (1985-2006)*, ed. Lawrence E. Stager, J. David Schloen, and Daniel M. Master (Leon Levy Expedition to Ashkelon; Winona Lake: Eisenbrauns, 2008) 354; Saul M. Olyan, "Some Observations Concerning the Identity of the Queen of Heaven," *UF* 19 (1987) 161-74; Susan Ackerman, *Under Every Green Tree: Popular Religion in Sixth-Century Judah* (HSM 46; Atlanta: Scholars, 1992); "'And the Women Knead Dough': The Worship of the Queen of Heaven in Sixth-Century Judah," in *Gender and Difference in Ancient Israel*, 109-24; Smith, *The Early History of God*, 126-32; *God in Translation: Deities in Cross-Cultural Discourse in the Biblical World* (FAT 57; Tübingen: Mohr Siebeck, 2008; Grand Rapids: Eerdmans, 2010) 162 n. 113. For alternative views, see Herbert Cohn, "Is the 'Queen of Heaven' in Jeremiah the Goddess Anat?" *JBQ* 32 (2004) 55-57; Teresa Ann Ellis, "Jeremiah 44: What if 'the Queen of Heaven' Is YHWH?" *JSOT* 33 (2009) 465-88. Cross notes the attestation of the word *ʿgm*, "cookies," the single word in an inscription written on a Persian period "East Greek" bowl in Phoenician characters from Ashqelon; Cross believes these to be the cakes of the Queen of Heaven, aka ʿAshtart/Ishtar of the Hurrians. The identity of ʿAthtart *ḫr* has received a number of proposals: "Hurrian Ishtar" (Dennis Pardee, *RCU*, 275, among many commentators; see below); "ʿAthtartu of the tomb(s)" (Gregorio del Olmo Lete, *Canaanite Religion according to the Liturgical Texts of Ugarit*, trans. Wilfred G. E. Watson [Bethesda: CDL, 1999] 241 n. 77, based on Ugaritic *ḫrt* in KTU 1.5 VI 17-18); "Athtartu of the grotto/cavern" (Andrée Herdner, "Nouveaux textes alphabétiques de Ras Shamra," *Ugaritica* VII [1978] 21-26); or "Athtart of the window" (Émile Puech, "Le vocable d'*ʿAṯtart ḫurri — ʿštrt ḥr* à Ugarit et en Phénicie," *UF* 25 [1993] 327-30); or Astarte "of the estuary" (see Robert M. Kerr, "Notre-Dame-de-la-Ḥuronie?" *WO* 43 [2013] 206-12). The first view remains the most prominent in the scholarly literature. See Cross, *Leaves from an Epigrapher's Notebook*, 273-75; Pardee, *Les textes rituels* (Paris: Editions recherche sur les civilisations, 2000) 1:233-36 (with references); Corrine Bonnet, *Astarté: Dossier documentaire et perspectives historiques* (Contributi alla storia della religione fenicio-punica 2; Rome: Consiglio nazionale delle ricerche, 1996) 127-31; for a photograph, see Bonnet, *Astarté*, pl. X. In addition

to this evidence, Cross notes an Egyptian transcription from the Eighteenth Dynasty, *ʿa-s-ta-ra-ḫu-ru* (with bibliog.). For Puech, there is no *-y* gentilic, thus it does not mean "Hurrian" (as in KTU 1.40.29, 37; cf. "Kassite Yarihu *(yrḫ kṯy)* in 1.39.19; 1.102.14; *RCU,* 21, 69). Puech's view assumes a feminine adjectival form rather than a construct "Astarte of Hurri." Moreover, Puech's own proposal assumes *ḫr* as "window," which would otherwise be unattested in Ugaritic; cf. the common words for window or aperture, *ʾurbt* and *ḥln.* It might be expected that the meaning proposed would apply in Akkadian, but *ḫr* is not known in this meaning in Akkadian. See also Phoenician *ʿštrt ḥr* cited by Cross and Puech. It occurs twice, in an eighth-century inscription on a bronze statuette of a naked goddess in Sevilla and in an inscription on a Phoenician crater (see Puech, "Le vocable d'Aṯtart ḫurri"; Cross, *Leaves from an Epigrapher's Notebook,* 273-75; Pardee, *Les textes rituels,* 1:233-36 (with references); Bonnet, *Astarté,* 127-31 and pl. X. William F. Albright (*Yahweh and the Gods of Canaan: A Historical Analysis of Two Contrasting Faiths* [Jordan Lectures 1965; Garden City: Doubleday, 1968] 143, 149-50) and Cross (*Leaves from an Epigrapher's Notebook,* 274) propose that these references are to Ishtar of Nineveh. However, Ishtar of Nineveh is distinguished in the Akkadian textual record from Ugarit (e.g., RS 19.101.7; PRU IV, p. 288; cf. Shawushka of Nineveh in the Hurrian text, KTU 1:54.2-3).

124. As argued by Joseph N. Mavinga, "The Political Influence of Queen Mothers on Judean Kings in Jeremiah's Time," *JSem* 17 (2008) 266-88. A piece of Mavinga's claims is the assumption that Asherah is an Assyrian goddess.

125. Olyan, "Some Observations Concerning the Identity of the Queen of Heaven," 174.

126. Ackerman, "'And the Women Knead Dough,'" 109-24.

127. See Paul V. Mankowski, S.J., *Akkadian Loanwords in Biblical Hebrew* (HSS 47; Winona Lake: Eisenbrauns, 2000) 61-62; Cory Ke Michael Peacock, "Akkadian Loanwords in the Hebrew Bible: Social and Historical Implications" (Ph.D. diss., New York University, 2012) 79-80. Note also the older study of Moshe Held, "Studies in Biblical Lexicography in Light of Akkadian, Part I," *ErIsr* 16 (H. M. Orlinsky Volume; 1982) 76-85 (Heb.); Smith, *God in Translation,* 162 n. 113. Olyan ("Some Observations Concerning the Identity of the Queen of Heaven," 173) argues that such "cakes may also have been typical of the cultus of the West Semitic" goddess as well as Ishtar. While this claim about the cakes is possibly true, the word for the cakes itself is not typical West Semitic and is suggestive of a Mesopotamian background.

128. Tallay Ornan, "Ištar as Depicted on Finds from Israel," in *Studies in the Archaeology of the Iron Age in Israel and Jordan,* ed. Amihai Mazar (JSOTSup 331; Sheffield: Sheffield Academic, 2001) 235-56.

129. See also John Day, "Ashtoreth," 492.

130. This might account for the reference in 2 Kgs. 23:4 to Asherah as a goddess (as opposed to the symbol by the same name). The references to the asherah in 2 Kgs. 21:7; 23:6, 7 may refer to an elaborated, royal version of the symbol.

131. The issues about a/Asherah lie beyond the scope of this discussion. For the problems of seeing a goddess behind the inscriptional evidence or the biblical references to BH *ʾăšērâ,* see Shmuel Aḥituv, *Echoes from the Past: Hebrew and Cognate Inscriptions from the Biblical Period,* trans. and ed. Anson F. Rainey (Jerusalem: Carta, 2008) 221-24;

Frank Moore Cross, "The Phoenician Ostracon from Acco, the Ekron Inscriptions and אשרתה," *ErIsr* 29 (Ephraim Stern Festschrift; 2009) 20*-22*; Mark S. Smith, "The Blessing God and Goddess: A Longitudinal View from Ugarit to "Yahweh and . . . his asherah" at Kuntillet 'Ajrud," in *Enigmas and Images: Studies in Honor of Tryggve N. D. Mettinger,* ed. Göran Eidevall and Blazenka Scheuer (ConBOT 58; Winona Lake: Eisenbrauns, 2011) 213-26; Shmuel Aḥituv, Esther Eshel, and Ze'ev Meshel, in Meshel, *Kuntillet 'Ajrud (Ḥorvat Teman): An Iron Age II Religious Site on the Judah-Sinai Border* (Jerusalem: Israel Exploration Society, 2012) 127, 130-32, 138 n. 36. The presently available evidence (cf. 2 Kgs. 21:7; 23:6, 7; see note 130 above) reflects a symbol of Yahweh's cult and not of a goddess. However, this does not preclude the possibility of some devotion to the goddess, Asherah. Future discoveries may yet point in this direction. Cf. Mary Joan Leith, "Religious Continuity in Samaria/Israel: 800-335 BCE," in *Jewish 'Material' Otherness? Studies in the Formation of Persian Period Judaism(s),* ed. Christian Frevel and Izak Cornelius (OBO, in press); information courtesy of the author. If correct, the development of Asherah would generally parallel the situation of Astarte in Iron II Israel, as suggested here. The further issue of what or whom Judean pillar figurines represent remains open, despite identifications with various goddesses. For a critical discussion, see Erin Danielle Darby, "Interpreting Judean Pillar Figurines: Gender and Empire in Judean Apotropaic Ritual" (Ph.D. diss., Duke, 2011; FAT 2 [Tübingen: Mohr Siebeck, forthcoming]).

132. Cf. Jer. 16:16, which refers to hunting evidently in connection with non-Israelites. See McKane, *Jeremiah I,* 378.

133. Borowski, "Animals in the Religion of Syria-Palestine," in *A History of the Animal World in the Ancient Near East,* ed. Billie Jean Collins (HO 1/64; Leiden: Brill, 2002) 412.

134. For the identifications of the undomesticated species in Deut. 14:4-6, see Walter Houston, *Purity and Monotheism: Clean and Unclean Animals in Biblical Law* (JSOTSup 140; Sheffield: JSOT, 1993) 60-62.

135. Brian Hesse and Paula Wapnish, "An Archaeozoological Perspective on the Cultural Use of Mammals in the Levant," in Collins, *A History of the Animal World in the Ancient Near East,* 457-91. See also Hesse and Wapnish, "Can Pig Remains Be Used for Ethnic Diagnosis in the Ancient Near East?" in *The Archaeology of Israel: Constructing the Past, Interpreting the Present,* ed. Neil Asher Silberman and David B. Small (JSOTSup 237; Sheffield: Sheffield Academic, 1997) 238-39 n. 1.

136. For the evidence with discussion, see Smith, *The Early History of God,* 101-7.

137. Resheph appears as a divine figure as part of Yahweh's military retinue in Hab. 3:5, while the constellation of features associated in West Semitic literature with Baal is applied in biblical literature to Yahweh. Cf. the biblical title *yhwh ṣb'wt* and Ugaritic *ršp ṣb'i* (KTU 1.91.15). See Smith, *The Early History of God,* 80-101.

138. For this use of **lmd,* cf. Song 3:8; Isa. 2:4 = Mic. 4:3. See Chapter One, section 1 and Chapter Four, section 4 for the discussion of this root.

139. It has been proposed that in Jer. 16:16 Yahweh's "fishermen" and "hunters" are minor divinities. See Sang Youl Cho, "The Divine Title 'Fisherman' in Jer 16:16," *JNSL* 35 (2009) 97-105. If correct, it is to be noted that here these masculine figures show no vestige of the older role of the hunting goddesses in the divine household.

140. For this development, see Mark S. Smith, *The Origins of Biblical Monotheism:*

Israel's Polytheistic Background and the Ugaritic Texts (Oxford: Oxford University Press, 2001) 45-53, 163-78.

141. For another perspective, see Mobley, *The Empty Men,* 234-40. Mobley focuses attention on Joab rather than David, but some of his observations are pertinent to my remarks on David.

142. E.g., see the image in Ps. 19:5. See also Psalms 20; 44. Note as well the biblical passages noted in Chapter One's listing of features of warrior practices and values.

143. This point was drawn to my attention by my student, Cory Peacock. For discussion, see Duane L. Christensen, *Transformations of the War Oracle in Old Testament Prophecy: Studies in the Oracles Against the Nations* (Harvard Dissertations in Religion 3; Missoula: Scholars, 1975; repr. *Prophecy and War in Ancient Israel: Studies in the Oracles Against the Nations in Old Testament Prophecy* (Berkeley: BIBAL, 1989). Christensen dates biblical war oracles to the tenth to the eight centuries.

144. For this consideration, I wish to thank Corrine Carvalho.

145. See Kawashima, *Biblical Narrative and the Death of the Rhapsode,* 14-15; Dobbs-Allsopp, "Space, Line, and the Written Biblical Poem," 52. To account for this shift, both scholars emphasize what Kawashima calls "a shift from the medium of the spoken to the written word."

146. Niditch, *Oral World and Written Word;* Carr, *Writing on the Tablet of the Heart.* Note also Carr, *The Formation of the Hebrew Bible,* 4-7.

147. See Jer. 22:10 in possible connection with 2 Kgs. 23:29-30 (NJPS, 1063 n. a). In 2 Chr. 35:25, laments for Josiah are attributed to Jeremiah as well as male and female singers; these compositions are said to have been written. Cf. Jer. 22:18 for the laments that are not to be voiced for his son Jehoiakim.

148. I would not include in this point royal annalistic material as literature, yet even if one were to do so, the royal material in the Bible would be relatively small compared to prophetic, priestly, or wisdom materials.

149. See the useful survey of John J. Collins, in Adela Yarbro Collins and John J. Collins, *King and Messiah as Son of God: Divine, Human, and Angelic Messianic Figures in Biblical and Related Literature* (Grand Rapids: Eerdmans, 2008) 1-24.

150. See Carr, *The Formation of the Hebrew Bible,* 304-38.

151. See Mark S. Smith, *The Priestly Vision of Genesis 1* (Minneapolis: Fortress, 2010) 64-71.

152. See Jacob Wright, "The Commemoration of Defeat"; "Making a Name for Oneself: Martial Valor, Heroic Death, and Procreation in the Hebrew Bible," *JSOT* 38 (2011) 131-62. The author informs me that he has a book in progress on the topic: *A People-in-Arms: Military Organization and Peoplehood in Ancient Israel* (New York: Oxford University Press, in press).

153. This is not to minimize the later Persian period (and later) reception and compositional activity involved with these biblical works. It is beyond the scope of this study and impossible here to do justice to the subject of textual production in the Iron IIB-C and Persian periods. For Persian period revisions of older biblical literature, see Carr, *The Formation of the Hebrew Bible;* Erhard S. Gerstenberger, *Israel in the Persian Period: The Fifth and the Fourth Centuries* B.C.E., trans. Siegfried S. Schatzmann (Biblical Encyclopedia

8; Atlanta: Society of Biblical Literature, 2011) 274-425. See also the following important and very different surveys: Erich Zenger, ed., *Einleitung in das Alte Testament* (5th ed.; Stuttgart: Kohlhammer, 1995); Reinhard G. Kratz, *The Composition of the Narrative Books of the Old Testament*, trans. John Bowden (London: T. & T. Clark, 2005); Christoph Levin, *The Old Testament: A Brief Introduction*, trans. Margaret Kohl (Princeton: Princeton University, 2005); Rofé, *Introduction to the Literature of the Hebrew Bible.* For the complexities involved with Genesis–Kings, see also the essays in Thomas B. Dozeman, Thomas Römer, and Konrad Schmid, eds., *Pentateuch, Hexateuch, or Enneateuch? Identifying Literary Works in Genesis through Kings* (Ancient Israel and Its Literature 8; Atlanta: Society of Biblical Literature, 2011); Jean-Louis Ska, *The Exegesis of the Pentateuch: Exegetical Studies and Basic Questions* (FAT 66; Tübingen: Mohr Siebeck, 2009).

154. For the verb as signifying compilation or collection (possibly "from one place to another"), see Richard J. Clifford, *Proverbs* (OTL; Louisville: Westminster John Knox, 1999) 219-20. Clifford (p. 219) also notes that the verb "connotes more than collecting, for example, arranging and composing." In this vein, see also van der Toorn, *Scribal Culture and the Making of the Hebrew Bible*, 83; Carr, *The Formation of the Hebrew Bible*, 317-18, 350. Clifford's view is not entirely unlike the idea of "transferral," as argued based on an Akkadian parallel (with the same root in the same stem) by H. Louis Ginsberg, *The Israelian Heritage of Judaism* (New York: Jewish Theological Seminary of America, 1982) 36-38; Hayim ben Yosef Tawil, *An Akkadian Lexical Companion for Biblical Hebrew: Etymological-Semantic and Idiomatic Equivalents with Supplement on Biblical Aramaic* (Jersey City: Ktav, 2009) 287. For the notion as "transcription" (likewise supported with an Akkadian parallel), see the discussion in Michael V. Fox, *Proverbs 10–31* (AB 18B; New Haven: Yale University Press, 2009) 777-78.

155. Lord, *The Singer of Tales*, ed. Stephen Mitchell and Gregory Nagy (2nd ed.; Harvard Studies in Comparative Literature 24; Cambridge, MA: Harvard University Press, 2000) 156.

156. (Paris: Cerf, 1993; Eng. ed. *Religion as a Chain of Memory*, trans. Simon Lee [New Brunswick: Rutgers University Press, 2000]).

157. For a survey, see Mark S. Smith, *The Memoirs of God: History, Memory, and the Experience of the Divine in Ancient Israel* (Minneapolis: Fortress, 2004) 124-40.

158. Thus the date of the current forms of some of these poems may well be monarchic. For this issue, see Chapter Eight.

159. For more on these observations, see Smith, "Why Was 'Old Poetry' Used in Hebrew Narrative?" 197-210. In making this observation, I prescind from the question of older prose traditions in the Pentateuch or the so-called "Deuteronomistic History," as claimed in a number of studies; e.g., see Alexander Rofé, "Clan Sagas as a Source in Settlement Traditions," in *"A Wise and Discerning Mind": Essays in Honor of Burke O. Long*, ed. Saul M. Olyan and Robert C. Culley (BJS 325; Providence: Brown Judaic Studies, 2000) 191-203, esp. p. 199. The date of possibly most old prose traditions seems difficult to establish before the ninth century (if even then). The question lies beyond the scope of this discussion and remains an important desideratum for research.

Index of Subjects

abecedaries, 284, 295, 380, 542, 543, 550, 554. *See also* alphabet
Abimelekh, 23
Abinadab, 71
Abner, 271, 534
Absalom, 67, 411
Achilles, xii-xiii, 3, 4, 19, 20, 21, 22, 51, 54, 55, 59-64, 65, 66, 68, 69, 70, 71, 72, 73, 74, 75, 76, 77, 79, 81, 90, 177, 178, 270, 276, 277, 279, 280, 320, 335, 339, 340, 362, 385, 395, 396, 397, 398, 403, 405, 410, 413, 415, 443, 445, 540
  as "best of the Achaeans," 51, 64, 69, 71, 385
  as divine, 60
  as "god-like," 59
  lament over Patroklos, 60
  "noble," 59
  "pitiless," 59
  "swift-footed," 60, 534
  wrath of, 22, 59-61, 61-63, 362, 395, 443, 445. *See also* anger
Adad, 120, 444, 513, 536. *See also* Adodos
Addu-dûri of Mari, 462
Adodos, 198. *See also* Adad
Aeneas, 69, 396
afterlife, 104, 109, 110, 424, 430. *See also* warrior "afterlife"; warrior immortality
Agamemnon, xiii, 4, 21, 60, 61, 63, 64, 69, 70, 71, 74, 77, 177, 276, 397, 398, 403
Ahab, 272
Aiakides, 177, 277
Aias, 72, 77, 396
Ajax, 398
Akrotatos, 78, 79
Alexander the Great, xiii
alphabet, 30-31, 296, 342, 349, 368, 372, 428, 543, 550, 551. *See also* abecedaries
Amalek, 229, 232, 234, 255, 513
Amarna letters, 20, 41, 43, 205, 214, 380, 433, 499, 514
Amarna painting, 31, 178-79
Amasa, 397
Ammithtamru, 143, 155, 157
Ammurapi, 154, 155, 156, 158, 159, 461, 462
amulets, 25, 441, 493
Anat, 5, 6, 16, 17, 18, 19, 22, 23, 79, 94, 99, 100, 107-20, 124, 125, 126-36, 140, 141, 145, 148, 149, 150, 151, 153, 162, 163, 166, 168, 170-76, 179, 180, 182, 183, 186, 190-93, 195, 197, 200-201, 205, 206, 208, 271, 274, 308, 322, 323, 325, 326, 351, 352, 362, 396, 405, 407, 419-20, 425, 426, 427, 429, 432, 433, 435, 437, 439, 440, 443, 444, 449, 456, 470, 473, 476, 477, 481, 485, 486, 488, 494, 519, 534, 548, 570, 572

as warrior-teacher, 116, 134, 326, 350
"the strong," 173
winged, 117, 130
wrath of, 132, 396
Andromache, 77, 339
anger, 21-23, 59, 63, 65, 75, 360, 361, 362, 395, 396, 433, 445. *See also* Achilles, wrath of; Anat, wrath of; Yahweh, wrath of
"anti-epic," Israelite, 39-40, 378. *See also* "epic," Israelite
Anzu, 428
Aphrodite, 69, 74, 403
apocalyptic, xi, 37, 333
Apollo, 59, 68, 273, 395, 536
Aqhat, 5, 16, 19, 20, 21, 100-136, 137, 163, 174, 175, 193, 271, 274, 275, 326, 358, 359, 396, 419, 420, 421, 423, 429, 432, 435, 443, 445, 466
as "hero," 126, 128-29, 134
bow and arrows of, 100, 105, 106, 107, 108, 111, 117, 118, 118, 119, 129, 131, 132, 135
death of, 99, 100, 102, 103, 108-11, 113, 119, 120, 122, 123, 125, 129, 131, 132, 135, 136, 160, 241, 359, 396, 419, 420, 421, 435, 445, 535
name of, 425
Aqhat, story, 5-6, 27, 74, 99-136, 137, 139, 141, 142, 143, 145, 150, 153, 160, 177, 203, 208, 241, 267, 272, 273, 310, 311, 337, 402, 418, 419, 420, 423, 426, 434, 437, 442, 456, 466, 535, 536, 558, 559
Arbura, 31, 179, 474
archers, 26, 27, 32, 71, 129, 227, 296, 351, 360, 495, 544
Ares, 68, 69
armor, 24, 27
arrowheads, 25, 26-27, 169, 204, 205-6, 208, 228, 284, 295, 296, 322, 323, 358, 366, 367, 368, 449, 490, 493, 494, 512, 513, 528, 551, 552, 554
El-Khadr, 206, 228, 493
arrows, 17, 24, 25, 26, 27, 31, 32, 64, 72, 100, 105, 106, 107, 108, 111, 117, 118, 119, 129, 131, 132, 135, 164, 167, 171, 227, 351, 352, 409, 429, 442, 494, 544, 552
Arsay, 426, 474
Artemis, 350, 406
Aruru, 53, 75
Asahel, 270
Asher, 239, 249, 256, 549
asherah, 325, 574
Asherah, 43, 306, 324, 325, 382, 489, 494, 495, 573, 574. *See also* Athirat
Ashtarot (goddess), 6, 18, 131, 303
Ashtarot (place), 138, 151, 317-18, 319, 320, 566
Ashtoreth, 6, 324, 487. *See also* Astarte
Ashur-nerari V, 76, 428
assembly, 60, 62, 128, 142, 143, 156, 440, 451, 488
assinnu, 87, 88
Astarte, 6, 133, 169, 174, 175, 183-208, 308, 322, 323, 324, 352, 396, 407, 442, 443, 444, 473, 476, 477, 479, 486, 487, 488, 489, 490, 494, 495, 571, 572, 573, 574
as "face of Baal," 198-200
as lioness, 169, 202, 204-6, 359, 494
as "name of Baal," 198-200
astartes, 323, 571
Athena, 68, 69, 74, 404
Athirat, 115, 168, 176, 178, 205, 222, 427, 437, 462, 474, 479, 491, 494, 546. *See also* Asherah
Athtar, 6, 162, 168-69, 170, 184, 477, 478, 480, 487, 571
"of the heavens," 169
Athtart. *See* Astarte
attribute animal, 202, 204, 323, 359, 491. *See also* warrior animals
axe(s), 18, 25, 26, 31, 53, 83, 84, 85, 87, 131, 164, 221, 303, 364, 365

Baal, 6, 19, 21, 99, 100, 102, 103, 104, 109-12, 114, 120, 121, 123, 125, 133, 135, 139, 141, 145, 148, 149, 150, 151, 153, 164-68, 169, 170, 173-83, 189-90, 194, 195-200, 201, 202, 203, 205, 208, 238, 242, 270, 273, 337, 351, 353, 358, 360, 361, 373, 405, 409, 414, 419, 422, 427, 429, 430,

431, 439, 444, 446, 447, 448, 454, 456, 465, 466, 469, 470, 474, 476, 479, 480, 482, 488, 489, 490, 519, 525, 534, 535, 536, 574
as "Cloud-rider," 121, 189
as Dimaranu. *See* Demarous; Dimaranu
as "Lord of the Earth," 154, 165, 176, 270, 534
as "Mightiest Baal," 149, 164, 166, 167, 168, 172, 173, 176, 177, 179, 189, 270
as "Mightiest of Warriors," 167, 337
as Pidru. *See* Pidru
death of, 164, 165, 166, 270
fury of, 361
sexual relations, 414
Baal Cycle, 5, 6, 16, 17, 19, 20, 22, 38, 39, 115, 139, 140, 162-82, 183, 208, 224, 267, 273, 310, 377, 378, 385, 420, 464, 465, 470, 473, 475, 501, 556, 558, 559
Balaam, 287
Balaam inscription, 212, 517
Balaam oracles, 43, 211, 217, 219, 353, 497, 548
Balak, 221, 243, 287
Baraq, 20, 244, 246, 254, 255, 288, 358, 359
name of, 20, 358-59
Bashan, 151, 567
battle cry, 17
Bedan, 358, 359
Bedu, 559
bellomancy, 552
Benjamin, 238, 239, 255, 314, 359
Benob, 315, 563
Beowulf, 350, 392, 398, 404, 419, 544
Bethel, 196, 286, 323, 371, 489, 551
Bethsaida stele, 32, 373
"Biblical Archaeology," 42, 46
Beth Shan, 25
birds, 19
blessing, 17, 34, 75, 99, 102, 103, 111, 125, 129, 140, 148, 150, 155, 156, 159, 231, 241, 252, 289, 323, 325, 448, 452, 459, 501, 544, 566
blood. *See* warrior blood
bloodguilt, 124, 272, 339, 435
bones, animal, 27-29. *See also* deer; gazelle; ibex
Book of Yashar, 281, 300, 301, 539, 541
Booths. *See* Sukkot
bow(s), 16, 17, 27, 31, 32, 100, 105-8, 111, 113, 117, 118, 119, 129, 130, 131, 132, 133, 135, 163, 169, 170, 171, 174, 196, 226, 268, 273, 274, 278, 351, 352, 426, 428-29, 435, 442, 443
"Bow, The Song of the," 540-41
"Breasts and Womb," 43
Briseis, 60, 69, 70, 71, 77, 78, 403
Bull of Heaven, 54
burial(s), 18, 24-26, 570
Byblos, 111, 364, 532, 546, 568

Canaan(ite), 31, 37, 39, 41, 44, 145, 187, 198, 205, 228, 249, 250, 256, 264, 318, 320, 374, 378, 480, 569
captives, 17, 18, 19, 22, 32, 70, 77, 94, 131, 170, 172, 244, 255
Carchemish, 187, 194
chariotry, 346-347
Chemosh, 21
child sacrifice, 18
Chilionis, 78
Chronicles of Narnia, The, xi
clothing, 17, 57, 60, 66, 100, 102, 103, 105, 120, 121, 125, 127, 129, 136, 185, 190, 268, 271, 352, 423
and honor, 129
collective memory, 232, 248, 288, 330, 331, 332, 521, 522, 558, 576
"copulatory gaze," 180-81
corpse desecration, 18-19, 22-23, 24, 61-63, 356, 397
Covenant Code, 553-54
curse, 22, 76, 108, 114, 119, 120, 121, 123, 124, 127, 196, 198, 227, 231, 235, 240, 241, 252, 256, 262, 264, 269, 272, 343, 436, 437, 443, 505, 536
of Meroz. *See* Meroz
Cypro-Minoan, 341

Dagan, 168, 187, 201, 318, 447, 480. *See also* Dagon
dagger(s), 16, 24, 26, 31, 32, 179, 351, 352, 364, 365, 366, 368
Dagon, 165, 271, 318, 567. *See also* Dagan
Dan, 245, 256, 325, 359. *See also* Tel Dan
Danatayu, 99, 105, 106, 129, 426
  name of, 426
dance, 19, 93, 139, 172, 278, 293, 294, 356, 368, 471, 475
Daniel, 423, 434, 562
Danil, 5, 6, 99, 100, 101, 102, 103, 104, 105, 106, 109, 110, 112, 114, 119, 120, 121, 122, 123, 124, 125, 127, 128, 129, 136, 137, 141, 143, 144, 145, 147, 150, 151, 153, 203, 272, 317, 384, 419, 420, 421, 422, 424, 425, 426, 427, 434, 437, 438, 439, 499, 566
  as "hero," 102, 127-28
  as "man of the Harnamite," 102, 103, 124, 144
  as "man of Rp'u," 101-2, 109, 112, 121, 137, 208
  death of, 112, 141
  name of, 426
David, xii, xiii, 3, 4, 7, 11, 18, 19, 20, 39, 51, 53, 54, 55, 60, 63, 64-67, 69, 70, 71, 72, 73, 75, 78, 79, 80, 81, 82, 88, 89, 90, 94, 95, 131, 165, 166, 167, 174, 177, 179, 239, 246, 267, 270, 271, 274-83, 285, 292, 293, 294, 298, 300, 303, 309, 310, 311, 314-15, 316, 318, 322, 326, 327, 328, 329, 337, 340, 352, 356, 358, 359, 397, 399, 400, 401, 404, 409, 410, 411, 416, 423, 475, 539, 541, 546, 555, 563, 575
death, xi, 5, 6, 18, 21, 22, 26, 52, 90, 94, 104, 113, 137, 145, 151, 159, 164, 165, 166, 167, 269, 360, 361, 409, 417, 429, 431, 432, 439, 538. *See also* Mot; warrior death
  of Achilles, xiii, 64, 335, 397, 398
  of Asahel, 534
  of Baal, 164, 165, 166, 270
  of Aqhat, 99, 100, 102, 103, 108-11, 113, 119, 120, 122, 123, 125, 129, 131, 132, 135, 136, 160, 241, 359, 396, 419, 420, 421, 435, 445, 535
  of Danil, 112, 141
  of Enkidu, 54, 55, 56, 57, 58, 71, 85, 405
  of Gibeonites, 435
  of Jonathan, 51, 65, 66, 67, 268, 269, 270, 275-81, 314, 529
  of Josiah, 328
  of Mot, 439
  of Patroklos, 60, 61, 62, 63, 64, 397
  of Samson, 359, 432
  of Saul, 65, 268, 269, 270, 275-81, 314, 399, 529
  sleep as, 438
  social, 125, 291
Death. *See* Mot
Deborah, 20, 39, 244, 246, 250, 254, 255, 260, 288, 289, 353, 359, 377, 521, 525, 570
  as "mother" in Israel, 246, 254
deer, 27, 28, 29, 30, 33, 173, 368, 369, 370, 472
Demarous, 198. *See also* Dimaranu
Deber, 323, 571
Didanu, 154, 156, 353, 460
Dimaranu, 189, 190. *See also* Demarous
Diomedes, 77, 403
dishonor, 21, 61. *See also* shame
"disidentification," 12, 317
Ditanu, 156, 460
divination, 120, 139, 353, 412, 450. *See also* incantations; "magic"
DN-in-GN, 317, 566
dolmens. *See* megaliths
Dor, 29
Dothan, 551
dreams, 53, 56, 57, 71, 83, 84, 85, 86, 87, 89, 92, 93, 195, 340, 412, 413, 415, 421-22
drinking, 19
drinking blood, 17-18
"divine sons," 45
drunkenness, 103, 485. *See also* El, drunkenness of; warrior drunkenness
Dushara, 236
"dying and rising gods," 430

eating flesh, 17-18
Ebal. *See* Mount Ebal

Ebla, 30, 132, 184, 336, 358, 437, 463, 477, 478
Ecclesiastes, 502
Edom, 227, 228, 232, 234, 235, 237, 254, 511, 512, 517
Edrei, 138, 151, 318, 319, 449, 567
"egalitarianism," 42, 91, 298
Ekalte, 507, 554
El, 19, 99, 102, 103, 104, 109, 111, 115, 125, 129, 134, 140, 141, 145, 146, 147, 148, 150, 151, 153, 168, 189, 190, 191, 192, 193, 221, 222, 245, 427, 445, 452, 460, 470, 479, 484
  as "Bull," 460
  drunkenness of, 191, 192, 427, 484
elders, xii, 105, 128, 297, 420, 440, 553-54
Elhanan, 316
Elijah, 272, 361, 437, 502, 554, 560
  as "holy man," 361, 560
Elisha, 361, 554, 560
  as "holy man," 361, 560
El Shadday, 43, 382
Emar, 6, 43, 59, 118, 183, 185, 187, 194, 195, 196, 197, 200, 202, 394, 413, 437, 447, 448, 475, 476, 477, 478, 480, 481, 486, 487, 488, 493, 507, 554
emblem animal. *See* attribute animal
Enkidu, xii, 3, 4, 5, 20, 51, 52-59, 60, 61, 63, 65, 68, 70, 71, 72, 75, 78, 81-94, 134, 274, 278, 279, 334, 336, 337, 340, 389, 390, 391, 392, 394, 404, 405, 406, 409, 410, 413, 415, 417, 438, 444, 534, 539, 549, 550
  as "god-like," 54
  as "man of the wild," 55
  death of, 54, 55, 56, 57, 58, 71, 85, 405
  name of, 54
  sexual relations, 56
Enuma Elish, 76, 167, 304, 377, 385
Enyo, 74
Ephraim, 229, 240, 255, 363, 513
epic, 7, 9, 10, 22, 37-40, 52, 55, 59, 65, 72, 73, 77, 137, 167, 260, 271, 283, 321, 322, 336, 339, 340, 350, 377, 378, 387, 397-98, 399, 402, 404, 405, 408, 416, 419, 446, 464, 540, 541, 570
"epic," Israelite, 37, 38-40, 289, 343, 374, 376, 385, 399, 405. *See also* "anti-epic," Israelite
Epic of Zimri-Lim. *See* Zimri-Lim, Epic of
epic poetry, 7, 9, 39, 260, 317, 321, 335, 375, 378, 385, 419. *See also* epic; performance
Ereshkigal, 392
Erra, 356, 358, 360, 362, 363, 444
Esagila, 568
Esau, 129, 239, 325, 442
Eshbaal, 212, 316, 317
Eshmun, 195

"face of Baal," 195, 198
fame. *See* warrior fame
family, divine, 40
feasting, 19
feasting scene, 31
fierceness, 21
"fight or flight," 21
figurine(s), 206, 347, 374, 493, 494, 495, 529, 574
food, 19, 76, 106, 176, 178, 188, 191, 192, 360, 369, 451, 456, 473, 482
Fraser, James George, 110
Fravashis, 144-45

Gaal, 23
Gad, 240, 270, 274, 507
gazelle, 25, 27, 28, 29, 30, 32, 368, 369, 370, 371, 484, 485, 528, 534
gazelle (title), 268, 270, 274, 281, 527, 528. *See also* gazelle
gender, xiii, 3, 9, 20-21, 70, 74, 76, 82, 90, 92, 94, 95, 99, 115, 130, 131, 133, 136, 174, 175, 177, 178, 179, 182, 203, 204, 275, 278, 279, 334, 357, 358, 360, 391, 396, 401, 402, 405, 443, 445, 462-63, 464
gender polarity, 130, 178. *See also* warrior culture, inversion of gender
Gibeah, 286, 551
Gibeon, 25, 435, 551
Gideon, 20, 216, 239, 361, 439, 502, 510, 560

Gilboa, Mount, 18, 268, 278, 530
Gilead, 239, 240, 256, 286
Gilgamesh, xii, 4, 5, 23, 51, 52-59, 60, 61, 62, 65, 66, 69-71, 72, 74, 75, 78, 81-94, 112, 113, 116, 134, 168, 278, 334, 336, 340, 386-94, 404-5, 406, 407, 408, 410, 411, 413, 415, 416, 417, 429, 433, 434, 444, 539, 549
  as figuration of Enkidu, 56-57
  as "man of the city," 55, 79
  divinity of, 54
  his mourning of Enkidu, 56
  in the Dead Sea Scrolls, 340
  journeys of, 56-58
  name of, 53
  versions of, 53
Glaucus, 72
glory. *See* warrior glory
goddesses, warrior, 4, 12, 27. *See also* Anat; Astarte; Ishtar
  as patrons of human warriors, 16, 21, 27, 71, 74, 112-13, 130, 131, 134, 135, 150, 174, 206, 322, 495
  fading from Israel, 323, 331
Goliath, 18, 128, 131, 166, 167, 168, 271, 303, 316, 337, 385, 397, 564, 565

Hadad, 104, 121, 373
Hades, 64
hair, 17, 17, 45-46, 56, 57, 192, 193, 223, 224, 234, 264, 265, 354, 356, 416, 438, 485, 508
Hammurapi, 156, 460, 536
Hathor, 23, 208
Hauran stela, 373
heads (cut off), 30, 170, 172
Hebat, 187, 480
Hecabe, 78, 339
Hector, xiii, 19, 61, 62, 63, 64, 71, 72, 74, 77, 78, 273, 275, 396, 397, 398
  corpse of, 61, 62, 63, 74, 397
Helen of Troy, 69, 70, 77, 78, 403
Hera, 74, 403
ḥērem-warfare. See warfare *ḥērem*
hero cults, 320-22, 569, 570
  Greek, 320-22, 570
  lack in Israel, 321
heroic poetry, 7, 8, 9, 10, 11, 15, 39. *See also* warrior song
hero terms. *See* warrior terms
heroism, xi, 266, 337. *See also* warrior honor
Hesban, 29, 370. *See also* Heshbon
Heshbon, 291. *See also* Hesban
heterosexuality, 79, 412
Hezekiah, 111, 330, 358
holy men, 361, 560
homoeroticism, 80, 92, 400, 401, 402, 406, 411, 412, 414, 415, 416
homosexuality, 82, 83, 88, 340, 342, 385, 399, 401, 402, 406, 409, 410, 411, 412, 415, 416, 539
homosocial bonding, 90, 416
honor, xiii, 4, 5, 20, 26, 60, 62, 103, 108, 129, 131, 136, 359, 396, 429, 475, 546
Horan, 198
Horvat Rosh Zayet, 29
Hosea, 41, 216
"house of the father, the," 45, 159
"house of the mother, the," 159, 462-63
Humbaba, xii, 385, 387. *See also* Huwawa
hunter(s), 31, 32, 107, 116, 133, 175, 195, 350, 351, 368, 388, 442, 443, 574
  king as, 32, 388, 443
hunting, 3, 5, 16, 27-30, 31, 32, 33, 73, 117, 122, 128, 130, 131, 133, 149, 166, 173, 174, 175, 185, 187, 188, 189, 190, 192, 193, 194, 195, 201, 203, 218, 275, 297, 325, 326, 340, 350, 351, 365, 370, 371, 372, 373, 427, 442, 552, 574
  said not to be for women, 131-32, 174
hunting scene, 31, 32, 33
Huray, 129, 201
Huwawa, xii, 59, 340, 385, 386, 419. *See also* Humbaba

ibex, 30, 371
Idomeneus, 72
Iliad, xii, xiii, 1, 3, 4, 10, 22, 51, 60-64, 65, 68, 69, 70, 71, 72, 73, 74, 75, 76, 78, 82, 88, 93, 137, 139, 177, 260, 273, 330, 336,

339, 342, 348, 376, 385, 394, 395, 397, 398
date of, 394-95, 402, 403, 405, 414, 525, 532, 534, 536, 540, 560, 564
reception of, 560
immortality. *See* warrior immortality
Inanna, 172, 434, 548
incantations, 90, 132, 163, 186, 195, 200, 201, 323, 394, 417, 441, 444, 448, 449, 450, 465, 479, 485, 486, 490, 491, 559, 571. *See also* divination; "magic"
inversion. *See* warrior culture, inversion of gender
Isaiah, 216
Ishi, 315, 316, 563, 39
Israel, 2, 6-12, 15, 16, 19, 23, 25, 26, 27, 28, 29, 30, 33, 35-47, 65, 69, 73, 75, 76, 172, 179, 208, 211, 221, 223, 225, 226, 228, 229, 230, 231, 232, 245-50, 254, 258, 261, 263, 264, 265, 266, 269, 271, 278, 282, 283, 284, 285, 286, 287, 288, 290, 291, 293, 294, 295, 296, 297, 298, 299, 300, 301, 302, 304, 305, 307, 308, 309, 311, 312, 313, 319, 320, 321, 322, 323, 324, 325, 326, 327, 329, 330, 331, 332, 340, 349, 358, 375, 377, 379, 381, 383, 385, 404, 411, 417, 502, 514, 522, 526, 532, 534, 542, 543, 546, 553, 555, 558, 560, 562, 563, 569, 574
and Amalek, 229, 232, 234, 513
as "egalitarian," 42, 91, 298
as oral society, 285, 304, 542-43
as social collective, 232, 245, 247, 248-50, 251, 287, 299, 514, 553
Deborah, as mother in, 246, 254
literacy in, 543
putative earliest reference to, 382-83
Issachar, 222, 239, 255, 507, 508, 549
Ishtar, 4, 68-71, 75, 84, 93, 108, 112, 113, 115, 116, 118, 184, 186, 187, 194, 195, 196, 201, 205, 324, 404, 405, 406, 407, 411, 414, 433, 434, 442, 471, 473, 486, 491, 494, 539, 573
Izbet Sartah, 284, 295, 550, 551, 554

Jacob, 80, 129, 159, 230, 239, 243, 325, 442, 524
Jael, 231, 241, 242, 246, 248, 252, 254, 256, 258, 440, 519
javelin-heads, 25
Jehoiakim, 575
Jephthah, 128, 221, 359
Jeroboam I, 212
Jerubbaal, 358, 359, 565
Jerubeshet, 565
Jerusalem, 27, 103, 206, 239, 291, 303, 332, 349, 371, 404, 448
Joab, 67, 165, 239, 575
Job, 102, 434
Jonathan, xiii, 3, 4, 19, 39, 47, 51, 52, 53, 55, 60, 63, 64-67, 70, 71, 72, 73, 75, 79, 80, 82, 90, 94, 163, 166, 169, 174, 179, 268, 269, 270, 273, 274, 275, 276, 277, 278, 279, 280, 281, 282, 300, 314, 340, 352, 399, 401, 404, 410, 529, 533, 539, 542, 549, 570
bones of, 570
death of, 51, 65, 66, 67, 268, 269, 270, 275-81, 314, 529
Joseph, 103, 159, 240, 411
tribe of, 240
Josiah, 328, 330, 358, 550, 575
Judah, 12, 66, 80, 240, 303, 305, 309, 318, 321, 326, 329, 349, 358, 404, 411, 462, 509, 518, 555
Judeans, 281, 300, 303, 331, 541, 555
Judith, 313, 439, 440

Kaphtor, 341
Karatepe reliefs, 32
Khirbet al-Mudayna, 29
Khirbet el-Qom, 27
Khirbet Qeiyafa, 29, 348, 349, 355, 369, 543, 552
Khirbet Tannin, 551
kingship, 19, 65, 67, 73, 100, 112, 167, 168, 169, 175, 182, 276, 399, 406, 444, 474, 535
as patron of warrior literature, 11, 100, 102, 136, 297, 299, 339, 420, 453

royal ideology, 100, 111, 112, 167, 168, 339, 374, 388, 444, 558
Kinrot, 25, 29
Kirta, 6, 17, 109, 110, 113, 125, 129, 147, 156, 221, 222, 270, 310, 352, 420, 421, 437, 440, 462, 513, 558, 566
Kishon, Wadi, 236, 246, 256, 264, 265
kissing, 66, 86, 87, 89, 148, 414
knives, 26, 126, 127, 176, 366
Kothar, 99, 105, 106, 108, 138, 139, 140, 163, 273, 341, 419, 420, 427, 465, 481, 536
Kotharat, 105, 419, 425
Kuntillet ʿAjrud, 237, 351, 353, 373, 501, 530, 535, 544, 545, 561, 574

Labayu, 20
Lachish, 11, 29, 29, 295, 305, 306, 307, 325, 351, 364, 368
Lahmi, 316
lament, 19, 20
Lapiths, 72
Leah, 80
Lebanon, 149, 150, 151, 296, 310, 420, 455, 456, 572
Levi, 240, 524
Leviathan, 45, 381, 385
Linear B, 336, 398, 468
"life"//"nondeath," 108-10, 429
lion, 20, 56, 63, 164, 169, 202, 207, 208, 268, 270, 274, 323, 327, 354, 359, 371, 398, 466, 469, 491, 492, 493, 494, 532, 537, 552, 562
lionness, 86, 169, 204, 205-6, 359, 491, 494
literacy, 285, 543. *See also* abecedaries; scribes
love, 3, 63-67, 75, 78, 79, 80, 81, 82-85, 89-90, 92-94, 118, 179-81, 257, 275, 278-79, 300, 360, 397, 400, 404, 406, 407, 409, 410, 411, 415, 417, 482, 533, 537, 538, 539, 548
Lugale-e, 17, 167, 172, 273
Lycaon, 61

Machir, 240, 255
"magic," 139, 200, 361, 394, 443, 449, 450, 465, 470, 473, 482. *See also* divination; incantations
Malchi-shua, 71
Manahat, 551
Manasseh, 240, 249, 319
Maradona, Diego, 414
Marduk, 167, 407, 428, 568
Mari, 28, 43, 45, 59, 201, 353, 355, 357, 362, 389, 396, 426, 462, 468, 474, 477, 523, 546, 552, 557
marzeah, 147, 148, 450, 452, 453, 486
masculinity, 9, 81, 132, 334, 411, 441, 443
masks, 206, 207, 364, 439, 489
Mati-ilu, 76
Matrix, xi
medicinal plants, 485
megaliths, 317, 319, 321, 568
Megiddo, 19, 25, 32, 256, 289, 358, 364, 366, 371, 373, 473, 529
Megiddo ivory, 32, 358, 373, 529
Melanion, 391
Menelaus, 69, 77, 260, 350
Meqabelein, 27
Meriones, 72
Meroz, 227, 231, 232, 235, 240, 250, 252, 256, 262, 263, 265, 514
Mesha stele, 21, 240, 328, 355, 471, 560
messiah, xii
Michal, 65, 66, 69, 70, 78, 80, 279, 409, 475, 534
Mididi, 198
militia(s), 23, 45, 223, 226, 234, 254, 264, 265, 286, 288, 297, 328, 329, 511, 520, 521
Minet el-Bheida, 25
minor judges, 552
Mizpah, 286
Mlk, 148, 317, 447-48
Mordecai, 562
mortality. *See* warrior mortality
Moses, 237, 570
Mot, 6, 19, 21, 162, 163, 164-67, 168, 171, 173, 174, 175, 360, 361, 385, 439, 466, 468, 473, 525. *See also* Death
as "hero," 167
death of, 439

Mount Ebal, 28-29, 325, 369
mourning, 56, 79, 101, 114, 116, 120, 121, 124, 129, 135, 158, 159, 160, 271, 279, 374, 404, 413, 434, 437, 438, 458
Muse, 260, 395
myth, 37, 38, 40, 110, 196, 340, 350, 378, 446, 472, 521

Nahash, 20
nakedness, 19, 356, 391, 573
name, xii, 23, 480
name of Baal, 198-200, 205
Naphtali, 249, 256, 264, 507
Nastes, 77
Nephilim, 569
Nergal, 392, 447
netherworld. *See* underworld
nets, 27, 368
Nike, 93
Nikkal, 169
Ninsun, 53, 54, 74, 75, 83, 84, 85, 92, 388, 406, 413
Ninurta, 167, 436, 473
Nippur, 342, 388
Niqmaddu, 154, 155, 157, 158, 159, 458, 461
Noah, 102, 103, 423, 434
Nob, 18, 131, 303

Odysseus, xiii, 64, 69, 72, 177, 178, 276, 339, 396, 398, 404, 405, 408, 474, 539
Odyssey, 10, 51, 64, 127, 260, 330, 336, 350, 394, 404, 539, 548, 560, 563
  date of, 394-95
  reception of, 560
Og of Bashan, 138, 317, 319, 568-69
"old poetry," 7, 8, 11, 16, 21, 37, 38, 42-43, 46, 211-13, 216-20, 247, 259, 293, 300, 301, 302, 308, 309, 311, 312, 313, 327, 329, 332, 339, 345, 348, 375, 383, 384, 497, 498, 547, 559, 560, 576
  critique of dating, 216-20
  date of, 211-20
omens, 84, 90, 120, 360, 415, 513, 536
oral epic, 9, 37, 358
orality, 284, 294, 298, 541, 542, 543, 557, 562
oral poetry, 7, 9, 232, 239, 242, 247, 248, 261, 263, 277, 281, 282, 284, 285-88, 290-95, 298-300, 303-7, 310, 313, 327-30, 339, 358, 376, 394, 420, 421, 497, 539, 540-41, 542, 555, 556. *See also* performance
oral prose, 20, 315, 563
Oreb, 20

Panamuwa, 104
Paran, 227, 237
Paris, 64, 69, 74, 78, 398
Parry, Milman, 375, 376, 394
Patroklos, 3, 51, 52, 54, 59-64, 65, 70, 71, 72, 77, 78, 79, 90, 177, 178, 260, 273, 276, 277, 279, 280, 320, 340, 396, 397, 403, 408, 409, 410, 413, 415, 525
  death of, 60, 61, 62, 63, 64, 397
  ghost of, 61, 64
Peleus, 51, 60, 385
Pella, 207, 208, 366, 494
Penelope, 131, 405
Pentateuch sources, 37, 39, 330, 331, 375, 576
performance, 9, 11, 19, 38, 103, 259, 261, 271, 284, 286, 291, 294, 298, 299, 303, 304, 308, 310, 313, 339, 344, 357, 408, 457, 464, 515, 521, 525, 527, 541, 542, 549, 558, 560. *See also* "recomposition-in-performance"; warrior commemoration
  sites of, 285-90, 303-5, 549, 557
Philistine(s), 18, 25, 65, 71, 73, 179, 196, 198, 268, 271, 277, 290, 293, 294, 314, 316, 317, 318, 355, 359, 379, 380, 428, 432, 442, 467, 526, 529, 538, 540, 549, 550, 557, 564
Phinehas, 361
Phoenix, 177, 276
Phylarchos, 77, 78
Pidru, 177, 189, 190
Pidray, 167, 177, 179, 181, 426, 474
pilgrimage, 289, 361, 487, 490, 547, 554
pillar figurines, 574
plunder. *See* warfare plunder

women as. *See* women, as battle plunder
Priam, 62, 63, 64, 78, 396
prose, 7, 9, 11, 38, 39, 40, 45, 46, 54, 65, 66, 67, 71, 101, 147, 148, 160, 193, 211, 214, 244, 254, 257, 275, 276, 277, 281, 282, 286, 287, 288, 290, 293, 294, 299, 300, 301-2, 309, 310, 311-15, 320, 322, 326, 327, 328, 330, 332, 348, 352, 353, 356, 378, 379, 399, 410, 421, 464, 499, 518, 521, 538, 540, 541, 545, 548, 550, 558, 560, 562
Prousias II, 77
Pughat, 17, 99, 102, 103, 105, 114, 115, 119, 120, 122, 123, 124, 125, 126, 127, 129, 136, 241, 396, 409, 419, 421, 424, 425, 437, 440, 415, 446
as hero, 129
Pulp Fiction, xi

Qedeshet, 186, 372. *See also* Qudshu
Qudshu, 205, 493. *See also* Qedeshet
queen as mother, 462-63. *See also* "house of the mother"
queen mother, 462-63, 573
Queen of Heaven, 324, 572

Rachel, 80
Rashpu, 140, 175, 183, 202, 351, 454, 490. *See also* Resheph
Ras Shamra, 364, 371, 373, 386, 452, 518, 569. *See also* Ugarit
Rebecca, 129
"recomposition-in-performance," 261, 298, 339, 464. *See also* performance; "secondary unity"
relative particle, 215, 216, 500, 502, 529
Rephaim *(rp'um/rp'im)*, 6, 12, 20, 34, 110, 136-61, 208, 308, 310, 315-21, 331, 336, 407, 446-47, 450, 451, 452, 454, 456, 458, 461, 567, 569
as collective, 109, 143, 158-59
Rephaim texts, 5, 12, 138-61, 177, 208, 308, 310, 420, 453, 457, 559
Resheph, 183, 185, 201, 202, 323, 476, 484, 485, 490, 574. *See also* Rashpu
Resheps, 490, 491
Reuben, 223, 239, 240, 255, 256, 507, 518, 549
Rp'u (name), 6, 101-2, 124, 136, 137-40, 142, 150, 154, 447, 457, 565
Rp'u (title), 156-57, 316-17, 448
running, 17, 166, 168

Sahab, 27
Saltu, 539
Samson, 224, 359, 361, 431, 432, 508, 549
death of, 359, 432
"riddle" of, 547
wrath of, 361
Samuel, 287
bones of, 570
Saph, 315, 316
Sarpedon, 72, 396
Saul, xiii, 4, 18, 19, 23, 39, 51, 65, 66, 67, 69, 70, 71, 73, 78, 128, 131, 163, 166, 168, 169, 177, 179, 196, 246, 268, 269, 270, 271, 273, 275, 276, 277, 278, 279, 280, 282, 283, 292, 293, 294, 300, 303, 314, 356, 378, 397, 400, 435, 436, 514, 529, 531, 533, 537, 539, 540, 542, 549, 562, 565
armor of, 18, 131, 196, 303
bones of, 549
death of, 65, 268, 269, 270, 275-81, 314, 399, 529
"madness" of, 400
sayings, tribal, 219, 232, 239, 240, 517, 524, 549
scorpion, 25, 196
scorpion-man, 54
scorpion-spell, 489, 489
scribes, 38, 226, 229, 273, 295, 299, 300, 301, 303, 304, 316, 374, 375, 376, 420, 528, 542, 543, 554, 559
"secondary unity," 258, 522, 523. *See also* "recomposition-in-performance"
Seir, 227, 228, 232, 235, 237, 254, 511, 512
Sekhmet, 205, 206, 495
Seth, 197, 470, 487, 488
sex/sexuality, 5, 55, 56, 74, 75, 76, 77, 79-95, 104-5, 132, 133, 164, 177, 180-81, 197, 275, 279, 340, 354, 385, 390, 392, 401,

404, 406, 410, 411, 412, 414, 415, 416, 417, 434, 441, 470, 539
shades of the dead, 145, 156, 459
Shamash, 1, 54, 75, 406
shame, 19, 76, 108, 316, 324, 460, 531, 565. *See also* dishonor
Shamgar, 227, 228, 232, 234, 250, 254, 322
Shamhat, 55, 56, 68, 70, 81, 84, 134, 392, 404
Sharur, 163, 273
Shasu, 227, 228
Shechem, 20, 510, 514, 551
Sheol, 159, 409, 461, 466
shields, 17, 18, 131, 163, 221, 222, 255, 268, 270, 273, 274, 278, 303, 352, 354, 371, 442, 505, 506, 531, 536, 557
Shiloh, 29, 551
Sibbecai, 315
Sidon, 198, 323, 324, 364, 572
Siduri, 54, 56, 68, 70, 81, 404, 411
Simeon, 240, 524
Sinai, 227, 228, 236, 237, 254, 352, 489, 505, 516, 517, 560
Sinuhe, 167, 241
Sisera, 229, 242, 246, 252, 256, 257, 258, 264, 287, 288, 520
snake, 58, 127, 186, 201, 559
  incantations for, 186, 201, 559
social collective, 109, 125, 143, 158-59, 226, 231, 248-49, 251
  family as, 125
  Israel as, 248-49, 251, 287, 553
  militia as, 226, 245, 511
  Rephaim as, 109, 143, 158-59
  stars as, 231, 264
  women, 279, 463
social death. *See* death, social
Solomon, 168, 309, 323, 324, 329, 409, 430, 510, 546, 548, 558, 562
song, 3, 5, 9, 19, 20, 78, 178, 179, 182, 260, 266, 271, 276, 277, 281, 282, 283, 285, 288, 289, 293, 294, 295, 299, 302, 303, 307, 328, 335, 344, 354, 356, 357, 377, 429, 473, 521, 524, 525, 533, 539, 540, 541, 544, 548, 549, 558, 562, 570. *See also* warrior song; women, as performers of song; women, as producers of song
spears, 16, 25, 26, 31
spindle, associated with women, 132, 408, 443, 444
spoils of battle. *See* warfare plunder
stars, 122, 124, 125, 127, 166, 184, 189, 190, 227, 229, 230, 231, 234, 246, 256, 263, 264, 265, 437, 513
  as collective, 231, 264
  as divine army, 229, 230, 231, 234, 246, 256, 263, 264, 265
status, 4
strength. *See* warrior strength
subcultures, 2, 338
Sukkot, 143
Sunjata epic, 540-41
Sutu, Sutean, 117, 434, 435
swords, 16-17, 24, 25-26
  as trophies, 18

Taanach, 29, 256, 325, 369
Taanach stand, 32, 206, 208
Tall Abu Al-Kharaz, 29, 368, 370, 493, 495
Tallay, 167, 177, 179, 180, 426, 474
Tannit. *See* Tnt
Tarura, 31, 179, 474
Tas-Silg, 342
tears, 397-98
Teiman, 227, 237
Tel Dan, 29, 325, 370, 439, 472
Tel el-Oreimeh, 30, 371
Telemachus, 131
Tel es-Saidiyeh, 25, 30
Tel Halif, 33, 373
Tel Kinrot, 25, 29, 369
Tell el-Farah North, 551
Tell el-Farah South, 25, 27
Tell el-Umayri, 25, 370
Tell en-Nasbeh, 27, 286
Tell Hadidi, 507
Tell Husn. *See* Pella
Tell Qasile, 18, 131, 303, 355, 442, 557
Tell Rehov, 26, 359, 364, 365, 367, 495
Tell Taanach cult stands, 32, 206, 208

Tell Zeror, 25
Tel Nami, 25
Tel Qeiyafa. *See* Khirbet Qeiyafa
Tel Rehov model shrine, 32, 206-7, 208
Tel Zayit, 380, 542, 543, 550
Teucer, 72
Thariyelli, 155
Thersites, 76
Thetis, 51, 61, 64, 69, 74, 273, 385, 403
Tiamat, 167, 361, 385, 407, 467
Tikulti-Ninurta, 93, 224
Tiryns, 342
Tnt, 199, 489, 572
Tob, 286, 545
tools, 2, 25, 337
Trojan horse, 64, 548, 563
trophies (body parts), 18
Tros, 61
Troy, 64, 321, 336, 398, 403, 539
Tyre, 196, 273, 481, 489

Ugarit, 2, 3, 11-12, 15, 32, 33-34, 73, 102, 137, 139, 159, 185, 187, 195, 201, 225, 308, 309-12, 320
Ugarit gold plate hunting scene, 32
Ugaritic monarchy, 2, 6, 11, 12, 34
Ugaritic texts,
  relationship to biblical tradition, 43
Ugaritic verbal forms, 214-15
Ugarit royal bed panels, 32
underworld, xiii, 51, 53, 64, 113, 140, 154, 155, 155, 156, 157, 159, 164, 191, 392, 407, 458, 461, 466
undomesticated animals, 27-30
urban versus wild, 55
Uruk, 51, 55, 56, 57, 58, 89, 334, 338, 393, 404, 407
  walls of, 58
Utnapishti, 54, 56, 57, 392
Utshanabi, 57

veil, 86, 413
violence, xi, 3, 4, 63, 100, 114, 136, 162, 342, 419, 420, 445, 473. *See also* warfare
vows, 17

warfare, xi, xiii, 2, 3, 7, 11, 15, 16, 17, 18, 20, 22, 24, 27, 30, 31, 32, 35, 45, 59, 73, 74, 76, 77, 93, 94, 112, 117, 130, 131, 148, 162, 167, 172, 175, 185, 196, 202, 203, 208, 248, 266, 297, 310, 326, 327, 328, 329, 339, 340, 346-47, 355, 356, 359, 361, 362, 371, 396, 407, 409, 417, 442, 467, 526, 537, 561
  as dance, 93
  as feast, 93-94, 172
warfare cannibalism, 17-18, 23, 94
warfare *ḥērem*, 18, 45, 171-72, 355, 357, 471
warfare oracle(s), 17, 327, 335, 353, 513, 575
warfare plunder, xiii, 18, 19, 27, 30, 77, 78, 131, 177, 227, 251, 256, 257, 258, 271, 277, 296, 303, 356, 357, 408, 506, 544
warfare practices, post-battle, 11, 15, 17-20, 33, 328
warfare practices, pre-battle, 15, 16-17, 33, 45-46
warfare spoil. *See* warfare plunder
warrior aggression, 20, 21, 23
  terms for, 21-22
warrior "afterlife," 112, 137, 151, 336, 361. *See also* afterlife; warrior immortality; warrior spirits
warrior anger (fury), 21-22, 362, 396
warrior animals. *See* Anat, winged; Astarte, as lioness; attribute animals; gazelle; lion; lionness
warrior attitudes, 15, 20-21
warrior blood, 17, 18, 23, 72, 78, 79, 135, 170, 171, 172, 268, 289, 354, 408, 409, 471, 531, 547
  as cosmetic, 78-79
warrior "blood-lust," 22
warrior burials, 24-25, 570
warrior clothing, 17, 60, 66, 129, 136
warrior commemoration, xiii, 1, 2, 3, 6, 20, 35, 51, 58, 59, 62, 100, 112, 136, 154, 160, 161, 235, 266, 282, 283, 287, 288, 291, 303, 305, 319, 320, 322, 343, 387, 393, 433, 469, 517. *See also* performance
  palace's role in, 299, 301-3, 305, 309, 310, 325, 339, 557

temple's role in, 303
warrior corpses, 19, 24, 61, 62, 63, 272, 282, 356, 397, 413
desecration of, 18-19, 22-23, 24, 61-63, 356, 397
warrior culture, 2-3, 12, 15-23, 33, 34-35, 36
inversion, 3, 17, 56, 73, 74
inversion of gender, 3, 73, 74, 90, 133, 175, 203, 405, 408, 409. *See also* gender polarity
warrior death, xiii, 5, 6, 21, 26, 51, 52, 54, 55, 57, 58, 60, 61, 63, 64, 65, 66, 67, 69, 71, 85, 99, 100, 102, 103, 108, 109, 110, 119, 125, 129, 131, 137, 160, 270, 271, 272, 277, 281, 314, 335, 336, 359, 374, 431
as destiny, 160, 431
warrior dishonor, 21, 61, 108
warrior drunkenness, 19, 178
warrior fame, xii, 23, 139, 177, 277, 318, 393, 403. *See also* warrior glory
warrior glory, xii, xiii, 23, 60, 61, 126, 398, 403, 529. *See also* warrior fame
warrior goddesses as mentors for human warriors, 74, 116, 132, 133, 174, 175
warrior goddesses as models for human warriors, 74, 133, 150, 174, 175, 208, 396
warrior goddesses as patrons of human warriors, 16, 21, 27, 71, 74, 112-13, 130, 131, 134, 135, 150, 174, 206, 322, 495
warrior gods as models for human warriors, 150, 174, 175, 181, 444
warrior hair, 17, 45, 223-24, 234, 264, 265, 354, 356, 416, 508, 509
warrior hand-to-hand combat, 356
warrior honor, xiii, 4, 5, 20, 26, 60, 62, 63, 129, 121, 136, 258, 359, 396, 406, 429, 475, 546
warrior ideology in service to kings, 100, 111, 112, 167, 168, 388, 444
warrior immortality, 108-10, 113, 335, 405, 429. *See also* warrior "afterlife"
warrior insatiability, 22
warrior mortality, 20, 56, 63, 109, 359, 405
warrior nakedness, 19, 356
warrior nicknames, 20, 358-59, 528, 529, 533, 534
warrior painting, 31, 178-79
warrior poetry. *See* warrior song
warrior pairs, 3-4, 51-95, 174, 269, 385, 404, 416, 417, 539
lesser member in, 52, 53, 55, 58-59, 60
warrior size, 2, 17, 128, 168, 318, 319, 352, 569
warrior song (poetry), xii, 1, 2, 3, 4, 5, 9, 19, 304, 334, 335-36, 547, 540-41
the social dislocation of, 307, 308-32
warrior spirit, 69, 361, 560, 562
warrior spirits, 137, 144-45
warrior strength, 1, 2, 17, 21-22, 53, 81, 83, 125, 128, 134, 256, 336, 352, 439, 445, 475, 524, 526
warrior terms, 1-2, 17
warrior titles, 51, 59, 100, 101, 102, 109, 117, 127, 129, 131, 134, 135, 137, 150, 167, 169, 173, 190, 196, 205, 208, 270, 317, 337, 359, 411, 422, 446, 468, 529, 533, 566, 574
warrior training, 16, 17, 27, 63, 116, 129, 130, 135, 326, 350, 434, 442
warrior values, xiii, 1, 2, 15, 20-21, 33, 34, 99, 100, 101, 112, 127, 133-34, 138, 181, 182, 267, 350, 419, 575
warriors, as "brothers," 3, 53. *See also* warrior pairs
washing in blood, 17
washing in water, 17, 23
weapons, 16-17, 21, 23, 24, 25, 26, 30, 31, 32, 61, 67, 94, 100, 106, 107, 108, 114, 129, 130, 131, 136, 163, 168, 171, 172, 189, 268, 269, 270, 273, 278, 279, 303, 347, 350, 355, 358, 360, 362, 364, 365, 366, 367, 372, 395, 420, 427, 443, 479, 523, 533, 536, 557, 564, 568
as "extra-somatic body parts," 17, 108, 133, 273
as trophies, 130, 131, 303, 355, 367, 557
in burials, 24
names, 355
personified, 360, 362

said not to be for women, 21, 114, 274-75
washing, 17, 23, 354
wine, 19, 106, 107, 127, 130, 149, 151, 176, 178, 186, 191, 202, 372, 392, 440, 451, 455, 483. *See also* warrior drunkenness
women
as battle plunder (enslavement), 19, 70, 77, 257, 339, 408
as communication network, 19
as cultic participants, 464
as performers of song, 9, 19-20, 38-39, 271, 293-94, 298, 344, 525, 549, 550
as producers of song, 9, 19-20, 38-39, 271, 293-94, 298, 344, 358, 408, 525, 549
as social collective, 279, 463
clothing of, 125-26
dishonorable death by, 21
excluded, xiii, 9, 20-21, 79, 174, 178, 181, 274
goddesses as inversions of, 4, 20-21
in the military, xiii
mourning, 374, 413, 534. *See also* women, weeping
weeping, 19, 118, 120, 122, 124, 135, 271, 529. *See also* women, mourning

Yahweh, 16, 17, 21, 22, 23, 40, 76, 165, 222, 227, 228, 230, 231, 232, 234, 237, 238, 239, 241, 245, 246, 248, 249, 250, 251, 252, 255, 256, 257, 258, 259, 261, 262, 263, 264, 265, 271, 272, 286, 287, 288, 289, 299, 303, 305, 323, 325, 326, 351, 352, 359, 360, 403, 404, 405, 430, 434, 437, 441, 448, 520, 524, 531, 547, 574
as warrior-teacher, 16, 326, 350, 434
home of, 227-28
of hosts, 574
people of, 249, 250, 258, 286, 299
"the One of Sinai," 236, 254, 516
wrath of, 222, 355, 361
Yamm, 6, 21, 112, 162, 163, 164, 168, 176, 198, 200, 242, 273, 360, 385, 454, 468, 488
Yarih, 11, 135, 169, 188, 189, 191, 192, 201, 203
Yatpan, 99, 107, 114, 117, 118, 122, 125, 126, 127, 419, 420, 421, 434, 440, 456
Ydʿ-Ylḥn, 168
Yehawmilk, 111
Yhw3, 228

Zebulun, 239, 245, 249, 255, 256, 264, 284, 359, 549
Zeeb, 20, 359
Zeus, 74, 127, 198
Zimri-Lim, 353, 355, 362, 396, 443, 557
Epic of, 335, 353
Zinjirli, 104, 424
hunting scene, 32-33

Index of Texts

HEBREW BIBLE

Genesis

1 329
1:14 458
1:20 424
1:24 424
1:30 424
2:19 424
4:23-24 354
5:21-22 446
6:4 569
9 352
9:20-27 103
9:24 485
10:5 532
10:32 532
13:9 531
13:11 531
13:14 531
14:5 320
14:20 357
15:20 320
18 241, 426
18:18 241
21 442
21:12-21 351
22 18
24:11 544
24:28 463
25:13 314
25:23 532
25:27 239, 442
26:2 239
27 325
27:26-27 86
29:30 80
31:20 530
31:27 139
32:27 490
33:4 86
35:13 507
35:14 428
37 103
37:7 214
37:8 221
37:34 423
37:35 159, 458
38 423
39 103
39:2 411
39:23 411
41 103, 437
42:24 279
48:5 240
48:13-14 240
49 43, 211, 219, 239, 240, 243, 245, 289, 295, 504, 555
49:3 259
49:4 363, 403, 424, 524
49:4-7 23
49:6-7 259
49:7 21, 22
49:8-10 555
49:8-12 555
49:9 259, 524
49:10 217-18, 382, 503
49:11 18
49:12 19
49:13 239, 549
49:14 223, 239, 507, 549
49:15 239
49:16 245
49:17 359
49:18 245, 259
49:21 352
49:23-24 129
49:24 16
49:24-26 245
49:26 224
49:27 19, 359
50:23 240

Exodus
14–15 332
15 38, 43, 179, 211, 213, 219, 243, 263, 384, 385, 498, 500, 515, 519, 520, 558, 559
15:2 337
15:20-21 19
22:4 572
32 356, 473
32:17 17

Leviticus
3:1 505
11:10 424
11:46 424

Numbers
1:5 314
3:2 314
3:3 314
3:18 314
6:5 223, 416
11:25-26 560
11:29 520
13:4 314
13:16 314
13:22 317, 565
13:27 500
13:28 317, 565
13:29 569
13:33 569
16:29 432
16:30-33 466
18:12 427
21:14 547
21:27 289, 290, 547
21:27-30 547
21:29 520
21:30 529
21:33 318
22–24 287
22:8 517
22:19 239
22:21-33 546
23–24 43, 211, 259, 332
23:7 548
23:10 431, 541
23:18 243, 548
23:21 17
23:24 18, 172, 354
24:3 548
24:8 354
24:15 548
24:15-19 17, 555
24:17 230, 353
24:18 237
26:10 466
27:1 314
28:7 428
31:25-54 357
31:36 227
31:43 227
32:1 507
34:17 314
34:19 314

Deuteronomy
1:4 138
1:27 353
1:31 500
2–3 322
2:10-11 569
2:12 214
2:20 319
2:20-21 569
3:1 138, 318
3:5 226
3:10 138, 318
3:11 319
3:12-13 319
7:13 323, 571
8:15 500
11:6 466
12 28
12–26 330
12:15 28
13:6 400
13:17 549
14 28, 325
14:4-6 574
14:5 28
18:3 505
20:19-20 346
21 124
21:1 272
21:1-9 272
22:5 17, 136, 443, 445
23:9-14 17
26:2 426, 427
26:4 427
26:10 427
28:4 323, 571
28:18 323, 571
28:26 435
28:51 323, 571
29:10 544
32 213, 214, 243, 327, 346
32–33 211
32:2 272, 436
32:7 346, 558
32:8 532
32:8-9 40, 378
32:13 213
32:22 21
32:41 17, 358
32:42 17, 45, 46, 172, 223, 224, 356, 416, 508
33 240, 246, 289, 346
33:2 227, 228, 237, 246
33:2-5 561
33:7 246
33:11 246
33:12 239, 246
33:17 240, 292
33:20 17, 353
33:20-21 240
33:21 246, 356, 520
33:23 246
33:29 246

Joshua
1:14 336
3–4 287
3:5 17
6:2 336, 353
7:7 353

8:3 336
9:21 544
9:23 544
9:27 544
10:7 336
10:9-14 513, 514
10:12-13 281
10:13 282
10:26-27 18
10:28-39 352
15:8 320
17:1 337

Judges

1:2 353
1:33 570
2:1 214, 500
2:7 545
2:10 545
2:13 323, 324, 477
3:2 16, 434
3:10 22, 360
3:12 359
3:14 359
3:16 352
3:19 528
3:21 352
3:21-22 531
3:31 206, 228, 322
4 41, 287
4–5 20, 41, 332, 359, 440
4:9 17, 21, 76, 353
4:11 532
4:17 518, 523
4:17-21 126
4:19 518
4:19-21 127
4:21 17
5 8, 9, 20, 23, 38, 41, 42, 208, 212-66, 283, 284, 285, 287, 289, 294, 297, 298, 299, 300, 302, 303, 304, 305, 307, 309, 313, 328, 329, 377, 382, 384, 385, 497, 499, 514, 515, 523, 545, 558, 559
5:1 244, 254, 521
5:1-6 251
5:2 17, 42, 45, 46, 224, 232, 245, 251, 252, 253, 254, 257, 263, 264, 265, 356, 416, 508, 509
5:2-3 243
5:2-5 243, 251, 259
5:2-8 251, 252
5:2-9 243, 251, 257
5:2-13 232, 240, 243, 244, 245, 246, 247, 248, 250, 251, 253
5:3 42, 245, 246, 247, 251, 254, 259, 260, 261, 265, 290, 297, 305
5:3-5 251
5:4 227, 228, 236, 237, 238, 245, 250, 254, 260, 265, 517
5:4-5 227, 228, 232, 235-38, 243, 246, 250, 252, 262, 263, 265, 516, 520
5:5 236, 238, 245, 254, 265
5:6 206, 224-25, 228, 232, 248, 254, 264, 322
5:6-7 250, 520
5:6-8 243, 251
5:6-9 243, 253
5:7 244, 245, 246, 252, 254, 260, 264
5:7-8 246
5:8 222, 231, 243, 245, 253, 254, 255, 260, 264, 506
5:7 232, 253
5:9 17, 245, 251, 252, 253, 255, 257, 259, 260, 265, 290
5:9-11 42, 243, 251
5:9-12 251
5:9-13 251, 252
5:10 252, 253, 255, 260, 288, 289, 297, 351, 498, 546, 547
5:10-11 258
5:10-13 243, 251, 258, 259
5:10-14 243
5:11 232, 243, 245, 246, 250, 253, 255, 264, 265, 285, 286-90, 295, 544
5:12 243, 244, 246, 250, 251, 252, 253, 255, 260, 289, 377
5:12-13 258
5:12-15 251
5:12-17 243
5:12-18 251
5:12-22 243
5:12-23 243
5:13 242, 244, 245, 249, 252, 253, 255, 259, 260, 265, 288, 290
5:13-15 251
5:14 42, 229, 238, 252, 255, 260, 284, 542
5:14-16 251
5:14-17 258, 264
5:14-18 238-40, 248, 249, 252, 289, 520
5:14-30 232, 243, 244, 245, 247, 248
5:15 42, 239, 242, 246, 252, 253, 255, 259, 260
5:15-18 251
5:15-19 251
5:16 238, 239, 253, 256, 260, 549
5:16-17 260
5:17 239, 253, 256, 549
5:17-20 251
5:18 253, 256, 258, 264, 359, 530, 535
5:18-23 258
5:19 246, 249, 250, 253, 256, 264, 289, 356

5:19-21 251
5:19-22 243, 251
5:19-23 251, 252
5:20 230-31, 253, 256, 263-64, 265, 359
5:20-21 246, 520
5:21 243, 246, 256, 259, 260, 264, 290, 524
5:21-22 251
5:22 242, 252, 253, 256
5:22-23 251
5:23 128, 231, 240, 243, 250, 251, 252, 253, 256, 262, 263, 264, 265
5:23-24 231, 240-41, 252
5:23-27 251
5:23-31 252
5:24 252, 256
5:24-27 126, 241, 243, 246, 251, 258
5:24-30 243, 252, 258, 264
5:25 42, 241, 242, 252, 253, 256, 518
5:25-26 127
5:26 242, 252, 253, 257, 445
5:26-27 242
5:27 253, 257
5:28 253, 257
5:28-30 243, 251, 258
5:28-31 251
5:29 42, 252, 253, 257, 498
5:30 19, 77, 253, 257, 339
5:31 243, 251, 257
6–8 20, 502
6:2 360
6:12 336
6:13 545, 558
6:14 439
6:17 502
6:18 239
6:32 565
6:34 22, 361, 560
6:36-40 436
7:12 502
7:23 249
7:25 20
8:3 20, 363
8:14 554
8:26 502
8:32 570
9 23, 40
9:4 363
9:13 455
9:17 359
9:54 21, 76, 350
10 315
10:1 315
10:1-5 552
10:2 570
10:4 547, 562
10:5 570
10:6 323, 324, 477
10:34 562
11 18, 545
11:1 128, 336
11:1-3 286
11:11 286
11:25 221, 222
11:29 22
11:30 17
11:34 19, 179, 357, 550
11:40 215, 286, 501, 548
12 315
12:3 359
12:7 570
12:8 315
12:8-15 552
12:9 562
12:10 570
12:11 315
12:12 570
12:13 315
12:14 453
12:15 229, 570
13:1 353
13:5 224
13:7 224
13:25 22
14:3 529
14:6 22
14:19 22
15:14 22
15:18 529
15:20 529
16:16 359
16:17-20 224
16:22 224
16:23 318
16:28-30 224
16:30 359, 432
16:31 570
18 23
18:19 506
19:15 549
20:2 17
20:15 17
20:17 17, 337
20:25 17
20:35 17
20:46 17

Ruth

1:16 500
1:16-17 531
1:17 531
1:18 463
3:3 215
3:4 215

1 Samuel

1:13 432
1:22 443
2 43, 211, 219, 562
2:4 16
2:9 336
2:10 43, 562
5:1-7 318
5:3 165, 271
5:5 318
6:18 226
7:3 324
7:4 324, 477

7:7-11 353
9:1 336
9:1-2 128
9:2 168
9:22 562
10:5 139
10:23-24 17
11:1-2 20
11:6 22
12 288
12:7 287, 288, 520
12:7-12 287, 288
12:10 324
12:11 358-59
12:12 20
12:16-17 288
13:7 240
13:19-22 352
14:1 350, 529
14:9 400
14:27 352
14:35 356
14:43 352
14:52 23
15:33 179, 271
16 65
16:12-13 399
16:13-23 22
16:18 337
16:21 66, 80
17 316, 354, 468, 563
17:4 168, 467-68
17:7 316
17:23 468
17:26 529
17:33 128, 337
17:36 529
17:38-40 397
17:44 19, 435
17:46 19, 435
17:51 166, 271
18 65, 80
18:1 66, 80
18:1-4 66
18:3 66, 80
18:6 139, 293, 357
18:6-7 19, 179, 271
18:7 39, 73, 78, 246, 291-94, 356, 549
18:8 293
18:10 177, 276
18:11 16, 168
18:14 411
18:16 66, 80
18:20 66, 78, 80
18:22 80
18:28 66, 78, 80
19 73
19:15 563
20:16 66, 79
20:17 66
20:33 16, 168
20:34 363
20:41 66
20:41-42 66
21:4 74, 354
21:5 17, 74, 354
21:6 17
21:11 39, 73, 75, 246, 291-94, 356, 549
22:10 18, 131, 303
22:14 23
22:35 443
23:13 213, 500
23:18 79, 274
24:16 537
27:11 529, 550
28 353
28:4 530
28:15 457
28:16 xiii
28:16-19 xiii
28:19 xiii
28:21 359
29 356
29:5 39, 73, 78, 246, 291-94, 356, 549
30:2-3 19
30:16 356
31 71, 276
31:1 530
31:3 71
31:4 529
31:8 282, 530
31:8-13 19, 570
31:10 18, 131, 196, 198, 303, 318, 477

2 Samuel

1 9, 80, 211, 300, 305, 307
1:4-5 282
1:6 530
1:11-12 539
1:12 226, 520
1:18 281-82, 300, 302, 303, 541, 555
1:19 166, 268, 269, 270, 271, 277, 279, 280, 281, 466
1:19-25 19, 43, 269-70, 275, 277-78, 279, 280, 281
1:19-27 8, 42, 43, 65, 67, 71, 73, 139, 166, 267-83, 284, 285, 294, 295, 297, 298, 299, 303, 309, 328, 329, 357, 382, 384, 526-27, 539
1:20 19, 179, 268, 269, 271, 277, 278, 279, 285, 290-91, 379, 529
1:20-24 280
1:21 17, 120-21, 268, 269, 272-73, 277, 278, 279, 281, 290-91, 530, 535, 536
1:21-22 273
1:21-23 269, 278
1:22 16, 268, 269, 273, 278, 279
1:23 268, 269, 270, 274, 278, 279, 532
1:24 19, 78, 179, 268, 269, 271, 277, 278, 279, 281, 356-57, 548
1:25 166, 268, 269,

270, 277, 278, 279, 280, 466
1:26 79, 80, 94, 268, 269, 270, 274, 275, 278-79, 280, 282, 404, 539
1:26-27 667, 270, 279, 280, 357, 533
1:27 166, 268, 269, 270, 280, 466, 539
2:4 399
2:7 399
2:8 317
2:8-9 514
2:12-17 167
2:14 356
2:16 165, 271
2:17 21
2:18 270
2:19-23 534
2:32 570
3:7 403
3:29 76, 443
3:32-34 20, 280
3:33 528
3:34 165, 271, 534
3:39 23, 531
4:4 317
4:12 18
5:3 399
6:5 139
6:16 409
6:20 19, 409
6:22 475
8:13 23
10:6 545
11 327
11:1 239
11:4 89
11:11 354
11:11-13 74, 90, 414
11:21 565
12:16-18 423
12:22 423
12:24 89
14:25 411
14:33 87
15–19 555
15:1 17
15:7 317
15:21 505
16 69
16:12 81
16:16 315
16:18 81
17:8 337
17:10 532, 534
18:9 546
18:15 350
19 67
19:1-5 67
19:39 87
20:7 315
20:9 87
20:10-12 397
21 314-16, 436
21–24 562
21:1-4 435
21:1-14 356
21:6 317
21:10 435
21:11-14 570
21:12 530, 549
21:14 314, 562
21:15 315
21:15-17 315
21:15-22 314, 315, 317, 562, 563
21:16 352, 446
21:18 315, 317, 446
21:18-22 315, 327
21:19 315, 316
21:20 315, 319, 446
21:20-21 316
21:22 316, 317, 446
22 213, 313, 314, 327, 329, 383, 431, 498, 504, 505, 559, 562
22:2-51 314
22:7 431
22:8-16 329, 556
22:13 540
22:16 21
22:18 360
22:18-19 431
22:30 17
22:33 533, 561
22:34 17
22:35 16, 326, 350, 434
22:39 432
23 315, 327, 562
23:1 562
23:1-7 314, 556
23:7 562
23:8 16, 315, 562
23:8-9 315
23:8-39 314, 327, 562
23:9 314, 315
23:9-12 563
23:11-12 563
23:12 563
23:13 567
23:16-17 314
23:17 359
23:18 16, 168
23:18-19 314
23:19 23
23:20 314, 562
23:21 314
23:22 23
23:23 314
23:24 314
24–1 Kings 2 562
24:5-6 240
24:14 278

1 Kings

1:5 17
1:6 411
1:8 315, 562
1:10 315, 562
1:33 546
1:44 546
2:5 547
3:6 429
3:11 430
4:30 309

4:32 548
5:12 309
7:8 214, 500
8:12-13 309
8:13 281-82
9:15 510
10:16 533
10:17 533
11 324
11:5 323, 477
11:28 336
11:33 323, 477
14:11 435
16:4 435
17:1 121, 272, 436, 437, 536
18:46 361, 560
19:20 86
20:10 226
20:31 424
20:33 214
20:34 291
21:1-16 554
21:6 214
22 353
22:6 353
22:15 221
22:38 409

2 Kings
2:9 390
2:19-22 563
2:23-24 563
3 18
3:15 361, 560
3:18-19 353
4:1-7 563
4:7 215
4:16 215
4:21-24 546
4:23 215
4:38 506, 508
4:38-41 563
4:42-44 563
5:1 336
5:16 535
6:1-7 563
6:9-10 353
6:11 216, 502
6:27 506
8:1 215
8:4-5 557
8:4-6 563
8:29 214
9:5 528
9:15 214
13:15-19 443
13:20-21 361
15:20 336
16:13 428
18:30 353
23:5 230
23:13 324, 477
24:14 336

1 Chronicles
5:18 350
8:33 316
8:34 317
9:39 317
10:1 530
10:8 530
10:10 18, 196, 198
11:1 563
11:12 315
11:12-14 563
11:14 563
11:31 563
11:42 562
11:44 318
12:1 128
12:8 270, 274
12:22 128
13:8 139
18:11 357
20 315, 316, 317
20:4 318
20:4-8 315, 316, 336
20:5 316
20:5-8 317
20:6 137, 316
20:8 137, 316
21:13 278
27:6 562
29:24 562

2 Chronicles
19:2 400
35:25 328, 358, 550, 575

Nehemiah
8:3 549
10:38 427
11:8 563

Esther
9:19 226

Job
3:8 45
8:7 431
15:25-26 168
16:3 506
16:14 17, 168
19:24 304, 556
20:25 358
21:12 139
26:5 320
29:21 484
33:4 22
36:13 433
38:22 272
38:28 436, 506
38:32 230
38:40 484
40:4 484
40:10 533
41:1 45
41:14 524
42:12 431

Psalms
2 261, 305, 560
2:4 114
2:7 429
2:10 261
7:12 17

8:2 502
8:5 213
14:1 432
16:4 428, 469
18 213, 313, 314, 327, 329, 383, 431, 498, 504-5, 559, 562
18:2-51 314
18:7 431
18:8-16 313, 329, 556
18:13 540
18:16 21
18:18 360
18:18-19 431
18:30 17
18:32 533
18:33 533, 561
18:34 17
18:35 16, 326, 350, 434
18:39 432
19:5 17
20 555, 575
20:9 466
21:1 111
21:5 111
21:6 441
21:8 111
21:12 111
21:13 111
22:16 508
22:30 424, 450
23:5 139
29 211, 555
29:1 45
29:2 199
33:16 360
36:7 483
41:2 430
42–43 280
42:5 280
42:7 437
42:11 280
43:5 280
44 213, 575
44:18 531
45 302-3, 304-5, 409, 430, 555
45:1 302, 304
45:1-2 261, 304, 305, 409
45:2 307
45:3-5 329, 430
45:3-10 411
45:5 17
45:6 430
45:9 409
50:6 354
50:10 483
53:1 432
57:4 164, 169, 469, 552
58:7-10 547
58:10 17, 409, 471
58:11 354
59:8 114
68 43, 179, 211, 235, 237, 263, 292, 295, 302, 307, 309, 313, 382, 558, 559
68:5 536
68:8 558
68:8-9 227-28, 235-36, 516
68:9 235, 236, 238, 517
68:11-12 19
68:13-14 506
68:14 223
68:16 448
68:17 292
68:20 558
68:23 17, 409, 547
68:24-25 20
68:24-27 179
68:25 179
68:26 357, 548
68:30 217, 382
68:33 558
72:5 430
72:15 430
72:17 430
73:19 529
74:1 23
74:14 45
76:4 351
76:10 22
76:11-12 17
76:12 217, 382
78:65 19, 178, 485
79:5-6 22
83:2 530
83:9-11 545
88:10 320
89:8 451
89:14 360
89:19 128
89:19-37 430
91:3 368
91:7 292
103:20 360
104:15 455
110:5 21
112:2 541
118:14 498
124:7 368
127:4-5 443
129:5 531
144:1 16, 434
149:3 139
150:4 139

Proverbs

1:17 368
1:20 290
1:26 114
2:18 320
5:11 431
7:12 290
8:2 225
9 482
9:18 320
12:28 429
13:23 434
13:25 424
18:14 213
18:24 539
20:8 546
22:13 290

22:29 557
23:32 431
23:35 485
25–29 330
25:1 330
30:15 292
30:15-16 22
30:17 217, 218, 382
30:18 292
30:27 227, 544
30:29 292
30:30 532
31 502, 502
31:10-31 357-58
31:19 443
31:21 533
31:31 502

Song of Songs

1:1 158
2:8-9 534
2:13 455
3:4 463
3:7-11 409
3:8 16, 17, 434, 574
4:4 274
4:9 180, 181
6:5 181
6:13 278, 471
7:1 93, 278
8:2 463
8:6 351, 360, 409

Isaiah

1:21 529
2:4 16, 350, 434, 574
3:2 337
5:6 437
5:12 139
5:14 466
5:28 17
6:3 158
7 328
7:18 359
9 328
9:2 227, 356
9:3 544
10:15 221
10:19 542
10:30 570
11 328, 222
12:2 498
14:4 548
14:9 320, 461
15–16 529
15:3 291
16:5 557
18:7 217, 382
21:5 17, 531
21:7 546
24:8 139
24:11 291
24:19 424
26:12 508
26:14 320
27:1 45
28:10 441
29:11-12 543
30:28 361
30:32 139
32:6 432
34:6 531
38:16 111
40:9-10 19
40:22 547
41:1-5 213
42:13 22, 23, 408
42:17 531
51:17 485
51:17-18 103
51:20 368
55:1 451
57:6 428
58:2 354
59:17 22
62:6 530
63:1-6 409, 471
63:7 545

Jeremiah

1:7 213
2:8 313, 561
2:9 453
2:21 529
2:31 528
2:33 215
3:4 215
3:5 215
3:24 565
4:3 434
4:13 532
4:19 215
4:30 533
5:1 290
6:4 17
6:14 565
7:4 461
7:17 291
7:18 324, 428
8:8 313
8:11 565
9:8 164
14:14 530
9:17-19 124
9:17-20 271
9:18 529
9:20 290
9:25-26 529
11:13 565
13:23 492
15:3 435
15:12 366
15:17 361, 560
16:5-8 147
16:16 574
17:1 304, 556
18:18 313, 561
19:13 428
21:13 445
22:10 575
22:18 575
22:29 461
23:9 19, 178
23:18 451
23:22 451
23:32 363
27:7 453
29:27 570

31:21 215
31:32 76
32:29 428
37:21 291
38:10 562
38:22 531
44:15-30 324
44:17-25 428
46:5 531
46:6 532
46:10 22
47:15 445
48 529
48:41 76
48:46 520
49:4 445
49:22 76
51:30 76

Lamentations
1:1 529
1:20 278
2:3-4 23
3:66 23
4:11 23
4:19 532

Ezekiel
2:10 528
10:14 532
13:18-19 424
14 384
14:14 102
14:20 102, 505
16:18 215
17:2 290
18:2 290
18:27 424
19 327
19:2-3 327
19:5-6 327
20:28 428
20:49 290
21:9 17
21:11 17
21:15 358
21:20 358
21:21 552
21:33 358
23:25 22
24:3 506, 508
25:17 xi
26:7 158
26:11-12 291
27:10 273
27:11 273
28 384
28:3 102, 422
29:5 435
30:2 528
32:21 128
39:20 337
47:9 424

Daniel
3:20 336
4:33 272, 436
5:21 272, 436
6 562
7:10 292

Hosea
1:5 443
5:8 238
7:12 368
7:15 350
9:4 428
9:8 368
10:12 434

Joel
1:5 485
1:17 454
3:9 17

Amos
1:3 292
1:5 448
1:6 292
1:8 448
1:9 292
1:11 22, 23, 292
1:13 292
2:1 292
2:4 292
2:6 292
2:14-16 532
3:5 368
5:16 291, 528, 529
5:16-17 124
9:13 238

Micah
2:4 529, 530, 548
3:5 17
4:3 16, 350, 434
4:13 215
5:7 436, 535
6:5 287, 288, 520
6:6 213, 287
6:7 18, 292

Nahum
2:4 358
3:13 76

Habakkuk
2:5 22
2:6 548
2:15-16 22
3 43, 211, 219, 222, 261, 309, 313, 505, 560-61
3:2 346, 558
3:3 227, 237, 561
3:4 360
3:5 183
3:6 230
3:7 227
3:8 21, 22, 222
3:9 351, 352, 561
3:10 437
3:11 351, 352, 358
3:12 21
3:13 237, 561
3:14 226, 511

Zephaniah
2:3 354

3:3 532
3:4 363

Zechariah
9:9 546
13:8 390

Malachi
1:8 506
2:17 354

SECOND TEMPLE LITERATURE

Tobit
2:11 443

Judith
9:1 439
12–13 126, 127
12:5-9 125
12:13 440
12:15 125
12:17-20 440
13:7 439
13:15 21

Sirach (Ben Sira, Ecclessiasticus)
36:13 448

1 Maccabees
4:57 274
10:83-84 318

1 Esdras
7:6 557

Dead Sea Scrolls
1QM 12:9-10 436
4Q530 2:2 340
4Q531 17 340
4Q531 17.12 340
4QDeuteronomy[j] 40
4QSam[a] 564
4QSam[b] 363
4QSam[c] 399

WEST SEMITIC INSCRIPTIONS

Ahiqar
ll. 118-119 557

Ammonite seal (Astarte in Sidon) 572

Aramaic stele (from Egypt) 488

arrowhead inscriptions 27, 169, 204-6, 208, 228, 284, 295-97, 322, 323, 358, 367, 368, 449, 490, 492, 493, 494, 513, 528, 551, 552

Ashkelon 572

Bukan, Tell 112, 536

Deir Alla 212, 238, 351, 498, 517

Ekron, Tel 404

El-Hofra 489

Fekheriyeh, Tell 362, 430

Horvat Uzza ostracon 501, 545

Injirli 355

Izbet Sartah abecedary 284, 295, 550, 551, 554

Jerusalem seal inscription 352

Jerusalem stone inscription 348

KAI
10:8-9 111, 450
13 438
13:8 569
14:8 569
14:18 198
24:9 448
26A I 16-17 432
26A II 5-6 443
26A II 18-19 448
26A III 2-7 450
26C III 15-16 448
48:2 571
49:3 489
78:2 199
79:1 199
79:10-11 199
81:1 199, 572
85:1 199
86:1 199
87:2 199
88:1 199
94:1 199
97:1 199
102:1 199
105:1 199
117:1 569
137:1 199
175:2 199
176:2-3 199
181:5-6 21
181:7-8 240
181:15-18 355
202 353
214:16-17 104
214:21-22 104
222 A 21-24 22
222 A 31 492
222 C 3 453
222 C 8 453

223 A 9 492

Kuntillet 'Ajrud 17, 237, 353, 501, 530, 535, 544, 560, 561

Kuttamuwa 104, 424
line 5 104
lines 10-11 104

Mididi 198

Neirab 431

Nora 489

Qeiyafa, Tel 348, 349, 355, 543, 552

Rehov, Tel 349, 359

Sarepta 199

Sevilla statuette 573

Zayit, Tel, abecedary 380, 542, 543, 550

TEXTS FROM UGARIT

KTU
The Baal Cycle
1.1–1.6 162
1.1–1.2 162, 163, 164
1.1 III 1 341
1.1 III 17 452
1.1 III 18 341
1.1 IV 4 147, 452
1.1 IV 4-5 484
1.1 IV 5 460
1.1 IV 13 452
1.2 I 163-64, 182, 465
1.2 I 16 286, 501
1.2 I 19 122
1.2 I 21 439
1.2 I 22 180
1.2 I 31-32 163, 164
1.2 I 32 180
1.2 I 32-33 164
1.2 I 33 17
1.2 I 34-35 217, 382
1.2 I 38 21
1.2 I 39 122
1.2 I 40 195, 201
1.2 III 162, 168
1.2 III 12 469
1.2 III 18 452, 456, 469
1.2 III 20 169, 205
1.2 III 24 452
1.2 IV 112, 162-63, 175, 176, 182, 273, 355, 465, 536
1.2 IV 7-10 163
1.2 IV 7-27 162
1.2 IV 8-9 426, 447
1.2 IV 9 242
1.2 IV 11-15 163
1.2 IV 12-13 153
1.2 IV 13 456
1.2 IV 15-18 163
1.2 IV 17 360
1.2 IV 18-23 163
1.2 IV 18-26 242
1.2 IV 19-20 153
1.2 IV 22 242
1.2 IV 23-25 163
1.2 IV 25 242
1.2 IV 25-26 163
1.2 IV 27 163, 483
1.2 IV 28 200, 484, 204
1.3 I 6, 19, 20, 112, 162, 176-81, 431, 474
1.3 I 2-27 176-77
1.3 I 4-8 178
1.3 I 8-17 178-79, 456
1.3 I 12 475
1.3 I 13-15 181
1.3 I 18-22 177-78, 290
1.3 I 19 431
1.3 I 22 180, 190
1.3 I 22-25 180
1.3 I 22-27 179-80, 181
1.3 I 26 179
1.3 II 18, 22, 79, 162, 174, 176, 195
1.3 II 2-3 79, 354
1.3 II 3-16 171
1.3 II 4-5 177
1.3 II 5 171, 439
1.3 II 5-16 171
1.3 II 5-30 170-72
1.3 II 8 122
1.3 II 8-9 177
1.3 II 11-13 18, 172
1.3 II 12 178
1.3 II 13 178, 434
1.3 II 13-15 171, 456
1.3 II 15 352
1.3 II 15-16 131, 351
1.3 II 16 108
1.3 II 17 171
1.3 II 17-30 18, 94, 171, 172
1.3 II 18 177
1.3 II 18-21 178
1.3 II 18-22 177-78
1.3 II 19-20 22, 171, 396
1.3 II 20-22 171, 456
1.3 II 22-28 178
1.3 II 23 180
1.3 II 24 180
1.3 II 25 114, 432
1.3 II 27 434
1.3 II 27-28 171
1.3 II 29-30 22, 171, 396
1.3 II 30-35 547
1.3 II 34-35 17, 79
1.3 II 38-40 17
1.3 II 39 436, 535
1.3 II 40-41 436, 535
1.3 III 1-2 125

1.3 III 4-8 179, 357
1.3 III 5 456
1.3 III 5-7 180
1.3 III 12 286, 501
1.3 III 14 167
1.3 III 30-31 456
1.3 III 32–IV 4 425
1.3 III 33 107
1.3 III 33-35 123
1.3 III 35 107
1.3 III 38-47 174
1.3 III 43-46 203
1.3 III 45-46 125
1.3 IV 2-3 153
1.3 IV 5 122
1.3 IV 7-8 167
1.3 IV 20 456
1.3 IV 31-32 431
1.3 IV 38 549
1.3 IV 38-40 180
1.3 IV 43-44 436
1.3 IV 48-52 474
1.3 V 470
1.3 V 3-4 474
1.3 V 4-5 117
1.3 V 4-8 115
1.3 V 15 122
1.3 V 17-18 546
1.3 V 19-25 115
1.3 V 27-29 115
1.3 V 28-29 115
1.3 V 32-33 168
1.3 V 35-44 474
1.3 VI 105
1.3 VI 12 286, 501
1.3 VI 13 108
1.3 VI 14 341
1.3 VI 15-16 108
1.3 VI 17-18 549
1.3 VI 25 167
1.4 I 4-18 474
1.4 I 19-20 431
1.4 I 26-28 549
1.4 II 5-7 125
1.4 II 3-16 426
1.4 II 12-16 426
1.4 II 16-20 123
1.4 II 16-26 425
1.4 II 17 107
1.4 II 19 107-8
1.4 II 24-26 125
1.4 III 4-7 546
1.4 III 9-12 546
1.4 III 14 45
1.4 III 18-21 475
1.4 III 26-28 190
1.4 III 42 483
1.4 IV 2-7 122
1.4 IV 7 472
1.4 IV 12 472
1.4 IV 20-26 115
1.4 IV 27 439
1.4 IV 40-47 474
1.4 IV 43-44 168
1.4 IV 47-57 474
1.4 IV 58 452
1.4 IV 59-62 222
1.4 IV 62–V 1 474
1.4 V 179
1.4 V 5 456
1.4 V 9 358, 481
1.4 V 42-43 34, 421, 556, 559
1.4 V 43 122
1.4 V 45-46 505
1.4 V 58 452
1.4 V 63 452
1.4 VI 1 452
1.4 VI 14 452
1.4 VI 24-32 159
1.4 VI 42-43 482-83
1.4 VI 40-43 150
1.4 VI 41 432
1.4 VI 58 483
1.4 VII 7-13 174
1.4 VII 7-14 175
1.4 VII 14 452
1.4 VII 27 180
1.4 VII 37 452
1.4 VII 39 190
1.4 VII 45 45
1.4 VII 47 164, 167
1.4 VII 49 481, 485
1.4 VII 53-56 17, 224
1.4 VIII 558
1.4 VIII–1.6 162, 164
1.4 VIII 13 113
1.4 VIII 16 45
1.4 VIII 17 467
1.4 VIII 20 467
1.4 VIII 21-24 546
1.4 VIII 30 45
1.4 VIII 31 286, 501
1.4 VIII 32 164, 167
1.4 VIII 34-35 167
1.4 VIII 49 34
1.5 I 1 45
1.5 I 8 164, 167
1.5 I 11 452
1.5 I 14 164, 167, 197
1.5 I 14-16 466
1.5 II 2-3 166
1.5 II 6-7 499
1.5 II 9 164, 167, 286, 501
1.5 II 10-11 167
1.5 II 16 113
1.5 II 18 167
1.5 IV 18-21 107
1.5 IV 19-22 427
1.5 IV 21 427
1.5 V 164
1.5 V 6-9 465
1.5 V 19-22 414
1.5 V 23 105
1.5 V 25 456
1.5 VI 164, 437
1.5 VI 3-5 165
1.5 VI 5-7 164-65, 166
1.5 VI 5-10 164
1.5 VI 6-11 167
1.5 VI 8-10 135, 165-66, 270
1.5 VI 11-25 425
1.5 VI 17-18 572

1.5 VI 24 452
1.5 VI 30-31 270
1.6 I 162, 168, 169, 437, 469
1.6 I 8-31 19
1.6 I 15-29 172-73
1.6 I 19 173
1.6 I 20 173
1.6 I 22 173
1.6 I 24 173
1.6 I 26 173
1.6 I 49 452
1.6 I 50-52 168
1.6 I 51 16
1.6 I 52 17
1.6 I 53 180
1.6 I 53-61 168
1.6 I 56-62 17
1.6 I 61 452
1.6 II 162, 168
1.6 II 15-23 166
1.6 II 15-17 166
1.6 II 17-19 166
1.6 II 23 467
1.6 II 24-25 546
1.6 II 28-31 174
1.6 II 35-37 19, 118
1.6 III 6-7 238
1.6 III 12-13 238
1.6 III 19 456
1.6 V 8-9 437
1.6 V 9 361
1.6 V 20-21 21
1.6 V 23 452
1.6 VI 12 180
1.6 VI 14 180
1.6 VI 15 180
1.6 VI 16 180
1.6 VI 16-20 21, 409, 525
1.6 VI 16-22 162, 166-67
1.6 VI 17 180
1.6 VI 18 180
1.6 VI 19 428
1.6 VI 22-23 159
1.6 VI 22-35 168
1.6 VI 28 153, 456
1.6 VI 31 164, 167
1.6 VI 45-47 139-40
1.6 VI 46-47 336, 446
1.6 VI 49-50 449
1.6 VI 54-55 420
1.6 VI 54-58 34
1.6 VI 54-59 182
1.8 II 6-9 224
1.8 II 9 508
1.10 470
1.10 II 195
1.10 II 6 351
1.10 II 10-12 117
1.10 II 14-15 180
1.10 III 13-14 448
1.10 III 33-37 105
1.11 470
1.12 I 25-29 103
1.12 I 34-41 107
1.12 II 21-25 190
1.12 II 44-45 437
1.12 II 52-55 107
1.12 II 53 483
1.12 II 53-55 534
1.12 II 59 544
1.13 23, 171-72
1.13.3-5 172
1.13.3-7 18, 171-72
1.13.5-7 172

Kirta

1.14 I 28-30 122
1.14 I 39-40 549
1.14 I 41-43 221
1.14 II 9-11 125, 354
1.14 II 13-26 352
1.14 II 32 368
1.14 II 39-50 360
1.14 II 46 513
1.14 III 2-4 159
1.14 III 9 544
1.14 III 10-12 159
1.14 III 38 483
1.14 III 41-42 201
1.14 III 52-54 125, 354
1.14 III 55–IV 8 352
1.14 IV 17-18 549
1.14 IV 21-28 360
1.14 IV 25 513
1.14 IV 34-43 17
1.14 IV 55 190
1.14 V 1 544
1.14 V 6 426
1.14 VI 26-28 201
1.15 III 2-4 147, 156, 566
1.15 III 13-15 147, 156, 566
1.15 III 22 437
1.15 IV 7 270, 529
1.15 IV 18 270, 529
1.15 IV 28 110
1.15 V 20 110
1.16 I 3-5 357
1.16 I 14-15 109
1.16 I 17-18 110, 113
1.16 I 17-19 357
1.16 I 24-25 110
1.16 I 26-27 434
1.16 I 31-45 357
1.16 I 43 548
1.16 I 53 439
1.16 I 54 108
1.16 II 40 113
1.16 II 40-42 357
1.16 IV 9 452
1.16 VI 22-25 448
1.16 VI 23-24 153
1.16 VI 26 485
1.16 VI 28 286, 501
1.16 VI 32 432
1.16 VI 34 469
1.16 VI 44 432
1.16 VI 50 108
1.16 VI 55-57 198

Aqhat

1.17 101, 420, 425

1.17 I 101-2, 127, 137
1.17 I-II 100, 105
1.17 I 1-15 101, 102, 423
1.17 I 2 101, 317
1.17 I 15-16 426
1.17 I 15-33 102
1.17 I 16 423
1.17 I 16–II 23 100
1.17 I 17 101, 127, 317
1.17 I 18 101, 317
1.17 I 23-24 125
1.17 I 28 453
1.17 I 28-29 203
1.17 I 35 101, 127, 137, 317
1.17 I 36 101, 317
1.17 I 36-37 103
1.17 I 37 127, 137, 317
1.17 I 42 101, 137, 317
1.17 I 46 453
1.17 I 47 203
1.17 II 16, 104-5
1.17 II 1-8 104-5
1.17 II 2-3 203
1.17 II 8-23 105
1.17 II 13 456
1.17 II 14 103
1.17 II 18-19 203
1.17 II 24 499
1.17 II 24-25 105
1.17 II 26-27 105
1.17 II 27 101
1.17 II 27-40 105
1.17 II 28 101-2, 127, 137, 317
1.17 II 39 426
1.17 II 41-46 105
1.17 III 101
1.17 III-IV 105
1.17 IV 101
1.17 V 16, 100, 105-7, 129, 424
1.17 V 2-3 105
1.17 V 3-4 105
1.17 V 4 101
1.17 V 4-5 102, 317
1.17 V 4-8 105
1.17 V 4-13 119
1.17 V 5 127, 137
1.17 V 7 518
1.17 V 8 469
1.17 V 9 122, 180
1.17 V 9-13 106
1.17 V 12-13 447
1.17 V 14 102, 127, 137, 317
1.17 V 16 426
1.17 V 17 103
1.17 V 17-19 424
1.17 V 23 103
1.17 V 31 108
1.17 V 33-34 102, 317
1.17 V 34 127, 137
1.17 V 35-38 131
1.17 V 37 119
1.17 V 37-38 424
1.17 V 37-39 106, 129
1.17 V 39 427
1.17 V-VI 16
1.17 VI–18 IV 23, 101
1.17 VI 21, 107-15, 117, 127, 130, 163, 174, 558
1.17 VI 1-2 107
1.17 VI 1-4 107
1.17 VI 1-6 130
1.17 VI 3-9 107
1.17 VI 4-6 107
1.17 VI 4-7 108
1.17 VI 6-8 107
1.17 VI 6-9 107
1.17 VI 7-8 427
1.17 VI 8-9 107
1.17 VI 8-10 107
1.17 VI 9-10 107
1.17 VI 10-11 107
1.17 VI 11 358
1.17 VI 13 107, 130
1.17 VI 13-14 108
1.17 VI 13-18 107
1.17 VI 13-25 106
1.17 VI 15-16 108
1.17 VI 15-19 108
1.17 VI 17 134
1.17 VI 17-19 130
1.17 VI 20 127, 128, 452
1.17 VI 20-23 105
1.17 VI 20-25 108
1.17 VI 25-29 109
1.17 VI 26 127, 128, 134, 429
1.17 VI 26-33 106
1.17 VI 27 111
1.17 VI 28-29 111
1.17 VI 30 112
1.17 VI 30-33 109, 112
1.17 VI 32 111, 429
1.17 VI 33 127, 128, 452
1.17 VI 33-38 113
1.17 VI 33-39 193
1.17 VI 33-41 113
1.17 VI 34-35 113
1.17 VI 35-36 102, 113
1.17 VI 36-37 113
1.17 VI 38 102, 110, 113, 359
1.17 VI 38-39 110
1.17 VI 39 431
1.17 VI 39-41 21, 113, 174, 274
1.17 VI 40 174
1.17 VI 41 114
1.17 VI 42 117, 120, 127, 129
1.17 VI 42-43 133
1.17 VI 42-45 114, 133
1.17 VI 43-45 115
1.17 VI 44 432
1.17 VI 44-45 134
1.17 VI 45 134
1.17 VI 46 117
1.17 VI 46-49 115
1.17 VI 46–1.18 I 19 115, 134
1.17 VI 51 127, 129
1.17 VI 52 102, 317
1.18 101, 115-16
1.18 I 161, 193, 425
1.18 I 7-11 115
1.18 I 15 452
1.18 I 15-16 115

1.18 I 17-19 115
1.18 I 19 456
1.18 I 20-34 116
1.18 I 20-22 116
1.18 I 21 127, 129
1.18 I 22 114
1.18 I 22-23 116
1.18 I 23-31 134
1.18 I 24 116, 129, 132, 175, 193, 433
1.18 I 27 134, 175, 193
1.18 I 29 16, 134, 175, 193, 326, 350
1.18 I 30-31 116, 193
1.18 II 101, 135, 425
1.18 III 101, 135, 425
1.18 IV 107, 114, 116, 117-18, 135, 193, 425
1.18 IV 5-6 117
1.18 IV 5-37 117
1.18 IV 6-11 117
1.18 IV 7-8 116-17
1.18 IV 11 452
1.18 IV 11-15 117
1.18 IV 12-13 118
1.18 IV 14 127, 134, 135
1.18 IV 16-27 118
1.18 IV 17-18 118, 125
1.18 IV 17-27 117
1.18 IV 21-26 111
1.18 IV 22 466
1.18 IV 25 103, 125
1.18 IV 26-27 111
1.18 IV 27-29 125
1.18 IV 27-37 118
1.18 IV 33-37 135
1.18 IV 36 103, 125
1.18 IV 36-37 123
1.18 IV 38 135
1.18 IV 39 118, 135
1.18 IV 40 135
1.18 IV 40-41 118, 119, 135
1.18 IV 40-42 118
1.18 IV 42 135
1.19 I 119-22
1.19 I 1 421
1.19 I 1-6 123
1.19 I 1-19 119
1.19 I 2 119
1.19 I 3-38 114
1.19 I 4 119
1.19 I 13-16 119
1.19 I 15-16 111
1.19 I 17 119
1.19 I 18-19 119
1.19 I 19-20 119
1.19 I 19-25 128
1.19 I 19-37 119
1.19 I 20 102, 127, 129, 137, 317
1.19 I 28-29 122
1.19 I 29-30 124
1.19 I 29-31 119
1.19 I 32-33 120, 122
1.19 I 34 425
1.19 I 34-35 115, 119, 120
1.19 I 36-37 102, 120, 121, 122, 317
1.19 I 37 127, 129, 137
1.19 I 38-39 102, 121, 317
1.19 I 38-48 120
1.19 I 39 121, 137
1.19 I 40-46 121
1.19 I 42-46 121
1.19 I 44-45 535
1.19 I 44-46 120, 272, 536
1.19 I 45-46 120
1.19 I 46-48 121, 122
1.19 I 47 102, 137, 317
1.19 I 48 127, 129
1.19 II 122-23
1.19 II 1-3 122
1.19 II 1-5 122
1.19 II 3 230
1.19 II 5-7 122
1.19 II 7 230
1.19 II 8-10 122
1.19 II 12 122
1.19 II 13 180
1.19 II 12-25 122
1.19 II 17-18 121
1.19 II 18 127
1.19 II 19-20 119
1.19 II 26-27 122
1.19 II 27-28 122
1.19 II 27-36 122
1.19 II 27-44 121
1.19 II 28-29 122
1.19 II 31-32 122
1.19 II 32-34 122
1.19 II 34-36 122
1.19 II 37 122, 123
1.19 II 37-38 123
1.19 II 37-39 123
1.19 II 38 103, 123, 125
1.19 II 41 102, 137, 317
1.19 II 41-42 102
1.19 II 41-44 123
1.19 II 42 125, 127
1.19 II 44-47 123
1.19 II 44-49 123, 425
1.19 II 46 108
1.19 II 48 123, 129
1.19 II 56-57 123
1.19 II 57 123
1.19 III 123-24
1.19 III 1-28 123
1.19 III 1-38 114
1.19 III 19 501
1.19 III 28-39 123
1.19 III 33 180
1.19 III 39-40 123
1.19 III 40-41 123
1.19 III 40–IV 17 160
1.19 III 41 438
1.19 III 45–IV 7 123
1.19 III 47 124, 127
1.19 III 48 124
1.19 III 49 124
1.19 III 53 127
1.19 III 53-54 124
1.19 III 56 124
1.19 IV 17, 115, 124-26
1.19 IV 4 127

1.19 IV 7 124
1.19 IV 8-17 124
1.19 IV 9-17 120
1.19 IV 11-12 129
1.19 IV 12 127
1.19 IV 13 102, 137, 317
1.19 IV 15-16 129
1.19 IV 16 127
1.19 IV 17 102, 137, 317
1.19 IV 17-18 437
1.19 IV 17-25 124
1.19 IV 17-26 124
1.19 IV 18 102, 137, 317
1.19 IV 19 127, 129
1.19 IV 22-25 124
1.19 IV 23 559
1.19 IV 23-24 421
1.19 IV 26-27 139, 449
1.19 IV 28 124
1.19 IV 28-61 124
1.19 IV 29-31 124
1.19 IV 29-35 124-25
1.19 IV 32-33 102, 241
1.19 IV 34-35 125, 127
1.19 IV 35 452
1.19 IV 36 102, 103, 137, 317, 424
1.19 IV 36-38 125
1.19 IV 39 125
1.19 IV 39-40 125, 127
1.19 IV 40-41 125
1.19 IV 41-43 125, 354
1.19 IV 42 409
1.19 IV 43 129
1.19 IV 43-46 115, 125, 127, 136
1.19 IV 44-48 124
1.19 IV 46-61 118, 126
1.19 IV 50-51 126
1.19 IV 51 126, 434
1.19 IV 52 452
1.19 IV 52-54 126
1.19 IV 53-54 126
1.19 IV 54-56 440
1.19 IV 55 126
1.19 IV 56 452
1.19 IV 57 126
1.19 IV 58-59 126
1.19 IV 59-60 126
1.19 IV 60-61 127
1.19 IV 61 127, 128
1.19 IV 62 421
1.19 IV 63 34

The Rephaim Texts

1.20–1.22 138, 140-53, 420, 450, 559
1.20 142-45
1.20 I 142-43
1.20 I 1-2 142-43, 446
1.20 I 3 143
1.20 I 4 143
1.20 I 4-5 143
1.20 I 5 143
1.20 I 8-11 143
1.20 II 143-45
1.20 II 1 144
1.20 II 1-2 446
1.20 II 1-4 144
1.20 II 1-7 153
1.20 II 5-7 145
1.20 II 6-7 446
1.20 II 7 141, 452
1.20 II 8 141
1.20 II 8-9 145, 446
1.20 II 8-11 145
1.20 II 10-11 145
1.20 II 11 143, 145
1.21 I 146
1.21 II 146-48
1.21 II 1-3 153
1.21 II 3 144
1.21 II 3-4 147, 153, 446
1.21 II 7-8 153
1.21 II 8 147
1.21 II 11-12 147, 446
1.22 148-53
1.22 I 148-51
1.22 I 1 153
1.22 I 1-7 452
1.22 I 2-3 150
1.22 I 3 452
1.22 I 4-6 150
1.22 I 4-10 150
1.22 I 6-7 141, 150
1.22 I 8 141, 452
1.22 I 8-9 141, 150, 153
1.22 I 9 142
1.22 I 9-10 118, 150, 153, 456
1.22 I 9-12 452
1.22 I 10 138, 157
1.22 I 10-11 485
1.22 I 10-14 150
1.22 I 12 432
1.22 I 14-20 150
1.22 I 17 455
1.22 I 17-20 151
1.22 I 20 141, 310
1.22 I 21-26 143
1.22 I 24 435
1.22 I 24-25 150
1.22 I 25 426
1.22 I 26 141
1.22 II 151-53
1.22 II 2 141
1.22 II 2-4 153
1.22 II 3-4 153
1.22 II 5 147
1.22 II 5-6 446
1.22 II 5-11 153
1.22 II 7 141
1.22 II 7-8 150, 153
1.22 II 8 141, 142, 452
1.22 II 8-11 153
1.22 II 10-11 446
1.22 II 11 147
1.22 II 12 150, 153
1.22 II 13-14 446
1.22 II 15 143, 153
1.22 II 16 352
1.22 II 17-18 153
1.22 II 18-20 153, 446
1.22 II 18-26 153
1.22 II 20 144
1.22 II 20-21 446

1.22 II 20-26 153
1.22 II 25-26 446

The Rituals and Myths of the Goodly Gods

1.23 434, 452, 489
1.23.6 427, 451
1.23.8 448
1.23.10 432
1.23.14 241
1.23.51-52 105
1.23.52 105, 126
1.23.59 105, 126
1.23.66-67 437
1.23.71-76 451

Nikkal wa-Ib

1.24 169, 436
1.24.1 492
1.24.25-26 474
1.24.28-30 169
1.24.30 205
1.24.30-32 169
1.24.32-37 169
1.24.40 492

Rituals and Other Religious Texts

1.39.7 488
1.40 159, 463
1.40.7 45
1.40.8 45
1.40.18 472
1.40.26 472
1.40.29 573
1.40.35 374, 472
1.40.37 573
1.41 143
1.41.50 143
1.41.50-55 143
1.43.24 452
1.46.11 432
1.47.25 186
1.48.7 368
1.48.17 479
1.50.1 186
1.50.3 186
1.50.4 186
1.54.2-3 573
1.81.18 186
1.81.19 186
1.86 195
1.86.1 195
1.86.3 196
1.86.6 195
1.87 143
1.91 202, 490
1.91.10 186, 193, 571
1.91.10-11 202
1.91.15 574
1.92 188-90, 193, 194, 203, 481
1.92.2-3 189
1.92.4 189
1.92.5 189
1.92.6-13 189
1.92.7 352
1.92.12 352
1.92.14 189, 202
1.92.15 202
1.92.15-16 189, 192
1.92.20 189-90
1.92.20-25 189
1.92.22-23 190
1.92.24-25 190
1.92.26 197
1.92.26-27 189, 190
1.92.27 190, 201
1.92.31-32 190
1.92.32 197
1.92.33 197
1.92.33-37 190
1.100.6 439
1.100.20 186, 200, 201
1.100.34 201
1.100.35 201
1.100.41 317, 447, 566
1.100.46 341
1.100.77-79 200-201
1.100.78 186, 201, 559
1.101 179
1.101.7-8 481
1.101.15-18 357
1.103 + 1.145 360
1.106.15-17 177
1.106.16 548
1.107.32 460
1.107.39 186, 201
1.107.40 441
1.107.42 317, 447, 566
1.107.44 460

Feast of Rp'u

1.108 102, 138-40, 142, 150, 318, 321, 448, 452
1.108.1 138, 157, 448, 454
1.108.1-2 138, 153, 317, 447
1.108.1-5 138-40, 147
1.108.1-7 124
1.108.2-3 310, 567
1.108.3 469
1.108.4 139
1.108.5 139
1.108.6 173
1.108.6-10 140
1.108.8-9 117
1.108.11-14 140
1.108.15 140
1.108.18 140
1.108.18-27 448
1.108.19 140
1.108.20 428
1.108.21 140
1.108.22 140
1.108.23-27 140
1.108.26-27 111
1.109.4 432
1.111.15-22 478
1.111.17-18 571
1.111.20 436
1.112.13 186
1.113 139, 450
1.113.15 475

El's marzeah

1.114 103, 190-93, 194, 195, 200, 201, 203
1.114.1-2 192

1.114.1-24 559
1.114.1-28 559
1.114.2-3 192
1.114.4 189
1.114.9 193, 200
1.114.9-11 192
1.114.10-11 201
1.114.14 200
1.114.15 147, 452
1.114.16 192
1.114.17-28 192
1.114.22-23 193, 200
1.114.23-28 192-93
1.114.26 193, 200
1.114.26-27 193
1.114.27 426
1.114.28 446
1.114.29-31 559
1.115.6-8 474
1.118.9-10 186
1.118.24 186

Instructions for prayer to Baal

1.119.26-36 160
1.119.28-34 463
1.119.34 121
1.123.2 18, 131, 303, 536
1.124 156
1.124.3 353
1.124.12 353
1.127.8 464
1.127.32 180
1.132 181
1.132.1-3 181
1.133.4 197
1.148.1 156, 197
1.148.16 197
1.148.18 186, 193, 571
1.148.18-22 490
1.148.21 436, 535

Royal funerary ritual

1.161 34, 109, 138, 148, 154-60, 310, 457-59, 463
1.161.1 156, 190, 447, 541
1.161.2 157
1.161.2-3 156, 157, 158
1.161.2-12 156
1.161.4-5 156, 447
1.161.4-7 156, 157, 319
1.161.6-7 157
1.161.7 157, 454
1.161.8 157, 158
1.161.8-10 156, 157
1.161.9 157
1.161.9-10 158
1.161.11-12 157
1.161.13-16 158
1.161.13-17 158
1.161.17 158
1.161.18-26 159
1.161.20 452
1.161.20-21 110
1.161.23-24 157
1.161.27-30 159
1.161.27-31 156
1.161.27-34 159
1.161.31-33 463
1.161.31-34 158, 159
1.162.1 156
1.163.5 475
1.166 447
1.166.9 447
1.166.13 447, 448
1.169.1 441
1.169.5-6 483
1.169.9-11 449
1.169.10 450
1.170.2 460
1.170.3 428
1.170.8 189

Letters

2.7.9 111
2.10.11-13 167, 360
2.11.1 462
2.11.13 429
2.13.2 462
2.13.5 462
2.13.6 462
2.13.11 462
2.15.3 422
2.15.7 499
2.15.8 506
2.15.10 499
2.16.2 462
2.16.6 462
2.16.18 462
2.23.2 110
2.23.4 110
2.23.6 110
2.30.1 462
2.30.4 462
2.30.5 462
2.30.9 462
2.30.21 462
2.33.15 429
2.33.22 110
2.33.26 110
2.33.31 110
2.33.34 467
2.34.2 462
2.34.6 462
2.34.8 462
2.34.32-33 455
2.36 225
2.36.16 225
2.36.17 225
2.39.11 110
2.39.13 110
2.39.19 110
2.39.33-35 499
2.41.16 428
2.41.19 429
2.42 449
2.42.6-9 186
2.42.9 449
2.42.24 186, 428
2.42.25 186
2.42.26 186
2.61 356
2.61.6 356
2.70 554
2.70.16 527
2.72.1 462

2.72.2 462
2.72.5 462
2.72.15 462
2.72.20 506
2.72.31 462
2.72.33 462
2.80.1 462
2.82.20 499

Legal texts
3.1.15 475
3.9 147, 554
3.9.1 452
3.9.1-4 453
3.9.13 452

Administrative texts
4.63 III 38 205, 513
4.63 IV 13 205
4.69 II 9 460
4.69 VI 29 460
4.75 V 21 422, 446, 566
4.99.6 368
4.102.1 441
4.102.3 128
4.102.5 441
4.102.8 441
4.102.16 128
4.102.18 128
4.102.19 128
4.102.20 128
4.102.23 128
4.116.7 200, 205
4.126.25 368
4.127.7 190
4.130.10 422, 446, 566
4.141 I 1 189
4.141 I 19 337
4.141 III 16 189
4.141 III 16-17 189
4.141 III 17 189
4.168.3-4 185
4.172.6 509
4.182.9 108
4.182.26 108
4.182.55 186, 193, 571
4.182.58 186, 193, 571
4.182.59 499
4.219.1 202
4.219.2 185
4.219.2-3 202
4.245 I 1 186
4.245 I 11 186
4.262.2 175
4.266 225
4.266.5 509
4.270.11 190
4.275.4 190
4.279.1 435
4.307.6 494
4.309.17 337
4.310.4 422, 566
4.320.4 494
4.335.15 422, 566
4.336 225
4.339.14 286, 501
4.349.1 128
4.360.3 460
4.366.13 205
4.366.14 205
4.382.23-24 448
4.385.9 190
4.388 225
4.399.8 452
4.607.32 460
4.612.6 157
4.617.35 565
4.623.8 565
4.642.4-7 452
4.682.8 200, 205
4.730.6 337
4.760.5 460
4.767 485
4.785.12 422, 566
4.785.18 565
4.790.16 447

Scribal texts
5.9 I 2-6 111
5.9 I 5 549
5.9 I 7-16 428
5.9. I 9-15 440
5.10.2 111, 429
5.10.3 462
5.11.4 111, 429

Others
6.25.2 544
6.30.1 111
6.62 202
7.75.1 475
9.432.34 190

Ras Shamra (RS), texts and objects
5.031 373
5.032 32
15.70 453
15.70.3-18 453
15.88 453
16.386 509
17.87.21-23 185
17.352 186, 187
17.352.7 187
17.352.12 185, 193
18.01 453, 485
19.101.7 573
20.033.19 456
20.235.17-18 185
92.2016 479
94.2018 460
94.2050 + 94.2092.23 565
94.2050 + 94.2092.45 460
94.2064.50 422
94.2275 II 7 205, 513
94.2284.12 424
94.2284.32 424
94.2290.11 205, 513
94.2382.11′ 494
94.2519.5 474
94.2519.17 474
94.5002 460
94.5018 460
96.2020.27 460
98.02 202, 203-6, 208, 491-92
98.02.1 204

98.02.1-2 204
98.02.1-3 204
98.02.1-5 204
98.02.2 204, 205
98.02.3 203, 204, 207
98.02.4 204
98.02.4-5 204, 205
98.02.5 204
99.1072.32 157

Tiryns inscription (KTU, third edition, 6.104) 342

Ugaritica V polyglot 115, 436-37, 452

MESOPOTAMIAN SOURCES

Agushaya 93

Amarna letters (EA)
54 475
55 475
63:3 205
64:3 205
65:3 205
84:13 475
137 226
147 444

'Ana 323

Bilgames and the Netherworld
ll. 244-247 86

Descent of Ishtar to the Underworld 433

Emar
17.1 187
17.12 187
17.41 187
32.21 187
42 187
43 187
43.1 187
45 187
52 187
256.33 198
265.11 187
279.5 187
336.105 187
369.63-64 413
370 187
370.20 196
373 437
373.12 196
373.124 448
378.41 448
379.1 196
380.2 196
382.1 196
446 197
446.87-90 194
446.91-94 194
452.21 194
460 187, 196
460.1 196
460.6 196
460.9 196
472.62 447
473.15 447
495.3 196
767 394
Westenholz 30.1 196

Enlil and Ninlil 433

Enuma Elish
I.54 86
II.1-5 86
II.16-17 361
II.92 407
II.116 407
II.143-144 407
III.16-17 361
III.74-75 361
III.79-80 361
III.132 86
IV.86 167
IV.112 368
V 428
VII.147 304, 537

Enuma Anu Enlil
44.24 536
46 513

Erra and Ishum
I:5 358
I:26 362
I:46 407
I:49-51 360
I:50 407
I:51 94
III:20-21 356
III:168 358
IV:56 115
IV:94 368
V:19 360

Epic of Zimri-Lim 335, 353

Esarhaddon Monument A 536

Esarhaddon Vassal Treaties 487-88

Gilgamesh Emar fragment
2 118

Gilgamesh Old Babylonian version (OB)
II i 1 84
II i 1-35 340
II i 8-9 93
II i 17 57
II i 18 55
II i 22 86
II i 32-35 83
II i 35 85

II i 54 55
II ii 2 92
II ii 43 388
II ii 44 84
II ii 46-49 88
II ii 48 56
II iii 110 57
II v 198 89
III i 18 86
III i 18-19 86
III i 24-25 86
III iii 106 388
III iii 107 55
III iii 112-16 55
III iii 119 388
III iii 129 388
III iii 140 388
III iii 161 388

Gilgamesh
Old Babylonian Harmal-1
obv. 3 388
rev. 10 388
rev. 15 340

Old Babylonian Harmal-2
obv. 48 388

Old Babylonian IM (Baghdad)
17-18 456

Old Babylonian Ischali
obv.11′ 388
obv. 15′ 388
rev. 38′ 456

Old Babylonian Meissner (= Sippar)
i 8′ 56
ii 0′-5′ 411
ii 2′ 85, 92, 94

Old Babylonian Nippur
obv. 1 388
obv. 8 388
obv. 9 388

Old Babylonian Schøyen 1
obv. 6′ 388

Old Babylonian Schøyen 2
obv. 4 388
obv. 33 388
obv. 84 388

Gilgamesh Standard Babylonian Version (SBV)
I.1-28 393
I.2 58
I.4 58
I.6 58
I.18-23 58
I.29 81, 134, 393
I.35-36 388
I.37 81
I.41 57
I.48 54
I.61 87
I.61-62 81
I.62 81
I.72 77
I.75 81
I.76 77, 89
1.82 53
I.90 81
I.90-93 407
I.91 77, 89
I.94-104 53
I.98 53
I.105 56
I.106 87
I.150-152 83
I.164 81
I.181 81
I.186 84
I.191-195 88
I.194 56
I.202 56
I.211 81, 134
I.218 134
I.221 334
I.234-239 81
I.236 81
I.237 81
I.238 134
I.240 334
I.245 84
I.245-293 340
I.256 83
I.258 388
I.266 388
I.267 83
I.273 413
I.283-284 83
I.285 53, 57, 388
I.288-289 83
I.290 388
I.300 88
II.35 57
II.113 89
II.176 56
II.248 84
II.260 442
II.287-301 xii
II.289 89
III.23-115 75
III.56-58 406
III.74-79 406
III.120-127 75
III.125 89
IV 56
IV.1-2 56
IV.120-121 56
IV.163-164 56
IV.248 xii, 23
V.6 456
V.55 84
V.145 89
VI 388
VI.150 54
VI.158 390
VI.160-175 xii
VI.165 388
VI.171 77
VI.172 89
VI.174 89

VI.174-175 549
VI.180 89
VII.1 71
VII.85-89 71
VII.41 56
VII.139-140 54
VII.146-147 56
VII.165-210 71
VII.255-267 54, 71-72
VIII.3-56 xii
VIII.39 438
VIII.44-45 78, 413, 534
VIII.46 85
VIII.48 83
VIII.58-59 86
VIII.60-61 86
VIII.62-64 438
VIII.90-91 56
VIII.137 53
IX-X 392
IX.2 56
IX.3 57
IX.15 84-85
IX.51 54
X.7 54
X.29-52 xii
X.45 56
X.55 85, 92, 94
X.55-57 411
X.56 85, 92, 94
X.58 56
X.68-69 85, 92, 94
X.93 5
X.112-148 xii
X.132-133 278
X.132-134 411
X.135 58
X.227 391
X.232-234 411
X.233-234 278
X.235 56
X.245-246 278
X.259-260 56
X.268 54
XI 56
XI.3-4 57
XI.128 56
XI.213 89
XI.253-258 57
XI.263-270 57
XI.301-302 56
XI.319-320 56
XI.323-328 58
XII 392
XII.88 86
XII.96-97 86

Hazor tablet 494

Lion and the She-Goat, The 490

Mari (ARM)
I 76 27 557
XI 68 462
XII 141 462
XII 146 462
XII 242 462
XXI 112 12 462
XXIV 6 38′ 462
XXIV 6 40′ 462
XXV 382 462
XXVI 24 352

Lugale
IV 1 94

Tikulti-Ninurta Epic
ii 4 93
iv 20 93

EGYPTIAN SOURCES

Amarna warrior inscription 31, 179, 474

Astarte and the Sea 487

demotic incantations 195, 197, 485

Harris magical papyrus 473

Papyrus Anastasi
I 273
I,23.4 226
VI 228

Beit el-Wali relief inscription 469

Beth-Shean hieratic inscription 426

Chester Beatty VII verso 470

Destruction of Mankind 22-23, 362, 363

Papyrus Amherst 63 352, 476, 570

Sinuhe 167, 241, 468, 518

Tale of the Two Brothers 76, 396, 443

Tell el-Borg stele 199

Winchester plaque 205

AEGEAN/GREEK SOURCES

Aeschylus
Myrmidons 79

Cypro-Minoan inscriptions 341-42

Cyprus lead bullet inscription 77

Homeric Hymn to Apollo 230

Homer
Iliad
1.1 525
1.4-5 435
1.7 59
1.8-32 63
1.8-412 69
1.84 270
1.91 64
1.148 270
1.178-181 395
1.215 270
1.131 59
1.179 59
1.194-195 74
1.244 64
1.345 60, 63
1.357-358 74
1.412 64
1.488-492 60
1.489 270
1.673-674 81
2.161 403
2.177 403
2.212 76
2.225-229 77
2.279 69
2.235-236 76
2.484-493 260
2.589-590 403
2.761 260
2.872 77
3.37-38 74
3.84-94 403
3.154-160 403
3.161-242 78
3.189 77
3.206 69
3.301 77
3.374-376 69
3.426-436 78
3.438 69
3.457 69
4.19 403
4.75 230
4.127 260
4.146 260
4.150 69
4.174 403
4.197 403
4.207 403
4.415-416 403
4.439 68
4.450-451 72
4.825-834 68
5.3 403
5.51 350
5.35 68
5.181-183 536
5.273 403
5.299 274, 537
5.330-351 403
5.348-351 74
5.426-430 74
5.592 74
5.736-737 74
5.843 398
6.7 398
6.186 77
6.230-235 400
6.454-455 77
6.465 77
7.17-42 68
7.83 536
7.89-91 398
7.96 77
7.96-100 76
7.104 260
7.165-166 72
7.235-236 77
7.236 275
7.256 274
7.350-351 403
7.399-411 403
7.451-453 403
8.64-65 72
8.163 77
8.164-166 77
8.205 69
8.236-237 403
8.291 77
8.387 74
9 20, 178
9.129 77
9.131-134 69, 177
9.139 77
9.185-192 139, 276
9.190 60
9.273-274 69
9.302 396
9.308-429 xiii
9.339 69, 403
9.413 403
9.415 403
9.485 59
9.494 59
9.497 59
9.603 396
9.632 59
9.663-668 77, 79
10.112 396
10.212 403
10.243 396
10.297 274, 537
10.297-298 72
10.484 72
10.515-516 68
11 72
11.58 396
11.67-71 417
11.113 532
11.129 274, 537
11.140 396
11.173 274
11.218 260
11.239 537
11.288 398
11.383 532
11.389-390 408
11.454 356
11.612-848 60
11.644 396

11.785 396
11.786-787 60
11.838 60
12.40-50 532
12.42 274
12.127 72
12.176 260
12.292-293 274
12.293 532
12.299-308 532
12.307 396
12.307-330 72
12.344-370 72
13.291 93
13.603 260
15.282 398
15.441 16
15.610-614 403
15.715 72
16.20 260
16.33 59
16.84 403
16.129 273
16.204 59
16.255 356
16.278-283 273
16.584 260
16.692-693 260
16.744 260
16.752 532
16.754 260
16.756 532
16.787 260
16.798-799 273
16.812 260
16.818-822 71
16.818-828 273
16.843 260, 525
17.16 403
17.20-23 532
17.80 398
17.131 403
17.228 93
17.232 403
17.251 403
17.279-280 81
17.285-287 403
17.307 398
17.321-322 403
17.679 260
17.702 260
17.719 398
18.10 398
18.80-81 60
18.81 63
18.85-86 74
18.94-96 61
18.98 60
18.107-111 395
18.111-113 397
18.121 403
18.130-133 297
18.163 408
18.368-369 74
19 279
19.3-4 74
19.15-16 61
19.35-36 397
19.75 397
19.279 59
19.280 77, 407
19.282-301 408
19.282-302 78
19.287-300 19
19.315-337 280
19.325 403
20.251-252 408
20.252-253 408
20.467-468 61
20.494 72
21.34-96 339
21.95 397
21.97-119 61
21.98 61
21.99-106 397
21.110 61
21.112 61
21.147 61
21.189 396
21.297 403
21.324-382 403
21.542-543 61, 403
22.41 61
22.42 356
22.66 356
22.111-130 403
22.124-125 77
22.130 396
23.222-225 413
22.260 63
22.315 78
22.324 273
22.326-330 71, 297
22.344 63
22.355-360 397
23.19-23 540
23.20-31 61
23.43-53 540
23.54-107 540
23.66-67 51
23.83-84 64, 398
23.85 60
23.95-96 61
23.137 74
23.180 61
23.243-244 398
23.391 540
23.395 19
23.448 62
23.600 260
23.746-747 397
23.798-799 62
23.824 62
23.896 62
24.3 62
24.3-21 62
24.6 79
24.15-17 397
24.22 397
24.59 59
24.159-484 62
24.274 60
24.384 398
24.483 396
24.485-506 62
24.486 59
24.504 62
24.506-509 62

24.507-516 397
24.512 62
24.559 63
24.571 63
24.591 63
24.592 63
24.725-745 78, 339
24.746-747 78
24.748-759 339

Odyssey
1.1 260
3.236-238 113
4.667-668 127
8.499-520 398, 548
8.499-534 539
8.523-553 339
9.2-10 474
14.133-134 435
15.299 431
21.350 132
22.30 435
23.259-262 397
23.271-273 397

Linear B 336, 398, 468

Mycenae Grave Circle A inscription 321

Philo of Byblos
The Phoenician History 18, 190, 198, 482, 489

Plato
Symposium
179e-180b 79

Polybius 77

Xenophon
Symposium 79

LATIN SOURCES

Cicero
Pro Archia xiii

Diodorus Siculus 356

Josephus
Antiquities 572
Contra Apionem 481, 572

Index of West Semitic Key Words, Grammatical Features, and Poetic Terms

KEY WORDS

'hb, "to love," 66, 67, 80, 279, 400, 410, 482, 537
'ḥrt, "end, destiny" (mortality of warriors), 113, 160, 431
'p, "anger," 21, 22, 23
'ṯr, "place; after (?)," 146, 147, 150, 452, 453, 500
'l, "god; El," 141, 446
bĕrît, "covenant," 53, 389
bn 'nt, "son of Anat," 206, 228, 322, 494
b'l, "Baal; lord," 110, 112, 129, 155, 188, 189, 191, 429, 535 (see also *b'l 'arṣ*)
b'l 'arṣ, "lord of the earth," 164, 165, 176, 270, 534
gbr, "warrior," 1, 16, 17, 128, 136, 166, 252, 271, 277, 336, 532
zbl, "prince," 454
ḥbr, "to divine," 138-140, 449, 450
ḥēmâ, "heat" (for anger), 21, 22, 362
ḥûṣ, "plaza, square," 290-291, 548-549
ḥyy, "to live" (*ḥwy*, "to let live"), 103, 108, 109, 110, 111, 424, 429, 430
ḥym, "life"//*blmt*, "nondeath," 108-110, 429
ḥnt, "favor," 422
ḥry 'p, for "burning anger," 21
ḥērem (*ḫrm), "ban" (type of warfare), 18, 45, 171-172, 355, 357, 471
yld, "to bear (children)" (used of votaries), 317, 441
yṯb, "to sit, be enthroned," 138, 317, 448
kbd, "glory" (for warriors), 23
lb't, "lioness; Lion Lady" (title of goddess), 169, 204, 205, 206, 228, 494, 513 (see also *'bdlb't*)
lmd, "to teach, train" (warriors), 16, 116, 134, 326, 350, 376, 434, 574
mdbr, "outback, desert," 165
mhr, "expert" (used for soldiers), 117, 135, 148, 150, 151, 170, 296, 431, 445, 456, 537, 557
mōšĕlîm, "oral composers, poets," 290, 547-548
m(w)t, "to die," 102, 113, 131, 140, 142, 148, 164, 165, 191, 270, 277, 359, 429
mzlt, "stars (constellations)," 230, 512
mspr, "account," 463 (see also *spr*)
mt, "man; devotee," 176, 178, 422, 466, 566 (see also *mt rp'i*)
mt rp'i, "man of Rapi'u," 101-2, 103, 109, 112, 137, 144, 317. *See also mt*

mtpṭ, "judgment, ruling," 353. *See also* **ṯpṭ*
**nṭp*, "drip" (of rain, used of theophany), 238
**nʿm*, "lovely, attractive, desirable" (used of warriors), 112, 134, 165, 201, 274, 444, 531, 537
**nʿr*, "young person; retainer," 128, 350, 441
**npl*, "to fall" (used for warrior death), 164, 165-166, 253, 270-271, 279, 466, 534
npš/nbš, "self, life-breath, appetite," 103, 104, 125, 166, 169, 359, 424, 431, 432, 439, 466
ntbt, "route," (purchased for concessions), 224-225, 232, 509
sd, "assembly," 142, 143, 451
**spr* (noun), "document, record; scribe," 154, 281, 284, 297, 463, 528, 541, 542, 544
**spr* (verb), "to tell," 558
ʿbdlbʾt, "servant of the Lioness," 205-6, 228, 512 (see also *lbʾt*)
ʿbrh, "overflow" (for anger), 22
**ʿyn*, "to eye-ball" (for male sexual gaze), 179-180
**ʿly*, "above," 469
**ʿm*, "people; fighting force," 245, 253, 258, 288, 520
ʿz, "strength, fierceness," 21, 166, 167, 360, 409, 524
**ʿtq* (C-stem), "to transfer" (?), used of texts, 576
**ǵll*, "to glean" (of grapes; also of warfare), 149, 171, 434, 455
ǵzr, "hero," 1, 102, 127-128, 131, 135, 137, 139, 144, 148, 164, 167, 171, 176, 177, 337, 441, 454, 468, 526, 528
pĕrāzôn, "village militia," 225-226, 232, 234, 288
**pḥz*, "to be unsteady; boil over," 23, 363
pǵt, "girl," also name of Pughat, 126
pn bʿl, "face of Baal," 198-200
**prd*, "to divide, branch off, disaffiliate," 531
**prʿ*, "to grow" (uncut hair), 45, 224, 232, 234, 264, 265, 356, 508
**prʿ*, "first, best," 106
**ṣby*, "to covet, desire," 107-8, 427
**ṣ(w)d*, "to hunt," 106, 134, 149, 166, 188, 192, 480, 485, 486
ṣdqt, "victories" (used of Yahweh), 287-288
**ṣḥq*, "to sport," 356
**ṣly*, "to curse; to pray, implore, abjure," 121
qdš/qdšt, "Holy One" (divine title), 185, 186, 205, 372, 493
qinʾâ, "(warrior) zeal," 21
rûaḥ, "spirit," 21, 361, 362, 363, 560
**rpʾ*, "to heal," 139, 193, 446-447, 449. *See also* Rpʾu and Rephaim in the Subject Index
**śbʿ/šbʿ*, "to be sated, satisfied," 21, 22
šlm, "well-being, peace," 155, 156, 159, 459
šm bʿl, "name of Baal," 198-200
**ṯny*, "to recite (song)," 215, 286, 287, 501-2, 545
ṯpṭ* (špṭ*), "to rule, judge," 138, 296, 353, 468-469, 552. *See also mtpṭ*

Grammatical Features

archaism, 212
bn + noun, 475
definite article, 527, 528, 533
DN of GN, 317, 566
DN *b-* (in) GN, 317, 566
double questions, 220-21, 505, 506
energic indicative, 212-13, 499
-în masculine plural noun ending, 498
m- preformative nouns, 285, 544, 546
"old poetry," 7, 8, 11, 16, 21, 37, 38, 42-43, 46, 211-13, 216-20, 247, 259, 293, 300, 301, 302, 308, 309, 311, 312, 313, 327, 329, 332, 339, 345, 348, 375, 383, 384, 497, 498, 547, 559, 560, 576
  critique of dating, 216-20
  date of, 211-20

performative perfect verbs, 157, 158, 457
Phoenician /a/ > /o/ vowel shift, 324
qal passive, 461
š (relative particle), 215-216, 502-3
semantic fields, 347, 351, 352, 426
-*tî* second person fem. sg. suffix-verb ending, 212, 215, 244
Ugaritic verbal forms, 214-215
-*y* fem. noun ending, 426
**yqtl*, 497
"*yaqtul* preterite," 213, 214, 384, 467, 500

Poetic Terms

alliteration, 252, 529, 531
chiasm, 252, 267, 277, 278, 387, 523, 562
coda, 533
inclusion, 120, 278, 279, 280, 523
parallelism, 56, 101, 110, 139, 145, 159, 160, 180, 201, 204, 244, 251, 252, 263, 272, 278, 292, 293, 313, 336, 382, 423, 429, 431, 437, 446, 456, 459, 483, 484, 499, 503, 507, 508, 523, 524, 530, 549
  "distant inverted parallelism," 278, 530
  internal parallelism, 523, 549
  morphological parallelism, 229, 292, 547
  parallelism of numerals, 144, 292, 437, 549
  personal names in parallelism, 201, 293
  semantic parallelism, 272, 523
  sonant parallelism, 229, 230, 292, 524, 530, 457
  synonymous parallelism, 292, 293
  syntactical parallelism, 523
  yqtl*/qtl* parallelism, 484
paronomasia, 252, 277
"recomposition-in-performance," 261, 298, 339, 464. *See also* "secondary unity"; voice, "I"-voice
refrain, 280, 523, 540
reprise, 268, 270, 277, 279, 280, 281, 533
"secondary unity," 258, 522, 523. *See also* "recomposition-in-performance"
rhyme, 292, 422, 531
voice
  court voice, 304, 305, 557
  "epic 'I'-voice," 260
  first-person voice, 204. *See also* "I-voice"
  "I-voice," 244, 259-261, 265, 270, 279, 288, 289, 290, 302, 304, 305, 339, 464, 521, 524, 525, 545
  multiple voices, 267, 275, 277
  private voice, 278, 280
  public voice, 278, 280
  warrior voice, 60, 61, 354, 464. *See also* "I-voice"
wordplay, 53, 87, 88, 102, 116, 270, 273, 292, 422, 434, 441, 529, 531, 547

Index of Select Iconography

DEITIES

Deities, stand (Tell Taanach), 32, 206-7, 496
Goddesses in Iron II Israel, 323
Goddess on horseback (Egypt), 196
Warrior animal-god, stele (Bethsaida), 32, 373
Warrior animal-god, stele (Hauran), 373
Warrior-deities, with worshippers presenting a stag, silver cup (Hatti), 372
Warrior deities (Ugarit), 371
Warrior deities (Levant), 371-72
Warrior deities, West Semitic (Egypt), 371-72
  Anat, 476
  Astarte, 196, 206-8, 477, 487, 495
  Athirat (Asherah), 495
  Baal, 476
  Ishtar, 324, 478
  Resheph, 476, 484-85
  Shed, 485

ANIMALS

(*See also* warrior animal-god, above under *Deities*)

Animal, with fronts limbs extending, cult shrine (?)(Pella), 207
Animal, in prone position, with front limbs extending, with human pipe-layer below, chalice (Cyprus), 207
Bull of Heaven, 387
Figurine, leonine face and female body (Beth-Shean), 206
Figurine, leonine face and female body (Jerusalem), 206
Figurine, leonine face and female body (Tel Rehov), 206
Figurine, leonine face and female body (Tel el-Zira'a), 206
Gazelle head (Tell es-Sa'idiyeh), 30
Horned animals, seals, 30
Humbaba, 387
Leonine, 207-8, 491, 492, 532
Leonine, with claws extending on human heads, Late Bronze terracotta model shrine (Tel Rehov), 32, 206-7
Stag, incised sherd (Tel el-'Oreimeh), 30

HUMANS

(*See also* figurine, leonine face and female body, above under *Animals*)

Achilles and Priam, bronze relief, 103
Archer (in Assyrian style), seal with Hebrew owner inscription (Jerusalem), 352
Archer, on pithos B (Kuntillet Ajrud), 351
Archers, seals (Iron Age Israel), 32
Battle scenes with chariots, ivory (Late Bronze Megiddo), 32, 373
Combat scenes, seals (Iron Age), 32
Gilgamesh, 3, 40, 386-87, 388
  in the Levant, 394
Hunting (Egypt), 371
Hunting and warrior scenes, inlays of royal bed (Ugarit), 32
Hunting scene, dagger hilt (Syria), 351
Hunting scene, Early Bronze rock art (Negev), 30, 372
Hunting scene, gold bowl (Ugarit), 32
Hunting scene, incense altar (Tell Halif), 33, 373-374
Hunting scene, Late Bronze seal, 31
Hunting scene, relief (Karatepe), 32
Hunting scene, relief (Zinjirl), 32-33
Hunting scene, with hounds pursuing wild goats (Cyprus), 373
Hunting scenes, vases (Cyprus), 351
Kuttamuwa feasting, stele (Zinjirl), 424
Warfare (Egypt), 371
War prisoners, heads, and spoils, inlays (Ebla), 30, 372
War prisoners before the king, Late Bronze ivory plaque (Megiddo), 32, 373
Warrior (Syrian), wall-painting (Egypt), 31
Warrior, wife and child, limestone-painting (Amarna), 31
Warrior pair, OB terracotta plaque (British Museum), 55. *See also* Gilgamesh
Warrior pairs in combat, cylinder seal (Syria), 356
Weapons, bulla (Jerusalem), 351
Weapons, reliefs (Lachish), 351, 367
Woman mourning figurine (Lachish), 374
Woman warriors with bows, 443
Woman's face, relief (Dan), 439

OBJECTS

Alphabet pictographs (Egypt), 30-31, 372, 428
Bows, 428
Chariots, seals (Iron Age Israel), 32
Cosmetics, 439

Index of Modern Authors

Aartun, Kjell, 483
Aboud, J., 418, 422
Abusch, Tzvi, 341, 404, 407, 411, 433, 465
Achenbach, Reinhard, 355, 471
Ackerman, James S., 353
Ackerman, Susan, 4, 81, 82, 84, 89-91, 230, 279, 324, 326, 342, 357, 385, 390, 392, 400, 401, 402, 410, 411, 412, 413, 414, 415, 416, 417, 462, 508, 513, 514, 519, 520, 521, 537, 539, 572, 573
Ackroyd, Peter, 231, 234, 240, 246, 250, 252, 514, 516, 518, 522
Adam, Klaus-Peter, 399, 538
Adams, James Noel, 489
Agius, Dionisius A., 437
Aḥituv, Shmuel, 349, 359, 501, 505, 512, 519, 544, 545, 550, 560, 573
Ahlström, Gösta, 509, 510, 520, 556
Aitken, Kenneth T., 418
Albright, William Foxwell, 184, 211, 226, 238, 371, 381, 417, 428, 467, 478, 496, 510, 511, 517, 528, 544, 545, 546, 547, 573
Alexander, Caroline, 334
d'Alfonso, Lorenzo, 480
Allen, James, 226, 510
Allen, Spencer L., 566
Alonso Schökel, Luis, 258, 522, 523
Alster, Bendt, 394, 490, 532
Ames, Frank Ritchel, 338, 343
Amiet, Pierre, 491
Amit, Yairah, 249, 520, 522, 525
Amzallag, Nissim, 527
Andersen, Francis I., 561
Anderson, Gary A., 271, 535
Anderson, John E., 561
Andreasen, Niels-Eric A., 462
Antonaccio, Carla M., 569, 570
Appadurai, Arjun, 337
Appleby, Joyce, 344, 345
Arbeli-Raveh, Shoshana, 435
Archi, Alfonso, 447, 448, 478
Arnaud, Daniel, 386, 393, 394, 480, 507, 559, 569
Asher, Jeffrey R., 536
Astour, Michael C., 341, 509
Ataç, Mehmet-Ali, 387
Attridge, Harold W., 482, 489
Aufrecht, Walter E., 566, 571, 572
Avigad, Nahman, 351, 371, 449, 494
Avioz, Michael, 565
Avriel, Mikhal, 527
Axelsson, Lars Eric, 511, 512
Ayali-Darshan, Noga, 478, 488

Baden, Joel, 400, 538
Bahrani, Zainab, 91, 347, 355, 363, 416
Baises, B. Q., 441
Baker, Jill, 365

Index of Modern Authors

Bakker, Jan Albert, 568
Bakker, Egbert J., 339, 394, 464
Bang, Seung Ho, 374
Barkay, Gabriel, 343, 351, 441
Barker, Kenneth L., 473
Barnes, Timothy D., 334
Barnett, Richard D., 318, 319, 565, 568
Bar-Oz, Guy, 369
Barré, Michael L., 205, 337, 430, 431, 450, 479, 494, 566
Barrett, John C., 365
Barrick, W. Boyd, 527
Barton, John, 383
Basetti, S., 477
Bataille, Georges, 340
Bauks, Michaela, 545
Bean, Adam L., 566
Bechmann, Ulrike, 251, 514, 522
Beck, Deborah, 72, 339, 397, 403, 405, 525
Beck, Pirhiya, 351, 373, 495, 496, 497
Beckman, Gary, 390, 414, 477, 480, 481, 507
Beeston, A. F. L., 487
Beissinger, Margaret, 340, 377
Belcher, Stephen Paterson IV, 540
Benardete, Seth, 59, 61, 72, 333, 334, 339, 396, 397, 398, 403, 405, 408, 411, 525, 532, 534, 536
Ben-Barak, Zafrira, 462
Benz, Brendon, 226, 510, 514
Bergmann, Claudia D., 408
Bergsträsser, Gotthelf, 502
Berlin, Adele, 524
Berman, Joshua, 465
Bernat, David A., 530
Beye, C., 341
Bhayro, Siam, 400
Biella, Joan Copeland, 389, 478, 486, 492
Biggs, Robert D., 417
Biran, Avraham, 549
Blair, Judit M., 571
Blau, Joshua, 459
Blenkinsopp, Joseph, 251, 253, 258, 514, 522, 524
Blétry, Silvie, 493
Bloch, Yigal, 213, 500, 501, 502, 505
Bloch-Smith, Elizabeth, 25, 27, 350, 366, 367, 381, 424, 495, 570
Blum, Erhard, 559
Bodi, Daniel, 335, 415
Boehringer, Sandra, 402
Boessneck, Joachim, 370
Bohak, Gideon, 571
Boling, Robert, 226, 251, 502, 507, 510, 511, 519, 520, 521, 522, 544, 546, 547
Bonfil, Ruhama, 365
Bonjour, Loyse, 4, 80, 82, 340, 342, 385, 399, 401, 404, 410, 412
Bonnet, Corinne, 488, 489, 572, 573
Bordreuil, Pierre, 158, 338, 410, 421, 422, 447, 456, 457, 458, 459, 461, 474, 491, 493, 494, 513, 527, 537, 565
Borgman, Paul, 400, 538
Borowski, Oded, 325, 370, 373, 574
Bosworth, David, 339, 356, 400, 467, 538
Bottéro, Jean, 412
Bourke, Stephen J., 366
Bowen, Nancy R., 556
Bowra, C. M., 335
Brandfon, Frederic, 380
Braudel, Fernand, 10, 345
Braun, Joachim, 473
Bravo, Jorge J., III, 336
Brenner, Athalya, 293, 357, 358, 534, 546
Bretschneider, Joachim, 492
Brettler, Marc Zvi, 521
Bright, John, 374
Brown, Bill, 337
Brown, John Pairman, 335, 341, 356, 560, 564
Brown, William, 548
Brulé, Pierre, 396, 403, 408
Bruno, D. Arvid, 378
Buchholz, H.-G., 532
Bunimovitz, Shlomo, 42, 379, 381
Burney, C. F., 212, 215, 220, 226, 227, 229, 230, 251, 288, 497, 501, 502, 505, 506, 508, 510, 511, 513, 516, 522, 523, 544, 546, 547
Butler, S. A. L., 412, 422
Byrne, Ryan, 295, 296, 297, 367, 542, 550, 551, 552, 554

Caca, Kathy L., 408
Cantrell, Deborah O'Daniel, 346
Capomacchia, Anna Maria G., 416
Caquot, André, 304, 418, 455, 479, 514, 522, 556, 557
Carmignac, Jean, 468
Carr, David M., 8, 284, 327, 343, 375, 542, 543, 553, 555, 556, 560, 561, 562, 563, 575, 576
Carroll, John T., 548
Carvalho, Corrine, 333
Cassuto, Umberto, 39, 40, 216, 377, 378
Cathcart, Kevin, 482
Cavignaux, Antoine, 571
Chadwick, John, 336, 468
Chaiken, Miriam S., 339
Chaniotis, Angelos, 77, 78, 348, 402, 407, 408, 409, 416, 417, 442, 445
Chapman, Cynthia R., 76, 408, 463
Charpin, Dominique, 435, 543, 570
Chavel, Simeon, 490
Cho, Sang Youl, 574
Choi, John H., 485
Christensen, Duane L., 335, 353, 541, 575
Clanton, Dan W., 334
Clemens, David M., 185, 479, 509
Clifford, Richard J., 357, 429, 432, 451, 502, 509, 539, 576
Coben, Lawrence S., 541
Coetzee, J. M., xii, 334
Cohen, Chaim, 213, 281, 342, 500, 540
Cohen, Ronald, 526
Cohen, Susan L., 365
Cohen, Yoram, 480
Cohn, Carol, 334
Cohn, Herbert, 572
Colani, Madeleine, 568
Coldstream, J. N., 320, 321, 398, 570
Collins, Adela Yarbro, 536
Collins, John J., 536, 575
Collon, Dominique, 387
Condor, Claude Reignier, 567
Conklin, Blane, 505, 535
Conroy, Charles, 374, 376
Considine, Patrick, 395
Coogan, Michael David, 38, 226, 234, 235, 238, 239, 243, 244, 246, 248, 251, 252, 253, 254, 258, 344, 377, 418, 421, 439, 444, 450, 489, 508, 510, 513, 514, 516, 517, 519, 520, 522, 523
Cook, John, 383, 503
Cook, Steven, 505
Cooper, Alan, 123, 324, 435, 438, 449, 477, 572
Cooper, Jerrold S., 53, 85, 386, 388, 390, 392, 412, 414, 415
Cornelius, Izak, 371, 372, 443, 476, 477, 484, 487, 532
Craigie, Peter C., 504, 508, 509, 514, 519, 525
Crawford, Sidnie Ann White, 440
Creangă, Ovidiu, 402, 411
Creed, Robert P., 539, 544
Creveld, Martin van, 337, 344, 348
Croft, Paul, 29, 370
Cross, Frank Moore, 8, 26, 36, 37, 38, 39, 40, 42, 44, 205, 211, 212, 216, 218, 219, 230, 231, 236, 237, 238, 239, 240, 241, 249, 289, 296, 313, 319, 341, 343, 353, 357, 363, 367, 368, 374, 375, 376, 377, 378, 379, 383, 389, 399, 431, 433, 435, 439, 440, 445, 446, 448, 460, 469, 489, 493, 494, 497, 500, 504, 505, 506, 507, 508, 511, 512, 513, 514, 516, 517, 518, 520, 522, 523, 524, 525, 526, 528, 533, 540, 547, 550, 551, 552, 555, 556, 559, 560, 568, 572, 573, 574
Crouch, C. L., 343
Culley, Robert C., 541
Cunchillos, J. L., 468, 509
Cunningham, Graham, 444
Currie, Bruno, 569

Dahood, Mitchell J., 469
Dalby, Andrew, 540
Dalix, Anne-Sophie, 455, 479
Dalley, Stephanie, 390, 394, 413, 414, 439, 445, 467
Darby, Erin Danielle, 574
Da Silva, Aldina, 465
Dassow, Eva von, 339
Davenport, Tracy, 407, 415

Davidson, Richard M., 402
Davis, Thomas W., 381
Day, John, 318, 326, 358, 476, 487, 488, 511, 512, 567, 572, 573
Day, Peggy L., 175, 401, 470, 473, 476, 545, 570
Dayagi-Mendels, Michal, 439, 489
De Backer, Fabrice, 347
Debord, Guy, 525
Degen, Davida Eisenberg, 372
Démare-Lafont, Sophie, 554
Demsky, Aaron, 349, 434, 543, 550, 564
Deoudi, Maria, 570
Dessel, J. P., 553
Deutsch, Robert, 493, 494
Dever, William G., 345, 380
Dhorme, Edouard, 564
Dietrich, Manfried, 158, 173, 342, 418, 421, 431, 434, 435, 440, 447, 455, 456, 458, 459, 470, 472, 482, 484, 509, 510, 567
Dijk-Hemmes, Fokkelien van, 78, 293, 357, 358, 377, 409, 525, 534, 549
Dijkstra, Meindert, 190, 418, 481, 482, 509
Dimock, George E., 442
Dion, Paul E., 523, 545
Doak, Brian R., 363, 446, 567, 569
Doan, William, 284, 515, 521, 527, 541, 542
Dobbs-Allsopp, F. W., 311, 559, 575
Dorsey, David A., 509
Dothan, Trude, 374, 494
Doumet-Serhal, Claude, 364
Downes, Jeremy M., 358
Downs, Laura Lee, 344
Dozeman, Thomas B., 576
Dressler, H. H. P., 427, 430
Driesch, Angela von den, 370
Driver, G. R., 502
Driver, Samuel Rolles, 496, 563, 565
Dundes, Alan, 414
Dupont-Sommer, André, 488
Durand, Jean-Marie, 335, 389
Duranti, Alessandro, 337, 338

Echols, Charles L., 220, 499, 505, 515
Edelman, Diana Vikander, 280, 363, 379, 527, 539, 540
Ehrensvärd, Martin, 383, 499, 503
Eidelstein, Gershon, 366
Eitan, Avraham, 366
Elayi, Josette, 367
Ellis, Teresa Ann, 572
Ellwood, Robert, 337
Emerton, John A., 348, 352, 470, 513
Emery, Allan Comstock, III, 347, 364
Engberg, Robert M., 496
Eph'al, Israel, 346, 347
Epstein, Claire, 567, 568
Eskhult, Mats, 483
Esler, Philip E., 335
Estes, Todd, 344
Exum, J. Cheryl, 345

Fantar, M'hamed Hassine, 488
Fassberg, Steven E., 486, 493, 504
Faust, Avraham, 37, 40, 41, 42, 44, 46, 349, 379, 380, 381, 385, 530
Feliu, Lluis, 480
Fijałkowska, Lena, 554
Fink, Amir, 373, 424
Finkelstein, Israel, 349, 350, 379, 510
Finkelstein, J. J., 389, 460
Fischer, Peter M., 368, 370, 493, 495
Fishbane, Michael, 235, 236, 516, 517
Fisher, Helen E., 475
Fitzgerald, Aloysius, F.S.C., 384, 517, 561
Fleishman, Joseph, 441
Fleming, Daniel E., 52, 55, 187, 194, 197, 198, 353, 386, 388, 390, 391, 392, 399, 413, 416, 417, 437, 469, 480, 486, 487, 488, 520, 521, 538, 540, 541, 552, 553, 554, 555
Flourentzos, Pavlos, 496
Fokkelman, Jan P., 253, 515, 523, 524, 527
Ford, James N., 446, 449, 450, 467, 482, 484, 485
Forstner-Müller, Irene, 365
Foster, Benjamin, 53, 55, 57, 58, 89, 92, 351, 356, 360, 361, 362, 387, 388, 390, 394, 406, 407, 411, 414, 415, 416, 430, 433, 467, 539, 540

Fox, Michael V., 509, 576
Franken, H. J., 366
Frankfort, Henri, 351, 429
Frantsouzoff, S. A., 487
Franzaroli, Pelio, 463
Fraser, James A., 568
Fraser, James George, 110
Frayne, Douglas, 387, 388, 393
Frechette, Christopher G., 430
Freedberg, Christine Thomas, 462
Freedman, David Noel, 8, 211, 218, 230, 293, 343, 344, 353, 357, 383, 497, 505, 508, 513, 514, 523, 526, 527, 530, 531, 533, 534, 535, 540, 544, 546, 550, 555, 556
Freedman, R. David, 461
Freedman, Sally M., 393
Frendo, Anthony J., 494
Fretz, Mark J., 347
Freu, Jacques, 462
Frick, Frank S., 369, 496
Fritz, Volkmar, 38, 243, 244, 245, 247, 249, 376, 515, 519, 520, 521, 522
Frolov, Serge, 358, 468, 503, 564
Frymer-Kensky, Tikva, 278, 353, 406, 417, 444, 491, 539
Futato, Mark, 437

Gai, Amikam, 425
Galil, Gershom, 543, 552
Galpaz-Feller, Pnina, 359
Galter, Hannes D., 565
Ganor, Saar, 348, 543, 552
Garbini, Giovanni, 212, 483, 498, 515
Gardiner, Alan, 428
Garfinkel, Yosef, 25, 348, 364, 365, 543, 552
Garr, W. Randall, 351, 498, 571
Garsiel, Moshe, 563
Gaster, T. H., 436, 471, 477, 535, 547, 556
Geertz, Clifford, 338, 346
Gehlken, Erlend, 513, 536
Gelb, Ignace J., 477, 481, 493
Gelder, Ken, 338
Geller, Stephen A., 497
Genz, Hermann, 351, 365, 428
Geoghagen, Jeffrey C., 497
George, A. R., 52, 53, 55, 58, 81, 84, 86, 87, 334, 340, 386, 387, 388, 389, 390, 391, 392, 393, 394, 406, 409, 411, 412, 413, 414, 432, 435, 437, 438, 442, 444, 445, 456, 527, 531, 537, 550
George, Mark, 527
Gerhards, Meik, 558
Gerig, Bruce L., 402
Gerleman, Gillis, 515
Gerstenberger, Erhard S., 575
Gevirtz, Stanley, 273, 354, 502, 508, 526, 529, 530, 531, 532, 533, 536, 540
Gianto, Agustinus, 393, 395, 396, 445
Gibson, J. C. L., 180, 367, 449, 466, 472, 475, 495, 551
Giles, Terry, 284, 515, 521, 527, 541, 542
Gilmour, Rachelle, 399, 538
Ginsberg, H. L., 44, 120, 122, 128, 211, 223, 224, 272, 273, 416, 418, 422, 423, 424, 429, 436, 437, 438, 439, 441, 455, 466, 470, 472, 475, 497, 498, 502, 508, 526, 535, 576
Gitin, Seymour, 380, 494
Giveon, Raphael, 512
Gleason, Maud W., 411
Globe, Alexander, 515
Gnuse, Robert K., 375
Goerwitz, Richard L., 509
Goff, Matthew, 340
Gogel, Sandra Landis, 557
Goitein, S. D., 78, 408
Goldenberg, David M., 423
Goldstein, Ronnie, 378
González de Canales, F., 349
Good, Edwin M., 432, 442
Good, Robert M., 224, 455, 509, 520, 546
Gordon, Cyrus, 39, 341, 351, 357, 361, 377, 462, 518
Gordon, Milton M., 338
Gottschall, Jonathan, 396, 397, 403
Görg, Manfred, 383, 449, 511, 512, 516, 567
Gransard-Desmond, J. O., 532
Grant, Deena, 360, 362
Gray, John, 472, 476, 508, 515, 520
Grayson, A. Kirk, 351, 352, 354, 355, 432, 444

Green, Alberto R. W., 476
Green, Anthony, 387
Greenberg, Moshe, 357
Greenblatt, Stephen, 345, 346
Greene, Thomas M., 19, 271, 357, 397, 408, 535
Greenfield, Jonas C., 134, 362, 363, 377, 384, 424, 430, 434, 437, 445, 450, 455, 469, 543, 546
Greenstein, Edward L., 214, 344, 360, 378, 384, 449, 451, 457, 466, 467, 481, 485, 500, 503, 506, 521, 523, 531, 535, 540, 567
Greer, Jonathan, 370
Grether, Oscar, 515
Greve, Julia M. Asher, 391
Grimme, Hubert, 517
Gröndahl, Frauke, 493
Groneberg, Brigitte, 406, 479
Gross, Walter, 251, 499, 517, 519, 522, 525, 556
Gruber, Mayer I., 425, 441, 455
Gruntfest, Yaakov, 501
Gubel, Eric, 373
Guichard, Michael, 335
Guigues, M. P.-E., 367
Guillaume, Philippe, 501, 526, 545
Guinan, Ann Kessler, 415
Güterbock, Hans, 372
Gzella, Holger, 214, 378, 444, 458, 501, 523, 528, 552

Haak, Robert D., 511, 560
Hachlili, R., 424
Hackett, Jo Ann, 363, 382, 501, 517
Hadley, Judith M., 494, 496
Haenfler, Ross, 338
Hallo, W. W., 428, 458, 490, 494
Halperin, David M., 402, 412
Halpern, Baruch, 212, 213, 215, 242, 253, 341, 371, 379, 400, 497, 499, 500, 501, 502, 515, 519, 538, 544
Hamblin, William J., 347
Hamilton, Gordon J., 31, 372, 380, 428, 550, 565
Hamilton, Mark W., 276, 399, 531, 535, 538
Hamori, Esther J., 340, 413
Harcourt, Hugh R., 407
Harlé, Paul, 524
Harris, Rivkah, 53, 56, 75, 82, 89, 90, 392, 405, 406, 414, 415, 417, 434, 444, 471, 473, 539
Hartenstein, Friedhelm, 490
Hartley, John E., 546
Hasel, Michael G., 347
Häser, Jutta, 495
Hatto, A. T., 335
Haupt, Paul, 211, 497, 507
Hauser, Alan, 515, 520
Hawk, L. Daniel, 356
Hawley, Robert, 491
Hays, Christopher B., 446, 457, 460
Heacock, Anthony, 341, 401
Healey, John F., 318, 422, 447, 460, 565, 567, 568
Heaton, Anthony, 401
Hebdige, Dick, 338
Hedges, Chris, xi, 333, 339, 521, 537
Heimpel, Wolfgang, 389, 435, 478, 479
Held, Moshe, 128, 221, 389, 441, 458, 506, 526, 573
Heltzer, Michael, 367, 371, 435, 449, 493, 494, 551
Hendel, Ronald, 226, 286, 497, 503, 510, 511, 521, 522, 544
Henderson, Jeffrey, 391, 398
Henle, Jane, 397
Herdner, Andrée, 418, 572
Herold, Anja, 490
Herr, Larry G., 366, 370, 381, 521, 548
Herrmann, Virginia Rimmer, 424
Herrmann, W., 479, 481
Hervieu-Léger, Danièle, 331, 345, 558, 576
Herzog, Ze'ev, 529, 548, 549
Hess, Richard, 358, 367, 493, 512, 542, 543, 550, 551
Hesse, Brian, 28, 29, 369, 370, 371, 574
Hestrin, Ruth, 24, 364, 496
Hexter, Ralph, 260, 525
Hiebert, Theodore, 560

Higham, Thomas, 511
Hillers, Delbert, 132, 374, 376, 427, 438, 443, 546
Hoch, James E., 226, 286, 350, 389, 442, 444, 486, 508, 510, 518, 537, 544
Hoenig, Sidney B., 549
Hoffmeier, James K., 199, 354, 489, 491, 564
Hoffner, Harry, 167, 356, 443, 467
Höfner, Maria, 486
Holladay, Jack S., Jr., 510
Holladay, William L., 527
Holloway, Steven W., 354, 442, 557
Holmstedt, Robert, 383, 503
Hoop, Raymond de, 504, 555
Horowitz, Wayne, 380, 392, 494
Horwitz, Liora Kolska, 369, 370
Horwitz, William J., 144, 451, 452, 456
Hostetter, Edwin C., 318, 568, 569
Houston, Walter, 574
Huehnergard, John, 436, 452, 454, 456, 461, 479, 500, 502
Huffmon, Herbert B., 493
Hulin, Linda Carless, 487
Hundley, Michael, 490
Hunt, Lynn, 344
Hurowitz, Victor Avigdor, 351, 390, 392, 393, 406, 414, 502
Hurvitz, Avi, 211, 219, 383, 503, 504
Husser, Jean-Marie, 132, 133, 405, 418, 421, 444, 509

Iggers, Georg G., 344, 345
Ikeda, Yutaka, 515
Inomata, Takeshi, 541
Ismail, Bahija Khalil, 571
Isser, Stanley, 7, 335, 343, 542, 555

Jackson, D. R., 340
Jacob, Margaret, 344
Jacobsen, Thorkild, 52, 82, 83, 89, 386, 387, 392, 404, 405, 412, 415, 433, 440, 465, 468, 471, 473, 475, 536, 549
Jamieson-Drake, David W., 542
Jamme, Albert, 477, 478, 492, 534
Janko, Richard, 376, 394
Janzen, David, 545
Janzen, J. Gerald, 356, 357
Japhet, Sara, 316, 563, 565
Jean, Cynthia, 394
Jennings, Theodore W., Jr., 402, 403, 404
Jeyes, Ulla, 445
Johansen, K. Friis, 395, 397, 398, 570
Johnson, Benjamin J. M., 564
Jones, Christopher P., 336, 468
Jones, Meriel, 411
Jongeling, Karel, 489
Joosten, Jan, 213, 214, 383, 500, 503, 504, 532, 572

Kaddari, Menahem Zevi, 508
Kalsbeek, J., 366
Kapelrud, Arvid S., 436
Karageorghis, Vassos, 373, 474
Karge, Paul, 567
Kaufman, Stephen A., 355
Kawashima, Robert S., 311, 359, 375, 376, 515, 559, 575
Keel, Othmar, 323, 371, 372, 373, 380, 487, 489, 571
Kelle, Brad E., 343, 344, 553
Kempinsky, Aaron, 28, 369
Kerr, Robert M., 489, 572
Kettenhofen, Erich, 567
Kilmer, Anne D., 87, 88, 409, 414
Kim, Dong-Hyuk, 504
Kim, Koowon, 421, 423, 425
Kim, Yoo-Ki, 523
King, Katherine Callen, 334, 395, 396, 397
King, Philip J., 345, 346, 352, 363, 529, 564
Kister, Menahem, 431
Kitchen, Kenneth A., 199, 389, 489, 491
Kivilo, Maarit, 395
Klein, Ralph, 316, 563, 564, 565
Kletter, Raz, 357, 496
Knapp, A. Bernard, 449, 479
Knauf, Ernest Axel, 42, 212, 215, 220, 382, 498, 499, 502, 505, 512, 525, 554, 556
Knight, Douglas A., 553
Knohl, Israel, 235, 382, 516
Koch, Klaus, 423, 511, 520
Koch-Westenholz, Ula, 390

Koenen, Klaus, 369
Kogan, Leonid, 230, 231, 514
Kogut, Simcha, 503, 505
Koitabashi, Matahisa, 473
Koller, Aaron J., 347, 351, 352, 474, 504, 562, 565
Kompaoré, Garber, 505
Kosmala, Hans, 336, 562
Kosman, Admiel, 569
Kotzé, Zacharias, 360, 362
Krahmalkov, Charles R., 448, 480, 571, 572
Kramer, Samuel N., 434
Kratz, Reinhard G., 355, 471, 553, 576
Krebernik, Manfred, 336
Kruger, Hennie, 513
Kruger, Paul A., 360, 362
Kugel, James L., 529
Kutler, Lawrence, 520
Kutscher, E. Y., 211, 212, 215, 497, 499, 502, 509
Kutter, Juliane, 467
Kyle, Donald G., 397

Lackenbacher, Sylvie, 341, 479, 486
Lambert, Wilfred, 55, 89, 347, 350, 387, 390, 393, 408, 415, 422, 435
Landy, Francis, 419, 440, 527
Langlois, Michael, 335
Lapinkivi, Pirjo, 390, 413, 415
Lapsley, Jacqueline E., 410, 537
Lattimore, Richard, 63, 398, 474, 539
Launderville, Dale, 334, 402, 406, 408, 410, 413, 415
Lawrence, Paul J. N., 389
Leclant, Jean, 487, 512
LeDoux, Joseph, 475
Lee, S. Noah, 530
Le Goff, Jacques, 345, 558
Lehmann, Gunnar, 513
Leichty, Erle, 435, 442, 536
Leick, Gwendolyn, 181, 475
Leith, Mary Joan, 574
Lemaire, André, 349, 371, 394, 449, 469, 494, 511, 543
Lemardèle, Christophe, 508
Lendon, J. E., 347
Lepre, Cesare, 515
Leslau, Wolf, 477, 492, 511, 544
Leuchter, Mark, 378, 379, 508, 515, 526
Leuenberger, Martin, 430
Leven, Dan, 366
Levene, Dan, 571
Levin, Christoph, 212, 375, 497, 498, 502, 511, 515, 516, 519, 520, 524, 576
Levin, Yigal, 348
Levine, Baruch, 43, 159, 216, 219, 230, 334, 354, 356, 361, 383, 384, 432, 457, 458, 459, 461, 462, 463, 464, 502, 504, 508, 513, 523, 525, 529, 541, 547, 548, 555, 560
Levinson, Bernard M., 553
Lev-Tov, Justin, 30, 369, 370
Levtow, Nathaniel B., 338
Levy, Thomas E., 511
Lewis, Theodore J., 142, 144, 158, 159, 200, 205, 423, 449, 450, 451, 452, 453, 455, 456, 457, 458, 459, 460, 461, 479, 482, 484, 485, 486, 490, 491
L'Heureux, Conrad, 316, 317, 564, 565
Lichtenstein, Murray H., 482
Lichtheim, Miriam, 362, 363, 407, 468
Linafelt, Tod, 275, 276, 527, 529, 538
Lincoln, Bruce, 338
Lindars, Barnabas, 508
Lindquist, Maria, 569
Lipiński, Edward, 202, 476, 491, 492, 493, 496
Liverani, Mario, 479, 509, 553
Llompart, Jorge, 349
Lloyd-Jones, Hugh, 394
Loewenstamm, S. E., 473
Løland, Hanne, 91, 416
Long, Burke O., 541, 550
López-Ruiz, Carolina, 340, 342
Lord, Albert B., 37, 38, 330, 375, 376, 394, 576
Loretz, Oswald, 158, 173, 342, 418, 421, 431, 434, 435, 440, 447, 449, 458, 459, 470, 482, 484, 509, 510, 567
Loud, Gordon, 373
Louden, Bruce, 398, 402, 404, 406
Loulloupos, M. C., 251

Lundberg, Marilyn J., 441
Lundin, A. G., 487

Macchi, Jean-Daniel, 504
MacDonald, Burton, 567
Macgregor, Sherry Lou, 358
Machinist, Peter, 260, 363, 525
Maeir, Aren, 367, 564
Mafico, Temba L. J., 469
Magee, Peter, 368
Malamat, Abraham, 18, 303, 353, 355, 357, 381, 384, 385, 400, 451, 557
Malul, M., 443
Mankowski, Paul, 230, 513, 573
Manor, Dale W., 510
Maran, Joseph, 342
Marcus, David, 429, 461
Marcus, Ralph, 572
Marello, Pierre, 391
Margalit, Baruch, 100, 138, 342, 418, 419, 421, 425, 427, 432, 434, 438, 449, 464, 471, 472, 567
Marsman, Hennie J., 462
Martin, Richard P., 440
Matthews, Victor H., 348
Matthiae, Paolo, 372
Mavinga, Joseph N., 573
Mayer, Werner, 342
Mayer-Opificius, Ruth, 371
Mazar, Amihai, 28, 169, 207, 349, 350, 355, 359, 382, 442, 469, 495, 512, 550, 557
Mazar, Benjamin, 169, 296, 494, 512, 552, 563
Mazar, Eilat, 26, 349, 366, 371, 495
McAlpine, Thomas H., 438
McCall, Marsh H., Jr., 376
McCarter, P. Kyle, 26, 27, 199, 200, 275, 276, 296, 317, 318, 358, 361, 362, 368, 401, 456, 470, 490, 528, 530, 531, 533, 535, 538, 551, 552, 564, 565, 566, 572
McCorriston, Joy, 487, 547
McEwen, Edward, 428
McGeough, Kevin, 128, 441, 509, 510, 562
McKane, William, 363, 565, 574
McKenzie, Steven L., 400, 538, 556
McLaughlin, John L., 453, 486
McLeod, W., 428
Meier, Samuel A., 358
Mellaart, James, 368
Mendenhall, George E., 428, 550
Merwe, Christo H. J. van der, 516
Meshel, Naphtali S., 369
Meshel, Ze'ev, 353, 501, 530, 535, 545, 561, 574
Mettinger, T. N. D., 109, 429, 430
Meyers, Carol L., 344, 357, 363, 385, 549, 553, 562
Michalowski, Piotr, 58, 387, 444
Milgrom, Jacob, 370
Milik, J. T., 26, 296, 340, 368, 494
Millard, Alan, 167, 290, 299, 348, 356, 468, 531, 548, 550, 551, 555, 564
Miller, Cynthia L., 528, 529, 542
Miller, Patrick D., 128, 270, 337, 441, 526, 528, 529, 533
Miller, Robert D., II, 277, 285, 296, 297, 338, 350, 367, 376, 508, 534, 539, 542, 543, 545, 551, 552, 553
Milstein, Sara J., 52, 55, 386, 388, 390, 391, 392, 393, 413, 416, 417
Miron, Eli, 347
Mitchell, T. C., 494
Mittermayer, Catherine, 386
Mobley, Gregory, 7, 335, 337, 343, 346, 356, 358, 363, 563, 575
Monroe, Christopher, 341
Monroe, Lauren Shedletsky, 159, 355, 462, 464, 471
Montrose, Louis A., 346
Moor, Johannes C. de, 8, 109, 112, 212, 229, 253, 288, 343, 345, 353, 376, 418, 429, 430, 431, 440, 451, 455, 464, 472, 477, 479, 481, 497, 507, 513, 518, 520, 522, 546
Moore, George Foot, 220, 229, 505, 506, 513, 516, 547
Moore, Megan Bishop, 343, 344
Moore, Michael S., 387
Morag, Shelomo, 211, 217, 445, 456, 497, 503
Moran, William L., 52, 53, 56, 57, 58, 81, 212, 214, 380, 382, 386, 387, 391, 392,

393, 394, 400, 410, 411, 433, 435, 444, 475, 499, 503, 510, 537
Mori, Lucia, 507
Morris, Ian, 399
Morris, Sarah P., 63, 341, 398
Morrow, William, 553
Mowinckel, Sigmund, 211, 497
Mozan, Zvi, 527
Muellner, Leonard, 362, 395
Müller, Hans Peter, 243, 519
Müller, Reinhard, 565
Müller, Vera, 472
Münnich, Maciej M., 476
Muraoka, Takamitsu, 501
Murphy, Kelly J., 132, 418, 443, 444, 470, 473
Murray, A. T., 63, 398, 431, 440, 442
Murray, Oswyn, 453
Muscarella, Oscar White, 372

Na'aman, Nadav, 226, 349, 441, 510, 515, 522, 523, 524
Nagy, Gregory, 60, 260, 261, 298, 320, 339, 385, 395, 397, 398, 464, 525, 526, 555, 562, 570
Najjar, Mohammad, 511
Nakhai, Beth Alpert, 381
Nardelli, Jean-Fabrice, 4, 81, 342, 385, 399, 401, 410, 416
Nash, Harriet, 437
Natan-Yulzary, Shirly, 99, 120, 121, 130, 131, 418, 419, 432, 433, 436, 437, 442, 536
Naudé, Jacobus A., 383, 503
Naveh, Joseph, 359, 494, 571
Nebes, Norbert, 483
Neef, Heinz-Dieter, 212, 243, 498, 515, 519
Negbi, Ora, 371, 529
Niccacci, Alviero, 213, 500
Niditch, Susan, xi, 7, 260, 285, 304, 327, 333, 334, 335, 342, 343, 354, 374, 378, 392, 417, 509, 525, 539, 541, 542, 556, 557, 561, 562, 575
Niehr, Herbert, 235, 456, 516, 517, 552
Nihan, Christophe, 66, 400, 537, 538
Niles, John D., 544
Nissinen, Martti, 82, 88, 90, 353, 362, 396, 400, 401, 406, 411, 412, 414, 415, 416, 443, 467, 475, 488, 513
Noble, John T., 293, 549
Notarius, Tania, 214, 492, 497, 500, 506
Noth, Martin, 37
Notley, R. S., 369
Nowack, Wilhelm, 516
Nys, Nadine, 492
Nysse, Richard W., 526

Oakley, John H., 417
Oberhelman, Steven M., 402, 415
Obermann, Julius, 465
O'Connell, Mary Ellen, 338
O'Connell, Robert H., 513, 515, 516
O'Connor, Michael Patrick, 213, 214, 292, 422, 425, 426, 497, 500, 527, 530, 533, 539, 549, 550
Oden, Daniel, 554
Oden, Robert A., Jr., 482, 489, 494
Ogden, Daniel, 79, 402, 410, 415, 420
Olmo Lete, Gregorio del, 343, 420, 450, 459, 460, 471, 479, 490, 496, 558, 569, 572
Olyan, Saul M., 80, 274, 278, 324, 401, 404, 405, 410, 411, 448, 489, 530, 537, 539, 540, 572, 573
Oppenheim, A. Leo, 83, 84, 392, 412, 413
Ornan, Tallay, 373, 387, 573
Oshima, Takayoshi, 380, 494
Otto, A., 480
Otto, Eckart, 560

Pagan, Joseph Martin, 337, 360, 437, 460, 477, 503, 552
Pakman, Dalia, 439
Palva, Heikki, 540
Panitz-Cohen, Nava, 207, 495
Pardee, Dennis, 104, 126, 135, 141, 147, 150, 156, 158, 159, 160, 187, 188, 190, 194, 200, 201, 203, 204, 205, 306, 339, 344, 354, 360, 374, 376, 378, 396, 410, 421, 422, 424, 425, 426, 427, 429, 430, 431, 432, 433, 434, 435, 437, 438, 439, 441, 442, 444, 446, 447, 450, 451, 452, 453, 454, 456, 457, 458, 459, 460, 461, 464,

465, 468, 469, 471, 473, 474, 475, 478, 479, 480, 481, 482, 484, 485, 486, 489, 490, 491, 492, 493, 494, 499, 503, 509, 513, 527, 537, 548, 550, 554, 557, 558, 559, 565, 568, 572, 573
Parker, Julie Faith, 440
Parker, Robert, 320, 336, 446, 569, 570
Parker, Simon B., 38, 100, 126, 344, 350, 374, 376, 378, 418, 419, 420, 421, 422, 426, 427, 428, 429, 430, 433, 434, 435, 436, 437, 438, 439, 440, 442, 444, 451, 518, 535
Parpola, Simo, 428, 433, 436, 443, 475, 487, 492, 503, 539, 557
Pat-El, Na'ama, 382, 501
Patrich, Joseph, 424
Paul, Shalom M., 528
Paz, Sarit, 357
Peacock, Cory Ke Michael, 230, 513, 573, 575
Pearson, Mike Parker, 365
Peled, Ilan, 411, 415
Pennacchietti, Fabrizio A., 484
Perdue, Leo, 473
Person, Raymond F., Jr., 376
Peterson, Jeremiah, 392
Petschow, H., 412
Pfeiffer, Henrik, 243, 244, 247, 511, 515, 519, 520, 521
Pfoh, Emanuel, 385
Philip, Graham, 24, 25, 347, 364, 365
Philip, Tarja, 408
Piasetzky, Eli, 350
Pinnock, Frances, 478
Pinsky, Robert, 400
Piquer Otero, Andrés, 38, 377, 499, 501
Pitard, Wayne T., 141, 438, 448, 450, 451, 459, 461, 552
Poethig, Eunice, 357
Pohlig, James N., 504
Polak, Frank H., 375, 378, 503, 541, 560
Pollitt, Jerome J., 442
Pomponio, Francesco, 478
Pope, Marvin H., 113, 117, 135, 147, 211, 360, 409, 417, 422, 423, 424, 429, 430, 431, 432, 434, 439, 445, 448, 450, 451, 453, 455, 461, 463, 466, 471, 475, 481, 505, 536, 566
Porter, Benjamin, 30, 369, 370
Pritchard, James, 199, 366, 371, 489
Pritchett, W. Kendrick, 408
Propp, William C., 304, 511, 529, 530, 556, 557
Pruzsinsky, Regine, 477, 480, 481, 487, 493
Puech, Émile, 26, 348, 355, 367, 368, 493, 494, 528, 543, 551, 552, 553, 554, 572, 573

Qimron, Elisha, 534

Raabe, Paul R., 540
Raaflaub, Kurt A., 395, 570
Rabin, Chaim, 509, 568
Rahmani, Levy Yitzhaq, 205, 206, 494, 495
Rahmouni, Aicha, 336, 441, 444, 445, 449, 456, 468, 473, 567
Rainey, Anson, 28, 228, 369, 380, 382, 429, 433, 499, 500, 512, 518
Rechenmacher, Hans, 492
Redfield, James, 395
Redford, Donald, 380, 487, 512
Reese, David S., 532
Reeves, Edward B., 361, 554
Rendsburg, Gary A., 215, 498, 499, 502, 518, 555
Renfroe, Fred, 431, 432, 436, 437, 438, 481, 485, 507, 535
Renz, Johannes, 557
Rezetko, Robert, 383, 499, 503
Richter, Wolfgang, 251, 522
Roberts, J. J. M., 184, 478, 479
Roberts, John, 334, 397, 398
Robertson, David A., 211, 212, 213, 217, 218, 380, 382, 383, 499, 500, 503
Robin, Christian, 491
Rochberg, Francesca, 84, 412, 413
Rofé, Alexander, 7, 219, 235, 315, 343, 375, 504, 516, 517, 518, 557, 562, 563, 564, 576
Rogland, Max, 501
Rollinger, Robert, 341

Rollston, Christopher, 26, 296, 348, 367, 368, 542, 543, 550, 551, 552, 561
Römer, Thomas, 4, 80, 82, 335, 340, 342, 385, 399, 401, 404, 410, 412, 576
Ronzevalle, Sebastien, 368
Rosen, Steven, 28, 369
Roth, Martha T., 427, 436, 536
Rothenberg, Beno, 366
Rougemont, Françoise, 340
Rouillard-Bonraisin, Hedwige, 567, 569
Routledge, Bruce, 30, 369, 370
Rowan, Yorke M., 24, 364
Rowe, Ignacio Márquez, 510
Rowson, Everett, 411
Rubin, Aaron D., 363
Rubio, Gonzalo, 388
Runciman, W. G., 337
Russell, Brian D., 384
Russell, Stephen C., 356, 384
Rütersworden, Udo, 352
Ryckmans, Jacques, 478, 487, 492

Saarelainen, Katri, 357
Saarisalo, Aapeli, 507, 508
Sader, Hélène, 551
Sallaberger, Walther, 386
Sanders, Seth L., 380, 424, 542
Sanmartín, Joaquín Ascaso, 173, 472, 567
Santos-Granero, Fernando, 337, 352, 427, 444, 461, 536
Sass, Benjamin, 368, 449, 550, 551
Sasson, Jack M., 340, 353, 385, 509
Sauvage, Caroline, 342, 462
Savage, Stephen H., 568
Sawyer, J. F. A., 231, 514
Schaeffer, C. F. A., 465
Schaper, Joachim, 542
Schaudig, Hanspeter, 393
Schein, Seth L., 320, 335, 336, 340, 395, 396, 397, 398, 402, 569
Schick, Tamar, 24, 364
Schley, Donald G., 563
Schlimm, Matthew R., 361
Schloen, J. David, 128, 229, 253, 289, 345, 350, 373, 378, 380, 424, 460, 507, 508, 510, 513, 515, 547
Schmid, Konrad, 8, 343, 511, 576
Schmidt, Brian B., 457
Schmitt, Rüdiger, 355, 471, 526
Schmitz, Philip C., 424
Schmuttermayr, Georg, 383, 505
Schnapp, Alain, 442
Schneider, Jane, 338
Schneider, Thomas, 337, 470
Schniedewind, William, 215, 216, 284, 502, 503, 541, 542
Schorch, Stefan, 425, 453, 503
Schroeder, Christoph, 556
Schroer, Silvia, 401, 410
Schwartz, Baruch, 369
Schwemer, Daniel, 476
Seeden, Helga, 371
Seeligmann, Isac Leo, 36, 337, 386, 526, 541, 545
Seevers, Boyd, 346
Segal, Charles, 539
Segal, Robert A., 391
Seidl, Ursula, 388
Seow, C. Leong, 199, 353, 489
Sergent, Bernard, 409
Serjeant, R. B., 486, 492
Serrano, Leonardo, 349
Setzer, Claudia, 333
Shaffer, Aaron, 362
Shahid, Irfan, 512
Shai, Itzhaq, 349
Shalev, Sariel, 347, 364
Shapiro, H. A., 402, 560
Sharer, Robert J., 339
Shaw, I., 428
Shaw, Jane, 515
Shea, William H., 527
Shefferman, David A., 333
Shiloh, Yigal, 548
al-Shorman, Abdulla, 568
Short, J. Randall, 400, 538
Shreckhise, Robert, 500
Shuval, Menakhen, 371, 373
Silver, Edward, 221, 506
Simiand, François, 10
Singer, Itamar, 432, 449, 462, 559
Sinos, Rebecca H., 417, 514

Sivan, Daniel, 215, 216, 433, 437, 441, 447, 460, 461, 502, 503, 506
Ska, Jean-Louis, 576
Skinner, John, 507
Slanski, Kathryn E., 354
Slatkin, Laura M., 402
Slavitt, David R., 334
Slotki, Israel W., 496
Smend, Rudolph, 35, 36, 374, 516, 520
Smith, Adam T., 525, 526
Smith, Jonathan Z., 412, 430
Smith, Mark S., 344, 345, 354, 355, 360, 361, 373, 374, 376, 378, 384, 407, 417, 418, 421, 424, 425, 430, 439, 444, 449, 450, 452, 457, 458, 460, 465, 466, 467, 470, 471, 474, 476, 477, 478, 482, 489, 490, 491, 496, 501, 503, 511, 512, 518, 519, 520, 521, 525, 531, 533, 542, 557, 558, 560, 566, 567, 569, 571, 572, 573, 574, 575, 576
Smith, William Robertson, 477
Smith, William Stevenson, 371
Soggin, J. Alberto, 212, 251, 253, 498, 502, 520, 522
Sparks, Kenton, 516
Sperling, S. David, 531
Spiegel, Shalom, 116, 434
Spronk, Klaas, 109, 353, 430
Stadelmann, Rainer, 487
Stager, Lawrence E., 226, 253, 272, 341, 345, 364, 373, 384, 428, 507, 510, 512, 516, 535
Staubli, Thomas, 401, 410
Steiner, Margreet, 349
Steiner, Richard C., 195, 199, 382, 452, 476, 486, 489, 503, 504, 517, 529, 555, 570
Steinkeller, Piotr, 460
Steymans, Hans Ulrich, 340, 394
Stoebe, Hans J., 540
Stone, Jon R., 333
Stone, Lawson, 378
Strauss, Barry, 347
Stavrakopoulou, Francesca, 567, 570
Strawn, Brent A., 532, 534
Strenski, Ivan, 333
Struble, Eudora J., 424
Stuart, Douglas K., 497
Stuckenbruck, Loren T., 340
Studer, Gottlieb Ludwig, 212, 215, 251, 253, 497, 498, 502, 506, 511, 520, 522
Such-Gutiérrez, M., 393
Sun, Chloe, 100, 418, 419, 420, 443
Suriano, Matthew J., 446, 457, 569
Sweeney, Deborah, 371

Tadmor, Hayim, 389, 494
Talmon, Shemaryahu, 38, 278, 518, 527, 530, 535, 539, 567
Tarragon, Jean-Michel de, 457, 458, 459, 461, 462
Tawil, Hayim ben Yosef, 454, 492, 576
Taylor, J. Glenn, 158, 457, 458, 519
Taylor, Rabun, 338
Tazawa, Keiko, 360, 361, 362, 469, 470, 473, 476, 478, 489, 490, 491, 549
Teissier, Beatrice, 356, 371, 372
Thackeray, H. St. John, 561, 572
Thalmann, Jean-Paul, 364
Theis, Christopher, 383
Thompson, R. Campbell, 485
Thornton, Sarah, 338
Tickner, J. Ann, 334
Tigay, Jeffrey H., 52, 376, 386, 445
Toorn, Karel van der, 345, 352, 388, 406, 413, 423, 443, 512, 556, 561, 562, 576
Tournay, Raymond, 229, 513
Tov, Emanuel, 513, 564
Trible, Phyllis, 357
Tritle, Lawrence A., 397
Tromp, Nicholas J., 450
Tropper, Josef, 361, 499
Trotter, James M., 556
Tryfonidou, Marina, 453
Tsagalis, Christos C., 403, 537
Tsevat, Matitiahu, 565
Tsumura, David, 425, 457, 459, 461
Tuell, Steven, 481
Tugendhaft, Aaron, 377, 464, 465
Tylus, Jane, 340, 377

Uehlinger, Christoph, 323, 372, 380, 487, 489, 571
Uziel, Joe, 349

Vainstub, Daniel, 359
Van Leeuwen, Raymond C., 394
Van Siclen, Charles C., III, 487
Vaughan, Andrew G., 367, 441, 552
Vaux, Roland de, 356, 467
Vedeler, Harold Torger, 443, 445
Veen, Peter van der, 383
Vendler, Helen, 422
Vermaak, P. S., 414
Vermeule, Emily, 63, 93, 335, 339, 340, 350, 356, 398, 405, 408, 417, 534
Vermeylen, Jacques, 399, 414, 538
Vern, Robyn, 212, 213, 383, 499, 500
Vetters, Melissa, 342
Vidal, Jordi, 18, 347, 354, 355, 435, 523
Vieweger, Dieter, 495
Vincent, John, 345
Vincent, Mark A., 516, 523
Vita, Juan-Pablo, 340, 468

Wachsman, Shelley, 428
Wagner, Volker, 553
Walls, Neal, 81, 82, 91, 93, 94, 405, 407, 411, 412, 413, 414, 416, 417, 443, 470, 476, 488
Walsh, Thomas R., 395
Waltisberg, Michael, 212, 215, 498, 502, 545
Waltke, Bruce K., 429, 509, 532
Wapnish, Paula, 28, 29, 369, 370, 472, 574
Watanabe, Chikako E., 390, 428, 436, 443, 487
Watson, Wilfred G. E., 344, 361, 418, 428, 432, 434, 435, 436, 440, 451, 455, 456, 471, 474, 481, 482, 483, 485, 492
Watts, James W., 422
Wazana, Nili, 346, 362, 363, 569
Way, Kenneth C., 472
Wees, Hans van, 4, 10, 79, 93, 137, 336, 340, 342, 345, 347, 362, 367, 374, 384, 395, 397, 402, 403, 404, 407, 408, 410, 417, 419, 446, 536, 570
Weiner, Annette B., 338
Weinfeld, Moshe, 230, 389, 513
Weippert, Manfred, 512
Weiser, Arthur, 508, 516
Weiss, Meir, 523
Weitzman, Steven, 275, 276, 513, 527, 534, 538, 540
Wente, Edward F., 488
West, David R., 385, 403
West, Martin Litchfield, 336, 341, 376, 394, 395, 398
Westbrook, Raymond, 553
Westenholz, Aage, 390
Westenholz, Joan Goodnick, 196, 478, 480, 487, 490, 514
Westermann, Claus, 423
Wheeler, Everett L., 348
White, Marsha, 378, 379
Whitley, James, 321, 570
Wierling, Dorothee, 10, 345
Wiggerman, Franz A. M., 460
Wiggins, Steve A., 205, 474, 475, 494
Wijngaarden, Gert Jan van, 342
Wikander, Ola, 501
Wilkinson, Richard H., 428, 443
Wilks, Ivor, 540, 541
Williams, P. J., 447
Williams, Ronald J., 461, 466
Williams-Forte, Elizabeth, 442
Wilson, J., 341
Wilson, John A., 510
Wilson, Robert R., 361, 560
Wimmer, Stefan J., 426, 564
Winter, Irene J., 81, 410, 411
Wiseman, Donald J., 477, 487
Wofford, Susanne, 340, 377
Wolde, Ellen van, 360, 410, 435, 504
Wolff, Hope Nash, 350, 392, 393, 404, 416, 419, 446
Wolff, Samuel, 25, 366
Wolters, Albert M., 357, 502
Wong, Gregory T. K., 516, 521, 522, 523
Wright, Allen, 468, 564
Wright, David P., 100, 106, 107, 115, 116, 120, 131, 132, 418, 419, 420, 421, 423, 425, 426, 427, 428, 432, 433, 434, 435,

436, 437, 438, 439, 440, 442, 443, 445, 553
Wright, G. Ernest, 381
Wright, Jacob L., 7, 343, 347, 400, 433, 517, 519, 526, 538, 569, 575
Wright, J. W., Jr., 411
Wyatt, Nicolas, 122, 184, 420, 426, 427, 430, 437, 438, 477, 478, 567, 571

Xella, Paolo, 426, 478

Yadin, Azzan, 547, 564
Yadin, Yigael, 202, 346, 491
Yaqub, Nadia G., 540
Yardeni, Ada, 355
Yee, Gale A., 527
Yon, Marguerite, 25, 32, 342, 365, 373, 465
Young, Ian, 212, 218, 383, 498, 499, 503, 543
Younger, K. Lawson, 436, 536

Zakovitch, Yair, 376, 377
Zamora, José-Angel, 453, 468
Zapletal, Vincenz, 251, 516, 522
Zehnder, Markus, 401, 410
Zenger, Erich, 576
Zertal, Adam, 28, 369, 537
Zevit, Ziony, 355, 370, 424, 471, 493, 498
Zewi, Tamar, 499
Zhou, Yiqun, 358
Ziegler, Nele, 388, 390, 410, 474
Ziffer, Irit, 496
Zijl, Peter J. van, 464, 471, 472
Zobel, Hans-Jürgen, 239, 516, 517
Zohar, Mattanyah, 568
Zorn, Jeffrey, 445, 456, 467, 537, 557, 564
Zsolnay, Ilona, 444, 491
Zuckerman, Bruce, 441
Zuckerman, Sharon, 532
Zukerman, Alexander, 341, 564
Zwickel, Wolfgang, 496

www.ingramcontent.com/pod-product-compliance
Lightning Source LLC
Chambersburg PA
CBHW031538300426
44111CB00006BA/91
* 9 7 8 0 8 0 2 8 6 7 9 2 6 *